Hege... ...
against idealist philosophy ... ...egan
to develop his theory of historical
materialism. He related the state of
society to its economic foundations
and mode of production, and
recommended armed revolution on the
part of the proletariat. In Paris in
1844 Marx met Friedrich Engels, with
whom he formed a life-long partnership.
Together they prepared the *Manifesto
of the Communist Party* (1848) as a
statement of the Communist League's
policy. In 1848 Marx returned to
Germany and took an active part in
the unsuccessful democratic revolution.
The following year he arrived in
England as a refugee and lived in
London until his death in 1883.
Helped financially by Engels, Marx and
his family nevertheless lived in great
poverty. After years of research
(mostly carried out in the British
Museum), he published in 1867 the
first volume of his great work, *Capital*.
From 1864 to 1872 Marx played a
leading role in the International
Working Men's Association, and his
last years saw the development of the
first mass workers' parties founded on
avowedly Marxist principles. Besides
the two posthumous volumes of
Capital compiled by Engels, Karl
Marx's other writings include *The
German Ideology*, *The Poverty of
Philosophy*, *A Contribution to the
Critique of Political Economy* and
Theories of Surplus-Value.

KARL MARX

Capital

A Critique of
Political Economy

Volume One

Introduced by
Ernest Mandel

Translated by
Ben Fowkes

Penguin Books
in association with New Left Review

Penguin Books Ltd, Harmondsworth, Middlesex, England
Penguin Books, 625 Madison Avenue, New York, New York 10022, U.S.A.
Penguin Books Australia Ltd, Ringwood, Victoria, Australia
Penguin Books Canada Ltd, 2801 John Street, Markham, Ontario, Canada L3R 1B4
Penguin Books (N.Z.) Ltd, 182–190 Wairau Road, Auckland 10, New Zealand

New Left Review, 7 Carlisle Street, London W1

This edition first published 1976
Reprinted 1979, 1982

Made and printed in Great Britain by
Hazell Watson & Viney Ltd,
Aylesbury, Bucks
Set in Monotype Times Roman

Contents

Introduction

When Volume 1 of *Capital* was first published, capitalist industry, though predominant in a few Western European countries, still appeared as an isolated island encircled by a sea of independent farmers and handicraftsmen which covered the whole world, including the greater part even of Europe. What Marx's *Capital* explained, however, was above all the ruthless and irresistible impulse to growth which characterizes production for private profit and the predominant use of profit for capital accumulation. Since Marx wrote, capitalist technology and industry have indeed spread all over the world. As they have done so, moreover, not only have material wealth and the possibilities for freeing mankind definitively from the burden of meaningless, repetitive and mechanical work increased, but so too has the polarization of society between fewer and fewer owners of capital and more and more workers of hand and brain, forced to sell their labour-power to these owners. The concentration of wealth and power in a small number of giant industrial and financial corporations has brought with it an increasingly universal struggle between Capital and Labour.

Periodically the bourgeois class and its ideologues have thought they have found the stone of wisdom; have felt able, accordingly, to announce the end of crises and socio-economic contradictions in the capitalist system. But despite Keynesian techniques, notwithstanding all the various attempts to integrate the working class into late capitalism, for over a decade now the system has appeared if anything more crisis-ridden than when Marx wrote *Capital*. From the Vietnam war to the turmoil of the world monetary system; from the upsurge of radical workers' struggles in Western Europe since 1968 to the rejection of bourgeois values and culture by large numbers of young people throughout the world; from the ecology and energy crises to the recurrent economic recessions: there is no need to look very far for indications that capitalism's heyday is over. *Capital* explains why the sharpening contradictions of the system were as inevitable as its impetuous growth. In that sense, contrary to a generally accepted belief, Marx is much more an economist of the twentieth century than of the nineteenth. Today's Western world is much nearer to the 'pure' model of *Capital* than was the world in which it was composed.

I. THE PURPOSE OF *CAPITAL*

In *Capital* Marx's fundamental aim was to lay bare the laws of motion which govern the origins, the rise, the development, the decline and the disappearance of a given social form of economic organization: the capitalist mode of production. He was not seeking *universal* laws of economic organization. Indeed, one of the essential theses of *Capital* is that no such laws exist. For Marx, there are no economic laws valid for each and every basically different form of society (aside from trivialities like the formula which points out that no society can consume more than it produces without reducing its stock of wealth – whether the natural fertility of the land, the total population, the mass of means of production, or several of these). Each specific social form of economic organization has its own specific economic laws. *Capital* limits itself to examining those which govern the capitalist mode of production.

Capital is therefore not 'pure' economic theory at all. For Marx, 'pure' economic theory, that is economic theory which abstracts from a specific social structure, is impossible. It would be similar to 'pure' anatomy, abstracted from the specific species which is to be examined. We can push the analogy further. Although, of course, *comparative anatomy* is a branch of natural science, useful for increasing our knowledge of human and animal physiology, it can be only a by-product of the development of the anatomical understanding of specific given species. In the same way, Marx's theory of historical materialism does indeed include comparative economic analysis – for example an examination of the evolution of human labour, human labour productivity, social surplus product and economic growth, from slave society through feudalism to capitalism. But such comparison can result only from the analysis of specific modes of production, each with its own economic logic and its own laws of motion. These cannot be superseded by or subsumed under 'eternal' economic laws. We can even push the analogy to its final conclusion. If one tries to find some basic common kernel in 'all' anatomy, one leaves the realm of that specific science and enters another: biology or biochemistry. In the same way, if one tries to discover basic working hypotheses valid for 'all' economic systems, one passes from the realm of economic theory to that of the science of social structures: historical materialism.

In this way, Marx's economic theory and its crowning work *Capital* are based upon an understanding of the *relativity, social determination and historical limitation* of all economic laws. In the socio-economic development of mankind, commodity production, market economy or the distribution of social resources among different branches of production by 'objective economic laws' operating 'behind the back of the producers' do not correspond to 'human nature', have not always existed and will not always exist. *Capital*, explaining the origins of the capitalist mode of production, points towards the inevitable historical decline and fall of this same social system. An economic theory based upon the historical relativity of every economic system, its strict limitation in time, tactlessly reminds Messrs the capitalists, their hangers-on and their apologists that capitalism itself is a product of history. It will perish in due course as it once was born. A new social form of economic organization will then take the place of the capitalist one: it will function according to other laws than those which govern the capitalist economy.

Nevertheless, *Capital* does not deal exclusively with the capitalist mode of production, although the discovery of the laws which govern this mode of production is its fundamental objective. Capitalist production is generalized commodity production. Generalized commodity production fully unfolds trends and contradictions which are latent in every one of its basic 'cells', the commodities. It is no accident that Marx starts *Capital* Volume 1 with an analysis neither of 'the capitalist mode of production', nor of capital, nor of wage-labour, nor even of the relations between wage-labour and capital. For it is impossible to analyse any of these basic concepts or categories – which correspond to the basic structure of capitalist society – scientifically, totally and adequately without a previous analysis of value, exchange-value and surplus-value. But these latter categories in turn hinge upon an analysis of the commodity and of commodity-producing labour.

Just as surplus-value and capital emerge *logically* from an analysis of value and exchange-value, so too does the capitalist mode of production emerge *historically* from the growth of commodity production: without simple commodity production no capitalism can come into existence. *Capital*, the *Grundrisse* and the other basic economic writings of Karl Marx therefore include many analyses of simple commodity production, a form of production which existed in manifold ways for nearly 10,000 years before modern capitalism was born, but which found its fullest flowering only between the thirteenth and sixteenth centuries A.D. in the Low Countries, northern Italy, and later Britain (and to a lesser degree in Japan before the Meiji revolution).

Objections have been advanced – by early Russian Marxist authors like Bogdanov, by later commentators like Rubin and by contemporary Marxists like Lucio Colletti and Louis Althusser[1] – to the view, originating with Engels and held by Rosa Luxemburg, to which I subscribe,[2] that Marx's *Capital* provides not only a basic analysis of the capitalist mode of production, but also significant comments upon the whole historical period which includes essential phenomena of petty commodity production. These objections, however, are based upon a double confusion. It is true that the capitalist mode of production is the only social organization of the economy which implies *generalized* commodity production. It would thus be completely mistaken to consider, for example, Hellenistic slave society or the classical Islamic Empire – two forms of society with strongly developed petty commodity production, money economy and international trade – as being *ruled* by the 'law of value'. Commodity production in these precapitalist modes of production is intertwined with, and in the last analysis subordinated to, organizations of production (in the first

1. I. I. Rubin, *Essays on Marx's Theory of Value*, Detroit, 1972, pp. 254–6; Lucio Colletti, *Marxism and Hegel*, NLB, London, 1973, pp. 131–2; Louis Althusser, 'The Object of *Capital*', in *Reading Capital*, NLB, London, 1970, pp. 113–17, 124–6. There is also a very illuminating remark by Marx himself, from 'Chapter 6' of *Capital*, Vol. 1 (see Appendix to this volume): 'Nevertheless, within certain limits both goods and money were circulated and hence there was a certain evolution of trade: this was the *premiss* and *point of departure for the formation of capital* and the capitalist mode of production' (pp. 1059–60 below).
2. Karl Marx, *Capital*, Moscow, 1962, Vol. 3, pp. 172–4; Friedrich Engels, 'Law of Value and Rate of Profit', ibid. (appendix), pp. 873–6; Rosa Luxemburg, *Einführung in die Nationalökonomie*, Berlin, 1925, pp. 199–232; Ernest Mandel, *Marxist Economic Theory*, London, 1969, Vol. 1, pp. 65–8.

place agricultural production) of a clearly non-capitalist nature, which follow a different economic logic from that which governs exchanges between commodities or the accumulation of capital.

But this in no way implies that in societies in which petty commodity production has already become the *predominant* mode of production (that is where the majority of the producers are free peasants and free handicraftsmen who own and exchange the products of their labour), the laws governing the exchange of commodities and the circulation of money do not strongly influence the economic dynamic. Indeed, it is precisely the *unfolding* of the law of value which leads in such societies to the separation of the direct producers from their means of production, although a whole series of social and political developments influences this birth-process of modern capitalism, hastening it, slowing it down, or combining it with trends going in different directions.

On the other hand, if it is true that fully-fledged 'economic accounting based upon quantities of socially equalized labour' comes into its own only under capitalism, and this only as an objective economic law and not as conscious decisions of owners of commodities, it does not follow at all from this statement that 'labour quantities accounting' cannot *begin* to appear in pre-capitalist societies, in which commodity production becomes a regular institution. Indeed, it is precisely when petty commodity production is already largely developed, but at the same time still intertwined with traditional forms of 'natural' economic organization, which imply conscious allocations of economic resources and social labour between different forms of production (through customs, habits, rites, religion, deliberation of elders, assemblies of participants etc.), that the need for a conscious accounting of 'labour quantities' can and must appear, in order to avoid basic injustices and inequalities in social organizations still based upon a high degree of social equality and coherence. I have tried to prove by empirical data that this has in fact been the case, at different historical periods, in different parts of the world.[3]

This does not mean that the 'law of value' is a 'product of pre-capitalist history'. Nor does it mean that such still relatively primitive societies were burdened with the same manic pursuit of material rewards, and measurement of labour-time expenditure down to fractions of seconds, as our own; for these are, indeed, 'pure' products of bourgeois society. It only means that the em-

3. Mandel, op. cit., pp. 59–65.

bryonic forms of the 'law of value' can be discovered in the embryonic developments of commodity production, just as the 'elementary cell' of capital, the commodity, contains in an embryonic way all the inner qualities and contradictions of that social category. To deny this historical dimension of Marx's analysis is to transform the origins of capitalism into an insoluble mystery.

One could argue that this is rather a moot point for economists, interesting only for anthropologists, ethnologists or historians. But its implications are in fact extremely far-reaching. By stating that the analysis of the laws of motion governing the capitalist mode of production necessarily includes at least some essential elements of an analysis of economic phenomena valid for the whole historical epoch encompassing economic organizations in which commodity production exists, one extends the validity of parts of Marx's *Capital* not only into the past but also into the future. For phenomena of commodity production obviously survive, at least partially, in those societies in which the rule of capital has already been overthrown, but which are not yet fully-fledged classless, that is socialist, societies: the USSR and the People's Republics of Eastern Europe, China, North Vietnam, North Korea and Cuba. *Capital* is no more a guide to understanding the laws of motion of these societies than it is a guide to understanding the laws of motion of developed late medieval society based upon petty commodity production. But it can tell us a lot about the dynamics (and disintegrating logic) of commodity production and money economy in such non-capitalist societies, and the contradictions which these introduce into the specific and 'pure' laws of motion of the latter.

If *Capital* is not a treatise on eternal economic laws, does it at least contain a science of the capitalist economy? Some Marxists, in the first place the German Karl Korsch, have denied this.[4] For them – as for so many bourgeois critics of Marx – *Capital* is essentially an instrument for the revolutionary overthrow of capitalism by the proletariat. According to them, it is impossible to separate the 'scientific' content of *Capital* from its 'revolutionary' intention, as the Austro-German Marxist Rudolf Hilferding tried to do.[5] This contention overlooks a basic distinction which Marx and Engels introduced between utopian and scientific socialism. Marx remained indeed a revolutionary during the whole of his

4. Karl Korsch, *Marxism and Philosophy*, NLB, London, 1970, pp. 54–60·
5. Rudolf Hilferding, *Das Finanzkapital*, Vienna, 1923, p. x.

adult life after 1843. But he considered it essential to base socialism (communism) upon a scientific foundation. The scientific analysis of the capitalist mode of production was to be the cornerstone of that foundation, showing why and how capitalism created, through its own development, the economic, material and social pre-conditions for a society of associated producers. In that sense, Marx strove, not indeed in contradiction to, but precisely as a function of this intention, to analyse capitalism in an objective and strictly scientific way. In other words, he did not simply give vent to an aggressive hostility towards a particular form of economic organization, for reasons of revolutionary passion and compassion for the downtrodden and oppressed; nor, it hardly needs to be said, was he motivated by personal spite, material failure or psychotic imbalance. Marx sought to discover objective laws of motion. There was nobody – not even the typical bourgeois *Spiesser* – whom he despised more than the man with scientific pretensions who nevertheless deliberately twists empirical data or falsifies research results to suit some subjective purpose. Precisely because Marx was convinced that the cause of the proletariat was of decisive importance for the whole future of mankind, he wanted to create for that cause not a flimsy platform of rhetorical invective or wishful thinking, but the rock-like foundation of scientific truth.

2. THE METHOD OF *CAPITAL*

The purpose of *Capital* is itself a clear reminder of the method of knowledge applied by Marx to his main work: the method of the materialist dialectic. Marx left no doubt that this was indeed how he himself understood his labours. In a letter sent to Maurice Lachâtre, the editor of the first French edition of *Capital* Volume 1, he insisted on the fact that he was the first person to have applied this method to the study of economic problems.[6] Again in his own postface to the second German edition of *Capital* Volume 1, Marx specified this use of the dialectical method as the *differentia specifica* of *Capital*, which distinguished it from all other economic analyses.[7]

6. Marx, letter to Maurice Lachâtre of 18 March 1872; see 'Preface to the French Edition', p. 104 below.
7. See below, pp. 102–3.

When the dialectical method is applied to the study of economic problems, economic phenomena are not viewed separately from each other, by bits and pieces, but in their inner connection as an integrated totality, structured around, and by, a basic predominant mode of production. This totality is analysed in all its aspects and manifestations, as determined by certain given laws of motion, which relate also to its origins and its inevitable disappearance. These laws of motion of the given mode of production are discovered to be nothing but the unfolding of the inner contradictions of that structure, which define its very nature. The given economic structure is seen to be characterized at one and the same time by the unity of these contradictions and by their struggle, both of which determine the constant changes which it undergoes. The (quantitative) changes which constantly occur in the given mode of production, through adaptation, integration of reforms and self-defence (evolution), are distinguished from those (qualitative) changes which, by sudden leaps, produce a different structure, a new mode of production (revolution).

Marx clearly opposes his own dialectical method of investigation and knowledge to that of Hegel, although he never hesitates to recognize his debt of gratitude to the German philosopher who, spurred on by the French Revolution, catapulted dialectical thought back into the modern world. Hegel's dialectics were idealist: the basic motion was that of the Absolute Idea; material reality was only the outward appearance of ideal essence. For Marx, on the contrary, the dialectic is materialist, 'the ideal is nothing but the material world reflected in the mind of man, and translated into forms of thought'.[8] The basic laws of motion of history are those of real men, themselves producing their own material existence in a given social framework. The development of thought corresponds in the final analysis to that basic movement, and reflects it, albeit through many mediations. Thus the scientific thought process through which Marx came to understand the operations of the capitalist mode of production was itself a product of that mode of production, of bourgeois society and its contradictions. Only secondarily can it be seen as a product of the development of many human sciences and ideologies: classical German philosophy; English political economy; French historiography and political science; pre-Marxian socialism. Only the

8. ibid., p. 102.

growth of bourgeois society and its contradictions, above all the struggle between capital and labour, enabled Marx to assimilate, combine and transform these sciences in the specific way and the specific direction he did. Nevertheless, while the materialist dialectic is Hegel's (idealist) dialectic 'turned right side up again', both have basic common traits. Dialectics as the logic of motion presupposes that *all* motion, *all* evolution, whether of nature, society or human thought, adopts certain general forms which are called 'dialectical'.[9] Engels and Lenin both saw, in the very way in which *Capital* Volume 1 was constructed, a striking application of this general dialectical method; thus Lenin wrote that although Marx had never written his projected short treatise on dialectics, he had nevertheless left us *Capital*, which is the application of the materialist dialectic in the field of economic phenomena.[10]

Precisely because Marx's dialectic is a materialist one, however, it does not start from intuition, preconceptions or mystifying schemes, but from a full assimilation of scientific data. The method of investigation must differ from the method of exposition. Empirical facts have to be gathered first, the given state of knowledge has to be fully grasped. Only when this is achieved can a dialectical reorganization of the material be undertaken in order to understand the given totality. If this is successful, the result is a 'reproduction' in man's thought of this material totality: the capitalist mode of production.

The main danger for any scientist involved in the study of social phenomena is that of taking anything for granted, of 'problem-blindness'. The distinction between appearance and essence, which Marx inherited from Hegel[11] and which is part and parcel of the dialectical method of investigation, is nothing but a constant attempt to pierce farther and farther through successive layers of phenomena, towards laws of motion which *explain* why these phenomena evolve in a certain direction and in certain ways. Con-

9. Engels, letter to Conrad Schmidt of 1 November 1891, in Marx/Engels, *Selected Correspondence*, Moscow, 1965, p. 439.

10. Lenin, 'Plan of Hegel's Dialectics (Logic)', *Collected Works*, Vol. 38, p. 319.

11. 'There it will be seen what the philistine's and vulgar economist's *way of looking at things* stems from, namely, from the fact that it is only the direct *form of manifestation* of relations that is reflected in their brains and not their *inner connection*. Incidentally, if the latter were the case what need would there be of *science*?' (letter from Marx to Engels, 27 June 1867, *Selected Correspondence*, p. 191). See also *Capital*, Vol. 3, p. 307.

stantly searching for questions – calling into question! – where others only see ready-made answers and vulgar 'evidence': this is certainly one of Marx's main merits as a revolutionary innovator in economic science.

But for Marx, the materialist dialectician, the distinction between 'essence' and 'appearance' in no sense implies that 'appearance' is less 'real' then 'essence'. Movements of value determine in the last analysis movements of prices; but Marx the materialist would have laughed at any 'Marxist' who suggested that prices were 'unreal', because in the last analysis *determined* by value movements. The distinction between 'essence' and 'appearance' refers to different levels of determination, that is in the last analysis to the process of cognition, not to different degrees of reality. To explain the capitalist mode of production in its totality it is wholly insufficient to understand simply the 'basic essence', the 'law of value'. It is necessary to integrate 'essence' and 'appearance' through all their intermediate mediating links, to explain how and why a given 'essence' appears in given concrete forms and not in others. For these 'appearances' themselves are neither accidental nor self-evident. They pose problems, they have to be explained in their turn, and this very explanation helps to pierce through new layers of mystery and brings us again nearer to a full understanding of the specific form of economic organization which we want to understand. To deny this need to reintegrate 'essence' and 'appearance' is as un-dialectical and as mystifying as to accept 'appearances' as they are, without looking for the basic forces and contradictions which they tend to hide from the superficial and empiricist observer.

The way in which *Capital* starts with an analysis of the basic categories of commodity production, with the 'basic unit' (fundamental cell) of capitalist economic life, the commodity, has often been cited as a model application of this materialist dialectic. Marx himself makes it clear that he does not start from a basic concept – value – but from an elementary material phenomenon – the commodity – which is at the basis of capitalism, as the only economic organization based upon generalized commodity production.[12] It is therefore correct but incomplete, strictly speaking, to say that Marx's method consists of 'rising from the abstract to the con-

12. Karl Marx, 'Randglossen zu A. Wagners "Lehrbuch der politischen Oekonomie"', *MEW* 19, pp. 364, 368–9 (English translation in *Theoretical Practice*, No. 5, London, 1972).

crete'.[13] In fact, he starts from elements of the material concrete to go to the theoretical abstract, which helps him then to reproduce the concrete totality in his theoretical analysis. In its full richness and deployment, the concrete is always a combination of innumerable theoretical 'abstractions'. But the material concrete, that is, real bourgeois society, exists before this whole scientific endeavour, determines it in the last instance, and remains a constant practical point of reference to test the validity of the theory. Only if the reproduction of this concrete totality in man's thought comes nearer to the real material totality is thought really scientific. At first sight, the movement which dominates *Capital* Volume 1 appears as a movement of economic 'categories', from the commodity and its inner contradictions to the accumulation of capital and its breakdown. The question has often been asked: is this movement just an abstract synopsis of the 'essence' of capitalism, or is it a greatly simplified reflection of real economic development, that is, the real history leading from the first appearance of commodity production up to full-scale capitalist production in the West, purified of all secondary and combined forms which would only obscure the basic nature of this movement?

It is impossible to answer this question simply with a 'yes' or a 'no'. Commodities produced accidentally in pre-capitalist societies, at the very margin of the basic processes of production and consumption, obviously cannot trigger off the striking and terrifying logic of the 'law of value' which Marx majestically unfolds in *Capital*. Commodity production as a basic and dominant feature of economic life presupposes capitalism, that is a society in which labour-power and instruments of labour have themselves become commodities. In that sense it is true that the analysis of Volume 1 of *Capital* is logical (based upon dialectical logic) and not historical.

13. Marx, *Grundrisse*, Pelican Marx Library, p. 101. See on the contrary Lenin (op. cit., p. 171): 'Thought proceeding from the concrete to the abstract ... does not get away *from* the truth but comes closer to it.' In his comments on the three volumes of *Capital* written in the early thirties, D. I. Rosenberg makes the interesting point that Marx's abstractions are in their turn concrete, inasmuch as they are related to a concrete economic formation and as they are historically determined. They are neither arbitrary nor *a priori* abstractions. (See the Spanish translation of the original Russian text, published by *Seminario de 'El Capital'*, Escuela Nacional de Economia, UNAM, Mexico, Cuaderno I, p. 46.)

But dialectics imply that every phenomenon has an origin and an end, that nothing is either eternal or finished once and for all. Hence the historical cell of capital is at the same time the key to the logical analysis of capital: phylogenesis and embryology cannot be completely separated. Within capital accumulation in contemporary everyday capitalist life, some aspects of primitive capital accumulation are reproduced: without that primitive capital accumulation, there would be no capitalist mode of production. So the logical analysis does reflect some basic trends of historical development after all. The simplest forms of appearance of the 'economic categories' (which are just forms of material existence, of material reality as perceived and simplified by the human mind) are often also their primitive, that is their original, form. However controversial this interpretation may be, it is difficult to deny that this unity of historical and logical analysis is the way in which Marx and Engels understood their own method.[14]

A whole literature has been produced, from Bernstein to Popper and on to contemporary academic economists, on the subject of the 'useless', 'metaphysical' or even 'mystifying' nature of the dialectical method which Marx borrowed from Hegel.[15] The positivist narrowness of outlook of these critics themselves generally bears eloquent testimony to the contrary, that is to the broad historical vision and the piercing lucidity which the dialectical method helped Marx to achieve. Thanks to that method, Marx's *Capital* appears as a giant compared to any subsequent or contemporary work of economic analysis. It was never intended as a handbook to help governments to solve such problems as balance-of-payments deficits, nor yet as a learned, if somewhat trite, explanation of all the exciting happenings in the market place when

14. See on this and related subjects, among others: Otto Morf, *Geschichte und Dialektik in der politischen Oekonomie*, Frankfurt, 1970; Evald Vasiljevic Iljenkov, *La dialettica dell' astratto e del concreto nel Capitale di Marx*, Milan, 1961; Karel Kosík, *Die Dialektik des Konkreten*, Frankfurt, 1967; Jindřich Zelený, *Die Wissenschaftslogik und 'Das Kapital'*, Frankfurt, 1969; Leo Kofler, *Geschichte und Dialektik*, Hamburg, 1955, etc.

15. For example, Eugen von Böhm-Bawerk, *Karl Marx and the Close of his System*, New York, 1949, p. 117; Eduard Bernstein, *Die Voraussetzungen des Sozialismus und die Aufgaben der Sozialdemokratie*, Stuttgart, 1899, pp. 51–71; Karl Popper, *The Open Society and its Enemies*, London, 1962, Vol. 2, p. 82; Vassily Leontief, 'The Significance of Marxian Economics for Present-Day Economic Theory', *American Economic Review Supplement*, March 1938, reprinted in Horowitz, *Marx and Modern Economics*, London, 1968, p. 95, etc.

Mr Smith finds no buyer for the last of his 1,000 tons of iron. It was intended as an explanation of what would happen to labour, machinery, technology, the size of enterprises, the social structure of the population, the discontinuity of economic growth, and the relations between workers and work, as the capitalist mode of production unfolded all its terrifying potential. From that point of view, the achievement is truly impressive. It is precisely because of Marx's capacity to discover the long-term laws of motion of the capitalist mode of production in its essence, irrespective of thousands of 'impurities' and of secondary aspects, that his long-term predictions – the laws of accumulation of capital, stepped-up technological progress, accelerated increase in the productivity and intensity of labour, growing concentration and centralization of capital, transformation of the great majority of economically active people into sellers of labour-power, declining rate of profit, increased rate of surplus value, periodically recurrent recessions, inevitable class struggle between Capital and Labour, increasing revolutionary attempts to overthrow capitalism – have been so strikingly confirmed by history.[16]

This judgement has generally been challenged on two grounds. The easiest way out for critics of Marx is simply to deny that the laws of motion of the capitalist mode of production which he discovered have been verified at all. This is generally done by reducing them to a couple of misstated and oversimplified formulae (see below): 'progressive immiseration of the working class' and 'ever-worsening economic crisis'.[17] A more sophisticated objec-

16. 'However important these technical contributions to the progress of economic theory in the present-day appraisal of Marxian achievements, they are overshadowed by his brilliant analysis of the long-term tendencies of the capitalist system. The record is indeed impressive: increasing concentration of wealth, rapid elimination of small and medium-sized enterprise, progressive limitation of competition, incessant technological progress accompanied by the ever-growing importance of fixed capital, and, last but not least, the un-diminishing amplitude of recurrent business cycles – an unsurpassed series of prognostications fulfilled, against which modern economic theory with all its refinements has little to show indeed.' (Leontief, op. cit., p. 94.)

17. A classical example of such over simplification is given by Paul Samuelson. He reduces the laws of motion of the capitalist mode of production to two (!): 'the immiseration of the working class', and 'the growing monopolization under capitalism', and concludes on the first that 'it simply never took place', while declaring on the second that 'for thirty years Marx seemed to have been right in this prophecy, even though for the next seventy years he does not seem to be borne out by the most careful researches on industrial

tion was advanced by Karl Popper, who denied the very possibility, or rather the scientific nature, of such 'laws', calling them 'unconditional historical prophecies' to be clearly distinguished from 'scientific predictions'. 'Ordinary predictions in science,' says Popper, 'are conditional. They assert that certain changes (say, of the temperature of water in a kettle) will be accompanied by other changes (say the boiling of the water).'[18] Popper denies the scientific nature of *Capital* by asserting that, unlike scientific theories, its hypotheses cannot be scientifically tested.[19]

This is obviously based upon a misunderstanding of the very nature of the materialist dialectic, which, as Lenin pointed out, requires constant verification through praxis to increase its cognition content.[20] In fact, it would be very easy to 'prove' Marx's analysis to have been wrong, if experience had shown, for example, that the more capitalist industry develops, the smaller and smaller the average factory becomes, the less it depends upon new technology, the more its capital is supplied by the workers themselves, the more workers become owners of their factories, the less the part of wages taken by consumer goods becomes (and the greater becomes the part of wages used for buying the workers' own means of production). If, in addition, there had been decades without economic fluctuations and a full-scale disappearance of trade unions and employers' associations (all flowing from the disappearance of contradictions between Capital and Labour, inasmuch as workers increasingly become the controllers of their own means and conditions of production), then one could indeed say that *Capital* was so much rubbish and had dismally failed to predict what would happen in the real capitalist world a century after its publication. It is sufficient to compare the real history of the

---

concentration'. Everything is then capped by the final statement that Marx thought there was an 'inevitable law of capitalist development that the business cycle should be getting worse and worse' and that this was not true either (Paul A. Samuelson, 'Marxian Economics as Economics', *American Economic Review*, Vol. 57 (1967), pp. 622–3).

18. Karl K. Popper, 'Predictions and Prophecy in the Social Sciences', in *Conjectures and Refutations – The Growth of Scientific Knowledge*, London, 1963, p. 339.

19. Popper, *The Open Society and its Enemies*, Vol. 2, the whole of Chapter 23, especially p. 210.

20. Lenin, op. cit., p. 319: 'All these moments (steps, stages, processes) of cognition move in the direction from the subject to the object, being tested in practice and arriving through this test at truth . . .'

period since 1867 on the one hand with what Marx predicted it would be, and on the other with any such alternative 'laws of motion', to understand how remarkable indeed was Marx's theoretical achievement and how strongly it stands up against the experimental test of history.[21]

3. THE PLAN OF *CAPITAL*

Capital was not the result of spontaneous generation nor was it the product of a sudden interest of Marx in economic problems. Ever since this doctor in philosophy (Jena, 1841) had become a communist in the course of the eighteen-forties under the pressure of current experience with social problems (the treatment of wood-thieves in the Rhine provinces of Prussia; the uprising of the Silesian textile workers; the strikes in England; the class struggle in France), he had turned towards economic studies. But his first encounter with modern political economy (which left its main results in the *Economic and Philosophical Manuscripts, The Poverty of Philosophy, Wage Labour and Capital* and *The Communist Manifesto*) was roughly interrupted by the pressure of external events. Participating actively in politics, Marx returned from Paris to Germany at the outbreak of the revolutionary movement in 1848. There he founded and directed a daily paper. When counter-revolutionary reaction submerged Europe after the revolutions collapsed, he emigrated to London and had to struggle for his livelihood as a journalist. These current pressures, together with the

21. An amusing aside to this seemingly absurd hypothesis of 'other' imaginable laws of motion is provided by Vilfredo Pareto's 'critique' of Marx's theory of value. In order to prove that Marx had a built-in *petitio principis* in the labour theory of value, Pareto stated that we might as well assume that the seamstress hires her machine, and her own subsistence, which would then lead to the conclusion that the machine has 'produced' the surplus-value ('Introduction à K. Marx *Le Capital*, extraits faits par P. Lafargue', in *Marxisme et économie pure*, Geneva, 1966, pp. 47–8). Leaving aside the fact that his example 'proves' nothing of the kind, it is significant what this counter-model implies: that workers hire their own means of production and, as a result of this, *own the products of their labour*, sell them on the market, and thereby appropriate the profits (surplus-value) produced in the course of the process of production. Now it is evident that this has in no way been the predominant trend of industrial development in the last 150 years. But, even at the end of the nineteenth century, the question seemed so 'open' in Pareto's mind that he could advance such an hypothesis without being struck by its evident absurdity. This all the more underlines the profundity of Marx's insight into the operations of capitalism.

burden of émigré politics in London, delayed the possibility of a systematic presentation of his economic theory for a whole decade.

Only when, through Lassalle, a publisher pressed him to explain his economic ideas in a fully-fledged way did he return to a full-scale encounter with Adam Smith and Malthus, Ricardo and J.-B. Say, Simonde de Sismondi and Tooke, together with the famous British government *Blue Books* which were to become an invaluable source of factual material about the conditions of British industry, trade, finance and working-class life. The systematic study of economic facts and thoughts about capitalism, resumed by Marx around 1857, produced the following works:

(a) a first rough draft of *Capital*, published posthumously under the title *Grundrisse der Kritik der politischen Oekonomie* (Foundations of the Critique of Political Economy), written in 1857–8;
(b) the uncompleted book *Zur Kritik der politischen Oekonomie* (A Contribution to the Critique of Political Economy), published in 1859;
(c) the 1861–3 manuscripts, twenty-three enormous notebooks, from which Kautsky extracted *Theories of Surplus-Value* (also known as Volume 4 of *Capital*). This however encompasses only notebooks VI–XV inclusive. Notebooks I–V deal with matters generally encompassed in *Capital* Volume 1; notebooks XVI, XVII and XVIII deal with matters in *Capital* Volume 3; notebooks XIX–XXIII again deal with matters related to *Capital* Volume 1, and include a lengthy treatment of the history of techniques and the use of machines under capitalism;
(d) a manuscript of 1864–5, mostly dealing with matters taken up in *Capital* Volume 3;
(e) four manuscripts written between 1865 and 1870, from which Engels extracted most of the material for *Capital* Volume 2;
(f) the final version of *Capital* Volume 1, written in 1866–7.

Of the six basic economic writings of the mature Marx, Volume 1 is therefore the only one which the author completed and edited himself, and of which he even made available corrected editions in German and in French.[22] Volumes 2 and 3 of *Capital*, left un-

22. The two most accurate, scientific editions of *Capital* Vol. 1 are that of the Institute for Marxism-Leninism of the Central Committee of the SED (*MEW* 23) and that of H. J. Lieber and Benedikt Kautsky (Stuttgart, 1962), both of which indicate the variations of the text between the various German editions and the French edition edited by Marx and Engels themselves. The

finished, were posthumously and laboriously published by Marx's life-long friend Friedrich Engels. *Theories of Surplus-Value* was rearranged and published by Kautsky. The *Grundrisse* was presented to the public for the first time only in 1939. A considerable part of the 1861–3 manuscripts still remains unpublished.

The initial plan of *Capital* was drawn up in 1857; the final plan dates from 1865–6. Between these two dates there lay nine years of intense study, especially in the British Museum, realized under very difficult circumstances. Marx was burdened by constant financial troubles; by the illness and death of three of his children, among them his beloved son Edgar; and by his growing re-involvement in current political and social studies, especially through his activity in the International Working Men's Association (the so-called First International). The need to answer a sharp and slanderous attack by a German political opponent, a certain Herr Vogt, cost Marx nearly half a year's delay in the production of *Capital* Volume 1. Finally, illness and bad health became increasing obstacles. He himself spoke sarcastically of his 'carbuncles', the effects of which the bourgeoisie would not forget for a long time. But in fact it is his strikingly stoical attitude towards all the miseries surrounding him, rather than any special bitterness born from material hardship, that permeates his mature work.

From the beginning, Marx wanted to present an all-round analysis of capitalism in its totality. The initial plan of *Capital* already bears witness to this intention and reads as follows:

1. *Volume on Capital*
   (a) Capital in general
       (1) Process of production of capital
       (2) Process of circulation of capital
       (3) Profit and interest
   (b) On competition
   (c) On credit
   (d) On joint stock companies
2. *Volume on landed property*

Lieber edition is somewhat more complete, because it indicates all these variations in the text itself. I have counted at least one hundred textual variations in the Lieber edition, some of which are important, but only a few sufficiently so to be mentioned in this introduction. [The present translation was made from *MEW* 23. Significant divergences between this and the earlier editions in German and French are indicated in the text.]

3. *Volume on wage labour*
4. *Volume on the State*
5. *Volume on international trade*
6. *Volume on the world market and crises*[23]

The 1865–6 version of *Capital*, however, falls into four volumes:

Volume 1: Process of production of capital
Volume 2: Process of circulation of capital
Volume 3: Forms of the process in its totality
Volume 4: History of the theory

Roman Rosdolsky, who has made the most extensive study to date of this problem, has isolated no less than fourteen different versions of the plan for *Capital* between September 1857 and April 1868.[24]

Two questions are raised by these changes. First, why did Marx modify his initial plan, and what implications do the modifications have for an understanding of Marx's method and for the content of *Capital*? Second, does the 1865–6 version imply that the four volumes which we possess today represent the full – although in the case of all save the first volume unedited – work as finally intended by Marx? The answer to each of those questions has many interesting implications both for the discussion of Marx's economic theory itself and for the light it throws on the contributions made by some of his gifted followers and disciples.

In fact, what we today call *Capital* is the third attempt by Marx to present his views on the capitalist mode of production in its totality. The first attempt, the *Grundrisse* of 1857–8, follows exactly the initial plan of *Capital*, but stops at point 1 (a) (3) of that plan. The second attempt, dating from 1861–3, is still unpublished, except for the part on *Theories of Surplus-Value*. The third attempt is the 1865–6 one, of which we have Volumes 1–4. We know that, as early as January 1863, Marx had already decided to deal with land rent as an element of distribution of total surplus-value among different sectors of the ruling classes. However, he still seemed to stick at that time to a separate volume on wage-labour, a separate volume on landed property, and separate

23. Karl Marx, letter to Engels of 2 April 1858, in *Selected Correspondence,* p. 104.
24. Roman Rosdolsky, *Zur Entstehungsgeschichte des Marx'schen Kapital,* Frankfurt, 1968, Vol. 1, p. 78.

volumes on credit, competition and joint-stock companies.[25] The logic of this plan implied the desire to deal with the basic social classes of bourgeois society in a separate way: first the industrial capitalists; then the landowners; finally the proletariat. It implied also the desire to separate sharply the problems of production of value, surplus-value and capital from the problems of capitalist competition, which can only be understood as arising out of processes of redistribution of previously produced surplus-value.

However, if this original plan was clearly a necessary stepping stone towards the final analysis of the capitalist mode of production, as Marx's analysis progressed it proved itself increasingly an obstacle to a rigorous and consistent *exposé* of the laws of motion of that mode of production. It had therefore to be discarded in the end. The volume on wage-labour became integrated into Volume 1, 'The Process of Production of Capital'. It appeared impossible to deal with wage-labour separately and apart from the production of surplus-value, that is from the capitalist process of production (Marx probably intended to deal with the fluctuations of wages in Volume 6 on the world market and crises). The volume on landed property became integrated, together with those on profit and interest, on competition and on joint-stock companies, into the new Volume 3, which examines key forms of the capitalist mode of production in its totality, from the point of view of redistribution of the total surplus-value produced among various sectors of the propertied class.

Looking at this transformation of the initial plan of *Capital*, we can, however, also understand what did *not* change. Volumes 1 and 2 of *Capital* can still be subsumed under the heading of 'Capital in General'. Only Volume 3, like the originally planned 4, 5 and 6, which were never written, falls under the heading of 'many capitals'. This means concretely that a certain number of problems, such as, for instance, the problem of the origin and mechanics of the 'trade cycle' (of capitalist crises of overproduction), have no place in Volumes 1 and 2 and can be dealt with only when one descends from the highest level of abstraction, where capital is dealt with in its global relationship to wage-labour, to an examination of the interactions of various capitals upon each other. Because she did not take this specific structure of the successive volumes of *Capital* into account, Rosa Luxemburg was

25. Karl Marx, letter to Kugelmann of 28 December 1862, *MEW* 30, pp. 639–40; *Theories of Surplus-Value*, London, 1969, Part One, p. 404.

methodologically mistaken in accusing Marx of having constructed his reproduction schemes of Volume 2 without solving the 'realization problem' or without formulating a theory of crises.[26] I shall return to this interesting problem in my introduction to *Capital* Volume 2.

A similar mistake is made by Joan Robinson, in her Preface to the second edition of *An Essay on Marxian Economics*, where she construes a contradiction between the assumptions regarding real wages of *Capital* Volume 1 and those of Volume 3. In Volume 1, she says, Marx assumes that a rising labour productivity leads to a rising rate of exploitation, whereas in Volume 3 he assumes that rising labour productivity could lead, through a stable rate of exploitation, to a rising rate of real wages and a declining rate of profit.[27] Joan Robinson does not understand that Volumes 1 and 3 of *Capital* are at different levels of abstraction, deal with different questions, and make different assumptions in order to clarify the *specific dynamics* which allow answers to these questions.

In Volume 1, Marx examines the relations between Capital and Labour in general, abstracting from the effects of competition between capitalists on the distribution of surplus-value and on the variations of real wages. He therefore assumes initially stable real subsistence wages, in order to show through what mechanics surplus-value is produced, appropriated and increased by capital. In Volume 3 he examines the effects of capitalist competition upon the distribution and redistribution of surplus-value among capitalists, and therefore has to integrate into the analysis the effects of this competition on the rate of exploitation (for example in periods of boom, with a high level of employment). In order to work out the basic answers to these questions, it is perfectly logical to abstract *initially* from fluctuations in the rate of profit and wages in Volume 1, and to assume *initially* a stable rate of exploitation in Volume 3, but subsequently to abandon these simplifying hypotheses (Volume 1, Chapter 17; Volume 3, Chapter 14).

Finally, it seems clear from many remarks interspersed throughout the manuscript of Volume 3 that Marx maintained his intention of completing *Capital* with volumes on the state, foreign trade, the world market and crises, although he placed these problems

26. Rosa Luxemburg, *The Accumulation of Capital*, London, 1956, pp. 329–47; Rosdolsky, op. cit., Vol. 1, pp. 86–97.
27. Joan Robinson, *An Essay on Marxian Economics*, London, 1949, pp. viii–ix.

clearly outside the final plan of *Capital* itself.[28] Only when the un-published manuscript of 1861–3 becomes available will we know whether some rough draft of what he intended to develop in these three books does indeed exist somewhere, or whether it was intended as a completely new and further development of his study of bourgeois society.

In view of these changes in the plan of *Capital* as a whole, the final version of the plan of Volume 1 is all the more striking. We should not forget that Volume 1, as edited by Marx, is largely *posterior* to the original and incomplete drafts of Volumes 2 and 3 later to be edited by Engels.[29] It is therefore Volume 1 which allows us the best insight into Marx's view of capitalism.

From the place of Volume 1 in the total final plan of *Capital*, we can immediately draw an answer to two misconceptions which occur again and again in discussion of Marx's economic theory. It is true that according to Marx and Engels capitalists do not exchange the commodities they own on the basis of their value, whereas under petty commodity production exchange of commodities is roughly based upon their value.[30] But it does not follow at all that *Capital* Volume 1, which assumes the exchange of commodities according to their value, is concerned with pre-capitalist commodity production and exchange, and that only in Volume 3 do we start to examine what capitalist commodity circulation is all about. On the contrary, Marx abstracts from the problem of re-distribution of surplus-value among competing capitalists – that is, the problem of the equalization of the rate of profit – in Volume 1 precisely in order to isolate and demonstrate the laws of *capitalist* commodity production and circulation in their 'purest', most fundamental way.

In the same way it is wrong to assume that Volume 1 deals only

28. Karl Marx, *Capital*, Vol. 3, pp. 232, 392, etc.; Rosdolsky, op. cit., Vol. 1, p. 76.
29. According to Maximilien Rubel, the manuscripts for *Capital* Vol. 2 originated between 1865 and 1870, apart from a new version of the first four chapters written in 1877 and a short manuscript of 1879; the manuscripts for Vol. 3 date from 1861–3 and 1865–70 (*Bibliographie des œuvres de Karl Marx*, Paris, 1956, p. 22). We are therefore justified in assuming that, except for the short passages changed in 1877 and 1879, the manuscripts used for editing Vol. 2 and 3 of *Capital* are anterior to the final version of Vol. 1. (See also Engels' introduction to Vol. 2, *MEW* 24, pp. 8–13.)
30. Karl Marx, *Capital*, Vol. 3, pp. 174–5; Friedrich Engels, 'Law of Value and Rate of Profit', ibid. (appendix), p. 876.

with the 'essence' or with 'abstractions', whereas 'concrete' capitalism is analysed only in Volume 3. Nothing could be more 'concrete' and closer to immediately perceived economic data ('appearances') than the analysis of the working day, of wages and of machinery in Volume 1. Commentators here confuse the *type of question* solved in Volume 1 with the *method of answering*. Volume 1 abstracts from capitalist competition, from uneven and combined development and *therefore* from prices of production and equalization of the rate of profit and even more from market prices, in order to reveal the *basic* origin of surplus-value in the process of production, which is a process of consumption of labour-power by capital. But this problem is dealt with by a combination of theoretical insight and empirical verification, by a constant attempt to discover the mediating links between 'essence' and 'appearance', by a thorough analysis of how and why the 'essence' (the value of labour-power) is manifesting itself through the 'appearances' (the fluctuations of real wages).

4. THE PLAN OF VOLUME I

Volume 1 of *Capital* presents itself as a rigorously logical construction. We start from the elementary form of capitalist wealth – the commodity – and its inner contradiction – the contradiction between use-value and exchange-value. Because it is produced by *private* labour, whose social character can no longer be recognized automatically, immediately and directly by society, the commodity can exist only together with a necessary corollary, money, a universal means of exchange. But the analysis of the circulation of commodities accompanied by circulation of money leads to the unfolding of the inner potentialities and contradictions of money: the possibility of exchange-value embodied in money becoming an autonomous economic agent; of money appearing as starting and final point, and not simply intermediary, of a process of circulation; of money bent upon accretion of money, that is of capital.

In pre-capitalist societies, capital appears outside the sphere of production, and hardly ever enters that sphere. It feeds parasitically upon the social surplus product produced and originally appropriated by non-capitalist classes. Here Marx comes to his central point. A basic difference between the capitalist and pre-capitalist modes of production is that under capitalism capital not only appropriates surplus-value; it produces surplus-value. Because he considered this fundamental to an understanding of all aspects of bourgeois society – incidentally, not only the economic but also the political – Marx starts *Capital* with a whole volume devoted to a lengthy analysis of the process of production. For the capitalist process of production is at one and the same time a process of production of value, a process of production of surplus-value, a process of production of capital, and a process of production and constant reproduction of the basic antagonistic social relations: the relation between wage-labour and capital, the compulsion for the proletariat to sell its labour-power to the capitalists, the compulsion for the capitalists to accumulate capital and therefore to maximize the extortion of surplus-value from the workers.

Volume 1 of *Capital* is centred around Marx's basic discovery, the explanation of the 'secret' of surplus-value. There exists one commodity, to wit labour-power, whose use-value for the capitalist is its ability to produce new value larger than its own exchange-value. The 'process of production' which Marx analyses in Volume 1 is, therefore, essentially the process of production of surplus-value.

The production of surplus-value can, however, be examined in a more detailed way only if capital itself is subdivided into constant capital and variable capital. *Constant capital* represents that part of the wealth of the capitalist class with which it acquires and maintains a monopoly of property and access to the material means of production. Thereby it cuts the working class off from any possibility of producing its own livelihood in an independent way. It is a necessary precondition for the production of surplus-value. But it does not produce that surplus-value in and by itself. Only the labour-power of living labour produces additional value, including surplus-value. That is why Marx calls that portion of capital by which the capitalists buy the labour-power of the workers *variable capital*, for only that portion actually produces surplus-value.

The next step in the analysis is the distinction between the production of absolute and of relative surplus-value. Absolute surplus-value is produced by a lengthening of the working day beyond that number of hours during which the worker produces the value which is only the equivalent of his wages. Relative surplus-value is produced by increasing the productivity of labour in the wage-goods industry sector, which enables the worker to reproduce the equivalent of his wages in a shorter portion of the working day, thereby increasing surplus-value without a lengthening of the working day. Marx notes that while the production of absolute surplus-value predominated in the early centuries of the capitalist mode of production (in England, roughly speaking, between the sixteenth century and the first half of the nineteenth), the production of relative surplus-value becomes predominant once the logic of the industrial revolution (of the development of machinery) and the logic of the class struggle between labour and capital fully unfold themselves.

A central section of Part Four of Volume 1 ('The Production of Relative Surplus-Value') is taken up by a lengthy and minute analysis of manufacture and of the modern factory (Chapters 14 and 15). Here the production of surplus-value takes on an important additional dimension. During the stage of manufacturing industry, capital exploits the fruits of an increase in the productivity of labour born from more and more advanced forms of the division of labour. But the *technique of production* remains fundamentally the same. Labour is subdivided in function of the subdivision of the final product produced by manufacture. But beyond these subdivisions no changes occur in the labour process. The main interest for the capitalist during the stage of manufacture is, therefore, the constant direct *control of capital over labour* in order to secure a maximum expenditure of surplus labour with a given level of technique. It is like a workhouse in which the workers lose their freedom to determine their own work rhythm, in which work becomes unfree, forced labour from that point of view also. Many initial manufacturing concerns were indeed literally that: workhouses, filled with labourers who to various degrees had lost their individual freedom.

With the industrial revolution and the emergence of the modern factory, this process of the submission of labour to capital in the course of the process of production is rooted, not only in the hierarchical forms of labour organization, but in the very nature of the production process itself. Inasmuch as production becomes mechanized, it becomes reorganized around machinery. The work rhythm and work content of living labour are subordinated to the mechanical needs of machinery itself. Alienation of labour is no longer only alienation of the products of labour, but alienation of the forms and contents of the work itself.

The explosive potentialities of modern machinery are developed by Marx in three directions simultaneously. Machines are capital's main weapon for subordinating labour to capital in the course of the process of production. Machines are the main weapon for increasing the production of relative surplus-value, thereby relentlessly spurring on the process of accumulation of capital. And labour-saving machines are the main weapon for producing and reproducing the industrial 'reserve army of labour', through which wages are kept fluctuating around the value of the commodity labour-power, and through which the appropriation of surplus-value is normally guaranteed to the capitalists.

Marx, therefore, logically integrates the development of the class struggle between capital and labour into his analysis of the production of surplus-value, inasmuch as he sees that class struggle as originating in that process of production. The extortion of surplus-value from living labour means a struggle by the capitalists to lengthen the working day, to increase the work-load of the workers without increasing wages, to appropriate for capital all the benefits of increased productivity of labour. Conversely, the struggle against capitalist exploitation means, for the workers, a struggle to reduce the working day without any reduction of wages, a struggle for cuts in the work-load, a struggle for increased real wages. How this class struggle against the immediate aspects of capitalist exploitation transforms itself into a struggle for the overthrow of the capitalist system – this question is briefly taken up in the eighth and final part of Volume 1. Part Seven, meanwhile, deals basically with the accumulation of capital, the goal of the whole infernal logic which Marx has laid bare so far. Capital produces surplus-value which in turn is, to a large extent, transformed into additional capital, which in turn produces additional surplus-value. And so on, with all its subsequent contradictory effects for mankind.

If we list the contents of the successive parts of Volume 1, subdividing Part One into its three constituent chapters, we can see how this flawless logic of the analysis unfolds and how it roughly corresponds to the historical process 'stripped of the historical form and diverting chance occurrences'.[31]

I. Starting point: elementary form of capitalist wealth: the commodity

31. Friedrich Engels' review of Marx's *A Contribution to the Critique of Political Economy*. See appendix to volume of that name, London, 1971, p. 225.

(a) the commodity and the realization of its exchange-value, or the process of exchange

(b) the process of exchange and the means of exchange: money

(c) money, necessary mediator of the process of circulation of commodities

II. Money transforming itself into capital, i.e. value searching for an accretion of value, surplus-value; the nature of surplus-value

III. The production of surplus-value: absolute surplus-value

IV. The production of surplus-value: relative surplus-value (from manufacturing to the modern factory system)

V. Relations between wages, productivity of labour and surplus-value; the rate of surplus-value

VI. How the value of labour-power is transformed into wages, their different forms and variations

VII./VIII. The accumulation of capital, i.e. capitalist wealth in its totality: its consequences for labour. The origins of capitalism (the 'primitive accumulation of capital')

At the end of Volume 1 we are back where we started from: capitalist wealth. But now we no longer understand it simply as a sum of 'elementary elements', a mountain of commodities (although it is this mountain also!). We see it now also as the result of a gigantic process of value *production*, of surplus-value *extraction*, out of living labour; as a gigantic movement constantly revolutionizing the means of production, the organization of production, the labour process and the producers themselves. The formula 'capital-value in search of additional value' is now understood as capital organizing a process of self-valorization (*Verwertung*), a process of constant searching for increases in its own value through the unity of the labour process and the process of production of increased value (*Einheit von Arbeitsprozess und Verwertungsprozess*). We thus understand more fully why an analysis of capitalism *has* first to clarify everything which happens in the course of the process of production.[32]

32. The Pelican Marx Library edition of the *Grundrisse* contains a grave and regrettable error of translation. Marx's concept of *Verwertung* (valorization, process of accretion of value) is translated throughout as 'realization of capital'. Marx uses the concept of realization generally only in relation to the realization of the value of commodities (containing, of course, surplus-value). But this problem has its place in the realm of the circulation of commodities and capital, whereas the problem of valorization of capital (the problem of surplus-value or profit in relation to, or as a proportion of, capital) is a basic aspect of the capitalist process of production.

Marx's attitude towards technology, machinery and the factory system has often been misinterpreted, even by authors favourably inclined towards him. It is obviously true that more than any other contemporary economist, sociologist or philosopher, he was aware of the long-range revolutionary effects of machinery upon all aspects of life in bourgeois society. It is also true that his indictment of the inhuman results of the capitalist use of machinery cannot escape anyone who reads Chapters 10, 15 and 25 of *Capital* Volume 1 with a minimum of attention. Is it therefore appropriate to see in Marx a latter-day Luddite, a forerunner of the zero-growth prophets? Or is it true, as others have argued,[33] that Marx was a deep admirer of capitalist technology and put all his hopes in the long-run emancipatory effects of that technology, alone capable of reducing the unavoidable work-load and work-fatigue to which man is condemned?

Marx the dialectician, bent upon an all-sided analysis of capitalism and capitalist technology, avoids both these pitfalls, the conservatively romantic as well as the inhumanly mechanistic one. In classic passages of the *Grundrisse*[34] he underlines the civilizing and progressive aspects of capitalism, its giant impulse to develop the social forces of production, its relentless search for new ways and means to economize on labour, for new needs and new sectors of mass production, which help to unfold man's unlimited possibilities. But simultaneously he shows how the *specific capitalist form* of this development increases tenfold the inhuman potentiality of technology, machinery and exchange-value 'gone mad' (that is, becoming goals in themselves). Capitalism subordinates men to machines instead of using machines to liberate men from the burden of mechanical and repetitive work. It subordinates all social activities to the imperatives of an incessant drive for individual enrichment in terms of money, instead of gearing social life to the development of rich individualities and their social relations. The contradiction between use-value and exchange-value, inherent in every commodity, fully unfolds itself in this contradictory nature of *capitalist* machinery. When capitalism is not overthrown once it has created the material and social preconditions for a classless society of associated producers, this

33. See among others, Kostas Axelos, *Marx, penseur de la technique*, Paris, 1963.
34. Karl Marx, *Grundrisse*, Pelican Marx Library, pp. 325, 527–9, 707–12, etc.

contradiction implies the possibility of a steadily increasing *trans-formation of the forces of production into forces of destruction*, in the most literal sense of the word: not only forces of destruction of wealth (crises and wars), of human wealth and human happiness, but also forces of destruction of life *tout court*.

5. THE MARXIST LABOUR THEORY OF VALUE

No part of Marx's theory has been more assaulted in the academic world during the last seventy-five years than his theory of value. His bourgeois critics show a sharp class instinct here, for this theory is indeed the corner-stone of the whole system. But no contemporary intellectual endeavour has been so obviously based upon a basic misunderstanding as the repeated attacks on the Marxist labour theory of value.[35]

That theory recognizes two aspects of the problem of value, a quantitative and a qualitative one. From a quantitative point of view, the value of a commodity is the quantity of simple labour (skilled labour being reduced to simple labour through a given coefficient) socially necessary for its production (that is, at a given average productivity of labour). From a qualitative point of view, the value of a commodity is determined by *abstract* human labour – commodities which have been produced by *private* labour become commensurate only inasmuch as society abstracts from the concrete and specific aspect of each individual private craft or branch of industry and equalizes all these labours as abstract social labour, regardless of the specific use-value of each commodity.

In order to understand this theory, it is sufficient to formulate the question to which Marx tried to give an answer. The problem is as follows. Man has to work in order to satisfy his material needs, to 'produce his material life'. The way in which the labour of all producers in a given society is divided among different branches of material production will determine the extent to which different needs can be fulfilled. Hence, given a certain set of needs, a rough equilibrium between needs and output requires a

35. The 'classical' attack by Böhm-Bawerk was answered by Hilferding (both are printed together in Böhm-Bawerk, op. cit.). Other similar attacks were made by Pareto (op. cit., pp. 40 ff.), Michael von Tugan-Baranovsky (*Theoretische Grundlagen des Marxismus*, Leipzig, 1905, pp. 139 ff.), and others. A more recent one is contained in Joan Robinson, op. cit., and is effectively answered by Rosdolsky, op. cit., Vol. 2, pp. 626–40.

distribution of labour (of 'labour inputs') between these various branches of production in a given proportion, and in that only. In a primitive society, or in a fully developed socialist one, this distribution of labour inputs occurs in a consciously planned way: in a primitive society, on the basis of habits, custom, tradition, magico-ritual processes, decisions by elders etc.; in a socialist one, on the basis of a democratic selection of priorities by the mass of the associated producers-consumers themselves. But under capitalism, where labour has become private labour, where products of labour are commodities produced independently from each other by thousands of independent firms, no conscious decision pre-establishes such an equilibrium of inputs of labour and socially recognized needs (under capitalism this implies, of course, that only those needs expressed through effective demand are socially recognized). Equilibrium is reached only accidentally, through the operation of blind market forces. Price fluctuations, to which academic economists remain glued, are in the most favourable hypothesis only signals which indicate whether this equilibrium is being shaken, by what pressure and in what direction. They do not explain *what* is being equilibrated and *which* is the driving force behind all these myriad fluctuations. It is precisely this question which Marx tried to answer with his perfected labour theory of value.

From this approach it is immediately clear that, contrary to what so many of his critics starting with the Austrian Böhm-Bawerk assumed, Marx never intended to explain short-term price fluctuations on the market with his theory of value.[36] (Probably he intended to raise some of the problems involved in short-term price fluctuations in the never-written Volume 6 of the original plan for *Capital*.) Nor does it make any sense to speak of the labour theory of value, as explained in Volume 1 of *Capital*, as a 'micro-economic theory' allegedly in contrast with the 'macro-economic' labour theory of value in Volume 3. What Marx tried to discover was a *hidden key behind price fluctuations*, the atoms inside the molecule so to speak. He moved the whole economic analysis to a different and higher level of abstraction. His question was not: *how does* Sammy run (what movements do his legs and body make while running), but *what makes* Sammy run.

It follows that 99 per cent of the criticism directed against the

36. Böhm-Bawerk, op. cit., pp. 29–30; Samuelson, op. cit., p. 620; Tugan-Baranovsky, op. cit., p. 141.

Marxist labour theory of value is entirely beside the point, especially when it tries to 'refute' the first pages of Chapter 1 of *Capital* Volume 1, which have sometimes been construed as a 'proof' of that theory.[37] To say that commodities have qualities in common other than the fact that they are products of social labour transforms an analysis of social relations into a logical parlour game. Obviously, these 'other qualities' have nothing to do with the *nexus* between members of society in an anarchic market economy. The fact that both bread and aeroplanes are 'scarce' does not make them commensurable. Even when thousands of people are dying of hunger, and the 'intensity of need' for bread is certainly a thousand times greater than the 'intensity of need' for aeroplanes, the first commodity will remain immensely cheaper than the second, because much less socially necessary labour has been spent on its production.

The question has often been asked: why bother at all with this type of inquiry? Why can one not restrict 'economics' to the analysis of what actually occurs in day-to-day economic life (under capitalism, it goes without saying) – the ups and downs of prices, wages, interest rates, profits etc., instead of trying to discover mysterious 'forces beneath the surface of the economy' which are supposed to govern actual economic events, but only on a very high level of abstraction and in the very final analysis?

This neo-positivist approach is curiously and typically unscientific. Nobody dealing with medicine, not to speak of other physical sciences, would dare for fear of becoming a laughing stock to ask: 'Why bother to look for the "deeper causes" of diseases, when one can collect symptoms to establish a diagnosis?' Obviously no real understanding of economic development is possible if one does not try to discover precisely what 'lies behind' immediate appearances. Laws about immediate short-term fluctuations of prices on the market cannot explain why, to give an interesting example, one kilogram of gold buys in 1974 nearly twice as many given baskets of American consumer commodities as seventy years ago (the average consumer price index has risen somewhat more than fivefold compared to 1904, whereas the price of gold on the free market has risen nine times). Obviously this basic movement of prices in the long run has something to do with the different dynamics of the long-term social productivity of

37. Böhm-Bawerk, op. cit., pp. 65–80; Joseph Schumpeter, *Capitalism, Socialism and Democracy*, London, 1962, pp. 23–4.

labour in the various consumer industries on the one hand and in the gold-mining industry on the other; that is, with the laws of value as formulated by Marx.

Once we understand that the famous 'invisible hand' which is supposed to regulate supply and demand on the market is nothing but the operation of that same law of value, we can tie together a whole series of economic processes which otherwise remain disconnected pieces of analysis. Money born out of exchange can serve as a universal equivalent of the value of commodities only because it is itself a commodity with its own intrinsic value (or, in the case of paper money, represents a commodity with its own intrinsic value). Monetary theory is re-united with the theory of value and the theory of capital accumulation. The ups and downs of the trade cycle appear as the mechanism through which upheavals in the value of commodities end by asserting themselves, with the painful devalorization (loss of value) this entails, not only for the 'infantry' of the commodity army, the individual mass of finished consumer goods sold on a day-to-day basis, but also for its 'heavy artillery', that is, large-scale machinery, fixed capital. The theory of economic growth, of the 'trade cycle', of capitalist crises, the theory of the rate of profit and of its tendency to decline – everything flows in the last analysis from this operation of the law of value. So the question whether it has any use at all in economic analysis is, therefore, as meaningless as the question whether you need the concept of basic particles (atoms, etc.) in physics. Indeed, no coherent and consistent analysis of the capitalist economy in its totality, explaining all the basic laws of motion of that system, is possible without 'elementary principles' organized around the value of commodities.

In Marxist economic theory, the 'law of value' fulfils a triple function. In the first place it *governs* (which does not mean that it determines here and now) the exchange relations between commodities; that is to say, it establishes the *axis* around which *long-term changes* in relative prices of commodities oscillate. (This includes under capitalism also the exchange relation between capital and labour, an extremely important point to which we shall return presently.) In the second place it determines the relative proportions of total social labour (and this implies, in the last analysis, total material resources of society) devoted to the output of different groups of commodities. In this way, the law of value distributes in the final analysis material resources over different branches of production (and of social activity in general) according to the division of 'effective demand' for different groups of commodities, it being always understood that this occurs within the framework of antagonistic class relations of production and distribution. In the third place it rules economic growth, by determining the average rate of profit and directing investment towards those firms and sectors of production where profit is above average, and away from those firms and sectors where profit is below average. Again, these movements of capital and investment correspond in the final analysis to conditions of 'economy' and 'waste' of social labour, that is to the workings of the law of value.

Marx's labour theory of value is a further development and perfection of the labour theory of value as it emanated from the 'classical' school of political economy, and especially of Ricardo's version. But the changes Marx brought into that theory were manifold. One especially was to be decisive: the use of the concept of *abstract social labour* as the foundation of his theory of value. It is for this reason that Marx cannot be considered as in any way an 'advanced neo-Ricardian'. 'Labour quantities as the essence of value' is something quite different from 'labour quantities as *numéraire*' – a common measuring rod of the value of all commodities. The distinction between concrete labour, which determines the use-value of commodities, and abstract labour, which determines their value, is a revolutionary step forward beyond Ricardo of which Marx was very proud; indeed he considered it his main achievement, together with the discovery of the *general* category of surplus-value, encompassing profit, rent and interest. It is based on an understanding of the peculiar structure of a society of commodity-producers, that is of the key problem of how to relate to each other the segments of the global labour potential of society which have taken the form of private labour. It represents, therefore, together with Marx's concept of necessary labour and surplus labour (necessary product and surplus product), the key nexus between economic theory and the science of social revolution, historical materialism.

The way in which the Marxist labour theory of value sharply excludes use-value from any direct determination of value and exchange-value has often been interpreted as a rejection by Marx of use-value beyond the boundary of economic analysis and theory altogether. This does not correspond at all to the rich dialectical complexity of *Capital*. When we deal with the problems of reproduction, in the introduction to Volume 2, we shall have occasion to dwell on the specific way in which the contradiction between use-value and exchange-value *has* to be bridged under capitalism, in order to make economic growth at all possible. Here, we only want to stress that, for Marx, the commodity was understood as encompassing *both* a unity and a contradiction between use-value and exchange-value: a good with no use-value for any potential buyer could not realize its exchange-value; and the specific *use-value* of two categories of commodities, means of production and labour-power, played a key role in his analysis of the capitalist mode of production.

As has already been stated, the law of value fundamentally expresses the fact that in a society based upon private property and private labour (in which economic decision-making is fragmented between thousands of independent firms and millions of independent 'economic agents') social labour cannot immediately be recognized as such. If Mr Jones has his workers produce 100,000 pairs of shoes a year he knows that people need shoes and buy them; he even knows, if he bothers to do his homework, that the annual number of shoes sold in the United Kingdom (and all those countries to which he intends to export his output) vastly outdistances the modest figure of 100,000 pairs. But he has no way of knowing whether the *specific* 100,000 pairs of shoes he owns will find specific customers willing and able to buy them. Only after selling his shoes and receiving their equivalent can he say (provided he has realized the average rate of profit on his invested capital): my workers have truly spent socially necessary labour in my factory. If part of the produced shoes remain unsold, or if they are sold at a loss or at a profit significantly less than the average, this means that part of the labour spent on their production has not been recognized by society as socially necessary labour, has in fact been wasted labour from the point of view of society as a whole.

But this 'recognition of' or 'refusal to recognize' a given quantity of labour by society occurs exclusively in function of meeting effective demand on the market, that is it is independent of the use-value or social usefulness of the specific physical qualities of a given commodity. Society recognizes quantities of labour spent in its production, making abstraction of these considerations. That is why Marx called these quantities, quantities of abstract socially necessary labour. If a pound of opium, a box of dum-dum bullets or a portrait of Hitler find customers on the market, the labour which has been spent on their output is socially necessary labour; its production has been value-production. If, on the contrary, an exquisite piece of china or a new pharmaceutical product for some reason does not find customers, its production has created no value, has been equivalent to a waste of social labour – even if, in some distant future, their creators will be celebrated as geniuses or benefactors of mankind. The labour theory of value has nothing to do with judgements on the usefulness of things from the point of view of human happiness or social progress. It has even less to do with establishing 'conditions for justice in exchange'. It simply recognizes the deeper meaning of the actual act of exchange and of the output of commodities under capitalism, and what governs the distribution of income between social classes which results from these acts, independently of any moral, aesthetic or political judgement. Indeed, if one were to look for such 'judgements', one would have to say that Marx, while understanding why the law of value has to operate as it does under commodity production, did not at all strive to 'defend' that law, but on the contrary to build a society in which its operations would be totally abolished.

One of the most common and innocuous objections made against Marx's labour theory of value runs along these lines: if prices are governed in the last analysis by value (socially necessary quantities of abstract labour), how can goods have prices if they are not products of labour, that is if they have no value? Marx himself in fact answered that objection long before drafting *Capital* Volume 1.[38] Products of nature ('free goods'), which have indeed no value since no social labour has been spent on their production, can get a price through private appropriation, through the social institution of private property. Land on which no human hand has ever worked to increase its fertility has no value. But it can get a price if it is surrounded by a fence upon which is put a placard 'Private property: Trespassing forbidden', and if people are ready to pay that price because they need that land as a source of livelihood. This price will in reality be the capitalization of the net income (land rent) accruing to its owner, income produced by those who will farm it and draw material resources (goods for self-consumption or commodities) from it through their toil.[39]

38. See *A Contribution to the Critique of Political Economy*, p. 62.
39. Again and again the objection has been raised against the Marxist labour theory of value that it 'assumes' labour to be the only scarce factor of

In reaction against all those who mistakenly claimed that Volume 1 of *Capital* was concerned with showing that commodities actually exchange under capitalism according to the quantities of abstract socially necessary labour they contain, some authors have contended that the labour theory of value is concerned only with a *qualitative* problem and not with a *quantitative* one, the 'socially necessary' labour content of commodities being unmeasurable. This bends the stick too far in the other direction. It is true that the quantitative measurement of the labour quantities in commodities is difficult. But the difficulty is not so much a conceptual one (one could, for example, start from macro-economic aggregates, the total sum of man-hours spent in the whole realm of material production – industry, agriculture and commodity transport – in a given country, its division between different branches of industry and key groups of commodities, their interrelationship through an input-output table, the labour spent for the average unit produced in 'autarchic' branches where no raw material has to be imported from foreign lands, and so climb up towards an estimate of total labour expenditure per branch and per commodity produced . . .) as one stemming from a lack of accurate information. It will be necessary to 'open the books' of all capitalist enterprises and to verify these figures on the basis of shop-floor evidence in order to approach a quantitative

---

production and supposes either that land and machines are abundant or that they can be excluded altogether from value analysis. This is obviously nonsense. Leontief makes the correct point that Marx was probably the first economist to give fixed capital a central importance in the process of production, as against, for example, Böhm-Bawerk (op. cit., p. 93). What Marx does assume is that machines cannot in and by themselves 'command' portions of the total available labour-power of society to be additionally expended or to move from one sector of production to another – a proposition which is rather self-evident, besides having been scientifically proved by Marx. Once one understands that, for Marx, value is in the last analysis assignment of portions of the socially available labour-power, total value newly produced being equal to total expenditure of living labour in a given period, one solves the riddle. Incidentally, one should also understand that Marx, advancing beyond classical economy, did not 'dissolve' the value of the annual product into wages and surplus-value (profits, rents and interests), but added to this the value of raw materials and machinery used up in the process of production. His only point was that this part of the annual product's value did not increase in the process of production but was only maintained, the only source of *new* value being living labour.

measurement of the labour content of commodities in capitalist countries.[40]

6. MARX'S KEY DISCOVERY: HIS THEORY OF SURPLUS-VALUE

The classical school of political economy, including Ricardo, saw profits as a residual net income, once wages had been paid. Indeed, so strict was their adherence to this concept that Ricardo believed that only increases or decreases in production costs in the wage-good industries could influence the rate of profit. Whatever happened to the luxury goods industry, or even to raw materials, would not affect the global rate of profit.

This view is incomplete and therefore incorrect, But it was at least an attempt to come to grips with the problem of income distribution between social classes as a function of what happens in the course of production. The exponents of post-Ricardian 'vulgar' economic theory, and especially the neo-classical marginalists, do not bother to ask the question 'why?', they are content just to answer the question 'how?'. They simply note that 'factors' (labour, capital, land) get different 'prices' on the market, and limit themselves to a study of how these prices fluctuate. To consider the *origins* of profit, interest and rent; to ask whether workers *must* abandon part of the product of their labour when they work for an alien entrepreneur; to examine the mechanisms through which this appropriation occurs as a result of an honest-to-god act of exchange, without any cheating or plotting: it was left to Marx to unravel these basic questions about the capitalist mode of production.

The origin of the income and consumption of the ruling classes in pre-capitalist societies is no matter of speculation. Anybody knows that, from an economic point of view, they were the results of appropriation of part of the fruits of the producers' labour by the ruling class. When the medieval serf worked half the week for his own livelihood on the land of his manse, and the other half of the week without remuneration on the estate of the noble or the church, one could argue that, from a 'moral' point of view, he was offering unpaid labour 'in exchange' for the 'service' of profane or divine protection. But nobody would confuse this 'exchange' with what goes on in the market place. It was in fact no economic

40. Friedrich Engels' insert in *Capital*, Vol. 3, pp. 74–6.

exchange at all, in any sense of the word, no give-and-take of anything which can be 'priced', in even the most indirect way. The 'service of protection' is not 'bought' by the serf any more than a small Chicago businessman 'buys a service' from a gang of hoodlums. It is an extortion imposed upon him by the social set-up, whether he likes it or not. The origin of the social surplus product accruing to the pre-capitalist ruling class is, therefore, obviously unpaid labour (whether in the form of labour services, or of physical products of these labour services, or even of money-rent) expended by the producers.

In the case of slavery, the context is as clear if not clearer, especially in those extreme examples where even the miserable pittance of the slave was not provided by the masters, but had to be provided by the slave himself on the seventh day of the week. Indeed, regarding these slave plantations, even the most sceptical critics of historical materialism will find it hard to doubt that the whole social product, the part which fed the slaves as well as the part which fed the masters, had but one origin: social labour expended by the slaves and by them alone.

When, however, we look at the capitalist mode of production, everything seems much more complicated and much more obscure, to say the least. No brutal force, personified by an overseer with a whip or some group of armed men, appears to force the worker to give up anything he has produced or owns himself. His relationship with the capitalist appears to be based upon an act of exchange which is identical to that of a small artisan or a farmer, owners of commodities they themselves have produced, who meet in the market place. The worker appears to sell his 'labour' in exchange for a wage. The capitalist 'combines' that labour with machines, raw material and the labour of other men to produce finished products. As the capitalist owns these machines and raw materials, as well as the money to pay the wages, is it not 'natural' that he should also own the finished products which result from the 'combination of these factors'?

This is what *appears* to occur under capitalism. However, probing below the surface, Marx comes up with a series of striking observations which can only be denied if one deliberately refuses to examine the unique social conditions which create the very peculiar and exceptional 'exchange' between labour and capital. In the first place, there is an institutional inequality of conditions between capitalists and workers. The capitalist is not *forced* to buy labour-power on a continuous basis. He does it only if it is profitable to him. If not, he prefers to wait, to lay off workers, or even to close his plant down till better times. The worker, on the other hand (the word is used here in the social meaning made clear precisely by this sentence, and not necessarily in the stricter sense of manual labourer), is *under economic compulsion* to sell his labour-power. As he has no access to the means of production, including land, as he has no access to any large-scale free stock of food, and as he has no reserves of money which enable him to survive for any length of time while doing nothing, he *must* sell his labour-power to the capitalist on a continuous basis and at the current rate. Without such institutionalized compulsion, a fully developed capitalist society would be impossible. Indeed, once such compulsion is absent (for example where large tracts of free land subsist), capitalism will remain dwarfed until, by hook or by crook, the bourgeois class suppresses access to that free land. The last chapter of *Capital* Volume 1, on colonization, develops this point to great effect. The history of Africa, especially of South Africa, but also of the Portuguese, Belgian, French and British colonies, strikingly confirms this analysis.[41] If people are living under conditions where there is no *economic* compulsion to sell their labour-power, then repressive *juridical* and *political* compulsion has to deliver the necessary manpower to the entrepreneurs; otherwise capitalism could not survive under these circumstances.

The function of trade unions, be it said in passing, is immediately clarified in the light of this analysis. Workers who combine to set up a reserve fund can be freed at least for some weeks from the compulsion to sell their labour-power on a continuous basis at the given market rate. Capitalism does not like that at all. It is contrary to 'nature'; if not to human nature, then at least to the deeper nature of bourgeois society. That is why, under robust nascent capitalism, trade unions were simply banned. That is also why, under senile capitalism, we are gradually returning to a situation in which workers are denied the right to strike – the

41. We refer here to the large-scale appropriation of land by white settlers and colonial companies, the herding together of Africans into 'reserves', the imposition of money taxes in essentially non-monetary economies, forcing the Africans to sell their labour-power in order to get the necessary money to pay taxes, the imposition of large-scale money fines, or even direct forced labour penalties for innumerable transgressions of laws specially designed to furnish the settlers with labour-power, etc., etc.

right to abstain from selling their labour-power at the offered price whenever they like. In this instance, Marx's insight is clearly confirmed by the highest authorities of the bourgeois state: under capitalism, labour is fundamentally *forced* labour. Whenever possible, capitalists prefer hypocritically to cloak the compulsion under a smokescreen of 'equal and just exchange' on the 'labour market'. When hypocrisy is no longer possible, they return to what they began with: naked coercion.

Marx, of course, was perfectly well aware of the fact that, in order to organize production in modern factories, it was not enough to combine the social labour-power of manual and intellectual workers. It was necessary to provide for land, buildings, energy, infrastructural elements like roads and water, machinery, a given fabric of organized society, means of communication, etc. But it is obviously absurd to presume that, because factory production is impossible without these conditions of production, roads and canals therefore 'produce value'. It is no more logical to assume that machines 'produce' any value, in and by themselves. Of all these 'factors' it can be said only that their given value has to be maintained and reproduced, through incorporation of part of it in the current output of living labour, during the production process.

We come nearer to the truth when we note that *property titles* (private appropriation rights) to land and machinery lead to a situation where these 'factors' will not be incorporated into the process of production without their proprietors receiving an expected 'return' over and above the compensation for the wear and tear of the 'factors'. This is obviously true. But it does not follow at all that such 'returns' are then 'produced' by the property titles. Nor does it imply that owners of such property titles meet the owners of labour-power on an equal footing. Only if we were in a 'capitalistic slave society', where owners of slaves hired out labour-power to owners of factories renting land from landed proprietors, could one say that institutional equality existed between all owners – though, of course, not between owners and slaves! Obviously, in that case, the slave owners would hire out their slaves only if they received a 'net return' *over and above the upkeep of the slaves*.

In the second place, the social situation in which a small part of society has monopolized property and access to the means of production, to the exclusion of all or nearly all direct producers, is in no way a product of 'natural inequality of talents and inclinations' among human beings. Indeed, it did not exist for tens of thousands of years of social life on the part of *homo sapiens*. Even in the relatively recent past, say 150 years ago, nine-tenths of the producers on this planet – who were in their overwhelming majority agricultural producers – did have direct access, in one way or another, to their means of production and livelihood. The separation of the producer from his means of production was a long and bloody historical process, analysed in detail by Marx in Part Eight of *Capital* Volume 1, 'So-Called Primitive Accumulation'.

In the third place, the worker does not sell the capitalist his labour, but his *labour-power*, his capacity to work for a given period of *time*. This labour-power becomes a commodity under capitalism.[42] As such it has a specific value (exchange-value), as any other commodity does: the quantity of social labour necessary to reproduce it – that is to say the value of the consumer goods necessary to keep the worker and his children in condition to continue to work at a given level of intensity of effort. But it has a

42. Obviously Marx did not 'transform' men into 'commodities', as so many of his 'ethical' opponents accuse him of doing. He noted that *capitalism* had operated such a transformation and therefore condemned capitalism. Popper significantly contends that 'the value theory [of Marx] . . . considers human labour as fundamentally different from all other processes in nature, for example from the labour of animals. This shows clearly that the theory is based ultimately upon a moral theory, the doctrine that human suffering and a human lifetime spent is a thing [!] fundamentally different from all natural processes . . . I do not deny that this theory is right in the moral sense . . . But I also think that an economic analysis should not be based upon a moral or metaphysical or religious doctrine of which the holder is unconscious' (*The Open Society*, Vol. 2, p. 329). In the first place, Marx was not at all unconscious of the differences between human labour and the endeavours of animals such as ants; he comments on it in the first chapter of *Capital* Vol. 1. In the second place, there is nothing metaphysical about the fact that, when men engage in mutual social relations in order to produce their livelihood, they will certainly consider human labour, as the basis of this social organization, quite differently from natural processes, fertility of the soil or of cattle, etc. There is nothing metaphysical about the distinction, *from man's point of view*, between chemical processes in trees and the necessary arrangements to divide the total labour time available to the community between different types of human activity. Two thousand years ago, defenders of the institution of slavery used to equate slaves with 'speaking instruments', or 'speaking beasts of toil'. We know very well that Popper does not condone slavery. Would he then say that this condemnation of slavery is purely 'metaphysical', or would he admit that it is based upon a scientific, anthropological distinction between man and animals?

special quality, a special 'use-value' for the capitalist. When the capitalist 'consumes' labour-power in the process of production, the *worker produces value*. His labour has the double capacity to *conserve value* – that is, to transfer into the finished product the value of the raw material and of a fraction of the machinery used up in this process of production – and to *create new value*, by spending itself. The whole mystery of the origin of profits and rents is over once one understands that, in the process of production, the workers can (and must – otherwise the capitalist would not hire them) produce value over and above the value of their own labour-power, over and above the equivalent of the wages which they receive. We are back where we started in pre-capitalist societies, and we have been able to eliminate the cobweb of apparent 'exchange equality': like feudal rent or the slave-owner's livelihood, capitalist profits, interests and rents originate from the *difference between what the workers produce and what they receive for their upkeep*. Under capitalism this difference appears in the form of value, and not of physical output. This fact prevents the process from being immediately transparent. But it does not make it fundamentally different from the 'exchange' taking place between feudal lord and serf.

It is therefore incorrect to state, as does Blaug, following other academic critics of Marx, that Marx's theory of surplus-value is a theory of 'unearned increment'.[43] It is an *appropriation* or *deduction theory* of the capitalists' income, as was the classical labour theory of value. Capitalists appropriate value which the workers have already produced, prior to the process of circulation of commodities and of distribution of income. No value can be distributed – from a macro-economic point of view, in other words viewing bourgeois society as a whole – which has not been previously produced.

Marx himself considered the discovery of the concept of surplus-value, representing the sum total of profits, interests and rents of all parts of the bourgeois class, as his main theoretical discovery.[44]

43. Mark Blaug, 'Technical Change and Marxian Economics', *Kyklos* Vol. 3, 1960, quoted in Horowitz, op. cit., p. 227.

44. 'Das Beste an meinem Buch ist 1. (darauf beruht *alles* Verständnis der facts) der gleich im *Ersten* Kapitel hervorgehobne *Doppelcharakter der Arbeit*, je nachdem sie sich in Gebrauchswert oder Tauschwert ausdrückt; 2. die Behandlung des *Mehrwerts unabhängig von seinen besondren* Formen als Profit, Zins, Grundrente etc. Namentlich in 2. Band wird dies sich zeigen' (Marx, letter to Engels of 24 August 1868, *MEW* 31, p. 326).

It ties together the historical science of society and the science of the capitalist economy, explaining both the origins and content of the class struggle and the dynamic of capitalist society.[45]

For once we understand that surplus-value is *produced* by workers, that surplus-value is nothing but the age-old social surplus product *in money form*, in the form of value, we understand the historical leap which occurred when that social surplus product no longer appeared essentially in the form of luxury goods (of which consumption is necessarily limited, even under conditions of such extreme extravagance as during the Roman Empire or in the eighteenth-century French court) but in the form of money. More money means not only additional purchasing power for such luxury goods, but additional purchasing power for more machines, more raw materials, more labour-power. Here too Marx discovered an economic compulsion. Private property, the fragmentation of social labour among various firms, that is, the very nature of generalized commodity production – capitalism – implies a compulsion to compete for shares of the market. The need to accumulate capital, the need to increase the extraction of surplus-value, the unquenchable thirst for surplus-value which characterizes capitalism, it is all here: the accumulation of capital=the transformation of surplus-value into additional capital.

Again, as for value, we should note what this is all about: command over fractions of the total disposable quantity of social labour. It is sufficient to recall this basic fact to understand how misplaced are criticisms of the theory of surplus-value which speak about the 'productivity of capital', capital being understood as machines.[46] Machines can never, in and by themselves, hire any

45. Popper (*The Open Society*, Vol. 2, p. 160) contends that Marx did not discover the general category of surplus-value at all, but inherited it from Ricardo. He quotes Engels' introduction to Vol. 2 of *Capital* in that respect. Engels says nothing of the kind. He states, as any student of economic doctrines knows, that a long series of economists, from Adam Smith and the physiocrats to Ricardo and the post-Ricardian anti-capitalists of the eighteen twenties and thirties in Britain, considered profits and rents to be subtractions from the products of 'productive labour'. But only Marx succeeded in showing *what kind of labour* produces surplus-value and what the real content of the process of surplus-value production is, irrespective of its specific forms, and in *explaining* this process.

46. Samuelson, following Böhm-Bawerk, derives this 'productivity of capital' from the fact that 'you can get more future consumption product by using indirect or roundabout methods' (*Economics, an Introductory Analysis*, New York, 4th edition, pp. 576–7). In the explanation which follows, the

fraction of the disposable social labour force, except in science fiction. In the more prosaic world in which we live, *men* owning machines can, for that reason, hire and fire other men. How the product of the labour of these men is then divided, and why, is what Marx seeks to explain.

Of course, Marx did not 'deny' that machinery could increase the social productivity of labour. On the contrary, if one reads Chapter 15 of *Capital* Volume 1, one will see immediately that he was more aware of that potential of technology than any economist among his contemporaries. But the question which most of his critics and other exponents of 'vulgar' economics overlook is very simple, namely, why should the results of the increased productivity of labour be appropriated by the capitalist? Why should the combined productivity of many men working together – the famous 'collective labour potential of the factory' to which a key analysis is devoted in the original Part Seven ('Chapter Six') omitted from the published version of *Capital* Volume 1 (see appendix to this volume, pp. 943–1084) – the combined productivity of scientists and technologists, workers by hand and brain, inventors of machinery and flexers of muscle, increase the profit of the owners of machinery? Surely not because that machinery has some mysterious quality of 'creating' value, that is of 'creating' quantities of socially necessary labour?[47] Surely rather because the owners are in a position to appropriate the products of that combination. So we are back to Marx's theory of surplus-value.

An interesting, if somewhat astounding, innovation in apologetics for capitalist profits has recently occurred in the form of the theory of the firm developed by Alchian and Demsetz.[48] Owners of different 'co-operating inputs' are supposed to have a natural tendency to shirk, because they give some preference to 'non-

'increment', however, originates from the fact that 'current consumption' is 'sacrificed' for the production of 'intermediate goods'. But it is *people* who forgo consumption (we leave aside *which* people really are forced into abstinence). People *produce* intermediate goods. People increase the productivity of their *labour*. How all these *human* operations suddenly lead to value oozing out of 'intermediate goods' (called 'productivity of capital') is a mystifying secret which Samuelson does not solve.

47. The only quality machines have 'in and of themselves' is to increase the productivity of labour and thereby to *decrease* the value of commodities – not to 'create' value.

48. A. Alchian and H. Demsetz, 'Production, Information Costs and Economic Organisation', *American Economic Review*, 1972.

pecuniary goods' (!) such as leisure, attractive working conditions and time to converse with fellow workers. It follows, according to Alchian and Demsetz, that if shirking is to be checked someone must have both the right to monitor the performance of team members and the disinclination to shirk himself. To this end he must have the right to receive the *residue* after all other inputs have been paid contractual amounts, the right to terminate membership of the team and the right to sell these rights. After having received with great joy the good tidings that he has now been promoted to the status of member of a 'co-operative team', on an equal footing with the capitalist, the average worker cannot fail to wonder for what mysterious reason the 'someone' who gets all these 'economically necessary rights' is *always* the owner of the 'input – means of production' and *never* the owner of the 'input – labour-power'. Would it be because the capitalist is free from the human vice of shirking, or has no inclination to leisure or attractive working conditions? Or is it perhaps because Messrs Apologists for Capitalism are trying to argue away the fact of surplus-value appropriation through monopoly ownership of the means of production?

7. MARX'S THEORY OF CAPITAL

Capital is thus, from the Marxist point of view, a *social relation between men* which appears as a relation between things or between men and things. Flowing logically from Marx's labour theory of value and theory of surplus-value, this is another of the key discoveries which opposes his economic theory radically to all forms of academic 'economics'.

Marx energetically rejects the idea, as expounded by 'vulgar' and neo-classical economists, that 'capital' is just 'any stock of wealth' or 'any means to increase labour productivity'.[49] A chimpanzee using a stick to get at bananas is no more the first capitalist than a tribal community learning to accrue its wealth through animal husbandry or land irrigation is 'accumulating capital'. Capital presupposes that goods are not being produced for direct consumption by the producing communities, but are sold as commodities; that the total labour potential of society has become fragmented into private labours conducted independently

49. Joseph Schumpeter, *History of Economic Analysis*, New York, 1954, pp. 558–9.

of each other; that commodities therefore have value; that this value is realized through exchange with a special commodity called money; that it can therefore start an independent process of circulation, being property of a given class of society whose members operate as owners of value looking for increments of value. If, as Adam Smith explained to successive generations of students of economic phenomena, productive (technical) *division of labour* is a source of increased labour productivity – to a large extent independently from the specific social form of organization of the economy – then capital is not a product of that division of labour, but of a *social division of labour*, in which owners of accumulated value face non-owners.

Joseph Schumpeter reproached Marx with having elaborated a theory of capital which was unable to explain the origins of capital.[50] Nothing is further from the truth. Marx the dialectician perfectly understood the difference between, on the one hand, the production and reproduction of capital on the basis of the capitalist mode of production and, on the other, the origins and development of capital in pre-capitalist modes of production. Indeed, one of the essential objections to the imprecise and unscientific handling of categories by 'vulgar' economists was their undifferentiated use of the terms 'capital' and 'capitalism' as more or less synonymous. *Capitalism* is the capitalist mode of production, the seizure of the means of production by capital, which has become predominant in the sphere of production. *Capital* is value (initially in the form of money) becoming an independent operator in the pores of a non-capitalist mode of production. Capital appears initially as usury and merchant (long-distance trade) capital. After a long historical process, and only under specific social conditions, does capital victoriously penetrate the sphere of production in the form of manufacturing capital. (This occurred in the late fifteenth and sixteenth centuries in Western Europe; in the eighteenth century in Japan. In China, *isolated elements* of manufacturing capital had probably already appeared more than a thousand years earlier.)

In simple commodity production, capital does not *produce* surplus-value. It simply transforms into surplus-value parts of current output and revenue which originate independently from capital. It can appropriate part of the social surplus product normally passing into the hands of pre-capitalist ruling classes (for

50. Schumpeter, *Capitalism, Socialism and Democracy*, pp. 15–18.

instance the appropriation, through usury, of part of the feudal land rent). It can appropriate part of the product which normally serves as a consumption fund for the producers themselves. The basic characteristic of these operations of capital under pre-capitalist relations of production is that it will barely increase the global wealth of society; it will neither significantly develop productive forces nor stimulate economic growth. It can only have a disintegrating effect on the given pre-capitalist social order, precipitating the ruin of several social classes. However, by accelerating the transformation of goods produced and consumed as use-values only into commodities, that is by accelerating the spread of money economy, it can historically prepare the ground for an eventual appearance of the capitalist mode of production.

Capital operating in pre-capitalist modes of production refers essentially to a theory of money circulation and appropriation. This is why in Volume 1 of *Capital* Marx first introduces capital in Part Two, *after* having explained the nature of money. Indeed, Part Two is entitled 'The Transformation of Money into Capital'. Here again, the logical analysis corresponds to the historical process, to which Marx continually refers, albeit for the most part in footnotes. On the other hand, capital operating in the capitalist mode of production, the real object of study of *Capital*, refers obviously to a theory of production and appropriation of value and surplus-value. Marx explains in Volume 1, Chapter 24, how the law of appropriation of commodities is transformed when we pass from a society of petty commodity producers to a capitalist society. In the first case, the direct producers are owners of the products of their labour; in the second, the owners of capital become the owners of the products of the labour of the direct producers. Apologists for capitalism try to justify this fact by the argument that, after all, capitalists 'place at the disposal' of the workers the tools with which production occurs.[51] But again history allows us to pierce through the hypocrisy of the argument. For capitalism was not born – in the days of manufacturing – with the capitalist 'putting at the disposal of the producers' any new machinery. It was born with the capitalists *expropriating* the tools

51. For example, MacCord Wright, *Capitalism*, New York, 1951, p. 135. In the 'Results of the Immediate Process of Production', Marx shows how mystifyingly capitalism represents increases in the *social productivity of labour*, through *social* developments like scientific progress, co-operation of many workers, etc. as results of the 'productivity of capital'.

owned by the producers themselves and assembling these very tools under a common roof.[52]

Capital, under the capitalist mode of production, is therefore value constantly increased by surplus-value, which is produced by productive labour and appropriated by capitalists through the appropriation of the commodities produced by the workers in factories owned by capitalists. The way in which this analysis of capital and capitalism hinges on the institution of private property has often been misunderstood or (and) misrepresented, both by critics and by disciples of Marx. It therefore merits some comment.

Historically and logically, capitalism is tied to the private ownership of the means of production, which allows private appropriation of produced commodities, thus private appropriation of surplus-value, and thus private accumulation of capital. It is surely not accidental that the 'rights of private property' are thus at the bottom of the whole constitutional and juridical superstructure which centuries of law-making have erected upon the basis of commodity production.

But what we confront when we examine the social relations which lie behind these juridical forms is, of course, something which is not simply formal private property; otherwise the analysis would be reduced to simple tautology. When Marx states that commodity production is only possible because social labour has been fragmented into *private labours conducted independently from each other*,[53] he refers to a *socio-economic* and *not* a juridical reality; the latter is only a reflection – and sometimes a very imperfect one! – of the former. What capitalism is about, then, is a specific relation between wage-labour and capital, a social organization in which social labour is fragmented into firms independent of each other, which take independent decisions about investment, prices and forms of financing growth, which compete with each other for shares of markets and profits (of the total surplus-value produced

52. On this aspect of the development of home industries and of the first manufactures in the fifteenth and sixteenth centuries, see, among other sources, N. W. Posthumus, *De Geschiedenis van de Leidsche Lakenindustrie*, 's-Gravenhage, 1908.

53. See below, p. 165. In a note added by Engels in the fourth German edition of *Capital* Vol. 1 (see p. 138 below), he makes the point that in English there are two different words to express the two different aspects of labour: use-value-producing labour is called *work*, exchange-value-producing labour, which is only quantitatively measured, is called labour.

by productive labour in its totality), and which *therefore* buy and exploit wage-labour under specific economic conditions, compulsions and constraints. It is not simply a general relationship between 'producers' and 'accumulators', or 'producers' and 'administrators', for such a relationship is in the last analysis characteristic of all class societies and not specific to capitalism at all.

The *content* of the *economic* institution of private capital is therefore the *independent firm* (whether a small manufacturer or a giant multi-national corporation). Whether the *juridical form* strictly conforms to that content or not is irrelevant, and often poses complex legal problems. Are stockholders only owners of income titles, or are they owners of fractions of the firm's 'assets' or 'property'? The bankruptcy laws – which differ in different capitalist countries – can go into the most sophisticated nuances imaginable on this subject. But the vital economic decisions (key investment decisions, for example) are taken by all those firms which are really independent and not subordinate companies. The basic fact of life of the capitalist economy is the fact that these vital decisions are not taken by society as a whole or by the 'associated producers'.

Again, the content of this *economic* institution of private property (fragmented social labour) should not be confused with the question of the precise *agents* who take the independent firms' decisions. Whether those who take the decisions are individual owners, or representatives of stockholders, or so-called managers, does not in the least change the fact that they are working under the same previously analysed economic compulsion. Some economists today, such as Galbraith and even some Marxists, contend that the contemporary giant corporation has largely freed itself from these constraints.[54] This is an illusion, born of an extrapolation from conditions prevailing during a rather lengthy boom. In fact, the idea that any giant corporation, whatever its dimensions or power, could emancipate itself definitively from the compulsion of (monopolistic) competition, that is, could have a guaranteed specific demand for its products, independently of the trade cycle and from technological innovation, could make sense only if it were insulated both from economic fluctuations and

54. John Kenneth Galbraith, *The New Industrial State*, New York, 1967, Chapter 18.

from economic uncertainty, that is if the very nature of its output as commodity production was denied. Experience does not confirm such a contention.

The basic distinction which Galbraith, following Baumol, Kaysen and others, introduces between compulsion to profit maximization (true for yesterday's firms) and compulsion to growth maximization (true for today's corporations)[55] becomes devoid of practical long-term significance once we understand that growth remains essentially a function of profit, that capital accumulation can result in the last analysis only from surplus-value production and realization. The only kernel of truth which remains, then, is the difference between short-term and long-term profit maximization, which is indeed one of the basic differences between competitive capitalism and monopoly capitalism.

The debate on the nature of capital has received a new and significant impetus with the 'internal' critique of the theory of the marginal productivity of capital by Piero Sraffa and the Cambridge school. The latter have demonstrated convincingly that the measurement of capital inputs in the neo-classical 'production function' is based upon circular reasoning.[56] For if the effect of marginal increases or decreases of capital inputs upon output has to be *measured*, this can only be done in money terms, given the heterogeneous nature of so-called 'capital goods'. 'But this process of pricing or valuation of capital inputs presupposes a rate of return on the plant and equipment in question, of which the latter value is the capitalization'; that is 'one has to *assume* a rate of interest in order to demonstrate how this equilibrium rate of return is determined'.[57] The way out, obviously, is to look for a common substance in all the 'capital goods' independent of money, that is to return to socially necessary labour as the measurable substance of the value of all commodities.

55. ibid., Chapter 10.

56. Joan Robinson, *The Accumulation of Capital*, London, 1956; Piero Sraffa, *Production of Commodities by Means of Commodities*, Cambridge, 1960.

57. Maurice Dobb, 'The Sraffa System and the Critique of the Neo-Classical Theory of Distribution', reprinted in E. K. Hunt and Jesse G. Swartz (ed.), *A Critique of Economic Theory*, Harmondsworth, 1972, p. 207. One should note, however, that, to use the Schumpeterian jargon, Dobb thus only justifies the use of labour as a *numéraire* (a unit of account), in a typically neo-Ricardian way, and not at all on the basis of the Marxist labour theory of value.

8. MARX'S THEORY OF ACCUMULATION OF CAPITAL

Capital is thus, by definition, value looking for accretion, for sur-plus-value. But if capital produces surplus-value, surplus-value also produces additional capital. Under capitalism, economic growth therefore appears in the form of accumulation of capital. The basic drive of the capitalist mode of production is the drive to accumulate capital. This is not so because of some mysterious and tautological 'accumulative passion' or inclination on the part of capitalists. It is essentially explained by competition, that is by the phenomenon of 'various capitals'. Without competition, Marx states categorically, the 'driving fire' of growth would become extinguished.[58] Totally monopolized capital ('a single world trust') would essentially be stagnating capital.

But competition is combined with the trend to replace labour by machinery as a driving force for capital accumulation and eco-nomic growth under capitalism. If the extension of output maintained the given relationship between inputs of living labour and inputs of dead labour (machinery and raw materials), it would rapidly reach both a physical limit (the total available manpower) and hence a profit limit. Under conditions of permanent full employment, wages would tend to increase and erode profits to the point where capital accumulation and economic growth would gradually disappear.

Under capitalism, however, economic growth is not 'neutral' with respect to the relationship between living and dead labour inputs (between variable and constant capital). It is heavily loaded in favour of an expansion of labour-saving devices. Indeed, a permanent tendency to increase the social productivity of labour is the main civilizing by-product of capital accumulation, the main objective service which capitalism has rendered mankind. Capital accumulation takes on the primary form of an increase in the value of plant and equipment, as well as of the stock of raw materials available in industrialized capitalist countries. On a long-term basis, this accumulation is as impressive as Marx could have imagined. The value of all accumulated private non-farm producer durables multiplied more than tenfold in constant dollars between 1900 and 1965 in the U.S.A., and this estimate is certainly undervalued as it is based upon official records biased for reasons of tax evasion.

58. Karl Marx, *Capital*, Vol. 3, p. 254.

Capital accumulation is, of course, distinct from the behaviour of pre-capitalist ruling classes. If all surplus-value were to be consumed in the form of luxury goods, no capital accumulation would take place at all. Capital would then be maintained at the level it had already reached. This special 'limiting' case was indeed presented by Marx under the name of 'simple reproduction', for purely analytical reasons. It does not, of course, correspond to any 'real' stage or situation of a normally functioning capitalist mode of production.[59] As we pointed out, what characterizes capitalism is precisely the compulsion to accumulate, that is 'enlarged reproduction'.

Enlarged reproduction presupposes that not all surplus-value produced by productive labour, and appropriated by the capitalist class, is unproductively consumed. Part of it is transformed into luxury goods and disappears from the process of reproduction. Part of it is transformed into additional capital by being used to buy additional plant and equipment, additional raw materials and additional labour-power. This, then, is the process of accumulation of capital: the transformation of surplus-value into additional capital, which can produce new increments of surplus-value, leading to new increments of capital. The movement develops in the form of a spiral, as Simonde de Sismondi, one of the early 'romantic' critics of capitalism, whom Marx quotes approvingly on this question, already understood.

The fact that capital accumulation is possible only because part of the surplus-value appropriated by the capitalist class is not socially squandered in luxury goods constitutes the starting point for the so-called 'abstinence' theory (more accurately, justification) of profits and capitalist exploitation.[60] Historically, there is not an atom of evidence for the assumption that capital somehow grew out of the 'frugal habits' of some members of the community, as opposed to the 'improvidence' of others, each of them having equal access to resources that were initially com-

59. One could say that it corresponds to a border case of stagnation in a given phase of the trade cycle.

60. Even Schumpeter still largely defended this 'abstinence' theory of profit, although giving it a less vulgar character than in the case of Senior. 'The capitalist ... exchanges a fund against a flow. The "abstinence" for which ... he is being paid enters into the accumulation of the fund. There is no additional payment for refraining from consuming it even in cases in which this would be physically possible' (*History of Economic Analysis*, p. 661). See also *Capitalism, Socialism and Democracy*, p. 16.

parable. On the contrary, all historical evidence confirms that the sudden appearance of large amounts of 'capital' (in the form of a stock of precious metals and other treasure) in a society previously confined almost exclusively to natural economy (to the output of goods possessing only use-value) was the result not of 'frugality' and 'thrift' but of large-scale piracy, robbery, violence, theft, enslavement of men and trade in slaves. The history of the origins of West European usury and merchant capital between the tenth and the thirteenth centuries, from the piracy in the Mediterranean through the plundering of Byzantium by the Fourth Crusade to the regular plundering razzias into the Slav territories of Central and Eastern Europe, is very eloquent in this respect.

What is unconfirmed by history is even more absurd in the light of contemporary economic analysis. Nobody could seriously argue that Messrs Rockefeller, Morgan and Mellon have to be compensated for their virtue in not squandering tens of billions of dollars on additional yachts, mansions and private jets – the vulgar version of the abstinence theory. But its more sophisticated version, namely the idea that the profits of the owners of capital are just the way in which their 'fund' is transformed into the 'flow' of long-term capital investment, provides a nice piece of circular reasoning. For whence does the 'fund' originate, if not precisely from the 'flow', that is to say what else is capital if not accumulated profits? To deny that profits originate in the process of production flies in the face of all scientific as well as practical observation of what goes on in a capitalist economy. Once we understand this, there is no room left for any abstinence theory of profit – only for a subtraction one.

The process of capital accumulation is viewed by Marx in *Capital* at two different and successive levels of abstraction. In Volume 1, in the framework of 'Capital in general', he examines it essentially in the light of what occurs in and flows from the exchange between wage-labour and capital. In Volume 3, he examines capital accumulation (economic growth under capitalism) in the light of what occurs in the sphere of 'many capitals', that is of capitalist competition. I shall therefore leave to the introduction to Volume 3 an examination of the main criticisms made of Marx by those who question the validity of the laws of motion of capital accumulation set out in that volume. Here, I shall limit myself to examining the basic effects of capital accumulation on wage-labour.

Unlike many of his contemporaries, including some of the sternest non-Marxist critics of capitalism, Marx did not consider that capital accumulation had a simple and unequivocally detrimental effect upon the situation of wage-labour. Marx had studied the movement of real wages during the trade cycle, and the fact that wages were at their highest level when capital accumulation was progressing at the quickest pace by no means escaped him.[61] But, once again, he tried to go beyond such evident facts to study the *fundamental modifications in value terms* which capital accumulation would exercise upon labour.

It thus became his contention that the very way in which capital accumulation proceeds, the very motive force of capitalist progress – the development of fixed capital, of machinery – contains a powerful dynamic to reduce the *value* of labour-power. For as this value is the equivalent of the value of a *given* quantity of consumer goods, supposed to be necessary to restore the capacity of a worker to produce at a given level of intensity, a decrease in the value of these consumer goods resulting from an increase in the productivity of labour in the consumer goods industry leads to a decrease in the value of labour-power, all other things remaining equal.

This argument implies neither any tendency to a decrease in real wages (on the contrary, it is based upon the assumption of *stable* real wages in the short and medium term), nor any trend towards 'growing absolute misery' of the working class. We shall deal with this theory falsely attributed to Marx in the next section of this introduction. But it does imply that the favourable results of the increase in productivity of labour end by falling, to a large extent, into the hands of the capitalist class, by transforming themselves into supplementary 'relative surplus-value', provided that the long-term trend of the industrial reserve army of labour is either stable or increasing.

On a world scale this has certainly been true for as long as capitalism has existed. As Marx predicted, capitalism spread not only by creating new jobs but also by creating new unemployed (by destroying employment of previous wage earners, and especially of previously self-employed small farmers and handicraftsmen). But to calculate a 'world average value of labour-power' is of course a meaningless abstraction. Indeed, ever since industrial capitalism

61. Karl Marx, 'Wages, Price and Profit', in *Selected Works* in one volume, London, 1970, pp. 220–21.

in the West started to swamp the rest of the world with its cheap, mass-produced commodities, and at the latest since the eighteen-seventies, a *divergent* trend has appeared in the world economy: a long-term decline of the reserve army of labour in Western Europe (as a result of exports of both emigrants and commodities) and a rise in the reserve army of labour in the underdeveloped countries. (This latter process included, of course, the transformation of masses of pre-capitalist farmers, cattle-raisers and artisans into uprooted 'marginalized' vagrants, migrant seasonal labourers, and forced labourers, following a pattern similar to what had happened a few centuries earlier in Western Europe.)

The dynamics of 'capital accumulation on a world scale' have therefore to be seen as those of an organic whole, and not as the simple sum of capital accumulation processes in distinct countries. The operation of the world market as a gigantic syphon to transfer value from the south to the north of our planet (from the countries with lower to the countries with higher productivity of labour) lies at the very root of the imperialist system. While the debate on the theoretical explanation of this phenomenon is still in its initial stages,[62] it is important to note that the phenomenon itself is based upon uneven movements (uneven mobility) of capital and labour, and introduces all those dimensions into the analysis of capitalism which Marx reserved for the never-written Volumes 4, 5 and 6 in the original plan of *Capital*.

The accumulation of capital is the accumulation of wealth in the form of commodities, of value. Value production becomes a goal in itself. Work is degraded to the level of a means by which to receive money incomes. One of the most striking and most 'modern' parts of *Capital* is that which examines the inhuman consequences of capital accumulation for the workers and for work itself. Marx himself added to the second German edition of Volume 1 the note

62. See, among other writings: Samir Amin, *L'Accumulation à l'échelle mondiale*, Paris, 1970; Arghiri Emmanuel, *Unequal Exchange* (including a discussion with Charles Bettelheim), London, 1972; Christian Palloix, *L'Économie mondiale capitaliste*, Paris, 1971; and the discussion of these books by Ernest Mandel in *Late Capitalism*, London, 1975. Interestingly enough, W. Arthur Lewis, in his 'Development with Unlimited Supplies of Labour' (Manchester School of Economic and Social Studies, Vol. XXII, May 1954), tries to show that stepped-up capital accumulation implies a large industrial reserve army; but he limits this case exclusively to initial industrialization and does not admit Marx's assumption of permanent reconstitution of this reserve army through the mechanization process.

that, under capitalism, labour-power not only becomes a commodity for the capitalist but also receives this form *for the worker himself*, implying that this degradation of work is both objectively and subjectively the fate of the industrial proletariat. It took 'official' political economy a long time, indeed until after the growing revolt of the workers against assembly line speed-ups, to discover what Marx had anticipated from a thorough understanding of the fundamental mechanisms which govern the capitalist mode of production.

Because capital accumulation presupposes production for profit, because it has profit maximization as its very *rationale*, exact and minute cost calculations entail constant reorganizations of the production process with the single purpose of reducing costs. From the point of view of the single capitalist firm, a worker cannot be seen as a human being endowed with elementary rights, dignity, and needs to develop his personality. He is a 'cost element' and this 'cost' must be constantly and exclusively measured in money terms, in order to be reduced to the utmost. Even when 'human relations' and 'psychological considerations' are introduced into labour organization, they are all centred in the last analysis upon 'economies of cost' (of those 'overhead costs' called excessive labour turnover, too many work interruptions, absenteeism, strikes, etc.).[63]

Capitalist economy is thus a gigantic enterprise of dehumanization, of transformation of human beings from goals in themselves into instruments and means for money-making and capital accumulation. It is not the machine, nor any technological compulsion, which inevitably transforms workers and men and women in general into appendices and slaves of monstrous equipment. It is the capitalist principle of profit maximization by individual firms which unleashes this terrifying trend. Other types of technology and other types of machine are perfectly conceivable – provided that the guiding principle of investment is no longer 'cost-saving' by individual competing firms, but the optimum development of all human beings.

63. The most extreme case is that of 'globalization of costs' in cost-benefit analysis, in which human illness and death are likewise computed in the form of money costs.

9. MARX'S THEORY OF WAGES

Strangely enough, the idea of an ever-increasing decline in the standard of living of the working class, which has often been falsely attributed to Marx, originated with those economists against whom he maintained a constant barrage of polemics after perfecting his own economic theories. It originated with Malthus and, via Ricardo, reached several socialists of Marx's generation, such as Ferdinand Lassalle. Whether under the guise of a 'stable wage fund' or under the guise of an 'iron law of wages', it is essentially a *population growth theory of wages*. Whenever wages rise sufficiently above the physiological minimum, labourers are supposed to have more children, who then in turn create large-scale unemployment and depress wages back to the minimum.

The logical shortcomings of this theory are glaring. It examines only what happens on the supply side of labour-power; it does not examine at all what happens on the demand side. It presupposes that the potential working population is a linear function of population increase, and that the demographic movement is in turn a linear function of real income. All the intermediate links – like the effects of increases of income not only upon the child mortality rate but also upon birth rates, not to speak of the effects of increases of income and of the organized strength of the working class on the length of the working week, the duration of training and the moment of retiring from the work process – are eliminated from the chain of reasoning, thereby leading to wrong and indeed absurd results.

If one compares Marx's own theory of wages to the opinions held by academic economists of his time, one sees at once the step forward which he accomplished. For he points out not only that labour-power, having been transformed by capitalism into a commodity, has a value which is objectively determined like the value of all other commodities, but also that the value of labour-power has a characteristic distinct from that of all other commodities – to wit that it is dependent on two elements: the *physiological* needs and the *historical-moral* needs of the working class.

This distinction is closely linked with the peculiar nature of labour-power: a commodity inseparable from and integrated with human beings, who are not only endowed with muscles and a stomach, but also with consciousness, nerves, desires, hopes and potential rebelliousness. The *physical capacity* to work can be measured by the calory inputs that have to compensate losses of energy. But the *willingness* to work at a given rhythm, a given intensity, under given conditions, with a given equipment of higher and higher value and increasing vulnerability, presupposes a level of consumption which is not simply equivalent to a sum-total of calories, but is also a function of what is commonly considered by the working class to be its 'current', 'habitual' standard of living.[64] Marx notes that these habitual standards differ greatly from country to country, and are generally higher in those countries which have an advanced, developed capitalist industry than in those which are still at pre-industrial levels, or are going through the throes of 'primitive' industrial capital accumulation.[65]

We thus reach an unexpected conclusion: according to this aspect of Marx's work, real wages would actually have to be higher in more advanced capitalist countries – and therefore also in more advanced stages of capitalism – than in less developed countries. This would also imply that they would tend to increase in time, as the level of industrialization increases. On the other hand, we have noted earlier that Marx explained fluctuation of wages during the trade cycle, that is of the price and not of the value of labour-power, as being governed essentially by the movements of the industrial reserve army. Real wages would tend to increase in times of boom and full employment and to decline in times of depression and large-scale unemployment. He indicated, however, that there was nothing automatic about this movement, and that the actual class *struggle* – including trade-union action, which he considered indispensable for this very reason – was the instrument through which workers could take advantage of more

64. Lenin makes the point that with the development of capitalist industry there is a progressive increase in the workers' needs ('On the So-Called Market Question', in *Collected Works*, Vol. 1, pp. 106–7). See also Marx: 'This much, however, can even now be mentioned in passing, namely that the relative restriction on the sphere of the workers' consumption (which is only quantitative, not qualitative, or rather, only qualitative as posited through the quantitative) gives them as consumers ... an entirely different importance as agents of production from that which they possessed e.g. in antiquity or in the Middle Ages, or now possess in Asia' (*Grundrisse*, Pelican Marx Library, p. 283). Also ibid., pp. 186–7, 409.

65. Karl Marx, 'Wages, Price and Profit', *Selected Works* in one volume, p. 223; *Capital*, Vol. 1, Chapter 22 (see below, pp. 702–5). The most categorical statement in that respect is to be found in *Theories of Surplus-Value*, Part II, pp. 16–17: 'The more productive one country is relative to another in the world market, the higher will be its wages, as compared with the other.'

favourable conditions on the 'labour market' somewhat to increase their wages, whereas the main effect of depression was that it would weaken the resistence of the working class to wage-cuts.

But Marx stuck to his theory of value with regard to wages. Wages are the prices of the commodity labour-power. Like all other prices, they do not fluctuate at random, but around an axis which is the value of that commodity. The movements of wages that are influenced by the ups and downs of the trade cycle explain only short-term fluctuations: these have to be integrated within a wider analysis, explaining the long-term fluctuations of wages in function of the *changes in the value of labour-power*.

We can thus formulate Marx's theory of wages as an *accumulation of capital wage theory*, in opposition to the crude demographic wage theory of the Malthus–Ricardo–Lassalle school. Long-term movements of wages are a function of the accumulation of capital in a fivefold sense:

– Accumulation of capital implies a decline in value of a given basket of consumer goods included in the given standard of living of the working class (with the given reproduction costs of labour-power). In this sense, the development of capitalism tends to *depress the value* of labour-power, all other things remaining equal. Let us repeat: such a decline in the value of labour-power does not imply a decline, but only a stability, of real wages.

– Accumulation of capital implies a decline in the value and an expansion of the output (mass production) of consumer goods previously not included in the reproduction costs of labour-power. If objective and subjective conditions are favourable, the working class *can force* the inclusion of these goods into the accepted minimum standard of living, can expand the 'moral-historical' component of the value of labour-power, thereby *increasing its value*. This again does not happen automatically, but essentially as a result of the class struggle.

– Accumulation of capital will favour the increase in value of labour-power if the *long-term structural supply* of labour-power does not strongly exceed demand, or is even below demand. This explains why wages in the U.S.A. were from the beginning significantly higher than in Europe, why wages started rising significantly in the latter part of the nineteenth century in Europe as a result of massive overseas emigration of the reserve army of labour, and why persistent massive unemployment and underemployment in the underdeveloped countries has implied a tendentially declining value of labour-power (often even accompanied by declining real wages) in the last two decades.

– Accumulation of capital forms the upper *barrier* which no increase in the value or the price of labour-power can break under capitalism. If and when the increase in the value of labour-power implies a strong decline in surplus-value, accumulation of capital slows down, large-scale unemployment reappears, and wages are 'readjusted' to a level compatible with capital accumulation. In other words, under capitalism, wages *can* fall to the point where the 'historical-moral' ingredient of the value of labour-power completely disappears, where they are actually reduced to the bare physiological minimum. They *cannot* rise to the point where the 'historical-moral' ingredient of the value of labour-power wipes out surplus-value as the source of capital accumulation.

– Accumulation of capital implies increased exploitation of the workers, including an increased *attrition of labour-power*, especially through intensification of the production process. But this in turn implies the *need for higher consumption* just to reproduce labour-power even physiologically. So one can say that, in this sense, capitalism increases the value of labour-power by making its exploitation more intensive.[66] One can especially find negative confirmation of this effect of the accumulation of capital on the value of labour-power. Once wages decline below a certain level (especially under the effects of wars or reactionary dictatorships), the productive effort of the workers will decline and labour-power will not be reconstituted to its full productive capacity, as a result of too low a level of wages.

How, then, has it been possible for so many writers, for so long, to have attributed to Marx a 'theory of absolute impoverishment

66. We have noted that the *value* of labour-power is an objective category. This implies, among other phenomena, that an important increase in the intensity of the labour process leads to an increase in the value of labour-power, all other things remaining equal. A higher expenditure of labour-power implies the need for higher consumption, for example, food of higher calory content, to avoid an erosion of the capacity to work. Rosdolsky (op. cit., Vol. 1, p. 331) in this respect draws attention to a distinction made by Otto Bauer between 'physiological needs' born from the simple life process of the worker, and those needs born from the work process, the second expanding progressively compared with the first in step precisely with the growing intensification of work under capitalism.

of the workers under capitalism' which obviously implied a theory of tendential fall in the value not only of labour-power but even of real wages?[67] In the first place because Marx, in his youthful writings, did in fact hold such a theory – for example, in the Communist Manifesto.[68] But this was formulated before he had brought his theoretical understanding of the capitalist mode of production to its final, mature conclusion. It is only in the years 1857–8 that we have the birth of Marx's economic theory in its rounded, consistent form. After he had written *A Contribution to the Critique of Political Economy* and the *Grundrisse*, there was no longer a trace of any such historical trend towards absolute impoverishment in his economic analysis.

In the second place, because so many writers confuse Marx's treatment of the *value* of labour-power (which depends upon the *value* of the consumer goods the worker buys with his wages) with the category of real wages (determined by the *mass* of consumer goods his wages buy). Under capitalism, given the constant increase in the productivity of labour, these categories can move in opposite directions.[69]

67. See, among others: Pareto, op. cit., p. 63; Ludwig von Mises, *Le Socialisme*, Paris, 1938, p. 438; Schumpeter, *Capitalism, Socialism and Democracy*, pp. 34–8; Karl Popper, *The Open Society*, Vol. 2, pp. 155–8; W. Arthur Lewis, *Theory of Economic Growth*, London, 1955, p. 298; Eric Roll, *A History of Economic Thought* (2nd edition), London, 1954, pp. 284, 293, etc. Two authors who, though they have studied Marx closely and call themselves Marxists, nevertheless repeat the same mistaken view are John Strachey in *Contemporary Capitalism*, London, 1956, pp. 101–8 and Fritz Sternberg in *Der Imperialismus*, Berlin, 1962, pp. 57–60. More objective are Paul M. Sweezy's account in *The Theory of Capitalist Development*, Oxford, 1943, pp. 87–92, and J. Steindl's in *Maturity and Stagnation in the American Economy*, Chapter 14, Oxford, 1952.

68. 'Manifesto of the Communist Party', *The Revolutions of 1848*, Pelican Marx Library, 1973, pp. 74–5, 78.

69. *Capital*, Vol. 1, Chapter 17 (see below, p. 659), contains the key formula in that respect: 'In this way it is possible, given increasing productivity of labour, for the *price* of labour-power to fall constantly and for this fall to be accompanied by a constant growth in the *mass* of the worker's means of subsistence' (our stress). In the same way, in a famous passage at the end of 'Wages, Price and Profit', Marx says that: '... consequently the general tendency of capitalistic production is not to raise but to sink the average standard of wages, or to push the *value of labour* to its minimum limit' (*Selected Works* in one volume, p. 225) and he adds that efforts to *increase wages* 99 times out of 100 only tend to maintain the value of labour-power. This whole argument applies to the trend of the *value* of labour-power, not to that of real wages.

In the third place, because two famous passages in *Capital* Volume 1 have been consistently misinterpreted.[70] In both these passages Marx does speak about 'increasing misery' and pauperism, and about 'accumulation of misery'. But the context indicates clearly that what he is referring to is the poverty and misery of the 'surplus population', of the 'Lazarus layer of the working class', that is, of the *unemployed or semi-employed poor*. Revealing studies on poverty in rich countries like the United States and Great Britain[71] have strikingly confirmed that the misery of these old-age pensioners, unemployed, sick, homeless, degraded or irregularly working lower layers of the proletariat *is* indeed a permanent feature of capitalism, including the capitalism of the 'welfare state'. The truth is simply that in passages such as these Marx uses formulations that are ambiguous and so lend weight to confusion on the question.

Does this mean that Marx did not formulate any theory of impoverishment of the working class, or that he made optimistic predictions about the general trend of working-class conditions under capitalism? This would of course be a complete paradox, in the light of what he wrote in Chapter 25 of *Capital* Volume 1. The point to be made is simply that this chapter – like all of Marx's mature writings on this subject – *is not concerned with movements of real wages at all*, any more than the chapters on value are about movements of market prices of commodities other than the commodity labour-power. This is clearly indicated in the very passage in question by Marx's statement that as capital accumulates the situation of workers becomes worse *irrespective of whether their wages are high or low.*[72]

What we in fact have here is a theory of a tendency towards *relative impoverishment* of the working class under capitalism in a

70. See below, Chapter 25, Section 4, pp. 797–8, 799.

71. See, for example, Michael Harrington's already classic *The Other America*, Harmondsworth, 1963, and the equivalent British study by Brian Abel Smith and Peter Townsend, *The Poor and the Poorest*, London, 1963, which estimates that 14 per cent of the British population (7 million people!) were living in, or on the margin of, poverty twenty years after the establishment of the welfare state! To have revealed that such poverty is rooted in the *system* of wage-labour, and that no permanent elimination of it (i.e. a guaranteed standard of living for all human beings, irrespective of how much they work or indeed whether they work at all) is possible without upsetting the economic compulsion to sell the proletarian's labour-power, is one of Marx's most epoch-making discoveries and fundamental to his economic theory.

72. See below, p. 799.

double sense. Firstly, in the sense that productive workers tend to get a smaller part of the new value they produce: in other words there is a trend towards an increase in the rate of surplus-value. Secondly, in the sense that *even when wages rise* the needs of the workers as human beings are denied. This applies even to their additional consumer needs that grow out of the very increase in the productivity of labour which results from the accumulation of capital. One has only to think of the unfulfilled needs of workers in the fields of education, health, skill acquisition and differentiation, leisure, culture, housing, even in the richest capitalist countries of today, to see how this assumption remains accurate in spite of the so-called 'consumer society'. But it applies much more to the needs of the worker as a producer and a citizen – his need to develop a full personality, to become a rich and creative human being, etc.; these needs are brutally crushed by the tyranny of meaningless, mechanical, parcellized work, alienation of productive capacities and alienation of real human wealth.

In addition to this law of *general relative* impoverishment of workers under capitalism, Marx also notes a trend towards *periodic absolute* impoverishment, essentially in function of the movement of unemployment. This is closely linked to the inevitability of cyclical fluctuations under capitalism, that is the inevitability of periodic crises of overproduction, or 'recessions' as they are called today with less provocative connotations.

There is also another aspect of Marx's theory of wages over which, for almost a century, controversy has raged. This is the question of the different values of 'skilled labour-power' and 'unskilled labour-power' (whether related or not to the question of whether Marx gives a satisfactory explanation of the fact that, according to his labour theory of value, skilled labour produces more value in an hour of work than unskilled labour). Starting with Böhm-Bawerk, some critics have claimed to discover here one of the basic inconsistencies in Marx's economic theory.[73] For if the greater productivity, in value terms, of skilled as opposed to unskilled workers is a function of the higher wages of the former, are we not back at Adam Smith's famous circular argument, in

73. For example Böhm-Bawerk, op. cit., pp. 80–85; Pareto, op. cit., pp. 52–3; Schumpeter, *Capitalism, Socialism and Democracy*, p. 24, etc. An interesting discussion of this problem was recently provided by Bob Rowthorn, 'Skilled Labour in the Marxist System', in *Bulletin of the Conference of Socialist Economists*, Spring 1974.

which the 'price of labour' determines the 'natural price' of goods but is in turn determined by the 'natural price' of one category of goods, so-called wage goods, that is food?

But in fact Marx avoided such circular reasoning, contrary to what his critics mistakenly assume. He never explained the higher value content of an hour of skilled labour as compared to an hour of unskilled labour by the higher wages which skilled labour receives. This higher content is explained strictly in terms of the labour theory of value, by the additional labour costs necessary for producing the skill, in which are also included the total costs of schooling spent on those who do not successfully conclude their studies.[74] The higher value produced by an hour of skilled labour, as compared to an hour of unskilled labour, results from the fact that skilled labour participates in the 'total labour-power' (*Gesamtarbeitsvermögen*) of society (or of a given branch of industry) not only with its own labour-power but also with a fraction of the labour-power necessary to produce its skill. In other words, each hour of skilled labour can be considered as an hour of unskilled labour multiplied by a coefficient dependent on this cost of schooling.[75] Marx speaks in this context of 'composite labour' as against 'simple labour'. The skill, by analogy, can be compared to an additional tool, which is in itself not value-producing, but which transfers part of its own value into the value of the product produced by the skilled worker.

74. This solution was first formulated by Hilferding in his answer to Böhm-Bawerk (op. cit., pp. 136–46), then worked out more explicitly by Hans Deutsch (*Qualifizierte Arbeit und Kapitalismus*, Vienna, 1904) and Otto Bauer ('Qualifizierte Arbeit und Kapitalismus', in *Die Neue Zeit*, 1905–6, No. 20). Deutsch differs from Hilferding in that according to Hilferding only the cost of production of skill (the work of the teacher, etc.) adds to the value of skilled labour-power, whereas for Deutsch the time spent by the apprentice (or student) himself while learning has to be added to those costs. Bauer supports Deutsch's thesis that the 'labour' of the apprentice (student) creates supplementary value and enters the process of value production of the skilled worker, but contrary to Deutsch (and together with Hilferding) he contends that this value increases the surplus-value produced by the skilled worker, not the value of his own labour-power. See on this controversy also Rubin, op. cit., pp. 159–71, and Rosdolsky, op. cit., Vol. 2, pp. 597–614.

75. Rubin, op. cit., pp. 165–6.

10. MARX'S THEORY OF MONEY

Marx's attempt to formulate his own theory of money originates in a significant flaw in Ricardo's economic system.[76] While Ricardo adheres to a strict labour theory of value concerning commodities, he contends that this is true for gold only if the quantity in circulation remains in exact proportion to the mass and prices of other commodities. Increases or decreases in this money circulation would provoke an increase or decrease in commodity prices and this in turn would provoke a further decrease or increase in the value of gold. Marx tries to overcome this inconsistency by integrating his theory of money into his general explanation of value, value production and autonomous value circulation (money circulation, capital circulation), on the basis of a rigorous application of the labour theory of value.

As with the theory of value, the most important aspect of this monetary theory is the qualitative one, which has hitherto received too little attention from either the critics or the disciples of Marx. The fact that social labour, in a society based upon generalized commodity production, is fragmented into many segments of private labour executed independently of each other leads, as we have seen, to the result that its social character can only be recognized *post festum*, through the sale of the commodity and depending upon the amount of equivalent it receives in this sale. The social character of the labour embedded in the commodity, therefore, can only appear as *a thing* outside the commodity – that is, money. The fact that relations between human beings appear under capitalism (generalized commodity production) as relations between things – a phenomenon which Marx analysed at length in the fourth section on 'The Fetishism of the Commodity' of Chapter 1 of *Capital* Volume 1 (see pp. 163–77 below) – should, therefore, not be understood in the sense that people under capitalism, being in the grip of false consciousness, have the illusion of being confronted with things when in reality they are confronted with specific social relations of production. It is also an objective necessity and compulsion. Under conditions of generalized commodity production, social labour *cannot* be immediately recognized otherwise than through its exchange against money. The circulation of commodities cannot but produce its own

76. Karl Marx, *A Contribution to the Critique of Political Economy*, pp. 170–79.

counterpart in the circulation of the medium of exchange, money.[77] Money is the necessary materialization of abstract social labour: that is the qualitative determinant in Marxist monetary theory.

It is by losing sight of this fundamental social nature of money, rooted in specific social relations of production, that so many authors, including Marxist ones,[78] have been tempted to give money, and money-creation, functions which they cannot fulfil in a society based upon private property. To assume an 'automatic' realization of the exchange-value of commodities through the creation of an 'adequate' volume of money presupposes that that value is pre-established, that all labour expended on the production of these commodities was socially necessary labour. In other words, it presupposes that there exists a permanent equilibrium of supply with effective demand and, therefore, that there is no commodity production at all but *a priori* adaptation of production to consciously registered needs. Under capitalism, including monopoly capitalism, this can never be achieved.

Money born from the process of exchange, from the circulation of commodities, can realize the value of these commodities only because it itself has value, because it itself is a commodity produced by socially necessary abstract labour. Marx's theory of money is, therefore, above all a *commodity theory of money* in which the monetary standards (precious metals) enter the process of circulation with an intrinsic value of their own. From that point of view, Marx must reject any quantity theory of money applied to money

77. See Marx's footnote at the beginning of Chapter 3 on Money (below, p. 188): 'The question why money does not itself directly represent labour-time, so that a piece of paper may represent, for instance, x hours' labour, comes down simply to the question why, on the basis of commodity production, the products of labour must take the form of commodities. This is obvious, because their taking the form of commodities implies their differentiation into commodities [on the one hand] and the money commodity [on the other]. It is also asked why private labour cannot be treated as its opposite, directly social labour.'

78. For example, Hilferding's proposal (*Das Finanzkapital*, pp. 29–30) for a category called 'socially necessary value of circulation' (*gesellschaftlich notwendiger Zirkulationswert*), established by dividing the sum of *values* of all commodities by the velocity of circulation of money. Hilferding does not notice the incongruity of dividing quantities of value, i.e. socially necessary labour quanta, by the velocity of circulation media. Only prices (the *monetary* expression of value) can, of course, be so divided. Commodities cannot enter the circulation process except with (preliminary) prices. (See *A Contribution to the Critique of Political Economy*, pp. 66–8.)

based upon a gold or gold-and-silver basis. When, with a given velocity of circulation, a given amount of gold has a value higher than that of the total mass of commodities against which it exchanges itself, it can no more 'lose' value (that is, provoke an increase of prices through abundance of bullion) in the circulation process than any other commodity. What happens is simply that part of it will be withdrawn from circulation and hoarded, until such time as the need for circulation again increases.

But if such a commodity theory of money implies a straight rejection of the quantity theory, as long as money is directly based upon precious metals, it points in the opposite direction as soon as we are faced with paper bank notes which function in reality as *representatives* of, and tokens for, precious metals. In this case, quite independently of whether or not there is legal convertibility of paper into gold,[79] emission of paper money to the amount which, at a given value of gold and a given velocity of circulation of the bank notes, enables it to realize the prices of all the commodities in circulation, will leave these prices unaffected. But if this amount of paper money in circulation is doubled at its face value, all other things remaining equal, prices expressed in that currency will also double, not in contradiction with, but in application of, the labour theory of value. To simplify, if we presume that each unit of gold circulates only once a year, the equation 1,000,000 tons of steel = 1,000 kilos of gold means that the same quantity of socially necessary abstract labour (say 100,000,000 man hours) has been necessary to produce the respective quantities of steel and gold. If £1,000,000 represents 1,000 kilos of gold, then the fact that the price of 1 ton of steel is £1 is just a straight expression of the equality in value (in quantities of abstract labour) between 1 ton of steel and 1 kilo of gold. But if, through additional issuing of paper money, 1,000 kilos of gold is now represented by £2,000,000 instead of £1,000,000, then, all other things remaining equal, the price of steel will rise from £1 to £2 in strict application of the labour theory of value.

This does not mean that, with regard to paper money, Marx was the proponent of any mechanistic quantity theory. There is an evident analogy between his theory and the traditional forms of

79. This was, for example, the case in France after its military defeat by Germany in 1870–71, when the payment of a heavy gold war indemnity to the Reich imposed a temporary suspension of convertibility of the franc without provoking any inflationary price movement in the Third Republic.

the quantity of money; but this analogy is limited by two essential factors. In the first place, for Marx, with paper money as with metallic money, it is the movement of the value of commodities, that is fluctuations of material production and of productivity of labour, which remains the *primum movens* of price fluctuations, not the ups and downs of the quantity of paper money in circulation.[80] In that respect, in *Capital* Volume 3, Marx examines the need to increase money circulation at the moment of the outbreak of the crisis, and he sharply criticizes the role which the Bank of England played, through the application of the 'currency principle', in accentuating money panics and monetary crises as accelerators of crises of overproduction when these coincided with an outflow of gold from England. In the same way, however, he denied any possibility of preventing recessions by issuing additional money.[81]

In the second place, Marx understood perfectly that the dialectical interrelationship of all the elements of a mechanistic quantity theory equation excludes the possibility of simply deriving conclusions from independent variations of a single one of these elements. He knew, for example, that the velocity of circulation of money was co-determined by the trade cycle, and could not be considered stable in a given phase when only the quantity of money was supposed to change. But an analysis of his opinions on all these subjects as well as a short comment on his whole theory of the role of money in the trade cycle and of fictitious capital has its place in the introduction to Volume 3 rather than Volume 1 of *Capital*.

With the development and generalization of commodity production, money becomes more and more transformed into money capital. It is more and more replaced by 'monetary signs' in the process of circulation, and becomes more and more transformed from a means of exchange into a means of payment, that is into the counterpart of debts, into an instrument of credit. But in examining the credit role of money Marx maintains a rigorous adherence to the labour theory of value, so that his whole economic system is thoroughly 'monistic'. Money as the general equivalent of the

80. Except in cases of galloping inflation.
81. See Karl Marx, *Capital*, Vol. 3, p. 503. In the margin of the first edition of *Capital* Vol. 1, Marx added a note to Chapter 3, converted by Engels in subsequent editions into a footnote (see below, p. 236n.), in which he indicated the distinction between monetary crises as expressions of general crises of overproduction, and autonomous monetary crises.

exchange value of all commodities and money as the means to settle debts (resulting out of the generalization of sales on credit) are both claims on a given fraction of the total labour expenditure of society in a given period. Whatever the 'nominal' value of the currency, and whatever the 'standard of measurement' of prices, it is obviously impossible to distribute more labour quantities than have been produced and stocked within the same period of time. On the other hand, given the very nature of commodity production, no general increase of money circulation (no increase of 'aggregate demand') can in the long run prevent the eventuality that a whole series of commodities produced will not meet the 'specific demand' they need to allow their proprietors to realize at least the average rate of profit. Technological changes, differences in productivity between different plants and firms, changes in real wages and in the structure of consumer expenditures, changes in the rate of profit entailing changes in the direction and structure of investment: all these complex movements which make the trade cycle and periodic recessions possible and indeed unavoidable under conditions of generalized commodity production cannot be eliminated by manipulation of currency volume or currency units. Experience since Marx's death, and especially since the 'Keynesian revolution', fully confirms the correctness of this diagnosis, although it also confirms that, under specific conditions and within specific limits, monetary policies can reduce the *amplitude* of economic fluctuations, a fact of which Marx was perfectly aware.[82]

Marx's short comments on the dual nature of gold, as the basis 'in the last resort' of all paper money systems and as the only possible 'world currency' acceptable for final settlement of accounts between the central banks (and bourgeois classes) of different nations, make especially interesting reading today, when the Bretton Woods monetary system has broken down because of the inconvertibility of the dollar into gold. It is interesting to note that Marx, while rejecting all theories which explain the 'value' of money by convention or state compulsion,[83] does relate this role of gold as a means of final settlement of accounts on an international scale to the specific role of the bourgeois state. Among the functions of the state is that of creating the 'general conditions for capitalist production'. A coherent and accepted currency cer-

82. Karl Marx, *Capital*, Vol. 3, Chapter 34, especially p. 539.
83. Karl Marx, *Grundrisse*, p. 165; *A Contribution to the Critique of Political Economy*, p. 116.

tainly belongs to these 'general conditions'. Paper money with a fixed rate of exchange (*Zwangskurs*) can be imposed only *through the authority of the state* within given limits.[84] But where this authority is absent, proprietors of commodities cannot be forced to accept in exchange for their goods paper money whose rate they consider inflated. 'Paper gold' as a universal means of exchange and payment on the world market presupposes, therefore, a world government, in other words the absence of inter-imperialist competition and, therefore, in the last analysis the withering away of private property. To expect such a situation to occur under capitalism is utopian.

Marx's theory of money has been much less analysed, criticized and discussed by later Marxists than other parts of his economic theory.[85] An interesting discussion did, however, occur on the eve of the First World War between Hilferding, Kautsky and Varga, on the possibility of deducing from the *value* of commodities a 'socially necessary volume of money' – a hypothesis which is obviously mistaken since it confuses the *value* of commodities with their *price*.[86] Varga, moreover, in a series of polemics which were continued in the early twenties, persisted in maintaining that, as central banks bought gold at a fixed price, the fluctuations of the intrinsic value of gold would not influence the general level of prices, but only govern the ups and downs of the differential rent commanded by gold mines with a productivity above the level allowing the average rate of profit at the given price of gold.[87] Subsequent developments, especially in the last four or five years, have confirmed that both these attempted corrections of Marx's theory of money were unfounded and wrong.

84. Karl Marx, *Grundrisse*, pp. 121–35; *A Contribution to the Critique of Political Economy*, pp. 116, 119–22, 149–53.

85. A rare exception is the book by Bruno Fritsch, *Die Geld- und Kredittheorie von Karl Marx*, Frankfurt, 1968, which, although very critical, recognizes Marx's merit as the 'first real theoretician of credit'. Much weaker was an earlier book by H. Block, *Die Marxsche Geldtheorie*, Jena, 1926.

86. Karl Kautsky, 'Geld, Papier und Ware', in *Die Neue Zeit*, 1911–12, Nos. 24, 25.

87. Eugen Varga, 'Goldproduktion und Teuerung', in *Die Neue Zeit*, 1911–12, I, No. 7, and 1912–13, I, No. 16; Rudolf Hilferding, 'Geld und Ware', ibid., 1911–12, I, No. 22; Karl Kautsky, 'Die Wandlungen der Goldproduktion und der wechselnde Charakter der Teuerung', Erganzungschaft No. 16, *Die Neue Zeit*, 1912–13; Otto Bauer, 'Goldproduktion und Teuerung', *Die Neue Zeit*, 1912–13, II, Nos. 1 and 2. This discussion continued between Varga and E. Ludwig in 1923, in the theoretical organ of the KPD, *Die Internationale*.

II. *CAPITAL* AND THE DESTINY OF CAPITALISM

It is above all through its integration of theory and history that Marxism manifests its superiority in the economic domain over classical and neo-classical political economy. It is through its ability to foresee correctly long-term trends of capitalist development, including the main inner contradictions of the capitalist mode of production which propel this long-term development forward, that *Capital* continues to fascinate friend and foe alike. Those who, generation after generation, continue to accuse Marx of 'unscientific' *parti pris* or speculative excursions into the realms of prophecy[88] cannot escape the burden of proof. It is up to them to account for the mysterious fact that a thinker according to them so devoid of analytical tools should have been able unfailingly to work out the long-term laws of motion that have determined the development of capitalism for a century and a half.

Apart from the so-called law of increasing absolute impoverishment of the working class wrongly attributed to Marx, the aspect of the latter's theoretical conclusions concerning the capitalist mode of production which has been most consistently under attack since *Capital* Volume 1 first appeared has been the so-called 'theory of the inevitable collapse of capitalism' (*Zusammenbruchstheorie*). First strongly challenged by the Bernsteinian 'revisionists' within the socialist movement, and only weakly defended by most orthodox Marxists of the epoch,[89] the theory has been exposed to ridicule by a monotonous succession of authors in the last decades. All have asked the ritual rhetorical question: has not the capitalist mode of production shown a capacity of adaptation and self-reform far beyond anything which Marx foresaw?[90]

88. The most outstanding example is that of Popper, *The Open Society and its Enemies*, Vol. 2. See also, by the same author, *Conjectures and Refutations*, pp. 336–46, quoted above.

89. For Bernstein's questioning of the breakdown theory see, for example, op. cit., pp. 113–28. For a very mild reply see Heinrich Cunow, 'Zur Zusammenbruchstheorie' in *Die Neue Zeit*, 1898–9, I, pp. 424–30. In *Das Finanzkapital* Hilferding already raised the theoretical possibility of an 'organized' capitalism without crises, through the operations of a 'general cartel' (op. cit., p. 372).

90. See, for example, Tugan-Baranovsky, op. cit., pp. 236–9; Schumpeter, *Capitalism, Socialism and Democracy*, p. 42; Popper, *The Open Society and its Enemies*, Vol. 2, p. 155 et al.; C.A.R. Crosland, *The Future of Socialism*,

Arguments along these lines usually contain a basic flaw: they try to prove too much. They contend that capitalism has survived so many crises that nobody can seriously challenge its capacity to survive future ones. But at the same time they also contend that the present economic system in the West cannot any longer be characterized as 'capitalist'; and that through successive self-reform and adaptation, in order to overcome crises which threatened to wreck it, capitalism has transformed itself into a new social organization of the economy. This they most often characterize by the term 'mixed economy', although a host of other formulas such as 'managerial capitalism', 'organized capitalism', 'managerial society', 'technostructure rule', etc. have at times been devised to describe it.[91]

But *Capital* is not simply a powerful tool for understanding the great lines of world development since the industrial revolution. It also furnishes us with a clear and unequivocal definition of what the capitalist mode of production essentially represents. Capitalism is neither a society of 'perfect competition', nor a society of 'increasing pauperism', nor a society where 'private entrepreneurs rule the factories', nor even a society in which 'money is the one and only master'. Vague and imprecise definitions of this type, which allow evasion of the *basic* issues, lead to endless confusion about the relationship of today's economic system in the West with the economic system analysed by *Capital*.[92] *Capital* shows that the capitalist mode of production is fundamentally determined by

---

London, 1956, pp. 3–5, etc. An interesting and voluminous anthology of texts related to the *Zusammenbruchstheorie* has been published in Italy by Lucio Colletti and Claudio Napoleoni, *Il futuro del capitalismo – crollo o sviluppo?*, Bari, 1970.

91. It is impossible to list all the important authors who have evolved this type of analysis. It is sufficient to indicate the main trends: that of James Burnham's 'Managerial Revolution'; that of the social democrats and Samuelson's 'mixed economy' (see Crosland, op. cit., pp. 29–35); that of Robin Morris's 'Managerial Capitalism'; and that of Galbraith's 'technostructure' (*The New Industrial State*) which follows, perhaps unknowingly, the analysis of the German Social Democrat Richard Loewenthal (writing under the pen-name Paul Sering), in *Jenseits des Kapitalismus*, Nuremberg, 1946.

92. Here a characteristic statement by Popper: 'How utterly absurd it is to identify the economic system of the modern democracies with the system Marx called "capitalism" can be seen at a glance, by comparing it with his ten-point programme for the communist revolution' (in the Communist Manifesto of 1848) (*The Open Society and its Enemies*, Vol. 2, p. 129).

three conditions and three only: (1) the fact that the mass of producers are not owners of the means of production in the economic
sense of the word, but have to sell their labour-power to the owners; (2) the fact that these owners are organized into separate firms
which compete with each other for shares of the market on which
commodities are sold, for profitable fields of investment for capital,
for sources of raw materials, etc. (that is, the institution of private
property in the economic sense of the word); (3) the fact that these
same owners of the means of production (different firms) are,
therefore, compelled to extort the maximum surplus-value from
the producers, in order to accumulate more and more capital –
which leads, under conditions of generalized commodity production and generalized alienation, to constantly growing mechanization of labour, concentration and centralization of capital, growing organic composition of capital, the tendency for the rate of
profit to fall, and periodically recurrent crises of over-production.

If these are the criteria, there can be no question that Western
society is still capitalist; that wage-labour and capital are still the
two antagonistic classes of society; that accumulation of capital is
more than ever the basic motive force of that society; and that the
extortion and realization of private profit governs the basic drive
of separate firms.

Such aspects of contemporary Western society as the fact that
some of these firms are nationalized; that there is growing state
intervention in the economy; that competition has become 'imperfect' (that it is no longer essentially fought by cutting prices,
but rather by reducing production costs and increasing distribution and sales); that workers have strong trade unions (except
when, under conditions of violent social crisis, bourgeois democratic freedoms are abolished) and that their standard of living has
risen far more than Marx expected it to rise – all this in no way
abolishes or reduces the relevance of the basic structural features
of capitalism, as defined by *Capital*, from which all the basic laws
of motion of the system flow. These basic laws of motion thus
continue to remain valid.

Without courting paradox one could even contend that, from a
structural point of view, the 'concrete' capitalism of the final
quarter of the twentieth century is much closer to the 'abstract'
model of *Capital* than was the 'concrete' capitalism of 1867, when
Marx finished correcting the proofs of Volume 1. Firstly, because
the intermediate class of small independent producers, proprietors

of their own means of production, which was still a significant social layer a century ago, has today nearly been eroded out of existence; dependent wage and salary earners, compelled to sell their labour-power, now amount to over 80 per cent of the economically active population in most Western countries and in several to over 90 per cent. Secondly, because concentration and centralization of capital has led to a situation where not only do a couple of hundred giant corporations dominate the economy of each imperialist country, but a few hundred multi-national corporations also concentrate in their hands one third of all the wealth of the capitalist *world* economy. Thirdly, because the productivity and the objective socialization of labour have increased to such an extent that production of value for private enrichment has become absurd beyond anything Marx could have foreseen a century ago and the world cries out so compellingly for a planned husbanding of resources to satisfy needs on the basis of consciously and democratically chosen priorities that even opponents of socialism cannot fail to understand the message.[93]

Why then, one might ask, have the expropriators not yet become the expropriated, and why does capitalism still survive in the highly industrialized countries? The answer to that question would involve a detailed critical review of twentieth-century political and social history. But the whole point is, of course, that Marx never predicted any sudden and automatic collapse of the capitalist system in one 'final' crisis, due to a single economic 'cause'. In the famous Chapter 32 of *Capital* Volume 1, 'The Historical Tendency of Capitalist Accumulation', Marx describes economic tendencies provoking a reaction from social forces. The growth of the proletariat, of its exploitation, and of organized revolt against that exploitation, are the main levers for the overthrow of capitalism. Centralization of the means of production and objective socialization of labour create the economic preconditions for a society based upon collective property and free co-operation by associated producers. But they do not automatically produce such a society on some universal day of victory. They have to be consciously utilized, at privileged moments of *social* crisis, to bring about the revolutionary overthrow of the system.

Marx was as far removed from any fatalistic belief in the automatic effects of economic determinism as any social thinker could

93. See, for example, the reaction of scholars like Barry Commoner (*The Closing Cycle*, London, 1972) to the ecological crisis.

be. He repeated over and over again that men made and had to make their own history, only not in an arbitrary way and independently from the material conditions in which they found themselves.[94] Any theory of the collapse of capitalism, therefore, can only present itself as Marxist if it is a theory of conscious overthrow of capitalism, that is, a theory of socialist revolution.[95] Chapter 32, at the end of *Capital* Volume 1, only indicates in very general terms how and why objective inner contradictions of the capitalist mode of production make this overthrow both possible and necessary. The rest has to result, in Marx's words, from the growth of 'the revolt of the working class, a class constantly increasing in numbers, and trained, united and organized by the very mechanism of the capitalist process of production'.

In other words, between the growing economic contradictions of the capitalist mode of production on the one hand, and the collapse of capitalism on the other hand, there is a necessary mediation: the development of the class consciousness, organized strength and capacity for revolutionary action of the working class (including revolutionary leadership). *That* chapter of Marxist theory is not incorporated into *Capital*. Perhaps Marx intended to discuss it in the book on the State which he wanted to write but never came even to draft. At all events, he left no systematic exposition of his thought in this respect, although many ideas on the subject are to be found scattered throughout his articles and letters. It was up to his most gifted followers, foremost among them Lenin, Trotsky and Rosa Luxemburg, to deal systematically with what one might call 'the Marxist theory of the subjective factor'.

94. See, for instance, the end of Marx's remarkable letter to Friedrich Bolte of 23 November 1871 (*Selected Correspondence*, pp. 269–71) in which he explains the necessity for previous organization of the working class in order for it to be able to challenge the bourgeoisie for political power, and the fact that without such systematic education through propaganda, agitation and action, the working class remains a captive of bourgeois politics.

95. Rosa Luxemburg admirably synthesized the contradictory trends as early as 1899: 'The production relations of capitalist society approach more and more the production relations of socialist society. But on the other hand, its political and juridical relations [and, one might add, their ideological reflections in the minds of men as well] establish between capitalist society and socialist society a steadily rising wall. This wall is not overthrown but on the contrary strengthened and consolidated by the development of social reforms and the course of [bourgeois parliamentary] democracy' ('Reform or Revolution', in Mary Alice Waters (ed.), *Rosa Luxemburg Speaks*, New York, 1970, p. 57).

The survival of capitalism to this day in the most industrialized countries has certainly given it a life-span far beyond what Marx expected. But this is not because the system has developed in essentially other directions than those predicted by *Capital*. Nor is it because it has been able to avoid a periodic repetition of explosive social crises. On the contrary, since the Russian revolution of 1905, and certainly since the outbreak of the First World War, such crises have become recurrent features of contemporary history.

In the course of such crises, capitalism has indeed been overthrown in many countries, Russia and China being the most important. But contrary to what Marx expected, this overthrow occurred not so much where the proletariat was most strongly developed numerically and economically, as a result of the greatest possible extension of capitalist industry, that is, in those countries which also have a powerful bourgeois class. It occurred rather in those countries where the bourgeoisie was weakest and where, therefore, the political relationship of forces was favourable for a young proletariat capable of gaining the support of a strongly rebellious peasantry. This historical detour can be understood only if one integrates into the analysis two key factors: on the one hand, the development of imperialism and its effect on the large part of the human race which lives in socially and economically underdeveloped societies (the law of uneven and combined development); on the other hand, the interrelationship between the lack of revolutionary experience on the part of the Western working class during the long period of 'organic growth' of imperialism (1890–1914) and the growing reformism and integration of social democracy into bourgeois society and the bourgeois state which were responsible for the failure of the first large-scale revolutionary crises in the West, in 1918–23 (above all in Germany and Italy). As a result of this failure, the victorious Russian revolution itself became isolated, and the international working-class movement went through the dark interlude of Stalinism, from which it only slowly began to emerge in the nineteen-fifties. This brings us back to what I have called the Marxist theory of the subjective factor – and incidentally explains why, after the rich flowering of Marxist economic theory in the period 1895–1930, a quarter of a century of almost total stagnation occurred in that field too.

The debate around the *Zusammenbruchstheorie* has suffered from a confusion between two different questions: the question whether the replacement of capitalism by socialism is inevitable (an inevitable result of the inner economic contradictions of the capitalist mode of production); and the question whether, in the absence of a socialist revolution, capitalism would live on for ever. A negative answer to the first question in no way implies a positive one to the second. Indeed, classical Marxists, following the young Marx, formulated their prognosis in the form of a dilemma: socialism or barbarism.

The social catastrophes which mankind has witnessed since Auschwitz and Hiroshima indicate that there was nothing 'romantic' in such a prognosis, but that it expressed a clear insight into the terrifying destructive potential of exchange-value production, capital accumulation, and the struggle for personal enrichment as ends in themselves. The concrete mechanics of the economic breakdown of capitalist economy may be open to conjecture. The interrelationship of the downturn of value production (decline of the total number of labour hours produced as a result of semi-automation), of the increasing difficulty of realizing surplus-value, of increasing output of waste not entering the reproduction process, of increasing depletion of national resources and, above all, of longterm decline of the rate of profit, is still far from clear.[96] But a very strong case can be made for the thesis that there are definite limits to the adaptability of capitalist relations of production, and that these limits are being progressively attained in one field after another.

It is most unlikely that capitalism will survive another halfcentury of the crises (military, political, social, monetary, cultural) which have occurred uninterruptedly since 1914. It is most probable, moreover, that *Capital* and what it stands for – namely a scientific analysis of bourgeois society which represents the proletariat's class consciousness at its highest level – will in the end prove to have made a decisive contribution to capitalism's replacement by a classless society of associated producers.

96. I shall return to this whole subject, and especially to the relationship of the breakdown controversy to the tendency for the average rate of profit to decline, in the introduction to *Capital*, Vol. 3.

ERNEST MANDEL

Translator's Preface

The original English translation of the first volume of *Capital*, by Samuel Moore and Edward Aveling, was edited by Engels. His letters show that he took the task very seriously, and, as Marx's friend and collaborator for forty years, he was certainly in a position to make the translation an authoritative presentation of Marx's thought in English.

So why is a new translation necessary? Firstly, the English language itself has changed. A translation made in the nineteenth century can hardly survive this change intact. Think only of the pejorative sense the word 'labourer' has taken on, making its replacement by 'worker' essential.

Secondly, Engels always tried to spare Marx's readers from grappling with difficult passages. In this, he was following his friend's example. In the Postface to the French edition, written in 1875, Marx explains that he has revised the French text in order to make it 'more accessible to the reader', even though the rendering presented to him by Roy was 'scrupulously exact', referring in justification to the French public's impatience with theoretical discussion. In 1975, however, after the immense effort of critical investigation into Marxism made in the last few decades, and the publication of hitherto unavailable texts, it is no longer necessary to water down *Capital* in order to spare the reader (who was, in any case, generally put off by the bulk of the book rather than its difficulty). Hence whole sentences omitted by Engels can be restored, and theoretical difficulties, instead of being swept under the carpet, can be exposed to the daylight, in so far as the English language is capable of this. This comment relates above all to German philosophical terms, used repeatedly by Marx in *Capital*, as indeed elsewhere. In translating these, I have tried not to prejudge the philosophical questions, the question of Marx's relation to Hegel and that of the relation between his philosophy and his political economy, but rather to present a text which would permit the reader to form his own view.

Thirdly, it is generally agreed that Marx was a master of literary German. A translation which overlooks this will not do justice to his vivid use of the language and the startling and strong images which abound in *Capital*. In my translation, I have always tried to bear this element in mind. How successfully, the reader must judge.

BEN FOWKES

NOTE

In compiling the editorial footnotes, indicated by asterisks etc., the translator has derived much assistance from the *Marx-Engels Werke* (*MEW*) edition of *Capital*.

Preface to the First Edition

This work, whose first volume I now submit to the public, forms the continuation of my book *Zur Kritik der Politischen Ökonomie*, published in 1859.* The long pause between the first part and the continuation is due to an illness of many years' duration, which interrupted my work again and again.

The substance of that earlier work is summarized in the first chapter† of this volume. This is done not merely for the sake of connectedness and completeness. The presentation is improved. As far as circumstances in any way permit, many points only hinted at in the earlier book are here worked out more fully, while, conversely, points worked out fully there are only touched upon in this volume. The sections on the history of the theories of value and of money are now, of course, left out altogether. However, the reader of the earlier work will find new sources relating to the history of those theories in the notes to the first chapter.

Beginnings are always difficult in all sciences. The understanding of the first chapter, especially the section that contains the analysis of commodities, will therefore present the greatest difficulty. I have popularized the passages concerning the substance of value and the magnitude of value as much as possible.‡[1] The

1. This is the more necessary, in that even the section of Ferdinand Lassalle's work against Schulze-Delitzsch in which he professes to give 'the intellectual quintessence' of my explanations on these matters, contains important mistakes. If Ferdinand Lassalle has borrowed almost literally from my writings, and without any acknowledgement, all the general theoretical propositions in

*English translation: *A Contribution to the Critique of Political Economy*, tr. S. W. Ryazanskaya, London, 1971.

†The first chapter in the first edition. In subsequent editions this was expanded to three chapters, as in this edition.

‡In this edition, numbered footnotes are Marx's own. Those marked by asterisks etc. are the translator's.

value-form, whose fully developed shape is the money-form, is very simple and slight in content. Nevertheless, the human mind has sought in vain for more than 2,000 years to get to the bottom of it, while on the other hand there has been at least an approximation to a successful analysis of forms which are much richer in content and more complex. Why? Because the complete body is easier to study than its cells. Moreover, in the analysis of economic forms neither microscopes nor chemical reagents are of assistance. The power of abstraction must replace both. But for bourgeois society, the commodity-form of the product of labour, or the value-form of the commodity, is the economic cell-form. To the superficial observer, the analysis of these forms seems to turn upon minutiae. It does in fact deal with minutiae, but so similarly does microscopic anatomy.

With the exception of the section on the form of value, therefore, this volume cannot stand accused on the score of difficulty. I assume, of course, a reader who is willing to learn something new and therefore to think for himself.

The physicist either observes natural processes where they occur in their most significant form, and are least affected by disturbing influences, or, wherever possible, he makes experiments under conditions which ensure that the process will occur in its pure state. What I have to examine in this work is the capitalist mode of production, and the relations of production and forms of intercourse [*Verkehrsverhältnisse*] that correspond to it. Until now, their *locus classicus* has been England. This is the reason why England is used as the main illustration of the theoretical developments I make. If, however, the German reader pharisaically shrugs his shoulders at the condition of the English industrial and agricultural workers, or optimistically comforts himself with the thought that in Germany things are not nearly so bad, I must plainly tell him: *De te fabula narratur!**

Intrinsically, it is not a question of the higher or lower degree of

his economic works, for example those on the historical character of capital, on the connection between the relations of production and the mode of production, etc., etc., even down to the terminology created by me, this may perhaps be due to purposes of propaganda. I am of course not speaking here of his detailed working-out and application of these propositions, which I have nothing to do with.

---

* 'The tale is told of you' (Horace, *Satires*, Bk I, Satire 1).

development of the social antagonisms that spring from the natural laws of capitalist production. It is a question of these laws themselves, of these tendencies winning their way through and working themselves out with iron necessity. The country that is more developed industrially only shows, to the less developed, the image of its own future.

But in any case, and apart from all this, where capitalist production has made itself fully at home amongst us,* for instance in the factories properly so called, the situation is much worse than in England, because the counterpoise of the Factory Acts is absent. In all other spheres, and just like the rest of Continental Western Europe, we suffer not only from the development of capitalist production, but also from the incompleteness of that development. Alongside the modern evils, we are oppressed by a whole series of inherited evils, arising from the passive survival of archaic and outmoded modes of production, with their accompanying train of anachronistic social and political relations. We suffer not only from the living, but from the dead. *Le mort saisit le vif!*†

The social statistics of Germany and the rest of Continental Western Europe are, in comparison with those of England, quite wretched. But they raise the veil just enough to let us catch a glimpse of the Medusa's head behind it. We should be appalled at our own circumstances if, as in England, our governments and parliaments periodically appointed commissions of inquiry into economic conditions; if these commissions were armed with the same plenary powers to get at the truth; if it were possible to find for this purpose men as competent, as free from partisanship and respect of persons as are England's factory inspectors, her medical reporters on public health, her commissioners of inquiry into the exploitation of women and children, into conditions of housing and nourishment, and so on. Perseus wore a magic cap so that the monsters he hunted down might not see him. We draw the magic cap down over our own eyes and ears so as to deny that there are any monsters.

Let us not deceive ourselves about this. Just as in the eighteenth century the American War of Independence sounded the tocsin for the European middle class, so in the nineteenth century the American Civil War did the same for the European working class. In England the process of transformation is palpably evident. When it has reached a certain point, it must react on the Continent.

*i.e. amongst the Germans.   †'The dead man clutches onto the living!'

There it will take a form more brutal or more humane, according to the degree of development of the working class itself. Apart from any higher motives, then, the most basic interests of the present ruling classes dictate to them that they clear out of the way all the legally removable obstacles to the development of the working class. For this reason, among others, I have devoted a great deal of space in this volume to the history, the details, and the results of the English factory legislation. One nation can and should learn from others. Even when a society has begun to track down the natural laws of its movement – and it is the ultimate aim of this work to reveal the economic law of motion of modern society – it can neither leap over the natural phases of its development nor remove them by decree. But it can shorten and lessen the birth-pangs.

To prevent possible misunderstandings, let me say this. I do not by any means depict the capitalist and the landowner in rosy colours. But individuals are dealt with here only in so far as they are the personifications of economic categories, the bearers [*Träger*] of particular class-relations and interests. My standpoint, from which the development of the economic formation of society is viewed as a process of natural history, can less than any other make the individual responsible for relations whose creature he remains, socially speaking, however much he may subjectively raise himself above them.

In the domain of political economy, free scientific inquiry does not merely meet the same enemies as in all other domains. The peculiar nature of the material it deals with summons into the fray on the opposing side the most violent, sordid and malignant passions of the human breast, the Furies of private interest. The Established Church, for instance, will more readily pardon an attack on thirty-eight of its thirty-nine articles than on one thirty-ninth of its income. Nowadays atheism itself is a *culpa levis*,* as compared with the criticism of existing property relations. Nevertheless, even here there is an unmistakable advance. I refer, as an example, to the Blue Book published within the last few weeks: 'Correspondence with Her Majesty's Missions Abroad, Regarding Industrial Questions and Trades' Unions'. There the representatives of the English Crown in foreign countries declare in plain language that in Germany, in France, in short in all the civilized states of the European Continent, a radical change in the existing relations

* 'Venial sin'.

between capital and labour is as evident and inevitable as in England. At the same time, on the other side of the Atlantic Ocean, Mr Wade, Vice-President of the United States, has declared in public meetings that, after the abolition of slavery, a radical transformation in the existing relations of capital and landed property is on the agenda. These are signs of the times, not to be hidden by purple mantles or black cassocks. They do not signify that tomorrow a miracle will occur. They do show that, within the ruling classes themselves, the foreboding is emerging that the present society is no solid crystal, but an organism capable of change, and constantly engaged in a process of change.

The second volume of this work will deal with the process of the circulation of capital (Book II) and the various forms of the process of capital in its totality (Book III), while the third and last volume (Book IV) will deal with the history of the theory.*

I welcome every opinion based on scientific criticism. As to the prejudices of so-called public opinion, to which I have never made concessions, now, as ever, my maxim is that of the great Florentine:

'*Segui il tuo corso, e lascia dir le genti.*'†

Karl Marx

London, 25 July 1867

*Books II and III were issued by Engels after Marx's death as separate volumes, and are referred to below as Volumes 2 and 3, as they are generally known. This would have made Book IV Volume 4, but the manuscript for this was eventually published by Kautsky as *Theories of Surplus-Value*.

†'Go on your way, and let the people talk.' Marx altered Dante's words to make them fit in here. The original is '*Vien retro a me, e lascia dir le genti*' ('Follow me, and let the people talk'), in *Divina Commedia*, *Purgatorio*, Canto V, line 13.

Postface to the Second Edition

I must start by informing the readers of the first edition about the alterations made in the second edition. The clearer arrangement of the book will be immediately apparent. Additional notes are everywhere marked as notes to the second edition. The following are the most important points with regard to the text itself:

In Chapter 1, Section 1, the derivation of value by analysis of the equations in which every exchange-value is expressed has been carried out with greater scientific strictness; similarly, the connection between the substance of value and the determination of the magnitude of value by the labour-time socially necessary, which was only alluded to in the first edition, is now expressly emphasized. Chapter 1, Section 3 (on the form of value), has been completely revised, a task which was made necessary by the two-fold presentation of it in the first edition, if by nothing else. Let me remark in passing that this twofold presentation was occasioned by my friend Dr L. Kugelmann, in Hanover. I was visiting him in the spring of 1867 when the first proof-sheets arrived from Hamburg, and he convinced me that most readers needed a supplementary, more didactic exposition of the form of value. The last section of the first chapter, 'The Fetishism of Commodities, etc.', has been altered considerably. Chapter 3, Section 1 (on the measure of values), has been carefully revised, because in the first edition this section was treated carelessly, the reader having been referred to the explanation already given in *Zur Kritik der Politischen Ökonomie*, Berlin, 1859. Chapter 7, particularly Section 2, has been re-worked to a great extent.

It would be pointless to go into all the partial textual changes, which are often purely stylistic. They occur throughout the book. Nevertheless, I find now, on revising the French translation which is appearing in Paris, that several parts of the German original stand in need of a rather thorough re-working, while other parts require rather heavy stylistic editing, and still others require the painstaking elimination of occasional slips. But there was no time for that. For I was informed only in the autumn of 1871, when in the midst of other urgent work, that the book was sold out and the printing of the second edition was to begin in January 1872.

The appreciation which *Das Kapital* rapidly gained in wide circles of the German working class is the best reward for my labours. A man who in economic matters represents the bourgeois standpoint, the Viennese manufacturer Herr Mayer, in a pamphlet published during the Franco-German War,* aptly expounded the idea that the great capacity for theory, which used to be considered a hereditary German attribute, had almost completely disappeared amongst the so-called educated classes in Germany, but that amongst the working class, on the contrary, it was enjoying a revival.

Political economy remains a foreign science in Germany, up to this very moment. In his *Geschichtliche Darstellung des Handels, der Gewerbe, usw.*,† especially in the first two volumes, published in 1830, Gustav von Gülich has already examined, for the most part, the historical circumstances that prevented the development of the capitalist mode of production in Germany, and consequently the construction there of modern bourgeois society. Thus the living soil from which political economy springs was absent. It had to be imported from England and France as a ready-made article; its German professors always remained pupils. The theoretical expression of an alien reality turned in their hands into a collection of dogmas, interpreted by them in the sense of the petty-bourgeois world surrounding them, and therefore misinterpreted. The feeling of scientific impotence, a feeling which could not entirely be suppressed, and the uneasy awareness that they had to master an area in fact entirely foreign to them, was only imperfectly concealed beneath a parade of literary and historical erudition, or by an admixture of extraneous material borrowed from the so-called *kameral* sciences,‡ a medley of smatterings through whose pur-

*Sigmund Mayer, *Die Sociale Frage in Wien*, Vienna, 1871.

† *Historical Description of Commerce, Industry, etc.*, 5 vols., Jena, 1830–45.

‡ *Kameralwissenschaft*, or Cameralism, was the German version of Mercantilism. It tended to see political economy in narrow terms as a matter of finance and administration, since it arose as a set of ideas as to how the rulers of German princely states could use their revenues to promote the state's well being. Notable Cameralists were von Hörnigkh in the seventeenth and Justi in the eighteenth century.

gatory the hopeful candidate for the German bureaucracy has to pass.

Since 1848 capitalist production has developed rapidly in Germany, and at the present time it is in the full bloom of speculation and swindling. But fate is still unpropitious to our professional economists. At the time when they were able to deal with political economy in an unprejudiced way, modern economic conditions were absent from the reality of Germany. And as soon as these conditions did come into existence, it was under circumstances that no longer permitted their impartial investigation within the bounds of the bourgeois horizon. In so far as political economy is bourgeois, i.e. in so far as it views the capitalist order as the absolute and ultimate form of social production, instead of as a historically transient stage of development, it can only remain a science while the class struggle remains latent or manifests itself only in isolated and sporadic phenomena.

Let us take England. Its classical political economy belongs to a period in which the class struggle was as yet undeveloped. Its last great representative, Ricardo, ultimately (and consciously) made the antagonism of class interests, of wages and profits, of profits and rent, the starting-point of his investigations, naïvely taking this antagonism for a social law of nature. But with this contribution the bourgeois science of economics had reached the limits beyond which it could not pass. Already in Ricardo's lifetime, and in opposition to him, it was met by criticism in the person of Sismondi.[1]

The succeeding period, from 1820 to 1830, was notable in England for the lively scientific activity which took place in the field of political economy. It was the period of both the vulgarizing and the extending of Ricardo's theory, and of the contest of that theory with the old school. Splendid tournaments were held. What was achieved at that time is little known on the European Continent, because the polemic is for the most part scattered over articles in reviews, *pièces d'occasion* and pamphlets. The unprejudiced character of this polemic – although Ricardo's theory already serves, in exceptional cases, as a weapon with which to attack the bourgeois economic system – is explained by the circumstances of the time. On the one hand, large-scale industry itself

1. See my work *Zur Kritik der Politischen Ökonomie*, p. 39 [English translation, p. 61].

was only just emerging from its childhood, as is shown by the fact that the periodic cycle of its modern life opens for the first time with the crisis of 1825. On the other hand, the class struggle between capital and labour was forced into the background, politically by the discord between the governments and the feudal aristocracy gathered around the Holy Alliance, assembled in one camp, and the mass of the people, led by the bourgeoisie, in the other camp, and economically by the quarrel between industrial capital and aristocratic landed property. This latter quarrel was concealed in France by the antagonism between small-scale, fragmented property and big landownership, but in England it broke out openly after the passing of the Corn Laws. The literature of political economy in England at this time calls to mind the economic 'storm and stress period' which in France followed the death of Dr Quesnay,* but only as an Indian summer reminds us of spring. With the year 1830 there came the crisis which was to be decisive, once and for all.

In France and England the bourgeoisie had conquered political power. From that time on, the class struggle took on more and more explicit and threatening forms, both in practice and in theory. It sounded the knell of scientific bourgeois economics. It was thenceforth no longer a question whether this or that theorem was true, but whether it was useful to capital or harmful, expedient or inexpedient, in accordance with police regulations or contrary to them. In place of disinterested inquirers there stepped hired prize-fighters; in place of genuine scientific research, the bad conscience and evil intent of apologetics. Still, even the importunate pamphlets with which the Anti-Corn Law League, led by the manufacturers Cobden and Bright, deluged the world offer a historical interest, if no scientific one, on account of their polemic against the landed aristocracy. But since then the free-trade legislation inaugurated by Sir Robert Peel has deprived vulgar economics even of this, its last sting.

The Continental revolution of 1848 also had its reaction in

---

*Dr Quesnay died in 1774. His death was immediately followed by Turgot's attempt to put Physiocratic ideas into practice, while he was Louis XVI's Controller-General (1774–6). His fall in 1776 opened a period of political and economic crisis which culminated in the French Revolution. It is this which Marx has in mind, rather than the (somewhat exiguous) theoretical writings of the period after 1774.

England. Men who still claimed some scientific standing and aspired to be something more than mere sophists and sycophants of the ruling classes tried to harmonize the political economy of capital with the claims, no longer to be ignored, of the proletariat. Hence a shallow syncretism, of which John Stuart Mill is the best representative. This is a declaration of bankruptcy by 'bourgeois' economics, an event already illuminated in a masterly manner by the great Russian scholar and critic N. Chernyshevsky, in his *Outlines of Political Economy According to Mill*.

In Germany, therefore, the capitalist mode of production came to maturity after its antagonistic character had already been revealed, with much sound and fury, by the historical struggles which took place in France and England. Moreover, the German proletariat had in the meantime already attained a far clearer theoretical awareness than the German bourgeoisie. Thus, at the very moment when a bourgeois science of political economy at last seemed possible in Germany, it had in reality again become impossible.

Under these circumstances its spokesmen divided into two groups. The one set, prudent, practical business folk, flocked to the banner of Bastiat, the most superficial and therefore the most successful representative of apologetic vulgar economics; the other set, proud of the professorial dignity of their science, followed John Stuart Mill in his attempt to reconcile the irreconcilable. Just as in the classical period of bourgeois economics, so also in the period of its decline, the Germans remained mere pupils, imitators and followers, petty retailers and hawkers in the service of the great foreign wholesale concern.

The peculiar historical development of German society therefore excluded any original development of 'bourgeois' economics there, but did not exclude its critique. In so far as such a critique represents a class, it can only represent the class whose historical task is the overthrow of the capitalist mode of production and the final abolition of all classes – the proletariat.

The learned and unlearned spokesmen of the German bourgeoisie tried at first to kill *Das Kapital* with silence, a technique which had succeeded with my earlier writings. As soon as they found that these tactics no longer fitted the conditions of the time, they wrote prescriptions 'for tranquillizing the bourgeois mind', on the pretext of criticizing my book. But they found in the workers' press – see for example Joseph Dietzgen's articles in the

Volksstaat* – champions stronger than themselves, to whom they still owe a reply even now.[2]

An excellent Russian translation of *Capital* appeared in the spring of 1872 in St Petersburg. The edition of 3,000 copies is already nearly exhausted. As early as 1871, N. Sieber, Professor of Political Economy in the University of Kiev, in his work *David Ricardo's Theory of Value and of Capital*, referred to my theory of value, money and capital as in its fundamentals a necessary sequel to the teaching of Smith and Ricardo. What astonishes a Western European when he reads this solid piece of work is the author's consistent and firm grasp of the purely theoretical position.

That the method employed in *Capital* has been little understood is shown by the various mutually contradictory conceptions that have been formed of it.

Thus the Paris *Revue Positiviste*† reproaches me for, on the one hand, treating economics metaphysically, and, on the other hand – imagine this! – confining myself merely to the critical analysis of the actual facts, instead of writing recipes (Comtist ones?) for the cook-shops of the future. Professor Sieber has already given the answer to the reproach about metaphysics: 'In so far as it deals

2. The mealy-mouthed babblers of German vulgar economics grumbled about the style of my book. No one can feel the literary shortcomings of *Capital* more strongly than I myself. Yet I will quote in this connection one English and one Russian notice, for the benefit and enjoyment of these gentlemen and their public. The *Saturday Review*, an entirely hostile journal, said in its notice of the first edition: 'The presentation of the subject invests the driest economic questions with a certain peculiar charm.' The *St Petersburg Journal* (*Sankt-Peterburgskye Vyedomosty*), in its issue of 20 April 1872, says: 'The presentation of the subject, with the exception of one or two excessively specialized parts, is distinguished by its comprehensibility to the general reader, its clearness, and, in spite of the high scientific level of the questions discussed, by an unusual liveliness. In this respect the author in no way resembles ... the majority of German scholars, who ... write their books in a language so dry and obscure that the heads of ordinary mortals are cracked by it.'

*Dietzgen's articles on *Capital* actually appeared in Nos. 31, 34, 35 and 36 of the *Demokratisches Wochenblatt* in 1868. After the founding congress of the German Social Democratic Workers' Party in 1869 the paper was made its official organ, and renamed *Der Volksstaat*.

† *La Philosophie Positive*. *Revue* was the journal of the followers of Auguste Comte. It appeared in Paris between 1867 and 1883, under the editorship of E. Littré.

with actual theory, the method of Marx is the deductive method of the whole English school, a school whose failings and virtues are common to the best theoretical economists.' Mr M. Block – in *Les Théoriciens du socialisme en Allemagne. Extrait du Journal des économistes, Juillet et Août 1872* – makes the discovery that my method is analytic, and says: 'With this work, M. Marx can be ranged among the most eminent analytical thinkers.' The German reviewers, of course, cry out against my 'Hegelian sophistry'. The *European Messenger* (*Vyestnik Evropy*) of St Petersburg, in an article dealing exclusively with the method of *Capital* (May 1872 issue, pp. 427–36), finds my method of inquiry severely realistic, but my method of presentation, unfortunately, German-dialectical. It says: 'At first sight, if the judgement is made on the basis of the external form of the presentation, Marx is the most idealist of philosophers, and indeed in the German, i.e. the bad sense of the word. But in point of fact he is infinitely more realistic than all his predecessors in the business of economic criticism . . . He can in no sense be called an idealist.' I cannot answer the writer of this review* in any better way than by quoting a few extracts from his own criticism, which may, apart from this, interest some of my readers for whom the Russian original is inaccessible.

After a quotation from the preface to my *Zur Kritik der Politischen Ökonomie*, Berlin, 1850, p. iv–vii,† where I have discussed the materialist basis of my method, the reviewer goes on: 'The one thing which is important for Marx is to find the law of the phenomena with whose investigation he is concerned; and it is not only the law which governs these phenomena, in so far as they have a definite form and mutual connection within a given historical period, that is important to him. Of still greater importance to him is the law of their variation, of their development, i.e. of their transition from one form into another, from one series of connections into a different one. Once he has discovered this law, he investigates in detail the effects with which it manifests itself in social life . . . Consequently, Marx only concerns himself with one thing: to show, by an exact scientific investigation, the necessity of successive determinate orders of social relations, and to establish, as impeccably as possible, the facts from which he starts out and

---

*I. I. Kaufman (1848–1916), Russian economist, Professor of Political Economy at the University of St Petersburg, and author of numerous works on money and credit.

†English translation, pp. 19–23.

on which he depends. For this it is quite enough, if he proves, at the same time, both the necessity of the present order of things, and the necessity of another order into which the first must inevitably pass over; and it is a matter of indifference whether men believe or do not believe it, whether they are conscious of it or not. Marx treats the social movement as a process of natural history, governed by laws not only independent of human will, consciousness and intelligence, but rather, on the contrary, determining that will, consciousness and intelligence ... If the conscious element plays such a subordinate part in the history of civilization, it is self-evident that a critique whose object is civilization itself can, less than anything else, have for its basis any form or any result of consciousness. This means that it is not the idea but only its external manifestation which can serve as the starting-point. A critique of this kind will confine itself to the confrontation and comparison of a fact, not with ideas, but with another fact. The only things of importance for this inquiry are that the facts be investigated as accurately as possible, and that they actually form different aspects of development *vis-à-vis* each other. But most important of all is the precise analysis of the series of successions, of the sequences and links within which the different stages of development present themselves. It will be said, against this, that the general laws of economic life are one and the same, no matter whether they are applied to the present or the past. But this is exactly what Marx denies. According to him, such abstract laws do not exist ... On the contrary, in his opinion, every historical period possesses its own laws ... As soon as life has passed through a given period of development, and is passing over from one given stage to another, it begins to be subject also to other laws. In short, economic life offers us a phenomenon analogous to the history of evolution in other branches of biology ... The old economists misunderstood the nature of economic laws when they likened them to the laws of physics and chemistry. A more thorough analysis of the phenomena shows that social organisms differ among themselves as fundamentally as plants or animals. Indeed, one and the same phenomenon falls under quite different laws in consequence of the different general structure of these organisms, the variations of their individual organs, and the different conditions in which those organs function. Marx denies, for example, that the law of population is the same at all times and in all places. He asserts, on the contrary, that every stage of development has its own law of population ... With the varying degrees of development of productive power, social conditions and the laws governing them vary too. While Marx sets himself the task of following and explaining the capitalist economic order from this point of view, he is only formulating, in a strictly scientific manner, the aim that every accurate investigation into economic life must have ... The scientific value of such an inquiry lies in the illumination of the special laws that regulate the origin, existence, development and death of a given social organism and its replacement by another, higher one. And in fact this is the value of Marx's book.'

Here the reviewer pictures what he takes to be my own actual method, in a striking and, as far as concerns my own application of it, generous way. But what else is he depicting but the dialectical method?

Of course the method of presentation must differ in form from that of inquiry. The latter has to appropriate the material in detail, to analyse its different forms of development and to track down their inner connection. Only after this work has been done can the real movement be appropriately presented. If this is done successfully, if the life of the subject-matter is now reflected back in the ideas, then it may appear as if we have before us an *a priori* construction.

My dialectical method is, in its foundations, not only different from the Hegelian, but exactly opposite to it. For Hegel, the process of thinking, which he even transforms into an independent subject, under the name of 'the Idea', is the creator of the real world, and the real world is only the external appearance of the idea. With me the reverse is true: the ideal is nothing but the material world reflected in the mind of man, and translated into forms of thought.

I criticized the mystificatory side of the Hegelian dialectic nearly thirty years ago, at a time when it was still the fashion. But just when I was working at the first volume of *Capital*, the ill-humoured, arrogant and mediocre epigones who now talk large in educated German circles began to take pleasure in treating Hegel in the same way as the good Moses Mendelssohn treated Spinoza in Lessing's time, namely as a 'dead dog'.* I therefore openly

---

*Moses Mendelssohn (1729–86) was a philosopher who popularized the ideas of the Enlightenment in Germany, and a friend of Lessing. Marx refers here to Mendelssohn's controversy with Jacobi over the alleged Spinozism of

avowed myself the pupil of that mighty thinker, and even, here and there in the chapter on the theory of value, coquetted with the mode of expression peculiar to him. The mystification which the dialectic suffers in Hegel's hands by no means prevents him from being the first to present its general forms of motion in a comprehensive and conscious manner. With him it is standing on its head. It must be inverted, in order to discover the rational kernel within the mystical shell.

In its mystified form, the dialectic became the fashion in Germany, because it seemed to transfigure and glorify what exists. In its rational form it is a scandal and an abomination to the bourgeoisie and its doctrinaire spokesmen, because it includes in its positive understanding of what exists a simultaneous recognition of its negation, its inevitable destruction; because it regards every historically developed form as being in a fluid state, in motion, and therefore grasps its transient aspect as well; and because it does not let itself be impressed by anything, being in its very essence critical and revolutionary.

The fact that the movement of capitalist society is full of contradictions impresses itself most strikingly on the practical bourgeois in the changes of the periodic cycle through which modern industry passes, the summit of which is the general crisis. That crisis is once again approaching, although as yet it is only in its preliminary stages, and by the universality of its field of action and the intensity of its impact it will drum dialectics even into the heads of the upstarts in charge of the new Holy Prussian-German Empire.

Karl Marx

London, 24 January 1873

Lessing. In the pamphlet 'Moses Mendelssohn to the Friends of Lessing' (1786), he defends the latter against this 'accusation' and the related one of atheism.

Preface to the French Edition

To citizen Maurice La Châtre

Dear Citizen,

I applaud your idea of publishing the translation of *Capital* as a serial. In this form the book will be more accessible to the working class, a consideration which to me outweighs everything else.

That is the good side of your suggestion, but here is the reverse of the medal: the method of analysis which I have employed, and which had not previously been applied to economic subjects, makes the reading of the first chapters rather arduous, and it is to be feared that the French public, always impatient to come to a conclusion, eager to know the connection between general principles and the immediate questions that have aroused their passions, may be disheartened because they will be unable to move on at once.

That is a disadvantage I am powerless to overcome, unless it be by forewarning and forearming those readers who zealously seek the truth. There is no royal road to science, and only those who do not dread the fatiguing climb of its steep paths have a chance of gaining its luminous summits.

Believe me, dear citizen,

Your devoted,
Karl Marx

London, 18 March 1872

Postface to the French Edition

To the Reader

Mr J. Roy set himself the task of producing a version that would be as exact and even literal as possible, and has scrupulously fulfilled it. But his very scrupulousness has compelled me to modify his text, with a view to rendering it more intelligible to the reader. These alterations, introduced from day to day, as the book was published in parts, were not made with equal care and were bound to result in a lack of harmony in style.

Having once undertaken this work of revision, I was led to apply it also to the basic original text (the second German edition), to simplify some arguments, to complete others, to give additional historical or statistical material, to add critical suggestions, etc. Hence, whatever the literary defects of this French edition may be, it possesses a scientific value independent of the original and should be consulted even by readers familiar with German.

Below I give the passages in the Postface to the second German edition which treat of the development of political economy in Germany and the method employed in the present work.*

Karl Marx

London, 28 April 1875

* See above, pp. 95–103.

Preface to the Third Edition

Marx was not destined to get this, the third edition, ready for the press himself. The powerful thinker, to whose greatness even his opponents now make obeisance, died on 14 March 1883.

Upon me who, in Marx, lost the best, the truest friend I had – and had for forty years – the friend to whom I am more indebted than can be expressed in words – upon me now devolved the duty of attending to the publication of this third edition, as well as of the second volume, which Marx had left behind in manuscript. I must now account here to the reader for the way in which I discharged the first part of my duty.

It was Marx's original intention to re-write a great part of the text of the first volume, to formulate many theoretical points more exactly, to insert new ones, and to bring historical and statistical materials up to date. But his ailing condition and the urgent need to do the final editing of the second volume* induced him to give up this scheme. Only the most necessary alterations were to be made, only the insertions which the French edition (*Le Capital*, par Karl Marx, Paris, Lachâtre, 1873†) already contained were to be put in.

Among the books left by Marx there was a German copy which he himself had corrected here and there and provided with references to the French edition; also a French copy in which he had indicated the exact passages to be used. These alterations and additions are confined, with few exceptions, to Part Seven of the book, entitled 'The Process of Accumulation of Capital'. Here the previous text followed the original draft more closely than elsewhere, while the preceding sections had been gone over more thoroughly. The style was therefore more vivacious, more of a single cast, but also more careless, studded with Anglicisms and

*See above, p. 93, first note.
†The French edition appeared in instalments between 1872 and 1875.

in parts unclear; there were gaps here and there in the presentation of arguments, some important particulars being merely alluded to.

With regard to the style, Marx had himself thoroughly revised several sub-sections and had thereby indicated to me here, as well as in numerous oral suggestions, the length to which I could go in eliminating English technical terms and other Anglicisms. Marx would in any event have gone over the additions and supplementary texts and have replaced the smooth French with his own terse German; I had to be satisfied, when transferring them, with bringing them into maximum harmony with the original text.

Thus not a single word was changed in this third edition without my firm conviction that the author would have altered it himself. It would never occur to me to introduce into *Capital* the current jargon in which German economists are wont to express themselves – that gibberish in which, for instance, one who has others give him their labour for cash is called a labour-*giver* [*Arbeitgeber*] and one whose labour is taken away from him for wages is called a labour-*taker* [*Arbeitnehmer*]. In French, too, the word '*travail*' is used in every-day life in the sense of 'occupation'. But the French would rightly consider any economist crazy should he call the capitalist a *donneur de travail* (labour-giver) or the worker a *receveur de travail* (labour-taker).

Nor have I taken the liberty of converting the English coins and money, weights and measures used throughout the text into their new German equivalents. When the first edition appeared there were as many kinds of weights and measures in Germany as there are days in the year. Apart from this, there were two kinds of mark (the *Reichsmark* only existed at the time in the imagination of Soetbeer, who had invented it in the late thirties), two kinds of guilder, and at least three kinds of thaler, including one called the *neues Zweidrittel*.* In the natural sciences the metric system prevailed, in the world market – English weights and measures. Under such circumstances, English units of measurement were quite natural for a book which had to take its factual proofs almost exclusively from the conditions prevailing in English industry. The last-named reason is decisive even today, especially as the corresponding conditions in the world market have hardly

* 'New two-thirds': a silver coin worth $\frac{2}{3}$ of a thaler, which circulated in a number of German principalities between the seventeenth and the nineteenth centuries.

changed and English weights and measures almost entirely predominate, particularly in the key industries, iron and cotton.

In conclusion, a few words on Marx's manner of quoting, which is so little understood. When they are pure statements of fact or descriptions, the quotations, from the English Blue Books, for example, serve of course as simple documentary proof. But this is not so when the theoretical views of other economists are cited. Here the quotation is intended merely to state where, when and by whom an economic idea conceived in the course of development was first clearly enunciated. Here the only consideration is that the economic conception in question must be of some significance to the history of the science, that it is the more or less adequate theoretical expression of the economic situation of its time. But whether this conception still possesses any absolute or relative validity from the standpoint of the author or whether it has already become wholly past history is quite immaterial. Hence these quotations are only a running commentary to the text, a commentary borrowed from the history of economic science. They establish the dates and originators of certain of the more important advances in economic theory. And that was a very necessary thing in a science whose historians have so far distinguished themselves only by the tendentious ignorance characteristic of place-hunters. It will now be understood why Marx, in consonance with the Postface to the second edition, only had occasion to quote German economists in very exceptional cases.

There is hope that the second volume will appear in the course of 1884.

Frederick Engels

London, 7 November 1883

Preface to the English Edition

The publication of an English version of *Das Kapital* needs no apology. On the contrary, an explanation might be expected why this English version has been delayed until now, seeing that for some years past the theories advocated in this book have been constantly referred to, attacked and defended, interpreted and misinterpreted, in the periodical press and the current literature of both England and America.

When, soon after the author's death in 1883, it became evident that an English edition of the work was really required, Mr Samuel Moore, for many years a friend of Marx and of the present writer, and than whom, perhaps, no one is more conversant with the book itself, consented to undertake the translation which the literary executors of Marx were anxious to lay before the public. It was understood that I should compare the MS. with the original work, and suggest such alterations as I might deem advisable. When, by and by, it was found that Mr Moore's professional occupations prevented him from finishing the translation as quickly as we all desired, we gladly accepted Dr Aveling's offer to undertake a portion of the work; at the same time Mrs Aveling, Marx's youngest daughter, offered to check the quotations and to restore the original text of the numerous passages taken from English authors and Blue Books and translated by Marx into German. This has been done throughout, with but a few unavoidable exceptions.

The following portions of the book have been translated by Dr Aveling: (1) Chapters 10 ('The Working Day') and 11 ('Rate and Mass of Surplus-Value'); (2) Part Six ('Wages', comprising Chapters 19 to 22); (3) from Chapter 24, Section 4 ('Circumstances which' etc.) to the end of the book, comprising the latter part of Chapter 24, Chapter 25, and the whole of Part Eight (Chapters 26 to 33); (4) the two author's Prefaces.* All the rest of the book has been done by Mr Moore. While, thus, each of the translators is responsible for his share of the work only, I bear a joint responsibility for the whole.

The third German edition, which has been made the basis of our work throughout, was prepared by me, in 1883, with the assistance of notes left by the author, indicating the passages of the second edition to be replaced by designated passages from the French text published in 1873.[1] The alterations thus effected in the text of the second edition generally coincided with changes prescribed by Marx in a set of MS. instructions for an English translation that was planned, about ten years ago, in America, but abandoned chiefly for want of a fit and proper translator. This MS. was placed at our disposal by our old friend Mr F. A. Sorge of Hoboken, N.J. It designates some further interpolations from the French edition; but, being so many years older than the final instructions for the third edition, I did not consider myself at liberty to make use of it otherwise than sparingly, and chiefly in cases where it helped us over difficulties. In the same way, the French text has been referred to in most of the difficult passages, as an indicator of what the author himself was prepared to sacrifice wherever something of the full import of the original had to be sacrificed in the rendering.

1. *Le Capital, par Karl Marx. Traduction de M. J. Roy, entièrement revisée par l'auteur*, Paris, Lachâtre. This translation, especially in the latter part of the book, contains considerable alterations in and additions to the text of the second German edition.

---

*For the English edition of *Capital*, Engels changed Marx's earlier division of the book into chapters and parts, making the three sections of what was Chapter 4 and the seven sections of what was Chapter 24 into separate chapters. For reasons of convenience to English readers, we have held to Engels's arrangement. We have also followed Engels in presenting the chapters on 'So-called Primitive Accumulation' as a separate Part VIII, which is certainly justifiable in view of its special subject matter. The following table shows the relation between parts and chapters in English and German editions:

	German	English
Chapters	1–3	1–3
	4	4–6
	5–23	7–25
	24	26–32
	25	33
Parts	One–Six	One–Six
	Seven	Seven–Eight

There is, however, one difficulty we could not spare the reader: the use of certain terms in a sense different from what they have, not only in common life, but in ordinary political economy. But this was unavoidable. Every new aspect of a science involves a revolution in the technical terms of that science. This is best shown by chemistry, where the whole of the terminology is radically changed about once in twenty years, and where you will hardly find a single organic compound that has not gone through a whole series of different names. Political economy has generally been content to take, just as they were, the terms of commercial and industrial life, and to operate with them, entirely failing to see that by so doing it confined itself within the narrow circle of ideas expressed by those terms. Thus, though perfectly aware that both profits and rent are but sub-divisions, fragments of that unpaid part of the product which the labourer has to supply to his employer (its first appropriator, though not its ultimate exclusive owner), yet even classical political economy never went beyond the received notions of profits and rents, never examined this unpaid part of the product (called by Marx surplus product) in its integrity as a whole, and therefore never arrived at a clear comprehension, either of its origin and nature, or of the laws that regulate the subsequent distribution of its value. Similarly all industry, not agricultural or handicraft, is indiscriminately comprised in the term of manufacture, and thereby the distinction is obliterated between two great and essentially different periods of economic history: the period of manufacture proper, based on the division of manual labour, and the period of modern industry based on machinery. It is, however, self-evident that a theory which views modern capitalist production as a mere passing stage in the economic history of mankind, must make use of terms different from those habitual to writers who look upon that form of production as imperishable and final.

A word respecting the author's method of quoting may not be out of place. In the majority of cases, the quotations serve, in the usual way, as documentary evidence in support of assertions made in the text. But in many instances, passages from economic writers are quoted in order to indicate when, where and by whom a certain proposition was for the first time clearly enunciated. This is done in cases where the proposition quoted is of importance as being a more or less adequate expression of the conditions of social production and exchange prevalent at the time, and quite irrespective of Marx's recognition, or otherwise, of its general validity. These quotations, therefore, supplement the text by a running commentary taken from the history of the science.

Our translation comprises the first book of the work only. But this first book is in a great measure a whole in itself, and has for twenty years ranked as an independent work. The second book, edited in German by me in 1885, is decidedly incomplete without the third, which cannot be published before the end of 1887. When Book III has been brought out in the original German, it will then be soon enough to think about preparing an English edition of both.

Capital is often called, on the Continent, 'the Bible of the working class'. That the conclusions arrived at in this work are daily more and more becoming the fundamental principles of the great working-class movement, not only in Germany and Switzerland, but in France, in Holland and Belgium, in America, and even in Italy and Spain, that everywhere the working class more and more recognizes, in these conclusions, the most adequate expression of its condition and of its aspirations, nobody acquainted with that movement will deny. And in England, too, the theories of Marx, even at this moment, exercise a powerful influence upon the socialist movement which is spreading in the ranks of 'cultured' people no less than in those of the working class. But that is not all. The time is rapidly approaching when a thorough examination of England's economic position will impose itself as an irresistible national necessity. The working of the industrial system of this country, impossible without a constant and rapid extension of production, and therefore of markets, is coming to a dead stop. Free-trade has exhausted its resources; even Manchester doubts this its *quondam* economic gospel.[2] Foreign industry, rapidly developing, stares English production in the face everywhere, not only in protected, but also in neutral markets, and even on this side of the Channel. While the productive power increases in a geometric ratio, the extension of markets proceeds at

2. 'At the quarterly meeting of the Manchester Chamber of Commerce, held this afternoon, a warm discussion took place on the subject of Free-trade. A resolution was moved to the effect that "having waited in vain forty years for other nations to follow the Free-trade example of England, this Chamber thinks the time has now arrived to reconsider that position". The resolution was rejected by a majority of one only, the figures being 21 for, and 22 against' (*Evening Standard*, 1 November 1886).

best in an arithmetic one. The decennial cycle of stagnation, prosperity, overproduction and crisis, ever recurrent from 1825 to 1867, seems indeed to have run its course; but only to land us in the slough of despond of a permanent and chronic depression. The sighed-for period of prosperity will not come; as often as we seem to perceive its heralding symptoms, so often do they again vanish into air. Meanwhile, each succeeding winter brings up afresh the great question, 'what to do with the unemployed'; but while the number of the unemployed keeps swelling from year to year, there is nobody to answer that question; and we can almost calculate the moment when the unemployed, losing patience, will take their own fate into their own hands. Surely, at such a moment, the voice ought to be heard of a man whose whole theory is the result of a life-long study of the economic history and condition of England, and whom that study led to the conclusion that, at least in Europe, England is the only country where the inevitable social revolution might be effected entirely by peaceful and legal means. He certainly never forgot to add that he hardly expected the English ruling classes to submit, without a 'pro-slavery rebellion',* to this peaceful and legal revolution.

Frederick Engels

5 November 1886

*This is Marx's and Engels' usual description of the American Civil War of 1861 to 1865, which was set off by the revolt of the slave-owners of the Southern states.

Preface to the Fourth Edition

The fourth edition required that I should establish in final form, as nearly as possible, both text and footnotes. The following brief explanation will show how I have fulfilled this task.

After again comparing the French edition and Marx's manuscript remarks I have made some further additions to the German text from that translation. They will be found on p. 212, pp. 624–6, pp. 730–4, pp. 777–80 and on p. 783 in note 13.* I have also followed the example of the French and English editions by putting the long footnote on the miners into the text (pp. 626–34). Other small alterations are of a purely technical nature.

Further, I have added a few more explanatory notes, especially where changed historical conditions seemed to demand this. All these additional notes are enclosed in square brackets and marked either with my initials or 'D.H.'.†

In the meantime, a complete revision of the numerous quotations had been made necessary by the publication of the English edition. For this edition Marx's youngest daughter, Eleanor, undertook to compare all the quotations with their originals, so that those taken from English sources, which constitute the vast majority, are given there not as re-translations from the German but in the original English form. In preparing the fourth edition it was therefore incumbent upon me to consult this text. The comparison revealed various small inaccuracies: page numbers wrongly indicated, owing partly to mistakes in copying from note-books, and partly to the accumulated misprints of three editions; misplaced quotation or omission marks, which cannot be avoided when a mass of quotations is copied from note-book

---

* The page numbers in the present edition have been inserted in place of Engels' references to the third and fourth German editions.

† *Der Herausgeber*, i.e. the editor. In this edition all of Engels' additions are integrated into the text but indicated as such.

extracts; here and there some rather unhappy translation of a word; particular passages quoted from the old Paris note-books of 1843–5, when Marx did not know English and was reading English economists in French translations, so that the double translation yielded a slightly different shade of meaning, as in the case of Steuart, Ure, etc., where the English text had now to be used – and other similar instances of trifling inaccuracy or negligence. But anyone who compares the fourth edition with the previous ones can convince himself that all this laborious process of emendation has not produced the smallest change in the book worth speaking of. There was only one quotation which could not be traced – the one from Richard Jones (p. 746, note 35). Marx probably slipped up when writing down the title of the book.* All the other quotations retain their cogency in full, or have had their cogency enhanced by being put into their present exact form.

Here, however, I am obliged to revert to an old story.

I know of only one case in which the accuracy of a quotation given by Marx has been called in question. But as the issue dragged on beyond his lifetime I cannot well ignore it here.

On 7 March 1872 there appeared in the Berlin *Concordia*, the organ of the Association of German Manufacturers, an anonymous article entitled 'How Karl Marx Quotes'. It was asserted there, with an excessive display of moral indignation and unparliamentary language, that the quotation from Gladstone's Budget Speech of 16 April 1863 (in the Inaugural Address of the International Working Men's Association, 1864,† and repeated in *Capital*, Vol. 1, pp. 805–6) had been falsified; that not a single word of the sentence: 'this intoxicating augmentation of wealth and power ... is ... entirely confined to classes of property' was to be found in the (semi-official) stenographic report in *Hansard*. 'But this sentence is nowhere to be found in Gladstone's speech. Exactly the opposite is stated there.' (In bold type): 'THIS SENTENCE, BOTH IN FORM AND SUBSTANCE, IS A LIE INSERTED BY MARX.'

Marx, to whom this issue of *Concordia* was sent the following May, answered the anonymous author in the *Volksstaat* of 1

* This quotation was in fact later successfully traced. Cf. below, p. 746, last note.

† See Karl Marx, *The First International and After*, Pelican Marx Library, 1974, p. 75.

June. As he could not recall which newspaper report he had used for the quotation, he limited himself to citing, first the equivalent quotation from two English publications, and then the report in *The Times*, according to which Gladstone says:

'That is the state of the case as regards the wealth of this country. I must say for one, I should look almost with apprehension and pain upon this intoxicating augmentation of wealth and power, if it were my belief that it was confined to classes who are in easy circumstances. This takes no cognizance at all of the condition of the labouring population. The augmentation I have described and which is founded, I think, upon accurate returns, is an augmentation entirely confined to classes possessed of property.'

Thus Gladstone says here that he would be sorry if this were so, but it *is* so: this intoxicating augmentation of wealth and power *is* entirely confined to classes of property. And, as for the semi-official *Hansard*, Marx goes on to say: 'In the version he manipulated afterwards, Mr Gladstone was astute enough to obliterate this passage, which, coming from an English Chancellor of the Exchequer, was certainly compromising. This, by the way, is a traditional custom in the English parliament, and not an invention got up by little Lasker against Bebel.'*

The anonymous writer gets angrier and angrier. In his rejoinder, in the *Concordia* of 4 July, he sweeps aside second-hand sources and demurely suggests that it is the 'custom' to quote parliamentary speeches from the stenographic report; adding, however, that the report in *The Times* (which includes the 'falsified' sentence) and the report in *Hansard* (which omits it) are 'substantially in complete agreement', and also that the report in *The Times* contains 'the exact opposite to that notorious passage in the *Inaugural Address*'. The fellow carefully conceals the fact that the report in *The Times* explicitly includes that self-same 'notorious passage', side by side with its alleged 'opposite'. Despite all this, however, the anonymous writer feels that he is stuck fast and that he can only save himself by some new dodge. Thus, although his article bristles, as we have just shown, with 'impudent mendacity' and is

---

*In the *Reichstag* sitting of 8 November 1871 the National Liberal deputy Lasker declared in the course of a speech against the Social Democrat Bebel that if the German workers tried to follow the example of the Paris Commune 'the honest, propertied citizens would beat them to death with cudgels'. But in the stenographic report he had the words 'beat them to death with cudgels' replaced with 'hold them down with their own strength'. Bebel immediately revealed that this was a falsification.

interlarded with such edifying terms of abuse as 'bad faith', 'dishonesty', 'lying allegation', 'that spurious quotation', 'impudent mendacity', 'a quotation entirely falsified', 'this falsification', 'simply infamous', etc., he finds it necessary to divert the issue to another domain, and therefore promises 'to explain in a second article the meaning which we' (the non-mendacious anonymous one) 'attribute to the content of Gladstone's words'. As if his particular opinion, unauthoritative as it is, had anything whatever to do with the matter! This second article was printed in the *Concordia* of 11 July.

Marx replied again in the *Volksstaat* of 7 August, now giving in addition the reports of the passage in question from the *Morning Star* and *Morning Advertiser* of 17 April 1863. According to both reports, Gladstone said that he would look with apprehension, etc. upon this intoxicating augmentation of wealth and power if he believed it to be confined to 'classes in easy circumstances'. But this augmentation *was* in fact, he said, 'entirely confined to classes possessed of property'. So these reports too reproduced word for word the sentence alleged to have been 'lyingly inserted'. Marx further established once more, by comparing the texts in *The Times* and in *Hansard*, that this sentence, which three newspaper reports of identical content, appearing independently of one another the next morning, proved to have been really uttered, was missing from the *Hansard* report, revised according to the familiar 'custom', and that Gladstone, to use Marx's words, 'had afterwards conjured it away'. In conclusion Marx stated that he had no time to enter into any further discussions with the anonymous one. The latter also seems to have had enough; at any rate Marx received no further issues of *Concordia*.

With this the matter appeared to be dead and buried. True, once or twice later on there reached us, from persons in touch with the University of Cambridge, mysterious rumours of an unspeakable literary crime which Marx was supposed to have committed in *Capital*; but despite all investigation nothing more definite could be learned. Then, on 29 November 1883, eight months after Marx's death, there appeared in *The Times* a letter headed Trinity College, Cambridge, and signed Sedley Taylor, in which this little man, who dabbles in the mildest sort of co-operative activities,* seized upon some chance pretext or other to

---

*Sedley Taylor (1834–1920), Fellow of Trinity College, Cambridge, and author of a book entitled *Profit Sharing between Capital and Labour* (1884).

enlighten us at last, not only about those vague Cambridge rumours, but also about the anonymous fellow in the *Concordia*.

'What appears extremely singular,' says the little man from Trinity College, 'is that it was reserved for *Professor Brentano* (then of the University of Breslau, now of that of Strassburg) to expose ... the bad faith which had manifestly dictated the citation made from Mr Gladstone's speech in the [Inaugural] Address. Herr Karl Marx, who ... attempted to defend the citation, had the hardihood, in the deadly shifts to which Brentano's masterly conduct of the attack speedily reduced him, to assert that Mr Gladstone had "manipulated" the report of his speech in *The Times* of 17 April 1863, before it appeared in *Hansard*, in order to "obliterate" a passage which "was certainly compromising" for an English Chancellor of the Exchequer. On Brentano's showing, by a detailed comparison of texts, that the reports of *The Times* and of *Hansard* agreed in utterly excluding the meaning which craftily isolated quotation had put upon Mr Gladstone's words, Marx withdrew from further controversy under the plea of "want of time".'

So that was at the bottom of the whole business! And thus was the anonymous campaign of Herr Brentano* in the *Concordia* gloriously reflected in the imagination of the producers' co-operatives of Cambridge. There he stood, sword in hand, and thus he battled, in his 'masterly conduct of the attack', this St George of the Association of German Manufacturers, while the infernal dragon Marx, 'in deadly shifts', 'speedily' breathed his last at his feet.

A battle-scene worthy of Ariosto! But the whole thing only served to conceal the further dodges of our St George. Here there is no longer talk of 'lying insertion' or 'falsification', but of 'craftily isolated quotation'. The whole issue was shifted, and St George and his Cambridge shield-bearer were very well aware why they had done this.

Eleanor Marx replied in the monthly journal *To-day* (February 1884), as *The Times* refused to publish her letter. She once more focused the debate on the sole question at issue: had Marx 'lyingly inserted' that sentence or not? To this Mr Sedley Taylor answered that 'the question whether a particular sentence did or

* Lujo Brentano (1844–1931), 'Professorial socialist', founder of the Verein für Sozialpolitik, liberal advocate of social reform, and Professor at various German universities from 1872 until 1914.

did not occur in Mr Gladstone's speech' had been, in his opinion, 'of very subordinate importance' in the Brentano–Marx controversy, 'compared to the issue whether the quotation in dispute was made with the intention of conveying, or of perverting Mr Gladstone's meaning'. He then admits that the report in *The Times* contained 'a verbal contrariety'; but, if the context is rightly interpreted, i.e., in the Gladstonian Liberal sense, it shows what Mr Gladstone *meant* to say (*To-day*, March 1884). The most comic point here is that our little Cambridge man now insists upon quoting the speech *not* from *Hansard*, as, according to the anonymous Brentano, it is 'customary' to do, but from the report in *The Times*, which the same Brentano had characterized as 'of necessity botched'. Naturally so, for in *Hansard* the vexatious sentence is missing.

Eleanor Marx had no difficulty (in the same issue of *To-day*) in dissolving all this argumentation into thin air. Either Mr Taylor had read the controversy of 1872, in which case he was now making not only 'lying insertions' but also 'lying' suppressions; or he had not read it and ought to remain silent. In either case it was certain that he did not dare for a moment to maintain the accusation of his friend Brentano that Marx had made a 'lying' addition. On the contrary, Marx, it now seems, had not lyingly added but suppressed an important sentence. But this same sentence is quoted on page 5 of the *Inaugural Address*, a few lines before the alleged 'lying insertion',* and as to the 'contrariety' in Gladstone's speech, is it not Marx himself who refers in *Capital* (p. 806, note 40) to 'the continual crying contradictions in Gladstone's Budget speeches of 1863 and 1864'? Only he does not venture, *à la* Sedley Taylor, to resolve them into complacent Liberal sentiments. Eleanor Marx, in concluding her reply, sums up as folows:

'Marx has not suppressed anything worth quoting, neither has he "lyingly" added anything. But he has restored, rescued from oblivion, a particular sentence of one of Mr Gladstone's speeches, a sentence which had indubitably been pronounced, but which somehow or other had found its way – out of *Hansard*.'

With that, Mr Sedley Taylor too had had enough, and the result of this whole professorial cobweb, spun out over two

---

*Karl Marx, op. cit. The sentence is this: 'The average condition of the British labourer has improved to a degree we know to be extraordinary and unexampled in the history of any country or any age.'

decades and two great countries, is that nobody has since dared to cast any other aspersion upon Marx's literary honesty; while Mr Sedley Taylor, no doubt, will after this put as little confidence in the literary war bulletins of Herr Brentano as Herr Brentano will in the papal infallibility of *Hansard*.*

Frederick Engels

London, 25 June 1890

* This was not in fact the end of this controversy. Brentano came back into the fray once again, which led Engels to publish a more comprehensive refutation of Brentano's charges, with all the documents concerned appended in pamphlet form: *Brentano Contra Marx*, reprinted in *MEW* 22.

Capital

Volume One

Part One

Commodities and Money

Chapter 1: The Commodity

I. THE TWO FACTORS OF THE COMMODITY: USE-VALUE AND VALUE (SUBSTANCE OF VALUE, MAGNITUDE OF VALUE)

The wealth of societies in which the capitalist mode of production prevails appears as an 'immense collection of commodities'[1]; the individual commodity appears as its elementary form. Our investigation therefore begins with the analysis of the commodity.

The commodity is, first of all, an external object, a thing which through its qualities satisfies human needs of whatever kind. The nature of these needs, whether they arise, for example, from the stomach, or the imagination, makes no difference.[2] Nor does it matter here how the thing satisfies man's need, whether directly as a means of subsistence, i.e. an object of consumption, or indirectly as a means of production.

Every useful thing, for example, iron, paper, etc., may be looked at from the two points of view of quality and quantity. Every useful thing is a whole composed of many properties; it can therefore be useful in various ways. The discovery of these ways and hence of the manifold uses of things is the work of history.[3] So also is the invention of socially recognized standards of measurement for the quantities of these useful objects. The diversity of the

1. Karl Marx, *Zur Kritik der Politischen Ökonomie*, Berlin, 1859, p. 3 [English translation, p. 27].

2. 'Desire implies want; it is the appetite of the mind, and as natural as hunger to the body . . . The greatest number (of things) have their value from supplying the wants of the mind' (Nicholas Barbon, *A Discourse on Coining the New Money Lighter. In Answer to Mr Locke's Considerations etc.*, London, 1696, pp. 2, 3).

3. 'Things have an intrinsick vertue' (this is Barbon's special term for use-value) 'which in all places have the same vertue; as the loadstone to attract iron' (op. cit., p. 6). The magnet's property of attracting iron only became useful once it had led to the discovery of magnetic polarity.

measures for commodities arises in part from the diverse nature of the objects to be measured, and in part from convention.

The usefulness of a thing makes it a use-value.[4] But this usefulness does not dangle in mid-air. It is conditioned by the physical properties of the commodity, and has no existence apart from the latter. It is therefore the physical body of the commodity itself, for instance iron, corn, a diamond, which is the use-value or useful thing. This property of a commodity is independent of the amount of labour required to appropriate its useful qualities. When examining use-values, we always assume we are dealing with definite quantities, such as dozens of watches, yards of linen, or tons of iron. The use-values of commodities provide the material for a special branch of knowledge, namely the commercial knowledge of commodities.[5] Use-values are only realized [*verwirklicht*] in use or in consumption. They constitute the material content of wealth, whatever its social form may be. In the form of society to be considered here they are also the material bearers [*Träger*] of . . . exchange-value.

Exchange-value appears first of all as the quantitative relation, the proportion, in which use-values of one kind exchange for use-values of another kind.[6] This relation changes constantly with time and place. Hence exchange-value appears to be something accidental and purely relative, and consequently an intrinsic value, i.e. an exchange-value that is inseparably connected with the commodity, inherent in it, seems a contradiction in terms.[7] Let us consider the matter more closely.

4. 'The natural worth of anything consists in its fitness to supply the necessities, or serve the conveniences of human life' (John Locke, 'Some Considerations on the Consequences of the Lowering of Interest' (1691), in *Works*, London, 1777, Vol. 2, p. 28). In English writers of the seventeenth century we still often find the word 'worth' used for use-value and 'value' for exchange-value. This is quite in accordance with the spirit of a language that likes to use a Teutonic word for the actual thing, and a Romance word for its reflection.

5. In bourgeois society the legal fiction prevails that each person, as a buyer, has an encyclopedic knowledge of commodities.

6. 'Value consists in the exchange relation between one thing and another, between a given amount of one product and a given amount of another' (Le Trosne, *De l'intérêt social*, in *Physiocrates*, ed. Daire, Paris, 1846, p. 889).

7. 'Nothing can have an intrinsick value' (N. Barbon, op. cit., p. 6); or as Butler says:

'The value of a thing
Is just as much as it will bring.'*

*Samuel Butler, *Hudibras*, Part 2, Canto 1, lines 465–6, 'For what is worth in any thing, but so much money as 'twill bring?'

A given commodity, a quarter of wheat for example, is exchanged for x boot-polish, y silk or z gold, etc. In short, it is exchanged for other commodities in the most diverse proportions. Therefore the wheat has many exchange values instead of one. But x boot-polish, y silk or z gold, etc., each represent the exchange-value of one quarter of wheat. Therefore x boot-polish, y silk, z gold, etc., must, as exchange-values, be mutually replaceable or of identical magnitude. It follows from this that, firstly, the valid exchange-values of a particular commodity express something equal, and secondly, exchange-value cannot be anything other than the mode of expression, the 'form of appearance',* of a content distinguishable from it.

Let us now take two commodities, for example corn and iron. Whatever their exchange relation may be, it can always be represented by an equation in which a given quantity of corn is equated to some quantity of iron, for instance 1 quarter of corn = x cwt of iron. What does this equation signify? It signifies that a common element of identical magnitude exists in two different things, in 1 quarter of corn and similarly in x cwt of iron. Both are therefore equal to a third thing, which in itself is neither the one nor the other. Each of them, so far as it is exchange-value, must therefore be reducible to this third thing.

A simple geometrical example will illustrate this. In order to determine and compare the areas of all rectilinear figures we split them up into triangles. Then the triangle itself is reduced to an expression totally different from its visible shape: half the product of the base and the altitude. In the same way the exchange values of commodities must be reduced to a common element, of which they represent a greater or a lesser quantity.

This common element cannot be a geometrical, physical, chemical or other natural property of commodities. Such properties come into consideration only to the extent that they make the commodities useful, i.e. turn them into use-values. But clearly, the exchange relation of commodities is characterized precisely by its abstraction from their use-values. Within the exchange relation, one use-value is worth just as much as another, provided only that it is present in the appropriate quantity. Or, as old Barbon says: 'One sort of wares are as good as another, if the value be equal. There is no difference or distinction in things of equal value ...

* *Erscheinungsform*. This word appears in inverted commas in the original.

One hundred pounds worth of lead or iron, is of as great a value as one hundred pounds worth of silver and gold.'[8]

As use-values, commodities differ above all in quality, while as exchange-values they can only differ in quantity, and therefore do not contain an atom of use-value.

If then we disregard the use-value of commodities, only one property remains, that of being products of labour. But even the product of labour has already been transformed in our hands. If we make abstraction from its use-value, we abstract also from the material constituents and forms which make it a use-value. It is no longer a table, a house, a piece of yarn or any other useful thing. All its sensuous characteristics are extinguished. Nor is it any longer the product of the labour of the joiner, the mason or the spinner, or of any other particular kind of productive labour. With the disappearance of the useful character of the products of labour, the useful character of the kinds of labour embodied in them also disappears; this in turn entails the disappearance of the different concrete forms of labour. They can no longer be distinguished, but are all together reduced to the same kind of labour, human labour in the abstract.

Let us now look at the residue of the products of labour. There is nothing left of them in each case but the same phantom-like objectivity; they are merely congealed quantities of homogeneous human labour, i.e. of human labour-power expended without regard to the form of its expenditure. All these things now tell us is that human labour-power has been expended to produce them, human labour is accumulated in them. As crystals of this social substance, which is common to them all, they are values – commodity values [*Warenwerte*].

We have seen that when commodities are in the relation of exchange, their exchange-value manifests itself as something totally independent of their use-value. But if we abstract from their use-value, there remains their value, as it has just been defined. The common factor in the exchange relation, or in the exchange-value of the commodity, is therefore its value. The progress of the investigation will lead us back to exchange-value as the necessary mode of expression, or form of appearance, of value. For the present, however, we must consider the nature of value independently of its form of appearance [*Erscheinungs form*].

8. N. Barbon, op. cit., pp. 53 and 7.

A use-value, or useful article, therefore, has value only because abstract human labour is objectified [*vergegenständlicht*] or materialized in it. How, then, is the magnitude of this value to be measured? By means of the quantity of the 'value-forming substance', the labour, contained in the article. This quantity is measured by its duration, and the labour-time is itself measured on the particular scale of hours, days etc.

It might seem that if the value of a commodity is determined by the quantity of labour expended to produce it, it would be the more valuable the more unskilful and lazy the worker who produced it, because he would need more time to complete the article. However, the labour that forms the substance of value is equal human labour, the expenditure of identical human labour-power. The total labour-power of society, which is manifested in the values of the world of commodities, counts here as one homogeneous mass of human labour-power, although composed of innumerable individual units of labour-power. Each of these units is the same as any other, to the extent that it has the character of a socially average unit of labour-power and acts as such, i.e. only needs, in order to produce a commodity, the labour time which is necessary on an average, or in other words is socially necessary. Socially necessary labour-time is the labour-time required to produce any use-value under the conditions of production normal for a given society and with the average degree of skill and intensity of labour prevalent in that society. The introduction of power-looms into England, for example, probably reduced by one half the labour required to convert a given quantity of yarn into woven fabric. In order to do this, the English hand-loom weaver in fact needed the same amount of labour-time as before; but the product of his individual hour of labour now only represented half an hour of social labour, and consequently fell to one half its former value.

What exclusively determines the magnitude of the value of any article is therefore the amount of labour socially necessary, or the labour-time socially necessary for its production.[9] The individual

9. 'The value of them' (the necessaries of life) 'when they are exchanged the one for another, is regulated by the quantity of labour necessarily required, and commonly taken in producing them' (*Some Thoughts on the Interest of Money in General, and Particularly in the Publick Funds*, London, pp. 36, 37). This remarkable anonymous work of the eighteenth century bears no date. However, it is clear from its contents that it appeared in the reign of George II, about 1739 or 1740.

commodity counts here only as an average sample of its kind.[10] Commodities which contain equal quantities of labour, or which can be produced in the same time, have therefore the same value. The value of a commodity is related to the value of any other commodity as the labour-time necessary for the production of the one is related to the labour-time necessary for the production of the other. 'As exchange-values, all commodities are merely definite quantities of *congealed labour-time*.'[11]

The value of a commodity would therefore remain constant, if the labour-time required for its production also remained constant. But the latter changes with every variation in the productivity of labour. This is determined by a wide range of circumstances; it is determined amongst other things by the workers' average degree of skill, the level of development of science and its technological application, the social organization of the process of production, the extent and effectiveness of the means of production, and the conditions found in the natural environment. For example, the same quantity of labour is present in eight bushels of corn in favourable seasons and in only four bushels in unfavourable seasons. The same quantity of labour provides more metal in rich mines than in poor. Diamonds are of very rare occurrence on the earth's surface, and hence their discovery costs, on an average, a great deal of labour-time. Consequently much labour is represented in a small volume. Jacob questions whether gold has ever been paid for at its full value.* This applies still more to diamonds. According to Eschwege, the total produce of the Brazilian diamond mines for the eighty years ending in 1823 still did not amount to the price of $1\frac{1}{2}$ years' average produce of the sugar and coffee plantations of the same country,† although the diamonds represented much more labour, therefore more value. With richer mines, the same quantity of labour would be embodied in more diamonds, and their value would fall. If man succeeded, without much labour, in transforming carbon into diamonds,

10. 'Properly speaking, all products of the same kind form a single mass, and their price is determined in general and without regard to particular circumstances' (Le Trosne, op. cit., p. 893).

11. Karl Marx, op. cit., p. 6 [English translation, p. 30].

* William Jacob, *An Historical Enquiry into the Production and Consumption of the Precious Metals*, London, 1831, Vol. 2, p. 101.

† This information comes from H. A. M. Merivale, *Lectures on Colonization and Colonies*, London, 1841. Cf. *Grundrisse*, p. 833.

their value might fall below that of bricks. In general, the greater the productivity of labour, the less the labour-time required to produce an article, the less the mass of labour crystallized in that article, and the less its value. Inversely, the less the productivity of labour, the greater the labour-time necessary to produce an article, and the greater its value. The value of a commodity, therefore, varies directly as the quantity, and inversely as the productivity, of the labour which finds its realization within the commodity. (Now we know the *substance* of value. It is *labour*. We know the *measure of its magnitude*. It is *labour-time*. The *form*, which stamps *value* as *exchange-value*, remains to be analysed. But before this we need to develop the characteristics we have already found somewhat more fully.)*

A thing can be a use-value without being a value. This is the case whenever its utility to man is not mediated through labour. Air, virgin soil, natural meadows, unplanted forests, etc. fall into this category. A thing can be useful, and a product of human labour, without being a commodity. He who satisfies his own need with the product of his own labour admittedly creates use-values, but not commodities. In order to produce the latter, he must not only produce use-values, but use-values for others, social use-values. (And not merely for others. The medieval peasant produced a corn-rent for the feudal lord and a corn-tithe for the priest; but neither the corn-rent nor the corn-tithe became commodities simply by being produced for others. In order to become a commodity, the product must be transferred to the other person, for whom it serves as a use-value, through the medium of exchange.)† Finally, nothing can be a value without being an object of utility. If the thing is useless, so is the labour contained in it; the labour does not count as labour, and therefore creates no value.

2. THE DUAL CHARACTER OF THE LABOUR EMBODIED IN COMMODITIES

Initially the commodity appeared to us as an object with a dual character, possessing both use-value and exchange-value. Later

* The passage in parentheses occurs only in the first edition.

† [Note by Engels to the fourth German edition:] I have inserted the passage in parentheses because, through its omission, the misconception has very frequently arisen that Marx regarded every product consumed by someone other than the producer as a commodity.

on it was seen that labour, too, has a dual character: in so far as it finds its expression in value, it no longer possesses the same characteristics as when it is the creator of use-values. I was the first to point out and examine critically this twofold nature of the labour contained in commodities.[12] As this point is crucial to an understanding of political economy, it requires further elucidation.

Let us take two commodities, such as a coat and 10 yards of linen, and let the value of the first be twice the value of the second, so that, if 10 yards of linen = W, the coat = $2W$.

The coat is a use-value that satisfies a particular need. A specific kind of productive activity is required to bring it into existence. This activity is determined by its aim, mode of operation, object, means and result. We use the abbreviated expression 'useful labour' for labour whose utility is represented by the use-value of its product, or by the fact that its product is a use-value. In this connection we consider only its useful effect.

As the coat and the linen are qualitatively different use-values, so also are the forms of labour through which their existence is mediated – tailoring and weaving. If the use-values were not qualitatively different, hence not the products of qualitatively different forms of useful labour, they would be absolutely incapable of confronting each other as commodities. Coats cannot be exchanged for coats, one use-value cannot be exchanged for another of the same kind.

The totality of heterogeneous use-values or physical commodities reflects a totality of similarly heterogeneous forms of useful labour, which differ in order, genus, species and variety: in short, a social division of labour. This division of labour is a necessary condition for commodity production, although the converse does not hold; commodity production is not a necessary condition for the social division of labour. Labour is socially divided in the primitive Indian community, although the products do not thereby become commodities. Or, to take an example nearer home, labour is systematically divided in every factory, but the workers do not bring about this division by exchanging their individual products. Only the products of mutually independent acts of labour, performed in isolation, can confront each other as commodities.

To sum up, then: the use-value of every commodity contains

12. Karl Marx, op. cit., pp. 12, 13, and passim [English translation, pp. 41, 42].

useful labour, i.e. productive activity of a definite kind, carried on with a definite aim. Use-values cannot confront each other as commodities unless the useful labour contained in them is qualitatively different in each case. In a society whose products generally assume the form of commodities, i.e. in a society of commodity producers, this qualitative difference between the useful forms of labour which are carried on independently and privately by individual producers develops into a complex system, a social division of labour.

It is moreover a matter of indifference whether the coat is worn by the tailor or by his customer. In both cases it acts as a use-value. So, too, the relation between the coat and the labour that produced it is not in itself altered when tailoring becomes a special trade, an independent branch of the social division of labour. Men made clothes for thousands of years, under the compulsion of the need for clothing, without a single man ever becoming a tailor. But the existence of coats, of linen, of every element of material wealth not provided in advance by nature, had always to be mediated through a specific productive activity appropriate to its purpose, a productive activity that assimilated particular natural materials to particular human requirements. Labour, then, as the creator of use-values, as useful labour, is a condition of human existence which is independent of all forms of society; it is an eternal natural necessity which mediates the metabolism between man and nature, and therefore human life itself.

Use-values like coats, linen, etc., in short, the physical bodies of commodities, are combinations of two elements, the material provided by nature, and labour. If we subtract the total amount of useful labour of different kinds which is contained in the coat, the linen, etc., a material substratum is always left. This substratum is furnished by nature without human intervention. When man engages in production, he can only proceed as nature does herself, i.e. he can only change the form of the materials.[13] Furthermore,

13. 'All the phenomena of the universe, whether produced by the hand of man or indeed by the universal laws of physics, are not to be conceived of as acts of creation but solely as a reordering of matter. Composition and separation are the only elements found by the human mind whenever it analyses the notion of reproduction; and so it is with the reproduction of value' (use-value, although Verri himself, in this polemic against the Physiocrats, is not quite certain of the kind of value he is referring to) 'and wealth, whether earth, air and water are turned into corn in the fields, or the secretions of an insect are turned into silk by the hand of man, or some small pieces of metal are

even in this work of modification he is constantly helped by natural forces. Labour is therefore not the only source of material wealth, i.e. of the use-values it produces. As William Petty says, labour is the father of material wealth, the earth is its mother.*

Let us now pass from the commodity as an object of utility to the value of commodities.

We have assumed that the coat is worth twice as much as the linen. But this is merely a quantitative difference, and does not concern us at the moment. We shall therefore simply bear in mind that if the value of a coat is twice that of 10 yards of linen, 20 yards of linen will have the same value as a coat. As values, the coat and the linen have the same substance, they are the objective expressions of homogeneous labour. But tailoring and weaving are qualitatively different forms of labour. There are, however, states of society in which the same man alternately makes clothes and weaves. In this case, these two different modes of labour are only modifications of the labour of the same individual and not yet fixed functions peculiar to different individuals, just as the coat our tailor makes today, and the pair of trousers he makes tomorrow, require him only to vary his own individual labour. Moreover, we can see at a glance that in our capitalist society a given portion of labour is supplied alternately in the form of tailoring and in the form of weaving, in accordance with changes in the direction of the demand for labour. This change in the form of labour may well not take place without friction, but it must take place.

If we leave aside the determinate quality of productive activity, and therefore the useful character of the labour, what remains is its quality of being an expenditure of human labour-power. Tailoring and weaving, although they are qualitatively different productive activities, are both a productive expenditure of human brains, muscles, nerves, hands etc., and in this sense both human labour. They are merely two different forms of the expenditure of human labour-power. Of course, human labour-power must itself

---

arranged together to form a repeating watch' (Pietro Verri, *Meditazioni sulla economia politica* – first printed in 1771 – in Custodi's edition of the Italian economists, *Parte moderna*, Vol. 15, pp. 21, 22).

---

* *A Treatise of Taxes and Contributions*, published anonymously by William Petty, London, 1667, p. 47.

have attained a certain level of development before it can be expended in this or that form. But the value of a commodity represents human labour pure and simple, the expenditure of human labour in general. And just as, in civil society, a general or a banker plays a great part but man as such plays a very mean part,[14] so, here too, the same is true of human labour. It is the expenditure of simple labour-power, i.e. of the labour-power possessed in his bodily organism by every ordinary man, on the average, without being developed in any special way. *Simple average labour*, it is true, varies in character in different countries and at different cultural epochs, but in a particular society it is given. More complex labour counts only as *intensified*, or rather *multiplied* simple labour, so that a smaller quantity of complex labour is considered equal to a larger quantity of simple labour. Experience shows that this reduction is constantly being made. A commodity may be the outcome of the most complicated labour, but through its *value* it is posited as equal to the product of simple labour, hence it represents only a specific quantity of simple labour.[15] The various proportions in which different kinds of labour are reduced to simple labour as their unit of measurement are established by a social process that goes on behind the backs of the producers; these proportions therefore appear to the producers to have been handed down by tradition. In the interests of simplification, we shall henceforth view every form of labour-power directly as simple labour-power; by this we shall simply be saving ourselves the trouble of making the reduction.

Just as, in viewing the coat and the linen as values, we abstract from their different use-values, so, in the case of the labour represented by those values, do we disregard the difference between its useful forms, tailoring and weaving. The use-values coat and linen are combinations of, on the one hand, productive activity with a definite purpose, and, on the other, cloth and yarn; the values coat and linen, however, are merely congealed

14. Cf. Hegel, *Philosophie des Rechts*, Berlin, 1840, p. 250, para. 190.*

15. The reader should note that we are not speaking here of the wages or value the worker receives for (e.g.) a day's labour, but of the value of the commodity in which his day of labour is objectified. At this stage of our presentation, the category of wages does not exist at all.

*Hegel says here: 'In civil society as a whole, at the standpoint of needs, what we have before us is the composite idea which we call man. Thus this is the first time, and indeed the only time, to speak of man in this sense' (*Hegel's Philosophy of Right*, tr. T. M. Knox, Oxford, 1952, p. 127).

quantities of homogeneous labour. In the same way, the labour contained in these values does not count by virtue of its productive relation to cloth and yarn, but only as being an expenditure of human labour-power. Tailoring and weaving are the formative elements in the use-values coat and linen, precisely because these two kinds of labour are of different qualities; but only in so far as abstraction is made from their particular qualities, only in so far as both possess the same quality of being human labour, do tailoring and weaving form the substance of the values of the two articles mentioned.

Coats and linen, however, are not merely values in general, but values of definite magnitude, and, following our assumption, the coat is worth twice as much as the 10 yards of linen. Why is there this difference in value? Because the linen contains only half as much labour as the coat, so that labour-power had to be expended twice as long to produce the second as to produce the first.

While, therefore, with reference to use-value, the labour contained in a commodity counts only qualitatively, with reference to value it counts only quantitatively, once it has been reduced to human labour pure and simple. In the former case it was a matter of the 'how' and the 'what' of labour, in the latter of the 'how much', of the temporal duration of labour. Since the magnitude of the value of a commodity represents nothing but the quantity of labour embodied in it, it follows that all commodities, when taken in certain proportions, must be equal in value.

If the productivity of all the different sorts of useful labour required, let us say, for the production of a coat remains unchanged, the total value of the coats produced will increase along with their quantity. If one coat represents x days' labour, two coats will represent $2x$ days' labour, and so on. But now assume that the duration of the labour necessary for the production of a coat is doubled or halved. In the first case, one coat is worth as much as two coats were before; in the second case two coats are only worth as much as one was before, although in both cases one coat performs the same service, and the useful labour contained in it remains of the same quality. One change has taken place, however: a change in the quantity of labour expended to produce the article.

In itself, an increase in the quantity of use-values constitutes an increase in material wealth. Two coats will clothe two men, one coat will only clothe one man, etc. Nevertheless, an increase in the amount of material wealth may correspond to a simultaneous fall in the magnitude of its value. This contradictory movement arises out of the twofold character of labour. By 'productivity' of course, we always mean the productivity of concrete useful labour; in reality this determines only the degree of effectiveness of productive activity directed towards a given purpose within a given period of time. Useful labour becomes, therefore, a more or less abundant source of products in direct proportion as its productivity rises or falls. As against this, however, variations in productivity have no impact whatever on the labour itself represented in value. As productivity is an attribute of labour in its concrete useful form, it naturally ceases to have any bearing on that labour as soon as we abstract from its concrete useful form. The same labour, therefore, performed for the same length of time, always yields the same amount of value, independently of any variations in productivity. But it provides different quantities of use-values during equal periods of time; more, if productivity rises; fewer, if it falls. For this reason, the same change in productivity which increases the fruitfulness of labour, and therefore the amount of use-values produced by it, also brings about a reduction in the value of this increased total amount, if it cuts down the total amount of labour-time necessary to produce the use-values. The converse also holds.

On the one hand, all labour is an expenditure of human labour-power, in the physiological sense, and it is in this quality of being equal, or abstract, human labour that it forms the value of commodities. On the other hand, all labour is an expenditure of human labour-power in a particular form and with a definite aim, and it is in this quality of being concrete useful labour that it produces use-values.[16]

16. In order to prove that 'labour alone is the ultimate and real standard by which the value of all commodities can at all times and places be estimated and compared', Adam Smith* says this: 'Equal quantities of labour, at all times and places, must have the same value for the labourer. In his ordinary state of health, strength and activity; in the ordinary degree of his skill and dexterity, he must always lay down the same portion of his ease, his liberty, and his happiness' (*Wealth of Nations*, Bk I, Ch. 5 [pp. 104–5]). On the one hand, Adam Smith here (but not everywhere) confuses his determination of value by the quantity of labour expended in the production of commodities with the determination of the values of commodities by the value of labour, and therefore endeavours to prove that equal quantities of labour always have the same

*Here, as elsewhere occasionally, Marx quotes an English author in German. This explains certain slight divergences from the original English text.

3. THE VALUE-FORM, OR EXCHANGE-VALUE

Commodities come into the world in the form of use-values or material goods, such as iron, linen, corn, etc. This is their plain, homely, natural form. However, they are only commodities because they have a dual nature, because they are at the same time objects of utility and bearers of value. Therefore they only appear as commodities, or have the form of commodities, in so far as they possess a double form, i.e. natural form and value form.

The objectivity of commodities as values differs from Dame Quickly in the sense that 'a man knows not where to have it'.* Not an atom of matter enters into the objectivity of commodities as values; in this it is the direct opposite of the coarsely sensuous objectivity of commodities as physical objects. We may twist and turn a single commodity as we wish; it remains impossible to grasp it as a thing possessing value. However, let us remember that commodities possess an objective character as values only in so far as they are all expressions of an identical social substance, human labour, that their objective character as values is therefore

---

value. On the other hand, he has a suspicion that, in so far as labour manifests itself in the value of commodities, it only counts as an expenditure of labour-power; but then again he views this expenditure merely as the sacrifice of rest, freedom and happiness, not as also man's normal life-activity. Of course, he has the modern wage-labourer in mind. Adam Smith's anonymous predecessor, cited in note 9, is much nearer the mark when he says: 'One man has employed himself a week in providing this necessary of life . . . and he that gives him some other in exchange, cannot make a better estimate of what is a proper equivalent, than by computing what cost him just as much labour and time: which in effect is no more than exchanging one man's labour in one thing for a time certain, for another man's labour in another thing for the same time' (*Some Thoughts on the Interest of Money in General etc.*, p. 39). [Note by Engels to the fourth German edition:] The English language has the advantage of possessing two separate words for these two different aspects of labour. Labour which creates use-values and is qualitatively determined is called 'work' as opposed to 'labour'; labour which creates value and is only measured quantitatively is called 'labour', as opposed to 'work'.†

† Unfortunately, English usage does not always correspond to Engels' distinction. We have tried to adopt it where possible.

---

* Falstaff: Why, she's neither fish nor flesh; a man knows not where to have her.
Dame Quickly: Thou art an unjust man in saying so: thou or any man knows where to have me, thou knave, thou!
(*Henry IV*, Part 1, Act 3, Scene 3.)

purely social. From this it follows self-evidently that it can only appear in the social relation between commodity and commodity. In fact we started from exchange-value, or the exchange relation of commodities, in order to track down the value that lay hidden within it. We must now return to this form of appearance of value.

Everyone knows, if nothing else, that commodities have a common value-form which contrasts in the most striking manner with the motley natural forms of their use-values. I refer to the money-form. Now, however, we have to perform a task never even attempted by bourgeois economics. That is, we have to show the origin of this money-form, we have to trace the development of the expression of value contained in the value-relation of commodities from its simplest, almost imperceptible outline to the dazzling money-form. When this has been done, the mystery of money will immediately disappear.

The simplest value-relation is evidently that of one commodity to another commodity of a different kind (it does not matter which one). Hence the relation between the values of two commodities supplies us with the simplest expression of the value of a single commodity.

(a) The Simple, Isolated, or Accidental Form of Value

x commodity A $= y$ commodity B or: x commodity A is worth y commodity B.
(20 yards of linen $=$ 1 coat, or: 20 yards of linen are worth 1 coat)

(1) *The two poles of the expression of value: the relative form of value and the equivalent form*

The whole mystery of the form of value lies hidden in this simple form. Our real difficulty, therefore, is to analyse it.

Here two different kinds of commodities (in our example the linen and the coat) evidently play two different parts. The linen expresses its value in the coat; the coat serves as the material in which that value is expressed. The first commodity plays an active role, the second a passive one. The value of the first commodity is represented as relative value, in other words the commodity is in the relative form of value. The second commodity fulfils the function of equivalent, in other words it is in the equivalent form.

The relative form of value and the equivalent form are two

inseparable moments, which belong to and mutually condition each other; but, at the same time, they are mutually exclusive or opposed extremes, i.e. poles of the expression of value. They are always divided up between the different commodities brought into relation with each other by that expression. I cannot, for example, express the value of linen in linen. 20 yards of linen = 20 yards of linen is not an expression of value. The equation states rather the contrary: 20 yards of linen are nothing but 20 yards of linen, a definite quantity of linen considered as an object of utility. The value of the linen can therefore only be expressed relatively, i.e. in another commodity. The relative form of the value of the linen therefore presupposes that some other commodity confronts it in the equivalent form. On the other hand, this other commodity, which figures as the equivalent, cannot simultaneously be in the relative form of value. It is not the latter commodity whose value is being expressed. It only provides the material in which the value of the first commodity is expressed.

Of course, the expression 20 yards of linen = 1 coat, or 20 yards of linen are worth 1 coat, also includes its converse: 1 coat = 20 yards of linen, or 1 coat is worth 20 yards of linen. But in this case I must reverse the equation, in order to express the value of the coat relatively; and, if I do that, the linen becomes the equivalent instead of the coat. The same commodity cannot, therefore, simultaneously appear in both forms in the same expression of value. These forms rather exclude each other as polar opposites.

Whether a commodity is in the relative form or in its opposite, the equivalent form, entirely depends on its actual position in the expression of value. That is, it depends on whether it is the commodity whose value is being expressed, or the commodity in which value is being expressed.

(2) *The relative form of value*

(i) *The content of the relative form of value* In order to find out how the simple expression of the value of a commodity lies hidden in the value-relation between two commodities, we must, first of all, consider the value-relation quite independently of its quantitative aspect. The usual mode of procedure is the precise opposite of this: nothing is seen in the value-relation but the proportion in which definite quantities of two sorts of commodity count as equal to each other. It is overlooked that the magnitudes of different things only become comparable in quantitative terms when they have been reduced to the same unit. Only as expressions of the same unit do they have a common denominator, and are therefore commensurable magnitudes.[17]

Whether 20 yards of linen = 1 coat or = 20 coats or = x coats, i.e. whether a given quantity of linen is worth few or many coats, it is always implied, whatever the proportion, that the linen and the coat, as magnitudes of value, are expressions of the same unit, things of the same nature. Linen = coat is the basis of the equation.

But these two qualitatively equated commodities do not play the same part. It is only the value of the linen that is expressed. And how? By being related to the coat as its 'equivalent', or 'the thing exchangeable' with it. In this relation the coat counts as the form of existence of value, as the material embodiment of value, for only as such is it the same as the linen. On the other hand, the linen's own existence as value comes into view or receives an independent expression, for it is only as value that it can be related to the coat as being equal in value to it, or exchangeable with it. In the same way, butyric acid is a different substance from propyl formate. Yet both are made up of the same chemical substances, carbon (C), hydrogen (H) and oxygen (O). Moreover, these substances are combined together in the same proportions in each case, namely $C_4H_8O_2$. If now butyric acid were to be equated with propyl formate, then, in the first place, propyl formate would count in this relation only as a form of existence of $C_4H_8O_2$; and in the second place, it would thereby be asserted that butyric acid also consists of $C_4H_8O_2$. Thus by equating propyl formate with butyric acid one would be expressing their chemical composition as opposed to their physical formation.

If we say that, as values, commodities are simply congealed quantities of human labour, our analysis reduces them, it is true, to the level of abstract value, but does not give them a form of value distinct from their natural forms. It is otherwise in the value relation of one commodity to another. The first commodity's

17. The few economists, such as S. Bailey, who have concerned themselves with the analysis of the form of value have been unable to arrive at any result, firstly because they confuse the form of value with value itself, and secondly because, under the coarse influence of the practical bourgeois, they give their attention from the outset, and exclusively, to the quantitative aspect of the question. 'The command of quantity ... constitutes value' (*Money and Its Vicissitudes*, London, 1837, p. 11). Written by S. Bailey.

value character emerges here through its own relation to the
second commodity.

By equating, for example, the coat as a thing of value to the
linen, we equate the labour embedded in the coat with the labour
embedded in the linen. Now it is true that the tailoring which
makes the coat is concrete labour of a different sort from the
weaving which makes the linen. But the act of equating tailoring
with weaving reduces the former in fact to what is really equal in
the two kinds of labour, to the characteristic they have in common of being human labour. This is a roundabout way of saying
that weaving too, in so far as it weaves value, has nothing to distinguish it from tailoring, and, consequently, is abstract human
labour. It is only the expression of equivalence between different
sorts of commodities which brings to view the specific character
of value-creating labour, by actually reducing the different kinds
of labour embedded in the different kinds of commodity to their
common quality of being human labour in general.[18]

However, it is not enough to express the specific character of
the labour which goes to make up the value of the linen. Human
labour-power in its fluid state, or human labour, creates value,
but is not itself value. It becomes value in its coagulated state, in
objective form. The value of the linen as a congealed mass of
human labour can be expressed only as an 'objectivity' [*Gegenständlichkeit*], a thing which is materially different from the linen
itself and yet common to the linen and all other commodities.
The problem is already solved.

When it is in the value-relation with the linen, the coat counts
qualitatively as the equal of the linen, it counts as a thing of the
same nature, because it is a value. Here it is therefore a thing in

18. One of the first economists, after William Petty,* to have seen through
the nature of value, the famous Franklin, says this: 'Trade in general being
nothing else but the exchange of labour for labour, the value of all things is . . .
most justly measured by labour' (*The Works of B. Franklin etc.*, edited by
Sparks, Boston, 1836, Vol. 2, p. 267). Franklin is not aware that in measuring
the value of everything 'in labour' he makes abstraction from any difference
in the kinds of labour exchanged – and thus reduces them all to equal human
labour. Yet he states this without knowing it. He speaks first of 'the one
labour', then of 'the other labour', and finally of 'labour', without further
qualification, as the substance of the value of everything.

* Sir William Petty (1623–87), English economist and statistician, regarded
by Marx as the founder of modern political economy (see below, p. 174, n. 34).
'Petty recognizes labour as the source of material wealth' but misapprehends
the source of exchange-value (Karl Marx, op. cit., pp. 52–4).

which value is manifested, or which represents value in its tangible natural form. Yet the coat itself, the physical aspect of the coat-commodity, is purely a use-value. A coat as such no more expresses value than does the first piece of linen we come across. This proves only that, within its value-relation to the linen, the coat signifies more than it does outside it, just as some men count for more when inside a gold-braided uniform than they do otherwise.

In the production of the coat, human labour-power, in the shape of tailoring, has in actual fact been expended. Human labour has therefore been accumulated in the coat. From this point of view, the coat is a 'bearer of value', although this property never shows through, even when the coat is at its most threadbare. In its value-relation with the linen, the coat counts only under this aspect, counts therefore as embodied value, as the body of value [*Wertkörper*]. Despite its buttoned-up appearance, the linen recognizes in it a splendid kindred soul, the soul of value. Nevertheless, the coat cannot represent value towards the linen unless value, for the latter, simultaneously assumes the form of a coat. An individual, A, for instance, cannot be 'your majesty' to another individual, B, unless majesty in B's eyes assumes the physical shape of A, and, moreover, changes facial features, hair and many other things, with every new 'father of his people'.

Hence, in the value-relation, in which the coat is the equivalent of the linen, the form of the coat counts as the form of value. The value of the commodity linen is therefore expressed by the physical body of the commodity coat, the value of one by the use-value of the other. As a use-value, the linen is something palpably different from the coat; as value, it is identical with the coat, and therefore looks like the coat. Thus the linen acquires a value-form different from its natural form. Its existence as value is manifested in its equality with the coat, just as the sheep-like nature of the Christian is shown in his resemblance to the Lamb of God.

We see, then, that everything our analysis of the value of commodities previously told us is repeated by the linen itself, as soon as it enters into association with another commodity, the coat. Only it reveals its thoughts in a language with which it alone is familiar, the language of commodities. In order to tell us that labour creates its own value in its abstract quality of being human labour, it says that the coat, in so far as it counts as its equal, i.e. is value, consists of the same labour as it does itself. In order to inform us that its sublime objectivity as a value differs from its stiff and starchy existence as a body, it says that value has the appearance of a coat, and therefore that in so far as the linen itself is an object of value [*Wertding*], it and the coat are as like as two peas. Let us note, incidentally, that the language of commodities also has, apart from Hebrew, plenty of other more or less correct dialects. The German word '*Wertsein*' (to be worth), for instance, brings out less strikingly than the Romance verb '*valere*', '*valer*', '*valoir*' that the equating of commodity B with commodity A is the expression of value proper to commodity A. *Paris vaut bien une messe!**

By means of the value-relation, therefore, the natural form of commodity B becomes the value-form of commodity A, in other words the physical body of commodity B becomes a mirror for the value of commodity A.[19] Commodity A, then, in entering into a relation with commodity B as an object of value [*Wertkörper*], as a materialization of human labour, makes the use-value B into the material through which its own value is expressed. The value of commodity A, thus expressed in the use-value of commodity B, has the form of relative value.

(ii) *The quantitative determinacy of the relative form of value*
Every commodity whose-value is to be expressed is a useful object of a given quantity, for instance 15 bushels of corn, or 100 lb. of coffee. A given quantity of any commodity contains a definite quantity of human labour. Therefore the form of value must not only express value in general, but also quantitatively determined value, i.e. the magnitude of value. In the value-relation of commodity A to commodity B, of the linen to the coat, therefore, not only is the commodity-type coat equated with the linen in qualitative terms as an object of value as such, but also a definite quantity of the object of value or equivalent, 1 coat for example, is equated with a definite quantity of linen, such as 20 yards. The equation 20

19. In a certain sense, a man is in the same situation as a commodity. As he neither enters into the world in possession of a mirror, nor as a Fichtean philosopher who can say 'I am I', a man first sees and recognizes himself in another man. Peter only relates to himself as a man through his relation to another man, Paul, in whom he recognizes his likeness. With this, however, Paul also becomes from head to toe, in his physical form as Paul, the form of appearance of the species man for Peter.

---

*'Paris is certainly worth a mass.' Henry IV's supposed words on his conversion to Roman Catholicism in 1593.

yards of linen = 1 coat, or 20 yards of linen are worth 1 coat, presupposes the presence in 1 coat of exactly as much of the substance of value as there is in 20 yards of linen, implies therefore that the quantities in which the two commodities are present have cost the same amount of labour or the same quantity of labour-time. But the labour-time necessary for the production of 20 yards of linen or 1 coat varies with every change in the productivity of the weaver or the tailor. The influence of such changes on the relative expression of the magnitude of value must now be investigated more closely.

I. Let the value of the linen change[20] while the value of the coat remains constant. If the labour-time necessary for the production of linen be doubled, as a result of the increasing infertility of flax-growing soil for instance, its value will also be doubled. Instead of the equation 20 yards of linen = 1 coat, we should have 20 yards of linen = 2 coats, since 1 coat would now contain only half as much labour-time as 20 yards of linen. If, on the other hand, the necessary labour-time be reduced by one half, as a result of improved looms for instance, the value of the linen will fall by one half. In accordance with this the equation will now read 20 yards of linen = $\frac{1}{2}$ coat. The relative value of commodity A, i.e. its value expressed in commodity B, rises and falls in direct relation to the value of A, if the value of B remains constant.

II. Let the value of the linen remain constant, while the value of the coat changes. If, under these circumstances, the labour-time necessary for the production of a coat is doubled, as a result, for instance, of a poor crop of wool, we should have, instead of 20 yards of linen = 1 coat, 20 yards of linen = $\frac{1}{2}$ coat. If, on the other hand, the value of the coat sinks by one half, then 20 yards of linen = 2 coats. Hence, if the value of commodity A remains constant, its relative value, as expressed in commodity B, rises and falls in inverse relation to the change in the value of B.

If we compare the different cases examined under headings I and II, it emerges that the same change in the magnitude of relative value may arise from entirely opposed causes. Thus the equation 20 yards of linen = 1 coat becomes 20 yards of linen = 2 coats, either because the value of the linen has doubled or because the value of the coat has fallen by one half, and it becomes 20

20. Here, as occasionally also on previous pages, we use the expression 'value' for quantitatively determined values, i.e. for the magnitude of value.

yards of linen $= \frac{1}{2}$ coat, either because the value of the linen has fallen by one half, or because the value of the coat has doubled.

III. Let the quantities of labour necessary for the production of the linen and the coat vary simultaneously in the same direction and the same proportion. In this case, 20 yards of linen $= 1$ coat, as before, whatever change may have taken place in their respective values. Their change of value is revealed only when they are compared with a third commodity, whose value has remained constant. If the values of all commodities rose or fell simultaneously, and in the same proportion, their relative values would remain unaltered. The change in their real values would be manifested by an increase or decrease in the quantity of commodities produced within the same labour-time.

IV. The labour-time necessary for the production respectively of the linen and the coat, and hence their values, may vary simultaneously in the same direction, but to an unequal degree, or in opposite directions, and so on. The influence of all possible combinations of this kind on the relative value of a commodity can be worked out simply by applying cases I, II and III.

Thus real changes in the magnitude of value are neither unequivocally nor exhaustively reflected in their relative expression, or, in other words, in the magnitude of the relative value. The relative value of a commodity may vary, although its value remains constant. Its relative value may remain constant, although its value varies; and finally, simultaneous variations in the magnitude of its value and in the relative expression of that magnitude do not by any means have to correspond at all points.[21]

21. The vulgar economists* have exploited this lack of congruence between the magnitude of value and its relative expression with their customary ingenuity. For example: 'Once admit that A falls, because B, with which it is exchanged, rises, while no less labour is bestowed in the meantime on A, and your general principle of value falls to the ground ... If he [Ricardo] allowed that when A rises in value relatively to B, B falls in value relatively to A, he cut away the ground on which he rested his grand proposition, that the value of a commodity is ever determined by the labour embodied in it; for if a change in the cost of A alters not only its own value in relation to B, for which it is exchanged, but also the value of B relatively to that of A, though no change has taken place in the quantity of labour to produce B, then not only the doctrine falls to the ground which asserts that the quantity of labour bestowed on an article regulates its value, but also that which affirms the cost of an article to

* Marx explains his use of the term 'vulgar economists' in Section 4 of this chapter, pp. 174–5, n. 34.

(iii) *The equivalent form* We have seen that a commodity A (the linen), by expressing its value in the use-value of a commodity B of a different kind (the coat), impresses upon the latter a form of value peculiar to it, namely that of the equivalent. The commodity linen brings to view its own existence as a value through the fact that the coat can be equated with the linen although it has not assumed a form of value distinct from its own physical form. The coat is directly exchangeable with the linen; in this way the linen in fact expresses its own existence as a value [*Wertsein*]. The equivalent form of a commodity, accordingly, is the form in which it is directly exchangeable with other commodities.

If one kind of commodity, such as a coat, serves as the equivalent of another, such as linen, and coats therefore acquire the characteristic property of being in a form in which they can be directly exchanged with linen, this still by no means provides us with the proportion in which the two are exchangeable. Since the magnitude of the value of the linen is a given quantity, this proportion depends on the magnitude of the coat's value. Whether the coat is expressed as the equivalent and the linen as relative value, or, inversely, the linen is expressed as equivalent and the coat as relative value, the magnitude of the coat's value is determined, as ever, by the labour-time necessary for its production, independently of its value-form. But as soon as the coat takes up the position of the equivalent in the value expression, the magnitude of its value ceases to be expressed quantitatively. On the contrary, the coat now figures in the value equation merely as a definite quantity of some article.

For instance, 40 yards of linen are 'worth' – what? 2 coats. Because the commodity coat here plays the part of equivalent, because the use-value coat counts as the embodiment of value *vis-à-vis* the linen, a definite number of coats is sufficient to express a definite quantity of value in the linen. Two coats can therefore express the magnitude of value of 40 yards of linen, but they can

---

regulate its value' (J. Broadhurst, *Political Economy*, London, 1842, pp. 11 and 14).

Mr Broadhurst might just as well say: consider the fractions 10/20, 10/50, 10/100 etc. The number 10 remains unchanged, and yet its proportional magnitude, its magnitude in relation to the numbers 20, 50, 100 continually diminishes. Therefore, the great principle that the magnitude of a whole number, such as 10, is 'regulated' by the number of times the number 1 is contained in it falls to the ground.

never express the magnitude of their own value. Because they had a superficial conception of this fact, i.e. because they considered that in the equation of value the equivalent always has the form of a simple quantity of some article, of a use-value, Bailey and many of his predecessors and followers were misled into seeing the expression of value as merely a quantitative relation;* whereas in fact the equivalent form of a commodity contains no quantitative determinant of value.

The first peculiarity which strikes us when we reflect on the equivalent form is this, that use-value becomes the form of appearance of its opposite, value.

The natural form of the commodity becomes its value-form. But, note well, this substitution only occurs in the case of a commodity B (coat, or maize, or iron, etc.) when some other commodity A (linen etc.) enters into a value-relation with it, and then only within the limits of this relation. Since a commodity cannot be related to itself as equivalent, and therefore cannot make its own physical shape into the expression of its own value, it must be related to another commodity as equivalent, and therefore must make the physical shape of another commodity into its own value-form.

Let us make this clear with the example of a measure which is applied to commodities as material objects, i.e. as use-values. A sugar-loaf, because it is a body, is heavy and therefore possesses weight; but we can neither take a look at this weight nor touch it. We then take various pieces of iron, whose weight has been determined beforehand. The bodily form of the iron, considered for itself, is no more the form of appearance of weight than is the sugar-loaf. Nevertheless, in order to express the sugar-loaf as a weight, we put it into a relation of weight with the iron. In this relation, the iron counts as a body representing nothing but weight. Quantities of iron therefore serve to measure the weight of the sugar, and represent, in relation to the sugar-loaf, weight in its pure form, the form of manifestation of weight. This part is played by the iron only within this relation, i.e. within the relation into which the sugar, or any other body whose weight is to be found, enters with the iron. If both objects lacked weight, they

*'The most superficial form of exchange-value, that is the *quantitative relation* in which commodities exchange with one another, *constitutes*, according to Bailey, their value' (Karl Marx, *Theories of Surplus-Value*, Part III, London, 1972, p. 129).

could not enter into this relation, hence the one could not serve to express the weight of the other. When we throw both of them into the scales, we see in reality that considered as weight they are the same, and therefore that, taken in the appropriate proportions, they have the same weight. Just as the body of the iron, as a measure of weight, represents weight alone, in relation to the sugar-loaf, so, in our expression of value, the body of the coat represents value alone.

Here, however, the analogy ceases. In the expression of the weight of the sugar-loaf, the iron represents a natural property common to both bodies, their weight; but in the expression of value of the linen the coat represents a supra-natural property: their value, which is something purely social.

The relative value-form of a commodity, the linen for example, expresses its value-existence as something wholly different from its substance and properties, as the quality of being comparable with a coat for example; this expression itself therefore indicates that it conceals a social relation. With the equivalent form the reverse is true. The equivalent form consists precisely in this, that the material commodity itself, the coat for instance, expresses value just as it is in its everyday life, and is therefore endowed with the form of value by nature itself. Admittedly, this holds good only within the value-relation, in which the commodity linen is related to the commodity coat as its equivalent.[22] However, the properties of a thing do not arise from its relations to other things, they are, on the contrary, merely activated by such relations. The coat, therefore, seems to be endowed with its equivalent form, its property of direct exchangeability, by nature, just as much as its property of being heavy or its ability to keep us warm. Hence the mysteriousness of the equivalent form, which only impinges on the crude bourgeois vision of the political economist when it confronts him in its fully developed shape, that of money. He then seeks to explain away the mystical character of gold and silver by substituting for them less dazzling commodities, and, with ever-renewed satisfaction, reeling off a catalogue of all the

22. Determinations of reflection [*Reflexionsbestimmungen*] of this kind are altogether very curious. For instance, one man is king only because other men stand in the relation of subjects to him. They, on the other hand, imagine that they are subjects because he is king.*

*Cf. Hegel, *Science of Logic*, tr. A. V. Miller, London, 1969, pp. 409–11, where the determinations of reflection are stated to be 'not of a qualitative kind . . . but determinatenesses which are themselves relations'.

inferior commodities which have played the role of the equivalent at one time or another. He does not suspect that even the simplest expression of value, such as 20 yards of linen = 1 coat, already presents the riddle of the equivalent form for us to solve.

The body of the commodity, which serves as the equivalent, always figures as the embodiment of abstract human labour, and is always the product of some specific useful and concrete labour. This concrete labour therefore becomes the expression of abstract human labour. If the coat is merely abstract human labour's realization, the tailoring actually realized in it is merely abstract human labour's form of realization. In the expression of value of the linen, the usefulness of tailoring consists, not in making clothes, and thus also people, but in making a physical object which we at once recognize as value, as a congealed quantity of labour, therefore, which is absolutely indistinguishable from the labour objectified in the value of the linen. In order to act as such a mirror of value, tailoring itself must reflect nothing apart from its own abstract quality of being human labour.

Human labour-power is expended in the form of tailoring as well as in the form of weaving. Both therefore possess the general property of being human labour, and they therefore have to be considered in certain cases, such as the production of value, solely from this point of view. There is nothing mysterious in this. But in the value expression of the commodity the question is stood on its head. In order to express the fact that, for instance, weaving creates the value of linen through its general property of being human labour rather than in its concrete form as weaving, we contrast it with the concrete labour which produces the equivalent of the linen, namely tailoring. Tailoring is now seen as the tangible form of realization of abstract human labour.

The equivalent form therefore possesses a second peculiarity: in it, concrete labour becomes the form of manifestation of its opposite, abstract human labour.

But because this concrete labour, tailoring, counts exclusively as the expression of undifferentiated human labour, it possesses the characteristic of being identical with other kinds of labour, such as the labour embodied in the linen. Consequently, although, like all other commodity-producing labour, it is the labour of private individuals, it is nevertheless labour in its directly social form. It is precisely for this reason that it presents itself to us in the shape of a product which is directly exchangeable with other commodities.

Thus the equivalent form has a third peculiarity: private labour takes the form of its opposite, namely labour in its directly social form.

The two peculiarities of the equivalent form we have just developed will become still clearer if we go back to the great investigator who was the first to analyse the value-form, like so many other forms of thought, society and nature. I mean Aristotle.

In the first place, he states quite clearly that the money-form of the commodity is only a more developed aspect of the simple form of value, i.e. of the expression of the value of a commodity in some other commodity chosen at random, for he says:

$$5 \text{ beds} = 1 \text{ house}$$

(Κλῖναι πέντε ἀντὶ οἰκίας)

is indistinguishable from

$$5 \text{ beds} = \text{a certain amount of money}$$

(Κλῖναι πέντε ἀντὶ . . . ὅσου αἱ πέντε κλῖναι)

He further sees that the value-relation which provides the framework for this expression of value itself requires that the house should be qualitatively equated with the bed, and that these things, being distinct to the senses, could not be compared with each other as commensurable magnitudes if they lacked this essential identity. 'There can be no exchange,' he says, 'without equality, and no equality without commensurability' ('οὔτ' ἰσοτης μὴ οὔσης συμμετρίας'). Here, however, he falters, and abandons the further analysis of the form of value. 'It is, however, in reality, impossible ("τῇ μὲν οὖν ἀληθείᾳ ἀδύνατον") that such unlike things can be commensurable,' i.e. qualitatively equal. This form of equation can only be something foreign to the true nature of the things, it is therefore only 'a makeshift for practical purposes'.*

Aristotle therefore himself tells us what prevented any further analysis: the lack of a concept of value. What is the homogeneous element, i.e. the common substance, which the house represents from the point of view of the bed, in the value expression for the bed? Such a thing, in truth, cannot exist, says Aristotle. But why not? Towards the bed, the house represents something equal, in so far as it represents what is really equal, both in the bed and the house. And that is – human labour.

However, Aristotle himself was unable to extract this fact, that,

*The quotations in this paragraph are from Aristotle, *Nicomachean Ethics*, Bk V, Ch. 5 (Loeb edition, London, 1926, pp. 287–9).

in the form of commodity-values, all labour is expressed as equal human labour and therefore as labour of equal quality, by inspection from the form of value, because Greek society was founded on the labour of slaves, hence had as its natural basis the inequality of men and of their labour-powers. The secret of the expression of value, namely the equality and equivalence of all kinds of labour because and in so far as they are human labour in general, could not be deciphered until the concept of human equality had already acquired the permanence of a fixed popular opinion. This however becomes possible only in a society where the commodity-form is the universal form of the product of labour, hence the dominant social relation is the relation between men as possessors of commodities. Aristotle's genius is displayed precisely by his discovery of a relation of equality in the value-expression of commodities. Only the historical limitation inherent in the society in which he lived prevented him from finding out what 'in reality' this relation of equality consisted of.

(iv) *The simple form of value considered as a whole*   A commodity's simple form of value is contained in its value-relation with another commodity of a different kind, i.e. in its exchange relation with the latter. The value of commodity A is qualitatively expressed by the direct exchangeability of commodity B with commodity A. It is quantitatively expressed by the exchangeability of a specific quantity of commodity B with a given quantity of A. In other words, the value of a commodity is independently expressed through its presentation [*Darstellung*] as 'exchange-value'. When, at the beginning of this chapter, we said in the customary manner that a commodity is both a use-value and an exchange-value, this was, strictly speaking, wrong. A commodity is a use-value or object of utility, and a 'value'. It appears as the twofold thing it really is as soon as its value possesses its own particular form of manifestation, which is distinct from its natural form. This form of manifestation is exchange-value, and the commodity never has this form when looked at in isolation, but only when it is in a value-relation or an exchange relation with a second commodity of a different kind. Once we know this, our manner of speaking does no harm; it serves, rather, as an abbreviation.

Our analysis has shown that the form of value, that is, the expression of the value of a commodity, arises from the nature of commodity-value, as opposed to value and its magnitude arising from their mode of expression as exchange-value. This second view is the delusion both of the Mercantilists (and people like Ferrier, Ganilh, etc.,[23] who have made a modern rehash of Mercantilism) and their antipodes, the modern bagmen of free trade, such as Bastiat and his associates. The Mercantilists place their main emphasis on the qualitative side of the expression of value, hence on the equivalent form of the commodity, which in its finished form is money. The modern pedlars of free trade, on the other hand, who must get rid of their commodities at any price, stress the quantitative side of the relative form of value. For them, accordingly, there exists neither value, nor magnitude of value, anywhere except in its expression by means of the exchange relation, that is, in the daily list of prices current on the Stock Exchange. The Scotsman Macleod,* whose function it is to trick out the confused ideas of Lombard Street in the most learned finery, is a successful cross between the superstitious Mercantilists and the enlightened pedlars of free trade.

A close scrutiny of the expression of the value of commodity A contained in the value-relation of A to B has shown that within that relation the natural form of commodity A figures only as the aspect of use-value, while the natural form of B figures only as the form of value, or aspect of value. The internal opposition between use-value and value, hidden within the commodity, is therefore represented on the surface by an external opposition, i.e. by a relation between two commodities such that the one commodity, *whose own* value is supposed to be expressed, counts directly only as a use-value, whereas the other commodity, *in which* that value is to be expressed, counts directly only as exchange-value. Hence the simple form of value of a commodity is the simple form of appearance of the opposition between use-value and value which is contained within the commodity.

The product of labour is an object of utility in all states of society; but it is only a historically specific epoch of development which presents the labour expended in the production of a useful

23. F. L. A. Ferrier (*sous-inspecteur des douanes*), *Du gouvernement considéré dans ses rapports avec le commerce*, Paris, 1805; and Charles Ganilh, *Des systèmes d'économie politique*, 2nd edn, Paris, 1821.

---

*H. D. Macleod (1821–1902), opponent of the classical economists, who, Marx says, 'misinterprets the most elementary economic relations to such an extent that he asserts that money in general arises from its most advanced form, that is means of payment' (Karl Marx, *A Contribution to the Critique of Political Economy*, p. 143).

article as an 'objective' property of that article, i.e. as its value. It is only then that the product of labour becomes transformed into a commodity. It therefore follows that the simple form of value of the commodity is at the same time the simple form of value of the product of labour, and also that the development of the commodity-form coincides with the development of the value-form.

We perceive straight away the insufficiency of the simple form of value: it is an embryonic form which must undergo a series of metamorphoses before it can ripen into the price-form.

The expression of the value of commodity A in terms of any other commodity B merely distinguishes the value of A from its use-value, and therefore merely places A in an exchange-relation with any particular single different kind of commodity, instead of representing A's qualitative equality with all other commodities and its quantitative proportionality to them. To the simple relative form of value of a commodity there corresponds the single equivalent form of another commodity. Thus, in the relative expression of value of the linen, the coat only possesses the form of equivalent, the form of direct exchangeability, in relation to this one individual commodity, the linen.

Nevertheless, the simple form of value automatically passes over into a more complete form. Admittedly, this simple form only expresses the value of a commodity A in one commodity of another kind. But what this second commodity is, whether it is a coat, iron, corn, etc., is a matter of complete indifference. Therefore different simple expressions of the value of one and the same commodity arise according to whether that commodity enters into a value-relation with this second commodity or another kind of commodity.[24] The number of such possible expressions is limited only by the number of the different kinds of commodities distinct from it. The isolated expression of A's value is thus transformed into the indefinitely expandable series of different simple expressions of that value.

(b) The Total or Expanded Form of Value

z commodity A $= u$ commodity B or $= v$ commodity C or $= w$ commodity D or $= x$ commodity E or $=$ etc.

24. In Homer, for instance (*Iliad*, VII, 472–5), the value of a thing is expressed in a series of different things.

(20 yards of linen = 1 coat or = 10 lb. tea or = 40 lb. coffee or = 1 quarter of corn or = 2 ounces of gold or = $\frac{1}{2}$ ton of iron or = etc.)

(1) *The expanded relative form of value*

The value of a commodity, the linen for example, is now expressed in terms of innumerable other members of the world of commodities. Every other physical commodity now becomes a mirror of the linen's value.[25] It is thus that this value first shows itself as being, in reality, a congealed quantity of undifferentiated human labour. For the labour which creates it is now explicitly presented as labour which counts as the equal of every other sort of human labour, whatever natural form it may possess, hence whether it is objectified in a coat, in corn, in iron, or in gold. The linen, by virtue of the form of value, no longer stands in a social relation with merely one other kind of commodity, but with the whole world of commodities as well. As a commodity it is a citizen of that world. At the same time, the endless series of expressions of its value implies that, from the point of view of the value of the commodity, the particular form of use-value in which it appears is a matter of indifference.

In the first form, 20 yards of linen = 1 coat, it might well be a purely accidental occurrence that these two commodities are ex-

25. For this reason we can speak of the coat-value of the linen when its value is expressed in coats, or of its corn-value when expressed in corn, and so on. Every such expression tells us that it is the value of the linen which appears in the use-values coat, corn etc. 'The value of any commodity denoting its relation in exchange, we may speak of it as . . . corn-value, cloth-value, according to the commodity with which it is compared; and hence there are a thousand different kinds of value, as many kinds of value as there are commodities in existence, and all are equally real and equally nominal' (*A Critical Dissertation on the Nature, Measure, and Causes of Value: Chiefly in Reference to the Writings of Mr Ricardo and His Followers. By the Author of Essays on the Formation, etc., of Opinions,* London, 1825, p. 39). S. Bailey, the author of this anonymous work, which in its day created a considerable stir in England, was under the delusion that by pointing to the multiplicity of the relative expressions of the same commodity-value he had obliterated any possibility of a conceptual determination of value. Still, despite the narrowness of his own outlook he was able to put his finger on some serious defects in the Ricardian theory, as is demonstrated by the animosity with which he was attacked by Ricardo's followers, in the *Westminster Review* for example.*

*The *Westminster Review* was founded in 1824 by Bentham and Bowring, as a quarterly journal of orthodox Radicalism. It was Ricardian in economic theory.

changeable in a specific quantitative relation. In the second form, on the contrary, the background to this accidental appearance, essentially different from it, and determining it, immediately shines through. The value of the linen remains unaltered in magnitude, whether expressed in coats, coffee, or iron, or in innumerable different commodities, belonging to as many different owners. The accidental relation between two individual commodity-owners disappears. It becomes plain that it is not the exchange of commodities which regulates the magnitude of their values, but rather the reverse, the magnitude of the value of commodities which regulates the proportion in which they exchange.

(2) *The particular equivalent form*

Each commodity, such as coat, tea, iron, etc., figures in the expression of value of the linen as an equivalent, hence as a physical object possessing value. The specific natural form of each of these commodities is now a particular equivalent form alongside many others. In the same way, the many specific, concrete, and useful kinds of labour contained in the physical commodities now count as the same number of particular forms of realization or manifestation of human labour in general.

(3) *Defects of the total or expanded form of value*

Firstly, the relative expression of value of the commodity is incomplete, because the series of its representations never comes to an end. The chain, of which each equation of value is a link, is liable at any moment to be lengthened by a newly created commodity, which will provide the material for a fresh expression of value. Secondly, it is a motley mosaic of disparate and unconnected expressions of value. And lastly, if, as must be the case, the relative value of each commodity is expressed in this expanded form, it follows that the relative form of value of each commodity is an endless series of expressions of value which are all different from the relative form of value of every other commodity. The defects of the expanded relative form of value are reflected in the corresponding equivalent form. Since the natural form of each particular kind of commodity is one particular equivalent form amongst innumerable other equivalent forms, the only equivalent forms which exist are limited ones, and each of them excludes all the others. Similarly, the specific, concrete, useful kind of labour contained in each particular commodity-equivalent is only a particular kind of labour and therefore not an exhaustive form of appearance of human labour in general. It is true that the completed or total form of appearance of human labour is constituted by the totality of its particular forms of appearance. But in that case it has no single, unified form of appearance.

The expanded relative form of value is, however, nothing but the sum of the simple relative expressions or equations of the first form, such as:

20 yards of linen = 1 coat
20 yards of linen = 10 lb. of tea, etc.

However, each of these equations implies the identical equation in reverse:

1 coat = 20 yards of linen
10 lb. of tea = 20 yards of linen, etc.

In fact, when a person exchanges his linen for many other commodities, and thus expresses its value in a series of other commodities, it necessarily follows that the other owners of commodities exchange them for the linen, and therefore express the values of their various commodities in one and the same third commodity, the linen. If, then, we reverse the series 20 yards of linen = 1 coat, or = 10 lb. of tea, etc., i.e. if we give expression to the converse relation already implied in the series, we get:

(c) The General Form of Value

$$
\left.
\begin{array}{l}
\text{1 coat} \\
\text{10 lb. of tea} \\
\text{40 lb. of coffee} \\
\text{1 quarter of corn} \\
\text{2 ounces of gold} \\
\tfrac{1}{2} \text{ ton of iron} \\
x \text{ commodity A etc.}
\end{array}
\right\} = \text{20 yards of linen}
$$

(1) *The changed character of the form of value*

The commodities now present their values to us, (1) in a simple form, because in a single commodity; (2) in a unified form, because in the same commodity each time. Their form of value is simple and common to all, hence general.

The two previous forms (let us call them A and B) only amounted to the expression of the value of a commodity as something distinct from its own use-value or its physical shape as a commodity.

The first form, A, produced equations like this: 1 coat = 20 yards of linen, 10 lb. of tea = $\frac{1}{2}$ ton of iron. The value of the coat is expressed as comparable with linen,* that of the tea as comparable with iron. But to be comparable with linen and with iron, these expressions of the value of coat and tea, is to be as different as linen is from iron. This form, it is plain, appears in practice only in the early stages, when the products of labour are converted into commodities by accidental occasional exchanges.

The second form, B, distinguishes the value of a commodity from its own use-value more adequately than the first, for the value of the coat now stands in contrast with its natural form in all possible shapes, in the sense that it is equated with linen, iron, tea, in short with everything but itself. On the other hand any expression of value common to all commodities is directly excluded; for, in the expression of value of each commodity, all other commodities now appear only in the form of equivalents. The expanded form of value comes into actual existence for the first time when a particular product of labour, such as cattle, is no longer exceptionally, but habitually, exchanged for various other commodities.

The new form we have just obtained expresses the values of the world of commodities through one single kind of commodity set apart from the rest, through the linen for example, and thus represents the values of all commodities by means of their equality with linen. Through its equation with linen, the value of every commodity is now not only differentiated from its own use-value, but from all use-values, and is, by that very fact, expressed as that which is common to all commodities. By this form, commodities are, for the first time, really brought into relation with each other as values, or permitted to appear to each other as exchange-values.

The two earlier forms express the value of each commodity either in terms of a single commodity of a different kind, or in a series of many commodities which differ from the first one. In both cases it is the private task, so to speak, of the individual

* 'Comparable with linen' is the expression we have chosen to render *Leinwandgleiches*, 'comparable with iron' renders *Eisengleiches*, and so on. These circumlocutions are unavoidable here.

commodity to give itself a form of value, and it accomplishes this task without the aid of the others, which play towards it the merely passive role of equivalent. The general form of value, on the other hand, can only arise as the joint contribution of the whole world of commodities. A commodity only acquires a general expression of its value if, at the same time, all other commodities express their values in the same equivalent; and every newly emergent commodity must follow suit. It thus becomes evident that because the objectivity of commodities as values is the purely 'social existence' of these things, it can only be expressed through the whole range of their social relations; consequently the form of their value must possess social validity.

In this form, when they are all counted as comparable with the linen, all commodities appear not only as qualitatively equal, as values in general, but also as values of quantitatively comparable magnitude. Because the magnitudes of their values are expressed in one and the same material, the linen, these magnitudes are now reflected in each other. For instance, 10 lb. of tea = 20 yards of linen, and 40 lb. of coffee = 20 yards of linen. Therefore 10 lb. of tea = 40 lb. of coffee. In other words, 1 lb. of coffee contains only a quarter as much of the substance of value, that is, labour, as 1 lb. of tea.

The general relative form of value imposes the character of universal equivalent on the linen, which is the commodity excluded, as equivalent, from the whole world of commodities. Its own natural form is the form assumed in common by the values of all commodities; it is therefore directly exchangeable with all other commodities. The physical form of the linen counts as the visible incarnation, the social chrysalis state, of all human labour. Weaving, the private labour which produces linen, acquires as a result a general social form, the form of equality with all other kinds of labour. The innumerable equations of which the general form of value is composed equate the labour realized in the linen with the labour contained in every other commodity in turn, and they thus convert weaving into the general form of appearance of undifferentiated human labour. In this manner the labour objectified in the values of commodities is not just presented negatively, as labour in which abstraction is made from all the concrete forms and useful properties of actual work. Its own positive nature is explicitly brought out, namely the fact that it is the reduction of all kinds of actual labour to their common character of being human labour in general, of being the expenditure of human labour-power.

The general value-form, in which all the products of labour are presented as mere congealed quantities of undifferentiated human labour, shows by its very structure that it is the social expression of the world of commodities. In this way it is made plain that within this world the general human character of labour forms its specific social character.

(2) *The development of the relative and equivalent forms of value:*
    their interdependence

The degree of development of the relative form of value, and that of the equivalent form, correspond. But we must bear in mind that the development of the equivalent form is only the expression and the result of the development of the relative form.

The simple or isolated relative form of value of one commodity converts some other commodity into an isolated equivalent. The expanded form of relative value, that expression of the value of one commodity in terms of all other commodities, imprints those other commodities with the form of particular equivalents of different kinds. Finally, a particular kind of commodity acquires the form of universal equivalent, because all other commodities make it the material embodiment of their uniform and universal form of value.

But the antagonism between the relative form of value and the equivalent form, the two poles of the value-form, also develops concomitantly with the development of the value-form itself.

The first form, 20 yards of linen = 1 coat, already contains this antagonism, without as yet fixing it. According to whether we read the same equation forwards or backwards, each of the two commodity poles, such as the linen and the coat, is to be found in the relative form on one occasion, and in the equivalent form on the other occasion. Here it is still difficult to keep hold of the polar antagonism.

In form B, only one commodity at a time can completely expand its relative value, and it only possesses this expanded relative form of value because, and in so far as, all other commodities are, with respect to it, equivalents. Here we can no longer reverse the equation 20 yards of linen = 1 coat without altering its whole character, and converting it from the expanded form into the general form of value.

Finally, the last form, C, gives to the world of commodities a general social relative form of value, because, and in so far as, all commodities except one are thereby excluded from the equivalent form. A single commodity, the linen, therefore has the form of direct exchangeability with all other commodities, in other words it has a directly social form because, and in so far as, no other commodity is in this situation.[26]

The commodity that figures as universal equivalent is on the other hand excluded from the uniform and therefore universal relative form of value. If the linen, or any other commodity serving as universal equivalent, were, at the same time, to share in the relative form of value, it would have to serve as its own equivalent. We should then have: 20 yards of linen = 20 yards of linen, a tautology in which neither the value nor its magnitude is expressed. In order to express the relative value of the universal equivalent, we must rather reverse the form C. This equivalent has no relative form of value in common with other commodities; its value is, rather, expressed relatively in the infinite series of all other physical commodities. Thus the expanded relative form of value, or form B, now appears as the specific relative form of value of the equivalent commodity.

---

26. It is by no means self-evident that the form of direct and universal ex changeability is an antagonistic form, as inseparable from its opposite, the form of non-direct exchangeability, as the positivity of one pole of a magnet is from the negativity of the other pole. This has allowed the illusion to arise that all commodities can simultaneously be imprinted with the stamp of direct exchangeability, in the same way that it might be imagined that all Catholics can be popes. It is, of course, highly desirable in the eyes of the petty bourgeois, who views the production of commodities as the absolute summit of human freedom and individual independence, that the inconveniences resulting from the impossibility of exchanging commodities directly, which are inherent in this form, should be removed. This philistine utopia is depicted in the socialism of Proudhon, which, as I have shown elsewhere,* does not even possess the merit of originality, but was in fact developed far more successfully long before Proudhon by Gray, Bray and others. Even so, wisdom of this kind is still rife in certain circles under the name of 'science'. No school of thought has thrown around the word 'science' more haphazardly than that of Proudhon, for '*wo Begriffe fehlen, da stellt zur rechten Zeit ein Wort sich ein*'.†

*In Chapter 1 of Marx's 1847 polemic against Proudhon, *The Poverty of Philosophy*.

†'Where thoughts are absent, words are brought in as convenient replacements.' A slightly altered quotation from Goethe, *Faust*, Part I, Scene 4, Faust's Study, lines 1995–6.

(3) *The transition from the general form of value to the money form*

The universal equivalent form is a form of value in general. It can therefore be assumed by any commodity. On the other hand, a commodity is only to be found in the universal equivalent form (form C) if, and in so far as, it is excluded from the ranks of all other commodities, as being their equivalent. Only when this exclusion becomes finally restricted to a specific kind of commodity does the uniform relative form of value of the world of commodities attain objective fixedness and general social validity.

The specific kind of commodity with whose natural form the equivalent form is socially interwoven now becomes the money commodity, or serves as money. It becomes its specific social function, and consequently its social monopoly, to play the part of universal equivalent within the world of commodities. Among the commodities which in form B figure as particular equivalents of the linen, and in form C express in common their relative values in linen, there is one in particular which has historically conquered this advantageous position: gold. If, then, in form C, we replace the linen by gold, we get:

(d) The Money Form

$$\left.\begin{array}{l}\text{20 yards of linen}\\\text{1 coat}\\\text{10 lb. of tea}\\\text{40 lb. of coffee}\\\text{1 quarter of corn}\\\tfrac{1}{2}\text{ ton of iron}\\x\text{ commodity A}\end{array}\right\}=\text{2 ounces of gold}$$

Fundamental changes have taken place in the course of the transition from form A to form B, and from form B to form C. As against this, form D differs not at all from form C, except that now instead of linen gold has assumed the universal equivalent form. Gold is in form D what linen was in form C: the universal equivalent. The advance consists only in that the form of direct and universal exchangeability, in other words the universal equivalent form, has now by social custom finally become entwined with the specific natural form of the commodity gold.

Gold confronts the other commodities as money only because it previously confronted them as a commodity. Like all other commodities it also functioned as an equivalent, either as a single equivalent in isolated exchanges or as a particular equivalent alongside other commodity-equivalents. Gradually it began to serve as universal equivalent in narrower or wider fields. As soon as it had won a monopoly of this position in the expression of value for the world of commodities, it became the money commodity, and only then, when it had already become the money commodity, did form D become distinct from form C, and the general form of value come to be transformed into the money form.

The simple expression of the relative value of a single commodity, such as linen, in a commodity which is already functioning as the money commodity, such as gold, is the price form. The 'price form' of the linen is therefore: 20 yards of linen = 2 ounces of gold, or, if 2 ounces of gold when coined are £2, 20 yards of linen = £2.

The only difficulty in the concept of the money form is that of grasping the universal equivalent form, and hence the general form of value as such, form C. Form C can be reduced by working backwards to form B, the expanded form of value, and its constitutive element is form A: 20 yards of linen = 1 coat or x commodity A = y commodity B. The simple commodity form is therefore the germ of the money-form.

4. THE FETISHISM OF THE COMMODITY AND ITS SECRET

A commodity appears at first sight an extremely obvious, trivial thing. But its analysis brings out that it is a very strange thing, abounding in metaphysical subtleties and theological niceties. So far as it is a use-value, there is nothing mysterious about it, whether we consider it from the point of view that by its properties it satisfies human needs, or that it first takes on these properties as the product of human labour. It is absolutely clear that, by his activity, man changes the forms of the materials of nature in such a way as to make them useful to him. The form of wood, for instance, is altered if a table is made out of it. Nevertheless the table continues to be wood, an ordinary, sensuous thing. But as soon as it emerges as a commodity, it changes into a thing which transcends sensuousness. It not only stands with its feet on the ground, but, in relation to all other commodities, it stands on its head, and evolves out of its wooden brain grotesque ideas, far more wonderful than if it were to begin dancing of its own free will.[27]

The mystical character of the commodity does not therefore arise from its use-value. Just as little does it proceed from the nature of the determinants of value. For in the first place, however varied the useful kinds of labour, or productive activities, it is a physiological fact that they are functions of the human organism, and that each such function, whatever may be its nature or its form, is essentially the expenditure of human brain, nerves, muscles and sense organs. Secondly, with regard to the foundation of the quantitative determination of value, namely the duration of that expenditure or the quantity of labour, this is quite palpably different from its quality. In all situations, the labour-time it costs to produce the means of subsistence must necessarily concern mankind, although not to the same degree at different stages of development.[28] And finally, as soon as men start to work for each other in any way, their labour also assumes a social form.

Whence, then, arises the enigmatic character of the product of labour, as soon as it assumes the form of a commodity? Clearly, it arises from this form itself. The equality of the kinds of human labour takes on a physical form in the equal objectivity of the products of labour as values; the measure of the expenditure of human labour-power by its duration takes on the form of the magnitude of the value of the products of labour; and finally the relationships between the producers, within which the social characteristics of their labours are manifested, take on the form of a social relation between the products of labour.

The mysterious character of the commodity-form consists therefore simply in the fact that the commodity reflects the social characteristics of men's own labour as objective characteristics of

27. One may recall that China and the tables began to dance when the rest of the world appeared to be standing still – *pour encourager les autres*.*

28. Among the ancient Germans the size of a piece of land was measured according to the labour of a day; hence the acre was called *Tagwerk, Tagwanne* (*jurnale*, or *terra jurnalis*, or *diornalis*), *Mannwerk, Mannskraft, Mannsmaad, Mannshauet*, etc. See Georg Ludwig von Maurer, *Einleitung zur Geschichte der Mark-, Hof-, usw. Verfassung*, Munich, 1854, p. 129 ff.

* 'To encourage the others'. A reference to the simultaneous emergence in the 1850s of the Taiping revolt in China and the craze for spiritualism which swept over upper-class German society. The rest of the world was 'standing still' in the period of reaction immediately after the defeat of the 1848 Revolutions.

the products of labour themselves, as the socio-natural properties of these things. Hence it also reflects the social relation of the producers to the sum total of labour as a social relation between objects, a relation which exists apart from and outside the producers. Through this substitution, the products of labour become commodities, sensuous things which are at the same time suprasensible or social. In the same way, the impression made by a thing on the optic nerve is perceived not as a subjective excitation of that nerve but as the objective form of a thing outside the eye. In the act of seeing, of course, light is really transmitted from one thing, the external object, to another thing, the eye. It is a physical relation between physical things. As against this, the commodity-form, and the value-relation of the products of labour within which it appears, have absolutely no connection with the physical nature of the commodity and the material [*dinglich*] relations arising out of this. It is nothing but the definite social relation between men themselves which assumes here, for them, the fantastic form of a relation between things. In order, therefore, to find an analogy we must take flight into the misty realm of religion. There the products of the human brain appear as autonomous figures endowed with a life of their own, which enter into relations both with each other and with the human race. So it is in the world of commodities with the products of men's hands. I call this the fetishism which attaches itself to the products of labour as soon as they are produced as commodities, and is therefore inseparable from the production of commodities.

As the foregoing analysis has already demonstrated, this fetishism of the world of commodities arises from the peculiar social character of the labour which produces them.

Objects of utility become commodities only because they are the products of the labour of private individuals who work independently of each other. The sum total of the labour of all these private individuals forms the aggregate labour of society. Since the producers do not come into social contact until they exchange the products of their labour, the specific social characteristics of their private labours appear only within this exchange. In other words, the labour of the private individual manifests itself as an element of the total labour of society only through the relations which the act of exchange establishes between the products, and, through their mediation, between the producers. To the producers, therefore, the social relations between their private labours appear as what they are, i.e. they do not appear as direct social relations between persons in their work, but rather as material [*dinglich*] relations between persons and social relations between things.

It is only by being exchanged that the products of labour acquire a socially uniform objectivity as values, which is distinct from their sensuously varied objectivity as articles of utility. This division of the product of labour into a useful thing and a thing possessing value appears in practice only when exchange has already acquired a sufficient extension and importance to allow useful things to be produced for the purpose of being exchanged, so that their character as values has already to be taken into consideration during production. From this moment on, the labour of the individual producer acquires a twofold social character. On the one hand, it must, as a definite useful kind of labour, satisfy a definite social need, and thus maintain its position as an element of the total labour, as a branch of the social division of labour, which originally sprang up spontaneously. On the other hand, it can satisfy the manifold needs of the individual producer himself only in so far as every particular kind of useful private labour can be exchanged with, i.e. counts as the equal of, every other kind of useful private labour. Equality in the full sense between different kinds of labour can be arrived at only if we abstract from their real inequality, if we reduce them to the characteristic they have in common, that of being the expenditure of human labour-power, of human labour in the abstract. The private producer's brain reflects this twofold social character of his labour only in the forms which appear in practical intercourse, in the exchange of products. Hence the socially useful character of his private labour is reflected in the form that the product of labour has to be useful to others, and the social character of the equality of the various kinds of labour is reflected in the form of the common character, as values, possessed by these materially different things, the products of labour.

Men do not therefore bring the products of their labour into relation with each other as values because they see these objects merely as the material integuments of homogeneous human labour. The reverse is true: by equating their different products to each other in exchange as values, they equate their different kinds of labour as human labour. They do this without being aware of it.[29] Value, therefore, does not have its description branded on its forehead; it rather transforms every product of labour into a social hieroglyphic. Later on, men try to decipher the hieroglyphic, to get behind the secret of their own social product: for the characteristic which objects of utility have of being values is as much men's social product as is their language. The belated scientific discovery that the products of labour, in so far as they are values, are merely the material expressions of the human labour expended to produce them, marks an epoch in the history of mankind's development, but by no means banishes the semblance of objectivity possessed by the social characteristics of labour. Something which is only valid for this particular form of production, the production of commodities, namely the fact that the specific social character of private labours carried on independently of each other consists in their equality as human labour, and, in the product, assumes the form of the existence of value, appears to those caught up in the relations of commodity production (and this is true both before and after the above-mentioned scientific discovery) to be just as ultimately valid as the fact that the scientific dissection of the air into its component parts left the atmosphere itself unaltered in its physical configuration.

What initially concerns producers in practice when they make an exchange is how much of some other product they get for their own; in what proportions can the products be exchanged? As soon as these proportions have attained a certain customary stability, they appear to result from the nature of the products, so that, for instance, one ton of iron and two ounces of gold appear to be equal in value, in the same way as a pound of gold and a pound of iron are equal in weight, despite their different physical and chemical properties. The value character of the products of labour becomes firmly established only when they act as magnitudes of value. These magnitudes vary continually, independently of the will, foreknowledge and actions of the exchangers. Their own movement within society has for them the form of a movement made by things, and these things, far from being under

29. Therefore, when Galiani said: Value is a relation between persons ('*La Ricchezza è una ragione tra due persone*') he ought to have added: a relation concealed beneath a material shell. (Galiani, *Della Moneta*, p. 221, Vol. 3 of Custodi's collection entitled *Scrittori classici italiani di economia politica, Parte moderna*, Milan, 1803.)

their control, in fact control them. The production of commodities must be fully developed before the scientific conviction emerges, from experience itself, that all the different kinds of private labour (which are carried on independently of each other, and yet, as spontaneously developed branches of the social division of labour, are in a situation of all-round dependence on each other) are continually being reduced to the quantitative proportions in which society requires them. The reason for this reduction is that in the midst of the accidental and ever-fluctuating exchange relations between the products, the labour-time socially necessary to produce them asserts itself as a regulative law of nature. In the same way, the law of gravity asserts itself when a person's house collapses on top of him.[30] The determination of the magnitude of value by labour-time is therefore a secret hidden under the apparent movements in the relative values of commodities. Its discovery destroys the semblance of the merely accidental determination of the magnitude of the value of the products of labour, but by no means abolishes that determination's material form.

Reflection on the forms of human life, hence also scientific analysis of those forms, takes a course directly opposite to their real development. Reflection begins *post festum*,* and therefore with the results of the process of development ready to hand. The forms which stamp products as commodities and which are therefore the preliminary requirements for the circulation of commodities, already possess the fixed quality of natural forms of social life before man seeks to give an account, not of their historical character, for in his eyes they are immutable, but of their content and meaning. Consequently, it was solely the analysis of the prices of commodities which led to the determination of the magnitude of value, and solely the common expression of all commodities in money which led to the establishment of their character as values. It is however precisely this finished form of the world of commodities – the money form – which conceals the social character of private labour and the social relations between the individual

30. 'What are we to think of a law which can only assert itself through periodic crises? It is just a natural law which depends on the lack of awareness of the people who undergo it' (Friedrich Engels, *Umrisse zu einer Kritik der Nationalökonomie*, in the *Deutsch-Französische Jahrbücher*, edited by Arnold Ruge and Karl Marx, Paris, 1844) [English translation in Marx/Engels' *Collected Works*, Vol. 3, London, 1975, p. 433].

* 'After the feast', i.e. after the events reflected on have taken place.

workers, by making those relations appear as relations between material objects, instead of revealing them plainly. If I state that coats or boots stand in a relation to linen because the latter is the universal incarnation of abstract human labour, the absurdity of the statement is self-evident. Nevertheless, when the producers of coats and boots bring these commodities into a relation with linen, or with gold or silver (and this makes no difference here), as the universal equivalent, the relation between their own private labour and the collective labour of society appears to them in exactly this absurd form.

The categories of bourgeois economics consist precisely of forms of this kind. They are forms of thought which are socially valid, and therefore objective, for the relations of production belonging to this historically determined mode of social production, i.e. commodity production. The whole mystery of commodities, all the magic and necromancy that surrounds the products of labour on the basis of commodity production, vanishes therefore as soon as we come to other forms of production.

As political economists are fond of Robinson Crusoe stories,[31] let us first look at Robinson on his island. Undemanding though he is by nature, he still has needs to satisfy, and must therefore perform useful labours of various kinds: he must make tools, knock together furniture, tame llamas, fish, hunt and so on. Of his prayers and the like, we take no account here, since our friend takes pleasure in them and sees them as recreation. Despite the diversity of his productive functions, he knows that they are only different forms of activity of one and the same Robinson, hence only different modes of human labour. Necessity itself compels him to divide his time with precision between his different func-

31. Even Ricardo has his Robinson Crusoe stories. 'Ricardo makes his primitive fisherman and primitive hunter into owners of commodities who immediately exchange their fish and game in proportion to the labour-time which is materialized in these exchange-values. On this occasion he slips into the anachronism of allowing the primitive fisherman and hunter to calculate the value of their implements in accordance with the annuity tables used on the London Stock Exchange in 1817. Apart from bourgeois society, the "parallelograms of Mr Owen" seem to have been the only form of society Ricardo was acquainted with' *(Karl Marx, *Zur Kritik etc.*, pp. 38–9) [English translation, p. 60].

*The 'parallelograms' were the utopian socialist Robert Owen's suggestion for the most appropriate layout for a workers' settlement, made in *A New View of Society* (1813) and immediately seized on by his critics. Ricardo's reference to them is from his *On Protection of Agriculture*, London, 1822, p. 21.

tions. Whether one function occupies a greater space in his total activity than another depends on the magnitude of the difficulties to be overcome in attaining the useful effect aimed at. Our friend Robinson Crusoe learns this by experience, and having saved a watch, ledger, ink and pen from the shipwreck, he soon begins, like a good Englishman, to keep a set of books. His stock-book contains a catalogue of the useful objects he possesses, of the various operations necessary for their production, and finally of the labour-time that specific quantities of these products have on average cost him. All the relations between Robinson and these objects that form his self-created wealth are here so simple and transparent that even Mr Sedley Taylor* could understand them. And yet those relations contain all the essential determinants of value.

Let us now transport ourselves from Robinson's island, bathed in light, to medieval Europe, shrouded in darkness. Here, instead of the independent man, we find everyone dependent – serfs and lords, vassals and suzerains, laymen and clerics. Personal dependence characterizes the social relations of material production as much as it does the other spheres of life based on that production. But precisely because relations of personal dependence form the given social foundation, there is no need for labour and its products to assume a fantastic form different from their reality. They take the shape, in the transactions of society, of services in kind and payments in kind. The natural form of labour, its particularity – and not, as in a society based on commodity production, its universality – is here its immediate social form. The *corvée* can be measured by time just as well as the labour which produces commodities, but every serf knows that what he expends in the service of his lord is a specific quantity of his own personal labour-power. The tithe owed to the priest is more clearly apparent than his blessing. Whatever we may think, then, of the different roles in which men confront each other in such a society, the social relations between individuals in the performance of their labour appear at all events as their own personal relations, and are not disguised as social relations between things, between the products of labour.

* The original German has here 'Herr M. Wirth', chosen by Marx as a run-of-the-mill vulgar economist and propagandist familiar to German readers. Engels introduced 'Mr Sedley Taylor', a Cambridge don against whom he polemicized in his preface to the fourth German edition (see above, p. 117).

For an example of labour in common, i.e. directly associated labour, we do not need to go back to the spontaneously developed form which we find at the threshold of the history of all civilized peoples.[32] We have one nearer to hand in the patriarchal rural industry of a peasant family which produces corn, cattle, yarn, linen and clothing for its own use. These things confront the family as so many products of its collective labour, but they do not confront each other as commodities. The different kinds of labour which create these products – such as tilling the fields, tending the cattle, spinning, weaving and making clothes – are already in their natural form social functions; for they are functions of the family, which, just as much as a society based on commodity production, possesses its own spontaneously developed division of labour. The distribution of labour within the family and the labour-time expended by the individual members of the family, are regulated by differences of sex and age as well as by seasonal variations in the natural conditions of labour. The fact that the expenditure of the individual labour-powers is measured by duration appears here, by its very nature, as a social characteristic of labour itself, because the individual labour-powers, by their very nature, act only as instruments of the joint labour-power of the family.

Let us finally imagine, for a change, an association of free men, working with the means of production held in common, and expending their many different forms of labour-power in full self-awareness as one single social labour force. All the characteristics of Robinson's labour are repeated here, but with the difference that they are social instead of individual. All Robinson's products were exclusively the result of his own personal labour and they were therefore directly objects of utility for him personally. The total product of our imagined association is a social product. One part of this product serves as fresh means of production and re-

32. 'A ridiculous notion has spread abroad recently that communal property in its natural, spontaneous form is specifically Slav, indeed exclusively Russian. In fact, it is the primitive form that we can prove to have existed among Romans, Teutons and Celts, and which indeed still exists to this day in India, in a whole range of diverse patterns, albeit sometimes only as remnants. A more exact study of the Asiatic, and specifically of the Indian form of communal property would indicate the way in which different forms of spontaneous, primitive communal property give rise to different forms of its dissolution. Thus the different original types of Roman and Germanic private property can be deduced from the different forms of Indian communal property' (Karl Marx, *Zur Kritik, etc.*, p. 10) [English translation, p. 33].

mains social. But another part is consumed by the members of the association as means of subsistence. This part must therefore be divided amongst them. The way this division is made will vary with the particular kind of social organization of production and the corresponding level of social development attained by the producers. We shall assume, but only for the sake of a parallel with the production of commodities, that the share of each individual producer in the means of subsistence is determined by his labour-time. Labour-time would in that case play a double part. Its apportionment in accordance with a definite social plan maintains the correct proportion between the different functions of labour and the various needs of the associations. On the other hand, labour-time also serves as a measure of the part taken by each individual in the common labour, and of his share in the part of the total product destined for individual consumption. The social relations of the individual producers, both towards their labour and the products of their labour, are here transparent in their simplicity, in production as well as in distribution.

For a society of commodity producers, whose general social relation of production consists in the fact that they treat their products as commodities, hence as values, and in this material [*sachlich*] form bring their individual, private labours into relation with each other as homogeneous human labour, Christianity with its religious cult of man in the abstract, more particularly in its bourgeois development, i.e. in Protestantism, Deism, etc., is the most fitting form of religion. In the ancient Asiatic, Classical-antique, and other such modes of production, the transformation of the product into a commodity, and therefore men's existence as producers of commodities, plays a subordinate role, which however increases in importance as these communities approach nearer and nearer to the stage of their dissolution. Trading nations, properly so called, exist only in the interstices of the ancient world, like the gods of Epicurus in the *intermundia*,* or Jews in the pores of Polish society. Those ancient social organisms of production are much more simple and transparent than those of bourgeois society.

---

*According to the Greek philosopher Epicurus (*c*. 341–*c*. 270 B.C.), the gods existed only in the *intermundia*, or spaces between different worlds, and had no influence on the course of human affairs. Very few of the writings of Epicurus have been preserved in the original Greek, and this particular idea survived only by being included in Cicero, *De natura deorum*, Book I, Section 18.

But they are founded either on the immaturity of man as an individual, when he has not yet torn himself loose from the umbilical cord of his natural species-connection with other men, or on direct relations of dominance and servitude. They are conditioned by a low stage of development of the productive powers of labour and correspondingly limited relations between men within the process of creating and reproducing their material life, hence also limited relations between man and nature. These real limitations are reflected in the ancient worship of nature, and in other elements of tribal religions. The religious reflections of the real world can, in any case, vanish only when the practical relations of everyday life between man and man, and man and nature, generally present themselves to him in a transparent and rational form. The veil is not removed from the countenance of the social life-process, i.e. the process of material production, until it becomes production by freely associated men, and stands under their conscious and planned control. This, however, requires that society possess a material foundation, or a series of material conditions of existence, which in their turn are the natural and spontaneous product of a long and tormented historical development.

Political economy has indeed analysed value and its magnitude, however incompletely,[33] and has uncovered the content concealed

33. The insufficiency of Ricardo's analysis of the magnitude of value – and his analysis is by far the best – will appear from the third and fourth books of this work.* As regards value in general, classical political economy in fact nowhere distinguishes explicitly and with a clear awareness between labour as it appears in the value of a product, and the same labour as it appears in the product's use-value. Of course the distinction is made in practice, since labour is treated sometimes from its quantitative aspect, and at other times qualitatively. But it does not occur to the economists that a purely quantitative distinction between the kinds of labour presupposes their qualitative unity or equality, and therefore their reduction to abstract human labour. For instance, Ricardo declares that he agrees with Destutt de Tracy when the latter says: 'As it is certain that our physical and moral faculties are alone our original riches, the employment of those faculties, labour of some kind, is our original treasure, and it is always from this employment that all those things are created which we call riches ... It is certain too, that all those things only represent the labour which has created them, and if they have a value, or even two distinct values, they can only derive them from that' (the value) 'of the labour from which they emanate' (Ricardo, *The Principles of Political Economy*, 3rd edn, London, 1821, p. 334).† We would here only point out that

*These are the books that appeared, respectively, as Volume 3 of *Capital*, and *Theories of Surplus-Value* (3 volumes).

†Destutt de Tracy, *Élémens d'idéologie*, Parts 4 and 5, Paris, 1826, pp. 35–6.

within these forms. But it has never once asked the question why this content has assumed that particular form, that is to say, why labour is expressed in value, and why the measurement of labour by its duration is expressed in the magnitude of the value of the product.[34] These formulas, which bear the unmistakable stamp of

Ricardo imposes his own more profound interpretation on the words of Destutt. Admittedly Destutt does say that all things which constitute wealth 'represent the labour which has created them', but, on the other hand, he also says that they acquire their 'two different values' (use-value and exchange-value) from 'the value of labour'. He thus falls into the commonplace error of the vulgar economists, who assume the value of one commodity (here labour) in order in turn to use it to determine the values of other commodities. But Ricardo reads him as if he had said that labour (not the value of labour) is represented both in use-value and in exchange-value. Nevertheless, Ricardo himself makes so little of the dual character of the labour represented in this twofold way that he is forced to spend the whole of his chapter 'Value and Riches, their Distinctive Properties' on a laborious examination of the trivialities of a J. B. Say. And at the end he is therefore quite astonished to find that while Destutt agrees with him that labour is the source of value, he nevertheless also agrees with Say about the concept of value.*

34. It is one of the chief failings of classical political economy that it has never succeeded, by means of its analysis of commodities, and in particular of their value, in discovering the form of value which in fact turns value into exchange-value. Even its best representatives, Adam Smith and Ricardo, treat the form of value as something of indifference, something external to the nature of the commodity itself. The explanation for this is not simply that their attention is entirely absorbed by the analysis of the magnitude of value. It lies deeper. The value-form of the product of labour is the most abstract, but also the most universal form of the bourgeois mode of production; by that fact it stamps the bourgeois mode of production as a particular kind of social production of a historical and transitory character. If then we make the mistake of treating it as the eternal natural form of social production, we necessarily overlook the specificity of the value-form, and consequently of the commodity-form together with its further developments, the money form, the capital form, etc. We therefore find that economists who are entirely agreed that labour-time is the measure of the magnitude of value, have the strangest and most contradictory ideas about money, that is, about the universal equivalent in its finished form. This emerges sharply when they deal with banking, where the commonplace definitions of money will no longer hold water. Hence there has arisen in opposition to the classical economists a restored Mercantilist System (Ganilh etc.), which sees in value only the social form, or rather its insubstantial semblance. Let me point out once and for all that by classical political economy I mean all the economists who, since the time of W. Petty, have investigated the real internal framework [*Zusammenhang*] of bourgeois

* 'I am sorry to be obliged to add that M. de Tracy supports, by his authority, the definitions which M. Say has given of the words "value", "riches", and "utility" ' (Ricardo, op. cit., p. 334).

belonging to a social formation in which the process of production has mastery over man, instead of the opposite, appear to the political economists' bourgeois consciousness to be as much a self-evident and nature-imposed necessity as productive labour itself. Hence the pre-bourgeois forms of the social organization of production are treated by political economy in much the same way as the Fathers of the Church treated pre-Christian religions.[35]

---

relations of production, as opposed to the vulgar economists who only flounder around within the apparent framework of those relations, ceaselessly ruminate on the materials long since provided by scientific political economy, and seek there plausible explanations of the crudest phenomena for the domestic purposes of the bourgeoisie. Apart from this, the vulgar economists confine themselves to systematizing in a pedantic way, and proclaiming for everlasting truths, the banal and complacent notions held by the bourgeois agents of production about their own world, which is to them the best possible one.

35. 'The economists have a singular way of proceeding. For them, there are only two kinds of institutions, artificial and natural. The institutions offeud alism are artificial institutions, those of the bourgeoisie are natural institutions. In this they resemble the theologians, who likewise establish two kinds of religion. Every religion which is not heirs is an invention of men, while their own is an emanation of God . . . Thus there has been history, but there is no longer any' (Karl Marx, *Misère de la philosophie. Réponse à la philosophie de la misère de M. Proudhon*, 1847, p. 113).* Truly comical is M. Bastiat, who imagines that the ancient Greeks and Romans lived by plunder alone. For if people live by plunder for centuries there must, after all, always be something there to plunder; in other words, the objects of plunder must be continually reproduced. It seems, therefore, that even the Greeks and the Romans had a process of production, hence an economy, which constituted the material basis of their world as much as the bourgeois economy constitutes that of the present-day world. Or perhaps Bastiat means that a mode of production based on the labour of slaves is based on a system of plunder? In that case he is on dangerous ground. If a giant thinker like Aristotle could err in his evaluation of slave-labour, why should a dwarf economist like Bastiat be right in his evaluation of wage-labour? I seize this opportunity of briefly refuting an objection made by a German–American publication to my work *Zur Kritik der Politischen Ökonomie*, 1859. My view is that each particular mode of production, and the relations of production corresponding to it at each given moment, in short 'the economic structure of society', is 'the real foundation, on which arises a legal and political superstructure and to which correspond definite forms of social consciousness', and that 'the mode of production of material life conditions the general process of social, political and intellectual life'.†

*English translation: Karl Marx, *The Poverty of Philosophy*, London, 1966, p. 105.

†These passages are taken from the Preface to *A Contribution to the Critique of Political Economy*, written in January 1859 (English translation, pp. 20–21).

The degree to which some economists are misled by the fetish-ism attached to the world of commodities, or by the objective appearance of the social characteristics of labour, is shown, among other things, by the dull and tedious dispute over the part played by nature in the formation of exchange-value. Since exchange-value is a definite social manner of expressing the labour bestowed on a thing, it can have no more natural content than has, for ex-ample, the rate of exchange.

As the commodity-form is the most general and the most un-developed form of bourgeois production, it makes its appearance at an early date, though not in the same predominant and there-fore characteristic manner as nowadays. Hence its fetish character is still relatively easy to penetrate. But when we come to more concrete forms, even this appearance of simplicity vanishes. Where did the illusions of the Monetary System come from? The adherents of the Monetary System did not see gold and silver as representing money as a social relation of production, but in the form of natural objects with peculiar social properties. And what of modern political economy, which looks down so disdainfully on the Mone-tary System? Does not its fetishism become quite palpable when it deals with capital? How long is it since the disappearance of the Physiocratic illusion that ground rent grows out of the soil, not out of society?

But, to avoid anticipating, we will content ourselves here with one more example relating to the commodity-form itself. If com-modities could speak, they would say this: our use-value may interest men, but it does not belong to us as objects. What does belong to us as objects, however, is our value. Our own inter-

---

In the opinion of the German–American publication this is all very true for our own times, in which material interests are preponderant, but not for the Middle Ages, dominated by Catholicism, nor for Athens and Rome, domi-nated by politics. In the first place, it strikes us as odd that anyone should sup-pose that these well-worn phrases about the Middle Ages and the ancient world were unknown to anyone else. One thing is clear: the Middle Ages could not live on Catholicism, nor could the ancient world on politics. On the contrary, it is the manner in which they gained their livelihood which explains why in one case politics, in the other case Catholicism, played the chief part. For the rest, one needs no more than a slight acquaintance with, for example, the history of the Roman Republic, to be aware that its secret history is the history of landed property. And then there is Don Quixote, who long ago paid the penalty for wrongly imagining that knight errantry was compatible with all economic forms of society.

course as commodities proves it. We relate to each other merely as exchange-values. Now listen how those commodities speak through the mouth of the economist:

'Value (i.e. exchange-value) is a property of things, riches (i.e. use-value) of man. Value, in this sense, necessarily implies exchanges, riches do not.'[36]

'Riches (use-value) are the attribute of man, value is the attribute of commodities. A man or a community is rich, a pearl or a diamond is valuable . . . A pearl or a diamond is valuable as a pearl or diamond.'[37]

So far no chemist has ever discovered exchange-value either in a pearl or a diamond. The economists who have discovered this chemical substance, and who lay special claim to critical acumen, nevertheless find that the use-value of material objects belongs to them independently of their material properties, while their value, on the other hand, forms a part of them as objects. What confirms them in this view is the peculiar circumstance that the use-value of a thing is realized without exchange, i.e. in the direct relation between the thing and man, while, inversely, its value is realized only in exchange, i.e. in a social process. Who would not call to mind at this point the advice given by the good Dogberry to the night-watchman Seacoal?*

'To be a well-favoured man is the gift of fortune; but reading and writing comes by nature.'[38]

36. *Observations on Some Verbal Disputes in Pol. Econ., Particularly Relating to Value, and to Supply and Demand*, London, 1821, p. 16.

37. S. Bailey, op. cit., p. 165.

38. Both the author of *Observations etc.*, and S. Bailey accuse Ricardo of converting exchange-value from something relative into something absolute. The reverse is true. He has reduced the apparent relativity which these things (diamonds, pearls, etc.) possess to the true relation hidden behind the appearance, namely their relativity as mere expressions of human labour. If the followers of Ricardo answer Bailey somewhat rudely, but by no means convincingly, this is because they are unable to find in Ricardo's own works any elucidation of the inner connection between value and the form of value, or exchange-value.

_____

*In Shakespeare's comedy *Much Ado About Nothing*, Act 3, Scene 3.

Chapter 2: The Process of Exchange

Commodities cannot themselves go to market and perform exchanges in their own right. We must, therefore, have recourse to their guardians, who are the possessors of commodities. Commodities are things, and therefore lack the power to resist man. If they are unwilling, he can use force; in other words, he can take possession of them.[1] In order that these objects may enter into relation with each other as commodities, their guardians must place themselves in relation to one another as persons whose will resides in those objects, and must behave in such a way that each does not appropriate the commodity of the other, and alienate his own, except through an act to which both parties consent. The guardians must therefore recognize each other as owners of private property. This juridical relation, whose form is the contract, whether as part of a developed legal system or not, is a relation between two wills which mirrors the economic relation. The content of this juridical relation (or relation of two wills) is itself determined by the economic relation.[2] Here the persons exist for one another merely

1. In the twelfth century, so renowned for its piety, very delicate things often appear among these commodities. Thus a French poet of the period enumerates among the commodities to be found in the fair of Lendit, alongside clothing, shoes, leather, implements of cultivation, skins, etc., also *'femmes folles de leur corps'*.*

2. Proudhon creates his ideal of justice, of *'justice éternelle'*, from the juridical relations that correspond to the production of commodities: he thereby proves, to the consolation of all good petty bourgeois, that the production of commodities is a form as eternal as justice. Then he turns round and seeks to reform the actual production of commodities, and the corresponding legal system, in accordance with this ideal. What would one think of a chemist who, instead of studying the actual laws governing molecular interactions, and on that basis solving definite problems, claimed to regulate

*'Wanton women'. This passage comes from the *Dit du Lendit*, a satirical poem by the medieval French poet Guillot de Paris.

as representatives and hence owners, of commodities. As we proceed to develop our investigation, we shall find, in general, that the characters who appear on the economic stage are merely personifications of economic relations; it is as the bearers* of these economic relations that they come into contact with each other.

What chiefly distinguishes a commodity from its owner is the fact that every other commodity counts for it only as the form of appearance of its own value. A born leveller and cynic, it is always ready to exchange not only soul, but body, with each and every other commodity, be it more repulsive than Maritornes herself.† The owner makes up for this lack in the commodity of a sense of the concrete, physical body of the other commodity, by his own five and more senses. For the owner, his commodity possesses no direct use-value. Otherwise, he would not bring it to market. It has use-value for others; but for himself its only direct use-value is as a bearer of exchange-value, and consequently, a means of exchange.[3] He therefore makes up his mind to sell it in return for commodities whose use-value is of service to him. All commodities are non-use-values for their owners, and use-values for their non-owners. Consequently, they must all change hands. But this changing of hands constitutes their exchange, and their exchange puts them in relation with each other as values and realizes them as values. Hence commodities must be realized as values before they can be realized as use-values.

On the other hand, they must stand the test as use-values before they can be realized as values. For the labour expended on them only counts in so far as it is expended in a form which is useful

those interactions by means of the 'eternal ideas' of *'naturalité'* and *'affinité'*? Do we really know any more about 'usury', when we say it contradicts *'justice éternelle'*, *'équité éternelle'*, *'mutualité éternelle'*, and other *'vérités éternelles'* than the fathers of the church did when they said it was incompatible with *'grâce éternelle'*, *'foi éternelle'*, and *'la volunté éternelle de Dieu'*?

3. 'For twofold is the use of every object ... The one is peculiar to the object as such, the other is not, as a sandal which may be worn and is also exchangeable. Both are uses of the sandal, for even he who exchanges the sandal for the money or food he is in need of, makes use of the sandal as a sandal. But not in its natural way. For it has not been made for the sake of being exchanged' (Aristotle, *Republic*, I, i, c. 9).

---

*The concept of an object (or person) as the receptacle, repository, bearer [*Träger*] of some thing or tendency quite different from it appears repeatedly in *Capital*, and I have tried to translate it uniformly as 'bearer'.

† Maritornes: a character from Cervantes' novel *Don Quixote*.

for others. However, only the act of exchange can prove whether that labour is useful for others, and its product consequently capable of satisfying the needs of others.

The owner of a commodity is prepared to part with it only in return for other commodities whose use-value satisfies his own need. So far, exchange is merely an individual process for him. On the other hand, he desires to realize his commodity, as a value, in any other suitable commodity of the same value. It does not matter to him whether his own commodity has any use-value for the owner of the other commodity or not. From this point of view, exchange is for him a general social process. But the same process cannot be simultaneously for all owners of commodities both exclusively individual and exclusively social and general.

Let us look at the matter a little more closely. To the owner of a commodity, every other commodity counts as the particular equivalent of his own commodity. Hence his own commodity is the universal equivalent for all the others. But since this applies to every owner, there is in fact no commodity acting as universal equivalent, and the commodities possess no general relative form of value under which they can be equated as values and have the magnitude of their values compared. Therefore they definitely do not confront each other as commodities, but as products or use-values only.

In their difficulties our commodity-owners think like Faust: 'In the beginning was the deed.'* They have therefore already acted before thinking. The natural laws of the commodity have manifested themselves in the natural instinct of the owners of commodities. They can only bring their commodities into relation as values, and therefore as commodities, by bringing them into an opposing relation with some one other commodity, which serves as the universal equivalent. We have already reached that result by our analysis of the commodity. But only the action of society can turn a particular commodity into the universal equivalent. The social action of all other commodities, therefore, sets apart the particular commodity in which they all represent their values. The natural form of this commodity thereby becomes the socially recognized equivalent form. Through the agency of the social process it becomes the specific social function of the commodity

_____

* '*Im Anfang war die Tat*' (Goethe, *Faust*, Part I, Scene 3, Faust's Study, line 1237).

which has been set apart to be the universal equivalent. It thus becomes – money.

'*Illi unum consilium habent et virtutem et potestatem suam bestiae tradunt . . . Et ne quis possit emere aut vendere, nisi qui habet characterem aut nomen bestiae, aut numerum nominis eius*' (Apocalypse).*

Money necessarily crystallizes out of the process of exchange, in which different products of labour are in fact equated with each other, and thus converted into commodities. The historical broadening and deepening of the phenomenon of exchange develops the opposition between use-value and value which is latent in the nature of the commodity. The need to give an external expression to this opposition for the purposes of commercial intercourse produces the drive towards an independent form of value, which finds neither rest nor peace until an independent form has been achieved by the differentiation of commodities into commodities and money. At the same rate, then, as the transformation of the products of labour into commodities is accomplished, one particular commodity is transformed into money.[4]

The direct exchange of products has the form of the simple expression of value in one respect, but not as yet in another. That form was x commodity A $= y$ commodity B. The form of the direct exchange of products is x use-value A $= y$ use-value B.[5] The articles A and B in this case are not as yet commodities, but become so only through the act of exchange. The first way in which

4. From this we may form an estimate of the craftiness of petty-bourgeois socialism, which wants to perpetuate the production of commodities while simultaneously abolishing the 'antagonism between money and commodities', i.e. abolishing money itself, since money only exists in and through this antagonism.* One might just as well abolish the Pope while leaving Catholicism in existence. For more on this point see my work *Zur Kritik der Politischen Ökonomie*, p. 61 ff. [English translation, pp. 83–6].

5. So long as a chaotic mass of articles is offered as the equivalent for a single article (as is often the case among savages), instead of two distinct objects of utility being exchanged, we are only at the threshold of even the direct exchange of products.

*This is directed at the proposal of John Gray, in *The Social System* (1831), for the introduction of labour-money, later taken up by Proudhon.

———

*'These have one mind, and shall give their power and strength unto the beast' (Revelation 17: 13). 'And that no man might buy or sell, save that he had the mark, or the name of the beast, or the number of his name' (Revelation 13: 17).

an object of utility attains the possibility of becoming an exchange-value is to exist as a non-use-value, as a quantum of use-value superfluous to the immediate needs of its owner. Things are in themselves external to man, and therefore alienable. In order that this alienation [*Veräusserung*] may be reciprocal, it is only neces-sary for men to agree tacitly to treat each other as the private owners of those alienable things, and, precisely for that reason, as persons who are independent of each other. But this relationship of reciprocal isolation and foreignness does not exist for the mem-bers of a primitive community of natural origin, whether it takes the form of a patriarchal family, an ancient Indian commune or an Inca state. The exchange of commodities begins where com-munities have their boundaries, at their points of contact with other communities, or with members of the latter. However, as soon as products have become commodities in the external re-lations of a community, they also, by reaction, become com-modities in the internal life of the community. Their quantitative exchange-relation is at first determined purely by chance. They become exchangeable through the mutual desire of their owners to alienate them. In the meantime, the need for others' objects of utility gradually establishes itself. The constant repetition of ex-change makes it a normal social process. In the course of time, therefore, at least some part of the products must be produced intentionally for the purpose of exchange. From that moment the distinction between the usefulness of things for direct consumption and their usefulness in exchange becomes firmly established. Their use-value becomes distinguished from their exchange-value. On the other hand, the quantitative proportion in which the things are exchangeable becomes dependent on their production itself. Custom fixes their values at definite magnitudes.

In the direct exchange of products, each commodity is a direct means of exchange to its owner, and an equivalent to those who do not possess it, although only in so far as it has use-value for them. At this stage, therefore, the articles exchanged do not acquire a value-form independent of their own use-value, or of the in-dividual needs of the exchangers. The need for this form first develops with the increase in the number and variety of the com-modities entering into the process of exchange. The problem and the means for its solution arise simultaneously. Commercial inter-course, in which the owners of commodities exchange and com-pare their own articles with various other articles, never takes place unless different kinds of commodities belonging to different owners are exchanged for, and equated as values with, one single further kind of commodity. This further commodity, by becoming the equivalent of various other commodities, directly acquires the form of a universal or social equivalent, if only within narrow limits. The universal equivalent form comes and goes with the momentary social contacts which call it into existence. It is transiently attached to this or that commodity in alternation. But with the development of exchange it fixes itself firmly and exclusively onto particular kinds of commodity, i.e. it crystallizes out into the money-form. The particular kind of commodity to which it sticks is at first a matter of accident. Nevertheless there are two circumstances which are by and large decisive. The money-form comes to be attached either to the most important articles of exchange from outside, which are in fact the primitive and spontaneous forms of manifestation of the exchange-value of local products, or to the object of utility which forms the chief element of indigenous alienable wealth, for example cattle. Nomadic peoples are the first to develop the money-form, because all their worldly possessions are in a movable and therefore directly alienable form, and because their mode of life, by continually bringing them into contact with foreign communities, encourages the exchange of products. Men have often made man himself into the primitive material of money, in the shape of the slave, but they have never done this with the land and soil. Such an idea could only arise in a bourgeois society, and one which was already well developed. It dates from the last third of the seventeenth century, and the first attempt to implement the idea on a national scale was made a century later, during the French bourgeois revolution.*

In the same proportion as exchange bursts its local bonds, and the value of commodities accordingly expands more and more into the material embodiment of human labour as such, in that proportion does the money-form become transferred to commodities which are by nature fitted to perform the social function of a universal equivalent. Those commodities are the precious metals.

The truth of the statement that 'although gold and silver are not by nature money, money is by nature gold and silver',[6] is

6. Karl Marx, op. cit., p. 135 [English translation, p. 155]. 'The metals . . . are by their nature money' (Galiani, *Della Moneta*, in Custodi's collection, *Parte moderna*, Vol. 3, p. 137).

─────────────

*The issue of the *assignats* in 1789, backed by confiscated Church lands.

shown by the appropriateness of their natural properties for the functions of money.[7] So far, however, we are acquainted with only one function of money, namely to serve as the form of appearance of the value of commodities, that is as the material in which the magnitudes of their values are socially expressed. Only a material whose every sample possesses the same uniform quality can be an adequate form of appearance of value, that is a material embodiment of abstract and therefore equal human labour. On the other hand, since the difference between the magnitudes of value is purely quantitative, the money commodity must be capable of purely quantitative differentiation, it must therefore be divisible at will, and it must also be possible to assemble it again from its component parts. Gold and silver possess these properties by nature.

The money commodity acquires a dual use-value. Alongside its special use-value as a commodity (gold, for instance, serves to fill hollow teeth, it forms the raw material for luxury articles, etc.) it acquires a formal use-value, arising out of its specific social function.

Since all other commodities are merely particular equivalents for money, the latter being their universal equivalent, they relate to money as particular commodities relate to the universal commodity.[8]

We have seen that the money-form is merely the reflection thrown upon a single commodity by the relations between all other commodities. That money is a commodity[9] is therefore only a discovery for those who proceed from its finished shape in order to analyse it afterwards. The process of exchange gives to the com-

7. For further details on this subject see the chapter on 'The Precious Metals' in my work cited above [English translation, pp. 153–7].
8. 'Money is the universal commodity' (Verri, op. cit., p. 16).
9. 'Silver and gold themselves, which we may call by the general name of Bullion, are ... commodities ... rising and falling in ... value ... Bullion then may be reckoned to be of higher value, where the smaller weight will purchase the greater quantity of the product or manufacture of the country etc.' (S. Clement, *A Discourse of the General Notions of Money, Trade, and Exchange, as They Stand in Relations to Each Other. By a Merchant*, London, 1695, p. 7). 'Silver and gold, coined or uncoined, tho' they are used for a measure of all other things, are no less a commodity than wine, oyl, tobacco, cloth or stuffs' (J. Child, *A Discourse Concerning Trade, and That in Particular of the East-Indies etc.*, London, 1689, p. 2). 'The stock and riches of the kingdom cannot properly be confined to money, nor ought gold and silver to be excluded from being merchandize' (T. Papillon, *The East-India Trade a Most Profitable Trade*, London, 1677, p. 4).

modity which it has converted into money not its value but its specific value-form. Confusion between these two attributes has misled some writers into maintaining that the value of gold and silver is imaginary.[10] The fact that money can, in certain functions, be replaced by mere symbols of itself, gave rise to another mistaken notion, that it is itself a mere symbol. Nevertheless, this error did contain the suspicion that the money-form of the thing is external to the thing itself, being simply the form of appearance of human relations hidden behind it. In this sense every commodity is a symbol, since, as value, it is only the material shell of the human labour expended on it.[11] But if it is declared that the social characteristics assumed by material objects, or the material charac-

10. 'Gold and silver have value as metals before they are money' (Galiani, op. cit., p. 72). Locke says, 'The universal consent of mankind gave to silver, on account of its qualities which made it suitable for money, an imaginary value' (John Locke, *Some Considerations etc.*, 1691, in *Works*, ed. 1777, Vol. 2, p. 15). Law, on the other hand, says 'How could different nations give an imaginary value to any single thing ... or how could this imaginary value have maintained itself?' But he himself understood very little of the matter, for example 'Silver was exchanged in proportion to the use-value it possessed, consequently in proportion to its real value. By its adoption as money it received an additional value (*une valeur additionnelle*)' (Jean Law, *Considérations sur le numéraire et le commerce*, in E. Daire's edition of *Économistes financiers du XVIII siècle*, pp. 469–70).

11. 'Money is their (the commodities') symbol' (V. de Forbonnais, *Élémens du commerce*, new edn, Leyden, 1776, Vol. 2, p. 143). 'As a symbol it is attracted by the commodities' (ibid. p. 155). 'Money is a symbol of a thing and represents it' (Montesquieu, *Esprit des lois*, *Œuvres*, London, 1767, Vol. 2, p. 3). 'Money is not a mere symbol, for it is itself wealth; it does not represent the values, it is their equivalent' (Le Trosne, op. cit., p. 910). 'If we consider the concept of value, we must look on the thing itself only as a symbol; it counts not as itself, but as what it is worth' (Hegel, op. cit., p. 100).* Long before the economists, lawyers made fashionable the idea that money is a mere symbol, and that the value of the precious metals is purely imaginary. This they did in the sycophantic service of the royal power, supporting the right of the latter to debase the coinage, during the whole of the Middle Ages, by the traditions of the Roman Empire and the conceptions of money to be found in the Digest. 'Let no one call into question,' says their apt pupil, Philip of Valois, in a decree of 1346, 'that the trade, the composition, the supply, and the power of issuing ordinances on the currency ... belongs exclusively to us and to our royal majesty, to fix such a rate and at such a price as it shall please us and seem good to us.' It was a maxim of Roman Law that the value of money was fixed by Imperial decree. It was expressly forbidden to treat money as a commodity. '*Pecunias vero nulli emere fas erit, nam in usu publico constitutas*

* This is a reference to the *Philosophy of Right*, para. 63, Addition (English translation, p. 240).

teristics assumed by the social determinations of labour on the basis of a definite mode of production, are mere symbols, then it is also declared, at the same time, that these characteristics are the arbitrary product of human reflection. This was the kind of explanation favoured by the eighteenth century: in this way the Enlightenment endeavoured, at least temporarily, to remove the appearance of strangeness from the mysterious shapes assumed by human relations whose origins they were unable to decipher.

It has already been remarked above that the equivalent form of a commodity does not imply that the magnitude of its value can be determined. Therefore, even if we know that gold is money, and consequently directly exchangeable with all other commodities, this still does not tell us how much 10lb. of gold is worth, for instance. Money, like every other commodity, cannot express the magnitude of its value except relatively in other commodities. This value is determined by the labour-time required for its production, and is expressed in the quantity of any other commodity in which the same amount of labour-time is congealed.[12] This establishing of its relative value occurs at the source of its production by means of barter. As soon as it enters into circulation as money, its value is already given. In the last decades of the seventeenth century the first step in the analysis of money, the discovery that money is a commodity, had already been taken; but this was merely the first step, and nothing more. The difficulty lies not in comprehending that money is a commodity, but in discovering how, why and by what means a commodity becomes money.[13]

---

oportet non esse mercem.'* There is a good discussion of this by G. F. Pagnini, in *Saggio sopra il giusto pregio delle cose*, 1751, printed in Custodi's collection, *Parte moderna*, Vol. 2. In the second part of his work Pagnini directs his polemic especially against the legal gentlemen.

12. 'If a man can bring to London an ounce of silver out of the Earth of Peru, in the same time that he can produce a bushel of corn, then the one is the natural price of the other: now, if by reason of new or more easie mines a man can procure two ounces of silver as easily as he formerly did one, the corn will be as cheap at ten shillings the bushel as it was before at five shillings, *caeteris paribus*' (William Petty, *A Treatise of Taxes and Contributions*, London, 1667, p. 32).

13. The learned Professor Roscher, after first informing us that 'the false definitions of money may be divided into two main groups: those which make

*'However, it shall not be lawful for anyone to buy money, for, as it was created for public use, it is not permissible for it to be a commodity' (*Codex Theodosianus*, lib. 9, tit. 23).

We have already seen, from the simplest expression of value, x commodity $A = y$ commodity B, that the thing in which the magnitude of the value of another thing is represented appears to have the equivalent form independently of this relation, as a social property inherent in its nature. We followed the process by which this false semblance became firmly established, a process which was completed when the universal equivalent form became identified with the natural form of a particular commodity, and thus crystallized into the money-form. What appears to happen is not that a particular commodity becomes money because all other commodities express their values in it, but, on the contrary, that all other commodities universally express their values in a particular commodity because it is money. The movement through which this process has been mediated vanishes in its own result, leaving no trace behind. Without any initiative on their part, the commodities find their own value-configuration ready to hand, in the form of a physical commodity existing outside but also alongside them. This physical object, gold or silver in its crude state, becomes, immediately on its emergence from the bowels of the earth, the direct incarnation of all human labour. Hence the magic of money. Men are henceforth related to each other in their social process of production in a purely atomistic way. Their own relations of production therefore assume a material shape which is independent of their control and their conscious individual action. This situation is manifested first by the fact that the products of men's labour universally take on the form of commodities. The riddle of the money fetish is therefore the riddle of the commodity fetish, now become visible and dazzling to our eyes.

---

it more, and those which make it less, than a commodity', gives us a motley catalogue of works on the nature of money, which does not provide even the glimmer of an insight into the real history of the theory. He then draws this moral: 'For the rest, it is not to be denied that most of the later economists do not bear sufficiently in mind the peculiarities that distinguish money from other commodities' (it is then, after all, either more or less than a commodity!) . . . 'So far, the semi-mercantilist reaction of Ganilh is not altogether without foundation' (Wilhelm Roscher, *Die Grundlagen der Nationalökonomie*, 3rd edn, 1858, pp. 207–10). More! Less! Not sufficiently! So far! Not altogether! What a way of determining one's concepts! And this eclectic professorial twaddle is modestly baptized by Herr Roscher 'the anatomico-physiological method' of political economy! However, he does deserve credit for one discovery, namely, that money is 'a pleasant commodity'.

Chapter 3: Money, or the Circulation of Commodities

1. THE MEASURE OF VALUES

Throughout this work I assume that gold is the money commodity, for the sake of simplicity.

The first main function of gold is to supply commodities with the material for the expression of their values, or to represent their values as magnitudes of the same denomination, qualitatively equal and quantitatively comparable. It thus acts as a universal measure of value, and only through performing this function does gold, the specific equivalent commodity, become money.

It is not money that renders the commodities commensurable. Quite the contrary. Because all commodities, as values, are objectified human labour, and therefore in themselves commensurable, their values can be communally measured in one and the same specific commodity, and this commodity can be converted into the common measure of their values, that is into money. Money as a measure of value is the necessary form of appearance of the measure of value which is immanent in commodities, namely labour-time.[1]

1. The question why money does not itself directly represent labour-time, so that a piece of paper may represent, for instance, x hours' labour, comes down simply to the question why, on the basis of commodity production, the products of labour must take the form of commodities. This is obvious, because their taking the form of commodities implies their differentiation into commodities [on the one hand] and the money commodity [on the other]. It is also asked why private labour cannot be treated as its opposite, directly social labour. I have elsewhere discussed exhaustively the shallow utopianism of the idea of 'labour-money' in a society founded on the production of commodities (op. cit., p. 61 ff.).* On this point I will only say further that Owen's 'labour money', for instance, is no more 'money' than a theatre ticket is. Owen presupposes directly socialized labour, a form of production diametrically opposed to the production of commodities. The certificate of labour is merely

* English translation, pp. 83 ff.

The expression of the value of a commodity in gold – x commodity A $= y$ money commodity – is its money-form or price. A single equation, such as 1 ton of iron $=$ 2 ounces of gold, now suffices to express the value of the iron in a socially valid manner. There is no longer any need for this equation to figure as a link in the chain of equations that express the values of all other commodities, because the equivalent commodity, gold, already possesses the character of money. The general relative form of value of commodities has therefore resumed its original shape of simple or individual relative value. On the other hand, the expanded relative expression of value, the endless series of equations, has now become the specific relative form of value of the money commodity. However, the endless series itself is now a socially given fact in the shape of the prices of the commodities. We have only to read the quotations of a price-list backwards, to find the magnitude of the value of money expressed in all sorts of commodities. As against this, money has no price. In order to form a part of this uniform relative form of value of the other commodities, it would have to be brought into relation with itself as its own equivalent.

The price or money-form of commodities is, like their form of value generally, quite distinct from their palpable and real bodily form; it is therefore a purely ideal or notional form. Although invisible, the value of iron, linen and corn exists in these very articles: it is signified through their equality with gold, even though this relation with gold exists only in their heads, so to speak. The guardian of the commodities must therefore lend them his tongue, or hang a ticket on them, in order to communicate their prices to the outside world.[2] Since the expression of the value of commodi-

---

evidence of the part taken by the individual in the common labour, and of his claim to a certain portion of the common product which has been set aside for consumption. But Owen never made the mistake of presupposing the production of commodities, while, at the same time, by juggling with money, trying to circumvent the necessary conditions of that form of production.

2. Savages and semi-savages use the tongue differently. Captain Parry says of the inhabitants of the west coast of Baffin's Bay: 'In this case (the case of barter) they licked it (the thing represented to them) twice to their tongues, after which they seemed to consider the bargain satisfactorily concluded.'* In the same way, among the Eastern Eskimo, the exchanger licked each article on

*W. E. Parry, *Journal of a Voyage for the Discovery of a North-West Passage*, London, 1821, p. 227.

ties in gold is a purely ideal act,* we may use purely imaginary or ideal gold to perform this operation. Every owner of commodities knows that he is nowhere near turning them into gold when he has given their value the form of a price or of imaginary gold, and that it does not require the tiniest particle of real gold to give a valuation in gold of millions of pounds' worth of commodities. In its function as measure of value, money therefore serves only in an imaginary or ideal capacity. This circumstance has given rise to the wildest theories.[3] But, although the money that performs the functions of a measure of value is only imaginary, the price depends entirely on the actual substance that is money. The value, i.e. the quantity of human labour, which is contained in a ton of iron is expressed by an imaginary quantity of the money commodity which contains the same amount of labour as the iron. Therefore, according to whether it is gold, silver or copper which is serving as the measure of value, the value of the ton of iron will be expressed by very different prices, or will be represented by very different quantities of those metals.

If therefore two different commodities, such as gold and silver, serve simultaneously as measures of value, all commodities will have two separate price-expressions, the price in gold and the price in silver, which will quietly co-exist as long as the ratio of the value of silver to that of gold remains unchanged, say at 15 to 1. However, every alteration in this ratio disturbs the ratio between the gold-prices and the silver-prices of commodities, and thus proves in fact that a duplication of the measure of value contradicts the function of that measure.[4]

---

receiving it. If the tongue is thus used in the North as the organ of appropriation, it is no wonder that in the South the stomach serves as the organ of accumulated property, and that a Kaffir estimates the wealth of a man by the size of his belly. The Kaffirs know what they are doing, for at the same time as the official British Health Report of 1864 was bemoaning the deficiency of fat-forming substances among a large part of the working class, a certain Dr Harvey (not, however, the man who discovered the circulation of the blood) was doing well by advertising recipes for reducing the surplus fat of the bourgeoisie and the aristocracy.

3. See Karl Marx, *Zur Kritik etc.*, 'Theories of the Standard of Money', pp. 53 ff. [English translation, pp. 76 ff.].

4. 'Wherever silver and gold exist side by side as legal money, i.e. as measure of value, the vain attempt has always been made to treat them as one and the

---

*In other words, it is an act which takes place entirely in the mind, and involves no physical transaction.

Commodities with definite prices all appear in this form: *a* commodity A = *x* gold; *b* commodity B = *y* gold; *c* commodity C = *z* gold, etc., where *a*, *b*, *c* represent definite quantities of the commodities A, B, C and *x*, *y*, *z* definite quantities of gold. The values of these commodities are therefore changed into imaginary quantities of gold of different magnitudes. Hence, in spite of the confusing variety of the commodities themselves, their values become magnitudes of the same denomination, gold-magnitudes. As such, they are now capable of being compared with each other and measured, and the course of development produces the need to compare them, for technical reasons, with some fixed quantity of gold as their unit of measurement. This unit, by subsequent division into aliquot parts, becomes itself the standard of measurement. Before they become money, gold, silver and copper already possess such standards in their weights, so that, for example, a pound, which serves as a unit of measurement, can on the one hand be divided into ounces, and on the other hand be

---

same substance. If one assumes that a given labour-time must invariably be objectified in the same proportion in silver and gold, then one assumes, in fact, that gold and silver are the same substance, and that silver, the less valuable metal, represents a constant fraction of gold. From the reign of Edward III to the time of George II, the history of money in England consists of one long series of perturbations caused by the clash between the legally fixed ratio between the values of gold and silver, and the fluctuations in their real values. At one time gold was too high, at another, silver. The metal that was estimated below its value was withdrawn from circulation, melted down and exported. The ratio between the two metals was then again altered by law, but the new nominal ratio soon came into conflict, in its turn, with the real ratio. In our own times, the slight and transient fall in the value of gold compared with silver, which was a consequence of the Indian and Chinese demand for silver, produced on a far more extended scale in France the same phenomena, export of silver, and its expulsion from circulation by gold. During the years 1855, 1856 and 1857, the excess in France of gold-imports over gold-exports amounted to £41,580,000, while the excess of silver-exports over silver-imports came to £34,704,000. In fact, in countries in which both metals are legally measures of value, and therefore both legal tender, so that everyone has the option of paying in either metal, the metal that rises in value is at a premium, and, like every other commodity, measures its price in the over-valued metal which alone serves in reality as the measure of value. All the experience of history in this area can be reduced simply to this fact, that where two commodities perform by law the functions of a measure of value, in practice only one maintains that position' (Karl Marx, op. cit., pp. 52–3) [English edition, pp. 75–6].

combined with others to make up hundredweights.[5] It is owing to this that, in all metallic currencies, the names given to the standards of money or of price were originally taken from the pre-existing names of the standards of weight.

As measure of value, and as standard of price, money performs two quite different functions. It is the measure of value as the social incarnation of human labour; it is the standard of price as a quantity of metal with a fixed weight. As the measure of value it serves to convert the values of all the manifold commodities into prices, into imaginary quantities of gold; as the standard of price it measures those quantities of gold. The measure of values measures commodities considered as values; the standard of price measures, on the contrary, quantities of gold by a unit quantity of gold, not the value of one quantity of gold by the weight of another. For the standard of price, a certain weight of gold must be fixed as the unit of measurement. In this case, as in all cases where quantities of the same denomination are to be measured, the stability of the measurement is of decisive importance. Hence the less the unit of measurement (here a quantity of gold) is subject to variation, the better the standard of price fulfils its office. But gold can serve as a measure of value only because it is itself a product of labour, and therefore potentially variable in value.[6]

It is, first of all, quite clear that a change in the value of gold in no way impairs its function as a standard of price. No matter how the value of gold varies, different quantities of gold always remain in the same value-relation to each other. If the value of gold fell by 1,000 per cent, 12 ounces of gold would continue to have twelve times the value of one ounce of gold, and when we are dealing with prices we are only concerned with the relation between different quantities of gold. Since, on the other hand, an ounce of gold undergoes no change in weight when its value rises or falls, no

5. The peculiar circumstance that while the ounce of gold serves in England as the unit of the standard of money, it is not divided up into aliquot parts, has been explained as follows: 'Our coinage was originally adapted to the employment of silver only, hence an ounce of silver can always be divided into a certain adequate number of pieces of coin; but as gold was introduced at a later period into a coinage adapted only to silver, an ounce of gold cannot be coined into an aliquot number of pieces' (Maclaren, *A Sketch of the History of the Currency*, London, 1858, p. 16).

6. With English writers the confusion over measure of value and standard of price ('standard of value') is indescribable. Their functions, and therefore their names, are constantly interchanged.

change can take place in the weight of its aliquot parts. Thus gold always renders the same service as a fixed measure of price, however much its value may vary. Moreover, a change in the value of gold does not prevent it from fulfilling its function as measure of value. The change affects all commodities simultaneously, and therefore, other things being equal, leaves the mutual relations between their values unaltered, although those values are now all expressed in higher or lower gold-prices than before.

Just as in the case of the estimation of the value of a commodity in the use-value of any other commodity, so also in this case, where commodities are valued in gold, we assume nothing more than that the production of a given quantity of gold costs, at a given period, a given amount of labour. As regards the fluctuations of commodity prices in general, they are subject to the laws of the simple relative expression of value which we developed in an earlier chapter.

A general rise in the prices of commodities can result either from a rise in their values, which happens when the value of money remains constant, or from a fall in the value of money, which happens when the values of commodities remain constant. The process also occurs in reverse: a general fall in prices can result either from a fall in the values of commodities, if the value of money remains constant, or from a rise in the value of money, if the values of commodities remain constant. It therefore by no means follows that a rise in the value of money necessarily implies a proportional fall in the prices of commodities, or that a fall in the value of money implies a proportional rise in prices. This would hold only for commodities whose value remains constant. But commodities whose value rises simultaneously with and in proportion to that of money would retain the same price. And if their value rose either slower or faster than that of money, the fall or rise in their prices would be determined by the difference between the path described by their value and that described by the value of money. And so on.

Let us now go back to considering the price-form. For various reasons, the money-names of the metal weights are gradually separated from their original weight-names, the historically decisive reasons being: (1) The introduction of foreign money among less developed peoples. This happened at Rome in its early days, where gold and silver coins circulated at first as foreign commodities. The names of these foreign coins were different from those of the indigenous weights. (2) With the development of material wealth, the more precious metal extrudes the less precious from its function as measure of value. Silver drives out copper, gold drives out silver, however much this sequence may contradict the chronology of the poets.[7] The word pound, for instance, was the money-name given to an actual pound weight of silver. As soon as gold had driven out silver as a measure of value, the same name became attached to, say, one fifteenth of a pound of gold, depending on the ratio between the values of gold and silver. Pound as a money-name and pound as the ordinary weight-name of gold are now two different things.[8] (3) Centuries of continuous debasement of the currency by kings and princes have in fact left nothing behind of the original weights of gold coins but their names.[9]

These historical processes have made the separation of the money-name from the weight-name into a fixed popular custom. Since the standard of money is on the one hand purely conventional, while on the other hand it must possess universal validity, it is in the end regulated by law. A given weight of one of the precious metals, an ounce of gold for instance, becomes officially divided into aliquot parts, baptized by the law as a pound, a thaler, etc. These aliquot parts, which then serve as the actual units of money, are subdivided into other aliquot parts with legal names, such as a shilling, a penny etc.[10] But, despite this, a definite weight of metal remains the standard of metallic money. All that has changed is the subdivision and the denomination of the money.

The prices, or quantities of gold, into which the values of commodities are ideally changed are therefore now expressed in the money-names, or the legally valid names of the subdivisions of the

7. In any case, its historical validity is not entirely universal.

8. Thus the pound sterling denotes less than one-third of its original weight, the 'pound Scots' before the Union,* only one 36th, the French livre one 74th, the Spanish maravedi, less than one 1,000th, and the Portuguese rei a still smaller fraction.

9. 'The coins which today have a merely ideal denomination are in all nations the oldest; once upon a time they were all real, and because they were real people reckoned with them' (Galiani, *Della Moneta*, op. cit., p. 153).

10. David Urquhart remarks in his 'Familiar Words' on the monstrosity (!) that nowadays a pound (sterling), which is the unit of the English standard of money, is equal to about a quarter of an ounce of gold. 'This is falsifying a measure, not establishing a standard.'† In this 'false denomination' of the weight of gold, he finds what he finds everywhere else, the falsifying hand of civilization.

* The Union of Scotland with England in 1707.

† David Urquhart, *Familiar Words as Affecting England and the English*, London, 1855, p. 105.

gold standard made for the purpose of reckoning. Hence, instead of saying that a quarter of wheat is worth an ounce of gold, people in England would say that it was worth £3 17s. 10½d. In this way commodities express by their money-names how much they are worth, and money serves as money of account whenever it is a question of fixing a thing as a value and therefore in its money-form.[11]

The name of a thing is entirely external to its nature. I know nothing of a man if I merely know his name is Jacob. In the same way, every trace of the money-relation disappears in the money-names pound, thaler, franc, ducat, etc. The confusion caused by attributing a hidden meaning to these cabalistic signs is made even greater by the fact that these money-names express both the values of commodities and, simultaneously, aliquot parts of a certain weight of metal, namely the weight of the metal which serves as the standard of money.[12] On the other hand, it is in fact necessary that value, as opposed to the multifarious objects of the world of commodities, should develop into this form, a material and non-mental one, but also a simple social form.[13]

Price is the money-name of the labour objectified in a com-

11. 'When Anacharsis was asked what the Greeks used money for, he replied: for reckoning' (Athenaeus, *Deipnosophistae*, Bk IV, 49, v. 2, ed. Schweighäuser, 1802).

12. 'Because as standard of price gold is expressed by the same names of account as the prices of commodities – for example £3 17s. 10½d. may denote an ounce of gold just as well as a ton of iron – these names of account are called the *mint-price* of gold. Thus the extraordinary notion arose that gold is estimated in its own material and that, unlike all other commodities, its price is fixed by the State. The establishing of names of account for definite weights of gold was mistaken for the establishing of the value of these weights' (Karl Marx, op. cit., p. 52) [English edition, p. 74].

13. Cf. 'Theories of the Standard of Money', in *Zur Kritik etc.*, pp. 53 ff. [English edition, pp. 76 ff.]. Some theorists had fantastic notions of raising or lowering the 'mint-price' of money by getting the state to transfer to greater or smaller weights of gold or silver the names already legally appropriated to fixed weights of those metals, so that for example ¼ ounce of gold could be minted into 40 shillings in the future instead of 20. However, Petty dealt with these so exhaustively in his *Quantulumcunque Concerning Money: To the Lord Marquis of Halifax*, 1682, at least in those cases where they aimed not at clumsy financial operations against public and private creditors but rather at economic quack remedies, that even his immediate followers, Sir Dudley North and John Locke, not to mention later ones, could only repeat what he said more shallowly. 'If the wealth of a nation,' he remarks, 'could be decupled by a proclamation, it were strange that such proclamations have not long since been made by our Governors' (Petty, op. cit., p. 36).

modity. Hence the expression of the equivalence of a commodity with the quantity of money whose name is that commodity's price is a tautology,[14] just as the expression of the relative value of a commodity is an expression of the equivalence of two commodities. But although price, being the exponent of the magnitude of a commodity's value, is the exponent of its exchange-ratio with money, it does not follow that the exponent of this exchange-ratio is necessarily the exponent of the magnitude of the commodity's value. Suppose two equal quantities of socially necessary labour are respectively represented by 1 quarter of wheat and £2 (approximately $\frac{1}{2}$ ounce of gold). £2 is the expression in money of the magnitude of the value of the quarter of wheat, or its price. If circumstances now allow this price to be raised to £3, or compel it to be reduced to £1, then although £1 and £3 may be too small or too large to give proper expression to the magnitude of the wheat's value, they are nevertheless prices of the wheat, for they are, in the first place, the form of its value, i.e. money, and, in the second place, the exponents of its exchange-ratio with money. If the conditions of production, or the productivity of labour, remain constant, the same amount of social labour-time must be expended on the reproduction of a quarter of wheat, both before and after the change in price. This situation is not dependent either on the will of the wheat producer or on that of the owners of the other commodities. The magnitude of the value of a commodity therefore expresses a necessary relation to social labour-time which is inherent in the process by which its value is created. With the transformation of the magnitude of value into the price this necessary relation appears as the exchange-ratio between a single commodity and the money commodity which exists outside it. This relation, however, may express both the magnitude of value of the commodity and the greater or lesser quantity of money for which it can be sold under the given circumstances. The possibility, therefore, of a quantitative incongruity between price and magnitude of value, i.e. the possibility that the price may diverge from the magnitude of value, is inherent in the price-form itself. This is not a defect, but, on the contrary, it makes this form the adequate one for a mode of production whose laws can only assert themselves as blindly operating averages between constant irregularities.

14. 'Or indeed it must be admitted that a million in money is worth more than an equal value in commodities' (Le Trosne, op. cit., p. 919), and hence 'that one value is worth more than another value which is equal to it'.

The price-form, however, is not only compatible with the possibility of a quantitative incongruity between magnitude of value and price, i.e. between the magnitude of value and its own expression in money, but it may also harbour a qualitative contradiction, with the result that price ceases altogether to express value, despite the fact that money is nothing but the value-form of commodities. Things which in and for themselves are not commodities, things such as conscience, honour, etc., can be offered for sale by their holders, and thus acquire the form of commodities through their price. Hence a thing can, formally speaking, have a price without having a value. The expression of price is in this case imaginary, like certain quantities in mathematics. On the other hand, the imaginary price-form may also conceal a real value-relation or one derived from it, as for instance the price of uncultivated land, which is without value because no human labour is objectified in it.

Like the relative form of value in general, price expresses the value of a commodity (for instance a ton of iron) by asserting that a given quantity of the equivalent (for instance an ounce of gold) is directly exchangeable with iron. But it by no means asserts the converse, that iron is directly exchangeable with gold. In order, therefore, that a commodity may in practice operate effectively as exchange-value, it must divest itself of its natural physical body and become transformed from merely imaginary into real gold, although this act of transubstantiation may be more 'troublesome' for it than the transition from necessity to freedom for the Hegelian 'concept', the casting of his shell for a lobster, or the putting-off of the old Adam for Saint Jerome.[15] Though a commodity may, alongside its real shape (iron, for instance), possess an ideal value-shape or an imagined gold-shape in the form of its price, it cannot simultaneously be both real iron and real gold. To establish its price it is sufficient for it to be equated with gold in the imagination. But to enable it to render its owner the service of a universal equivalent, it must be actually replaced by gold. If the owner of the iron were to go to the owner of some other earthly

15. If Jerome had to wrestle hard in his youth with the material flesh, as is shown by his fight in the desert with visions of beautiful women, he had also to wrestle in his old age with the spiritual flesh. 'I thought', he says, 'I was in the spirit before the Judge of the Universe.' 'Who art thou?' asked a voice. 'I am a Christian.' 'Thou liest,' thundered back the great Judge, 'thou art nought but a Ciceronian' [*Letter XXII, Ad Eustochium*].

commodity, and were to refer him to the price of iron as proof that it was already money, his answer would be the terrestrial equivalent of the answer given by St Peter in heaven to Dante, when the latter recited the creed:

> *'Assai bene è trascorsa*
> *D'esta moneta già la lega e il peso,*
> *Ma dimmi se tu l'hai nella tua borsa.'**

The price-form therefore implies both the exchangeability of commodities for money and the necessity of exchanges. On the other hand, gold serves as an ideal measure of value only because it has already established itself as the money commodity in the process of exchange. Hard cash lurks within the ideal measure of value.

2. THE MEANS OF CIRCULATION

(a) The Metamorphosis of Commodities

We saw in a former chapter that the exchange of commodities implies contradictory and mutually exclusive conditions. The further development of the commodity does not abolish these contradictions, but rather provides the form within which they have room to move. This is, in general, the way in which real contradictions are resolved. For instance, it is a contradiction to depict one body as constantly falling towards another and at the same time constantly flying away from it. The ellipse is a form of motion within which this contradiction is both realized and resolved.

In so far as the process of exchange transfers commodities from hands in which they are non-use-values to hands in which they are use-values, it is a process of social metabolism.† The product of one kind of useful labour replaces that of another. Once a commodity has arrived at a situation in which it can serve as a use-value, it falls out of the sphere of exchange into that of consumption. But the former sphere alone interests us here. We therefore have to consider the whole process in its formal aspect, that is to

---

* 'Right well hath now been tested this coin's alloy and weight; but tell me if thou hast it in thy purse' (Dante, *Divina Commedia, Paradiso*, Canto XXIV, lines 84–5).

† Here Marx introduces for the first time the concept of 'metabolism' (*Stoffwechsel*). This biological analogy plays a considerable part in his analysis of circulation and the labour process.

say, the change in form or the metamorphosis of commodities through which the social metabolism is mediated.

This change of form has been very imperfectly grasped as yet, owing to the circumstance that, quite apart from the lack of clarity in the concept of value itself, every change of form in a commodity results from the exchange of two commodities, namely an ordinary commodity and the money commodity. If we keep in mind only this material aspect, that is, the exchange of the commodity for gold, we overlook the very thing we ought to observe, namely what has happened to the form of the commodity. We do not see that gold, as a mere commodity, is not money, and that the other commodities, through their prices, themselves relate to gold as the medium for expressing their own shape in money.

Commodities first enter into the process of exchange ungilded and unsweetened, retaining their original home-grown shape. Exchange, however, produces a differentiation of the commodity into two elements, commodity and money, an external opposition which expresses the opposition between use-value and value which is inherent in it. In this opposition, commodities as use-values confront money as exchange-value. On the other hand, both sides of this opposition are commodities, hence themselves unities of use-value and value. But this unity of differences is expressed at two opposite poles, and at each pole in an opposite way. This is the alternating relation between the two poles: the commodity is in reality a use-value; its existence as a value appears only ideally, in its price, through which it is related to the real embodiment of its value, the gold which confronts it as its opposite. Inversely, the material of gold ranks only as the materialization of value, as money. It is therefore in reality exchange-value. Its use-value appears only ideally in the series of expressions of relative value within which it confronts all the other commodities as the totality of real embodiments of its utility. These antagonistic forms of the commodities are the real forms of motion of the process of exchange.

Let us now accompany the owner of some commodity, say our old friend the linen weaver, to the scene of action, the market. His commodity, 20 yards of linen, has a definite price, £2. He exchanges it for the £2, and then, being a man of the old school, he parts for the £2 in return for a family Bible of the same price. The linen, for him a mere commodity, a bearer of value, is alienated in exchange for gold, which is the shape of the linen's value, then it is taken out of this shape and alienated again in exchange for another commodity, the Bible, which is destined to enter the weaver's house as an object of utility and there to satisfy his family's need for edification. The process of exchange is therefore accomplished through two metamorphoses of opposite yet mutually complementary character – the conversion of the commodity into money, and the re-conversion of the money into a commodity.[16] The two moments of this metamorphosis are at once distinct transactions by the weaver – selling, or the exchange of the commodity for money, and buying, or the exchange of the money for a commodity – and the unity of the two acts: selling in order to buy.

The end result of the transaction, from the point of view of the weaver, is that instead of being in possession of the linen, he now has the Bible; instead of his original commodity, he now possesses another of the same value but of different utility. He procures his other means of subsistence and of production in a similar way. For the weaver, the whole process accomplishes nothing more than the exchange of the product of his labour for the product of someone else's, nothing more than an exchange of products.

The process of exchange is therefore accomplished through the following changes of form:

Commodity–Money–Commodity

C–M–C

As far as concerns its material content, the movement is C–C, the exchange of one commodity for another, the metabolic interaction of social labour, in whose result the process itself becomes extinguished.

C–M. First metamorphosis of the commodity, or sale. The leap taken by value from the body of the commodity into the body of the gold is the commodity's *salto mortale*, as I have called it elsewhere.* If the leap falls short, it is not the commodity which is de-

---

16. 'ἐκ δὲ τοῦ . . . πυρὸς τ'ἀνταμείβεσθαι πάντα, φησὶν ὁ 'Ηράκλειτος, καὶ πῦρ ἀπαντων, ὥσπερ χρυσοῦ χρήματα καί χρημάτων χρυσός' (F. Lassalle, *Die Philosophie Herakleitos des Dunkeln*, Berlin, 1858, Vol. 1, p. 222).* Lassalle, in his note on this passage, p. 224, n. 3, erroneously makes money a mere symbol of value.

*'As Heracleitus says, all things exchange for fire, and fire for all things, just as gold does for goods and goods for gold' (Plutarch, *Moralia*, 'The E at Delphi', 388D).

---

* See *A Contribution to the Critique of Political Economy*, p. 88.

frauded but rather its owner. The social division of labour makes the nature of his labour as one-sided as his needs are many-sided. This is precisely the reason why the product of his labour serves him solely as exchange-value. But it cannot acquire universal social validity as an equivalent-form except by being converted into money. That money, however, is in someone else's pocket. To allow it to be drawn out, the commodity produced by its owner's labour must above all be a use-value for the owner of the money. The labour expended on it must therefore be of a socially useful kind, i.e. it must maintain its position as a branch of the social division of labour. But the division of labour is an organization of production which has grown up naturally, a web which has been, and continues to be, woven behind the backs of the producers of commodities. Perhaps the commodity is the product of a new kind of labour, and claims to satisfy a newly arisen need, or is even trying to bring forth a new need on its own account. Perhaps a particular operation, although yesterday it still formed one out of the many operations conducted by one producer in creating a given commodity, may today tear itself out of this framework, establish itself as an independent branch of labour, and send its part of the product to market as an independent commodity. The circumstances may or may not be ripe for such a process of separation. Today the product satisfies a social need. Tomorrow it may perhaps be expelled partly or completely from its place by a similar product. Moreover, although our weaver's labour may be a recognized branch of the social division of labour, yet that fact is by no means sufficient to guarantee the utility of his 20 yards of linen. If the society's need for linen – and such a need has a limit like every other need – has already been satisfied by the products of rival weavers, our friend's product is superfluous, redundant and consequently useless. Although people do not look a gift-horse in the mouth, our friend does not frequent the market to make presents of his products. Let us assume, however, that the use-value of his product does maintain itself, and that the commodity therefore attracts money. Now we have to ask: how much money? No doubt the answer is already anticipated in the price of the commodity, which is the exponent of the magnitude of its value. We leave out of consideration here any possible subjective errors in calculation by the owner of the commodity, which will immediately be corrected objectively in the market. We suppose him to have spent on his product only the average socially necessary quantity of labour-time. The price of the commodity, therefore, is merely the money-name of the quantity of social labour objectified in it. But now the old-established conditions of production in weaving are thrown into the melting-pot, without the permission of, and behind the back of, our weaver. What was yesterday undoubtedly labour-time socially necessary to the production of a yard of linen ceases to be so today, a fact which the owner of the money is only too eager to prove from the prices quoted by our friend's competitors. Unluckily for the weaver, people of his kind are in plentiful supply. Let us suppose, finally, that every piece of linen on the market contains nothing but socially necessary labour-time. In spite of this, all these pieces taken as a whole may contain superfluously expended labour-time. If the market cannot stomach the whole quantity at the normal price of 2 shillings a yard, this proves that too great a portion of the total social labour-time has been expended in the form of weaving. The effect is the same as if each individual weaver had expended more labour-time on his particular product than was socially necessary. As the German proverb has it: caught together, hung together. All the linen on the market counts as one single article of commerce, and each piece of linen is only an aliquot part of it. And in fact the value of each single yard is also nothing but the materialization of the same socially determined quantity of homogeneous human labour.*

We see then that commodities are in love with money, but that 'the course of true love never did run smooth'. The quantitative articulation [*Gliederung*] of society's productive organism, by which its scattered elements are integrated into the system of the division of labour, is as haphazard and spontaneous as its qualitative articulation. The owners of commodities therefore find out that the same division of labour which turns them into independent private producers also makes the social process of production and the relations of the individual producers to each other within that process independent of the producers themselves; they also find out that the independence of the individuals from each other has as

---

*In a letter of 28 November 1878 to N. F. Danielson, the Russian translator of *Capital*, Marx made the following alteration to this sentence: 'And in fact the value of each single yard is also nothing but the materialization of a part of the quantity of social labour expended in the whole amount of the linen.' An analogous correction was made in a copy of the second German edition of the first volume of *Capital* which belonged to Marx; however this was not in his handwriting. [Note by the Institute of Marxism-Leninism]

its counterpart and supplement a system of all-round material dependence.

The division of labour converts the product of labour into a commodity, and thereby makes necessary its conversion into money. At the same time, it makes it a matter of chance whether this transubstantiation succeeds or not. Here, however, we have to look at the phenomenon in its pure shape, and must therefore assume it has proceeded normally. In any case, if the process is to take place at all, i.e. if the commodity is not impossible to sell, a change of form must always occur, although there may be an abnormal loss or accretion of substance – that is, of the magnitude of value.

The seller has his commodity replaced by gold, the buyer has his gold replaced by a commodity. The striking phenomenon here is that a commodity and gold, 20 yards of linen and £2, have changed hands and places, in other words that they have been exchanged. But what is the commodity exchanged for? For the universal shape assumed by its own value. And what is the gold exchanged for? For a particular form of its own use-value. Why does gold confront the linen as money? Because the linen's price of £2, its money-name, already brings it into relation with the gold as money. The commodity is divested of its original form through its sale, i.e. the moment its use-value actually attracts the gold, which previously had a merely imaginary existence in its price. The realization of a commodity's price, or of its merely ideal value-form, is therefore at the same time, and inversely, the realization of the merely ideal use-value of money; the conversion of a commodity into money is the conversion of money into a commodity. This single process is two-sided: from one pole, that of the commodity-owner, it is a sale, from the other pole, that of the money-owner, it is a purchase. In other words, a sale is a purchase, C–M is also M–C.[17]

Up to this point we have considered only one economic relation between men, a relation between owners of commodities in which they appropriate the produce of the labour of others by alienating [*entfremden*] the produce of their own labour. Hence, for one com-

---

17. 'Every sale is a purchase' (Dr Quesnay, *Dialogues sur le commerce et les travaux des artisans, Physiocrates,* ed. Daire, Part 1, Paris, 1846, p. 170), or, as Quesnay says in his *Maximes générales*, 'To sell is to buy.'*

*This quotation appears in Dupont de Nemours, *Maximes du docteur Quesnay*, printed in *Physiocrates*, ed. Daire, Part 1, Paris, 1846, p. 392.

modity-owner to meet with another, in the form of a money-owner, it is necessary either that the product of the latter should possess by its nature the form of money, i.e. it should be gold, the material of which money consists, or that his product should already have changed its skin and stripped off its original form of a useful object. In order to function as money, gold must of course enter the market at some point or other. This point is to be found at its source of production, where the gold is exchanged, as the immediate product of labour, for some other product of equal value. But from that moment onwards, it always represents the realized price of some commodity.[18] Leaving aside its exchange for other commodities at the source of production, gold is, in the hands of every commodity-owner, his own commodity divested [*entäussert*] of its original shape by being alienated [*veräussert*];* it is the product of a sale or of the first metamorphosis C–M.[19] Gold, as we saw, became ideal money, or a measure of value, because all commodities measured their values in it, and thus made it the imaginary opposite of their natural shape as objects of utility, hence the shape of their value. It became real money because the commodities, through their complete alienation, suffered a divestiture or transformation of their real shapes as objects of utility, thus making it the real embodiment of their values. When they thus assume the shape of values, commodities strip off every trace of their natural and original use-value, and of the particular kind of useful labour to which they owe their creation, in order to pupate into the homogeneous social materialization of undifferentiated human labour. From the mere look of a piece of money, we cannot tell what breed of commodity has been transformed into it. In their money-form all commodities look alike. Hence money may be dirt, although dirt is not money. We will assume that the two golden coins in return for which our weaver has parted with his linen are the metamorphosed shape of a quarter of wheat. The sale of the linen, C–M, is at the same time its purchase, M–C. But this process, considered as the sale of the linen, starts off a move-

18. 'The price of one commodity can only be paid by the price of another commodity' (Mercier de la Rivière, *L'Ordre naturel et essentiel des sociétés politiques, Physiocrates*, ed. Daire, Part 2, p. 554).
19. 'In order to have this money, one must have made a sale' (ibid., p. 543).

* Cf. *Grundrisse*, p. 196: 'Appropriation through and by means of divestiture [*Entäusserung*] and alienation [*Veräusserung*] is the fundamental condition of commodity circulation.'

ment which ends with its opposite: the purchase of a Bible. Considered as purchase of the linen, on the other hand, the process completes a movement which began with its opposite, the sale of the wheat. C–M (linen–money), which is the first phase of C–M–C (linen–money–Bible), is also M–C (money–linen), the last phase of another movement C–M–C (wheat–money–linen). The first metamorphosis of one commodity, its transformation from the commodity-form into money, is therefore also invariably the second, and diametrically opposite, metamorphosis of some other commodity, the retransformation of the latter from money into a commodity.[20]

M–C. The second or concluding metamorphosis of the commodity: purchase. Money is the absolutely alienable commodity, because it is all other commodities divested of their shape, the product of their universal alienation. It reads all prices backwards, and thus as it were mirrors itself in the bodies of all other commodities, which provide the material through which it can come into being as a commodity. At the same time the prices, those wooing glances cast at money by commodities, define the limit of its convertibility, namely its own quantity. Since every commodity disappears when it becomes money it is impossible to tell from the money itself how it got into the hands of its possessor, or what article has been changed into it. *Non olet*,* from whatever source it may come. If it represents, on the one hand, a commodity which has been sold, it also represents, on the other hand, a commodity which can be bought.[21]

M–C, a purchase, is at the same time C–M, a sale; the concluding metamorphosis of one commodity is the first metamorphosis of another. For our weaver, the life of his commodity ends with the Bible into which he has reconverted his £2. But suppose the seller of the Bible turns the £2 set free by the weaver into brandy. M–C, the concluding phase of C–M–C (linen–money–Bible), is also C–M, the first phase of C–M–C (Bible–money–

20. As remarked previously, the actual producer of gold or silver forms an exception. He exchanges his product without having first sold it.

21. 'If money represents, in our hands, the things we can wish to buy, it also represents the things we have sold for this money' (Mercier de la Rivière, op. cit., p. 586).

*'It (money) has no smell.' This is alleged to have been the reply of the Roman Emperor Vespasian to his son Titus, when the latter reproached him for obtaining money by taxing the public lavatories.

brandy). Since the producer of the commodity offers only a single product, he often sells it in large quantities, whereas the fact that he has many needs compels him to split up the price realized, the sum of money set free, into numerous purchases. Hence a sale leads to many purchases of different commodities. The concluding metamorphosis of a commodity thus constitutes an aggregate of the first metamorphoses of other commodities.

If we now consider the completed metamorphosis of a commodity as a whole, it appears in the first place that it is made up of two opposite and complementary movements, C–M and M–C. These two antithetical transmutations of the commodity are accomplished through two antithetical social processes in which the commodity-owner takes part, and are reflected in the antithetical economic characteristics of the two processes. By taking part in the act of sale, the commodity-owner becomes a seller; in the act of purchase, he becomes a buyer. But just as, in every transmutation of a commodity, its two forms, the commodity-form and the money-form, exist simultaneously but at opposite poles, so every seller is confronted with a buyer, every buyer with a seller. While the same commodity is successively passing through the two inverted transmutations, from a commodity into money and from money into another commodity, the owner of the commodity successively changes his role from seller to buyer. Being a seller and being a buyer are therefore not fixed roles, but constantly attach themselves to different persons in the course of the circulation of commodities.

The complete metamorphosis of a commodity, in its simplest form, implies four *dénouements* and three *dramatis personae*. First, a commodity comes face to face with money; the latter is the form taken by the value of the former, and exists over there in someone else's pocket in all its hard, material reality. A commodity-owner is thus confronted with a money-owner. Now as soon as the commodity has been changed into money, the money becomes its vanishing equivalent-form, whose use-value or content exists here on the spot, in the bodies of other commodities. Money, the final stage of the first transformation, is at the same time the starting-point for the second. The person who is a seller in the first transaction thus becomes a buyer in the second, in which a third commodity-owner comes to meet him as a seller.[22]

22. 'There are accordingly . . . four final terms and three contracting parties, one of whom intervenes twice' (Le Trosne, op. cit., p. 909).

The two inverted phases of the movement which makes up the metamorphosis of a commodity constitute a circuit: commodity-form, stripping off of this form, and return to it. Of course, the commodity itself is here subject to contradictory determinations. At the starting-point it is a non-use-value to its owner; at the end it is a use-value. So too the money appears in the first phase as a solid crystal of value into which the commodity has been transformed, but afterwards it dissolves into the mere equivalent-form of the commodity.

The two metamorphoses which constitute the commodity's circular path are at the same time two inverse partial metamorphoses of two other commodities. One and the same commodity (the linen) opens the series of its own metamorphoses, and completes the metamorphosis of another (the wheat). In its first transformation, the sale, the linen plays these two parts in its own person. But then it goes the way of all flesh, enters the chrysalis state as gold, and thereby simultaneously completes the first metamorphosis of a third commodity. Hence the circuit made by one commodity in the course of its metamorphoses is inextricably entwined with the circuits of other commodities. This whole process constitutes the circulation of commodities.

The circulation of commodities differs from the direct exchange of products not only in form, but in its essence. We have only to consider the course of events. The weaver has undoubtedly exchanged his linen for a Bible, his own commodity for someone else's. But this phenomenon is only true for him. The Bible-pusher, who prefers a warming drink to cold sheets, had no intention of exchanging linen for his Bible; the weaver did not know that wheat had been exchanged for his linen. B's commodity replaces that of A, but A and B do not mutually exchange their commodities. It may in fact happen that A and B buy from each other, but a particular relationship of this kind is by no means the necessary result of the general conditions of the circulation of commodities. We see here, on the one hand, how the exchange of commodities breaks through all the individual and local limitations of the direct exchange of products, and develops the metabolic process of human labour. On the other hand, there develops a whole network of social connections of natural origin, entirely beyond the control of the human agents. Only because the farmer has sold his wheat is the weaver able to sell his linen, only because the weaver has sold his linen is our rash and intemperate friend able to sell his Bible, and only because the latter already has the water of everlasting life is the distiller able to sell his *eau-de-vie*. And so it goes on.

The process of circulation, therefore, unlike the direct exchange of products, does not disappear from view once the use-values have changed places and changed hands. The money does not vanish when it finally drops out of the series of metamorphoses undergone by a commodity. It always leaves behind a precipitate at a point in the arena of circulation vacated by the commodities. In the complete metamorphosis of the linen, for example, linen–money–Bible, the linen first falls out of circulation, and money steps into its place. Then the Bible falls out of circulation, and again money takes its place. When one commodity replaces another, the money commodity always sticks to the hands of some third person.[23] Circulation sweats money from every pore.

Nothing could be more foolish than the dogma that because every sale is a purchase, and every purchase a sale, the circulation of commodities necessarily implies an equilibrium between sales and purchases. If this means that the number of actual sales accomplished is equal to the number of purchases, it is a flat tautology. But its real intention is to show that every seller brings his own buyer to market with him. Sale and purchase are one identical act, considered as the alternating relation between two persons who are in polar opposition to each other, the commodity-owner and the money-owner. They constitute two acts, of polar and opposite character, considered as the transactions of one and the same person. Hence the identity of sale and purchase implies that the commodity is useless if, when it is thrown into the alchemist's retort of circulation, it does not come out again as money; if, in other words, it cannot be sold by its owner, and therefore bought by the owner of the money. This identity further implies that the process, if it reaches fruition, constitutes a point of rest, an interval, long or short, in the life of the commodity. Since the first metamorphosis of a commodity is at once a sale and a purchase, this partial process is at the same time an independent process in itself. The buyer has the commodity, the seller has the money, i.e. a commodity which remains in a form capable of circulating, whether it reappears on the market at an earlier or later date. No one can sell unless someone else purchases. But no one directly needs to

23. This phenomenon may be self-evident, but it is in most cases overlooked by political economists, especially by the average free-trader.

purchase because he has just sold. Circulation bursts through all the temporal, spatial and personal barriers imposed by the direct exchange of products, and it does this by splitting up the direct identity present in this case between the exchange of one's own product and the acquisition of someone else's into the two antithetical segments of sale and purchase. To say that these mutually independent and antithetical processes form an internal unity is to say also that their internal unity moves forward through external antitheses. These two processes lack internal independence because they complement each other. Hence, if the assertion of their external independence [*äusserliche Verselbständigung*] proceeds to a certain critical point, their unity violently makes itself felt by producing – a crisis. There is an antithesis, immanent in the commodity, between use-value and value, between private labour which must simultaneously manifest itself as directly social labour, and a particular concrete kind of labour which simultaneously counts as merely abstract universal labour, between the conversion of things into persons and the conversion of persons into things*; the antithetical phases of the metamorphosis of the commodity are the developed forms of motion of this immanent contradiction. These forms therefore imply the possibility of crises, though no more than the possibility. For the development of this possibility into a reality a whole series of conditions is required, which do not yet even exist from the standpoint of the simple circulation of commodities.[24]

24. See my observations on James Mill in *Zur Kritik etc.*, pp. 74–6 [English translation, pp. 96–8]. There are two points here which are characteristic of the method of the bourgeoisie's economic apologists. The first is the identification of the circulation of commodities with the direct exchange of products, achieved simply by abstracting from their differences. The second is the attempt to explain away the contradictions of the capitalist process of production by dissolving the relations between persons engaged in that process of production into the simple relations arising out of the circulation of commodities. The production and circulation of commodities are however phenomena which are to be found in the most diverse modes of production, even if they vary in extent and importance. If we are only familiar with the abstract categories of circulation, which are common to all of them, we cannot know anything of their *differentia specifica*, and we cannot therefore pronounce judgement on them. In no science other than political economy does there prevail such a combina-

*'*Personifizierung der Sachen und Versachlichung der Personen*'. More succinctly, 'Personification of things and reification of persons'.

(b) The Circulation of Money

The change of form through which the metabolism of the products of labour is accomplished, C–M–C, requires that a given value shall form the starting-point of the process, in the shape of a commodity, and that it shall return to the same point in the shape of a commodity. This movement of commodities is therefore a circuit. On the other hand, the form of this movement excludes money from the circuit. The result of the movement is not the return of the money, but its continued removal further and further away from its starting-point. As long as the seller sticks fast to his money, which is the transformed shape of his commodity, that commodity is still at the stage of the first metamorphosis, in other words it has completed only the first half of its circulatory course. Once the process of selling in order to buy is complete the money again leaves the hands of its original possessor. Of course, if the weaver, having bought the Bible, sells more linen, money comes back into his hands. But this return is not a result of the circulation of the first 20 yards of linen; that circulation rather removed money from the hands of the weaver and placed it in those of the Bible-pusher. The return of money to the weaver results only from the renewal or repetition of the same process of circulation with a fresh commodity, and it ends in the same way as the previous process. Hence the movement directly imparted to money by the circulation of commodities takes the form of a constant removal from its starting-point, a path followed from the hands of one commodity-owner into those of another. This path is its circulation (currency, *cours de la monnaie*).*

The circulation of money is the constant and monotonous re-

---

tion of great self-importance with the mouthing of elementary commonplaces. For instance, J. B. Say sets himself up as a judge of crises because he knows that a commodity is a product.*

*'The conception adopted by Ricardo from the tedious Say, that overproduction is not possible or at least that no general glut of the market is possible, is based on the proposition that products are exchanged against products' (*Theories of Surplus-Value*, Part 2, p. 493). In his *Traité d'économie politique*, Vol. 2, Paris, 1814, p. 382, Say writes: 'Products can only be bought with products.'

---

*We have chosen to regard the words in parentheses as explanatory synonyms rather than suggested translations of the German word '*Umlauf*'. The use of the word 'currency' for 'circulation of money' was old-fashioned even in 1867.

petition of the same process. The commodity is always in the hands of the seller; the money, as a means of purchase, always in the hands of the buyer. And money serves as a means of purchase by realizing the price of the commodity. By doing this, it transfers the commodity from the seller to the buyer, and removes the money from the hands of the buyer into those of the seller, where it again goes through the same process with another commodity. That this one-sided form of motion of the money arises out of the two-sided form of motion of the commodity is a circumstance which is hidden from view. The very nature of the circulation of commodities produces a semblance of the opposite. The first metamorphosis of a commodity is visibly not only the money's movement, but also that of the commodity itself; in the second metamorphosis, on the contrary, the movement appears to us as the movement of the money alone. In the first phase of its circulation the commodity changes places with the money. Thereupon the commodity, in its shape as an object of utility, falls out of circulation into consumption.[25] Its value-shape or monetary larva steps into its shoes. It then passes through the second phase of its circulation, no longer in its own natural shape, but in its monetary shape. With this, the continuity of the movement depends entirely on the money, and the same movement which, for the commodity, in-cludes two opposed processes, is, when considered as the move-ment of the money, always one and the same process, a constant change of places with commodities which are always different. Hence the result of the circulation of commodities, namely the re-placement of one commodity by another, appears not to have been mediated by its own change of form, but rather by the func-tion of money as means of circulation. As means of circulation, money circulates commodities, which in and for themselves lack the power of movement, and transfers them from hands in which they are non-use-values into hands in which they are use-values; and this process always takes the opposite direction to the path of the commodities themselves. Money constantly removes com-modities from the sphere of circulation, by constantly stepping into their place in circulation, and in this way continually moving away from its own starting-point. Hence although the movement

25. Even when the commodity is sold over and over again, a situation we are not yet concerned with, it falls, when definitely sold for the last time, out of the sphere of circulation into that of consumption, where it serves either as means of subsistence or means of production.

of money is merely the expression of the circulation of commodities, the situation appears to be the reverse of this, namely the circulation of commodities seems to be the result of the movement of money.[26]

Again, money functions as a means of circulation only because in it the value possessed by commodities has taken on an independent shape. Hence its movement, as the medium of circulation, is in fact merely the movement undergone by commodities while changing their form. This fact must therefore make itself plainly visible in the circulation of money. (Thus the linen, for instance, first of all changes its commodity-form into its money-form. The final term of its first metamorphosis C–M, the money-form, then becomes the first term of its final metamorphosis M–C, its transformation back into the shape of the Bible. But each of these two changes of form is accomplished by an exchange between commodity and money, by their reciprocal displacement. The same pieces of coin come into the seller's hand as the alienated form of the commodity and leave it as the commodity in its absolutely alienable form. They are displaced twice. The first metamorphosis of the linen puts these coins into the weaver's pocket, the second draws them out of it. The two opposite changes undergone by the same commodity are reflected in the displacement, twice repeated but in opposite directions, of the same pieces of coin.

If however only a one-sided metamorphosis takes place, if there are only sales or only purchases, then a given piece of money changes its place only once. Its second change of place always expresses the second metamorphosis of the commodity, its reconversion from money. The frequently repeated displacement of the same coins reflects not only the series of metamorphoses undergone by a single commodity, but also the mutual entanglement of the innumerable metamorphoses in the whole world of commodities.)* It is in any case evident that all this is valid only for the simple circulation of commodities, the form we are considering here.

Every commodity, when it first steps into circulation and under-

26. 'It [money] has no other motion than that with which it is endowed by the products' (Le Trosne, op. cit., p. 885).

---

*The passage in parentheses is an expanded version of Marx's original argument, inserted by Engels into the fourth German edition.

goes its first change of form, does so only to fall out of circulation once more and be replaced again and again by fresh commodities. Money, on the contrary, as the medium of circulation, haunts the sphere of circulation and constantly moves around within it. The question therefore arises of how much money this sphere continuously absorbs.

In a given country there take place every day at the same time, though in different places, numerous one-sided metamorphoses of commodities; in other words, simple sales on one hand, simple purchases on the other. In their prices, the commodities have already been equated with definite but imaginary quantities of money. And since, in the direct form of circulation being considered here, money and commodities always come into physical confrontation with each other, one at the positive pole of purchase, the other at the negative pole of sale, it is clear that the amount of means of circulation required is determined beforehand by the sum of the prices of all these commodities. As a matter of fact, the money is only the representation in real life of the quantity of gold previously expressed in the imagination by the sum of the prices of the commodities. It is therefore self-evident that these two quantities are equal. We know however that, the values of commodities remaining constant, their prices vary with the value of gold (the material of money), rising in proportion as it falls, and falling in proportion as it rises. Given that the sum of the prices of commodities falls or rises in this way, it follows that the quantity of money in circulation must fall or rise to the same extent. This change in the quantity of the circulating medium is certainly caused by the money itself, yet not in virtue of its function as a medium of circulation, but rather in virtue of its function as a measure of value. First the price of the commodities varies inversely as the value of the money, and then the quantity of the medium of circulation varies directly as the price of the commodities. Exactly the same phenomenon would arise if, for instance, instead of the value of gold falling, silver were to replace it as the measure of value, or if, instead of the value of silver rising, it were to be driven out of its function as measure of value by gold. In the one case, more silver would be in circulation than there was previously gold, and in the other case, less gold would be in circulation than there was previously silver. In each case the value of the money material, i.e. the value of the commodity serving as the measure of value, would have undergone a change, and so too, therefore, would the prices of commodities which express their values in money, as well as the quantity of money which would need to be in circulation to realize those prices. We have already seen that the sphere of circulation has a gap in it, through which gold (or silver, or the money material in general) enters as a commodity with a given value. Hence, when money begins to function as a measure of value, when it is used to determine prices, its value is presupposed. If that value falls, the fall first shows itself in a change in the prices of those commodities which are directly exchanged with the precious metals at their source. The greater part of all other commodities, especially at the less developed stages of bourgeois society, will continue for a long time to be estimated in terms of the former value of the measure of value, which has now become antiquated and illusory. Nevertheless, one commodity infects another through their common value-relation, so that their prices, expressed in gold or silver, gradually settle down into the proportions determined by their comparative values, until finally the values of all commodities are estimated in terms of the new value of the monetary metal. This process of equalization is accompanied by a continued increase in the quantity of the precious metals, owing to the influx needed to replace the commodities directly exchanged with them. In proportion therefore as the adjusted prices of the commodities become universal, in proportion as their values come to be estimated according to the new value of the metal (which has fallen and may, up to a certain point, continue to fall), in that same proportion does the increased mass of metal which is necessary for the realization of the new prices become available. A one-sided observation of the events which followed the discovery of fresh supplies of gold and silver led some people in the seventeenth and more particularly in the eighteenth century to the false conclusion that the prices of commodities had risen because there was more gold and silver acting as the means of circulation. Henceforth we shall assume the value of gold as a given factor, as in fact it is if we take it at the moment when we estimate the price of a commodity.

On this assumption, then, the quantity of the medium of circulation is determined by the sum of the prices to be realized. If we now further assume that the price of each commodity is given, the sum of the prices clearly depends on the total amount of commodities found in circulation. We do not need to rack our brains to grasp that if our quarter of wheat costs £2, 100 quarters will cost

£200, 200 quarters £400, and so on, and therefore that the quantity of money which changes places with the wheat, when it is sold, must increase as the quantity of the wheat increases.

If the mass of commodities remains constant, the quantity of money in circulation surges up or down according to the fluctuations in the prices of the commodities. It rises and falls because the sum of the prices increases or diminishes as a result of the change of price. For this it is by no means necessary that the prices of all commodities should rise or fall simultaneously. A rise or a fall in the prices of a number of leading articles is sufficient in the one case to increase, in the other to diminish, the sum of the prices of all commodities, and therefore to put more or less money in circulation. Whether the change in the price reflects an actual change in the value of the commodities, or merely fluctuations in their market prices, the effect on the quantity of the medium of circulation remains the same.

Let us assume that there occur a number of unconnected and simultaneous sales, or partial metamorphoses, in different localities; sales of, say, 1 quarter of wheat, 20 yards of linen, 1 Bible and 4 gallons of brandy. If the price of each article is £2, and the sum of the prices to be realized is consequently £8, it follows that £8 in money must enter into circulation. If, on the other hand, these same articles are links in the following chain of metamorphoses: 1 quarter of wheat – £2 – 20 yards of linen – £2 – 1 Bible – £2 – 4 gallons of brandy – £2, a chain which is already well known to us, in that case the £2 causes the different commodities to circulate after realizing their prices successively, and therefore realizing the sum of those prices, which is £8, the £2 finally comes to rest in the hands of the distiller. The £2 has turned over four times. It has performed four acts of circulation. This repeated change of place of the same pieces of money corresponds to the double change of form undergone by the commodities, it corresponds to their movement through two diametrically opposed stages of circulation, and the intertwining of the metamorphoses of different commodities.[27] These antithetical and mutually complementary phases, through which the process passes, cannot take place alongside each other. They must follow in temporal succession. It is segments of time

27. 'It is products which set it' (money) 'in motion and make it circulate . . . The velocity of its' (money's) 'motion supplements its quantity. When necessary, it does nothing but slide from hand to hand, without stopping for a moment' (Le Trosne, op. cit., pp. 915–16).

216 Commodities and Money

therefore which form the measure of the duration of the process, in other words, the velocity of the circulation of money is measured by the number of times the same piece of money turns over within a given period. Suppose the process of circulation of the four articles takes a day. The sum of prices to be realized is £8, the number of times the £2 turns over during the day is four, and the quantity of money in circulation is £2. Hence, for a given interval of time during the process of circulation, we have the following equation: the quantity of money functioning as the circulating medium = the sum of the prices of the commodities divided by the number of times coins of the same denomination turn over. This law holds generally. The process of circulation in a given country is made up, on the one hand, of numerous isolated and simultaneous partial metamorphoses, sales (and purchases) running parallel to each other in which each coin changes its position only once, or performs only one act of circulation; on the other hand, it is made up of many distinct series of metamorphoses, partly running parallel, partly coalescing with each other, and in each of these series each coin turns over a number of times. How often each coin turns over varies according to the circumstances. Given the total number of times all the circulating coins of one denomination turn over, we can arrive at the average number of times a single coin turns over, or, in other words, the average velocity of circulation of money. The quantity of money thrown into the process of circulation at the beginning of each day is of course determined by the sum of the prices of all the commodities circulating simultaneously and side by side. But within that process coins are, so to speak, made responsible for each other. If one increases its velocity of circulation, the other slows down or completely leaves the sphere of circulation. This is because the sphere of circulation can absorb only the amount of gold which, multiplied by the average number of times its basic unit turns over, is equal to the sum of prices to be realized. Hence, if the number of acts of circulation performed by the separate pieces increases, the total number of those pieces in circulation diminishes. If the number of acts of circulation diminishes, the total number of pieces increases. Since the quantity of money which can function as means of circulation is fixed for a given average velocity of circulation, one has only to throw a given quantity of £1 notes into circulation in order to extract the same number of sovereigns from it. This trick is well known to all banks.

Just as the circulation of money is in general merely a reflection of the process of circulation of commodities, i.e. their circular path through diametrically opposed metamorphoses, so too the velocity of circulation of money is merely a reflection of the rapidity with which commodities change their forms, the continuous interlocking of the series of metamorphoses, the hurried nature of society's metabolic process, the quick disappearance of commodities from the sphere of circulation, and their equally quick replacement by fresh commodities. In the velocity of circulation, therefore, there appears the fluid unity of the antithetical and complementary phases, i.e. the transformation of the commodities from the form of utility into the form of value and their re-transformation in the reverse direction, or the two processes of sale and purchase. Inversely, when the circulation of money slows down, the two processes become separated, they assert their independence and mutual antagonism; stagnation occurs in the changes of form, and hence in the metabolic process. The circulation itself, of course, gives no clue to the origin of this stagnation; it merely presents us with the phenomenon. Popular opinion is naturally inclined to attribute this phenomenon to a quantitative deficiency in the circulating medium, since it sees money appear and disappear less frequently at all points on the periphery of circulation, in proportion as the circulation of money slows down.[28]

The total quantity of money functioning during a given period as the circulating medium is determined on the one hand by the sum of the prices of the commodities in circulation, and on the other hand by the rapidity of alternation of the antithetical pro-

28. 'Money being ... the common measure of buying and selling, every body who hath anything to sell, and cannot procure chapmen for it, is presently apt to think, that want of money in the kingdom, or country, is the cause why his goods do not go off; and so, want of money is the common cry; which is a great mistake ... What do these people want, who cry out for money? ... The farmer complains ... he thinks that were more money in the country, he would have a price for his goods. Then it seems money is not his want, but a price for his corn and cattel, which he would sell, but cannot ... Why cannot he get a price? ... (1) Either there is too much corn and cattel in the country, so that most who come to market have need of selling, as he hath, and few of buying; or (2) there wants the usual vent abroad by transportation ... ; or (3) the consumption fails, as when men, by reason of poverty, do not spend so much in their houses as formerly they did; wherefore it is not the increase of specific money, which would at all advance the farmer's goods, but the removal of any of these three causes, which do truly keep down the market ... The merchant and shopkeeper want money in the same manner, that is, they want a vent for the goods they deal in, by reason that the markets fail ... [A nation]

cesses of circulation. The proportion of the sum of the prices which can on average be realized by each single coin depends on this rapidity of alternation. But the sum of the prices of the commodities depends on the quantity, as well as on the price, of each kind of commodity. These three factors, the movement of prices, the quantity of commodities in circulation, and the velocity of circulation of money, can all vary in various directions under different conditions. Hence the sum of the prices to be realized, and consequently the quantity of the circulating medium conditioned by that sum, will vary with the very numerous variations of the three factors in combination. Here we shall outline only the most important variations in the history of commodity prices.

While prices remain constant, the quantity of the circulating medium may increase owing to an increase in the number of commodities in circulation, or a decrease in the velocity of circulation of money, or a combination of the two. On the other hand, the quantity of the circulating medium may decrease with a decreasing number of commodities, or with an increasing rapidity of circulation.

With a general rise in the prices of commodities, the quantity of the circulating medium will remain constant, if the number of commodities in circulation decreases proportionally to the increase in their prices, or if the velocity of monetary circulation increases at the same rate as prices rise, the number of commodities in circulation remaining constant. The quantity of the circulating medium may decrease, owing to a more rapid decrease in the number of commodities, or to a more rapid increase in the velocity of monetary circulation, in comparison with the fall in the prices of commodities.

---

never thrives better, than when riches are tost from hand to hand' (Sir Dudley North, *Discourses upon Trade*, London, 1691, pp. 11–15 passim). Herrenschwand's fanciful notions* amount merely to this, that the contradictions which arise from the nature of commodities, and therefore come to the surface in their circulation, can be removed by increasing the amount of the medium of circulation. It should be mentioned in passing that it by no means follows, from the fact that the popular ascription of stagnation in the processes of production and circulation to an insufficiency of the circulating medium is a delusion, that an actual shortage of the circulating medium resulting from, say, bungling government interference with the 'regulation of currency' may not for its part give rise to stagnation.

*Jean Herrenschwand (1728–1812), Swiss economist, author of *De l'économie politique moderne*, London, 1786, and *De l'économie politique et morale de l'espèce humaine*, London, 1796.

With a general fall in the prices of commodities, the quantity of the circulating medium will remain constant, if the number of commodities increases proportionally to their fall in price, or if the velocity of monetary circulation decreases in the same proportion. The quantity of the circulating medium will increase, if the number of commodities increases more quickly, or the rapidity of circulation decreases more quickly, than the prices fall.

The variations of the different factors may be mutually compensatory, so that notwithstanding their continued instability, the sum of the prices to be realized and the quantity of money in circulation remains constant; consequently, we find, especially if we take long periods into consideration, that the quantity of money in circulation in each country diverges far less from its average level than we should at first sight have expected, with the exception of the violent perturbations which arise periodically, either from crises in production and commerce, or, more rarely, from changes in the value of money itself.

The law that the quantity of the circulating medium is determined by the sum of the prices of the commodities in circulation, and the average velocity of the circulation of money,[29] may also be stated as follows: given the sum of the values of commodities, and the average rapidity of their metamorphoses, the quantity of money or of the material of money in circulation depends on its

29. 'There is a certain measure and proportion of money requisite to drive the trade of a nation, more or less than which would prejudice the same. Just as there is a certain proportion of farthings necessary in a small retail trade, to change silver money, and to even such reckonings as cannot be adjusted with the smallest silver pieces ... Now, as the proportion of the number of farthings requisite in commerce is to be taken from the number of people, the frequency of their exchanges: as also, and principally, from the value of the smallest silver pieces of money; so in like manner, the proportion of money (gold and silver specie) requisite in our trade, is to be likewise taken from the frequency of commutations, and from the bigness of the payments' (William Petty, *A Treatise of Taxes and Contributions*, London, 1667, p. 17). Hume's theory* was defended against the attacks of J. Steuart and others by A. Young, in his *Political Arithmetic*, London, 1774, where there is a special chapter on this, entitled 'Prices Depend on Quantity of Money', pp. 112 ff. I stated in *Zur Kritik etc.*, p. 149 [English edition, p. 168], 'He' (Adam Smith) 'quietly eliminates the question about the amount of coin in circulation

*Hume's theory, first advanced in *Essays Moral, Political, and Literary*, Part II, London, 1752, was that the prices of commodities depend on the amount of money in circulation, rather than the amount of money in circulation depending on the prices of commodities. It is criticized in detail in *A Contribution to the Critique of Political Economy*, pp. 160–64.

own value. The illusion that it is, on the contrary, prices which are determined by the quantity of the circulating medium, and that the latter for its part depends on the amount of monetary material which happens to be present in a country,[30] had its roots in the absurd hypothesis adopted by the original representatives of this view that commodities enter into the process of circulation without a price, and money enters without a value, and that, once they have entered circulation, an aliquot part of the medley of commodities is exchanged for an aliquot part of the heap of precious metals.[31]

---

by quite improperly regarding money as a simple commodity.' This is only true in so far as Adam Smith treats of money while developing his own theories. Occasionally, however, for example in criticizing earlier systems of political economy, he takes the correct view: 'The quantity of coin in every country is regulated by the value of the commodities which are to be circulated by it ... The value of the goods annually bought and sold in any country requires a certain quantity of money to circulate and distribute them to their proper consumers, and can give employment to no more. The channel of circulation necessarily draws to itself a sum sufficient to fill it, and never admits any more' (*Wealth of Nations*, Bk IV, Ch. 1). In similar fashion Smith begins his work in the official manner with an apotheosis of the division of labour. Later on, in the last book, on the sources of the public revenue,* he occasionally reproduces the denunciations of the division of labour made by his teacher, A. Ferguson.†

30. 'The prices of things will certainly rise in every nation, as the gold and silver increase amongst the people; and consequently, where the gold and silver decrease in any nation, the prices of all things must fall proportionately to such decrease of money' (Jacob Vanderlint, *Money Answers All Things*, London, 1734, p. 5). A close comparison of this book with Hume's *Essays* leaves not the slightest doubt in my mind that Hume knew and used Vanderlint's work, which is certainly an important one. The opinion that prices are determined by the quantity of the circulating medium was also held by Barbon and other much earlier writers. 'No inconvenience,' says Vanderlint, 'can arise by an unrestrained trade, but very great advantage; since, if the cash of the nation be decreased by it, which prohibitions are designed to prevent, those nations that get the cash will certainly find everything advance in price, as the cash increases amongst them. And ... our manufactures, and everything else, will soon become so moderate as to turn the balance of trade in our favour, and thereby fetch the money back again' (op. cit., pp. 43, 44).

31. That each single kind of commodity, through its price, forms an element in the sum of the prices of all the commodities in circulation, is self-evident. But how mutually incommensurable use-values are to be exchanged, *en masse*,

*Bk V, Ch. 2, of the *Wealth of Nations* is entitled 'Of the Sources of the General or Public Revenue of the Society'.

†For Adam Ferguson's denunciation of the division of labour, see below, p. 474.

(c) Coin. The Symbol of Value

Money takes the shape of coin because of its function as the circulating medium. The weight of gold represented in the imagination by the prices or money-names of the commodities has to confront those commodities, within circulation, as coins or pieces of gold of the same denomination. The business of coining, like

---

for the total sum of gold or silver in a country is quite incomprehensible. If we can perform the swindle of converting the world of commodities into one single total commodity, of which each commodity is merely an aliquot part, we arrive at this beautiful calculation: the total commodity = x cwt of gold; commodity A = an aliquot part of the total commodity = the same aliquot part of x cwt of gold. This is stated in all seriousness by Montesquieu: 'If one compares the amount of gold and silver in the world with the sum of the commodities available, it is certain that each product or commodity, taken in isolation, could be compared with a certain portion of the total amount of money. Let us suppose that there is only one product, or commodity, in the world, or only one that can be purchased, and that it can be divided in the same way as money: a certain part of this commodity would then correspond to a part of the total amount of money; half the total of the one would correspond to half the total of the other, etc. . . . the determination of the prices of things always depends, fundamentally, on the relation between the total amount of things and the total amount of their monetary symbols' (Montesquieu, op. cit., Vol. 3, pp. 12, 13). As to the further development of this theory by Ricardo and his disciples, James Mill, Lord Overstone and others, see *Zur Kritik, etc.*, pp. 140–46, and pp. 150 ff. [English edition, pp. 179–85 and 169–77]. John Stuart Mill, with his usual eclectic logic, understands how to hold at the same time the view of his father, James Mill, and the opposite view. When we compare the text of his compendium *Principles of Political Economy* with the Preface to the first edition, where he announces himself as the Adam Smith of his day, we do not know what we should be most astonished at, the naïveté of the man or that of the public which accepted him in good faith as the new Adam Smith, for he bears about as much resemblance to Adam Smith as General Williams 'of Kars'* does to the Duke of Wellington. The original researches of Mr J. S. Mill in the domain of political economy, which are neither extensive nor profound, will all be found drawn up in neat and disciplined columns in his little pamphlet *Some Unsettled Questions of Political Economy*, which appeared in 1844. Locke expressly asserts that there is a connection between the absence of value in gold and silver, and the determination of their value by their quantity. 'Mankind having consented to put an imaginary value upon gold and silver . . . the intrinsick value, regarded in these metals, is nothing but the quantity' (*Some Considerations, etc.*, 1691, in *Works*, ed. 1777, Vol. 2, p. 15).

*Colonel Fenwick Williams (1800–83) was a British commissioner in charge of Turkish troops defending the fortress of Kars, in Armenia, in 1855, during the Crimean War. The fortress fell to the Russians in November 1855, but Williams was made a General and a baronet for his defence of it.

the establishing of a standard measure of prices, is an attribute proper to the state. The different national uniforms worn at home by gold and silver as coins, but taken off again when they appear on the world market, demonstrate the separation between the internal or national spheres of commodity circulation and its universal sphere, the world market.

The only difference, therefore, between coin and bullion lies in their physical configuration, and gold can at any time pass from one form to the other.[32] For a coin, the road from the mint is also the path to the melting pot. In the course of circulation, coins wear down, some to a greater extent, some to a lesser. The denomination of the gold and its substance, the nominal content and the real content, begin to move apart. Coins of the same denomination become different in value, because they are different in weight. The weight of gold fixed upon as the standard of prices diverges from the weight which serves as the circulating medium, and the latter thereby ceases to be a real equivalent of the commodities whose prices it realizes. The history of these difficulties constitutes the history of the coinage throughout the Middle Ages and in modern times down to the eighteenth century. The natural and spontaneous tendency of the process of circulation to transform the coin from its metallic existence as gold into the semblance of gold, or to transform the coin into a symbol of its official metallic content, is itself recognized by the most recent laws on the degree of metal loss which demonetizes a gold coin, i.e. renders it incapable of being circulated.

The fact that the circulation of money itself splits the nominal

32. It lies of course entirely beyond my purpose to deal with such details as the seigniorage on minting. I will however cite against the romantic sycophant Adam Müller, who admires the 'magnificent liberality' with which 'the English government coins for nothing',* the following opinion of Sir Dudley North: 'Silver and gold, like other commodities, have their ebbings and flowings. Upon the arrival of quantities from Spain ... it is carried into the Tower, and coined. Not long after there will come a demand for bullion to be exported again. If there is none, but all happens to be in coin, what then? Melt it down again; there's no loss in it, for the coining costs the owner nothing. Thus the nation has been abused, and made to pay for the twisting of straw for asses to eat. If the merchant' (North was himself one of the biggest merchants at the time of Charles II) 'were made to pay the price of the coinage, he would not have sent his silver to the Tower without consideration; and coined money would always keep a value above uncoined silver' (North, op. cit., p. 18).

* A. H. Müller, *Die Elemente der Staatskunst*, Part 2, Berlin, 1809, p. 280.

content of coins away from their real content, dividing their metallic existence from their functional existence, this fact implies the latent possibility of replacing metallic money with tokens made of some other material, i.e. symbols which would perform the function of coins. The technical obstacles to coining extremely minute quantities of gold or silver, and the circumstance that at first the less precious metal is used as a measure of value instead of the more precious, copper instead of silver, silver instead of gold, and that the less precious circulates as money until dethroned by the more precious – these facts provide a historical explanation for the role played by silver and copper tokens as substitutes for gold coins. Silver and copper coins replace gold in those regions of the circulation of commodities where coins pass from hand to hand most rapidly, and are therefore worn out most quickly. This happens where sales and purchases on a very small scale recur unceasingly. In order to prevent these satellites from establishing themselves permanently in the place of gold, the law determines the very minute proportions in which alone they can be accepted as alternative payment. The particular tracks pursued by the different sorts of coin in circulation naturally run into each other. Small change appears alongside gold for the payment of fractional parts of the smallest gold coin; gold constantly enters into retail circulation, although it is just as constantly being thrown out again by being exchanged with small change.[33]

The metallic content of silver and copper tokens is arbitrarily determined by law. In the course of circulation they wear down even more rapidly than gold coins. Their function as coins is therefore in practice entirely independent of their weight, i.e. it is independent of all value. In its form of existence as coin, gold becomes completely divorced from the substance of its value. Relatively valueless objects, therefore, such as paper notes, can serve as

33. 'If silver never exceed what is wanted for the smaller payments, it cannot be collected in sufficient quantities for the larger payments ... the use of gold in the main payments necessarily implies also its use in the retail trade: those who have gold coins offering them for small purchases, and receiving with the commodity purchased a balance of silver in return; by which means the surplus of silver that would otherwise encumber the retail dealer is drawn off and dispersed into general circulation. But if there is as much silver as will transact the small payments independent of gold, the retail trader must then receive silver for small purchases; and it must of necessity accumulate in his hands' (David Buchanan, *Inquiry into the Taxation and Commercial Policy of Great Britain*, Edinburgh, 1844, pp. 248–9).

coins in place of gold. This purely symbolic character of the currency is still somewhat disguised in the case of metal tokens. In paper money it stands out plainly. But we can see: everything depends on the first step.

Here we are concerned only with inconvertible paper money issued by the state and given forced currency. This money emerges directly out of the circulation of metallic money. Credit-money on the other hand implies relations which are as yet totally unknown, from the standpoint of the simple circulation of commodities. But it may be noted in passing that just as true paper money arises out of the function of money as the circulating medium, so does credit-money take root spontaneously in the function of money as the means of payment.[34]

Pieces of paper on which money-names are printed, such as £1, £5, etc., are thrown into the circulation process from outside by the state. In so far as they actually circulate in place of the same amount of gold, their movement is simply a reflection of the laws of monetary circulation itself. A law peculiar to the circulation of paper money can only spring up from the proportion in which that paper money represents gold. In simple terms the law referred to is as follows: the issue of paper money must be restricted to the quantity of gold (or silver) which would actually be in circulation, and which is represented symbolically by the paper money. Now it is true that the quantity of gold which can be absorbed by the sphere of circulation constantly fluctuates above and below a certain average level. But despite this, the mass of the circulating

---

34. The financial mandarin Wan Mao-in took it into his head one day to lay before the Son of Heaven a proposal which had the secret purpose of transforming the *assignats* of the Chinese Empire into convertible banknotes. The Committee on the *assignats*, in its report of April 1854, severely rebuked him for this. Whether he also received the traditional thrashing with bamboo-sticks is not stated. The concluding part of the report is as follows: 'The Committee has carefully examined his proposal and finds that it is entirely in the interests of the merchants, and in no respect advantageous to the Crown' (*Arbeiten der Kaiserlich Russischen Gesandschaft zu Peking über China*, aus dem Russischen von Dr K. Abel und F. A. Mecklenburg, Erster Band, Berlin, 1858, p. 54). In his evidence before the Committee of the House of Lords on the Bank Acts, a governor of the Bank of England says, with regard to the abrasion of gold coins in the course of their circulation: 'Every year a fresh class of sovereigns' (this is not a political statement, for 'sovereign' is a name for the pound sterling) 'becomes too light. The class which one year passes with full weight, loses enough by wear and tear to draw the scales next year against it' (House of Lords Committee, 1848, n. 429).

medium in a given country never sinks below a certain minimum, which can be ascertained by experience. The fact that this minimum mass continually undergoes changes in its constituent parts, or that the pieces of gold of which it consists are constantly being replaced by other pieces, naturally causes no change either in its amount or in the continuity with which it flows around the sphere of circulation. It can therefore be replaced by paper symbols. If however all the channels of circulation were today filled with paper money to the full extent of their capacity for absorbing money, they might the next day be over-full owing to the fluctuations in the circulation of commodities. There would no longer be any standard. If the paper money exceeds its proper limit, i.e. the amount in gold coins of the same denomination which could have been in circulation, then, quite apart from the danger of becoming universally discredited, it will still represent within the world of commodities only that quantity of gold which is fixed by its immanent laws. No greater quantity is capable of being represented. If the quantity of paper money represents twice the amount of gold available, then in practice £1 will be the money-name not of $\frac{1}{4}$ of an ounce of gold, but $\frac{1}{8}$ of an ounce. The effect is the same as if an alteration had taken place in the function of gold as the standard of prices. The values previously expressed by the price of £1 would now be expressed by the price of £2.

Paper money is a symbol of gold, a symbol of money. Its relation to the values of commodities consists only in this: they find imaginary expression in certain quantities of gold, and the same quantities are symbolically and physically represented by the paper. Only in so far as paper money represents gold, which like all other commodities has value, is it a symbol of value.[35]

Finally, one may ask why gold is capable of being replaced by

35. The following passage from Fullarton shows how unclear even the best writers on money are about its different functions: 'That, as far as concerns our domestic exchanges, all the monetary functions which are usually performed by gold and silver coins, may be performed as effectually by a circulation of inconvertible notes, having no value but that factitious and conventional value . . . they derive from the law, is a fact which admits, I conceive, of no denial. Value of this description may be made to answer all the purposes of intrinsic value, and supersede even the necessity for a standard, provided only the quantity of issues be kept under due limitation' (Fullarton, *Regulation of Currencies*, 2nd edn, London, 1845, p. 21). In other words, because the money commodity is capable of being replaced in circulation by mere symbols of value, it is superfluous as a measure of value and a standard of prices!

valueless symbols of itself. As we have already seen, it is capable of being replaced in this way only if its function as coin or circulating medium can be singled out or rendered independent. Now this function of being the circulating medium does not attain an independent position as far as the individual gold coins are concerned, although that independent position does appear in the case of the continued circulation of abraded coins. A piece of money is a mere coin, or means of circulation, only as long as it is actually in circulation. But what is not valid for the individual gold coin is valid for that minimum mass of gold which is capable of being replaced by paper money. That mass constantly haunts the sphere of circulation, continually functions as a circulating medium, and therefore exists exclusively as the bearer of this function. Its movement therefore represents nothing but the continued alternation of the inverse phases of the metamorphosis C–M–C, phases in which the commodity's shape as a value confronts it only to disappear again immediately. The presentation of the exchange-value of a commodity as an independent entity is here only a transient aspect of the process. The commodity is immediately replaced again by another commodity. Hence in this process which continually makes money pass from hand to hand, it only needs to lead a symbolic existence. Its functional existence so to speak absorbs its material existence. Since it is a transiently objectified reflection of the prices of commodities, it serves only as a symbol of itself, and can therefore be replaced by another symbol.[36] One thing is necessary, however: the symbol of money must have its own objective social validity. The paper acquires this by its forced currency. The state's compulsion can only be of any effect within that internal sphere of circulation which is circumscribed by the boundaries of a given community, but it is also only within that sphere that money is completely absorbed in its function as medium of circulation, and is therefore able to receive, in the form of paper

36. From the fact that gold and silver themselves become their own symbols, in so far as they are coins, i.e. exclusively have the function of the medium of circulation, Nicholas Barbon deduces the right of governments 'to raise money', i.e. to give to the quantity of silver called a shilling the name of a greater quantity, such as a crown, and so to pay back shillings to creditors instead of crowns. 'Money does wear and grow lighter by often telling over ... It is the denomination and currency of the money that men regard in bargaining, and not the quantity of silver ... 'Tis the public authority upon the metal that makes it money' (N. Barbon, op. cit., p. 29, 30, 25).

money, a purely functional mode of existence in which it is externally separated from its metallic substance.

3. MONEY

The commodity which functions as a measure of value and therefore also as the medium of circulation, either in its own body or through a representative, is money. Gold (or silver) is therefore money. It functions as money, on the one hand, when it has to appear in person as gold. It is then the money commodity, neither merely ideal, as when it is the measure of value, nor capable of being represented, as when it is the medium of circulation. On the other hand, it also functions as money when its function, whether performed in person or by a representative, causes it to be fixed as the sole form of value, or, in other words, as the only adequate form of existence of exchange value in the face of all the other commodities, here playing the role of use-values pure and simple.

(a) Hoarding

The continuous circular movement of the two antithetical metamorphoses of commodities, or the repeated alternating flow of sale and purchase, is reflected in the unceasing turnover of money, in the function it performs of a *perpetuum mobile* of circulation. But as soon as the series of metamorphoses is interrupted, as soon as sales are not supplemented by subsequent purchases, money is immobilized. In other words, it is transformed, as Boisguillebert says, from '*meuble*' into '*immeuble*',* from coin into money.

When the circulation of commodities first develops, there also develops the necessity and the passionate desire to hold fast to the product of the first metamorphosis. This product is the transformed shape of the commodity, or its gold chrysalis.[37] Commodities are thus sold not in order to buy commodities, but in

37. 'Monetary wealth is nothing but ... wealth in products, transformed into money' (Mercier de la Rivière, op. cit., p. 573). 'A value in the form of a product has merely changed its form' (ibid., p. 486).

---

* From movable into immovable. (Boisguillebert, *Le Détail de la France*, in *Économistes financiers du XVIIIe siècle*, ed. E. Daire, Paris, 1843, p. 213.)

order to replace their commodity-form by their money-form. Instead of being merely a way of mediating the metabolic process [*Stoffwechsel*], this change of form becomes an end in itself. The form of the commodity in which it is divested of content is prevented from functioning as its absolutely alienable form, or even as its merely transient money-form. The money is petrified into a hoard, and the seller of commodities becomes a hoarder of money.

In the very beginnings of the circulation of commodities, it is only the excess amounts of use-value which are converted into money. Gold and silver thus become of themselves social expressions for superfluity or wealth. This naïve form of hoarding is perpetuated among those peoples whose traditional mode of production, aimed at fulfilling their own requirements, corresponds to a fixed and limited range of needs. This is true of the Asiatics, particularly the Indians. Vanderlint, who imagines that the prices of commodities in a country are determined by the quantity of gold and silver to be found in it, asks himself why Indian commodities are so cheap. Answer: because the Indians bury their money. From 1602 to 1734, he remarks, they buried 150 million pounds worth of silver, which originally came from America to Europe.[38] From 1856 to 1866, in other words in ten years, England exported to India (and China, but most of the metal exported to China flows back again to India) £120,000,000 in silver, which had been received in exchange for Australian gold.

With more developed commodity production, every producer is compelled to secure for himself the *nexus rerum*,* the 'social pledge'.[39] His needs are ceaselessly renewed, and necessitate the continual purchase of other people's commodities, whereas the production and sale of his own commodity costs time and is subject to various accidents. In order then to be able to buy without selling, he must have sold previously without buying. This operation, conducted on a general scale, seems to involve a self-contradiction. But at the sources of their production the precious metals are directly exchanged for other commodities. And here we have sales (by the owners of commodities) without purchases (by

38. ''Tis by this practice they keep all their goods and manufactures at such low rates' (Vanderlint, op. cit., pp. 95–6).

39. 'Money . . . is a pledge' (John Bellers, *Essays about the Poor, Manufactures, Trade, Plantations, and Immorality*, London, 1699, p. 13)

*In Roman law, the obligation of the debtor to the creditor.

the owners of gold or silver).[40] And later sales, again without subsequent purchases, merely bring about a further distribution of the precious metals among all the owners of commodities. In this way, hoards of gold and silver of the most various sizes are piled up at all the points of commercial intercourse. With the possibility of keeping hold of the commodity as exchange-value, or exchange-value as a commodity, the lust for gold awakens. With the extension of commodity circulation there is an increase in the power of money, that absolutely social form of wealth which is always ready to be used. 'Gold is a wonderful thing! Its owner is master of all he desires. Gold can even enable souls to enter Paradise' (Columbus, in his letter from Jamaica, 1503). Since money does not reveal what has been transformed into it, everything, commodity or not, is convertible into money. Everything becomes saleable and purchaseable. Circulation becomes the great social retort into which everything is thrown, to come out again as the money crystal. Nothing is immune from this alchemy, the bones of the saints cannot withstand it, let alone more delicate *res sacrosanctae, extra commercium hominum*.*[41] Just as in money every qualitative differen~e between commodities is extinguished, so too for its part, as a radical leveller, it extinguishes all distinctions.[42] But money is itself a commodity, an external object

40. A purchase, in the strict sense, implies that gold and silver are already the transformed shape of commodities, in other words the product of a sale.

41. Henry III, *roi très chrétien*,* robbed monasteries etc. of their relics and turned them into money. It is well known what part the despoiling of the Delphic temple by the Phocians† played in the history of Greece. Among the ancients, temples served as the dwellings of the gods of commodities. They were 'sacred banks'. With the Phoenicians, a trading people *par excellence*, money was the transmuted shape of everything. It was, therefore, quite in order that the virgins who at the feast of the goddess of love gave themselves to strangers should offer to the goddess the piece of money they received in payment.

42. 'Gold? yellow, glittering, precious gold? . . .
Thus much of this, will make black, white; foul, fair;
Wrong, right; base, noble; old, young; coward, valiant.
. . . What this, you gods? Why, this
Will lug your priests and servants from your sides,
Pluck stout men's pillows from below their heads;

*'Most Christian King'. The official title of the kings of France.
† In 457 B.C. the Phocians, in alliance with Athens, seized Delphi.

---

*'Consecrated objects, beyond human commerce.' In this case, the Phoenician virgins.

capable of becoming the private property of any individual. Thus the social power becomes the private power of private persons. Ancient society therefore denounced it as tending to destroy the economic and moral order.[43] Modern society, which already in its infancy had pulled Pluto by the hair of his head from the bowels of the earth,[44] greets gold as its Holy Grail, as the glittering incarnation of its innermost principle of life.

The commodity, as a use-value, satisfies a particular need and forms a particular element of material wealth. But the value of a commodity measures the degree of its attractiveness for all other elements of material wealth, and therefore measures the social wealth of its owner. To the simple owner of commodities among the barbarians, and even to the peasant of Western Europe, value is inseparable from the value-form, hence an increase in his hoard of gold and silver is an increase in value. It is true that the value of money varies, whether as a result of a variation in its own value, or of a change in the values of commodities. But this on the one hand does not prevent 200 ounces of gold from continuing to contain more value than 100 ounces, nor on the other hand does it prevent the metallic natural form of this object from continuing to be the universal equivalent form of all other commodities, and the directly social incarnation of all human labour. The hoarding drive is boundless in its nature. Qualitatively or formally considered, money is independent of all limits, that is it is the universal representative of material wealth because it is directly convertible into

---

This yellow slave
Will knit and break religions; bless the accursed;
Make the hoar leprosy adored; place thieves,
And give them title, knee and approbation,
With senators on the bench; this is it,
That makes the wappen'd widow wed again:
... Come damned earth,
Thou common whore of mankind.'
(Shakespeare, *Timon of Athens*, Act 4, Scene 3)

43. 'Nothing so evil as money ever grew to be current among men. This lays cities low, this drives men from their homes, this trains and warps honest souls till they set themselves to works of shame; this still teaches folk to practise villanies, and to know every godless deed' (Sophocles, *Antigone*).*

44. 'Avarice hopes to drag Pluto himself out of the bowels of the earth' (Athenaeus, *Deipnosophistae*).†

*Lines 295 to 301, pp. 64–5 of the edition by Sir R. Jebb, *Sophocles, the Plays and Fragments, Part III, The Antigone*, Cambridge, 1928.

† Bk VI, para. 233.

any other commodity. But at the same time every actual sum of money is limited in amount, and therefore has only a limited efficacy as a means of purchase. This contradiction between the quantitative limitation and the qualitative lack of limitation of money keeps driving the hoarder back to his Sisyphean task: accumulation. He is in the same situation as a world conqueror, who discovers a new boundary with each country he annexes.

In order that gold may be held as money, and made to form a hoard, it must be prevented from circulating, or from dissolving into the means of purchasing enjoyment. The hoarder therefore sacrifices the lusts of his flesh to the fetish of gold. He takes the gospel of abstinence very seriously. On the other hand, he cannot withdraw any more from circulation, in the shape of money, than he has thrown into it, in the shape of commodities. The more he produces, the more he can sell. Work, thrift and greed are therefore his three cardinal virtues, and to sell much and buy little is the sum of his political economy.[45]

Alongside the direct form of the hoard there runs its aesthetic form, the possession of commodities made out of gold and silver. This grows with the wealth of civil society. 'Let us be rich, or let us appear rich' (Diderot). In this way there is formed, on the one hand, a constantly extending market for gold and silver which is independent of their monetary functions, and on the other hand a latent source of monetary inflow which is used particularly in periods of social disturbance.

Hoarding serves various purposes in an economy where metallic circulation prevails. Its first function arises out of the conditions of the circulation of gold and silver coins. We have seen how, owing to the continual fluctuations in the extent and rapidity of the circulation of commodities and in their prices, the quantity of money in circulation unceasingly ebbs and flows. This quantity must therefore be capable of expansion and contraction. At one time money must be attracted as coin, at another time coin must be repelled as money. In order that the mass of money actually in circulation may always correspond to the saturation level of the sphere of circulation, it is necessary for the quantity of gold and silver available in a country to be greater than the quantity

45. 'These are the pivots around which all the measures of political economy turn: the maximum possible increase in the number of sellers of each commodity, and the maximum possible decrease in the number of buyers' (Verri, op. cit., pp. 52–3).

required to function as coin. The reserves created by hoarding
serve as channels through which money may flow in and out
of circulation, so that the circulation itself never overflows its
banks.[46]

(b) Means of Payment

In the direct form of commodity circulation hitherto considered,
we found a given value always presented to us in a double shape,
as a commodity at one pole, and money at the opposite pole. The
owners of commodities therefore came into contact as the representatives of equivalents which were already available to each of
them. But with the development of circulation, conditions arise
under which the alienation of the commodity becomes separated
by an interval of time from the realization of its price.* It will be
sufficient to indicate the most simple of these conditions. One sort
of commodity requires a longer, another a shorter time for its
production. The production of different commodities depends on
different seasons of the year. One commodity may be born in the
market place, another must travel to a distant market. One commodity-owner may therefore step forth as a seller before the other
is ready to buy. When the same transactions are continually
repeated between the same persons, the conditions of sale are
regulated according to the conditions of production. On the other

46. 'There is required for carrying on the trade of the nation a determinate
sum of specifick money, which varies, and is sometimes more, sometimes less,
as the circumstances we are in require . . . This ebbing and flowing of money
supplies and accommodates itself, without any aid of Politicians . . . The
buckets work alternately; when money is scarce, bullion is coined; when
bullion is scarce, money is melted' (Sir D. North, op. cit., postscript, p. 3).
John Stuart Mill, who was for a long time an official of the East India Company, confirms that in India silver ornaments still continue to perform directly
the functions of a hoard: 'Silver ornaments are brought out and coined when
there is a high rate of interest, and go back again when the rate of interest
falls' (J. S. Mill's evidence, in *Report from the Select Committee on the Bank
Acts*, 1857, n. 2084, 2101). According to a parliamentary document of 1864
on the gold and silver import and export of India,* the import of gold and
silver in 1863 exceeded the export by £19,367,764. During the eight years up
to 1864, the excess of imports over exports of the precious metals amounted to
£109,652,917. During this century far more than £200,000,000 has been
coined in India.
    * *East India (Bullion). Return to the House of Commons*, 8 February 1864.

*The commodity can be *alienated*, that is it can leave the hands of the seller,
before it is *sold*, which happens when its price is paid over.

hand, the use of certain kinds of commodity (houses, for instance) is sold for a definite period. Only after the lease has expired has the buyer actually received the use-value of the commodity. He therefore buys it before he pays for it. The seller sells an existing commodity, the buyer buys as the mere representative of money, or rather as the representative of future money. The seller becomes a creditor, the buyer becomes a debtor. Since the metamorphosis of commodities, or the development of their form of value, has undergone a change here, money receives a new function as well. It becomes the means of payment.[47]

The role of creditor or of debtor results here from the simple circulation of commodities. The change in its form impresses this new stamp on seller and buyer. At first, therefore, these new roles are just as transient as those of seller and buyer, and are played alternately by the same actors. Nevertheless, this opposition now looks less pleasant from the very outset, and it is capable of a more rigid crystallization.[48] However, the same characteristics can emerge independently of the circulation of commodities. The class struggle in the ancient world, for instance, took the form mainly of a contest between debtors and creditors, and ended in Rome with the ruin of the plebeian debtors, who were replaced by slaves. In the Middle Ages the contest ended with the ruin of the feudal debtors, who lost their political power together with its economic basis. Here, indeed, the money-form – and the relation between creditor and debtor does have the form of a money-relation – was only the reflection of an antagonism which lay deeper, at the level of the economic conditions of existence.

Let us return to the sphere of circulation. The two equivalents, commodities and money, have ceased to appear simultaneously at the two poles of the process of sale. The money functions now,

47. [Note by Engels to the fourth German edition:] Luther distinguishes between money as means of purchase and means of payment: 'You have caused me to suffer two-fold damage, because I cannot pay on the one hand and cannot buy on the other' (Martin Luther, *An die Pfarrherrn, wider den Wucher zu predigen*, Wittenberg, 1540 [without pagination]).*

48. The following shows the relations existing between debtors and creditors among English traders at the beginning of the eighteenth century: 'Such a spirit of cruelty reigns here in England among the men of trade, that is not to be met with in any other society of men, nor in any other kingdom of the world' (*An Essay on Credit and the Bankrupt Act*, London, 1707, p. 2).

* This passage occurs in the context of an attack on the theory that interest could be taken in compensation for the loss of an opportunity on the part of the lender to buy something with the money loaned. Cf. *Theories of Surplus-Value*, Part III, p. 535.

first as a measure of value in the determination of the price of the commodity sold; the price fixed by contract measures the obligation of the buyer, i.e. the sum of money he owes at a particular time. Secondly it serves as a nominal means of purchase. Although existing only in the promise of the buyer to pay, it causes the commodity to change hands. Not until payment falls due does the means of payment actually step into circulation, i.e. leave the hand of the buyer for that of the seller. The circulating medium was transformed into a hoard because the process stopped short after the first phase, because the converted shape of the commodity was withdrawn from circulation. The means of payment enters circulation, but only after the commodity has already left it. The money no longer mediates the process. It brings it to an end by emerging independently, as the absolute form of existence of exchange-value, in other words the universal commodity. The seller turned his commodity into money in order to satisfy some need; the hoarder in order to preserve the monetary form of his commodity, and the indebted purchaser in order to be able to pay. If he does not pay, his goods will be sold compulsorily. The value-form of the commodity, money, has now become the self-sufficient purpose of the sale, owing to a social necessity springing from the conditions of the process of circulation itself.

The buyer converts money back into commodities before he has turned commodities into money: in other words, he achieves the second metamorphosis of commodities before the first. The seller's commodity circulates, and realizes its price, but only as a title to money in civil law. It is converted into a use-value before it has been converted into money. The completion of its first metamorphosis occurs only subsequently.[49]

The obligations falling due within a given period of the circulation process represent the sum of the prices of the commodities

49. The reason why I take no notice in the text of an opposite form will be seen from the following quotation from my book which appeared in 1859: 'Conversely, in the transaction M–C, money as a real means of purchase may be alienated, thus realizing the price of the commodity before the use-value of the money is realized, or before the commodity is handed over. This happens, for instance, in the well-known form of advance-payment. Or in the form of payment used by the English government to buy opium from Indian ryots . . . In these cases, however, money functions only in the familiar form of means of purchase . . . Of course capital, too, is advanced in the form of money . . . but this aspect does not lie within the scope of simple circulation' (*Zur Kritik, etc.*, pp. 119, 120) [English edition, p. 140 and n.].

whose sale gave rise to those obligations. The quantity of money necessary to realize this sum depends in the first instance on the rapidity of circulation of the means of payment. The quantity is conditioned by two factors: first, the way in which relations between creditors and debtors interlock, as when A receives money from B, who is in debt to him, and then pays it out to his creditor C; and second, the length of time between the different days in which the obligations fall due. The chain of payments, or retarded first metamorphoses, which participate in the process, is essentially different from that intertwining of the series of metamorphoses considered earlier. The flow of the circulating medium does not merely express the connection between buyers and sellers: the connection itself arises within, and exists through, the circulation of money. The movement of the means of payment, however, expresses a social connection which was already present independently.

The fact that sales take place simultaneously and side by side limits the extent to which the rapidity of turnover can make up for the quantity of currency available. On the other hand, this fact gives a new impulse towards the economical use of the means of payment. With the concentration of payments in one place, special institutions and methods of liquidation develop spontaneously. For instance, the *virements*** in medieval Lyons. The debts due to A from B, to B from C, to C from A, and so on, have only to be brought face to face in order to cancel each other out, to a certain extent, as positive and negative amounts. There remains only a single debit balance to be settled. The greater the concentration of the payments, the less is this balance in relation to the total amount, hence the less is the mass of the means of payment in circulation.

There is a contradiction immanent in the function of money as the means of payment. When the payments balance each other, money functions only nominally, as money of account, as a measure of value. But when actual payments have to be made, money does not come onto the scene as a circulating medium, in its merely transient form of an intermediary in the social metabolism, but as the individual incarnation of social labour, the independent presence of exchange-value, the universal commodity.†

* 'Clearing-houses'.
† Marx gave a slightly different, but illuminating, formulation of this rather difficult idea in the original draft of *Zur Kritik der Politischen Ökono-*

This contradiction bursts forth in that aspect of an industrial and commercial crisis which is known as a monetary crisis.[50] Such a crisis occurs only where the ongoing chain of payments has been fully developed, along with an artificial system for settling them. Whenever there is a general disturbance of the mechanism, no matter what its cause, money suddenly and immediately changes over from its merely nominal shape, money of account, into hard cash. Profane commodities can no longer replace it. The use-value of commodities becomes valueless, and their value vanishes in the face of their own form of value. The bourgeois, drunk with prosperity and arrogantly certain of himself, has just declared that money is a purely imaginary creation. 'Commodities alone are money,' he said. But now the opposite cry resounds over the markets of the world: only money is a commodity. As the hart pants after fresh water, so pants his soul after money, the only wealth.[51] In a crisis, the antithesis between commodities and their value-form, money, is raised to the level of an absolute contradiction. Hence money's form of appearance is here also a matter of indifference. The monetary famine remains whether payments

50. [Note by Engels to the third German edition:] The monetary crisis, defined in the text as a particular phase of every general industrial and commercial crisis, must be clearly distinguished from the special sort of crisis, also called a monetary crisis, which may appear independently of the rest, and only affects industry and commerce by its backwash. The pivot of these crises is to be found in money capital, and their immediate sphere of impact is therefore banking, the stock exchange and finance.

51. 'This sudden transformation of the credit system into a monetary system adds theoretical dismay to the actually existing panic, and the agents of the circulation process are overawed by the impenetrable mystery surrounding their own relations' (Karl Marx, *Zur Kritik, etc.*, p. 126) [English edition, p. 146]. 'The poor stand still, because the rich have no money to employ them, though they have the same land and hands to provide victuals and clothes, as ever they had; . . . which is the true Riches of a Nation, and not the money' (John Bellers, *Proposals for Raising a Colledge of Industry*, London, 1696, pp. 3–4).

mie: 'In times of actual monetary crisis, a contradiction appears which is immanent in the development of money as universal means of payment. It is not required as measure; nor as coin . . .; but as exchange value become independent, as the physically available universal equivalent, as the materialization of abstract wealth, in short, entirely in the form in which it is the object of actual hoarding, as money' (*Grundrisse der Kritik der politischen Ökonomie*, Heft B. Berlin, 1953, p. 876).

have to be made in gold or in credit-money, such as bank-notes.[52]

If we now consider the total amount of money in circulation during a given period, we find that, for any given turnover rate of the medium of circulation and the means of payment, it is equal to the sum of prices to be realized, plus the sum of the payments falling due, minus the payments which balance each other out, and, finally, minus the number of circuits in which the same piece of coin serves alternately as medium of circulation and means of payment. The farmer, for example, sells his wheat for £2, and this money serves thus as the medium of circulation. On the day when the payment falls due, he uses it to pay for linen which the weaver has delivered. The same £2 now serves as the means of payment. The weaver now buys a Bible for cash. This serves again as the medium of circulation, and so on. Therefore, even when prices, speed of monetary circulation and economies in the use of the means of payment are given, the quantity of money in circulation no longer corresponds with the mass of commodities in circulation during a given period, such as a day. Money which represents commodities long since withdrawn from circulation continues to circulate. Commodities circulate, but their equivalent in money does not appear until some future date. Moreover, the debts contracted each day, and the payments falling due on the same day, are entirely incommensurable magnitudes.[53]

52. The following shows how such occasions are exploited by the 'friends of commerce': 'On one occasion (1839) an old, grasping banker (in the city) in his private room raised the lid of the desk he sat over, and displayed to a friend rolls of bank-notes, saying with intense glee there were £600,000 of them, they were held to make money tight, and would all be let out after three o'clock on the same day' (*The Theory of Exchange. The Bank Charter Act of 1844*, London, 1864, p. 81) [by H. Roy]. The *Observer*, a semi-official government organ, remarked on 24 April 1864: 'Some very curious rumours are current of the means which have been resorted to in order to create a scarcity of bank-notes . . . Questionable as it would seem, to suppose that any trick of the kind would be adopted, the report has been so universal that it really deserves mention.'

53. 'The amount of purchases or contracts entered upon during the course of any given day, will not affect the quantity of money afloat on that particular day, but, in the vast majority of cases, will resolve themselves into multifarious drafts upon the quantity of money which may be afloat at subsequent dates more or less distant . . . The bills granted or credits opened, today, need have no resemblance whatever, either in quantity, amount, or duration, to those granted or entered upon tomorrow or next day; nay, many of today's bills, and credits, when due, fall in with a mass of liabilities whose origins traverse a range of antecedent dates altogether indefinite, bills at 12, 6, 3

Credit-money springs directly out of the function of money as a means of payment, in that certificates of debts owing for already purchased commodities themselves circulate for the purpose of transferring those debts to others. On the other hand, the function of money as a means of payment undergoes expansion in proportion as the system of credit itself expands. As the means of payment money takes on its own peculiar forms of existence, in which it inhabits the sphere of large-scale commercial transactions. Gold and silver coin, on the other hand, are mostly relegated to the sphere of retail trade.[54]

When the production of commodities has attained a certain level and extent, the function of money as means of payment begins to spread out beyond the sphere of the circulation of commodities. It becomes the universal material of contracts.[55] Rent, taxes and so on are transformed from payments in kind to payments in money. The great extent to which this transformation is conditioned by the total shape of the process of production is shown for example by the twice-repeated failure of the Roman

---

months or 1 often aggregating together to swell the common liabilities of one particular day . . .' (*The Currency Theory Reviewed: A Letter to the Scotch People. By a Banker in England*, Edinburgh, 1845, pp. 29, 30 passim).

54. As an example of how little real money enters into true commercial operations, I give below a statement by one of the largest London merchant banks (Morrison, Dillon & Co.) of its yearly receipts and payments. Its transactions during the year 1856, extending in fact to many millions of pounds, are here reduced to the scale of one million.

Receipts		*Payments*	
Bankers' and merchants' bills payable after date	£533,596	Bills payable after date	£302,674
Cheques on bankers, etc., payable on demand	£357,715	Cheques on London bankers	£663,672
Country notes	£9,627	Bank of England notes	£22,743
Bank of England notes	£68,554	Gold	£9,427
Gold	£28,089	Silver and copper	£1,484
Silver and copper	£1,486		
Post Office orders	£933		
Total:	£1,000,000	Total:	£1,000,000

(*Report from the Select Committee on the Bank Acts*, July 1858, p. lxxi)

55. 'The course of trade being thus turned, from exchanging of goods for goods, or delivering and taking, to selling and paying, all the bargains . . . are now stated upon the foot of a Price in money' ([Daniel Defoe], *An Essay upon Publick Credit*, 3rd edn, London, 1710, p. 8).

Empire to levy all contributions in money. The unspeakable misery of the French agricultural population under Louis XIV, a misery so eloquently denounced by Boisguillebert, Marshall Vauban and others, was due not only to the weight of the taxes but also to the conversion of taxes in kind into taxes in money.[56] In Asia, on the other hand, the form of ground rent paid in kind, which is at the same time the main element in state taxation, is based on relations of production which reproduce themselves with the immutability of natural conditions. And this mode of payment in its turn acts to maintain the ancient form of production. It forms one of the secrets of the self-preservation of the Ottoman Empire. If the foreign trade imposed on Japan by Europe brings with it the transformation of rents in kind into money rents, then the exemplary agriculture of that country will be done for. Its narrowly based economic conditions of existence will be swept away.

In every country, certain days become established as the dates on which general settlements are made. They depend in part, leaving aside other circular movements described by reproduction, upon the natural conditions of production, which are bound up with the alternation of the seasons. They also regulate the dates for payments which have no direct connection with the circulation of commodities, such as taxes, rents and so on. The fact that the quantity of money required to make these isolated payments over the whole surface of society falls due on certain days of the year causes periodic, but entirely superficial, perturbations in the economy of the means of payment.[57] From the law of the rapidity

56. 'Money . . has become the executioner of everything.' Finance is 'the alembic in which a frightful quantity of goods and commodities has been distilled in order to extract that unholy essence.' 'Money declares war on the whole of humanity' (Boisguillebert, *Dissertation sur la nature des richesses, de l'argent et des tributs*, ed. Daire, *Économistes financiers*, Paris, 1843, Vol. 1, pp. 413, 419, 417, 418).

57. 'On Whitsuntide, 1824,' said Mr Craig before the Commons Committee of 1826, 'there was such an immense demand for notes upon the banks of Edinburgh, that by 11 o'clock we had not a note left in our custody. We sent round to all the different banks to borrow, but could not get them, and many of the transactions were adjusted by slips of paper only; yet by three o'clock the whole of the notes were returned into the banks from which they had issued! It was a mere transfer from hand to hand.' Although the average effective circulation of bank-notes in Scotland is less than £3m., yet on certain settlement days in the year every single note in the possession of the bankers, amounting altogether to about £7m., is called into activity. On these occasions the notes have a single and specific function to perform, and as

of circulation of the means of payment, it follows that the quantity of the means of payment required for all periodic payments, whatever their source, is in direct* proportion to the length of the periods.[58]

The development of money as a means of payment makes it necessary to accumulate it in preparation for the days when the sums which are owing fall due. While hoarding, considered as an independent form of self-enrichment, vanishes with the advance of bourgeois society [*die bürgerliche Gesellschaft*], it grows at the same time in the form of the accumulation of a reserve fund of the means of payment.

(c) World Money

When money leaves the domestic sphere of circulation it loses the local functions it has acquired there, as the standard of prices, coin, and small change, and as a symbol of value, and falls back into its original form as precious metal in the shape of bullion. In world trade, commodities develop their value universally. Their independent value-form thus confronts them here too as world money. It is in the world market that money first functions to its

---

soon as they have performed it they flow back into the various banks from which they issued. (See John Fullarton, *Regulation of Currencies*, London, 1845, p. 86, note.) In explanation it should be added that in Scotland, at the time of Fullarton's work, notes and not cheques were used to withdraw deposits.

58. To the question 'if there were occasion to raise 40 millions p.a., whether the same 6 millions (gold) . . . would suffice for such revolutions and circulations thereof, as trade requires,' Petty replies in his usual masterly manner, 'I answer yes: for the expense being 40 millions, if the revolutions were in such short circles, viz., weekly, as happens among poor artisans and labourers, who receive and pay every Saturday, then $\frac{40}{52}$ parts of 1 million of money would answer these ends; but if the circles be quarterly, according to our custom of paying rent, and gathering taxes, then 10 million were requisite. Wherefore, supposing payments in general to be of a mixed circle between one week and 13, then add 10 millions to $\frac{40}{52}$, the half of which will be $5\frac{1}{2}$, so as if we have $5\frac{1}{2}$ millions we have enough' (William Petty, *Political Anatomy of Ireland, 1672*, London edition, 1691, pp. 13, 14) [what Marx cites here is Petty's essay *Verbum Sapienti*, which appeared as a supplement to the *Political Anatomy of Ireland*].

---

*All previous editions have the word 'inverse' here. Yet it is quite apparent from the discussion in note 58 that Marx meant to write 'direct'. In short, the longer the *period*, the more money is needed, and *vice versa*.

full extent as the commodity whose natural form is also the directly social form of realization of human labour in the abstract. Its mode of existence becomes adequate to its concept.

Within the sphere of domestic circulation, there can only be one commodity which by serving as a measure of value becomes money. On the world market a double standard prevails, both gold and silver.[59]

59. Hence the absurdity of all legislation laying down that the banks of a country should form reserves only of the particular precious metal circulating within the country as money. The 'pleasant difficulties' created in this way by the Bank of England for itself are a well-known example. On the subject of the major historical epochs in the relative value of gold and silver, see Karl Marx, op. cit., pp. 136 ff. [English edition, pp. 155 ff.]. Sir Robert Peel, by his Bank Act of 1844, sought to tide over the difficulty by allowing the Bank of England to issue notes against silver bullion, on condition that the reserve of silver should never exceed more than one fourth of the reserve of gold. For that purpose, the value of silver is estimated according to its market price (in gold) on the London market.

[The following was added by Engels to the fourth German edition:] We find ourselves once more in a period of serious change in the relative values of gold and silver. About twenty-five years ago the ratio expressing the relative value of gold and silver was $15\frac{1}{2}:1$; now it is approximately $22:1$, and silver is still constantly falling as against gold. This is essentially the result of a revolution in the mode of production of both metals. Formerly gold was obtained almost exclusively by washing it out from gold-bearing alluvial deposits, products of the weathering of auriferous rocks. Now this method has become inadequate and has been forced into the background by the processing of quartz lodes themselves, a mode of extraction which formerly was only of secondary importance, although well known to the ancients (Diodorus, III, 12–14). Moreover, not only were huge new silver deposits discovered in North America, in the western part of the Rocky Mountains, but these and the Mexican silver mines were really opened up by the laying of railways, which made possible the shipment of modern machinery and fuel and in consequence the mining of silver on a very large scale at low cost. However, there is a great difference in the way the two metals occur in the quartz lodes. The gold is mostly native, but disseminated throughout the quartz in minute quantities. The whole mass of the vein must therefore be crushed and the gold either washed out or extracted by means of mercury. Often 1,000,000 grammes of quartz barely yield 1–3 grammes of gold, and very seldom do they yield 30–60 grammes. Silver is seldom found native: however, it occurs in special quartz that is separated from the lode with comparative ease and contains mostly 40–90 per cent silver, and is also contained, in smaller quantities, in copper, lead and other ores which in themselves are worthwhile working. From this alone it is apparent that the labour expended on the production of gold is tending to increase, while that expended on silver production has decidedly decreased, which quite naturally explains the drop in the value of the latter. This fall in value would express itself in a still greater fall in price if the price of silver were not pegged even today by artificial means. But America's rich silver

World money serves as the universal means of payment, as the universal means of purchase, and as the absolute social materialization of wealth as such (universal wealth).* Its predominant function is as means of payment in the settling of international balances. Hence the slogan of the Mercantile System: balance of trade.⁶⁰ Gold and silver serve essentially as international means of purchase when the customary equilibrium in the interchange of products between different nations is suddenly disturbed. And,

---

deposits have so far barely been tapped, and thus the prospects are that the value of this metal will keep on dropping for rather a long time to come. A still greater contributing factor here is the relative decrease in the need for silver for articles of general use and for luxuries, that is its replacement by plated goods, aluminium, etc. One may thus gauge the utopianism of the bimetallist idea that compulsory international quotation will raise silver again to the old value ratio of $1:15\frac{1}{2}$. It is more likely that silver will forfeit its money function more and more in the world market.

60. The opponents of the Mercantile System, a system which considered the settlement of surplus trade balances in gold and silver as the aim of international trade, were for their part entirely mistaken as to the function of world money. I have thoroughly demonstrated elsewhere, taking Ricardo as an example, the way in which a false conception of the laws which regulate the quantity of the circulating medium is reflected in a false conception of the international movement of the precious metals (op. cit., pp. 150 ff.) [English edition, p. 174]. His erroneous dogma: 'An unfavourable balance of trade never arises but from a redundant currency . . . The exportation of the coin is caused by its cheapness, and is not the effect, but the cause of an unfavourable balance,'* already occurs in Barbon: 'The balance of Trade, if there be one, is not the cause of sending away the money out of a nation; but that proceeds from the difference of the value of bullion in every country' (N. Barbon, op. cit., pp. 59, 60). MacCulloch, in *The Literature of Political Economy: A Classified Catalogue*, London, 1845, praises Barbon for this anticipation, but very wisely avoids even mentioning the naïve forms in which the absurd presuppositions of the 'currency principle'† appear in Barbon's work. The uncritical and even dishonest nature of MacCulloch's catalogue reaches its summit in the sections devoted to the history of the theory of money, where he is flattering Lord Overstone (ex-banker Loyd), whom he describes as *'facile princeps argentariorum'* [the recognized king of the money merchants].‡

*David Ricardo, *The High Price of Bullion, a Proof of the Depreciation of Bank Notes*, 4th edn, London, 1811, pp. 11, 12, 14.

†'Currency principle': the principle, implemented in the Bank Act of 1844, that the amount of currency in circulation should always correspond to the quantity of gold in the country. See Karl Marx, op. cit., English edition, p. 185.

‡Samuel Jones Loyd (1796–1883). Rich and influential banker, witness before two Parliamentary committees on banking (those of 1833 and 1840). Main advocate of the 'currency principle'. Created Baron Overstone in 1860.

---

*The words in parentheses were added in English by Marx.

lastly, world money serves as the universally recognized social materialization of wealth, whenever it is not a matter of buying or paying, but of transferring wealth from one country to another, and whenever its transfer in the form of commodities is ruled out, either by the conjuncture of the market, or by the purpose of the transfer itself.[61]

Just as every country needs a reserve fund for its internal circulation, so too it requires one for circulation in the world market. The functions of hoards, therefore, arise in part out of the function of money as medium of payment and circulation internally, and in part out of its function as a world currency.[62] In this latter role it is always the genuine money-commodity, gold and silver in their physical shape, which is required. For that reason Sir James Steuart expressly characterizes gold and silver as 'money of the world'* in order to distinguish them from their merely local representatives.

The stream of gold and silver has a twofold motion. On the one hand, it spreads out from its sources all over the world, and is absorbed to various extents into the different national spheres of circulation, where it enters into the various channels of internal circulation. There it replaces abraded gold and silver coins, supplies the material for articles of luxury, and petrifies into hoards.[63]

61. For instance, in the case of subsidies, money loans for carrying on wars or for enabling banks to resume cash payments, etc., value may be required precisely in the money-form.

62. 'I would desire, indeed, no more convincing evidence of the competency of the machinery of the hoards in specie-paying countries to perform every necessary office of international adjustment, without any sensible aid from the general circulation, than the facility with which France, when but just recovering from the shock of a destructive foreign invasion, completed within the space of 27 months the payment of her forced contribution of nearly 20 millions to the allied powers, and a considerable proportion of the sum in specie, without any perceptible contraction or derangement of her domestic currency, or even any alarming fluctuation of her exchanges' (Fullarton, op. cit., p. 141). [Added by Engels to the fourth German edition:] We have a still more striking example in the facility with which the same France was able in 1871-3 to pay off within 30 months a forced contribution more than ten times as great, a considerable part of it likewise in specie.

63. 'Money is shared among the nations in accordance with their need for it . . . as it is always attracted by the products' (Le Trosne, op. cit., p. 916). 'The mines which are continually giving gold and silver, do give sufficient to supply such a needful balance to every nation' (J. Vanderlint, op. cit., p. 40).

*Sir James Steuart, *An Inquiry into the Principles of Political Economy*, Dublin, 1770, Vol. 2, p. 370. Cf. *Zur Kritik etc.*, English translation, p. 167.

This first movement is transmitted through the medium of the direct exchange of the labour of individual countries which has been realized in commodities for the labour realized in the precious metals by the gold- and silver-producing countries. On the other hand, gold and silver continually flow backwards and forwards between the different national spheres of circulation, and this movement follows the unceasing fluctuations of the rate of exchange.[64]

Countries with developed bourgeois production limit the hoards concentrated in the strong rooms of the banks to the minimum required for the performance of their specific functions.[65] Whenever these hoards are strikingly above their average level, this is, with some exceptions, an indication of stagnation in the circulation of commodities, i.e. of an interruption in the flow of their metamorphoses.[66]

64. 'Exchanges rise and fall every week, and at some particular times in the year run high against a nation, and at other times run as high on the contrary' (N. Barbon, op. cit., p. 39).

65. These different functions can come dangerously into conflict whenever gold and silver have also to serve as a fund for the conversion of bank notes.

66. 'What money is more than of absolute necessity for a Home Trade, is dead stock . . . and brings no profit to that country it's kept in, but as it is transported in trade, as well as imported' (John Bellers, *Essays, etc.*, p. 13). 'What if we have too much coin? We may melt down the heaviest and turn it into the splendour of plate, vessels or utensils of gold or silver; or send it out as a commodity, where the same is wanted or desired; or let it out at interest, where interest is high' (W. Petty, *Quantulumcunque*, p. 39). 'Money is but the fat of the Body Politick, whereof too much doth as often hinder its agility, as too little makes it sick . . . as fat lubricates the motion of the muscles, feeds in want of victuals, fills up the uneven cavities, and beautifies the body; so doth money in the state quicken its action, feeds from abroad in time of dearth at home; evens accounts . . . and beautifies the whole; altho' more especially the particular persons that have it in plenty' (W. Petty, *Political Anatomy of Ireland*, pp. 14, 15) [in fact, this is again the supplement, *Verbum Sapienti*].

Part Two

The Transformation
of Money into Capital

Chapter 4: The General Formula for Capital

The circulation of commodities is the starting-point of capital. The production of commodities and their circulation in its developed form, namely trade, form the historic presuppositions under which capital arises. World trade and the world market date from the sixteenth century, and from then on the modern history of capital starts to unfold.

If we disregard the material content of the circulation of commodities, i.e. the exchange of the various use-values, and consider only the economic forms brought into being by this process, we find that its ultimate product is money. This ultimate product of commodity circulation is the first form of appearance of capital.

Historically speaking, capital invariably first confronts landed property in the form of money; in the form of monetary wealth, merchants' capital and usurers' capital.[1] However, we do not need to look back at the history of capital's origins in order to recognize that money is its first form of appearance. Every day the same story is played out before our eyes. Even up to the present day, all new capital, in the first instance, steps onto the stage – i.e. the market, whether it is the commodity-market, the labour-market, or the money-market – in the shape of money, money which has to be transformed into capital by definite processes.

The first distinction between money as money and money as capital is nothing more than a difference in their form of circulation. The direct form of the circulation of commodities is C–M–C, the transformation of commodities into money and the re-conversion of money into commodities: selling in order to buy.

1. The antagonism between the power of landed property, based on personal relations of domination and servitude, and the power of money, which is impersonal, is clearly expressed by the two French proverbs, 'Nulle terre sans seigneur', and 'L'argent n'a pas de maître'.*
* 'No land without its lord' and 'Money has no master'.

But alongside this form we find another form, which is quite distinct from the first: M–C–M, the transformation of money into commodities, and the re-conversion of commodities into money: buying in order to sell. Money which describes the latter course in its movement is transformed into capital, becomes capital, and, from the point of view of its function, already is capital.

Let us examine the circular movement M–C–M a little more closely. Just as in the case of simple circulation, it passes through two antithetical phases. In the first phase, M–C (the purchase), the money is changed into a commodity. In the second phase, C–M (the sale), the commodity is changed back again into money. These two phases, taken together in their unity, constitute the total movement which exchanges money for a commodity, and the same commodity for money, which buys a commodity in order to sell it, or, if one neglects the formal distinction between buying and selling, buys a commodity with money and then buys money with a commodity.[2] The result, in which the whole process vanishes, is the exchange of money for money, M–M. If I purchase 2,000 lb. of cotton for £100, and resell the 2,000 lb. of cotton for £110, I have in fact exchanged £100 for £110, money for money.

Now it is evident that the circulatory process M–C–M would be absurd and empty if the intention were, by using this roundabout route, to exchange two equal sums of money, £100 for £100. The miser's plan would be far simpler and surer: he holds on to his £100 instead of exposing it to the dangers of circulation. And yet, whether the merchant who has paid £100 for his cotton sells it for £110, or lets it go for £100, or even £50, his money has at all events described a characteristic and original path, quite different in kind from the path of simple circulation, as for instance in the case of the peasant who sells corn, and with the money thus set free buys clothes. First, then, we have to characterize the formal distinctions between the two circular paths M–C–M and C–M–C. This will simultaneously provide us with the difference in content which lies behind these formal distinctions.

Let us first see what the two forms have in common.

Both paths can be divided into the same two antithetical phases, C–M, sale, and M–C, purchase. In each phase the same material elements confront each other, namely a commodity and money,

2. 'With money one buys commodities, and with commodities one buys money' (Mercier de la Rivière, *L'Ordre naturel et essentiel des sociétés politiques*, p. 543).

and the same economic *dramatis personae*, a buyer and a seller. Each circular path is the unity of the same two antithetical phases, and in each case this unity is mediated through the emergence of three participants in a contract, of whom one only sells, another only buys and the third both buys and sells.

What however first and foremost distinguishes the two paths C–M–C and M–C–M from each other is the inverted order of succession of the two opposed phases of circulation. The simple circulation of commodities begins with a sale and ends with a purchase, while the circulation of money as capital begins with a purchase and ends with a sale. In the one case both the starting-point and the terminating-point of the movement are commodities, in the other they are money. The whole process is mediated in the first form by money, and in the second, inversely, by a commodity.

In the circulation C–M–C, the money is in the end converted into a commodity which serves as a use-value; it has therefore been spent once and for all. In the inverted form M–C–M, on the contrary, the buyer lays out money in order that, as a seller, he may recover money. By the purchase of his commodity he throws money into circulation, in order to withdraw it again by the sale of the same commodity. He releases the money, but only with the cunning intention of getting it back again. The money therefore is not spent, it is merely advanced.[3]

In the form C–M–C, the same piece of money is displaced twice. The seller gets it from the buyer and pays it away to another seller. The whole process begins when money is received in return for commodities, and comes to an end when money is given up in return for commodities. In the form M–C–M this process is inverted. Here it is not the piece of money which is displaced twice, but the commodity. The buyer takes it from the hands of the seller and passes it into the hands of another buyer. Whilst in the simple circulation of commodities the twofold displacement of the same piece of money effects its definitive transfer from one hand into another, here the twofold displacement of the same commodity causes the money to flow back to its initial point of departure.

3. 'When a thing is bought in order to be sold again, the sum employed is called money advanced; when it is bought not to be sold, it may be said to be expended' (James Steuart, *Works, etc.*, edited by General Sir James Steuart, his son, London, 1805, Vol. 1, p. 274).

This reflux of money to its starting-point does not depend on the commodity's being sold for more than was paid for it. That only has a bearing on the amount of money which flows back. The phenomenon of reflux itself takes place as soon as the purchased commodity is resold, i.e. as soon as the cycle M–C–M has been completed. We have here, therefore, a palpable difference between the circulation of money as capital, and its circulation as mere money.

The cycle C–M–C reaches its conclusion when the money brought in by the sale of one commodity is withdrawn again by the purchase of another. If there follows a reflux of money to its starting-point, this can happen only through a renewal or repetition of the whole course of the movement. If I sell a quarter of corn for £3, and with this £3 buy clothes, the money, so far as I am concerned, is irreversibly spent. I have nothing more to do with it. It belongs to the clothes merchant. If I now sell a second quarter of corn, money indeed flows back to me, not however as a result of the first transaction, but of its repetition. The money again leaves me as soon as I complete this second transaction by a fresh purchase. In the cycle C–M–C, therefore, the expenditure of money has nothing to do with its reflux. In M–C–M on the other hand the reflux of the money is conditioned by the very manner in which it is expended. Without this reflux, the operation fails, or the process is interrupted and incomplete, owing to the absence of its complementary and final phase, the sale.

The path C–M–C proceeds from the extreme constituted by one commodity, and ends with the extreme constituted by another, which falls out of circulation and into consumption. Consumption, the satisfaction of needs, in short use-value, is therefore its final goal. The path M–C–M, however, proceeds from the extreme of money and finally returns to that same extreme. Its driving and motivating force, its determining purpose, is therefore exchange-value.

In the simple circulation of commodities the two extremes have the same economic form. They are both commodities, and commodities of equal value. But they are also qualitatively different use-values, as for example corn and clothes. The exchange of products, the interchange carried out between the different materials in which social labour is embodied, forms here the content of the movement. It is otherwise in the cycle M–C–M. At first sight this appears to lack any content, because it is tautological. Both extremes have the same economic form. They are both money, and therefore are not qualitatively different use-values, for money is precisely the converted form of commodities, in which their particular use-values have been extinguished. To exchange £100 for cotton, and then to exchange this same cotton again for £100, is merely a roundabout way of exchanging money for money, the same for the same, and appears to be an operation as purposeless as it is absurd.[4] One sum of money is distinguishable from another only by its amount. The process M–C–M does not therefore owe its content to any qualitative difference between its extremes, for they are both money, but solely to quantitative changes. More money is finally withdrawn from circulation than was thrown into it at the beginning. The cotton originally bought for £100 is for example re-sold at £100+£10, i.e. £110. The complete form of this process is therefore M–C–M′, where M′ = M + Δ M, i.e. the original sum advanced plus an increment. This increment or excess over the original value I call 'surplus-value'.*

4. 'One does not exchange money for money,' exclaims Mercier de la Rivière to the Mercantilists (op. cit., p. 486). In a work which professes to deal with 'trade' and 'speculation' there occurs the following: 'All trade consists in the exchange of things of different kinds; and the advantage' (to the merchant?) 'arises out of this difference. To exchange a pound of bread against a pound of bread . . . would be attended with no advantage; . . . Hence trade is advantageously contrasted with gambling, which consists in a mere exchange of money for money' (Th. Corbet, *An Inquiry into the Causes and Modes of the Wealth of Individuals; or the Principles of Trade and Speculation Explained*, London, 1841, p. 5). Although Corbet does not see that M–M, the exchange of money for money, is the characteristic form of circulation, not only of merchants' capital, but of all capital, yet at least he acknowledges that this form is common to gambling and to one species of trade, namely speculation. Then, however, MacCulloch comes on the scene, and asserts that to buy in order to sell is to speculate, and thus the distinction between speculation and trade vanishes. 'Every transaction in which an individual buys produce in order to sell it again is in fact a speculation' (MacCulloch, *A Dictionary, Practical etc., of Commerce*, London, 1847, p. 1009). With much more naïveté, Pinto, the Pindar of the Amsterdam Stock Exchange,* remarks: 'Trade is a game' (this phrase is borrowed from Locke) 'and nothing can be won from beggars. If one won everything from everybody for long, it would be necessary to give back voluntarily the greater part of the profit in order to begin the game again' (Pinto, *Traité de la circulation et du crédit*, Amsterdam, 1771, p. 231).

*Pindar (522–442 B.C.) composed odes in praise of Olympic victors; Pinto (A.D. 1715–87), rich Amsterdam speculator and merchant, wrote books in praise of his country's financial system.

---

*In both German (*Mehrwert*) and English in the original.

The value originally advanced, therefore, not only remains intact while in circulation, but increases its magnitude, adds to itself a surplus-value, or is valorized [*verwertet sich*].* And this movement converts it into capital.

Of course, it is also possible that in C–M–C the two extremes C and C, say corn and clothes, may represent quantitatively different magnitudes of value. The peasant may sell his corn above its value, or may buy the clothes at less than their value. He may, on the other hand, be cheated by the clothes merchant. Yet, for this particular form of circulation, such differences in value are purely accidental. The fact that the corn and the clothes are equivalents does not deprive the process of all sense and meaning, as it does in M–C–M. The equivalence of their values is rather a necessary condition of its normal course.

The repetition or renewal of the act of selling in order to buy finds its measure and its goal (as does the process itself) in a final purpose which lies outside it, namely consumption, the satisfaction of definite needs. But in buying in order to sell, on the contrary, the end and the beginning are the same, money or exchange-value and this very fact makes the movement an endless one. Certainly M becomes M + Δ M, £100 becomes £110. But, considered qualitatively, £100 is the same as £110, namely money; while, from the quantitative point of view, £110 is, like £100, a sum of definite and limited value. If the £110 is now spent as money, it ceases to play its part. It is no longer capital. Withdrawn from circulation, it is petrified into a hoard, and it could remain in that position until the Last Judgement without a single farthing accruing to it. If, then, we are concerned with the valorization [*Verwertung*] of value, the value of the £110 has the same need for valorization as the value of the £100, for they are both limited expressions of exchange-value, and therefore both have the same vocation, to approach, by quantitative increase, as near as possible to absolute wealth. Momentarily, indeed, the value originally advanced, the £100, is distinguishable from the surplus-value of £10, added to it during circulation; but the distinction vanishes immediately. At the end of the process, we do not receive on one hand the original £100, and on the other the surplus-value

* Along with the concept of surplus-value, the concept of *Verwertung* is introduced here for the first time. Since there is no extant English word which adequately conveys Marx's meaning, we have adopted throughout the word 'valorization'.

of £10. What emerges is rather a value of £110, which is in exactly the same form, appropriate for commencing the valorization process, as the original £100. At the end of the movement, money emerges once again as its starting-point.[5] Therefore the final result of each separate cycle, in which a purchase and consequent sale are completed, forms of itself the starting-point for a new cycle. The simple circulation of commodities – selling in order to buy – is a means to a final goal which lies outside circulation, namely the appropriation of use-values, the satisfaction of needs. As against this, the circulation of money as capital is an end in itself, for the valorization of value takes place only within this constantly renewed movement. The movement of capital is therefore limitless.[6]

5. 'Capital is divided . . . into the original capital and profit – the incre-ment of capital . . . although in practice profit is immediately lumped to-gether with capital and set into motion with it' (F. Engels, *Umrisse zu einer Kritik der Nationalökonomie*, in *Deutsch-Französische Jahrbücher*, edited by Arnold Ruge and Karl Marx, Paris, 1844, p. 99) [English translation, p. 430].
6. Aristotle contrasts economics with 'chrematistics'. He starts with eco-nomics. So far as it is the art of acquisition, it is limited to procuring the articles necessary to existence and useful either to a household or the state. 'True wealth (ὁ ἀληθινὸς πλοῦτος) consists of such use-values; for the amount of property which is needed for a good life is not unlimited . . . There is, how-ever, a second mode of acquiring things, to which we may by preference and with correctness give the name of chrematistics, and in this case there appear to be no limits to riches and property. Trade (ἡ καπηλική is literally retail trade, and Aristotle chooses this form because use-values predominate in it) does not in its nature belong to chrematistics, for here the exchange only has reference to what is necessary for (the buyer or the seller) themselves.' Therefore, as he goes on to show, the original form of trade was barter, but with the extension of the latter there arose the necessity for money. With the discovery of money, barter of necessity developed into καπηλική, into trading in commodities, and this again, in contradiction with its original tendency, grew into chrematistics, the art of making money. Now chrematistics can be distinguished from eco-nomics in that 'for chrematistics, circulation is the source of riches (ποιητικὴ χρημάτων . . . διὰ χρημάτων μεταβολῆς). And it appears to revolve around money, for money is the beginning and the end of this kind of exchange (τὸ γὰρ νόμισμα στοιχεῖον καὶ πέρας τῆς ἀλλαγῆς ἐστιν). Therefore also riches, such as chrematistics strives for, are unlimited. Just as every art which is not a means to an end, but an end in itself, has no limit to its aims, because it seeks constantly to approach nearer and nearer to that end, while those arts which pursue means to an end are not boundless, since the goal itself imposes a limit on them, so with chrematistics there are no bounds to its aims, these aims being absolute wealth. Economics, unlike chrematistics, has a limit . . . for the object of the former is something different from money, of the latter the augmentation of money . . . By confusing these two forms, which overlap each

As the conscious bearer [*Träger*] of this movement, the possessor
of money becomes a capitalist. His person, or rather his pocket,
is the point from which the money starts, and to which it returns.
The objective content of the circulation we have been discussing –
the valorization of value – is his subjective purpose, and it is only
in so far as the appropriation of ever more wealth in the abstract
is the sole driving force behind his operations that he functions as
a capitalist, i.e. as capital personified and endowed with consciousness and a will. Use-values must therefore never be treated as the
immediate aim of the capitalist;[7] nor must the profit on any single
transaction. His aim is rather the unceasing movement of profit-
making.[8] This boundless drive for enrichment, this passionate
chase after value,[9] is common to the capitalist and the miser; but
while the miser is merely a capitalist gone mad, the capitalist is
a rational miser. The ceaseless augmentation of value, which the
miser seeks to attain by saving[10] his money from circulation, is

---

other, some people have been led to look upon the preservation and increase of
money *ad infinitum* as the final goal of economics' (Aristotle, *De Republica*, ed.
Bekker, lib. I, c. 8, 9, passim).*
   7. 'Commodities' (here used in the sense of use-values) 'are not the terminating object of the trading capitalist, money is his terminating object' (T.
Chalmers, *On Political Economy etc.*, 2nd edn, Glasgow, 1832, pp. 165–6).
   8. 'Though the merchant does not count the profit he has just made as
nothing, he nevertheless always has his eye on his future profit' (A. Genovesi,
Lezioni di economia civile (1765), printed in Custodi's edition of the Italian
economists, *Parte moderna*, Vol. 8, p. 139).
   9. 'The inextinguishable passion for gain, the *auri sacra fames*,† will always
lead capitalists' (MacCulloch, *The Principles of Political Economy*, London,
1830, p. 179). This view, of course, does not prevent the same MacCulloch
and his associates, when they are in theoretical difficulties, as for example in the
treatment of over-production, from transforming the same capitalist into a
good citizen, whose sole concern is for use-values, and who even develops an
insatiable hunger for boots, hats, eggs, calico and other extremely common
kinds of use-value.
   10. Σώζειν [to save] is a characteristic Greek expression for hoarding. So in
English the word 'to save' means both *retten* [to rescue] and *sparen* [to save].
   *English edition: *Works of Aristotle*, Vol. X, Oxford, 1921, 'Politica', trs.
B. Jowett, paras. 1256 and 1257. Much of this differs significantly from Marx's
translation into German, as a result of his practice of quoting so as to bring
out the meaning relevant to his argument. Thus 'gaining wealth through exchange' turns in Marx's hands into 'circulation', 'the art of household management' into 'economics', and 'the art of getting wealth' into 'chrematistics'.
   † 'Accursed hunger for gold'.

achieved by the more acute capitalist by means of throwing his money again and again into circulation.[11]

The independent form, i.e. the monetary form, which the value of commodities assumes in simple circulation, does nothing but mediate the exchange of commodities, and it vanishes in the final result of the movement. On the other hand, in the circulation M–C–M both the money and the commodity function only as different modes of existence of value itself, the money as its general mode of existence, the commodity as its particular or, so to speak, disguised mode.[12] It is constantly changing from one form into the other, without becoming lost in this movement; it thus becomes transformed into an automatic subject. If we pin down the specific forms of appearance assumed in turn by self-valorizing value in the course of its life, we reach the following elucidation: capital is money, capital is commodities.[13] In truth, however, value is here the subject* of a process in which, while constantly assuming the form in turn of money and commodities, it changes its own magnitude, throws off surplus-value from itself considered as original value, and thus valorizes itself independently. For the movement in the course of which it adds surplus-value is its own movement, its valorization is therefore self-valorization [*Selbstverwertung*]. By virtue of being value, it has acquired the occult ability to add value to itself. It brings forth living offspring, or at least lays golden eggs.

As the dominant subject [*übergreifendes Subjekt*] of this process, in which it alternately assumes and loses the form of money and the form of commodities, but preserves and expands itself through all these changes, value requires above all an independent form by means of which its identity with itself may be asserted. Only in the shape of money does it possess this form. Money therefore forms the starting-point and the conclusion of every valorization process.

11. 'Things possess an infinite quality when moving in a circle which they lack when advancing in a straight line' (Galiani, op. cit., p. 156).

12. 'It is not the material which forms capital, but the value of that material' (J. B. Say, *Traité d'économie politique*, 3rd edn, Paris, 1817, Vol. 2, p. 429).

13. 'Currency (!) employed in producing articles . . . is capital' (Macleod, *The Theory and Practice of Banking*, London, 1855, Vol. 1, Ch. 1, p. 55). 'Capital is commodities' (James Mill, *Elements of Political Economy*, London, 1821, p. 74).

---

*i.e. the independently acting agent.

It was £100, and now it is £110, etc. But the money itself is only one of the two forms of value. Unless it takes the form of some commodity, it does not become capital. There is here no antagonism, as in the case of hoarding, between the money and commodities. The capitalist knows that all commodities, however tattered they may look, or however badly they may smell, are in faith and in truth money, are by nature circumcised Jews, and, what is more, a wonderful means for making still more money out of money.

In simple circulation, the value of commodities attained at the most a form independent of their use-values, i.e. the form of money. But now, in the circulation M–C–M, value suddenly presents itself as a self-moving substance which passes through a process of its own, and for which commodities and money are both mere forms. But there is more to come: instead of simply representing the relations of commodities, it now enters into a private relationship with itself, as it were. It differentiates itself as original value from itself as surplus-value, just as God the Father differentiates himself from himself as God the Son, although both are of the same age and form, in fact one single person; for only by the surplus-value of £10 does the £100 originally advanced become capital, and as soon as this has happened, as soon as the son has been created and, through the son, the father, their difference vanishes again, and both become one, £110.

Value therefore now becomes value in process, money in process, and, as such, capital. It comes out of circulation, enters into it again, preserves and multiplies itself within circulation, emerges from it with an increased size, and starts the same cycle again and again.[14] M–M, 'money which begets money', such is the description of capital given by its first interpreters, the Mercantilists.

Buying in order to sell, or, more accurately, buying in order to sell dearer, M–C–M, seems admittedly to be a form peculiar to one kind of capital alone, merchants' capital. But industrial capital too is money which has been changed into commodities, and reconverted into more money by the sale of these commodities. Events which take place outside the sphere of circulation, in the interval between buying and selling, do not affect the form of this movement. Lastly, in the case of interest-bearing capital, the cir-

14. 'Capital ... permanent self-multiplying value' (Sismondi, *Nouveaux Principes d'économie politique*, Vol. 1, p. 89) [cited in German in the original, and slightly altered].

culation M–C–M' presents itself in abridged form, in its final result and without any intermediate stage, in a concise style, so to speak, as M–M', i.e. money which is worth more money, value which is greater than itself.

M–C–M' is in fact therefore the general formula for capital, in the form in which it appears directly in the sphere of circulation.

Chapter 5: Contradictions in the General Formula

The form of circulation within which money is transformed into capital contradicts all the previously developed laws bearing on the nature of commodities, value, money and even circulation itself. What distinguishes this form from that of the simple circulation of commodities is the inverted order of succession of the two antithetical processes, sale and purchase. How can this purely formal distinction change the nature of these processes, as if by magic?

But that is not all. This inversion has no existence for two of the three persons who transact business together. As a capitalist, I buy commodities from A and sell them again to B, but as a simple owner of commodities I sell them to B and then purchase further commodities from A. For A and B this distinction does not exist. They step forth only as buyers or sellers of commodities. I myself confront them each time as a mere owner of either money or commodities, as a buyer or a seller, and what is more, in both sets of transactions I confront A only as a buyer and B only as a seller. I confront the one only as money, the other only as commodities, but neither or them as capital or a capitalist, or a representative of anything more than money or commodities, or of anything which might produce any effect beyond that produced by money or commodities. For me the purchase from A and the sale to B are part of a series. But the connection between these two acts exists for me alone. A does not trouble himself about my transaction with B, nor does B about my business with A. And if I offered to explain to them the meritorious nature of my action in inverting the order of succession, they would probably point out to me that I was mistaken as to that order, and that the whole transaction, instead of beginning with a purchase and ending with a sale, began, on the contrary, with a sale and was concluded with a purchase. In truth, my first act, the purchase, was from the standpoint of A a sale, and my second act, the sale, was from the standpoint of B a purchase. Not content with that, A and B would declare that the whole series was superfluous and nothing but hocus-pocus; that for the future A would buy direct from B, and B sell direct to A. With this the whole transaction would shrink down to a single, one-sided phase of the ordinary circulation of commodities, a mere sale from A's point of view, and from B's, a mere purchase. Thus the inversion of the order of succession does not take us outside the sphere of the simple circulation of commodities, and we must rather look to see whether this simple circulation, by its nature, might permit the valorization of the values entering into it and consequently the formation of surplus-value.

Let us take the process of circulation in a form in which it presents itself to us as the exchange of commodities pure and simple. This is always the case when two owners of commodities buy from each other, and on the date of settlement the amounts they owe to each other balance out equally. Money serves here as money of account, and expresses the values of the commodities in their prices, but does not itself confront the commodities in a material shape. In so far as use-values are concerned, it is clear that both parties may gain. Both of them part with commodities which are of no service to them as use-values, and receive others they need to use. And this may not be the only advantage gained. A, who sells wine and buys corn, possibly produces more wine in the same labour-time than B, the corn-farmer, could produce, and B, on the other hand, may produce more corn than A, the wine-grower, could produce. A may therefore get more corn for the same exchange-value, and B more wine, than each would respectively get without any exchange if they had to produce their own corn and wine. With reference, therefore, to use-value, it can indeed be said that 'exchange is a transaction by which both sides gain'.[1] It is otherwise with exchange-value.

'A man who has plenty of wine and no corn treats with a man who has plenty of corn and no wine; an exchange takes place between them of corn to the value of 50, for wine of the same value. This act produces no increase of exchange-value either for

---

1. 'Exchange is an admirable transaction by which both sides gain – always (!)' (Destutt de Tracy, *Traité de la volonté et de ses effets*, Paris, 1826, p. 68). This work appeared afterwards as *Traité d'économie politique*. [In 1823; the first edition of the *Traité de la volonté* was published in 1815.]

the one or the other; for each of them already possessed, before the exchange, a value equal to that which he acquired by means of that operation.'[2]

This situation is not altered by placing money, as a medium of circulation, between the commodities, and making the sale and the purchase into two physically distinct acts.[3] The value of a commodity is expressed in its price before it enters into circulation, and it is therefore a pre-condition of circulation, not its result.[4]

If we consider this in the abstract, i.e. disregarding circumstances which do not flow from the immanent laws of simple commodity circulation, all that happens in exchange (if we leave aside the replacing of one use-value by another) is a metamorphosis, a mere change in the form of the commodity. The same value, i.e. the same quantity of objectified social labour, remains throughout in the hands of the same commodity-owner, first in the shape of his own commodity, then in the shape of the money into which the commodity has been transformed, and finally in the shape of the commodity into which this money has been re-converted. This change of form does not imply any change in the magnitude of the value. But the change which the value of the commodity undergoes in this process is limited to a change in its money-form. This form exists first as the price of the commodity offered for sale, then as an actual sum of money, which was, however, already expressed in the price, and lastly as the price of an equivalent commodity. This change of form no more implies, taken alone, a change in the quantity of value than does the changing of a £5 note into sovereigns, half-sovereigns and shillings. In so far, therefore, as the circulation of commodities involves a change only in the form of their values, it necessarily involves the exchange of equivalents, provided the phenomenon occurs in its purity. The vulgar economists have practically no inkling of the nature of value; hence, whenever they wish to consider the phenomenon in its purity, after their fashion, they assume that supply and demand are equal, i.e. that they cease to have any effect at all. If, then, as

2. Mercier de la Rivière, op. cit., p. 544.
3. 'Whether one of these two values is money, or whether they are both ordinary commodities, is in itself a matter of complete indifference' (Mercier de la Rivière, op. cit., p. 543).
4. 'It is not the parties to a contract who decide on the value; that has been decided before the contract' (Le Trosne, op. cit., p. 906).

regards the use-values exchanged, both buyer and seller may possibly gain something, this is not the case as regards exchange-values. Here we must rather say: 'Where equality exists there is no gain.'[5] It is true that commodities may be sold at prices which diverge from their values, but this divergence appears as an infringement of the laws governing the exchange of commodities.[6] In its pure form, the exchange of commodities is an exchange of equivalents, and thus it is not a method of increasing value.[7]

Hence we see that behind all attempts to represent the circulation of commodities as a source of surplus-value, there lurks an inadvertent substitution, a confusion of use-value and exchange-value. In Condillac, for instance: 'It is not true that in an exchange of commodities we give value for value. On the contrary, each of the two contracting parties in every case gives a less for a greater value . . . If we really exchanged equal values, neither party could make a profit. And yet they both gain, or ought to gain. Why? The value of a thing consists solely in its relation to our needs. What is more to the one is less to the other, and *vice versa* . . . It is not to be assumed that we offer for sale articles essential for our own consumption . . . We wish to part with a useless thing, in order to get one that we need; we want to give less for more . . . It was natural to think that, in an exchange, one value was given for another equal to it whenever each of the articles exchanged was of equal value with the same quantity of gold . . . But there is another point to be considered in our calculation. The question is, whether we both exchange something superfluous for something necessary.'[8] We see in this passage how Condillac not only confuses use-value with exchange-value, but in a really childish manner assumes that, in a society in which the production of commodities is well developed, each producer produces his own means

5. '*Dove è egualità non è lucro*' (Galiani, *Della Moneta*, in Custodi, *Parte moderna*, Vol. 4, p. 244).

6. 'The exchange becomes unfavourable for one of the parties when some external circumstance comes to lessen or increase the price; then equality is infringed; but this infringement arises from that cause and not from the exchange itself' (Le Trosne, op. cit., p. 904).

7. 'Exchange is by its nature a contract which rests on equality, i.e. it takes place between two equal values. It is therefore not a means of self-enrichment, since as much is given as is received' (Le Trosne, op. cit., p. 903).

8. Condillac, *Le Commerce et le gouvernement* (1776), ed. Daire and Molinari, in the *Mélanges d'économie politique*, Paris, 1847, pp. 267, 291.

of subsistence, and throws into circulation only what is super-fluous, the excess over his own requirements.[9] Still, Condillac's argument is frequently repeated by modern economists, especially when the point is to show that the exchange of commodities in its developed form, commerce, is productive of surplus-value. For instance, 'Commerce . . . adds value to products, for the same products in the hands of consumers are worth more than in the hands of producers, and it may strictly be considered an act of production.'[10] But commodities are not paid for twice over, once on account of their use-value, and a second time on account of their value. And though the use-value of a commodity is more serviceable to the buyer than to the seller, its money-form is more so to the seller. Would he sell it otherwise? We might therefore just as well say that the buyer performs what is 'strictly' an 'act of production' by converting stockings, for example, into money.

If commodities, or commodities and money, of equal exchange-value, and consequently equivalents, are exchanged, it is plain that no one abstracts more value from circulation than he throws into it. The formation of surplus-value does not take place. In its pure form, the circulation process necessitates the exchange of equiva-lents, but in reality processes do not take place in their pure form. Let us therefore assume an exchange of non-equivalents.

In any case the market for commodities is frequented only by owners of commodities, and the power which these persons exercise over each other is no other than the power of their com-modities. The material variety of the commodities is the material driving force behind their exchange, and it makes buyers and sellers mutually dependent, because none of them possesses the object of his own need, and each holds in his own hand the object of another's need. Apart from this material variety in their use-values, there is only one other mark of distinction between com-

9. Le Trosne therefore answers his friend Condillac quite correctly as follows: 'In a developed society absolutely nothing is superfluous.' At the same time he teases him by saying that 'If both the persons who exchange receive more in return for an equal amount, and part with less in return for an equal amount, they both get the same.'* It is because Condillac has not the remotest idea of the nature of exchange-value that he has been chosen by Herr Professor Wilhelm Roscher as a suitable guarantor of the soundness of his own childish notions. See Roscher's *Die Grundlagen der Nationalökonomie*, 3rd edn, 1858.

10. S. P. Newman, *Elements of Political Economy*, Andover and New York, 1835, p. 175.

*Le Trosne, op. cit., pp. 907, 904.

modities, the distinction between their natural form and their converted form, between commodities and money. Consequently, the owners of commodities can be differentiated only into sellers, those who own commodities, and buyers, those who own money.

Suppose then that some inexplicable privilege allows the seller to sell his commodities above their value, to sell what is worth 100 for 110, therefore with a nominal price increase of 10 per cent. In this case the seller pockets a surplus-value of 10. But after he has sold he becomes a buyer. A third owner of commodities now comes to him as seller, and he too, for his part, enjoys the privilege of selling his commodities 10 per cent too dear. Our friend gained 10 as a seller only to lose it again as a buyer.[11] In fact the net result is that all owners of commodities sell their goods to each other at 10 per cent above their value, which is exactly the same as if they sold them at their true value. A universal and nominal price increase of this kind has the same effect as if the values of commodities had been expressed for example in silver instead of in gold. The money-names or prices of the commodities would rise, but the relations between their values would remain unchanged.

Let us make the opposite assumption, that the buyer has the privilege of purchasing commodities below their value. In this case we do not even need to recall that he in his turn will become a seller. He was a seller before he became a buyer; he had already lost 10 per cent as a seller before he gained 10 per cent as a buyer.[12] Everything remains as it was before.

The formation of surplus-value, and therefore the transformation of money into capital, can consequently be explained neither by assuming that commodities are sold above their value, nor by assuming that they are bought at less than their value.[13]

11. 'By the augmentation of the nominal value of the produce ... sellers [are] not enriched ... since what they gain as sellers, they precisely expend in the quality of buyers' ([J. Gray],* *The Essential Principles of the Wealth of Nations etc.*, London, 1797, p. 66).

12. 'If one is compelled to sell a quantity of a certain product for 18 livres when it has a value of 24 livres, then, when one employs the same amount of money in buying, one will receive for 18 livres the same quantity of the product as 24 livres would have bought otherwise' (Le Trosne, op. cit., p. 897).

13. 'A seller can normally only succeed in raising the prices of his commodities if he agrees to pay, by and large, more for the commodities of the

* John Gray, eighteenth-century writer on economic and political questions. Not to be confused with John Gray (1798–1850), utopian socialist and follower of Robert Owen.

The problem is in no way simplified if extraneous matters are smuggled in, as with Colonel Torrens: 'Effectual demand consists in the power and inclination (!), on the part of consumers, to give for commodities, either by immediate or circuitous barter, some greater portion of . . . capital than their production costs.'[14] In circulation, producers and consumers confront each other only as buyers and sellers. To assert that the surplus-value acquired by the producer has its origin in the fact that consumers pay for commodities more than their value is only to disguise the following simple phrase: the owner of commodities possesses, as a seller, the privilege of selling too dear. The seller has himself produced the commodities or represents their producer, but the buyer has to no less an extent produced the commodities represented by his money, or represents the producer of those commodities. One producer is therefore confronted with another producer. The distinction between them is that one buys and the other sells. The fact that the owner of the commodities sells them at more than their value, under the designation of producer, and pays too much for them, under the designation of consumer, does not carry us a single step further.[15]

The consistent upholders of the mistaken theory that surplus-value has its origin in a nominal rise of prices or in the privilege which the seller has of selling too dear assume therefore that there exists a class of buyers who do not sell, i.e. a class of consumers who do not produce. The existence of such a class is inexplicable from the standpoint we have so far reached, that of simple circulation. But let us anticipate. The money with which such a class is constantly making purchases must constantly flow into its coffers without any exchange, *gratis*, whether by might or by right, from the pockets of the commodity-owners themselves. To sell commodities at more than their value to such a class is only to get back again, by swindling, a part of the money previously

other sellers; and for the same reason a consumer can normally only pay less for his purchases if he submits to a similar reduction in the prices of the things he sells' (Mercier de la Rivière, op. cit., p. 555).

14. R. Torrens, *An Essay on the Production of Wealth*, London, 1821, p. 349.

15. 'The idea of profits being paid by the consumers, is, assuredly, very absurd. Who are the consumers?' (G. Ramsay, *An Essay on the Distribution of Wealth*, Edinburgh, 1836, p. 183).

handed over for nothing.[16] Thus, the towns of Asia Minor paid a yearly money tribute to ancient Rome. With this money Rome bought commodities from them, and bought them too dear. The provincials cheated the Romans, and in this way swindled back from their conquerors a portion of the tribute in the course of trade. Yet, for all that, the provincials remained the ones who had been cheated. Their goods were still paid for with their own money. That is not the way to get rich or to create surplus-value.

Let us therefore keep within the limits of the exchange of commodities, where sellers are buyers, and buyers are sellers. Our perplexity may perhaps have arisen from conceiving people merely as personified categories, instead of as individuals.

A may be clever enough to get the advantage of B and C without their being able to take their revenge. A sells wine worth £40 to B, and obtains from him in exchange corn to the value of £50. A has converted his £40 into £50, has made more money out of less, and has transformed his commodities into capital. Let us examine this a little more closely. Before the exchange we had £40 of wine in the hands of A, and £50 worth of corn in those of B, a total value of £90. After the exchange we still have the same total value of £90. The value in circulation has not increased by one iota; all that has changed is its distribution between A and B. What appears on one side as a loss of value appears on the other side as surplus-value; what appears on one side as a minus appears on the other side as a plus. The same change would have taken place if A, without the disguise provided by the exchange, had directly stolen the £10 from B. The sum of the values in circulation can clearly not be augmented by any change in their distribution, any more than a Jew can increase the quantity of the precious metals in a country by selling a farthing from the time of Queen Anne for

---

16. 'When a man is in want of a demand, does Mr Malthus recommend him to pay some other person to take off his goods?' is a question put by an infuriated Ricardian to Malthus, who, like his disciple Parson Chalmers,* economically glorifies this class of simple buyers or consumers. See *An Inquiry into Those Principles, Respecting the Nature of Demand and the Necessity of Consumption, Lately Advocated by Mr Malthus etc.*, London, 1821, p. 55.

*The Reverend Thomas Chalmers (1780–1847) was a Scottish Presbyterian minister who taught moral philosophy and divinity, as well as writing books on political economy. 'Malthus's theory is expressed in an exaggerated and even more nauseating form by Thomas Chalmers (Professor of Divinity)' (*Theories of Surplus-Value*, Part 3, p. 56).

a guinea. The capitalist class of a given country, taken as a whole, cannot defraud itself.[17]

However much we twist and turn, the final conclusion remains the same. If equivalents are exchanged, no surplus-value results, and if non-equivalents are exchanged, we still have no surplus-value.[18] Circulation, or the exchange of commodities, creates no value.[19]

It can be understood, therefore, why, in our analysis of the primary form of capital, the form in which it determines the economic organization of modern society, we have entirely left out of consideration its well-known and so to speak antediluvian forms, merchants' capital and usurers' capital.

The form M–C–M', buying in order to sell dearer, is at its purest in genuine merchants' capital. But the whole of this movement takes place within the sphere of circulation. Since, however, it is impossible, by circulation alone, to explain the transformation of money into capital, and the formation of surplus-value, merchants' capital appears to be an impossibility, as long as equivalents are exchanged;[20] it appears, therefore, that it can

17. Destutt de Tracy, although, or perhaps because, he was a *Membre de l'Institut*,* held the opposite view. The industrial capitalists, he says, make profits because 'they all sell for more than it has cost to produce. And to whom do they sell? In the first instance to one another' (op. cit., p. 239).

18. 'The exchange of two equal values neither increases nor diminishes the amount of the values present in society. Equally, the exchange of two unequal values . . . effects no change in the sum of social values, although it adds to the wealth of one person what it removes from the wealth of another' (J. B. Say, op. cit., Vol. 2, pp. 443–4). Say, who is of course untroubled by the consequences of this statement, borrows it almost word for word from the Physiocrats. The following example will show how Monsieur Say exploited the writings of the Physiocrats, in his day quite forgotten, for the purpose of increasing the 'value' of his own. His 'most celebrated' saying, 'Products can only be bought with products' (op. cit., Vol. 2, p. 441), runs as follows in the original Physiocratic work: 'Products can only be paid for with products' (Le Trosne, op. cit., p. 899).

19. 'Exchange confers no value at all upon products' (F. Wayland, *The Elements of Political Economy*, Boston, 1843, p. 169).

20. 'Under the rule of invariable equivalents commerce would be impossible' (G. Opdyke, *A Treatise on Political Economy*, New York, 1851, pp. 66–9). 'The difference between real value and exchange-value is based on one fact –

*That is, a member of the Institut de France, the government-financed and run association which was established in 1793 to 'promote the arts and sciences' and still groups beneath its aegis the five great French literary and scientific academies (Académie Française, Académie des Inscriptions, Académie des Sciences, Académie des Beaux-arts, Académie des Sciences Morales et Politiques).

only be derived from the twofold advantage gained, over both the selling and the buying producers, by the merchant who parasitically inserts himself between them. It is in this sense that Franklin says 'war is robbery, commerce is cheating'.[21] If the valorization of merchants' capital is not to be explained merely by frauds practised on the producers of commodities, a long series of intermediate steps would be necessary, which are as yet entirely absent, since here our only assumption is the circulation of commodities and its simple elements.

What we have said with reference to merchants' capital applies still more to usurers' capital. In merchants' capital the two extremes, the money which is thrown upon the market and the augmented money which is withdrawn from the market, are at least mediated through a purchase and a sale, through the movement of circulation. In usurers' capital the form M–C–M' is reduced to the unmediated extremes M–M', money which is exchanged for more money, a form incompatible with the nature of money and therefore inexplicable from the standpoint of the exchange of commodities. Hence Aristotle says: 'Since chrematistics is a double science, one part belonging to commerce, the other to economics, the latter being necessary and praiseworthy, the former based on circulation and with justice disapproved (for it is not based on Nature, but on mutual cheating), the usurer is most rightly hated, because money itself is the source of his gain, and is not used for the purposes for which it was invented. For it originated for the exchange of commodities, but interest makes out of money, more money. Hence its name.' (τόχος interest and offspring.) 'For the offspring resembles the parent. But interest is money, so that of all modes of making a living, this is the most contrary to Nature.'[22]

In the course of our investigation, we shall find that both merchants' capital and interest-bearing capital are derivative forms, and at the same time it will become clear why, historically, these two forms appear before the modern primary form of capital.

---

namely, that the value of a thing differs from the so-called equivalent given for it in trade, i.e. that this equivalent is not an equivalent' (F. Engels, op. cit., p. 96) [English translation, p. 427].

21. Benjamin Franklin, *Positions to be Examined, Concerning National Wealth*, in *Works*, Vol. 2, ed. Sparks, p. 376.

22. Aristotle, op. cit., c. 10 [English translation, para. 1258b].

We have shown that surplus-value cannot arise from circulation, and therefore that, for it to be formed, something must take place in the background which is not visible in the circulation itself.[23] But can surplus-value originate anywhere else than in circulation, which is the sum total of all the mutual relations of commodity-owners? Outside circulation, the commodity-owner only stands in a relation to his own commodity. As far as the value of that commodity is concerned, the relation is limited to this, that the commodity contains a quantity of his own labour which is measured according to definite social laws. This quantity of labour is expressed by the magnitude of the value of his commodity, and since the value is reckoned in money of account, this quantity is also expressed by the price, £10 for instance. But his labour does not receive a double representation: it is not represented both in the value of the commodity and in an excess quantity over and above that value, it is not represented in a price of 10 which is simultaneously a price of 11, i.e. in a value which is greater than itself. The commodity-owner can create value by his labour, but he cannot create values which can valorize themselves. He can increase the value of his commodity by adding fresh labour, and therefore more value, to the value in hand, by making leather into boots, for instance. The same material now has more value, because it contains a greater quantity of labour. The boots have therefore more value than the leather, but the value of the leather remains what it was. It has not valorized itself, it has not annexed surplus-value during the making of the boots. It is therefore impossible that, outside the sphere of circulation, a producer of commodities can, without coming into contact with other commodity-owners, valorize value, and consequently transform money or commodities into capital.

Capital cannot therefore arise from circulation, and it is equally impossible for it to arise apart from circulation. It must have its origin both in circulation and not in circulation.

We therefore have a double result.

The transformation of money into capital has to be developed on the basis of the immanent laws of the exchange of commodities, in such a way that the starting-point is the exchange of equi-

23. 'Profit, in the usual condition of the market, is not made by exchanging. Had it not existed before, neither could it after that transaction' (Ramsay, op. cit., p. 184).

valents.[24] The money-owner, who is as yet only a capitalist in larval form, must buy his commodities at their value, sell them at their value, and yet at the end of the process withdraw more value from circulation than he threw into it at the beginning. His emergence as a butterfly must, and yet must not, take place in the sphere of circulation. These are the conditions of the problem. *Hic Rhodus, hic salta!**

24. The reader will see from the foregoing discussion that the meaning of this statement is only as follows: the formation of capital must be possible even though the price and the value of a commodity be the same, for it cannot be explained by referring to any divergence between price and value. If prices actually differ from values, we must first reduce the former to the latter, i.e. disregard this situation as an accidental one in order to observe the phenomenon of the formation of capital on the basis of the exchange of commodities in its purity, and to prevent our observations from being interfered with by disturbing incidental circumstances which are irrelevant to the actual course of the process. We know, moreover, that this reduction is not limited to the field of science. The continual oscillations in prices, their rise and fall, compensate each other, cancel each other out, and carry out their own reduction to an average price which is their internal regulator. This average price is the guiding light of the merchant or the manufacturer in every undertaking of a lengthy nature. The manufacturer knows that if a long period of time is considered, commodities are sold neither over nor under, but at, their average price. If, therefore, he were at all interested in disinterested thinking, he would formulate the problem of the formation of capital as follows: How can we account for the origin of capital on the assumption that prices are regulated by the average price, i.e. ultimately by the value of the commodities? I say 'ultimately' because average prices do not directly coincide with the values of commodities, as Adam Smith, Ricardo, and others believe.*

*'Ricardo accepts Smith's confusion or identification of exchange-value with cost-price or natural price,' a confusion based on the notion that exchange-value is formed by putting together the values of wages, profit and rent (*Theories of Surplus-Value*, Part II, p. 217).

---

*This is the reply made, in one of Aesop's fables, to a boaster who claimed he had once made an immense leap in Rhodes. 'Rhodes is here. Leap here and now.' But it is also a reference back to the *Preface* to Hegel's *Philosophy of Right*, where he uses the quotation to illustrate his view that the task of philosophy is to apprehend and comprehend what is, rather than what ought to be.

Chapter 6: The Sale and Purchase of Labour-Power

The change in value of the money which has to be transformed into capital cannot take place in the money itself, since in its function as means of purchase and payment it does no more than realize [*realisieren*] the price of the commodity it buys or pays for, while, when it sticks to its own peculiar form, it petrifies into a mass of value of constant magnitude.[1] Just as little can this change originate in the second act of circulation, the resale of the commodity, for this act merely converts the commodity from its natural form back into its money-form. The change must therefore take place in the commodity which is bought in the first act of circulation, M–C, but not in its value, for it is equivalents which are being exchanged, and the commodity is paid for at its full value. The change can therefore originate only in the actual use-value of the commodity, i.e. in its consumption. In order to extract value out of the consumption of a commodity, our friend the money-owner must be lucky enough to find within the sphere of circulation, on the market, a commodity whose use-value possesses the peculiar property of being a source of value, whose actual consumption is therefore itself an objectification [*Vergegenständlichung*] of labour, hence a creation of value. The possessor of money does find such a special commodity on the market: the capacity for labour [*Arbeitsvermögen*], in other words labour-power [*Arbeitskraft*].

We mean by labour-power, or labour-capacity, the aggregate of those mental and physical capabilities existing in the physical form, the living personality, of a human being, capabilities which he sets in motion whenever he produces a use-value of any kind.

But in order that the owner of money may find labour-power on the market as a commodity, various conditions must first be fulfilled. In and for itself, the exchange of commodities implies

1. 'In the form of money. . . capital is productive of no profit' (Ricardo, *Principles of Political Economy*, p. 267).

no other relations of dependence than those which result from its own nature. On this assumption, labour-power can appear on the market as a commodity only if, and in so far as, its possessor, the individual whose labour-power it is, offers it for sale or sells it as a commodity. In order that its possessor may sell it as a commodity, he must have it at his disposal, he must be the free proprietor of his own labour-capacity, hence of his person.[2] He and the owner of money meet in the market, and enter into relations with each other on a footing of equality as owners of commodities, with the sole difference that one is a buyer, the other a seller; both are therefore equal in the eyes of the law. For this relation to continue, the proprietor of labour-power must always sell it for a limited period only, for if he were to sell it in a lump, once and for all, he would be selling himself, converting himself from a free man into a slave, from an owner of a commodity into a commodity. He must constantly treat his labour-power as his own property, his own commodity, and he can do this only by placing it at the disposal of the buyer, i.e. handing it over to the buyer for him to consume, for a definite period of time, temporarily. In this way he manages both to alienate [*veräussern*] his labour-power and to avoid renouncing his rights of ownership over it.[3]

2. In encyclopedias of classical antiquity one can read such nonsense as this: In the ancient world capital was fully developed, 'except for the absence of the free worker* and of a system of credit'. Mommsen too, in his *History of Rome,* commits one blunder after another in this respect.

3. Hence legislation in various countries fixes a maximum length for labour contracts. Wherever free labour is the rule, the law regulates the conditions for terminating this contract. In some states, particularly in Mexico (and before the American Civil War in the territories taken by the United States from Mexico, as also in practice in the Danubian Principalities until Cuza's *coup d'état†*), slavery is hidden under the form of peonage. By means of advances

* Just as the word '*Arbeit*' can be rendered both as 'work' and as 'labour', so also the word '*Arbeiter*' can be rendered as 'worker' and as 'labourer'. We prefer 'worker' to 'labourer' in general, although in the case of 'agricultural labourer' we have made an exception. This is because the word 'labourer' has an old-fashioned and indeed a somewhat bourgeois flavour.

† Prince Alexander Cuza, Hospodar of the Danubian Principalities (Romania) from 1859 to 1866, in April 1864 proposed a land reform which was rejected by the Assembly, dominated as that was by the magnates. In May 1864 he dissolved the Assembly and issued a new Constitutional Statute, endorsed by a popular plebiscite. This allowed him to impose the Agrarian Law of August 1864 on the country. By this law, all feudal dues and tithes were swept away (with generous compensation of course) and the serfs were legally enfranchised.

The second essential condition which allows the owner of money to find labour-power in the market as a commodity is this, that the possessor of labour-power, instead of being able to sell commodities in which his labour has been objectified, must rather be compelled to offer for sale as a commodity that very labour-power which exists only in his living body.

In order that a man may be able to sell commodities other than his labour-power, he must of course possess means of production, such as raw materials, instruments of labour, etc. No boots can be made without leather. He requires also the means of subsistence. Nobody – not even a practitioner of *Zukunftsmusik** – can live on the products of the future, or on use-values whose production has not yet been completed; just as on the first day of his appearance on the world's stage, man must still consume every day, before and while he produces. If products are produced as commodities, they must be sold after they have been produced, and they can only satisfy the producer's needs after they have been sold. The time necessary for sale must be counted as well as the time of production.

For the transformation of money into capital, therefore, the owner of money must find the free worker available on the commodity-market; and this worker must be free in the double sense that as a free individual he can dispose of his labour-power as his own commodity, and that, on the other hand, he has no other commodity for sale, i.e. he is rid of them, he is free of all the

---

repayable in labour, which are handed down from generation to generation, not only the individual worker, but also his family, become in fact the property of other persons and their families. Juarez abolished peonage, but the so-called Emperor Maximilian re-established it by a decree which was aptly denounced in the House of Representatives in Washington as a decree for the re-introduction of slavery into Mexico. 'Single products of my particular physical and mental skill and of my power to act I can alienate to someone else and I can give him the use of my abilities for a restricted period, because, on the strength of this restriction, my abilities acquire an external relation to the totality and universality of my being. By alienating the whole of my time, as crystallized in my work, and everything I produced, I would be making into another's property the substance of my being, my universal activity and actuality, my personality' (Hegel, *Philosophie des Rechts*, Berlin, 1840, p. 104, para. 67) [English translation, p. 54].

---

*'Music of the future', in other words castles in the air, or dreams which may or may not be realized.

objects needed for the realization [*Verwirklichung*] of his labour-power.

Why this free worker confronts him in the sphere of circulation is a question which does not interest the owner of money, for he finds the labour-market in existence as a particular branch of the commodity-market. And for the present it interests us just as little. We confine ourselves to the fact theoretically, as he does practically. One thing, however, is clear: nature does not produce on the one hand owners of money or commodities, and on the other hand men possessing nothing but their own labour-power. This relation has no basis in natural history, nor does it have a social basis common to all periods of human history. It is clearly the result of a past historical development, the product of many economic revolutions, of the extinction of a whole series of older formations of social production.

The economic categories already discussed similarly bear a historical imprint. Definite historical conditions are involved in the existence of the product as a commodity. In order to become a commodity, the product must cease to be produced as the immediate means of subsistence of the producer himself. Had we gone further, and inquired under what circumstances all, or even the majority of products take the form of commodities, we should have found that this only happens on the basis of one particular mode of production, the capitalist one. Such an investigation, however, would have been foreign to the analysis of commodities. The production and circulation of commodities can still take place even though the great mass of the objects produced are intended for the immediate requirements of their producers, and are not turned into commodities, so that the process of social production is as yet by no means dominated in its length and breadth by exchange-value. The appearance of products as commodities requires a level of development of the division of labour within society such that the separation of use-value from exchange-value, a separation which first begins with barter, has already been completed. But such a degree of development is common to many economic formations of society [*ökonomische Gesellschaftsformationen*], with the most diverse historical characteristics.

If we go on to consider money, its existence implies that a definite stage in the development of commodity exchange has been reached. The various forms of money (money as the mere equivalent of commodities, money as means of circulation, money as means of payment, money as hoard, or money as world currency) indicate very different levels of the process of social production, according to the extent and relative preponderance of one function or the other. Yet we know by experience that a relatively feeble development of commodity circulation suffices for the creation of all these forms. It is otherwise with capital. The historical conditions of its existence are by no means given with the mere circulation of money and commodities. It arises only when the owner of the means of production and subsistence finds the free worker available, on the market, as the seller of his own labour-power. And this one historical pre-condition comprises a world's history. Capital, therefore, announces from the outset a new epoch in the process of social production.[4]

This peculiar commodity, labour-power, must now be examined more closely. Like all other commodities it has a value.[5] How is that value determined?

The value of labour-power is determined, as in the case of every other commodity, by the labour-time necessary for the production, and consequently also the reproduction, of this specific article. In so far as it has value, it represents no more than a definite quantity of the average social labour objectified in it. Labour-power exists only as a capacity of the living individual. Its production consequently presupposes his existence. Given the existence of the individual, the production of labour-power consists in his reproduction of himself or his maintenance. For his maintenance he requires a certain quantity of the means of subsistence. Therefore the labour-time necessary for the production of labour-power is the same as that necessary for the production of those means of subsistence; in other words, the value of labour-power is the value of the means of subsistence necessary for the maintenance of its owner. However, labour-power becomes a reality only by being expressed; it is activated only through labour. But in the course of this activity, i.e. labour, a definite quantity of human muscle, nerve, brain, etc. is expended, and these things have to be re-

4. The capitalist epoch is therefore characterized by the fact that labour-power, in the eyes of the worker himself, takes on the form of a commodity which is his property; his labour consequently takes on the form of wage-labour. On the other hand, it is only from this moment that the commodity-form of the products of labour becomes universal.

5. 'The value or worth of a man, is as of all other things his price – that is to say, so much as would be given for the use of his power' (T. Hobbes, *Leviathan*, in *Works*, ed. Molesworth, London, 1839–44, Vol. 3, p. 76).

placed. Since more is expended, more must be received.[6] If the owner of labour-power works today, tomorrow he must again be able to repeat the same process in the same conditions as regards health and strength. His means of subsistence must therefore be sufficient to maintain him in his normal state as a working individual. His natural needs, such as food, clothing, fuel and housing vary according to the climatic and other physical peculiarities of his country. On the other hand, the number and extent of his so-called necessary requirements, as also the manner in which they are satisfied, are themselves products of history, and depend therefore to a great extent on the level of civilization attained by a country; in particular they depend on the conditions in which, and consequently on the habits and expectations with which, the class of free workers has been formed.[7] In contrast, therefore, with the case of other commodities, the determination of the value of labour-power contains a historical and moral element. Nevertheless, in a given country at a given period, the average amount of the means of subsistence necessary for the worker is a known *datum*.

The owner of labour-power is mortal. If then his appearance in the market is to be continuous, and the continuous transformation of money into capital assumes this, the seller of labour-power must perpetuate himself 'in the way that every living individual perpetuates himself, by procreation'.[8] The labour-power withdrawn from the market by wear and tear, and by death, must be continually replaced by, at the very least, an equal amount of fresh labour-power. Hence the sum of means of subsistence necessary for the production of labour-power must include the means necessary for the worker's replacements, i.e. his children, in order that this race of peculiar commodity-owners may perpetuate its presence on the market.[9]

In order to modify the general nature of the human organism in

6. In ancient Rome, therefore, the *villicus*, as the overseer of the agricultural slaves, received 'more meagre fare than working slaves, because his work was lighter' (T. Mommsen, *Römische Geschichte*, 1856, p. 810).

7. Cf. W. T. Thornton, *Over-Population and Its Remedy*, London, 1846.

8. Petty.

9. 'Its' (labour's) 'natural price ... consists in such a quantity of necessaries and comforts of life, as, from the nature of the climate, and the habits of the country, are necessary to support the labourer, and to enable him to rear such a family as may preserve, in the market, an undiminished supply of labour' (R. Torrens, *An Essay on the External Corn Trade*, London, 1815, p. 62). The word labour is here wrongly used for labour-power.

such a way that it acquires skill and dexterity in a given branch of industry, and becomes labour-power of a developed and specific kind, a special education or training is needed, and this in turn costs an equivalent in commodities of a greater or lesser amount. The costs of education vary according to the degree of complexity of the labour-power required. These expenses (exceedingly small in the case of ordinary labour-power) form a part of the total value spent in producing it.

The value of labour-power can be resolved into the value of a definite quantity of the means of subsistence. It therefore varies with the value of the means of subsistence, i.e. with the quantity of labour-time required to produce them.

Some of the means of subsistence, such as food and fuel, are consumed every day, and must therefore be replaced every day. Others, such as clothes and furniture, last for longer periods and need to be replaced only at longer intervals. Articles of one kind must be bought or paid for every day, others every week, others every quarter and so on. But in whatever way the sum total of these outlays may be spread over the year, they must be covered by the average income, taking one day with another. If the total of the commodities required every day for the production of labour-power = A, and of those required every week = B, and of those required every quarter = C, and so on, the daily average of these commodities = $\dfrac{365A + 52B + 4C + \cdots}{365}$. Suppose that this mass of commodities required for the average day contains 6 hours of social labour, then every day half a day of average social labour is objectified in labour-power, or in other words half a day of labour is required for the daily production of labour-power. This quantity of labour forms the value of a day's labour-power, or the value of the labour-power reproduced every day. If half a day of average social labour is present in 3 shillings, then 3 shillings is the price corresponding to the value of a day's labour-power. If its owner therefore offers it for sale at 3 shillings a day, its selling price is equal to its value, and according to our original assumption the owner of money, who is intent on transforming his 3 shillings into capital, pays this value.

The ultimate or minimum limit of the value of labour-power is formed by the value of the commodities which have to be supplied every day to the bearer of labour-power, the man, so that he can renew his life-process. That is to say, the limit is formed by the value of the physically indispensable means of subsistence. If the price of labour-power falls to this minimum, it falls below its value, since under such circumstances it can be maintained and developed only in a crippled state, and the value of every commodity is determined by the labour-time required to provide it in its normal quality.

It is an extraordinarily cheap kind of sentimentality which declares that this method of determining the value of labour-power, a method prescribed by the very nature of the case, is brutal, and which laments with Rossi in this matter: 'To conceive capacity for labour (*puissance de travail*) in abstraction from the workers' means of subsistence during the production process is to conceive a phantom (*être de raison*). When we speak of labour, or capacity for labour, we speak at the same time of the worker and his means of subsistence, of the worker and his wages.'[10] When we speak of capacity for labour, we do not speak of labour, any more than we speak of digestion when we speak of capacity for digestion. As is well known, the latter process requires something more than a good stomach. When we speak of capacity for labour, we do not abstract from the necessary means of subsistence. On the contrary, their value is expressed in its value. If his capacity for labour remains unsold, this is of no advantage to the worker. He will rather feel it to be a cruel nature-imposed necessity that his capacity for labour has required for its production a definite quantity of the means of subsistence, and will continue to require this for its reproduction. Then, like Sismondi, he will discover that 'the capacity for labour . . . is nothing unless it is sold'.[11]

One consequence of the peculiar nature of labour-power as a commodity is this, that it does not in reality pass straight away into the hands of the buyer on the conclusion of the contract between buyer and seller. Its value, like that of every other commodity, is already determined before it enters into circulation, for a definite quantity of social labour has been spent on the production of the labour-power. But its use-value consists in the subsequent exercise of that power. The alienation [*Veräusserung*] of labour-power and its real manifestation [*Äusserung*], i.e. the period of its existence as a use-value, do not coincide in time. But in those cases in which the formal alienation by sale of the use-value of a

10. Rossi, *Cours d'économie politique*, Brussels, 1842, pp. 370–71.
11. Sismondi, *Nouvelles Principes etc.*, Vol. 1, p. 113.

commodity is not simultaneous with its actual transfer to the buyer, the money of the buyer serves as means of payment.[12]

In every country where the capitalist mode of production prevails, it is the custom not to pay for labour-power until it has been exercised for the period fixed by the contract, for example, at the end of each week. In all cases, therefore, the worker advances the use-value of his labour-power to the capitalist. He lets the buyer consume it before he receives payment of the price. Everywhere the worker allows credit to the capitalist. That this credit is no mere fiction is shown not only by the occasional loss of the wages the worker has already advanced, when a capitalist goes bankrupt,[13] but also by a series of more long-lasting consequences.[14]

12. 'All labour is paid after it has ceased' (*An Inquiry into Those Principles, Respecting the Nature of Demand, etc.*, p. 104). 'The system of commercial credit had to start at the moment when the worker, the prime creator of products, could, thanks to his savings, wait for his wages until the end of the week, the fortnight, the month, the quarter, etc.' (C. Ganilh, *Des systèmes de l'économie politique*, 2nd edn, Paris, 1821, Vol. 1, p. 150).

13. 'The worker lends his industry,' says Storch. But he slyly adds to this the statement that the worker 'risks nothing', except 'the loss of his wages . . . The worker does not hand over anything of a material nature' (Storch, *Cours d'économie politique*, St Petersburg, 1815, Vol. 2, pp. 36–7).

14. One example. In London there are two sorts of bakers, the 'full priced', who sell bread at its full value, and the 'undersellers', who sell it at less than its value. The latter class comprises more than three-quarters of the total number of bakers (p. xxxii in the Report of H. S. Tremenheere, the commissioner appointed to examine 'the grievances complained of by the journeymen bakers', etc., London, 1862). The undersellers, almost without exception, sell bread adulterated with alum, soap, pearl-ash, chalk, Derbyshire stonedust and other similar agreeable, nourishing and wholesome ingredients. (See the above-cited Blue Book, as also the report of the select committee of 1855 on the adulteration of food, and Dr Hassall's *Adulterations Detected*, 2nd edn, London, 1861.) Sir John Gordon stated before the committee of 1855 that 'in consequence of these adulterations, the poor man, who lives on two pounds of bread a day, does not now get one-fourth part of nourishing matter, let alone the deleterious effects on his health'. Tremenheere states (op. cit., p. xlviii) as the reason why a 'very large part of the working class', although well aware of this adulteration, nevertheless accept the alum, stone-dust, etc. as part of their purchase, that it is for them 'a matter of necessity to take from their baker or from the chandler's shop such bread as they choose to supply'. As they are not paid their wages before the end of the week, they in their turn are unable 'to pay for the bread consumed by their families during the week, before the end of the week', and Tremenheere adds on the evidence of witnesses, 'it is notorious that bread composed of those mixtures is made expressly for sale in this manner'. 'In many English agricultural districts' (and still more in Scottish)

Whether money serves as a means of purchase or a means of payment, this does not alter the nature of the exchange of commodities. The price of the labour-power is fixed by the contract, although it is not realized till later, like the rent of a house. The labour-power is sold, although it is paid for only at a later period. It will therefore be useful, if we want to conceive the relation in its pure form, to presuppose for the moment that the possessor of labour-power, on the occasion of each sale, immediately receives the price stipulated in the contract.

We now know the manner of determining the value paid by the owner of money to the owner of this peculiar commodity, labour-power. The use-value which the former gets in exchange manifests itself only in the actual utilization, in the process of the consumption of the labour-power. The money-owner buys everything necessary for this process, such as raw material, in the market, and pays the full price for it. The process of the consumption of labour-power is at the same time the production process of commodities and of surplus-value. The consumption of labour-power is completed, as in the case of every other commodity, outside the market or the sphere of circulation. Let us therefore, in company with the owner of money and the owner of labour-power, leave this noisy sphere, where everything takes place on the surface and in full view of everyone, and follow them into the hidden abode of production,

---

'wages are paid fortnightly and even monthly; with such long intervals between the payments, the agricultural labourer is obliged to buy on credit . . . He must pay higher prices, and is in fact tied to the shop which gives him credit. Thus at Horningham in Wilts., for example, where the wages are monthly, the same flour that he could buy elsewhere at 1s. 10d. per stone, costs him 2s. 4d. per stone' (*Public Health, Sixth Report* of the Medical Officer of the Privy Council, etc., 1864, p. 264). 'The block-printers of Paisley and Kilmarnock' (Western Scotland) 'enforced in 1833 by a strike the reduction of the period of payment from monthly to fortnightly' (*Reports of the Inspectors of Factories . . . 31 October 1853,* p. 34). As a further nice development from the credit given by the workers to the capitalist, we may refer to the method adopted by many English coal-owners whereby the worker is not paid till the end of the month, and in the meantime receives sums on account from the capitalist, often in goods for which the miner is obliged to pay more than the market price (truck system). 'It is a common practice with the coal masters to pay once a month, and advance cash to their workmen at the end of each intermediate week. The cash is given in the shop' (i.e. the tommy-shop which belongs to the master); 'the men take it on one side and lay it out on the other' (*Children's Employment Commission, Third Report,* London, 1864, p. 38, n. 192).

on whose threshold there hangs the notice 'No admittance except on business'. Here we shall see, not only how capital produces, but how capital is itself produced. The secret of profit-making must at last be laid bare.

The sphere of circulation or commodity exchange, within whose boundaries the sale and purchase of labour-power goes on, is in fact a very Eden of the innate rights of man. It is the exclusive realm of Freedom, Equality, Property and Bentham. Freedom, because both buyer and seller of a commodity, let us say of labour-power, are determined only by their own free will. They contract as free persons, who are equal before the law. Their contract is the final result in which their joint will finds a common legal expression. Equality, because each enters into relation with the other, as with a simple owner of commodities, and they exchange equivalent for equivalent. Property, because each disposes only of what is his own. And Bentham, because each looks only to his own advantage. The only force bringing them together, and putting them into relation with each other, is the selfishness, the gain and the private interest of each. Each pays heed to himself only, and no one worries about the others. And precisely for that reason, either in accordance with the pre-established harmony of things, or under the auspices of an omniscient providence, they all work together to their mutual advantage, for the common weal, and in the common interest.

When we leave this sphere of simple circulation or the exchange of commodities, which provides the 'free-trader *vulgaris*' with his views, his concepts and the standard by which he judges the society of capital and wage-labour, a certain change takes place, or so it appears, in the physiognomy of our *dramatis personae*. He who was previously the money-owner now strides out in front as a capitalist; the possessor of labour-power follows as his worker. The one smirks self-importantly and is intent on business; the other is timid and holds back, like someone who has brought his own hide to market and now has nothing else to expect but – a tanning.

Part Three

The Production of Absolute
Surplus-Value

Chapter 7: The Labour Process and the Valorization Process

I. THE LABOUR PROCESS

The use of labour-power is labour itself. The purchaser of labour-power consumes it by setting the seller of it to work. By working, the latter becomes in actuality what previously he only was potentially, namely labour-power in action, a worker. In order to embody his labour in commodities, he must above all embody it in use-values, things which serve to satisfy needs of one kind or another. Hence what the capitalist sets the worker to produce is a particular use-value, a specific article. The fact that the production of use-values, or goods, is carried on under the control of a capitalist and on his behalf does not alter the general character of that production. We shall therefore, in the first place, have to consider the labour process independently of any specific social formation.

Labour is, first of all, a process between man and nature, a process by which man, through his own actions, mediates, regulates and controls the metabolism between himself and nature. He confronts the materials of nature as a force of nature. He sets in motion the natural forces which belong to his own body, his arms, legs, head and hands, in order to appropriate the materials of nature in a form adapted to his own needs. Through this movement he acts upon external nature and changes it, and in this way he simultaneously changes his own nature. He develops the potentialities slumbering within nature, and subjects the play of its forces to his own sovereign power. We are not dealing here with those first instinctive forms of labour which remain on the animal level. An immense interval of time separates the state of things in which a man brings his labour-power to market for sale as a commodity from the situation when human labour had not yet cast off its first instinctive form. We presuppose labour in a form in which it is an exclusively human characteristic. A spider conducts operations which resemble those of the weaver, and a bee would put many a human architect to shame by the construction of its honeycomb cells. But what distinguishes the worst architect from the best of bees is that the architect builds the cell in his mind before he constructs it in wax. At the end of every labour process, a result emerges which had already been conceived by the worker at the beginning, hence already existed ideally. Man not only effects a change of form in the materials of nature; he also realizes [*verwirklicht*] his own purpose in those materials. And this is a purpose he is conscious of, it determines the mode of his activity with the rigidity of a law, and he must subordinate his will to it. This subordination is no mere momentary act. Apart from the exertion of the working organs, a purposeful will is required for the entire duration of the work. This means close attention. The less he is attracted by the nature of the work and the way in which it has to be accomplished, and the less, therefore, he enjoys it as the free play of his own physical and mental powers, the closer his attention is forced to be.

The simple elements of the labour process are (1) purposeful activity, that is work itself, (2) the object on which that work is performed, and (3) the instruments of that work.

The land (and this, economically speaking, includes water) in its original state in which it supplies[1] man with necessaries or means of subsistence ready to hand is available without any effort on his part as the universal material for human labour. All those things which labour merely separates from immediate connection with their environment are objects of labour spontaneously provided by nature, such as fish caught and separated from their natural element, namely water, timber felled in virgin forests, and ores extracted from their veins. If, on the other hand, the object of labour has, so to speak, been filtered through previous labour, we call it raw material. For example, ore already extracted and ready for washing. All raw material is an object of labour [*Arbeitsgegenstand*], but not every object of labour is raw material; the object of

1. 'The earth's spontaneous productions being in small quantity, quite independent of man, appear, as it were, to be furnished by Nature, in the same way as a small sum is given to a young man, in order to put him in a way of industry, and of making his fortune' (James Steuart, *Principles of Political Economy*, Dublin, 1770, Vol. 1, p. 116).

labour counts as raw material only when it has already undergone some alteration by means of labour.*

An instrument of labour is a thing, or a complex of things, which the worker interposes between himself and the object of his labour and which serves as a conductor, directing his activity onto that object. He makes use of the mechanical, physical and chemical properties of some substances in order to set them to work on other substances as instruments of his power, and in accordance with his purposes.[2] Leaving out of consideration such ready-made means of subsistence as fruits, in gathering which a man's bodily organs alone serve as the instruments of his labour, the object the worker directly takes possession of is not the object of labour but its instrument. Thus nature becomes one of the organs of his activity, which he annexes to his own bodily organs, adding stature to himself in spite of the Bible. As the earth is his original larder, so too it is his original tool house. It supplies him, for instance, with stones for throwing, grinding, pressing, cutting, etc. The earth itself is an instrument of labour, but its use in this way, in agriculture, presupposes a whole series of other instruments and a comparatively high stage of development of labour-power.[3] As soon as the labour process has undergone the slightest development, it requires specially prepared instruments. Thus we find stone implements and weapons in the oldest caves. In the earliest period of human history, domesticated animals, i.e. animals that have undergone modification by means of labour, that

2. 'Reason is as cunning as it is powerful. Cunning may be said to lie in the intermediative action which, while it permits the objects to follow their own bent and act upon one another till they waste away, and does not itself directly interfere in the process, is nevertheless only working out its own aims' (Hegel, *Enzyklopädie, Erster Theil, Die Logik*, Berlin, 1840, p. 382) [Para. 209, Addition. English translation: *Hegel's Logic*, tr. W. V. Wallace (revised by J. N. Findlay), Oxford, 1975, pp. 272–3].

3. In his otherwise miserable work *Théorie de l'économie politique*, Paris, 1815, Ganilh enumerates in a striking manner in opposition to the Physiocrats* the long series of labour processes which form the presupposition for agriculture properly so called.

*'For the Physiocrats, the productivity of labour appeared as a *gift of nature, a productive power of nature* . . . Surplus-value therefore appeared as a *gift of nature*' (*Theories of Surplus-Value*, Part 1, pp. 49–51).

---

* Marx thus uses the term 'raw material' in a technical sense, narrower than that of standard English usage.

have been bred specially, play the chief part as instruments of labour along with stones, wood, bones and shells, which have also had work done on them.[4] The use and construction of instruments of labour, although present in germ among certain species of animals, is characteristic of the specifically human labour process, and Franklin therefore defines man as 'a tool-making animal'. Relics of bygone instruments of labour possess the same importance for the investigation of extinct economic formations of society as do fossil bones for the determination of extinct species of animals. It is not what is made but how, and by what instruments of labour, that distinguishes different economic epochs.[5] Instruments of labour not only supply a standard of the degree of development which human labour has attained, but they also indicate the social relations within which men work. Among the instruments of labour, those of a mechanical kind, which, taken as a whole, we may call the bones and muscles of production, offer much more decisive evidence of the character of a given social epoch of production than those which, like pipes, tubs, baskets, jars etc., serve only to hold the materials for labour, and may be given the general denotation of the vascular system of production. The latter first begins to play an important part in the chemical industries.[6]

In a wider sense we may include among the instruments of labour, in addition to things through which the impact of labour on its object is mediated, and which therefore, in one way or another, serve as conductors of activity, all the objective conditions necessary for carrying on the labour process. These do not enter directly into the process, but without them it is either impossible for it to take place, or possible only to a partial extent. Once again, the earth itself is a universal instrument of this kind, for it provides

4. In his *Réflexions sur la formation et la distribution des richesses* (1766), Turgot gives a good account of the importance of domesticated animals for the beginnings of civilization.

5. The least important commodities of all for the technological comparison of different epochs of production are articles of real luxury.

6. The writers of history have so far paid very little attention to the development of material production, which is the basis of all social life, and therefore of all real history. But prehistoric times at any rate have been classified on the basis of the investigations of natural science, rather than so-called historical research. Prehistory has been divided, according to the materials used to make tools and weapons, into the Stone Age, the Bronze Age and the Iron Age.

the worker with the ground beneath his feet and a 'field of employment' for his own particular process. Instruments of this kind, which have already been mediated through past labour, include workshops, canals, roads, etc.

In the labour process, therefore, man's activity, *via* the instruments of labour, effects an alteration in the object of labour which was intended from the outset. The process is extinguished in the product. The product of the process is a use-value, a piece of natural material adapted to human needs by means of a change in its form. Labour has become bound up in its object: labour has been objectified, the object has been worked on. What on the side of the worker appeared in the form of unrest [*Unruhe*] now appears, on the side of the product, in the form of being [*Sein*], as a fixed, immobile characteristic. The worker has spun, and the product is a spinning.*

If we look at the whole process from the point of view of its result, the product, it is plain that both the instruments and the object of labour are means of production[7] and that the labour itself is productive labour.[8]

Although a use-value emerges from the labour process, in the form of a product, other use-values, products of previous labour, enter into it as means of production. The same use-value is both the product of a previous process, and a means of production in a later process. Products are therefore not only results of labour, but also its essential conditions.

With the exception of the extractive industries, such as mining, hunting, fishing (and agriculture, but only in so far as it starts by breaking up virgin soil), where the material for labour is provided directly by nature, all branches of industry deal with raw material, i.e. an object of labour which has already been filtered through labour, which is itself already a product of labour. An example is seed in agriculture. Animals and plants which we are accustomed to consider as products of nature, may be, in their present form,

7. It appears paradoxical to assert that uncaught fish, for instance, are a means of production in the fishing industry. But hitherto no one has discovered the art of catching fish in waters that contain none.

8. This method of determining what is productive labour, from the standpoint of the simple labour process, is by no means sufficient to cover the capitalist process of production.

---

*'Spinning': a quantity of thread or spun yarn (*O.E.D.*).

not only products of, say, last year's labour, but the result of a gradual transformation continued through many generations under human control, and through the agency of human labour. As regards the instruments of labour in particular, they show traces of the labour of past ages, even to the most superficial observer, in the great majority of cases.

Raw material may either form the principal substance of a product, or it may enter into its formation only as an accessory. An accessory may be consumed by the instruments of labour, such as coal by a steam-engine, oil by a wheel, hay by draft-horses, or it may be added to the raw material in order to produce some physical modification of it, as chlorine is added to unbleached linen, coal to iron, dye to wool, or again it may help to accomplish the work itself, as in the case of the materials used for heating and lighting workshops. The distinction between principal substance and accessory vanishes in the chemical industries proper, because there none of the raw material re-appears, in its original composition, in the substance of the product.[9]

Every object possesses various properties, and is thus capable of being applied to different uses. The same product may therefore form the raw material for very different labour processes. Corn, for example, is a raw material for millers, starch-manufacturers, distillers and cattle-breeders. It also enters as raw material into its own production in the shape of seed; coal both emerges from the mining industry as a product and enters into it as a means of production.

Again, a particular product may be used as both instrument of labour and raw material in the same process. Take, for instance, the fattening of cattle, where the animal is the raw material, and at the same time an instrument for the production of manure.

A product, though ready for immediate consumption, may nevertheless serve as raw material for a further product, as grapes do when they become the raw material for wine. On the other hand, labour may release its product in such a form that it can only be used as raw material. Raw material in this condition, such as

9. Storch distinguishes between raw material ('*matière*') and accessory materials ('*matériaux*'). Cherbuliez describes accessories as '*matières instrumentales*'.*

*H. Storch, *Cours d'économie politique*, Vol. 1, St Petersburg, 1815, p. 228; A. Cherbuliez, *Richesse ou pauvreté*, Paris, 1841, p. 14.

cotton, thread and yarn, is called semi-manufactured, but should rather be described as having been manufactured up to a certain level. Although itself already a product, this raw material may have to go through a whole series of different processes, and in each of these it serves as raw material, changing its shape constantly, until it is precipitated from the last process of the series in finished form, either as means of subsistence or as instrument of labour.

Hence we see that whether a use-value is to be regarded as raw material, as instrument of labour or as product is determined entirely by its specific function in the labour process, by the position it occupies there: as its position changes, so do its determining characteristics.

Therefore, whenever products enter as means of production into new labour processes, they lose their character of being products and function only as objective factors contributing to living labour. A spinner treats spindles only as a means for spinning, and flax as the material he spins. Of course it is impossible to spin without material and spindles; and therefore the availability of these products is presupposed at the beginning of the spinning operation. But in the process itself, the fact that they are the products of past labour is as irrelevant as, in the case of the digestive process, the fact that bread is the product of the previous labour of the farmer, the miller and the baker. On the contrary, it is by their imperfections that the means of production in any process bring to our attention their character of being the products of past labour. A knife which fails to cut, a piece of thread which keeps on snapping, forcibly remind us of Mr A, the cutler, or Mr B, the spinner. In a successful product, the role played by past labour in mediating its useful properties has been extinguished.

A machine which is not active in the labour process is useless. In addition, it falls prey to the destructive power of natural processes. Iron rusts; wood rots. Yarn with which we neither weave nor knit is cotton wasted. Living labour must seize on these things, awaken them from the dead, change them from merely possible into real and effective use-values. Bathed in the fire of labour, appropriated as part of its organism, and infused with vital energy for the performance of the functions appropriate to their concept and to their vocation in the process, they are indeed consumed, but to some purpose, as elements in the formation of new use-values, new products, which are capable of entering into individual consumption as means of subsistence or into a new labour process as means of production.

If then, on the one hand, finished products are not only results of the labour process, but also conditions of its existence, their induction into the process, their contact with living labour, is the sole means by which they can be made to retain their character of use-values, and be realized.

Labour uses up its material elements, its objects and its instruments. It consumes them, and is therefore a process of consumption. Such productive consumption is distinguished from individual consumption by this, that the latter uses up products as means of subsistence for the living individual; the former, as means of subsistence for labour, i.e. for the activity through which the living individual's labour-power manifests itself. Thus the product of individual consumption is the consumer himself; the result of productive consumption is a product distinct from the consumer.

In so far then as its instruments and its objects are themselves products, labour consumes products in order to create products, or in other words consumes one set of products by turning them into means of production for another set. But just as the labour process originally took place only between man and the earth (which was available independently of any human action), so even now we still employ in the process many means of production which are provided directly by nature and do not represent any combination of natural substances with human labour.

The labour process, as we have just presented it in its simple and abstract elements, is purposeful activity aimed at the production of use-values. It is an appropriation of what exists in nature for the requirements of man. It is the universal condition for the metabolic interaction [*Stoffwechsel*] between man and nature, the everlasting nature-imposed condition of human existence, and it is therefore independent of every form of that existence, or rather it is common to all forms of society in which human beings live. We did not, therefore, have to present the worker in his relationship with other workers; it was enough to present man and his labour on one side, nature and its materials on the other. The taste of porridge does not tell us who grew the oats, and the process we have presented does not reveal the conditions under which it takes place, whether it is happening under the slave-owner's brutal lash or the anxious eye of the capitalist, whether Cincinnatus undertakes it in tilling his couple of acres,* or a savage, when he lays low a wild beast with a stone.[10]

Let us now return to our would-be capitalist. We left him just after he had purchased, in the open market, all the necessary factors of the labour process; its objective factors, the means of production, as well as its personal factor, labour-power. With the keen eye of an expert, he has selected the means of production and the kind of labour-power best adapted to his particular trade, be it spinning, bootmaking or any other kind. He then proceeds to consume the commodity, the labour-power he has just bought, i.e. he causes the worker, the bearer of that labour-power, to consume the means of production by his labour. The general character of the labour process is evidently not changed by the fact that the worker works for the capitalist instead of for himself; moreover, the particular methods and operations employed in bootmaking or spinning are not immediately altered by the intervention of the capitalist. He must begin by taking the labour-power as he finds it in the market, and consequently he must be satisfied with the kind of labour which arose in a period when there were as yet no capitalists. The transformation of the mode of production itself which results from the subordination of labour to capital can only occur later on, and we shall therefore deal with it in a later chapter.

The labour process, when it is the process by which the capitalist consumes labour-power, exhibits two characteristic phenomena.

First, the worker works under the control of the capitalist to whom his labour belongs; the capitalist takes good care that the work is done in a proper manner, and the means of production are applied directly to the purpose, so that the raw material is not wasted, and the instruments of labour are spared, i.e. only worn to the extent necessitated by their use in the work.

10. By a wonderful feat of logical acumen, Colonel Torrens has discovered, in this stone of the savage, the origin of capital. 'In the first stone which the savage flings at the wild animal he pursues, in the first stick that he seizes to strike down the fruit which hangs above his reach, we see the appropriation of one article for the purpose of aiding in the acquisition of another, and thus discover the origin of capital' (R. Torrens, *An Essay on the Production of Wealth, etc.*, pp. 70–71). No doubt this 'first stick' [*Stock*] would also explain why 'stock' in English is synonymous with capital.

---

* The Roman patrician Lucius Quinctius Cincinnatus (dictator of Rome from 458 to 439 B.C.) was reputed to have lived a simple and exemplary life, cultivating his own small farm in person.

Secondly, the product is the property of the capitalist and not that of the worker, its immediate producer. Suppose that a capitalist pays for a day's worth of labour-power; then the right to use that power for a day belongs to him, just as much as the right to use any other commodity, such as a horse he had hired for the day. The use of a commodity belongs to its purchaser, and the seller of labour-power, by giving his labour, does no more, in reality, than part with the use-value he has sold. From the instant he steps into the workshop, the use-value of his labour-power and therefore also its use, which is labour, belongs to the capitalist. By the purchase of labour-power, the capitalist incorporates labour, as a living agent of fermentation, into the lifeless constituents of the product, which also belong to him. From his point of view, the labour process is nothing more than the consumption of the commodity purchased, i.e. of labour-power; but he can consume this labour-power only by adding the means of production to it. The labour process is a process between things the capitalist has purchased, things which belong to him. Thus the product of this process belongs to him just as much as the wine which is the product of the process of fermentation going on in his cellar.[11]

11. 'Products are appropriated before they are transformed into capital; this transformation does not withdraw them from that appropriation' (Cherbuliez, *Richesse ou pauvreté*, Paris, 1841, p. 54). 'The proletarian, by selling his labour for a definite quantity of the means of subsistence (*approvisionnement*),* renounces all claim to a share in the product. The products continue to be appropriated as before: this is in no way altered by the bargain we have mentioned. The product belongs exclusively to the capitalist, who supplied the raw materials and the *approvisionnement*. This follows rigorously from the law of appropriation, a law whose fundamental principle was the exact opposite, namely that every worker has an exclusive right to the ownership of what he produces' (ibid., p. 58). 'When the labourers receive wages for their labour . . . the capitalist is then the owner not of the capital only' (i.e. the means of production) 'but of the labour also. If what is paid as wages is included, as it commonly is, in the term capital, it is absurd to talk of labour separately from capital. The word capital as thus employed includes labour and capital both' (James Mill, *Elements of Political Economy*, London, 1821, pp. 70–71).

*See the discussion of Cherbuliez's notion of *approvisionnement* in *Grundrisse* (English edition), pp. 299–300: 'The economists, incidentally, introduce the *product* as third element of the substance of capital . . . This is the product [as] . . . immediate object of individual consumption; *approvisionnement*, as Cherbuliez calls it.'

2. THE VALORIZATION PROCESS

The product – the property of the capitalist – is a use-value, as yarn, for example, or boots. But although boots are, to some extent, the basis of social progress, and our capitalist is decidedly in favour of progress, he does not manufacture boots for their own sake. Use-value is certainly not *la chose qu'on aime pour lui-même** in the production of commodities. Use-values are produced by capitalists only because and in so far as they form the material substratum of exchange-value, are the bearers of exchange-value. Our capitalist has two objectives: in the first place, he wants to produce a use-value which has exchange-value, i.e. an article destined to be sold, a commodity; and secondly he wants to produce a commodity greater in value than the sum of the values of the commodities used to produce it, namely the means of production and the labour-power he purchased with his good money on the open market. His aim is to produce not only a use-value, but a commodity; not only use-value, but value; and not just value, but also surplus-value.

It must be borne in mind that we are now dealing with the production of commodities, and that up to this point we have considered only one aspect of the process. Just as the commodity itself is a unity formed of use-value and value, so the process of production must be a unity, composed of the labour process and the process of creating value [*Wertbildungsprozess*].

Let us now examine production as a process of creating value.

We know that the value of each commodity is determined by the quantity of labour materialized in its use-value, by the labour-time socially necessary to produce it. This rule also holds good in the case of the product handed over to the capitalist as a result of the labour-process. Assuming this product to be yarn, our first step is to calculate the quantity of labour objectified in it.

For spinning the yarn, raw material is required; suppose in this case 10 lb. of cotton. We have no need at present to investigate the value of this cotton, for our capitalist has, we will assume, bought it at its full value, say 10 shillings. In this price the labour required for the production of the cotton is already expressed in terms of average social labour. We will further assume that the wear and tear of the spindle, which for our present purpose may represent all other instruments of labour employed, amounts to

*'The thing desired for its own sake'.

the value of 2 shillings. If then, twenty-four hours of labour, or two working days, are required to produce the quantity of gold represented by 12 shillings, it follows first of all that two days of labour are objectified in the yarn.

We should not let ourselves be misled by the circumstance that the cotton has changed its form and the worn-down portion of the spindle has entirely disappeared. According to the general law of value, if the value of 40 lb. of yarn = the value of 40 lb. of cotton + the value of a whole spindle, i.e. if the same amount of labour-time is required to produce the commodities on either side of this equation, then 10 lb. of yarn are an equivalent for 10 lb. of cotton, together with a quarter of a spindle. In the case we are considering, the same amount of labour-time is represented in the 10 lb. of yarn on the one hand, and in the 10 lb. of cotton and the fraction of a spindle on the other. It is therefore a matter of indifference whether value appears in cotton, in a spindle or in yarn: its amount remains the same. The spindle and cotton, instead of resting quietly side by side, join together in the process, their forms are altered, and they are turned into yarn; but their value is no more affected by this fact than it would be if they had been simply exchanged for their equivalent in yarn.

The labour-time required for the production of the cotton, the raw material of the yarn, is part of the labour necessary to produce the yarn, and is therefore contained in the yarn. The same applies to the labour embodied in the spindle, without whose wear and tear the cotton could not be spun.[12]

Hence in determining the value of the yarn, or the labour-time required for its production, all the special processes carried on at various times and in different places which were necessary, first to produce the cotton and the wasted portion of the spindle, and then with the cotton and the spindle to spin the yarn, may together be looked on as different and successive phases of the same labour process. All the labour contained in the yarn is past labour; and it is a matter of no importance that the labour expended to produce its constituent elements lies further back in the past than the labour expended on the final process, the spinning. The former stands, as it were, in the pluperfect, the latter in the perfect tense, but this does not matter. If a definite quantity of labour, say thirty

12. 'Not only the labour applied immediately to commodities affects their value, but the labour also which is bestowed on the implements, tools, and buildings with which such labour is assisted' (Ricardo, op. cit., p. 16).

days, is needed to build a house, the total amount of labour incorporated in the house is not altered by the fact that the work of the last day was done twenty-nine days later than that of the first. Therefore the labour contained in the raw material and instruments of labour can be treated just as if it were labour expended in an earlier stage of the spinning process, before the labour finally added in the form of actual spinning.

The values of the means of production which are expressed in the price of 12 shillings (the cotton and the spindle) are therefore constituent parts of the value of the yarn, i.e. of the value of the product.

Two conditions must nevertheless be fulfilled. First, the cotton and the spindle must genuinely have served to produce a use-value; they must in the present case become yarn. Value is independent of the particular use-value by which it is borne, but a use-value of some kind has to act as its bearer. Second, the labour-time expended must not exceed what is necessary under the given social conditions of production. Therefore, if no more than 1 lb. of cotton is needed to spin 1 lb. of yarn, no more than this weight of cotton may be consumed in the production of 1 lb. of yarn. The same is true of the spindle. If the capitalist has a foible for using golden spindles instead of steel ones, the only labour that counts for anything in the value of the yarn remains that which would be required to produce a steel spindle, because no more is necessary under the given social conditions.

We now know what part of the value of the yarn is formed by the means of production, namely the cotton and the spindle. It is 12 shillings, i.e. the materialization of two days of labour. The next point to be considered is what part of the value of the yarn is added to the cotton by the labour of the spinner.

We have now to consider this labour from a standpoint quite different from that adopted for the labour process. There we viewed it solely as the activity which has the purpose of changing cotton into yarn; there, the more appropriate the work was to its purpose, the better the yarn, other circumstances remaining the same. In that case the labour of the spinner was specifically different from other kinds of productive labour, and this difference revealed itself both subjectively in the particular purpose of spinning, and objectively in the special character of its operations, the special nature of its means of production, and the special use-value of its product. For the operation of spinning, cotton and spindles are a necessity, but for making rifled cannon they would be of no use whatever. Here, on the contrary, where we consider the labour of the spinner only in so far as it creates value, i.e. is a source of value, that labour differs in no respect from the labour of the man who bores cannon, or (what concerns us more closely here) from the labour of the cotton-planter and the spindle-maker which is realized in the means of production of the yarn. It is solely by reason of this identity that cotton planting, spindle-making and spinning are capable of forming the component parts of one whole, namely the value of the yarn, differing only quantitatively from each other. Here we are no longer concerned with the quality, the character and the content of the labour, but merely with its quantity. And this simply requires to be calculated. We assume that spinning is simple labour, the average labour of a given society. Later it will be seen that the contrary assumption would make no difference.

During the labour process, the worker's labour constantly undergoes a transformation, from the form of unrest [*Unruhe*] into that of being [*Sein*], from the form of motion [*Bewegung*] into that of objectivity [*Gegenständlichkeit*]. At the end of one hour, the spinning motion is represented in a certain quantity of yarn; in other words, a definite quantity of labour, namely that of one hour, has been objectified in the cotton. We say labour, i.e. the expenditure of his vital force by the spinner, and not spinning labour, because the special work of spinning counts here only in so far as it is the expenditure of labour-power in general, and not the specific labour of the spinner.

In the process we are now considering it is of extreme importance that no more time be consumed in the work of transforming the cotton into yarn than is necessary under the given social conditions. If under normal, i.e. average social conditions of production, x pounds of cotton are made into y pounds of yarn by one hour's labour, then a day's labour does not count as 12 hours' labour unless 12x lb. of cotton have been made into 12y lb. of yarn; for only socially necessary labour-time counts towards the creation of value.

Not only the labour, but also the raw material and the product now appear in quite a new light, very different from that in which we viewed them in the labour process pure and simple. Now the raw material merely serves to absorb a definite quantity of labour. By being soaked in labour, the raw material is in fact changed into yarn, because labour-power is expended in the form of spinning and added to it; but the product, the yarn, is now nothing more than a measure of the labour absorbed by the cotton. If in one hour 1⅔ lb. of cotton can be spun into 1⅔ lb. of yarn, then 10 lb. of yarn indicate the absorption of 6 hours of labour. Definite quantities of product, quantities which are determined by experience, now represent nothing but definite quantities of labour, definite masses of crystallized labour-time. They are now simply the material shape taken by a given number of hours or days of social labour.

The fact that the labour is precisely the labour of spinning, that its material is cotton, its product yarn, is as irrelevant here as it is that the object of labour is itself already a product, hence already raw material. If the worker, instead of spinning, were to be employed in a coal-mine, the object on which he worked would be coal, which is present in nature; nevertheless, a definite quantity of coal, when extracted from its seam, would represent a definite quantity of absorbed labour.

We assumed, on the occasion of its sale, that the value of a day's labour-power was 3 shillings, and that 6 hours of labour was incorporated in that sum; and consequently that this amount of labour was needed to produce the worker's average daily means of subsistence. If now our spinner, by working for one hour, can convert 1⅔ lb. of cotton into 1⅔ lb. of yarn,[13] it follows that in 6 hours he will convert 10 lb. of cotton into 10 lb. of yarn. Hence, during the spinning process, the cotton absorbs 6 hours of labour. The same quantity of labour is also embodied in a piece of gold of the value of 3 shillings. A value of 3 shillings, therefore, is added to the cotton by the labour of spinning.

Let us now consider the total value of the product, the 10 lb. of yarn. Two and a half days of labour have been objectified in it. Out of this, two days were contained in the cotton and the worn-down portion of the spindle, and half a day was absorbed during the process of spinning. This two and a half days of labour is represented by a piece of gold of the value of 15 shillings. Hence 15 shillings is an adequate price for the 10 lb. of yarn, and the price of 1 lb. is 1s. 6d.

Our capitalist stares in astonishment. The value of the product is equal to the value of the capital advanced. The value advanced has not been valorized, no surplus-value has been created, and

13. These figures are entirely arbitrary.

consequently money has not been transformed into capital. The price of the yarn is 15 shillings, and 15 shillings were spent in the open market on the constituent elements of the product or, what amounts to the same thing, on the factors of the labour process; 10 shillings were paid for the cotton, 2 shillings for the wear of the spindle and 3 shillings for the labour-power. The swollen value of the yarn is of no avail, for it is merely the sum of the values formerly existing in the cotton, the spindle and the labour-power: out of such a simple addition of existing values, no surplus-value can possibly arise.[14] These values are now all concentrated in one thing; but so they were in the sum of 15 shillings, before it was split up into three parts by the purchase of the commodities.

In itself this result is not particularly strange. The value of one pound of yarn is 1s. 6d., and our capitalist would therefore have to pay 15 shillings for 10 lb. of yarn on the open market. It is clear that whether a man buys his house ready built, or has it built for him, neither of these operations will increase the amount of money laid out on the house.

Our capitalist, who is at home in vulgar economics, may perhaps say that he advanced his money with the intention of making more money out of it. The road to hell is paved with good intentions, and he might just as well have intended to make money without producing at all.[15] He makes threats. He will not be caught napping again. In future he will buy the commodities in the market, instead of manufacturing them himself. But if all his brother capitalists were to do the same, where would he find his commodities on the market? And he cannot eat his money. He recites the catechism: 'Consider my abstinence. I might have

14. This is the fundamental proposition which forms the basis of the doctrine of the Physiocrats that all non-agricultural labour is unproductive. For the professional economist it is irrefutable. 'This method of adding to one particular object the value of numerous others' (for example adding the living costs of the weaver to the flax) 'of as it were heaping up various values in layers on top of one single value, has the result that this value grows to the same extent . . . The expression "addition" gives a very clear picture of the way in which the price of a manufactured product is formed; this price is only the sum of a number of values which have been consumed, and it is arrived at by adding them together; however, addition is not the same as multiplication' (Mercier de la Rivière, op. cit., p. 599).

15. Thus from 1844 to 1847 he withdrew part of his capital from productive employment in order to throw it away in railway speculations; and so also, during the American Civil War, he closed his factory and turned the workers onto the street in order to gamble on the Liverpool cotton exchange.

squandered the 15 shillings, but instead I consumed it productively and made yarn with it.' Very true; and as a reward he is now in possession of good yarn instead of a bad conscience. As for playing the part of a miser, it would never do for him to relapse into such bad ways; we have already seen what such asceticism leads to. Besides, where there is nothing, the king has lost his rights; whatever the merits of his abstinence there is no money there to recompense him, because the value of the product is merely the sum of the values thrown into the process of production. Let him therefore console himself with the reflection that virtue is its own reward. But no, on the contrary, he becomes insistent. The yarn is of no use to him, he says. He produced it in order to sell it. In that case let him sell it, or, easier still, let him in future produce only things he needs himself, a remedy already prescribed by his personal physician MacCulloch as being of proven efficacy against an epidemic of over-production. Now our capitalist grows defiant. 'Can the worker produce commodities out of nothing, merely by using his arms and legs? Did I not provide him with the materials through which, and in which alone, his labour could be embodied? And as the greater part of society consists of such impecunious creatures, have I not rendered society an incalculable service by providing my instruments of production, my cotton and my spindle, and the worker too, for have I not provided him with the means of subsistence? Am I to be allowed nothing in return for all this service?' But has the worker not performed an equivalent service in return, by changing his cotton and his spindle into yarn? In any case, here the question of service does not arise.[16] A service is nothing other than the useful effect of a use-value, be it that of a com-

---

16. 'Let whoever wants to do so extol himself, put on finery and adorn himself [but pay no heed and keep firmly to the scriptures] . . . Whoever takes more or better than he gives, that is usury and does not signify a service but a wrong done to his neighbour, as when one steals and robs. Not everything described as a service and a benefit to one's neighbour is in fact a service and a benefit. An adulteress and an adulterer do each other a great service and pleasure. A horseman does great service to a robber by helping him to rob on the highway, and attack the people and the land. The papists do our people a great service in that they do not drown, burn, or murder them all, or let them rot in prison, but let some live and drive them out or take from them what they have. The devil himself does his servants a great, inestimable service . . . To sum up: the world is full of great, excellent daily services and good deeds' (Martin Luther, *An die Pfarrherrn, wider den Wucher zu predigen. Vermanung*, Wittenberg, 1540).

modity, or that of the labour.[17] But here we are dealing with exchange-value. The capitalist paid to the worker a value of 3 shillings, and the worker gave him back an exact equivalent in the value of 3 shillings he added to the cotton: he gave him value for value. Our friend, who has up till now displayed all the arrogance of capital, suddenly takes on the unassuming demeanour of one of his own workers, and exclaims: 'Have I myself not worked? Have I not performed the labour of superintendence, of overseeing the spinner? And does not this labour, too, create value?' The capitalist's own overseer and manager shrug their shoulders. In the meantime, with a hearty laugh, he recovers his composure. The whole litany he has just recited was simply meant to pull the wool over our eyes. He himself does not care twopence for it. He leaves this and all similar subterfuges and conjuring tricks to the professors of political economy, who are paid for it. He himself is a practical man, and although he does not always consider what he says outside his business, within his business he knows what he is doing.

Let us examine the matter more closely. The value of a day's labour-power amounts to 3 shillings, because on our assumption half a day's labour is objectified in that quantity of labour-power, i.e. because the means of subsistence required every day for the production of labour-power cost half a day's labour. But the past labour embodied in the labour-power and the living labour it can perform, and the daily cost of maintaining labour-power and its daily expenditure in work, are two totally different things. The former determines the exchange-value of the labour-power, the latter is its use-value. The fact that half a day's labour is necessary to keep the worker alive during 24 hours does not in any way prevent him from working a whole day. Therefore the value of labour-power, and the value which that labour-power valorizes [*verwertet*] in the labour-process, are two entirely different magnitudes; and this difference was what the capitalist had in mind when he was purchasing the labour-power. The useful quality of labour-power, by virtue of which it makes yarn or boots, was to the capitalist merely the necessary condition for his activity; for in order to create value labour must be expended in a useful manner. What

17. In *Zur Kritik der politischen Ökonomie*, p. 14 [English edition, p. 37], I make the following remark on this point: 'It is easy to understand what "service" the category "service" must render to economists like J. B. Say and F. Bastiat.'

was really decisive for him was the specific use-value which this commodity possesses of being a source not only of value, but of more value than it has itself. This is the specific service the capitalist expects from labour-power, and in this transaction he acts in accordance with the eternal laws of commodity-exchange. In fact, the seller of labour-power, like the seller of any other commodity, realizes [*realisiert*] its exchange-value, and alienates [*veräussert*] its use-value. He cannot take the one without giving the other. The use-value of labour-power, in other words labour, belongs just as little to its seller as the use-value of oil after it has been sold belongs to the dealer who sold it. The owner of the money has paid the value of a day's labour-power; he therefore has the use of it for a day, a day's labour belongs to him. On the one hand the daily sustenance of labour-power costs only half a day's labour, while on the other hand the very same labour-power can remain effective, can work, during a whole day, and consequently the value which its use during one day creates is double what the capitalist pays for that use; this circumstance is a piece of good luck for the buyer, but by no means an injustice towards the seller.

Our capitalist foresaw this situation, and that was the cause of his laughter. The worker therefore finds, in the workshop, the means of production necessary for working not just 6 but 12 hours. If 10 lb. of cotton could absorb 6 hours' labour, and become 10 lb. of yarn, now 20 lb. of cotton will absorb 12 hours' labour and be changed into 20 lb. of yarn. Let us examine the product of this extended labour-process. Now five days of labour are objectified in this 20 lb. of yarn; four days are due to the cotton and the lost steel of the spindle, the remaining day has been absorbed by the cotton during the spinning process. Expressed in gold, the labour of five days is 30 shillings. This is therefore the price of the 20 lb. of yarn, giving, as before, 1s. 6d. as the price of 1 lb. But the sum of the values of the commodities thrown into the process amounts to 27 shillings. The value of the yarn is 30 shillings. Therefore the value of the product is one-ninth greater than the value advanced to produce it; 27 shillings have turned into 30 shillings; a surplus-value of 3 shillings has been precipitated. The trick has at last worked: money has been transformed into capital.

Every condition of the problem is satisfied, while the laws governing the exchange of commodities have not been violated in any way. Equivalent has been exchanged for equivalent. For the capitalist as buyer paid the full value for each commodity, for the cotton, for the spindle and for the labour-power. He then did what is done by every purchaser of commodities: he consumed their use-value. The process of consuming labour-power, which was also the process of producing commodities, resulted in 20 lb. of yarn, with a value of 30 shillings. The capitalist, formerly a buyer, now returns to the market as a seller. He sells his yarn at 1s. 6d. a pound, which is its exact value. Yet for all that he withdraws 3 shillings more from circulation than he originally threw into it. This whole course of events, the transformation of money into capital, both takes place and does not take place in the sphere of circulation. It takes place through the mediation of circulation because it is conditioned by the purchase of the labour-power in the market; it does not take place in circulation because what happens there is only an introduction to the valorization process, which is entirely confined to the sphere of production. And so 'everything is for the best in the best of all possible worlds'.

By turning his money into commodities which serve as the building materials for a new product, and as factors in the labour process, by incorporating living labour into their lifeless objectivity, the capitalist simultaneously transforms value, i.e. past labour in its objectified and lifeless form, into capital, value which can perform its own valorization process, an animated monster which begins to 'work', 'as if its body were by love possessed'.*

If we now compare the process of creating value with the process of valorization, we see that the latter is nothing but the continuation of the former beyond a definite point. If the process is not carried beyond the point where the value paid by the capitalist for the labour-power is replaced by an exact equivalent, it is simply a process of creating value; but if it is continued beyond that point, it becomes a process of valorization.

If we proceed further, and compare the process of creating value with the labour process, we find that the latter consists in the useful labour which produces use-values. Here the movement of production is viewed qualitatively, with regard to the particular kind of article produced, and in accordance with the purpose and content of the movement. But if it is viewed as a value-creating process the same labour process appears only quantitatively. Here it is a question merely of the time needed to do the work, of the period, that is, during which the labour-power is usefully expended.

---

*Goethe, *Faust*, Part I, Auerbach's Cellar in Leipzig, line 2141 ('*als hätt' es Lieb' im Leibe*').

Here the commodities which enter into the labour process no longer count as functionally determined and material elements on which labour-power acts with a given purpose. They count merely as definite quantities of objectified labour. Whether it was already contained in the means of production, or has just been added by the action of labour-power, that labour counts only according to its duration. It amounts to so many hours, or days, etc.

Moreover, the time spent in production counts only in so far as it is socially necessary for the production of a use-value. This has various consequences. First, the labour-power must be functioning under normal conditions. If a self-acting mule is the socially predominant instrument of labour for spinning, it would be impermissible to supply the spinner with a spinning-wheel. The cotton too must not be such rubbish as to tear at every other moment, but must be of suitable quality. Otherwise the spinner would spend more time than socially necessary in producing his pound of yarn, and in this case the excess of time would create neither value nor money. But whether the objective factors of labour are normal or not does not depend on the worker, but rather on the capitalist. A further condition is that the labour-power itself must be of normal effectiveness. In the trade in which it is being employed, it must possess the average skill, dexterity and speed prevalent in that trade, and our capitalist took good care to buy labour-power of such normal quality. It must be expended with the average amount of exertion and the usual degree of intensity; and the capitalist is as careful to see that this is done, as he is to ensure that his workmen are not idle for a single moment. He has bought the use of the labour-power for a definite period, and he insists on his rights. He has no intention of being robbed. Lastly – and for this purpose our friend has a penal code of his own – all wasteful consumption of raw material or instruments of labour is strictly forbidden, because what is wasted in this way represents a superfluous expenditure of quantities of objectified labour, labour that does not count in the product or enter into its value.[18]

18. This is one of the circumstances which make production based on slavery more expensive. Under slavery, according to the striking expression employed in antiquity, the worker is distinguishable only as *instrumentum vocale* from an animal, which is *instrumentum semi-vocale*, and from a lifeless implement, which is *instrumentum mutum*.* But he himself takes care to let

*The slave was the 'speaking implement', the animal the 'semi-mute implement' and the plough the 'mute implement' (Varro, *Rerum Rusticarum Libri Tres*, I, 17).

We now see that the difference between labour, considered on the one hand as producing utilities, and on the other hand as creating value, a difference which we discovered by our analysis of a commodity, resolves itself into a distinction between two aspects of the production process.

The production process, considered as the unity of the labour process and the process of creating value, is the process of production of commodities; considered as the unity of the labour process and the process of valorization, it is the capitalist process of production, or the capitalist form of the production of commodities.

We stated on a previous page that in the valorization process it does not in the least matter whether the labour appropriated by the capitalist is simple labour of average social quality, or more complex labour, labour with a higher specific gravity as it were.

---

both beast and implement feel that he is none of them, but rather a human being. He gives himself the satisfaction of knowing that he is different by treating the one with brutality and damaging the other *con amore*. Hence the economic principle, universally applied in this mode of production, of employing only the rudest and heaviest implements, which are difficult to damage owing to their very clumsiness. In the slave states bordering on the Gulf of Mexico, down to the date of the Civil War, the only ploughs to be found were those constructed on the old Chinese model, which turned up the earth like a pig or a mole, instead of making furrows. Cf. J. E. Cairnes, *The Slave Power*, London, 1862, pp. 46 ff. In his *Seaboard Slave States*, Olmsted says, among other things, 'I am here shown tools that no man in his senses, with us, would allow a labourer, for whom he was paying wages, to be encumbered with; and the excessive weight and clumsiness of which, I would judge, would make work at least ten per cent greater than with those ordinarily used with us. And I am assured that, with the careless and clumsy treatment they always must get from the slaves, anything lighter or less rude could not be furnished them with good economy, and that such tools as we constantly give our labourers and find our profit in giving them, would not last a day in a Virginia cornfield – much lighter and more free from stones though it be than ours. So, too, when I ask why mules are so universally substituted for horses on the farm, the first reason given, and confessedly the most conclusive one, is that horses are always soon foundered or crippled by them, while mules will bear cudgelling, or lose a meal or two now and then, and not be materially injured, and they do not take cold or get sick, if neglected or overworked. But I do not need to go further than to the window of the room in which I am writing, to see at almost any time, treatment of cattle that would ensure the immediate discharge of the driver by almost any farmer owning them in the North.'*

*F. L. Olmsted, *A Journey in the Seaboard Slave States*, New York, 1856, pp. 46–7.

All labour of a higher, or more complicated, character than average labour is expenditure of labour-power of a more costly kind, labour-power whose production has cost more time and labour than unskilled or simple labour-power, and which therefore has a higher value. This power being of higher value, it expresses itself in labour of a higher sort, and therefore becomes objectified, during an equal amount of time, in proportionally higher values. Whatever difference in skill there may be between the labour of a spinner and that of a jeweller, the portion of his labour by which the jeweller merely replaces the value of his own labour-power does not in any way differ in quality from the additional portion by which he creates surplus-value. In both cases, the surplus-value results only from a quantitative excess of labour, from a lengthening of one and the same labour-process: in the one case, the process of making jewels, in the other, the process of making yarn.[19]

19. The distinction between higher and simple labour, 'skilled labour' and 'unskilled labour', rests in part on pure illusion or, to say the least, on distinctions that have long since ceased to be real, and survive only by virtue of a traditional convention; and in part on the helpless condition of some sections of the working class, a condition that prevents them from exacting equally with the rest the value of their labour-power. Accidental circumstances here play so great a part that these two forms of labour sometimes change places. Where, for instance, the physique of the working class has deteriorated and is, relatively speaking, exhausted, which is the case in all countries where capitalist production is highly developed, the lower forms of labour, which demand great expenditure of muscle, are in general considered as higher forms, compared with much more delicate forms of labour; the latter sink down to the level of simple labour. Take as an example the labour of a bricklayer, which in England occupies a much higher level than that of a damask-weaver. Again, although the labour of a fustian-cutter demands greater bodily exertion, and is at the same time unhealthy, it counts only as simple labour. Moreover, we must not imagine that so-called 'skilled' labour forms a large part of the whole of the nation's labour. Laing estimates that in England (and Wales) the livelihood of 11,300,000 people depends on unskilled labour. If from the total population of 18,000,000 living at the time when he wrote, we deduct 1,000,000 for the 'genteel population', 1,500,000 for paupers, vagrants, criminals and prostitutes, and 4,650,000 who compose the middle class, there remain the above-mentioned 11,000,000. But in his middle class he includes people who live on the interest of small investments, officials, men of letters, artists, schoolmasters and the like, and in order to swell the number he also includes in these 4,650,000 the better paid portion of the 'factory workers'! The bricklayers, too, figure amongst these 'high-class workers' (S. Laing, *National Distress etc.*, London, 1844). 'The great class who have nothing to give for food but ordinary labour, are the great bulk of the people' (James Mill, in the article 'Colony', *Supplement to the Encyclopaedia Britannica*, 1831).

But, on the other hand, in every process of creating value the reduction of the higher type of labour to average social labour, for instance one day of the former to x days of the latter, is unavoidable.[20] We therefore save ourselves a superfluous operation, and simplify our analysis, by the assumption that the labour of the worker employed by the capitalist is average simple labour.

20. 'Where reference is made to labour as a measure of value, it necessarily implies labour of one particular kind . . . the proportion which the other kinds bear to it being easily ascertained' ([J. Cazenove], *Outlines of Political Economy*, London, 1832, pp. 22–3).

Chapter 8: Constant Capital and Variable Capital

The various factors of the labour process play different parts in forming the value of the product.

The worker adds fresh value to the material of his labour by expending on it a given amount of additional labour, no matter what the specific content, purpose and technical character of that labour may be. On the other hand, the values of the means of production used up in the process are preserved, and present themselves afresh as constituent parts of the value of the product; the values of the cotton and the spindle, for instance, re-appear again in the value of the yarn. The value of the means of production is therefore preserved by being transferred to the product. This transfer takes place during the conversion of those means into a product, in other words during the labour process. It is mediated through labour. But how is this done?

The worker does not perform two pieces of work simultaneously, one in order to add value to the cotton, the other in order to preserve the value of the means of production, or, what amounts to the same thing, to transfer to the yarn, as product, the value of the cotton on which he works, and part of the value of the spindle with which he works. But by the very act of adding new value he preserves their former values. Since however the addition of new value to the material of his labour, and the preservation of its former value, are two entirely distinct results, it is plain that this twofold nature of the result can be explained only by the twofold nature of his labour; it must at the same time create value through one of its properties and preserve or transfer value through another.

Now how does every worker add fresh labour-time and therefore fresh value? Evidently, only by working productively in a particular way. The spinner adds labour-time by spinning, the weaver by weaving, the smith by forging. But although these operations add labour as such, and therefore new values, it is only through the agency of labour directed to a particular purpose, by means of the spinning, the weaving and the forging respectively, that the means of production, the cotton and the spindle, the yarn and the loom, and the iron and the anvil, become constituent elements of the product, of a new use-value.[1] The old form of the use-value disappears, but it is taken up again in a new form of use-value. We saw, when we were considering the process of creating value, that if a use-value is effectively consumed in the production of a new use-value, the quantity of labour expended to produce the article which has been consumed forms a part of the quantity of labour necessary to produce the new use-value; this portion is therefore labour transferred from the means of production to the new product. Hence the worker preserves the values of the already consumed means of production or transfers them to the product as portions of its value, not by virtue of his additional labour as such, but by virtue of the particular useful character of that labour, by virtue of its specific productive form. Therefore, in so far as labour is productive activity directed to a particular purpose, in so far as it is spinning, weaving or forging, etc., it raises the means of production from the dead merely by entering into contact with them, infuses them with life so that they become factors of the labour process, and combines with them to form new products.

If the specific productive labour of the worker were not spinning, he could not convert the cotton into yarn, and therefore he could not transfer the values of the cotton and spindle to the yarn. Suppose the same worker were to change his trade to that of a joiner, he would still by a day's labour add value to the material he worked on. We see therefore that the addition of new value takes place not by virtue of his labour being spinning in particular, or joinery in particular, but because it is labour in general, abstract social labour; and we see also that the value added is of a certain definite amount, not because his labour has a particular useful content, but because it lasts for a definite length of time. On the one hand, it is by virtue of its general character as expenditure of human labour-power in the abstract that spinning adds new value to the values of the cotton and the spindle; and on the other hand, it is by virtue of its special character as a concrete, useful process that the same labour of spinning both transfers the values of the means of production to the product and preserves them in the

1. 'Labour gives a new creation for one extinguished' (*An Essay on the Political Economy of Nations*, London, 1821, p. 13).

product. Hence a twofold result emerges within the same period of time.

By the simple addition of a certain quantity of labour, new value is added, and by the quality of this added labour, the original values of the means of production are preserved in the product. This twofold effect, resulting from the twofold character of labour, appears quite plainly in numerous phenomena.

Let us assume that some invention enables the spinner to spin as much cotton in 6 hours as he was able to spin before in 36 hours. His labour is now six times as effective as it was, considered as useful productive activity directed to a given purpose. The product of 6 hours' labour has increased sixfold, from 6 lb. to 36 lb. But now the 36 lb. of cotton absorb only the same amount of labour as did the 6 lb. formerly. One-sixth as much new labour is absorbed by each pound of cotton, and consequently the value added by the labour to each pound is only one-sixth of what it formerly was. On the other hand, in the product (the 36 lb. of yarn) the value transferred from the cotton is six times as great as before. The value of the raw material preserved and transferred to the product by the 6 hours of spinning is six times as great as before, although the new value added by the labour of the spinner to each pound of the very same raw material is one-sixth of what it was formerly. This shows that the two properties of labour, by virtue of which it is enabled in one case to preserve value and in the other to create value, within the same indivisible process, are different in their very essence. On the one hand, the longer the time necessary to spin a given weight of cotton into yarn, the greater the amount of fresh value added to the cotton; but, on the other hand, the greater the weight of the cotton spun in a given time, the greater is the value preserved, by being transferred from it to the product.

Let us now assume that the productivity of the spinner's labour, instead of varying, remains constant, that he therefore requires the same time as he formerly did to convert one pound of cotton into yarn, but that the exchange-value of the cotton varies, either by rising to six times its former value or by falling to one-sixth of that value. In both these cases, the spinner puts the same quantity of labour into a pound of cotton, and therefore adds as much value, as he did before the change in the value; he also produces a given weight of yarn in the same time as he did before. Nevertheless, the value he transfers from the cotton to the yarn is either six times what it was before, or, in the second case, one-sixth as much. The same result occurs when the value of the instruments of labour rises or falls, while their usefulness in the labour process remains unaltered.

Again, if the technical conditions of the spinning process remain unchanged, and no change of value takes place in the means of production, the spinner continues to consume in equal working-times equal quantities of raw material and equal quantities of machinery of unvarying value. The value preserved in the product is directly proportional to the new value added to the product. In two weeks the spinner adds twice as much labour, and therefore twice as much value, as in one week, and during the same time he consumes twice as much material, and wears out twice as much machinery, of double the value in each case; he therefore preserves, in the product of two weeks, twice as much value as in the product of one week. As long as the conditions of production remain the same, the more value the worker adds by fresh labour, the more value he transfers and preserves. However, this does not happen because he adds new value, but because the addition of new value takes place under unvaried conditions which are independent of his own labour.

Of course it may be said, in a relative sense, that the worker always preserves old value in proportion to the added quantity of new value. Whether the value of cotton rises from one shilling to two shillings, or falls to sixpence, the worker invariably preserves in the product of one hour only half as much value as he preserves in two hours. Similarly, if the productivity of his own labour rises or falls, he will in the course of one hour spin either more or less cotton then he did before, and will consequently preserve more or less of the value of the cotton in the product of one hour; but, all the same, he will preserve twice as much value by two hours' labour as he will by one.

Value exists only in use-values, in things, if we leave aside its purely symbolic representation in tokens. (Man himself, viewed merely as the physical existence of labour-power, is a natural object, a thing, although a living, conscious thing, and labour is the physical manifestation [*dingliche Aüsserung*] of that power.) If therefore an article loses its use-value it also loses its value. The reason why means of production do not lose their value at the same time as they lose their use-value is that they lose in the labour process the original form of their use-value only to assume in the product the form of a new use-value. But however important it may be to value that it should have some use-value to exist in, it is still a matter of complete indifference what particular object serves this purpose. We saw this when dealing with the metamorphosis of commodities. Hence it follows that in the labour process the means of production transfer their value to the product only in so far as they lose their exchange-value along with their independent use-value. They only give up to the product the value they themselves lose as means of production. But in this respect the objective factors of the labour process do not all behave in the same way.

The coal burnt under the boiler vanishes without leaving a trace; so too the oil with which the axles of wheels are greased. Dye-stuffs and other auxiliary substances also vanish, but re-appear in the properties of the product. The raw material forms the substance of the product, but only after it has undergone a change in its form. Hence raw material and auxiliary substances lose the independent form with which they entered into the labour process. It is otherwise with the actual instruments of labour. Tools, machines, factory buildings and containers are only of use in the labour process as long as they keep their original shape, and are ready each morning to enter into it in the same form. And just as during their lifetime, that is to say during the labour process, they retain their shape independently of the product, so too after their death. The mortal remains of machines, tools, workshops etc., always continue to lead an existence distinct from that of the product they helped to turn out. If we now consider the case of any instrument of labour during the whole period of its service, from the day of its entry into the workshop to the day of its banishment to the lumber room, we find that during this period its use-value has been completely consumed, and therefore its exchange-value completely transferred to the product. For instance, if a spinning machine lasts for ten years, it is plain that during that working period its total value is gradually transferred to the product of the ten years. The lifetime of an instrument of labour is thus spent in the repetition of a greater or lesser number of similar operations. The instrument suffers the same fate as the man. Every day brings a man twenty-four hours nearer to his grave, although no one can tell accurately, merely by looking at a man, how many days he has still to travel on that road. This difficulty, however, does not prevent life insurance companies from using the theory of averages to draw very accurate, and what is more, very profitable conclusions about the length of a man's life. So it is with the instruments of labour. It is known by experience how long on the average a machine of a particular kind will last. Suppose its use-value in the labour process lasts only six days. It then loses on average one-sixth of its use-value every day, and therefore parts with one-sixth of its value to each day's product. The deterioration of all instruments, their daily loss of use-value, and the corresponding quantity of value they part with to the product, are accordingly calculated on this basis.

It is thus strikingly clear that means of production never transfer more value to the product than they themselves lose during the labour process by the destruction of their own use-value. If an instrument of production has no value to lose, i.e. if it is not the product of human labour, it transfers no value to the product. It helps to create use-value without contributing to the formation of exchange-value. This is true of all those means of production supplied by nature without human assistance, such as land, wind, water, metals in the form of ore, and timber in virgin forests.

Here we are confronted with another interesting phenomenon. Suppose a machine is worth £1,000, and wears out in 1,000 days. Then every day one-thousandth of the value of the machine is transferred to the day's product. At the same time the machine as a whole continues to take part in the labour process, though with diminishing vitality. Thus it appears that one factor of the labour process, a means of production, continually enters as a whole into that process, while it only enters in parts into the valorization process. The distinction between the labour process and the valorization process is reflected here in their objective factors, in that one and the same means of production, in one and the same process of production, counts in its totality as an element in the labour process, but only piece by piece as an element in the creation of value.[2]

2. We are not concerned here with repairs to the instruments of labour. A machine under repair is no longer an instrument of labour, but its material. Work is no longer done with it, but upon it, in order to patch up its use-value. It is quite permissible for our purpose to assume that the labour expended on the repair of instruments is included in the labour necessary for their original production. But in the text we deal with that deterioration which no doctor can cure, and which little by little brings about death, with 'that kind of wear which cannot be repaired from time to time, and which, in the case of a knife, would ultimately reduce it to a state in which the cutler would say of it, it is not worth a new blade'. We have shown in the text that a machine participates in every labour process as a whole, but enters into the

On the other hand a means of production may enter as a whole into the valorization process, although it enters only piece by piece into the labour process. Suppose that in spinning cotton, the waste for every 115 lb. used amounts to 15 lb., which is converted, not into yarn, but into 'devil's dust'.* Now, although this amount of waste is normal and inevitable under average conditions of spinning, the value of the 15 lb. of cotton is just as surely transferred to the value of the yarn as is the value of the 100 lb. that form the substance of the yarn. The use-value of 15 lb. of cotton must vanish into dust before 100 lb. of yarn can be made. The destruction of this cotton is therefore a necessary condition for the production of the yarn. And because it is a necessary condition, and for no other reason, the value of that cotton is transferred to the product. The same holds good for every kind of refuse resulting from a labour process, where that refuse cannot be further employed as a means in the production of new and independent use-values. Such an employment of refuse can be seen in the large machine-building factories at Manchester, where mountains of iron turnings are carted away to the foundry in the evening, only to re-appear the next morning in the workshops as solid masses of iron.

We have seen that the means of production transfer value to the new product only when during the labour process they lose value in the shape of their old use-value. The maximum loss of value the means of production can suffer in the process is plainly limited by the amount of the original value with which they entered into it, or,

---

simultaneous process of valorization only in parts. How great, then, is the confusion of ideas exhibited in the following extract! 'Mr Ricardo says a portion of the labour of the engineer in making stocking machines' is contained for example in the value of a pair of stockings. 'Yet the total labour that produced each single pair of stockings . . . includes the whole labour of the engineer, not a portion; for one machine makes many pairs, and none of those pairs could have been done without any part of the machine' (*Observations on Certain Verbal Disputes in Political Economy, Particularly Relating to Value*, p. 54). The author, an uncommonly self-satisfied 'wiseacre', is justified in his confusion, and therefore in his polemic, only to the extent that neither Ricardo nor any other economist before or since has accurately distinguished the two aspects of labour, and still less, therefore, analysed the part played by each of these aspects in the formation of value.

---

*The name given to flock made out of cotton scraps by a machine known as the 'devil'.

in other words, by the labour-time required to produce them. Therefore the means of production can never add more value to the product than they themselves possess independently of the process in which they assist. However useful a given kind of raw material, or a machine, or other means of production may be, even if it cost £150 or, say, 500 days of labour, it cannot under any circumstances add more than £150 to the value of the product. Its value is determined not by the labour process into which it enters as a means of production, but by that out of which it has issued as a product. In the labour process it serves only as a use-value, a thing with useful properties, and cannot therefore transfer any value to the product unless it possessed value before its entry into the process.[3]

While productive labour is changing the means of production into constituent elements of a new product, their value undergoes a metempsychosis. It deserts the consumed body to occupy the newly created one. But this transmigration takes place, as it were, behind the back of the actual labour in progress. The worker is unable to add new labour, to create new value, without at the same

3. This shows the absurdity and triviality of the view adopted by J. B. Say, who claims to derive surplus-value (interest, profit, rent) from the '*services productifs*' rendered by the means of production (land, instruments of labour, raw material) in the labour process *via* their use-values. Mr Wilhelm Roscher, who seldom loses the opportunity of rushing into print with ingenious apologetic fantasies, records the following example: 'J. B. Say (*Traité*, Vol. I, Ch. 4) very truly remarks: the value produced by an oil mill, after deduction of all costs, is something new, something quite different from the labour by which the oil mill itself was erected' (op. cit., p. 82, note). Very true! The oil produced by the oil mill is indeed something very different from the labour expended in constructing the mill! By 'value' Mr Roscher means such stuff as 'oil', because oil has value, despite the fact that 'in nature' petroleum is to be found, although in relatively 'small quantities', which is what he appears to refer to when he says 'It (nature!) produces scarcely any exchange-value' [ibid., p. 79]. Mr Roscher's 'nature' and the exchange-value it produces are rather like the foolish virgin who admitted that she had had a child, but 'only a very little one'. This 'man of learning' ('*savant sérieux*') continues on the same subject: 'Ricardo's school is in the habit of including capital as accumulated labour under the heading of labour. This is unskilful (!), because (!) indeed the owner of capital (!) has after all (!) done more than merely (!?) create (?) and preserve (??) the same (what same?): namely (?!?) the abstention from the enjoyment of it, in return for which he demands, for instance (!!!) interest' (ibid. [p. 82]). How very 'skilful' is this 'anatomico-physiological method' of political economy, which converts a mere 'demand' into a source of value!

time preserving old values, because the labour he adds must be of a specific useful kind, and he cannot do work of a useful kind without employing products as the means of production of a new product, and thereby transferring their value to the new product. The property therefore which labour-power in action, living labour, possesses of preserving value, at the same time that it adds it, is a gift of nature which costs the worker nothing, but is very advantageous to the capitalist since it preserves the existing value of his capital.[4] As long as trade is good, the capitalist is too absorbed in making profits to take notice of this gratuitous gift of labour. Violent interruptions of the labour process, crises, make him painfully aware of it.[5]

As regards the means of production, what is really consumed is their use-value, and the consumption of this use-value by labour results in the product. There is in fact no consumption of their value[6] and it would therefore be inaccurate to say that it is reproduced. It is rather preserved; not by reason of any operation it itself undergoes in the labour process but because the use-value in which it originally existed vanishes (although when it vanishes, it does so into another use-value). Hence the value of the means of

4. 'Of all the instruments of the farmer's trade, the labour of man ... is that on which he is most to rely for the re-payment of his capital. The other two ... the working stock of the cattle and the ... carts, ploughs, spades, and so forth, without a given portion of the first, are nothing at all' (Edmund Burke, *Thoughts and Details on Scarcity, Originally Presented to the Rt. Hon. W. Pitt in the Month of November 1795*, London, 1800, p. 10).

5. In *The Times* of 26 November 1862, a manufacturer whose mill employs 800 workers and consumes a yearly average of 150 bales of East Indian cotton, or 130 bales of American, complains dolefully of the overhead expenses of his factory when it is not in use. He estimates these at £6,000 a year. Among them are a number of items not relevant here, such as rent, rates, taxes, insurance, the salaries of the manager, the accountant, the engineer and others. But on top of that he reckons £150 for coal used to heat the mill occasionally, and to set the steam-engine in motion. In addition, he includes the wages of the people employed at odd times to keep the machinery in working order. Lastly, he puts down £1,200 for depreciation of machinery, because 'the weather and the natural principles of decay do not suspend their operations because the steam-engine ceases to revolve'. He expressly states that he does not estimate his depreciation at more than the small sum of £1,200 because his machinery is already nearly worn out.

6. 'Productive Consumption: where the consumption of a commodity is a part of the process of production ... In these instances there is no consumption of value' (S. P. Newman, op. cit., p. 296).

production re-appears in the value of the product, but it is not strictly speaking reproduced in that value. What is produced is a new use-value in which the old exchange-value re-appears.[7]

It is otherwise with the subjective factor of the labour process, labour-power, which sets itself in motion independently. While labour, because it is directed to a specific purpose, preserves and transfers to the product the value of the means of production, at the same time, throughout every instant it is in motion, it is creating an additional value, a new value. Suppose the process of production breaks off just when the worker has produced an equivalent for the value of his own labour-power, when for example by six hours of labour he has added a value of three shillings. This value is the excess of the total value of the product over the portion of its value contributed by the means of production. It is the only original value formed during this process, the only portion of the value of the product created by the process itself. Of course, we do not forget that this new value only replaces the money advanced by the capitalist in purchasing labour-power, and spent by the worker on means of subsistence. With regard to the three shillings which have been expended, the new value of three shillings appears merely as a reproduction. Nevertheless, it is a real reproduction, and not, as in the case of the value of the means of production, simply an apparent one. The replacement of one value by another is here brought about by the creation of new value.

We know however from what has gone before that the labour process may continue beyond the time necessary to reproduce and

7. In an American compendium, which has gone through perhaps twenty editions, the following passage occurs: 'It matters not in what form capital re-appears.' Then, after a lengthy enumeration of all the possible ingredients of production whose value re-appears in the product, the author reaches this conclusion: 'The various kinds of food, clothing, and shelter necessary for the existence and comfort of the human being are also changed. They are consumed from time to time, and their value re-appears in that new vigour imparted to his body and mind, forming fresh capital, to be employed again in the work of production' (F. Wayland, op. cit., pp. 31, 32). Without pointing out other oddities, let us just note for example that what re-appears in the new vigour is not the bread's price, but its body-building substance. What, on the other hand, re-appears in the value of that vigour is not the means of subsistence but their value. The same means of subsistence, at half the price, would form just as much muscle and bone, just as much vigour, but not vigour of the same value. This confusion of 'value' and 'vigour', coupled with the author's pharisaical vagueness, conceals an attempt, an inevitably vain attempt, to squeeze an explanation of surplus-value out of the mere re-appearance of pre-existing values.

incorporate in the product a mere equivalent for the value of the labour-power. For this, six hours alone would be sufficient: but the process lasts longer, say for twelve hours. The activity of labour-power, therefore, not only reproduces its own value, but produces value over and above this. This surplus-value is the difference between the value of the product and the value of the elements consumed in the formation of the product, in other words the means of production and the labour-power.

In presenting the different parts played by the various factors of the labour process in the formation of the product's value, we have in fact characterized the different functions allotted to the different elements of capital in its own valorization process. The excess of the total value of the product over the sum of the values of its constituent elements is the excess of the capital which has been valorized over the value of the capital originally advanced. The means of production on the one hand, labour-power on the other, are merely the different forms of existence which the value of the original capital assumed when it lost its monetary form and was transformed into the various factors of the labour process.

That part of capital, therefore, which is turned into means of production, i.e. the raw material, the auxiliary material and the instruments of labour, does not undergo any quantitative alteration of value in the process of production. For this reason, I call it the constant part of capital, or more briefly, constant capital.

On the other hand, that part of capital which is turned into labour-power does undergo an alteration of value in the process of production. It both reproduces the equivalent of its own value and produces an excess, a surplus-value, which may itself vary, and be more or less according to circumstances. This part of capital is continually being transformed from a constant into a variable magnitude. I therefore call it the variable part of capital, or more briefly, variable capital. The same elements of capital which, from the point of view of the labour process, can be distinguished respectively as the objective and subjective factors, as means of production and labour-power, can be distinguished, from the point of view of the valorization process, as constant and variable capital.

The definition of constant capital given above by no means excludes the possibility of a change of value in its elements. Suppose that the price of cotton is one day sixpence a pound, and the next day, as a result of a failure of the cotton crop, a shilling a pound. Each pound of the cotton bought at sixpence, and worked up after the rise in value, transfers to the product a value of one shilling; and the cotton already spun before the rise, and perhaps circulating in the market as yarn, similarly transfers to the product twice its original value. It is plain, however, that these changes of value are independent of the valorization of the cotton in the spinning process itself. If the old cotton had never been spun, it could be resold at a shilling a pound after the rise, instead of at sixpence. Further, the fewer the processes the cotton has gone through, the more certain is this result. We therefore find that speculators make it a rule, when such sudden changes in value occur, to speculate in the raw material in its least worked-up form: to speculate, therefore, in yarn rather than in cloth, and indeed in cotton itself rather than in yarn. The change of value in the case we have been considering originates not in the process in which the cotton plays the part of a means of production, and in which it therefore functions as constant capital, but in the process in which the cotton itself is produced. The value of a commodity is certainly determined by the quantity of labour contained in it, but this quantity is itself socially determined. If the amount of labour-time socially necessary for the production of any commodity alters – and a given weight of cotton represents more labour after a bad harvest than after a good one – this reacts back on all the old commodities of the same type, because they are only individuals of the same species,[8] and their value at any given time is measured by the labour socially necessary to produce them, i.e. by the labour necessary under the social conditions existing at the time.

As the value of the raw material may change, so too may that of the instruments of labour, the machinery, etc. employed in the process; and consequently that portion of the value of the product transferred to it from them may also change. If, as a result of a new invention, machinery of a particular kind can be produced with a lessened expenditure of labour, the old machinery undergoes a certain amount of depreciation, and therefore transfers proportionately less value to the product. But here too the change in value originates outside the process in which the machine is acting as a means of production. Once engaged in this process the machine cannot transfer more value than it possesses independently of the process.

8. 'Properly speaking, all products of the same kind form a single mass, and their price is determined in general and without regard to particular circumstances' (Le Trosne, op. cit., p. 893).

Just as a change in the value of the means of production, even after they have begun to take part in the labour process, does not alter their character as constant capital, so too a change in the proportion of constant to variable capital does not affect the distinction in their functions. The technical conditions of the labour process may be revolutionized to such an extent that where formerly ten men using ten implements of small value worked up a relatively small quantity of raw material, one man may now, with the aid of one expensive machine, work up one hundred times as much raw material. In the latter case we have an enormous increase in the constant capital, i.e. the total value of the means of production employed, and at the same time a great reduction in the variable part of the capital, which has been laid out in labour-power. This change however alters only the quantitative relation between the constant and the variable capital, or the proportion in which the total capital is split up into its constant and variable constituents; it has not in the least degree affected the essential difference between the two.

Chapter 9: The Rate of Surplus-Value

I. THE DEGREE OF EXPLOITATION OF LABOUR-POWER

The surplus-value generated in the production process by C, the capital advanced, i.e. the valorization of the value of the capital C, presents itself to us first as the amount by which the value of the product exceeds the value of its constituent elements.

The capital C is made up of two components, one the sum of money c laid out on means of production, and the other the sum of money v expended on labour-power; c represents the portion of value which has been turned into constant capital, v that turned into variable capital. At the beginning, then, $C = c + v$: for example, if £500 is the capital advanced, its components may be such that the £500 = £410 constant + £90 variable. When the process of production is finished, we get a commodity whose value $= (c + v) + s$, where s is the surplus-value; or, taking our former figures, the value of this commodity is (£410 constant + £90 variable) + £90 surplus. The original capital has now changed from C to C', from £500 to £590. The difference is s, or a surplus-value of £90. Since the value of the constituent elements of the product is equal to the value of the capital advanced, it is a mere tautology to say that the excess of the value of the product over the value of its constituent elements is equal to the valorization of the value of the capital advanced, or to the surplus-value produced.

Nevertheless, we must examine this tautology a little more closely. The equation being made is between the value of the product and the value of its constituents consumed in the process of production. Now we have seen how that portion of the constant capital which consists of the instruments of labour transfers to the product only a fraction of its value, while the remainder of that value continues in its old form of existence. Since this remainder plays no part in the formation of value, we may at present leave it on one side. To introduce it into the calculation would make no difference. For instance, taking our former example, $c = £410$: assume that this sum consists of £312 value of raw material, £44 value of auxiliary material and £54 value of the machinery worn away in the process; and assume that the total value of the machinery employed is £1,054. Out of this latter sum, then, we reckon as advanced for the purpose of turning out the product the sum of £54 alone, which the machinery loses by wear and tear while performing its function, and therefore parts with to the product. Now if we also reckoned the remaining £1,000, which continues to exist in its old form in the machinery, as transferred to the product, we would also have to reckon it as part of the value advanced, and thus make it appear on both sides of our calculation.[1] We should, in this way, get £1,500 on one side and £1,590 on the other. The difference between these two sums, or the surplus-value, would still be £90. When we refer, therefore, to constant capital advanced for the production of value, we always mean the value of the means of production actually consumed in the course of production, unless the context demonstrates the reverse.

This being so, let us return to the formula $C = c + v$, which we saw was transformed into $C' = (c + v) + s$, C becoming C'. We know that the value of the constant capital is transferred to the product, and merely re-appears in it. The new value actually created in the process, the 'value-product', is therefore not the same as the value of the product; it is not, as it would at first sight appear, $(c + v) + s$ or £140 constant + £90 variable + £90 surplus, but rather $v + s$ or £90 variable + £90 surplus. In other words, not £590 but £180. If c, the constant capital, $= O$, in other words if there were branches of industry in which the capitalist could dispense with all means of production made by previous labour, whether raw material, auxiliary material, or instruments, employing only labour-power and materials supplied by nature, if that were the case, there would be no constant capital to transfer to the product. This component of the value of the product, i.e. the £410 in our example, would be eliminated, but the sum of £180, the amount of new value created, or the value produced, which contains £90 of surplus-value, would remain just as great as if c repre-

1. 'If we reckon the value of the fixed capital employed as a part of the advances, we must reckon the remaining value of such capital at the end of the year as a part of the annual return' (Malthus, *Principles of Political Economy*, 2nd edn, London, 1836, p. 269).

sented the highest value imaginable. We should have $C = (O + v)$ $= v$, and C' the valorized capital $= v + s$, and therefore $C' - C = s$ as before. On the other hand, if $s = O$, in other words if the labour-power whose value is advanced in the form of variable capital were to produce only its equivalent, we should have $C = c + v$, and C' (the value of the product) $= (c + v) + O$, hence $C = C'$. In this case the capital advanced would not have valorized its value.

From what has gone before we know that surplus-value is purely the result of an alteration in the value of v, of that part of the capital which was converted into labour-power; consequently, $v + s = v + \Delta v$ (v plus an increment of v). But the fact that it is v alone that varies, and the conditions of that variation, are obscured by the circumstance that in consequence of the increase in the variable component of the capital, there is also an increase in the sum total of the capital advanced. It was originally £500 and becomes £590. Therefore, in order that our investigation may lead to accurate results, we must make abstraction from that portion of the value of the product in which constant capital alone appears, and thus posit the constant capital as zero or make $c = O$. This is merely an application of a mathematical rule, employed whenever we operate with constant and variable magnitudes, related to each other only by the symbols of addition and subtraction.

A further difficulty is caused by the original form of the variable capital. In our example, $C' =$ £410 constant + £90 variable + £90 surplus; but £90 is a given and therefore a constant quantity and hence it appears absurd to treat it as variable. In fact, however, the £90 variable is here merely a symbol for the process undergone by this value. The portion of the capital invested in the purchase of labour-power is a definite quantity of objectified labour, a constant value like the value of the labour-power purchased. But in the process of production the place of the £90 is taken by labour-power which sets itself in motion, dead labour is replaced by living labour, something stagnant by something flowing, a constant by a variable. The result is the reproduction of v plus an increment of v. From the point of view of capitalist production, therefore, the whole process appears as the independent motion of what was originally constant value, but has now been transformed into labour-power. Both the process and its result are ascribed to this independent motion of value. If, therefore, such expressions as '£90 variable capital' or 'such and such a quantity of self-valorizing value' appear to contain contradictions, this is only because they express a contradiction immanent in capitalist production.

At first sight it appears strange to equate the constant capital to zero. But we do this every day. If, for example, we want to calculate the amount of profit gained by England from the cotton industry, we first of all deduct the sums paid for cotton to the United States, India, Egypt and various other countries, i.e. we posit the value of the capital that merely re-appears in the value of the product as a zero magnitude.

Of course, the ratio of surplus-value not only to that portion of the capital from which it directly arises, and whose change in value it represents, but also to the sum total of the capital advanced, is economically of very great importance. We shall therefore deal exhaustively with this ratio in our third book.* In order to enable one portion of capital to realize its value by being converted into labour-power, it is necessary that another portion be converted into means of production. In order that variable capital may perform its function, constant capital must be advanced to an adequate proportion, the proportion appropriate to the special technical conditions of each labour process. However, the fact that retorts and other vessels are necessary to a chemical process does not prevent the chemist from ignoring them when he undertakes his analysis of the results. If we look at the creation and the alteration of value for themselves, i.e. in their pure form, then the means of production, this physical shape taken on by constant capital, provides only the material in which fluid, value-creating labour-power has to be incorporated. Neither the nature nor the value of this material is of any importance. All that is needed is a sufficient supply of material to absorb the labour expended in the process of production. That supply once given, the material may rise or fall in value, or even be without any value in itself, like the land and the sea; but this will have no influence on the creation of value or on the variation in the quantity of value.[2]

In the first place, therefore, we equate the constant part of

2. What Lucretius says is self-evident: '*nil posse creari de nihilo*', out of nothing, nothing can be created.* 'Creation of value' is the transposition of labour-power into labour. Labour-power itself is, above all else, the material of nature transposed into a human organism.

* Lucretius, *De rerum Natura*, Bk I, verses 156–7.

* The ratio to which Marx refers here, rather obliquely, is in fact the rate of profit (s/C). See *Capital*, Vol. 3, Ch. 2, 'The Rate of Profit'.

capital with zero. The capital advanced is consequently reduced from $c+v$ to v, and instead of the value of the product $(c+v)+s$ we now have the value produced $(v+s)$. Given that the new value produced $= £180$, a sum which consequently represents the whole of the labour expended during the process, if we subtract £90 from it, being the value of the variable capital, we have £90 left, the amount of the surplus-value. This sum of £90, or s, expresses the absolute quantity of surplus-value produced. The relative quantity produced, or the ratio in which the variable capital has valorized its value, is plainly determined by the ratio of the surplus-value to the variable capital, and expressed by s/v. In our example this ratio is 90/90, or 100 per cent. This relative increase in the value of the variable capital, or the relative magnitude of the surplus-value, is called here the rate of surplus-value.[3]

We have seen that the worker, during one part of the labour process, produces only the value of his labour-power, i.e. the value of his means of subsistence. Since his work forms part of a system based on the social division of labour, he does not directly produce his own means of subsistence. Instead of this, he pro-duces a particular commodity, yarn for example, with a value equal to the value of his means of subsistence, or of the money for it. The part of his day's labour devoted to this purpose will be greater or less, in proportion to the value of his average daily requirements or, what amounts to the same thing, in proportion to the labour-time required on average to produce them. If the value of his daily means of subsistence represents an average of 6 hours' objectified labour, the worker must work an average of 6 hours to produce that value. If, instead of working for the capitalist, he worked independently on his own account, he would, other things being equal, still be obliged to work for the same number of hours in order to produce the value of his labour-power, and thereby to gain the means of subsistence necessary for his own preservation or continued reproduction. But as we have seen, during that part of his day's labour in which he pro-duces the value of his labour-power, say 3 shillings, he produces only an equivalent for the value of his labour-power already

3. The English use the terms 'rate of profit', 'rate of interest' to express this proportion. We shall see in Volume 3 that the rate of profit is no mystery, when one knows the laws of surplus-value.* But if one works in the reverse direction, one comprehends neither the one nor the other.

*See p. 323, last note, above.

advanced[4] by the capitalist; the new value created only replaces the variable capital advanced. It is owing to this fact that the production of the new value of 3 shillings has the appearance of a mere reproduction. I call the portion of the working day during which this reproduction takes place necessary labour-time, and the labour expended during that time necessary labour;[5] necessary for the worker, because independent of the particular social form of his labour; necessary for capital and the capitalist world, because the continued existence of the worker is the basis of that world.

During the second period of the labour process, that in which his labour is no longer necessary labour, the worker does indeed expend labour-power, he does work, but his labour is no longer necessary labour, and he creates no value for himself. He creates surplus-value which, for the capitalist, has all the charms of something created out of nothing. This part of the working day I call surplus labour-time, and to the labour expended during that time I give the name of surplus labour. It is just as important for a correct understanding of surplus-value to conceive it as merely a congealed quantity of surplus labour-time, as nothing but objectified surplus labour, as it is for a proper comprehension of value in general to conceive it as merely a congealed quantity of so many hours of labour, as nothing but objectified labour. What distinguishes the various economic formations of society – the distinction between for example a society based on slave-labour and a society based on wage-labour – is the form in which this surplus labour is in each case extorted from the immediate producer, the worker.[6]

4. [Note added by Engels to the third German edition:] Here the author uses the current economic language. It will be remembered that on p. 278 it was shown that in reality it is the worker who does the 'advancing' to the capitalist, not the capitalist to the worker.

5. In this work we have up to now used the term 'necessary labour-time' to designate the time necessary under given social conditions for the production of any commodity. Henceforward we use it to designate as well the time necessary for the production of the particular commodity labour-power. The use of the same technical term in different senses is inconvenient, but it cannot be entirely avoided in any science. Compare, for instance, the higher with the lower branches of mathematics.

6. With an originality worthy of Gottsched* himself, Herr Wilhelm

*The literary critic Johann Christoph Gottsched (1700–1766), famous for the unoriginality with which he translated the ideas of the French Enlightenment into German terms. In German literary history, however, he holds an important place for this very reason.

Since, on the one hand, the variable capital and the labour-power purchased by that capital are equal in value, and the value of this labour-power determines the necessary part of the working day; and since, on the other hand, the surplus-value is determined by the surplus part of the working day, it follows that surplus-value is in the same ratio to variable capital as surplus labour is to necessary labour. In other words, the rate of surplus value, $\frac{s}{v}$ = $\frac{\text{surplus labour}}{\text{necessary labour}}$. Both ratios, $\frac{s}{v}$ and $\frac{\text{surplus labour}}{\text{necessary labour}}$, express the same thing in different ways; in the one case in the form of objectified labour, in the other in the form of living, fluid labour.

The rate of surplus-value is therefore an exact expression for the degree of exploitation of labour-power by capital, or of the worker by the capitalist.[7]

We assumed in our example that the value of the product = £410 constant+£90 variable+£90 surplus, and that the capital advanced = £500. Since the surplus-value = £90, and the capital advanced = £500, we should, according to the usual way

---

Thucydides Roscher* has discovered that if, on the one hand, the formation of surplus-value or a surplus product, and the consequent accumulation of capital, is nowadays due to the 'thrift' of the capitalist, who 'demands his interest in return', on the other hand, 'in the lowest stages of civilization it is the strong who compel the weak to be thrifty' (op. cit., p. 78). To be thrifty with what? With labour? With the surplus products which are not even available? What is it that makes such men as Roscher account for the origin of surplus-value by drawing on the more or less plausible excuses offered by the capitalist for his appropriation of the available surplus-value? It is, besides their real ignorance, an apologetic dread of a scientific analysis of value and surplus-value which might produce a result unpalatable to the powers that be.

7. Although the rate of surplus-value is an exact expression for the degree of exploitation of labour-power, it is in no sense an expression for the absolute magnitude of the exploitation. For example, if necessary labour = 5 hours and surplus labour = 5 hours, the degree of exploitation is 100 per cent. The amount of exploitation is here measured by 5 hours. If, on the other hand, the necessary labour = 6 hours and the surplus labour = 6 hours, the degree of exploitation remains as before 100 per cent, while the actual amount of exploitation has increased by 20 per cent, namely from 5 to 6 hours.

*Professor Wilhelm Roscher (1817–94) proclaimed that he was the 'Thucydides of political economy' in the preface to his book *Die Grundlagen der Nationalökonomie* (1854). Marx on the other hand describes him as 'the master of the academic form' and his works as 'the graveyard of the science of political economy' (*Theories of Surplus-Value*, Part 3, p. 502).

of reckoning, get 18 per cent as the rate of surplus-value (because it is generally confused with the rate of profit), a rate so low it might well cause a pleasant surprise to Mr Carey and other harmonizers.* But in fact the rate of surplus-value is not equal to $\frac{s}{C}$ or $\frac{s}{c+v}$ but to $\frac{s}{v}$; thus it is not $\frac{90}{500}$ but $\frac{90}{90} = 100$ per cent, which is more than five times the apparent degree of exploitation. Although, in the case we have supposed, we do not know the actual length of the working day, or the duration in days and weeks of the labour process, or the number of workers set in motion simultaneously by the variable capital of £90, the rate of surplus-value $\frac{s}{v}$ accurately discloses to us, by means of its equivalent expression, $\frac{\text{surplus labour}}{\text{necessary labour}}$, the relation between the two parts of the working day. This relation is here one of equality, being 100 per cent. Hence the worker in our example works one half of the day for himself, the other half for the capitalist.

The method of calculating the rate of surplus-value is therefore, in brief, as follows. We take the total value of the product and posit the constant capital which merely re-appears in it as equal to zero. What remains is the only value that has actually been created in the process of producing the commodity. If the amount of surplus-value is given, we have only to deduct it from this remainder to find the variable capital. And *vice versa* if the latter is given and we need to find the surplus-value. If both are given, we have only to perform the concluding operation, namely calculate $\frac{s}{v}$, the ratio of the surplus-value to the variable capital.

Simple as the method is, it may not be amiss, by means of a few examples, to exercise the reader in the application of the novel principles underlying it.

First we will take the case of a spinning mill containing 10,000 mule spindles, spinning No. 32 yarn from American cotton, and producing 1 lb. of yarn weekly per spindle. We assume the waste to be 6 per cent: accordingly 10,600 lb. of cotton are consumed

---

* Exponents of the view that the relations of production within bourgeois society are inherently harmonious, and that the antagonisms described by the classical political economists are superficial and accidental rather than intrinsic to the system. Marx devoted a section of the *Grundrisse* (English edition, pp. 883–93) to a critique of the 'harmonizers'.

weekly, of which 600 lb. go to waste. The price of the cotton in April 1871 was 7¾d. per lb.; the raw material therefore costs approximately £342. The 10,000 spindles, including machinery for preparation and motive power, cost, we will assume, £1 per spindle, amounting to a total of £10,000. Depreciation we put at 10 per cent, or £1,000 a year = £20 a week. The rent of the building we suppose to be £300 a year, or £6 a week. The amount of coal consumed (for 100 h.p. indicated, at 4 lb. of coal per horse-power per hour during 60 hours, and including coal consumed in heating the mill) is 11 tons a week at 8s. 6d. a ton, and therefore comes to about £4½ a week; gas, £1 a week, oil etc., £4½ a week. Total cost of the above auxiliary materials, £10 a week. Therefore the constant part of the value of the week's product is £378. Wages amount to £52 a week. The price of the yarn is 12¼d. per lb., which gives, for the value of 10,000 lb., the sum of £150. The surplus-value is therefore in this case £510— £430 = £80. We put the constant part of the value of the product equal to zero, as it plays no part in the creation of value. There remains £132 as the weekly value created, which = £52 variable + £80 surplus. The rate of surplus-value is therefore $\frac{80}{52} = 153\frac{11}{13}$ per cent. In a working day of 10 hours with average labour the result is: necessary labour = $3\frac{31}{33}$ hours, and surplus labour = $6\frac{2}{33}$.[8]

One more example. Jacob gives the following calculation for the year 1815. Owing to the previous adjustment of several items it is very imperfect; nevertheless it is sufficient for our purpose. In it he assumes that the price of wheat is 8s. a quarter, and that the average yield per acre is 22 bushels.*

Here the assumption is always made that the price of the product is the same as its value, and, moreover, surplus-value is distributed under the various headings of profit, interest, rent etc. To us these headings are irrelevant. We simply add them together, and the sum is a surplus-value of £3 11s. 0d. The sum of £3 19s. 0d.

8. The example in the first edition, taken from a spinning mill for the year 1860, contained a number of factual errors. The data given in the present text, which are entirely accurate, were given to me by a Manchester manufacturer. It should be noted that in England the horse-power of an engine was formerly calculated from the diameter of its cylinders, but now the actual horse-power shown on the indicator is taken.

*William Jacob, *A Letter to Samuel Whitbread, being a Sequel to Considerations on the Protection Required by British Agriculture*, London, 1815, p. 33.

Value Produced Per Acre

Seed	£1	9	0	Tithes, rates and taxes £1	1 0
Manure	£2	10	0	Rent £1	8 0
Wages	£3	10	0	Farmer's profit and	
				interest £1	2 0
Total	£7	9	0	Total £3	11 0

paid for seed and manure is constant capital, and we put it equal
to zero. There is left the sum of £3 10s. 0d., which is the variable
capital advanced, and we see that a new value of £3 10s. 0d.+
£3 11s. 0d. has been produced in its place. Therefore $\dfrac{s}{v} = \dfrac{£3\ 11s.\ 0d.}{£3\ 10s.\ 0d.}$
i.e. more than 100 per cent. The worker employs more than half his
working day in producing the surplus-value, which different persons then share amongst themselves, on different pretexts.[9]

2. THE REPRESENTATION OF THE VALUE OF THE PRODUCT BY CORRESPONDING PROPORTIONAL PARTS OF THE PRODUCT

Let us now return to the example which showed us how the capitalist
converts money into capital. The necessary labour of his spinning
worker amounted to 6 hours, surplus labour was the same, the
degree of exploitation of labour-power was therefore 100 per cent.
The product of a working day of 12 hours is 20 lb. of yarn,
having a value of 30s. No less than eight-tenths of this value, or
24s., is formed by the mere re-appearance in it of the value of the
means of production (20 lb. of cotton, value 20s., and the worn
part of the spindle, 4s.). In other words, this part consists of
constant capital. The remaining two-tenths, or 6s., is the new
value created during the spinning process; one half of this replaces
the value of the day's labour-power, or the variable capital, the
remaining half constitutes a surplus-value of 3s. The total value
of the 20 lb. of yarn is thus made up as follows:

30s. value of yarn = 24s. constant + 3s. variable + 3s. surplus.

9. The calculations given in the text are intended merely as illustrations.
We have in fact assumed that prices = values. We shall, however, see in
Volume 3 that even in the case of average prices the assumption cannot be
made in this very simple manner.*
   * See *Capital*, Vol. 3, Ch. 1, 'Cost-Price and Profit'.

Since the whole of this value is contained in the 20 lb. of yarn produced, it follows that the various component parts of this value can be represented as being contained respectively in proportional parts of the product.

If the value of 30s. is contained in 20 lb. of yarn, then eight-tenths of this value, or the 24s. that forms its constant part, is contained in eight-tenths of the product, or in 16 lb. of yarn. Of the latter, $13\frac{1}{3}$ lb. represent the value of the raw material, the 20s. worth of cotton spun, and $2\frac{2}{3}$ lb. represent the 4s. worth of spindle etc. worn away in the process.

Hence the whole of the cotton used up in spinning the 20 lb. of yarn is represented by $13\frac{1}{3}$ lb. of yarn. This latter weight of yarn admittedly contains by weight no more than $13\frac{1}{3}$ lb. of cotton, worth $13\frac{1}{3}$s.; but the $6\frac{2}{3}$s. additional value contained in it is the equivalent for the cotton consumed in spinning the remaining $6\frac{2}{3}$ lb. of yarn. The effect is the same as if these $6\frac{2}{3}$ lb. of yarn contained no cotton at all, and the whole 20 lb. of cotton were concentrated in the $13\frac{1}{3}$ lb. of yarn. The latter weight, on the other hand, does not contain an atom of the value of the auxiliary materials and instruments of labour, or of the value newly created in the process.

In the same way, the $2\frac{2}{3}$ lb. of yarn in which the 4s., the remainder of the constant capital, is embodied represent nothing but the value of the auxiliary materials and instruments of labour consumed in producing the 20 lb. of yarn.

We have therefore arrived at this result: although eight-tenths of the product, or 16 lb. of yarn, seen in its physical existence as a use-value, is just as much the fabric of the spinner's labour as the remainder of the same product, yet when viewed in this connection it does not contain and has not absorbed any labour expended during the process of spinning. It is just as if the cotton had converted itself into yarn without any help, it is just as if the shape it had assumed was mere trickery and deceit. In fact, when the capitalist has sold it for 24s. and, with the money, replaced his means of production it becomes evident that the 16 lb. of yarn is nothing more than cotton, spindle-waste and coal in disguise.

On the other hand, the remaining two-tenths of the product, or 4 lb. of yarn, represent nothing but the new value of 6s. created during the 12 hours' spinning process. All the value transferred to those 4 lb. from the raw material and instruments of labour consumed was so to speak intercepted in order to be incorporated in the 16 lb. first spun. In this case, it is as if the spinner had spun 4 lb. of yarn out of air, or as if he had spun it with the aid of cotton and spindles which were available in nature, without human intervention, and therefore transferred no value to the product.

Of this 4 lb. of yarn, in which the whole of the value created in the daily process of spinning is condensed, one half represents the equivalent for the value of the labour consumed, or the 3s. of variable capital, the other half represents the 3s. of surplus-value.

Since 12 hours' labour put in by the spinner are objectified in 6s., it follows that 60 hours' labour are objectified in yarn of the value of 30s. And this quantity of labour-time does in fact exist in the 20 lb. of yarn; for eight-tenths of the yarn, or 16 lb., is a materialization of the 48 hours' labour expended before the beginning of the spinning process on the means of production; the other two-tenths, or 4 lb., is a materialization of the 12 hours' labour expended during the process itself.

On a former page* we saw that the value of the yarn is equal to the new value created during the production of that yarn plus the value previously existing in the means of production. It has now been shown how the different constituents of the value of the product, distinguished according to their function or according to their concept, may be represented by corresponding proportional parts of the product itself.

In this way, the product, i.e. the result of the process of production, is split up into different parts, one part representing only the labour previously spent on the means of production, or the constant capital, another part only the necessary labour spent during the process of production, or the variable capital, and another and last part only the surplus labour expended during the process, or the surplus-value. The decomposition of the product is as simple a task as it is important; this will be seen later when we apply it to complex and hitherto unsolved problems.

So far we have treated the total product as the final result, ready for use, of a working day of 12 hours. We can, however, also follow this total product through all the stages of its production; and in this way we shall arrive at the same result as before if we represent the partial products, precipitated at different stages, as functionally distinct parts of the final or total product.

The spinner produces 20 lb. of yarn in 12 hours. Hence he pro-

* In the discussion of the valorization process, p. 297.

duces 1⅔ lb. in 1 hour, and 13⅓ lb. in 8 hours, or a partial product equal in value to all the cotton that is spun in a whole day. Similarly, the partial product of the next period of 1 hour and 36 minutes is 2⅔ lb. of yarn. This represents the value of the instruments of labour that are consumed in 12 hours. In the following hour and 12 minutes the spinner produces 2 lb. of yarn worth 3s., a value equal to the whole value he creates in his 6 hours of necessary labour. Finally, in the last hour and 12 minutes he produces another 2 lb. of yarn, whose value is equal to the surplus-value created by his surplus labour in the course of half a day. This method of calculation serves the English manufacturer for everyday use; it shows, he will say, that in the first 8 hours, or ⅔ of the working day, he gets back the value of his cotton; and so on for the remaining hours. It is also a perfectly correct method, since it is in fact the first method given above, only transferred from the spatial sphere, in which the different parts of the completed product lie side by side, to the temporal sphere, in which those parts are produced in succession. But it can also be accompanied by very barbaric notions, especially in the heads of people who are as much interested, practically, in the valorization process, as they are, theoretically, in misunderstanding it. It may be imagined, for instance, that our spinner produces or replaces in the first 8 hours of the working day the value of the cotton, in the following hour and 36 minutes the value of the deterioration in the instruments of labour, in the next hour and 12 minutes the value of his wages, and finally that he devotes only the famous 'last hour' to the production of surplus-value for the factory-owner. In this way the spinner is made to perform the twofold miracle not only of producing cotton, spindles, steam-engine, coal, oil, etc., at the same time as he is using them to spin, but also of turning one working day of a given level of intensity into five similar days. For, in the example we are considering, the production of the raw material and the instruments of labour requires 24 divided by 6 = 4 working days of 12 hours each, and their conversion into yarn requires another such day. That the love of profit induces an easy belief in such miracles, and that there is no lack of sycophantic doctrinaires to prove their existence is demonstrated by the following famous historical example.

3. SENIOR'S 'LAST HOUR'

One fine morning, in the year 1836, Nassau W. Senior, who may be called the Clauren* of the English economists, a man famed both for his economic science and his beautiful style, was summoned from Oxford to Manchester, to learn in the latter place the political economy he taught in the former. The manufacturers chose him as their prize-fighter, not only against the newly passed Factory Act† but against the Ten Hours' Agitation which aimed to go beyond it. With their usual practical acuteness they had realized that the learned professor 'wanted a good deal of finishing'; that is why they invited him to Manchester. For his part, the professor has embodied the lecture he received from the Manchester manufacturers in a pamphlet entitled *Letters on the Factory Act, as it Affects the Cotton Manufacture* (London, 1837). Here we find, amongst other things, the following edifying passage:

'Under the present law, no mill in which persons under 18 years of age are employed . . . can be worked more than 11½ hours a day, that is, 12 hours for 5 days in the week, and 9 on Saturday. Now the following analysis (!) will show that in a mill so worked, the whole net profit is derived from the last hour. I will suppose a manufacturer to invest £100,000 – £80,000 in his mill and machinery, and £20,000 in raw material and wages. The annual return of that mill, supposing the capital to be turned once a year, and gross profits to be 15 per cent, ought to be goods worth £115,000 . . . Of this £115,000 each of the twenty-three half-hours of work produces five 115ths, or one 23rd. Of these twenty-three 23rds (constituting the whole £115,000), twenty, that is to say £100,000 out of the £115,000, simply replace the capital; one 23rd (or £5,000 out of the £115,000) makes up for the deterioration of the mill and machinery. The remaining two 23rds, that is the last two of the twenty-three half-hours of every day, produce the net profit of 10 per cent. If, therefore (prices remaining the same), the factory could be kept at work 13 hours instead of 11½, with an addition of about £2,600 to the circulating capital, the net profit would be more than doubled. On the other hand, if the hours of working were reduced by one hour per day (prices remaining the same), the net profit

---

* Heinrich Clauren (1771–1854) was a writer of sentimental novels and short stories.
† The reference here is to the Factory Act of 1833, discussed in detail below, on pp. 390–93.

would be destroyed – if they were reduced by one hour and a half, even the gross profit would be destroyed.'[10]

And the professor calls this an 'analysis'! If he believed the outcries of the manufacturers to the effect that the workers spent the best part of the day in the production, i.e. the reproduction or replacement, of the value of the buildings, machinery, cotton, coal, etc., then his analysis was superfluous. His answer could simply have been this: 'Gentlemen! If you work your mills for 10 hours instead of 11½, then, other things being equal, the daily consumption of cotton, machinery etc. will decrease in proportion. You gain just as much as you lose. Your workpeople will in future spend one hour and a half less time in reproducing or replacing the capital advanced.' If, on the other hand, he did not take them at their word but, being an expert in such matters, considered it necessary to undertake an analysis, then he ought, in a question which turns exclusively on the relation of the net profit to the length of the working day, above all to have asked the manufacturers to be careful not to lump together machinery, workshops, raw material and labour, but to be good enough to place the constant capital, invested in buildings, machinery, raw material

10. Senior, op. cit., pp. 12–13. We let pass such extraordinary notions as are of no importance here; for instance, the assertion that manufacturers reckon as part of their profit, gross or net, dirty or pure, the amount required to make good wear and tear of machinery, or in other words to replace a part of the capital. So too, we pass over any question as to the accuracy of Senior's figures. Leonard Horner has shown in *A Letter to Mr Senior etc.*, London, 1837, that they are worth no more than the so-called 'analysis'. Leonard Horner was one of the Factory Inquiry Commissioners in 1833, and Inspector, or rather Censor of Factories, till 1859. His services to the English working class will never be forgotten. He carried on a life-long contest, not only with the embittered manufacturers, but also with the Cabinet, to whom the number of votes cast in their favour by the masters in the House of Commons was a matter of far greater importance than the number of hours worked by the 'hands' in the mills. Apart from errors in its content, Senior's presentation is confused. What he really intended to say was this: The manufacturer employs the worker for 11½ hours, or 23 half hours, but each multiplied by the number of working days in the year. On this assumption, the 23 half hours yield an annual product of £115,000; one half hour yields $1/23 \times$ £115,000; 20 half hours yield $20/23 \times$ £115,000 = £100,000, i.e. they simply replace the capital advanced. There remain 3 half hours, which yield $3/23 \times$ £115,000 = £15,000, or the gross profit. Of these 3 half hours, one yields $1/23 \times$ £115,000 = £5,000; i.e. it makes up for the wear and tear of the machinery; the remaining 2 half hours, i.e. the last hour, yield $2/23 \times$ £115,000 = £10,000, or the net profit. In the text Senior converts the last 2/23 of the product into portions of the working day itself.

etc., on one side of the account and the capital advanced in wages on the other side. If it then turned out that, according to the calculations of the manufacturers, the worker reproduced or replaced his wages in 2 half hours, in that case, he should have continued his analysis as follows: 'According to your figures, the workman produces his wages in the last hour but one, and your surplus-value, or net profit, in the last hour. Now, since in equal periods he produces equal values, the product of the last hour but one must have the same value as that of the last hour. Further, it is only while he works that he produces any value at all, and the quantity of work he does is measured by his labour-time. This you say amounts to 11½ hours a day. He employs one portion of these 11½ hours in producing or replacing his wages, and the remaining portion in producing your net profit. Beyond this he does absolutely nothing. But since, on your assumption, his wages and the surplus-value he provides are of equal value, it is clear that he produces his wages in 5¾ hours, and your net profit in the other 5¾ hours. Again, since the value of the yarn produced in 2 hours is equal to the sum of the value of his wages and of your net profit, the measure of the value of this yarn must be 11½ working hours, of which 5¾ hours measure the value of the yarn produced in the last hour but one, and 5¾ hours the value of the yarn produced in the last hour of all. We now come to a ticklish point, so watch out! The last working hour but one is, like the first, an ordinary working hour, neither more nor less. How then can the spinner produce in one hour, in the shape of yarn, a value that embodies 5¾ hours' labour? The truth is that he does not perform any such miracle. The use-value produced by him in one hour is a definite quantity of yarn. The value of this yarn is measured by 5¾ working hours, of which 4¾ were, without any assistance from him, previously embodied in the means of production, in the cotton, the machinery, and so on; the remaining one hour alone is added by him. Therefore, since his wages are produced in 5¾ hours, and the yarn produced in one hour also contains 5¾ hours' work, there is no witchcraft in the result that the value created by his 5¾ hours of spinning is equal to the value of the product spun in one hour. You are altogether on the wrong track, if you think that he loses a single moment of his working day in reproducing or replacing the values of the cotton, the machinery and so on. On the contrary, it is because his labour converts the cotton and the spindles into yarn, because he spins, that the values of the cotton and spindles go over to the yarn of their own accord. This is a result of the quality of his labour, not its quantity. It is true that he will transfer to the yarn more value, in the shape of cotton, in one hour than he will in half an hour. But that is only because in one hour he spins up more cotton than in half an hour. You see then that your assertion that the workman produces, in the last hour but one, the value of his wages, and in the last hour your net profit, amounts to no more than this, that in the yarn produced by him in 2 working hours, whether they are the 2 first or the 2 last hours of the working day, there are incorporated 11½ working hours, i.e. precisely as many hours as there are in his working day. And my assertion that in the first 5¾ hours he produces his wages, and in the last 5¾ hours your net profit, amounts only to this, that you pay him for the former, but not for the latter. In speaking of payment of labour, instead of payment of labour-power, I am only using your own slang expression. Now gentlemen, if you compare the working time you pay for with the working time you do not pay for, you will find that they are related to each other as half a day is to half a day; this gives a rate of 100 per cent, and a very pretty percentage it is. Further, there is not the least doubt that if you make your "hands" toil for 13 hours instead of 11½, and as may be expected from you, if you treat the work done in that extra one hour and a half as pure surplus labour, then the latter will be increased from 5¾ hours' labour to 7¼ hours' labour, and the rate of surplus-value will go up from 100 per cent to $126\frac{2}{23}$ per cent. So that you are altogether too sanguine in expecting that by such an addition of 1½ hours to the working day the rate will rise from 100 per cent to 200 per cent and more, in other words that it will be "more than doubled". On the other hand – the heart of man is a wonderful thing, especially when it is carried in his wallet – you take too pessimistic a view when you fear that a reduction of the hours of labour from 11½ to 10 will sweep away the whole of your net profit. Not at all. All other conditions remaining the same, the surplus labour will fall from 5¾ hours to 4¾ hours, a period that still gives a very profitable rate of surplus-value, namely $82\frac{14}{23}$ per cent. But this fateful "last hour" about which you have invented more stories than the millenarians about the Day of Judgement, is "all bosh". If it goes, it will not cost you your "pure profit", nor will it cost the boys and girls you employ their "pure minds".[11]

11. If, on the one hand, Senior demonstrated that the net profit of the manufacturer, the existence of the English cotton industry and England's

command of the markets of the world depend on 'the last hour of work', on the other hand Dr Andrew Ure showed that if children and young persons under 18 years of age, instead of being kept the full 12 hours in the warm and pure moral atmosphere of the factory, are turned out an hour sooner into the heartless and frivolous outer world, they will be deprived, owing to idleness and vice, of all hope of salvation for their souls.* Since 1848, the factory inspectors have never tired of teasing the factory-owners about this 'last', this 'fatal hour'. Thus Mr Howell says in his report of the 21 May 1855: 'Had the following ingenious calculation' (he quotes Senior) 'been correct, every cotton factory in the United Kingdom would have been working at a loss since the year 1850' (*Reports of the Inspectors of Factories ... 30 April 1855*, pp. 19–20). In the year 1848, after the passing of the Ten Hours' Bill, the masters of a number of flax-spinning mills, which lie scattered over the countryside on the borders of Dorset and Somerset, foisted a petition against the bill onto a few of their workers. One of the clauses of this petition is as follows: 'Your petitioners, as parents, conceive that an additional hour of leisure will tend more to demoralize the children than otherwise, believing that idleness is the parent of vice.' On this the factory report of 31 October 1848 says: 'The atmosphere of the flax mills, in which the children of these virtuous and tender parents work, is so loaded with dust and fibre from the raw material that it is exceptionally unpleasant to stand even 10 minutes in the spinning rooms for you are unable to do so without the most painful sensation, owing to the eyes, the ears, the nostrils, and the mouth being immediately filled by the clouds of flax dust from which there is no escape. The labour itself, owing to the feverish haste of the machinery, demands unceasing application of skill and movement, under the control of a watchfulness that never tires, and it seems somewhat hard, to let parents apply the term "idling" to their own children, who, after allowing for meal-times, are fettered for 10 whole hours to such an occupation, in such an atmosphere ... These children work longer than the labourers in the neighbouring villages ... Such cruel talk about "idleness and vice" ought to be branded as the purest cant, and the most shameless hypocrisy ... That portion of the public, who, about twelve years ago, were struck by the assurance with which, under the sanction of high authority, it was publicly and most earnestly proclaimed, that the whole net profit of the manufacturer flows from the labour of the last hour, and that, therefore, the reduction of the working day by one hour would destroy his net profit, that portion of the public, we say, will hardly believe its eyes, when it now finds that the original discovery of the virtues of 'the last hour' has since been so far improved as to include morals as well as profit; so that, if the duration of the labour of children is reduced to a full 10 hours, their morals together with the net profits of their employers, will vanish, both being dependent on this last, this fatal hour' (see *Reports of the Inspectors of Factories ... 31 October 1848*, p. 101). The same report then gives some examples of the morality and virtue of these same manufacturers, of the tricks, artifices, temptations, threats and falsifications they made use of in order, first, to compel a few defenceless workers to sign petitions of such a kind, and then to impose them on Parliament as the petitions of a whole branch of industry, or of whole counties. It is highly characteristic of the

*A. Ure, *The Philosophy of Manufactures*, London, 1835, p. 406.

Whenever your "last hour" strikes in earnest, think of the Oxford professor. And now, gentlemen, farewell, and may we meet again in a better world, but not before.'[12] . . . The battle-cry of the 'last hour', invented by Senior in 1836, was raised once again in the London *Economist* of 15 April 1848 by James Wilson, an economic mandarin of high standing, in a polemic against the Ten Hours' Bill.*

4. THE SURPLUS PRODUCT

We call the portion of the product that represents surplus-value (i.e. one-tenth of the 20 lb., or 2 lb. of yarn, in the example given above) by the name of 'surplus product' (*Mehrprodukt, produit net*). Just as the rate of surplus-value is determined by its relation, not to the sum total of the capital, but to its variable part, in the same way, the relative amount of the surplus product is determined by its ratio, not to the remaining part of the total product, but to that part of it in which necessary labour is incorporated. Since the production of surplus-value is the determining purpose of capitalist production, the size of a given quantity of wealth

---

present status of so-called economic 'science' that neither Senior himself, who at a later period, be it said to his credit, energetically supported the factory legislation, nor his opponents, have ever at any time been able to explain why the 'original discovery' led to false conclusions. They appealed to actual experience, hence the 'why and wherefore' of the matter remained a mystery.

12. Nevertheless, the learned professor did profit to some extent from his journey to Manchester. In his *Letters on the Factory Act* he makes the whole net gain, including 'profit' and 'interest', and even 'something more', depend on a single hour of unpaid labour put in by the worker. One year previously, in his *Outline of Political Economy* written for the instruction of Oxford students and cultivated philistines, he had also 'discovered', in opposition to Ricardo's determination of value by labour, that profit is derived from the labour of the capitalist, and interest from his asceticism, in other words from his 'abstinence'. The dodge was an old one, but the word 'abstinence' was new. Roscher translated it correctly into German with the word '*Enthaltung*'. But some of his countrymen, not so well versed in Latin, have produced a version with a monkish flavour: *Entsagung.**

* 'Renunciation (of worldly pleasures)'.

---

*James Wilson (1805–60), founder in 1843 of the *Economist*, a strongly free-trade organ. He opposed the Bank Act of 1844, was an M.P. between 1847 and 1859, Financial Secretary to the Treasury between 1853 and 1858, and a financial member of the Council of India between 1859 and 1860.

must be measured, not by the absolute quantity produced, but by the relative magnitude of the surplus product.[13]

The sum of the necessary labour and the surplus labour, i.e. the sum of the periods of time during which the worker respectively replaces the value of his labour-power and produces the surplus-value, constitutes the absolute extent of his labour-time, i.e. the working day.

13. 'To an individual with a capital of £20,000, whose profits were £2,000 per annum, it would be a matter quite indifferent whether his capital would employ a hundred or a thousand men, whether the commodity produced sold for £10,000 or £20,000, provided, in all cases, his profit were not diminished below £2,000. Is not the real interest of the nation similar? Provided its net real income, its rent and profits, be the same, it is of no importance whether the nation consists of 10 or of 12 millions of inhabitants' (Ricardo, op. cit., p. 416). Long before Ricardo, Arthur Young, a fanatical advocate of the surplus product, and apart from that a rambling, uncritical writer whose reputation is inversely related to his merits, said this: 'Of what use, in a modern kingdom, would be a whole province thus divided, in the old Roman manner, by small independent peasants, however well cultivated, except for the mere purpose of breeding men, which taken singly is a most useless purpose?' (Arthur Young, *Political Arithmetic, etc.*, London, 1774, p. 47). Very curious is 'the strong inclination . . . to represent net wealth as beneficial to the labouring class . . . though it is evidently not on account of being net' (T. Hopkins, *On Rent of Land, etc.*, London, 1828, p. 126).

Chapter 10: The Working Day

1. THE LIMITS OF THE WORKING DAY

We began with the assumption that labour-power is bought and sold at its value. Its value, like that of all other commodities, is determined by the labour-time necessary to produce it. If it takes 6 hours to produce the average daily means of subsistence of the worker, he must work an average of 6 hours a day to produce his daily labour-power, or to reproduce the value received as a result of its sale. The necessary part of his working day amounts to 6 hours, and is therefore, other things being equal, a given quantity. But with this the extent of the working day itself is not yet given.

Let us assume that a line A – – – – – – B represents the length of the necessary labour-time, say 6 hours. If the labour is prolonged beyond AB by 1, 3 or 6 hours, we get three other lines:

Working day I: A – – – – – – B – C
Working day II: A – – – – – – B – – – C
Working day III: A – – – – – – B – – – – – – C

which represent three different working days of 7, 9 and 12 hours. The extension BC of the line AB represents the length of the surplus labour. As the working day is AB + BC, or AC, it varies with the variable magnitude BC. Since AB is constant, the ratio of BC to AB can always be calculated. In working day I, it is one-sixth, in working day II, three-sixths, in working day III, six-sixths of AB. Since, further, the ratio of surplus labour-time to necessary labour-time determines the rate of surplus-value, the latter is given by the ratio of BC to AB. It amounts in the three different working days respectively to $16\frac{2}{3}$, 50 and 100 per cent. On the other hand, the rate of surplus-value alone would not give us the extent of the working day. If this rate were 100 per cent, the working day might be of 8, 10, 12 or more hours. It would indicate that the two constituent parts of the working day, necessary labour-time and surplus labour-time, were equal in extent, but not how long each of these two constituent parts was. The working day is thus not a constant, but a variable quantity. One of its parts, certainly, is determined by the labour-time required for the reproduction of the labour-power of the worker himself. But its total amount varies with the duration of the surplus labour. The working day is therefore capable of being determined, but in and for itself indeterminate.[1]

Although the working day is not a fixed but a fluid quantity, it can, on the other hand, vary only within certain limits. The minimum limit, however, cannot be determined. Of course, if we make the extension line BC, or the surplus labour, equal to zero, we have a minimum limit, i.e. the part of the day in which the worker must necessarily work for his own maintenance. Under the capitalist mode of production, however, this necessary labour can form only a part of the working day; the working day can never be reduced to this minimum. On the other hand, the working day does have a maximum limit. It cannot be prolonged beyond a certain point. This maximum limit is conditioned by two things. First by the physical limits to labour-power. Within the 24 hours of the natural day a man can only expend a certain quantity of his vital force. Similarly, a horse can work regularly for only 8 hours a day. During part of the day the vital force must rest, sleep; during another part the man has to satisfy other physical needs, to feed, wash and clothe himself. Besides these purely physical limitations, the extension of the working day encounters moral obstacles. The worker needs time in which to satisfy his intellectual and social requirements, and the extent and the number of these requirements is conditioned by the general level of civilization. The length of the working day therefore fluctuates within boundaries both physical and social. But these limiting conditions are of a very elastic nature, and allow a tremendous amount of latitude. So we find working days of many different lengths, of 8, 10, 12, 14, 16 and 18 hours.

The capitalist has bought the labour-power at its daily value. The use-value of the labour-power belongs to him throughout one working day. He has thus acquired the right to make the

1. 'A day's labour is vague, it may be long or short' (*An Essay on Trade and Commerce, Containing Observations on Taxes, etc.*, London, 1770, p. 73).

worker work for him during one day. But what is a working day?[2] At all events, it is less than a natural day. How much less? The capitalist has his own views of this point of no return, the necessary limit of the working day. As a capitalist, he is only capital personified. His soul is the soul of capital. But capital has one sole driving force, the drive to valorize itself, to create surplus-value, to make its constant part, the means of production, absorb the greatest possible amount of surplus labour.[3] Capital is dead labour which, vampire-like, lives only by sucking living labour, and lives the more, the more labour it sucks. The time during which the worker works is the time during which the capitalist consumes the labour-power he has bought from him.[4] If the worker consumes his disposable time for himself, he robs the capitalist.[5]

The capitalist therefore takes his stand on the law of commodity-exchange. Like all other buyers, he seeks to extract the maximum possible benefit from the use-value of his commodity. Suddenly, however, there arises the voice of the worker, which had previously been stifled in the sound and fury of the production process:

'The commodity I have sold you differs from the ordinary crowd of commodities in that its use creates value, a greater value than it costs. That is why you bought it. What appears on your side as the valorization of capital is on my side an excess expenditure of labour-power. You and I know on the market only one

2. This question is far more important than the celebrated question of Sir Robert Peel to the Birmingham Chamber of Commerce: What is a pound? Peel was able to pose this question only because he was as much in the dark about the nature of money as the 'little shilling men'* of Birmingham.

3. 'It is the aim of the capitalist to obtain with his expended capital the greatest possible quantity of labour (*d'obtenir du capital dépensé la plus forte somme de travail possible*)' (J. G. Courcelle-Seneuil, *Traité théorique et pratique des entreprises industrielles*, 2nd edn, Paris, 1857, p. 63).

4. 'An hour's labour lost in a day is a prodigious injury to a commercial State . . . There is a very great consumption of luxuries among the labouring poor of this kingdom: particularly among the manufacturing populace, by which they also consume their time, the most fatal of consumptions' (*An Essay on Trade and Commerce, etc.*, pp. 47, 153).

5. 'If the free worker rests for an instant, the base and petty management which watches over him with wary eyes claims he is stealing from it' (N. Linguet, *Théorie des lois civiles, etc.*, London, 1767, Vol. 2, p. 466).

*The followers of the banker and Radical M.P. Thomas Attwood (1783–1856) of Birmingham, so called because they advocated the repayment of creditors in shillings of a reduced gold content, as a way of solving the currency problems incurred at the end of the Napoleonic Wars. See *A Contribution to the Critique of Political Economy*, English edition, pp. 81–3.

law, that of the exchange of commodities. And the consumption of the commodity belongs not to the seller who parts with it, but to the buyer who acquires it. The use of my daily labour-power therefore belongs to you. But by means of the price you pay for it every day, I must be able to reproduce it every day, thus allowing myself to sell it again. Apart from natural deterioration through age etc., I must be able to work tomorrow with the same normal amount of strength, health and freshness as today. You are constantly preaching to me the gospel of "saving" and "abstinence". Very well! Like a sensible, thrifty owner of property I will husband my sole wealth, my labour-power, and abstain from wasting it foolishly. Every day I will spend, set in motion, transfer into labour only as much of it as is compatible with its normal duration and healthy development. By an unlimited extension of the working day, you may in one day use up a quantity of labour-power greater than I can restore in three. What you gain in labour, I lose in the substance of labour. Using my labour and despoiling it are quite different things. If the average length of time an average worker can live (while doing a reasonable amount of work) is 30 years, the value of my labour-power, which you pay me from day to day,

is $\dfrac{1}{365 \times 30}$ or $\dfrac{1}{10,950}$ of its total value. But if you consume it in 10 years, you pay me daily $\dfrac{1}{10,950}$ instead of $\dfrac{1}{3,650}$ of its total value, i.e. only one-third of its daily value, and you therefore rob me every day of two-thirds of the value of my commodity. You pay me for one day's labour-power, while you use three days of it. That is against our contract and the law of commodity exchange. I therefore demand a working day of normal length, and I demand it without any appeal to your heart, for in money matters sentiment is out of place. You may be a model citizen, perhaps a member of the R.S.P.C.A., and you may be in the odour of sanctity as well; but the thing you represent when you come face to face with me has no heart in its breast. What seems to throb there is my own heartbeat. I demand a normal working day because, like every other seller, I demand the value of my commodity.'[6]

6. During the great strike of the London building workers [1859–60] for the reduction of the working day to 9 hours, their committee published a manifesto that contained, to some extent, the plea of our worker. The manifesto alludes, not without irony, to the fact that the greatest profit-

We see then that, leaving aside certain extremely elastic restrictions, the nature of commodity exchange itself imposes no limit to the working day, no limit to surplus labour. The capitalist maintains his rights as a purchaser when he tries to make the working day as long as possible, and, where possible, to make two working days out of one. On the other hand, the peculiar nature of the commodity sold implies a limit to its consumption by the purchaser, and the worker maintains his right as a seller when he wishes to reduce the working day to a particular normal length. There is here therefore an antinomy, of right against right, both equally bearing the seal of the law of exchange. Between equal rights, force decides. Hence, in the history of capitalist production, the establishment of a norm for the working day presents itself as a struggle over the limits of that day, a struggle between collective capital, i.e. the class of capitalists, and collective labour, i.e. the working class.

2. THE VORACIOUS APPETITE FOR SURPLUS LABOUR. MANUFACTURER AND BOYAR

Capital did not invent surplus labour. Wherever a part of society possesses the monopoly of the means of production, the worker, free or unfree, must add to the labour-time necessary for his own maintenance an extra quantity of labour-time in order to produce the means of subsistence for the owner of the means of production,[7] whether this proprietor be an Athenian καλὸς κ'ἀγαθός,* an Etruscan theocrat, a *civis romanus*, a Norman baron, an American slave-owner, a Wallachian boyar, a modern landlord or a capital-

---

monger among the building masters, a certain Sir M. Peto, was in the 'odour of sanctity'.* (The same Peto, after 1867, came to an end *à la* Strousberg.)†

7. 'Those who labour ... in reality feed both the pensioners, called the rich, and themselves' (Edmund Burke, op. cit., pp. 2–3).

*Peto was a Baptist, a benefactor to various chapels, and the author in 1842 of a pamphlet entitled *Divine Support in Death*.

†The bankruptcy of Peto's firm was in fact in 1866; the allusion here is to the bankruptcy of the German financier and speculator B. H. Strousberg in St Petersburg in 1875 and his subsequent expulsion from Russia after being charged with fraud.

---

*'Handsome and good': ancient Greek expression for an aristocrat.

ist.[8] It is however clear that in any economic formation of society where the use-value rather than the exchange-value of the product predominates, surplus labour will be restricted by a more or less confined set of needs, and that no boundless thirst for surplus labour will arise from the character of production itself. Hence in antiquity over-work becomes frightful only when the aim is to obtain exchange-value in its independent monetary shape, i.e. in the production of gold and silver. The recognized form of over-work here is forced labour until death. One only needs to read Diodorus Siculus.[9] Nevertheless, these are exceptions in antiquity. But as soon as peoples whose production still moves within the lower forms of slave-labour, the *corvée*, etc. are drawn into a world market dominated by the capitalist mode of production, whereby the sale of their products for export develops into their principal interest, the civilized horrors of over-work are grafted onto the barbaric horrors of slavery, serfdom etc. Hence the Negro labour in the southern states of the American Union preserved a moderately patriarchal character as long as production was chiefly directed to the satisfaction of immediate local requirements. But in proportion as the export of cotton became of vital interest to those states, the over-working of the Negro, and sometimes the consumption of his life in seven years of labour, became a factor in a calculated and calculating system. It was no longer a question of obtaining from him a certain quantity of useful products, but rather of the production of surplus-value itself. The same is true of the *corvée*, in the Danubian Principalities for instance.

The comparison of the appetite for surplus labour in the Danubian Principalities with the same appetite as found in English factories has a special interest, because the *corvée* presents surplus labour in an independent and immediately perceptible form.

Suppose the working day consists of 6 hours of necessary

8. Niebuhr remarks very naïvely in his *Roman History*: 'It is evident that monuments like those of the Etruscans, which astound us even in their ruins, presuppose lords and vassals in small (!) states.' Sismondi, with deeper insight, says that 'Brussels lace' presupposes wage-lords and wage-slaves.

9. 'One cannot see these unfortunates' (in the gold mines between Egypt, Ethiopia and Arabia) 'who are unable even to keep their bodies clean or to clothe their nakedness, without pitying their miserable lot. There is no indulgence, no forbearance for the sick, the feeble, the aged, or for feminine weaknesses. All, forced by blows, must work on until death puts an end to their sufferings and their distress' (Diodorus Siculus, *Historische Bibliothek*, Bk III, Ch. 13).

labour and 6 hours of surplus labour. Then the free worker gives the capitalist 6×6 or 36 hours of surplus labour every week. It is the same as if he worked 3 days in the week for himself and 3 days in the week gratis for the capitalist. But this fact is not directly visible. Surplus labour and necessary labour are mingled together. I can therefore express the same relation by saying for instance that in every minute the worker works 30 seconds for himself and 30 seconds for the capitalist, etc. It is otherwise with the *corvée*. The necessary labour which the Wallachian peasant performs for his own maintenance is distinctly marked off from his surplus labour on behalf of the boyar. The one he does on his own field, the other on the seignorial estate. Both parts of the labour-time thus exist independently, side by side with each other. In the *corvée* the surplus labour is accurately marked off from the necessary labour. However, this clearly alters nothing in the quantitative relation of surplus labour to necessary labour. Three days' surplus labour in the week remain three days that yield no equivalent to the worker himself, whether the surplus labour is called *corvée* or wage-labour. But in the capitalist the appetite for surplus labour appears in the drive for an unlimited extension of the working day, while in the boyar it appears more simply in a direct hunt for days of *corvée*.[10]

In the Danubian Principalities the *corvée* was linked with rents in kind and other appurtenances of serfdom, but it formed the most important tribute paid to the ruling class. Where this was the case, the *corvée* rarely arose from serfdom; instead serfdom arose, inversely, from the *corvée*.[11] This is what took place in the

10. What follows refers to the situation in the Romanian provinces before the transformations which have occurred since the Crimean War.*

11. [Note by Engels to the third German edition:] This is also true of Germany, and especially of Prussia east of the Elbe. In the fifteenth century the German peasant was nearly everywhere a man who, though subject to certain obligations in the form of produce and labour, was otherwise at least in practice free. The German colonists in Brandenburg, Pomerania, Silesia and East Prussia were even legally acknowledged as free men. The victory of the nobility in the Peasants' War put an end to that. Not only were the conquered South German peasants again enslaved, but also, after the middle of the sixteenth century, the peasants of East Prussia, Brandenburg, Pomerania and Silesia were degraded to the condition of serfs. Soon afterwards the free peasants of Schleswig-Holstein followed them. (Maurer, *Fronhöfe*, Vol. 4; Meitzen, *Der Boden des Preussischen Staates*; Hanssen, *Leibeigenschaft in Schleswig-Holstein*.)

*The agrarian reforms of the 1860s, which included the abolition of serfdom (see p. 271, last note).

Romanian provinces. Their original mode of production was based on communal property, but not communal property in its Slav or Indian form. Part of the land was cultivated independently as free private property by the members of the commune, another part – the *ager publicus* – was cultivated by them in common. The products of this common labour served partly as a reserve fund against bad harvests and other misfortunes, partly as a kind of state treasury to cover the costs of war, religion and other communal expenses. In the course of time military and clerical dignitaries usurped the communal land, and along with this the obligations owed to it. The labour of the free peasants on their communal land was transformed into *corvée* performed for the thieves who had taken that land. This *corvée* soon developed into a servile relationship existing in point of fact, though not legally, until Russia, the liberator of the world, raised it to the level of a law on the pretext of abolishing serfdom.* The code of the *corvée*, which the Russian General Kiselev proclaimed in 1831, was of course dictated by the boyars themselves. Thus, at one stroke, Russia both conquered the magnates of the Danubian Principalities and earned the applause of cretinous liberals throughout Europe.

According to the *Règlement organique*, as this code of the *corvée* is called, every Wallachian peasant owes to the so-called landlord, besides a mass of payments in kind, which are specified in detail, the following: (1) 12 days of labour in general, (2) 1 day of field labour, (3) 1 day of wood-carrying. Taken together, this is 14 days in the year. However, with deep insight into political economy, the working day is not taken in its ordinary sense, but as the working day necessary to the production of an average daily product; and that average daily product is determined in such a sly manner than even a Cyclops would be unable to finish the job within 24 hours. Therefore the *Règlement* itself declares, dryly and with true Russian irony, that by 12 working days one must understand the product of the manual labour of 36 days, by 1 day of field labour 3 days, and by 1 day of wood-carrying, similarly, 3 times as much. The sum total is now 42 days of *corvée*. To this had to be added the so-called *jobbagio*, service due to the lord for emergency requirements. In proportion to the size of its population, every village has to furnish annually a definite contingent to the *jobbagio*. This additional *corvée* is estimated at 14 days for each Wallachian

* The Danubian Principalities were under Russian occupation between 1828 and 1834. General P. D. Kiselev was the viceroy.

peasant. Thus the prescribed *corvée* amounts to 56 working days every year. But because of the severe climate the agricultural year in Wallachia numbers only 210 days, of which 40 for Sundays and holidays, and 30 on an average for bad weather, together 70 days, do not count. 140 working days remain. The ratio of the *corvée* to the necessary labour 56/84, or 66⅔ per cent, gives a much smaller rate of surplus-value than that which regulates the work of the English agricultural labourer or factory worker. This is, however, only the legally prescribed *corvée*. And in a spirit yet more 'liberal' than the English Factory Acts, the *Règlement organique* was able to facilitate its own evasion. After it has made 56 days out of 12, the nominal day's work of each of the 56 *corvée* days is again so arranged that a portion of it must fall on the next day. In one day, for instance, an amount of land must be weeded which would require twice as much time for this work, particularly on the maize plantations. The legal day's work for some kinds of agricultural labour can be interpreted in such a way that the day begins in the month of May and ends in the month of October. For Moldavia the regulations are even stricter. 'The 12 *corvée* days of the *Règlement organique*,' cried a boyar, drunk with victory, 'amount to 365 days in the year.'[12]

If the *Règlement organique* of the Danubian Principalities was a positive expression of the appetite for surplus labour which every paragraph legalized, the English Factory Acts are the negative expression of the same appetite. These laws curb capital's drive towards a limitless draining away of labour-power by forcibly limiting the working day on the authority of the state, but a state ruled by capitalist and landlord. Apart from the daily more threatening advance of the working-class movement, the limiting of factory labour was dictated by the same necessity as forced the manuring of English fields with guano. The same blind desire for profit that in the one case exhausted the soil had in the other case seized hold of the vital force of the nation at its roots. Periodical epidemics speak as clearly on this point as the diminishing military standard of height in France and Germany.[13]

12 Further details are to be found in É. Regnault's *Histoire politique et sociale des principautés danubiennes,* Paris, 1855 [pp. 304 ff.].

13. 'In general and within certain limits, evidence of the prosperity of organic beings is provided by their exceeding the medium size of their kind. As for man, his bodily height diminishes if his due growth is interfered with, either by physical or by social conditions. In all European countries in which

The Factory Act of 1850 now in force (1867) allows 10 hours for the average working day, i.e. for the first five days 12 hours from 6 a.m. to 6 p.m., including half an hour for breakfast, and an hour for dinner, thus leaving 10½ working hours, and 8 hours for Saturday, from 6 a.m. to 2 p.m., of which half an hour is subtracted for breakfast. 60 working hours are left, 10½ for each of the first 5 days, 7½ for the last.[14] Certain guardians of these laws are appointed, factory inspectors, directly under the Home Secretary, and their reports are published every six months by order of Parliament. They therefore provide regular and official statistics of the voracious appetite of the capitalists for surplus labour.

Let us listen for a moment to the factory inspectors.[15] 'The fraudulent mill-owner begins work a quarter of an hour (some-

---

there is conscription, the medium height of adult men, and in general their fitness for military service, has diminished since it was introduced. Before the revolution of 1789 the minimum for the infantry in France was 165 cm.; in 1818 (law of 10 March), 157 cm.; by the law of 21 March 1832, 156 cm.; on an average in France more than half of all the conscripts are rejected on account of deficient height or bodily weakness. The military standard of height in Saxony in 1780 was 178 cm. It is now 155. In Prussia it is 157. According to Dr Meyer's statement of 9 May 1862 in the *Bayrische Zeitung*, taking an average over nine years, in Prussia 716 out of every 1,000 conscripts were unfit for military service, 317 because of deficiency in height, and 399 because of bodily defects . . . Berlin in 1858 could not provide its contingent of recruits; it was 156 men short' (J. von Liebig, *Die Chemie in ihrer Anwendung auf Agrikultur und Physiologie*, 7th edn, Vol. 1, pp. 117–18).

14. The history of the Factory Act of 1850 will be found later in this chapter

15. I only touch here and there on the period from the beginning of modern industry in England to 1845, concerning which I would refer the reader to *Die Lage der arbeitenden Klasse in England*, by Friedrich Engels, Leipzig, 1845 [English translation: *The Condition of the Working Class in England*, Panther, 1969]. How well Engels understood the spirit of the capitalist mode of production is shown by the Factory Reports, Reports on Mines, etc. which have appeared since 1845, and how wonderfully he painted the circumstances in detail is seen on the most superficial comparison of his work with the official reports of the Children's Employment Commission, published eighteen to twenty years later (1863–7). These deal especially with the branches of industry in which the Factory Acts had not, up to 1862, been introduced, and in part remain unintroduced up to the present. Here then, little or no alteration had been enforced by authority in the conditions depicted by Engels. I have taken my examples chiefly from the free-trade period after 1848, that paradisiac age whose commercial travellers spin such fabulous tales to the Germans, so blatantly and with such a total neglect of economic science. In passing, let us note that England figures in the foreground here because it is the classic representative of capitalist production, and is the only country to possess a continuous set of official statistics relating to the matters we are considering.

times more, sometimes less) before 6 a.m., and leaves off a quarter of an hour (sometimes more, sometimes less) after 6 p.m. He takes 5 minutes from the beginning and from the end of the half hour nominally allowed for breakfast, and 10 minutes at the beginning and end of the hour nominally allowed for dinner. He works for a quarter of an hour (sometimes more, sometimes less) after 2 p.m. on Saturday. Thus his gain is:

Before 6 a.m.	15 minutes
After 6 p.m.	15 minutes
At breakfast time	10 minutes
At dinner time	20 minutes
	60 minutes
Total for five days	300 minutes
On Saturday before 6 a.m.	15 minutes
At breakfast time	10 minutes
After 2 p.m.	15 minutes
	40 minutes
Weekly total	340 minutes

Or 5 hours and 40 minutes weekly, which, multiplied by 50 working weeks in the year (allowing two for holidays and occasional stoppages), is equal to 27 working days.'[16]

'Five minutes a day's increased work, multiplied by weeks, are equal to two and a half days of produce in the year.'[17] 'An additional hour a day gained by small instalments before 6 a.m., after 6 p.m., and at the beginning and end of the times nominally fixed for meals, is nearly equivalent to working 13 months in the year.'[18]

Crises during which production is interrupted and the factories work 'short time', i.e. for only a part of the week, naturally do not affect the tendency to extend the working day. The less business there is, the more profit has to be made on the business done. The less time spent in work, the more of that time has to be turned into surplus labour-time. This is how the factory inspectors report on the period of crisis from 1857 to 1858:

16. 'Suggestions, etc., by Mr L. Horner, Inspector of Factories', in *Factories Regulation Acts*. Ordered by the House of Commons to be printed, 9 August 1859, pp. 4–5.

17. *Reports of the Inspectors of Factories for the Half Year, October 1856*, p. 35.

18. *Reports, etc. . . . . 30 April 1858*, p. 9.

'It may seem inconsistent that there should be any over-working at a time when trade is so bad; but that very badness leads to the transgression by unscrupulous men, they get the extra profit of it ... In the last half year,' says Leonard Horner, '122 mills in my district have been given up; 143 were found standing, yet over-work is continued beyond the legal hours.'[19] 'For a great part of the time,' says Mr Howell, 'owing to the depression of trade, many factories were altogether closed, and a still greater number were working short time. I continue, however, to receive about the usual number of complaints that half, or three-quarters of an hour in the day, are snatched from the workers by encroaching upon the times professedly allowed for rest and refreshment.'[20]

The same phenomenon was repeated on a smaller scale during the frightful cotton crisis from 1861 to 1865.[21] 'It is sometimes advanced by way of excuse, when persons are found at work in a factory, either at a meal hour, or at some illegal time, that they will not leave the mill at the appointed hour, and that compulsion is necessary to force them to cease work' (cleaning their machinery, etc.) 'especially on Saturday afternoons. But, if the hands remain in a factory after the machinery has ceased to revolve ... they would not have been so employed if sufficient time had been set apart specially for cleaning, etc., either before 6 a.m. or before 2 p.m. on Saturday afternoons.'[22]

19. ibid., p. 10.
20. ibid., p. 25.
21. *Reports, etc., for the Half Year ending 30 April 1861*. See Appendix No. 2; *Reports, etc., 31 October 1862*, pp. 7, 52, 53. Violations of the Acts became more numerous during the last half of the year 1863. Cf. *Reports, etc., ending 31 October 1863*, p. 7.
22. *Reports, etc., 31 October 1860*, p. 23. With what fanaticism, according to the evidence of manufacturers given in courts of law, their hands set themselves against every interruption in factory labour, is shown by the following curious incident. At the beginning of June 1836, information reached the magistrates of Dewsbury (Yorkshire) that the owners of eight large mills in the neighbourhood of Batley had violated the Factory Act. Some of these gentlemen were accused of having kept five boys between 12 and 15 years of age at work from 6 a.m. on Friday to 4 p.m. on the following Saturday, not allowing them any respite except for meals and one hour for sleep at midnight. And these children had to do this ceaseless labour of 30 hours in the 'shoddy-hole', the name for the hole where the woollen rags are pulled to pieces, and where a dense atmosphere of dust, shreds, etc. forces even the adult worker to cover his mouth continually with handkerchiefs for the protection of his lungs! The accused gentlemen affirmed in lieu of taking an oath – as Quakers they were too scrupulously religious to take an oath – that they had, in their

'The profit to be gained by it' (over-working in violation of the Act) 'appears to be, to many, a greater temptation than they can resist; they calculate upon the chance of not being found out; and when they see the small amount of penalty and costs, which those who have been convicted have had to pay, they find that if they should be detected there will still be a considerable balance of gain . . . '[23] 'In cases where the additional time is gained by a multiplication of small thefts in the course of the day, there are insuperable difficulties to the inspectors making out a case.'[24]

These 'small thefts' of capital from the workers' meal-times and recreation times are also described by the factory inspectors as 'petty pilferings of minutes',[25] 'snatching a few minutes'[26] or, in the technical language of the workers, 'nibbling and cribbling at meal-times'.[27]

It is evident that in this atmosphere the formation of surplus-value by surplus labour is no secret. 'If you allow me (as I was informed by a highly respectable master) to work only ten minutes in the day over-time, you put one thousand a year in my pocket.'[28] 'Moments are the elements of profit.'[29]

In this connection, nothing is more characteristic than the designation of the workers who work full time as 'full-timers', and the children under 13 who are only allowed to work six hours as 'half-timers'.[30] The worker is here nothing more than personified

---

great compassion for the unhappy children, allowed them four hours for sleep, but the obstinate children absolutely would not go to bed. The Quaker gentlemen were fined £20. Dryden anticipated the attitude of these Quakers:

'Fox full fraught in seeming sanctity,
That feared an oath, but like the devil would lie,
That look'd like Lent, and had the holy leer,
And durst not sin! before he said his prayer!'*

23. *Reports, etc., 31 October 1856*, p. 34.
24. ibid., p. 35.
25. ibid., p. 48.
26. ibid., p. 48.
27. ibid., p. 48.
28. ibid., p. 48.
29. *Reports of the Inspectors of Factories for 30 April 1860*, p. 56.
30. This is the official expression both in the factories and in the reports.

*Dryden, 'The Cock and the Fox: or, the Tale of the Nun's Priest' (1700), lines 480–88. 'Fox' in the first line is presumably George Fox (1624–91), the founder of the Quaker sect.

labour-time. All individual distinctions are obliterated in that between 'full-timers' and 'half-timers'.

3. BRANCHES OF ENGLISH INDUSTRY WITHOUT LEGAL LIMITS TO EXPLOITATION

So far, we have observed the drive towards the extension of the working day, and the werewolf-like hunger for surplus labour, in an area where capital's monstrous outrages, unsurpassed, according to an English bourgeois economist, by the cruelties of the Spaniards to the American red-skins,[31] caused it at last to be bound by the chains of legal regulations. Now let us cast a glance at certain branches of production in which the exploitation of labour is either still unfettered even now, or was so yesterday.

'Mr Broughton Charlton, county magistrate, declared, as chairman of a meeting held at the Assembly Rooms, Nottingham, on 14 January 1860, that there was an amount of privation and suffering among that portion of the population connected with the lace trade, unknown in other parts of the kingdom, indeed, in the civilized world ... Children of nine or ten years are dragged from their squalid beds at two, three, or four o'clock in the morning and compelled to work for a bare subsistence until ten, eleven, or twelve at night, their limbs wearing away, their frames dwindling, their faces whitening, and their humanity absolutely sinking into a stone-like torpor, utterly horrible to contemplate ... We are not surprised, he went on, that Mr Mallett, or any other manufacturer, should stand forward and protest against discussion ... The system, as the Rev. Montagu Valpy describes it, is one of unmitigated slavery, socially, physically, morally, and spiritually ... What can be thought of a town which holds a public meeting to petition that the period of labour for men shall be diminished to eighteen hours a day? ... We declaim against the Virginian and Carolinian cotton-planters. Is their black-market, their lash, and their barter of human flesh more detestable than

31. 'The cupidity of mill-owners whose cruelties in the pursuit of gain have hardly been exceeded by those perpetrated by the Spaniards in the conquest of America in the pursuit of gold' (John Wade, *History of the Middle and Working Classes*, 3rd edn, London, 1835, p. 114). The theoretical part of this book, which is a kind of outline of political economy, contains, considering when it was published, certain original elements, for instance on commercial crises. The historical part suffers by being a shameless plagiarism of Sir F. M. Eden's *The State of the Poor*, London, 1797.

this slow sacrifice of humanity which takes place in order that veils and collars may be fabricated for the benefit of capitalists?'[32]

The potteries of Staffordshire have, during the last twenty-two years, formed the subject-matter of three Parliamentary inquiries. The results are embodied in Mr Scriven's Report of 1841 to the 'Children's Employment Commissioners', in Dr Greenhow's Report of 1860 published by order of the medical officer of the Privy Council (*Public Health, Third Report*, I, 102–13), and lastly in Mr Longe's Report of 1862, printed in the *Children's Employment Commission, First Report*, dated 13 June 1863. For my purpose it is enough to take some of the depositions of the exploited children themselves from the reports of 1860 and 1863. From the children we may deduce the situation of the adults, especially the girls and women, and in a branch of industry, indeed, alongside which cotton spinning appears as a very agreeable and healthy occupation.[33]

William Wood, 9 years old, 'was 7 years 10 months old when he began to work'. He 'ran moulds' (carried ready-moulded articles into the drying-room, afterwards bringing back the empty mould) from the very beginning. He came to work every day in the week at 6 a.m., and left off at about 9 p.m. 'I work till 9 o'clock at night six days in the week. I have done so for the last seven or eight weeks.' Fifteen hours of labour for a child of 7! J. Murray, 12 years of age, says: 'I turn jigger and run moulds. I come at 6. Sometimes I come at 4. I worked all night last night, till 6 o'clock this morning. I have not been in bed since the night before last. There were eight or nine other boys working last night. All but one have come this morning. I get 3 shillings and sixpence. I do not get any more for working at night. I worked two nights last week.' Fernyhough, a boy of 10: 'I have not always an hour (for dinner). I have only half an hour sometimes: on Thursday, Friday, and Saturday.'[34]

Dr Greenhow states that the average life-expectancy in the pottery districts of Stoke-on-Trent and Wolstanton is extraordinarily low. Although only 36·6 per cent of the male population over the age of 20 are employed in the potteries in the district of Stoke, and 30·4 per cent in Wolstanton, more than half the deaths

32. *Daily Telegraph*, 17 January 1860.
33. Cf. Engels, *Lage etc.*, pp. 249–51 [English translation, pp. 232–4].
34. *Children's Employment Commission, First Report, etc.*, 1863, Appendix, pp. 16, 19, 18.

among men of that age in the first district, and nearly two-fifths in the second district, are the result of pulmonary diseases among the potters. Dr Boothroyd, a medical practitioner at Hanley, says: 'Each successive generation of potters is more dwarfed and less robust than the preceding one.' Similarly another doctor, Mr McBean, states: 'Since I began to practise among the potters 25 years ago, I have observed a marked degeneration, especially shown in diminution of stature and breadth.' These statements are taken from Dr Greenhow's Report of 1860.[35]

From the report of the Commissioners in 1863, the following: Dr J. T. Arledge, senior physician of the North Staffordshire Infirmary, says: 'The potters as a class, both men and women, represent a degenerated population, both physically and morally. They are, as a rule, stunted in growth, ill-shaped, and frequently ill-formed in the chest; they become prematurely old, and are certainly short-lived; they are phlegmatic and bloodless, and exhibit their debility of constitution by obstinate attacks of dyspepsia, and disorders of the liver and kidneys, and by rheumatism. But of all diseases they are especially prone to chest-disease, to pneumonia, phthisis, bronchitis, and asthma. One form would appear peculiar to them, and is known as potter's asthma, or potter's consumption. Scrofula attacking the glands, or bones, or other parts of the body, is a disease of two-thirds or more of the potters ... That the "degenerescence" of the population of this district is not even greater than it is, is due to the constant re-cruiting from the adjacent country, and intermarriages with more healthy races.'[36]

Mr Charles Parsons, until recently the House Surgeon of the same hospital, writes in a letter to Commissioner Longe, amongst other things: 'I can only speak from personal observation and not from statistical data, but I do not hesitate to assert that my indignation has been aroused again and again at the sight of poor children whose health has been sacrificed to gratify the avarice of either parents or employers.' He enumerates the causes of the diseases of the potters, and sums them up in the phrase 'long hours'. In their report, the Commissioners express the hope that 'a manufacture which has assumed so prominent a place in the whole world, will not long be subject to the remark that its great success is accompanied with the physical deterioration, wide-

35. *Public Health, Third Report, etc.*, pp. 102, 104, 105.
36. *Children's Employment Commission, First Report, etc.*, 1863, p. 24.

spread bodily suffering, and early death of the workpeople . . . by whose labour and skill such great results have been achieved'.[37] And all that holds of the potteries in England is true of those in Scotland.[38]

The manufacture of matches dates from 1833, from the discovery of the method of applying phosphorus to the match itself. Since 1845 this branch of industry has developed rapidly in England, and has spread out from the thickly populated parts of London to the cities of Manchester, Birmingham, Liverpool, Bristol, Norwich, Newcastle and Glasgow. It has brought with it tetanus, a disease which a Vienna doctor already discovered in 1845 to be peculiar to the makers of matches. Half the workers are children under 13 and young persons under 18. The manufacture of matches, on account of its unhealthiness and unpleasantness, has such a bad reputation that only the most miserable part of the working class, half-starved widows and so forth, deliver up their children to it, their 'ragged, half-starved, untaught children'.[39] Of the witnesses examined by Commissioner White (1863), 270 were under 18, fifty under 10, ten only 8, and five only 6 years old. With a working day ranging from 12 to 14 or 15 hours, night-labour, irregular meal-times, and meals mostly taken in the workrooms themselves, pestilent with phosphorus, Dante would have found the worst horrors in his Inferno surpassed in this industry.

In the manufacture of wallpaper the coarser sorts are printed by machine; the finer by hand (block printing). The most active business months are from the beginning of October to the end of April. During this time the work often lasts, almost uninterruptedly, from 6 a.m. to 10 p.m. or further into the night.

J. Leach's deposition: 'Last winter six out of nineteen girls were away from ill-health at one time from over-work. I have to bawl at them to keep them awake.' W. Duffy: 'I have seen when the children could none of them keep their eyes open for the work; indeed, none of us could.' J. Lightbourne: 'Am 13 . . . We worked last winter till 9 (evening), and the winter before till 10. I used to cry with sore feet every night last winter.' G. Apsden: 'That boy of mine . . . when he was 7 years old I used to carry him on my back to and fro through the snow, and he used to have 16 hours a

37. *Children's Employment Commission, First Report, etc.*, 1863, p. 22, and xi.
38. ibid., p. xlvii.
39. ibid., p. liv.

day ... I have often knelt down to feed him as he stood by the machine, for he could not leave it or stop.' Smith, the managing partner of a Manchester factory: 'We (he means his "hands" who work for "us") work on, with no stoppage for meals, so that the day's work of 10½ hours is finished by 4.30 p.m., and all after that is overtime.'[40] (Does this Mr Smith take no meals himself during 10½ hours?) 'We' (this same Smith) 'seldom leave off working before 6 p.m.' (he means leave off from consuming 'our' labour-power machines), 'so that we' (the same man again) 'are really working overtime the whole year round ... For all these, children and adults alike (152 children and young persons and 140 adults), the average work for the last 18 months has been at the very least 7 days, 5 hours, or 78½ hours a week. For the six weeks ending 2 May this year (1862), the average was higher – 8 days or 84 hours a week.' Despite this, the same Mr Smith, who is so fond of the plural of majesty, adds, smirking with satisfaction, 'Machine-work is not great.' Similarly, the employers in the block printing trade say: 'Hand labour is more healthy than machine-work.' On the whole, manufacturers are indignantly opposed to the proposal 'to stop the machines at least during meal-times'.

'A clause which allowed work between say 6 a.m. and 9 p.m.,' says Mr Otley, manager of a wallpaper factory in the Borough (a district of London), 'would suit us (!) very well, but the factory hours, 6 a.m. to 6 p.m., are not suitable. Our machine is always stopped for dinner.' (What generosity!) 'There is no waste of paper and colour to speak of. But,' he adds sympathetically, 'I can understand the loss of time not being liked.' In the Commission's report the naïve opinion is expressed that the fear in some 'leading firms' of losing time, i.e. the time for appropriating the labour of others [*fremde Arbeit*],* and thereby 'losing profit', is not a 'sufficient reason' for 'allowing children under 13, and

40. This is not to be taken in the same sense as our surplus labour-time. These gentlemen consider 10½ hours of labour as the normal working day, and this of course includes the normal quantity of surplus labour. After this begins 'overtime', which is paid a little better. It will be seen later that the labour expended during the so-called normal day is paid below its value, so that overtime is merely a capitalist trick to extort more surplus labour. In any case, this would remain true of overtime even if the labour-power expended during the normal working day were paid for at its full value.

---

*Here, as elsewhere, we have opted for 'labour of others' rather than 'alien labour'.

young persons under 18, working 12 to 16 hours per day, to lose their dinner', nor for giving it to them as coal and water are supplied to the steam-engine, soap to wool, oil to the wheel – namely during the process of production itself, as merely auxiliary material for the instruments of labour.[41]

No other branch of industry in England has preserved up to the present day a method of production as archaic, as pre-christian (as we see from the poets of the Roman Empire) as baking has. (We shall disregard the practice of making bread by machinery, which has only recently begun to make its way here.) But capital, as we said earlier, is at first indifferent towards the technical character of the labour process it seizes control of. At the outset, it takes it as it finds it.

The incredible adulteration of bread, especially in London, was first revealed by the Committee of the House of Commons 'on the adulteration of articles of food' (1855–6), and by Dr Hassall's work *Adulterations Detected*.[42] The consequence of these revelations was the Act of 6 August 1860, 'for preventing the adulteration of articles of food and drink', an inoperative law, as it naturally shows the tenderest consideration for every 'freetrader' who decides 'to turn an honest penny' by buying and selling adulterated commodities.[43] The Committee itself more or less naïvely formulated its conviction that free trade essentially meant trade with adulterated, or as the English ingeniously put it, 'sophisticated' goods. In fact, this kind of 'sophistry' understands better than Protagoras how to make white black, and black white, and better than the Eleatics* how to demonstrate before your very eyes that everything real is merely apparent.[44]

41. *Children's Employment Commission, First Report, etc.*, 1863, Appendix pp. 123–5, 140, and lxiv.
42. Alum, either finely powdered or mixed with salt, is a normal article of commerce bearing the significant name of 'baker's stuff'.
43. Soot is a very active form of carbon, and provides a manure sold by capitalist chimney-sweeps to English farmers. Now, in 1862 the British 'jury-man' had to decide in a law-suit whether soot with which, unknown to the buyer, 90 per cent of dust and sand are mixed, is 'genuine' soot in the 'commercial' sense or 'adulterated' soot in the 'legal' sense. The 'friends of commerce' decided it was 'genuine' commercial soot, and rejected the suit of the plaintiff, a farmer, who had in addition to pay the costs of the proceedings.
44. The French chemist, Chevallier, in his treatise on the 'sophistications'

*The Eleatics were Greek philosophers of the sixth and fifth centuries B.C., who held that Being alone was true, and that everything outside the one fixed Being was merely apparent.

At all events the Committee had directed the attention of the public to its 'daily bread', and therefore to the baking trade. At the same time the cry of the London journeymen bakers against their over-work rose in public meetings and petitions to Parliament. The cry was so urgent that Mr H. S. Tremenheere, also a member of the above-mentioned Commission of 1863, was appointed a Royal Commissioner of Inquiry. His report,[45] together with the evidence given, moved the public not in its heart but in its stomach. Englishmen, with their good command of the Bible, knew well enough that man, unless by elective grace a capitalist, or a landlord, or the holder of a sinecure, is destined to eat his bread in the sweat of his brow, but they did not know that he had to eat daily in his bread a certain quantity of human perspiration mixed with the discharge of abscesses, cobwebs, dead cockroaches and putrid German yeast, not to mention alum, sand and other agreeable mineral ingredients. Without any regard for His Holiness 'Free Trade', the hitherto 'free' baking trade was therefore placed under the supervision of state-appointed inspectors (at the close of the Parliamentary session of 1863), and by the same Act of Parliament work from 9 in the evening to 5 in the morning was forbidden for journeymen bakers under 18. The last clause speaks volumes as to the over-work in this old-fashioned, homely line of business.

'The work of a London journeyman baker begins, as a rule, at about eleven at night. At that hour he "makes the dough" – a laborious process, which lasts from half an hour to three quarters of an hour, according to the size of the batch or the labour bestowed upon it. He then lies down upon the kneading-board, which is also the covering of the trough in which the dough is

---

of commodities,* enumerates, for many of the 600 or more articles he passes in review, 10, 20, 30 different methods of adulteration. He adds that he does not know all the methods, and does not mention all that he knows. He gives 6 kinds of adulteration of sugar, 9 of olive oil, 10 of butter, 12 of salt, 19 of milk, 20 of bread, 23 of brandy, 24 of meal, 28 of chocolate, 30 of wine, 32 of coffee, etc. Even God Almighty does not escape this fate. See Rouard de Card, *De la falsification des substances sacramentelles*, Paris, 1856.

45. *Report, etc., Relative to the Grievances Complained of by the Journeymen Bakers, etc.*, London, 1862, and *Second Report, etc.*, London, 1863.

* Jean Baptiste Alphonse Chevallier (1793–1879) was a chemist who wrote extensively on adulterations. His main work is *Dictionnaire des altérations et falsifications des substances alimentaires, médicamenteuses et commerciales, avec l'indication des moyens de les reconnaître* (Paris, 1850–52, 2 vols).

"made"; and with a sack under him, and another rolled up as a pillow, he sleeps for about a couple of hours. He is then engaged in a rapid and continuous labour for about five hours – throwing out the dough, "scaling it off", moulding it, putting it into the oven, preparing and baking rolls and fancy bread, taking the batch bread out of the oven, and up into the shop, etc., etc. The temperature of a bakehouse ranges from about 75 to upwards of 90 degrees, and in the smaller bakehouses approximates usually to the higher rather than to the lower degree of heat. When the business of making the bread, rolls, etc., is over, that of its distribution begins, and a considerable proportion of the journeymen in the trade, after working hard in the manner described during the night, are upon their legs for many hours during the day, carrying baskets, or wheeling hand-carts, and sometimes again in the bakehouse, leaving off work at various hours between 1 and 6 p.m. according to the season of the year, or the amount and nature of their master's business; while others are again engaged in the bakehouse in "bringing out" more batches until late in the afternoon.'[46] ... 'During what is called "the London season", the operatives belonging to the "full-priced" bakers at the West End of the town generally begin work at 11 p.m., and are engaged in making the bread, with one or two short (sometimes very short) intervals of rest, up to 8 o'clock the next morning. They are then engaged all day long, up to 4, 5, 6, and as late as 7 o'clock in the evening carrying out bread, or sometimes in the afternoon in the bakehouse again, assisting in the biscuit-baking. They may have, after they have done their work, sometimes 5 or 6, sometimes only four or five hours' sleep before they begin again. On Fridays they always begin sooner, some about 10 o'clock, and continue in some cases, at work, either in making or delivering the bread up to 8 p.m. on Saturday night, but more generally up to 4 or 5 o'clock, Sunday morning. On Sundays the men must attend twice or three times during the day for an hour or two to make preparations for the next day's bread ... The men employed by the underselling masters (who sell their bread under the "full price", and who, as already pointed out, comprise three-fourths of the London bakers) have not only to work on the average longer hours, but their work is almost entirely confined to the bakehouse. The underselling masters generally sell their bread ... in the shop. If they send it out, which is not common, except as supplying

46. *First Report, etc.*, pp. vi–vii.

chandlers' shops, they usually employ other hands for that purpose. It is not their practice to deliver bread from house to house. Towards the end of the week . . . the men begin on Thursday night at 10 o'clock, and continue on with only slight intermission until late on Saturday evening.'[47]

Even the bourgeois, from his standpoint, grasps the position of the 'underselling masters': 'The unpaid labour of the men was made the source whereby the competition was carried on.'[48] And the 'full-priced baker' denounces his 'underselling' competitors to the Commission of Inquiry as thieves of other people's labour and adulterators of the product. 'They only exist now by first defrauding the public, and next getting 18 hours' work out of their men for 12 hours' wages.'[49]

The adulteration of bread, and the formation of a class of bakers who sell bread for less than its full price, are developments which have taken place in England since the beginning of the eighteenth century, i.e. as soon as the corporate character of the trade was lost, and the capitalist stepped behind the nominal master baker in the shape of a miller or a flour factor.[50] This laid the foundation for capitalist production in this trade, for the unlimited extension of the working day, and for night work, although the last-mentioned has secured a real foothold only since 1824, even in London.[51]

After what has just been said, it will be understood that the Commission's report classes journeymen bakers among the short-lived workers, who, having by good luck escaped the normal decimation of the children of the working class, rarely reach the age of 42. Nevertheless, the baking trade is always overwhelmed with applicants. The sources for the supply of these 'labour-powers' to London are Scotland, the agricultural districts of the West of England, and – Germany.

47. ibid., p. lxxi.

48. George Read, *The History of Baking*, London, 1848, p. 16.

49. *First Report, etc.* Evidence of the 'full-priced baker' Cheeseman, p. 108.

50. George Read, op. cit. At the end of the seventeenth and the beginning of the eighteenth century the factors (i.e. agents) who crowded into every possible trade were still denounced as 'public nuisances'. For example, the Grand Jury at the quarter session of the Justices of the Peace for the County of Somerset addressed a 'presentment' to the House of Commons which states, among other things, 'that these factors of Blackwell Hall are a Public Nuisance and Prejudice to the Clothing Trade, and ought to be put down as a Nuisance' (*The Case of our English Wool, etc.*, London, 1685, pp. 6, 7).

51. *First Report, etc.*, p. viii.

In the years 1858–60 the journeymen bakers of Ireland organized, at their own expense, huge meetings to agitate against night work and Sunday work. The public – for example at the Dublin meeting of May 1860 – supported them with typically Irish warmth. As a result of this movement, a rule of exclusive day-labour was successfully established in Wexford, Kilkenny, Clonmel, Waterford, etc. 'In Limerick, where the grievances of the journeymen are demonstrated to be excessive, the movement has been defeated by the opposition of the master bakers, the miller bakers being the greatest opponents. The example of Limerick led to a retrogression in Ennis and Tipperary. In Cork, where the strongest possible demonstration of feeling took place, the masters, by exercising their power of turning the men out of employment, have defeated the movement. In Dublin, the master bakers have offered the most determined opposition to the movement, and by discountenancing as much as possible the journeymen promoting it, have succeeded in leading the men into acquiescence in Sunday work and night work, contrary to the convictions of the men.'[52]

The Committee of the English government, a government which, in Ireland, is armed to the teeth, merely remonstrates, in funereal tones it is true, against the implacable master bakers of Dublin, Limerick, Cork, etc.: 'The Committee believe that the hours of labour are limited by natural laws, which cannot be violated with impunity. That for master bakers to induce their workmen, by the fear of losing employment, to violate their religious convictions and their better feelings, to disobey the laws of the land, and to disregard public opinion' (this all refers to Sunday labour) 'is calculated to provoke ill-feeling between workmen and masters ... and affords an example dangerous to religion, morality, and social order ... The Committee believe that any constant work beyond 12 hours a day encroaches on the domestic and private life of the working man, and so leads to disastrous moral results, interfering with each man's home, and the discharge of his family duties as a son, a brother, a husband, a father. That work beyond 12 hours has a tendency to undermine the health of the working man, and so leads to premature old age and death, to the great injury of families of working men, thus deprived of the care and support of the head of the family when most required.'[53]

52. *Report of the Committee on the Baking Trade in Ireland for 1861.*
53. ibid.

We have just been in Ireland. On the other side of the channel, in Scotland, the agricultural labourer, the man of the plough, is protesting against his 13 to 14 hours' work in a very severe climate, with 4 hours' additional work on Sunday (in that land of Sabbatarians!),[54] while simultaneously in London three railwaymen – a guard, an engine-driver, and a signalman – are up before a coroner's jury. A tremendous railway accident has dispatched hundreds of passengers into the next world. The negligence of the railway workers is the cause of the misfortune. They declare with one voice before the jury that ten or twelve years before their labour lasted only 8 hours a day. During the last five or six years, they say, it has been screwed up to 14, 18 and 20 hours, and when the pressure of holiday travellers is especially severe, when excursion trains are put on, their labour often lasts for 40 or 50 hours without a break. They are ordinary men, not Cyclops. At a certain point their labour-power ran out. Torpor seized them. Their brains stopped thinking, their eyes stopped seeing. The thoroughly 'respectable British Juryman' replied with a verdict that sent them to the Assizes on a charge of manslaughter; in a mild rider to the verdict the jury expressed the pious hope that the capitalist railway magnates would in future be more extravagant in the purchase of the necessary number of 'labour-powers', and more 'abstemious', more 'self-denying', more 'thrifty', in the extortion of paid labour-power.[55]

54. Public meeting of agricultural labourers at Lasswade, near Edinburgh, 5 January 1866. (See *Workman's Advocate*, 13 January 1866.) The formation since the end of 1865 of a trade union among the agricultural labourers, first of all in Scotland, is a historic event. In one of the most oppressed agricultural districts of England, Buckinghamshire, in March 1867, the labourers carried through a great strike to raise their weekly wage from 9–10 shillings to 12 shillings. (It will be seen from the preceding passage that the movement of the English agricultural proletariat, entirely crushed since the suppression of its violent manifestations after 1830, and especially since the introduction of the new Poor Laws, begins again in the sixties, until it finally becomes epochmaking in 1872. I return to this in Volume 2, and also deal there with the Blue Books which have appeared since 1867 on the position of the English agricultural labourers. – Addendum to the third edition.)*

55. *Reynolds' Newspaper*, 21 January 1866. Every week this same paper brings a whole list of fresh railway catastrophes under the sensational headings 'Fearful and fatal accidents', 'Appalling tragedies', etc. This is the answer of a worker on the North Staffordshire Line: 'Everyone knows the consequences

*Marx appears not to have pursued this idea, as nothing on the subject appears either in Volume 2 or Volume 3.

From the motley crowd of workers of all callings, ages and sexes, who throng around us more urgently than did the souls of the slain around Ulysses, on whom we see at a glance the signs of over-work, without referring to the Blue Books under their arms, let us select two more figures, whose striking contrast proves that all men are alike in the face of capital – a milliner and a blacksmith.

In the last week of June 1863, all the London daily papers published a paragraph with the 'sensational' heading, 'Death from simple over-work'. It dealt with the death of the milliner, Mary Anne Walkley, 20 years old, employed in a highly respectable dressmaking establishment, exploited by a lady with the pleasant name of Elise. The old, often-told story was now revealed once again.[56] These girls work, on an average, $16\frac{1}{2}$ hours without a break, during the season often 30 hours, and the flow of their failing 'labour-power' is maintained by occasional supplies of sherry, port or coffee. It was the height of the season. It was necessary, in the twinkling of an eye, to conjure up magnificent dresses for the noble ladies invited to the ball in honour of the newly imported Princess of Wales. Mary Anne Walkley had worked uninterruptedly for $26\frac{1}{2}$ hours, with sixty other girls, thirty in each room. The rooms provided only $\frac{1}{3}$ of the necessary quantity of air, measured in cubic feet. At night the girls slept in pairs in the stifling holes into which a bedroom was divided by

---

that may occur if the driver and fireman of a locomotive engine are not continually on the look-out. How can that be expected from a man who has been at such work for 29 or 30 hours, exposed to the weather, and without rest? The following is an example which is of very frequent occurrence: One fireman commenced work on the Monday morning at a very early hour. When he had finished what is called a day's work, he had been on duty 14 hours 50 minutes. Before he had time to get his tea, he was again called on for duty . . . The next time he finished he had been on duty 14 hours 25 minutes, making a total of 29 hours 15 minutes without intermission. The rest of the week's work was made up as follows: Wednesday, 15 hours; Thursday, 15 hours 35 minutes; Friday, $14\frac{1}{2}$ hours; Saturday, 14 hours 10 minutes, making a total for the week of 88 hours 40 minutes. Now, sir, fancy his astonishment on being paid $6\frac{1}{4}$ days for the whole. Thinking it was a mistake, he applied to the time-keeper . . . and inquired what they considered a day's work, and was told 13 hours for a goods man (i.e. 78 hours) . . . He then asked for what he had made over and above the 78 hours per week, but was refused. However, he was at last told they would give him another quarter, i.e. 10d.' (ibid., 4 February 1866).

56. Cf. F. Engels, op. cit., pp. 253–4 [English edition, pp. 235–8].

wooden partitions.[57] And this was one of the better millinery establishments in London. Mary Anne Walkley fell ill on the Friday and died on Sunday, without, to the astonishment of Madame Elise, having finished off the bit of finery she was working on. The doctor, a Mr Keys, called too late to the girl's deathbed, made his deposition to the coroner's jury in plain language: 'Mary Anne Walkley died from long hours of work in an overcrowded work-room, and a too small and badly ventilated bedroom.' In order to give the doctor a lesson in good manners, the coroner's jury thereupon brought in the verdict that 'the deceased had died of apoplexy, but there was reason to fear that her death had been accelerated by over-work in an overcrowded work-room, etc.'.

'Our white slaves,' exclaimed the *Morning Star*, the organ of the free-trading gentlemen Cobden and Bright, 'our white slaves, who are toiled into the grave, for the most part silently pine and die.'[58]

57. Dr Letheby, Consulting Physician of the Board of Health, declared: 'The minimum of air for each adult ought to be in a sleeping room 300, and in a dwelling room 500 cubic feet.' Dr Richardson, Senior Physician at one of the London hospitals: 'With needlewomen of all kinds, including milliners, dressmakers, and ordinary sempstresses, there are three miseries – over-work, deficient air, and either deficient food or deficient digestion . . . Needlework, in the main . . . is infinitely better adapted to women than to men. But the mischiefs of the trade, in the metropolis especially, are that it is monopolised by some twenty-six capitalists, who, under the advantages that spring from capital, can bring in capital to force economy out of labour. This power tells throughout the whole class. If a dressmaker can get a little circle of customers, such is the competition that, in her home, she must work to the death to hold it together, and this same over-work she must of necessity inflict on any who may assist her. If she fail, do not try independently, she must join an establishment, where her labour is not less, but where her money is safe. Placed thus, she becomes a mere slave, tossed about with the variations of society. Now at home, in one room, starving, or near to it, then engaged 15, 16, aye, even 18 hours out of the 24, in an air that is scarcely tolerable, and on food which, even if it be good, cannot be digested in the absence of pure air. On these victims, consumption, which is purely a disease of bad air, feeds' (Dr Richardson, 'Work and Over-Work', in *Social Science Review*, 18 July 1863).

58. *Morning Star*, 23 June 1863. *The Times* used this opportunity to defend the American slave-owners against Bright etc. 'Very many of us think,' says a leading article of 2 July 1863, 'that, while we work our own young women to death, using the scourge of starvation, instead of the crack of the whip, as the instrument of compulsion, we have scarcely a right to hound on fire and slaughter against families who were born slave-owners, and who, at least,

'It is not only in dressmakers' rooms that working to death is the order of the day, but in a thousand other places; in every place I had almost said, where "a thriving business" has to be done . . . We will take the blacksmith as a type. If the poets were true, there is no man so hearty, so merry, as the blacksmith; he rises early and strikes his sparks before the sun; he eats and drinks and sleeps as no other man. Working in moderation, he is, in fact, in one of the best of human positions, physically speaking. But we follow him into the city or town, and we see the stress of work on that strong man, and what then is his position in the death-rate of his country. In Marylebone, blacksmiths die at the rate of 31 per thousand per annum, or 11 above the mean of the male adults of the country in its entirety. The occupation, instinctive almost as a portion of human art, unobjectionable as a branch of human industry, is made by mere excess of work the destroyer of the man. He can strike so many blows per day, walk so many steps, breathe so many breaths, produce so much work, and live an average, say, of fifty years; he is made to strike so many more blows, to walk so many more steps, to breathe so many more breaths per day, and to increase altogether a fourth

---

feed their slaves well, and work them lightly.' In the same manner, the *Standard*, a Tory paper, delivered a rebuke to the Rev. Newman Hall*: 'He excommunicated the slave owners, but prays with the fine folk who, without remorse, make the omnibus drivers and conductors of London, etc., work 16 hours a day for the wages of a dog' (*Standard*, 15 August 1863). Finally, the oracle spoke, Thomas Carlyle, the man of whom I already wrote in 1850: 'The Genius has gone to the devil; the Cult has remained.'† In a short parable, he reduces the one great event of contemporary history, the American Civil War, to this level, that the Peter of the North wants to break the head of the Paul of the South with all his might, because the Peter of the North hires his labour by the day, and the Paul of the South hires his 'for life' ('Ilias Americana in Nuce', *Macmillan's Magazine*, August 1863). Thus the bubble of Tory sympathy for the urban workers – not, by God, for the rural workers! – has burst at last. The kernel of it is – slavery!

*Rev. Christopher Newman Hall (1816–1902), Congregationalist minister, Liberal in politics, a prominent advocate of the Northern cause during the American Civil War.

†Marx refers here to his review of Carlyle's book *Latter-Day Pamphlets*, in the *Neue Rheinische Zeitung. Revue*, April 1850. The quotation should run, in full, 'in these pamphlets, the cult of genius, which Carlyle shares with Strauss, has lost what genius it possessed; the cult has remained' (*MEW* 7, p. 256).

The Working Day 367

of his life. He meets the effort; the result is, that producing for a limited time a fourth more work, he dies at 37 for 50.'[59]

4. DAY-WORK AND NIGHT-WORK. THE SHIFT-SYSTEM

Constant capital, the means of production, only exist, considered from the standpoint of the process of valorization, in order to absorb labour and, with every drop of labour, a proportional quantity of surplus labour. In so far as the means of production fail to do this, their mere existence forms a loss for the capitalist, in a negative sense, for while they lie fallow they represent a useless advance of capital. This loss becomes a positive one as soon as the interruption of employment necessitates an additional outlay when the work begins again. The prolongation of the working day beyond the limits of the natural day, into the night, only acts as a palliative. It only slightly quenches the vampire thirst for the living blood of labour. Capitalist production therefore drives, by its inherent nature, towards the appropriation of labour throughout the whole of the 24 hours in the day. But since it is physically impossible to exploit the same individual labour-power constantly, during the night as well as the day, capital has to overcome this physical obstacle. An alternation becomes necessary, between the labour-powers used up by day and those used up by night. This can be accomplished in various ways; for instance it may be arranged that part of the working personnel is employed for one week on day-work, and for the next week on night-work. It is well known that this shift-system, this alternation of two sets of workers, predominated in the full-blooded springtime of the English cotton industry, and that at the present time it still flourishes, among other places, in the cotton-spinning factories of the Moscow *gubernia*.* This 24-hour process of production exists today as a system in many of the as yet 'free' branches of industry in Great Britain, in the blast-furnaces, forges, rolling mills and other metallurgical establishments of England, Wales and Scotland. Here the labour process includes a great part of the 24 hours of Sunday, in addition to the 24 hours of the 6 working days. The

59. Dr Richardson, op. cit., pp. 476 ff.

*'Government'; the largest administrative subdivision of the Russian Empire.

workers consist of men and women, adults and children of both sexes. The ages of the children and young persons run through all the intermediate grades, from 8 (in some cases from 6) to 18.[60] In some branches of industry, the girls and women work through the night together with the male personnel.[61]

Leaving aside the generally harmful effects of night labour,[62] the duration of the process of production, unbroken for 24 hours, offers very welcome opportunities for exceeding the limits of the normal working day, for example in the branches of industry already mentioned, which are themselves very strenuous; the official working day usually comes to 12 hours by night or day for all workers. But the amount of over-work done in excess of

60. *Children's Employment Commission, Third Report*, London, 1864, pp. iv–vi.

61. 'Both in Staffordshire and in South Wales young girls and women are employed on the pit banks and on the coke heaps, not only by day but also by night. This practice has been often noticed in Reports presented to Parliament, as being attended with great and notorious evils. These females employed with the men, hardly distinguished from them in their dress, and begrimed with dirt and smoke, are exposed to the deterioration of character, arising from their loss of self-respect, which can hardly fail to follow from their unfeminine occupation' (ibid., pp. 194, xxvi. Cf. *Fourth Report* (1865), 61, p. xiii). It is the same in the glass-works.

62. A steel manufacturer who employs children in night labour remarks: 'It seems but natural that boys who work at night cannot sleep and get proper rest by day, but will be running about' (*Fourth Report*, 63, p. xiii). A doctor has this to say on the importance of sunlight for the maintenance and growth of the body: 'Light also acts upon the tissues of the body directly in hardening them and supporting their elasticity. The muscles of animals, when they are deprived of a proper amount of light, become soft and inelastic, the nervous power loses its tone from defective stimulation, and the elaboration of all growth seems to be perverted ... In the case of children, constant access to plenty of light during the day, and to the direct rays of the sun for a part of it, is most essential to health. Light assists in the elaboration of good plastic blood, and hardens the fibre after it has been laid down. It also acts as a stimulus upon the organs of sight, and by this means brings about more activity in the various cerebral functions.' Dr W. Strange, Senior Physician at the Worcester General Hospital, from whose work on *Health* (1864) this passage is taken, writes in a letter to Mr White, one of the Commissioners: 'I have had opportunities formerly, when in Lancashire, of observing the effects of night-work upon children, and I have no hesitation in saying, contrary to what *some* employers were fond of asserting, those who were subjected to it soon suffered in their health' (*Children's Employment Commission, Fourth Report*, 284, p. 55). That such a question could provide the material for a serious controversy is the best demonstration of the way capitalist production acts on the mental functions of the capitalists and their retainers.

this limit is in many cases, to use the words of the official English report, 'truly fearful'.[63]

'It is impossible,' says the report, 'for any mind to realize the amount of work described in the following passages as being performed by boys of from 9 to 12 years of age . . . without coming irresistibly to the conclusion that such abuses of the power of parents and of employers can no longer be allowed to exist.'[64]

'The practice of boys working at all by day and night turns either in the usual course of things, or at pressing times, seems inevitably to open the door to their not infrequently working unduly long hours. These hours are, indeed, in some cases, not only cruelly, but even incredibly long for children. Amongst a number of boys it will, of course, not infrequently happen that one or more are from some cause absent. When this happens, their place is made up by one or more boys, who work in the other turn. That this is a well-understood system is plain . . . from the answer of the manager of some large rolling-mills, who, when I asked him how the place of the boys absent from their turn was made up, "I daresay, sir, you know that as well as I do", and admitted the fact.'[65]

'At a rolling-mill where the proper hours were from 6 a.m. to 5.30 p.m., a boy worked about four nights every week till 8.30 p.m. at least . . . and this for six months. Another, at 9 years old, sometimes made three 12-hour shifts running, and, when 10, has made two days and two nights running.' A third, 'now 10 . . . worked from 6 a.m. till 12 p.m. three nights, and till 9 p.m. the other nights'. 'Another, now 13, . . . worked from 6 p.m. till 12 noon next day, for a week together, and sometimes for three shifts together, e.g., from Monday morning till Tuesday night.' 'Another, now 12, has worked in an iron foundry at Staveley from 6 a.m. till 12 p.m. for a fortnight on end; could not do it any more.' 'George Allinsworth, age 9, came here as cellar-boy last Friday; next morning we had to begin at 3, so I stopped here all night. Live five miles off. Slept on the floor of the furnace, over head, with an apron under me, and a bit of a jacket over me. The two other days I have been here at 6 a.m. Aye! it *is* hot in here. Before I came here I was nearly a year at the same work at some works in the country. Began there, too, at 3 on Saturday morning – always did, but was very gain (near) home, and could sleep at

63. ibid., 57, p. xii.   64. ibid., 58, p. xii.   65. ibid.

home. Other days I began at 6 in the morning, and gi'en over at 6 or 7 in the evening,' etc.[66]

Let us now hear how capital itself regards this 24-hour system. The extreme forms of the system, its abuse in the 'cruel and

66. ibid., p. xiii. The level of education of these 'labour-powers' must naturally be such as appears in the following dialogues with one of the Commissioners: Jeremiah Haynes, age 12 – 'Four times four is eight; four fours are sixteen. A king is him that has all the money and gold. We have a King (told it is a Queen), they call her the Princess Alexandra. Told that she married the Queen's son. The Queen's son is the Princess Alexandra. A Princess is a man.' William Turner, age 12 – 'Don't live in England. Think it *is* a country, but didn't know before.' John Morris, age 14 – 'Have heard say that God made the world, and that all the people was drowned but one; heard say that one was a little bird.' William Smith, age 15 – 'God made man, man made woman.' Edward Taylor, age 15 – 'Do not know of London.' Henry Matthewman, age 17 – 'Had been to chapel, but missed a good many times lately. One name that they preached about was Jesus Christ, but I cannot say any others, and I cannot tell anything about him. He was not killed, but died like other people. He was not the same as other people in some ways, because he was religious in some ways, and others isn't' (loc. cit., p. xv). 'The devil is a good person. I don't know where he lives.' 'Christ was a wicked man.' 'This girl spelt God as dog, and did not know the name of the queen' (*Children's Employment Commission, Fifth Report*, 1866, p. 55, n. 278). The same system obtains in the glass and paper works as in the metallurgical establishments already cited. In the paper factories, where the paper is made by machinery, night-work is the rule for all processes, except rag-sorting. In some cases night-work is carried on incessantly through the whole week, by means of shifts, and thus continues from Sunday night until midnight of the following Saturday. The men on day-work work five days of 12 hours, and one day of 18 hours; those on night-work work five nights of 12 hours, and one of 6 hours in each week. In other cases each group works 24 hours consecutively on alternate days, one group working 6 hours on Monday, and 18 on Saturday, to make up the 24 hours. In other cases an intermediate system prevails, by which all those employed on the paper-making machinery work 15 or 16 hours every day in the week. This system, says Commissioner Lord, 'seems to combine all the evils of both the 12 hours' and the 24 hours' relays'. Children under 13, young persons under 18, and women, work under this night system. Sometimes, under the 12-hour system, they are forced to work a double shift of 24 hours, owing to the failure of their counterparts to turn up. The evidence proves that boys and girls very often work overtime, which not infrequently extends to 24 or even 36 hours of uninterrupted toil. In the 'continuous and unvarying' process of glazing there are to be found girls of 12 who work 14 hours a day for the whole month, 'without any regular relief or cessation beyond two, or, at most, three breaks of half an hour each for meals'. In some factories, where regular night-work has been entirely given up, a frightful amount of overtime is put in, 'and that often in the dirtiest, and in the hottest, and in the most monotonous of the various processes' (*Children's Employment Commission, Fourth Report*, 1865, pp. xxxviii and xxxix).

incredible' extension of the working day, are naturally passed over in silence. Capital only speaks of the system in its 'normal' form.

Messrs Naylor and Vickers, steel manufacturers, who employ between 600 and 700 persons, among whom only 10 per cent are under 18, with only twenty boys under 18 working on the night shift, have the following comments to make: 'The boys do not suffer from the heat. The temperature is probably from 86 degrees to 90 degrees . . . At the forges and in the rolling-mills the hands work night and day, in relays, but all the other parts of the work are day-work, i.e. from 6 a.m. to 6 p.m. In the forge the hours are from 12 to 12. Some of the hands always work in the night, without any alternation of day and night work . . . We do not find any difference in the health of those who work regularly by night and those who work by day, and probably people can sleep better if they have the same period of rest than if it is changed . . . About twenty of the boys under the age of 18 work in the night sets . . . We could not well do without lads under 18 working by night. The objection would be the increase in the cost of production . . . Skilled hands and the heads in every department are difficult to get, but of lads we could get any number . . . But from the small proportion of boys that we employ, the subject' (i.e. the subject of restrictions on night-work) 'is of little importance or interest to us.'[67]

Mr J. Ellis, from the firm of Messrs John Brown & Co., steel and iron works, employing about 3,000 men and boys, part of whose operations, namely iron and heavier steel work, goes on night and day in shifts, states 'that in the heavier steel work one or two boys are employed to a score or two men'. Their business employs 500 boys under 18, and of these about a third, or 170, are under the age of 13. With reference to the proposed alteration of the law, Mr Ellis says: 'I do not think it would be very objectionable to require that no person under the age of 18 should work more than 12 hours in the 24. But we do not think that any line could be drawn over the age of 12, at which boys could be dispensed with for night-work. But we would sooner be prevented from employing boys under the age of 13, or even so high as 14, at all, than not be allowed to employ boys that we do have at night. Those boys who work in the day sets must take their turn in the night sets also, because the men could not work in the night sets

67. *Fourth Report, etc.*, 1865, 79, p. xvi.

only; it would ruin their health . . . We think, however, that night-work in alternate weeks is no harm.' (Messrs Naylor & Vickers, on the other hand, in line with the best interests of their business, took the opposite view, that periodic alternations of night and day-labour might well do more harm than continual night-labour.) 'We find the men who do it, as well* as the others who do other work only by day . . . Our objections to not allowing boys under 18 to work at night, would be on account of the increase of expense, but this is the only reason.' (What cynical naïveté!) 'We think that the increase would be more than the trade, with due regard to its being successfully carried out, could fairly bear.' (What mealy-mouthed phraseology!) 'Labour is scarce here, and might fall short if there were such a regulation.' (In other words, Ellis, or Brown & Co., might be subjected to the fatal embarrassment of having to pay labour-power at its full value.)[68]

The 'Cyclops Steel and Iron Works' of Messrs Cammell & Co. is conducted on the same large scale as the works of the above-mentioned John Brown & Co. The managing director had handed in his evidence to the Government Commissioner, Mr White, in writing. Later he found it convenient to suppress the manuscript when it was returned to him for revision. But Mr White has a retentive memory. He recalled quite clearly that for these Cyclopean gentlemen the prohibition of the night-labour of children and young persons 'would be impossible, it would be tantamount to stopping their works', and yet their business employs little more than 6 per cent of boys under 18, and less than 1 per cent under 13.[69]

On the same question, Mr E. F. Sanderson, of the firm of Sanderson Bros. & Co., steel rolling-mills and forges, Attercliffe, says: 'Great difficulty would be caused by preventing boys under 18 from working at night. The chief would be the increase of cost from employing men instead of boys. I cannot say what this would be, but probably it would not be enough to enable the manufacturers to raise the price of steel, and consequently it would fall on them, as of course the men' (how wrong-headed these people are!) 'would refuse to pay it.' Mr Sanderson does not know how much he pays the children, but 'perhaps the younger

68. *Fourth Report, etc.*, 1865, 80, p. xvi.   69. ibid., 82, p. xvii.

---

*That is, as healthy.

boys get from 4s. to 5s. a week . . . The boys' work is of a kind for which the strength of boys is generally' ('generally', but of course not always 'in particular') 'quite sufficient, and consequently there would be no gain in the greater strength of the men to counterbalance the loss, or it would be only in the few cases in which the metal is heavy. The men would not like so well not to have boys under them, as men would be less obedient. Besides, boys must begin young to learn the trade. Leaving day-work alone open to boys would not answer the purpose.'

And why not? Why could the boys not learn their craft in the daytime? Your reason? 'Owing to the men working days and nights in alternate weeks, the men would be separated half the time from their boys, and would lose half the profit which they make from them. The training which they give to an apprentice is considered as part of the return for the boys' labour, and thus enables the men to get it at a cheaper rate. Each man would want half of this profit.' In other words, Messrs Sanderson would have to pay part of the wages of the adult men out of their own pockets instead of by the night-work of the boys. Messrs Sanderson's profit would thus fall to some extent, and this is the good Sandersonian reason why boys cannot learn their craft by day.[70] Apart from this, it would throw night-work on the men alone, who are at present relieved by the boys, and they would not be able to stand it. In short, the difficulties would be so great as to lead in all likelihood to the total suppression of night-work. 'As far as the work itself is concerned,' says E. F. Sanderson, 'this would suit as well, but – ' But Messrs Sanderson have something else to make besides steel. Steel-making is simply a pretext for profit-making. The steel furnaces, rolling-mills, etc., the buildings, machinery, iron, coal, etc., have something more to do than transform themselves into steel. They are there to absorb surplus labour, and they naturally absorb more in 24 hours than in 12. In fact, both by the sanction of the law and the grace of God, they give to the Sandersons a draft on the labour-time of a certain number of hands for all the 24 hours of the day, and as soon as there is an interruption in their function of absorbing labour they

70. 'In a time so rich in reflection and so devoted to *raisonnement* as our own, he must be a poor creature who cannot advance a good ground for everything, even for what is worst and most depraved. Everything in the world that has become corrupt, has had good ground for its corruption' (Hegel, op. cit., p. 249) [*Logic*, para. 121, Addition. English translation, p. 178].

lose their character as capital, and are therefore a pure loss for the Sandersons. 'But then there would be the loss from so much expensive machinery, lying idle half the time, and to get through the amount of work which we are able to do on the present system, we should have to double our premises and plant, which would double the outlay.' But why should these Sandersons pretend to a privilege not enjoyed by the other capitalists who only work during the day, and whose buildings, machinery, raw material, therefore lie 'idle' during the night? E. F. Sanderson answers in the name of all the Sandersons: 'It is true that there is this loss from machinery lying idle in those manufactories in which work only goes on by day. But the use of furnaces would involve a further loss in our case. If they were kept up these would be a waste of fuel' (instead of the present waste of the living substance of the workers) 'and if they were not, there would be loss of time in laying the fires and getting the heat up' (whereas a loss of sleeping time, even that of 8-year-olds, is a gain of working time for the Sanderson clan), 'and the furnaces themselves would suffer from the changes of temperature' (whereas those same furnaces suffer nothing from the alternation of day-work and night-work).[71]

71. *Children's Employment Commission, Fourth Report,* 1865, 85, p. xvii. Commissioner White has an answer to similar tender scruples of the glass manufacturers, who maintain that 'regular meal-times' for the children are impossible because this would lead to a 'pure loss' or a 'waste' of a certain quantity of heat, radiated by the furnaces. His answer is quite unlike that of Ure, Senior etc., and their puny German imitators, like Roscher, who are moved by the 'abstinence', the 'self-denial' and the 'saving' of the capitalists in the expenditure of their money, and by their Timurlane-like 'prodigality' in human lives! 'A certain amount of heat beyond what is usual at present might also be going to waste, if meal-times were secured in these cases, but it seems likely not equal in money-value to the waste of animal power now going on in glass-houses throughout the kingdom from growing boys not having enough quiet time to eat their meals at ease, with a little rest afterwards for digestion' (ibid., p. xlv). And this in 1865, 'the year of progress'! Without considering the strength expended in lifting and carrying, these children, in the sheds where bottle and flint glass are made, walk 15 to 20 miles in every 6 hours, performing their work continuously. And it often lasts for 14 or 15 hours! In many of these glass works, as in the Moscow spinning mills, the 6-hour shift system is in force. 'During the working part of the week six hours is the utmost unbroken period ever attained at any one time for rest and out of this has to come the time spent in coming and going to and from work, washing, dressing, and meals, leaving a very short period indeed for rest, and none for fresh air and play, unless at the expense of the sleep necessary for young boys, especially at such hot and fatiguing work . . . Even the short sleep is obviously liable to be broken by a boy having to wake himself

5. THE STRUGGLE FOR A NORMAL WORKING DAY. LAWS FOR THE COMPULSORY EXTENSION OF THE WORKING DAY, FROM THE MIDDLE OF THE FOURTEENTH TO THE END OF THE SEVENTEENTH CENTURY

'What is a working day? What is the length of time during which capital may consume the labour-power whose daily value it has paid for? How far may the working day be extended beyond the amount of labour-time necessary for the reproduction of labour-power itself?' We have seen that capital's reply to these questions is this: the working day contains the full 24 hours, with the deduction of the few hours of rest without which labour-power is absolutely incapable of renewing its services. Hence it is self-evident that the worker is nothing other than labour-power for the duration of his whole life, and that therefore all his disposable time is by nature and by right labour-time, to be devoted to the self-valorization of capital. Time for education, for intellectual development, for the fulfilment of social functions, for social intercourse, for the free play of the vital forces of his body and his mind, even the rest time of Sunday (and that in a country of Sabbatarians!)[72] – what foolishness! But in its blind and measureless drive, its insatiable appetite for surplus labour, capital oversteps not only the moral but even the merely physical limits of the working day. It usurps the time for growth, development and healthy maintenance of the body. It steals

---

if it is night, or by the noise, if it is day.' Mr White gives cases where a boy worked for 36 consecutive hours, and others where boys of 12 drudged on until 2 in the morning, and then slept in the works till 5 a.m. (3 hours!) only to resume their work. 'The amount of work,' say Tremenheere and Tufnell, who drafted the general report, 'done by boys, youths, girls, and women, in the course of their daily or nightly spell of labour, is certainly extraordinary' (ibid., pp. xliii and xliv). Meanwhile, late at night perhaps, Mr Glass-Capital, stuffed full with abstinence, and primed with port wine, reels home from his club, droning out idiotically 'Britons never, never shall be slaves!'

72. In England even now in rural districts a labourer is occasionally condemned to imprisonment for desecrating the Sabbath by working in his front garden. The same man would be punished for breach of contract if he remained away from his metal, paper or glass works on Sunday, even on account of some religious foible. The orthodox Parliament will entertain no complaint of Sabbath-breaking if it occurs in the 'process of valorization' of capital. A petition of August 1863 in which the London day-labourers in fish and poultry shops asked for the abolition of Sunday labour states that their work lasts an average of 16 hours a day for the first 6 days of the week, 8 to 10 hours on Sunday. We also learn from this petition that the delicate gourmands among

the time required for the consumption of fresh air and sunlight. It haggles over the meal-times, where possible incorporating them into the production process itself, so that food is added to the worker as to a mere means of production, as coal is supplied to the boiler, and grease and oil to the machinery. It reduces the sound sleep needed for the restoration, renewal and refreshment of the vital forces to the exact amount of torpor essential to the revival of an absolutely exhausted organism. It is not the normal maintenance of labour-power which determines the limits of the working day here, but rather the greatest possible daily expenditure of labour-power, no matter how diseased, compulsory and painful it may be, which determines the limits of the workers' period of rest. Capital asks no questions about the length of life of labour-power. What interests it is purely and simply the maximum of labour-power that can be set in motion in a working day. It attains this objective by shortening the life of labour-power, in the same way as a greedy farmer snatches more produce from the soil by robbing it of its fertility.

By extending the working day, therefore, capitalist production, which is essentially the production of surplus-value, the absorption of surplus labour, not only produces a deterioration of human labour-power by robbing it of its normal moral and physical conditions of development and activity, but also produces the premature exhaustion and death of this labour-power itself.[73] It

the aristocratic hypocrites of Exeter Hall* particularly encourage this 'Sunday labour'. These 'saints', so zealous *in cute curanda*,† show they are Christians by the humility with which they bear the over-work, the deprivation and the hunger of others. *Obsequium ventris istis* (the workers') *perniciosius est.*‡

73. 'We have given in our previous reports the statements of several experienced manufacturers to the effect that over-hours ... certainly tend prematurely to exhaust the working power of the men' (op. cit., 64, p. xiii).

* A large hall on the north side of the Strand, built in 1831, and pulled down in 1907. It was used throughout its existence for meetings by religious bodies of various kinds, but especially by the Church Missionary Society. 'Exeter Hall' was in Marx's time a shorthand expression for that tendency among the English ruling classes which stood for the extension of English power in Africa with the aim of converting the 'natives' to Christianity, and at the same time stamping out the slave trade. It is associated with the name of Wilberforce.

† 'In attending to their bodily pleasures' (Horace, *Epistles*, 1, 2, 29).

‡ Horace's actual words were: '*obsequium ventris mihi perniciosius est cur*?' ('why is gluttony more ruinous to my stomach?'). Hence, here, 'gluttony is more ruinous to their (the workers') stomachs'. (Horace, *Satires*, Bk II, Satire 7, line 104.)

extends the worker's production-time within a given period by shortening his life.

But the value of labour-power includes the value of the commodities necessary for the reproduction of the worker, for continuing the existence of the working class. If then the unnatural extension of the working day, which capital necessarily strives for in its unmeasured drive for self-valorization, shortens the life of the individual worker, and therefore the duration of his labour-power, the forces used up have to be replaced more rapidly, and it will be more expensive to reproduce labour-power, just as in the case of a machine, where the part of its value that has to be reproduced daily grows greater the more rapidly the machine is worn out. It would seem therefore that the interest of capital itself points in the direction of a normal working day.

The slave-owner buys his worker in the same way as he buys his horse. If he loses his slave, he loses a piece of capital, which he must replace by fresh expenditure on the slave-market. But take note of this: 'The rice-grounds of Georgia, or the swamps of the Mississippi, may be fatally injurious to the human constitution; but the waste of human life which the cultivation of these districts necessitates, is not so great that it cannot be repaired from the teeming preserves of Virginia and Kentucky. Considerations of economy, moreover, which, under a natural system, afford some security for humane treatment by identifying the master's interest with the slave's preservation, when once trading in slaves is practised, become reasons for racking to the uttermost the toil of the slave; for, when his place can at once be supplied from foreign preserves, the duration of his life becomes a matter of less moment than its productiveness while it lasts. It is accordingly a maxim of slave management, in slave-importing countries, that the most effective economy is that which takes out of the human chattel in the shortest space of time the utmost amount of exertion it is capable of putting forth. It is in tropical culture, where annual profits often equal the whole capital of plantations, that negro life is most recklessly sacrificed. It is the agriculture of the West Indies, which has been for centuries prolific of fabulous wealth, that has engulfed millions of the African race. It is in Cuba, at this day, whose revenues are reckoned by millions, and whose planters are princes, that we see in the servile class, the coarsest fare, the most exhausting and unremitting toil, and even the absolute destruction of a portion of its numbers every year.'[74]

74. Cairnes, op. cit., pp. 110–11.

Mutato nomine de te fabula narratur.* For slave trade, read labour-market, for Kentucky and Virginia, Ireland and the agricultural districts of England, Scotland and Wales, for Africa, Germany. We have heard how over-work has thinned the ranks of the bakers in London. Nevertheless, the London labour-market is always over-stocked with German and other candidates for death in the bakeries. Pottery, as we saw, is one of the branches of industry with the lowest life-expectancy. Does this lead to any shortage of potters? Josiah Wedgwood, the inventor of modern pottery, and himself an ordinary worker by origin, said in 1785 before the House of Commons that the whole trade employed from 15,000 to 20,000 people.[75] In 1861 the population of the urban centres alone of this industry in Great Britain numbered 101,302. 'The cotton trade has existed for ninety years ... It has existed for three generations of the English race, and I believe I may safely say that during that period it has destroyed nine generations of factory operatives.'[76]

Admittedly the labour-market shows significant gaps in certain epochs of feverish expansion. In 1834 for example. But then the manufacturers proposed to the Poor Law Commissioners that they should send the 'surplus population' of the agricultural districts to the north, with the explanation 'that the manufacturers would absorb and use it up'.[77] 'Agents were appointed with the consent of the Poor Law Commissioners ... An office was set up in Manchester, to which lists were sent of those workpeople in the agricultural districts wanting employment, and their names were registered in books. The manufacturers attended at these offices, and selected such persons as they chose; when they had selected such persons as their "wants required", they gave instructions to have them forwarded to Manchester, and they were sent, ticketed like bales of goods, by canals, or with carriers, others tramping on the road, and many of them were found on the way lost and half-starved. This system had grown up into a regular trade. This House will hardly

75. John Ward, *The Borough of Stoke-upon-Trent*, London, 1843, p. 42.
76. Ferrand's* speech in the House of Commons, 27 April 1863.
77. 'Those were the very words used by the cotton manufacturers' (op. cit.).
*William Busfeild Ferrand, of Keighley in Yorkshire (1809–89). An 'Oastlerite' Tory, who agitated against the Poor Law of 1834 and in favour of the Factory Acts. He played an important part in passing the 1847 Factory Act. M.P. between 1841 and 1847, and between 1863 and 1866.

*'The name is changed, but the tale is told of you!' (Horace, *Satires*, Bk I, Satire 1).

believe it, but I tell them, that this traffic in human flesh was as well kept up, they were in effect as regularly sold to these manufacturers as slaves are sold to the cotton-grower in the United States . . . In 1860, the cotton trade was at its zenith. . . . The manufacturers again found that they were short of hands . . . They applied to the "flesh agents", as they are called. Those agents sent to the southern downs of England, to the pastures of Dorsetshire, to the glades of Devonshire, to the people tending kine in Wiltshire, but they sought in vain. The surplus population was "absorbed".'

The *Bury Guardian* lamented that, after the conclusion of the Anglo-French commercial treaty,* '10,000 additional hands could be absorbed by Lancashire, and that 30,000 or 40,000 will be needed'. After the 'flesh agents and sub-agents' had vainly combed through the agricultural districts 'a deputation came up to London, and waited on the right hon. gentleman (Mr Villiers, President of the Poor Law Board) with a view of obtaining poor children from certain union houses for the mills of Lancashire'.[78]

78. op. cit. Mr Villiers, despite the best of intentions on his part, was 'legally' obliged to refuse the requests of the manufacturers. These gentlemen nevertheless achieved their aims owing to the complaisance of the local poor law boards. Mr A. Redgrave, inspector of factories, assures us that this time the system under which orphans and the children of paupers were treated 'legally' as apprentices 'was not accompanied with the old abuses' (on these 'abuses' see Engels, op. cit.), although in one case there certainly was 'abuse of this system in respect to a number of girls and young women brought from the agricultural districts of Scotland into Lancashire and Cheshire'. Under this 'system' the manufacturer entered into a contract with the workhouse authorities for a certain period. He fed, clothed and lodged the children, and gave them a small allowance of money. The following remark by Mr Redgrave sounds very peculiar, especially if we consider that the year 1860 was quite unparalleled, even among the years of prosperity of the English cotton trade, and that, apart from this, wages were exceptionally high. For this extraordinary demand for labour had to contend with the depopulation of Ireland, with unequalled emigration from the English and Scottish agricultural districts to Australia and America, and with an actual fall in the population of some of the English agricultural districts, resulting partly from a collapse of the workers' powers of reproduction, which was deliberately aimed at and successfully attained, and partly from the already completed dispersal of the disposable population by the dealers in human flesh. Despite all this, Mr Redgrave says: 'This kind of labour, however' (i.e. the labour of the poor-house children) 'would only be sought after when none other could be procured, for it is a high-priced labour. The ordinary wages of a boy of 13

*The Anglo-French Treaty of Commerce of 1860, by which tariff barriers between Britain and France were lowered on both sides.

What experience generally shows to the capitalist is a constant excess of population, i.e. an excess in relation to capital's need for valorization at a given moment, although this throng of people is made up of generations of stunted, short-lived and rapidly replaced human beings, plucked, so to speak, before they were ripe.[79] And indeed, experience shows to the intelligent observer how rapidly and firmly capitalist production has seized the vital forces of the people at their very roots, although historically speaking it hardly dates from yesterday. Experience shows too how the degeneration of the industrial population is retarded only by the constant absorption of primitive and natural elements from the countryside, and how even the agricultural labourers, in spite of the fresh air and the 'principle of natural selection' that works so powerfully amongst them, and permits the survival of only the strongest individuals, are already beginning to die off.[80] Capital, which has such 'good

would be about 4s. per week, but to lodge, to clothe, to feed, and to provide medical attendance and proper superintendence for 50 or 100 of these boys, and to set aside some remuneration for them, could not be accomplished for 4s. a head per week' (*Reports of the Inspectors of Factories . . . 30 April 1860*, p. 27). Mr Redgrave forgets to tell us how the worker himself can do all this for his children out of their 4s. a week wages, when the manufacturer cannot do it for the 50 or 100 children lodged, boarded and superintended all together. To guard against false conclusions from the text, I should add here that the English cotton industry, after being placed under the Factory Act of 1850, with its regulation of working hours etc., must be regarded as England's model industry. The English cotton worker is in every respect better off than the man who shares his fate on the Continent. 'The Prussian factory operative labours at least ten hours per week more than his English competitor, and if employed at his own loom in his own house, his labour is not restricted to even those additional hours' (*Reports of the Inspectors of Factories . . . 31 October 1855*, p. 103). After the Industrial Exhibition of 1851 Redgrave travelled on the Continent, particularly in France and Germany, in order to investigate factory conditions there. He says this of the Prussian factory worker: 'He receives a remuneration sufficient to procure the simple fare, and to supply the slender comforts to which he has been accustomed . . . he lives upon his coarse fare, and works hard, wherein his position is subordinate to that of the English operative' (*Reports of the Inspectors of Factories . . . 31 October 1853*, p. 85).

79. The over-worked 'die off with strange rapidity; but the places of those who perish are instantly filled, and a frequent change of persons makes no alteration in the scene' (*England and America*, London, 1833, Vol. 1, p. 55. Author E. G. Wakefield).

80. See *Public Health. Sixth Report of the Medical Officer of the Privy Council*, 1863, published in London, 1864. This report deals particularly with the agricultural labourers. 'Sutherland . . . is commonly represented as a

reasons' for denying the sufferings of the legions of workers surrounding it, allows its actual movement to be determined as much and as little by the sight of the coming degradation and final depopulation of the human race, as by the probable fall of the earth into the sun. In every stock-jobbing swindle everyone knows that some time or other the crash must come, but everyone hopes that it may fall on the head of his neighbour, after he himself has caught the shower of gold and placed it in secure hands. *Après moi le déluge!* is the watchword of every capitalist and of every capitalist nation. Capital therefore takes no account of the health and the length of life of the worker, unless society forces it to do so.[81] Its answer to the outcry about the physical and mental degradation, the premature death, the torture of over-work, is this: Should that pain trouble us, since it increases our pleasure (profit)? * But looking at these things as a whole, it is evident that this does not depend on the will, either good or bad, of the individual capitalist. Under free competition, the immanent laws of capitalist production confront the individual capitalist as a coercive force external to him.[82]

---

highly improved county ... but ... recent inquiry has discovered that even there, in districts once famous for fine men and gallant soldiers, the inhabitants have degenerated into a meagre and stunted race. In the healthiest situations, on hill sides fronting the sea, the faces of their famished children are as pale as they could be in the foul atmosphere of a London alley' (W. T. Thornton, *Over-Population and Its Remedy*, op. cit., pp. 74, 75). They resemble in fact the 30,000 'gallant Highlanders' whom Glasgow herds together with prostitutes and thieves in its wynds and closes.

81. 'But though the health of a population is so important a fact of the national capital, we are afraid it must be said that the class of employers of labour have not been the most forward to guard and cherish this treasure ... The consideration of the health of the operatives was forced upon the mill-owners' (*The Times*, 5 November 1861). 'The men of the West Riding became the clothiers of mankind ... the health of the workpeople was sacrificed, and the race in a few generations must have degenerated. But a reaction set in. Lord Shaftesbury's Bill limited the hours of children's labour, etc' (*Twenty-Second Annual Report of the Registrar-General*, 1861).

82. We therefore find, for example, that at the beginning of 1863 twenty-six firms owning extensive potteries in Staffordshire, including Josiah Wedgwood & Sons, presented a petition for 'some legislative enactment'. Competition with other capitalists, they said, did not allow them to limit the hours worked by children voluntarily, etc. 'Much as we deplore the evils before mentioned, it would not be possible to prevent them by any scheme

---

*'*Sollte jene Qual uns quälen, da sie unsre Lust vermehrt?*' (Goethe, 'An Suleika', from *West-östlicher Diwan*, Bk VII, 1815).

The establishment of a normal working day is the result of centuries of struggle between the capitalist and the worker. But the history of this struggle displays two opposite tendencies. Compare, for example, the English factory legislation of our time with the English Labour Statutes from the fourteenth century to well into the middle of the eighteenth.[83] While the modern Factory Acts compulsorily shorten the working day, the earlier statutes tried forcibly to lengthen it. Of course, the pretensions of capital in its embryonic state, in its state of becoming, when it cannot yet use the sheer force of economic relations to secure its right to absorb a sufficient quantity of surplus labour, but must be aided by the power of the state – its pretensions in this situation appear very modest in comparison with the concessions it has to make, complainingly and unwillingly, in its adult condition. Centuries are required before the 'free' worker, owing to the greater development of the capitalist mode of production, makes a voluntary agreement, i.e. is compelled by social conditions to sell the whole of his active life, his very capacity for labour, in return for the price of his customary means of subsistence, to sell his birthright for a mess of pottage. Hence it is natural that the longer working day which capital tried to impose on adult workers by acts of state power from the middle of the fourteenth to the end of the seventeenth century is approximately of the same length as the shorter working day which, in the second half of the nineteenth century, the state has here and there interposed as a barrier to the transformation of children's blood into capital. What has now been proclaimed, for instance in the State of Mas-

---

of agreement between the manufacturers ... Taking all these points into consideration, we have come to the conviction that some legislative enactment is wanted' (*Children's Employment Commission, First Report*, 1863, p. 322). The recent past [1873] offers a much more striking example. The high level of the price of cotton, during a period of feverish activity, induced the manufacturers of Blackburn to shorten the hours worked in their mills for a certain fixed period, by mutual consent. This period expired at around the end of November 1871. Meanwhile, the wealthier manufacturers, who combined spinning with weaving, used the fall in production following this agreement to extend their own business and thus make great profits at the expense of the small employers. Thereupon the latter, in their hour of need, turned to the – factory workers, urged them to mount a serious agitation for the 9-hour system, and promised them monetary contributions for the purpose!

83. These Labour Statutes (which had their counterparts in France, the Netherlands, and elsewhere at the same epoch) were first formally repealed in England in 1813, when they had long since been set aside by the relations of production.

sachusetts, until recently the freest state of the North American republic, as the statutory limit of the labour of children under 12, was in England, even in the middle of the seventeenth century, the normal working day of able-bodied artisans, robust ploughmen and gigantic blacksmiths.[84]

The first 'Statute of Labourers' (23 Edward III, 1349) found its immediate pretext (not its cause, for legislation of this kind outlives its pretext by centuries) in the great plague that decimated the population, so that, as a Tory writer says, 'The difficulty of getting men to work on reasonable terms' (i.e. at a price that left their employers a reasonable quantity of surplus labour) 'grew to such a height as to be quite intolerable.'[85] Reasonable wages were therefore fixed by law as well as the limits of the working day. The latter point, the only one that interests us here, is repeated in the Statute of 1496 (Henry VII). The working day for all craftsmen ('artificers') and field labourers from March to September was supposed to last from 5 in the morning to between 7 and 8 in the evening, although this was never enforced. The meal-times, however, consisted of 1 hour for breakfast, 1½ hours for dinner, and half an hour for 'noonmeate', i.e. exactly twice as much as under the Factory Acts now in force.[86] In winter, work was to last from 5 in the morning until

84. 'No child under 12 years of age shall be employed in any manufacturing establishment more than 10 hours in one day' (*General Statutes of Massachusetts*, 63, Ch. 12. These statutes were passed between 1836 and 1858.) 'Labour performed during a period of 10 hours in any day in all cotton, woollen, silk, paper, glass, and flax factories, or in manufactories of iron and brass, shall be considered a legal day's labour. And be it enacted, that hereafter no minor engaged in any factory shall be holden or required to work more than 10 hours in any day, or 60 hours in any week; and that hereafter no minor shall be admitted as a worker under the age of 10 years in any factory within this State' (*State of New Jersey. An Act to Limit the Hours of Labour, etc.*, paras. 1 and 2. Law of 18 March 1851). 'No minor who has attained the age of 12 years, and is under the age of 15 years, shall be employed in any manufacturing establishment more than 11 hours in any one day, nor before 5 o'clock in the morning, nor after 7.30 in the evening' (*Revised Statutes of the State of Rhode Island, etc.*, Ch. 139, para. 23, 1 July 1857).

85. [J. B. Byles], *Sophisms of Free Trade*, 7th edn, London, 1850, p. 205, 9th edn, p. 253. This same Tory, moreover, admits that 'Acts of Parliament regulating wages, but against the labourer and in favour of the master, lasted for the long period of 464 years. Population grew. These laws were then found, and really became, unnecessary and burdensome' (op. cit., p. 206).

86. On this statute, J. Wade remarks correctly: 'From the statement above' (i.e. with regard to the Statute of 1496) 'it appears that in 1496 the diet was considered equivalent to one-third of the income of an artificer and

dark, with the same intervals. A statute of Elizabeth of 1562 leaves the length of the working day for all labourers 'hired for daily or weekly wages' untouched, but seeks to limit the intervals to 2½ hours in the summer and 2 in the winter. Dinner is to last only 1 hour, and the 'afternoon-sleep of half an hour' is only allowed between the middle of May and the middle of August. For every hour of absence 1d. is to be subtracted from the wage. In practice, however, the conditions were much more favourable to the labourers than in the statute-book. William Petty, the father of political economy, and to some extent the founder of statistics, says in a work he published in the last third of the seventeenth century: 'Labouring men' (the meaning then was 'agricultural labourers') 'work ten hours *per diem*, and make twenty meals per week, viz., three a day for working days, and two on Sundays; whereby it is plain, that if they could fast on Friday nights, and dine in one hour and an half, whereas they take two, from eleven to one; thereby thus working $\frac{1}{20}$ more, and spending $\frac{1}{20}$ less, the above-mentioned tax might be raised.'[87] Was Dr Andrew Ure not right when he deplored the Twelve Hours' Bill of 1833 as a retrogression to the age of darkness? It is true that the regulations contained in the statutes and mentioned by Petty apply also to apprentices. But the situation with respect to child labour, even at the end of the seventeenth century, is shown by the following complaint: 'Our youth, here in England, do absolutely nothing before they come to be apprentices, and then they naturally require a long time – seven years – to be formed into complete craftsmen.'* Germany, on the other hand, is praised, because the children there are educated from their cradle at least to 'something of employment'.[88]

---

one-half the income of a labourer, which indicates a greater degree of inde‐ pendence among the working-classes than prevails at present; for the board, both of labourers and artificers, would now be reckoned at a much higher proportion of their wages' (J. Wade, *History of the Middle and Working Classes*, pp. 24–5, 577). The opinion that this difference is due to the difference between the relative prices of food and clothing then and now is refuted by the most superficial glance at Bishop Fleetwood's *Chronicon Preciosum* (1st edn, London, 1707; 2nd edn, London, 1745).

87. W. Petty, *Political Anatomy of Ireland*, 1672, edition of 1691, p. 10. [This page reference is actually to the supplement, *Verbum Sapienti*.]

88. *A Discourse on the Necessity of Encouraging Mechanick Industry*, London, 1690, p. 13. Macaulay, who has falsified English history in the

---

*This is not strictly a quotation, but a compressed version of the text indicated in n. 88.

Still, during the greater part of the eighteenth century, up to the epoch of large-scale industry, capital in England had not succeeded in gaining control of the worker's whole week by paying the weekly value of his labour-power. (The agricultural labourers, however, formed an exception.) The fact that they could live for a whole week on the wage of four days did not appear to the workers to be a sufficient reason for working for the capitalist for the other two days. One party of English economists, in the service of capital, denounced this obstinacy in the most violent manner, another party defended the workers. Let us listen for example to the polemic between Postlethwayt,* whose Dictionary of Trade then enjoyed the same reputation as similar works by MacCulloch and Mac-

interest of the Whigs and the bourgeoisie, declaims as follows: 'The practice of setting children prematurely to work ... prevailed in the seventeenth century to an extent which, when compared with the extent of the manufacturing system, seems almost incredible. At Norwich, the chief seat of the clothing trade, a little creature of six years old was thought fit for labour. Several writers of that time, and among them some who were considered as eminently benevolent, mention with exultation the fact that in that single city, boys and girls of very tender age create wealth exceeding what was necessary for their own subsistence by twelve thousand pounds a year. The more carefully we examine the history of the past, the more reason shall we find to dissent from those who imagine that our age has been fruitful of new social evils ... That which is new is the intelligence and the humanity which remedies them' (*History of England*, Vol. 1, p. 417). Macaulay might have reported further that 'extremely well-disposed' friends of commerce in the seventeenth century recount with 'exultation' how in a workhouse in Holland a child of four was employed, and that this example of 'applied virtue' is accepted as adequate evidence in all the writings of humanitarians *à la* Macaulay, up to the time of Adam Smith. It is true that with the rise of manufacture [*Manufaktur*] as opposed to handicrafts [*Handwerk*],* traces of the exploitation of children begin to appear. This exploitation always existed to a certain extent among the peasants, and was the more developed, the heavier the yoke pressing on the countryman. The tendency of capital is unmistakable; but the facts themselves are as isolated as the phenomenon of a two-headed baby. Hence they were noted with 'exultation' as especially peculiar and remarkable, and recommended as models for their own time and for posterity by the far-seeing 'friends of commerce'. This same Scottish sycophant and fine talker, Macaulay, says: 'We hear today only of retrogression and see only progress.' What eyes, and above all, what ears!

*Marx distinguishes between three forms of industrial organization. In chronological order, these are *Handwerk* (handicrafts), *Manufaktur* (manufacture) and large-scale industry (*die grosse Industrie*).

*Malachy Postlethwayt (1707–67), English economist.

Gregor do today, and the author of the *Essay on Trade and Commerce* cited earlier.[89]

Postlethwayt says among other things: 'We cannot put an end to these few observations, without noticing that trite remark in the mouth of too many; that if the industrious poor can obtain enough to maintain themselves in five days, they will not work the whole six. Whence they infer the necessity of even the necessaries of life being made dear by taxes, or any other means, to compel the working artisan and manufacturer to labour the whole six days in the week, without ceasing. I must beg leave to differ in sentiment from those great politicians, who contend for the perpetual slavery of the working people of this kingdom; they forget the vulgar adage, all work and no play. Have not the English boasted of the ingenuity and dexterity of her working artists and manufacturers which have heretofore given credit and reputation to British wares in general? What has this been owing to? To nothing more probably than the relaxation of the working people in their own way. Were they obliged to toil the year round, the whole six days in the week, in a repetition of the same work, might it not blunt their ingenuity, and render them stupid instead of alert and dexterous; and might not our workmen lose their reputation instead of maintaining it by such eternal slavery? . . . And what sort of workmanship could we expect from such hard-driven animals? . . . Many of them will execute as much work in four days as a Frenchman will in five or six. But if Englishmen are to be eternal drudges, 'tis to be feared they will degenerate below the Frenchmen. As our people are famed for

89. The most ferocious of the accusers of the workers is the anonymous author of *An Essay on Trade and Commerce, Containing Observations on Taxes, etc.*, London, 1770, quoted above. He had already touched on the matter in his earlier work, *Considerations on Taxes*, London, 1765. That unspeakable statistical prattler Arthur Young, the Polonius of political economy, is on the same side of the fence.* The foremost of the defenders of the workers are: Jacob Vanderlint, in *Money Answers All Things*, London, 1734; the Rev. Nathaniel Forster, D.D., in *An Enquiry into the Causes of the Present High Price of Provisions*, London, 1767; Dr Price; and in particular Postlethwayt himself, both in a supplement to his *Universal Dictionary of Trade and Commerce* and in his *Great Britain's Commercial Interest Explained and Improved*, 2nd edn, London, 1759. The facts themselves are confirmed by many other writers of the time, including, among others, Josiah Tucker.†
*In his *Political Arithmetic*, London, 1774.
†Josiah Tucker (1712–99), Dean of Gloucester, was a forerunner of Adam Smith in political economy and wrote in favour of American independence and of free-trade.

bravery in war, do we not say that it is owing to good English roast beef and pudding in their bellies, as well as their constitutional spirit of liberty? And why may not the superior ingenuity and dexterity of our artists and manufacturers be owing to that freedom and liberty to direct themselves in their own way, and I hope we shall never have them deprived of such privileges and that good living from whence their ingenuity no less than their courage may proceed.'[90] To this the author of the *Essay on Trade and Commerce* replies: 'If the making of every seventh day an holiday is supposed to be of divine institution, as it implies the appropriating the other six days to labour' (he means capital, as we shall soon see) 'surely it will not be thought cruel to enforce it ... That mankind in general, are naturally inclined to ease and indolence, we fatally experience to be true, from the conduct of our manufacturing populace, who do not labour, upon an average, above four days in a week, unless provisions happen to be very dear ... Put all the necessaries of the poor under one denomination; for instance, call them all wheat, or suppose that... the bushel of wheat shall cost five shillings and that he' (the worker) 'earns a shilling a day by his labour, he then would be obliged to work five days only in a week. If the bushel of wheat should cost but four shillings, he would be obliged to work but four days; but as wages in this kingdom are much higher in proportion to the price of necessaries... the manufacturer' [i.e. the manufacturing worker], 'who labours four days, has a surplus of money to live idle with the rest of the week ... I hope I have said enough to make it appear that the moderate labour of six days in a week is no slavery. Our labouring people' [i.e. the agricultural labourers] 'do this, and to all appearance are the happiest of all our labouring poor,[91] but the Dutch do this in manufactures, and appear to be a very happy people. The French do so, when holidays do not intervene.[92] But our populace have adopted a notion, that as Englishmen they enjoy a birthright privilege of being more free and independent than in any country in Europe. Now this idea, as far as it may affect the bravery of our troops, may be of some use; but the less the manufacturing poor have of it, certainly the better for them-

90. Postlethwayt, op. cit., 'First Preliminary Discourse', p. 14.

91. *An Essay, etc.* On p. 96 he himself tells us what the 'happiness' of the English agricultural labourer in 1770 actually consisted in. 'Their powers are always upon the stretch, they cannot live cheaper than they do, nor work harder.'

92. Protestantism, by changing almost all the traditional holidays into working days, played an important part in the genesis of capital.

selves and for the State. The labouring people should never think
themselves independent of their superiors ... It is extremely
dangerous to encourage mobs in a commercial state like ours,
where, perhaps, seven parts out of eight of the whole, are people
with little or no property. The cure will not be perfect, till our
manufacturing poor are contented to labour six days for the same
sum which they now earn in four days.'[93] To this end, and for 'ex-
tirpating idleness, debauchery and excess', promoting a spirit of
industry, 'lowering the price of labour in our manufactories, and
easing the lands of the heavy burden of poor's rates', our 'faithful
Eckart' of capital proposes the well-tried method of locking up
workers who become dependent on public support (in one word,
paupers) in 'an ideal workhouse'. Such an ideal workhouse must
be made a 'House of Terror', and not an asylum for the poor
'where they are to be plentifully fed, warmly and decently clothed,
and where they do but little work'.[94] In this 'House of Terror', this
'ideal workhouse, the poor shall work 14 hours in a day, allowing
proper time for meals, in such manner that there shall remain 12
hours of neat labour.'[95]

Twelve working hours a day in the 'Ideal Workhouse', the 'House
of Terror' of 1770! 63 years later, in 1833, when the English Parliament reduced the working day for children of 13 to 18 years to 12
full hours, in four branches of industry, the Day of Judgement
seemed to have dawned for English industry! In 1852, when Louis
Bonaparte sought to secure his position with the bourgeoisie by
tampering with the legal working day, the people of France cried
out with one voice 'the law that limits the working day to 12 hours
is the one good that has remained to us of the legislation of the
Republic'.[96] At Zurich the work of children over 10 is limited to

93. *An Essay, etc.*, pp. 15, 41, 96, 97, 55, 57, 69. Jacob Vanderlint declared
as early as 1734 that the secret of the capitalists' complaints about the laziness
of the working people was simply this, that they claimed six days' labour instead of four for the same wages.
94. ibid., pp. 242–3.
95. ibid., p. 260. 'The French,' he says, 'laugh at our enthusiastic ideas of
liberty' (ibid., p. 78).
96. 'They especially objected to work beyond the 12 hours per day, because
the law which fixed those hours, is the only good which remains to them of the
legislation of the Republic' (*Reports of the Inspectors of Factories ... 31
October 1855*, p. 80). The French Twelve Hours' Bill of 5 September 1850, a
bourgeois edition of the Provisional Government's decree of 2 March 1848,
holds in all workshops without exception. Before this law, the working day in
France was without a definite limit. It lasted 14, 15 or more hours in the

12 hours; in Aargau in 1862, the work of children between 13 and 16 was reduced from 12½ to 12 hours; in Austria in 1860, for children between 14 and 16, the same reduction was made.[97] 'What progress since 1770,' Macaulay might shout 'with exultation'.

The 'House of Terror' for paupers, only dreamed of by the capitalist mind in 1770, was brought into being a few years later in the shape of a gigantic 'workhouse' for the industrial worker himself. It was called the factory. And this time the ideal was a pale shadow compared with the reality.

6. THE STRUGGLE FOR A NORMAL WORKING DAY. LAWS FOR THE COMPULSORY LIMITATION OF WORKING HOURS. THE ENGLISH FACTORY LEGISLATION OF 1833–64

After capital had taken centuries to extend the working day to its normal maximum limit, and then beyond this to the limit of the natural day of 12 hours,[98] there followed, with the birth of large-

factories. See *Des classes ouvrières en France, pendant l'année 1848*, by Monsieur Blanqui. M. Blanqui, the economist, not the revolutionary, had been given the task of inquiring into the condition of the working class by the government.

97. Belgium has proved itself to be the model bourgeois state in regard to the regulation of the working day. Lord Howard de Walden, English Plenipotentiary at Brussels,* reported to the Foreign Office on 12 May 1862: 'M. Rogier, the minister, informed me that children's labour is limited neither by a general law nor by any local regulations; that the Government, during the last three years, intended in every session to propose a bill on the subject, but always found an insuperable obstacle in the jealous opposition which was made to any legislation in contradiction with the principle of complete freedom of labour.'

98. 'It is certainly much to be regretted that any class of persons should toil 12 hours a day, which, including the time for their meals and for going to and returning from their work, amounts, in fact, to 14 of the 24 hours ... Without entering into the question of health, no one will hesitate, I think, to admit that, *in a moral point of view*, so entire an absorption of the time of the working classes, without intermission, from the early age of 13, and in trades not subject to restriction, much younger, must be extremely prejudicial, and is an evil greatly to be deplored ... For the sake, therefore, of public morals, of bringing up an orderly population, and of giving the great body of the people a reasonable enjoyment of life, it is much to be desired that in all trades some portion of every working day should be reserved for rest and leisure' (Leonard Horner, in *Reports of the Inspectors of Factories ... 31 December 1841*).

*Charles Augustus Ellis, Lord Howard de Walden and Seaford (1799–1868), diplomat. Minister Plenipotentiary at Brussels from 1846 to 1868.

scale industry in the last third of the eighteenth century, an ava-
lanche of violent and unmeasured encroachments. Every boundary
set by morality and nature, age and sex, day and night, was broken
down. Even the ideas of day and night, which in the old statutes
were of peasant simplicity, became so confused that an English
judge, as late as 1860, needed the penetration of an interpreter of
the Talmud to explain 'judicially' what was day and what was
night.[99] Capital was celebrating its orgies.

As soon as the working class, stunned at first by the noise and
turmoil of the new system of production, had recovered its senses
to some extent, it began to offer resistance, first of all in England,
the native land of large-scale industry. For three decades, however,
the concessions wrung from industry by the working class remained purely nominal. Parliament passed five Labour Laws
between 1802 and 1833, but was shrewd enough not to vote a
penny for their compulsory implementation, for the necessary
official personnel, etc.[1] They remained a dead letter. 'The fact is,
that prior to the Act of 1833, young persons and children were
worked all night, all day, or both *ad libitum*.'[2]

A normal working day for modern industry dates only from the
Factory Act of 1833, which included cotton, wool, flax and silk
factories. Nothing characterizes the spirit of capital better than the
history of English factory legislation from 1833 to 1864.

The Act of 1833 lays down that the ordinary factory working day
should begin at 5.30 in the morning and end at 8.30 in the evening,
and within these limits, a period of 15 hours, it is lawful to employ
young persons (i.e. persons between 13 and 18 years of age), at any
time of the day, provided that no one individual young person works

99. See *Judgment of Mr J. H. Otway, Belfast. Hilary Sessions, County
Antrim, 1860*.
1. It is very characteristic of the regime of Louis Philippe, the bourgeois king,
that the one Factory Act passed during his reign, that of 22 March 1841,
was never put into force. And this law only dealt with child-labour. It fixed
8 hours a day for children between 8 and 12, 12 hours for children between 12
and 16, etc., with many exceptions which allow night-work even for children
of 8 years. The supervision and enforcement of this law, in a country
where even the mice are administered by the police, is left to the goodwill of
the 'friends of commerce'. Only since 1853, and in one single department –
the Nord – has a paid government inspector been appointed. Not less characteristic of the development of French society in general is the fact that
until the Revolution of 1848 Louis Philippe's law stood alone amid the all-
embracing network of French legislation.
2. *Reports of the Inspectors of Factories . . . 30 April 1860*, p. 50.

more than 12 hours in any one day, except in certain cases especially provided for. The sixth chapter of the Act provided: 'That there shall be allowed in the course of every day not less than one and a half hours for meals to every such person restricted as hereinbefore provided.' The employment of children under 9, with exceptions mentioned later, was forbidden; the work of children between 9 and 13 was limited to 8 hours a day; night-work, i.e., according to this Act, work between 8.30 p.m. and 5.30 a.m., was forbidden for all persons between 9 and 18.

The law-makers were so far from wishing to interfere with the freedom of capital to exploit adult labour-power, or, as they called it, 'the freedom of labour', that they created a special system in order to prevent the Factory Acts from having such a frightful consequence.

'The great evil of the factory system as at present conducted,' says the first report of the Central Board of the Commission, on 28 June 1833, 'has appeared to us to be that it entails the necessity of continuing the labour of children to the utmost length of that of the adults. The only remedy for this evil, short of the limitation of the labour of adults, which would, in our opinion, create an evil greater than that which is sought to be remedied, appears to be the plan of working double sets of children.'* Under the name of the 'system of relays' ('relay' means, in English as also in French, the changing of the post-horses at each different halting-place), this 'plan' was therefore carried out, so that, for example, one set of children of between 9 and 13 years were put into harness from 5.30 a.m. until 1.30 p.m., another set from 1.30 p.m. until 8.30 p.m., and so on.

In order to reward the manufacturers for having, in the most impudent way, ignored all the Acts relating to child labour passed during the previous twenty-two years, the pill was yet further gilded for them. Parliament decreed that after 1 March 1834 no child under 11, after 1 March 1835 no child under 12, and after 1 March 1836 no child under 13 was to work more than 8 hours in a factory. This 'liberalism', so full of consideration for 'capital', was the more noteworthy in that Dr Farre, Sir A. Carlisle, Sir B. Brodie, Sir C. Bell, Mr Guthrie etc., in a word, the most distinguished physicians and surgeons in London, had declared in their evidence

* *Factories Inquiry Commission. First Report of the Central Board of His Majesty's Commissioners.* Ordered by the House of Commons to be printed, 28 June 1833, p. 53.

before the House of Commons that there was danger in delay. Dr Farre was still blunter: 'Legislation is necessary for the prevention of death, in any form in which it can be prematurely inflicted, and certainly this' (the factory method) 'must be viewed as a most cruel mode of inflicting it.'*

The same 'reformed' Parliament which in its delicate consideration for the manufacturers condemned children under 13, for years to come, to the hell of 72 hours of factory labour every week, this same Parliament, in the Emancipation Act (which also administered freedom drop by drop), forbade the planters, from the very beginning, to work any Negro slave for more than 45 hours a week.

But capital was by no means soothed; it now began a noisy and long-lasting agitation. This turned on the age-limit of the category of human beings who, under the name 'children', were restricted to 8 hours of work and were subject to a certain amount of compulsory education. According to the anthropology of the capitalists, the age of childhood ended at 10, or, at the outside, 11. The nearer the deadline approached for the full implementation of the Factory Act, the fatal year 1836, the wilder became the rage of the mob of manufacturers. They managed in fact to intimidate the government to such an extent that in 1835 it proposed to lower the limit of the age of childhood from 13 to 12. But now the 'pressure from without' became more threatening. The House of Commons lost its nerve. It refused to throw children of 13 under the Juggernaut wheels of capital for more than 8 hours a day, and the Act of 1833 came into full operation. It remained unaltered till June 1844.

During the decade in which it regulated factory work, at first in part, and then entirely, the official reports of the factory inspectors teem with complaints about the impossibility of enforcing it. The point of time within the 15 hours from 5.30 a.m. to 8.30 p.m. at which each 'young person' and each 'child' was to begin, break off, resume, or end his 12 or 8 hours of labour was left by the Act of 1833 to the free decision of the lords of capital; similarly, the Act also permitted them to assign different meal-times to different persons. Thanks to this provision, the capitalists soon discovered a new 'system of relays', by which the work-horses were not changed at fixed stations, but were always re-harnessed at different stations.

* *Report from the Committee on the Bill to Regulate the Labour of Children in the Mills and Factories of the United Kingdom: with the Minutes of Evidence.* Ordered by the House of Commons to be printed, 8 August 1832. Evidence of Dr J. R. Farre, pp. 598–602.

We shall not pause here to reflect on the beauty of this system, as we shall have to return to it later. But this much is clear at first glance: it annulled the whole Factory Act, not only in the spirit, but in the letter. How could the factory inspectors, with this complex bookkeeping in respect of each individual child or young person, enforce the legally determined hours of work, and compel the employers to grant the legal meal-times? In many of the factories, the old and scandalous brutalities soon blossomed again unpunished. In an interview with the Home Secretary (1844), the factory inspectors demonstrated the impossibility of any control under the newly invented relay system.[3] In the meantime, however, circumstances had greatly changed. The factory workers, especially since 1838, had made the Ten Hours' Bill their economic, as they had made the Charter* their political, election cry. Some of the manufacturers, even, who had run their factories in conformity with the Act of 1833, overwhelmed Parliament with representations on the immoral 'competition' of their 'false brethren', who were able to break the law because of their greater impudence or their more fortunate local circumstances. Moreover, however much the individual manufacturer might like to give free rein to his old lust for gain, the spokesmen and political leaders of the manufacturing class ordered a change in attitude and in language towards the workers. They had started their campaign to repeal the Corn Laws, and they needed the workers to help them to victory! They promised, therefore, not only that the loaf of bread would be twice its size, but also that the Ten Hours' Bill would be enacted in the free trade millennium.[4] Thus they were even less inclined, and less able, to oppose a measure intended only to make the law of 1833 a reality. And finally, the Tories, threatened in their most sacred interest, the rent of land, thundered with philanthropic indignation against the 'nefarious practices'[5] of their foes.

This was the origin of the additional Factory Act of 7 June 1844,

3. *Reports of the Inspectors of Factories . . . 31 October 1849*, p. 6.
4. *Reports of the Inspectors of Factories . . . 31 October 1848*, p. 98.
5. Let us note in passing that Leonard Horner makes use of this expression in his official reports. (*Reports of the Inspectors of Factories . . . 31 October 1859*, p. 7.)

---

* Better known as the 'People's Charter', the manifesto issued in May 1838 by a number of groups, including the London Working Men's Association, which called for universal male suffrage and various related electoral reforms. Hence 'Chartism'.

which came into effect on 10 September 1844. It placed under protection a new category of workers, namely women over 18. They were placed in every respect on the same footing as young persons, their working hours limited to 12, and night-work forbidden to them. For the first time it was found necessary for the labour of adults to be controlled directly and officially by legislation. The Factory Report of 1844–5 states ironically: 'No instances have come to my knowledge of adult women having expressed any regret at their rights being thus far interfered with.'[6] The working hours of children under 13 were reduced to 6½, and in certain circumstances to 7.[7]

To get rid of the abuses of the spurious 'system of relays', the law established among other things the following important regulations: 'The hours of work of children and young persons shall be reckoned from the time when any child or young person shall begin to work in the morning.' So that if A, for example, begins work at 8 in the morning, and B at 10, B's working day must nevertheless end at the same hour as A's. 'The time shall be regulated by a public clock,' for example the nearest railway clock, by which the factory clock is to be set. The manufacturer has to hang up a 'legible' printed notice stating the hours for the beginning and ending of work and the pauses allowed for meals. Children beginning work before 12 noon may not be again employed after 1 p.m. The afternoon shift must therefore consist of other children than those employed in the morning. Of the hour and a half for meal-times, 'one hour thereof at the least shall be given before three of the clock in the afternoon . . . and at the same period of the day. No child or young person shall be employed more than five hours before 1 p.m. without an interval for meal-time of at least 30 minutes. No child or young person (or female) shall be employed or allowed to remain in any room in which any manufacturing process is then' (i.e. at meal-times) 'carried on.'

It has been seen that these highly detailed specifications, which regulate, with military uniformity, the times, the limits and the pauses of work by the stroke of the clock, were by no means a product of the fantasy of Members of Parliament. They developed gradually out of circumstances as natural laws of the modern mode

6. *Reports of the Inspectors of Factories . . . 30 September 1844*, p. 15.
7. The Act allows children to be employed for 10 hours if they do not work day after day, but only on alternate days. In the main, this clause remained inoperative.

of production. Their formulation, official recognition and proclamation by the state were the result of a long class struggle. One of
their first consequences was that in practice the working day of
adult males in factories became subject to the same limitations,
since in most processes of production the co-operation of children,
young persons and women is indispensable. On the whole, therefore,
during the period from 1844 to 1847, the 12 hours' working day
became universal and uniform in all branches of industry under the
Factory Act.

The manufacturers, however, did not allow this 'progress' without a compensating 'retrogression'. At their instigation the House
of Commons reduced the minimum age for exploitable children
from 9 to 8, in order to ensure that 'additional supply of factory
children'[8] which is owed to the capitalists, according to divine and
human law.

The years 1846 to 1847 are epoch-making in the economic history
of England. The Corn Laws were repealed; the duties on cotton and
other raw materials were removed; free trade was proclaimed as the
guiding star of legislation; in short, the millennium had arrived.
On the other hand, in the same years the Chartist movement and the
ten hours' agitation reached their highest point. They found allies
in the Tories, who were panting for revenge. Despite the fanatical
opposition of the army of perjured Freetraders, headed by Bright
and Cobden, the Ten Hours' Bill, so long struggled for, made its
way through Parliament.

The new Factory Act of 8 June 1847 enacted that on 1 July 1847
there should be a preliminary reduction of the working day for
'young persons' (from 13 to 18) and all females to 11 hours, but that
on 1 May 1848 there should be a definite limitation of the working
day to 10 hours. For the rest, the Act was only an emendatory supplement to the Acts of 1833 and 1844.

Capital now undertook a preliminary campaign to prevent the
Act from coming into full force on 1 May 1848. And the workers
themselves, under the pretence that they had been taught by experience, were to help in the destruction of their own work. The
moment was cleverly chosen. 'It must be remembered, too, that there
has been more than two years of great suffering (in consequence of

8. 'As a reduction in their hours of work would cause a larger number'
(of children) 'to be employed, it was thought that the additional supply of
children from 8 to 9 years of age would meet the increased demand' (ibid.,
p. 13).

the terrible crisis of 1846–7) among the factory operatives, from many mills having worked short time, and many being altogether closed. A considerable number of the operatives must therefore be in very narrow circumstances; many, it is to be feared, in debt; so that it might fairly have been presumed that at the present time they would prefer working the longer time, in order to make up for past losses, perhaps to pay off debts, or get their furniture out of pawn, or replace that sold, or to get a new supply of clothes for themselves and their families.'[9]

The manufacturers tried to aggravate the natural impact of these circumstances by a general 10 per cent reduction in wages. This was done in order, as it were, to celebrate the inauguration of the new free-trade era. Then followed a further reduction of 8⅓ per cent as soon as the working day was shortened to 11 hours, and a reduction of twice that amount as soon as it was finally shortened to 10. Therefore, wherever circumstances permitted, a reduction in wages of at least 25 per cent took place.[10] Under these favourably prepared conditions the agitation among the factory workers for the repeal of the Act of 1847 was begun. No method of deceit, seduction or intimidation was left unused; but all in vain. In relation to the half-dozen petitions in which the workers were made to complain of 'their oppression by the Act', the petitioners themselves declared under oral examination that their signatures had been extorted. They felt themselves oppressed, but by something different from the Factory Act.[11] But if the manufacturers did not succeed in getting the workers to speak as they wished, they themselves shrieked all the louder in the press and in Parliament in the name of the workers. They denounced the factory inspector as a species of revolutionary commissioner reminiscent of the Convention,* who would ruthlessly sacrifice the unfortunate factory workers to his

9. *Reports of the Inspectors of Factories . . . 31 October 1848*, p. 16.

10. 'I found that men who had been getting 10s. a week, had had 1s. taken off for a reduction in the rate of 10 per cent, and 1s. 6d. off the remaining 9s. for the reduction in time, together 2s. 6d., and notwithstanding this, many of them said they would rather work 10 hours' (ibid.).

11. '"Though I signed it" (the petition) "I said at the time I was putting my hand to a wrong thing." "Then why did you put your hand to it?" "Because I should have been turned off if I had refused." Whence it would appear that this petitioner felt himself "oppressed", but not exactly by the Factory Act' (ibid., p. 102).

_____

*The French revolutionary assembly of 1792 to 1795, which presided over the Terror.

mania for improving the world. This manoeuvre also failed. Leonard Horner, himself a factory inspector, conducted many examinations of witnesses in the factories of Lancashire, both personally and through sub-inspectors. About 70 per cent of the workers examined declared in favour of 10 hours, a much smaller percentage in favour of 11, and an altogether insignificant minority for the old 12 hours.[12]

Another 'friendly' dodge was to make the adult males work 12 to 15 hours, and then to declare that this fact was a fine demonstration of what the proletariat really wanted. But the 'ruthless' factory inspector Leonard Horner was again on the spot. The majority of the 'overtimers' declared: 'They would much prefer working 10 hours for less wages, but they had no choice; so many were out of employment (so many spinners getting very low wages by having to work as piecers, being unable to do better), that if they refused to work the longer time, others would immediately get their places, so that it was a question with them of agreeing to work the longer time, or of being thrown out of employment altogether.'[13]

The preliminary campaign of capital thus came to grief, and the Ten Hours' Act came into force on 1 May 1848. Meanwhile, however, the fiasco of the Chartist party, whose leaders had been imprisoned and whose organization dismembered, had shattered the self-confidence of the English working class. Soon after this the June insurrection in Paris and its bloody suppression united, in England as on the Continent, all fractions of the ruling classes, landowners and capitalists, stock-exchange sharks and small-time shopkeepers, Protectionists and Freetraders, government and opposition, priests and free-thinkers, young whores and old nuns, under the common slogan of the salvation of property, religion, the family and society. Everywhere the working class was outlawed, anathematized, placed under the '*loi des suspects*'.* The manu-

12. ibid., p. 17. In Mr Horner's district 10,270 adult male labourers were examined in 181 factories. Their evidence is to be found in the appendix to the Factory Reports for the half-year ending October 1848. These examinations provide material which is valuable in other connections as well.

13. ibid. See the statements collected by Leonard Horner himself, Nos. 69, 70, 71, 72, 92, 93, and those collected by Sub-Inspector A, Nos. 51, 52, 58, 59, 62, 70, of the Appendix. A manufacturer, too, told the plain unvarnished truth in one instance. See No. 14, after No. 265 (ibid.).

*The law against all those suspected of assisting the counter-revolution, passed on 17 September 1793 by the Convention. It formed the legal basis

facturers no longer needed to restrain themselves. They broke out in open revolt, not only against the Ten Hours' Act, but against all the legislation since 1833 that had aimed at restricting to some extent the 'free' exploitation of labour-power. It was a pro-slavery rebellion* in miniature, carried on for over two years with a cynical recklessness and a terroristic energy which were so much the easier to achieve in that the rebel capitalist risked nothing but the skin of his workers.

To understand what follows, we must remember that all three Factory Acts, those of 1833, 1844 and 1847, were in force, in so far as the one did not amend the others; that not one of these limited the working day of the male worker of over 18; and that since 1833 the 15 hours from 5.30 a.m. until 8.30 p.m. had remained the legal 'day', within the limits of which the 12 hours, and later the 10 hours, of labour by young persons and women had to be performed under the prescribed conditions.

The manufacturers began by here and there dismissing a number of the young persons and women they employed, in many cases half of them, and then, for the adult males, restoring night-work, which had almost disappeared. The Ten Hours' Act, they cried, leaves us no other alternative.[14]

The second step they took related to the legal pauses for meals. Let us listen to the factory inspectors. 'Since the restriction of the hours of work to ten, the factory occupiers maintain, although they have not yet practically gone the whole length, that supposing the hours of work to be from 9 a.m. to 7 p.m. they fulfil the provisions of the statutes by allowing an hour before 9 a.m. and half an hour after 7 p.m. (for meals). In some cases they now allow an hour, or half an hour for dinner, insisting at the same time, that they are not bound to allow any part of the hour and a half in the course of the factory working-day.'[15] Thus the manufacturers maintained that the scrupulously strict provisions of the Act of 1844 with regard to meal-times only gave the workers permission to eat and drink before coming into the factory, and after leaving it – i.e. at home! And why indeed should the workers not eat their dinner before 9 o'clock in

14. *Reports of the Inspectors of Factories . . . 31 October 1848*, pp. 133–4.
15. *Reports of the Inspectors of Factories . . . 30 April 1848*, p. 47.

for the Terror. As applied here, however, the expression refers to repressive laws passed in various countries after 1848.
*This is Marx's usual term for the American Civil War of 1861 to 1865.

the morning? The crown lawyers, however, decided that the prescribed meal-times 'must be in the interval during the working-hours, and that it will not be lawful to work for 10 hours continuously, from 9 a.m. to 7 p.m., without any interval'.[16]

After these pleasant demonstrations, capital commenced its real revolt by taking a step which agreed with the letter of the law of 1844, and was therefore legal.

The Act of 1844 certainly prohibited the employment after 1 p.m. of children aged from 8 to 13 who had been employed before noon. But it did not regulate in any way the 6½ hours' work of the children whose working day began at 12 midday or later. Children of 8 might, if they began work at noon, be employed from 12 till 1 (1 hour); from 2 till 4 in the afternoon (2 hours); and from 5 till 8.30 in the evening (3½ hours). Taken together, this made up a legal 6½ hours! But they could do even better. In order to make the children's work coincide with that of the adult male labourers up to 8.30 p.m., the manufacturers only had to give them no work till 2 in the afternoon; they could then keep them in the factory until 8.30 in the evening without intermission. 'And it is now expressly admitted that the practice exists in England from the desire of mill-owners to have their machinery at work for more than 10 hours a day, to keep the children at work with male adults after all the young persons and women have left, and until 8.30 p.m. if the factory-owners choose.'[17] Workers and factory inspectors protested on hygienic and moral grounds, but Capital answered:

> 'My deeds upon my head! I crave the law,
> The penalty and forfeit of my bond.'*

In fact, according to statistics laid before the House of Commons on 26 July 1850, 3,742 children were still being subjected to this 'practice' in 257 factories on 15 July 1850, despite all the protests.[18] But this was not enough. Lynx-eyed capital discovered that although the Act of 1844 did not allow 5 hours' work before midday without a pause of at least 30 minutes for refreshment, it prescribed nothing like this for afternoon work. Hence capital demanded and ob-

16. *Reports of the Inspectors of Factories* ... *31 October 1848*, p. 130.
17. ibid., p. 142.
18. *Reports of the Inspectors of Factories* ... *31 October 1850*, pp. 5–6.

---

*This quotation, and the one following, are from *The Merchant of Venice*, Act 4, Scene 1 (Shylock's speech).

tained the satisfaction not only of making children of 8 drudge without any interval from 2 to 8.30 p.m., but also of letting them go hungry.

> 'Ay, his breast,
> So says the bond.'[19]

This Shylock-like clinging to the letter of the law of 1844, in so far as it regulated child-labour, was, however, only a way of introducing an open revolt against the same law, in so far as it regulated the labour of 'young persons and women'. It will be remembered that the abolition of the 'false relay system' was the main aim of that law, and formed its main content. The manufacturers began their revolt simply by declaring that the sections of the Act of 1844 which prohibited the unrestricted use of young persons and women in such short fractions of the day of 15 hours as the employer chose had been 'comparatively harmless' as long as working hours were limited to 12 hours, but that under the Ten Hours' Act they were a 'grievous hardship'.[20] They informed the inspectors very coolly that they would set themselves above the letter of the law, and re-

19. The nature of capital remains the same in its developed as it is in its undeveloped forms. In the code of law which was imposed on the Territory of Mexico under the influence of the slave-owners, shortly before the outbreak of the American Civil War, it is asserted that the worker 'is his' (the capitalist's) 'money' since the capitalist has bought his labour-power. The same view was current among the Roman patricians. The money they advanced to the plebeian debtor became transformed, through his consumption of the means of subsistence, into his flesh and blood. This 'flesh and blood' was therefore 'their money'. Hence the law of the Ten Tables,* which is worthy of Shylock. Linguet's theory† that the patrician creditors from time to time prepared banquets of debtors' flesh on the other side of the Tiber remains as doubtful as Daumer's theory about the Lord's Supper.‡

20. *Reports of the Inspectors of Factories . . . 31 October 1848*, p. 133.

*The Law of the Twelve Tables (ten tables plus two supplementary ones) is the earliest Roman code of laws, drawn up in 450 B.C. Table III.6 states: 'On the third market day the creditors shall cut shares. If they have cut more or less than their shares it shall be without prejudice.' All the writers of classical antiquity who dealt with this passage interpreted it to mean an actual division of the debtor's body, not his property, and Marx follows them here (as did Hegel).

† Linguet stated his theory in the book *Théorie des lois civiles, ou principes fondamentaux de la société*, London, 1767, Vol. 2, Bk 5, Ch. 20.

‡ G. F. Daumer (1800–1875), writer on religious history, had a theory, put forward in *Die Geheimnisse des christlichen Altertums* (2 vols., Hamburg, 1847), that the early Christians consumed human flesh when they celebrated the Lord's Supper.

introduce the old system on their own account.[21] This would, they said, be in the interests of the ill-advised operatives themselves, 'as it would allow them to pay higher wages'. 'This was the only possible plan by which to maintain, under the Ten Hours' Act, the industrial supremacy of Great Britain.' 'Perhaps it may be a little difficult to detect irregularities under the relay system; but what of that? Is the great manufacturing interest of this country to be treated as a secondary matter in order to save some little trouble to Inspectors and Sub-Inspectors of Factories?'[22]

All these dodges were of course of no avail. The factory inspectors appealed to the courts. But the Home Secretary, Sir George Grey, was soon so overwhelmed by the clouds of dust arising from the manufacturers' petitions that in a circular of 5 August 1848 he recommended the inspectors not 'to lay informations against mill-owners for a breach of the letter of the Act, or for employment of young persons by relays in cases in which there is no reason to believe that such young persons have been actually employed for a longer period than that sanctioned by law'. At this, Factory Inspector J. Stuart allowed the so-called relay system for the 15-hour period of the factory day to be restored throughout Scotland, where it soon flourished again as of old. The English factory inspectors, on the other hand, declared that the Home Secretary had no dictatorial powers enabling him to suspend the laws, and continued their legal proceedings against the 'pro-slavery rebellion'.

But what was the point of summoning the manufacturers to appear before the courts when the courts, in this case the county magistrates,[23] acquitted them? In these tribunals the manufacturers sat in judgement on themselves. An example. A certain Eskrigge, a cotton-spinner, of the firm of Kershaw, Leese & Co., had laid before the factory inspector of his district the details of a relay system intended for his mill. Receiving a refusal, he at first kept quiet. A few months later, an individual named Robinson, also a cotton-spinner, and if not Eskrigge's Man Friday at

21. Thus, among others, the philanthropist Ashworth, in a letter to Leonard Horner which is repulsive in its Quaker manner. (*Reports of the Inspectors of Factories . . . 30 April 1849*, p. 4.)

22. *Reports of the Inspectors of Factories . . . 30 April 1849*, pp. 138, 140.

23. These 'county magistrates', the 'Great Unpaid' as William Cobbett described them, are unpaid judges chosen from the most eminent people in each county. They constitute in fact the patrimonial jurisdiction of the ruling classes.

least his relative, appeared before the borough magistrates of Stockport on a charge of introducing the very plan of relays Eskrigge had devised. The bench consisted of four Justices, three of them cotton-spinners, and was headed by this same inevitable Eskrigge. Eskrigge acquitted Robinson, and now decided that what was right for Robinson was fair for Eskrigge. Supported by his own legal decision, he at once introduced the new relay system into his own factory.[24] Of course, the composition of this tribunal was in itself a blatant violation of the law.[25] 'These judicial farces,' exclaims Inspector Howell, 'urgently call for a remedy – either that the law should be so altered as to be made to conform to these decisions, or that it should be administered by a less fallible tribunal, whose decisions would conform to the law . . . when these cases are brought forward. I long for a stipendiary magistrate.'[26]

The Crown lawyers declared that the manufacturers' interpretation of the Act of 1848 was absurd. But the saviours of society would not allow themselves to be turned from their purpose. Leonard Horner reports: 'Having endeavoured to enforce the Act . . . by ten prosecutions in seven magisterial divisions, and having been supported by the magistrates in one case only . . . I considered it useless to prosecute more for this evasion of the law. That part of the Act of 1848 which was framed for securing uniformity in the hours of work . . . is thus no longer in force in my district (Lancashire). Neither have the sub-inspectors or myself any means of satisfying ourselves, when we inspect a mill working by shifts, that the young persons and women are not working more than 10 hours a day . . . In a return of the 30 April . . . of mill-owners working by shifts, the number amounts to 114, and has been for some time rapidly increasing. In general, the time of working the mill is extended to $13\frac{1}{2}$ hours, from 6 a.m. to $7\frac{1}{2}$ p.m., . . . in some instances it amounts to 15 hours, from $5\frac{1}{2}$ a.m. to $8\frac{1}{2}$ p.m.'[27] Leonard Horner already possessed by December 1848 a list of 65 manufacturers and 29 factory overseers who

24. *Reports of the Inspectors of Factories . . . 30 April 1849*, pp. 21–2. Cf. similar examples in ibid., pp. 4, 5.

25. By Section 10 of I. and II. William IV, c. 24, known as Sir John Hobhouse's Factory Act, it was forbidden to any owner of a cotton-spinning or weaving mill, or the father, son or brother of such an owner, to act as Justice of the Peace in any inquiries concerning the Factory Act.

26. *Reports of the Inspectors of Factories . . . 30 April 1849*, p. 22.

27. *Reports of the Inspectors of Factories . . . 30 April 1849*, p. 5.

unanimously declared that no system of supervision could, under this relay system, prevent the most extensive amount of over-work.[28] Sometimes the same children and young persons were shifted from the spinning-room to the weaving-room, sometimes, in the course of 15 hours, they were shifted from one factory to another.[29] How was it possible to control a system which 'under the guise of relays, is some one of the many plans for shuffling "the hands" about in endless variety, and shifting the hours of work and of rest for different individuals throughout the day, so that you may never have one complete set of hands working together in the same room at the same time'?[30]

But even if we entirely leave aside actual over-work, this so-called relay system was an offspring of capital's imagination never surpassed even by Fourier in his humorous sketches of the '*courtes séances*',* except that the 'attraction of labour' is here transformed into the attraction of capital. Look, for example, at those schemes praised by the 'respectable press' as models of 'what a reasonable degree of care and method can accomplish'. The working personnel was sometimes divided into from twelve to fifteen categories, and these categories themselves constantly underwent changes in their composition. During the 15 hours of the factory day, capital dragged in the worker now for 30 minutes, now for an hour, and then pushed him out again, to drag him into the factory and thrust him out afresh, hounding him hither and thither, in scattered shreds of time, without ever letting go until the full 10 hours of work was done. As on the stage, the same persons had to appear in turn in the different scenes of the different acts. And just as an actor is committed to the stage throughout the whole course of the play, so the workers were committed to the factory for the whole 15 hours, without reckoning the time taken in coming and going. Thus the hours of rest were turned into hours of enforced idleness, which drove the young men to the taverns and the young girls to the brothels.

28. *Reports of the Inspectors of Factories . . . 31 October 1849*, p. 6.
29. *Reports of the Inspectors of Factories . . . 30 April 1849*, p. 21.
30. *Reports of the Inspectors of Factories . . . 31 October 1848*, p. 95.

---

*'Short sessions', the brief periods of labour Fourier envisaged for his ideal society. They corresponded to the eleventh human passion, the passion for variety, and without them labour would not be 'attractive'. Cf. *Le Nouveau Monde industriel et sociétaire*, 2nd edn, Paris, 1845, p. 67.

Every new trick the capitalist hit upon from day to day for keeping his machinery going for 12 or 15 hours without increasing the number of the personnel meant that the worker had to gulp down his meals in a different fragment of time. During the 10 hours' agitation, the manufacturers cried out that the mob of workers were petitioning in the hope of obtaining 12 hours' wages for 10 hours' work. Now they reversed the medal. They paid 10 hours' wages for 12 or 15 hours' disposition over the workers' labour-power.[31] This was the heart of the matter, this was the manufacturers' edition of the ten hours' law! These were the same unctuous Free traders, dripping with the milk of human kindness, who for ten whole years, during the agitation against the Corn Laws, had demonstrated to the workers, by making precise calculations in pounds, shillings and pence, that with corn freely imported 10 hours of labour would be quite sufficient, given the existing means of English industry, to enrich the capitalists.[32]

This revolt of capital was after two years finally crowned with victory by a decision handed down by one of the four highest courts in England, the Court of Exchequer, which, in a case brought before it on 8 February 1850, decided that the manufacturers were certainly acting against the sense of the Act of 1844, but that this Act itself contained certain words that rendered it meaningless. 'This verdict was tantamount to an abrogation of the Ten Hours' Bill.'[33] A great number of manufacturers, who

31. See *Reports of the Inspectors of Factories . . . 30 April 1849*, p. 6, and the detailed explanation of the 'shifting system' given by Factory Inspectors Howell and Saunders in the *Reports of the Inspectors of Factories . . . 31 October 1848*. See also the petition to the Queen from the clergy of Ashton* and vicinity, in the spring of 1849, against the 'shift system'.

32. Cf. for example R. H. Greg, *The Factory Question and the Ten Hours' Bill*, London, 1837.

33. F. Engels' 'Die englische Zehnstundenbill', in the *Neue Rheinische Zeitung. Politisch-ökonomische Revue*, edited by myself, p. 13 of the issue for April 1850 [English translation: Marx and Engels, *Articles on Britain*, London, 1971, p. 105] During the American Civil War the same 'High' Court of Justice discovered a verbal twist which exactly reversed the meaning of the law against the arming of pirate ships.†

*Ashton-under-Lyne, in Lancashire. A cotton town, and a main centre of the agitation which had led up to the Factory Act of 1847.

†This law was the Foreign Enlistment Act of 1819 (59 George III, c. 69). It forbade the fitting-out of vessels to engage in military operations against states with which Britain was not at war. In November 1863 the Court of Exchequer held that the British government had no justification under the Act for its seizure of the *Alexandra*, a ship intended for the Confederate States.

until then had been afraid to use the shift system for young persons and women, now seized on it enthusiastically.[34]

But this apparently decisive victory of capital was immediately followed by a counter-stroke. So far, the workers had offered a resistance which was passive, though inflexible and unceasing. They now protested in Lancashire and Yorkshire in threatening meetings. The so-called Ten Hours' Act, they said, was thus mere humbug, a parliamentary fraud. It had never existed! The factory inspectors urgently warned the government that class antagonisms had reached an unheard-of degree of tension. Some of the manufacturers themselves grumbled: 'On account of the contradictory decisions of the magistrates, a condition of things altogether abnormal and anarchical obtains. One law holds in Yorkshire, another in Lancashire; one law in one parish of Lancashire, another in its immediate neighbourhood. The manufacturer in large towns could evade the law, the manufacturer in country districts could not find the people necessary for the relay system, still less for the shifting of hands from one factory to another, etc.' And the most fundamental right under the law of capital is the equal exploitation of labour-power by all capitalists.

Under these circumstances, it came to a compromise between manufacturers and men, given the seal of parliamentary approval in the supplementary Factory Act of 5 August 1850. The working day for 'young persons and women' was lengthened from 10 to 10½ hours for the first five days of the week, and shortened to 7½ hours on Saturdays. The work had to take place between 6 a.m. and 6 p.m.,[35] with pauses of not less than 1½ hours for meal-times, these meal-times to be allowed at exactly the same time for all, and in accordance with the regulations laid down in 1844. By this the relay system was ended once and for all.[36] For child labour, the Act of 1844 remained in force.

One set of manufacturers secured to themselves special seigniorial rights over the children of the proletariat, just as they had done before. These were the silk manufacturers. In 1833 they had

34. *Reports of the Inspectors of Factories . . . 30 April 1850.*

35. In winter the period from 7 a.m. to 7 p.m. can be substituted for this.

36. 'The present law' (of 1850) 'was a compromise whereby the employed surrendered the benefit of the Ten Hours' Act for the advantage of one uniform period for the commencement and termination of the labour of those whose labour is restricted' (*Reports of the Inspectors of Factories . . . 30 April 1852,* p. 14).

howled threateningly that 'if the liberty of working children of any age for 10 hours a day were taken away, it would stop their works'.[37] It would be impossible for them to buy a sufficient number of children over 13. They extorted the privilege they desired. Subsequent investigation showed that the pretext was a deliberate lie. This did not, however, prevent them, throughout the following decade, from spinning silk for 10 hours a day out of the blood of little children who had to be put on stools to perform their work.[38] The Act of 1844 certainly 'robbed' the silk manufacturers of the 'liberty' of employing children under 11 for longer than 6½ hours each day. But as against this, it secured them the privilege of working children between 11 and 13 for 10 hours a day, and annulling in their case the education which had been made compulsory for all other factory children. This time the pretext was 'the delicate texture of the fabric in which they were employed, requiring a lightness of touch, only to be acquired by their early introduction to these factories'.[39] The children were quite simply slaughtered for the sake of their delicate fingers, just as horned cattle are slaughtered in southern Russia for their hides and their fat. Finally, in 1850, the privilege granted in 1844 was limited to the departments of silk-twisting and silk-winding. But here, in order to compensate capital for the loss of its 'liberty', the hours of labour for children aged from 11 to 13 were increased from 10 to 10½. Pretext: 'Labour in silk mills was lighter than in mills for other fabrics, and less likely in other respects also to be prejudicial to health.'[40] Official medical inquiries proved afterwards that, on the contrary, 'the average death-rate is exceedingly high in the silk districts, and amongst the female part of the population is higher even than it is in the cotton districts of Lancashire'.[41] Despite the protests of the factory inspectors,

37. *Reports of the Inspectors of Factories . . . 30 September 1844*, p. 13.
38. ibid.
39. *Reports of the Inspectors of Factories . . . 31 October 1846*, p. 20.
40. *Reports of the Inspectors of Factories . . . 31 October 1861*, p. 26.
41. ibid., p. 27. In general, the working population has greatly improved physically under the regime of the Factory Act. All medical testimony agrees on this point, and my own personal observation on various occasions has convinced me this is true. Nevertheless, and leaving aside the terrible death-rate of children in the first years of their life, the official reports of Dr Greenhow show the unfavourable health conditions of the manufacturing districts as compared with 'agricultural districts of normal health'. As evidence, take the following table from his 1861 report:

repeated every 6 months, this evil has lasted to the present day.[42] The Act of 1850 replaced the 15-hour period from 6 a.m. to 8.30 p.m. by a 12-hour period from 6 a.m. to 6 p.m., but only for 'young persons and women'. It did not therefore affect children, who could always be employed for half an hour before this period, and 2½ hours after it, provided the total duration of their labour did not exceed 6½ hours. While the bill was under discussion, the factory inspectors laid before Parliament statistics relating to the infamous abuses which had arisen from this anomaly. But in vain. In the background lurked the intention of using the children to force the working day of adult males up to 15 hours, in years of prosperity. The experience of the three years which followed demonstrated that such an attempt was bound to fail in face of

Percentage of adult males engaged in manufactures	Death-rate from pulmonary affections per 100,000 males	Name of District	Death-rate from pulmonary affections per 100,000 females	Percentage of adult females engaged in manufactures	Kind of female occupation
14·9	598	Wigan	644	18·0	Cotton
42·6	708	Blackburn	734	34·9	Ditto
37·3	547	Halifax	564	20·4	Worsted
41·9	611	Bradford	603	30·0	Ditto
31·0	691	Macclesfield	804	26·0	Silk
14·9	588	Leek	705	17·2	Ditto
36·6	721	Stoke-upon-Trent	665	19·3	Earthenware
30·4	726	Woolstanton	727	13·9	Ditto
	305	Eight healthy agricultural districts	340		

42. The reluctance with which the English 'Free traders' gave up the protective duty on silk manufacture is well known. The absence of protection for English factory children now serves in place of protection against French imports.

the resistance of the adult male workers.[43] The Act of 1850 was therefore finally completed in 1853 by the prohibition of the 'employment of children in the morning before and in the evening after young persons and women'. Henceforth, with few exceptions, the Factory Act of 1850 regulated the working day of all workers in the branches of industry subject to it.[44] By then, half a century had elapsed since the passing of the first Factory Act.[45]

Factory legislation went beyond its original sphere of application for the first time in the Printworks Act of 1845. The unwillingness with which capital accepted this new 'extravagance' speaks through every line of the Act. It limits the working day for children from 8 to 13, and for women, to 16 hours between 6 a.m. and 10 p.m. without any legal pause for meal-times. It allows males over 13 to be worked at will day and night.[46] It is a parliamentary abortion.[47]

Nevertheless, the principle had triumphed with its victory in those great branches of industry which form the most characteristic creation of the modern mode of production. Their wonderful development from 1853 to 1860, hand-in-hand with the physical and moral regeneration of the factory workers, was visible to the weakest eyes. The very manufacturers from whom the legal

43. *Reports of the Inspectors of Factories . . . 30 April 1853*, p. 30.

44. During the years 1859 and 1860, when the English cotton industry was at its zenith, the manufacturers tried to reconcile the adult male workers to an extension of the working day by using the bait of higher wages for overtime. The hand-mule spinners and self-actor minders put an end to the experiment by sending a petition to their employers, in which they said: 'Plainly speaking, our lives are to us a burthen; and, while we are confined to the mills nearly two days a week' (20 hours) 'more than the other operatives of the country, we feel like helots in the land, and that we are perpetuating a system injurious to ourselves and future generations . . . This, therefore, is to give you most respectful notice that when we commence work again after the Christmas and New Year holidays, we shall work 60 hours per week, and no more, or from six to six, with one hour and a half out' (*Reports of the Inspectors of Factories . . . 30 April 1860*, p. 30).

45. On the means provided by the wording of this Act for its own violation, see the Parliamentary Return *Factories Regulation Acts* (6 August 1859), and in it Leonard Horner's 'Suggestions for Amending the Factory Acts to Enable the Inspectors to Prevent Illegal Working, Now Become Very Prevalent'.

46. 'Children of the age of 8 years and upwards, have, indeed, been employed from 6 a.m. to 9 p.m. during the last half year in my district' (*Reports of the Inspectors of Factories . . . 31 October 1857*, p. 39).

47. 'The Printworks Act is admitted to be a failure, both with reference to its educational and protective provisions' (*Reports of the Inspectors of Factories . . . 31 October 1862*, p. 52).

limitation and regulation of the working day had been wrung step by step in the course of a civil war lasting half a century now pointed boastfully to the contrast with the areas of exploitation which were still 'free'.[48] The Pharisees of 'political economy' now proclaimed that their newly won insight into the necessity for a legally regulated working day was a characteristic achievement of their 'science'.[49] It will easily be understood that after the factory magnates had resigned themselves and submitted to the inevitable, capital's power of resistance gradually weakened, while at the same time the working class's power of attack grew with the number of its allies in those social layers not directly interested in the question. Hence the comparatively rapid progress since 1860.

Dye-works and bleach-works were brought under the Factory Act of 1850 in 1860;[50] lace and stocking factories in 1861. As a result of the first report of the Commission on the Employment of Children (1863) the same fate was shared by the manufacturers of all earthenware products (not just the potteries), matches,

48. Thus E. Potter, for example, in a letter of 24 March 1863 to *The Times*. *The Times* reminded him of the manufacturers' revolt against the Ten Hours' Bill.

49. Thus, among others, Mr W. Newmarch, collaborator and editor of Tooke's *History of Prices*. Is it a scientific advance to make cowardly concessions to public opinion?

50. The Act passed in 1860 laid down for dye-works and bleach-works that the working day should be provisionally fixed, on 1 August 1861, at 12 hours, and definitively fixed, on 1 August 1862, at 10 hours, i.e. at 10½ hours for ordinary days and 7½ for Saturday. Now when the fatal year arrived, in 1862, the old farce was repeated. The manufacturers petitioned Parliament to allow the employment of young persons and women for 12 hours a day for yet one more year. 'In the existing condition of the trade' (at the time of the cotton famine) 'it was greatly to the advantage of the operatives to work 12 hours per day, and make wages when they could.' A bill to this effect was brought in 'and it was mainly due to the action of the operative bleachers in Scotland that the bill was abandoned' (*Reports of the Inspectors of Factories . . . 31 October 1862*, pp. 14, 15). Defeated in this way by the very workers in whose name it pretended to speak, capital discovered, with the help of the judicial magnifying-glass, that the Act of 1860, drawn up in equivocal phrases, like all the Acts of Parliament for the 'protection of labour', provided them with a pretext for excluding from its operation the 'calenderers' and the 'finishers'. English jurisprudence, always the faithful servant of capital, sanctioned this piece of pettifogging in the Court of Common Pleas. 'The operatives have been greatly disappointed . . . they have complained of over-work, and it is greatly to be regretted that the clear intention of the legislature should have failed by reason of a faulty definition' (ibid., p. 18).

percussion-caps, cartridges, carpets and fustian cuttings, and the employers of people engaged in the many processes included under the name of 'finishing'. In the year 1863 bleaching in the open air[51] and baking were placed under special Acts by which, in the former

51. The 'open-air bleachers' had evaded the law of 1860 with the lie that no women worked at bleaching during the night. This lie was exposed by the factory inspectors, and at the same time Parliament was robbed of its illusions as to the pleasant atmosphere of fields and meadows in which the open-air bleaching was supposed to take place by petitions from the workers themselves. In this aerial bleaching, drying-rooms with temperatures of from 90° to 100° Fahrenheit were used, and the work there was mainly done by girls. 'Cooling' is the technical expression for their occasional escape from the drying-rooms into the fresh air. 'Fifteen girls in stoves. Heat from 80° to 90° for linens, and 100° and upwards for cambrics. Twelve girls ironing and doing-up in a small room about 10 feet square, in the centre of which is a close stove. The girls stand round the stove, which throws out a terrific heat, and dries the cambrics rapidly for the ironers. The hours of work for these hands are unlimited. If busy, they work till 9 or 12 at night for successive nights' (*Reports of the Inspectors of Factories . . . 31 October 1862*, p. 56). A medical man states: 'No special hours are allowed for cooling, but if the temperature gets too high, or the workers' hands get soiled from perspiration, they are allowed to go out for a few minutes . . . My experience, which is considerable, in treating the diseases of stove workers, compels me to express the opinion that their sanitary condition is by no means so high as that of the operatives in a spinning factory' (and capital, in its representations to Parliament, had painted them as rubicund and healthy, in the manner of Rubens!). 'The diseases most observable amongst them are phthisis, bronchitis, irregularity of uterine functions, hysteria in its most aggravated forms, and rheumatism. All of these, I believe, are either directly or indirectly induced by the impure, overheated air of the apartments in which the hands are employed, and the want of sufficient comfortable clothing to protect them from the cold, damp atmosphere, in winter, when going to their homes' (ibid., pp. 56–7). The factory inspectors remark, on the subject of the law of 1863,* extracted subsequently from these jovial 'open-air bleachers' [i.e. the employers], 'The Act has not only failed to afford that protection to the workers which it appears to offer, but contains a clause . . . apparently so worded that, unless persons are detected working after 8 o'clock at night, they appear to come under no protective provisions at all, and if they do so work, the mode of proof is so doubtful that a conviction can scarcely follow' (ibid., p. 52). 'To all intents and purposes, therefore, as an Act for any benevolent or educational purpose, it is a failure; since it can scarcely be called benevolent to permit, which is tantamount to compelling, women and children to work 14 hours a day with or without meals, as the case may be, and perhaps for longer hours than these, without limit as to age, without reference to sex, and without regard to the social habits of the families of the neighbourhood, in which such works (bleaching and dyeing) are situated' (*Reports of the Inspectors of Factories . . . 30 April 1863*, p. 40).

*The law Marx refers to here is in fact the Open Air Bleach-works Act of April 1862, which came into force on 1 January 1863.

case, the labour of young persons and women at night was forbidden (from 8 in the evening to 6 in the morning), and in the latter, the employment of journeymen bakers under 18 between 9 in the evening and 5 in the morning. We shall return to the later proposals of the same Commission, which threaten to deprive all the important branches of English industry of their 'freedom', with the exception of agriculture, mining and transport.[52]

7. THE STRUGGLE FOR A NORMAL WORKING DAY. IMPACT OF THE ENGLISH FACTORY LEGISLATION ON OTHER COUNTRIES

The reader will recall that the production of surplus-value, or the extraction of surplus labour, forms the specific content and purpose of capitalist production, quite apart from any reconstruction of the mode of production itself which may arise from the subordination of labour to capital. He will remember that, from the standpoint so far developed here, it is only the independent worker, a man who is thus legally qualified to act for himself, who enters into a contract with the capitalist as the seller of a commodity. So if our historical sketch has shown the prominent part played by modern industry on the one hand, and the labour of those who are physically and legally minors on the other, the former is still for us only a particular department of the exploitation of labour, and the latter only a particularly striking example of it. Without anticipating subsequent developments, the following points can be derived merely by connecting together the historical facts:

First. Capital's drive towards a boundless and ruthless extension of the working day is satisfied first in those industries which were first to be revolutionized by water-power, steam and machinery, in those earliest creations of the modern mode of production, the spinning and weaving of cotton, wool, flax and silk. The changed material mode of production, and the correspondingly changed social relations of the producers,[53] first gave rise to outrages without measure, and then called forth, in opposition to

52. Since 1866, when I wrote the above passages, a reaction has set in once again.

53. 'The conduct of each of these classes' (capitalists and workers) 'has been the result of the relative situation in which they have been placed' (*Reports of the Inspectors of Factories . . . 31 October 1848*, p. 113).

this, social control, which legally limits, regulates and makes uniform the working day and its pauses. During the first half of the nineteenth century, this control therefore appears simply as legislation for exceptions.[54] As soon as the Factory Acts had conquered the original domain of the new mode of production, it was found that in the meantime many other branches of production had made their entry into the factory system properly so called, that manufactures* with more or less obsolete methods, such as potteries, glass-making etc., that old-fashioned handicrafts like baking, and finally that even the scattered so-called domestic industries, such as nail-making,[55] had long since fallen as completely under capitalist exploitation as the factories themselves. Factory legislation was therefore compelled gradually to strip itself of its exceptional character, or to declare that any house in which work was done was a factory, as in England, where the law proceeds in the manner of the Roman Casuists.[56]†

Second. The history of the regulation of the working day in certain branches of production, and the struggle still going on in others over this regulation, prove conclusively that the isolated worker, the worker as 'free' seller of his labour-power, succumbs without resistance once capitalist production has reached a certain stage of maturity. The establishment of a normal working day is therefore the product of a protracted and more or less concealed civil war between the capitalist class and the working

54. 'The employments, placed under restriction, were connected with the manufacture of textile fabrics by the aid of steam or water-power. There were two conditions to which an employment must be subject to cause it to be inspected, viz., the use of steam or water-power, and the manufacture of certain specified fibres' (*Reports of the Inspectors of Factories . . . 31 October 1864*, p. 8).

55. The latest reports of the Children's Employment Commission contain especially valuable material on the situation in this so-called domestic industry.

56. 'The Acts of last Session (1864) . . . embrace a diversity of occupations, the customs in which differ greatly, and the use of mechanical power to give motion to machinery is no longer one of the elements necessary, as formerly, to constitute, in legal phrase, a "Factory"' (*Reports of the Inspectors of Factories . . . 31 October 1864*, p. 8).

---

*More idiomatic would be 'industries', but these are industries with obsolete methods, and they belong to the age of 'manufacture'.

†The Roman Catholic Casuists of the seventeenth century, especially the Jesuits, were famed for using refined and tortuous arguments so as to preserve intact the formal framework of inconvenient doctrines while abolishing them in substance.

class. Since the contest takes place in the arena of modern industry, it is fought out first of all in the homeland of that industry – England.[57] The English factory workers were the champions, not only of the English working class, but of the modern working class in general, just as their theorists were the first to throw down the gauntlet to the theory of the capitalists.[58] Hence the philosopher of the factory, Ure, considers it a mark of inextinguishable disgrace on the part of the English working class that they wrote 'the slavery of the Factory Acts' on their banners, as opposed to capital, which was striving manfully for the 'perfect freedom of labour'.[59]

France limps slowly behind England. The French twelve hours' law needed the February revolution to bring it into the world,[60]

57. Belgium, the paradise of Continental liberalism, shows no trace of this movement. Even in the coal and metal mines, workers of both sexes and all ages are consumed, in perfect 'freedom', at any period, and through any length of time. Out of every 1,000 persons employed there, 733 are men, 88 women, 135 boys and 44 girls under 16; in the blast-furnaces, etc., out of 1,000 employed, 668 are men, 149 women, 98 boys and 85 girls under 16. Add to this the low wages paid in return for the enormous exploitation of mature and immature labour-power. The average daily pay for a man is 2s. 8d., for a woman 1s. 8d., for a boy, 1s. 2½d. As a result, Belgium nearly doubled the amount and the value of its exports of coal, iron, etc. between 1850 and 1863.

58. Robert Owen, soon after 1810, not only maintained the necessity of a limitation of the working day in theory, but actually introduced the 10-hour day into his factory at New Lanark. This was laughed at as a communist utopia; so was his 'combination of children's education with productive labour', as well as the workers' co-operative societies he was the first to set up. Today, the first utopia is a Factory Act, the second figures as an official phrase in all Factory Acts, and the third is already being used as a cloak for reactionary swindles.

59. Ure (French translation), *Philosophie des manufactures*, Paris, 1836, Vol. 2, pp. 39–40, 67, 77, etc.

60. We read in the *Compte Rendu* of the International Statistical Congress held in Paris in 1855: 'The French law, which limits the length of daily labour in factories and workshops to 12 hours, does not confine this work to definite fixed hours. For children's labour only the working time is prescribed as between 5 a.m. and 9 p.m. Therefore, some of the manufacturers use the right which this fatal silence gives them to keep their works going without intermission, day in, day out, with the possible exception of Sunday. For this purpose they use two different sets of workers, of whom neither is in the workshop more than 12 hours at a time, but the work of the establishment lasts day and night. The law is satisfied, but is humanity?' Besides 'the destructive influence of night-labour on the human organism', stress is also laid upon 'the fatal influence of the association of the two sexes by night in the same badly lighted workshops'.

and it has far more loopholes than its English model. Nevertheless, the French revolutionary method has its own peculiar advantages. At one stroke it dictates the same limits to the working day in all shops and factories without distinction, whereas the English legislation yields reluctantly to the pressure of circumstances, now on this point, now on that, and is well on the way to creating an inextricable tangle of contradictory enactments.[61] Moreover, the French law proclaims as a principle what in England was only won in the name of children, minors and women, and has only recently been claimed, for the first time, as a universal right.[62]

In the United States of America, every independent workers' movement was paralysed as long as slavery disfigured a part of the republic. Labour in a white skin cannot emancipate itself where it is branded in a black skin. However, a new life immediately arose from the death of slavery. The first fruit of the American Civil War was the eight hours' agitation, which ran from the Atlantic to the Pacific, from New England to California, with the seven-league boots of the locomotive. The General Congress of Labour held at Baltimore in August 1866 declared: 'The first and great necessity of the present, to free the labour of this country from capitalistic slavery, is the passing of a law by which eight hours shall be the normal working day in all States of the American Union. We are resolved to put forth all our strength until this glorious result is attained.'[63] At the same time (the beginning of

61. 'For instance, there is within my district one occupier who, within the same curtilage, is at the same time a bleacher and dyer under the Bleaching and Dyeing Works Act, a printer under the Print Works Act, and a finisher under the Factory Act' (Report of Mr Baker, in *Reports of the Inspectors of Factories . . . 31 October 1861*, p. 20). After enumerating the different provisions of these Acts, and the complications arising from them, Mr Baker says: 'It will hence appear that it must be very difficult to secure the execution of these three Acts of Parliament where the occupier chooses to evade the law.' But one thing *is* secured by this means: law-suits for the gentlemen of the law.

62. Thus the factory inspectors at last venture to say: 'These objections' (objections of capital to the legal limitation of the working day) 'must succumb before the broad principle of the rights of labour . . . There is a time when the master's right in his workman's labour ceases, and his time becomes his own, even if there were no exhaustion in the question' (*Reports of the Inspectors of Factories . . . 31 October 1862*, p. 54).

63. 'We, the workers of Dunkirk, declare that the length of time of labour required under the present system is too great, and that, far from leaving the worker time for rest and education, it plunges him into a condition of servitude but little better than slavery. That is why we decide that eight hours are

September 1866), the Congress of the International Working Men's Association, held at Geneva, passed the following resolution, proposed by the London General Council: 'We declare that the limitation of the working day is a preliminary condition without which all further attempts at improvement and emancipation must prove abortive ... the Congress proposes eight hours as the legal limit of the working day.'*

Thus the working-class movement on both sides of the Atlantic, which had grown instinctively out of the relations of production themselves, set its seal on the words of the English factory inspector, R. J. Saunders; 'Further steps towards a reformation of society can never be carried out with any hope of success, unless the hours of labour be limited, and the prescribed limit strictly enforced.'[64]

It must be acknowledged that our worker emerges from the process of production looking different from when he entered it. In the market, as owner of the commodity 'labour-power', he stood face to face with other owners of commodities, one owner against another owner. The contract by which he sold his labour-power to the capitalist proved in black and white, so to speak, that he was free to dispose of himself. But when the transaction was concluded, it was discovered that he was no 'free agent', that the period of time for which he is free to sell his labour-power is the period of time for which he is forced to sell it,[65] that

enough for a working day, and ought to be legally recognized as enough; why we call to our help that powerful lever, the press; .. and why we shall consider all those that refuse us this help as enemies of the reform of labour and of the rights of the labourer' (Resolution of the Working Men of Dunkirk, State of New York, 1866).

64. *Reports of the Inspectors of Factories ... 31 October 1848*, p. 112.

65. 'The proceedings' (the manoeuvres of capital, for instance from 1848 to 1850) 'have afforded, moreover, incontrovertible proof of the fallacy of the assertion so often advanced, that operatives need no protection, but may be considered as free agents in the disposal of the only property which they possess – the labour of their hands and the sweat of their brows' (*Reports of the Inspectors of Factories ... 30 April 1850*, p. 45). 'Free labour (if so it may be termed) even in a free country, requires the strong arm of the law to protect it' (*Reports of the Inspectors of Factories ... 31 October 1864*, p. 34). 'To permit, which is tantamount to compelling ... to work 14 hours a day without meals etc.' (*Reports of the Inspectors of Factories ... 30 April 1863*, p. 40).

*This resolution was drafted by Marx himself. (See 'Instructions for Delegates to the Geneva Conference', printed in *The First International and After*, Pelican Marx Library, 1973, p. 87.)

in fact the vampire will not let go 'while there remains a single muscle, sinew or drop of blood to be exploited'.[66] For 'protection' against the serpent of their agonies, the workers have to put their heads together and, as a class, compel the passing of a law, an all-powerful social barrier by which they can be prevented from selling themselves and their families into slavery and death by voluntary contract with capital.[67] In the place of the pompous catalogue of the 'inalienable rights of man' there steps the modest Magna Carta of the legally limited working day, which at last makes clear 'when the time which the worker sells is ended, and when his own begins'.[68] *Quantum mutatus ab illo!**

66. F. Engels, 'Die englische Zehnstundenbill', op. cit., p. 5 [English translation, p. 97].

67. The Ten Hours' Act, in the branches of industry subject to it, has 'put an end to the premature decrepitude of the former long-hour workers' (*Reports of the Inspectors of Factories . . . 31 October 1859*, p. 47). 'Capital' (in factories) 'can never be employed in keeping the machinery in motion beyond a limited time, without certain injury to the health and morals of the labourers employed; and they are not in a position to protect themselves' (ibid., p. 8).

68. 'A still greater boon is the distinction at last made clear between the worker's own time and his master's. The worker knows now when that which he sells is ended, and when his own begins; and by possessing a sure fore-knowledge of this, is enabled to pre-arrange his own minutes for his own purposes' (ibid., p. 52). 'By making them masters of their own time' (the Factory Acts) '. . . have given them a moral energy which is directing them to eventual possession of political power' (ibid., p. 47). With suppressed irony, and using very cautious expressions, the factory inspectors hint that the present Ten Hours' Act also frees the capitalist from some of the brutality natural to a man who is merely an embodiment of capital, and that it has given him time for a little 'culture'. 'Formerly the master had no time for anything but money; the servant had no time for anything but labour' (ibid., p. 48).

---

* 'What a great change from that time' (Virgil, *Aeneid*, Bk 2, line 274).

Chapter 11: The Rate and Mass of Surplus-Value

In this chapter, as hitherto, the value of labour-power, and therefore the part of the working day necessary for the reproduction or maintenance of that labour-power, is assumed to be a given, constant magnitude.

With this presupposition, the rate of surplus-value directly gives us the mass of surplus-value furnished to the capitalist by the worker within a definite period of time. If, for example, the necessary labour amounts to 6 hours a day, expressed in a quantity of gold equal to 3 shillings, then 3 shillings is the daily value of one labour-power, or the value of the capital advanced to buy one labour-power. If, further, the rate of surplus-value is 100 per cent, this variable capital of 3 shillings produces a mass of surplus-value of 3 shillings, in other words, the worker supplies every day a mass of surplus labour of 6 hours.

But the variable capital is the monetary expression for the total value of all the labour-powers the capitalist employs simultaneously. Its value is therefore equal to the average value of one labour-power multiplied by the number of labour-powers employed. With a given value of labour-power, therefore, the magnitude of the variable capital varies directly with the number of workers employed simultaneously. If the daily value of one labour-power is 3 shillings, then a capital of 300 shillings must be advanced in order to exploit 100 labour-powers every day, and a capital of $n \times 3$ shillings must be advanced in order to exploit n labour-powers every day.

In the same way, if a variable capital of 3 shillings, being the daily value of one labour-power, produces a daily surplus-value of 3 shillings, a variable capital of 300 shillings will produce a daily surplus-value of 300 shillings, and one of $n \times 3$ shillings will produce a daily surplus-value of $n \times 3$ shillings. The mass of surplus-value produced is therefore equal to the surplus-value provided by the working day of one worker multiplied by the number of workers employed. But as the mass of surplus-value which a single worker produces (the value of labour-power being given) is determined by the rate of surplus-value, this first law follows: the mass of surplus-value produced is equal to the amount of the variable capital advanced multiplied by the rate of surplus-value; in other words: the mass of surplus-value is determined by the product of the number of labour-powers simultaneously exploited by the same capitalist and the degree of exploitation of each individual labour-power.

Let the mass of the surplus value be S, the surplus-value supplied by the individual worker in the average day s, the variable capital advanced daily in the purchase of one individual labour-power v, the sum total of the variable capital V, the value of an average labour-power P, its degree of exploitation $\dfrac{a'}{a}$ $\left(\dfrac{\text{surplus labour}}{\text{necessary labour}}\right)$ and the number of workers employed, n; we have, then:

$$S = \begin{cases} \dfrac{s}{v} \times V \\[2mm] P \times \dfrac{a'}{a} \times n \end{cases}$$

We assume throughout, not only that the value of an average labour-power is constant, but that the workers employed by a capitalist are reduced to average workers. There do exist exceptional cases in which the surplus-value produced does not increase in proportion to the number of workers being exploited, but then the value of the labour-power does not remain constant.

In the production of a definite mass of surplus-value, therefore, a decrease in one factor may be compensated for by an increase in the other. If the variable capital diminishes, and at the same time the rate of surplus-value increases in the same ratio, the mass of surplus-value remains unaltered. If, on our earlier assumption, the capitalist has to advance 300 shillings in order to exploit 100 workers each day, and if the rate of surplus-value amounts to 50 per cent, this variable capital of 300 shillings yields a surplus-value of 150 shillings, or 100×3 working hours. If the rate of surplus-value doubles, or the working day, instead of being extended from 6 to 9, is extended from 6 to 12 hours, and at the same time variable capital is reduced by half, i.e. to 150 shillings, it too yields a surplus-value of 150 shillings, or 50×6 working hours. A decrease in the variable capital may therefore be compensated for by a proportionate rise in the degree of exploitation of labour-power, or a decrease in the number of workers employed by a proportionate extension of the working day. Within certain limits, therefore, the supply of labour exploitable by capital is independent of the supply of workers.[1] And, inversely, a fall in the rate of surplus-value leaves the mass of surplus-value which has been produced unaltered, if the amount of the variable capital, i.e. the number of workers employed, increases in the same proportion.

Nevertheless there are limits, which cannot be overcome, to the compensation for a decrease in the number of workers employed, i.e. a decrease in the amount of variable capital advanced, provided by a rise in the rate of surplus-value, i.e. the lengthening of the working day. Whatever the value of labour-power may be, whether the labour-time necessary for the maintenance of the worker is 2 hours or 10, the total value a worker can produce, day in, day out, is always less than the value in which 24 hours of labour are objectified. For instance, it is less than 12 shillings, if 12 shillings is the monetary expression for 24 hours of objectified labour. On our former assumption, according to which 6 hours of labour every day are necessary in order to reproduce the labour-power itself or to replace the value of the capital advanced to purchase it, a variable capital of 1,500 shillings, employing 500 workers at a rate of surplus-value of 100 per cent with a 12-hour working day, produces every day a surplus-value of 1,500 shillings, or 6×500 working hours. A capital of 300 shillings, employing 100 workers a day with a rate of surplus value of 200 per cent, or with a working day of 18 hours, only produces a mass of surplus-value of 600 shillings, or 12×100 working hours; and its total value-product, the equivalent of the variable capital advanced plus the surplus-value, can, day in, day out, never reach the sum of 1,200 shillings or 24×100 working hours. The absolute limit of the average working day – this being by nature always less than 24 hours – sets an absolute limit to the compensation for a reduction of variable capital by a higher rate of surplus-value, or for the decrease of the number of workers exploited by a

1. This elementary law appears to be unknown to the vulgar economist, who imagines, like an inverted Archimedes, that in the determination of the market price of labour by supply and demand he has found the fulcrum by means of which he cannot so much move the world, as bring it to a standstill.

higher degree of exploitation of labour-power. This self-evident second law is of importance for the explanation of many phenomena, arising from the tendency of capital to reduce as much as possible the number of workers employed, i.e. the amount of its variable component, the part which is changed into labour-power (we shall develop this tendency later on),* which stands in contradiction with its other tendency to produce the greatest possible mass of surplus-value. On the other hand, if the mass of labour-power employed or the amount of variable capital increases, but not in proportion to the fall in the rate of surplus-value, a diminution occurs in the mass of surplus-value produced.

A third law results from the determination by the following two factors of the mass of surplus-value produced: rate of surplus-value and the amount of variable capital advanced. The rate of surplus-value, i.e. the degree of exploitation of labour-power, and the value of labour-power, i.e. the amount of the necessary labour-time, being given, it is self-evident that the greater the variable capital, the greater would be the mass of the value produced and of the surplus-value. If the limit of the working day is given, and also the limit of its necessary part, the mass of value and surplus-value produced by the individual capitalist is clearly exclusively dependent on the mass of labour that he sets in motion. But this, on the assumptions we have made above, depends on the mass of labour-power, or the number of workers he exploits, and this number in its turn is determined by the amount of the variable capital advanced. With a given rate of surplus-value, and a given value of labour-power, therefore, the masses of surplus-value produced vary directly as the amounts of the variable capitals advanced. Now we know that the capitalist divides his capital into two parts. He lays out one part on means of production. This is the constant part of his capital. He lays out the other part on living labour-power. This part forms his variable capital. On the basis of the same mode of production, the division of capital into constant and variable differs in different branches of production, and within the same branch of production, too, this relation changes with changes in the technical foundations and in the ways of linking together the processes of production in society. But whatever the proportion between the constant and the variable part of a given capital, whether it is $1:2$, or $1:10$ or $1:x$, the law

* See Chapter 25, Sections 2 and 3 (pp. 772–94).

just laid down is not affected by this. For, according to our previous analysis, the value of the constant capital re-appears in the value of the product, but does not enter into the newly produced value, the newly created value-product. To employ 1,000 spinners, more raw material, spindles, etc. are of course required than to employ 100. The value of these additional means of production, however, may rise, fall, remain unaltered, be large or small; it has no influence on the valorization process performed by the labour-powers which set the means of production in motion. The law demonstrated above therefore takes this form: the masses of value and of surplus-value produced by different capitals – the value of labour-power being given and its degree of exploitation being equal – vary directly as the amounts of the variable components of these capitals, i.e. the parts which have been turned into living labour-power.

This law clearly contradicts all experience based on immediate appearances. Everyone knows that a cotton spinner, who, if we consider the percentage over the whole of his applied capital, employs much constant capital and little variable capital, does not, on account of this, pocket less profit or surplus-value than a baker, who sets in motion relatively much variable capital and little constant capital. For the solution of this apparent contradiction, many intermediate terms are still needed, just as, from the standpoint of elementary algebra, many intermediate terms are needed before we can understand that 0/0 may represent an actual magnitude. Classical economics holds instinctively to this law, although it has never actually formulated it, because it is a necessary consequence of the law of value. It tries to rescue the law from the contradictions of immediate experience by making a violent abstraction. We shall see later[2] how the school of Ricardo came to grief on this stumbling-block. Vulgar economics, which like the Bourbons 'has really learnt nothing', relies here as elsewhere on the mere semblance as opposed to the law which

2. This point will be examined more closely in Book 4.*
*See *Theories of Surplus-Value*, Part III, London, 1972, Chapter 20, 'Disintegration of the Ricardian School', and in particular the very clear formulation on p. 117: 'The difficulty arose because capitals of equal magnitude, but of unequal composition ... containing unequal proportions of constant and variable capital ... set in motion unequal quantities of ... unpaid labour; consequently they cannot appropriate equal quantities of surplus-value ... But capitals of equal magnitude, no matter what their organic composition, yield equal profits.'

regulates and determines the phenomena. In antithesis to Spinoza, it believes that 'ignorance is a sufficient reason'.*

The labour which is set in motion by the total capital of a society, day in, day out, may be regarded as a single working day. If, for example, the number of workers is a million, and the average working day is 10 hours, the social working day will consist of 10 million hours. With a given length of this working day, whether its limits are fixed physically or socially, the mass of surplus-value can be increased only by increasing the number of workers, i.e. the size of the working population. The growth of population here forms the mathematical limit to the production of surplus-value by the total social capital. And, inversely, with a given population this limit is formed by the possible lengthening of the working day.[3] It will however be seen in the next chapter that this law holds only for the form of surplus-value dealt with up to the present.

From the foregoing treatment of the production of surplus-value it follows that not every sum of money, or value, can be transformed into capital at will. In fact, it is a presupposition of this transformation that a certain minimum of money or of exchange-value is in the hands of the individual possessor of money or commodities. The minimum of variable capital is the cost price of a single labour-power employed the whole year through, day in, day out, for the production of surplus-value. If this worker were in possession of his own means of production, and were satisfied to live as a worker, he could make do with the amount of labour-time necessary to reproduce his means of subsistence, say 8 hours a day. In addition to this, he would only need means of production sufficient for 8 working hours. The capitalist, on the other hand, who makes him do, besides these 8 hours, say 4 hours of surplus labour, requires an additional sum of money for furnishing the additional means of production. On our assump-

3. 'The Labour, that is the economic time, of society, is a given portion, say ten hours a day of a million people, or ten million hours . . . Capital has its boundary of increase. This boundary may, at any given period, be attained in the actual extent of economic time employed' (*An Essay on the Political Economy of Nations*, London, 1821, pp. 47, 49).

*Spinoza, in the appendix to Part I of his *Ethics*, rejects the teleological argument for the existence of God, stating that ignorance of other causes is not a sufficient reason for the view that God created nature with some particular end in view.

tion, however, he would have to employ not one but two workers in order to live, on the surplus-value appropriated daily, as well as and no better than a worker, i.e. in order to be able to satisfy his needs. In this case the mere maintenance of life would be the purpose of his production, not the increase of wealth. But capitalist production presupposes the increase of wealth. To live only twice as well as an ordinary worker and, as well as that, turn half of the surplus-value produced into capital, he would have to multiply the number of workers and the minimum of the capital advanced by eight. Of course he can, like the man who is working for him, participate directly in the process of production, but then he is only a hybrid, a man between capitalist and worker, a 'small master'. A certain stage of capitalist production necessitates that the capitalist be able to devote the whole of the time during which he functions as a capitalist, i.e. as capital personified, to the appropriation and therefore the control of the labour of others [*fremde Arbeit*], and to the sale of the products of that labour.[4] The guild system of the Middle Ages therefore tried forcibly to prevent the transformation of the master of a craft into a capitalist, by limiting the number of workers a single master could employ to a very low maximum. Hence the possessor of money or commodities actually turns into a capitalist only where the minimum sum advanced for production greatly exceeds the known medieval maximum. Here, as in natural science, is shown the correctness of the law discovered by Hegel, in his *Logic*, that at a certain point merely quantitative differences pass over by a dialectical inversion into qualitative distinctions.[5]

4. 'The farmer cannot rely on his own labour, and if he does, I will maintain that he is a loser by it. His employment should be a general attention to the whole: his thresher must be watched, or he will soon lose his wages in corn not threshed out; his mowers, reapers, etc., must be looked after; he must constantly go round his fences; he must see there is no neglect; which would be the case if he was confined to any one spot' (*An Inquiry into the Connection between the Present Price of Provisions, and the Size of Farms, etc. By a Farmer* [J. Arbuthnot], London, 1773, p. 12). This book is very interesting. In it, one may study the genesis of the 'capitalist farmer' or 'merchant farmer', as he is explicitly called, and observe his self-glorification at the expense of the 'small farmer', who is concerned essentially with his own subsistence. 'The class of capitalists are from the first partially, and they become ultimately completely, discharged from the necessity of manual labour' (*Textbook of Lectures on the Political Economy of Nations*, by the Reverend Richard Jones, Hertford, 1852, Lecture III, p. 39).
5. The molecular theory of modern chemistry, first scientifically worked

The minimum sum of value the individual possessor of money or commodities must command in order to metamorphose himself into a capitalist changes with the different stages of development of capitalist production, and is at given stages different in different spheres of production, according to their special technical conditions. Certain spheres, even at the beginnings of capitalist production, require a minimum of capital which is not yet to be found in the hands of single individuals. This situation gives rise partly to state subsidies to private persons, as in France in the time of Colbert and in some German states right into our own epoch, and partly to the formation of companies with a legally secured monopoly over the conduct of certain branches of industry and commerce[6] – the forerunners of the modern joint-stock companies.

We shall not examine in detail the changes which take place in the relation between the capitalist and the wage-labourer in the course of the process of production, nor shall we deal any further with the characteristics of capital itself. Here we shall only emphasize certain main points.

Capital developed within the production process until it acquired command over labour, i.e. over self-activating labour-power, in other words the worker himself. The capitalist, who is capital personified, now takes care that the worker does his work regularly and with the proper degree of intensity.

Capital also developed into a coercive relation, and this compels

---

out by Laurent and Gerhardt, rests on no other law. [Addition to the third edition by Engels:] For the explanation of this statement, which is not very clear to non-chemists, we remark that the author speaks here of the homologous series of carbon compounds, first so named by C. Gerhardt in 1843, each series of which has its own general algebraic formula. Thus the series of paraffins: $C_nH_{2n+2}O$, that of the normal alcohols: $C_nH_{2n+2}O$; of the normal fatty acids: $C_nH_{2n}O_2$, and many others. In the above examples, by the simply quantitative addition of CH_2 to the molecular formula, a qualitatively different body is each time formed. On the share (overestimated by Marx) of Laurent and Gerhardt in the determination of this important fact see Kopp, *Entwickelung der Chemie*, Munich, 1873, pp. 709, 716, and Schorlemmer, *The Rise and Development of Organic Chemistry*, London, 1879, p. 54.

6. Martin Luther calls these institutions 'The Company Monopolia'.*

*'Who is so stupid that he cannot see that the trading companies are nothing but pure monopolies?' (*Von Kaufshandlung und Wucher*, 1524, in *Dr Martin Luthers Werke, Kritische Gesamtausgabe*, Vol. 15, Weimar, 1899, p. 312).

the working class to do more work than would be required by the narrow circle of its own needs. As an agent in producing the activity of others, as an extractor of surplus labour and an exploiter of labour-power, it surpasses all earlier systems of production, which were based on directly compulsory labour, in its energy and its quality of unbounded and ruthless activity.

At first capital subordinates labour on the basis of the technical conditions within which labour has been carried on up to that point in history. It does not therefore directly change the mode of production. The production of surplus-value in the form we have so far considered, by means of simple extension of the working day, appeared therefore independently of any change in the mode of production itself. It was no less effective in the old-fashioned bakeries than in the modern cotton factories.

If we consider the process of production from the point of view of the simple labour-process, the worker is related to the means of production, not in their quality as capital, but as being the mere means and material of his own purposeful productive activity. In tanning, for example, he deals with the skins as his simple object of labour. It is not the capitalist whose skin he tans. But it is different as soon as we view the production process as a process of valorization. The means of production are at once changed into means for the absorption of the labour of others. It is no longer the worker who employs the means of production, but the means of production which employ the worker. Instead of being consumed by him as material elements of his productive activity, they consume him as the ferment necessary to their own life-process, and the life-process of capital consists solely in its own motion as self-valorizing value. Furnaces and workshops that stand idle by night, and absorb no living labour, are 'a mere loss' to the capitalist. Hence furnaces and workshops constitute 'lawful claims upon the night-labour' of the labour-powers. As soon as a certain sum of money is transformed into means of production, i.e. into the objective factors of the production process, the means of production themselves are transformed into a title, both by right and by might, to the labour and surplus labour of others. An example will show, in conclusion, how this inversion, indeed this distortion, which is peculiar to and characteristic of capitalist production, of the relation between dead labour and living labour, between value and the force that creates value, is mirrored in the consciousness of the capitalist. During the English manufacturers' revolt of

1848–50, 'the head of one of the oldest and most respectable houses in the West of Scotland, Messrs Carlile Sons & Co., of the linen and cotton thread factory at Paisley, a company which has now existed for about a century, which was in operation in 1752, and four generations of the same family have conducted it . . . ', this 'very intelligent gentleman' wrote a letter printed in the *Glasgow Daily Mail* of 25 April 1849,[7] under the heading 'The Relay System', where the following grotesquely naïve passage, among others, crept in: 'Let us now . . . see what evils will attend the limiting to 10 hours the working of the factory . . . They amount to the most serious damage to the mill-owner's prospects and property. If he' (i.e. his 'hands') 'worked 12 hours before, and is limited to 10, then every 12 machines or spindles in his establishment shrink to 10, and should the works be disposed of, they will be valued only as 10, so that a sixth part would thus be deducted from the value of every factory in the country.'[8]

In this West of Scotland bourgeois brain, which has inherited the capitalist qualities of 'four generations', the value of the means of production, spindles, etc., is so inextricably confused with the quality they possess, as capital, of valorizing themselves, or swallowing up every day a definite quantity of the unpaid labour of others, that the head of the firm of Carlile & Co. actually imagines that if he sells his factory, not only will the value of the spindles be paid to him, but, in addition, their power of self-valorization, not only the labour contained in them, which is necessary to the production of spindles of this kind, but also the surplus labour which they help to pump out daily from the brave Scots of Paisley. This is why he thinks that with the shortening of the working day by 2 hours, the selling-price of 12 spinning machines dwindles to that of 10!

7. *Reports of the Inspectors of Factories* . . . *30 April 1849*, p. 59.

8. ibid., p. 60. Factory Inspector Stuart, himself a Scotsman and, unlike the English factory inspectors, a complete prisoner of the capitalist mode of thought, remarks expressly on this letter which he incorporates in his report that it is 'the most useful of the communications which any of the factory-owners working with relays have given to those engaged in the same trade, and which is the most calculated to remove the prejudices of such of them as have scruples respecting any change of the arrangement of the hours of work'.

Part Four

The Production of Relative Surplus-Value

Chapter 12: The Concept of Relative Surplus-Value

That portion of the working day which merely produces an equivalent for the value paid by the capitalist for his labour-power has up to this point been treated by us as a constant magnitude. And so it is, under given conditions of production and at a given stage in the economic development of society. As we saw, the worker could continue to work for 2, 3, 4, 6, etc. hours beyond this, his necessary labour-time. The rate of surplus-value and the length of the working day depended on how far this extra time was prolonged. Although the necessary labour-time was constant, we saw, on the other hand, that the total working day was variable. Now suppose we have a working day whose length and whose division between necessary labour and surplus labour are given. Let the whole line AC,

A ---------- B -- C

represent, for example, a working day of 12 hours; the section AB represents 10 hours of necessary labour, and the section BC represents 2 hours of surplus labour. How can the production of surplus-value be increased, i.e. how can surplus labour be prolonged, without any prolongation, or independently of any prolongation, of the line AC?

Although the boundaries of the working day, A and C, are given, it would seem possible to lengthen the line BC, other than by extension beyond its end point C, which is also the end of the working day AC, by pushing back its starting point B in the direction of A. Assume that B′B in the line

A --------- B′ - B -- C

is equal to half of BC, or to 1 hour's labour-time. If now, in AC, the working day of 12 hours, we move point B to B′, then BC becomes B′C; the surplus labour increases by one half, from 2 hours to 3 hours, although the working day remains 12 hours as before. This extension of the surplus labour-time from BC to B′C, from 2 hours to 3 hours, is however evidently impossible without a simultaneous contraction of the necessary labour-time from AB to AB', from 10 hours to 9 hours. The prolongation of surplus labour would correspond to a shortening of necessary labour; i.e. a portion of the labour-time previously consumed, in reality, for the worker's own benefit would be converted into labour-time expended for the capitalist. There would be an alteration, not in the length of the working day, but in its division into necessary labour-time and surplus labour-time.

On the other hand, it is evident that the duration of surplus labour is given when the length of the working day and the value of labour-power are given. The value of labour-power, i.e. the labour-time necessary to produce labour-power, determines the labour-time necessary for the reproduction of the value of labour-power. If 1 hour of work is embodied in sixpence, and the value of a day's labour-power is 5 shillings, the worker must work for 10 hours a day in order to replace the value paid by capital for his labour-power, or to produce an equivalent for the value of the means of subsistence he needs to consume every day. Given the value of these means of subsistence, the value of his labour-power can be calculated;[1] and given the value of his labour-power, the duration of his necessary labour-time. The duration of the surplus labour, however, is arrived at by subtracting the necessary labour-time from the total working day: 10 from 12 leaves 2, and it is not easy to see how, under the given conditions, the surplus labour can possibly be prolonged beyond 2 hours. No doubt the capitalist could, instead of 5s., pay the worker 4s. 6d. or even less. 9 hours' labour-time would be sufficient to reproduce this value of 4s. 6d.; and consequently 3 hours of surplus labour, instead of 2, would accrue to the capitalist, and the surplus-value would rise from 1s.

1. The value of his average daily wages is determined by what the worker needs 'so as to live, labour, and generate' (William Petty, *Political Anatomy of Ireland*, 1672, p. 64). 'The price of Labour is always constituted of the price of necessaries . . . Whenever . . . the labouring man's wages will not, suitably to his low rank and station, as a labouring man, support such a family as is often the lot of many of them to have', he is not receiving the proper wages (J. Vanderlint, op. cit., p. 15). 'The simple worker, who possesses nothing but his arms and his industriousness, has nothing unless he manages to sell his labour to others . . . In every kind of labour, it must happen, and it does in fact happen, that the wage of the worker is limited to what he needs to secure his own subsistence' (Turgot, *Réflexions, etc.*, in *Œuvres*, ed. Daire, Vol. I, p. 10). 'The price of the necessaries of life is, in fact, the cost of producing labour' (Malthus, *Inquiry into, etc., Rent*, London, 1815, p. 48, note).

to 1s. 6d. This result, however, could be attained only by pushing the wage of the worker down below the value of his labour-power. With the 4s. 6d. which he produces in 9 hours, he commands one-tenth less of the means of subsistence than before, and consequently the reproduction of his labour-power can take place only in a stunted form. The surplus labour would in this case be prolonged only by transgressing its normal limits; its domain would be extended only by a usurpation of part of the domain of necessary labour-time. Despite the important part which this method plays in practice, we are excluded from considering it here by our assumption that all commodities, including labour-power, are bought and sold at their full value. If we once assume this, it follows that the labour-time necessary for the production of labour-power, or for the reproduction of its value, cannot be lessened by a fall in the worker's wages below the value of his labour-power, but only by a fall in this value itself. Given the length of the working day, the prolongation of the surplus labour must of necessity originate in the curtailment of the necessary labour-time; the latter cannot arise from the former. In the example we chose, the value of labour-power had to fall in fact by one-tenth in order for the necessary labour-time to be diminished by one-tenth, i.e. from 10 hours to 9, and for the surplus labour to consequently be prolonged from 2 hours to 3.

A fall of this kind in the value of labour-power implies, however, that the same means of subsistence formerly produced in 10 hours can now be produced in 9 hours. But this is impossible without an increase in the productivity of labour. For example, suppose a cobbler, with a given set of tools, makes one pair of boots in one working day of 12 hours. If he is to make two pairs in the same time, the productivity of his labour must be doubled; and this cannot be done except by an alteration in his tools or in his mode of working, or both. Hence the conditions of production of his labour, i.e. his mode of production, and the labour process itself, must be revolutionized. By an increase in the productivity of labour, we mean an alteration in the labour process of such a kind as to shorten the labour-time socially necessary for the production of a commodity, and to endow a given quantity of labour with the power of producing a greater quantity of use-value.[2] Hitherto, in

2. 'When the crafts assume a more perfect form, this means nothing other than the discovery of new ways of making a product with fewer people, or (which is the same thing) in a shorter time, than previously' (Galiani, op. cit.,

dealing with the production of surplus-value in the above form, we have assumed that the mode of production is given and invariable. But when surplus-value has to be produced by the conversion of necessary labour into surplus labour, it by no means suffices for capital to take over the labour process in its given or historically transmitted shape, and then simply to prolong its duration. The technical and social conditions of the process and consequently the mode of production itself must be revolutionized before the productivity of labour can be increased. Then, with the increase in the productivity of labour, the value of labour-power will fall, and the portion of the working day necessary for the reproduction of that value will be shortened.

I call that surplus-value which is produced by the lengthening of the working day, *absolute surplus-value*. In contrast to this, I call that surplus-value which arises from the curtailment of the necessary labour-time, and from the corresponding alteration in the respective lengths of the two components of the working day, *relative surplus-value*.

In order to make the value of labour-power go down, the rise in the productivity of labour must seize upon those branches of industry whose products determine the value of labour-power, and consequently either belong to the category of normal means of subsistence, or are capable of replacing them. But the value of a commodity is determined not only by the quantity of labour which gives it its final form, but also by the quantity of labour contained in the instruments by which it has been produced. For instance, the value of a pair of boots depends not only on the labour of the cobbler, but also on the value of the leather, wax, thread, etc. Hence a fall in the value of labour-power is also brought about by an increase in the productivity of labour, and by a corresponding cheapening of commodities in those industries which supply the instruments of labour and the material for labour, i.e. the physical elements of constant capital which are required for producing the means of subsistence. But an increase in the productivity of labour in those branches of industry which supply neither the necessary means of subsistence nor the means by which they are produced leaves the value of labour-power undisturbed.

The cheapening of the commodity, of course, causes only a

---

p. 159). 'Economies in the cost of production can only be economies in the quantity of labour employed in production' (Sismondi, *Études*, Vol. I, p. 22).

relative fall in the value of labour-power, a fall proportional to the extent to which that commodity enters into the reproduction of labour-power. Shirts, for instance, are a necessary means of subsistence, but are only one out of many. The total sum of the necessary means of subsistence, however, consists of various commodities, each the product of a distinct industry; and the value of each of those commodities enters as a component part into the value of labour-power. The latter value decreases with the decrease of the labour-time necessary for its reproduction. The total decrease of necessary labour-time is equal to the sum of all the different reductions in labour-time which have occurred in those various distinct branches of production. Here we treat this general result as if it were the direct result and the direct purpose in each individual case. When an individual capitalist cheapens shirts, for instance, by increasing the productivity of labour, he by no means necessarily aims to reduce the value of labour-power and shorten necessary labour-time in proportion to this. But he contributes towards increasing the general rate of surplus-value only in so far as he ultimately contributes to this result.[3] The general and necessary tendencies of capital must be distinguished from their forms of appearance.

While it is not our intention here to consider the way in which the immanent laws of capitalist production manifest themselves in the external movement of the individual capitals, assert themselves as the coercive laws of competition, and therefore enter into the consciousness of the individual capitalist as the motives which drive him forward, this much is clear: a scientific analysis of competition is possible only if we can grasp the inner nature of capital, just as the apparent motions of the heavenly bodies are intelligible only to someone who is acquainted with their real motions, which are not perceptible to the senses. Nevertheless, for the understanding of the production of relative surplus-value, and merely on the basis of the results already achieved, we may add the following remarks.

If 1 hour's labour is embodied in 6d., a value of 6s. will be produced in a working day of 12 hours. Suppose that with labour of

---

3. 'Let us suppose . . . the products . . . of the manufacturer are doubled by improvement in machinery . . . he will be able to clothe his workmen by means of a smaller proportion of the entire return . . . and thus his profit will be raised. But in no other way will it be influenced' (Ramsay, op. cit., pp. 168–9).

the currently prevailing productivity twelve articles are produced in these 12 hours. Let the value of the means of production used up in each article be 6d. Under these circumstances, each article costs 1s.: 6d. for the value of the means of production, and 6d. for the value newly added in working with those means. Now let some one capitalist contrive to double the productivity of labour, and to produce twenty-four instead of twelve articles in the course of a working day of 12 hours. The value of the means of production remaining the same, the value of each article will fall to 9d., made up of 6d. for the value of the means of production and 3d. for the value newly added by the labour. Even though the productivity of labour has been doubled, the day's labour creates, as before, a new value of 6s. and no more, which is now however spread over twice as many articles. Each article now has embodied in it $\frac{1}{24}$th of this value instead of $\frac{1}{12}$th, 3d. instead of 6d.; or, what amounts to the same thing, only half an hour of labour-time, instead of a whole hour, is now added to the means of production while they are being transformed into each article. The individual value of these articles is now below their social value; in other words, they have cost less labour-time than the great bulk of the same article produced under the average social conditions. Each article costs, on an average, 1s., and represents 2 hours of social labour; but under the altered mode of production it costs only 9d., or contains only 1½ hours' labour. The real value of a commodity, however, is not its individual, but its social value; that is to say, its value is not measured by the labour-time that the article costs the producer in each individual case, but by the labour-time socially required for its production. If, therefore, the capitalist who applies the new method sells his commodity at its social value of one shilling, he sells it for 3d. above its individual value, and thus he realizes an extra surplus-value of 3d. On the other hand, the working day of 12 hours is now represented, for him, by twenty-four articles instead of twelve. Hence, in order to get rid of the product of one working day, the demand must be double what it was, i.e. the market must become twice as extensive. Other things being equal, the capitalist's commodities can only command a more extensive market if their prices are reduced. He will therefore sell them above their individual but below their social value, say at 10d. each. By this means he still squeezes an extra surplus-value of one penny out of each. This augmentation of surplus-value is pocketed by the capitalist himself, whether or not his commodities belong to the class of necessary means of subsistence, and therefore participate in determining the general value of labour-power. Hence, quite independently of this, there is a motive for each individual capitalist to cheapen his commodities by increasing the productivity of labour.

Nevertheless, even in this case, the increased production of surplus-value arises from the curtailment of the necessary labour-time, and the corresponding prolongation of the surplus labour.[4] Let the necessary labour-time amount to 10 hours, the value of a day's labour-power to 5s., the surplus labour-time to 2 hours, and the daily surplus-value to 1s. But the capitalist now produces 24 articles, which he sells at 10d. each, making 20s. in all. Since the value of the means of production is 12s., $14\frac{2}{5}$ of these articles merely replace the constant capital advanced. The labour of the 12-hour working day is represented by the remaining $9\frac{3}{5}$ articles. Since the price of the labour-power is 5s., 6 articles represent the necessary labour-time, and $3\frac{3}{5}$ articles the surplus labour. The ratio of necessary labour to surplus labour, which under average social conditions was 5:1, is now only 5:3. We may arrive at the same result in the following way. The value of the product of the working day of 12 hours is 20s. Of this sum, 12s. represent the value of the means of production, a value that merely re-appears in the finished product. There remain 8s., which are the expression in money of the value newly created during the working day. This sum is greater than the sum in which average social labour of the same kind is expressed: 12 hours of the latter labour are expressed by only 6s. The exceptionally productive labour acts as intensified labour; it creates in equal periods of time greater values than average social labour of the same kind.* But our capitalist still continues to pay as before only 5s. as the daily value of labour-power. Hence, instead of 10 hours, the worker now needs to work for only $7\frac{1}{5}$ hours in order to reproduce this value. His

---

4. 'A man's profit does not depend upon his command of the produce of other men's labour, but upon his command of labour itself. If he can sell his goods at a higher price, while his workmen's wages remain unaltered, he is clearly benefited . . . A smaller proportion of what he produces is sufficient to put that labour into motion, and a larger proportion consequently remains for himself' ([J. Cazenove] *Outlines of Political Economy*, London, 1832, pp. 49–50).

---

* See above, Section 2 of Chapter 1 (pp. 135–6), for Marx's discussion of intensified labour.

surplus labour is therefore increased by $2\frac{4}{5}$ hours, and the surplus-value he produces grows from one into 3s. Hence the capitalist who applies the improved method of production appropriates and devotes to surplus labour a greater portion of the working day than the other capitalists in the same business. He does as an individual what capital itself taken as a whole does when engaged in producing relative surplus-value. On the other hand, however, this extra surplus-value vanishes as soon as the new method of production is generalized, for then the difference between the individual value of the cheapened commodity and its social value vanishes. The law of the determination of value by labour-time makes itself felt to the individual capitalist who applies the new method of production by compelling him to sell his goods under their social value; this same law, acting as a coercive law of competition, forces his competitors to adopt the new method.[5] The general rate of surplus-value is therefore ultimately affected by the whole process only when the increase in the productivity of labour has seized upon those branches of production and cheapened those commodities that contribute towards the necessary means of subsistence, and are therefore elements of the value of labour-power.

The value of commodities stands in inverse ratio to the productivity of labour. So, too, does the value of labour-power, since it depends on the values of commodities. Relative surplus-value, however, is directly proportional to the productivity of labour. It rises and falls together with productivity. The value of money being assumed to be constant, an average social working day of 12 hours always produces the same new value, 6s., no matter how this sum may be apportioned between surplus-value and wages. But if, as a result of an increase in productivity, there is a fall in the value of the means of subsistence, and the daily value of labour-power is thereby reduced from 5s. to 3, the surplus-value will increase from 1s. to 3. 10 hours were necessary for the reproduction of the value of the labour-power; now only 6 are required. 4 hours have been set free, and can be annexed to the domain of surplus labour. Capital therefore has an immanent drive, and a constant

5. 'If my neighbour by doing much with little labour, can sell cheap, I must contrive to sell as cheap as he. So that every art, trade, or engine, doing work with labour of fewer hands, and consequently cheaper, begets in others a kind of necessity and emulation, either of using the same art, trade, or engine, or of inventing something like it, that every man may be upon the square, that no man may be able to undersell his neighbour' (*The Advantages of the East-India Trade to England*, London, 1720, p. 67).

tendency, towards increasing the productivity of labour, in order to cheapen commodities and, by cheapening commodities, to cheapen the worker himself.[6]

The absolute value of a commodity is, in itself, of no interest to the capitalist who produces it. All that interests him is the surplus-value present in it, which can be realized by sale. Realization [*Realisierung*] of the surplus-value necessarily carries with it the replacement of the value advanced. Now, since relative surplus-value increases in direct proportion to the development of the productivity of labour, while the value of commodities stands in precisely the opposite relation to the growth of productivity; since the same process both cheapens commodities and augments the surplus-value contained in them, we have here the solution of the following riddle: Why does the capitalist, whose sole concern is to produce exchange-value, continually strive to bring down the exchange-value of commodities? One of the founders of political economy, Quesnay, used to torment his opponents with this question, and they could find no answer to it. 'You acknowledge,' he says, 'that the more one can reduce the expenses and costs of labour in the manufacture of industrial products, without injury to production, the more advantageous is that reduction, because it diminishes the price of the finished article. And yet you believe that the production of wealth, which arises from the labour of the craftsmen, consists in the augmentation of the exchange-value of their products.'[7]

The shortening of the working day, therefore, is by no means

6. 'In whatever proportion the expenses of a labourer are diminished, in the same proportion will his wages be diminished, if the restraints upon industry are at the same time taken off' (*Considerations Concerning Taking Off the Bounty on Corn Exported, etc.*, London, 1753, p. 7). 'The interest of trade requires, that corn and all provisions should be as cheap as possible; for whatever makes them dear, must make labour dear also . . . in all countries, where industry is not restrained, the price of provisions must affect the price of labour. This will always be diminished when the necessaries of life grow cheaper' (ibid., p. 3). 'Wages are decreased in the same proportion as the powers of production increase. Machinery, it is true, cheapens the necessaries of life, but it also cheapens the labourer' (*A Prize Essay on the Comparative Merits of Competition and Co-operation*, London, 1834, p. 27).

7. '*Ils conviennent que plus on peut, sans préjudice, épargner de frais ou de travaux dispendieux dans la fabrication des ouvrages des artisans, plus cette épargne est profitable par la diminution des prix de ces ouvrages. Cependant ils croient que la production de richesse qui résulte des travaux des artisans consiste dans l'augmentation de la valeur vénale de leurs ouvrages*' (Quesnay, *Dialogues sur le commerce et sur les travaux des artisans*, pp. 188–9).

what is aimed at in capitalist production, when labour is economized by increasing its productivity.[8] It is only the shortening of the labour-time necessary for the production of a definite quantity of commodities that is aimed at. The fact that the worker, when the productivity of his labour has been increased, produces say ten times as many commodities as before, and thus spends one-tenth as much labour-time on each, by no means prevents him from continuing to work 12 hours as before, nor from producing in those 12 hours 1,200 articles instead of 120. Indeed, his working day may simultaneously be prolonged, so as to make him produce say 1,400 articles in 14 hours. Therefore in the treatises of economists of the stamp of MacCulloch, Ure, Senior and the like, we may read on one page that the worker owes a debt of gratitude to capital for developing his productivity, because the necessary labour-time is thereby shortened, and on the next page that he must prove his gratitude by working in future for 15 hours instead of 10. The objective of the development of the productivity of labour within the context of capitalist production is the shortening of that part of the working day in which the worker must work for himself, and the lengthening, thereby, of the other part of the day, in which he is free to work for nothing for the capitalist. How far this result can also be attained without cheapening commodities will appear from the following chapters, where we examine the particular methods of producing relative surplus-value.

8. 'These speculators, who are so economical of the labour of the workers they would have to pay' (J. N. Bidaut, *Du monopole qui s'établit dans les arts industriels et le commerce*, Paris, 1828, p. 13). 'The employer will be always on the stretch to economise time and labour' (Dugald Stewart, *Lectures on Political Economy*, in *Works*, ed. by Sir W. Hamilton, Vol. 8, Edinburgh, 1855, p. 318). 'Their' (the capitalists') 'interest is that the productive powers of the labourers they employ should be the greatest possible. On promoting that power their attention is fixed and almost exclusively fixed' (R. Jones, op. cit., Lecture III [p. 38]).

Chapter 13: Co-operation

Capitalist production only really begins, as we have already seen, when each individual capital simultaneously employs a comparatively large number of workers, and when, as a result, the labour-process is carried on on an extensive scale, and yields relatively large quantities of products. A large number of workers working together, at the same time, in one place (or, if you like, in the same field of labour), in order to produce the same sort of commodity under the command of the same capitalist, constitutes the starting-point of capitalist production. This is true both historically and conceptually. With regard to the mode of production itself, manufacture [*Manufaktur*] can hardly be distinguished, in its earliest stages, from the handicraft trades [*Handwerksindustrie*] of the guilds, except by the greater number of workers simultaneously employed by the same individual capital. It is merely an enlargement of the workshop of the master craftsman of the guilds.

At first, then, the difference is purely quantitative. We have shown that the surplus-value produced by a given capital is equal to the surplus-value produced by each worker multiplied by the number of workers simultaneously employed. The number of workers does not in itself affect either the rate of surplus-value or the degree of exploitation of labour-power, and, with regard to the production of commodity-values in general, every qualitative alteration in the labour process appears to be irrelevant. If a working day of 12 hours is objectified in 6 shillings, 1,200 working days of 12 hours will be objectified in 1,200 times 6 shillings. In one case $12 \times 1,200$ working-hours are incorporated in the products, and in the other case 12 working-hours. In the production of value a number of workers merely rank as so many individual workers, and it therefore makes no difference in the value produced whether the 1,200 men work separately or united under the command of one capitalist.

Nevertheless, within certain limits, a modification does take place. The labour objectified in value is labour of an average social quality, it is an expression of average labour-power. Any average magnitude, however, is merely the average of a number of separate magnitudes all of one kind, but differing in quantity. In every industry, each individual worker differs from the average worker. These individual differences, or 'errors' as they are called in mathematics, compensate each other and vanish whenever a certain minimum number of workers are employed together. Edmund Burke, that famous sophist and sycophant, goes so far as to make the following assertion, based on his practical observations as a farmer: that 'in so small a platoon' as that of five farm labourers, all individual differences in the labour vanish, and that consequently any given five adult farm labourers taken together will do as much work in the same time as any other five.[1] But however that may be, it is clear that the collective working day of a large number of workers employed simultaneously, divided by the number of these workers, gives one day of average social labour. For example, let the working day of each individual be 12 hours. Then the collective working day of twelve men simultaneously employed consists of 144 hours; and although the labour of each of the dozen men may diverge more or less from average social labour, each of them requiring a different amount of time for the same operation, the working day of every one possesses the qualities of an average social working day, because it forms one-twelfth of the collective working day of 144 hours. From the point of view of the capitalist who employs these twelve men, the working day is that of the whole dozen. Each individual man's day is an aliquot

1. 'Unquestionably, there is a good deal of difference between the value of one man's labour and that of another from strength, dexterity, and honest application. But I am quite sure, from my best observation, that any given five men will, in their total, afford a proportion of labour equal to any other five within the periods of life I have stated; that is, that among such five men there will be one possessing all the qualifications of a good workman, one bad, and the other three middling, and approximating to the first and the last. So that in so small a platoon as that of even five, you will find the full complement of all that five men can earn' (E. Burke, op. cit., pp. 15–16). Cf. Quételet on the average individual.*

    * Jacques Quételet (1796–1874) was a Belgian statistician and astronomer. In the 1840s he developed the theory, based on his statistical investigations, that there was an 'average man' who could be derived by applying the theory of probabilities to statistical data. Cf. in particular his *Du Système social et des lois qui la régissent*, Paris, 1848.

part of the collective working day, no matter whether the twelve men help each other in their work, or whether the connection between their operations consists merely in the fact that the men are all working for the same capitalist. But if the twelve men are employed in six pairs, by six different 'small masters', it will be entirely a matter of chance whether each of these masters produces the same value, and consequently whether he secures the general rate of surplus-value. Divergences would occur in individual cases. If one worker required considerably more time for the production of a commodity than was socially necessary, the duration of the necessary labour-time would, in his case, diverge significantly from the labour-time socially necessary, the average labour-time. His labour would therefore not count as average labour, and his labour-power would not count as average labour-power. It would either be unsaleable, or saleable only at less than the average value of labour-power. A fixed minimum of efficiency in all labour is therefore assumed, and we shall see later on that capitalist pr duction provides the means of fixing this minimum. Neverthel this minimum diverges from the average, although on the ꜱ͟ꜱ͟ ꜱ͟er hand the capitalist has to pay the average value of labour-power. Of the six small masters, then, one would squeeze out more than the average rate of surplus-value, another less. The inequalities would cancel out for the society as a whole, but not for the individual masters. The law of valorization therefore comes fully into its own for the individual producer only when he produces as a capitalist and employs a number of workers simultaneously, i.e. when from the outset he sets in motion labour of a socially average character.[2]

Even without an alteration in the method of work, the simultaneous employment of a large number of workers produces a revolution in the objective conditions of the labour process. The buildings where the workers actually work, the store-houses for the raw material, the implements and utensils they use simultaneously or in turns; in short, a portion of the means of production, are now consumed jointly in the labour process. On the one hand,

2. Professor Roscher claims to have discovered that one needlewoman employed by his wife during two days does more work than two needlewomen employed together on the same day.* The learned professor ought not to study the capitalist process of production in the nursery, nor under circumstances where the protagonist of the drama, the capitalist, is missing.

* W. Roscher, *Die Grundlagen der Nationalökonomie*, 3rd edn, Stuttgart, 1858, pp. 88–9.

the exchange-value of these means of production is not increased; for the exchange-value of a commodity is not raised by any increase in the exploitation of its use-value. On the other hand, they are used in common, and therefore on a larger scale than before. A room where twenty weavers work at twenty looms must be larger than the room of a single weaver with two assistants. But it costs less labour to build one workshop for twenty persons than to build ten to accommodate two weavers each; thus the value of the means of production concentrated for use in common on a large scale does not increase in direct proportion to their extent and useful effect. When consumed in common, they give up a smaller part of their value to each single product; partly because the total value they part with is spread over a greater number of products, and partly because their value, although it is greater in absolute terms, is relatively less, looked at from the point of view of their sphere of action, than the value of separate means of production. Owing to this, the value of a part of the constant capital falls, and, in proportion to the size of this fall, the total value of the commodity also falls. The effect is the same as if the means of production had cost less. This economy in the application of the means of production arises entirely out of their joint consumption in the labour process by many workers. Moreover, this character of being necessary conditions of social labour, a character that distinguishes them from the dispersed and relatively more costly means of production of isolated, independent workers or small masters, is maintained even when the numerous workers assembled together do not assist each other but merely work side by side. A portion of the instruments of labour acquires this social character before the labour process itself does so.

Economy in the use of the means of production has to be considered from two points of view. Firstly, in so far as it cheapens commodities, and thereby brings about a fall in the value of labour-power. Secondly, in so far as it alters the ratio of surplus-value to the total capital advanced, i.e. to the sum of the values of its constant and variable components. The latter aspect will not be considered until the first section of Volume 3 of this work.* In

* Cf. *Capital*, Vol. 3, Ch. 2, 'The Rate of Profit'. The ratio mentioned in the text, namely $\frac{s}{c + v}$, is the rate of profit (since $c + v = C$), as opposed to the rate of surplus-value, which is $\frac{s}{v}$.

order that we may treat them in their proper context, many other points relevant here have also been relegated to the third volume. The particular course taken by our analysis forces this tearing apart of the object under investigation; this corresponds also to the spirit of capitalist production. Here the worker finds the instruments of labour existing independently of him as another man's property, hence economy in their use appears, from his standpoint, to be a separate operation, one that does not concern him, and therefore has no connection with the methods by which his own personal productivity is increased.

When numerous workers work together side by side in accordance with a plan, whether in the same process, or in different but connected processes, this form of labour is called co-operation.[3]

Just as the offensive power of a squadron of cavalry, or the defensive power of an infantry regiment, is essentially different from the sum of the offensive or defensive powers of the individual soldiers taken separately, so the sum total of the mechanical forces exerted by isolated workers differs from the social force that is developed when many hands co-operate in the same undivided operation, such as raising a heavy weight, turning a winch or getting an obstacle out of the way.[4] In such cases the effect of the combined labour could either not be produced at all by isolated individual labour, or it could be produced only by a great expenditure of time, or on a very dwarf-like scale. Not only do we have here an increase in the productive power of the individual, by means of co-operation, but the creation of a new productive power, which is intrinsically a collective one.[5]

Apart from the new power that arises from the fusion of many forces into a single force, mere social contact begets in most industries a rivalry and a stimulation of the 'animal spirits', which heightens the efficiency of each individual worker. This is why a dozen people working together will produce far more, in their

3. '*Concours de forces*' (Destutt de Tracy, op. cit., p. 80).
4. 'There are numerous operations of so simple a kind as not to admit a division into parts, which cannot be performed without the co-operation of many pairs of hands. I would instance the lifting of a large tree on to a wain . . . everything, in short, which cannot be done unless a great many pairs of hands help each other in the same undivided employment and at the same time' (E. G. Wakefield, *A View of the Art of Colonization*, London, 1849, p. 168).
5. 'As one man cannot, and ten men must strain to lift a ton of weight, yet 100 men can do it only by the strength of a finger of each of them' (John Bellers, *Proposals for Raising a Colledge of Industry*, London, 1696, p. 21).

collective working day of 144 hours than twelve isolated men each working for 12 hours, and far more than one man who works 12 days in succession.[6] This originates from the fact that man, if not as Aristotle thought a political animal,[7] is at all events a social animal.

Although a number of men may be simultaneously occupied together on the same work, or the same kind of work, the labour of each, as a part of the labour of all, may correspond to a distinct phase of the labour process; and as a result of the system of co-operation, the object of labour passes through the phases of the process more quickly than before. For instance, if a dozen masons place themselves in a row, so as to pass stones from the foot of a ladder to its summit, each of them does the same thing; and yet their separate acts form connected parts of one total operation; these acts are particular phases which each stone must go through, and the stones are thus carried up more quickly by the twenty-four hands of the row of men than they could be if each man went separately up and down the ladder with his load.[8] The

6. 'There is also' (when the same number of men are employed by one farmer on 300 acres, instead of by ten farmers with 30 acres apiece) 'an advantage in the proportion of servants, which will not so easily be understood but by practical men; for it is natural to say, as 1 is to 4, so are 3 to 12: but this will not hold good in practice; for in harvest time and many other operations which require that kind of despatch by the throwing many hands together, the work is better and more expeditiously done: f.i. in harvest, 2 drivers, 2 loaders, 2 pitchers, 2 rakers, and the rest at the rick, or in the barn, will despatch double the work that the same number of hands would do if divided into different gangs on different farms' (*An Inquiry into the Connection between the Present Price of Provisions, and the Size of Farms*, by a farmer [J. Arbuthnot], London, 1773, pp. 7–8).

7. The real meaning of Aristotle's definition is that man is by nature citizen of a town.* This is quite as characteristic of classical antiquity as Franklin's definition of man as a tool-making animal is characteristic of Yankeedom.

8. 'It should be noted further that this partial division of labour can occur even when the workers are engaged in the same task. Masons, for example, engaged in passing bricks from hand to hand to a higher stage of the building, are all performing the same task, and yet there does exist amongst them a sort of division of labour. This consists in the fact that each of them passes the brick to a given space, and, taken together, they make it arrive much more quickly at the required spot than they would do if each of them carried his brick separately to the upper storey' (F. Skarbek, *Théorie des richesses sociales*, 2nd edn, Paris, 1839, Vol. 1, pp. 97–8).

*'It is evident that the state (πόλις) is a creation of nature, and that man is by nature a political animal (πολιτικὸν ζῷον)' (Aristotle, *Politics*, Book 1, 2).

object of labour is carried over the same distance in a shorter time. Again, a combination of labour occurs whenever a building, for instance, is taken in hand on different sides simultaneously; although here too the co-operating masons are doing the same work, or the same kind of work. The twelve masons, in their collective working day of 144 hours, make much more progress with the building than one mason could make working for 12 days, or 144 hours. The reason for this is that a body of men working together have hands and eyes both in front and behind, and can be said to be to a certain extent omnipresent. The various parts of the product come to fruition simultaneously.

In the above instances we stressed the point that the men do the same work, or the same kind of work, because this, the most simple form of common labour, plays a great part in co-operation, even at its most fully developed stage. If the labour process is complicated, then the sheer number of the co-operators permits the apportionment of various operations to different hands, and consequently their simultaneous performance. The time necessary for the completion of the whole work is thereby shortened.[9]

In many industries there are critical moments, that is to say periods of time determined by the nature of the labour process itself, during which certain definite results must be obtained. For instance, if a flock of sheep has to be shorn or a field of wheat has to be cut and harvested, the quantity and quality of the product depends on the initiation and the completion of the work at certain definite points in time. In these cases, the time the labour process may take is laid down in advance, just as it is in fishing for herrings. A single person cannot carve a working day of more than say, 12 hours, out of the natural day, but 100 men co-operating can extend the working day to 1,200 hours. The shortness of the time allowed for the work is compensated for by the large mass of labour thrown into the field of production at the decisive moment. The completion of the task within the proper time depends on the simultaneous application of numerous combined working days; the amount of useful effect depends on the number of workers;

9. 'If it is a question of undertaking a complex piece of labour, different things must be done simultaneously. One person does one thing, while another does something else, and they all contribute to the effect that a single man would be unable to produce. One rows while another holds the rudder, and a third casts the net or harpoons the fish; in this way fishing enjoys a success that would be impossible without this co-operation' (Destutt de Tracy, op. cit., p. 78).

this number, however, is always smaller than the number of isolated workers that would be required to do the same amount of
work in the same period.[10] It is owing to the absence of this kind
of co-operation that a great quantity of corn is wasted every year
in the western part of the United States, and the same thing happens to cotton in those eastern parts of India where English rule
has destroyed the old communities.[11]

On the one hand, co-operation allows work to be carried on over
a large area; for certain labour processes, therefore, it is required
simply by the physical constitution of the object of labour. Examples of this are the draining of marshes, the construction of
dykes, irrigation, and the building of canals, roads and railways.
On the other hand, while extending the scale of production it
renders possible a relative contraction of its arena. This simultaneous restriction of space and extension of effectiveness, which
allows a large number of incidental expenses (*faux frais**) to be
spared, results from the massing together of workers and of various
labour processes, and from the concentration of the means of
production.[12]

10. 'The doing of it' (agricultural labour) 'at the critical juncture is of so
much the greater consequence' (*An Inquiry into the Connection between the
Present Price, etc.* [J. Arbuthnot], p. 7). 'In agriculture, there is no more
important factor than that of time' (Liebig, *Über Theorie und Praxis in der
Landwirtschaft*, 1856, p. 23).

11. 'The next evil is one which one would scarcely expect to find in a country
which exports more labour than any other in the world, with the exception
perhaps of China and England – the impossibility of procuring a sufficient
number of hands to clean the cotton. The consequence of this is that large
quantities of the crop are left unpicked, while another portion is gathered
from the ground when it has fallen, and is of course discoloured and partially
rotted, so that for want of labour at the proper season the cultivator is actually
forced to submit to the loss of a large part of that crop for which England is
so anxiously looking' (*Bengal Hurkaru. Bi-monthly Overland Summary of
News*, 22 July 1861).

12. In the progress of cultivation, 'all, and perhaps more than all, the
capital and labour which once loosely occupied 500 acres, are now concentrated
for the more complete tillage of 100'. Although 'relatively to the amount of
capital and labour employed, space is concentrated, it is an enlarged sphere of
production, as compared to the sphere of production formerly occupied or
worked upon by one single independent agent of production' (R. Jones, *An
Essay on the Distribution of Wealth*, Part I, 'On Rent', London, 1831, p.191).

---

* Literally 'false costs'; but *faux frais* is a technical expression used by the
French economists of the early nineteenth century (for example Garnier and
Say) to cover expenses not directly incurred in the course of production. The

The combined working day produces a greater quantity of use-values than an equal sum of isolated working days, and consequently diminishes the labour-time necessary for the production of a given useful effect. Whether the combined working day, in a given case, acquires this increased productivity because it heightens the mechanical force of labour, or extends its sphere of action over a greater space, or contracts the field of production relatively to the scale of production, or at the critical moment sets large masses of labour to work, or excites rivalry between individuals and raises their animal spirits, or impresses on the similar operations carried on by a number of men the stamp of continuity and many-sidedness, or performs different operations simultaneously, or economizes the means of production by use in common, or lends to individual labour the character of average social labour – whichever of these is the cause of the increase, the special productive power of the combined working day is, under all circumstances, the social productive power of labour, or the productive power of social labour. This power arises from co-operation itself. When the worker co-operates in a planned way with others, he strips off the fetters of his individuality, and develops the capabilities of his species.[13]

As a general rule, workers cannot co-operate without being brought together: their assembly in one place is a necessary condition for their co-operation. Hence wage-labourers cannot co-operate unless they are employed simultaneously by the same capital, the same capitalist, and therefore unless their labour-powers are bought simultaneously by him. The total value of these labour-powers, or the amount of the wages of these workers for a day or a week, as the case may be, must be ready in the pocket of the capitalist before the workers themselves are ready to start the process of production. The payment of 300 workers at once, even though only for one day, requires a greater outlay of capital than the payment of a smaller number of men, week by week, during a

13. 'The strength of the individual man is very small, but the union of a number of very small forces produces a collective force which is greater than the sum of all the partial forces, so that merely by being joined together these forces can reduce the time required, and extend the field of their action' (G. R. Carli, note to P. Verri, op. cit., Vol. 15, p. 196).

idea of *faux frais de production* originated in Adam Smith's distinction between productive and unproductive labour. Cf. *Theories of Surplus-Value*, Part I, p. 167.

whole year. Hence the number of the workers that co-operate, or the scale of co-operation, depends in the first instance on the amount of capital that the individual capitalist can spare for the purchase of labour-power; in other words, on the extent to which a single capitalist has command over the means of subsistence of a number of workers.

And as with variable capital, so also with constant capital. For example, the outlay on raw material is thirty times as great for the capitalist who employs 300 men as it is for each of the thirty capitalists who employ ten men. The value and quantity of the instruments of labour used in common does not, it is true, increase at the same rate as the number of workers, but it does increase very considerably. Hence, concentration of large masses of the means of production in the hands of individual capitalists is a material condition for the co-operation of wage-labourers, and the extent of co-operation, or the scale of production, depends on the extent of this concentration.

We saw in a former chapter that a certain minimum amount of capital was necessary in order that the number of workers simultaneously employed, and consequently the amount of surplus-value produced, might suffice to liberate the employer himself from manual labour, to convert him from a small master into a capitalist, and thus formally to establish the capital-relation. We now see that a certain minimum amount is a material condition for the conversion of numerous isolated and independent processes into one combined social process.

We also saw that, at first, the subjection of labour to capital was only a formal result of the fact that the worker, instead of working for himself, works for, and consequently under, the capitalist. Through the co-operation of numerous wage-labourers, the command of capital develops into a requirement for carrying on the labour process itself, into a real condition of production. That a capitalist should command in the field of production is now as indispensable as that a general should command on the field of battle.

All directly social or communal labour on a large scale requires, to a greater or lesser degree, a directing authority, in order to secure the harmonious co-operation of the activities of individuals, and to perform the general functions that have their origin in the motion of the total productive organism, as distinguished from the motion of its separate organs. A single violin player is his own conductor: an orchestra requires a separate one. The work of directing, superintending and adjusting becomes one of the functions of capital, from the moment that the labour under capital's control becomes co-operative. As a specific function of capital, the directing function acquires its own special characteristics.

The driving motive and determining purpose of capitalist production is the self-valorization of capital to the greatest possible extent,[14] i.e. the greatest possible production of surplus-value, hence the greatest possible exploitation of labour-power by the capitalist. As the number of the co-operating workers increases, so too does their resistance to the domination of capital, and, necessarily, the pressure put on by capital to overcome this resistance. The control exercised by the capitalist is not only a special function arising from the nature of the social labour process, and peculiar to that process, but it is at the same time a function of the exploitation of a social labour process, and is consequently conditioned by the unavoidable antagonism between the exploiter and the raw material of his exploitation. Similarly, as the means of production extend, the necessity increases for some effective control over the proper application of them, because they confront the wage-labourer as the property of another [*fremdes Eigentum*].[15] Moreover, the co-operation of wage-labourers is entirely brought about by the capital that employs them. Their unification into one single productive body, and the establishment of a connection between their individual functions, lies outside their competence. These things are not their own act, but

14. 'Profits . . . is the sole end of trade' (J. Vanderlint, op. cit., p. 11).

15. On 26 May 1866, a philistine English periodical, the *Spectator*, reported that after the introduction of a sort of partnership between the capitalist and the workers in the 'Wirework Company of Manchester', 'the first result was a sudden decrease in waste, the men not seeing why they should waste their own property any more than any other master's, and waste is, perhaps, next to bad debts, the greatest source of manufacturing loss'. The same paper finds that the main defect in the Rochdale co-operative experiments* is this: 'They showed that associations of workmen could manage shops, mills, and almost all forms of industry with success, and they immediately improved the condition of the men, but then they did not leave a clear place for masters.' *Quelle horreur!*

*The first co-operative society was set up by the workers of Rochdale in 1844, under the influence of utopian socialist ideas. At first a society of consumers alone, it later entered into production on its own account.

the act of the capital that brings them together and maintains them in that situation. Hence the interconnection between their various labours confronts them, in the realm of ideas, as a plan drawn up by the capitalist, and, in practice, as his authority, as the powerful will of a being outside them, who subjects their activity to his purpose.

If capitalist direction is thus twofold in content, owing to the twofold nature of the process of production which has to be directed – on the one hand a social labour process for the creation of a product, and on the other hand capital's process of valorization – in form it is purely despotic. As co-operation extends its scale, this despotism develops the forms that are peculiar to it. Just as at first the capitalist is relieved from actual labour as soon as his capital has reached that minimum amount with which capitalist production, properly speaking, first begins, so now he hands over the work of direct and constant supervision of the individual workers and groups of workers to a special kind of wage-labourer. An industrial army of workers under the command of a capitalist requires, like a real army, officers (managers) and N.C.O.s (foremen, overseers), who command during the labour process in the name of capital. The work of supervision becomes their established and exclusive function. When comparing the mode of production of isolated peasants or independent artisans with the plantation economy which rests on slavery, political economists count this labour of superintendence as part of the *faux frais de production*.[16] But when considering the capitalist mode of production they on the contrary identify the function of direction which arises out of the nature of the communal labour process with the function of direction which is made necessary by the capitalist and therefore antagonistic character of that process.[17] It is not because he is a leader of industry that a man is a capitalist; on the contrary, he is a leader of industry because he is a capitalist. The leadership of

16. Professor Cairnes, after stating that the 'superintendence of labour' is a leading feature of production by slaves in the southern states of the U.S.A., continues: 'The peasant proprietor' (of the North) 'appropriating the whole produce of his toil, needs no other stimulus to exertion. Superintendence is here completely dispensed with' (Cairnes, op. cit., pp. 48–9).

17. Sir James Steuart, a writer altogether remarkable for his quick eye for the characteristic social distinctions between different modes of production, says: 'Why do large undertakings in the manufacturing way ruin private industry, but by coming nearer to the simplicity of slaves?' (*Principles of Political Economy*, London, 1767, Vol. 1, pp. 167–8).

industry is an attribute of capital, just as in feudal times the functions of general and judge were attributes of landed property.[18]

The worker is the owner of his labour-power until he has finished bargaining for its sale with the capitalist, and he can sell no more than what he has – i.e. his individual, isolated labour-power. This relation between capital and labour is in no way altered by the fact that the capitalist, instead of buying the labour-power of one man, buys that of 100, and enters into separate contracts with 100 unconnected men instead of with one. He can set the 100 men to work, without letting them co-operate. He pays them the value of 100 independent labour-powers, but he does not pay for the combined labour-power of the 100. Being independent of each other, the workers are isolated. They enter into relations with the capitalist, but not with each other. Their co-operation only begins with the labour process, but by then they have ceased to belong to themselves. On entering the labour process they are incorporated into capital. As co-operators, as members of a working organism, they merely form a particular mode of existence of capital. Hence the productive power developed by the worker socially is the productive power of capital. The socially productive power of labour develops as a free gift to capital whenever the workers are placed under certain conditions, and it is capital which places them under these conditions. Because this power costs capital nothing, while on the other hand it is not developed by the worker until his labour itself belongs to capital, it appears as a power which capital possesses by its nature – a productive power inherent in capital.

The colossal effects of simple co-operation are to be seen in the gigantic structures erected by the ancient Asiatics, Egyptians, Etruscans, etc. 'It has happened in times past that these Oriental States, after supplying the expenses of their civil and military establishments, have found themselves in possession of a surplus which they could apply to works of magnificence or utility and in the construction of these their command over the hands and arms of almost the entire non-agricultural population has produced stupendous monuments which still indicate their power. The teeming valley of the Nile ... produced food for a swarming non-agricultural population, and this food, belonging to the monarch

18. Hence Auguste Comte and his school might just as well have shown that feudal lords are an eternal necessity, in the same way as they have done in the case of the lords of capital.

and the priesthood, afforded the means of erecting the mighty monuments which filled the land ... In moving the colossal statues and vast masses of which the transport creates wonder, human labour almost alone was prodigally used ... The number of the labourers and the concentration of their efforts sufficed. We see mighty coral reefs rising from the depths of the ocean into islands and firm land, yet each individual depositor is puny, weak, and contemptible. The non-agricultural labourers of an Asiatic monarchy have little but their individual bodily exertions to bring to the task, but their number is their strength, and the power of directing these masses gave rise to the palaces and temples, the pyramids, and the armies of gigantic statues of which the remains astonish and perplex us. It is that confinement of the revenues which feed them, to one or a few hands, which makes such undertakings possible.'[19] This power of Asiatic and Egyptian kings, of Etruscan theocrats, etc. has in modern society been transferred to the capitalist, whether he appears as an isolated individual or, as in the case of joint-stock companies, in combination with others.

Co-operation in the labour process, such as we find it at the beginning of human civilization, among hunting peoples[20] or, say, as a predominant feature of the agriculture of Indian communities, is based on the one hand on the common ownership of the conditions of production, and on the other hand on the fact that in those cases the individual has as little torn himself free from the umbilical cord of his tribe or community as a bee has from his hive. Both of these characteristics distinguish this form of co-operation from capitalist co-operation. The sporadic application of co-operation on a large scale in ancient times, in the Middle Ages, and in modern colonies, rests on direct relations of domination and servitude, in most cases on slavery. As against this, the capitalist form presupposes from the outset the free wage-labourer who sells his labour-power to capital. Historically, however, this form is developed in opposition to peasant agriculture and independent handicrafts, whether in guilds or not.[21]

19. R. Jones, *Textbook of Lectures, etc.*, pp. 77–8. The ancient Assyrian, Egyptian and similar collections in London and the other European capitals allow us to witness those co-operative labour processes with our own eyes.

20. Linguet is probably right in his *Théorie des lois civiles* when he declares that hunting was the first form of co-operation, and that the man-hunt (war) was one of the earliest forms of hunting.

21. Peasant agriculture on a small scale and production by independent artisans, both of which, on the one hand, form the basis of the feudal mode of

From the standpoint of the peasant and the artisan, capitalist co-operation does not appear as a particular historical form of co-operation; instead, co-operation itself appears as a historical form peculiar to, and specifically distinguishing, the capitalist process of production.

Just as the social productive power of labour that is developed by co-operation appears to be the productive power of capital, so co-operation itself, contrasted with the process of production carried on by isolated independent workers, or even by small masters, appears to be a specific form of the capitalist process of production. It is the first change experienced by the actual labour process when subjected to capital. It takes place spontaneously and naturally. The simultaneous employment of a large number of wage-labourers in the same labour process, which is a necessary condition for this change, also forms the starting-point of capitalist production. This starting-point coincides with the birth of capital itself. If then, on the one hand, the capitalist mode of production is a historically necessary condition for the transformation of the labour process into a social process, so, on the other hand, this social form of the labour process is a method employed by capital for the more profitable exploitation of labour, by increasing its productive power.

In its simple shape, as investigated so far, co-operation is a necessary concomitant of all production on a large scale, but it does not in itself represent a fixed form characteristic of a particular epoch in the development of the capitalist mode of production. At the most it appears to do so, and then only approximately, in the handicraft-like beginnings of manufacture[22] and in that kind of large-scale agriculture which corresponds to the period of manufacture, and is distinguished from peasant agriculture mainly by the number of workers simultaneously employed and the mass of means of production concentrated for their

---

production, and, on the other hand, appear alongside capitalist production after the dissolution of the feudal mode, equally form the economic foundation of the communities of classical antiquity at their best period, after the primitive oriental system of common ownership of land had disappeared, and before slavery had seized on production in earnest.

22. 'Whether the united skill, industry, and emulation of many together on the same work be not the way to advance it? And whether it had been otherwise possible for England to have carried on her Woollen Manufacture to so great a perfection?' (Berkeley, *The Querist*, London, 1750, p. 56, query No. 521).

use. Simple co-operation has always been, and continues to be, the predominant form in those branches of production in which capital operates on a large scale, but the division of labour and machinery play only an insignificant part.

Co-operation remains the fundamental form of the capitalist mode of production, although in its simple shape it continues to appear as one particular form alongside the more developed ones.

Chapter 14: The Division of Labour and Manufacture

I. THE DUAL ORIGIN OF MANUFACTURE

That form of co-operation which is based on division of labour assumes its classical shape in manufacture. As a characteristic form of the capitalist process of production it prevails throughout the manufacturing period properly so called, which extends, roughly speaking, from the middle of the sixteenth century to the last third of the eighteenth century.

Manufacture originates in two ways:

1. By the assembling together in one workshop, under the control of a single capitalist, of workers belonging to various independent handicrafts, through whose hands a given article must pass on its way to completion. A carriage, for example, was formerly the product of a great number of independent craftsmen, such as wheelwrights, harness-makers, tailors, locksmiths, upholsterers, turners, fringe-makers, glaziers, painters, polishers, gilders, etc. In the *manufacture* of carriages, however, all these different craftsmen are assembled in one building where the unfinished product passes from hand to hand. It is true that a carriage cannot be gilded before it has been made. But if a number of carriages are being made simultaneously, some may be in the hands of the gilders while others are going through an earlier process. So far, we are still on the footing of simple co-operation, which finds its materials ready to hand in the shape of men and things. But very soon an important change takes place. The tailor, the locksmith and the other craftsmen are now exclusively occupied in the making of carriages; they therefore gradually lose the habit, and therefore the ability, of carrying on their old trade in all its ramifications. But on the other hand, their activity, which is now entirely one-sided, assumes the form most appropriate to its narrowed sphere of effectiveness. At first, the manufacture of carriages appeared as a combination of

various independent handicrafts. But it gradually began to signify the splitting-up of carriage production into its various detailed operations, and each single operation crystallized into the exclusive function of a particular worker, the manufacture as a whole being performed by these partial workers in conjunction. In the same way, cloth manufacture, as also a whole series of other manufactures, arose from combining together different handicrafts under the command of a single capitalist.[1]

2. Manufacture can also arise in exactly the opposite way. One capitalist simultaneously employs in one workshop a number of craftsmen who all do the same work, or the same kind of work, such as making paper, type or needles. This is co-operation in its simplest form. Each of these craftsmen (with the help, perhaps, of one or two apprentices) makes the entire commodity, and he consequently performs in succession all the operations necessary to produce it. He still works in his old handicraft-like way. But very soon external circumstances cause a different use to be made of the concentration of the workers on one spot and the simultaneousness of their work. An increased quantity of the article has perhaps to be delivered within a given time. The work is therefore divided up. Instead of each man being allowed to perform all the various operations in succession, these operations are changed into disconnected, isolated ones, carried on side by side; each is assigned to a different craftsman, and the whole of them together are performed simultaneously by the co-operators. This accidental division is repeated, develops advantages of its own and gradually ossifies into a systematic division of labour.

1. The following quotation provides a more modern example of this mode of formation of manufacture: The silk spinning and weaving of Lyons and Nîmes 'is entirely patriarchal; it employs a large number of women and children, but without exhausting or ruining them; it allows them to stay in their beautiful valleys of the Drôme, the Var, the Isère, the Vaucluse, cultivating their silkworms and unwinding their cocoons; it never becomes a true factory industry. However, the principle of the division of labour takes on a special character . . . so that it can be applied to the high degree required here. There do indeed exist winders, throwsters, dyers, sizers, and finally weavers; but they are not assembled in the same workshop, nor are they dependent on a single master; they are all independent' (A. Blanqui, *Cours d'économie industrielle, recueilli par A. Blaise*, Paris, 1838–9, p. 79). Since Blanqui wrote this, the various independent workers have to some extent been united in factories. [Addition by Engels to the fourth German edition:] And since Marx wrote the above, the power-loom has invaded these factories, and is now rapidly superseding the hand-loom. The Krefeld silk industry also has a tale to tell about this.

The commodity, from being the individual product of an independent craftsman, becomes the social product of a union of craftsmen, each of whom performs one, and only one, of the constituent partial operations. The same operations which, in the case of a papermaker belonging to a guild in Germany, merged into each other as the successive acts of one craftsman became in Dutch paper manufacture a number of partial operations performed side by side by numerous workers acting in cooperation. The needlemaker of Nuremberg, organized in his guild, laid the foundation for English needle manufacture. But while in Nuremberg that single craftsman performed a series of perhaps twenty operations one after the other, in England it was not long before there were twenty needlemakers side by side, each performing only one operation of the twenty. Finally, as a result of further experience, each of those twenty operations was again split up, isolated and made entirely independent, so that it became the exclusive function of a separate worker.

The mode in which manufacture arises, its growth out of handicrafts, is therefore twofold. On the one hand it arises from the combination of various independent trades, which lose that independence and become specialized to such an extent that they are reduced to merely supplementary and partial operations in the production of one particular commodity. On the other hand, it arises from the co-operation of craftsmen in one particular handicraft; it splits up that handicraft into its various detailed operations, isolating these operations and developing their mutual independence to the point where each becomes the exclusive function of a particular worker. On the one hand, therefore, manufacture either introduces division of labour into a process of production, or further develops that division; on the other hand it combines together handicrafts that were formerly separate. But whatever may have been its particular starting-point, its final form is always the same – a productive mechanism whose organs are human beings.

For a proper understanding of the division of labour in manufacture, it is essential to keep the following points firmly in mind. Firstly, the analysis of a process of production into its particular phases here coincides completely with the decomposition of a handicraft into its different partial operations. Whether complex or simple, each operation has to be done by hand, retains the character of a handicraft, and is therefore dependent on the strength, skill, quickness and sureness with which the individual worker manipulates his tools. Handicraft remains the basis, a technically narrow basis which excludes a really scientific division of the production process into its component parts, since every partial process undergone by the product must be capable of being done by hand, and of forming a separate handicraft. It is precisely because the skill of the craftsman thus continues to be the foundation of the production process that every worker becomes exclusively assigned to a partial function and that his labour-power becomes transformed into the life-long organ of this partial function. Secondly, this division of labour is a particular sort of co-operation, and many of its advantages spring from the nature of co-operation in general, not from this particular form of it.

2. THE SPECIALIZED WORKER AND HIS TOOLS

If we now go into more detail, it is firstly clear that a worker who performs the same simple operation for the whole of his life converts his body into the automatic, one-sided implement of that operation. Consequently, he takes less time in doing it than the craftsman who performs a whole series of operations in succession. The collective worker, who constitutes the living mechanism of manufacture, is made up solely of such one-sidedly specialized workers. Hence, in comparison with the independent handicraft, more is produced in less time, or in other words the productivity of labour is increased.[2] Moreover, once this partial labour is established as the exclusive function of one person, the methods it employs become perfected. The worker's continued repetition of the same narrowly defined act and the concentration of his attention on it teach him by experience how to attain the desired effect with the minimum of exertion. But since there are always several generations of workers living at one time, and working together at the manufacture of a given article, the technical skill, the tricks of the trade thus acquired, become established, and are accumulated and handed down.[3]

Manufacture, in fact, produces the skill of the specialized worker

2. 'The more any manufacture of much variety shall be distributed and assigned to different artists, the same must needs be better done and with greater expedition, with less loss of time and labour' (*The Advantages of the East-India Trade*, London, 1720, p. 71).

3. 'Easy labour is transmitted skill' (T. Hodgskin, *Popular Political Economy*, p. 48).

by reproducing and systematically driving to an extreme within the workshop the naturally developed differentiation which it found ready to hand in society. On the other hand, the conversion of a partial task into the life-long destiny of a man corresponds to the tendency shown by earlier societies towards making trades hereditary. The trades either became petrified into castes, or, in cases where definite historical conditions produced a variability in the individual which was incompatible with a caste system, they hardened into guilds. Castes and guilds arise from the action of the same natural law that regulates the differentiation of plants and animals into species and varieties, except that, when a certain degree of development has been reached, the heredity of castes and the exclusiveness of guilds are ordained as a law of society.[4] 'The muslins of Dacca in fineness, the calicoes and other piece goods of Coromandel in brilliant and durable colours, have never been surpassed. Yet they are produced without capital, machinery, division of labour, or any of those means which give such facilities to the manufacturing interest of Europe. The weaver is merely a detached individual, working a web when ordered of a customer, and with a loom of the rudest construction, consisting sometimes of a few branches or bars of wood, put roughly together. There is even no expedient for rolling up the warp; the loom must therefore be kept stretched to its full length, and becomes so inconveniently large that it cannot be contained within the hut of the manufacturer, who is therefore compelled to ply his trade in the open air, where it is interrupted by every vicissitude of the weather.'[5] It is only the special skill accumulated from generation

---

4. 'The arts too, in Egypt, have ... reached the requisite degree of perfection. For it is the only country where craftsmen may not in any way interfere in the affairs of other classes of citizen, but must follow that calling alone which by law is hereditary in their clan ... Among other peoples it is found that tradesmen divide their attention between too many objects. At one time they try agriculture, at another they take to commerce, at another they busy themselves with two or three occupations at once. In free countries they mostly frequent the popular assemblies ... In Egypt, on the contrary, a craftsman is severely punished if he meddles with affairs of State, or carries on several trades at once. Thus there is nothing to disturb their application to their calling ... Moreover, they inherit from their forefathers numerous rules of their trade, and they are eager to discover still more advantageous ways of practising it' (Diodorus Siculus, *Historische Bibliothek*, Bk I, Ch. 74).

5. H. Murray and J. Wilson, etc., *Historical and Descriptive Account of British India, etc.*, Edinburgh, 1832, Vol. 2, pp. 449–50. The Indian loom is upright, i.e. the warp is stretched vertically.

to generation, and transmitted from father to son, that gives to the Hindu, as it gives to the spider, this virtuosity. And yet the work of such a Hindu weaver is very complicated, in comparison with that of the majority of workers under the system of manufacture.

A craftsman who performs the various partial operations in the production of a finished article one after the other must at one time change his place, at another time his tools. The transition from one operation to another interrupts the flow of his labour and creates gaps in his working day, so to speak. These close up when he is tied to the same operation the whole day long; they vanish in the same proportion as the changes in his work diminish. The resulting increase of productivity is due either to an increased expenditure of labour-power in a given time – i.e. increased intensity of labour – or to a decrease in the amount of labour-power unproductively consumed. The extra expenditure of power required by every transition from rest to motion is compensated for by prolonging the duration of the normal speed of work, when once acquired. As against this, however, constant labour of one uniform kind disturbs the intensity and flow of a man's vital forces, which find recreation and delight in the change of activity itself.

The productivity of labour depends not only on the proficiency of the worker, but also on the quality of his tools. Tools of the same kind, such as knives, drills, gimlets, hammers, etc., may be employed in different processes; and the same tool may serve various purposes in a single process. But as soon as the different operations of a labour process are disconnected from each other, and each partial operation acquires in the hands of the worker a suitable form peculiar to it, alterations become necessary in the tools which previously served more than one purpose. The direction taken by this change of form is determined by the particular difficulties put in the worker's way by the unchanged form of the old tool. Manufacture is characterized by the differentiation of the instruments of labour – a differentiation whereby tools of a given sort acquire fixed shapes, adapted to each particular application – and by the specialization of these instruments, which allows full play to each special tool only in the hands of a specific kind of worker. In Birmingham alone 500 varieties of hammer are produced, and not only is each one adapted to a particular process, but several varieties often serve exclusively for the different operations in the same process. The manufacturing period simplifies, improves and multiplies the implements of labour by adapting them to the exclusive and special functions of each kind of worker.[6] It thus creates at the same time one of the material conditions for the existence of machinery, which consists of a combination of simple instruments.

The specialized worker and his instruments are the simplest elements of manufacture. Let us now turn to look at manufacture as a whole.

3. THE TWO FUNDAMENTAL FORMS OF MANUFACTURE – HETEROGENEOUS AND ORGANIC

Manufacture has two fundamental forms of articulation which, although occasionally intertwined, are essentially different in kind, and moreover play very different roles in the later transformation of manufacture into large-scale industry carried on by machinery. This double character arises from the nature of the article produced, which either results from the merely mechanical assembling of partial products made independently, or owes its completed shape to a series of connected processes and manipulations.

A locomotive, for instance, consists of more than 5,000 independent parts. It cannot however serve as an example of the first kind of genuine manufacture, for it is a creation of large-scale industry. But a watch can, and William Petty used it to illustrate the division of labour in manufacture. Formerly the individual creation of a craftsman from Nuremberg, the watch has been transformed into the social product of an immense number of specialized workers, such as mainspring makers, dial makers, spiral-spring makers, jewelled hole makers, ruby lever makers, hand makers, case makers, screw makers, gilders. Then there are numerous subdivisions, such as wheel makers (with a further division between brass and steel), pin makers, movement makers, *acheveurs de pignon* (who fix the wheels on the axles and polish the

6. In his epoch-making work on the origin of species, Darwin remarks with reference to the natural organs of plants and animals: 'As long as the same part has to perform diversified work, we can perhaps see why it should remain variable, that is, why natural selection should not have preserved or rejected each little deviation of form so carefully as when the part has to serve for some one special purpose. In the same way that a knife which has to cut all sorts of things may be of almost any shape; whilst a tool for some particular purpose must be of some particular shape' [Charles Darwin, *The Origin of Species*, Ch. 5, 'Laws of Variation'].

facets), pivot makers, *planteurs de finissage* (who put the wheels and springs in the works), *finisseurs de barillet* (who cut teeth in the wheels, make the holes of the right size, etc.), escapement makers, cylinder makers for cylinder escapements, escapement wheel makers, balance-wheel makers, makers of the *raquette* (the apparatus for regulating the watch), *planteurs d'échappement* (escapement makers proper); then *repasseurs de barillet* (who finish the box for the spring), steel polishers, wheel polishers, screw polishers, figure painters, dial enamellers (who melt the enamel on the copper), *fabricants de pendants* (who make the ring by which the case is hung), *finisseurs de charnière* (who put the brass hinges in the cover), *graveurs, ciseleurs, polisseurs de boîte*, etc., etc., and last of all the *repasseurs*, who fit together the whole watch and hand it over in a going state. Only a few parts of the watch pass through several hands; and all these *membra disjecta* come together for the first time in the hand that binds them into one mechanical whole. This external relation between the finished product and its various and diverse elements makes it a matter of chance in this case as in the case of all similar finished articles, whether the specialized workers are brought together in one workshop or not. The subdivided operations themselves may be carried on like so many independent handicrafts, as they are in the Cantons of Vaud and Neuchâtel; while in Geneva there exist large watch factories, i.e. establishments where the specialized workers directly co-operate under the control of a single capitalist. Even in the latter case the dial, springs and case are seldom made in the factory itself. To carry on the trade as a manufacture, with concentration of workers, is profitable only under exceptional conditions, because competition is at its greatest between those workers who desire to work at home, because the splitting-up of the work into a number of heterogeneous processes scarcely permits the use of instruments of labour common to all, and because the capitalist, by scattering the work around, saves any outlay on workshops, etc.[7] Nevertheless, the position of this specialized

7. In the year 1854 Geneva produced 80,000 watches, which is not one-fifth of the production in the Canton of Neuchâtel. La Chaux-de-Fonds alone, which one may look upon as a huge watch factory, produces twice as many as Geneva every year. From 1850 to 1861 Geneva produced 720,000 watches. See 'Report from Geneva on the Watch Trade' in *Reports by H.M.'s Secretaries of Embassy and Legation, on the Manufactures, Commerce, etc.*, No. 6, 1863. When the production of articles that merely consist of parts fitted together is split up into different processes, the lack of connection between

worker, who, although he works at home, does so for a capitalist (manufacturer, *établisseur*), is very different from that of the independent craftsman, who works for his own customers.[8]

The second kind of manufacture, its perfected form, produces articles that go through connected phases of development, go step by step through a series of processes, like the wire in the manufacture of needles, which passes through the hands of seventy-two, and sometimes even ninety-two, different specialized workers.

In so far as such a manufacture, when first started, combines scattered handicrafts, it lessens the space by which the various phases of production are separated from each other. The time taken in passing from one stage to another is shortened, and so is the labour by means of which these transitions are made.[9] In comparison with a handicraft, productive power is gained, and this gain arises from the general co-operative character of manufacture. On the other hand, division of labour, which is the principle peculiar to manufacture, requires the isolation of the various stages of production and their independence of each other. The establishment and maintenance of a connection between the isolated functions requires that the article be transported incessantly from one hand to another, and from one process to another. From the standpoint of large-scale industry, this requirement emerges as a characteristic and costly limitation, and one that is inherent in the principle of manufacture.[10]

If we confine our attention to some determinate quantity of

---

these processes in itself makes it very difficult to convert a manufacture of this kind to large-scale industrial production by means of machines; but in the case of a watch there are two extra impediments, namely the minuteness and delicacy of its parts, and its character as an article of luxury. Hence their variety, which is such that in the best London houses scarcely a dozen watches are made alike in the course of a year. The watch factory of Messrs Vacheron and Constantin, in which machinery has been employed with success, produces at the most three or four different varieties of size and form.

8. In watchmaking, that classical example of heterogeneous manufacture, we may study with great accuracy the above-mentioned differentiation and specialization of the instruments of labour which arises from the decomposition of the craftsman's activity.

9. 'In so close a cohabitation of the people, the carriage must needs be less' (*The Advantages of the East-India Trade*, p. 106).

10. 'The isolation of the different stages of manufacture, consequent upon the employment of manual labour, adds immensely to the cost of production, the loss mainly arising from the mere removals from one process to another' (*The Industry of Nations*, London, 1855, Part II, p. 200).

raw material, to a heap of rags, for instance, in paper manufacture, or a length of wire in needle manufacture, we perceive that it passes successively through a series of stages in the hands of the various specialized workers, until it takes on its final shape. On the other hand, if we look at the workshop as a complete mechanism, we see the raw material in all stages of its production at the same time. The collective worker, formed from the combination of the many specialized workers, draws the wire with one set of tooled-up hands, straightens the wire with another set, armed with different tools, cuts it with another set, points it with another set, and so on. The different stages of the process, previously successive in time, have become simultaneous and contiguous in space. Hence a greater quantity of finished commodities is produced within the same period.[11] This simultaneity, it is true, arises from the general co-operative form of the process as a whole; but manufacture not only finds the conditions for co-operation ready to hand; it also, to some extent, creates them by subdividing handicraft labour. On the other hand, it only accomplishes the social organization of the labour process by riveting each worker to a single fraction of the work.

Since the product of each specialized worker is, at the same time, only a particular stage in the development of a finished article which is the same in each case, each worker, or group of workers, prepares the raw material for another worker or group of workers. The result of the labour of the one is the starting-point for the labour of the other. One worker therefore directly sets the other to work. The labour-time necessary to attain the desired effect in each partial process is learnt by experience, and the mechanism of manufacture, taken as a whole, is based on the assumption that a given result will be obtained in a given time. It is only on this assumption that the various supplementary labour processes can proceed uninterruptedly, simultaneously, and side by side. It is clear that the direct mutual interdependence of the different pieces of work, and therefore of the workers,

11. 'It' (the division of labour) 'produces also an economy of time by separating the work into its different branches, all of which may be carried on into execution at the same moment . . . By carrying on all the different processes at once, which an individual must have executed separately, it becomes possible to produce a multitude of pins completely finished in the same time as a single pin might have been either cut or pointed' (Dugald Stewart, op. cit., p. 319).

compels each one of them to spend on his work no more than the necessary time. This creates a continuity, a uniformity, a regularity, an order,[12] and even an intensity of labour, quite different from that found in an independent handicraft or even in simple co-operation. The rule that the labour-time expended on a commodity should not exceed the amount socially necessary to produce it is one that appears, in the production of commodities in general, to be enforced from outside by the action of competition: to put it superficially, each single producer is obliged to sell his commodity at its market price. In manufacture, on the contrary, the provision of a given quantity of the product in a given period of labour is a technical law of the process of production itself.[13]

Different operations, however, require unequal lengths of time, and therefore, in equal lengths of time, yield unequal quantities of the specialized products. Thus if the same worker has to perform the same operation day after day, there must be a different number of workers for each operation; for instance, in type manufacture there are four founders and two breakers to one rubber: the founder casts 2,000 type an hour, the breaker breaks up 4,000, and the rubber polishes 8,000. Here we have again the principle of co-operation in its simplest form, the simultaneous employment of many people doing the same thing; only now this principle is the expression of an organic relation. The division of labour under the system of manufacture not only simplifies and multiplies the qualitatively different parts of society's collective worker, but also creates a fixed mathematical relation or ratio which regulates the quantitative extent of those parts – i.e. the relative number of workers, or the relative size of the group of workers, for each special function. Thus alongside the qualitative articulation, the division of labour develops a quantitative rule and a proportionality for the social labour process.

Once the most fitting proportion has been established by experience for the number of specialized workers in the various groups producing on a given scale, that scale can be extended only

12. 'The more variety of artists to every manufacture ... the greater the order and regularity of every work, the same must needs be done in less time, the labour must be less' (*The Advantages of the East-India Trade*, p. 68).

13. Nevertheless, in many branches of production the system of manufacture attains this result only very imperfectly, owing to the absence of the knowledge necessary to control with certainty the general chemical and physical conditions of the production process.

by employing a multiple of each particular group.[14] Moreover, the same individual can do certain kinds of work just as well on a large as on a small scale; for instance the labour of superintendence, the transportation of the parts of the product from one stage to the next, etc. The isolation of such functions, their allotment to a particular worker, becomes advantageous only with an increase in the number of workers employed; but this increase must affect every group proportionally.

The isolated group of workers to whom any particular specialized function is assigned is made up of homogeneous elements, and is one of the constituent organs of the total mechanism. In many manufactures, however, the group itself is an organized body of labour, the total mechanism being a repetition or multiplication of these elementary organisms of production. Let us take, for example, the manufacture of glass bottles. It may be resolved into three essentially different stages. First, the preliminary stage, which consists of preparing the components of the glass, mixing the sand and lime, etc. and melting them into a fluid mass of glass.[15] Various specialized workers are employed in this first stage, as also in the final one of removing the bottles from the drying furnace, sorting and packing them, etc. In the middle, between these two stages, comes the glass-melting proper, the manipulation of the fluid mass. At each mouth of the furnace there works a group called 'the hole', consisting of one bottle-maker or finisher, one blower, one gatherer, one putter-up or whetter-off, and one taker-in. These five specialized workers are special organs of a single working organism that only acts as a whole, and therefore can operate only by the direct co-operation of all five. The whole body is paralysed if only one of its members is missing. But a glass furnace has several openings (in England from four to six), each of which contains an earthenware melting-pot full of molten glass, and employs a similar five-man group of

14. 'When (from the peculiar nature of the produce of each manufactory) the number of processes into which it is most advantageous to divide it is ascertained, as well as the number of individuals to be employed, then all other manufactories which do not employ a direct multiple of this number will produce the article at a greater cost . . . Hence arises one of the causes of the great size of manufacturing establishments' (C. Babbage, *On the Economy of Machinery*, 1st edn, London, 1832, Ch. 21, pp. 172–3).

15. In England, the melting furnace is different from the glass furnace in which the glass is manipulated. In Belgium, the same furnace serves for both processes.

workers. The organization of each group is based on the division of labour, but the bond between the different groups is simple co-operation, which, by using in common one of the means of production, namely the furnace, causes it to be consumed more economically. A furnace of this kind, with its four to six groups, constitutes a glass house; and a glass factory comprises a number of such glass houses, together with the apparatus and the workers required for the preparatory and the final phases of production.

Finally, just as manufacture arises in part from the combination of various handicrafts, so too it develops into a combination of various manufactures. The larger English glass manufacturers, for instance, make their own earthenware melting-pots, because the success or failure of the process depends to a great extent on their quality. The manufacture of one of the means of production is here united with that of the product. On the other hand, the manufacture of the product may be united with other manufactures, in which the very same product serves in turn as raw material, or with whose products the original product is itself subsequently mixed. Thus we find the manufacture of flint glass combined with glass-cutting and brass-founding, brass being needed for the metal settings of various articles of glass. The various manufactures which have been combined together in this way form more or less separate departments of a complete manufacture, but they are at the same time independent processes, each with its own division of labour. In spite of the many advantages offered by this combination of manufactures, it never attains a complete technical unity on its own foundation. This unity only arises when it has been transformed into an industry carried on by machinery.

Early in the period of manufacture, the principle of lessening the labour-time necessary for the production of commodities[16] was consciously formulated and expressed; and the use of machines also appeared sporadically, especially for certain simple primary processes that have to be conducted on a very large scale and with the application of great force. Thus, at an early period in paper manufacture, the tearing-up of the rags was done by paper-mills; and in metal works the pounding of the ores was done by stamp-

16. This can be seen from W. Petty, John Bellers, Andrew Yarranton, the anonymous author of *The Advantages of the East-India Trade* and J. Vanderlint, not to mention others.

ing-mills.[17] The Roman Empire handed down the elementary form of all machinery in the shape of the water-wheel.[18] The handicraft period bequeathed to us the great inventions of the compass, gunpowder, type-printing and the automatic clock. But on the whole, machinery played that subordinate part which Adam Smith assigns to it in comparison with division of labour.[19] In the seventeenth century, the sporadic use of machinery was of the greatest importance, because it supplied the great mathematicians of that time with a practical basis and an incentive towards the creation of modern mechanics.

The collective worker, formed out of the combination of a number of individual specialized workers, is the item of machinery specifically characteristic of the manufacturing period. The various operations performed in turn by the producer of a commodity, which coalesce during the labour process, make demands of various kinds upon him. In one operation he must exert more strength, in another more skill, in another more attention; and the same individual does not possess all these qualities in an equal degree. After the various operations have been separated, made independent and isolated, the workers are divided, classified

17. Towards the end of the sixteenth century, mortars and sieves were still used in France for the pounding and washing of ores.

18. The whole history of the development of machinery can be traced in the history of the corn mill. The factory is still described in English as a 'mill'. In German technological writings of the first decade of the nineteenth century the term *'Mühle'* is still found in use, not only for all machinery driven by the forces of nature, but also for all manufactories where any machine-like apparatus is employed.

19. As will be seen in more detail in the fourth volume of this work, Adam Smith said nothing at all new about the division of labour. What characterizes him as the quintessential political economist of the period of manufacture is rather the stress he lays on it. The subordinate part he assigned to machinery provoked a polemic from Lauderdale in the early days of large-scale industry, and from Ure at a later and more developed stage.* Smith also confuses the differentiation of the instruments of labour, in which the specialized workers of the manufacturing epoch themselves took an active part, with the invention of machinery; in the latter case it is not the workers but men of learning, artisans and even peasants (Brindley)† who play the main role.

*Lauderdale's polemic against Smith is quoted in *Grundrisse*, pp. 688–9; Ure's is to be found in *The Philosophy of Manufactures*, p. 19. Lauderdale was writing in 1804, Ure in 1835.

† James Brindley (1716–72), civil engineer. Son of a small farmer in Derbyshire. Responsible for the first important canal in Britain, that between Worsley and Manchester, and for many others in the course of the 1760s.

and grouped according to their predominant qualities. If their natural endowments are the foundation on which the division of labour is built up, manufacture, once introduced, develops in them new powers that are by nature fitted only for limited and special functions. The collective worker now possesses all the qualities necessary for production in an equal degree of excellence, and expends them in the most economical way by exclusively employing all his organs, individualized in particular workers or groups of workers, in performing their special functions.[20] The one-sidedness and even the deficiencies of the specialized individual worker become perfections when he is part of the collective worker.[21] The habit of doing only one thing converts him into an organ which operates with the certainty of a force of nature, while his connection with the whole mechanism compels him to work with the regularity of a machine.[22]

Since the various functions performed by the collective worker can be simple or complex, high or low, the individual labour-powers*, his organs, require different degrees of training, and must therefore possess very different values. Manufacture therefore develops a hierarchy of labour-powers, to which there corresponds a scale of wages. The individual workers are appropriated and annexed for life by a limited function; while the various operations of the hierarchy of labour-powers are parcelled out among the workers according to both their natural and their acquired cap-

20. 'The master manufacturer, by dividing the work to be executed into different processes, each requiring different degrees of skill or of force, can purchase exactly that precise quantity of both which is necessary for each process; whereas, if the whole work were executed by one workman, that person must possess sufficient skill to perform the most difficult, and sufficient strength to execute the most laborious of the operations into which the art is divided' (C. Babbage, op. cit., Ch. 19) [pp. 175–6].

21. For instance, abnormal development of some muscles, curvature of bones, etc.

22. The question put by one of the Inquiry Commissioners, 'How are the young persons kept steadily to their work?', is very correctly answered by Mr William Marshall, the general manager of a glass works: 'They cannot well neglect their work; when they once begin, they must go on; they are just the same as parts of a machine' (*Children's Employment Commission, Fourth Report*, 1865, p. 247).

* *Arbeitskräfte*. These are in fact none other than the workers, but the term 'labour-powers' is deliberately employed here to show that, for capital, the worker is merely the repository of labour-power.

acities.[23] Every process of production, however, requires certain simple manipulations, which every man is capable of doing. These actions too are now separated from their constant interplay with those aspects of activity which are richer in content, and ossified into the exclusive functions of particular individuals.

Hence in every craft it seizes, manufacture creates a class of so-called unskilled labourers, a class strictly excluded by the nature of handicraft industry. If it develops a one-sided speciality to perfection, at the expense of the whole of a man's working capacity, it also begins to make a speciality of the absence of all development. Alongside the gradations of the hierarchy, there appears the simple separation of the workers into skilled and unskilled. For the latter, the cost of apprenticeship vanishes; for the former, it diminishes, compared with that required of the craftsman, owing to the simplification of the functions. In both cases the value of labour-power falls.[24] An exception to this law occurs whenever the decomposition of the labour process gives rise to new and comprehensive functions, which either did not appear at all in handicrafts or not to the same extent. The relative devaluation of labour-power caused by the disappearance or reduction of the expenses of apprenticeship directly implies a higher degree of valorization of capital; for everything that shortens the necessary labour-time required for the reproduction of labour-power, extends the domain of surplus labour.

4. THE DIVISION OF LABOUR IN MANUFACTURE, AND THE DIVISION OF LABOUR IN SOCIETY

We first considered the origin of manufacture, then its simple elements, the specialized worker and his tools, and finally the

23. Dr Ure, in his apotheosis of large-scale industry, brings out the peculiar character of manufacture more sharply than previous economists, who did not have his polemical interest in the matter, and more sharply even than his contemporaries – for instance Babbage, who, although much his superior in mathematics and mechanics, treated large-scale industry from the standpoint of manufacture alone. Ure says: 'To each [task], a workman of appropriate value and cost was naturally assigned. This appropriation forms the very essence of the division of labour.' On the other hand, he describes this division as 'adaptation of labour to the different talents of men', and, lastly, characterizes the whole manufacturing system as 'a system for the division or gradation of labour', and as 'the division of labour into degrees of skill', etc. (Ure, op. cit., pp. 19–23 passim).

24. 'Each handicraftsman being . . . enabled to perfect himself by practice in one point, became . . . a cheaper workman' (Ure, op. cit., p. 19).

total mechanism. We shall now lightly touch on the relation between the division of labour in manufacture, and the social division of labour which forms the foundation of all commodity production.

If we keep labour alone in view, we may designate the division of social production into its main *genera* such as agriculture, industry, etc. as division of labour in general, and the splitting-up of these broad divisions into species and sub-species as division of labour in particular. Finally, we may designate the division of labour within the workshop as division of labour in detail.[25]

The division of labour within society develops from one starting-point; the corresponding restriction of individuals to particular vocations or callings develops from another starting-point, which is diametrically opposed to the first. This second starting-point is also that of the division of labour within manufacture. Within a family[26] and, after further development, within a tribe, there springs up naturally a division of labour caused by differences of sex and age, and therefore based on a purely physiological foundation. More material for this division of labour is then provided by the expansion of the community, the increase of its population and, in particular, conflicts between the different tribes and the subjugation of one tribe by another. On the other hand, as I have already remarked,* the exchange of products springs up at

25. 'Division of labour proceeds from the separation of the most widely different professions to that division where several workers divide between them the preparation of one and the same product, as in manufacture' (Storch, *Cours d'économie politique*, Paris edition, Vol. 1, p. 173). 'Among peoples which have reached a certain level of civilization, we meet with three kinds of division of labour: the first, which we shall call general, brings about the division of the producers into agriculturalists, manufacturers, and shopkeepers, it corresponds to the three main branches of the nation's labour; the second, which one could call particular, is the division of each branch of labour into species . . . the third division of labour, which one should designate as a division of tasks, or of labour properly so called, is that which grows up in the individual crafts and trades . . . and takes root in the majority of the workshops and factories' (Skarbek, op. cit., pp. 84–5).

26. [Note by Engels to the third German edition:] Subsequent and very thorough investigations into the primitive condition of man led the author to the conclusion that it was not the family that originally developed into the tribe, but that, on the contrary, the tribe was the primitive and spontaneously developed form of human association, based on consanguinity, and that out of the first incipient loosening of the tribal bonds, the many and various forms of the family were afterwards developed.

*See above, p. 182.

the points where different families, tribes or communities come into contact; for at the dawn of civilization it is not private individuals but families, tribes, etc. that meet on an independent footing. Different communities find different means of production and different means of subsistence in their natural environment. Hence their modes of production and living, as well as their products, are different. It is this spontaneously developed difference which, when different communities come into contact, calls forth the mutual exchange of products and the consequent gradual conversion of those products into commodities. Exchange does not create the differences between spheres of production but it does bring the different spheres into a relation, thus converting them into more or less interdependent branches of the collective production of a whole society. In this case, the social division of labour arises from the exchange between spheres of production which are originally distinct from and independent of one another. In the other case, where the physiological division of labour is the starting-point, the particular organs of a compact whole become separated from each other and break off. This process of disintegration receives its main impetus from the exchange of commodities with foreign communities. Afterwards, these organs attain such a degree of independence that the sole bond still connecting the various kinds of work is the exchange of the products as commodities. In the one case, what was previously independent has been made dependent; in the other case, what was previously dependent has been made independent.

The foundation of every division of labour which has attained a certain degree of development, and has been brought about by the exchange of commodities, is the separation of town from country.[27] One might well say that the whole economic history of society is summed up in the movement of this antithesis. However, for the moment we shall not go into this.

Just as a certain number of simultaneously employed workers is the material pre-condition for the division of labour within manufacture, so the number and density of the population, which here corresponds to the collection of workers together in one workshop,

27. Sir James Steuart has provided the best treatment of this question. How little his book, which appeared ten years before the *Wealth of Nations*,* is known, even at the present time, may be judged from the fact that the

*Steuart's *Inquiry into the Principles of Political Economy* was first published in 1767, the *Wealth of Nations* in 1776.

is a pre-condition for the division of labour within society,[28] Nevertheless, this density is more or less relative. A relatively thinly populated country, with well-developed means of communication, has a denser population than a more numerously populated country with badly developed means of communication. In this sense, the northern states of the U.S.A. for instance, are more thickly populated than India.[29]

Since the production and the circulation of commodities are the general prerequisites of the capitalist mode of production, division of labour in manufacture requires that a division of labour within society should have already attained a certain degree of development. Inversely, the division of labour in manufacture reacts back upon that in society, developing and multiplying it further. With the differentiation of the instruments of labour, the trades which produce these instruments themselves become more and more differentiated.[30] If the system of manufacture seizes upon a trade which was previously carried on in connection with others, either as a chief or a subordinate trade, and by one producer, these trades immediately break their connection and assert their independence

admirers of Malthus do not know that the first edition of the latter's work on population contains, except in the purely declamatory part, very little but extracts from Steuart, as well as from the clerics Wallace* and Townsend.†

28. 'There is a certain density of population which is convenient, both for social intercourse, and for that combination of powers by which the produce of labour is increased' (James Mill, op. cit., p. 50). 'As the number of labourers increases, the productive power of society augments in the compound ratio of that increase, multiplied by the effects of the division of labour' (Thomas Hodgskin, op. cit., pp. 125–6).

29. As a result of the great demand for cotton after 1861, its production was extended at the expense of rice cultivation in some otherwise thickly populated districts of eastern India. In consequence there arose local famines, because, owing to deficiencies in the means of communication, and hence the absence of physical links, failures of the rice crop in one district could not be compensated for by importing supplies from other districts.

30. Thus the manufacture of shuttles formed a special branch of industry in Holland as early as the seventeenth century.

*Robert Wallace (1697–1771) was a Scottish Presbyterian minister, and author of treatises on population which are reputed to have influenced Malthus, namely *A Dissertation on the Numbers of Mankind in Ancient and Modern Times* (1753), and *Various Prospects of Mankind, Nature, and Providence* (1761).

†Rev. Joseph Townsend (1739–1816) was a Methodist clergyman who, in *A Dissertation on the Poor Laws* (1786), advanced a theory of population later taken over by Malthus.

of each other. If it seizes upon a particular stage in the production of a commodity, the other stages of its production become converted into as many independent trades. It has already been stated that where the finished article consists merely of a number of parts fitted together, the specialized operations may re-establish themselves as genuine and separate handicrafts. In order to accomplish the division of labour in manufacture more completely, a single branch of production is split up into numerous and to some extent entirely new manufactures, according to the varieties of its raw material or the various forms that the same piece of raw material may assume. Thus in France alone, in the first half of the eighteenth century, over 100 different kinds of silk stuffs were woven, and in Avignon, for instance, it was legally required that 'every apprentice should devote himself to only one sort of fabrication, and should not learn the preparation of several kinds of stuff at once'. The territorial division of labour, which confines special branches of production to special districts of a country, acquires fresh stimulus from the system of manufacture, which exploits all natural peculiarities.[31] The colonial system and the extension of the world market, both of which form part of the general conditions for the existence of the manufacturing period, furnish us with rich materials for displaying the division of labour in society. This is not the place, however, for us to show how division of labour seizes upon, not only the economic, but every other sphere of society, and everywhere lays the foundation for that specialization, that development in a man of one single faculty at the expense of all others, which already caused Adam Ferguson, the master of Adam Smith, to exclaim: 'We make a nation of Helots, and have no free citizens.'[32]

But in spite of the numerous analogies and links connecting them, the division of labour in the interior of a society, and that in the interior of a workshop, differ not only in degree, but also in kind. The analogy appears most indisputable where there is an invisible bond uniting the various branches of trade. For instance the cattle-breeder produces hides, the tanner makes the hides into

31. 'Whether the Woollen Manufacture of England is not divided into several parts or branches, appropriated to particular places, where they are only or principally manufactured; fine cloths in Somersetshire, coarse in Yorkshire, long ells at Exeter, saies [serges] at Sudbury, crapes at Norwich, linseys at Kendal, blankets at Witney, and so forth?' (Berkeley, *The Querist*, 1750, query No. 520).

32. A. Ferguson, *History of Civil Society*, Edinburgh, 1767, Part IV, Section ii, p. 285.

leather and the shoemaker makes the leather into boots. Here the product of each man is merely a step towards the final form, which is the combined product of their specialized labours. There are, besides, all the various trades which supply the cattle-breeder, the tanner and the shoemaker with their means of production. Now it is quite possible to imagine, with Adam Smith, that the difference between the above social division of labour, and the division in manufacture, is merely subjective, exists merely for the observer, who in the case of manufacture can see at a glance all the numerous operations being performed on one spot, while in the instance given above, the spreading-out of the work over great areas and the great number of people employed in each branch of labour obscure the connection.[33] But what is it that forms the bond between the independent labours of the cattle-breeder, the tanner and the shoemaker? It is the fact that their respective products are commodities. What, on the other hand, characterizes the division of labour in manufacture? The fact that the specialized worker produces no commodities.[34] It is only the common product of all the specialized workers that becomes a commodity.[35] The division

33. In manufacture proper, Smith says, the division of labour appears to be greater, because 'those employed in every different branch of the work can often be collected into the same workhouse, and placed at once under the view of the spectator. In those great manufactures (!), on the contrary, which are destined to supply the great wants of the great body of the people, every different branch of the work employs so great a number of workmen that it is impossible to collect them all into the same workhouse . . . the division is not near so obvious' (A. Smith, *Wealth of Nations*, Bk I, Ch. 1). The famous passage in the same chapter, which begins with the words, 'Observe the accommodation of the most common artificer or day-labourer in a civilized and thriving country', and then proceeds to depict what an enormous number and variety of industries contribute to the satisfaction of the needs of an ordinary worker, is copied almost word for word from the 'Remarks' added by B. de Mandeville to his *Fable of the Bees, or Private Vices, Publick Benefits* (first edition, without the remarks, 1706; with the remarks, 1714).

34. 'There is no longer anything which we can call the natural reward of individual labour. Each labourer produces only some part of a whole, and each part, having no value or utility in itself, there is nothing on which the labourer can seize, and say: It is my product, this I will keep to myself' (*Labour Defended against the Claims of Capital*, London, 1825, p. 25). The author of this admirable work is Thomas Hodgskin.

35. This distinction between the division of labour in society and in manufacture has been illustrated to the Yankees in practice. One of the new taxes devised at Washington during the Civil War was the duty of 6 per cent 'on all industrial products'. Question: What is an industrial product? Answer of the legislature: A thing is produced 'when it is made', and it is made when it is

of labour within society is mediated through the purchase and sale of the products of different branches of industry, while the connection between the various partial operations in a workshop is mediated through the sale of the labour-power of several workers to one capitalist, who applies it as combined labour-power. The division of labour within manufacture presupposes a concentration of the means of production in the hands of one capitalist; the division of labour within society presupposes a dispersal of those means among many independent producers of commodities. While, within the workshop, the iron law of proportionality subjects definite numbers of workers to definite functions, in the society outside the workshop, the play of chance and caprice results in a motley pattern of distribution of the producers and their means of production among the various branches of social labour. It is true that the different spheres of production constantly tend towards equilibrium, for the following reason. On the one hand, every producer of a commodity is obliged to produce a use-value, i.e. he must satisfy a particular social need (though the extent of these needs differs quantitatively, and there exists an inner bond which attaches the different levels of need to a system which has grown up spontaneously); on the other hand, the law of the value of commodities ultimately determines how much of its disposable labour-time society can expend on each kind of commodity. But this constant tendency on the part of the various spheres of production towards equilibrium comes into play only as a reaction against the constant upsetting of this equilibrium. The planned and regulated *a priori* system on which the division of labour is implemented within the workshop becomes, in the division of labour within society, an *a posteriori* necessity imposed by nature, controlling the unregulated caprice of the producers, and perceptible in the fluctuations of the barometer of market prices. Division of

---

ready for sale. Now for one example out of many. The New York and Philadelphia manufacturers had previously been in the habit of 'making' umbrellas with all their accessories. But since an umbrella is a composite mixture of very heterogeneous parts, these parts by degrees became the products of various separate industries, carried on independently in different places. They entered as separate commodities into the manufacture of umbrellas, so that all the umbrella manufacturers had to do was fit them together. The Yankees have given the name 'assembled articles' to articles of this kind, and they deserve this name, for they allow taxes to be assembled together as well. Thus an umbrella 'assembles', first 6 per cent on the price of each of its elements, and a further 6 per cent on its own total price.

labour within the workshop implies the undisputed authority of the capitalist over men, who are merely the members of a total mechanism which belongs to him. The division of labour within society brings into contact independent producers of commodities, who acknowledge no authority other than that of competition, of the coercion exerted by the pressure of their reciprocal interests, just as in the animal kingdom the 'war of all against all' more or less preserves the conditions of existence of every species. The same bourgeois consciousness which celebrates the division of labour in the workshop, the lifelong annexation of the worker to a partial operation, and his complete subjection to capital, as an organization of labour that increases its productive power, denounces with equal vigour every conscious attempt to control and regulate the process of production socially, as an inroad upon such sacred things as the rights of property, freedom and the self-determining 'genius' of the individual capitalist. It is very characteristic that the enthusiastic apologists of the factory system have nothing more damning to urge against a general organization of labour in society than that it would turn the whole of society into a factory.

If, in the society where the capitalist mode of production prevails, anarchy in the social division of labour and despotism in the manufacturing division of labour mutually condition each other, we find, on the contrary, in those earlier forms of society in which the separation of trades has been spontaneously developed, then crystallized, and finally made permanent by law, on the one hand, a specimen of the organization of the labour of society in accordance with an approved and authoritative plan, and, on the other, the entire exclusion of division of labour in the workshop or, at the least, its development on a minute scale, sporadically and accidentally.[36]

Those small and extremely ancient Indian communities, for example, some of which continue to exist to this day, are based on the possession of the land in common, on the blending of agricul-

36. 'It can . . . be laid down as a general rule that the less authority presides over the division of labour inside society, the more the division of labour develops inside the workshop, and the more it is subjected there to the authority of a single person. Thus authority in the workshop and authority in society, in relation to the division of labour, are in *inverse ratio* to each other' (Karl Marx, *Misère de la philosophie*, pp. 130–31) [English edition, p. 118].

ture and handicrafts and on an unalterable division of labour, which serves as a fixed plan and basis for action whenever a new community is started. The communities occupy areas of from 100 up to several thousand acres, and each forms a compact whole producing all it requires. Most of the products are destined for direct use by the community itself, and are not commodities. Hence production here is independent of that division of labour brought about in Indian society as a whole by the exchange of commodities. It is the surplus alone that becomes a commodity, and a part of that surplus cannot become a commodity until it has reached the hands of the state, because from time immemorial a certain quantity of the community's production has found its way to the state as rent in kind. The form of the community varies in different parts of India. In the simplest communities, the land is tilled in common, and the produce is divided among the members. At the same time, spinning and weaving are carried on in each family as subsidiary industries. Alongside the mass of people thus occupied in the same way, we find the 'chief inhabitant', who is judge, police authority and tax-gatherer in one; the book-keeper, who keeps the accounts of the tillage and registers everything relating to this; another official, who prosecutes criminals, protects strangers travelling through and escorts them to the next village; the boundary man, who guards the boundaries against neighbouring communities; the water-overseer, who distributes the water from the common tanks for irrigation; the Brahmin, who conducts the religious services; the schoolmaster, who on the sand teaches the children reading and writing; the calendar-Brahmin, or astrologer, who makes known the lucky or unlucky days for seed-time and harvest, and for every other kind of agricultural work; a smith and a carpenter, who make and repair all the agricultural implements; the potter, who makes all the pottery of the village; the barber, the washerman, who washes clothes, the silversmith, here and there the poet, who in some communities replaces the silversmith, in others the schoolmaster. This dozen or so of individuals is maintained at the expense of the whole community. If the population increases, a new community is founded, on the pattern of the old one, on unoccupied land. The whole mechanism reveals a systematic division of labour; but a division like that in manufacture is impossible, since the smith, the carpenter, etc. find themselves faced with an unchanging market, and at the most there occur, according to the sizes of the villages, two or three smiths or carpenters, instead of one.[37] The law that regulates the division of labour in the community acts with the irresistible authority of a law of nature, while each individual craftsman, the smith, the carpenter and so on, conducts in his workshop all the operations of his handicraft in the traditional way, but independently, and without recognizing any authority. The simplicity of the productive organism in these self-sufficing communities which constantly reproduce themselves in the same form and, when accidentally destroyed, spring up again on the same spot and with the same name[38] – this simplicity supplies the key to the riddle of the unchangeability of Asiatic societies, which is in such striking contrast with the constant dissolution and refounding of Asiatic states, and their never-ceasing changes of dynasty. The structure of the fundamental economic elements of society remains untouched by the storms which blow up in the cloudy regions of politics.

The rules of the guilds, as I have said before, deliberately hindered the transformation of the single master into a capitalist, by placing very strict limits on the number of apprentices and journeymen he could employ. Moreover, he could employ his journeymen only in the handicraft in which he was himself a master. The guilds zealously repelled every encroachment by merchants' capital, the only free form of capital which confronted them. A merchant could buy every kind of commodity, but he could not buy labour as a commodity. He existed only on sufferance, as a dealer in the products of the handicrafts. If circumstances called for a further division of labour, the existing guilds split themselves up into subordinate sections, or founded new guilds by the side of the old ones. But they did this without concentrating different handicrafts in one workshop. Hence the guild

37. Lieut.-Col. Mark Wilks, *Historical Sketches of the South of India*, London, 1810–17, Vol. 1, pp. 118–20. A good account of the various forms of the Indian community is to be found in George Campbell's *Modern India*, London, 1852.

38. 'Under this simple form ... the inhabitants of the country have lived from time immemorial. The boundaries of the villages have been but seldom altered, and though the villages themselves have been sometimes injured, and even desolated by war, famine, and disease, the same name, the same limits, the same interests, and even the same families, have continued for ages. The inhabitants give themselves no trouble about the breaking up and division of kingdoms; while the village remains entire, they care not to what power it is transferred, or to what sovereign it devolves; its internal economy remains unchanged' (T. Stamford Raffles, late Lieut.-Gov. of Java, *The History of Java*, London, 1817, Vol. 1, p. 285).

organization, however much it may have contributed to creating the material conditions for the existence of manufacture by sepa-rating, isolating and perfecting the handicrafts, excluded the kind of division of labour characteristic of manufacture. On the whole, the worker and his means of production remained closely united, like the snail with its shell, and therefore the principal basis of manufacture was absent, namely the autonomy of the means of production, as capital, *vis-à-vis* the worker.

While the division of labour in society at large, whether mediated through the exchange of commodities or not, can exist in the most diverse economic formations of society, the division of labour in the workshop, as practised by manufacture, is an entirely specific creation of the capitalist mode of production.

5. THE CAPITALIST CHARACTER OF MANUFACTURE

An increased number of workers under the control of one capi-talist is the natural starting-point, both of co-operation in general and of manufacture in particular. But the division of labour in manufacture makes this increase in the number of workers a technical necessity. The minimum number that any given capi-talist is bound to employ is here prescribed by the previously established division of labour. On the other hand, the advantages of further division can be obtained only by adding to the number of workers, and this means adding not single individuals but mul-tiples. However, an increase in the variable component of the capital employed necessitates an increase in its constant component too, i.e. both in the available extent of the conditions of produc-tion, such as workshops, implements, etc., and, in particular, in raw material, the demand for which grows much more quickly than the number of workers. The quantity of it consumed in a given time, by a given amount of labour, increases in the same ratio as does the productive power of that labour through its division. Hence it is a law, springing from the technical character of manufacture, that the minimum amount of capital which the capitalist must possess has to go on increasing. In other words, the transformation of the social means of production and subsistence into capital must keep extending.[39]

39. 'It is not sufficient that the capital' (he should have said the necessary means of subsistence **and** of production) 'required for the subdivision of

In manufacture, as well as in simple co-operation, the collective working organism is a form of existence of capital. The social mechanism of production, which is made up of numerous individual specialized workers, belongs to the capitalist. Hence the productive power which results from the combination of various kinds of labour appears as the productive power of capital. Manufacture proper not only subjects the previously independent worker to the discipline and command of capital, but creates in addition a hierarchical structure amongst the workers themselves. While simple co-operation leaves the mode of the individual's labour for the most part unchanged, manufacture thoroughly revolutionizes it, and seizes labour-power by its roots. It converts the worker into a crippled monstrosity by furthering his particular skill as in a forcing-house, through the suppression of a whole world of productive drives and inclinations, just as in the states of La Plata* they butcher a whole beast for the sake of his hide or his tallow. Not only is the specialized work distributed among the different individuals, but the individual himself is divided up, and transformed into the automatic motor of a detail operation,[40] thus realizing the absurd fable of Menenius Agrippa,† which

---

handicrafts should be in readiness in the society: it must also be accumulated in the hands of the employers in sufficiently large quantities to enable them to conduct their operations on a large scale ... The more the division increases, the more does the constant employment of a given number of workers require a greater outlay of capital in tools, raw material, etc.' (Storch, *Cours d'économie politique*, Paris edition, Vol. I, pp. 250–51). 'The concentration of the instruments of production and the division of labour are as inseparable one from the other as are, in the political sphere, the concentration of public authority and the division of private interests' (Karl Marx, *Misère de la philosophie*, p. 134) [English edition, p. 121].

40. Dugald Stewart calls manufacturing workers 'living automatons ... *employed in the details of the work*' (op. cit., p. 318).

---

*This clearly refers to Argentina, Paraguay and Uruguay, the three republics which border the river Plate.

†Menenius Agrippa (d. 493 B.C.) was a Roman patrician who, according to the legend, persuaded the plebeians to refrain from overthrowing patrician rule by using the analogy between the state and the human body. The patricians represented the stomach, the plebeians the limbs; the limbs were required to feed the stomach, and, conversely, if the stomach were not fed, the limbs themselves would soon wither.

presents man as a mere fragment of his own body.[41] If, in the first place, the worker sold his labour-power to capital because he lacked the material means of producing a commodity, now his own individual labour-power withholds its services unless it has been sold to capital. It will continue to function only in an environment which first comes into existence after its sale, namely the capitalist's workshop. Unfitted by nature to make anything independently, the manufacturing worker develops his productive activity only as an appendage of that workshop.[42] As the chosen people bore in their features the sign that they were the property of Jehovah, so the division of labour brands the manufacturing worker as the property of capital.

The knowledge, judgement and will which, even though to a small extent, are exercised by the independent peasant or handicraftsman, in the same way as the savage makes the whole art of war consist in the exercise of his personal cunning, are faculties now required only for the workshop as a whole. The possibility of an intelligent direction of production expands in one direction, because it vanishes in many others. What is lost by the specialized workers is concentrated in the capital which confronts them.[43] It is a result of the division of labour in manufacture that the worker is brought face to face with the intellectual potentialities [*geistige Potenzen*] of the material process of production as the property of another and as a power which rules over him. This process of separation starts in simple co-operation, where the capitalist represents to the individual workers the unity and the will of the whole body of social labour. It is developed in manufacture, which mutilates the worker, turning him into a fragment of himself. It is completed in large-scale industry, which makes science a potentiality for production which is distinct from labour and presses it into the service of capital.[44]

41. In corals, each individual is, in fact, the stomach of the whole group; but it supplies the group with nourishment instead of extracting it, like the Roman patrician.

42. 'The worker who is the master of a whole craft can work and find means of subsistence anywhere: the other' (the manufacturing worker) 'is only an appendage who, when he is separated from his fellows, possesses neither capability nor independence, and finds himself forced to accept any law it is thought fit to impose' (Storch, op. cit., St Petersburg edition, 1815, Vol. 1, p. 204).

43. 'The former may have gained what the other has lost' (A. Ferguson, op. cit., p. 281).

44. 'The man of knowledge and the productive labourer come to be widely

In manufacture, the social productive power of the collective worker, hence of capital, is enriched through the impoverishment of the worker in individual productive power. 'Ignorance is the mother of industry as well as of superstition. Reflection and fancy are subject to err; but a habit of moving the hand or the foot is independent of either. Manufactures, accordingly, prosper most where the mind is least consulted, and where the workshop may . . . be considered as an engine, the parts of which are men.'[45] As a matter of fact, in the middle of the eighteenth century some manufacturers preferred to employ semi-idiots for certain operations which, though simple, were trade secrets.[46]

'The understandings of the greater part of men,' says Adam Smith, 'are necessarily formed by their ordinary employments. The man whose whole life is spent in performing a few simple operations . . . has no occasion to exert his understanding . . . He generally becomes as stupid and ignorant as it is possible for a human creature to become.' After describing the stupidity of the specialized worker, he goes on: 'The uniformity of his stationary life naturally corrupts the courage of his mind . . . It corrupts even the activity of his body and renders him incapable of exerting his strength with vigour and perseverance in any other employments than that to which he has been bred. His dexterity at his own particular trade seems in this manner to be acquired at the expense of his intellectual, social, and martial virtues. But in every improved and civilized society, this is the state into which the labouring poor, that is, the great body of the people, must necessarily fall.'[47]

---

divided from each other, and knowledge, instead of remaining the handmaid of labour in the hand of the labourer to increase his productive powers . . . has almost everywhere arrayed itself against labour.' 'Knowledge' becomes 'an instrument, capable of being detached from labour and opposed to it' (W. Thompson, *An Inquiry into the Principles of the Distribution of Wealth*, London, 1824, p. 274).

45. A. Ferguson, op. cit., p. 280.

46. J. D. Tuckett, *A History of the Past and Present State of the Labouring Population*, London, 1846, Vol. 1, p. 148.

47. A. Smith, *Wealth of Nations*, Bk V, Ch. I [Part III], Art. 2. As a pupil of Adam Ferguson, who had pointed out the harmful effects of the division of labour, Smith was perfectly clear on this point. In the Introduction to his work, where he professedly praises the division of labour, he indicates only in passing that it is the source of social inequalities. It is not till the fifth book, on the 'Revenue of the State', that he reproduces Ferguson. In my *Misère de la philosophie* [*The Poverty of Philosophy*], I have sufficiently explained the historical relation between Ferguson, Adam Smith, Lemontey and Say as

For preventing the complete deterioration of the great mass of the people which arises from the division of labour, Adam Smith recommends education of the people by the state, but in prudently homoeopathic doses. Garnier, his French translator and commentator, who quite naturally developed into a senator under the first French Empire,* is entirely consistent in opposing Smith on this point. Education of the people, he urges, violates the first law of the division of labour, and with it 'our whole social system would be proscribed'. 'Like all other divisions of labour,' he says, 'that between hand labour and head labour[48] is more pronounced and decided in proportion as society' (he rightly uses this word to describe capital, landed property and the state that belongs to them) 'becomes richer. The division of labour, like every other, is an effect of past, and a cause of future progress ... ought the government then to work in opposition to this division of labour, and to hinder its natural course? Ought it to expend a part of the public money in the attempt to confound and blend together two classes of labour which are striving after division and separation?'[49]

Some crippling of body and mind is inseparable even from the division of labour in society as a whole. However, since manufacture carries this social separation of branches of labour much further, and also, by its peculiar division, attacks the individual at the very roots of his life, it is the first system to provide the materials and the impetus for industrial pathology.[50]

'To subdivide a man is to execute him, if he deserves the sent-

---

regards their criticisms of the division of labour, and also shown, for the first time, that the division of labour in manufacture is a specific form of the capitalist mode of production (pp. 122 ff.) [English edition, pp. 112–15].

48. Ferguson had already said (op. cit., p. 281): 'And thinking itself, in this age of separations, may become a peculiar craft.'

49. G. Garnier, Vol. 5 of his translation of Adam Smith, pp. 4–5.

50. Ramazzini, professor of practical medicine at Padua, published in 1713 his work *De morbis artificum*, which was translated into French in 1777, and reprinted in 1841 in the *Encyclopédie des sciences médicales. 7me Div. Auteurs classiques*. The period of large-scale industry has of course very much enlarged this catalogue of the diseases of the workers. See, among others, the work *Hygiène physique et morale de l'ouvrier dans les grandes villes en général, et dans la ville de Lyon en particulier*, by Dr A.-L. Fonteret, Paris, 1858, and

---

*Germain Garnier (1754–1821) was secretary to Louis XV's daughter in the 1780s, emigrated in 1792, returned in 1795, declared for Bonaparte, was made a Prefect in 1799, Count and senator in 1804, and President of the Senate in 1809. His translation of Adam Smith came out in 1802.

ence, to assassinate him if he does not ... The subdivision of labour is the assassination of a people.'[51]

Co-operation based on the division of labour, in other words manufacture, begins as a spontaneous formation. As soon as it attains a degree of consistency and extension, it becomes the conscious, methodical and systematic form of capitalist production. The history of manufacture proper shows how the division of labour which is peculiar to it acquires the most appropriate form at first by experience, as it were behind the backs of the actors, and then, like the guild handicrafts, strives to hold fast to that form when once it has been found, and here and there succeeds in keeping it for centuries. Any alteration in this form, except in trivial matters, never results from anything but a revolution in the instruments of labour. Modern manufacture – I am not referring here to large-scale industry, which is based on machinery – either finds the *disjecta membra poetae** ready to hand, and only waiting to be collected together, as is the case in the manufacture of clothes in large towns, or it can easily apply the principles of division, simply by exclusively assigning the various operations of a handicraft (such as book-binding) to particular men. In such cases, a week's experience is enough to determine the proportion between the numbers of the 'hands' necessary for the various functions.[52]

Die Krankheiten, welche verschiedenen Ständen, Altern, und Geschlechtern eigenthümlich sind, 6 vols., Ulm, 1860 [by R. H. Rohatzsch]. In 1854 the Society of Arts appointed a Commission of Inquiry into industrial pathology. The list of documents collected by this commission is to be seen in the catalogue of the Twickenham Economic Museum. Very important are the official *Reports on Public Health*. See also Eduard Reich, M.D., *Über die Entartung des Menschen*, Erlangen, 1868.

51. D. Urquhart, *Familiar Words*, London, 1855, p. 119. Hegel held very heretical views on the division of labour. In his *Philosophy of Right* he says: 'By educated men we may *prima facie* understand those who ... can do what others do.'*

52. The pleasant belief in the inventive genius displayed *a priori* by the individual capitalist in the division of labour exists nowadays only among German professors of the stamp of Herr Roscher, who, to recompense the capitalist from whose Jovian head the division of labour sprang ready formed, dedicates to him 'various wages'. The more or less extensive application of the division of labour depends on the length of the purse, not on the magnitude of the genius.

Philosophy of Right, para. 187, addition. English edition, p. 268.

---

*'The scattered members of the poet' (Horace, *Satires*, Bk I, Satire 4, line 62). The quotation has been changed slightly.

By dissection of handicraft activity into its separate components, by specialization of the instruments of labour, by the formation of specialized workers and by grouping and combining the latter into a single mechanism, the division of labour in manufacture provides the social process of production with a qualitative articulation and a quantitative proportionality. It thereby creates a definite organization of social labour and at the same time develops new, and social, productive powers of labour. As a specifically capitalist form of the process of social production – and, on the foundations available to it, it could not develop in any other form than a capitalist one – the division of labour in manufacture is merely a particular method of creating relative surplus-value, or of augmenting the self-valorization of capital – usually described as social wealth, 'wealth of nations', etc. – at the expense of the worker. Not only does it increase the socially productive power of labour for the benefit of the capitalist instead of the worker; it also does this by crippling the individual worker. It produces new conditions for the domination of capital over labour. If, therefore, on the one hand, it appears historically as an advance and a necessary aspect of the economic process of the formation of society, on the other hand, it appears as a more refined and civilized means of exploitation.

Political economy, which first emerged as an independent science during the period of manufacture, is only able to view the social division of labour in terms of the division found in manufacture,[53] i.e. as a means of producing more commodities with a given quantity of labour, and consequently of cheapening commodities and accelerating the accumulation of capital. In most striking contrast with this accentuation of quantity and exchange-value is the attitude of the writers of classical antiquity, who are exclusively concerned with quality and use-value.[54] As a result of

53. The older writers, like Petty and the anonymous author of *Advantages of the East-India Trade*, bring out the capitalist character of the division of labour as applied to manufacture more clearly than Adam Smith does.

54. A few eighteenth-century writers such as Beccaria and James Harris form an exception among the moderns and on the division of labour they almost entirely follow the ancients. Thus Beccaria: 'Everyone knows from experience that if the hands and the intelligence are always applied to the same kind of work and the same products, these will be produced more easily, in greater abundance, and in higher quality than if each individual makes for himself the things he needs . . . In this way, men are divided up into various classes and conditions, to their own advantage and to that of the community' (Cesare Beccaria, *Elementi di economia pubblica*, edited by Custodi, *Parte moderna*, Vol. II, p. 28). James Harris, later Earl of Malmesbury, famous for

the separation of the social branches of production, commodities are better made, men's various inclinations and talents select suitable fields of action,[55] and without some restriction no important results can be obtained anywhere.[56] Hence both product and producer are improved by the division of labour. If the growth of the quantity produced is occasionally mentioned, this is only done with reference to the greater abundance of use-values. There is not a word alluding to exchange-value, or to the cheapening of commodities. This standpoint, the standpoint of use-value, is adopted by Plato,[57] who treats the division of labour as the foundation on

---

the *Diaries* he wrote about his embassy at St Petersburg, says in a note to his *Dialogue Concerning Happiness*, London, 1741,* later reprinted in *Three Treatises, etc.*, 3rd edn, London, 1772: 'The whole argument to prove society natural (i.e. by division of employments) . . . is taken from the second book of Plato's *Republic.*'

55. Thus, in the *Odyssey*, XIV, 228, 'ἄλλος γὰρ τ'ἄλλοισιν ἀνὴρ ἐπιτέρπεται ἔργοις'† and the statement of Archilochus quoted by Sextus Empiricus, 'ἄλλος ἄλλῳ ἐπ' ἔργῳ καρδίην ἰαίνεται'.‡

56. 'πολλ' ἠπίστατο ἔργα, κακῶς δ' ἠπίστατο πάντα' ['He could do many works, but all of them badly']. The Athenian considered himself superior as a producer of commodities to the Spartan; for in time of war the latter had plenty of men at his disposal, but could not command money, as Thucydides makes Pericles say in the speech inciting the Athenians to the Peloponnesian War: 'σώμασι τε ἑτοιμότεροι οἱ αὐτουργοὶ τῶν ἀνθρώπων ἢ χρήμασι πολεμεῖν' (Thucydides, *History of the Peloponnesian War*, Bk I, para. 141). Nevertheless, even with regard to material production, αὐταρκεία [self-sufficiency], as opposed to the division of labour, remained their ideal, 'παρ' ὧν γὰρ τὸ εὖ, παρὰ τούτων καὶ τὸ αὔταρκες.'§ It should be mentioned here that at the date of the fall of the thirty Tyrants‖ there were still less than 5,000 Athenians without landed property.

57. With Plato, the division of labour within the community develops from the many-sidedness of the needs of individuals, and the one-sidedness of their capabilities. The main point with him is that the labourer must adapt himself to the work, not the work to the labourer, a thing which would be unavoidable if the labourer carried on several trades at once, thus making one or the other of them subordinate. 'Οὐ γὰρ . . . ἐθέλει τὸ πραττόμενον τὴν

---

*This was written, not by the diplomat James Harris (1746–1820), later Earl of Malmesbury, but by his father, the philosopher James Harris (1709–80). The quotation here is from *Three Treatises, etc.*, p. 292.

†'For different men take joy in different works.'

‡'Men differ as to what things cheer their hearts' (*Adversus mathematicos*, Bk xi, para. 44).

§'For with the latter there is well-being, but with the former there is independence' (Thucydides, op. cit.).

‖In 404 B.C., at the end of the Peloponnesian War.

which the division of society into estates is based, and also by Xenophon,[58] who with his characteristic bourgeois instinct already comes closer to the division of labour within the workshop. Plato's *Republic*, in so far as the division of labour is treated in it as the

---

τοῦ πράττοντος σχολὴν περιμένειν, ἀλλ' ἀνάγκη τὸν πράττοντα τῷ πραττομένῳ ἐπακολευθεῖν μὴ ἐν παρέργου μέρει. 'Ανάγκη. 'Εκ δὴ τούτων πλείω τε ἕκαστα γίγνεται καὶ κάλλιον καὶ ῥᾷον, ὅταν εἷς ἕν κατὰ φύσιν καὶ ἐν καιρῷ, σχολὴν τῶν ἄλλων ἄγων, πράττῃ.'* Similarly in Thucydides, loc. cit., para. 142: 'Sea-faring is an art like any other, and cannot, as circumstances require, be carried on as a subsidiary occupation; rather is it true that other subsidiary occupations cannot be carried on alongside it.' If the work, says Plato, has to wait for the labourer, the critical point in the process of production is often missed, and the article is spoiled, 'ἔργου καιρόν, διόλλυται.'† The same Platonic idea recurs in the protest of the English bleachers against the clause in the Factory Act providing for fixed meal-times for all the workers. Their business cannot await the convenience of the workmen, they say, because 'in the various operations of singeing, washing, bleaching, mangling, calendering, and dyeing, none of them can be stopped at a given moment without risk of damage ... to enforce the same dinner hour for all the workpeople might occasionally subject valuable goods to the risk of damage by incomplete operations.' *Le platonisme où va-t-il se nicher!*‡

58. Xenophon says that it is not only an honour to receive food from the table of the King of Persia, but such food is much more tasty than other food. 'And there is nothing wonderful in this, for as the other arts are brought to special perfection in the great towns, so the royal food is prepared in a special way. For in the small towns the same man makes bedsteads, doors, ploughs and tables: often, too, he builds houses into the bargain, and is quite content if he finds custom sufficient for his sustenance. It is altogether impossible for a man who does so many things to do them all well. But in the great towns, where each can find many buyers, one trade is sufficient to maintain the man who carries it on. Indeed, not even one complete trade is needed, but one man makes shoes for men, another for women. Here and there one man gets a living by sewing, another by cutting out shoes; one does nothing but cut out clothes, another nothing but sew the pieces together. It follows necessarily then, that he who does the simplest kind of work undoubtedly does it better than anyone else. So it is with the art of cooking' (Xenophon, *Cyropaedia*, Bk VIII, Ch. 2). Xenophon here lays stress exclusively on the excellence to be attained in the quality of the use-value, although he is already aware that the degree of division of labour reached is dependent on the extent of the market.

*'That ... is because the work will not wait for the leisure of the workman, but the workman must attend to it as his main affair, and not treat it as a subsidiary occupation.' 'He must indeed.' 'The result, then, is that more things are produced, and better, and more easily, when one man performs one task according to his nature, at the right moment, and at leisure from other occupations' (Plato, *Republic*, Bk II, para. 2).

†'[If someone lets slip] the right moment for the work, it is spoiled.'

‡'Where will Platonism be found next!'

formative principle of the state,* is merely an Athenian idealiza-
tion of the Egyptian caste system, Egypt having served as the
model of an industrial country to others of his contemporaries,
e.g. Isocrates.[59] It retained this importance for the Greeks even
at the time of the Roman Empire.[60]

During the manufacturing period proper, i.e. the period in which
manufacture is the predominant form taken by capitalist production, the full development of its own peculiar tendencies comes up
against obstacles from many directions. Although, as we have
already seen, manufacture creates a simple division of the workers
into skilled and unskilled, at the same time as it inserts them into a
hierarchical structure, the number of unskilled workers remains
very limited owing to the preponderant influence of the skilled.
Although it adapts the particular operations to the various degrees of maturity, strength and development of the living instruments of labour, and thus tends towards the exploitation of
women and children in production, this tendency is largely defeated by the habits and the resistance of the male workers.
Although the splitting-up of handicrafts lowers the cost of forming the worker, and thereby lowers his value, a long period of
apprenticeship is still necessary for certain more difficult kinds of
work; moreover, even where it would be superfluous, the workers
jealously retain it. In England, for instance, we find the laws of
apprenticeship, with their seven years' probation, in full force
down to the end of the manufacturing period; they are not entirely
thrown aside until the advent of large-scale industry. Since
handicraft skill is the foundation of manufacture, and since the
mechanism of manufacture as a whole possesses no objective
framework which would be independent of the workers themselves,

59. 'He' (Busiris) 'divided them all into special castes ... commanded
that the same individuals should always carry on the same trade, for he knew
that they who change their occupations become skilled in none; but that
those who constantly stick to one occupation bring it to the highest perfection. In truth, we shall also find that in relation to the arts and handicrafts,
they have outstripped their rivals more than a master does a bungler; and the
contrivances for maintaining the monarchy and the other institutions of their
state are so admirable that the famous philosophers who have dealt with this
subject have praised the constitution of the Egyptian state above all others'
(Isocrates, *Busiris*, para. 15).

60. Diodorus Siculus, op. cit. [Bk I, Ch. 74].

* Plato, *Republic*, Bk II, para. 2.

capital is constantly compelled to wrestle with the insubordination of the workers. 'By the infirmity of human nature,' says our friend Ure, 'it happens that the more skilful the workman, the more self-willed and intractable he is apt to become, and of course the less fit a component of a mechanical system in which . . . he may do great damage to the whole.'[61] Hence the complaint that the workers lack discipline runs through the whole of the period of manufacture.[62] Even if we did not have the testimony of contemporary writers on this, we have two simple facts which speak volumes: firstly, during the period between the sixteenth century and the epoch of large-scale industry capital failed in its attempt to seize control of the whole disposable labour-time of the manufacturing workers, and secondly, the manufactures are short-lived, changing their locality from one country to another with the emigration or immigration of workers. 'Order must in one way or another be established,' exclaims in 1770 the often-cited author of the *Essay on Trade and Commerce*. 'Order,' echoes Dr Andrew Ure sixty-six years later, was lacking in the system of manufacture, based as it was on 'the scholastic dogma of the division of labour', and 'Arkwright created order'.

At the same time, manufacture was unable either to seize upon the production of society to its full extent, or to revolutionize that production to its very core. It towered up as an artificial economic construction, on the broad foundation of the town handicrafts and the domestic industries of the countryside. At a certain stage of its development, the narrow technical basis on which manufacture rested came into contradiction with requirements of production which it had itself created.

One of its most finished products was the workshop for the production of the instruments of labour themselves, and particularly the complicated pieces of mechanical apparatus already being employed. 'A machine-factory,' says Ure, 'displayed the division of labour in manifold gradations – the file, the drill, the lathe, having each its different workmen in the order of skill.'* This workshop, the product of the division of labour in manufacture, produced in

61. Ure, op. cit., p. 20.
62. This is more true for England than for France, and more true for France than for Holland.

---

*Ure, op. cit., p. 21. The 'machine-factory' referred to by Ure is the same thing as Marx's 'workshop for the production of the instruments of labour'.

its turn – machines. It is machines that abolish the role of the handicraftsman as the regulating principle of social production. Thus, on the one hand, the technical reason for the lifelong attachment of the worker to a partial function is swept away. On the other hand, the barriers placed in the way of the domination of capital by this same regulating principle now also fall.

Chapter 15: Machinery and Large-Scale Industry

1. THE DEVELOPMENT OF MACHINERY

John Stuart Mill says in his *Principles of Political Economy*: 'It is questionable if all the mechanical inventions yet made have lightened the day's toil of any human being.'[1] That is, however, by no means the aim of the application of machinery under capitalism. Like every other instrument for increasing the productivity of labour, machinery is intended to cheapen commodities and, by shortening the part of the working day in which the worker works for himself, to lengthen the other part, the part he gives to the capitalist for nothing. The machine is a means for producing surplus-value.

In manufacture the transformation of the mode of production takes labour-power as its starting-point. In large-scale industry, on the other hand, the instruments of labour are the starting-point. We have first to investigate, then, how the instruments of labour are converted from tools into machines, or what the difference is between a machine and an implement used in a handicraft. We are concerned here only with broad and general characteristics, for epochs in the history of society are no more separated from each other by strict and abstract lines of demarcation than are geological epochs.

Mathematicians and experts on mechanics – and they are occasionally followed in this by English economists – call a tool a simple machine and a machine a complex tool. They see no essential difference between them, and even give the name of machine to simple mechanical aids such as the lever, the inclined plane, the screw, the wedge, etc.[2] As a matter of fact, every machine is a

---

1. Mill should have said, 'of any human being not fed by other people's labour', for there is no doubt that machinery has greatly increased the number of distinguished idlers.

2. See, for instance, Hutton's *Course of Mathematics*.

combination of these simple aids, or powers, no matter how they may be disguised. From the economic standpoint however, this explanation is worth nothing, because the historical element is missing from it. Again, some people try to explain the difference between a tool and a machine by saying that in the case of the tool, man is the motive power, whereas the power behind the machine is a natural force independent of man, as for instance an animal, water, wind and so on.[3] According to this, a plough drawn by oxen, which is common to the most diverse epochs of production, would be a machine, while Claussen's circular loom, which weaves 96,000 picks a minute, though it is set in motion by the hand of one single worker, would be a mere tool. Indeed, this same loom, though a tool when worked by hand, would be a machine if worked by steam. And since the application of animal power is one of man's earliest inventions, production by machinery would have preceded production by handicrafts. When in 1735 John Wyatt announced his spinning machine, and thereby started the industrial revolution of the eighteenth century, he nowhere mentioned that a donkey would provide the motive power instead of a man, yet this is what actually happened. In his programme it was called a machine 'to spin without fingers'.[4]

3. 'From this point of view we may draw a sharp line of demarcation between a tool and a machine: spades, hammers, chisels, etc., combinations of levers and of screws, in all of which, no matter how complicated they may be in other respects, man is the motive power ... all this falls under the category of tool; but the plough, which is drawn by animal power, and windmills, etc. must be classed among machines' (William Schulz, *Die Bewegung der Produktion*, Zürich, 1843, p. 38). In many respects a book to be recommended.
4. Spinning machines had already been used before his time, although very imperfect ones, and Italy was probably the country where they first appeared. A critical history of technology would show how little any of the inventions of the eighteenth century are the work of a single individual. As yet such a book does not exist. Darwin has directed attention to the history of natural technology, i.e. the formation of the organs of plants and animals, which serve as the instruments of production for sustaining their life. Does not the history of the productive organs of man in society, of organs that are the material basis of every particular organization of society, deserve equal attention? And would not such a history be easier to compile, since, as Vico says, human history differs from natural history in that we have made the former, but not the latter? Technology reveals the active relation of man to nature, the direct process of the production of his life, and thereby it also lays bare the process of the production of the social relations of his life, and of the mental conceptions that flow from those relations. Even a history of religion that is

All fully developed machinery consists of three essentially different parts, the motor mechanism, the transmitting mechanism and finally the tool or working machine. The motor mechanism acts as the driving force of the mechanism as a whole. It either generates its own motive power, like the steam-engine, the caloric-engine, the electro-magnetic machine, etc., or it receives its impulse from some already existing natural force, like the water-wheel from the descent of water down an incline, the windmill from the wind, and so on. The transmitting mechanism, composed of fly-wheels, shafting, toothed wheels, pulleys, straps, ropes, bands, pinions and gearing of the most varied kinds, regulates the motion, changes its form where necessary, as for instance from linear to circular, and divides and distributes it among the working machines. These two parts of the whole mechanism are there solely to impart motion to the working machine; using this motion the working machine then seizes on the object of labour and modifies it as desired. It is this last part of the machinery, the tool or working machine, with which the industrial revolution of the eighteenth century began. And to this day it constantly serves as the starting-point whenever a handicraft or a manufacture is turned into an industry carried on by machinery.

On a closer examination of the working machine proper we rediscover in it as a general rule, though often in highly modified forms, the very apparatus and tools used by the handicraftsman or the manufacturing worker*; but there is the difference that instead of being the tools of a man they are the implements of a mechanism, mechanical implements. Either the entire machine is only a more or less altered mechanical edition of the old handicraft tool, as for

---

written in abstraction from this material basis is uncritical. It is, in reality, much easier to discover by analysis the earthly kernel of the misty creations of religion than to do the opposite, i.e. to develop from the actual, given relations of life the forms in which these have been apotheosized. The latter method is the only materialist, and therefore the only scientific one. The weaknesses of the abstract materialism of natural science, a materialism which excludes the historical process, are immediately evident from the abstract and ideological conceptions expressed by its spokesmen whenever they venture beyond the bounds of their own speciality.

---

* Here, as elsewhere, the phrase 'manufacturing worker' is used to distinguish the worker under a system of manufacture from the industrial worker of modern times.

instance the power-loom,[5] or the working parts fitted in the frame of the machine are old acquaintances, as spindles are in a mule, needles in a stocking-loom, saw-blades in a sawing-machine and knives in a chopping-machine. The distinction between these tools and the actual framework of the working machine exists from their moment of entry into the world, because they continue for the most part to be produced by handicraft or by manufacture, and are afterwards fitted into the framework of the machine, which is produced by machinery.[6] The machine, therefore, is a mechanism that, after being set in motion, performs with its tools the same operations as the worker formerly did with similar tools. Whether the motive power is derived from man, or in turn from a machine, makes no difference here. From the moment that the tool proper is taken from man and fitted into a mechanism, a machine takes the place of a mere implement. The difference strikes one at once, even in those cases where man himself continues to be the prime mover. The number of implements that he himself can use simultaneously is limited by the number of his own natural instruments of production, i.e. his own bodily organs. In Germany they tried at first to make one spinner work two spinning-wheels, that is to work simultaneously with both hands and both feet. That proved to be too exhausting. Later, a treadle spinning-wheel with two spindles was invented, but adepts in spinning who could spin two threads at once were almost as scarce as two-headed men. The Jenny, on the other hand, even at the very beginning, spun with twelve to eighteen spindles, and the stocking-loom knits with many thousand needles at once. The number of tools that a machine can bring into play simultaneously is from the outset independent of the organic limitations that confine the tools of the handicraftsman.

In many manual implements the distinction between man as mere motive power and man as worker or operator properly so called is very striking indeed. For instance, the foot is merely the prime mover of the spinning-wheel, while the hand, working with

5. It is particularly in the original form of the power-loom that we recognize at first glance the old loom. In its modern form the power-loom has undergone essential alterations.

6. It is only since about 1850 that a constantly increasing portion of these machine tools have been made in England by machinery, and even then not by the same manufacturers as make the machines. Instances of machines for the production of these mechanical tools are the automatic bobbin-making engine, the card-setting engine, shuttle-making machines and machines for forging mule and throstle spindles.

the spindle, and drawing and twisting, performs the real operation of spinning. It is the second part of the handicraftsman's implement, in this case the spindle, which is first seized on by the industrial revolution, leaving to the worker, in addition to his new labour of watching the machine with his eyes and correcting its mistakes with his hands, the merely mechanical role of acting as the motive power. On the other hand, in cases where man has always acted as a simple motive power, as for instance by turning the crank of a mill,[7] by pumping, by moving the arm of a bellows up and down, by pounding with a mortar, etc., there is soon a call for the application of animals, water[8] and wind as motive powers. Here and there, long before the period of manufacture, and also to some extent during that period, these implements attain the stature of machines, but without creating any revolution in the mode of production. It becomes evident in the period of large-scale industry that these implements, even in the form of manual tools, are already machines. For instance, the pumps with which the Dutch emptied the Lake of Harlem in 1836-7 were constructed on the principle of ordinary pumps, the only difference being that their pistons were driven by Cyclopean steam-engines, instead of by men. In England, the common and very imperfect bellows of the blacksmith is occasionally converted into a blowing-engine by connecting its arm with a steam-engine. The steam-engine itself, such as it was at its invention during the manufacturing period

7. Moses said: 'Thou shalt not muzzle the ox when he treadeth out the corn' [Deuteronomy 25: 4]. But the Christian philanthropists of Germany fastened a wooden board round the necks of their serfs, whom they used as a motive power for grinding, in order to prevent them from putting flour into their mouths with their hands.

8. It was partly their lack of streams with a good fall on them, and partly their battles with superfluous quantities of water in other respects, that compelled the Dutch to resort to wind as a motive power. The windmill itself they got from Germany, where its invention called forth a pretty squabble between the nobility, the priests and the Emperor as to which of the three was the 'owner' of the wind. 'The air makes unfree' was the cry in Germany, at the same time as the wind was making Holland free.* What was reduced to bondage in the latter case was not the Dutchman but the land of Holland, in the interests of the Dutchman. In 1836, 12,000 windmills of a total of 6,000 horse-power were still being employed in Holland, to prevent two-thirds of the land from relapsing into a bog.

*'The air makes unfree' is a pun on the medieval German saying, 'town air makes free' (*Stadtluft macht frei*). This was based on the rule that if a serf could escape from his lord and stay within a town for a year and a day he became a free man.

at the close of the seventeenth century, and such as it continued to be down to 1780,[9] did not give rise to any industrial revolution. It was, on the contrary, the invention of machines that made a revolution in the form of steam-engines necessary. As soon as man, instead of working on the object of labour with a tool, becomes merely the motive power of a machine, it is purely accidental that the motive power happens to be clothed in the form of human muscles; wind, water or steam could just as well take man's place. Of course, this does not prevent such a change of form from producing great technical alterations in a mechanism which was originally constructed to be driven by man alone. Nowadays, all machines that have to break new ground, such as sewing-machines, bread-making machines, etc. are constructed to be driven by human as well as by purely mechanical motive power, unless they have special characteristics which exclude their use on a small scale.

The machine, which is the starting-point of the industrial revolution, replaces the worker, who handles a single tool, by a mechanism operating with a number of similar tools and set in motion by a single motive power, whatever the form of that power.[10] Here we have the machine, but in its first role as a simple element in production by machinery.

An increase in the size of the machine and the number of its working tools calls for a more massive mechanism to drive it; and this mechanism, in order to overcome its own inertia, requires a mightier moving power than that of man, quite apart from the fact that man is a very imperfect instrument for producing uniform and continuous motion. Now assuming that he is acting simply as a motor, that a machine has replaced the tool he was using, it is evident that he can also be replaced as a motor by natural forces. Of all the great motive forces handed down from the period of manufacture, horse-power is the worst, partly because a horse has a head of his own, partly because he is costly and the extent to which he can be used in factories is very limited.[11] Nevertheless,

9. It was indeed very much improved by Watt's first so-called single-acting engine, but even in this form it continued to be a mere machine for raising water and brine.

10. 'The union of all these simple instruments, set in motion by a single motor, constitutes a machine' (Babbage, op. cit., p. 136).

11. In January 1861, John C. Morton read before the Society of Arts a paper on 'The Forces Employed in Agriculture'. He states there: 'Every improvement that furthers the uniformity of the land makes the steam-

the horse was used extensively during the infancy of large-scale industry. This is proved both by the complaints of the agronomists of that epoch and by the way of expressing mechanical force in terms of 'horse-power', which survives to this day. The wind was too inconstant and uncontrollable and, apart from this, in England, the birthplace of large-scale industry, the use of water-power pre-ponderated even during the period of manufacture. In the seventeenth century attempts had already been made to turn two pairs of millstones with a single water-wheel. But the increased size of the transmitting mechanism came into conflict with the water-power, which was now insufficient, and this was one of the factors which gave the impulse for a more accurate investigation of the laws of friction. In the same way the irregularity caused by the motive power in mills that were set in motion by pushing and pulling a lever led to the theory, and the application, of the fly-wheel,[12] which later played such an important part in large-scale industry. In this way, the first scientific and technical elements of large-scale industry were developed during the period of manufacturing. Arkwright's throstle-spinning mill was from the very first turned by water. Despite this, the use of water-power as the main motive force brought with it various added difficulties. The flow of water could not be increased at will, it failed at certain seasons of the

---

engine more and more applicable to the production of pure mechanical force ... Horse-power is needed wherever crooked fences and other obstructions prevent uniform action. These obstructions are vanishing day by day. For operations that demand more exercise of will than actual force, the only power applicable is that controlled every instant by the human mind – in other words, man-power.' Mr Morton then reduces steam-power, horse-power and man-power to the unit in general use for steam-engines, namely the force required to raise 33,000 lb. one foot in one minute, and reckons the cost of one horse-power from a steam-engine to be 3d. per hour, and from a horse 5½d. Furthermore, a horse can work only eight hours a day if it is to maintain its health. At least three out of every seven horses used on cultivated land during the year can be dispensed with by the use of steam-power, at an expense not greater than the cost of the three during the three or four months in which alone they can be used effectively. Lastly, steam-power, in those agricultural operations in which it can be employed, improves the quality of the work in comparison with horse-power. To do the work of a steam-engine would require sixty-six men, at a total cost of 15s. an hour, and to do the work of a horse, thirty-two men, at a total cost of 8s. an hour.

12. Faulhaber, 1625; De Cous, 1688.*

*See the entries in the bibliography under Faulhaber and Hero Alexandrinus.

year, and above all it was essentially local.[13] Not till the invention of Watt's second and so-called double-acting steam-engine was a prime mover found which drew its own motive power from the consumption of coal and water, was entirely under man's control, was mobile and a means of locomotion, was urban and not – like the water-wheel – rural, permitted production to be concentrated in towns instead of – like the water-wheels – being scattered over the countryside[14] and, finally, was of universal technical application, and little affected in its choice of residence by local circumstances. The greatness of Watt's genius showed itself in the specification of the patent that he took out in April 1784. In that specification his steam-engine is described, not as an invention for a specific purpose, but as an agent universally applicable in industry. Many of the applications he points out in it, for instance the steam-hammer, were not introduced until half a century later. Even so he doubted the applicability of steam to navigation. Yet steam-engines of colossal size for ocean steamers were sent to the Great Exhibition of 1851 by his successors, the firm of Boulton and Watt.

As soon as tools had been converted from being manual implements of man into the parts of a mechanical apparatus, of a machine, the motive mechanism also acquired an independent form, entirely emancipated from the restraints of human strength. Thereupon the individual machine, which we have considered so far, sinks to a mere element in production by machinery. One motive mechanism was now able to drive many machines at once. The motive mechanism grows with the number of the machines that are turned simultaneously, and the transmitting mechanism becomes an extensive apparatus.

We have now to distinguish the co-operation of a number of machines of one kind from a complex system of machinery.

13. The modern invention of the turbine has freed the industrial exploitation of water-power from many of its former fetters.

14. 'In the early days of textile manufactures, the locality of the factory depended upon the existence of a stream having a sufficient fall to turn a water-wheel; and, although the establishment of the water-mills was the commencement of the breaking-up of the domestic system of manufacture, yet the mills necessarily situated upon streams, and frequently at considerable distances the one from the other, formed part of a rural, rather than an urban system; and it was not until the introduction of steam-power as a substitute for the stream that factories were congregated in towns, and localities where the coal and water required for the production of steam were found in sufficient quantities. The steam-engine is the parent of manufacturing towns' (A. Redgrave, in *Reports of the Inspectors of Factories . . . 30 April 1860*, p. 36).

In the one case, the product is entirely made by a single machine, which performs all the various operations previously done by one handicraftsman with his tool, by a weaver with his loom, for instance, or by several handicraftsmen successively, either separately or as members of a system of manufacture.[15] In the modern manufacture of envelopes, for example, one man folded the paper with the folder, another laid on the gum, a third turned over the flap on which the emblem is impressed, a fourth embossed the emblem and so on; and on each occasion the envelope had to change hands. One single envelope machine now performs all these operations at once, and makes more than 3,000 envelopes in an hour. In the London exhibition of 1862, there was an American machine for making paper cornets. It cut the paper, pasted, folded and finished 300 in a minute. Here the whole process, which under the manufacturing system was split up into a series of operations and carried out in that order, is completed by a single machine, operating a combination of different tools. Now whether such a machine is merely a reproduction of a complicated manual implement, or a combination of various simple implements specialized by manufacture, in both cases we meet again with simple co-operation in the factory, i.e. in the workshop in which machinery alone is used; and, leaving the worker out of consideration for the moment, this co-operation appears, in the first instance, as the assembling in one place of similar and simultaneously acting machines. Thus a weaving factory consists of a number of power-looms working side by side, and a sewing factory consists of a number of sewing-machines all in the same building. But there is here a technical unity in that all the machines receive their impulse simultaneously, and in an equal degree, from the pulsations of the common prime mover, which are imparted to them by the transmitting mechanism; and this mechanism, to a certain extent, is also common to them all, since only particular ramifications of it

15. From the standpoint of the division of labour in manufacture, weaving was not simple, but complicated manual labour, and consequently the power-loom is a machine that does very complicated work. It is quite wrong to suppose that modern machinery originally appropriated only those operations which the division of labour in manufacture had already simplified. Spinning and weaving were split up during the period of manufacture into new varieties, and the tools used were modified and improved; but the labour process itself was in no way split up, and it retained its handicraft-like character. It is not labour, but the instrument of labour, that serves as the starting-point of the machine.

branch off to each machine. Just as a number of tools, then, form the organs of a machine, so a number of machines of one kind constitute the organs of the motive mechanism.

A real machine system, however, does not take the place of these independent machines until the object of labour goes through a connected series of graduated processes carried out by a chain of mutually complementary machines of various kinds. Here we have again the co-operation by division of labour which is peculiar to manufacture, but now it appears as a combination of machines with specific functions. The tools peculiar to the various specialized workers, such as those of the beaters, combers, shearers, spinners, etc. in the manufacture of wool, are now transformed into the tools of specialized machines, each machine forming a special organ, with a special function in the combined mechanism. In those branches in which the machine system is first introduced, manufacture itself provides, in general, a natural basis for the division, and consequently the organization, of the process of production.[16] Nevertheless, an essential difference at once appears. In manufacture, it is the workers who, either singly or in groups, must carry on each particular process with their manual implements. The worker has been appropriated by the process; but the process had previously to be adapted to the worker. This subjective principle of the division of labour no longer exists in production by machinery. Here the total process is examined objectively, viewed in and for itself, and analysed into its constitutive phases.

16. Before the epoch of large-scale industry, the predominant manufacture in England was that of wool. Hence it was in this industry that, in the first half of the eighteenth century, the most experiments were made. Cotton, which required less careful preparation for its treatment by machinery, derived the benefit of the experience gained on wool, just as afterwards the treatment of wool by machinery was developed on the foundation laid by the use of machinery in spinning and weaving cotton. Certain isolated parts of the manufacture of wool, such as wool-combing, were only incorporated in the factory system during the last decade [i.e. up to 1867]. 'The application of power to the process of combing wool ... extensively in operation since the introduction of the combing-machine, especially Lister's ... undoubtedly had the effect of throwing a very large number of men out of work. Wool was formerly combed by hand, most frequently in the cottage of the comber. It is now very generally combed in the factory, and hand-labour is superseded, except in some particular kinds of work, in which hand-combed wool is still preferred. Many of the hand-combers found employment in the factories, but the produce of the hand-combers bears so small a proportion to that of the machine that the employment of a very large number of combers has passed away' (*Reports of the Inspectors of Factories ... 31 October 1856*, p. 16).

The problem of how to execute each particular process, and to bind the different partial processes together into a whole, is solved by the aid of machines, chemistry, etc.[17] But of course, in this case too, the theoretical conception must be perfected by accumulated experience on a large scale. Each particular machine supplies raw material to the machine next in line; and since they are all working at the same time, the product is always going through the various stages of its formation, and is also constantly in a state of transition from one phase of production to another. Just as in manufacture the direct co-operation of the specialized workers establishes a numerical proportion between the different groups, so in an organized system of machinery, where one machine is constantly kept employed by another, a fixed relation is established between their number, their size and their speed. The collective working machine, which is now an articulated system composed of various kinds of single machine, and of groups of single machines, becomes all the more perfect the more the process as a whole becomes a continuous one, i.e. the less the raw material is interrupted in its passage from the first phase to the last; in other words, the more its passage from one phase to another is effected not by the hand of man, but by the machinery itself. In manufacture, the isolation of each special process is a condition imposed by the division of labour itself, whereas in the fully developed factory the continuity of the special processes is the regulating principle.

A system of machinery, whether it is based simply on the co-operation of similar machines, as in weaving, or on a combination of different machines, as in spinning, constitutes in itself a vast automaton* as soon as it is driven by a self-acting prime mover. But although the whole system may for example be driven by a steam-engine, some of the individual machines may require the aid of the worker for some of their movements (such aid was necessary for the insertion of the mule carriage before the invention of the self-acting mule, and is still necessary in the fine-spinning mills). Equally, certain parts of the machine may have to be handled by the worker like a manual tool, if the machine is

17. 'The principle of the factory system, then, is to substitute ... the partition of a process into its essential constituents, for the division or graduation of labour among artisans' (Andrew Ure, *The Philosophy of Manufactures*, London, 1835, p. 20).

---

* The expression 'vast automaton' is taken from Ure. See below, p. 544.

to do its work. This was the case in machine-makers' workshops, before the conversion of the slide rest into a self-actor. As soon as a machine executes, without man's help, all the movements required to elaborate the raw material, and needs only supplementary assistance from the worker, we have an automatic system of machinery, capable of constant improvement in its details. Such improvements as the apparatus that stops a drawing frame whenever a sliver breaks, and the self-acting stop which stops the power-loom as soon as the shuttle bobbin is empty of weft, are quite modern inventions. As an example both of continuity of production and of the implementation of the automatic principle, we may take a modern paper-mill. In the paper industry generally, we may advantageously study in detail not only the distinctions between modes of production based on different means of production, but also the connection between the social relations of production and those modes of production. The old German paper-making trade provides an example of handicraft production; Holland in the seventeenth century and France in the eighteenth century provide examples of manufacture proper; and modern England provides the example of automatic fabrication. Besides these, there still exist, in India and China, two distinct ancient Asiatic forms of the same industry.

An organized system of machines to which motion is communicated by the transmitting mechanism from an automatic centre is the most developed form of production by machinery. Here we have, in place of the isolated machine, a mechanical monster whose body fills whole factories, and whose demonic power, at first hidden by the slow and measured motions of its gigantic members, finally bursts forth in the fast and feverish whirl of its countless working organs.

There were mules and steam-engines before there were any workers exclusively occupied in making mules and steam-engines, in the same way as men wore clothes before there were any tailors. However the inventions of Vaucanson, Arkwright, Watt and others could be put into practice only because each inventor found a considerable number of skilled mechanical workers available, placed at their disposal by the period of manufacture. Some of these workers were independent handicraftsmen of various trades, others were grouped together in manufactures, in which, as we have mentioned before, a division of labour of particular strictness prevailed. As inventions increased in number, and the demand for the newly discovered machines grew larger, the machine-making industry increasingly split up into numerous independent branches, and the division of labour within these manufactures developed accordingly. Here, therefore in manu-facture, we see the immediate technical foundation of large-scale industry. Manufacture produced the machinery with which large-scale industry abolished the handicraft and manufacturing systems in the spheres of production it first seized hold of. The system of machine production therefore grew spontaneously on a material basis which was inadequate to it. When the system had attained a certain degree of development, it had to overthrow this ready-made foundation, which had meanwhile undergone further development in its old form, and create for itself a new basis appropriate to its own mode of production. Just as the individual machine retains a dwarf-like character as long as it is worked by the power of man alone, and just as no system of machinery could be properly developed before the steam-engine took the place of the earlier motive powers, animals, wind and even water; so too large-scale industry was crippled in its whole development as long as its characteristic instrument of production, the machine, owed its existence to personal strength and personal skill, and depended on the muscular development, the keenness of sight and the manual dexterity with which the specialized workers, in manufacture, and the handicraftsmen outside manufacture, wielded their dwarf-like implements. Thus apart from the high cost of machines made in this way – a circumstance which forms the dominant motive for the capitalist's actions – the expansion of industries carried on by means of machinery and the invasion of fresh branches of production by machinery were dependent on the growth of a class of workers who, owing to the semi-artistic nature of their employment, could increase their numbers only gradually, and not by leaps and bounds. But, besides this, at a certain stage of its development large-scale industry also came into conflict with the technical basis provided for it by handicrafts and manufacture. A number of technical problems arose naturally and spontaneously from the very course of development: the size of the prime movers, of the transmitting mechanism and of the machines properly so called increased, the components of the machines became more complicated and diverse in form, they had to operate with stricter regularity, and they accordingly diverged more and more from the model which originally determined their construction under the handicraft system, and acquired an independent form restricted only by their mechanical task.[18] At the same time the automatic system was perfected, and it became more and more unavoidable to use materials which were difficult to work with, as for instance when iron replaced wood. In every case the solution of these problems met with a stumbling-block in the personal restrictions which even the collective worker of manufacture could not break through except to a limited extent. Such machines as the modern hydraulic press, the modern power-loom and the modern carding engine could never have been furnished by the manufacturing period.

The transformation of the mode of production in one sphere of industry necessitates a similar transformation in other spheres. This happens at first in branches of industry which are connected together by being separate phases of a process, and yet isolated by the social division of labour, in such a way that each of them produces an independent commodity. Thus machine spinning made machine weaving necessary, and both together made a mechanical and chemical revolution compulsory in bleaching, printing and dyeing. So too, on the other hand, the revolution in cotton-spinning called forth the invention of the gin, for separating the seeds from the cotton fibre; it was only by means of this invention that the production of cotton became possible on the enormous scale at present required.[19] But as well as this, the revolution in the modes of production of industry and agriculture made neces-

18. The power-loom was at first made chiefly of wood; in its improved modern form it is made of iron. To what an extent the old forms of the instruments of production influence their new forms at the beginning is shown, among other things, by the most superficial comparison of the present power-loom with the old one, of the modern blowing apparatus of a blast-furnace with the first inefficient mechanical reproduction of the ordinary bellows, and perhaps more strikingly than in any other way by the fact that, before the invention of the present locomotive, an attempt was made to construct a locomotive with two feet, which it raised from the ground alternately, like a horse. It is only after a considerable development of the science of mechanics, and an accumulation of practical experience, that the form of a machine becomes settled entirely in accordance with mechanical principles, and emancipated from the traditional form of the tool from which it has emerged.

19. The cotton gin invented by Eli Whitney had until very recent times undergone less essential changes than any other machine of the eighteenth century. It is only during the last decade (i.e. since 1856) that another American, Mr Emery of Albany, New York, has made Whitney's gin out of date by an improvement as simple as it is effective.

sary a revolution in the general conditions of the social process of production, i.e. in the means of communication and transport. In a society whose pivot, to use Fourier's expression,* was small-scale agriculture, with its subsidiary domestic industries and urban handicrafts, the means of communication and transport were so utterly inadequate to the needs of production in the period of manufacture, with its extended division of social labour, its concentration of instruments of labour and workers and its colonial markets, that they in fact became revolutionized. In the same way the means of communication and transport handed down from the period of manufacture soon became unbearable fetters on large-scale industry, given the feverish velocity with which it produces, its enormous extent, its constant flinging of capital and labour from one sphere of production into another and its newly created connections with the world market. Hence, quite apart from the immense transformation which took place in shipbuilding, the means of communication and transport gradually adapted themselves to the mode of production of large-scale industry by means of a system of river steamers, railways, ocean steamers and telegraphs. But the huge masses of iron that had now to be forged, welded, cut, bored and shaped required for their part machines of Cyclopean dimensions, which the machine-building trades of the period of manufacture were incapable of constructing.

Large-scale industry therefore had to take over the machine itself, its own characteristic instrument of production, and to produce machines by means of machines. It was not till it did this that it could create for itself an adequate technical foundation, and stand on its own feet. At the same time as machine production was becoming more general, in the first decades of the nineteenth century, it gradually took over the construction of the machines themselves. But it is only during the last few decades that the construction of railways and ocean steamers on a vast scale has called into existence the Cyclopean machines now employed in the construction of prime movers.

The most essential condition for the production of machines by machines was a prime mover capable of exerting any amount of force, while retaining perfect control. The steam-engine already

---

*In Fourier's table of 'successive characteristics of civilization' (op. cit., pp. 386–7), he describes four 'phases', each of which turns around a 'pivot', such as 'maritime monopoly' or 'industrial feudalism'.

fulfilled this condition. But at the same time it was necessary to produce the geometrically accurate straight lines, planes, circles, cylinders, cones and spheres for the individual parts of the machines. Henry Maudslay solved this problem in the first decade of the nineteenth century by the invention of the slide-rest, a tool that was soon made automatic, and was applied in a modified form to other machines for constructing machinery besides the lathe, for which it was originally intended. This mechanical appliance replaces not some particular tool but the hand itself, which produces a given form by holding and guiding the cutting tool along the iron or other material of labour. Thus it became possible to produce the geometrical shapes of the individual parts of machinery 'with a degree of ease, accuracy, and speed, that no accumulated experience of the hand of the most skilled workman could give'.[20]

If we now look at the part of the machinery which is employed in the construction of machines, and forms the actual operating tool, we find that the manual implements re-appear, but on a Cyclopean scale. The operating part of the boring machine is an immense drill driven by a steam-engine; without this machine, on the other hand, the cylinders of large steam-engines and of hydraulic presses could not be made. The mechanical lathe is only a Cyclopean reproduction of the ordinary foot-lathe; the planing machine is an iron carpenter that works on iron with the same tools as the human carpenter employs on wood; the instrument that cuts the veneers on the London wharves is a gigantic razor; the tool of the shearing machine, which shears iron as easily as a tailor's scissors cut cloth, is a monster pair of scissors; and the steam-hammer works with an ordinary hammer head, but of such a weight that even Thor himself could not wield it.[21] These steam-hammers are an invention of Nasmyth, and there is one that weighs over 6 tons and strikes with a vertical fall of 7

20. *The Industry of Nations*, London, 1855, Part II, p. 239. It is also re-marked, on the same page: 'Simple and outwardly unimportant as this appendage to lathes may appear, it is not, we believe, averring too much to state that its influence in improving and extending the use of machinery has been as great as that produced by Watt's improvements of the steam-engine itself. Its introduction went at once to perfect all machinery, to cheapen it, and to stimulate invention and improvement.'

21. One of these machines, used for forging paddle-wheel shafts in London, is in fact called 'Thor'. It forges a shaft of 16½ tons with as much ease as a blacksmith forges a horse-shoe.

feet, on an anvil weighing 36 tons. It is mere child's play for it to crush a block of granite into powder, yet it is no less capable of driving a nail into a piece of soft wood with a succession of light taps.[22]

As machinery, the instrument of labour assumes a material mode of existence which necessitates the replacement of human force by natural forces, and the replacement of the rule of thumb by the conscious application of natural science. In manufacture the organization of the social labour process is purely subjective: it is a combination of specialized workers. Large-scale industry, on the other hand, possesses in the machine system an entirely objective organization of production, which confronts the worker as a pre-existing material condition of production. In simple co-operation, and even in the more specialized form based on the division of labour, the extrusion of the isolated worker by the associated worker still appears to be more or less accidental. Machinery, with a few exceptions to be mentioned later, operates only by means of associated labour, or labour in common. Hence the co-operative character of the labour process is in this case a technical necessity dictated by the very nature of the instrument of labour.

2. THE VALUE TRANSFERRED BY THE MACHINERY TO THE PRODUCT

We saw that the productive forces resulting from co-operation and the division of labour cost capital nothing. They are natural forces of social labour. Other natural forces appropriated to productive processes, such as steam, water, etc., also cost nothing. But just as a man requires lungs to breathe with, so he requires something that is the work of human hands in order to consume the forces of nature productively. A water-wheel is necessary to exploit the force of water, and a steam-engine to exploit the elasticity of steam. Once discovered, the law of the deflection of a magnetic needle in the field of an electric current, or the law of the magnetization of iron by electricity, cost absolutely nothing.[23] But the exploitation of these laws for the purposes of

22. Wood-working machines that are also capable of being employed on a small scale are mostly American inventions.

23. Science, generally speaking, costs the capitalist nothing, a fact that by no means prevents him from exploiting it. 'Alien' science is incorporated by capital just as 'alien' labour is. But 'capitalist' appropriation and 'personal'

telegraphy, etc., necessitates costly and extensive apparatus. As we have seen, the machine does not drive out the tool. Rather does the tool expand and multiply, changing from a dwarf implement of the human organism to the implement of a mechanism created by man. Capital now sets the worker to work, not with a manual tool, but with a machine which itself handles the tools. Therefore, although it is clear at the first glance that large-scale industry raises the productivity of labour to an extraordinary degree by incorporating into the production process both the immense forces of nature and the results arrived at by natural science, it is by no means equally clear that this increase in productive force is not, on the other hand, purchased with an increase in the amount of labour expended. Machinery, like every other component of constant capital, creates no new value, but yields up its own value to the product it serves to beget. In so far as the machine has value and, as a result, transfers value to the product, it forms an element in the value of the latter. Instead of being cheapened, the product is made dearer in proportion to the value of the machine. And it is crystal clear that machines and systems of machinery, large-scale industry's characteristic instruments of labour, are incomparably more loaded with value than the implements used in handicrafts and in manufacture.

In the first place, it must be observed that machinery, while always entering as a whole into the labour process, enters only piece by piece into the process of valorization. It never adds more value than it loses, on an average, by depreciation. Hence there is a great difference between the value of a machine and the value transferred in a given time by the machine to the product. Equally, there is a great difference between the machine as a factor in the formation of value and as a factor in the formation of the product. The longer the period during which the machine serves in the same labour process, the greater are those differences. It is no doubt true, as we have seen, that every instrument of labour enters as a whole into the labour process, while only piecemeal, in proportion to its average daily depreciation, into the process of valorization. But this difference between the mere

appropriation, whether of science or of material wealth, are totally different things. Dr Ure himself deplores the gross ignorance of mechanical science which exists among his beloved machinery-exploiting manufacturers, and Liebig can tell us about the astounding ignorance of chemistry displayed by English chemical manufacturers.

utilization of the instrument and its depreciation is much greater in the case of machinery than it is with a tool, because the machine, being made from more durable material, has a longer life; because it can be employed more economically, from the point of view both of the deterioration of its own components and of its consumption of materials, as its use is regulated by strict scientific laws; and, finally, because its field of production is incomparably larger than that of a tool. Both in the case of the machine and of the tool, we find that after allowing for their average daily cost, that is for the value they transmit to the product by their average daily wear and tear, and for their consumption of auxiliary substances such as oil, coal and so on, they do their work for nothing, like the natural forces which are already available without the intervention of human labour. The greater the productive effectiveness of the machinery compared with that of the tool, the greater is the extent of its gratuitous service. Only in large-scale industry has man succeeded in making the product of his past labour, labour which has already been objectified, perform gratuitous service on a large scale, like a force of nature.[24]

When we considered co-operation and manufacture, we found that certain general conditions of production such as buildings could be consumed more economically than the scattered conditions of production of isolated craftsmen, because they could be consumed in common, and that they therefore made the product cheaper. In a system of machinery, not only is the framework of the machine consumed in common by its numerous working parts, but the prime mover, together with a part of the transmitting mechanism, is consumed in common by a large number of operating machines.

Given the difference between the value of the machinery and the

24. Ricardo lays such stress on this effect of machinery (of which, in other contexts, he takes no more notice than he does of the general distinction between the labour process and the valorization process) that he occasionally loses sight of the value given up by machines to the product, and puts them on the same footing as natural forces. Thus, for example, 'Adam Smith nowhere undervalues the services which these natural agents and machinery perform for us, but he very justly distinguishes the nature of the value which they add to commodities [by adding to value in use] . . . As they perform their work gratuitously [. . .] the assistance which they afford us adds nothing to value in exchange' (Ricardo, op. cit., pp. 336–7). This observation by Ricardo is of course correct in so far as it is directed against J. B. Say, who drivels on about the 'service' performed by machines when they create value which forms a part of 'profits'.

value transferred by it in a day to the product, the extent to which this latter value makes the product dearer depends in the first instance upon the size of the product, on its area, so to speak. Mr Baynes of Blackburn, in a lecture of 1857, estimates that 'each real[25] mechanical horse-power will drive 450 self-acting mule spindles, with preparation, or 220 throstle spindles, or 15 looms for 40-inch cloth with the appliances for warping, sizing, etc.'* In the first case, it is the daily product of 450 mule spindles, in the second, of 200 throstle spindles, and in the third, of 15 power-looms, over which is spread the daily cost of one horse-power and the deterioration of the machinery set in motion by that power. Hence this deterioration transfers only a minute amount of value to a pound of yarn or a yard of cloth. Similarly with the steam-hammer mentioned earlier. Since its daily deterioration, its consumption of coal, etc. are spread over the immense masses of iron hammered by it in a day, only a small value is added to a hundredweight of iron; but that value would be very great if the Cyclopean instrument were used to drive in small nails.

Given a machine's capacity for work, that is, the number of its

25. [Note by Engels to the third German edition:] A horse-power is equal to a force of 33,000 foot-pounds per minute, i.e. to a force that raises 33,000 pounds one foot in a minute, or one pound 33,000 feet. This is the horse-power meant in the text. In ordinary language, and also here and there in quotations in this work, a distinction is drawn between the 'normal' and the 'commercial' or 'indicated' horse-power of the same engine. The old or nominal horse-power is calculated exclusively from the length of the piston-stroke and the diameter of the cylinder, and leaves pressure of steam and piston speed out of consideration. What it expresses is in practice this: the engine would be one of, for example, 50 horse-power, if it were driven with the same low pressure of steam and the same slow piston speed as in the days of Boulton and Watt. But the two latter factors have increased enormously since those days. In order to measure the mechanical force exerted today by an engine, an indicator has been invented which shows the pressure of the steam in the cylinder. The piston speed is easily ascertained. Thus the 'indicated' or 'commercial' horse-power of an engine is expressed by a mathematical formula involving diameter of cylinder, length of stroke, piston speed and steam pressure simultaneously, and showing what multiple of 33,000 pounds is really raised by the engine in a minute. Hence, one 'nominal' horse-power may exert three, four or even five 'indicated' or 'real' horse-power. This observation is made for the purpose of explaining various quotations on subsequent pages.

* J. B. Baynes, *The Cotton Trade. Two lectures on the Above Subject, Delivered before the Members of the Blackburn Literary, Scientific, and Mechanics' Institution, Blackburn*, London, 1857, p. 48.

operating tools or, where it is a question of force, their size, the amount of its product will depend on the velocity of its working parts, on the speed, for instance, of the spindles, or on the number of blows given by the hammer in a minute. Many of these colossal hammers strike seventy times in a minute, and Ryder's patent machine for forging spindles with small hammers gives as many as 700 strokes per minute.

Given the rate at which machinery transfers its value to the product, the amount of value so transferred depends on the total value of the machinery.[26] The less labour it contains, the less value it contributes to the product. The less value it gives up, the more productive it is, and the more its services approach those rendered by natural forces. But the production of machinery lessens its value in relation to its extension and efficacy.

A comparative analysis of the prices of commodities produced by handicrafts or manufacture, and of the prices of the same commodities produced by machinery, shows in general that in the product of machinery the value arising out of the instrument of labour increases relatively, but decreases absolutely. In other words, its absolute amount decreases, but its amount in relation to the total value of the product – of a pound of yarn, for instance – increases.[27]

26. The reader who is imbued with capitalist notions will naturally miss here the 'interest' added by the machine to the product in proportion to its capital value. It is however easily seen that since a machine no more creates new value than any other part of constant capital, it cannot add any value under the heading of 'interest'. It is also evident that here, where we are dealing with the production of surplus-value, we cannot *a priori* presuppose the existence of any part of that value as interest. The capitalist mode of calculating, which seems on the face of it to be absurd, and to contradict the laws of the creation of value, will be explained in the third volume of this work.

27. The portion of value which is added by the machinery decreases both absolutely and relatively when the machinery drives out horses and other animals which are employed merely as motive forces and not as machines for inducing metabolic changes. We may remark here, incidentally, that Descartes, in defining animals as mere machines, saw with the eyes of the period of manufacture. The medieval view, on the other hand, was that animals were assistants to man, and this is also the view taken later by von Haller, in his *Restauration der Staatswissenschaften.** Descartes, like Bacon, thought that the

*Karl Ludwig von Haller (1768–1854) was a Swiss historian and the leading political theorist of the Reaction after 1815. His book, mentioned here, may be translated as 'The Restoration of Political Science'. It is a conscious attempt to return back beyond the eighteenth-century Enlightenment to monarchical absolutism based on natural law, and to adopt an explicitly 'medieval' standpoint.

It is evident that whenever it costs as much labour to produce a machine as is saved by the employment of that machine, all that has taken place is a displacement of labour. Consequently, the total labour required to produce a commodity has not been lessened, in other words, the productivity of labour has not been increased. However, the difference between the labour a machine costs and the labour it saves, in other words the degree of productivity the machine possesses, does not depend on the difference between its own value and the value of the tool it replaces. As long as the labour spent on a machine is such that the portion of its value added to the product remains smaller than the value added by the worker to the product with his tool, there is always a difference of labour saved in favour of the machine. The productivity of the machine is therefore measured by the human labour-power it replaces. According to Mr Baynes, $2\frac{1}{2}$ workers are required for the 450 mule spindles, including preparation machinery, that are driven by one horse-power[28]; each self-acting mule spindle, working 10 hours, produces 13 ounces of yarn

---

altered methods of thought would result in an alteration in the shape of production, and the practical subjugation of nature by man. This is shown by a passage in the *Discours de la méthode*: 'It is possible' (using the method he introduced in philosophy) 'to attain knowledge very useful in life and, in place of the speculative philosophy taught in the schools, one can find a practical philosophy by which, given that we know the powers and the effectiveness of fire, water, air, the stars, and all the other bodies that surround us, as well and as accurately as we know the various trades of our craftsmen, we shall be able to employ them in the same manner as the latter to all those uses to which they are adapted, and thus as it were make ourselves the masters and the possessors of nature', thereby contributing 'to the perfection of human life'.* In the preface to Sir Dudley North's *Discourses upon Trade* (1691) it is stated that the method of Descartes, as applied to political economy, had begun to free it from the old fables and superstitious notions about money, trade, etc. On the whole, however, the early English economists sided with Bacon and Hobbes as their philosophers, while, at a later period, Locke became 'the philosopher' κατ'ἐξοχήν† of political economy in England, France and Italy.

28. According to the annual report of the Essen Chamber of Commerce (October 1863), the Krupp steel works, with its 161 furnaces, 32 steam-engines (in the year 1800 this was roughly the total number of steam-engines working in Manchester), 14 steam-hammers (representing in all 1,236 horse-power), 49 forges, 203 tool-machines and approximately 2,400 workers, produced in 1862 thirteen million pounds of cast steel. Here there are less than two workers to each horse-power.

* Descartes, *Discours de la méthode* (1637), Part VI.
†*par excellence*.

(average thickness); consequently 2½ workers spin 365⅗ lb. of yarn per week. Hence, if we disregard waste to make the calculation simpler, 366 lb. of cotton absorb only 150 hours of labour during their conversion into yarn, in other words 15 working days of 10 hours each. But with a spinning-wheel, assuming that the hand-spinner produces 13 ounces of yarn in 60 hours, the same weight of cotton would absorb 2,700 working days of 10 hours each, or 27,000 hours of labour.[29] Where block-printing, the old method of printing calico by hand, has been driven out by machine-printing, a single machine, with the aid of one man or boy, prints as much calico of four colours in one hour as it formerly took 200 men to do.[30] Before Eli Whitney invented the cotton gin in 1793, the separation of the seed from a pound of cotton cost an average day's labour. By means of his invention it became possible for one black woman to clean 100 lb. a day, and since then the effectiveness of the gin has been increased considerably. A pound of raw cotton which previously cost 50 cents to produce could subsequently be sold for 10 cents at a greater profit, i.e. with more unpaid labour. In India they use an instrument called a churka, which is half machine and half tool, for separating the seeds from the cotton wool; with this one man and one woman can clean 28 lb. a day. With the churka invented some years ago by Dr Forbes, one man and a boy produce 250 lb. a day. If oxen, steam or water are used for driving it, only a few boys and girls are required, as feeders (providers of material for the machine). Sixteen of these machines driven by oxen do as much work in a day as 750 people did before, on average.[31]

As already stated,* a steam-plough does as much work in one hour at a cost of 3d. as 66 men at a cost of 15s. I come back to this example in order to clear up an erroneous notion. The 15s. are by no means the expression in money of all the labour expended in one hour by the 66 men. If the ratio of surplus

29. Babbage estimates that in Java 117 per cent is added to the value of cotton by the labour of spinning alone. At the same period (1832) the total value added to cotton by machinery and labour in the fine-spinning industry amounted to about 33 per cent of the initial value of the raw material (*On the Economy of Machinery*, pp. 165–6).

30. Machine-printing also economizes on colour.

31. See *Paper read by Dr Watson, Reporter on Products to the Government of India, before the Society of Arts*, 17 April 1860.

---

*See above, p. 498.

labour to necessary labour were 100 per cent, these 66 men would produce in one hour a value of 30s., although their wages, 15s., represented only their labour for half an hour. Let us suppose, then, that a machine costs as much as the wages for a year of the 150 men it displaces, say £3,000; this £3,000 is by no means the expression in money of the labour provided by these men and added to the object of labour before the introduction of the machine, but only the expression of that portion of their year's labour which was expended for themselves and is represented by their wages. On the other hand, the £3,000, the monetary value of the machine, expresses all the labour expended to produce it, whatever the proportion between the worker's wages and the capitalist's surplus-value. Therefore, even if the machine costs as much as the labour-power displaced by it, the labour objectified in it is still much smaller in quantity than the living labour it replaces.[32]

The use of machinery for the exclusive purpose of cheapening the product is limited by the requirement that less labour must be expended in producing the machinery than is displaced by the employment of that machinery. For the capitalist, however, there is a further limit on its use. Instead of paying for the labour, he pays only the value of the labour-power employed; the limit to his using a machine is therefore fixed by the difference between the value of the machine and the value of the labour-power replaced by it. Since the division of the day's work into necessary labour and surplus labour differs in different countries, and even in the same country at different periods, or in different branches of industry; and further, since the actual wage of the worker sometimes sinks below the value of his labour-power, and sometimes rises above it, it is possible for the difference between the price of the machinery and the price of the labour-power replaced by that machinery to undergo great variations, while the difference between the quantity of labour needed to produce the machine and the total quantity of labour replaced by it remains constant.[33] But it is only the former difference that determines the cost to the capitalist of producing a commodity, and influences his actions

32. 'These mute agents' (the machines) 'are always the produce of much less labour than that which they displace, even when they are of the same money-value' (Ricardo, op. cit., p. 40).

33. The field of application for machinery would therefore be entirely different in a communist society from what it is in bourgeois society.

through the pressure of competition. Hence the invention now-adays in England of machines that are employed only in North America; just as in the sixteenth and seventeenth centuries machines were invented in Germany for use exclusively in Holland, and just as many French inventions of the eighteenth century were exploited only in England. In the older countries, machinery itself, when employed in some branches of industry, creates such a superfluity of labour ('redundancy of labour' is how Ricardo puts it*) in other branches that the fall of wages below the value of labour-power impedes the use of machinery in those other branches and, from the standpoint of the capitalist, makes the use of machinery superfluous, and often impossible, because his profit comes from a reduction in the labour paid for, not in the labour employed. In some branches of the wool industry in England the employment of children has been considerably lessened during recent years, and in some cases entirely abolished. Why? Because the Factory Acts made two sets of children necessary, one set working six hours, the other four, or both sets working five hours. But the parents refused to sell the 'half-timers' cheaper than the 'full-timers'. Hence the substitution of machinery for the 'half-timers'.[34] Before the labour of women and children under 10 years old was forbidden in mines, the capitalists considered the employment of naked women and girls, often in company with men, so far sanctioned by their moral code, and especially by their ledgers, that it was only after the passing of the Act that they had recourse to machinery. The Yankees have invented a stone-breaking machine. The English

34. 'Employers of labour would not unnecessarily retain two sets of children under 13 . . . In fact one class of manufacturers, the spinners of woollen yarn, now rarely employ children under 13 years of age, i.e. half-timers. They have introduced improved and new machinery of various kinds, which altogether supersedes the employment of children' (i.e. of children under 13 years old); 'for instance, I will mention one process as an illustration of this diminution in the number of children, wherein by the addition of an apparatus, called a piecing machine, to existing machines, the work of six or four half-timers, according to the peculiarity of each machine, can be performed by one young person' (i.e. over 13 years old) . . . 'The half-time system "stimulated" the invention of the piecing machine' (*Reports of the Inspectors of Factories . . . 31 October 1858*) [pp. 42–3].

* Ricardo refers rather to 'redundancy of people' (op. cit., p. 472) although of course it is clear from the context that it is workers whose redundancy he has in mind.

do not make use of it because the 'wretch'[35] who does this work gets paid for such a small portion of his labour that machinery would increase the cost of production to the capitalist.[36] In England women are still occasionally used instead of horses for hauling barges,[37] because the labour required to produce horses and machines is an accurately known quantity, while that required to maintain the women of the surplus population is beneath all calculation. Hence we nowhere find a more shameless squandering of human labour-power for despicable purposes than in England, the land of machinery.

3. THE MOST IMMEDIATE EFFECTS OF MACHINE PRODUCTION ON THE WORKER

As we have shown, the starting-point of large-scale industry is the revolution in the instruments of labour, and this attains its most highly developed form in the organized system of machinery in the factory. Before we inquire how human material is incorporated with this objective organism, let us consider some general effects of the revolution on the worker himself.

(a) Appropriation of Supplementary Labour-Power by Capital. The Employment of Women and Children

In so far as machinery dispenses with muscular power, it becomes a means for employing workers of slight muscular strength, or whose bodily development is incomplete, but whose limbs are all the more supple. The labour of women and children was therefore the first result of the capitalist application of machinery! That mighty substitute for labour and for workers, the machine, was immediately transformed into a means for increasing the number of wage-labourers by enrolling, under the direct sway of capital, every member of the worker's family, without distinction of age or sex. Compulsory work for the capitalist usurped the place, not only of the children's play, but also of independent labour at home, within customary limits, for the family itself.[38]

35. 'Wretch' is the technical expression used in English political economy for the agricultural labourer.

36. 'Machinery . . . can frequently not be employed until labour' (he means wages) 'rises' (Ricardo, op. cit., p. 479).

37. See *Report of the Social Science Congress at Edinburgh,* October 1863.

38. During the cotton crisis caused by the American Civil War, Dr Edward Smith was sent by the English government to Lancashire, Cheshire and other

The value of labour-power was determined, not only by the labour-time necessary to maintain the individual adult worker, but also by that necessary to maintain his family. Machinery, by throwing every member of that family onto the labour-market, spreads the value of the man's labour-power over his whole family. It thus depreciates it. To purchase the labour-power of a family of four workers may perhaps cost more than it formerly did to purchase the labour-power of the head of the family, but, in return, four days' labour takes the place of one day's, and the price falls in proportion to the excess of the surplus labour of four over the surplus labour of one. In order that the family may live, four people must now provide not only labour for the capitalist, but also surplus labour. Thus we see that machinery, while augmenting the human material that forms capital's most characteristic field of exploitation,[39] at the same time raises the degree of that exploitation.

-----

places to report on the state of health of the cotton operatives. He reported that from a hygienic point of view, and apart from the banishment of the operatives from the factory atmosphere, the crisis had several advantages. The women now had sufficient leisure to give their infants the breast, instead of poisoning them with 'Godfrey's Cordial' (an opiate). They also had the time to learn to cook. Unfortunately, the acquisition of this art occurred at a time when they had nothing to cook. But from this we see how capital, for the purposes of its self-valorization, has usurped the family labour necessary for consumption. This crisis was also utilized to teach sewing to the daughters of the workers in sewing schools. An American revolution and a universal crisis were needed in order that working girls, who spin for the whole world, might learn to sew!

39. 'The numerical increase of labourers has been great, through the growing substitution of female for male, and above all, of childish for adult labour. Three girls of 13, at wages of from 6 shillings to 8 shillings a week, have replaced the one man of mature age, at wages varying from 18 shillings to 45 shillings' (Thomas de Quincey, *The Logic of Political Economy*, London, 1844, note to p. 147). Since certain family functions, such as nursing and suckling children, cannot be entirely suppressed, the mothers who have been confiscated by capital must try substitutes of some sort. Domestic work, such as sewing and mending, must be replaced by the purchase of ready-made articles. Hence the diminished expenditure of labour in the house is accompanied by an increased expenditure of money outside. The cost of production of the working-class family therefore increases, and balances its greater income. In addition to this, economy and judgement in the consumption and preparation of the means of subsistence become impossible. Abundant material on these facts, which are concealed by official political economy, is to be found in the *Reports of the Inspectors of Factories*, the *Reports of the Children's Employment Commission*, and particularly in the *Reports on Public Health*.

Machinery also revolutionizes, and quite fundamentally, the agency through which the capital-relation is formally mediated, i.e. the contract between the worker and the capitalist. Taking the exchange of commodities as our basis, our first assumption was that the capitalist and the worker confronted each other as free persons, as independent owners of commodities, the one possessing money and the means of production, the other labour-power. But now the capitalist buys children and young persons. Previously the worker sold his own labour-power, which he disposed of as a free agent, formally speaking. Now he sells wife and child. He has become a slave-dealer.[40] Notices of demand for children's labour often resemble in form the inquiries for Negro slaves that were formerly to be read among the advertisements in American journals. 'My attention,' says an English factory inspector, 'was drawn to an advertisement in the local paper of one of the most important manufacturing towns of my district, of which the following is a copy: "Wanted, 12 to 20 young persons, not younger than what can pass for 13 years. Wages, 4 shillings a week. Apply, etc." '[41] The phrase 'what can pass for 13 years' refers to the fact that, according to the Factory Act, children under 13 years old may only work 6 hours a day. An officially appointed doctor (the 'certifying surgeon') must certify their age. The manufacturer, therefore, asks for children who look as if they are already 13 years old. The decrease, often by leaps and bounds, in the number of children under 13 years employed in factories, a decrease that is shown in an astonishing manner by the English statistics of the last twenty years, was for the

40. The shortening of the hours of labour for women and children in English factories was exacted from capital by the adult male workers. In striking contrast with this great fact, we find in the most recent years of the Children's Employment Commission that, in relation to this traffic in children, working-class parents have assumed characteristics that are truly revolting and thoroughly like slave-dealing. But the pharisaical capitalist, as may be seen from the same reports, denounces this bestiality which he himself creates, perpetuates and exploits, and which, moreover, he baptizes 'freedom of labour'. 'Infant labour has been called into aid ... even to work for their own daily bread. Without strength to endure such disproportionate toil, without instruction to guide their future life, they have been thrown into a situation physically and morally polluted. The Jewish historian has remarked upon the overthrow of Jerusalem by Titus that it was no wonder it should have been destroyed, with such a signal destruction, when an inhuman mother sacrificed her own offspring to satisfy the cravings of absolute hunger' (*Public Economy Concentrated*, Carlisle, 1833, p. 66).

41. A. Redgrave, in *Reports of the Inspectors of Factories ... 31 October 1858*, pp. 40–41.

most part, according to the evidence of the factory inspectors themselves, the work of the certifying surgeons, who adjusted the children's ages in a manner appropriate to the capitalist's greed for exploitation and the parents' need to engage in this traffic. In the notorious London district of Bethnal Green a public market is held every Monday and Tuesday morning, at which children of both sexes, from 9 years of age upwards, hire themselves out to the silk manufacturers. 'The usual terms are 1s. 8d. a week (this belongs to the parents) and "2d. for myself and tea". The Contract is binding only for the week. The scene and language while this market is going on are quite disgraceful.'[42] It still happens in England that women 'take children from the workhouse and let any one have them out for 2s. 6d. a week'.[43] In spite of legislation, the number of boys sold in Great Britain by their parents to act as live chimney-sweeping machines (although machines exist to replace them) is at least 2,000.[44] The revolution effected by machinery in the legal relationship between buyer and seller of labour-power, causing the transaction as a whole to lose the appearance of a contract between free persons, later offered the English Parliament an excuse, founded on juristic principles, for state intervention into factory affairs. Whenever the law limits the labour of children to 6 hours in industries not previously touched, the complaints of the manufacturers resound yet again. They allege that numbers of parents withdraw their children from the industries brought under the Act in order to sell them where 'freedom of labour' still prevails, i.e. where children under 13 years are compelled to work like adults, and for that reason can be sold at a higher price. But since capital is by its nature a leveller, since it insists upon equality in the conditions of exploitation of labour in every sphere of production as its own innate right, the limitation by law of children's labour in one branch of industry results in its limitation in others.

We have already alluded to the physical deterioration of the children and young persons, as well as the women, whom machinery subjects to the exploitation of capital, first directly in the fac-

42. *Children's Employment Commission, Fifth Report*, London, 1866, p. 81, n. 31. [Added by Engels in the fourth German edition:] The Bethnal Green silk industry has now almost disappeared.

43. *Children's Employment Commission Third Report*, London, 1864, p. 53, n. 15.

44. ibid., *Fifth Report*, p. xxii, n. 137.

tories that sprout forth on the basis of machinery, and then indirectly in all the remaining branches of industry. Here we shall dwell on one point only, the enormous mortality of the children of the workers during the first few years of their life. In 16 of the registration districts into which England is divided, there are, for every 100,000 children alive under the age of one year, only 9,085 deaths in a year on an average (in one district only 7,047); in 24 districts the deaths are over 10,000 but under 11,000, in 39 districts over 11,000 but under 12,000; in 48 districts over 12,000 but under 13,000; in 22 districts over 20,000; in 25 districts over 21,000; in 17 over 22,000; in 11 over 23,000; in Hoo, Wolverhampton, Ashton-under-Lyne and Preston, over 24,000; in Nottingham, Stockport and Bradford, over 25,000; in Wisbeach, 26,000; and in Manchester, 26,125.[45] As was shown by an official medical inquiry in the year 1861, the high death-rates are, apart from local causes, principally due to the employment of the mothers away from their homes, and to the neglect and maltreatment arising from their absence, which consists in such things as insufficient nourishment, unsuitable food and dosing with opiates; besides this, there arises an unnatural estrangement between mother and child, and as a consequence intentional starving and poisoning of the children.[46] In those agricultural districts 'where a minimum in the employment of women exists, the death-rate is on the other hand very low'.[47] However, the 1861 Commission of Inquiry arrived at the unexpected conclusion that in some purely agricultural districts bordering on the North Sea, the death-rate of children under one year old almost equalled that of the worst factory districts. Dr Julian Hunter was therefore commissioned to investigate this phenomenon on the spot. His report is incorporated into the *Sixth Report on Public Health*.[48] Up to that time it was supposed that the children were decimated by malaria, and other diseases peculiar to low-lying and marshy districts. But the in-

45. *Public Health, Sixth Report*, London, 1864, p. 34.
46. 'It' (the inquiry of 1861) '... showed, moreover, that while, with the described circumstances, infants perish under the neglect and mismanagement which their mothers' occupations imply, the mothers become to a grievous extent denaturalized towards their offspring – commonly not troubling themselves much at the death, and even sometimes ... taking direct measures to insure it' (ibid.).
47. ibid., p. 454.
48. pp. 454–63. 'Reports by Dr Henry Julian Hunter on the Excessive Mortality of Infants in Some Rural Districts of England.'

quiry showed the very opposite, namely 'that the same cause which drove away malaria, the conversion of the land from a morass in winter and a scanty pasture in summer into fruitful corn land, created the exceptional death-rate of the infants'.[49] The seventy medical men whom Dr Hunter examined in those districts were 'wonderfully in accord' on this point. In fact, the revolution in cultivation had led to the introduction of the industrial system. 'Married women, who work in gangs along with boys and girls, are, for a stipulated sum of money, placed at the disposal of the farmer by a man called the "undertaker", who contracts for the whole gang. These gangs will sometimes travel many miles from their own village; they are to be met morning and evening on the roads, dressed in short petticoats, with suitable coats and boots, and sometimes trousers, looking wonderfully strong and healthy, but tainted with a customary immorality and heedless of the fatal results which their love of this busy and independent life is bringing on their unfortunate offspring who are pining at home.'[50] All the phenomena of the factory districts are reproduced here, including a yet higher degree of disguised infanticide and stupefaction of children with opiates.[51] 'My knowledge of such evils,' says Dr Simon, the medical officer of the Privy Council and editor-in-chief of the *Reports on Public Health*, 'may excuse the profound misgiving with which I regard any large industrial employment of adult women.'[52] 'Happy indeed', exclaims Mr Baker, the factory inspector, in his official report, 'happy indeed will it be for the manufacturing districts of England, when every married woman having a family is prohibited from working in any textile works at all.'[53]

The moral degradation which arises out of the exploitation by capitalism of the labour of women and children has been so ex-

49. *Public Health, Sixth Report*, London, 1864, pp. 35, 455–6.

50. ibid., p. 456.

51. In the agricultural as well as the factory districts of England the consumption of opium among adult workers, both male and female, is extending daily. 'To push the sale of opiate . . . is the great aim of some enterprising wholesale merchants. By druggists it is considered the leading article' (ibid., p. 459). Infants that received opiates 'shrank up into little old men', or 'wizened like little monkeys' (ibid., p. 460). We see here how India and China have taken their revenge on England.

52. ibid., p. 37.

53. *Reports of the Inspectors of Factories . . . 31 October 1862*, p. 59. This factory inspector was formerly a doctor.

haustively presented by F. Engels in his *Condition of the Working Class in England*, and by other writers too, that a mere mention will suffice here. But the intellectual degeneration artificially produced by transforming immature human beings into mere machines for the production of surplus-value (and there is a very clear distinction between this and the state of natural ignorance in which the mind lies fallow without losing its capacity for development, its natural fertility) finally compelled even the English Parliament to make elementary education a legal requirement before children under 14 years could be consumed 'productively' by being employed in those industries which are subject to the Factory Acts. The spirit of capitalist production emerges clearly from the ludicrous way the so-called education clauses of the Factory Acts have been drawn up, from the absence of any administrative machinery, whereby this compulsory education is once again made for the most part illusory, from the opposition of the manufacturers themselves to these education clauses, and from the tricks and dodges they use to evade them. 'For this the legislature is alone to blame, by having passed a delusive law, which, while it would seem to provide that the children employed in factories shall be *educated*, contains no enactment by which that professed end can be secured. It provides nothing more than that the children shall on certain days of the week, and for a certain number of hours (three) in each day, be inclosed within the four walls of a place called a school, and that the employer of the child shall receive weekly a certificate to that effect signed by a person designated by the subscriber as a schoolmaster or schoolmistress.'[54] Before the passing of the amended Factory Act of 1844, it happened not infrequently that the certificates of attendance at school were signed by the schoolmaster or schoolmistress with a cross, as they themselves were unable to write. 'On one occasion, on visiting a place called a school, from which certificates of school attendance had issued, I was so struck with the ignorance of the master, that I said to him: "Pray, sir, can you read?" His reply was "Aye, summat!" and as a justification of his right to grant certificates, he added: "At any rate, I am before my scholars."' The inspectors, when the Bill of 1844 was in preparation, did not fail to denounce the disgraceful state of the places called schools, certificates from which they were obliged to admit as a compliance with the laws,

54. Leonard Horner, in *Reports of the Inspectors of Factories* ... *30 April 1857*, p. 17.

but they were successful only in obtaining this, that since the passing of the Act of 1844, 'the figures in the school certificate must be filled up in the handwriting of the schoolmaster, who must also sign his Christian and surname in full'.[55]

Sir John Kincaid, factory inspector for Scotland, relates similar official experiences. 'The first school we visited was kept by a Mrs Ann Killin. Upon asking her to spell her name, she straightway made a mistake, by beginning with the letter C, but correcting herself immediately, she said her name began with a K. On looking at her signature, however, in the school certificate books. I noticed that she spelt it in various ways, while her handwriting left no doubt as to her unfitness to teach. She herself also acknowledged that she could not keep the register . . . In a second school I found the schoolroom 15 feet long, and 10 feet wide, and counted in this space 75 children, who were gabbling something unintelligible.'[56] 'But it is not only in the miserable places above referred to that the children obtain certificates of school attendance without having received instruction of any value, for in many schools where there is a competent teacher, his efforts are of little avail from the dis-tracting crowd of children of all ages, from infants of 3 years old and upwards; his livelihood, miserable at the best, depending on the pence received from the greatest number of children whom it is possible to cram into the space. To this is to be added scanty school furniture, deficiency of books, and other materials for teaching, and the depressing effect upon the poor children them-selves of a close, noisome atmosphere. I have been in many such schools, where I have seen rows of children doing absolutely nothing; and this is certified as school attendance, and, in statis-tical returns, such children are set down as being educated.'[57] In Scotland the manufacturers do their best to exclude from employ-ment the children who are obliged to attend school. 'It requires no further argument to prove that the educational clauses of the Factory Act, being held in such disfavour among mill-owners, tend in a great measure to exclude that class of children alike from the employment and the benefit of education contemplated by this

55. Leonard Horner, in *Reports of the Inspectors of Factories* ... *31 October 1855*, pp. 18–19.

56. Sir John Kincaid, in *Reports of the Inspectors of Factories* ... *31 October 1858*, pp. 31–2.

57. Leonard Horner, in *Reports of the Inspectors of Factories* ... *31 October 1857*, pp. 17–18.

Act.'⁵⁸ This situation appears at its most grotesque and repulsive in calico print works, which are regulated by a special Act.* This Act lays it down that 'every child, before being employed in a print works, must have attended school for at least 30 days, and not less than 150 hours, during the six months immediately preceding such first day of employment, and during the continuance of its employment in the print works, it must attend for a like period of 30 days, and 150 hours during every successive period of six months . . . The attendance at School must be between 8 a.m. and 6 p.m. No attendance of less than 2½ hours, nor more than 5 hours on any one day, shall be reckoned as part of the 150 hours. Under ordinary circumstances the children attend school morning and afternoon for 30 days, for at least 5 hours each day, and upon the expiration of the 30 days, the statutory total of 150 hours having been attained, having, in their language, made up their book, they return to the print works, where they continue until the six months have expired, when another instalment of school attendance becomes due, and they again seek the school until the book is again made up . . . Many boys having attended school for the required number of hours, when they return to school after the expiration of their six months' work in the print works, are in the same condition as when they first attended school as print-work boys, [and I have been assured] that they have lost all they gained by their previous school attendance . . . In other print works the children's attendance at school is made to depend altogether upon the exigencies of the work in the establishment. The requisite number of hours is made up each six months, by instalments consisting of from 3 to 5 hours at a time, spreading over, perhaps, the whole six months . . . For instance, the attendance on one day might be from 8 to 11 a.m., on another day from 1 p.m. to 4 p.m., and the child might not appear at school again for several days, when it would attend from 3 p.m. to 6 p.m.; then it might attend for 3 or 4 days consecutively, or for a week, then it would not appear in school for 3 weeks or a month, after that upon some odd days at some odd hours when the operative who employed it chose to spare it; and thus the child was, as it were, buffeted from

58. Sir John Kincaid, in *Reports of the Inspectors of Factories . . . 31 October 1856*, p. 66.

---

* The Printworks Act of 1845. See above, p. 408.

school to work, from work to school, until the tale of 150 hours was told.'[59]

Machinery, by this excessive addition of women and children to the working personnel, at last breaks the resistance which the male workers had continued to oppose to the despotism of capital throughout the period of manufacture.[60]

(b) The Prolongation of the Working Day

If machinery is the most powerful means of raising the productivity of labour, i.e. of shortening the working time needed to produce a commodity, it is also, as a repository of capital, the most powerful means of lengthening the working day beyond all natural limits in those industries first directly seized on by it. It creates, on the one hand, new conditions which permit capital to give free rein to this tendency, and on the other hand, new incentives which whet its insatiable appetite for the labour of others.

In the first place, in machinery the motion and the activity of the instrument of labour asserts its independence *vis-à-vis* the worker. The instrument of labour now becomes an industrial form of perpetual motion. It would go on producing for ever, if it did not come up against certain natural limits in the shape of the weak bodies and the strong wills of its human assistants. Because it is capital, the automatic mechanism is endowed, in the person of the

59. A. Redgrave, in *Reports of the Inspectors of Factories ... 31 October 1857*, pp. 41–2. In those industries where the Factory Act proper (not the Printworks Act referred to in the text) has been in force for some time, the obstacles in the way of the education clauses have been overcome in recent years. In industries not subject to the Act, the views of Mr Geddes, a glass manufacturer, still extensively prevail. He informed Mr White, one of the Commissioners of Inquiry, 'As far as I can see, the greater amount of education which a part of the working class has enjoyed for some years past is an evil. It is dangerous, because it makes them independent' (*Children's Employment Commission, Fourth Report*, London, 1865, p. 253).

60. 'Mr E., a manufacturer ... informed me that he employed females exclusively at his power-looms ... gives a decided preference to married females, especially those who have families at home dependent on them for support; they are attentive, docile, more so than unmarried females, and are compelled to use their utmost exertions to procure the necessaries of life. Thus are the virtues, the peculiar virtues of the female character to be perverted to her injury – thus all that is most dutiful and tender in her nature is made a means of her bondage and suffering' (*Ten Hours' Factory Bill. The Speech of Lord Ashley, 15 March*, London, 1844, p. 20).

capitalist, with consciousness and a will. As capital, therefore, it is animated by the drive to reduce to a minimum the resistance offered by man, that obstinate yet elastic natural barrier.[61] This resistance is moreover lessened by the apparently undemanding nature of work at a machine, and the more pliant and, docile character of the women and children employed by preference.[62]

The productivity of machinery is, as we saw, inversely proportional to the value transferred by it to the product. The longer the period during which it functions, the greater is the mass of the products over which the value transmitted by the machine is spread, and the smaller is the portion of that value added to each single commodity. The active lifetime of a machine, however, is clearly dependent on the length of the working day, or the duration of the daily labour process multiplied by the number of days for which the process is carried on.

The amount of deterioration suffered by a machine does not by any means exactly correspond to the length of time it has been in use. And even if it were so, a machine working 16 hours a day for $7\frac{1}{2}$ years covers as long a working period as the same machine working only 8 hours a day for 15 years and transmits to the total product no more value. Notwithstanding this, the value of the machine would be reproduced twice as quickly in the first case as in the second, and the capitalist, using the same machine, would

61. 'Since the general introduction of machinery, human nature has been forced far beyond its average strength' (Robert Owen, *Observations on the Effects of the Manufacturing System*, 2nd edn, London, 1817, p. 16).

62. The English, who are very willing to regard the first empirical form of appearance of a thing as its cause, often attribute the long hours of work in factories to the extensive Herod-like kidnappings perpetrated in the early days of the factory system, when children were stolen from the workhouses and the orphanages, and capital thereby incorporated a mass of unresisting human material. Fielden, for instance, himself an English manufacturer, says: 'It is evident that the long hours of work were brought about by the circumstance of so great a number of destitute children being supplied from different parts of the country, that the masters were independent of the hands, and that having once established the custom by means of the miserable materials they had procured in this way, they could impose it on their neighbours with the greater facility' (J. Fielden, *The Curse of the Factory System*, London, 1836, p. 11). With reference to female labour, the factory inspector Saunders says in his report of 1844: 'Amongst the female operatives there are some women who, for many weeks in succession, except for a few days, are employed from 6 a.m. till midnight, with less than 2 hours for meals, so that on 5 days of the week they have only 6 hours left out of the 24, for going to and from their homes and resting in bed.'

absorb in $7\frac{1}{2}$ years as much surplus-value as he would in 15 in the second case.

The physical deterioration of the machine is of two kinds. The one arises from use, as coins wear away by circulating, the other from lack of use, as a sword rusts when left in its scabbard. This second kind is its consumption by the elements. Deterioration of the first kind is more or less directly proportional, and that of the second kind to a certain extent inversely proportional, to the use of the machine.[63]

But in addition to the material wear and tear, a machine also undergoes what we might call a moral depreciation. It loses exchange-value, either because machines of the same sort are being produced more cheaply than it was, or because better machines are entering into competition with it.[64] In both cases, however young and full of life the machine may be, its value is no longer determined by the necessary labour-time actually objectified in it, but by the labour-time necessary to reproduce either it or the better machine. It has therefore been devalued to a greater or lesser extent. The shorter the period taken to reproduce its total value, the less is the danger of moral depreciation; and the longer the working day, the shorter that period in fact is. When machinery is first introduced into a particular branch of production, new methods of reproducing it more cheaply follow blow upon blow,[65] and so do improvements which relate not only to individual parts and details of the machine, but also to its whole construction. It is therefore in the early days of a machine's life that this special incentive to the prolongation of the working day makes itself felt most acutely.[66]

63. '[When they strike, the operatives] occasion ... injury to the delicate moving parts of metallic mechanisms by inaction' (Ure, op. cit., p. 28).

64. The 'Manchester Spinner' already referred to* (*The Times*, 26 November 1862) enumerates, as part of the cost of machinery, 'an allowance for deterioration of machinery'. 'It is also intended,' he says, 'to cover the loss which is constantly arising from the superseding of machines before they are worn out, by others of a new and better construction.'

65. 'It has been estimated, roughly, that the first individual of a newly-invented machine will cost about five times as much as the construction of the second' (Babbage, op. cit., pp. 211–12).

66. 'The improvement which took place not long ago in frames for making patent-net was so great that a machine in good repair which had cost £1,200 sold a few years later for £60 ... improvements succeeded each other so

*See above, p. 315.

Given the length of the working day, and in otherwise identical circumstances, the exploitation of double the number of workers requires not only a doubling of that part of constant capital which is invested in machinery and buildings, but also a doubling of the part laid out in raw material and auxiliary substances. The lengthening of the working day, on the other hand, permits an expansion of the scale of production without any change in the amount of capital invested in machinery and buildings.[67] Not only does surplus-value increase therefore, but the outlay necessary to obtain it diminishes. It is true that this takes place, more or less, with every lengthening of the working day; but here the change is of far greater importance because the part of the capital that has been converted into the instruments of labour now falls more decisively into the balance.[68] The development of machine production ties a constantly increasing portion of the capital to a form in which, on the one hand, it is constantly capable of valorization, and in which, on the other hand, it loses both use-value and exchange-value whenever it is deprived of contact with living labour. Mr Ashworth, an English cotton magnate, imparted the following lesson to Professor Nassau W. Senior: 'When a labourer lays down his spade, he renders useless, for that period, a capital worth eighteen-pence. When one of our people leaves the mill, he renders useless a capital that has cost £100,000.'[69] Just imagine that! Making 'useless', if only for a single moment, a piece of capital that has cost £100,000! It is in truth monstrous that a single one of our people should ever leave the factory! The increased use of

rapidly that machines which had never been finished were abandoned in the hands of their makers, because new improvements had superseded their utility' (Babbage, op. cit., p. 233). In these times of stormy and rapid progress, therefore, the tulle manufacturers soon extended the working day from its original 8 hours to 24, by using double sets of workers.

67. 'It is self-evident, that, amid the ebbings and flowings of the markets and the alternate expansions and contractions of demand, occasions will constantly recur, in which the manufacturer may employ additional floating capital without employing additional fixed capital . . . if additional quantities of raw material can be worked up without incurring an additional expense for buildings and machinery' (R. Torrens, *On Wages and Combination*, London, 1834, p. 64).

68. This circumstance is mentioned here only for the sake of completeness, as we shall only come to consider the rate of profit, i.e. the ratio of surplus-value to the total capital advanced, when we reach Volume 3.

69. Senior, *Letters on the Factory Act*, London, 1837, pp. 13–14.

machinery, as Senior now realizes, having been instructed by Mr Ashworth, makes a constantly increased prolongation of the working day 'desirable'.[70]

Machinery produces relative surplus-value, not only by directly reducing the value of labour-power, and indirectly cheapening it by cheapening the commodities that enter into its reproduction, but also, when it is first introduced sporadically into an industry, by converting the labour employed by the owner of that machinery into labour of a higher degree, by raising the social value of the article produced above its individual value, and thus enabling the capitalist to replace the value of a day's labour-power by a smaller portion of the value of a day's product. During this transitional period, while the use of machinery remains a sort of monopoly, profits are exceptional, and the capitalist endeavours to exploit thoroughly 'the sunny time of this his first love' by prolonging the working day as far as possible. The magnitude of the profit gives him an insatiable hunger for yet more profit.

As machinery comes into general use in a particular branch of production, the social value of the machine's product sinks down to its individual value, and the following law asserts itself : surplus-value does not arise from the labour-power that has been replaced by the machinery, but from the labour-power actually employed in working with the machinery. Surplus-value arises only from the variable part of capital, and we saw that the amount of surplus-value depends on two factors, namely the rate of surplus-value and the number of workers simultaneously employed.* Given the length of the working day, the rate of surplus-value is determined by the relative duration of the necessary labour and the surplus labour performed in the course of a working day. The number of

70. 'The great proportion of fixed to circulating capital . . . makes long hours of work desirable.' With the increased use of machinery, etc., 'the motives to long hours of work will become greater, as the only means by which a large proportion of fixed capital can be made profitable' (ibid., pp. 11–13). 'There are certain expenses upon a mill which go on in the same proportion whether the mill be running short or full time, as, for instance, rent, rates, and taxes, insurance against fire, wages of several permanent servants, deterioration of machinery, with various other charges upon a manufacturing establishment, the proportion of which to profits increases as the production decreases' (*Reports of the Inspectors of Factories . . . 31 October 1862*, p. 19).

---

*See above, p. 420.

workers simultaneously employed depends, for its part, on the ratio of the variable to the constant capital. Now, however much the use of machinery may increase surplus labour at the expense of necessary labour by raising the productive power of labour, it is clear that it attains this result only by diminishing the number of workers employed by a given amount of capital. It converts a portion of capital which was previously variable, i.e. had been turned into living labour, into machinery, i.e. into constant capital which does not produce surplus-value. It is impossible, for instance, to squeeze as much surplus-value out of two as out of twenty-four workers. If each of these twenty-four men gives only 1 hour of surplus labour in 12, the twenty-four men give together 24 hours of surplus labour, while 24 hours is the total labour of the two men. Hence there is an immanent contradiction in the application of machinery to the production of surplus-value, since, of the two factors of the surplus-value created by a given amount of capital, one, the rate of surplus-value, cannot be increased except by diminishing the other, the number of workers. This contradiction comes to light as soon as machinery has come into general use in a given industry, for then the value of the machine-produced commodity regulates the social value of all commodities of the same kind; and it is this contradiction which in turn drives the capitalist, without his being aware of the fact,[71] to the most ruthless and excessive prolongation of the working day, in order that he may secure compensation for the decrease in the relative number of workers exploited by increasing not only relative but also absolute surplus labour.

The capitalist application of machinery on the one hand supplies new and powerful incentives for an unbounded prolongation of the working day, and produces such a revolution in the mode of labour as well as the character of the social working organism that it is able to break all resistance to this tendency. But on the other hand, partly by placing at the capitalists' disposal new strata of the working class previously inaccessible to him, partly by setting free the workers it supplants, machinery produces a surplus working

71. Why it is that this immanent contradiction does not enter the head of the individual capitalist, or the political economists who are imbued with his views, will appear from the first part of Volume 3.*

*See *Capital*, Vol. 3, Chapter 15, Section 2, 'Conflict between Expansion of Production and Production of Surplus-Value'.

population,[72] which is compelled to submit to the dictates of capital. Hence that remarkable phenomenon in the history of modern industry, that machinery sweeps away every moral and natural restriction on the length of the working day. Hence too the economic paradox that the most powerful instrument for reducing labour-time suffers a dialectical inversion and becomes the most unfailing means for turning the whole lifetime of the worker and his family into labour-time at capital's disposal for its own valorization. 'If', dreamed Aristotle, the greatest thinker of antiquity, 'if every tool, when summoned, or even by intelligent anticipation, could do the work that befits it, just as the creations of Daedalus moved of themselves, or the tripods of Hephaestus went of their own accord to their sacred work, if the weavers' shuttles were to weave of themselves, then there would be no need either of apprentices for the master craftsmen, or of slaves for the lords.'[73] And Antipater,* a Greek poet of the time of Cicero, hailed the water-wheel for grinding corn, that most basic form of all productive machinery, as the liberator of female slaves and the restorer of the golden age.[74] Oh those heathens! They understood nothing of political economy and Christianity, as the learned Bastiat dis-

72. It is one of the greatest merits of Ricardo that he saw machinery not only as a means of producing commodities, but also a means of producing a 'redundant population'.*

73. F. Biese, *Die Philosophie des Aristoteles*, Vol. 2, Berlin, 1842, p. 408.†

74. I give here the translation of this poem by Stolberg, because, just like our earlier quotations about the division of labour,‡ it brings out the antithesis between the views of the ancients and the moderns. 'Spare the hand that grinds the corn, Oh miller girls, and softly sleep. Let Chanticleer announce the morn in vain! Deo has commanded the work of the girls to be done by the Nymphs, and now they skip lightly over the wheels, so that the shaken axles revolve with their spokes and pull round the load of the revolving stones. Let us live the life of our fathers, and let us rest from work and enjoy the gifts that the Goddess sends us' (*Gedichte aus dem Griechischen Übersetzt von Christian Graf zu Stolberg*, Hamburg, 1782).§

* Ricardo, *On the Principles of Political Economy and Taxation*, 3rd edn, London, 1821, p. 478.

† The passage is taken from Aristotle, *Politics*, Bk I, Ch. 4 (p. 10 of the translation by E. Barker, Oxford, 1946).

‡ See above, pp. 486–9.

§ The English translation has been taken from the Moore-Aveling version of *Capital*. The original Greek is in *The Greek Anthology*, Bk IX, No. 418.

* Antipater of Thessalonica, a minor Greek epigrammatist, fl. first century B.C.

covered, and before him the still wiser MacCulloch. They did not, for example, comprehend that machinery is the surest means of lengthening the working day. They may perhaps have excused the slavery of one person as a means to the full human development of another. But they lacked the specifically Christian qualities which would have enabled them to preach the slavery of the masses in order that a few crude and half-educated parvenus might become 'eminent spinners', 'extensive sausage-makers' and 'influential shoe-black dealers'.

(c) Intensification of Labour

As we have seen, the immoderate lengthening of the working day produced by machinery in the hands of capital leads later on to a reaction on the part of the society, which is threatened in the very sources of its life; and, from there, to a normal working day whose length is fixed by law. On the foundation laid by the latter, something we have already met with, namely the intensification of labour, develops into a phenomenon of decisive importance. Our analysis of absolute surplus-value dealt primarily with the extensive magnitude of labour, its duration, while its intensity was treated as a given factor. We have now to consider the inversion [*Umschlag*] of extensive magnitude into intensive magnitude, or magnitude of degree.

It is self-evident that in proportion as the use of machinery spreads, and the experience of a special class of worker – the machine-worker – accumulates, the rapidity and thereby the intensity of labour undergoes a natural increase. Thus in England, in the course of half a century, the lengthening of the working day has gone hand in hand with an increase in the intensity of factory labour. Nevertheless, the reader will clearly see that we are dealing here, not with temporary paroxysms of labour but with labour repeated day after day with unvarying uniformity. Hence a point must inevitably be reached where extension of the working day and intensification of labour become mutually exclusive so that the lengthening of the working day becomes compatible only with a lower degree of intensity, and inversely, a higher degree of intensity only with a shortening of the working day. As soon as the gradual upsurge of working-class revolt had compelled Parliament compulsorily to shorten the hours of labour, and to begin by imposing a normal working day on factories properly so called, i.e.

from the moment that it was made impossible once and for all to increase the production of surplus-value by prolonging the working day, capital threw itself with all its might, and in full awareness of the situation, into the production of relative surplus-value, by speeding up the development of the machine system. At the same time a change took place in the nature of relative surplus-value. In general, relative surplus-value is produced by raising the productivity of the worker, and thereby enabling him to produce more in a given time with the same expenditure of labour. The same amount of labour-time adds the same value as before to the total product, but this unchanged amount of exchange-value is spread over more use-values. Hence the value of each single commodity falls. But the situation changes with the compulsory shortening of the hours of labour. This gives an immense impetus to the development of productivity and the more economical use of the conditions of production. It imposes on the worker an increased expenditure of labour within a time which remains constant, a heightened tension of labour-power, and a closer filling-up of the pores of the working day, i.e. a condensation of labour, to a degree which can only be attained within the limits of the shortened working day. This compression of a greater mass of labour into a given period now counts for what it really is, namely an increase in the quantity of labour. In addition to the measure of its 'extensive magnitude', labour-time now acquires a measure of its intensity, or degree of density.[75] The denser hour of the 10-hour working day contains more labour, i.e. expended labour-power, than the more porous hour of the 12-hour working day. Thus the product of one of the 10 hours has has as much value as the product of $1\frac{1}{5}$ of the 12 hours, or even more. Apart from the increased yield of relative surplus-value which results from the heightened productivity of labour, the same mass of value is now produced for the capitalist by, say, $3\frac{1}{3}$ hours of surplus labour and $6\frac{2}{3}$ hours of necessary labour, as was previously produced by 4 hours of surplus labour and 8 hours of necessary labour.

We now come to the question of how the labour is intensified.

75. There are, of course, always differences in intensity in the labour performed in different industries. But, as Adam Smith has shown, these differences are compensated to a partial extent by attendant circumstances peculiar to each sort of labour. Labour-time as a measure of value, however, is not affected in this case, except in so far as intensive and extensive magnitude are two antithetical and mutually exclusive expressions for one and the same quantity of labour.

The first effect of shortening the working day results from the self-evident law that the efficiency of labour-power is in inverse ratio to the duration of its expenditure. Hence, within certain limits, what is lost by shortening the duration of labour is gained by increasing the degree of power exerted. Moreover, the capitalist ensures by his method of payment that the worker really does expend more labour-power.[76] In manufactures like potteries, where machinery plays little or no part, the introduction of the Factory Act has strikingly shown that the mere shortening of the working day increases to a wonderful degree the regularity, uniformity, order, continuity and energy of labour.[77] It seemed, however, doubtful whether this effect could be produced in the factory proper, because there the dependence of the worker on the continuous and uniform motion of the machinery had already created the strictest discipline. Hence, when in 1844 the reduction of the working day to less than twelve hours was being debated, the manufacturers declared almost unanimously 'that their overlookers in the different rooms took good care that the hands lost no time', that 'the extent of vigilance and attention on the part of the workmen was hardly capable of being increased', and therefore, assuming the speed of the machinery and other conditions remained constant, 'to expect in a well-managed factory any important result from increased attention of the workmen was an absurdity'.[78] This assertion was controverted by means of experiments. Mr Robert Gardner reduced the hours of work in his two large factories at Preston, on and after 20 April 1844, from 12 to 11 hours a day. The result of about a year on this system was that 'the same amount of product for the same cost was received, and the workpeople as a whole earned in 11 hours as much wages as they did before in 12'.[79] I shall pass over the experiments made in the spinning and carding rooms, because they were accompanied by an increase of 2 per cent in the speed of the machines. But in the weaving department, where moreover many sorts of figured fancy articles were woven, there was not the slightest alteration in the

76. Especially by piece-wages, a form we shall investigate in Part VI of this book.

77. See *Reports of the Inspectors of Factories . . . 31st October 1865.*

78. *Reports of the Inspectors of Factories for 1844, and the Quarter Ending 30 April 1845,* pp. 20–21.

79. ibid., p. 19. Since the wages for piece-work were unaltered, the weekly wage depended on the quantity produced.

objective conditions of production. The result was: 'From 6th January to 20th April 1844, with a 12 hours' day, average weekly wages of each hand 10s. 1½d., from 20th April to 29th June 1844, with a day of 11 hours, average weekly wages 10s. 3½d.'[80] Here we have more produced in 11 hours than previously in 12, entirely as a result of steadier application to the work and a more economical use of time on the part of the workers. While they got the same wages and gained one hour of spare time, the capitalist got the same amount produced and saved the cost of coal, gas and other such items for one hour. Similar equally successful experiments were carried out in the mills of Messrs Horrocks and Jacson.[81]

The shortening of the working day creates, to begin with, the subjective condition for the condensation of labour, i.e. it makes it possible for the worker to set more labour-power in motion within a given time. As soon as that shortening becomes compulsory, machinery becomes in the hands of capital the objective means, systematically employed, for squeezing out more labour in a given time. This occurs in two ways: the speed of the machines is increased, and the same worker receives a greater quantity of machinery to supervise or operate. Improved construction of the machinery is necessary, partly to allow greater pressure to be put on the worker, partly because it is an inevitable concomitant of intensification of labour, since the legal limitation of the working day compels the capitalist to exercise the strictest economy in the cost of production. The improvements in the steam-engine have increased the piston speed and at the same time have made it possible, by means of a greater economy of power, to drive more machinery with the same engine, while consuming the same amount of coal, or even a smaller amount. The improvements in the transmitting mechanism have lessened friction and reduced the diameter and weight of the shafts to a constantly decreasing minimum, something which strikingly distinguishes modern machinery from the older type. Finally, the improvements in the operative machines

80. ibid., p. 20.
81. ibid., p. 21. The moral element played an important part in the above experiments. The workers told the factory inspector: 'We work with more spirit, we have the reward ever before us of getting away sooner at night, and one active and cheerful spirit pervades the whole mill, from the youngest piecer to the oldest hand, and we can greatly help each other' (ibid.).

have, while reducing their size, increased their speed and efficiency, as in the modern power-loom; or, while increasing the size of their frames, they have also increased the extent and number of their working parts, as in spinning-mules, or added to the speed of those working parts by imperceptible alterations of detail, such as those which ten years ago increased the speed of the spindles in self-acting mules by one-fifth.

The reduction of the working day to 12 hours dates in England from 1832. In 1836 a manufacturer stated: 'The labour now undergone in the factories is much greater than it used to be . . . compared with thirty or forty years ago . . . owing to the greater attention and activity required by the greatly increased speed which is given to the machinery.'[82] In the year 1844, Lord Ashley, now Lord Shaftesbury, made in the House of Commons the following statements, which were supported by documentary evidence:

'The labour performed by those engaged in the processes of manufacture, is three times as great as in the beginning of such operations. Machinery has executed, no doubt, the work that would demand the sinews of millions of men; but it has also prodigiously multiplied the labour of those who are governed by its fearful movements . . . In 1815, the labour of following a pair of mules spinning cotton of No. 40 – reckoning 12 hours to the working day – involved a necessity of walking 8 miles. In 1832, the distance travelled in following a pair of mules, spinning cotton yarn of the same number, was 20 miles, and frequently more. In 1825 the spinner put up daily, on each of these mules, 208 stretches, making a total of 1,640 stretches in the course of the day. In 1832, the spinner put up on each mule 2,200 stretches, making a total of 4,400. In 1844, 2,400 stretches, making a total of 4,800; and in some cases the amount of labour required is even still greater . . . I have another document sent to me in 1842, stating that the labour is progressively increasing – increasing not only because the distance to be travelled is greater, but because the quantity of goods produced is multiplied, while the hands are fewer in proportion than before; and, moreover, because an inferior species of cotton is now often spun, which it is more difficult to work . . . In the carding-room there has also been a great increase of labour. One person there does the work formerly divided between two.

82. John Fielden, op. cit., p. 32.

In the weaving-room, where a vast number of persons are employed, and principally females ... the labour has increased within the last few years fully 10 per cent, owing to the increased speed of the machinery in spinning. In 1838, the number of hanks spun per week was 18,000, in 1843 it amounted to 21,000. In 1819, the number of picks in power-loom weaving per minute was 60 – in 1842 it was 140, showing a vast increase of labour.'[83]

In the face of this remarkable level of intensity, which labour had already reached in 1844 under the Twelve Hours' Act, there appeared to be a justification for the assertion made at that time by the English manufacturers that any further progress in that direction was impossible, and therefore that any further reduction in the hours of labour would necessarily bring with it a drop in production. The apparent correctness of their reasoning will best be shown by the following contemporary statement by Leonard Horner, the factory inspector and tireless censor of the manufacturers.

'Now, as the quantity produced must, in the main, be regulated by the speed of the machinery, it must be the interest of the mill-owner to drive it at the utmost rate of speed consistent with these following conditions, viz., the preservation of the machinery from too rapid deterioration; the preservation of the quality of the article manufactured; and the capability of the workman to follow the motion without a greater exertion than he can sustain for a constancy. One of the most important problems, therefore, which the owner of a factory has to solve, is to find out the maximum speed at which he can run, with a due regard to the above conditions. It frequently happens that he finds he has gone too fast, that breakages and bad work more than counterbalance the increased speed, and that he is obliged to slacken his pace. I therefore concluded, that as an active and intelligent mill-owner would find out the safe maximum, it would not be possible to produce as much in 11 hours as in 12. I further assumed that the operative paid by piece-work, would exert himself to the utmost consistent with the power of continuing at the same rate.'[84] Horner therefore came to the conclusion, despite the experiments of Gardner and others,

---

83. Lord Ashley, op. cit., pp. 6–9 passim.

84. *Reports of the Inspectors of Factories for the Quarter Ending 30 September 1844, and from 1 October 1844 to 30 April 1845*, p. 20.

that a further reduction of the working day below 12 hours would necessarily diminish the quantity of the product.[85] He himself cited his opinion of 1845 ten years later in order to show how much at that time he still under-estimated the elasticity of machinery and of human labour-power, both of which are simultaneously stretched to theif utmost by the compulsory shortening of the working day.

We now come to the period following the introduction of the Ten Hours' Act in 1847 into the English cotton, woollen, silk and flax mills.

'The speed of the spindles has increased upon throstles 500, and upon mules 1,000 revolutions a minute, i.e. the speed of the throstle spindle, which in 1839 was 4,500 times a minute, is now' (1862) '5,000; and of the mule spindle, that was 5,000, is now 6,000 times a minute, amounting in the former case to one-tenth; and in the second case to one-fifth additional increase.'[86] James Nasmyth, the eminent civil engineer of Patricroft, near Manchester, explained in a letter to Leonard Horner, written in 1852, the nature of the improvements in the steam-engine made between the years 1848 and 1852. After remarking that the horse-power of steam-engines, being always estimated in the official returns according to the power of similar engines in 1828,[87] is only nominal, and can serve only as an index of their real power, he goes on to say: 'I am confident that from the same weight of steam-engine machinery, we are now obtaining at least 50 per cent more duty or work performed on the average, and that in many cases the identical steam-engines which in the days of the restricted speed of 220 feet per minute, yielded 50 horse-power, are now yielding upwards of

85. ibid., p. 22.
86. *Reports of the Inspectors of Factories . . . 31 October 1862*, p. 62.
87. This changed with the 'Parliamentary Return' of 1862.* There the actual horse-power of the modern steam-engines and water-wheels appears in place of the nominal horse-power.† The doubling spindles, too, are no longer included with the actual spinning spindles (as they were in the 'Returns' of 1839, 1850 and 1856); further, in the case of woollen mills, the number of 'gigs' is added, a distinction is made between jute and hemp mills on the one hand, and flax mills on the other, and finally, stocking-weaving is for the first time inserted in the report.

*Full title: *Factories. Return to an Address of the Honourable House of Commons, Dated 24 April 1861. Ordered by the House of Commons to be Printed, 11 February 1862.*

†See above, p. 511, n. 25, for the distinction between 'nominal' and 'indicated' horse-power (called here 'actual' horse-power).

100 . . . The modern steam-engine of 100 horse-power is capable of being driven at a much greater force than formerly, arising from improvements in its construction, the capacity and construction of the boilers, etc. . . . Although the same number of hands are employed in proportion to the horse-power as at former periods, there are fewer hands employed in proportion to the machinery.'[88] In the year 1850, the factories of the United Kingdom employed 134,217 nominal horse-power to move 25,638,716 spindles and 301,445 looms. The number of spindles and looms in 1856 was, respectively, 33,503,580 and 369,205, which, if we reckon the nominal horse-power required to move them to be the same as in 1850, would call for a total horse-power of 175,000. But according to the official return for 1856 the actual horse-power was 161,435, in other words over 10,000 horse-power less than the result arrived at by calculating on the basis of the return of 1850.[89] 'The facts thus brought out by the Return' (of 1856) 'appear to be that the factory system is increasing rapidly; that although the same number of hands are employed in proportion to the horse-power as at former periods, there are fewer hands employed in proportion to the machinery; that the steam-engine is enabled to drive an increased weight of machinery by economy of force and other methods, and that an increased quantity of work can be turned off by improvements in machinery, and in methods of manufacture, by increase of speed of the machinery, and by a variety of other causes.'[90]

'The great improvements made in machines of every kind have raised their productive power very much. Without any doubt, the shortening of the hours of labour . . . gave the impulse to these improvements. The latter, combined with the more intense strain on the workman, have had the effect that at least as much is produced in the shortened working day' (shortened by two hours or one-sixth) 'as was previously produced during the longer one.'[91]

One fact is sufficient to show how greatly the wealth of the manufacturers increased along with the more intensive exploitation of labour-power. From 1838 to 1850 the average annual in-

88. *Reports of the Inspectors of Factories* . . . *31 October 1856*, pp. 13–14, 20, and *1852*, p. 23.

89. ibid., pp. 14–15.

90. ibid., p. 20.

91. *Reports of the Inspectors of Factories* . . . *31 October 1858*, pp. 9–10. Compare the *Reports* for 30 April 1860, pp. 30 ff.

crease in English cotton and other factories was 32, from 1850 to 1856 it was 86.*

But however great the progress of English industry had been during the eight years from 1848 to 1856 under the influence of a working day of 10 hours, it was far surpassed during the next period of six years from 1856 to 1862. In silk factories, for instance, there were 1,093,799 spindles in 1856, 1,388,544 spindles in 1862; 9,260 looms in 1856, 10,709 looms in 1862. The number of workers, however, was 56,131 in 1856 and 52,429 in 1862. The increase in spindles was therefore 26·9 per cent, and in looms 15·6 per cent, while the number of workers decreased by 7 per cent. In the year 1850, 875,830 spindles were used in worsted mills; in 1856 the figure was 1,324,549 (an increase of 51·2 per cent); and in 1862 it was 1,289,172 (a decrease of 2·7 per cent). But if we deduct the doubling spindles which figure in the total for 1856, but not in that for 1862, it will be found that after 1856 the number of spindles remained nearly stationary. On the other hand, after 1850 the speed of the spindles and looms was in many cases doubled. The number of power-looms in worsted mills was 32,617 in 1850, 38,956 in 1856, and 43,048 in 1862. The number of workers was 79,737 in 1850, 87,794 in 1856, and 86,063 in 1862. But the number of children under 14 years old included in these figures was 9,956 in 1850, 11,228 in 1856, and 13,178 in 1862. Thus in spite of the greatly increased number of looms in 1862, compared with 1856, the total number of workers employed decreased, and the number of children exploited increased.[92]

On the 27 April 1863, Mr Ferrand said in the House of Commons: 'I have been informed by delegates from sixteen districts of Lancashire and Cheshire, in whose behalf I speak, that the work in the factories is, in consequence of the improvements in machinery, constantly on the increase. Instead of as formerly one person with two helps tenting two looms, one person now tents three looms without helps, and it is no uncommon thing for one person to tent four. 12 hours' work, as is evident from the facts adduced,

92. *Reports of the Inspectors of Factories . . . 31 October 1862*, pp. 100, 103, 129–130.

Cf. Reports of the Inspectors of Factories . . . 31 October 1856, p. 12. This is not a percentage increase, but a figure arrived at by dividing the absolute increase in the number of factories (in one case 383, in the other case 517) by the number of years between each return.

is now compressed into less than 10 hours. It is therefore self-evident, to what an enormous extent the toil of the factory operative has increased during the last ten years.'[93]

Thus, although the factory inspectors unceasingly, and quite rightly, commend the results of the Acts of 1844 and 1850, they admit that the shortening of the working day has already produced such an intensification of the labour itself as is injurious to the health of the worker and therefore to his labour-power as well. 'In most of the cotton, worsted, and silk mills, an exhausting state of excitement necessary to enable the workers satisfactorily to mind the machinery, the motion of which has been greatly accelerated within the last few years, seems to me not unlikely to be one of the causes of that excess of mortality from lung disease, which Dr Greenhow has pointed out in his recent report on this subject.'[94] Capital's tendency, as soon as a prolongation of the hours of labour is once for all forbidden, is to compensate for this by systematically raising the intensity of labour, and converting every improvement in machinery into a more perfect means for soaking up labour-power. There cannot be the slightest doubt that this process must soon lead once again to a critical point at which a further reduction in the hours of labour will be inevitable.[95] On the other hand, the rapid advance of English industry between 1848 and the present time, i.e. during the period of the 10-hour working day, surpasses the advance made between 1833 and 1847, during the period of the 12-hour working day, by far more than the latter surpasses the advance made during the half century after the first introduction of the factory system, i.e. during the period of the unrestricted working day.[96]

93. A weaver, working with two modern power-looms, now makes in a week of 60 hours twenty-six pieces of a given quality, length and breadth, while on the old power-looms he could make no more than four similar pieces. The cost of weaving a piece of cloth of this kind had already fallen from 2s. 9d. to 5½d. at the beginning of the 1850s. 'Thirty years ago' (in 1841) 'one spinner with three piecers was not required to attend to more than one pair of mules with 300–324 spindles. At the present time' (the end of 1871) 'he has to mind with the help of five piecers 2,200 spindles, and produces not less than seven times as much yarn as in 1841' (Alexander Redgrave, factory inspector, writing in *Journal of the Society of Arts*, 5 January 1872).

94. *Reports of the Inspectors of Factories . . . 31 October 1861*, pp. 25–6.

95. Agitation for a working day of 8 hours has now (1867) begun in Lancashire among the factory workers.

96. The following few figures will show the progress of the actual 'factories' in the United Kingdom since 1848:

TABLE 1

	Quantity exported 1848	Quantity exported 1851	Quantity exported 1860	Quantity exported 1865
COTTON Cotton yarn (in lb.)	135,831,162	143,966,106	197,343,655	103,751,455
Sewing thread (in lb.)		4,392,176	6,297,554	4,648,611
Cotton cloth (in yds)	1,091,373,930	1,543,161,789	2,776,218,427	2,015,237,851
FLAX AND HEMP Yarn (in lb.)	11,722,182	18,841,326	31,210,612	36,777,334
Cloth (yds)	88,901,519	129,106,753	143,996,773	247,021,529
SILK Yarn (in lb.)	*466,825	462,513	897,402	812,589
Cloth (in lb.)		1,181,455	1,307,293	†2,869,837
WOOL Woollen and worsted yarns (in lb.)		14,670,880	27,533,968	31,669,267
Cloth (yds)		151,231,153	190,371,537	278,837,418

*1846.   † In yards.

TABLE 2

	Value exported 1848 £	Value exported 1851 £	Value exported 1860 £	Value exported 1865 £
COTTON Yarn	5,927,831	6,634,026	9,870,875	10,351,049
Cloth	16,753,369	23,454,810	42,141,505	46,903,796
FLAX AND HEMP Yarn	493,449	951,426	1,801,272	2,505,497
Cloth	2,802,789	4,107,396	4,804,803	9,155,318
SILK Yarn	77,789	196,380	826,107	768,064
Cloth		1,130,398	1,587,303	1,409,221
WOOL Yarn	776,975	1,484,544	3,843,450	5,424,017
Cloth	5,733,828	8,377,183	12,156,998	20,102,259

(See the two Blue Books, *Statistical Abstract for the United Kingdom*, No. 8, and No. 13, London, 1861, and 1866.) In Lancashire the number of mills

4. THE FACTORY

At the beginning of this chapter we considered the physical constituents of the factory, the organization of the system of machinery. We saw there how machinery, by appropriating the labour of
women and children, augments the quantity of human material for
capital to exploit, how it confiscates the whole of the worker's lifetime by its immoderate extension of the working day, and finally
how its progress, which permits an enormous increase in production within a shorter and shorter amount of time, serves as a
means of systematically getting more work done within a given
period of time, or, in other words, constantly exploiting labour-
power more intensively. We now turn to the factory as a whole,
and indeed in its most developed form.

Dr Ure, the Pindar of the automatic factory, describes it, on
the one hand, as 'combined co-operation of many orders of workpeople, adult and young, in tending with assiduous skill a system
of productive machines continuously impelled by a central power'
(the prime mover); and on the other hand as 'a vast automaton,
composed of various mechanical and intellectual organs, acting
in uninterrupted concert for the production of a common object,
all of them being subordinate to a self-regulated moving force'.*
These two descriptions are far from being identical. In one, the
combined collective worker appears as the dominant subject
[*übergreifendes Subjekt*], and the mechanical automaton as the
object; in the other, the automaton itself is the subject, and the
workers are merely conscious organs, co-ordinated with the unconscious organs of the automaton, and together with the latter

---

increased only 4 per cent between 1839 and 1850, 19 per cent between 1850
and 1856, and 33 per cent between 1856 and 1862; while the number of
persons employed in them during each of the above periods of 11 years increased absolutely, but diminished relatively. (See *Reports of the Inspectors
of Factories . . . 31 October 1862*, p. 63.) In Lancashire the cotton trade
predominates. But the very important role cotton plays in the textile
industry as a whole may be seen from the following comparative figures: the
cotton trade accounts for 45·2 per cent of the total number of textile factories
in the United Kingdom, 83·3 per cent of the spindles, 81·4 per cent of the
power-looms, 72·6 per cent of the horse-power that sets them in motion, and
58·2 per cent of the total number of persons employed (ibid., pp. 62–3).

---

*These quotations are from Ure, *Philosophy of Manufactures*, p. 13.

subordinated to the central moving force. The first description is applicable to every possible employment of machinery on a large scale, the second is characteristic of its use by capital, and therefore of the modern factory system. Ure therefore prefers to present the central machine from which the motion comes as not only an automaton but an autocrat. 'In these spacious halls the benignant power of steam summons around him his myriads of willing menials.'[97]

Along with the tool, the skill of the worker in handling it passes over to the machine. The capabilities of the tool are emancipated from the restraints inseparable from human labour-power. This destroys the technical foundation on which the division of labour in manufacture was based. Hence, in place of the hierarchy of specialized workers that characterizes manufacture, there appears, in the automatic factory, a tendency to equalize and reduce to an identical level every kind of work that has to be done by the minders of the machines;[98] in place of the artificially produced distinctions between the specialized workers, it is natural differences of age and sex that predominate.

In so far as the division of labour re-appears in the factory, it takes the form primarily of a distribution of workers among the specialized machines, and of quantities of workers, who do not however form organized groups, among the various departments of the factory, in each of which they work at a number of similar machines placed together; only simple co-operation therefore takes place between them. The organized group peculiar to manufacture is replaced by the connection between the head worker and his few assistants. The essential division is that between workers who are actually employed on the machines (among whom are included a few who look after the engine) and those who merely attend them (almost exclusively children). More or less all the 'feeders' who supply the machines with the material which is to be worked up are counted as attendants. In addition to these two principal classes, there is a numerically unimportant group whose occupation it is to look after the whole of the machinery and repair it from time to time, composed of engineers, mechanics, joiners etc. This is a superior class of workers, in part scientifically educated, in part trained in a handicraft; they stand outside the

97. Ure, op. cit., p. 18.
98. ibid., p. 20. Cf. Karl Marx, *Misère de la philosophie,* pp. 140–41 [English edition, pp. 124–5].

realm of the factory workers, and are added to them only to make up an aggregate.[99] This division of labour is purely technical.

All work at a machine requires the worker to be taught from childhood upwards, in order that he may learn to adapt his own movements to the uniform and unceasing motion of an automaton. Since the machinery, taken as a whole, forms a system of machines of various kinds, working simultaneously and in combination, co-operation based upon it requires the distribution of various groups of workers among the different kinds of machine. But machine production abolishes the necessity of fixing this distribution in the manner of manufacture, i.e. by constantly appropriating the same worker to the same function.[1] Since the motion of the whole factory proceeds not from the worker but from the machinery, the working personnel can continually be replaced without any interruption in the labour process. The most striking proof of this is afforded by the *relay system*, put into operation by the manufacturers during their revolt of 1848 to 1850.* Lastly, the speed with which machine work is learnt by young people does away with the need to bring up a special class of worker for exclusive employment by machinery.[2] The work of

99. It is characteristic of the English intention to deceive by use of statistics (and this is demonstrable in detail in other cases as well) that the English factory legislation expressly excludes from its area of competence, as being 'not factory workers', the class of workers last mentioned, while the 'Returns' published by Parliament just as expressly include in the category of factory workers not only engineers, mechanics, etc. but also managers, salesmen, messengers, warehousemen, packers etc., in short, everybody except the owner of the factory himself.

1. Ure concedes this. He says that 'in case of need' the workers can be moved at the will of the manager from one machine to another, and triumphantly exclaims: 'Such a change is in flat contradiction with the old routine, that divides the labour, and to one workman assigns the task of fashioning the head of a needle, to another the sharpening of the point.'* He ought rather to have asked himself why the 'old routine' is abandoned only 'in case of need' in the automatic factory.

2. When distress is very great, as for instance during the American Civil War, the factory worker is now and then, and by way of exception, employed by the bourgeois to do the roughest work, such as road-making, etc. The English *'ateliers nationaux'*† of 1862 and the following years, established for the unemployed cotton workers, differ from the French ones of 1848 in that in the latter the workers had to do unproductive work at the expense of the

*Ure, op. cit., p. 22.   †'National workshops'.

---

*See above, pp. 400–405.

those people who are merely attendants can, to some extent, be replaced in the factory by the use of machines.[3] In addition to this, the very simplicity of the work allows a rapid and constant turnover of the individuals burdened with this drudgery.

Thus although, from a technical point of view, the old system of· division of labour is thrown overboard by machinery, it hangs on in the factory as a tradition handed down from manufacture, and is then systematically reproduced and fixed in a more hideous form by capital as a means of exploiting labour-power. The lifelong speciality of handling the same tool now becomes the lifelong speciality of serving the same machine. Machinery is misused in order to transform the worker, from his very childhood, into a part of a specialized machine.[4] In this way, not only are the expenses necessary for his reproduction considerably lessened, but at the same time his helpless dependence upon the factory as a whole, and therefore upon the capitalist, is rendered complete. Here, as everywhere else, we must distinguish between the increased productivity which is due to the development of the social process of production, and that which is due to the exploitation by the capitalists of that development.

state, and in the former they had do to productive municipal work to the advantage of the bourgeois, and indeed more cheaply than the regular workers, with whom they were thus thrown into competition. 'The physical appearance of the cotton operatives is unquestionably improved. This I attribute . . . as do the men, to outdoor labour on public works' (*Reports of the Inspectors of Factories* . . . *31 October 1863*, p. 59). The reference here is to the factory workers of Preston, who were set to work on Preston Moor.

3. An example: the various pieces of mechanical apparatus introduced into woollen mills since the Act of 1844 in order to replace the labour of children. When the children of the manufacturers themselves have to go through a course of schooling as assistants in the factory, this hitherto almost unexplored area of mechanics will make remarkable progress. 'Of machinery, perhaps self-acting mules are as dangerous as any other kind. Most of the accidents from them happen to little children, from their creeping under the mules to sweep the floor whilst the mules are in motion. Several "minders" have been fined for this offence, but without much general benefit. If machine makers would only invent a self-sweeper, by whose use the necessity for these little children to creep under the machinery might be prevented, it would be a happy addition to our protective measures' (*Reports of the Inspectors of Factories* . . . *31 October 1866*, p. 63).

4. So much then for Proudhon's wonderful idea: he 'construes' machinery not as a synthesis of instruments of labour, but as a synthesis of instruments of different partial operations for the benefit of the worker himself.*

*See Marx, *Poverty of Philosophy*, pp. 116–17.

In handicrafts and manufacture, the worker makes use of a tool; in the factory, the machine makes use of him. There the movements of the instrument of labour proceed from him, here it is the movements of the machine that he must follow. In manufacture the workers are the parts of a living mechanism. In the factory we have a lifeless mechanism which is independent of the workers, who are incorporated into it as its living appendages. 'The wearisome routine of endless drudgery in which the same mechanical process is ever repeated, is like the torture of Sisyphus; the burden of toil, like the rock, is ever falling back upon the worn-out drudge.'[5]

Factory work exhausts the nervous system to the uttermost; at the same time, it does away with the many-sided play of the muscles, and confiscates every atom of freedom, both in bodily and in intellectual activity.[6] Even the lightening of the labour becomes an instrument of torture, since the machine does not free the worker from the work, but rather deprives the work itself of all content. Every kind of capitalist production, in so far as it is not only a labour process but also capital's process of valorization, has this in common, but it is not the worker who employs the conditions of his work, but rather the reverse, the conditions of work employ the worker. However, it is only with the coming of machinery that this inversion first acquires a technical and palpable reality. Owing to its conversion into an automaton, the instrument of labour confronts the worker during the labour process in the shape of capital, dead labour, which dominates and soaks up living labour-power. The separation of the intellectual faculties of the production process from manual labour, and the transformation of those faculties into powers exercised by capital over labour, is, as we have already shown, finally completed by large-scale

5. F. Engels, *Lage etc.*, p. 217 [English edition, p. 205].* Even a very ordinary and optimistic free-trader like Molinari makes this remark: 'A man becomes exhausted more quickly when he watches over the uniform motion of a mechanism for fifteen hours a day, than when he applies his physical strength throughout the same period of time. This labour of surveillance, which might perhaps serve as a useful exercise for the mind, if it did not go on too long, destroys both the mind and the body in the long run through excessive application' (G. de Molinari, *Études économiques*, Paris, 1846 [p. 49]).

6. F. Engels, op. cit., p. 216 [English edition, p. 204].

*This is in fact a quotation from Engels' footnote reference to a book by Dr J. P. Kay, *The Moral and Physical Condition of the Working Classes Employed in the Cotton Manufacture in Manchester* (1832).

industry erected on the foundation of machinery. The special skill of each individual machine-operator, who has now been deprived of all significance, vanishes as an infinitesimal quantity in the face of the science, the gigantic natural forces, and the mass of social labour embodied in the system of machinery, which, together with those three forces, constitutes the power of the 'master'. This 'master', therefore, in whose mind the machinery and his monopoly of it are inseparably united, contemptuously tells his 'hands', whenever he comes into conflict with them: 'The factory operatives should keep in wholesome remembrance the fact that theirs is really a low species of skilled labour; and that there is none which is more easily acquired, or of its quality more amply remunerated, or which by a short training of the least expert can be more quickly, as well as abundantly, acquired ... The master's machinery really plays a far more important part in the business of production than the labour and the skill of the operative, which six months' education can teach, and a common labourer can learn.'[7] The technical subordination of the worker to the uniform motion of the instruments of labour, and the peculiar composition of the working group, consisting as it does of individuals of both sexes and all ages, gives rise to a barrack-like discipline, which is elaborated into a complete system in the factory, and brings the previously mentioned labour of superintendence to its fullest development, thereby dividing the workers into manual labourers and overseers, into the private soldiers and the N.C.O.s of an industrial army. 'The main difficulty' (in the automatic factory) 'lay ... above all in training human beings to renounce their desultory habits of work, and to identify themselves with the unvarying regularity of the complex automaton. To devise and administer a successful code of factory discipline, suited to the necessities of factory diligence, was the Herculean enterprise, the noble achievement of Arkwright! Even at the present day, when the system is perfectly organized and its labour lightened to the utmost, it is found nearly impossible to convert persons past the age of puberty into useful factory hands.'[8] In the factory code, the capitalist formulates his autocratic power over his workers like

7. *The Master Spinners' and Manufacturers' Defence Fund. Report of the Committee*, Manchester, 1854, p. 17. We shall see later that the 'master' can sing quite a different tune when he is threatened with the loss of his 'living' automaton.

8. Ure, op. cit., p. 15. Anyone who knows Arkwright's biography will be

a private legislator, and purely as an emanation of his own will, unaccompanied by either that division of responsibility otherwise so much approved of by the bourgeoisie, or the still more approved representative system. This code is merely the capitalist caricature of the social regulation of the labour process which becomes necessary in co-operation on a large scale and in the employment in common of instruments of labour, and especially of machinery. The overseer's book of penalties replaces the slave-driver's lash. All punishments naturally resolve themselves into fines and deductions from wages, and the law-giving talent of the factory Lycurgus* so arranges matters that a violation of his laws is, if possible, more profitable to him than the keeping of them.[9]

---

unlikely to apply the epithet 'noble' to this barber-genius.* Of all the great inventors of the eighteenth century, he was unquestionably the greatest thief of other people's inventions and the meanest character.

9. 'The slavery in which the bourgeoisie holds the proletariat chained is nowhere more conspicuous than in the factory system. Here ends all freedom in law and in fact. The operative must be in the mill at half past five in the morning; if he comes a couple of minutes too late, he is fined; if he comes ten minutes too late, he is not let in until breakfast is over, and a quarter of the day's wages is withheld ... He must eat, drink and sleep at command ... The despotic bell calls him from his bed, his breakfast, his dinner. What a time he has of it, too, inside the factory! Here the employer is absolute law-giver; he makes regulations at will, changes and adds to his codex at pleasure; and even if he inserts the craziest stuff, the courts say to the working man: Since you have freely entered into this contract, you must be bound to it ... These operatives are condemned from their ninth year to their death to live under the sword, physically and mentally' (F. Engels, op. cit., p. 217 [English translation, pp. 205–7]). I shall illustrate 'what the courts say' with two examples. One case occurred at Sheffield at the end of 1866. In that town a worker had engaged himself for two years in a steelworks. As a result of a dispute with his employer he left the works, and declared that under no circumstances would he work for that master any more. He was prosecuted for breach of contract, and condemned to two months' imprisonment. (If the master breaks the contract, only a civil action can be

---

*Sir Richard Arkwright (1732–92) started out as a barber, and gleaned such mechanical knowledge as he had from conversations with customers. Despite this, he patented a spinning-frame in 1769. It was later claimed that he had thereby stolen the invention of a certain Thomas Highs. Then, in 1775, he patented a whole series of other inventions, none of which he had invented himself. Though deprived of his patents in 1781, a decision which was confirmed after a court action in 1785, he continued to develop new factories, and died leaving £500,000.

---

*The legendary author of the constitution of Sparta.

brought; all he risks is an award of damages.) After the worker had served his two months' imprisonment, the master invited him to return to the works, pursuant to the contract. The worker said no, he had already been punished for the breach of contract. The master prosecuted again, the court condemned again, although one of the judges, Mr Shee, publicly denounced it as a legal monstrosity that a man can periodically, as long as he lives, be punished over and over again for the same offence or crime. This judgement was handed down not by the 'Great Unpaid',* the provincial Dogberries, but by one of the highest courts of justice in London. [Added by Engels in the fourth German edition: This has now been done away with. With a few exceptions, such as when public gas-works are involved, the worker in England is now on an equal footing with the employer in case of breach of contract and can only be sued under civil law.] The second case occurred in Wiltshire at the end of November 1863. Around thirty power-loom weavers employed by one Harrup, a cloth manufacturer at Leower's Mill, Westbury Leigh, struck work because the same Harrup indulged in the agreeable habit of making deductions from their wages for being late in the morning; 6d. for two minutes; 1s. for three minutes, and 1s. 6d. for ten minutes. This is at the rate of 9s. per hour, and £4 10s. 0d. per day; whereas the annual average wage of the weavers never exceeded 10s. to 12s. a week. Harrup also appointed a boy to announce the starting time by a whistle, which he often did before six o'clock in the morning; and if the 'hands' were not all there at the moment the whistle ceased, the doors were closed and those who were shut out were fined. As there was no clock on the premises, the unfortunate workers were at the mercy of the young Harrup-inspired time-keeper. The striking 'hands', mothers of families as well as girls, offered to resume work if the time-keeper were replaced by a clock, and a more reasonable scale of fines introduced. Harrup summoned nineteen women and girls before the magistrates for breach of contract. To the utter indignation of all those present, they were each mulcted of 6d. and 2s. 6d. for costs. Harrup was followed from the court by a crowd of people who hissed him. A favourite operation with manufacturers is to punish workers by making deductions from their wages for faults in the material supplied to them. This method gave rise in 1866 to a widespread strike in the English pottery districts. The reports of the Childrens' Employment Commission (1863–6) give cases where the worker not only receives no wages, but becomes, by means of his labour, and owing to the penal regulations, the debtor of his worthy master. The recent cotton crisis has also furnished edifying examples of the sharp-wittedness shown by the factory autocrats in making deductions from wages. Mr R. Baker, the inspector of factories, says 'I have myself had lately to direct prosecutions against one cotton mill occupier for having in these pinching and painful times deducted 10d. a piece from some of the young workers employed by him, for the surgeon's certificate (for which he himself had only paid 6d.), when only allowed by the law to deduct 3d., and by custom nothing at all . . . And I have been informed of another, who, in order to keep within the law, but to attain the same object, charges the poor children who work for him a shilling each, as a fee for learning them the art and mystery of cotton spinning, so soon as they are declared by the surgeon fit and proper persons for that occupation. There

*See above, p. 401, n. 23.

Here we shall merely allude to the material conditions under which factory labour is performed. Every sense organ is injured by the artificially high temperatures, by the dust-laden atmosphere, by the deafening noise, not to mention the danger to life and limb among machines which are so closely crowded together, a danger which, with the regularity of the seasons, produces its list of those killed and wounded in the industrial battle.[10] The economical use of the social means of production, matured and forced as in a hothouse by the factory system, is turned in the hands of capital

---

may therefore be undercurrent causes for such extraordinary exhibitions as strikes, not only wherever they arise, but particularly at such times as the present, which without explanation, render them inexplicable to the public understanding.' He alludes here to a strike of power-loom weavers at Darwen, in June 1863. (*Reports of the Inspectors of Factories . . . 30 April 1863*, pp. 50–51.) The reports always go beyond their official dates.

10. The protection afforded by the Factory Acts against dangerous machinery has had a beneficial effect. 'But . . . there are other sources of accident which did not exist twenty years since; one especially, viz., the increased speed of the machinery. Wheels, rollers, spindles and shuttles are now propelled at increased and increasing rates; fingers must be quicker and defter in their movements to take up the broken thread, for, if placed with hesitation or carelessness, they are sacrificed . . . A large number of accidents are caused by the eagerness of the workpeople to get through their work expeditiously. It must be remembered that it is of the highest importance to manufacturers that their machinery should be in motion, i.e. producing yarns and goods. Every minute's stoppage is not only a loss of power, but of production, and the workpeople are urged by the overlookers, who are interested in the quantity of work turned off, to keep the machinery in motion; and it is no less important to those of the operatives who are paid by the weight or piece, that the machines should be kept in motion. Consequently, although it is strictly forbidden in many, nay in most factories, that machinery should be cleaned while in motion, it is nevertheless the constant practice in most, if not in all, that the workpeople do, unreproved, pick out waste, wipe rollers and wheels, etc., while their frames are in motion. Thus from this cause only, 906 accidents have occurred during the six months . . . Although a great deal of cleaning is constantly going on day by day, yet Saturday is generally the day set apart for the thorough cleansing of the machinery, and a great deal of this is done while the machinery is in motion. Since cleaning is not paid for, the workpeople seek to get done with it as speedily as possible. Hence the number of accidents which occur on Fridays, and especially on Saturdays, is much larger than on any other day. On the former day the excess is nearly 12 per cent over the average number of the four first days of the week, and on the latter day the excess is 25 per cent over the average of the preceding five or, if the number of working-hours on Saturday is taken into account – $7\frac{1}{2}$ hours on Saturday as compared with $10\frac{1}{2}$ on other days – there is an excess of 65 per cent on Saturdays over the average of the other five days' (*Reports of the Inspectors of Factories . . . 31 October 1866*, pp. 9, 15–17).

into systematic robbery of what is necessary for the life of the worker while he is at work, i.e. space, light, air and protection against the dangerous or the unhealthy concomitants of the production process, not to mention the theft of appliances for the comfort of the worker.[11] Was Fourier wrong when he called factories 'mitigated jails'?[12]*

5. THE STRUGGLE BETWEEN WORKER AND MACHINE

The struggle between the capitalist and the wage-labourer starts with the existence of the capital-relation itself. It rages throughout the period of manufacture.[13] But only since the introduction of

11. In Part I of Volume 3 I shall give an account of a recent campaign by the English manufacturers against the clauses in the Factory Acts that protect the 'hands' against dangerous machinery.* For the present, let this one quotation from the official report of Leonard Horner suffice: 'I have heard some mill-owners speak with inexcusable levity of some of the accidents; such, for instance, as the loss of a finger being a trifling matter. A working-man's living and prospects depend so much upon his fingers that any loss of them is a very serious matter to him. When I have heard such inconsiderate remarks made, I have usually put this question: Suppose you were in want of an additional workman, and two were to apply, both equally well qualified in other respects, but one had lost a thumb or a forefinger, which would you engage? There never was a hesitation as to the answer.' The manufacturers 'have mistaken prejudices against what they have heard represented as pseudo-philanthropic legislation' (*Reports of the Inspectors of Factories . . . 31 October 1855*). These manufacturers are 'clever folk' and it was not without reason that they were enthusiastically in favour of the Slave-holders' Rebellion.†

12. In those factories that have been longest subject to the Factory Acts, with their compulsory limitation of the hours of labour, and other regulations, many of the older abuses have vanished. The improvement of machinery in itself requires, to a certain extent, 'improved construction of the buildings', and this is of advantage to the workers. (See *Reports of the Inspectors of Factories . . . 31 October 1863*, p. 109.)

13. See, among others, John Houghton, *Husbandry and Trade Improved*, London, 1727; *The Advantages of the East-India Trade*, 1720; and John Bellers, *Essays about the Poor*, London, 1699. 'The masters and their workmen are, unhappily, in a perpetual war with each other. The invariable object of the former is to get their work done as cheaply as possible; and they do not

*See *Capital*, Vol. 3, Part I, Chapter 5, Section 2.
†The American Civil War.

* '*Les bagnes mitigés*'. The quotation is from Fourier, *La Fausse Industrie morcelée, répugnante, mensongère, et l'antidote, l'industrie naturelle, combinée, attrayante, véridique, donnant quadruple produit*, Paris, 1835, p. 59.

machinery has the worker fought against the instrument of labour itself, capital's material mode of existence. He is in revolt against this particular form of the means of production because it is the material foundation of the capitalist mode of production.

In the seventeenth century nearly all Europe experienced workers' revolts against the ribbon-loom, a machine for weaving ribbons and lace trimmings called in Germany *Bandmühle*, *Schnurmühle*, or *Mühlenstuhl*.[14] In the 1630s, a wind-driven saw-mill, erected near London by a Dutchman, succumbed to the rage of the mob. Even as late as the beginning of the eighteenth century, saw-mills driven by water overcame the opposition of the people only with great difficulty, supported as this opposition was by Parliament. No sooner had Everett constructed the first wool-shearing machine to be driven by water-power (1758) than it was set on fire by 100,000 people who had been thrown out of work. Fifty thousand workers, who had previously lived by carding wool, petitioned Parliament against Arkwright's scribbling mills and carding engines. The large-scale destruction of machinery which occurred in the English manufacturing districts during the first fifteen years of the nineteenth century, largely as a result of the employment of the power-loom, and known as the Luddite movement, gave the anti-Jacobin government, composed of such people as Sidmouth and Castlereagh, a pretext for the most violent and reactionary measures. It took both time and experience before the workers learnt to distinguish between machinery and its employment by capital, and therefore to transfer their attacks from the

---

fail to employ every artifice to this purpose, whilst the latter are equally attentive to every occasion of distressing their masters into a compliance with higher demands' (*An Enquiry into the Causes of the Present High Price of Provisions*, 1767, pp. 61–2. The author, the Reverend Nathaniel Forster, is entirely on the side of the workers).

14. The ribbon-loom was invented in Germany. The Italian abbé Lancellotti, in a work that appeared in Venice in 1637, but was written in 1623, says this: 'Anthony Müller of Danzig saw about fifty years ago in that town a very ingenious machine, which weaves four to six pieces at once. But the mayor of the town became apprehensive that this invention might throw a large number of workmen onto the streets, and therefore had the invention suppressed and the inventor secretly strangled or drowned.'* In Leyden, this machine was

---

*Marx is here citing the work by Secondo Lancellotti, *L'hoggidì, overo Gl'ingegni non inferiori à' passati*, Parte 2, Venice, 1637, on the basis of Johann Beckmann, *Beyträge zur Geschichte der Erfindungen*, Vol. I, Leipzig, 1786, pp. 125–32.

material instruments of production to the form of society which utilizes those instruments.[15]

The struggles over wages within the manufacturing system presuppose manufacture, and are in no sense directed against its existence. The opposition to the establishment of manufactures proceeds from the guild-masters and the privileged towns, not from the wage-labourers. Hence the writers of the manufacturing period treat the division of labour predominantly as a means of virtually making up for a shortage of workers, and not of actually displacing them. This distinction is very clear. If someone says that 100 million people would be required in England to spin with the old spinning-wheel the cotton that is now spun with mules by 500,000 people, this does not mean that the mules took the place of those millions who never existed. It means only that many million workers would be required to replace the spinning machinery. If, on the other hand, we say that in England the power-loom threw 800,000 weavers onto the streets, we do not refer to existing machinery, which would have to be replaced by a

---

not used until 1629; there riots by the lace-makers at length compelled the town council to prohibit it. The States General of Holland, after imposing various restrictions on its use by the decrees of 1623, 1639, etc., at length permitted it, still under certain conditions, by the decree of 15 December 1661. 'In this town', says Boxhorn (*Inst. Pol.*, 1663),* referring to the introduction of the ribbon-loom into Leyden, 'about twenty years ago certain people invented an instrument for weaving, with which a single person could weave more cloth, and more easily, than many others in the same length of time. As a result there arose disturbances and complaints from the weavers, until the town council finally prohibited the use of this instrument.' It was also prohibited in Cologne in 1676, at the same time as its introduction into England was causing disturbances among the workers. By an Imperial Edict of 19 February 1685, its use was forbidden throughout Germany. In Hamburg it was burnt in public by order of the Senate. The Emperor Charles VI, on 9 February 1719, renewed the edict of 1685, and not till 1765 was its use openly allowed in the Electorate of Saxony. This machine, which caused so much disturbance throughout Europe, was in fact the precursor of the mule and the power-loom, and of the industrial revolution of the eighteenth century. It enabled a boy with no previous experience of weaving to set the whole loom with all its shuttles in motion, simply by moving a rod backwards and forwards, and, in its improved form, it produced from forty to fifty pieces at once.

15. In old-fashioned manufactures the revolts of the workers against machinery, even to this day, occasionally take this crude form, as for instance in the case of the Sheffield file grinders in 1865.

*Full reference: M. Z. Boxhorn, *Marci Zuerii Boxhornii institutionum politicarum liber primus*, Amsterdam, 1663.

556 The Production of Relative Surplus-Value

certain number of workers, but to an actually existing number of workers who were in fact replaced or displaced by the looms. Handicraft labour, even if it was subdivided into many different parts, remained the basis throughout the period of manufacture. The demands of the new colonial markets could not be satisfied by the relatively small number of urban workers handed down from the Middle Ages, and the manufactures proper opened out new fields of production to the rural population which had been driven from the land by the dissolution of the feudal system. At that time, therefore, it was the positive side of the division of labour and co-operation in the workshops which emerged most clearly, i.e. the fact that they allowed the workers to be employed more productively.[16] Long before the period of large-scale industry, co-operation and the concentration of the instruments of labour in the hands of a few people gave rise, in numerous countries where these methods were applied to agriculture, to great, sudden and forcible revolutions in the mode of production, and, as a result, in the conditions of existence and the means of employment of the rural population. But here the struggle at first takes place more between large and small landed proprietors than between capital and wage-labour; on the other hand, when labourers are displaced by the instruments of labour, by sheep, horses, etc., in that case direct acts of violence are in the first instance the pre-condition of the industrial revolution. First the labourers are driven from the land, and then the sheep arrive. Very extensive thefts of land, as

16. This is also how Sir James Steuart conceives the impact of machinery. 'I consider machines, then, as means of securing a virtual increase in the number of working people, without being obliged to feed any more than before . . . In what way does the effect of a machine differ from that of new inhabitants?' (French translation, Vol. 1, Bk I, Ch. 19). More naïve is Petty, who says it replaces 'polygamy'.* That point of view is, at most, admissible only for certain parts of the United States. On the other hand, 'machinery can seldom be used with success to abridge the labour of an individual; more time would be lost in its construction than could be saved by its application. It is only really useful when it acts on great masses, when a single machine can assist the work of thousands. It is accordingly in the most populous countries, where there are most idle men, that it is most abundant . . . It is not called into use by a scarcity of men, but by the facility with which they can be brought to work in masses' (Piercy Ravenstone, *Thoughts on the Funding System, and Its Effects*, London, 1824, p. 45).

* 'Upon producing food and necessaries for the whole people of the land, by few hands; by introducing the Compendium and Facilitations of Art, which is equivalent to what men vainly hoped from Polygamy' (*Verbum Sapienti*, London, 1691, p. 22).

perpetrated in England for instance, are the means whereby large-scale agriculture first gains a field of application.[17] Hence this transformation in agriculture initially tends to have the appearance of a political revolution.

The instrument of labour, when it takes the form of a machine, immediately becomes a competitor of the worker himself.[18] The self-valorization of capital by means of the machine is related directly to the number of workers whose conditions of existence have been destroyed by it. The whole system of capitalist production is based on the worker's sale of his labour-power as a commodity. The division of labour develops this labour-power in a one-sided way, by reducing it to the highly particularized skill of handling a special tool. When it becomes the job of the machine to handle this tool, the use-value of the worker's labour-power vanishes, and with it its exchange-value. The worker becomes unsaleable, like paper money thrown out of currency by legal enactment. The section of the working class thus rendered superfluous by machinery, i.e. converted into a part of the population no longer directly necessary for the self-valorization of capital, either goes under in the unequal contest between the old handicraft and manufacturing production and the new machine production, or else floods all the more easily accessible branches of industry, swamps the labour-market, and makes the price of labour-power fall below its value. It is supposed to be a great consolation to the pauperized workers that, firstly, their sufferings are only temporary ('a temporary inconvenience') and, secondly, machinery only gradually seizes control of the whole of a given field of production, so that the extent and the intensity of its destructive effect is diminished. The first consolation cancels out the second. When machinery seizes on an industry by degrees, it produces chronic misery among the workers who compete with it. Where the transition is rapid, the effect is acute and is felt by great masses of people. World history offers no spectacle more frightful than the gradual extinction of the English hand-loom weavers; this tragedy dragged on for decades, finally coming to an

17. [Note by Engels to the fourth German edition:] This applies to Germany too. Wherever large-scale agriculture exists in our country, hence particularly in the East, it has become possible only through the clearing of peasants from the estates ('*Bauernlegen*'), a practice which became widespread after the sixteenth century, and especially after 1648.

18. 'Machinery and labour are in constant competition' (Ricardo, op. cit., p. 479).

end in 1838. Many of the weavers died of starvation, many vegetated with their families for a long period on 2½d. a day.[19] In India, on the other hand, the English cotton machinery produced an *acute* effect. The Governor General reported as follows in 1834–5: 'The misery hardly finds a parallel in the history of commerce. The bones of the cotton-weavers are bleaching the plains of India.' Of course, in turning the weavers out of this 'temporal' world, the machinery caused them a 'temporary inconvenience'.* But in any case, since machinery is continually seizing on new fields of production, its 'temporary' effect is really permanent. Hence the character of independence from and estrangement towards the worker, which the capitalist mode of production gives to the conditions of labour and the product of labour, develops into a complete and total antagonism with the advent of machinery.[20] It is therefore when machinery arrives on the scene that the

19. The competition between hand-weaving and power-weaving in England was prolonged before the introduction of the Poor Law of 1834 by the fact that wages, which had fallen considerably below the minimum, could be supplemented with parish relief. 'The Reverend Mr Turner was, in 1827, rector of Wilmslow, in Cheshire, a manufacturing district. The questions of the Committee on Emigration, and Mr Turner's answers, show how the competition of human labour is maintained against machinery. "Question: Has not the use of the power-loom superseded the use of the hand-loom? Answer: Undoubtedly; it would have superseded them much more than it has done, if the hand-loom weavers were not enabled to submit to a reduction of wages." "Question: But in submitting he has accepted wages which are insufficient to support him, and looks to parochial contribution as the remainder of his support? Answer: Yes, and in fact the competition between the hand-loom and the power-loom is maintained out of the poor-rates." Thus degrading pauperism or expatriation, is the benefit which the industrious receive from the introduction of machinery, to be reduced from the respectable and in some degree independent mechanic, to the cringing wretch who lives on the debasing bread of charity. This they call a temporary inconvenience' (*A Prize Essay on the Comparative Merits of Competition and Co-operation*, London, 1834, p. 29).

20. 'The same cause which may increase the [net] revenue of the country' (i.e., as Ricardo explains in the same passage, 'the revenues of landlords and capitalists', whose wealth, from the economic point of view, is equivalent to the wealth of the nation), 'may at the same time render the population redundant and deteriorate the condition of the labourer' (Ricardo, op. cit., p. 469). 'The constant aim and the tendency of every improvement in machinery is, in fact, to do away entirely with the labour of man, or to lessen its price by substituting the labour of women and children for that of grown-up men, or of unskilled for that of skilled workmen' (Ure, op. cit., p. 23).

* This play on the words 'temporal' and 'temporary' is possible because the German word *zeitlich* covers both senses.

worker for the first time revolts savagely against the instruments of labour.

The instrument of labour strikes down the worker. The direct antagonism between the two is at its most apparent whenever newly introduced machinery enters into competition with handicrafts or manufactures handed down from former times. But within large-scale industry itself the continual improvement of machinery and the development of the automatic system has an analogous effect. 'The object of improved machinery is to diminish manual labour, to provide for the performance of a process or the completion of a link in a manufacture by the aid of an iron instead of the human apparatus.'[21] 'The adaptation of power to machinery heretofore moved by hand is almost of daily occurrence ... the minor improvements in machinery having for their object economy of power, the production of better work, the turning off more work in the same time, or in supplying the place of a child, a female, or a man, are constant, and although sometimes apparently of no great moment, have somewhat important results.'[22] 'Whenever a process requires peculiar dexterity and steadiness of hand, it is withdrawn, as soon as possible, from the cunning workman, who is prone to irregularities of many kinds, and it is placed in charge of a peculiar mechanism, so self-regulating that a child can superintend it.'[23] 'On the automatic plan skilled labour gets progressively superseded.'[24] 'The effect of improvements in machinery, not merely in superseding the necessity for the employment of the same quantity of adult labour as before, in order to produce a given result, but in substituting one description of human labour for

21. *Reports of the Inspectors of Factories ... 31 October 1858*, p. 43.
22. *Reports of the Inspectors of Factories ... 31 October 1856*, p. 15.
23. Ure, op. cit., p. 19. 'The great advantage of the machinery employed in brick-making consists in this, that the employer is made entirely independent of skilled labourers' (*Children's Employment Commission, Fifth Report*, London, 1866, p. 130, n. 46). Mr A. Sturrock, superintendent of the machine department of the Great Northern Railway, says with regard to the building of machines (locomotives, etc.): 'Expensive English workmen are being less used every day. The production of the workshops of England is being increased by the use of improved tools and these tools are again served by a low class of labour ... Formerly their skilled labour necessarily produced all the parts of engines. Now the parts of engines are produced by labour with less skill, but with good tools. By tools, I mean engineer's machinery, lathes, planing machines, drills, and so on' (*Royal Commission on Railways, Minutes of Evidence*, n. 17862 and n. 17863, London, 1867).
24. Ure, op. cit., p. 20.

another, the less skilled for the more skilled, juvenile for adult, female for male, causes a fresh disturbance in the rate of wages.'[25] 'The effect of substituting the self-acting mule for the common mule, is to discharge the greater part of the men spinners, and to retain adolescents and children.'[26] The machine system's extraordinary capacity for expansion is a result of accumulated practical experience, the extent of the mechanical instruments already available for use, and the constant advance of technology; it has shown what giant strides it can take under the pressure of the shortened working day. But who in 1860, the year in which the English cotton industry reached its zenith, would have dreamt of the galloping pace of improvements in machinery, and the corresponding displacement of manual labour, which the stimulus of the American Civil War called forth in the following three years? A couple of examples from the *Reports of the Inspectors of Factories* will suffice on this point. A Manchester manufacturer states: 'We formerly had seventy-five carding engines, now we have twelve, doing the same quantity of work ... We are doing with fewer hands by fourteen, at a saving in wages of £10 a week. Our estimated saving in waste is about 10 per cent in the quantity of cotton consumed.' 'In another fine-spinning mill in Manchester, I was informed that through increased speed and the adoption of some self-acting processes, a reduction had been made, in number, of a fourth in one department, and of above half in another, and that the introduction of the combing machine in place of the second carding, had considerably reduced the number of hands formerly employed in the carding-room.' Another spinning-mill is estimated to effect a saving of 'hands' of 10 per cent. Messrs Gilmour, spinners at Manchester, make this statement: 'In our blowing-room department we consider our expense with new machinery is fully one-third less in wages and hands ... in the jack-frame and drawing-frame room, about one-third less in expense, and likewise one-third less in hands; in the spinning-room about one-third less in expenses. But this is not all; when our yarn goes to the manu-facturers, it is so much better by the application of our new machinery, that they will produce a greater quantity of cloth, and cheaper than from the yarn produced by old machinery.'[27] Mr Redgrave, the factory inspector, remarks in connection with this: 'The reduction of hands against increased production is, in fact,

25. Ure, op. cit., p. 321.   26. ibid., p. 23.
27. *Reports of the Inspectors of Factories ... 31 October 1863*, pp. 108–9.

constantly taking place; in woollen mills the reduction commenced some time since, and is continuing; a few days since, the master of a school in the neighbourhood of Rochdale said to me, that the great falling off in the girls' school is not only caused by the distress, but by the changes of machinery in the woollen mills, in consequence of which a reduction of seventy short-timers had taken place.'[28]

The following table shows the total result of the mechanical improvements in the English cotton industry resulting from the American Civil War*:

NUMBER OF FACTORIES

	1858	1861	1868
England and Wales	2,046	2,715	2,405
Scotland	152	163	131
Ireland	12	9	13
United Kingdom	2,210	2,887	2,549

NUMBER OF POWER-LOOMS

	1858	1861	1868
England and Wales	275,590	368,125	344,719
Scotland	21,624	30,110	31,864
Ireland	1,633	1,757	2,746
United Kingdom	298,847	399,992	379,329

28. ibid., p. 109. The rapid improvement of machinery during the crisis allowed the English manufacturers, immediately after the end of the American Civil War, and almost in no time, to glut the world market once again. During the last six months of 1866 cloth was almost unsaleable. This was followed by the sending of goods on consignment to India and China, which of course merely intensified the 'glut'. At the beginning of 1867 the manufacturers resorted to their usual way out of the difficulty: they reduced wages by 5 per cent. The workers resisted this, and made the theoretically quite correct assertion that the only remedy was to work short time, four days a week. After holding out for some time, the self-appointed captains of industry had to make up their minds to introduce short time, with reduced wages in some places, and in others without reduced wages.

*The table was compiled from the following three Parliamentary Returns: *Return to an Address of the Honourable the House of Commons*, 15 April 1856; *Return to an Address of the Honourable the House of Commons*, 24 April 1861; *Return to an Address of the Honourable the House of Commons*, 5 December 1867.

NUMBER OF SPINDLES

	1858	1861	1868
England and Wales	25,818,576	28,352,152	30,478,228
Scotland	2,041,129	1,915,398	1,397,546
Ireland	150,512	119,944	124,240
United Kingdom	28,010,217	30,387,494	32,000,014

NUMBER OF PERSONS EMPLOYED

	1858	1861	1868
England and Wales	341,170	407,598	357,052
Scotland	34,698	41,237	39,809
Ireland	3,345	2,734	4,203
United Kingdom	379,213	451,569	401,064

Hence, between 1861 and 1868, 338 cotton factories disappeared, in other words, more productive machinery on a larger scale was concentrated in the hands of a smaller number of capitalists. The number of power-looms decreased by 20,663; but since their product increased in the same period, an improved loom yielded more than an old one. Finally, the number of spindles increased by 1,612,541, while the number of workers employed decreased by 50,505. The 'temporary' misery inflicted on the workers by the cotton crisis was therefore heightened and made permanent by the rapid and continuous progress of machinery.

But machinery does not just act as a superior competitor to the worker, always on the point of making him superfluous. It is a power inimical to him, and capital proclaims this fact loudly and deliberately, as well as making use of it. It is the most powerful weapon for suppressing strikes, those periodic revolts of the working class against the autocracy of capital.[29] According to Gaskell, the steam-engine was from the very first an antagonist of 'human power', an antagonist that enabled the capitalists to tread underfoot the growing demands of the workers, which threatened to

29. 'The relation of master and man in the blown flint and bottle trades amounts to a chronic strike.' Hence the impetus given to the manufacture of pressed glass, in which the chief operations are done by machinery. One firm in Newcastle, which formerly produced 350,000 lb. of blown flint glass *per annum*, now produces instead 3,000,500 lb. of pressed glass. (*Children's Employment Commission, Fourth Report*, 1865, pp. 261–2.)

drive the infant factory system into crisis.[30] It would be possible to write a whole history of the inventions made since 1830 for the sole purpose of providing capital with weapons against working-class revolt. We would mention, above all, the self-acting mule, because it opened up a new epoch in the automatic system.[31]

Nasmyth, the inventor of the steam-hammer, gave the following evidence before the Commission on Trades Unions, with regard to the improvements in machinery he himself introduced as a result of the wide-spread and long-lasting strikes of the engineers in 1851. 'The characteristic feature of our modern mechanical improvements, is the introduction of self-acting tool machinery. What every mechanical workman has now to do, and what every boy can do, is not to work himself but to superintend the beautiful labour of the machine. The whole class of workmen that depend exclusively on their skill, is now done away with. Formerly, I employed four boys to every mechanic. Thanks to these new mechanical combinations, I have reduced the number of grown-up men from 1,500 to 750. The result was a considerable increase in my profits.'*

Ure says this of the colouring machines used in calico printing: 'At length capitalists sought deliverance from this intolerable bondage' (namely the terms of their contracts with the workers, which they saw as burdensome) 'in the resources of science, and were speedily re-instated in their legitimate rule, that of the head over the inferior members.' Then, speaking of an invention for dressing warps, whose immediate occasion was a strike, he says: 'The combined malcontents, who fancied themselves impregnably intrenched behind the old lines of division of labour, found their flanks turned and their defences rendered useless by the new mechanical tactics, and were obliged to surrender at discretion.' Of the invention of the self-acting mule, he says: 'A creation destined to restore order among the industrious classes . . . This invention confirms the great doctrine already propounded, that

30. Gaskell, *The Manufacturing Population of England*, London, 1833, pp. 11–12.

31. Mr Fairbairn* discovered several very important applications of machinery to the construction of machines as a result of strikes in his own factory.

*Sir Peter Fairbairn, 1799–1861, engineer and inventor. He set up a machine factory in Leeds in 1828.

Tenth Report of the Commissioners Appointed to Inquire into the Organization and Rules of Trades Unions and Other Associations: Together with Minutes of Evidence, London, 1868, pp. 63–4.

when capital enlists science into her service, the refractory hand of labour will always be taught docility.'[32] Although Ure's work appeared in 1835, at a time when the factory system was still comparatively little developed, it remains the classical expression of the spirit of the factory, not only because of its undisguised cynicism, but also because of the naïveté with which it blurts out the thoughtless contradictions of the capitalist brain. For instance, after unfolding the above-mentioned 'doctrine' that capital, with the aid of science, which has been taken onto the payroll, always reduces the refractory hand of labour to docility, he waxes indignant because 'physico-mechanical science ... has been accused of lending itself to the rich capitalist as an instrument for harassing the poor'. After preaching a long sermon to show how advantageous the rapid development of machinery is to the workers, he warns them that by their obstinacy and their strikes they hasten that development. 'Violent revulsions of this nature,' he says, 'display short-sighted man in the contemptible character of a self-tormentor.' A few pages before this he states the contrary: 'Had it not been for the violent collisions and interruptions resulting from erroneous views among the factory operatives, the factory system would have been developed still more rapidly and beneficially for all concerned.' Then he exclaims again: 'Fortunately for the state of society in the cotton districts of Great Britain, the improvements in machinery are gradual.' 'It' (the introduction of improvements in machinery) 'is said to lower the rate of earnings of adults by displacing a portion of them, and thus rendering their number superabundant as compared with the demand for their labour. It certainly augments the demand for the labour of children and increases the rate of *their* wages.' On the other hand, this same dispenser of consolation defends the lowness of the children's wages on the ground that it prevents parents from sending their children into the factory at too early an age. The whole of his book is a vindication of a working day of unrestricted length; that Parliament should forbid children of 13 years of age to be exhausted by working 12 hours a day reminds his liberal soul of the darkest days of the Middle Ages. This does not prevent him from calling upon the factory workers to thank Providence, which by means of machinery has given them 'the leisure to think of their immortal interests'.[33]

32. Ure, op. cit., pp. 367–70.
33. ibid., pp. 368, 7, 370, 280, 281, 321, 370, 475.

6. THE COMPENSATION THEORY, WITH REGARD TO THE WORKERS DISPLACED BY MACHINERY

A whole series of bourgeois political economists, including James Mill, MacCulloch, Torrens, Senior and John Stuart Mill, assert that all machinery that displaces workers simultaneously, and necessarily, sets free an amount of capital adequate to employ precisely those workers displaced.[34]

Let us assume that a capitalist employs 100 workers at £30 a year each in a carpet factory. The variable capital annually laid out therefore amounts to £3,000. Let us then assume that he dismisses fifty of his workers, and employs the remaining fifty with machinery that costs him £1,500. To simplify matters, we take no account of buildings, coal, etc. Finally, let the raw material annually consumed cost £3,000, both before and after the change.[35] Is any capital 'set free' by this metamorphosis? Before the change, the total sum of £6,000 consisted half of constant and half of variable capital. After the change it consists of £4,500 constant (£3,000 raw material and £1,500 machinery) and £1,500 variable capital. The variable capital, instead of being one-half, is only one-quarter of the total capital. Instead of being set free, a part of the capital is here locked up in such a way as to cease to be exchanged for labour-power; variable has been changed into constant capital. Other things being equal, the capital of £6,000 can now employ no more than fifty men. With each improvement in the machinery, it will employ fewer people. If the newly introduced machinery had cost less than the labour-power and implements displaced by it, if for instance instead of costing £1,500, it has cost only £1,000, a variable capital of £1,000 would have been converted into constant capital, and locked up in it, and a capital of £500 would have been set free. The latter sum, given the same annual wage-bill, would form a fund sufficient to employ about sixteen out of the fifty men dismissed, or rather less than sixteen, for, in order to be employed as capital, a part of this £500 must in its turn be transformed into constant capital, thus leaving only the remainder to be laid out in the purchase of labour-power.

34. Ricardo originally shared this view, but afterwards expressly disclaimed it, with the scientific impartiality and love of truth characteristic of him. See Ricardo, op. cit., Ch. 31, 'On Machinery'.

35. N. B. My illustration is entirely on the lines of those given by the above-mentioned economists.

But suppose, in addition to this, that the making of the new machinery employs an increased number of mechanics. Can this be regarded as compensation for the carpet-makers who have been thrown on the streets? At best, the construction of the machinery will still employ fewer men than its application displaces. The sum of £1,500, which previously represented the wages of the dismissed carpet-makers, now represents in the shape of machinery, (1) the value of the means of production used in the construction of that machinery, (2) the wages of the mechanics who constructed it and (3) the surplus-value falling to the share of their 'master'. Moreover, the machinery need not be renewed until it is worn out. Hence, in order to keep the increased number of mechanics in constant employment, one carpet manufacturer after another must replace workers with machines.

In fact the apologists for capitalism do not have in mind this sort of liberation of capital. They are thinking more of the means of subsistence of the workers who have been 'set free'. It cannot be denied in the above instance that the machinery not only liberates fifty men, thus placing them at the disposal of other capitalists, but also, at the same time, withdraws from their consumption, and sets free, £1,500 worth of means of subsistence. The simple and by no means new fact that machinery sets the workers free from their means of subsistence is expressed in economic language by saying that machinery sets free means of subsistence for the workers, or converts those means of subsistence into capital with which to employ them. Everything, as you see, depends on the way things are put, *Nominibus mollire licet mala*.*

This theory implies that the £1,500 worth of means of subsistence was capital that was being valorized by the labour of the fifty men dismissed. Accordingly, the capital ceases to be employed as soon as the workers begin their forced holiday, and never rests until it has found a new 'placing' in which the above-mentioned fifty can again consume it productively. On this theory, the capital and the workers must sooner or later come together again, and that is when the compensation will appear. Hence the sufferings of the workers displaced by machinery are as transient as worldly wealth.

But the £1,500 worth of means of subsistence never confronted the dismissed workers as capital. This role was reserved for the

* 'It is proper to lighten evils with words' (Ovid, *Artis Amatoriae*, Bk 2, line 657).

sum of £1,500 later on, when it had been transformed into machinery. If we look more closely, it will be seen that the initial sum of £1,500 represented only a portion of the carpets produced in a year by the fifty dismissed men, and they received this part as wages from their employer, paid in money instead of in kind. With the carpets thus transformed into £1,500 they bought means of subsistence to the same value. These means, therefore, were to them not capital but commodities, and they, as regards these commodities, were not wage-labourers, but buyers. The circumstance that they were 'set free' by the machinery from the means of purchase changed them from buyers into non-buyers. Hence a lessened demand for those commodities. *Voilà tout.* If this diminution of demand is not compensated for by an increase in demand from another direction, the market price of the commodities falls. If this state of things lasts for some time, and increases in extent, there follows the displacement of the workers employed in the production of those commodities. A part of the capital, which previously produced the necessary means of subsistence, is now reproduced in another form. While prices are falling, and capital is being displaced, the workers employed in the production of the necessary means of subsistence are in turn 'set free' from a part of their wages. Instead, therefore, of proving that when machinery frees the worker from his means of subsistence, it simultaneously converts those means into capital for his further employment, our friends the apologists, with their well-tried law of supply and demand, prove the opposite, namely that machinery throws workers onto the streets, not only in that branch of production into which it has been introduced, but also in branches into which it has not been introduced.

The real facts, which are travestied by the optimism of the economists, are these: the workers, when driven out of the workshop by the machinery, are thrown onto the labour-market. Their presence in the labour-market increases the number of labour-powers which are at the disposal of capitalist exploitation. In Part VII we shall see that this effect of machinery, which has been represented as a compensation for the working class, is, on the contrary, a most frightful scourge. For the present I will only say this: workers who have been thrown out of work in a given branch of industry can no doubt look for employment in another branch. If they find it, and thus renew the bond between them and the means of subsistence, this takes place only through the agency of a new, additional capital which is seeking investment, and in no way through the agency of the capital that was already functioning previously and was then converted into machinery. And even if they do find employment, what a miserable prospect they face! Crippled as they are by the division of labour, these poor devils are worth so little outside their old trade that they cannot find admission into any industries except a few inferior and therefore over-supplied and under-paid branches.[36] Furthermore, every branch of industry attracts each year a new stream of men, who furnish a contingent from which to fill up vacancies, and to draw a supply for expansion. As soon as machinery has set free a part of the workers employed in a given branch of industry, the reserve men are also diverted into new channels of employment, and become absorbed in other branches; meanwhile the original victims, during the period of transition, for the most part starve and perish.

It is an undoubted fact that machinery is not as such responsible for 'setting free' the worker from the means of subsistence. It cheapens and increases production in the branch it seizes on, and at first leaves unaltered the quantity of the means of subsistence produced in other branches. Hence, after the introduction of machinery, society possesses as much of the necessaries of life as before, if not more, for the workers who have been displaced, not to mention the enormous share of the annual product wasted by non-workers. And this is the point relied on by our economic apologists! The contradictions and antagonisms inseparable from the capitalist application of machinery do not exist, they say, because they do not arise out of machinery as such, but out of its capitalist application! Therefore, since machinery in itself shortens the hours of labour, but when employed by capital it lengthens them; since in itself it lightens labour, but when employed by

36. A disciple of Ricardo, in reply to the insipid nonsense uttered by J. B. Say,* remarks on this point: 'Where division of labour is well developed, the skill of the labourer is available only in that particular branch in which it has been acquired; he himself is a sort of machine. It does not therefore help matters one jot, to repeat in parrot fashion, that things have a tendency to find their level. On looking around us we cannot but see, that they are unable to find their level for a long time; and that when they do find it, the level is always lower than at the commencement of the process' (*An Inquiry into Those Principles Respecting the Nature of Demand, etc.*, London, 1821, p. 72).

*This passage is an attack on the view expressed by Say in *Traité d'économie politique*, Vol. 1, 4th edn, p. 60, that the workers derived an advantage, as consumers, from the introduction of machines.

capital it heightens its intensity; since in itself it is a victory of man over the forces of nature but in the hands of capital it makes man the slave of those forces; since in itself it increases the wealth of the producers, but in the hands of capital it makes them into paupers, the bourgeois economist simply states that the contemplation of machinery in itself demonstrates with exactitude that all these evident contradictions are a mere semblance, present in everyday reality, but not existing in themselves, and therefore having no theoretical existence either. Thus he manages to avoid racking his brains any more, and in addition implies that his opponent is guilty of the stupidity of contending, not against the capitalist application of machinery, but against machinery itself.

No doubt the bourgeois economist is far from denying that temporary inconveniences may result from the capitalist use of machinery. But where is the medal without its reverse side! Any other utilization of machinery than the capitalist one is to him impossible. Exploitation of the worker by the machine is therefore identical for him with exploitation of the machine by the worker. Therefore whoever reveals the real situation with the capitalist employment of machinery does not want machinery to be employed at all, and is an enemy of social progress![37] This is exactly the reasoning of Bill Sikes, the celebrated cut-throat.* 'Gentlemen of the jury, no doubt the throat of this commercial traveller has been cut. But that is not my fault, it is the fault of the knife. Must we, for such a temporary inconvenience, abolish the use of the knife? Only consider! Where would agriculture and trade be without the knife? Is it not as salutary in surgery, as it is skilled in anatomy? And a willing assistant at the festive table? If you abolish the knife – you hurl us back into the depths of barbarism.'[38]

37. MacCulloch, amongst others, is a past master at this kind of pretentious cretinism. 'If,' he says, with the affected naïveté of an eight-year-old, 'if it be advantageous, to develop the skill of the workman more and more, so that he is capable of producing, with the same or with a less quantity of labour, a constantly increasing quantity of commodities, it must also be advantageous that he should avail himself of the help of such machinery as will assist him most effectively in the attainment of this result' (MacCulloch, *Principles of Political Economy*, London, 1830, p. 182).

38. 'The inventor of the spinning machine has ruined India, a fact that is however of little concern to us' (A. Thiers, *De la propriété*, p. 275). M.

---

*This purported speech by Bill Sikes is a parody by Marx of Dickens' *Oliver Twist*. The Bill Sikes of the novel was not much given to ratiocination.

Although machinery necessarily throws men out of work in those industries into which it is introduced, it may, despite this, bring about an increase in employment in other industries. This effect of machinery, however, has nothing in common with the so-called theory of compensation. Since every article produced by a machine is cheaper than a similar article produced by hand, we deduce the following absolute law: if the total quantity of the article produced by machinery is equal to the total quantity of the article previously produced by a handicraft or by manufacture, and now made by machinery, then total labour expended is diminished. The increase in the labour required to produce the instruments of labour themselves, the machinery, coal, etc. must be less than the reduction in labour achieved by the employment of machinery; otherwise the product of the machine would be as dear as, or dearer than, the product of the manual labour. But as a matter of fact, the total quantity of the article produced by machinery with a diminished number of workers, instead of remaining equal to the total quantity of the hand-made article that has been displaced, exceeds this by far. Suppose that 400,000 yards of cloth have been produced on power-looms by fewer weavers than could weave 100,000 yards by hand. The quadrupled product contains four times as much raw material. Hence the production of raw material must be quadrupled. But as regards the instruments of labour consumed, such as buildings, coal, machinery and so on, it is different; the limit of the possible increase in the amount of additional labour required to produce them varies with the difference between the quantity of the machine-made article and the quantity of the same article that the same number of workers could make by hand.

Hence, as the use of machinery extends in a given industry, the immediate effect is to increase production in the other industries that provide the first with means of production. How far employment is thereby found for an increased number of workers depends, given the length of the working day and the intensity of

---

Thiers* here confuses the spinning machine with the power-loom, 'a fact that is however of little concern to us'.

*This is the French historian and politician Louis-Adolphe Thiers (1797–1877), representative *par excellence* of the French bourgeoisie, who accepted each of the successive governmental forms in nineteenth-century France, provided he could fill them with a bourgeois content, and finally presided over the crushing of the Paris Commune of 1871 as head of the French state.

labour, on the composition of the capital employed, i.e. on the ratio of its constant to its variable component.* This ratio, in its turn, varies considerably with the extent to which machinery has already penetrated, or is engaged in penetrating, those trades. The number of men condemned to work in coal and metal mines has been enormously swollen by the progress of machine production in England, although the growth in numbers has been slowed down during the last few decades by the introduction of new machinery into the mining industries.[39] Along with the machine, a new type of worker springs to life: the machine-maker. We have already learnt that machinery is seizing control even of this branch of production on an ever-increasing scale.[40] As to raw materials,[41] there can be no doubt that the rapid advance of cotton spinning not only promoted as if in a hot house the growing of cotton in the United States, and with it the African slave trade, but also made slave-breeding the chief business of the so-called border slave states.† In 1790, when the first census of slaves was taken in the United States, their number was 697,000; in 1861 it had nearly reached four millions. On the other hand, it is no less certain that the blossoming of the English woollen factories, together with the

39. According to the census of 1861 (Vol. 2, London, 1863) the number of people employed in coal-mines in England and Wales amounted to 246,613, of whom 73,546 were under 20, and 173,067 over 20. In the first category there were 835 between 5 and 10 years old, 30,701 between 10 and 15, and 42,010 between 15 and 19. The number of people employed in iron, copper, lead, tin and other mines was 319,222.

40. In England and Wales in 1861 the total number of people employed in the production of machinery was 60,807. This includes the manufacturers and their assistants, etc., as well as all the agents and business people connected with this industry, but it excludes the makers of small machines, such as sewing-machines, etc., and those who produce the operative parts of machines, such as spindles. The total number of civil engineers was 3,329.

41. Since iron is one of the most important raw materials, let me say here that in 1861, in England and Wales, there were 125,771 people working in iron foundries, of whom 123,430 were male and 2,341 female. Of the males, 30,810 were under 20 years old, and 92,620 over.

*This is the first mention of the concept of the '(organic) composition of capital', which plays such an important part in *Capital* later on. See below, p. 762, for a fuller definition.

† The states on the border between the South and North of the United States, where slavery co-existed with free labour until the American Civil War: Delaware, Maryland, Virginia, North Carolina, Kentucky, Tennessee, Missouri and Arkansas.

progressive transformation of arable land into sheep pasture, brought about the conversion of agricultural labourers into 'super-numeraries' and drove them in their masses from the land. Ireland, having during the last twenty years reduced its population by nearly one-half, is at this moment undergoing the process of still further reducing the number of its inhabitants to a level which will correspond exactly with the requirements of its landlords and the English woollen manufacturers.

When machinery penetrates into any of the preliminary or intermediate stages through which an object of labour has to pass on its way to its final form, there is an increased yield of material in those stages, and simultaneously an increased demand for labour in the handicrafts or manufactures supplied by the machines. Spinning by machinery, for example, supplied yarn so cheaply and so abundantly that the hand-loom weavers were at first able to work full-time without increased outlay. Their earnings accordingly rose.[42] This produced a flow of people into the cotton-weaving trade, until at length the 800,000 weavers called into existence by the jenny, the throstle and the mule were overwhelmed by the power-loom. So also, owing to the abundance of clothing materials produced by machinery, the number of tailors, seamstresses and needle-women went on increasing until the appearance of the sewing-machine.

In proportion as machinery, with the aid of a relatively small number of workers, increases the mass of raw materials, half-finished products and instruments of labour, the working-up of these raw materials and half-finished products becomes split up into innumerable subdivisions. There is thus an increase in the number of the branches of social production. Machine production drives the social division of labour immeasurably further than manufacture does, because it increases the productive power of the industries it seizes upon to a much greater degree.

The immediate result of machinery is to augment surplus-value and the mass of products in which surplus-value is embodied. It also increases the quantity of substances for the capitalists and their dependants to consume, and therefore the size of these

42. 'A family of four grown-up persons, with two children as winders, earned at the end of the last, and the beginning of the present century, by ten hours' daily labour, £4 a week. If the work was very pressing, they could earn more ... Before that, they had always suffered from a deficient supply of yarn' (Gaskell, op. cit., pp. 25–7).

social strata themselves. Their growing wealth, and the relatively diminished number of workers required to produce the means of subsistence, begets both new luxury requirements and the means of satisfying them. A larger portion of the social product is converted into surplus product, and a larger portion of the surplus product is reproduced and consumed in a multitude of refined shapes. In other words, the production of luxuries increases.[43] The products are also made more refined and more varied by the new world market relations created by large-scale industry. Not only are greater quantities of foreign luxury articles exchanged for home products, but a greater mass of foreign raw materials, ingredients and half-finished articles are used as means of production in the home industries. Owing to these relations with the world market, the demand for labour increases in the transport industry, and splits the latter into numerous extra subdivisions.[44]

The increase in means of production and subsistence, accompanied by a relative diminution in the number of workers, provides the impulse for an extension of work that can only bear fruit in the distant future, such as the construction of canals, docks, tunnels, bridges and so on. Entirely new branches of production, creating new fields of labour, are also formed as the direct result either of machinery or of the general industrial changes brought about by it. But the place occupied by these branches in total production is far from important, even in the most developed countries. The number of workers they employ is directly proportional to the demand created by these industries for the crudest form of manual labour. The chief industries of this kind are, at present, gas-works, telegraphy, photography, steam navigation and railways. According to the census of 1861 for England and Wales, we find in the gas industry (gas-works, production of mechanical apparatus, servants of the gas companies, etc.), 15,211 persons; in telegraphy, 2,399; in photography, 2,366; in steam navigation, 3,570; and in railways, 70,599, of whom the unskilled 'navvies', more or less permanently employed, and the whole administrative and commercial staff, make up about 28,000. The

43. F. Engels, in *Lage, etc.* [*Condition of the Working Class in England*], points out the miserable condition of a large number of precisely those luxury-workers. See also numerous instances in the Reports of the Children's Employment Commission.

44. In 1861, in England and Wales, there were 94,665 sailors in the merchant service.

total number of persons, therefore, employed in these five new industries amounts to 94,145.

Lastly, the extraordinary increase in the productivity of large-scale industry, accompanied as it is by both a more intensive and a more extensive exploitation of labour-power in all other spheres of production, permits a larger and larger part of the working class to be employed unproductively. Hence it is possible to reproduce the ancient domestic slaves, on a constantly extending scale, under the name of a servant class, including men-servants, women-servants, lackeys, etc. According to the census of 1861, the population of England and Wales was 20,066,224; 9,776,259 of these were males and 10,289,965 females. If we deduct from this population, firstly, all who are too old or too young for work, all 'unproductive' women, young persons and children; then the 'ideological' groups, such as members of the government, priests, lawyers, soldiers, etc.; then all the people exclusively occupied in consuming the labour of others in the form of ground rent, interest, etc.; and lastly, paupers, vagabonds and criminals, there remain in round numbers eight millions of the two sexes of every age, including in that number every capitalist who is in any way engaged in industry, commerce or finance. These eight millions are distributed as follows:

Agricultural labourers (including shepherds, farm servants and maidservants living in the houses of farmers)	1,098,261
Those employed in cotton, woollen, worsted, flax, hemp, silk and jute factories, in stocking-making and lace-making by machinery	642,607[45]
Those employed in coal-mines and metal mines	565,835
Those employed in metal works (blast-furnaces, rolling-mills, etc.) and metal manufactures of every kind	396,998[46]
The servant class	1,208,648[47]

45. Of these, only 177,596 are males above 13 years of age.

46. Of these, 30,501 are females.

47. Of these, 137,447 are males. Persons not serving in private houses are excluded from the total of 1,208,648. Between 1861 and 1870 the number of male servants nearly doubled, increasing to 267,671. In the year 1847 there were 2,694 gamekeepers (for the landlords' preserves), and in 1869 there were 4,921. The young servant girls in the houses of the London lower middle class are in common parlance called 'little slaveys'.

All the persons employed in textile factories and in mines, taken together, number 1,208,442; those employed in textile factories and metal industries, taken together, number 1,039,605; in both cases less than the number of modern domestic slaves. What an elevating consequence of the capitalist exploitation of machinery!

7. REPULSION AND ATTRACTION OF WORKERS THROUGH THE DEVELOPMENT OF MACHINE PRODUCTION. CRISES IN THE COTTON INDUSTRY

All the more respectable representatives of political economy concede that the introduction of new machinery has a baneful effect on the workers in the old handicrafts and manufactures with which this machinery at first competes. Almost all of them bemoan the slavery of the factory worker. And what is the great trump-card they play? That machinery, after the horrors of the period of its introduction and development have subsided, in the final analysis increases, rather than diminishing, the number of wage-slaves! Yes, political economy joyfully proclaims the theory, which is hideous to every 'philanthropist' who believes that the capitalist mode of production is an eternal necessity ordained by nature, that after a period of growth and transition, and even when it is already founded on production by machinery, the factory system grinds down more workers than it originally threw onto the streets.[48]

48. Ganilh, on the other hand, considers that the final result of machine production would be an absolute reduction in the number of wage-slaves, at whose expense an increased number of 'decent people' would live and develop their well-known 'perfectible perfectibility'. Little as he understands the movement of production, at least he feels that machinery must be a very fatal institution if its introduction converts busy workers into paupers and its development calls into existence more wage-slaves than it has suppressed. It is not possible to bring out the cretinous character of his standpoint except by quoting his own words: 'The classes which are condemned to produce and to consume grow smaller, and the classes which direct labour and bring relief, consolation and enlightenment to the whole population increase in size ... and appropriate all the advantages which result from the reduction in the cost of labour, from the abundant supply of commodities and from the low prices of consumer goods. Under this leadership, the human species rises to the highest creations of genius, penetrates the mysterious depths of religion and establishes the salutary principles of morality' (which consist in 'the appropriation of all the advantages etc.'), 'the laws for the protection of liberty' (the liberty of 'the classes condemned to produce'?) 'and power, of obedience and justice, of obligation and humanity.' This twaddle is to be found in C. Ganilh, *Des systèmes d'économie politique*, 2nd edn, Paris, 1821, Vol. 1, p. 224, and see p. 212.

It is true that in some cases, as we saw from the example of the English worsted and silk factories, an extraordinary extension of the factory system may, at a certain stage of its development, be accompanied not only by a relative, but by an absolute decrease in the number of workers employed.* In 1860, when a special census of all the factories in the United Kingdom was taken by order of Parliament, the factories in those parts of Lancashire, Cheshire and Yorkshire included in the district of Mr R. Baker, the factory inspector, numbered 652; 570 of these contained 85,622 power-looms and 6,819,146 spindles (not including doubling-spindles), utilized 27,439 horse-power in steam-engines and 1,390 horse-power in water-wheels, and employed 94,119 persons. In 1865, the same factories contained 95,163 looms and 7,025,031 spindles, utilized 28,925 horse-power in steam-engines and 1,445 horse-power in water-wheels, and employed 88,913 persons. Between 1860 and 1865, therefore, the increase in looms was 11 per cent, in spindles 3 per cent, and in engine-power 3 per cent, while the number of persons employed decreased $5\frac{1}{2}$ per cent.[49] Between 1852 and 1862 considerable growth occurred in English woollen manufacture, while the number of workers employed in that industry remained almost stationary. 'This shows to what a great extent the introduction of new machines had superseded the labour of preceding periods.'[50] In certain cases, the increase in the number of factory workers employed is only apparent, i.e. it is not due to the extension of industries already based on machine production but to the gradual annexation of neighbouring

49. *Reports of the Inspectors of Factories . . . 31 October 1865*, pp. 58 ff. At the same time, however, the material foundation had already been laid for the employment of a growing number of workers in 110 new factories, with 11,625 looms, 628,576 spindles and 2,695 horse-power in the form both of steam-engines and water-wheels (ibid.).

50. *Reports of the Inspectors of Factories . . . 31 October 1862*, p. 79. At the end of December 1871, Mr A. Redgrave, the factory inspector, in a lecture given at Bradford, in the New Mechanics' Institution, said, 'What has struck me for some time past is the altered appearance of the woollen factories. Formerly they were filled with women and children, now machinery seems to do all the work. At my asking for an explanation of this from a manufacturer, he gave me the following: "Under the old system I employed 63 persons; after the introduction of improved machinery I reduced my hands to 33, and lately, in consequence of new and extensive alterations, I have been in a position to reduce those 33 to 13."'

---

*See above, pp. 540–41.

branches of industry. For instance, the increase in power-looms and in the number of factory workers employed by them between 1838 and 1856 was, in the cotton trade, simply a result of the extension of this branch of industry; but in the other trades it resulted from the application of steam-power to the carpet-loom, the ribbon-loom and the linen-loom, which had previously been driven by muscle-power.[51] Hence the increase in the number of workers in these latter trades was merely an expression of the reduction in the total number of workers employed. Finally, we have considered this question entirely apart from the fact that everywhere, except in the metallurgical industries, young persons (under 18), women and children form by far the most preponderant element in the factory personnel.

Nevertheless, in spite of the mass of workers actually driven out and virtually replaced by machinery, we can understand how workers in factories may become more numerous than the manufacturing artisans and handicraftsmen they have displaced; their numbers grow through the building of more factories or the extension of old factories in a given industry. Suppose, for example, that under the old method of running the factory a capital of £500 is employed every week, two-fifths being constant and three-fifths variable capital, i.e. £200 being laid out in means of production, and £300, say £1 per man, in labour-power. With the introduction of machinery the composition of the total capital is altered. We will assume that it consists now of four-fifths constant and one-fifth variable, which means that only £100 is now laid out in labour-power. Consequently, two-thirds of the workers are dismissed. If now the business expands, and the total capital employed grows to £1,500, the other conditions of production remaining the same, the number of workers employed will increase to 300, just as many as before the introduction of the machinery. If the capital employed grows some more, to £2,000, 400 men will be employed, or one-third more than under the old system. Their numbers have in fact increased by 100, but in relative terms, i.e. in proportion to the total capital advanced, they have diminished by 800, for the £2,000 of capital would under the old method of running the enterprise have employed 1,200 instead of 400 workers. Hence a relative decrease in the number of workers employed is consistent with an actual increase in that number. We assumed above that while the total capital increased, its composi-

51. See *Reports of the Inspectors of Factories . . . 31 October 1856*, p. 16.

tion remained the same, because the conditions of production remained constant. But we have already seen that every advance in the use of machinery entails an increase in the constant component of capital, that part which consists of machinery, raw material, etc., and a decrease in its variable component, the part laid out in labour-power. We also know that in no other system of production is improvement so continuous and the composition of the capital employed so subject to variation as in the factory system. This constant variation is however equally constantly interrupted by periods of rest, during which there is a merely quantitative extension of factories on the existing technical basis. During such periods the number of workers employed increases. Thus in 1835 the total number of workers in the cotton, woollen, worsted, flax and silk factories of the United Kingdom was only 354,684; while in 1861 the number of power-loom weavers alone (of both sexes and all ages, from 8 years old upwards) was 230,654. Admittedly, this growth appears less significant when we consider that in 1838 the hand-loom weavers with their families (employed by the weavers themselves) still numbered 800,000,[52] not to mention those thrown out of work in Asia and on the European Continent.

In the few remarks I have still to make on this point, I shall refer in part to relations of a purely practical nature, the existence of which has not yet been revealed by our theoretical presentation.

As long as machine production expands in a given branch of industry at the expense of the old handicrafts or of manufacture, the result is as certain as is the result of an encounter between an army with breach-loading rifles and one with bows and arrows. This first period, during which machinery conquers its field of operations, is of decisive importance, owing to the extraordinary profits it helps to produce. These profits not only form a source of accelerated accumulation, they also attract into the favoured sphere of production a large part of the additional social capital that is constantly being created, and is always seeking out new areas of investment. The special advantages of this initial

52. 'The sufferings of the hand-loom weavers were the subject of an inquiry by a Royal Commission, but although their distress was acknowledged and lamented, the amelioration of their condition was left, and probably necessarily so, to the chances and changes of time, which it may now be hoped' (twenty years later!) 'have *nearly* obliterated those miseries, and not improbably by the present great extension of the power-loom'(*Reports of the Inspectors of Factories ... 31 October 1856*, p. 15).

period of furious activity are felt in every branch of production when it is newly penetrated by machinery. However, as soon as the factory system has attained a reasonable space to exist in, and reached a definite degree of maturity, and in particular as soon as the technical basis peculiar to it, machinery, is itself produced by machinery, as soon as coal-mining and iron-mining, the metallurgical industries, and the means of transport have been revolutionized; in short, as soon as the general conditions of production appropriate to large-scale industry have been established, this mode of production acquires an elasticity, a capacity for sudden extension by leaps and bounds, which comes up against no barriers but those presented by the availability of raw materials and the extent of sales outlets. On the one hand, the immediate effect of machinery is to increase the supply of raw material: thus, for example, the invention of the cotton gin increased the production of cotton.[53] On the other hand, the cheapness of the articles produced by machinery and the revolution in the means of transport and communication provide the weapons for the conquest of foreign markets. By ruining handicraft production of finished articles in other countries, machinery forcibly converts them into fields for the production of its raw material. Thus India was compelled to produce cotton, wool, hemp, jute and indigo for Great Britain.[54] By constantly turning workers into 'supernumeraries', large-scale industry, in all countries where it has taken root, spurs on rapid increases in emigration and the colonization of foreign lands, which are thereby converted into settlements for growing the raw material of the mother country, just as Australia, for example, was converted into a colony for growing wool.[55] A new and international division of labour

53. Other ways in which machinery affects the production of raw material will be mentioned in Volume 3.*

54. Export of cotton from India to Great Britain: 34,540,143 lb. in 1846; 204,141,168 lb. in 1860; 445,947,600 lb. in 1865.

Export of wool from India to Great Britain: 4,570,581 lb. in 1846; 20,214,173 lb. in 1860; 20,679,111 lb. in 1865.

55. Export of wool from the Cape of Good Hope to Great Britain: 2,958,457 lb. in 1846; 16,574,345 lb. in 1860; 29,920,623 lb. in 1865.

Export of wool from Australia to Great Britain: 21,789,346 lb. in 1846; 59,166,616 lb. in 1860; 109,734,261 lb. in 1865.

*As it turned out, Volume 3 of *Capital*, when published, contained nothing on this subject, although Chapters 40–44 (on the second form of differential rent) did deal with the related topic of the impact of extra amounts of capital directly invested in land.

springs up, one suited to the requirements of the main industrial countries, and it converts one part of the globe into a chiefly agricultural field of production for supplying the other part, which remains a pre-eminently industrial field. This revolution is linked with far-reaching changes in agriculture which we need not discuss any further at this point.[56]

On the motion of Mr Gladstone, the House of Commons ordered, on 17 February 1867, that a return be made of the total quantity of grain, corn and flour of all sorts imported into and exported from the United Kingdom between 1831 and 1866. I give on the opposite page a summary of the result. The flour is given in quarters of corn.

The factory system's tremendous capacity for expanding with sudden immense leaps, and its dependence on the world market, necessarily give rise to the following cycle: feverish production, a consequent glut on the market, then a contraction of the market, which causes production to be crippled. The life of industry becomes a series of periods of moderate activity, prosperity, over-production, crisis and stagnation. The uncertainty and instability to which machinery subjects the employment, and con-

56. The economic development of the United States is itself a product of the large-scale industry of Europe, or, to be more precise, of England. In its present form (1866) the United States must still be considered a European colony. [Added by Engels to the fourth German edition: 'Since then it has developed into a country whose industry holds second place in the world, without on that account entirely losing its colonial character.']

Export of Cotton from the United States to Great Britain

1846: 401,949,393 lb.	1852: 765,630,543 lb.
1859: 961,707,264 lb.	1860: 1,115,890,608 lb.

Export of Corn from the United States to Great Britain

	1850	1862
Wheat, cwt	16,202,312	41,033,503
Barley, cwt	3,669,653	6,624,800
Oats, cwt	3,174,801	4,426,994
Rye, cwt	388,749	7,108
Flour, cwt	3,819,440	7,207,113
Buckwheat, cwt	1,054	19,571
Maize, cwt	5,473,161	11,694,818
Bere or Bigg (kinds of Barley), cwt	2,039	7,675
Peas, cwt	811,620	1,024,722
Beans, cwt	1,822,972	2,037,137
Total exports of corn	34,365,801 cwt	74,083,351 cwt

QUINQUENNIAL PERIODS AND THE YEAR 1866

ANNUAL AVERAGE	1831–5	1836–40	1841–5	1846–50	1851–5	1856–60	1861–5	1866
Import (qrs)	1,096,373	2,389,729	2,843,865	8,776,552	8,345,237	10,913,612	15,009,871	16,457,340
Export (qrs)	225,263	251,770	139,056	155,461	307,491	341,150	302,754	216,218
Excess of import over export	871,110	2,137,959	2,704,809	8,621,091	8,037,746	10,572,462	14,707,117	16,241,122
POPULATION: Yearly average in each period	24,261,107	25,929,507	27,262,569	27,797,598	27,572,923	28,391,544	29,381,460	29,935,404
Average quantity of corn, etc., in quarters, consumed annually per head over and above the home produce consumed	0·036	·0082	0·099	0·310	0·291	0·372	0·501	0·543

sequently the living conditions, of the workers becomes a normal state of affairs, owing to these periodic turns of the industrial cycle. Except in the periods of prosperity, a most furious combat rages between the capitalists for their individual share in the market. This share is directly proportional to the cheapness of the product. Apart from the rivalry this struggle gives rise to in the use of improved machinery for replacing labour-power, and the introduction of new methods of production, there also comes a time in every industrial cycle when a forcible reduction of wages beneath the value of labour-power is attempted so as to cheapen commodities.[57]

A necessary condition for the growth of the number of factory

57. In an appeal made in July 1866 to the 'Trade Societies of England' by the shoemakers of Leicester, who had been thrown onto the streets by a lock-out, it is stated: 'Twenty years ago the Leicester shoe trade was revolu-tionized by the introduction of riveting in the place of stitching. At that time good wages could be earned. Great competition was shown between the different firms as to which could turn out the neatest article. Shortly after-wards, however, a worse kind of competition sprang up, namely, that of underselling one another in the market. The injurious consequences soon manifested themselves in reductions of wages, and so sweepingly quick was the fall in the price of labour, that many firms now pay only one half of the original wages. And yet, though wages sink lower and lower, profits appear, with each alteration in the scale of wages, to increase.' Even bad times are utilized by the manufacturers for making exceptional profits by excessive wage-reductions, i.e. by directly robbing the worker of his means of sub-sistence. Here is one example, relating to the crisis in the ribbon trade in Coventry:* 'From information I have received from manufacturers as well as workmen, there seems to be no doubt that wages have been reduced to a greater extent than either the competition of the foreign producers or other circumstances have rendered necessary ... the majority of weavers are work-ing at a reduction of 30 to 40 per cent in their wages. A piece of ribbon for making which the weaver got 6s. or 7s. five years back, now only brings them 3s. 3d. or 3s. 6d.; other work is now priced at 2s. and 2s. 3d. which was formerly priced at 4s. and 4s. 3d. The reduction in wage seems to have been carried to a greater extent than is necessary for increasing the demand. Indeed the reduction in the cost of weaving, in the case of many descriptions of ribbons, has not been accompanied by any corresponding reduction in the selling price of the manufactured article' (Report of Mr F. D. Longe, in *Children's Employment Commission, Fifth Report*, 1866, p. 114, n. 1).

* A severe recession in the Coventry ribbon trade began in 1857 under the impact of the general industrial and commercial crisis of that year, and deepened from 1860 onwards owing to the Anglo-French Trade Treaty, which opened the door to competition from Lyons. A further blow was struck to the trade by the fierce conflict of 1860 between the capitalists and the workers over the attempt of the former to replace the 'cottage factories' with factories proper (see below, p. 589).

workers is thus a proportionally much more rapid growth in the amount of capital invested in factories. But this process of growth takes place only within the ebbs and flows of the industrial cycle. It is, in addition, constantly interrupted by the technical progress that at one time virtually takes the place of additional workers, and at another time actually drives workers out of employment. This qualitative change in machine production continually removes workers from the factories, or closes their doors to the fresh stream of recruits, while the purely quantitative extension of the factories absorbs not only the men thrown out of work but also fresh contingents of workers. The latter are thus continually repelled and attracted, slung backwards and forwards, while, at the same time, constant changes take place in the sex, age and skill of the industrial conscripts.

The fate of the factory workers will best be depicted if we make a rapid survey of developments in the English cotton industry.

From 1770 until 1815 the cotton trade underwent only five years of depression or stagnation. During this period of forty-five years the English manufacturers had a monopoly of machinery and a monopoly of the world market. From 1815 to 1821 depression; 1822 and 1823 prosperity; 1824, repeal of the Combination Laws, great extension of factories everywhere; 1825, crisis; 1826, great misery and riots among the factory workers; 1827, slight improvement; 1828, great increase in power-looms, and in exports; 1829, exports, especially to India, surpass all former years; 1830, glutted markets, great distress; 1831 to 1833, continued depression, the monopoly of the trade with India and China withdrawn from the East India Company; 1834, great increase of factories and machinery, shortage of hands. The new poor law furthers the migration of agricultural labourers into the factory districts. The country districts swept clear of children. White slave trade; 1835, great prosperity, simultaneous starvation of the hand-loom weavers; 1836, great prosperity; 1837 and 1838, depression and crisis; 1839, revival; 1840, great depression, riots, the military called out to intervene; 1841 and 1842, frightful suffering among the factory workers; 1842, the manufacturers lock their hands out of the factories in order to enforce the repeal of the Corn Laws. Workers stream in their thousands into the towns of Lancashire and Yorkshire, are driven back by the military, and their leaders brought to trial at Lancaster; 1842, great misery; 1844, revival; 1845, great prosperity; 1846, continued improvement at first, then reaction. Repeal of the Corn Laws; 1847, crisis, general reduction of wages by 10 and more per cent in honour of the 'big loaf';* 1848, continued depression; Manchester under military protection; 1849, revival; 1850, prosperity; 1851, falling prices, low wages, frequent strikes; 1852, the situation begins to improve, strikes continue, the manufacturers threaten to import workers from abroad; 1853, increasing exports. Strike for three months, and great misery at Preston; 1854, prosperity, glutted markets; 1855, news of bankruptcies streams in from the United States, Canada and the markets of the Far East; 1856, great prosperity; 1857, crisis; 1858, improvement; 1859, great prosperity, increase in factories; 1860, zenith of the English cotton trade, the Indian, Australian and other markets so glutted with goods that even in 1863 they had not absorbed the whole lot; the French Treaty of Commerce, enormous growth of factories and machinery; 1861, prosperity continues for a time, reaction, the American Civil War, cotton famine; 1862 to 1863, complete collapse.

The history of the cotton famine is too typical for us not to dwell on it for a moment. From indications as to conditions in the world market in 1860 and 1861, we see that the cotton famine came in the nick of time for the manufacturers, and was to some extent advantageous to them, a fact acknowledged in the reports of the Manchester Chamber of Commerce, proclaimed in Parliament by Palmerston and Derby, and confirmed by events.[58] Of course, among the 2,887 cotton mills in the United Kingdom in 1861 there were many small ones. According to the report of the factory inspector, Mr A. Redgrave, 392 out of the 2,109 mills included in his district, or 19 per cent, employed less than 10 horse-power each; 345, or 16 per cent, employed between 10 and 20 horse-power; while 1,372 employed upwards of 20 horse-power.[59] The majority of the small mills were weaving sheds built during the period of prosperity after 1858, for the most part by speculators, of whom one supplied the yarn, another the machinery, a third the buildings, and they were run by men who

58. Compare *Reports of the Inspectors of Factories . . . 31 October 1862* p. 30.
59. ibid., p. 19.

---

*The supporters of the Anti-Corn Law League claimed that repeal would mean the replacement of the 'small loaf', provided to the workers under the existing system, with a 'big loaf', thanks to the advantages of free trade in corn.

had been overseers, or by other persons of small means. These small manufacturers mostly went to the wall. The same fate would have overtaken them in the commercial crisis which was staved off only by the cotton famine. Although they formed one-third of the total number of manufacturers, their mills absorbed much less than a third of the capital invested in the cotton trade. As to the extent of the stoppage, it appears from authentic estimates that in October 1862, 60·3 per cent of the spindles, and 58 per cent of the looms, were at a standstill. This refers to the cotton trade as a whole, and of course requires considerable modification for individual districts. Very few mills worked full time (60 hours a week); all the others worked at intervals. Even in those few cases where full time was worked, and at the customary piece-rate, the weekly wages of the workers necessarily shrank, because good cotton was replaced by bad, Sea Island by Egyptian (in fine-spinning mills), American and Egyptian by Surat (Indian) and pure cotton by a mixture of waste and Surat. The shorter fibre of the Surat cotton and its dirty condition, the greater fragility of the thread, the substitution of all sorts of heavy ingredients for flour in sizing the warps, all these things lessened the speed of the machinery, or the number of looms that could be superintended by one weaver, increased the amount of labour necessitated by defects in the machinery, and reduced the piece-wage by reducing the amount of the product actually leaving the mill. Where Surat cotton was used, the loss to the workers when on full time amounted to 20 per cent, 30 per cent or more. But on top of this, the majority of the manufacturers reduced the piece-rate by 5, 7½ and 10 per cent. We can therefore grasp the situation of these workers employed for only 3, 3½ or 4 days a week, or for only 6 hours a day. Even in 1863, after a comparative improvement had set in, the weekly wages of spinners and weavers were 3s. 4d., 3s. 10d., 4s. 6d. and 5s. 1d.[60] Even in this miserable state of affairs, however, the inventive spirit of the manufacturer did not stand still, but was exercised in making deductions from wages. These were to some extent inflicted as a penalty for defects in the finished article that were really due to his own bad cotton and his unsuitable machinery. Moreover, where the manufacturer owned the workers' cottages, he paid himself his rents by deducting the amount from these miserable wages. Mr Redgrave tells us of self-acting minders (i.e. workers in

60. *Reports of the Inspectors of Factories . . . 31 October 1863*, pp. 41–5.

charge of a pair of self-acting mules) 'earning at the end of a fortnight's full work 8s. 11d., and . . . from this sum was deducted the rent of the house, the manufacturer, however, returning half the rent as a gift. The minders took away the sum of 6s. 11d. In many places the self-acting minders ranged from 5s. to 9s. per week, and the weavers from 2s. to 6s. per week, during the latter part of 1862.'[61] Even when short time was being worked, the rent was frequently deducted from the workers' wages.[62] No wonder that in some parts of Lancashire a kind of famine fever broke out. But more characteristic than all this was the revolution that took place in the production process at the expense of the workers. *Experimenta in corpore vili*,* like those of anatomists on frogs, were actually being made here. 'Although,' says Mr Redgrave, 'I have given the actual earnings of the operatives in the several mills, it does not follow that they earn the same amount week by week. The operatives are subject to great fluctuation from the constant experimentalizing of the manufacturers . . . the earnings of the operatives rise and fall with the quality of the cotton mixings; sometimes they have been within 15 per cent of former earnings, and then, in a week or two, they have fallen off from 50 to 60 per cent.'[63] These experiments were not made just at the expense of the worker's means of subsistence. His five senses also had to pay the penalty. 'The people who are employed in making up Surat cotton complain very much. They inform me, on opening the bales of cotton there is an intolerable smell, which causes sickness . . . In the mixing, scribbling and carding rooms, the dust and dirt which are disengaged, irritate the air passages, and give rise to cough and difficulty of breathing. A disease of the skin, no doubt from the irritation of the dirt contained in the Surat cotton, also prevails . . . The fibre being so short, a great amount of size, both animal and vegetable, is used . . . Bronchitis is more prevalent owing to the dust. Inflammatory sore throat is common, from the same cause. Sickness and dyspepsia are produced by the frequent breaking of the weft, when the weaver sucks the weft through the eye of the shuttle.' On the other hand, these flour-substitutes were a Fortunatus's purse† to the manu-

61. *Reports of the Inspectors of Factories . . . 31 October 1863*, pp. 41–2.
62. ibid., p. 57.   63. ibid., pp. 50–51.

* 'Experiments on a worthless body'.
† Fortunatus was a figure of Teutonic legend, whose purse never became empty.

facturers because they increased the weight of the yarn. They caused '15 lb. of raw material to weigh 26 lb. after it was woven'.[64] In the *Reports of the Inspectors of Factories* for the half-year ending 30 April 1864, we read the following: 'The trade is availing itself of this resource at present to an extent which is even discreditable. I have heard on good authority of a cloth weighing 8 lb. which was made of $5\frac{1}{4}$ lb. cotton and $2\frac{3}{4}$ lb. size; and of another cloth weighing $5\frac{1}{4}$ lb., of which 2 lb. was size. These were ordinary export shirtings. In cloths of other descriptions, as much as 50 per cent size is sometimes added; so that a manufacturer may, and does truly boast, that he is getting rich by selling cloth for less money per pound than he paid for the mere yarn of which they [*sic*] are composed.'[65] But the workers did not just have to suffer from the experiments of the manufacturers inside the mills, and of the municipalities outside, from reduced wages and absence of work, from want and from charity, and from the eulogies uttered in the Lords and the Commons. 'Unfortunate females, in consequence of the cotton famine, were at its commencement thrown out of employment, and have thereby become outcasts of society; and now, though trade has revived, and work is plentiful, continue members of that unfortunate class, and are likely to continue so. There are also in the borough more youthful prostitutes than I have known for the last twenty-five years.'[66]

We find, then, in the first forty-five years of the English cotton industry, from 1770 to 1815, only five years of crisis and stagnation; but this was the period of monopoly. The second period from 1815 to 1863 counts, during its forty-eight years, only twenty years of revival and prosperity against twenty-eight of depression and stagnation. Between 1815 and 1830 competition with the continent of Europe and with the United States sets in. After 1833, the extension of the Asiatic markets is enforced by 'destruction of the human race'.* After the repeal of the Corn Laws, from 1846 to 1863, there are eight years of moderate

64. ibid., pp. 62–3.
65. *Reports of the Inspectors of Factories . . . 30 April 1864*, p. 27.
66. From a letter by Mr Harris, Chief Constable of Bolton, in *Reports of the Inspectors of Factories . . . 31 October 1865*, pp. 61–2.

*This is a reference to the opium trade with China, enforced by a series of measures, beginning with the appointment in 1833 of a British representative in Canton, and culminating in the Opium War of 1839 to 1842, after which the Chinese market was opened to British trade by the Treaty of Nanking.

activity and prosperity against nine years of depression and stagnation. The situation of the adult male workers, even during the years of prosperity, may be judged from the appended note.[67]

8. THE REVOLUTIONARY IMPACT OF LARGE-SCALE INDUSTRY ON MANUFACTURE, HANDICRAFTS AND DOMESTIC INDUSTRY

(a) Overthrow of Co-operation Based on Handicrafts and on the Division of Labour

We have seen how machinery does away with co-operation based on handicrafts, and with manufacture based on the handicraft division of labour. An example of the first sort is the reaping-machine; it replaces co-operation between reapers. A striking example of the second kind is the needle-making machine. According to Adam Smith, ten men in his time, using the system of the division of labour, made 48,000 sewing-needles every day.

67. In a proclamation issued in 1863 by some cotton workers, for the purpose of forming an emigration society, we find the following: 'That a large emigration of factory workers is now absolutely essential to raise them from their present prostrate condition, few will deny; but to show that a continuous stream of emigration is at all times demanded, without which it is impossible for them to maintain their position in ordinary times, we beg to call attention to the subjoined facts: In 1814 the official value of cotton goods exported was £17,665,378, whilst the real marketable value was £20,070,824. In 1858 the official value of cotton goods exported was £182,221,681; but the real or marketable value was only £43,001,322, being a ten-fold quantity sold for little more than double the former price. To produce results so disadvantageous to the country generally, and to the factory workers in particular, several causes have co-operated, which, had circumstances permitted, we should have brought more prominently under your notice; suffice it for the present to say that the most obvious one is the constant redundancy of labour, without which a trade so ruinous in its effects never could have been carried on, and which requires a constantly extending market to save it from annihilation. Our cotton mills may be brought to a stand by the periodical stagnations of trade, which, under present arrangements, are as inevitable as death itself; but the human mind is constantly at work, and although we believe we are under the mark in stating that six millions of persons have left these shores during the last 25 years, yet, from the natural increase of population, and the displacement of labour to cheapen production, a large percentage of the male adults in the most prosperous times find it impossible to obtain work in factories on any conditions whatever' (*Reports of the Inspectors of Factories . . . 30 April 1863*, pp. 51–2). We shall see in a later chapter how the manufacturers endeavoured, during the catastrophe in the cotton trade, to prevent the emigration of the factory workers by every means, including state intervention.

A single needle-making machine, however, makes 145,000 needles in a working day of 11 hours. One woman or one girl superintends four such machines, and so produces nearly 600,000 needles in a day, and over 3,000,000 in a week.[68] A single machine, when it takes the place of co-operation or of manufacture, may itself serve as the basis of an industry of a handicraft character. But this reproduction of the handicraft system on the basis of machinery only forms a transition to the factory system which, as a rule, makes its appearance as soon as human muscles are replaced, for the purpose of driving the machines, by a mechanical motive power such as steam or water. Here and there, but in any case only for a time, an industry may be carried on, on a small scale, by means of mechanical power. This is effected by hiring steam power, as is done in some of the Birmingham trades, or by the use of small caloric engines, as in some branches of weaving.[69] In the Coventry ribbon industry the experiment of 'cottage factories' was a quite natural and spontaneous development. In the centre of a square surrounded by rows of cottages, an engine-house was built and the engine was connected by shafts with the looms in the cottages. In all cases the power was hired out at so much per loom. The rent was payable weekly, whether the looms were working or not. Each cottage held from two to six looms; some belonged to the weaver, some were bought on credit, some were hired. The struggle between these cottage factories and the factory proper lasted over twelve years. It ended with the complete ruin of the 300 cottage factories.[70] Wherever the nature of the process has not necessitated production on a large scale, the new industries that have sprung up in the last few decades, such as envelope making, steel pen making, etc., have, as a general rule, first passed through the handicraft stage, and then the manufacturing stage, as short phases of transition to the factory stage. The transition is very difficult in those cases where the production of the article by manufacture consists, not of a series of graduated processes, but of a great number of dis-

---

68. *Children's Employment Commission, Third Report*, 1864, p. 108, n. 447.

69. In the United States the restoration in this way of handicrafts based on machinery is frequent; and therefore, when the inevitable transition to the factory system takes place, the process of concentration will, compared with Europe and even with England, stride forward in seven-league boots.

70. Compare *Reports of the Inspectors of Factories ... 31 October 1865*, p. 64.

connected ones. This circumstance formed a great hindrance to the establishment of steel pen factories. Nevertheless, about fifteen years ago a machine was invented that automatically performed six separate operations at once. The first steel pens were supplied by the handicraft system, in the year 1820, at £7 4s. the gross; in 1830 they were supplied by manufacture at 8s., and today the factory system supplies them at a wholesale price of from 2d. to 6d. the gross.[71]

(b) The Impact of the Factory System on Manufacture and Domestic Industries

With the development of the factory system and the revolution in agriculture that accompanies it, production in all the other branches of industry not only expands, but also alters its character. The principle of machine production, namely the division of the production process into its constituent phases, and the solution of the problems arising from this by the application of mechanics, chemistry and the whole range of the natural sciences, now plays the determining role everywhere. Hence machinery penetrates into manufacture for one specialized process after another. The solid crystallization of a hierarchy of specialized processes, which arose from the old division of labour, ceases to exist; it is dissolved, and makes way for constant changes. Quite apart from this, a fundamental transformation takes place in the composition of the collective labourer or, in other words, the combined working personnel. In contrast with the period of manufacture, the division of labour is now based, wherever possible, on the employment of women, of children of all ages and of unskilled workers, in short, of 'cheap labour', as the Englishman typically describes it. This is true not only for all large-scale production, whether machinery is employed or not, but also for the so-called domestic industries, whether carried on in the private dwellings of the workers, or in small workshops. This modern 'domestic industry' has nothing except the name in

71. Mr Gillott erected the first large-scale steel pen factory in Birmingham. As early as 1851 it was producing over 180,000,000 pens a year, and consuming 120 tons of steel. Birmingham has the monopoly of this industry in the United Kingdom, and at present produces thousands of millions of steel pens. According to the census of 1861, the number of persons employed was 1,428, of whom 1,268 were female workers, enrolled from 5 years of age upwards.

common with old-fashioned domestic industry, the existence of which presupposes independent urban handicrafts, independent peasant farming and, above all, a dwelling-house for the worker and his family. That kind of industry has now been converted into an external department of the factory, the manufacturing workshop, or the warehouse. Besides the factory worker, the workers engaged in manufacture, and the handicraftsmen, whom it concentrates in large masses at one spot, and directly commands, capital also sets another army in motion, by means of invisible threads: the outworkers in the domestic industries, who live in the large towns as well as being scattered over the countryside. An example: the shirt factory of Messrs Tillie at Londonderry, which employs 1,000 workers in the factory itself, and 9,000 outworkers spread over the country districts.[72]

The exploitation of cheap and immature labour-power is carried out in a more shameless manner in modern manufacture than in the factory proper. This is because the technical foundation of the factory system, namely the substitution of machines for muscular power, and the light character of the labour, is almost entirely absent in manufacture, and at the same time women and excessively young children are subjected quite unscrupulously to the influence of poisonous substances. In the so-called domestic industries this exploitation is still more shameless than in modern manufacture, because the workers' power of resistance declines with their dispersal; because a whole series of plundering parasites insinuate themselves between the actual employer and the worker he employs; because a domestic industry has always to compete either with the factory system, or with manufacturing in the same branch of production; because poverty robs the worker of the conditions most essential to his labour, of space, light and ventilation; because employment becomes more and more irregular; and, finally, because in these last places of refuge for the masses made 'redundant' by large-scale industry and agriculture, competition for work necessarily attains its maximum. Economical use of the means of production, first systematically carried out in the factory system and coinciding there, from the very beginning, with the most reckless squandering of labour-power, and the theft of the normal requirements for the labour-function, now, in a given branch of industry, turns

72. *Children's Employment Commission, Second Report*, 1864, p. lxviii, n. 415.

uppermost its antagonistic and murderous side; and the less the social productivity of labour and the technical basis for the combination of labour processes are developed in that branch, the more does the murderous side of this economy emerge.

(c) Modern Manufacture

I shall now illustrate the principles laid down above with a few examples. As a matter of fact, the reader is already familiar with a whole mass of instances given in the chapter on the working day. In the hardware manufactures of Birmingham and the neighbourhood, there are employed, mostly in very heavy work, 30,000 children and young persons, besides 10,000 women. They are to be found in a range of unhealthy jobs: in brass-foundries, button factories, and enamelling, galvanizing and lacquering works.[73] Owing to the excessive labour performed by their workers, both adult and non-adult, certain London firms where newspapers and books are printed have gained for themselves the honourable name of 'slaughter-houses'.[74] Similar excesses occur in book-binding, where the victims are chiefly women, girls and children; young persons have to do heavy work in rope-works, and night-work in salt mines, candle factories and chemical works; young people are worked to death at turning the looms in silk weaving, when it is not carried on by machinery.[75] One of the most shameful, dirtiest and worst paid jobs, a kind of labour on which women and young girls are by preference employed, is the sorting of rags. It is well known that Great Britain, apart from its own immense store of rags, is the emporium for the rag trade of the whole world. The rags flow in from Japan, from the most remote countries of South America, and from the Canary Islands. But the chief sources of supply are Germany, France, Russia, Italy, Egypt, Turkey, Belgium and Holland. They are used for manure, for making bed-flocks, for shoddy, and they serve as the raw material of paper. The rag-sorters are carriers for the spread of small-pox and other infectious diseases,

73. And now children are even employed at file-grinding in Sheffield!
74. *Children's Employment Commission, Fifth Report*, 1866, p. 3, n. 24; p. 6, n. 55, 56; p. 7, n. 59, 60.
75. ibid., pp. 114, 115, n. 6, 7. The commissioner rightly says that though as a rule machines take the place of men, here young persons literally replace machines.

and they themselves are the first victims.[76] A classic example of over-work, of hard and unsuitable labour, and of its brutalizing effects on the worker from his childhood upwards, is afforded not only by coal-mining and mining in general, but also by tile and brick making, in which industry the recently invented machinery is, in England, used only here and there. Between May and September the work lasts from 5 in the morning till 8 in the evening, and where the drying is done in the open air, it often lasts from 4 in the morning till 9 in the evening. Work from 5 in the morning till 7 in the evening is considered 'reduced' and 'moderate'. Boys and girls of 6 and even 4 years of age are employed. They work for the same number of hours as the adults, often longer. The work is hard and the summer heat increases the exhaustion. In a brickfield at Moxley, for example, a young woman (24 years old) was in the habit of making 2,000 bricks a day, with the assistance of two little girls who carried the clay for her and stacked the bricks. Every day these girls carried 10 tons up the slippery sides of the clay pits, from a depth of 30 feet, and then for a distance of 210 feet. 'It is almost impossible as things are for a child to pass through the ordeal of a brickfield without great moral degradation ... the low language, which they are accustomed to hear from their tenderest years, the filthy, indecent, and shameless habits, amidst which, unknowing, and half wild, they grow up, make them in after-life lawless, abandoned, dissolute ... A frightful source of demoralization is the mode of living. Each moulder, who is always a skilled labourer, and the chief of a group, supplies his seven subordinates with board and lodging in his cottage. Whether members of his family or not, the men, boys and girls all sleep in the cottage, which contains generally two, exceptionally three rooms, all on the ground floor, and badly ventilated. These people are so exhausted after the day's hard work, that neither the rules of health, of cleanliness, nor of decency are in the least observed. Many of these cottages are models of untidiness, dirt, and dust ... The greatest evil of the system that employs young girls on this sort of work, consists in this, that, as a rule, it chains them fast from childhood for the whole of their after-life to the most abandoned rabble. They become rough, foulmouthed boys, before Nature has taught them that they are women. Clothed in a few dirty rags,

76. See the report on the rag trade, with numerous examples, in *Public Health, Eighth Report*, London, 1866, pp. 196, 208.

the legs naked far above the knees, hair and face besmeared with dirt, they learn to treat all feelings of decency and shame with contempt. During meal-times they lie at full length in the fields, or watch the boys bathing in a neighbouring canal. Their heavy day's work at length completed, they put on better clothes, and accompany the men to the public houses.' That excessive drunkenness is prevalent from childhood upwards among the whole of this class, is only natural. 'The worst is that the brickmakers despair of themselves. You might as well, said one of the better kind to a chaplain of the Southall fields, try to raise and improve the devil as a brickie, sir!'[77]

There is a rich collection of official material to be found in the fourth and sixth *Public Health Reports* (1862 and 1864) on the way in which capital economizes on the requirements for labour in modern manufacture (in which I include all workshops on a large scale, except factories proper). The descriptions of the workshops, more especially those of the London printers and tailors, surpass the most loathsome fantasies of the novelists. The effect on the health of the workers is self-evident. Dr Simon, the chief medical officer of the Privy Council and the official editor of the *Public Health Reports*, says among other things: 'In my fourth report (1861) [published 1862] I showed, how it is practically impossible for the work-people to insist upon that which is their first sanitary right, viz., the right that, no matter what the work for which their employer brings them together, the labour, so far as it depends upon him, should be freed from all avoidably unwholesome conditions. I pointed out, that while the workpeople are practically incapable of doing themselves this sanitary justice, they are unable to obtain any effective support from the paid administrations of the sanitary policy . . . The life of myriads of workmen and workwomen is now uselessly tortured and shortened by the neverending physical suffering that their mere occupation begets,'[78] In illustration of the way in which the workrooms influence the state of health, Dr Simon gives the following table of mortality.[79]

77. *Children's Employment Commission, Fifth Report*, 1866, pp. xvi–xviii, n. 86–97, and pp. 130–33, n. 39–71. See also the *Third Report*, 1864, pp. 48, 56.

78. *Public Health, Sixth Report*, London, 1864, pp. 29, 31.

79. ibid., p. 30. Dr Simon remarks that mortality among the London tailors and printers between the ages of 25 and 35 is in fact much greater [than it appears], because employers in London obtain from the country a great number of young people up to 30 years of age, as 'apprentices' and 'improvers',

Number of persons of all ages employed in the respective industries	Industries compared as regards health	Death-rate per 100,000 men in the respective industries between the stated ages		
		Age 25–35	Age 35–45	Age 45–55
958,265	Agriculture in England and Wales	743	805	1,145
22,301 men ⎫ 12,379 women ⎬	London tailors	958	1,262	2,093
13,803 ⎭	London printers	894	1,747	2,367

(d) Modern Domestic Industry

I now come to so-called domestic industry. In order to get an idea of the horrors of this sphere, in which capital conducts its exploitation against the background of large-scale industry, one might well look, for instance, at the apparently idyllic trade of nail-making, carried on in a few remote villages of England.[80] Here, however, it will be enough to give a few examples from industries, some of whose branches are either not yet carried on with the aid of machinery, or do not as yet compete against machine and factory products: lace-making and straw-plaiting.

Of the 150,000 persons employed in England in the production of lace, about 10,000 fall within the sphere of the Factory Act of 1861. Almost the whole of the remaining 140,000 are women, young persons, and children of both sexes, although the male sex is only weakly represented here. The state of health of this 'cheap' material for exploitation can be seen from the following table, worked out by Dr Trueman, physician to the Nottingham General Dispensary. Out of 686 female patients who were lace-makers,

who come to perfect their skill in their trade. These figure in the census as Londoners, and they swell out the number of heads on which the London death-rate is calculated, without adding proportionally to the number of deaths there. The greater part of them in fact return to the country, and indeed especially in cases of severe illness (ibid.).

80. I refer here to hammered nails, as opposed to nails cut out and made by machinery. See *Children's Employment Commission, Third Report*, pp. xi, xix, n. 125–30, p. 52, n. 11, p. 114, n. 487, p. 137, n. 674.

most of them between the ages of 17 and 24, the proportion of consumptives was:

1852 – 1 in 45	1857 – 1 in 13
1853 – 1 in 28	1858 – 1 in 15
1854 – 1 in 17	1859 – 1 in 9
1855 – 1 in 18	1860 – 1 in 8
1856 – 1 in 15	1861 – 1 in 8[81]

This advance in the rate of consumption ought to suffice for the most optimistic advocate of progress, or for the most mendacious free-trade bagman in Germany.

The Factory Act of 1861 regulates the actual making of the lace, in so far as it is done by machinery, and it is done by machinery as a rule in England. The branches we are about to examine, solely with regard to those who work at home, and are not concentrated in workshops or warehouses, fall into two categories, namely (1) finishing, and (2) mending. The former gives the finishing touches to the machine-made lace, and includes numerous subdivisions.

The lace finishing is done either in what are called 'mistresses' houses', or by women in their own houses, with or without the help of their children. The women who keep the 'mistresses' houses' are themselves poor. The workroom is in a private house. The mistresses take orders from manufacturers, or from ware-housemen, and employ as many women, girls and young children as the size of their rooms and the fluctuating demand of the business will allow. The number of women employed in these work-rooms varies from twenty to forty in some, and from ten to twenty in others. The average age at which the children start work is 6 years, but in many cases it is below 5. The usual working hours are from 8 in the morning until 8 in the evening, with 1½ hours for meals, which are taken at irregular intervals, and often in the stinking workrooms. When business is brisk, the labour fre-quently lasts from 8 or even 6 o'clock in the morning until 10, 11 or 12 o'clock at night. In English barracks the regulation space allotted to each soldier is 500 to 600 cubic feet, and in the military hospitals 1,200 cubic feet. But in those finishing sties there are between 67 and 100 cubic feet for each person. At the same time the oxygen of the air is consumed by gas-lights. In order to keep the lace clean, the children are often compelled to pull off their shoes, even in winter, although the floor is tiled or flagged. 'It is not

81. *Children's Employment Commission, Second Report*, p. xxii, n. 166.

at all uncommon in Nottingham to find fourteen to twenty children huddled together in a small room, of, perhaps, not more than 12 feet square, and employed for 15 hours out of the 24, at work that of itself is exhausting, from its weariness and monotony, and is besides carried on under every possible unwholesome condition ... Even the very youngest children work with a strained attention and a rapidity that is astonishing, hardly ever giving their fingers rest or slowing their motion. If a question is asked them, they never raise their eyes from their work from fear of losing a single moment.' The 'long cane' is increasingly used as a stimulant by the mistresses as the working hours drag towards their close. 'The children gradually tire and become as restless as birds towards the end of their long detention at an occupation that is monotonous, eye-straining, and exhausting from the uniformity in the posture of the body. Their work is like slavery.'[82] When women and their children work at home, which nowadays means in a hired room, often in a garret, their situation is, if that is possible, still worse. This sort of work is given out within a radius of 80 miles from Nottingham. On leaving the warehouse at 9 or 10 o'clock at night, the children are often given a bundle of lace to take home with them and finish. The pharisee of a capitalist, represented by one of his paid lackeys, accompanies this action, of course, with the unctuous phrase 'That's for mother', yet he knows very well that the poor children must sit up and help.[83]

Pillow lace-making is chiefly carried on in England in two agricultural districts; one, the Honiton lace district, extending from 20 to 30 miles along the south coast of Devonshire, and including a few places in North Devon; the other comprising a great part of the counties of Buckingham, Bedford and Northampton, and also the adjoining portions of Oxfordshire and Huntingdonshire. The cottages of the agricultural labourers are the places where the work is usually carried on. Many manufacturers employ upwards of 3,000 of these lace-makers, who are chiefly children and young persons, and always female. The conditions we have just described for the lace-finishing trade also prevail here, except that instead of the 'mistresses' houses' we find what are called 'lace-schools' kept by poor women in their cottages. From their fifth year and often earlier, until their twelfth or fifteenth

82. *Children's Employment Commission, Second Report*, 1864, pp. xix, xx, xxi.

83. ibid., pp. xxi, xxii.

year, the children work in these schools; during the first year the
very young ones work from four to eight hours, and later on, from
six in the morning till eight and ten o'clock at night. 'These rooms
are generally the living rooms of small cottages, with the fireplace
stopped up to prevent draught, and sometimes even in winter, the
animal heat of the inmates being thought sufficient; in other cases,
they are small pantry-like rooms without any fireplaces . . . The
crowding in these rooms and the foulness of air produced by it are
sometimes extreme. Added to this is the injurious effect of drains,
privies, decomposing substances, and other filth usual in the pur-
lieus of the smaller cottages.' With regard to space: 'In one lace-
school eighteen girls and a mistress, 33 cubic feet to each person;
in another, where the smell was unbearable, eighteen persons and
24½ cubic feet per head. In this industry are to be found employed
children of 2 and 2½ years.'[84]

Where lace-making ends in the counties of Buckingham and
Bedford, straw-plaiting begins, and extends over a large part of
Hertfordshire and the westerly and northerly parts of Essex. In
1861, there were 40,043 persons employed in straw-plaiting and
straw-hat making; of these, 3,815 were males of all ages, the rest
females, of whom 14,913, including about 7,000 children, were
under 20 years of age. In the place of the lace-schools we find here
the 'straw-plait schools'. The children generally start to be
instructed in straw-plaiting at the age of 4, often between 3 and 4
years. They get no education, of course. The children themselves
call the elementary schools 'natural schools', distinguishing them
in this way from these blood-sucking institutions, in which they
are kept at work simply to get through the task, generally 30
yards a day, which is prescribed by their half-starved mothers.
These same mothers often make them work at home, after school
is over, till 10, 11 and 12 o'clock at night. The straw cuts their
mouths, with which they constantly moisten it, and their fingers.
Dr Ballard gives it as the general opinion of the whole body of
medical officers in London that 300 cubic feet is the minimum
space proper for each person in a bedroom or workroom. But
in the straw-plait schools space is more sparingly allotted than
in the lace-schools, '12¾, 17, 18½ and below 22 cubic feet for
each person'. The smaller of these numbers, says one of the
commissioners, Mr White, represents less space than the half of
what a child would occupy if packed in a box measuring 3 feet in

84. *Children's Employment Commission, Second Report,* 1864, pp. xxix–xxx.

each direction. Thus do the children enjoy life till the age of 12 or 14. The wretched half-starved parents think of nothing but getting as much as possible out of their children. The latter, as soon as they are grown up, do not care a farthing, and naturally so, for their parents, and leave them. 'It is no wonder that ignorance and vice abound in a population so brought up ... Their morality is at the lowest ebb ... a great number of the women have illegitimate children, and that at such an immature age that even those most conversant with criminal statistics are astounded.'[85] And the native land of these model families is itself the model Christian country in Europe; at least, this is what Count Montalembert says, and he is certainly a competent authority on Christianity!

Wages in the above industries, miserable as they are (the maximum wages of a child in the straw-plait schools rising in rare cases to 3 shillings), are reduced far below their nominal amount by the prevalence of the truck system everywhere, but especially in the lace districts.[86]

(e) Transition from Modern Manufacture and Domestic Industry to Large-Scale Industry. The Hastening of this Revolution by the Application of the Factory Acts to those Industries

The cheapening of labour-power, by sheer abuse of the labour of women and children, by sheer robbery of every normal condition needed for working and living, and by the sheer brutality of overwork and night-work, finally comes up against certain insuperable natural obstacles. This is also true of the cheapening of commodities, and of capitalist exploitation in general, which rest on these foundations. When this point has at last been reached – and this takes many years – the hour has struck for the introduction of machinery, and for a thenceforth rapid transformation of the scattered domestic industries, as well as the manufactures, into factory industries.

An example of this process, on the most colossal scale, is afforded by the production of 'wearing apparel'. This industry, according to the classification of the Children's Employment Commission, comprises straw-hat makers, ladies'-hat makers,

85. ibid., pp. xl–xli.
86. *Children's Employment Commission, First Report*, 1863, p. 185.

cap-makers, tailors, milliners and dressmakers, shirtmakers, corset-makers, glove-makers, shoemakers, besides many minor branches, such as the making of neck-ties, collars, etc. In 1861 the number of females employed in these industries, in England and Wales, amounted to 586,299, of whom 115,242 at least were under 20, and 16,650 under 15 years of age. The number of these working women in the United Kingdom in 1861 was 750,334. The number of males employed in England and Wales, in hat-making, shoemaking, glove-making and tailoring was 437,969; of these, 14,964 were under 15 years, 89,285 between 15 and 20, and 333,117 over 20 years. Many of the smaller branches are not included in these figures. But take the figures as they stand; we then have for England and Wales alone, according to the census of 1861, a total of 1,024,277 persons, about as many as are taken up by agriculture and cattle-breeding. We begin to understand the purpose for which machinery conjures up such immense quantities of goods, and 'sets free' such enormous masses of workers.

The production of 'wearing apparel' is carried on partly in manufacturing workshops within which there is merely a reproduction of the division of labour whose *membra disjecta** were already to hand; partly by small master-craftsmen, who do not, however, work as before for individual consumers, but for factories and warehouses, and to such an extent that often whole towns and stretches of country carry on certain branches, such as shoemaking, as a speciality; finally, on a very large scale, by the so-called domestic workers, who form an external department of the factories and warehouses, and even of the workshops of the smaller masters.[87]

The raw material for this labour, either in its raw shape or already semi-fabricated, is supplied by large-scale industry, and the mass of cheap human material (*taillable à merci et miséricorde*)† consists of the individuals 'set free' by large-scale industry and agriculture. The manufactures of this sphere owed their origin chiefly to the capitalists' need to have at hand an army equipped

87. In England millinery and dressmaking are for the most part carried on on the premises of the employer, by female workers who sometimes live there and sometimes elsewhere.

*'Scattered elements'.
†'Taxable at pleasure and mercy'. This was the term applied in France to serfs in the Middle Ages, and later, to express their lack of legal rights.

to respond to any increase in demand.[88] These manufactures, nevertheless, allowed the scattered handicrafts and domestic industries to continue to exist as a broad foundation. The great production of surplus-value in these branches of labour, and the progressive cheapening of their articles, were and are chiefly due to the minimum wages paid, which just sufficed for a miserable, vegetable existence, and to the extension of the hours of labour to the maximum endurable by the human organism. It was in fact the cheapness of the human sweat and the human blood which were converted into commodities, which permitted the constant extension of the market; this was especially true of England's colonial market where, besides, English tastes and habits prevail. At last the critical point was reached. The basis of the old method, sheer brutality in the exploitation of the workers, accompanied by a more or less systematic division of labour, no longer sufficed for the extending markets and for the still more rapidly extending competition of the capitalists. The hour of the machine had struck. The decisively revolutionary machine, the machine which attacks in an equal degree all the innumerable branches of this sphere of production, such as dressmaking, tailoring, shoemaking, sewing, hat-making and so on, is the sewing-machine.

Its immediate effect on the workers is like that of all machinery, which, during the epoch of large-scale industry, has seized on new branches of trade. Children who are too young are removed. The wage of those who work with machines rises compared with that of the domestic workers, many of whom belong among the 'poorest of the poor'. The wage of the better situated handicraftsmen sinks, however, since the machine is in competition with them. The new machine-minders are exclusively girls and young women. With the help of mechanical force, they destroy the monopoly that male labour had of the heavier work, and they drive off from the lighter work numbers of old women and very young children. The overpowering competition crushes the weakest manual workers. The fearful increase in death from starvation during the last ten years in London runs parallel with the extension of machine sewing.[89]

88. Commissioner White visited a military clothing factory that employed 1,000 to 1,200 persons, almost all females, and a shoe factory with 1,300 persons; of these nearly one-half were children and young persons (*Children's Employment Commission, Second Report*, p. xlvii, n. 319).

89. One example. The weekly report of deaths issued by the Registrar-General contains, under the date of 26 February 1864, five cases of death

The new female workers turn the machines by hand and foot, or by hand alone, sometimes sitting, sometimes standing, according to the weight, size and special make of the machine, and expend a great deal of labour-power. Their occupation is unwholesome, owing to the long hours, although in most cases these are not so long as under the old system. Wherever the sewing-machine is located in narrow and already over-crowded workrooms, it adds to the unwholesome influences. 'The effect,' says Mr Lord, 'of entering a low pitched room where thirty to forty machinists are working under such conditions . . . is almost overpowering . . . the heat, partly owing to gas stoves for heating irons, was dreadful . . . Even when moderate hours of work, i.e., from 8 in the morning till 6 in the evening, prevail in such places, yet three or four persons fall into a swoon regularly every day.'[90]

The revolution in the social mode of production which is the necessary product of the revolution in the means of production is accomplished through a variegated medley of transitional forms. These forms vary according to the extent to which the sewing-machine has become prevalent in one branch of industry or the other, the time during which it has been in operation, the previous condition of the workers, the degree to which manufacture, handicrafts or domestic industry preponderates, the level of rent of the workrooms,[91] and so on. In dress-making, for instance, where the labour for the most part was already organized, chiefly by simple co-operation, the sewing-machine at first formed nothing but a fresh element in the already existing system of manufacture. In tailoring, shirtmaking, shoemaking, etc., all the forms are intermingled. Here we see the factory system proper. We see middlemen receiving the raw material from the capitalist *en chef*, and setting to work at sewing-machines, in 'chambers' and 'garrets', groups of from ten to fifty or more female workers. Finally, as is always

---

from starvation. On the same day *The Times* reports another case. Six victims of starvation in one week!

90. *Children's Employment Commission, Second Report*, 1864, p. lxvii, n. 406–9, p. 84, n. 124, p. lxxiii, n. 441, p. 68, n. 6, p. 84, n. 126, p. 78, n. 85, p. 76, n. 69, p. lxxii, n. 438.

91. 'The rental of premises required for work-rooms seems to be the element which ultimately determines this point, and consequently it is in the metropolis that the old system of giving work out to small employers and families has been longest retained, or earliest returned to' (ibid., p. 83, n. 123).

the case with machinery when not organized into a system, and when it can also be used on a very small scale, handicraftsmen and domestic workers, along with their families, or with a little extra labour from outside, make use of their own sewing-machines.[92] The system actually prevalent in England is this: the capitalist concentrates a large number of machines on his premises, and then distributes the product of those machines amongst the domestic workers to work it up into its finished form.[93] The variety of these transitional forms does not, however, conceal the tendency operating to transform them into the factory system proper. This tendency is nurtured by the very nature of the sewing-machine, the manifold uses of which tend to compel the concentration, under one roof and one management, of previously separated branches of a trade. It is also favoured by the circumstance that preparatory needle-work and certain other operations are most conveniently done on the premises where the machine is at work, as well as by the inevitable expropriation of the hand sewers, and the domestic workers who work with their own machines. This fate has already in part overtaken them. The constantly increasing amount of capital invested in sewing-machines[94] spurs on the production of machine-made articles and gluts the market with them, thereby signalling to the domestic workers that they must sell their machines. The over-production of sewing-machines themselves causes their producers, who need to sell at all costs, to let them out for so much a week, thus crushing the small sewing-machine owners by their deadly competition.[95] Constant changes in the construction of the machines, and their ever-increasing cheapness, cause the older makes to depreciate daily and compel their sale in great numbers, at absurd prices, to large capitalists, who are now the only people who can employ them at a profit. Finally, the substitution of the steam-engine for man strikes the final blow in this, as in all similar processes of transformation. Initially the use of steam-power meets with certain technical difficulties, such as unsteadiness in the machines, difficulty in controlling their speed, rapid wear and tear

92. In glove-making and other industries where the condition of the workers is hardly to be distinguished from that of paupers, this does not happen.
93. ibid., p. 83, n. 122.
94. In the wholesale boot and shoe trade of Leicester alone, there were in 1864 800 sewing-machines already in use.
95. ibid., p. 84, n. 124.

of the lighter machines, etc. But these are all soon overcome by experience.[96] If, on the one hand, the concentration of many machines in large factories leads to the use of steam power, on the other hand the competition of steam with human muscles hastens on the concentration of workers and machines in large factories. Thus England is at present experiencing, not only in the colossal industry of making 'wearing apparel', but also in most of the other trades mentioned above, the conversion of manufacture, handicrafts and domestic work into the factory system, after each of those forms of production, totally changed and disorganized under the influence of large-scale industry, has long ago reproduced and even overdone all the horrors of the factory system, without reproducing any of the positive aspects of its development.[97]

This industrial revolution, which advances naturally and spontaneously, is also helped on artificially by the extension of the Factory Acts to all industries in which women, young persons and children are employed. The compulsory regulation of the working day, as regards its length, pauses, beginning and end, the introduction of the relay system for children, the exclusion from the factory of all children under a certain age, etc., necessitate on the one hand more machinery[98] and the substitution of steam as a motive power in the place of muscles.[99] On the other hand, in

96. Instances: the Army Clothing Depot at Pimlico, London, the shirt factory of Tillie and Henderson at Londonderry, and the clothes factory of Messrs Tait at Limerick, which employs about 1,200 'hands'.

97. 'Tendency to Factory System' (ibid., p. lxvii). 'The whole employment is at this time in a state of transition, and is undergoing the same change as that effected in the lace trade, weaving, etc.' (ibid., n. 405). 'A complete revolution' (ibid., p. xlvi, n. 318). At the time of the Children's Employment Commission report of 1840 stockings were still being made by manual labour. Since 1846 various sorts of machine have been introduced, and they are now driven by steam. The total number of persons of both sexes and all ages from 3 years upwards employed in the making of stockings in England was in 1862 about 129,000. Of these only 4,063 were, according to the Parliamentary Return of 11 February 1862, working under the Factory Acts.

98. Here is an example taken from the earthenware trade. Messrs Cochrane, of the Britannia Pottery, Glasgow, report: 'To keep up our quantity we have gone extensively into machines wrought by unskilled labour, and every day convinces us that we can produce a greater quantity than by the old method' (*Reports of the Inspectors of Factories . . . 31 October 1865*, p. 13). 'The effect of the Factory Acts is to force on the further introduction of machinery' (ibid., pp. 13–14).

99. Thus, after the extension of the Factory Act to the potteries, there was a great increase of power-jiggers in place of hand-moved jiggers.

order to make up for the loss of time, an expansion occurs of the means of production used in common, of the furnaces, buildings, etc., in one word, a greater concentration of the means of production and a corresponding increase in the number of workers conglomerated in one place. The chief objection, raised repeatedly and passionately on behalf of each manufacture threatened with the Factory Act, is in fact this, that in order to continue the business on the old scale a greater outlay of capital will be necessary. But, as regards labour in the so-called domestic industries and the intermediate forms between them and manufacture, as soon as limits are set to the working day and to the employment of children, those industries go to the wall. Unlimited exploitation of cheap labour-power is the sole foundation of their ability to compete.

One of the essential conditions for the existence of the factory system, especially when the length of the working day is fixed, is certainty in the result, i.e. the production in a given time of a given quantity of commodities, or of a given useful effect. The statutory pauses in the working day, moreover, imply the assumption that periodic and sudden cessations in the work do no harm to the article undergoing the process of production. This certainty in the result, and this possibility of interrupting the work, are of course more easily attained in the purely mechanical industries than in those in which chemical and physical processes play a part; as, for instance, in the earthenware trade, in bleaching, dyeing, baking, and in most of the metallurgical industries. Wherever there is a working day whose length is not restricted, wherever there is night-work and unrestricted waste of human life, there the slightest obstacle presented by the nature of the work to a change for the better is soon looked on as an eternal 'natural barrier' inherent in production. No poison kills vermin with more certainty than the Factory Act removes such 'natural barriers'. No one made a greater outcry over 'impossibilities' than the gentlemen who are involved in the manufacture of earthenware. In 1864, however, they were brought under the Act, and within sixteen months every 'impossibility' had vanished. 'The improved method', called forth by the Act, 'of making slip by pressure instead of by evaporation, the newly-constructed stoves for drying the ware in its green state, etc., are each events of great importance in the pottery art, and mark an advance which the preceding century could not rival ... It has even considerably reduced the temperature of the stoves themselves with a considerable saving of fuel, and with a readier effect on the ware.'[1] In spite of every prophecy, the cost price of earthenware did not rise, but the quantity produced did, and to such an extent that the export for the twelve months ending December 1865 exceeded in value by £138,628 the average of the preceding three years. In the manufacture of matches it was thought to be an indispensable requirement that boys, even while bolting their dinner, should go on dipping the matches in melted phosphorus, whose poisonous vapour rose into their faces. The Factory Act (1864) made the saving of time a necessity, and so forced into existence a dipping machine, whose vapour could not come into contact with the workers.[2] Similarly, at the present time, in those branches of lace manufacture not yet subject to the Factory Act, it is maintained that meal-times cannot be regular owing to the different periods required by the various kinds of lace for drying, periods which vary from three minutes to up to an hour and more. To this the Children's Employment Commissioners answer: 'The circumstances of this case are precisely analogous to that of the paper-stainers, dealt with in our first report. Some of the principal manufacturers in the trade urged that, in consequence of the nature of the materials used, and their various processes, they would be unable, without serious loss, to stop for meal-times at any given moment. But it was seen from the evidence that, by due care and previous arrangement, the apprehended difficulty could be got over; and accordingly by clause 6 of section 6 of the Factory Acts Extension Act passed during this Session of Parliament, an interval of eighteen months is given to them, from the passing of the Act, before they are required to conform to the meal hours specified by the Factory Acts.'[3] The Act had hardly received the sanction of Parliament when the manufacturers also discovered this: 'The inconveniences we expected to arise from the introduction of the Factory Acts into our branch of manufacture, I am happy to say, have not arisen. We do not find the production at all interfered with; in short we produce more in the same time.'[4] It is evident that the British Parliament, which no one will re-

1. *Reports of the Inspectors of Factories . . . 31 October 1865*, pp. 96 and 127.
2. The introduction of this and other machinery into match-making had the effect, in one department alone, that 230 young persons were replaced by 32 boys and girls of 14 to 17 years of age. This saving in labour was carried still further in 1865 by the employment of steam power.
3. *Children's Employment Commission, Second Report*, 1864, p. ix, n. 50.
4. *Reports of the Inspectors of Factories . . . 31 October 1865*, p. 22.

proach with being excessively endowed with genius, has been led by experience to the conclusion that a simple compulsory law is sufficient to enact away all the so-called impediments opposed by the nature of the process to the restriction and regulation of the working day. Hence, on the introduction of the Factory Act into a given industry, a period varying from six to eighteen months is fixed within which it is incumbent on the manufacturers to remove all technical impediments to the working of the Act. Mirabeau's '*Impossible! ne me dites jamais ce bête de mot!*'* is particularly applicable to modern technology. But though the Factory Acts thus artificially ripen the material elements necessary for the conversion of the manufacturing system into the factory system, yet at the same time, because they make it necessary to lay out a greater amount of capital, they hasten the decline of the small masters, and the concentration of capital.[5]

Apart from the purely technical impediments, which can be removed by technical means, the irregular habits of the workers themselves obstruct the regulation of the hours of labour. This is especially the case where piece-wages predominate, and where loss of time in one part of the day or week can be made good by subsequent overtime or by night-work, a process which brutalizes the adult worker and ruins his wife and children.[6] Although this

5. 'But it must be borne in mind that those improvements, though carried out fully in some establishments, are by no means general, and are not capable of being brought into use in many of the old manufactories without an expenditure of capital beyond the means of many of the present occupiers.' 'I cannot but rejoice,' writes Sub-Inspector May, 'that notwithstanding the temporary disorganization which inevitably follows the introduction of such a measure' (as the Factory Acts Extension Act) 'and is, indeed, directly indicative of the evils which it was intended to remedy, etc.' (*Reports of the Inspectors of Factories . . . 31 October 1865*, pp. 96–7).

6. With blast-furnaces, for instance, 'work towards the end of the week being generally much increased in duration, in consequence of the habit of the men of idling on Mondays and occasionally during a part of the whole of Tuesdays also' (*Children's Employment Commission, Third Report*, p. vi [n. 15]). 'The little masters generally have very irregular hours. They lose two or three days, and then work all night to make it up . . . They always employ their own children, if they have any' (ibid., p. vii [n. 19]). 'The want of regularity in coming to work, encouraged by the possibility and practice of making up for this by working longer hours' (ibid., p. xviii [n. 115]). 'In Birmingham . . . an enormous amount of time is lost . . . idling part of the time and slaving the rest' (ibid., p. xi [n. 61]).

*'Impossible! Never use that ridiculous word to me!'

absence of regularity in the expenditure of labour-power is a natural and crudely spontaneous reaction against the tedium of monotonous drudgery, it also originates, and to a much greater degree, from the anarchy in production itself, an anarchy that in its turn presupposes unbridled exploitation of labour-power by the capitalist. Alongside the general and periodic changes in the industrial cycle, and the special fluctuations in the markets to which each industry is subject, we may also reckon what is called 'the season', dependent either on the periodicity of favourable seasons of the year for navigation, or on fashion, and the sudden placing of large orders that have to be executed in the shortest possible time. The habit of giving such orders becomes more frequent with the extension of railways and telegraphs. 'The extension of the railway system throughout the country has tended very much to encourage giving short notice. Purchasers now come up from Glasgow, Manchester, and Edinburgh once every fortnight or so to the wholesale city warehouses which we supply, and give small orders requiring immediate execution, instead of buying from stock as they used to do. Years ago we were always able to work in the slack times so as to meet the demand of the next season, but now no one can say beforehand what will be in demand then.'[7]

In factories and places of manufacture which are not yet subject to the Factory Acts, the most fearful over-work prevails periodically during what is called the season, as a result of sudden orders. In the outside departments of factory, workshop and warehouse, the so-called domestic workers, whose employment is at best irregular, are entirely dependent for their raw material and their orders on the caprice of the capitalist, who, in this industry, is not hampered by any regard for depreciation of his buildings and machinery, and risks nothing by a stoppage of work but the skin of the worker himself. Here then he sets himself systematically to work to form an industrial reserve force that shall be ready at a moment's notice; during one part of the year he decimates this force by the most inhuman toil, during the other part he lets it starve for lack of work. 'Employers . . . avail themselves of the habitual irregularity [in work at home] when any extra work is wanted at a push, so that work goes on till 11 and 12 p.m., or 2

7. *Children's Employment Commission, Fourth Report*, p. xxxii [n. 202]. 'The extension of the railway system is said to have contributed greatly to this custom of giving sudden orders, and the consequent hurry, neglect of meal-times, and late hours of the workpeople' (ibid., p. xxxi [n. 202]).

a.m., or as the usual phrase is, "all hours",' and in places where 'the stench is enough to knock you down; you go to the door, perhaps, and open it, but shudder to go further'.[8] 'They are curious men,' said one of the witnesses, a shoemaker, speaking of the masters, 'and think it does a boy no harm to work too hard for half the year, if he is nearly idle for the other half.'[9]

Like the technical impediments, these 'usages which have grown with the growth of trade', or business customs, were also proclaimed by interested capitalists (and still are proclaimed) to be 'natural barriers' inherent in production. This was a favourite cry of the cotton lords at the time when they were first threatened with the Factory Acts. Although their industry depends, more than any other, on the world market, and therefore on shipping, experience showed they were lying. Since then, every pretended 'obstruction to business' has been treated by the Factory Inspectors as a mere sham.[10] The thoroughly conscientious investigations of the Children's Employment Commission prove that the effect of the regulation of the hours of work, in some industries, was to spread the mass of labour previously employed more evenly over the whole year;[11] that this regulation was the first rational bridle on the murderous, meaningless caprices of fashion,[12] caprices which fit in very badly with the system under which large-scale industry operates; that the development of ocean navigation

8. *Children's Employment Commission, Fourth Report*, p. xxxv, n. 235, 237.
9. ibid., p. 127, n. 56.
10. 'With respect to the loss of trade by non-completion of shipping orders in time, I remember that this was the pet argument of the factory masters in 1832 and 1833. Nothing that can be advanced now on this subject, could have the force that it had then, before steam had halved all distances and established new regulations for transit. It quite failed at that time of proof when put to the test, and again it will certainly fail should it have to be tried' (*Reports of the Inspectors of Factories ... 31 October 1862*, pp. 54–5).
11. *Children's Employment Commission, Third Report*, p. xviii, n. 118.
12. John Bellers remarked as long ago as 1699: 'The uncertainty of fashions does increase necessitous Poor. It has two great mischiefs in it. 1st). The journeymen are miserable in winter for want of work, the mercers and master-weavers not daring to lay out their stocks to keep the journeymen employed before the spring comes, and they know what the fashion will then be. 2ndly). In the spring the journeymen are not sufficient, but the master-weavers must draw in many prentices, that they may supply the trade of the kingdom in a quarter or half a year, which robs the plough of hands, drains the country of labourers, and in a great part stocks the city with beggars, and starves some in winter that are ashamed to beg' (*Essays about the Poor, Manufactures, etc.*, p. 9).

and of the means of communication in general has destroyed the actual technical foundation of seasonal labour,[13] and that all other so-called uncontrollable circumstances are swept away by the increased size of the buildings, the additional machinery, the increased number of workers employed simultaneously,[14] and the automatic impact of all these changes on the mode of conducting the wholesale trade.[15] But for all that, capital never becomes reconciled to such changes – and this is admitted over and over again by its own representatives – except 'under the pressure of a General Act of Parliament'[16] for the compulsory regulation of the hours of labour.

9. THE HEALTH AND EDUCATION CLAUSES OF THE FACTORY ACTS. THE GENERAL EXTENSION OF FACTORY LEGISLATION IN ENGLAND

Factory legislation, that first conscious and methodical reaction of society against the spontaneously developed form of its production process, is, as we have seen, just as much the necessary product of large-scale industry as cotton yarn, self-actors and the electric telegraph. Before we go on to consider the extension of that legislation in England, we shall briefly notice certain clauses contained in the Factory Acts which do not relate to the hours of work.

Quite apart from their wording, which makes it easy for the

13. *Children's Employment Commission, Fifth Report*, p. 171, n. 34.

14. The evidence of some Bradford export houses is as follows: 'Under these circumstances it seems clear that no boys need be worked longer than from 8 a.m. to 7 or 7.30 p.m. in making up . . . It is merely a question of extra hands and extra outlay; if some masters were not so greedy, the boys would not work late; an extra machine costs only £16 or £18 . . . Much of such overtime as does occur is to be referred to an insufficiency of appliances and a want of space' (*Children's Employment Commission, Fifth Report*, p. 171, n. 35, 36, 38).

15. ibid. (p. 81, n. 32). A London manufacturer, who by the way looks upon the compulsory regulation of the hours of labour as a protection for the workers against the manufacturers, and for the manufacturers themselves against the wholesale trade, states: 'The pressure in our trade is caused by the desire of shipping houses to send either by a sailing vessel in order to be in time for a particular season, and to save the difference in freight between that and steam, or by the earlier of two steamers so as to be the first in the foreign market.'

16. 'This could be obviated,' says a manufacturer, 'at the expense of an enlargement of the works under the pressure of a General Act of Parliament' (ibid., p. x, n. 38).

capitalist to evade them, the clauses relating to health are extremely meagre, and in fact limited to provisions for whitewashing the walls, for insuring cleanliness in some other matters, for ventilation and for protection against dangerous machinery. We shall return again in Volume 3* to the fanatical opposition of the manufacturers to those clauses which imposed on them a slight expenditure on appliances for protecting the arms and legs of their 'hands'. Here is yet another dazzling vindication of the free-trade dogma that, in a society of mutually antagonistic interests, each individual furthers the common welfare by seeking his own personal advantage! One example will suffice. It is a well-known fact that during the last twenty years the flax industry has expanded considerably, and that, with that expansion, the number of scutching mills in Ireland has increased. In 1864 there were in that country 1,800 of these mills. Regularly, in autumn and winter, women and 'young persons', the wives, sons and daughters of the neighbouring small farmers, a class of people entirely unaccustomed to machinery, are taken from field labour to feed the rollers of the scutching mills with flax. The accidents, both as regards number and kind, are wholly unparalleled in the history of machinery. In one scutching mill, at Kildinan, near Cork, there occurred between 1852 and 1856 six fatal accidents and sixty mutilations. Every one of these might have been prevented by the simplest appliances, costing a few shillings. Dr W. White, the certifying surgeon for factories at Downpatrick, states in his official report, dated 15 December 1865: 'The serious accidents at the scutching mills are of the most fearful nature. In many cases a quarter of the body is torn from the trunk, and either involves death or a future of wretched incapacity and suffering. The increase of mills in the country will of course extend these dreadful results, and it will be a great boon if they are brought under the legislature. I am convinced that by proper supervision of scutching mills a vast sacrifice of life and limb would be averted.'[17]

What could be more characteristic of the capitalist mode of production than the fact that it is necessary, by Act of Parliament, to force upon the capitalists the simplest appliances for maintaining cleanliness and health? In the potteries the Factory Act of

17. ibid., p. xv, n. 72 ff.

---

*Cf. *Capital*, Vol. 3, Part I, Chapter 5, Section II, 'Savings in Labour Conditions at the Expense of the Workers'.

1864 'has whitewashed and cleansed.upwards of 200 workshops, after a period of abstinence from any such cleaning, in many cases of 20 years, and in some entirely' (this is the 'abstinence' of the capitalist!), 'in which were employed 27,800 artisans, hitherto breathing through protracted days and often nights of labour, a mephitic atmosphere, and which rendered an otherwise comparatively innocuous occupation, pregnant with disease and death. The Act has improved the ventilation very much.'[18] At the same time, this part of the Act strikingly demonstrates that the capitalist mode of production, by its very nature, excludes all rational improvement beyond a certain point. It has been repeatedly noted that the English doctors are unanimous in declaring that where the work is continuous 500 cubic feet is the very smallest space that should be allowed for each person. Now, just as the Factory Acts, owing to their compulsory provisions, indirectly hasten the conversion of small workshops into factories, thus indirectly attacking the proprietary rights of the smaller capitalists, and assuring a monopoly to the big ones, so too, in the same way, thousands of small employers would be expropriated directly, at a single stroke, if it were made obligatory to provide the proper space for each worker in each workshop. This would strike at the very roots of the capitalist mode of production, i.e. the self-valorization of capital, whether on a small or a large scale, by means of the 'free' purchase and consumption of labour-power. Factory legislation is therefore brought to a dead halt before these 500 cubic feet of breathing space. The health officers, the industrial inquiry commissioners, the factory inspectors, all repeat, over and over again, that it is both necessary for the workers to have these 500 cubic feet, and impossible to impose this rule on capital. They are, in reality, declaring that consumption and the other pulmonary diseases of the workers are conditions necessary to the existence of capital.[19]

18. *Reports of the Inspectors of Factories . . . 31 October 1865*, p. 127.
19. It has been found out by experiment that with each breath of average intensity taken by an average, healthy individual, about 25 cubic inches of air are consumed, and that about twenty breaths are taken in each minute. Hence the air inhaled in 24 hours by each individual is about 720,000 cubic inches, or 416 cubic feet. It is clear, however, that air which has once been breathed cannot serve again for the same process until it has been purified in the great workshop of nature. According to the experiments of Valentin and Brunner, it appears that a healthy man gives off about 1,300 cubic inches of carbonic acid per hour; this would give about 8 ounces of solid carbon

Paltry as the education clauses of the Act appear on the whole, they do proclaim that elementary education is a compulsory precondition for the employment of children. [20] The success of those clauses proved for the first time the possibility of combining education and gymnastics[21] with manual labour, and consequently of combining manual labour with education and gymnastics. The factory inspectors soon found out, by questioning the schoolmasters, that the factory children, although they received only one half the education of the regular day students, yet learnt quite as much and often more. 'This can be accounted for by the simple fact that, with only being at school for one half of the day, they are always fresh, and nearly always ready and willing to receive instruction. The system on which they work, half manual labour, and half school, renders each employment a rest and a relief to the other; consequently, both are far more congenial to the child, than would be the case were he kept constantly at one. It is quite clear that a boy who has been at school all the morning, cannot (in hot weather particularly) cope with one who comes fresh and bright from his work.'[22] Further evidence of this will be found in Senior's speech at the Social Science Congress at Edinburgh in 1863. He shows there, amongst other things, how the monotonous,

---

thrown off from the lungs in 24 hours. 'Every man should have at least 800 cubic feet' (Huxley). [*Lessons in Elementary Physiology*, London, 1866, p. 105.]

20. According to the English Factory Act, parents cannot send their children under 14 years of age into factories under the control of the Act, unless at the same time they allow them to receive elementary education. The manufacturer is responsible for compliance with the Act. 'Factory education is compulsory, and it is a condition of labour' (*Reports of the Inspectors of Factories . . . 31 October 1865*, p. 111).

21. On the very advantageous results achieved by combining gymnastics (and military exercises in the case of boys) with compulsory education for factory children and pauper students, see the speech of N. W. Senior at the seventh annual congress of the National Association for the Promotion of Social Science, in *Report of Proceedings, etc.*, London, 1863, pp. 63–4, and also the *Reports of the Inspectors of Factories . . . 31 October 1865*, pp. 118–19, 120, 126 ff.

22. *Reports of the Inspectors of Factories . . . 31 October 1865*, pp. 118–19. A silk manufacturer naïvely stated to the Children's Employment Commissioners: 'I am quite sure that the true secret of producing efficient workpeople is to be found in uniting education and labour from a period of childhood. Of course the occupation must not be too severe, nor irksome or unhealthy. But of the advantage of the union I have no doubt. I wish my own children could have some work as well as play, to give variety to their schooling' (*Children's Employment Commission, Fifth Report*, p. 82, n. 36).

unproductive and long school day undergone by the children of the upper and middle classes uselessly adds to the labour of the teacher, 'while he not only fruitlessly but absolutely injuriously, wastes the time, health, and energy of the children'.[23] As Robert Owen has shown us in detail, the germ of the education of the future is present in the factory system; this education will, in the case of every child over a given age, combine productive labour with instruction and gymnastics, not only as one of the methods of adding to the efficiency of production, but as the only method of producing fully developed human beings.

As we have seen, large-scale industry sweeps away by technical means the division of labour characteristic of manufacture, under which each man is bound hand and foot for life to a single specialized operation. At the same time, the capitalist form of large-scale industry reproduces this same division of labour in a still more monstrous shape; in the factory proper, by converting the worker into a living appendage of the machine; and everywhere outside the factory by the sporadic use of machinery and machine workers,[24] or by the introduction of the labour of women,

23. Senior, op. cit., p. 66. The way in which large-scale industry, when it has reached a certain level, is capable of revolutionizing people's minds through the transformation it brings about in the material mode of production and the social relations of production, is strikingly demonstrated by a comparison of Senior's speech in 1863 with his philippic against the Factory Act of 1833. It could also be shown by a comparison of the views of the above-mentioned congress with the fact that in certain country districts of England poor parents are forbidden, on pain of death by starvation, to educate their children. Thus Mr Snell for example reports that it is a common occurrence in Somersetshire that, when a poor person claims parish relief, he is compelled to take his children out of school. Mr Wollaston, the clergyman at Feltham, also tells of cases where all relief was denied to certain families 'because they were sending their children to school!'

24. Wherever handicraft-machines, driven by men, compete directly or indirectly with more developed machines driven by mechanical power, a great change takes place with regard to the worker who drives the machine. At first the steam-engine replaces this worker, afterwards he must replace the steam-engine. Hence the tension and the amount of labour-power expended become monstrous. This is especially true in the case of the children who are condemned to this torture. Thus Mr Longe, one of the commissioners, found that in Coventry and the neighbourhood boys from 10 to 15 years were employed in turning the ribbon-looms, not to mention younger children who had to drive smaller machines. It is extraordinarily fatiguing work. 'The boy is a mere substitute for steam power' (*Children's Employment Commission, Fifth Report*, 1866, p. 114, n. 6). As to the fatal consequences of 'this system of slavery', as the official report styles it [p. 115, n. 63], see ibid., pp. 114 ff.

children and unskilled men as a new foundation for the division of labour. The contradiction between the division of labour under manufacture and the essential character of large-scale industry makes itself forcibly felt. It appears, for example, in the frightful fact that a great part of the children employed in modern factories and manufactures are from their earliest years riveted to the most simple manipulations, and exploited for years, without being taught a single kind of skill that would afterwards make them of use, even in the same factory. In the English letter-press printing trade, for example, there formerly existed a system, corresponding to that in the old manufactures and handicrafts, of advancing the apprentices from easy to more and more difficult work. They went through a course of teaching till they were finished printers. To be able to read and write was for every one of them a requirement of their trade. All this was changed by the printing machine. It employs two sorts of worker. On the one hand there are adults, tenters, and on the other hand there are boys, mostly from 11 to 17 years of age, whose sole occupation is either to spread the sheets of paper under the machine, or to take from it the printed sheets. They perform this weary task, in London especially, for 14, 15 and 16 hours at a stretch, during several days in the week, and frequently for 36 hours, with only 2 hours' rest for meals and sleep.[25] A great proportion of them cannot read, and they are, as a rule, utter savages and very extraordinary creatures. 'To qualify them for the work which they have to do they require no intellectual training; there is little room in it for skill, and less for judgement; their wages, though rather high for boys, do not increase proportionately as they grow up, and the majority of them cannot look for advancement to the better paid and more responsible post of machine minder, because, while each machine has but one minder, it has at least two, and often four boys attached to it.'[26] As soon as they get too old for such children's work, that is at about 17 years old, at the latest, they are discharged from the printing establishments. They become recruits for crime. Attempts to procure them employment elsewhere come to grief owing to their ignorance and brutality, their mental and bodily degradation.

What is true of the division of labour within the workshop under the system of manufacture is also true of the division of labour within society. As long as handicrafts and manufacture

25. ibid., p. 3, n. 24.   26. ibid., p. 7, n. 60.

form the universal basis of social production, the subjection of the producer to a single branch, the breaking-up of the originally multifarious parts of his employment,[27] is a necessary aspect of the process of development. It is on that basis that each separate branch of production acquires its technically appropriate shape empirically, and slowly perfects it. Then, as soon as a particular degree of maturity has been reached, it rapidly crystallizes. Once this has happened, the only thing that here and there gives rise to a change, apart from the provision of new materials for labour through the medium of trade, is the gradual alteration of the instruments of labour. But their form, too, once it has been definitively laid down by experience, undergoes a process of petrification, as is proved by their frequent transmission from one generation to another, unaltered, through thousands of years. It is characteristic of this situation that, right down to the eighteenth century, the different trades were called 'mysteries' (*mystères*),[28] into whose secrets none but those initiated by their profession and their practical experience could penetrate. Large-scale industry tore aside the veil that concealed from men their own social process of production and turned the various spontaneously divided branches of production into riddles, not only to outsiders but even to the initiated. Its principle, which is to view each process of production in and for itself, and to resolve it into its constituent elements without looking first at the ability of the human hand to perform the new processes, brought into existence the whole of the modern science of technology. The varied, apparently unconnected and petrified forms of the social production process

27. 'In some parts of the Highlands of Scotland ... not many years ago, every peasant, according to the Statistical Account, made his own shoes of leather tanned by himself. Many a shepherd and cottar too, with his wife and children, appeared at Church in clothes which had been touched by no hands but their own, since they were shorn from the sheep and sown in the flaxfield. In the preparation of these, it is added, scarcely a single article had been purchased, except the awl, needle, thimble, and a very few parts of the ironwork employed in the weaving. The dyes, too, were chiefly extracted by the women from trees, shrubs, and herbs' (Dugald Stewart, *Works*, ed. Hamilton, Vol. 8, p. 327–8).

28. In the famous *Livre des métiers* of Étienne Boileau, we find it prescribed that a journeyman, on being admitted among the masters, had to swear 'to love his brethren with brotherly love, to support them in their respective trades, not wilfully to betray the secrets of the trade, and besides, in the interests of all, not to recommend his own wares by calling the attention of the buyer to defects in the articles made by others.'

were now dissolved into conscious and planned applications of natural science, divided up systematically in accordance with the particular useful effect aimed at in each case. Similarly, technology discovered the few grand fundamental forms of motion which, despite all the diversity of the instruments used, apply necessarily to every productive action of the human body, just as the science of mechanics is not misled by the immense complication of modern machinery into viewing this as anything other than the constant re-appearance of the same simple mechanical processes.

Modern industry never views or treats the existing form of a production process as the definitive one. Its technical basis is therefore revolutionary, whereas all earlier modes of production were essentially conservative.[29] By means of machinery, chemical processes and other methods, it is continually transforming not only the technical basis of production but also the functions of the worker and the social combinations of the labour process. At the same time, it thereby also revolutionizes the division of labour within society, and incessantly throws masses of capital and of workers from one branch of production to another. Thus large-scale industry, by its very nature, necessitates variation of labour, fluidity of functions, and mobility of the worker in all directions. But on the other hand, in its capitalist form it reproduces the old division of labour with its ossified particularities. We have seen how this absolute contradiction* does away with all repose,

29. 'The bourgeoisie cannot exist without constantly revolutionizing the instruments of production, and thereby the relations of production, and with them the whole relations of society. Conservation of the old modes of production in unaltered form, was, on the contrary, the first condition of existence for all earlier industrial classes. Constant revolutionizing of production, uninterrupted disturbance of all social conditions, everlasting uncertainty and agitation distinguish the bourgeois epoch from all earlier ones. All fixed, fast-frozen relations, with their train of ancient and venerable prejudices and opinions, are swept away, all new-formed ones become antiquated before they can ossify. All that is solid melts into air, all that is holy is profaned, and man is at last compelled to face with sober senses, his real conditions of life, and his relations with his kind' (F. Engels and Karl Marx, *Manifest der Kommunistischen Partei*, London, 1848, p. 5) [English translation: 'Manifesto of the Communist Party', pp. 70–71, in Karl Marx, *The Revolutions of 1848*, Pelican Marx Library, 1973].

*Namely the contradiction between the revolutionary technical basis of large-scale industry and the form it takes under capitalism. The reference back is mainly to Section 3 of this chapter.

all fixity and all security as far as the worker's life-situation is concerned; how it constantly threatens, by taking away the instruments of labour, to snatch from his hands the means of subsistence,[30] and, by suppressing his specialized function, to make him superfluous. We have seen, too, how this contradiction bursts forth without restraint in the ceaseless human sacrifices required from the working class, in the reckless squandering of labour-powers, and in the devastating effects of social anarchy. This is the negative side. But if, at present, variation of labour imposes itself after the manner of an overpowering natural law, and with the blindly destructive action of a natural law that meets with obstacles everywhere,[31] large-scale industry, through its very catastrophes, makes the recognition of variation of labour and hence of the fitness of the worker for the maximum number of different kinds of labour into a question of life and death. This possibility of varying labour must become a general law of social production, and the existing relations must be adapted to permit its realization in practice. That monstrosity, the disposable working population held in reserve, in misery, for the changing requirements of capitalist exploitation, must be replaced by the individual man who is absolutely available for the different kinds of labour required of him; the partially developed individual, who is merely the bearer of one specialized social function, must be replaced by the totally developed individual, for whom the different social functions are different modes of activity he takes up in turn.

One aspect of this process of transformation, which has developed spontaneously from the foundation provided by large-scale industry, is the establishment of technical and agricultural schools. Another is the foundation of '*écoles d'enseignement pro-*

---

30. 'You take my life
When you do take the means whereby I live.'
(Shakespeare, *The Merchant of Venice*, Act 4, Scene 1)

31. A French worker wrote as follows on his return from San Francisco: 'I could never have believed that I was capable of working at all the trades I practised in California. I was firmly convinced that I was fit for nothing but the printing of books . . . Once I was in the midst of this world of adventurers, who change their jobs as often as their shirts, then, upon my faith, I did as the others. As mining did not pay well enough, I left it for the city, and there I became in succession a typographer, a slater, a plumber, etc. As a result of this discovery that I am fit for any sort of work, I feel less of a mollusc and more of a man' (A. Corbon, *De l'enseignement professionnel*, 2nd edn, p. 50).

fessionel,* in which the children of the workers receive a certain amount of instruction in technology and in the practical handling of the various implements of labour. Though the Factory Act, that first and meagre concession wrung from capital, is limited to combining elementary education with work in the factory, there can be no doubt that, with the inevitable conquest of political power by the working class, technological education, both theoretical and practical, will take its proper place in the schools of the workers. There is also no doubt that those revolutionary ferments whose goal is the abolition of the old division of labour stand in diametrical contradiction with the capitalist form of production, and the economic situation of the workers which corresponds to that form. However, the development of the contradictions of a given historical form of production is the only historical way in which it can be dissolved and then reconstructed on a new basis. '*Ne sutor ultra crepidam*',† a phrase which was the absolute summit of handicraft wisdom, became sheer nonsense from the moment the watchmaker Watt invented the steam-engine, the barber Arkwright the throstle and the jeweller Fulton the steamship.[32]

As long as factory legislation is confined to regulating the labour done in factories, etc., it is regarded only as an interference

32. John Bellers, a veritable phenomenon in the history of political economy, already saw very clearly, at the end of the seventeenth century, the need to abolish the present system of education and division of labour, which gives rise to hypertrophy and atrophy at the two opposite extremities of society. Amongst other things he says this: 'An idle learning being little better than the learning of idleness ... Bodily labour, it's a primitive institution of God ... Labour being as proper for the bodies' health as eating is for its living; for what pains a man saves by ease, he will find in disease ... Labour adds oil to the lamp of life, when thinking inflames it ... A childish silly employ' (an anticipatory warning against the Basedows* and their modern imitators) 'leaves the children's minds silly' (*Proposals for Raising a Colledge of Industry of All Useful Trades and Husbandry*, London, 1696, pp. 12, 14, 16, 18).
*J. B. Basedow (1724–90) was a German educational theorist, whose endeavours to reform the educational system were influenced by Rousseau and Comenius. He ran a school in which the children learned no Latin and came into closer contact with reality through practical activities.

_____
* 'Schools for vocational teaching'.
† 'Let the cobbler stick to his last,' the reply supposed to have been made by the Greek painter Apelles to a shoemaker who criticized one of his works. It is reported by Pliny the Elder, *Historia Naturalis*, Bk xxxv, para. 84.

with capital's rights of exploitation. But when it comes to regulating so-called 'domestic labour',[33] this is immediately viewed as
a direct attack on the *patria potestas*, or, in modern terms, parental
authority. The tender-hearted English Parliament long affected
to shrink from taking this step. The power of facts, however,
at last compelled it to acknowledge that large-scale industry, in
overturning the economic foundation of the old family system,
and the family labour corresponding to it, had also dissolved the
old family relationships. The rights of the children had to be proclaimed. The concluding report of the Children's Employment
Commission, published in 1866, says: 'It is, unhappily, to a
painful degree apparent throughout the whole of the evidence,
that against no persons do the children of both sexes so much
require protection as against their parents.' The system of unlimited
exploitation of children's labour in general and so-called domestic
labour in particular is 'maintained only because the parents are
able, without check or control, to exercise this arbitrary and
mischievous power over their young and tender offspring . . .
Parents must not possess the absolute power of making their
children mere machines to earn so much weekly wage . . . The
children and young persons, therefore, in all such cases may
justifiably claim from the legislature, as a natural right, that an
exemption should be secured to them, from what destroys
prematurely their physical strength, and lowers them in the scale
of intellectual and moral beings.'[34] It was not however the misuse of parental power that created the direct or indirect exploitation of immature labour-powers by capital, but rather the
opposite, i.e. the capitalist mode of exploitation, by sweeping
away the economic foundation which corresponded to parental
power, made the use of parental power into its misuse. However terrible and disgusting the dissolution of the old family
ties within the capitalist system may appear, large-scale industry,
by assigning an important part in socially organized processes
of production, outside the sphere of the domestic economy, to
women, young persons and children of both sexes, does never-

33. This sort of labour goes on mostly in small workshops, as we have seen
when dealing with the lace-making and straw-plaiting trades,* and as we
could demonstrate in more detail if we looked at the metal manufactures of
Sheffield, Birmingham, etc.

34. *Children's Employment Commission, Fifth Report*, p. xxv, n. 162, and
Second Report, p. xxxviii, n. 285, 289, p. xxv, pp. xxv–xxvi, n. 191.

* See above, pp. 596–9.

theless create a new economic foundation for a higher form of the family and of relations between the sexes. It is of course just as absurd to regard the Christian-Germanic form of the family as absolute and final as it would have been in the case of the ancient Roman, the ancient Greek or the Oriental forms, which, moreover, form a series in historical development. It is also obvious that the fact that the collective working group is composed of individuals of both sexes and all ages must under the appropriate conditions turn into a source of humane development, although in its spontaneously developed, brutal, capitalist form, the system works in the opposite direction, and becomes a pestiferous source of corruption and slavery, since here the worker exists for the process of production, and not the process of production for the worker.[35]

The necessity for a generalization of the Factory Acts, for transforming them from exceptional laws relating to mechanical spinning and weaving – those first creations of machinery – into the general law for all social production, arose, as we have seen, from the path of historical development taken by large-scale industry, for, in its wake, the traditional shape of manufacture, handicrafts and domestic industry is entirely revolutionized; manufactures are constantly passing over into the factory system, and handicrafts into manufactures; and, at the end, the spheres of handicrafts and domestic industry become, in what is relatively an amazingly short time, dens of misery where capitalist exploitation is given free rein to commit the most frightful iniquities. There are two circumstances which finally turn the scale: first, the constantly recurring experience that as soon as capital is subjected to state control, even at a handful of points on the periphery of society, it seeks compensation all the more unrestrainedly at all other points;[36] and second, the cry of the capitalists for equality in the conditions of competition, i.e. for equality of restraint on the exploitation of labour.[37] Let us listen to two heartfelt outpourings on this matter. Messrs W. Cooksley of Bristol, nail and chain manufacturers, voluntarily introduced the regulations

35. 'Factory labour may be as pure and as excellent as domestic labour, and perhaps more so' (*Reports of the Inspectors of Factories ... 31 October 1865*, p. 129).

36. *Reports of the Inspectors of Factories ... 31 October 1865*, pp. 27–32.

37. A large number of examples can be found in the *Reports of the Inspectors of Factories*.

of the Factory Acts into their business. 'As the old irregular system prevails in neighbouring works, the Messrs Cooksley are subject to the disadvantage of having their boys enticed to continue their labour elsewhere after 6 p.m. "This", they naturally say, "is an injustice and loss to us, as it exhausts a portion of the boy's strength of which we ought to have the full benefit."'[38] Mr J. Simpson (paper box and bagmaker, of London) states before the commissioners of the Children's Employment Commission: 'He would sign any petition for it' (legislative intervention) ... 'As it was, he always felt restless at night, when he had closed his place, lest others should be working later than him and getting away his orders.'[39] Summing up, the commissioners declare: 'It would be unjust to the larger employers that their factories should be placed under regulation, while the hours of labour in the small places in their own branch of business were under no legislative restriction. And to the injustice arising from the unfair conditions of competition, in regard to hours, that would be created if the smaller places of work were exempt, would be added the disadvantage to the larger manufacturers of finding their supply of juvenile and female labour drawn off to the places of work exempt from legislation. Further, a stimulus would be given to the multiplication of the smaller places of work, which are almost invariably the least favourable to the health, comfort, education, and general improvement of the people.'[40]

In its concluding report, the Children's Employment Commission proposes to subject to the Factory Act more than 1,400,000 children, young persons and women, of whom about one-half are exploited in small industries and in so-called domestic labour.[41] It says this: 'But if it should seem fit to Parliament to

38. *Children's Employment Commission, Fifth Report*, p. x, n. 35.
39. ibid., p. ix, n. 28.
40. ibid., p. xxv, n. 165–7. As to the advantages of large-scale, compared with small-scale, industries, see *Children's Employment Commission, Third Report*, p. 13, n. 144, p. 25, n. 121, p. 26, n. 125, p. 27, n. 140, etc.
41. The branches they propose to regulate are as follows: lace-making, stocking-weaving, straw-plaiting, the manufacture of wearing apparel with its numerous subdivisions, artificial flower-making, shoe-making, hat-making, glove-making, tailoring, all metal works, from blast-furnaces down to needle factories, etc., paper-mills, glass-works, tobacco factories, india-rubber works, braid-making (for weaving), hand carpet-making, umbrella and parasol making, the manufacture of spindles and spools, letterpress printing, book-binding, the manufacture of stationery (including paper bags, cards, coloured paper, etc.), rope-making, the manufacture of jet ornaments, brick-making,

place the whole of that large number of children, young persons and females under the protective legislation above adverted to ... it cannot be doubted that such legislation would have a most beneficent effect, not only upon the young and the feeble who are its more immediate objects, but upon the still larger body of adult workers who would, in all those employments, both directly and indirectly, come immediately under its influence. It would enforce upon them regular and moderate hours; it would lead to their places of work being kept in a healthy and cleanly state; it would therefore husband and improve that store of physical strength on which their own well-being and that of the country so much depends; it would save the rising generation from that over-exertion at an early age which undermines their constitutions and leads to premature decay; finally, it would ensure them – at least up to the age of 13 – the opportunity of receiving the elements of education, and would put an end to that utter ignorance ... which – as faithfully exhibited in the Reports of our Assistant Commissioners – cannot be regarded without the deepest pain, and a profound sense of national humiliation.'[42]

The Tory government announced on 5 February 1867, in the Speech from the Throne, that it had incorporated the proposals of the Children's Employment Commission into Bills.[43] To get that far, an extra twenty years of *experimenta in corpore vili** had been required. Already in 1840 a Parliamentary Commission of Inquiry into child labour had been appointed. Its report, issued in 1842, unfolded, in the words of Nassau W. Senior, 'the most frightful picture of avarice, selfishness and cruelty on the part of

---

silk-manufacture when carried on by hand, Coventry weaving, salt works, tallow chandlers, cement works, sugar refineries, biscuit-making, various industries connected with timber, and other mixed trades.

42. ibid., p. xxv, n. 169.

43. The Factory Acts Extension Act was passed on 12 August 1867. It regulates all foundries, smithies and metal works, including machine shops; and also glass-works, paper-mills, gutta-percha and india-rubber works, tobacco factories, letterpress printing and book-binding works. Finally it regulates all workshops in which more than fifty persons are employed. The Hours of Labour Regulation Act,* passed on 17 August 1867, regulates the smaller workshops and the so-called domestic industries. I shall revert to these Acts, and to the new Mining Act of 1872, in Volume 2.

* This is simply another way of describing the Workshops Regulation Act, cited on p. 624.

---

* 'Experiments on a worthless body'.

masters and parents, and of juvenile and infantile misery, degradation and destruction ever presented . . . It may be supposed that
it describes the horrors of a past age. But there is unhappily
evidence that those horrors continue as intense as they were. A
pamphlet [on the Lace Trade and Factory Act] published by Hard-
wicke in 1860 states that the abuses complained of in 1842 are in
full bloom at the present day [1863]. It is a strange proof of the
general neglect of the morals and health of the children of the
working class, that this report lay unnoticed for twenty years,
during which the children, "bred up without the remotest sign of
comprehension as to what is meant by the term morals, who had
neither knowledge, nor religion, nor natural affection", were
allowed to become the parents of the present generation.'[44]

In the meantime, the social situation had undergone a change.*
Parliament did not dare to shelve the demands of the Commission
of 1862 as it had done those of the Commission of 1840. Hence,
in 1864, when the Commission had not yet published more than
a part of its reports, the earthenware industries (including the
potteries), the manufacture of wallpaper, matches, cartridges, and
percussion caps, and the cutting of fustian were placed under the
Acts in force in the textile industry. It was then that the Tory
government which was now in power announced, in the Speech
from the Throne, the introduction of further Bills, founded on the
final recommendations of the Commission, which had completed
its labours in 1866.

The Factory Acts Extension Act received the royal assent on
15 August 1867, the Workshops Regulation Act on 21 August
1867; the first Act regulated the large industries, the second the
small.

The Factory Acts Extension Act applies to blast-furnaces, iron
and copper mills, foundries, machine shops, metal works, gutta-
percha works, paper-mills, glass-works, tobacco factories, letter-
press printing works, book-binding works, in short to all industrial
establishments of this kind, in which fifty individuals or more are
occupied simultaneously, and for not less than 100 days a year.

To give an idea of the extent of the sphere embraced by the

44. Senior, *Social Science Congress*, pp. 55–8.

*The following paragraphs, from 'In the meantime' to 'actually put these
measures into practice' (p. 626), were added by Engels to the fourth German
edition.

Workshops Regulation Act in its application, we shall cite the definitions it lays down:

'*Handicraft* shall mean any manual labour exercised by way of trade, or for purposes of gain in, or incidental to, the making any article or part of an article, or in, or incidental to, the altering, repairing, ornamenting, finishing, or otherwise adapting for sale any article.'

'*Workshop* shall mean any room or place whatever in the open air or under cover, in which any handicraft is carried on by any child, young person, or woman, and to which and over which the person by whom such child, young person, or woman is employed, has the right of access and control.'

'*Employed* shall mean occupied in any handicraft, whether for wages or not, under a master or under a parent as herein defined.'

'*Parent* shall mean parent, guardian, or person, having the custody of, or control over, any . . . child or young person.'

Clause 7, which imposes a penalty for the employment of children, young persons and women in contravention of the provisions of the Act, lays down fines, not only for the occupier of the workshop, whether a parent or not, but also for 'the parent of, or the person deriving any direct benefit from the labour of, or having the control over, the child, young person or woman'.

The Factory Acts Extension Act, which affects the large establishments, regresses from the Factory Act by a mass of vicious exceptions and cowardly compromises with the masters.

The Workshops Regulation Act, wretched as far as its detailed provisions were concerned, remained a dead letter in the hands of the municipal and local authorities who were charged with its execution. When in 1871, Parliament withdrew this power from them, in order to confer it on the factory inspectors, to whose province it thus added at a single stroke more than 100,000 workshops, as well as 300 brickworks, care was taken at the same time not to add more than eight assistants to their already undermanned staff.[45]

What strikes us, then, in the English legislation of 1867, is, on the one hand, the necessity imposed on the Parliament of the

45. The personnel of the factory inspectorate consisted of two inspectors, two assistant inspectors and forty-one sub-inspectors. Eight additional sub-inspectors were appointed in 1871. The total cost of administering the Acts in England, Scotland and Ireland amounted for the year 1871–2 to no more than £25,347, including legal expenses incurred in prosecuting offenders.

ruling classes of adopting, in principle, such extraordinary and extensive measures against the excesses of capitalist exploitation; and, on the other hand, the hesitation, the unwillingness and the bad faith with which it actually put these measures into practice.

The 1862 Inquiry Commission also proposed a renewed regulation of the mining industry,* an industry distinguished from all others by the fact that in it the interests of the landowner and the capitalist coincide. The antagonism between these two interests had been favourable to factory legislation, and the absence of that antagonism is sufficient to explain the delays and the chicanery surrounding the legislation on mines.

The 1840 Inquiry Commission had made revelations so terrible and shocking, and created such a scandal throughout Europe, that to salve its conscience Parliament passed the Mining Act of 1842. But this did no more than forbid the employment underground of children under 10 years of age and of females.

Then, in 1860, there came the Mines Inspection Act, which provides that mines shall be inspected by public officials appointed specially for that purpose, and that boys between the ages of 10 and 12 years shall not be employed, unless they have a school certificate, or go to school for a certain number of hours. This Act was a complete dead letter, owing to the ridiculously small number of inspectors, the meagreness of their powers, and other causes that will become apparent as we proceed.

One of the most recent Blue Books on mines is the *Report from the Select Committee on Mines, together with ... Evidence, 23 July 1866*. This is the work of a Parliamentary Committee selected from members of the House of Commons, and authorized to summon and examine witnesses. It is a thick folio volume, but the Report itself occupies only five lines, to this effect; the committee has nothing to say, and more witnesses must be examined!

The mode of examining the witnesses reminds one of the cross-examination of witnesses in English courts of justice, where the advocate tries, by means of impudent, confusing and unexpected questions, to intimidate and confound the witness, and to give a forced meaning to the answers thus extorted. In this inquiry the members of the committee themselves are the cross-examiners, and among them are to be found both mine-owners and mine-

*The following paragraphs, from 'an industry' to 'capitalist production' (p. 634), were transferred by Engels from a footnote to the text in the fourth German edition.

exploiters; the witnesses are mining workers, mostly coal miners. The whole farce is too characteristic of the spirit of capital not to call for a few extracts from this Report. For the sake of conciseness, I have classified them under headings. I should also add that every question and its obligatory answer are numbered in the English Blue Books, and that the witnesses whose depositions are cited here are all workers in coal mines.

1. *Employment in mines of boys of 10 years and upwards.* In the mines the work, including the obligatory journey to and from the mine, usually lasts 14 or 15 hours, in exceptional cases even longer, from 3, 4 and 5 a.m. until 5 and 6 p.m. in the evening (n. 6, 452, 83). The adults work in two shifts, of 8 hours each; but there is no such alternation with the boys, on account of the expense (n. 80, 203, 204). The younger boys are chiefly employed in opening and shutting the ventilating doors in the various parts of the mine; the older ones are employed on heavier work, in carrying coal, etc. (n. 122, 739, 740). They work these long hours underground until their 18th or 22nd year, when they are put to miner's work proper (n. 161). Children and young persons are at present worse treated and harder worked than at any previous period (n. 1663–7). The miners almost unanimously demand an Act of Parliament prohibiting the employment of children under 14 in mines. And now Hussey Vivian (himself a mine-owner) asks: 'Would not the opinion of the workman depend upon the poverty of the workman's family?' Mr Bruce: 'Do you not think it would be a very hard case, where a parent had been injured, or where he was sickly, or where a father was dead, and there was only a mother, to prevent a child between 12 and 14 earning 1s. 7d. a day for the good of the family? . . . You must lay down a general rule? . . . Are you prepared to recommend legislation which would prevent the employment of children under 12 and 14, whatever the state of their parents might be?' 'Yes' (n. 107–10). Vivian: 'Supposing that an enactment were passed preventing the employment of children under the age of 14, would it not be probable that . . . the parents of children would seek employment for their children in other directions, for instance, in manufacture?' 'Not generally I think' (n. 174). Kinnaird: 'Some of the boys are keepers of doors?' 'Yes'. 'Is there not generally a very great draught every time you open a door or close it?' 'Yes, generally there is.' 'It sounds a very easy thing, but it is in fact rather a painful one?' 'He is imprisoned there just the same as if he was in a cell of a gaol.' Bourgeois Vivian: 'Whenever a boy is furnished with a lamp

cannot he read?' 'Yes, he can read, if he finds himself in candles [i.e. if he buys himself candles] . . . I suppose he would be found fault with if he were discovered reading; he is there to mind his business, he has a duty to perform, and he has to attend to it in the first place, and I do not think it would be allowed down the pit' (n. 139, 141, 143, 158, 160).

2. *Education.* The mining workers want a law for the compulsory education of their children, as in factories. They declare that the clauses of the Act of 1860 which require a school certificate to be obtained before employing boys of 10 and 12 years of age are quite illusory. The 'painstaking' cross-examination conducted by the capitalist investigating magistrates on this subject is positively droll. 'Is it (the Act) required more against the masters or against the parents?' 'It is required against both I think.' 'You cannot say whether it is required against one more than against the other?' 'No; I can hardly answer that question' (n. 115, 116). 'Does there appear to be any desire on the part of the employers that the boys should have such hours as to enable them to go to school?' 'No; the hours are never shortened for that purpose' (n. 137). 'Should you say that the colliers generally improve their education; have you any instances of men who have, since they began to work, greatly improved their education, or do they not rather go back, and lose any advantage that they may have gained?' 'They generally become worse; they do not improve; they acquire bad habits; they get on to drinking and gambling and such like, and they go completely to wreck' (n. 211). 'Do they make any attempt of the kind' (for providing instruction) 'by having schools at night?' 'There are few collieries where night schools are held, and perhaps at those collieries a few boys do go to those schools; but they are so physically exhausted that it is to no purpose that they go there' (n. 454). 'You are then,' concludes the bourgeois, 'against education?' 'Most certainly not; but,' etc. (n. 443). 'But are they' (the employers) 'not compelled to demand them?' (school certificates) 'By law they are; but I am not aware they are demanded by the employers.' 'Then it is your opinion, that this provision of the Act as to requiring certificates, is not generally carried out in the collieries?' 'It is not carried out' (n. 443, 444). 'Do the men take a great interest in this question?' (of education) 'The majority of them do' (n. 717). 'Are they very anxious to see the law enforced?' 'The majority are' (n. 718). 'Do you think that in this country

any law that you pass . . . can really be effectual unless the population themselves assist in putting it into operation?' 'Many a man might wish to object to employing a boy, but he would perhaps become marked by it' (n. 720). 'Marked by whom?' 'By the employers' (n. 721). 'Do you think that the employers would find any fault with a man who obeyed the law . . .?' 'I believe they would' (n. 722). 'Have you ever heard of any workman objecting to employ a boy between 10 and 12, who could not write or read?' 'It is not left to men's option' (n. 123). 'Would you call for the interference of Parliament?' 'I think that if anything effectual is to be done in the education of the colliers' children, it will have to be made compulsory by Act of Parliament' (n. 1634). 'Would you lay that obligation upon the colliers only, or all the workpeople of Great Britain?' 'I came to speak for the colliers' (n. 1636). 'Why should you distinguish them' (the colliery boys) 'from other boys?' 'Because I think they are an exception to the rule' (n. 1638). 'In what respect?' 'In a physical respect' (n. 1639). 'Why should education be more valuable to them than to other classes of lads?' 'I do not know that it is more valuable; but through the over-exertion in mines there is less chance for the boys that are employed there to get education, either at Sunday schools, or at day schools' (n. 1640). 'It is impossible to look at a question of this sort absolutely by itself?' (n. 1644). 'Is there a sufficiency of schools?' 'No' (n. 1646). 'If the State were to require that every child should be sent to school, would there be schools for the children to go to?' 'No; but I think if the circumstances were to spring up, the schools would be forthcoming' (n. 1647). 'Some of them' (the boys) 'cannot read and write at all, I suppose?' 'The majority cannot . . . The majority of the men themselves cannot' (n. 705, 725).

3. *Employment of women.* Since 1842, women are no longer employed underground, but occupied on the surface in loading the coal, etc., in drawing the tubs to the canals and railway wagons, in sorting, etc. The numbers have increased considerably during the past three or four years (n. 1727). They are mostly the wives, daughters and widows of colliers, and their ages range from 12 to 50 or 60 years (n. 645, 1779). 'What is the feeling among the working miners as to the employment of women?' 'I think they generally condemn it' (n. 648). 'What objection do you see to it?' 'I think it is degrading to the sex' (n. 649). 'There is a peculiarity of dress?' 'Yes . . . it is rather a man's dress, and I believe in some

cases, it drowns all sense of decency.' 'Do the women smoke?' 'Some do.' 'And I suppose it is very dirty work?' 'Very dirty.' 'They get black and grimy?' 'As black as those who are down the mines . . . I believe that a woman having children (and there are plenty on the banks that have) cannot do her duty to her children' (n. 650–54, 710). 'Do you think that those widows could get employment anywhere else, which would bring them in as much wages as that?' (from 8s. to 10s. a week). 'I cannot speak to that' (n. 709). 'You would still be prepared, would you' (stony-hearted fellow!) 'to prevent their obtaining a livelihood by these means?' 'I would' (n. 710). 'What is the general feeling in the district . . . as to the employment of women?' 'The feeling is that it is degrading; and we wish as miners to have more respect to the fair sex than to see them placed on the pit bank . . . Some part of the work is very hard; some of these girls have raised as much as 10 tons of stuff a day' (n. 1715, 1717). 'Do you think that the women employed about the collieries are less moral than the women employed in the factories?' '. . . the percentage of bad ones may be a little more . . . than with the girls in the factories' (n. 1237). 'But you are not quite satisfied with the state of morality in the factories?' 'No' (n. 1733). 'Would you prohibit the employment of women in factories also?' 'No, I would not' (n. 1734). 'Why not?' 'I think it a more honourable occupation for them in the mills' (n. 1735). 'Still it is injurious to their morality, you think?' 'Not so much as working on the pit bank; but it is more on the social position I take it; I do not take it on its moral ground alone. The degradation, in its social bearing on the girls, is deplorable in the extreme. When these 400 or 500 girls become colliers' wives, the men suffer greatly from this degradation, and it causes them to leave their homes and drink' (n. 1736). 'You would be obliged to stop the employment of women in the ironworks as well, would you not, if you stopped it in the collieries?' 'I cannot speak for any other trade' (n. 1737). 'Can you see any difference in the circumstances of women employed in ironworks, and the circumstances of women employed above ground in collieries?' 'I have not ascertained anything as to that' (n. 1740). 'Can you see anything that makes a distinction between one class and the other?' 'I have not ascertained that, but I know from house to house visitation, that it is a deplorable state of things in our district . . .' (n. 1741). 'Would you interfere in every case with the employment of women where that employment was degrading?' 'It would become injurious, I think, in this way; the best feelings of Englishmen have been gained from the instruction of a mother . . .' (n. 1750). 'That equally applies to agricultural employments, does it not?' 'Yes, but that is only for two seasons, and they have work all the four seasons . . . They often work day and night, wet through to the skin, their constitution undermined and their health ruined' (n. 1751). 'You have not inquired more generally into that subject [i.e. the employment of women] perhaps?' 'I have certainly taken note of it as I have gone along, and certainly I have seen nothing parallel to the effects of the employment of women on the pit bank . . . It is the work of a man . . . a strong man' (n. 1753, 1793, 1794). 'Your feeling upon the whole subject is that the better class of colliers who desire to raise themselves and humanize themselves, instead of deriving help from the women, are pulled down by them?' 'Yes' (n. 1808).

After some further crooked questions from these bourgeois, the secret of their 'sympathy' for widows, poor families and so on emerges into the daylight. 'The coal proprietor appoints certain gentlemen to take the oversight of the workings, and it is their policy, in order to receive approbation, to place things on the most economical basis they can, and these girls are employed at from 1s. up to 1s. 6d. a day, where a man at the rate of 2s. 6d. a day would have to be employed' (n. 1816).

4. *Coroner's Juries.* 'With regard to coroner's inquests in your district, have the workmen confidence in the proceedings at those inquests when accidents occur?' 'No; they have not' (n. 360). 'Why not?' 'Chiefly because the men who are generally chosen, are men who know nothing about mines and such like.' 'Are not workmen summoned at all upon the juries?' 'Never but as witnesses to my knowledge.' 'Who are the people who are generally summoned upon these juries?' 'Generally tradesmen in the neighbourhood . . . from their circumstances they are sometimes liable to be influenced by their employers . . . the owners of the works. They are generally men who have no knowledge, and can scarcely understand the witnesses who are called before them, and the terms which are used and such like.' 'Would you have the jury composed of persons who had been employed in mining?' 'Yes, partly . . . they' (the workers) 'think that the verdict is not in accordance with the evidence given generally' (n. 361, 364, 366, 368, 371, 375). 'One great object in summoning a jury is to have an impartial one, is it not?' 'Yes, I should think so.' 'Do you think

that the juries would be impartial if they were composed to a considerable extent of workmen?' 'I cannot see any motive which the workmen would have to act partially ... they necessarily have a better knowledge of the operations in connection with the mine.' 'You do not think there would be a tendency on the part of the workmen to return unfairly severe verdicts?' 'No, I think not' (n. 378, 379, 380).

5. *False weights and measures.* The workers demand to be paid by the week instead of by the fortnight, and by weight instead of by the cubic content of the tubs; they also demand protection against the use of false weights, etc. (n. 1071). 'If the tubs were fraudulently increased, a man could discontinue working by giving 14 days' notice?' 'But if he goes to another place, there is the same thing going on there' (n. 1071). 'But he can leave that place where the wrong has been committed?' 'It is general; wherever he goes, he has to submit to it' (n. 1072). 'Could a man leave by giving 14 days' notice?' 'Yes' (n. 1073). So much for that!

6. *Inspection of mines.* Casualties from gas explosions are not the only things the workers suffer from (n. 234 ff.). 'Our men complained very much of the bad ventilation of the collieries ... the ventilation is so bad in general that the men can scarcely breathe; they are quite unfit for employment of any kind after they have been for a length of time in connection with their work; indeed, just at the part of the mine where I am working, men have been obliged to leave their employment and come home in consequence of that ... some of them have been out of work for weeks just in consequence of the bad state of the ventilation where there is not explosive gas ... there is plenty of air generally in the main courses, yet pains are not taken to get air into the workings where men are working.' 'Why do you not apply to the inspector?' 'To tell the truth there are many men who are timid on that point; there have been cases of men being sacrificed and losing their employment in consequence of applying to the inspector.' 'Why; is he a marked man for having complained?' 'Yes.' 'And he finds it difficult to get employment in another mine?' 'Yes.' 'Do you think the mines in your neighbourhood are sufficiently inspected to insure a compliance with the provisions of the Act?' 'No; they are not inspected at all ... the inspector has been down just once in the pit, and it has been going seven years ... In the district to which I belong there are not a sufficient

number of inspectors. We have one old man more than 70 years of age to inspect more than 130 collieries.' 'You wish to have a class of sub-inspectors?' 'Yes' (n. 234, 241, 251, 254, 274, 275, 554, 276, 293). 'But do you think it would be possible for Government to maintain such an army of inspectors as would be necessary to do all that you want them to do, without information from the men?' 'No, I should think it would be next to impossible.' 'It would be desirable the inspectors should come oftener?' 'Yes, and without being sent for' (n. 280, 277). 'Do you not think that the effect of having these inspectors examining the collieries so frequently would be to shift the responsibility (!) of supplying proper ventilation from the owners of the collieries to the Government officials?' 'No, I do not think that, I think that they should make it their business to enforce the Acts which are already in existence' (n. 285). 'When you speak of sub-inspectors, do you mean men at a less salary, and of an inferior stamp to the present inspectors?' 'I would not have them inferior, if you could get them otherwise' (n. 294). 'Do you merely want more inspectors, or do you want a lower class of men as an inspector?' 'A man who would knock about, and see that things are kept right; a man who would not be afraid of himself' (n. 295). 'If you obtained your wish in getting an inferior class of inspectors appointed, do you think that there would be no danger from want of skill, etc.?' 'I think not, I think that the Government would see after that, and have proper men in that position' (n. 297).

This kind of examination at last becomes too much even for the chairman of the investigating committee, and he interrupts with the observation: 'You want a class of men who would look into all the details of the mine, and would go into all the holes and corners, and go into the real facts ... they would report to the chief inspector, who would then bring his scientific knowledge to bear on the facts they had stated?' (n. 298, 299). 'Would it not entail very great expense if all these old workings were kept ventilated?' 'Yes, expense might be incurred, but life would be at the same time protected' (n. 531). A mining worker protests against Section 17 of the Act of 1860; he says: 'At the present time, if the inspector of mines finds a part of the mine unfit to work in, he has to report it to the mine-owner and the Home Secretary. After doing that, there is given to the owner 20 days to look over the matter; at the end of 20 days he has the power to refuse making any alteration in the mine; but, when he refuses, the mine-owner writes to the Home Secretary, at the same time nominating five engineers, and from those five engineers named by the mine-owner himself, the Home Secretary appoints one, I think, as arbitrator, or appoints arbitrators from them; now we think in that case the mine-owner virtually appoints his own arbitrator' (n. 581). Bourgeois examiner, himself a mine-owner: 'But ... is this a merely speculative objection?' (n. 586). 'Then you have a very poor opinion of the integrity of mining engineers?' 'It is most certainly unjust and inequitable' (n. 588). 'Do not mining engineers possess a sort of public character, and do not you think that they are above making such a partial decision as you apprehend?' 'I do not wish to answer such a question as that with respect to the personal character of those men. I believe that in many cases they would act very partially indeed, and that it ought not to be in their hands to do so, where men's lives are at stake' (n. 589). The same bourgeois has the impudence to put this question: 'Do you not think that the mine-owner also suffers loss from an explosion?' Finally, 'Are not you workmen in Lancashire able to take care of your own interests without calling in the Government to help you?' 'No' (n. 1042).

In the year 1865 there were 3,217 coal mines in Great Britain, and twelve inspectors. A Yorkshire mine-owner himself calculates (*The Times*, 26 January 1867) that, leaving aside the purely bureaucratic activities which absorb the whole of their time, each mine can be visited only once in ten years by an inspector. No wonder mining disasters have increased progressively, both in number and extent (sometimes with a loss of 200 to 300 men) during the last ten years. These are the beauties of 'free' capitalist production!

Defective* as it is, the Act passed in 1872 is the first that regulates the hours of labour of children employed in mines, and makes exploiters and owners, to a certain extent, responsible for so-called accidents.

The Royal Commission appointed in 1867 to inquire into the employment in agriculture of children, young persons and women has published some very important reports. Several attempts have been made to apply the principles of the Factory Acts, in a modified form, to agriculture, but so far these attempts have failed totally.

*The following two paragraphs were added by Engels in the fourth German edition to replace the sentence: 'Finally Professor Fawcett made similar proposals in the House of Commons (1867) for the agricultural labourers.'

However, all I wish to point out here is that there exists an irresistible tendency towards the general application of those principles.

If the general extension of factory legislation to all trades for the purpose of protecting the working class both in mind and body has become inevitable, on the other hand, as we have already pointed out, that extension hastens on the general conversion of numerous isolated small industries into a few combined industries carried on upon a large scale; it therefore accelerates the concentration of capital and the exclusive predominance of the factory system. It destroys both the ancient and the transitional forms behind which the dominion of capital is still partially hidden, and replaces them with a dominion which is direct and unconcealed. But by doing this it also generalizes the direct struggle against its rule. While in each individual workshop it enforces uniformity, regularity, order and economy, the result of the immense impetus given to technical improvement by the limitation and regulation of the working day is to increase the anarchy and the proneness to catastrophe of capitalist production as a whole, the intensity of labour, and the competition of machinery with the worker. By the destruction of small-scale and domestic industries it destroys the last resorts of the 'redundant population', thereby removing what was previously a safety-valve for the whole social mechanism. By maturing the material conditions and the social combination of the process of production, it matures the contradictions and antagonisms of the capitalist form of that process, and thereby ripens both the elements for forming a new society and the forces tending towards the overthrow of the old one.[46]

---

46. Robert Owen, who was the father of the co-operative factories and stores, but who, as we have remarked earlier, in no way shared the illusions of his followers about the field of effectiveness of these isolated elements of transformation, not only made the factory system in practice the sole foundation of his experiments, but also declared that system to be theoretically the point of departure for the social revolution. Herr Vissering, Professor of Political Economy in the University of Leyden, appears to have an inkling of the last point when, in his *Handboek van Praktische Staatshuishoudkunde*, 1860–62, which presents all the platitudes of vulgar economics in their most appropriate form, he expresses his enthusiasm for handicrafts as opposed to large-scale industry. [Added by Engels to the fourth German edition:] The 'inextricable tangle of contradictory enactments' (p. 414) which English legislation called into life by means of the mutually conflicting Factory Acts, the Factory Acts Extension Act and the Workshops Act, finally became intolerable, and thus all legislative enactments on this subject were codified in the Factory and Workshop Act of 1878. We cannot of course present here a

10. LARGE-SCALE INDUSTRY AND AGRICULTURE

The revolution called forth by large-scale industry in agriculture, and in the social relations of agricultural producers, will be investigated later on. Here we shall merely indicate a few results by way of anticipation. If the use of machinery in agriculture is for the most part free from the injurious physical effect it has on the factory worker,[47] its effect in making workers 'redundant' is more

_____

detailed critique of the English industrial code which is now in effect. The following remarks will have to suffice. The Act comprises:

(1) Textile mills. Here everything remains roughly as it was: children more than 10 years of age may work 5½ hours a day, or 6 hours and Saturday off; young persons and women, 10 hours on the five weekdays, and at most 6½ on Saturday.

(2) Non-textile factories. Here the regulations are brought closer than before to those of No. 1, but there are still several exceptions which favour the capitalists and which in certain cases may be expanded by special permission of the Home Secretary.

(3) Workshops, defined approximately as in the former Act. As for the children, young workers and women employed there, the workshops are roughly on a par with the non-textile factories, but again the regulations are made less stringent in certain cases.

(4) Workshops in which no children or young workers are employed, but only persons of both sexes above the age of 18. For this category the regulations are even less stringent.

(5) Domestic workshops, where only members of the family are employed, in the family dwelling. Still more elastic regulations and simultaneously the restriction that, without special permission from the Ministry or a Court, the inspector may only enter rooms which are not also used for dwelling purposes; lastly, unrestricted freedom for straw-plaiting and lace- and glove-making by members of the family. Yet, with all its defects, this Act shares with the Swiss Federal Factory Law of 23 March 1877 the honour of being by far the best piece of legislation in this field. A comparison of it with the said Swiss federal law is of particular interest because it clearly demonstrates the merits and demerits of the two legislative methods – the English, 'historical' method, which intervenes when occasion requires, and the Continental method, which is built up on the traditions of the French Revolution and attempts to frame more general regulations. Unfortunately the English code is still largely a dead letter as regards its application to workshops, owing to the insufficient numbers of inspecting personnel provided.

47. An exhaustive description of the machinery employed in agriculture in England is to be found in a book by Dr W. Hamm, *Die Landwirthschaftlichen Geräthe und Maschinen Englands*, 2nd edn, 1856. In his sketch of the course of development of English agriculture, the author follows Léonce de Lavergne too uncritically.* [Added by Engels to the fourth German edition:] The book is now out of date, of course.

*Léonce de Lavergne, *The Rural Economy of England, Scotland, and Ireland*, London, 1855, is the book Marx has in mind here.

intense and comes up against less resistance, as we shall see later in detail. In the counties of Cambridgeshire and Suffolk, for example, the area of cultivated land has been much extended within the last twenty years* while in the same period the rural population has diminished, not only relatively, but absolutely. In the United States of America the workers are as yet only virtually replaced by agricultural machinery, i.e. the machines allow the producer to cultivate a larger area, but do not actually expel any agricultural labourers employed. In 1861 the number of persons occupied in England and Wales in the manufacture of agricultural machinery was 1,034, while the number of agricultural labourers employed in using agricultural machinery and steam-engines was only 1,205.

In the sphere of agriculture, large-scale industry has a more re-volutionary effect than elsewhere, for the reason that it annihilates the bulwark of the old society, the 'peasant', and substitutes for him the wage-labourer. Thus the need for social transfor-mation, and the antagonism of the classes, reaches the same level in the countryside as it has attained in the towns. A conscious, technological application of science replaces the previous highly irrational and slothfully traditional way of working. The capitalist mode of production completes the disintegration of the primitive familial union which bound agriculture and manufacture together when they were both at an undeveloped and childlike stage. But at the same time it creates the material conditions for a new and higher synthesis, a union of agriculture and industry on the basis of the forms that have developed during the period of their an-tagonistic isolation. Capitalist production collects the population together in great centres, and causes the urban population to achieve an ever-growing preponderance. This has two results. On the one hand it concentrates the historical motive power of society; on the other hand, it disturbs the metabolic interaction between man and the earth, i.e. it prevents the return to the soil of its constituent elements consumed by man in the form of food and clothing; hence it hinders the operation of the eternal natural condition for the lasting fertility of the soil. Thus it destroys at the same time the physical health of the urban worker, and the in-tellectual life of the rural worker.[48] But by destroying the circum-

48. 'You divide the people into two hostile camps of clownish boors and emasculated dwarfs. Good heavens! a nation divided into agricultural and commercial interests, calling itself sane; nay, styling itself enlightened and

*i.e. from 1846 to 1866.

stances surrounding that metabolism, which originated in a merely natural and spontaneous fashion, it compels its systematic restoration as a regulative law of social production, and in a form adequate to the full development of the human race. In agriculture, as in manufacture, the capitalist transformation of the process of production also appears as a martyrology for the producer; the instrument of labour appears as a means of enslaving, exploiting and impoverishing the worker; the social combination of labour processes appears as an organized suppression of his individual vitality, freedom and autonomy. The dispersal of the rural workers over large areas breaks their power of resistance, while concentration increases that of the urban workers. In modern agriculture, as in urban industry, the increase in the productivity and the mobility of labour is purchased at the cost of laying waste and debilitating labour-power itself. Moreover, all progress in capitalist agriculture is a progress in the art, not only of robbing the worker, but of robbing the soil; all progress in increasing the fertility of the soil for a given time is a progress towards ruining the more long-lasting sources of that fertility. The more a country proceeds from large-scale industry as the background of its development, as in the case of the United States, the more rapid is this process of destruction.[49] Capitalist production, therefore, only develops the techniques and the degree of combination of the social process of production by simultaneously undermining the original sources of all wealth – the soil and the worker.

---

civilized, not only in spite of, but in consequence of this monstrous and unnatural division' (David Urquhart, op. cit., p. 119). This passage demonstrates both the strengths and the weaknesses of the kind of criticism which knows how to judge and condemn the present, but not how to comprehend it.

49. See Liebig, *Die Chemie in ihrer Anwendung auf Agricultur und Physiologie*, 7th edn, 1862, and especially the 'Einleitung in die Naturgesetze des Feldbaus' ['Introduction to the Natural Laws of Agriculture'] in Vol. 1. To have developed from the point of view of natural science the negative, i.e. destructive side of modern agriculture, is one of Liebig's immortal merits. Moreover, his brief comments on the history of agriculture, although not free from gross errors, contain flashes of insight. It is however to be regretted that he ventures quite at random on such assertions as the following: 'By greater pulverizing and more frequent ploughing, the circulation of air in the interior of porous soil is aided, and the surface exposed to the action of the atmosphere is increased and renewed; but it is easily seen that the increased yield of the land cannot be proportional to the labour spent on that land, but increases in a much smaller proportion. This law,' adds Liebig, 'was first enunciated by John Stuart Mill in his *Principles of Political Economy*, Vol. I,

p. 17, as follows: "That the produce of land increases, *caeteris paribus*, in a diminishing ratio to the increase of the labourers employed" (Mill here reproduces the law formulated by the Ricardian school in an erroneous form, for since the advance of agriculture in England was accompanied by a "*de-crease* of the labourers employed", this law, although discovered in, and applied to, England, could have no application in that country) "is the universal law of agricultural industry." This is very remarkable, since Mill was ignorant of the reason for this law' (Liebig, op. cit., Vol. 1, p. 143, and note). Apart from Liebig's incorrect interpretation of the word 'labour', a word used in quite a different sense from that adopted by political economy, it is, in any case, 'very remarkable' that he should make John Stuart Mill the first proponent of a theory which James Anderson was the first to publish, in the days of Adam Smith,* and which was repeated in various works down to the beginning of the nineteenth century; a theory which Malthus, that master in plagiarism (his whole population theory is a shameless plagiarism), appropriated in 1815;† which West‡ developed at the same time and independently of Anderson; which in the year 1817 was linked by Ricardo with the general theory of value, then made the round of the world as Ricardo's theory,§ and in 1820 was vulgarized by James Mill, the father of John Stuart Mill; and which was finally reproduced by John Stuart Mill and others as a dogma already quite commonplace, and known to every schoolboy. It is undeniable that the second Mill owes his certainly 'remarkable' authority almost entirely to such mistaken attributions.

*James Anderson (1739–1808), Scottish farmer and economist, first stated this theory in *An Enquiry into the Nature of the Corn Laws; with a View to the new Corn-Bill Proposed for Scotland*, Edinburgh, 1777.

† *An Inquiry into the Nature and Progress of Rent, and the Principles by Which It is Regulated*, London, 1815.

‡ Sir Edward West, *Essay on the Application of Capital to Land*, London, 1815.

§ Cf. *Theories of Surplus-Value*, Part 2, Ch. 9, 'History of the Ricardian Law of Rent', for a detailed exposition of these matters.

Part Five

The Production of Absolute and Relative Surplus-Value

Chapter 16: Absolute and Relative Surplus-Value

In considering the labour process, we began by treating it in the abstract, independently of its historical forms, as a process between man and nature (see Chapter 5). We stated there: 'If we look at the whole [labour] process from the point of view of its result, the product, it is plain that both the instruments of labour and the object of labour are means of production, and that the labour itself is productive labour.'* And in note 8 we added further: 'This method of determining what is productive labour, from the standpoint of the simple labour process, is by no means sufficient to cover the capitalist process of production.' We must now develop this point further.

In so far as the labour process is purely individual, the same worker unites in himself all the functions that later on become separated. When an individual appropriates natural objects for his own livelihood, he alone supervises his own activity. Later on he is supervised by others. The solitary man cannot operate upon nature without calling his own muscles into play under the control of his own brain. Just as head and hand belong together in the system of nature, so in the labour process mental and physical labour are united. Later on they become separate; and this separation develops into a hostile antagonism. The product is transformed from the direct product of the individual producer into a social product, the joint product of a collective labourer, i.e. a combination of workers, each of whom stands at a different distance from the actual manipulation of the object of labour. With the progressive accentuation of the co-operative character of the labour process, there necessarily occurs a progressive extension of the concept of productive labour, and of the concept of the bearer of that labour, the productive worker. In order to work productively, it is no longer necessary for the individual himself to

* See above, p. 287.

put his hand to the object; it is sufficient for him to be an organ of the collective labourer, and to perform any one of its subordinate functions. The definition of productive labour given above, the original definition, is derived from the nature of material production itself, and it remains correct for the collective labourer, considered as a whole. But it no longer holds good for each member taken individually.

Yet the concept of productive labour also becomes narrower. Capitalist production is not merely the production of commodities, it is, by its very essence, the production of surplus-value. The worker produces not for himself, but for capital. It is no longer sufficient, therefore, for him simply to produce. He must produce surplus-value. The only worker who is productive is one who produces surplus-value for the capitalist, or in other words contributes towards the self-valorization of capital. If we may take an example from outside the sphere of material production, a schoolmaster is a productive worker when, in addition to belabouring the heads of his pupils, he works himself into the ground to enrich the owner of the school. That the latter has laid out his capital in a teaching factory, instead of a sausage factory, makes no difference to the relation. The concept of a productive worker therefore implies not merely a relation between the activity of work and its useful effect, between the worker and the product of his work, but also a specifically social relation of production, a relation with a historical origin which stamps the worker as capital's direct means of valorization. To be a productive worker is therefore not a piece of luck, but a misfortune. In Volume 4 of this work, which deals with the history of the theory,* we shall show that the classical political economists always made the production of surplus-value the distinguishing characteristic of the productive worker. Hence their definition of a productive worker varies with their conception of the nature of surplus-value. Thus the Physiocrats insist that only agricultural labour is productive, since that alone, they say, yields a surplus-value. For the Physiocrats, indeed, surplus-value exists exclusively in the form of ground rent.

*The intended fourth volume was never published by Marx or by Engels, but the manuscripts on the history of the theory of surplus-value, written by Marx between January 1862 and July 1863, were preserved, and published by Kautsky between 1905 and 1910. The first complete English translation was issued in three parts between 1963 and 1972 by Lawrence and Wishart, under the title *Theories of Surplus-Value.*

The prolongation of the working day beyond the point at which the worker would have produced an exact equivalent for the value of his labour-power, and the appropriation of that surplus labour by capital – this is the process which constitutes the production of absolute surplus-value. It forms the general foundation of the capitalist system, and the starting-point for the production of relative surplus-value. The latter presupposes that the working day is already divided into two parts, necessary labour and surplus labour. In order to prolong the surplus labour, the necessary labour is shortened by methods for producing the equivalent of the wage of labour in a shorter time. The production of absolute surplus-value turns exclusively on the length of the working day, whereas the production of relative surplus-value completely revolutionizes the technical processes of labour and the groupings into which society is divided.

It therefore requires a specifically capitalist mode of production, a mode of production which, along with its methods, means and conditions, arises and develops spontaneously on the basis of the formal subsumption [*Subsumtion*]* of labour under capital. This formal subsumption is then replaced by a real subsumption.

It will be sufficient if we merely refer to certain hybrid forms, in which although surplus labour is not extorted by direct compulsion from the producer, the producer has not yet become formally subordinate to capital. In these forms, capital has not yet acquired a direct control over the labour process. Alongside the independent producers, who carry on their handicrafts or their agriculture in the inherited, traditional way, there steps the usurer or merchant with his usurer's capital or merchant's capital, which feeds on them like a parasite. The predominance of this form of exploitation in a society excludes the capitalist mode of production, although it may form the transition to capitalism, as in the later Middle Ages. Finally, as in the case of modern 'domestic industry', certain hybrid forms are reproduced here and there against the background of large-scale industry, though their physiognomy is totally changed.

A merely formal subsumption of labour under capital suffices for the production of absolute surplus-value. It is enough, for example, that handicraftsmen who previously worked on their own account, or as apprentices of a master, should become wage-labourers under the direct control of a capitalist. But we have seen

*See below, pp. 1019–38, for Marx's own exposition of the concepts of formal and real subsumption.

how methods of producing relative surplus-value are, at the same time, methods of producing absolute surplus-value. Indeed, the unrestricted prolongation of the working day turned out to be a very characteristic product of large-scale industry. The specifically capitalist mode of production ceases in general to be a mere means of producing relative surplus-value as soon as it has conquered an entire branch of production; this tendency is still more powerful when it has conquered all the important branches of production. It then becomes the universal, socially predominant form of the production process. It only continues to act as a special method of producing relative surplus-value in two respects: first, in so far as it seizes upon industries previously only formally subordinate to capital, that is, in so far as it continues to proselytize, and second, in so far as the industries already taken over continue to be revolutionized by changes in the methods of production.[8]

From one standpoint the distinction between absolute and relative surplus-value appears to be illusory. Relative surplus-value is absolute, because it requires the absolute prolongation of the working day beyond the labour-time necessary to the existence of the worker himself. Absolute surplus-value is relative, because it requires a development of the productivity of labour which will allow the necessary labour-time to be restricted to a portion of the working day. But if we keep in mind the movement of surplus-value, this semblance of identity vanishes. Once the capitalist mode of production has become the established and universal mode of production, the difference between absolute and relative surplus-value makes itself felt whenever there is a question of raising the rate of surplus-value. Assuming that labour-power is paid for at its value, we are confronted with this alternative: on the one hand, if the productivity of labour and its normal degree of intensity is given, the rate of surplus-value can be raised only by prolonging the working day in absolute terms; on the other hand, if the length of the working day is given, the rate of surplus-value can be raised only by a change in the relative magnitudes of the components of the working day, i.e. necessary labour and surplus labour, and if wages are not to fall below the value of labour-power, this change presupposes a change in either the productivity or the intensity of the labour.

If the worker needs to use all his time to produce the necessary means of subsistence for himself and his family, he has no time left in which to perform unpaid labour for other people. Unless labour has attained a certain level of productivity, the worker will have no such free time at his disposal, and without superfluous time there can be no surplus labour, hence no capitalists, as also no slave-owners, no feudal barons, in a word no class of large-scale landed proprietors.[1]

Thus we may say that surplus-value rests on a natural basis, but only in the very general sense that there is no natural obstacle absolutely preventing one man from lifting from himself the burden of the labour necessary to maintain his own existence, and imposing it on another, just as there is no unconquerable natural obstacle to the consumption of the flesh of one man by another.[2] It would be absolutely mistaken to attach mystical notions to this spontaneously developed productivity of labour, as is sometimes done. It is only when men have worked their way out of their initial animal condition, when therefore their labour has been to some extent socialized, that a situation arises in which the surplus labour of one person becomes a condition of existence for another. At the dawn of civilization, the productive powers acquired by labour are small, but so too are the needs which develop with and upon the means of their satisfaction. Furthermore, at that early period, the portion of society that lives on the labour of others is infinitely small compared with the mass of direct producers. As the social productivity of labour advances, this small portion of society increases both absolutely and relatively.[3] Besides, the capital-relation arises out of an economic soil that is the product of a long process of development. The existing productivity of labour, from which it proceeds as its basis, is a gift, not of nature, but of a history embracing thousands of centuries.

Even if we leave aside the question of the level of development attained by social production, the productivity of labour remains fettered by natural conditions. These conditions can all be traced back to the nature of man himself (his race, etc.) and to the natural

1. 'The very existence of the master-capitalists, as a distinct class, is dependent on the productiveness of industry' (Ramsay, op. cit., p. 206). 'If each man's labour were but enough to produce his own food, there could be no property' (Ravenstone, op. cit., pp. 14, 15).

2. According to a recent calculation there are still at least 4,000,000 cannibals in those parts of the earth which have so far been explored.

3. 'Among the wild Indians in America, almost everything is the labourer's, 99 parts of a hundred are to be put upon the account of labour. In England, perhaps, the labourer has not two thirds' (*The Advantages of the East-India Trade, etc.*, pp. 72, 73).

objects which surround him. External natural conditions can be divided from the economic point of view into two great classes, namely (1) natural wealth in the means of subsistence, i.e. a fruitful soil, waters teeming with fish, etc., and (2) natural wealth in the instruments of labour, such as waterfalls, navigable rivers, wood, metal, coal, etc. At the dawn of civilization, it is the first class that turns the scale; at a higher stage of development, it is the second. Compare for example England with India, or, in ancient times, Athens and Corinth with the shores of the Black Sea.

The smaller the number of natural requirements imperatively calling for satisfaction, and the greater the natural fertility of the soil and the kindness of the climate, the smaller the amount of labour-time necessary for the maintenance and reproduction of the producer. Hence the greater the quantity of excess labour the producer can perform for others, in addition to the labour he does for himself. This was pointed out long ago by Diodorus when discussing the ancient Egyptians: 'It is altogether incredible how little trouble and expense the bringing-up of their children causes them. They cook for them the first simple food at hand; they also give them the lower part of the papyrus stem to eat, if it can be roasted in the fire, and the roots and stalks of marsh plants, some raw, some boiled and roasted. Most of the children go without shoes and unclothed, since the air is very mild. Hence a child, until he is grown up, costs his parents not more than twenty drachmas altogether. This is the main reason why the population of Egypt is so numerous, and, therefore, why so many great works can be undertaken.'[4] Nevertheless, the gigantic building projects of ancient Egypt owed less to the size of the population than to the large proportion of it that was freely disposable. Just as, in the case of the individual worker, the less his necessary labour-time, the more surplus labour he can provide, so, in the case of the working population, the smaller the portion of it required for the production of the necessary means of subsistence, the greater the portion available for other work.

If we assume capitalist production, then, with all other circumstances remaining the same, and the length of the working day a given factor, the quantity of surplus labour will vary according to the natural conditions within which labour is carried on, in particular the fertility of the soil. But it by no means follows, in-

4. Diodorus Siculus, op. cit., Bk I, 80.

versely, that the most fertile soil is the most fitted for the growth of the capitalist mode of production. The latter presupposes the domination of man over nature. Where nature is too prodigal with her gifts, she 'keeps him in hand, like a child in leading-strings'. Man's own development is not in that case a nature-imposed necessity.[5] The mother country of capital is not the tropical region, with its luxuriant vegetation, but the temperate zone. It is not the absolute fertility of the soil but its degree of differentiation, the variety of its natural products, which forms the natural basis for the social division of labour, and which, by changes in the natural surroundings, spurs man on to the multiplication of his needs, his capacities, and the instruments and modes of his labour. It is the necessity of bringing a natural force under the control of society, of economizing on its energy, of appropriating or subduing it on a large scale by the work of the human hand, that plays the most decisive role in the history of industry. Thus, for example, the regulation of the flow of water in Egypt,[6] Lombardy and Holland. Or irrigation in India, Persia and so on, where artificial canals not only supply the soil with the water indispensable to it, but also carry down mineral fertilizers from the hills, in the shape of sediment. The secret of the flourishing state of industry in

5. 'The first' (natural wealth) 'as it is most noble and advantageous, so doth it make the people careless, proud, and given to all excesses; whereas the second [wealth acquired through labour] enforceth vigilancy, literature, arts, and policy' (*England's Treasure by Forraign Trade. Or the Balance of our Forraign Trade is the Rule of our Treasure*. Written by Thomas Mun of London, merchant, and now published for the common good by his son John Mun, London, 1669, pp. 181, 182). 'Nor can I conceive a greater curse upon a body of people, than to be thrown upon a spot of land, where the productions for subsistence and food were, in great measure, spontaneous, and the climate required or admitted little care for raiment and covering . . . there may be an extreme on the other side. A soil incapable of produce by labour is quite as bad as a soil that produces plentifully without any labour' ([N. Forster,] *An Enquiry into the Causes of the Present High Price of Provisions*, London, 1767, p. 10).

6. The necessity for predicting the rise and fall of the Nile created Egyptian astronomy, and with it the domination of the priests as the directors of agriculture. 'The solstice is the moment of the year when the Nile begins to rise, and it is the moment the Egyptians have had to watch for with the greatest attention . . . It was the evolution of this tropical year which they had to establish firmly so as to conduct their agricultural operations in accordance with it. They therefore had to search the heavens for a visible sign of the solstice's return' (Cuvier, *Discours sur les révolutions du globe*, ed. Hoefer, Paris, 1863, p. 141).

Spain and Sicily under the rule of the Arabs lay in their irrigation works.[7]

Favourable natural conditions can provide in themselves only the possibility, never the reality of surplus labour, nor, accordingly, the reality of surplus-value and a surplus product. The result of differences in the natural conditions of labour is this: the same quantity of labour satisfies a different mass of requirements[8] in different countries, and consequently under otherwise analogous circumstances, the quantity of necessary labour-time is different. These conditions affect surplus labour only as natural limits, i.e. by determining the point at which labour for others can begin. In proportion as industry advances these natural limits recede. In the midst of our Western European society, where the worker can only purchase the right to work for his own existence by performing surplus labour for others, it is very easy to imagine that it is an inherent quality of human labour to furnish a surplus product.[9] But consider, for example, an inhabitant of the islands of the East Indies, where sago grows wild in the forests. 'When the inhabi-

7. One of the material foundations of the power of the state over the small and unconnected producing organisms of India was the regulation of the water supply. Its Mohammedan rulers understood this better than their English successors. It is sufficient to recall the famine of 1866, which cost the lives of more than a million Hindus in the district of Orissa, in the Bengal Presidency.

8. 'There are no two countries which furnish an equal number of the necessaries of life in equal plenty, and with the same quantity of labour. Men's wants increase or diminish with the severity or temperateness of the climate they live in; consequently, the proportion of trade which the inhabitants of different countries are obliged to carry on through necessity cannot be the same, nor is it practicable to ascertain the degree of variation farther than by the degrees of Heat and Cold; from whence one may make this general conclusion, that the quantity of labour required for a certain number of people is greatest in cold climates, and least in hot ones; for in the former men not only want more clothes, but the earth more cultivating than in the latter' (*An Essay on the Governing Causes of the Natural Rate of Interest*, London, 1750, p. 59). The author of this epoch-making anonymous work, from which Hume took his theory of interest, was J. Massie.*

9. 'All labour must' (apparently this is also part of the 'rights and duties of the citizen') 'leave a surplus' (Proudhon).†

* Hume's essay, 'Of Interest', was published in 1752. In it he expressed the view that the rate of interest was dependent on 'the level of profits arising from commerce'. This was anticipated by Massie, in the work quoted. Cf. *Theories of Surplus-Value*, Part I, pp. 373–7.

† Proudhon, *Système des contradictions économiques, ou philosophie de la misère*, Vol. 1, Paris, 1846, p. 73.

tants have convinced themselves, by boring a hole in the tree, that the pith is ripe, the trunk is cut down and divided into several pieces, the pith is extracted, mixed with water and filtered: it is then quite fit for use as sago. One tree commonly yields 300 lb., and occasionally 500 to 600 lb. There, then, people go into the forests and cut bread for themselves, just as with us they cut fire-wood.'[10] Suppose now that an East Indian bread-cutter of this kind requires 12 working hours a week for the satisfaction of all his needs. Nature's direct gift to him is plenty of leisure time. Before he can apply this leisure time productively for himself, a whole series of historical circumstances is required; before he spends it in surplus labour for others, compulsion is necessary. If capitalist production were introduced, the good fellow would perhaps have to work six days a week, in order to appropriate to himself the product of one working day. In that case, the bounty of nature would not explain why he now has to work six days a week, or why he must provide five days of surplus labour. It explains only why his necessary labour-time would be limited to one day a week. But in no case would his surplus product arise from some innate, occult quality of human labour.

Thus both the historically developed productive forces of labour in society, and its naturally conditioned productive forces, appear as productive forces of the capital into which that labour is incorporated.

Ricardo never concerns himself with the origin of surplus-value. He treats it as an entity inherent in the capitalist mode of production, and in his eyes the latter is the natural form of social production. Whenever he discusses the productivity of labour, he seeks in it not the cause of the existence of surplus-value, but the cause that determines the magnitude of that value. On the other hand, his school has loudly proclaimed that the productive power of labour is the originating cause of profit (read: surplus-value). This is at least an advance in comparison with the Mercantilists, who derive the excess of the price of a product over its cost of production from the act of exchange, from the sale of the product above its value. Nevertheless, Ricardo's school also merely evaded the problem rather than solving it. In fact, these bourgeois economists instinctively and rightly saw that it was very dangerous to

10. F. Schouw, *Die Erde, die Pflanze und der Mensch*, 2nd edn, Leipzig, 1854, p. 148.

penetrate too deeply into the burning question of the origin of surplus-value. But what are we to think of John Stuart Mill, who, half a century after Ricardo, solemnly claims superiority over the Mercantilists by clumsily repeating the wretched evasions of Ricardo's earliest vulgarizers?

Mill says: 'The cause of profit is that labour produces more than is required for its support.' So far, nothing but the old story: but Mill, wishing to add something of his own, proceeds as follows: 'To vary the form of the theorem; the reason why capital yields a profit, is because food, clothing, materials and tools, last longer than the time which was required to produce them.' Here he confuses the duration of labour-time with the duration of its products. On this view, a baker, whose products last only a day, could never extract the same profit from his workers as a machine manufacturer, whose products last for twenty years or more. Of course, it is very true that if a bird's nest did not last longer than the time it takes to build, the birds would have to do without nests.

This fundamental truth once established, Mill asserts his own superiority over the Mercantilists: 'We thus see that profit arises, not from the incident of exchange, but from the productive power of labour; and the general profit of the country is always what the productive power of labour makes it, whether any exchange takes place or not. If there were no division of employments, there would be no buying or selling, but there would still be profit.' For Mill then, exchange, buying and selling, i.e. the general conditions of capitalist production, are a mere incident, and there would always be profits even without the purchase and sale of labour-power!

'If,' he continues, 'the labourers of the country collectively produce 20 per cent more than their wages, profits will be 20 per cent, whatever prices may or may not be.' This is, in one respect, a rare piece of tautology; for if the workers produce a surplus-value of 20 per cent for the capitalist, his profit will be related to their total wages in the proportion 20:100. Nevertheless, it is absolutely false to say that 'profits will be 20 per cent'. They will always be less, because they are calculated upon the sum total of the capital advanced. If, for example, the capitalist has advanced £500, of which £400 is laid out in means of production and £100 in wages, and if the rate of surplus-value is 20 per cent, the rate of profit will be 20:500, i.e. not 20 per cent but 4 per cent.

There follows a splendid example of Mill's way of handling the different historical forms of social production: 'I assume, throughout, the state of things which, [where the labourers and capitalists are separate classes], prevails, with few exceptions, universally; namely, that the capitalist advances the whole expenses, including the entire remuneration of the labourer.' Strange optical illusion, to see everywhere a situation which as yet exists only exceptionally on our earth! But let us proceed. Mill is good enough to make this concession: 'That he should do so is not a matter of inherent necessity.'* On the contrary, 'the labourer might wait, until the production is complete, for all that part of his wages which exceeds mere necessaries; and even for the whole, if he has funds in hand sufficient for his temporary support. But in the latter case, the labourer is to that extent really a capitalist in the concern, by supplying a portion of the funds necessary for carrying it on.' Mill might just as well have said that the worker who advances to himself not only the means of subsistence but also the means of production is in reality his own wage-labourer, or, indeed, that the American peasant is his own slave, because he does forced labour for himself instead of doing it for someone who is his master.

After thus proving clearly that capitalist production would still continue to exist even if it did not exist, Mill now proceeds, quite consistently, to show that it would not exist even if it did exist. 'And even in the former case' (where the worker is a wage-labourer to whom the capitalist advances the whole of his means of subsistence) 'he' (the worker) 'may be looked upon in the same light' (i.e. as a capitalist) 'since, contributing his labour at less than the market price (!), he may be regarded as lending the difference (?) to his employer and receiving it back with interest, etc.'[11] In

11. J. St. Mill, *Principles of Political Economy*, London, 1868, pp. 252–3 passim.

*If he had had the opportunity, Marx would certainly have altered this passage. The addition of the phrase in square brackets, 'where the labourers and capitalists are separate classes', omitted inadvertently by Marx, clears Mill, at least formally, from the charge of being guilty of an 'optical illusion'. Hence, in a letter of 28 November 1878 to N. F. Danielson, Marx proposed the replacement of the passage beginning 'Strange optical illusion' with this: 'Mr Mill is willing to concede that it is not absolutely necessary for it to be so, even under an economic system where workers and capitalists confront each other as separate classes.' [This note draws heavily on information provided in *MEW* 23, p. 540.]

reality, the worker advances his labour gratuitously to the capitalist during, say, one week, in order to receive its market price at the end of the week, etc.: according to Mill this makes him into a capitalist! On a level plain, simple mounds look like hills; and the insipid flatness of our present bourgeoisie is to be measured by the altitude of its 'great intellects'.

Chapter 17: Changes of Magnitude in the Price of Labour-Power and in Surplus-Value

The value of labour-power is determined by the value of the means of subsistence habitually required by the average worker. The quantity of the means of subsistence required is given at any particular epoch in any particular society, and can therefore be treated as a constant magnitude. What changes is the value of this quantity. There are, besides, two other factors that enter into the determination of the value of labour-power. One is the cost of developing that power, which varies with the mode of production. The other is the natural diversity of labour-power, the difference between the labour-power of men and women, children and adults. The utilization of these different sorts of labour-power, which is in turn conditioned by the mode of production, makes for great variations in the cost of reproducing the worker's family, and in the value of the labour-power of the adult male. Both these factors, however, are excluded in the following investigation.[1]

I assume (1) that commodities are sold at their value, (2) that the price of labour-power occasionally rises above its value, but never sinks below it.

On these assumptions, we have already found that the relative magnitudes of surplus-value and of price of labour-power are determined by three circumstances: (1) the length of the working day, or the extensive magnitude of labour, (2) the normal intensity of labour, or its intensive magnitude, whereby a given quantity of labour is expended in a given time and (3) the productivity of labour, whereby the same quantity of labour yields, in a given time, a greater or a smaller quantity of the product, depending on the degree of development attained by the conditions of production. Very different combinations are clearly pos-

1. [Note by Engels to the third German edition:] The case considered on pages 433–6 is also excluded here, of course.

sible, since one of the three factors can be constant while the other two vary, two factors can be constant while one varies, and, finally, all three may vary. In addition, the number of possible combinations is augmented by the fact that, when all these factors vary simultaneously, the amount and direction of their respective variations may differ. In what follows the chief combinations alone are considered.

I. THE LENGTH OF THE WORKING DAY AND THE INTENSITY OF LABOUR CONSTANT; THE PRODUCTIVITY OF LABOUR VARIABLE

On these assumptions the value of labour-power and the magnitude of surplus-value are determined by three laws.

Firstly, a working day of a given length always creates the same amount of value, no matter how the productivity of labour, and, with it, the mass of the product and the price of each single commodity produced may vary. If the value created by a working day of 12 hours is, say, 6 shillings, then, although the mass of the use-values produced varies with the productivity of labour, the value represented by 6 shillings will simply be spread over a greater or a less number of commodities.

Secondly, the value of labour-power and surplus-value vary in opposite directions. A variation in the productivity of labour, its increase or diminution, causes the value of labour-power to move in the opposite direction, while surplus-value moves in the same direction.

The value created by a working day of 12 hours is a constant quantity, say 6 shillings. This constant quantity is the sum of the surplus-value plus the value of the labour-power, the value of the labour-power being replaced with an equivalent by the worker himself. It is self-evident that if a constant quantity consists of two parts, neither of them can increase without the other diminishing. Let the two parts be equal at the beginning, and let 3 shillings be the value of the labour-power, and the same for the surplus-value. Then the value of the labour-power cannot rise from 3 shillings to 4 without the surplus-value falling from 3 shillings to 2; and the surplus-value cannot rise from 3 shillings to 4 without the value of the labour-power falling from 3 shillings to 2. Under these circumstances, then, no change can take place in the absolute magnitude either of the surplus-value or of the value of the labour-power without a simultaneous change in their relative magnitudes. It is impossible for them to rise or fall simultaneously.

Further, the value of the labour-power cannot fall, and consequently surplus-value cannot rise, without a rise in the productivity of labour. For instance, in the above case, the value of the labour-power cannot sink from 3 shillings to 2 unless an increase in the productivity of labour makes it possible to produce in 4 hours the same quantity of means of subsistence as could only be produced previously in 6 hours. On the other hand, the value of the labour-power cannot rise from 3 shillings to 4 without a decrease in the productivity of labour, so that 8 hours are required to produce the same quantity of means of subsistence as were previously produced in 6 hours. It follows from this that an increase in the productivity of labour causes a fall in the value of labour-power and a consequent rise in surplus-value, while, on the other hand, a decrease in the productivity of labour causes a rise in the value of labour-power and a fall in surplus-value.

In formulating this law,* Ricardo overlooked one thing: although a change in the magnitude of the surplus-value or surplus labour causes a change in the opposite direction in the magnitude of the value of labour-power, or in the quantity of necessary labour, it by no means follows that they vary in the same proportion. It is true that they increase or diminish by the same *quantity*. But their proportional increase or diminution depends on their original magnitude, before the change in the productivity of labour took place. If the value of the labour-power is 4 shillings, or the necessary labour-time is 8 hours, and the surplus-value is 2 shillings, or the surplus labour 4 hours, and if, owing to an increase in the productivity of labour, the value of the labour-power falls to 3 shillings, or the necessary labour-time to 6 hours, the surplus-value will rise to 3 shillings, or the surplus labour to 6 hours. The same quantity, 1 shilling or 2 hours, is added in one case, and subtracted in the other. But the proportional change of magnitude is different in the two cases. The value of the labour-power falls from 4 shillings to 3, i.e. it falls by $\frac{1}{4}$, or 25 per cent,

*Cf. Ricardo, *On the Principles of Political Economy*, p. 31, where the following formulation is given: 'There can be no rise in the value of labour without a fall of profits.' This could be re-formulated in Marxist terms as 'There can be no rise in the value of labour-power without a fall in surplus-value.' The whole question of Ricardo's theory of surplus-value is discussed in far more detail in *Theories of Surplus-Value*, Part 2, London, 1969, pp. 373–425.

but the surplus-value rises from 2 shillings to 3, i.e. it rises by $\frac{1}{2}$, or 50 per cent. It therefore follows that the proportional increase or diminution in surplus-value resulting from a given change in the productivity of labour depends on the original magnitude of that portion of the working day which is embodied in surplus-value; the smaller that portion, the greater the proportional change; the greater that portion, the less the proportional change.

(3) Increase or diminution in surplus-value is always the consequence, and never the cause, of the corresponding diminution or increase in the value of labour-power.[2]

Since the working day is constant in magnitude, and is represented by a value of constant magnitude, since there corresponds to every variation in the magnitude of surplus-value an inverse variation in the value of labour-power, and since the value of labour-power cannot change except as a result of a change in the productivity of labour, it clearly follows under these conditions that every change of magnitude in surplus-value arises from an inverse change of magnitude in the value of labour-power. If, then, as we have already seen, there can be no change of absolute magnitude in the value of labour-power, and in surplus-value, unaccompanied by a change in their relative magnitudes, it now follows that no change in their relative magnitudes is possible without a change in the absolute magnitude of the value of labour-power.

According to the third law, a change in the magnitude of surplus-value presupposes a movement in the value of labour-power, brought about by a change in the productivity of labour. The limit of this change is given by the altered value of labour-power. Nevertheless, even when circumstances allow the law to operate, subsidiary movements may occur. For example, if, as a result of an increase in the productivity of labour, the value of labour-power falls from 4 shillings to 3, or the necessary labour-

2. MacCulloch, among other people, has made the following absurd addition to this third law: he says that a rise in surplus-value which is not accompanied by a fall in the value of labour-power can occur as a result of the abolition of taxes formerly payable by the capitalist. But the abolition of such taxes makes no change whatever in the quantity of surplus-value extorted by the capitalist at first hand from the worker. It only alters the proportion in which that surplus-value is divided between the capitalist himself and third persons. It therefore produces no change whatsoever in the relation between surplus-value and the value of labour-power. MacCulloch's exception therefore proves only his failure to understand the rule, a misfortune that as often happens to him in the vulgarization of Ricardo as it does to J. B. Say in the vulgarization of Adam Smith.

time from 8 hours to 6, the price of labour-power might well fall only to 3s. 8d., 3s. 6d. or 3s. 2d., thus allowing the amount of surplus-value to rise only to 3s. 4d., 3s. 6d. or 3s. 10d. The amount of this fall, the lowest limit of which is 3 shillings (the new value of labour-power), depends on the relative weight thrown into the scale by the pressure of capital on the one side, and the resistance of the worker on the other.

The value of labour-power is determined by the value of a certain quantity of means of subsistence. It is the value and not the mass of these means of subsistence that varies with the productivity of labour. It is however possible that owing to an increase in the productivity of labour both the worker and the capitalist may simultaneously be able to appropriate a greater quantity of means of subsistence, without any change in the price of labour-power or in surplus-value. Let the value of labour-power be 3 shillings, and let the necessary labour-time amount to 6 hours. Let the surplus-value be, similarly, 3 shillings, and the surplus labour 6 hours. Now, if the productivity of labour were to be doubled without any alteration in the ratio between necessary labour and surplus labour, there would be no change in the magnitude either of the surplus-value or of the price of labour-power. The only result would be that each of these would represent twice as many use-values as before, and that each use-value would be twice as cheap as it was before. Although labour-power would be unchanged in price, it would have risen above its value. However, now assume a fall in the price of labour-power, not as far as 1s. 6d., the lowest possible point consistent with its new value, but to 2s. 10d. or 2s. 6d. This lower price would still represent an increased quantity of means of subsistence. In this way it is possible, given increasing productivity of labour, for the price of labour-power to fall constantly and for this fall to be accompanied by a constant growth in the mass of the worker's means of subsistence. But in relative terms, i.e. in comparison with surplus-value, the value of labour-power would keep falling, and thus the abyss between the life-situation of the worker and that of the capitalist would keep widening.[3]

3. 'When an alteration takes place in the productiveness of industry, so that either more or less is produced by a given quantity of labour and capital, the proportion of wages may obviously vary, whilst the quantity, which that proportion represents, remains the same, or the quantity may vary, whilst the proportion remains the same' ([J. Cazenove,] *Outlines of Political Economy, etc.* p. 67).

Ricardo was the first to give an accurate formulation of the three laws we have just stated. But his presentation of them suffers from the following defects: (1) he views the special conditions under which these laws hold good as the self-evident, universal, and exclusive conditions of capitalist production. He recognizes no change either in the length of the working day or in the intensity of labour, so that with him the productivity of labour becomes the only variable factor; (2), and this error vitiates his analysis much more than (1), he has not, any more than the other economists, investigated surplus-value as such, i.e. independently of its particular forms, such as profit, ground rent, etc. He therefore fails to differentiate between the laws governing the rate of surplus-value and those governing the rate of profit. The rate of profit is, as we have already said, the ratio of the surplus-value to the total capital advanced; the rate of surplus-value is the ratio of the surplus-value to the variable part of that capital. Assume that a capital C of £500 is made up of raw material, instruments of labour, etc. which, taken together, we shall call c, to the amount of £400, and of wages v, to the amount of £100; and assume, further, that the surplus value $s = $ £100. Then the rate of surplus-value will be $\frac{s}{v} = \frac{£100}{£100} = 100$ per cent. But the rate of profit will be $\frac{s}{C} = \frac{£100}{£500} = 20$ per cent. It is obvious, moreover, that the rate of profit may depend on circumstances which in no way affect the rate of surplus-value. I shall show in Volume 3 that the same rate of surplus-value may be expressed in the most diverse rates of profit, and that different rates of surplus-value may, under certain circumstances, be expressed in the same rate of profit.*

2. THE LENGTH OF THE WORKING DAY AND THE PRODUCTIVITY OF LABOUR CONSTANT; THE INTENSITY OF LABOUR VARIABLE

Increased intensity of labour means increased expenditure of labour in a given time. Hence a working day of more intense labour is embodied in more products than is one of less intense labour, the length of each working day being the same. Admit-

* Cf. *Capital*, Vol. 3, Chapter 3, 'The Relation of the Rate of Profit to the Rate of Surplus-Value'.

tedly, an increase in the productivity of labour will also supply more products in a given working day. But in that case the value of each single product falls, for it costs less labour than before, whereas in the case mentioned here that value remains unchanged, because each article costs the same amount of labour as before. Here we have an increase in the number of products unaccompanied by a fall in their individual prices: as their number increases, so does the sum of their prices, whereas in the case of an increase in productivity, a given value is spread over a greater mass of products. Hence, if the length of the working day remains constant, a day's labour of increased intensity will be incorporated in an increased amount of value, and, assuming no change in the value of money, in an increased amount of money. The value created varies with the extent to which the intensity of labour diverges from its normal social level of intensity. A given working day, therefore, no longer creates a constant value, but a variable one; in a day of 12 hours of ordinary intensity, the value created is, say, 6 shillings, but, with increased intensity, the value created may be 7, 8 or more shillings. It is clear that if the value created by a day's labour increases from, say, 6 to 8 shillings, then the two parts into which this value is divided, namely the price of labour-power and surplus-value, may both increase simultaneously, and either equally or unequally. They may both simultaneously increase from 3 shillings to 4. Here, the rise in the price of labour-power does not necessarily imply that it has risen above the value of labour-power. On the contrary, this rise in price may be accompanied by a fall below its value. This always occurs when the rise in the price of labour-power does not compensate for its more rapid deterioration.

We know that, with exceptions which are purely temporary, a change in the productivity of labour does not cause any change in the value of labour-power, nor, consequently, in the magnitude of surplus-value, unless the products of the industries affected are articles habitually consumed by the workers. But here this limitation falls to the ground. Whether the magnitude of the labour changes in extent or in intensity, there is always a corresponding change in the magnitude of the value created, independently of the nature of the article in which that value is embodied.

If the intensity of labour were to increase simultaneously and equally in every branch of industry, then the new and higher degree of intensity would become the normal social degree of intensity, and would therefore cease to count as an extensive magnitude. But even so, the intensity of labour would still be different in different countries, and would modify the application of the law of value to the working days of different nations. The more intensive working day of one nation would be represented by a greater sum of money than the less intensive day of another nation.[4]

3. THE PRODUCTIVITY AND INTENSITY OF LABOUR CONSTANT; THE LENGTH OF THE WORKING DAY VARIABLE

The working day may vary in two directions. It may be either shortened or lengthened. (From our present data, and within the limits of the assumptions made on p. 655, we obtain the following laws:

(1) The working day creates a greater or lesser amount of value in proportion to its length – thus, a variable and not a constant quantity of value.

(2) Every change in the relation between the magnitude of surplus-value and the value of labour-power arises from a change in the absolute magnitude of the surplus labour, and consequently of the surplus-value.

(3) The absolute value of labour-power can change only in consequence of the reaction exercised by the prolongation of surplus labour upon the wear and tear of labour-power. Every change in this absolute value is therefore the effect, but never the cause, of a change in the magnitude of surplus-value.

We begin with the case in which the working day is shortened.)*

(1) A shortening of the working day under the conditions given, i.e. with the productivity and the intensity of labour constant,

4. 'All things being equal, the English manufacturer can turn out a considerably larger amount of work in a given time than a foreign manufacturer, so much as to counterbalance the difference of the working days, between 60 hours a week here, and 72 or 80 elsewhere' (*Reports of the Inspectors of Factories . . . 31 October 1855*, p. 65). The most infallible means of reducing this difference between the product of the English and of the Continental working hour would be a law shortening the length of the working day in Continental factories.

---

*The passage in parentheses is not to be found in any of the German editions of *Capital*. It first appears in the French translation of 1872, and was presumably inserted by Engels into the first English translation.

leaves the value of labour-power, and therefore the necessary labour-time, as it was before. It reduces the surplus labour and the surplus-value. Along with the absolute magnitude of the latter, its relative magnitude also falls, i.e. its magnitude in relation to the magnitude of the value of labour-power, which remains constant. Only by reducing the price of labour-power below its value could the capitalist compensate himself for this fall.

All the usual arguments against the shortening of the working day depend on the assumption that the phenomenon occurs under the conditions presupposed here. But in reality the very opposite is the case: a shortening of the working day either follows upon, or immediately precedes, a change in the productivity and the intensity of labour.[5]

(2) Lengthening of the working day. Let the necessary labour-time be 6 hours, or the value of labour-power 3 shillings; also let the surplus labour be 6 hours, or the surplus-value 3 shillings. The whole working day then amounts to 12 hours and is embodied in a value of 6 shillings. If the working day is lengthened by 2 hours and the price of labour-power remains the same, the surplus-value increases both absolutely and relatively. Although there is no absolute change in the value of labour-power, it suffers a relative fall. Under the conditions assumed in I,* there could not be a change of relative magnitude in the value of labour-power without a change in its absolute magnitude. Here, on the contrary, the change of relative magnitude in the value of labour-power is the result of the change of absolute magnitude in surplus-value.

Since the value-product in which a day of labour is embodied increases with the length of that day, it is evident that the surplus-value and the price of labour-power may simultaneously increase, either by equal or unequal quantities. This simultaneous increase is therefore possible in two cases. The first case is an absolute increase in the length of the working day, and the second case is an increase in the intensity of labour unaccompanied by an increase in length.

5. 'There are compensating circumstances . . . which the working of the Ten Hours' Act has brought to light' (*Reports of the Inspectors of Factories . . . 31 October 1848*, p. 7).

---

* This refers to the case considered on pp. 656–60, i.e. when the length of the working day and the intensity of labour remain constant, and the productivity of labour is the only variable factor.

When the working day is prolonged, the price of labour-power may fall below its value, although that price nominally remains unchanged, or even rises. The value of a day's labour-power is estimated, as will be remembered, on the basis of its normal average duration, or the normal duration of the life of a worker, and on the basis of the appropriate normal standard of conversion of living substances into motion as it applies to the nature of man.[6] Up to a certain point, the increased deterioration of labour-power inseparable from a lengthening of the working day may be compensated for by making amends in the form of higher wages. But beyond this point deterioration increases in geometrical progression, and all the requirements for the normal reproduction and functioning of labour-power cease to be fulfilled. The price of labour-power and the degree of its exploitation cease to be commensurable quantities.

4. SIMULTANEOUS VARIATIONS IN THE DURATION, PRODUCTIVITY AND INTENSITY OF LABOUR

It is obvious that a large number of combinations are possible here. Any two of the factors may vary and the third remain constant, or all three may vary at once. They may vary equally or unequally, in the same direction or in opposed directions, with the result that the variations cancel each other out, either wholly or in part. Nevertheless, every possible case can easily be analysed by using the results obtained in cases I, II and III. The effect of every possible combination may be found by treating each factor in turn as variable, and the other two as constant for the time being. We shall therefore restrict ourselves here to a brief discussion of two important cases.

(1) *Diminishing productivity of labour with simultaneous lengthening of the working day*

In speaking here of diminishing productivity of labour, we are particularly concerned with those industries whose products determine the value of labour-power; we have in mind, for example,

6. 'The amount of labour which a man had undergone in the course of 24 hours might be approximately arrived at by an examination of the chemical changes which had taken place in his body, changed forms in matter indicating the anterior exercise of dynamic force' (Grove, *On the Correlation of Physical Forces* [pp. 308–9]).

diminishing productivity resulting from the decreasing fertility of the soil, and from the corresponding increase in the prices of its products. Assume a working day of 12 hours and a value-product of 6 shillings, half of which replaces the value of the labour-power, the other half forming the surplus-value. Then let a rise in the prices of the products of the soil occur, so that the value of labour-power goes up from 3 shillings to 4, and the necessary labour-time therefore rises from 6 hours to 8. If the length of the working day remains unaltered, the surplus labour will fall from 6 hours to 4, and the surplus-value from 3 shillings to 2. If the day is lengthened by 2 hours, i.e. from 12 hours to 14 hours, the surplus labour will remain at 6 hours, the surplus-value will remain at 6 shillings, but the relative magnitude of the surplus value will decrease in comparison with the magnitude of the value of labour-power, as measured by the necessary labour-time. If the day is lengthened by 4 hours, i.e. from 12 hours to 16, the proportional magnitudes of surplus-value and value of labour-power, of surplus labour and necessary labour, will continue unchanged, but the absolute magnitude of surplus-value will rise from 3 shillings to 4, and that of the surplus labour from 6 hours to 8, an increment of $\frac{1}{3}$ or $33\frac{1}{3}$ per cent. Therefore, with diminishing productivity of labour and a simultaneous lengthening of the working day, the absolute magnitude of surplus-value may continue unaltered, at the same time as its relative magnitude diminishes; its relative magnitude may continue unaltered at the same time as its absolute magnitude increases; and, finally, if the working day is lengthened to a sufficient extent, both may increase.

In the period between 1799 and 1815 an increase in the prices of the means of subsistence led in England to a nominal rise in wages, although there was a fall in real wages, as expressed in the quantity of the means of subsistence they would purchase. From this fact, West and Ricardo drew the conclusion that the diminution in the productivity of agricultural labour had brought about a fall in the rate of surplus-value, and they made this assumption (which was purely a product of their own imagination) the starting-point of important investigations into the relative magnitudes of wages, profits and ground rent.* But as a matter of fact surplus-

* West, *Essay on the Application of Capital to Land*, London, 1815; Ricardo, *An Essay on the Influence of a Low Price of Corn on the Profits of Stock*, London, 1815. These pamphlets were contributions to the controversy of 1815 over the Corn Laws.

value had at that time increased both in absolute and in relative magnitude, thanks to the increased intensity of labour, and to the prolongation of the working day which had been forced upon the workers. This was the period in which the right to prolong the working day without any restriction at all became accepted as one of the basic rights of the citizen[7]; it was also a period especially characterized, on the one hand, by a rapid growth of capital, and, on the other hand, by a rapid growth of pauperism.[8]

(2) *Increasing intensity and productivity of labour with simultaneous shortening of the working day*

Increased productivity and greater intensity of labour both have a similar effect. They both augment the mass of articles produced in a given time. Both therefore shorten that portion of the working

7. 'Corn and labour rarely march quite abreast; but there is an obvious limit, beyond which they cannot be separated. With regard to the unusual exertions made by the labouring classes in periods of dearness, which produce the fall of wages noticed in the evidence' (i.e. the evidence presented to the Parliamentary Committees of Inquiry held in 1814 and 1815) 'they are most meritorious in the individuals, and certainly favour the growth of capital. But no man of humanity could wish to see them constant and unremitted. They are most admirable as a temporary relief; but if they were constantly in action, effects of a similar kind would result from them, as from the population of a country being pushed to the very extreme limits of its food' (Malthus, *Inquiry into the Nature and Progress of Rent*, London, 1815, p. 48, n.). All honour to Malthus that he lays stress on the lengthening of the hours of labour, a fact to which he directly draws attention elsewhere in his pamphlet, whereas Ricardo and others, flying in the face of the most notorious facts, make invariability in the length of the working day the groundwork of all their investigations. Nevertheless the conservative interests Malthus served prevented him from seeing that unlimited prolongation of the working day, combined with an extraordinary development of machinery and the exploitation of the labour of women and children, inevitably made a great portion of the working class 'redundant', particularly after the cessation of wartime demand and the ending of the English monopoly of the world market. It was of course far more convenient, and much more in conformity with the interests of the ruling classes, whom Malthus idolized like a true priest, to explain this 'over-population' by the eternal laws of nature, rather than the merely historical laws of the nature of capitalist production.

8. 'A principal cause of the increase of capital, during the war, proceeded from the greater exertions, and perhaps the greater privations of the labouring classes, the most numerous in every society. More women and children were compelled by necessitous circumstances to enter upon laborious occupations, and former workmen, from the same cause, obliged to devote a greater portion of their time to increase production' (*Essays on Political Economy: In Which are Illustrated the Principal Causes of the Present National Distress*, London, 1830, p. 248).

day which the worker needs to produce his means of subsistence or their equivalent. The minimum length of the working day is fixed by this necessary component, which is however itself capable of further contraction. If the whole working day were to shrink to the length of its necessary component, surplus labour would vanish, something which is impossible under the regime of capital. Only the abolition of the capitalist form of production would permit the reduction of the working day to the necessary labour-time. But even in that case the latter would expand to take up more of the day, and for two reasons: first, because the worker's conditions of life would improve, and his aspirations become greater, and second, because a part of what is now surplus labour would then count as necessary labour, namely the labour which is necessary for the formation of a social fund for reserve and accumulation.

The more the productivity of labour increases, the more the working day can be shortened, and the more the working day is shortened, the more the intensity of labour can increase. From the point of view of society the productivity of labour also grows when economies are made in its use. This implies not only economizing on the means of production, but also avoiding all useless labour. The capitalist mode of production, while it enforces economy in each individual business, also begets, by its anarchic system of competition, the most outrageous squandering of labour-power and of the social means of production, not to mention the creation of a vast number of functions at present indispensable, but in themselves superfluous.

The intensity and productivity of labour being given, the part of the social working day necessarily taken up with material production is shorter and, as a consequence, the time at society's disposal for the free intellectual and social activity of the individual is greater, in proportion as work is more and more evenly divided among all the able-bodied members of society, and a particular social stratum is more and more deprived of the ability to shift the burden of labour (which is a necessity imposed by nature) from its own shoulders to those of another social stratum. The absolute minimum limit to the shortening of the working day is, from this point of view, the universality [*Allgemeinheit*] of labour. In capitalist society, free time is produced for one class by the conversion of the whole lifetime of the masses into labour-time.

Chapter 18: Different Formulae for the Rate of Surplus-Value

We have seen that the rate of surplus-value is represented by the following formulae:

I. $\dfrac{\text{Surplus-value}}{\text{Variable capital}} \left(\dfrac{s}{v}\right) = \dfrac{\text{Surplus-value}}{\text{Value of labour-power}}$

$= \dfrac{\text{Surplus labour}}{\text{Necessary labour}}$

The first two formulae represent, as a ratio of values, what is represented in the third formula as a ratio of the times during which those values are produced. These mutually replaceable formulae are rigorously definite and correct. We therefore find them worked out in classical political economy in substance, but not in a conscious form. Political economy in fact provides us with derivative formulae, as follows:

II. $\dfrac{\text{Surplus labour*}}{\text{Working day}} = \dfrac{\text{Surplus-value}}{\text{Value of the product}}$

$= \dfrac{\text{Surplus product}}{\text{Total product}}$

One and the same proportion is expressed here alternately in the form of labour-times, of the values in which those labour-times are embodied, and of the products in which those values exist. It is of course understood that by 'value of the product' the political economists mean only the value newly created in a working day, the constant part of the value of the product being excluded.

In all the formulae included under II the actual degree of exploitation of labour, or the rate of surplus-value, is falsely expressed. Let the working day be 12 hours long. Then, making

*In the French translation of *Capital* Marx placed parentheses round this formula, 'because the concept of surplus labour is not found clearly expressed in bourgeois political economy'.

the same assumptions as we have before, the real degree of exploitation of labour will be represented by the following proportions:

$$\frac{6 \text{ hours surplus labour}}{6 \text{ hours necessary labour}} = \frac{\text{Surplus-value of 3s.}}{\text{Variable capital of 3s.}}$$
$$= 100 \text{ per cent}$$

From the formulae included under II, we get, on the contrary:

$$\frac{6 \text{ hours surplus labour}}{\text{Working day of 12 hours}} = \frac{\text{Surplus-value of 3s.}}{\text{Value-product of 6s.}} = 50 \text{ per cent}$$

These derivative formulae express, in reality, only the proportion in which the working day, or the value produced by it, is divided between the capitalist and the worker. If they are to be treated as direct expressions of the degree of capital's self-valorization, the following erroneous law would hold good: surplus labour or surplus-value can never reach 100 per cent.[1] Since the surplus labour is only an aliquot part of the working day, or since surplus-value is only an aliquot part of the value-product, surplus labour must always be less than the working day,

1. Thus, for example, in Rodbertus, *Sociale Briefe an von Kirchmann, Dritter Brief: Widerlegung der Ricardo'schen Lehre von der Grundrente und Begründung einer neuen Rententheorie*, Berlin, 1851. I shall return to this pamphlet later on*; in spite of its erroneous theory of rent, it sees through the nature of capitalist production.

*Marx did so in *Theories of Surplus-Value*, Part 2, Ch. 8, pp. 15–114, Ch. 9, pp. 127–61.

[Added by Engels to the third German edition:] It may be seen from this how favourably Marx judged his predecessors, whenever he found in them a real advance, or new and sound ideas. In the meantime, the publication of Rodbertus's letters to Rudolf Meyer has shown that the above acknowledgement needs to be restricted to some extent. In those letters this passage occurs: 'Capital must be rescued not only from labour, but from itself, and that will be best effected by treating the acts of the industrial capitalist as economic and political functions that have been delegated to him with his capital, and by treating his profit as a form of salary, because we still know no other social organization. But salaries may be regulated, and may also be reduced if they take too much from wages. The irruption of Marx into society, as I may call his book, must be warded off ... Altogether, Marx's book is not so much an investigation of capital as a polemic against the present form of capital, a form which he confuses with the concept of capital itself' (*Briefe, etc., von Dr Rodbertus-Jagetzow*, ed. by Dr Rudolf Meyer, Berlin, 1881, Vol. 1, p. 111, 48th letter from Rodbertus). The bold onslaught mounted by Rodbertus in his 'social letters' finally dwindled down to ideological commonplaces of this kind.

or the surplus-value always less than the total value-product. In order, however, to attain the ratio of 100:100 they must be equal. In order for the surplus labour to absorb the whole day (i.e. an average day of any week or year) the necessary labour would have to sink to zero. But if necessary labour vanishes, surplus labour does as well, since it is only a function of the necessary labour. The ratio $\frac{\text{Surplus labour}}{\text{Working day}}$, or $\frac{\text{Surplus-value}}{\text{Value-product}}$ can therefore never reach the limit of $\frac{100}{100}$, still less rise to $\frac{100+x}{100}$. The rate of surplus-value, however, the real degree of exploitation of labour, is able to do this. Take, for example, the estimate of L. de Lavergne, according to which the English agricultural labourer gets only $\frac{1}{4}$ of the product[2] or of its value, while the capitalist farmer gets $\frac{3}{4}$, whatever the subsequent division of the booty between the capitalist, the landowner and others. On this calculation, the surplus labour of the English agricultural labourer is related to his necessary labour in the ratio of 3:1, which gives a rate of exploitation of 300 per cent.

Through the use of the formulae given under II, the political economists' favourite method of treating the working day as constant in magnitude became a fixed usage, because in those formulae surplus labour is always compared with a working day of a given length.

When the political economists treat surplus-value and the value of labour-power as fractions of the value-product – a mode of presentation which arises, by the way, out of the capitalist mode of production itself, and whose significance we shall unearth later on – they conceal the specific character of the capital-relation, namely the fact that variable capital is exchanged for living labour-power, and that the worker is accordingly excluded from the product. Instead of revealing the capital-relation they show us the false semblance of a relation of association, in which

2. That part of the product which merely replaces the constant capital advanced is of course left out in this calculation. De Lavergne, as a blind admirer of England, is inclined to estimate the share of the capitalist too low, rather than too high.*

*Léonce de Lavergne, *Rural Economy of England, Scotland, and Ireland*, London, 1855, p. 87. 'We find that in England a fourth only of gross production is appropriated to the payment of wages – whilst in France and Ireland one half is thus disposed of.'

worker and capitalist divide the product in proportion to the different elements which they respectively contribute towards its formation.[3]

But in any case, the formulae given under III can always be reconverted into the original formulae. If, for instance, we have

$$\frac{\text{Surplus labour of 6 hours}}{\text{Working day of 12 hours}}$$

then the necessary labour-time is the 12 hours of the working day minus the surplus labour of 6 hours, and we get the following result:

$$\frac{\text{Surplus labour of 6 hours}}{\text{Necessary labour of 6 hours}} = \frac{100}{100}$$

There is a third formula, which I have occasionally anticipated:

III. $\dfrac{\text{Surplus-value}}{\text{Value of labour-power}} = \dfrac{\text{Surplus labour}}{\text{Necessary labour}} = \dfrac{\text{Unpaid labour}}{\text{Paid labour}}$

After the analysis given above, it is no longer possible to be misled by the formula $\dfrac{\text{unpaid labour}}{\text{paid labour}}$ into concluding that the capitalist pays for labour and not for labour-power. $\dfrac{\text{Unpaid labour}}{\text{Paid labour}}$ is only a popular expression for $\dfrac{\text{surplus labour}}{\text{necessary labour}}$. The capitalist pays the value of the labour-power (or, if the price diverges from this, he pays the price) and receives in exchange the right to dispose of the living labour-power itself. The length of time during which he utilizes this labour-power is divided into two separate periods. During one period, the worker produces a value that is only equal to the value of his labour-power, i.e. he produces its equivalent. Thus the capitalist receives, in return for advancing the price of the labour-power, a product of the same price. It is the same as if he had bought the product ready-made in the market. During the other period, the period of surplus labour,

3. As all the developed forms of the capitalist process of production are forms of co-operation, nothing is easier, of course, than to make abstraction from their specifically antagonistic character, and, merely by verbal alterations, make them sound like forms of free association. This is what Count A. de Laborde does in *De l'esprit d'association dans tous les intérêts de la communauté*, Paris, 1818. H. Carey, the Yankee, occasionally performs this conjuring trick, with similar success, even with the relations prevailing under slavery.

the utilization of the labour-power creates a value for the capitalist without costing him any value in return[4]. He is thus able to set labour-power in motion without paying for it. It is in this sense that surplus labour can be called unpaid labour.

Capital, therefore, is not only the command over labour, as Adam Smith thought. It is essentially the command over unpaid labour. All surplus-value, whatever particular form (profit, interest or rent) it may subsequently crystallize into, is in substance the materialization of unpaid labour-time. The secret of the self-valorization of capital resolves itself into the fact that it has at its disposal a definite quantity of the unpaid labour of other people[*fremder Arbeit*].

4. Although the Physiocrats could not penetrate the mystery of surplus-value, this much was clear to them, that it was 'independent and disposable wealth, which he' (the possessor of the surplus value) 'has not bought, and nevertheless sells' (Turgot, *Réflexions sur la formation et la distribution des richesses*, p. 11).

Part Six

Wages

Chapter 19: The Transformation of the Value (and Respectively the Price) of Labour-Power into Wages

On the surface of bourgeois society the worker's wage appears as the price of labour, as a certain quantity of money that is paid for a certain quantity of labour. Thus people speak of the value of labour, and call its expression in money its necessary or natural price. On the other hand they speak of the market prices of labour, i.e. prices which oscillate above or below its necessary price.

But what is the value of a commodity? The objective form of the social labour expended in its production. And how do we measure the quantity of this value? By the quantity of the labour contained in it. How then is the value, e.g., of a 12-hour working day to be determined? By the 12 working hours contained in a working day of 12 hours, which is an absurd tautology.[1]

In order to be sold as a commodity in the market, labour must at all events exist before it is sold. But if the worker were able to endow it with an independent existence, he would be selling a commodity, and not labour.[2]

---

1. 'Mr Ricardo, ingeniously enough, avoids a difficulty which, on a first view, threatens to encumber his doctrine, that value depends on the quantity of labour employed in production. If this principle is rigidly adhered to, it follows that the value of labour depends on the quantity of labour employed in producing it – which is evidently absurd. By a dexterous turn, therefore, Mr Ricardo makes the value of labour depend on the quantity of labour required to produce wages; or, to give him the benefit of his own language, he maintains that the value of labour is to be estimated by the quantity of labour required to produce wages; by which he means the quantity of labour required to produce the money or commodities given to the labourer. This is similar to saying, that the value of cloth is estimated, not by the quantity of labour bestowed on its production, but by the quantity of labour bestowed on the production of the silver, for which the cloth is exchanged' ([S. Bailey,] *A Critical Dissertation on the Nature, etc., of Value*, pp. 50–51).

2. 'If you call labour a commodity, it is not like a commodity which is first produced in order to exchange, and then brought to market where it must exchange with other commodities according to the respective quantities

Apart from these contradictions, a direct exchange of money, i.e. of objectified labour, with living labour, would either supersede the law of value, which only begins to develop freely on the basis of capitalist production, or supersede capitalist production itself, which rests directly on wage-labour. The working day of 12 hours is represented in a monetary value of, for example, 6 shillings. There are two alternatives. Either equivalents are exchanged, and then the worker receives 6 shillings for 12 hours of labour; the price of his labour would be equal to the price of his product. In that case he produces no surplus-value for the buyer of his labour, the 6 shillings are not transformed into capital, and the basis of capitalist production vanishes. But it is precisely on that basis that he sells his labour and that his labour is wage-labour. Or else he receives, in return for 12 hours of labour, less than 6 shillings, i.e. less than 12 hours of labour. 12 hours of labour are exchanged for 10, 6, etc. hours of labour. But to equate unequal quantities in this way does not just do away with the determination of value. Such a self-destructive contradiction cannot be in any way even enunciated or formulated as a law.[3]

It is no use deducing the exchange of more labour against less from the differences in form in each case, one piece of labour being objectified, the other living.[4] In fact, this way out is even more absurd because the value of a commodity is determined not

---

of each which there may be in the market at the time; labour is created the moment it is brought to market; nay, it is brought to market before it is created' (*Observations on Certain Verbal Disputes, etc.*, pp. 75–6).

3. 'Treating labour as a commodity, and capital, the produce of labour, as another, then, if the value of these two commodities were regulated by equal quantities of labour, a given amount of labour would . . . exchange for that quantity of capital which had been produced by the same amount of labour; antecedent labour would . . . exchange for the same amount as present labour. But the value of labour in relation to other commodities . . . is not determined by equal quantities of labour' (E. G. Wakefield, in his edition of Adam Smith's *Wealth of Nations*, Vol. 1, London, 1835, pp. 230, 231, n.).

4. 'It was necessary to reach an agreement' (yet another edition of the *contrat social*!) 'that every time completed labour was exchanged for labour still to be performed, the latter' (the capitalist) 'would receive a higher value than the former' (the worker). Simonde (i.e. Sismondi),* *De la richesse commerciale* (Vol. 1, Geneva, 1803, p. 37).

* Jean-Charles-Léonard Simonde (1773–1842), the Swiss political economist and historian, in 1807 added the words de Sismondi to his name, having discovered a tenuous connection with an Italian aristocratic family called Sismondi, long resident in Pisa.

by the quantity of labour actually objectified in it, but by the quantity of living labour necessary to produce it. A commodity represents, say, 6 working hours. If an invention is made by which it can be produced in 3 hours, the value, even of the commodity already produced, falls by half. It now represents 3 hours of socially necessary labour instead of the 6 formerly required. It is therefore the quantity of labour required to produce it, not the objectified form of that labour, which determines the amount of the value of a commodity.

It is not labour which directly confronts the possessor of money on the commodity-market, but rather the worker. What the worker is selling is his labour-power. As soon as his labour actually begins, it has already ceased to belong to him; it can therefore no longer be sold by him. Labour is the substance, and the immanent measure of value, but it has no value itself.[5]

In the expression 'value of labour', the concept of value is not only completely extinguished, but inverted, so that it becomes its contrary. It is an expression as imaginary as the value of the earth. These imaginary expressions arise, nevertheless, from the relations of production themselves. They are categories for the forms of appearance of essential relations. That in their appearance things are often presented in an inverted way is something fairly familiar in every science, apart from political economy.[6]

Classical political economy borrowed the category 'price of

5. 'Labour the exclusive standard of value ... the creator of all wealth, no commodity' (Thomas Hodgskin, *Popular Political Economy*, p. 186).

6. On the other hand, the attempt to explain such expressions as merely poetic licence only shows the impotence of the analysis. Hence, in answer to Proudhon's phrase, 'Labour is said to *have value* not as a commodity itself, but in view of the values which it is supposed potentially to contain. The value of labour is a figurative expression', etc., I have remarked 'In labour as a commodity, which is a grim reality, he' (Proudhon) 'sees nothing but a grammatical ellipsis. Thus the whole of existing society, founded on labour as a commodity, is henceforth founded on a poetic licence, a figurative expression. If society wants to "eliminate all the drawbacks" that assail it, well, let it eliminate all the ill-sounding terms, change the language; and to this end it has only to apply to the *Académie* for a new edition of its dictionary' (Karl Marx, *Misère de la philosophie*, pp. 34–5) [*The Poverty of Philosophy*, pp. 49–50]. It is naturally still more convenient to understand by value nothing at all. Then one can without difficulty subsume everything under this category. Thus, for instance, J. B. Say asks 'What is value?' Answer: 'It is what a thing is worth.' What is price? 'The value of a thing expressed in money.' And why has 'labour on the land ... a value?' 'Because a price is put upon it.' Therefore value is what a thing is worth, and the land has its

labour' from everyday life without further criticism, and then simply asked the question, how is this price determined? It soon recognized that changes in the relation between demand and supply explained nothing, with regard to the price of labour or any other commodity, except those changes themselves, i.e. the oscillations of the market price above or below a certain mean. If demand and supply balance, the oscillation of prices ceases, all other circumstances remaining the same. But then demand and supply also cease to explain anything. The price of labour, at the moment when demand and supply are in equilibrium, is its natural price, determined independently of the relation of demand and supply. It was therefore found that the natural price was the object which actually had to be analysed. Or a longer period of oscillation in the market price was taken, for example a year, and the oscillations were found to cancel each other out, leaving a mean average quantity, a constant magnitude. This naturally had to be determined otherwise than by its own mutually compensatory variations. This price, which ultimately predominates over the accidental market prices of labour and regulates them, this 'necessary price' (according to the Physiocrats) or 'natural price' of labour (according to Adam Smith) can only be its value expressed in money, as with all other commodities. In this way, the political economists believed they could penetrate to the value of labour through the medium of the accidental prices of labour. As with other commodities, this value was then further determined by the cost of production. But what is the cost of production ... of the *worker*, i.e. the cost of producing or reproducing the worker himself? The political economists unconsciously substituted this question for the original one, for the search after the cost of production of labour as such turned in a circle, and did not allow them to get any further forward at all. Therefore what they called the 'value of labour' is in fact the value of labour-power, as it exists in the personality of the worker, and it is as different from its function, labour, as a machine is from the operations it performs. Because they were concerned with the difference between the market price of labour and its so-called value, with the relation of

'value' because its value is 'expressed in money'. This is, anyhow, a very simple way of explaining the why and wherefore of things.*

*J. B. Say, *Traité d'économie politique*, 4th edn, Paris, 1819, Vol. 2, pp. 486, 507. (These quotations are from a list of definitions added to editions from the fourth onwards.)

this value to the rate of profit and to the values of the commodities produced by means of labour, etc., they never discovered that the course of the analysis had led not only from the market prices of labour to its presumed value, but also to the resolution of this value of labour itself into the value of labour-power. Classical political economy's unconsciousness of this result of its own analysis and its uncritical acceptance of the categories 'value of labour', 'natural price of labour', etc. as the ultimate and adequate expression for the value-relation under consideration, led it into inextricable confusions and contradictions, as will be seen later,* while it offered a secure base of operations to the vulgar economists who, in their shallowness, make it a principle to worship appearances only.

Let us first see how the value (and the price) of labour-power is represented in its converted form as wages.

We know that the daily value of labour-power is calculated upon a certain length of the worker's life, and that this corresponds, in turn, to a certain length of the working day. Assume that the usual working day is 12 hours and the daily value of labour-power 3 shillings, which is the expression in money of a value embodying 6 hours of labour. If the worker receives 3 shillings, then he receives the value of his labour-power, which functions through 12 hours. If this value of a day's labour-power is now expressed as the value of a day's labour itself, we have the formula: 12 hours of labour has a value of 3 shillings. The value of labour-power thus determines the value of labour, or, expressed in money, its necessary price. If, on the other hand, the price of labour-power differs from its value, the price of labour will similarly differ from its so-called value.

As the value of labour is only an irrational expression for the value of labour-power, it follows of course that the value of labour must always be less than its value-product, for the capitalist always makes labour-power work longer than is necessary for the reproduction of its own value. In the above example, the value of the labour-power that functions through 12 hours is 3 shillings, which requires 6 hours for its reproduction. The value which the labour-power produces is however 6 shillings, because it in fact functions during 12 hours, and its value-product depends, not on its own value, but on the length of time it is in action. Thus

* A reference forward to the projected Volume 4, known now as *Theories of Surplus-Value*.

we reach a result which is at first sight absurd: labour which creates a value of 6 shillings possesses a value of 3 shillings.[7]

We see, further: the value of 3 shillings, which represents the paid portion of the working day, i.e. 6 hours of labour, appears as the value or price of the whole working day of 12 hours, which thus includes 6 hours which have not been paid for. The wage-form thus extinguishes every trace of the division of the working day into necessary labour and surplus labour, into paid labour and unpaid labour. All labour appears as paid labour. Under the *corvée* system it is different. There the labour of the serf for himself, and his compulsory labour for the lord of the land, are demarcated very clearly both in space and time. In slave labour, even the part of the working day in which the slave is only replacing the value of his own means of subsistence, in which he therefore actually works for himself alone, appears as labour for his master. All his labour appears as unpaid labour.[8] In wage-labour, on the contrary, even surplus labour, or unpaid labour, appears as paid. In the one case, the property-relation conceals the slave's labour for himself; in the other case the money-relation conceals the uncompensated labour of the wage-labourer.

We may therefore understand the decisive importance of the transformation of the value and price of labour-power into the form of wages, or into the value and price of labour itself. All the notions of justice held by both the worker and the capitalist, all the mystifications of the capitalist mode of production, all capitalism's illusions about freedom, all the apologetic tricks of vulgar economics, have as their basis the form of appearance discussed above, which makes the actual relation invisible, and indeed presents to the eye the precise opposite of that relation.

World history has taken a long time to get to the bottom of the

7. Cf. *Zur Kritik der Politischen Ökonomie*, p. 40 [*A Contribution to the Critique of Political Economy*, p. 62], where I state that, in my analysis of capital, I shall solve the following problem: 'how does production on the basis of exchange-value solely determined by labour-time lead to the result that the exchange-value of labour is less than the exchange-value of its product?'

8. The *Morning Star*, a London free-trade organ which is so naïve as to be positively foolish, protested again and again during the American Civil War, with all the moral indignation of which man is capable, that the Negroes in the 'Confederate States' worked absolutely for nothing. It should have compared the daily cost of a Negro in the southern states with that of a free worker in the East End of London.

mystery of wages; but, despite this, nothing is easier to understand than the necessity, the *raison d'être*, of this form of appearance.

The exchange between capital and labour at first presents itself to our perceptions in exactly the same way as the sale and purchase of all other commodities. The buyer gives a certain sum of money, the seller an article which is something other than money. The legal mind recognizes here at most a material difference, expressed in the legally equivalent formulae: '*Do ut des, do ut facias, facio ut des, facio ut facias.*'*

Further. Since exchange-value and use-value are in themselves incommensurable magnitudes, the expressions 'value of labour', 'price of labour', do not seem more irrational than the expressions 'value of cotton', 'price of cotton'. Moreover, the worker is paid after he has given his labour. In its function as a means of payment, money realizes, but only subsequently, the value or price of the article supplied – i.e. in this particular case, the value or price of the labour supplied. Finally, the use-value supplied by the worker to the capitalist is not in fact his labour-power but its function, a specific form of useful labour, such as tailoring, cobbling, spinning, etc. That this same labour is, on the other hand, the universal value-creating element, and thus possesses a property by virtue of which it differs from all other commodities, is something which falls outside the frame of reference of the everyday consciousness.

Let us put ourselves in the place of the worker who receives for 12 hours of labour the value-product of, say, 6 hours of labour, namely 2 shillings. For him, in fact, his 12 hours of labour is the means of buying the 3 shillings. The value of his labour-power may vary, with the value of his usual means of subsistence, from 3 to 4 shillings, or from 3 to 2 shillings; or, if the value of labour-power remains constant, its price may rise to 4 shillings or fall to 2 shillings as a result of changes in the relation of demand and supply. He always gives 12 hours of labour. Every change in the amount of the equivalent that he receives therefore necessarily appears to him as a change in the value or price of his 12 hours of labour. This circumstance misled Adam Smith, who treated the working day as a constant quantity,[9] into the opposite assertion

9. Adam Smith only incidentally alludes to the variation of the working day, when he is dealing with piece-wages.*

*In *Wealth of Nations*, Bk I, Ch. 8, 'Of the Wages of Labour'.

*'I give, that you may give; I give, that you may do; I do, that you may give; I do, that you may do.'

that the value of labour is constant, although the value of the means of subsistence may vary, and the same working day, therefore, may represent more or less money for the worker.

Let us consider, on the other hand, the capitalist. He wishes to receive as much labour as possible for as little money as possible. In practice, therefore, the only thing that interests him is the difference between the price of labour-power and the value which its function creates. But he tries to buy all commodities as cheaply as possible, and his own invariable explanation of his profit is that it is a result of mere sharp practice, of buying under the value and selling over it. Hence he never comes to see that if such a thing as the value of labour really existed, and he really paid this value, no capital would exist, and his money would never be transformed into capital.

Moreover, the actual movement of wages presents phenomena which seem to prove that it is not the value of labour-power which is paid, but the value of its function, of labour itself. We may reduce these phenomena to two great classes. (1) Changes in wages owing to changes in the length of the working day. One might as well conclude that it is not the value of a machine which is paid, but that of its operation, because it costs more to hire a machine for a week than for a day. (2) Individual differences between the wages of different workers who perform the same function. These individual differences also exist in the system of slavery, but there they do not give rise to any illusions, for labour-power is in that case itself sold frankly and openly, without any embellishment. Only, in the slave system, the advantage of a labour-power above the average, and the disadvantage of a labour-power below the average, affects the slave-owner; whereas in the system of wage-labour it affects the worker himself, because his labour-power is, in the one case, sold by himself, in the other, by a third person.

For the rest, what is true of all forms of appearance and their hidden background is also true of the form of appearance 'value and price of labour', or 'wages', as contrasted with the essential relation manifested in it, namely the value and price of labour-power. The forms of appearance are reproduced directly and spontaneously, as current and usual modes of thought; the essential relation must first be discovered by science. Classical political economy stumbles approximately onto the true state of affairs, but without consciously formulating it. It is unable to do this as long as it stays within its bourgeois skin.

Chapter 20: Time-Wages

Wages themselves again take many forms. This fact is not apparent from the ordinary economic treatises, which, in their crude obsession with the material side [*Stoff*], ignore all differences of form. An exposition of all these forms belongs to the special study of wage-labour, and not, therefore, to this work. Nevertheless, we shall have to give a brief description of the two fundamental forms here.

The sale of labour-power, as will be remembered, always takes place for definite periods of time. The converted form in which the daily value, weekly value, etc. of labour-power is directly presented is hence that of time-wages, therefore day-wages, etc.

Next it is to be noted that the laws set forth in Chapter 17, on the changes in the relative magnitudes of price of labour-power and surplus-value, can be transformed, by a simple alteration in their form, into laws of wages. Similarly, the distinction between the exchange-value of labour-power and the sum of means of subsistence into which this value is converted now appears as the distinction between nominal and real wages. It would be useless to repeat here, when dealing with the form of appearance, what we have already worked out in relation to the essential form. We shall therefore limit ourselves to a few points which characterize time-wages.

The sum of money[1] which the worker receives for his daily or weekly labour forms the amount of his nominal wages, or of his wages estimated in value. But it is clear that according to the length of the working day, that is, according to the amount of actual labour supplied every day, the same daily or weekly wage may represent very different prices of labour, i.e. very different sums of money for the same quantity of labour.[2] We must, there-

1. Here we always assume that the value of money itself remains constant.
2. 'The price of labour is the sum paid for a given quantity of labour' (Sir Edward West, *Price of Corn and Wages of Labour*, London, 1826, p. 67).

fore, in considering time-wages, again distinguish between the sum total of the daily or weekly wages, etc., and the price of labour. How then can we find this price, i.e. the money-value of a given quantity of labour? The average price of labour is the average daily value of labour-power divided by the average number of hours in the working day. If, for instance, the daily value of labour-power is 3 shillings, which is the value-product of 6 working hours, and if the working day is 12 hours, the price of 1 working hour is $\frac{3}{12}$ shillings, i.e. 3d. The price of the working hour thus found serves as the unit measure for the price of labour.

It follows therefore that daily and weekly wages may remain the same, although the price of labour falls constantly. If, for example, the usual working day is 10 hours and the daily value of labour-power 3 shillings, the price of the working hour is $3\frac{3}{5}$d. It falls to 3d. as soon as the working day rises to 12 hours, and to $2\frac{2}{5}$d. as soon as it rises to 15 hours. Despite all this, daily or weekly wages remain unchanged. Inversely, daily or weekly wages may rise, although the price of labour remains constant or even falls. If, for instance, the working day is 10 hours and the daily value of labour-power 3 shillings, the price of one working hour is $3\frac{3}{5}$d. If the worker, owing to an increase in the number of orders, works for 12 hours, and the price of labour remains the same, his daily wage now rises to 3s. $7\frac{1}{5}$d., without any variation having taken place in the price of labour. The same result might follow if, instead of the extensive magnitude of labour, its intensive magnitude increased.[3] The rise of nominal daily or weekly wages may therefore be unaccompanied by any change in the price of labour, or may even be accompanied by a fall in the latter. The same thing holds for the income of the worker's family, when the quantity of labour provided by the head of the family is augmented by the labour of the members of his family. There are therefore methods

---

West is the author of an epoch-making work in the history of political economy, published anonymously, the *Essay on the Application of Capital to Land, By a Fellow of the University College of Oxford*, London, 1815.

3. 'The wages of labour depend upon the price of labour and the quantity of labour performed ... An increase in the wages of labour does not necessarily imply an enhancement of the price of labour. From fuller employment, and greater exertions, the wages of labour may be considerably increased, while the price of labour may continue the same' (West, op. cit., pp. 67–8, 112). However, West dismisses the main question, 'How is the price of labour determined?', with mere banalities.

of lowering the price of labour which are independent of any reduction in the nominal daily or weekly wage.[4]

However, as a general law it follows that, given the amount of daily, weekly labour, etc., the daily or weekly wage depends on the price of labour, which itself varies either with the value of labour-power, or with the divergencies between its price and its value. Given the price of labour, on the other hand, the daily or weekly wage depends on the quantity of labour expended daily or weekly.

The unit of measurement for time-wages, the price of the working hour, is the value of a day's labour-power divided by the number of hours in the average working day. Let the latter be 12 hours, and the daily value of labour-power 3 shillings, the value-product of 6 hours of labour. Under these circumstances, the price of a working hour is 3d., and the value produced in it is 6d. If the worker is now employed for less than 12 hours a day (or for less than 6 days in the week), for instance only for 6 or 8 hours, he receives, at the price of labour just mentioned, only 2s. or 1s. 6d. a day.[5] As, on our hypothesis, he must work on average 6 hours a day in order to produce a day's wage which corresponds to nothing more than the value of his labour-power, and as, on the same hypothesis, he works only half of every hour for himself, and half for the capitalist, it is clear that he cannot obtain for himself the

4. This is perceived by the most fanatical representative of the eighteenth-century industrial bourgeoisie, the author of the *Essay on Trade and Commerce* we have often quoted already, although he puts the matter in a confused way: 'It is the quantity of labour and not the price of it' (he means by this the nominal daily or weekly wage) 'that is determined by the price of provisions and other necessaries: reduce the price of necessaries very low, and of course you reduce the quantity of labour in proportion. Master-manufacturers know that there are various ways of raising and falling the price of labour, besides that of altering its nominal amount' (op. cit., pp. 48, 61). N. W. Senior, in his *Three Lectures on the Rate of Wages*, London, 1830, where he uses West's work without mentioning it, has this to say: 'The labourer is principally interested in the amount of wages' (p. 15), that is to say, the worker is principally interested in what he receives, the nominal sum of his wages, not in what he gives, the quantity of labour!

5. The effect of such an abnormal under-employment is quite different from that of a general reduction of the working day, enforced by law. The former has nothing to do with the absolute length of the working day, and may just as well occur in a working day of 15 hours as in one of 6. The normal price of labour is in the first case calculated on the basis of an average working day of 15 hours, and in the second case a working day of 6 hours. The result is therefore the same if the worker is employed in the one case for only $7\frac{1}{2}$ hours, and in the other case for only 3 hours.

value-product of 6 hours if he is employed for less than 12 hours. In previous chapters we saw the destructive consequences of over-work; but here we come upon the origin of the sufferings which arise for the worker out of his being insufficiently employed.

If the hour's wage is fixed in such a way that the capitalist does not bind himself to pay a day's or a week's wage, but only to pay wages for the hours during which he chooses to employ the worker, he can employ him for a shorter time than that which is originally the basis of the calculation of the wages for the hour, or the unit of measurement of the price of labour. Since this unit is determined by the ratio of the daily value of labour-power to the working day of a given number of hours, it naturally loses all meaning as soon as the working day ceases to contain a definite number of hours. The connection between the paid and the unpaid labour is destroyed. The capitalist can now wring from the worker a certain quantity of surplus labour without allowing him the labour-time necessary for his own subsistence. He can annihilate all regularity of em-ployment, and according to his own convenience, caprice, and the interest of the moment, make the most frightful over-work alter-nate with relative or absolute cessation of work. He can abnormally lengthen the working day without giving the worker any corres-ponding compensation, under the pretence of paying 'the normal price of labour'. Hence the perfectly rational revolt of the London building workers in 1860* against the attempt of the capitalists to impose on them this sort of wage by the hour. The legal limitation of the working day puts an end to mischievous acts of this kind, though it does not of course end the diminution of employment caused by the competition of machinery, by changes in the quality of the workers employed, and partial or general crises.

With an increase in the daily or weekly wage, the price of labour may remain nominally constant, and yet fall below its normal level. This occurs every time the working day is prolonged beyond its customary length, while the price of labour (reckoned per working hour) remains constant. If, in the fraction $\frac{\text{daily value of labour-power}}{\text{working day}}$, the denominator increases, the numerator increases still more rapidly. The amount of de-terioration in labour-power, and therefore its value, increases with the duration of its functioning, and to a more rapid degree

---

* This strike began in fact in July 1859 and ended in February 1860.

than the increase of that duration. In many branches of industry, where time-wages are the general rule and there are no legal limits to the length of the working day, the habit has therefore spontaneously grown up of regarding the working day as normal only up to a point in time, for instance up to the expiration of the tenth hour ('normal working day', 'the day's work', 'the regular hours of work'). Beyond this limit the working time is overtime, and is paid at a better hourly rate ('extra pay)', although often in a proportion which is ridiculously small.[6] The normal working day exists here as a fraction of the actual working day, and over the year as a whole the latter is often more common than the former.[7] The increase in the price of labour when the working day is extended beyond a certain normal limit takes place in various British industries in such a way that the low price of labour during the so-called normal time compels the worker to work during the better paid overtime, if he wishes to obtain a sufficient wage at all.[8]

6. 'The rate of payment for overtime' (in lace-making) 'is so small, from $\frac{1}{2}$d. and $\frac{3}{4}$d. to 2d. per hour, that it stands in painful contrast to the amount of injury produced to the health and stamina of the workpeople ... The small amount thus earned is also often obliged to be spent in extra nourishment' (*Children's Employment Commission, Second Report*, p. xvi, n. 117).

7. As for instance in paper-staining until the recent introduction into this trade of the Factory Act. 'We work on with no stoppage for meals, so that the day's work of $10\frac{1}{2}$ hours is finished by 4.30 p.m., and all after that is overtime, and we seldom leave off working before 6 p.m., so that we are really working overtime the whole year round' (Mr Smith's evidence, in *Children's Employment Commission, First Report*, p. 125).

8. As for instance in the bleaching-works of Scotland. 'In some parts of Scotland this trade' (before the introduction of the Factory Act in 1862) 'was carried on by a system of overtime, i.e. ten hours a day were the regular hours of work, for which a nominal wage of 1s. 2d. per day was paid to a man, there being every day overtime for 3 or 4 hours, paid at the rate of 3d. per hour. The effect of this system' (was as follows:) 'a man could not earn more than 8s. per week when working the ordinary hours ... without overtime they could not earn a fair day's wages' (*Reports of the Inspectors of Factories ... 30 April 1863*, p. 10). 'The higher wages, for getting adult males to work longer hours, are a temptation too strong to be resisted' (*Reports of the Inspectors of Factories ... 30 April 1848*, p. 5). The book-binding trade in the city of London employs a large number of young girls from 14 to 15 years old, under indentures which prescribe certain definite hours of labour. Nevertheless, they work in the last week of each month until 10, 11, 12 or 1 o'clock at night, along with the older male workers, in very mixed company. 'The masters tempt them by extra pay and supper,' which they eat in neighbouring public houses. The great debauchery thus produced among these 'young immortals' (*Children's Employment Commission, Fifth Report*, p. 44,

Legal limitation of the working day puts an end to this pastime.[9]

It is a generally known fact that the longer the working day in a branch of industry, the lower the wages are.[10] The factory inspector Alexander Redgrave illustrates this by a comparative review of the twenty years from 1839 to 1859, according to which wages rose in the factories under the Ten Hours' Act, while they fell in the factories where the work went on for 14 and 15 hours every day.[11]

From the law stated above,* namely that the price of labour being given, the daily or weekly wage depends on the quantity of labour expended, it follows, first of all, that the lower the price of labour, the greater must be the quantity of labour, or the longer must be the working day, for the worker to secure even a miserable average wage. The low level of the price of labour acts here as a stimulus to the extension of the labour-time.[12]

However, the extension of the period of labour produces in its turn a fall in the price of labour, and with this a fall in the daily or the weekly wage.

---

n. 191) finds its compensation in the fact that, among other things, they bind many Bibles and other edifying books.

9. See *Reports of the Inspectors of Factories . . . 30 April 1863*, op. cit. The London building workers showed a very accurate appreciation of this state of affairs when, during the great strike and lock-out of 1860,* they declared that they would accept wages by the hour under only two conditions: (1) that, alongside the price of the working hour, a normal working day of 9 and 10 hours respectively should be laid down, and that the price of the hour for the 10-hour working day should be higher than that for an hour of the 9-hour working day; and (2) that every hour beyond the normal working day should be reckoned as overtime and proportionally more highly paid.

10. 'It is a very notable thing, too, that where long hours are the rule, small wages are also so' (*Reports of the Inspectors of Factories . . . 31 October 1863*, p. 9). 'The work which obtains the scanty pittance of food, is, for the most part, excessively prolonged' (*Public Health, Sixth Report*, 1864, p. 15).

11. *Reports of the Inspectors of Factories . . . 30 April 1860*, pp. 31–2.

12. The hand nail-makers of England, for example, have to work 15 hours a day, because of the low price of their labour, in order to hammer out an extremely wretched weekly wage. 'It's a great many hours in a day (6 a.m. to 8 p.m.), and he has to work hard all the time to get 11d. or 1s., and there is the wear of the tools, the cost of firing, and something for waste iron to go out

*See above, p. 686.

---

*See above, p. 685.

The determination of the price of labour by use of the ratio $\dfrac{\text{daily value of labour-power}}{\text{working day of a given number of hours}}$ shows that a mere prolongation of the working day lowers the price of labour, if no compensatory factor enters. But the same circumstances which allow the capitalist in the long run to prolong the working day also allow him at first, and compel him finally, to reduce the price of labour nominally as well until the total price of the increased number of hours goes down, and therefore the daily or weekly wage falls. Here we need only refer to two kinds of circumstance. If one man does the work of $1\frac{1}{2}$ or 2 men, the supply of labour increases, although the supply of labour-power on the market remains constant. The competition thus created between the workers allows the capitalist to force down the price of labour, while the fall in the price of labour allows him, on the other hand, to force up the hours of work still further.[13] Soon, however, this command over abnormal quantities of unpaid labour, i.e. quantities in excess of the average social amount, becomes a source of competition amongst the capitalists themselves. A part of the price of the commodity consists of the price of labour. The unpaid part of the price of labour does not need to be reckoned as part of the price of the commodity. It may be given to the buyer as a present. This is the first step taken under the impulse of competition. The second step, also compelled by competition, is the exclusion from the selling price of the commodity of at least a part of the abnormal surplus-value created by the extension of the working day. In this way, an abnormally low selling price of the commodity arises, at first sporadically, and becomes fixed by degrees; this lower selling price henceforward becomes the constant basis of a miserable wage for excessive hours of work, just as originally it was the product of those very circumstances. This movement is simply in-

of this, which takes off altogether $2\frac{1}{2}$d. or 3d' (*Children's Employment Commission, Third Report*, p. 136, n. 671). The women, although they work for the same length of time, earn a weekly wage of only 5s. (ibid., p. 137, n. 674).

13. For instance, if a factory worker refuses to work the long hours which are customary, 'he would very shortly be replaced by somebody who would work any length of time, and thus be thrown out of employment' (*Reports of the Inspectors of Factories . . . 30 April 1848*, Evidence, p. 39, n. 58). 'If one man performs the work of two . . . the rate of profits will generally be raised . . . in consequence of the additional supply of labour having diminished its price' (Senior, op. cit., p. 15).

dicated here, as the analysis of competition does not belong to this part of the investigation. Nevertheless, let the capitalist speak for himself, for a moment. 'In Birmingham there is so much competition of masters one against another, that many are obliged to do things as employers that they would otherwise be ashamed of; and yet no more money is made, but only the public gets the benefit.'[14] The reader will remember the two sorts of London bakers, of whom one sold the bread at its full price (the 'full-priced' bakers), the other below its normal price ('the underpriced', 'the undersellers').* The 'full-priced' denounced their rivals before the Parliamentary Committee of Inquiry: 'They only exist now by first defrauding the public, and next getting 18 hours' work out of their men for 12 hours' wages ... The unpaid labour of the men was made ... the source whereby the competition was carried on, and continues so to this day ... The competition among the master-bakers is the cause of the difficulty in getting rid of night-work. An underseller, who sells his bread below the cost-price according to the price of flour, must make it up by getting more out of the labour of the men ... If I got only 12 hours' work out of my men, and my neighbour got 18 or 20, he must beat me in the selling price. If the men could insist on payment for overwork, this would be set right ... A large number of those employed by the undersellers are foreigners and youths, who are obliged to accept almost any wages they can obtain.'[15]

This jeremiad is also interesting because it shows how it is only the semblance of the relations of production which is reflected by the brain of the capitalist. He does not know that the normal price of labour also includes a definite quantity of unpaid labour, and that this very unpaid labour is the normal source of his profits. The category of surplus labour-time does not exist at all for him, since it is included in the normal working day, which he thinks he

14. *Children's Employment Commission, Third Report*, Evidence, p. 66, n. 22.

15. *Report, etc., Relative to the Grievances Complained of by the Journeymen Bakers*, London, 1862, p. lii, and, in the same place, Evidence, notes 479, 359, 27. In any case, the 'full-priced' themselves, as was mentioned above, and as their spokesman, Bennett, himself admits, make their men 'generally begin work at 11 p.m. ... up to 8 o'clock the next morning ... they are then engaged all day long ... as late as 7 o'clock in the evening' (ibid., p. 22).

___

* See above, pp. 278–9, n. 14.

has paid for in the day's wages. But overtime, namely the prolongation of the working day beyond the limits corresponding to the usual price of labour, certainly does exist for him. When faced with his underselling competitor, he even insists upon extra pay for this overtime. Again, he does not know that this extra pay also includes unpaid labour, just as much as the price of the customary hour of labour does. For example, the price of one hour of the 12-hour working day is 3d., say the value-product of half a working hour, while the price of an overtime working hour is 4d., or the value-product of $\frac{2}{3}$ of a working hour. In the first case the capitalist appropriates one-half of the working hour, in the second case one third, without making any payment in return.

Chapter 21: Piece-Wages

The piece-wage is nothing but a converted form of the time-wage, just as the time-wage is a converted form of the value or price of labour-power.

In piece-wages it seems at first sight as if the use-value bought from the worker is not his labour-power as it actually functions, living labour, but labour already objectified in the product. It also seems as if the price of this labour is determined not, as with time-wages, by the fraction

$$\frac{\text{daily value of labour-power}}{\text{working day of a given number of hours}}$$

but by the producer's capacity for work.[1]

The confidence that trusts in this, the mere appearance of things, ought to receive an initial severe shock from the fact that both forms of wages exist side by side, at the same time, in the same branches of industry. For example, 'the compositors of London, as a general rule, work by the piece, time-work being the exception, while those in the country work by the day, the exception being work by the piece. The shipwrights of the port of London work by the job or piece, while those of all other ports work by the day.'[2]

In the same saddlery shops of London, often for the same work,

---

1. 'The system of piece-work illustrates an epoch in the history of the working-man; it is halfway between the position of the mere day-labourer depending upon the will of the capitalist and the co-operative artisan, who in the not distant future promises to combine the artisan and the capitalist in his own person. Piece-workers are in fact their own masters, even whilst working upon the capital of the employer' (John Watts, *Trade Societies and Strikes, Machinery and Co-operative Societies*, Manchester, 1865, pp. 52–3). I quote this little work because it is a veritable gutter full of long-decayed and apologetic commonplaces. The same Mr Watts previously dabbled in Owenism, and published in 1842 another pamphlet, *Facts and Fictions of Political Economy*, in which among other things he declared that 'property is robbery'. But that is already in the distant past.

2. T. J. Dunning, *Trades' Unions and Strikes*, London, 1860, p. 22.

piece-wages are paid to Frenchmen, and time-wages are paid to Englishmen. In the actual factories, where piece-wages are the general rule, certain specific operations have to be excepted from this form of evaluation on technical grounds, and they are therefore paid by time-wages.[3] However, it is in itself obvious that the difference of form in the payment of wages in no way alters their essential nature, although the one form may be more favourable to the development of capitalist production than the other.

Let the ordinary working day contain 12 hours, of which 6 are paid, 6 unpaid. Let its value-product be 6 shillings; the value-product of one hour of labour will therefore be 6d. Let us suppose that, as the result of experience, a worker, working with the average amount of intensity and skill, and therefore devoting to the production of an article only the amount of labour-time socially necessary, produces, in the course of 12 hours, twenty-four pieces, either distinct products or measurable parts of some integral construction. The value of these twenty-four pieces, after we have subtracted the amount of constant capital contained in them, will be 6 shillings, the value of a single piece will be 3d. The worker receives 1½d. per piece, and thus earns 3 shillings in 12 hours. Just as, with time-wages, it does not matter whether we assume that the worker works 6 hours for himself and 6 hours for the capitalist, or half of every hour for himself, and the other half for the capitalist, so here it does not matter whether we say that each individual piece is half paid for, and half unpaid for, or that the price of only twelve of the pieces is the equivalent of the value of the labour-power, while in the other twelve pieces surplus-value is incorporated.

The form of piece-wages is just as irrational as that of time-

3. Here is how the simultaneous coexistence of these two forms of wage favours cheating on the part of the manufacturers: 'A factory employs 400 people, the half of which work by the piece, and have a direct interest in working longer hours. The other 200 are paid by the day, work equally long with the others, and get no more money for their overtime . . . The work of these 200 people for half an hour a day is equal to one person's work for 50 hours, or ⅚ of one person's labour in a week, and is a positive gain to the employer' (*Reports of the Inspectors of Factories . . . 31 October 1860*, p. 9). 'Over-working to a very considerable extent still prevails; and, in most instances, with that security against detection and punishment which the law itself affords. I have in many former reports shown . . . the injury to workpeople who are not employed on piece-work, but receive weekly wages' (Leonard Horner, in *Reports of the Inspectors of Factories . . . 30 April 1859*, pp. 8–9).

wages. While, in our example, two pieces of a commodity, after subtraction of the value of the means of production consumed in them, are worth 6d., as the product of one hour of labour, the worker receives for them a price of 3d. Piece-wages are not in fact a direct expression of any relation of value. It is not, therefore, a question of measuring the value of the piece by the labour-time incorporated in it. It is rather the reverse: the labour the worker has expended must be measured by the number of pieces he has produced. In time-wages the labour is measured by its immediate duration, in piece-wages by the quantity of products in which the labour has become embodied during a given time.[4] The price of labour-time itself is finally determined by this equation: value of a day of labour = daily value of labour-power. The piece-wage is therefore only a modified form of the time-wage.

Let us now look a little more closely at the characteristic peculiarities of piece-wages.

The quality of the labour is here controlled by the work itself, which must be of good average quality if the piece-price is to be paid in full. Piece-wages become, from this point of view, the most fruitful source of reductions in wages, and of frauds committed by the capitalists.

This is because they provide an exact measure of the intensity of labour. Only the labour-time which is embodied in a quantity of commodities laid down in advance and fixed by experience counts as socially necessary labour-time and is paid as such. In the larger workshops of the London tailors, therefore, a certain piece of work, a waistcoat for instance, is called an hour, or half an hour, the hour being valued at 6d. Practice determines the size of the average product of one hour. With new fashions, repairs, etc. a contest arises between the employer and the worker as to whether a particular piece of work is one hour, and so on, until here also experience decides. Similarly in the London furniture workshops, etc. If the worker cannot provide labour of an average degree of efficiency, and if he cannot therefore supply a certain minimum of work per day, he is dismissed.[5]

4. 'Wages can be measured in two ways: either by the duration of the labour, or by its product' (*Abrégé élémentaire des principes de l'économie politique*, Paris, 1796, p. 32). The author of this anonymous work is G. Garnier.
5. 'So much weight of cotton is delivered to him' (the spinner) 'and he has to return by a certain time, in lieu of it, a given weight of twist or yarn, of a certain degree of fineness, and he is paid so much per pound for all that he so

Since the quality and intensity of the work are here controlled by the very form of the wage, superintendence of labour becomes to a great extent superfluous. Piece-wages therefore form the basis for the modern 'domestic labour' we described earlier,* as well as for a hierarchically organized system of exploitation and oppression. The latter has two fundamental forms. On the one hand piece-wages make it easier for parasites to interpose themselves between the capitalist and the wage-labourer, thus giving rise to the 'sub-letting of labour'. The profits of these middlemen come entirely from the difference between the price of labour which the capitalist pays, and the part of that price they actually allow the worker to receive.[6] In England, this system is called, characteristically, the 'sweating system'. On the other hand, piece-wages allow the capitalist to make a contract for so much per piece with the most important worker – in manufacture, with the chief of some group, in mines with the extractor of the coal, in the factory with the actual machine-worker – at a price for which this man himself undertakes the enlisting and the payment of his assistants. Here the exploitation of the worker by capital takes place through the medium of the exploitation of one worker by another.[7]

Given the system of piece-wages, it is naturally in the personal interest of the worker that he should strain his labour-power as intensely as possible; this in turn enables the capitalist to raise the normal degree of intensity of labour more easily.[8] Moreover, the

returns. If his work is defective in quality, the penalty falls on him, if less in quantity than the minimum fixed for a given time, he is dismissed and an abler operative procured' (Ure, op. cit., pp. 316–17).

6. 'It is when work passes through several hands, each of which is to take its share of profits, while only the last does the work, that the pay which reaches the workwoman is miserably disproportioned' (*Children's Employment Commission, Second Report*, p. lxx, n. 424).

7. Even the apologist Watts remarks: 'It would be a great improvement to the system of piece-work, if all the men employed on a job were partners in the contract, each according to his abilities, instead of one man being interested in over-working his fellows for his own benefit' (op. cit., p. 53). On the vile nature of the piece-work system, cf. *Children's Employment Commission, Third Report*, p. 66, n. 22, p. 11, n. 124, p. xi, n. 13, 53, 59, etc.

8. This spontaneous result is often artificially helped along, as for instance in London, in the engineering trade, where a customary trick is 'the selecting of a man who possesses superior physical strength and quickness, as the principal of several workmen, and paying him an additional rate, by the

*See above, pp. 595–9.

lengthening of the working day is now in the personal interest of the worker, since with it his daily or weekly wages rise.[9] This gradually brings on a reaction like that already described in time-wages, quite apart from the fact that the prolongation of the working day, even if the piece-wage remains constant, includes of necessity a fall in the price of the labour.

In time-wages, with few exceptions, the same wage is paid for the same function, while in piece-wages, although the price of the labour-time is measured by a definite quantity of the product, the daily or weekly wage will vary with the individual differences between the workers, one of whom will supply, within a given period, the minimum of product only, another the average, and a third more than the average. With regard to their actual income, then, there is great variety among the individual workers, according to their different degrees of skill, strength, energy and staying-power.[10] Of course, this does not alter the general relation between capital and wage-labour. First, the individual differences cancel each other out in the workshop as a whole, which thus supplies the average product within a given period of labour, and the total wages paid will be the average wage of that particular branch

quarter or otherwise, with the understanding that he is to exert himself to the utmost to induce the others, who are only paid the ordinary wages, to keep up to him ... without any comment this will go far to explain many of the complaints of stinting the action, superior skill, and working-power, made by the employers against the men' (i.e. when they are organized in trade unions) (Dunning, op. cit., pp. 22–3). As the author of this passage is himself a worker and the secretary of a trade union, this might be taken for an exaggeration. But compare, for example, the article 'Labourer' in the 'highly respectable' *Cyclopaedia of Agriculture*, ed. by J. C. Morton, where the method is recommended to the farmers as an approved one.

9. 'All those who are paid by piece-work ... profit by the transgression of the legal limits of work. This observation as to the willingness to work over-time is especially applicable to the women employed as weavers and reelers' (*Reports of the Inspectors of Factories ... 30 April 1858*, p. 9). 'This system' (piece-work) 'so advantageous to the employer ... tends directly to encourage the young potter greatly to over-work himself during the four or five years during which he is employed in the piece-work system, but at low wages ... This is ... another great cause to which the bad constitutions of the potters are to be attributed' (*Children's Employment Commission, First Report*, p. xiii).

10. 'Where the work in any trade is paid for by the piece at so much per job . . wages may very materially differ in amount ... But in work by the day there is generally an uniform rate ... recognized by both employer and employed as the standard of wages for the general run of workmen in the trade' (Dunning, op. cit., p. 17).

of industry. Second, the proportion between wages and surplus-value remains unaltered, since the mass of surplus labour supplied by each particular worker corresponds with the wage he receives. But the wider scope that piece-wages give to individuality tends to develop both that individuality, and with it the worker's sense of liberty, independence and self-control, and also the competition of workers with each other. The piece-wage therefore has a tendency, while raising the wages of individuals above the average, to lower this average itself. However, where a particular rate of piece-wage has for a long time been a fixed tradition, and its lowering, therefore, has presented especial difficulties, in such exceptional cases the masters have sometimes had recourse to the forcible transformation of piece-wages into time-wages. In 1860, for instance, this action set off a big strike among the ribbon-weavers of Coventry.[11] Finally, the piece-wage is one of the chief supports of the hour-system described in the preceding chapter.[12]

From what has been shown so far, it is apparent that the piece-

11. 'The labour of the journeymen-craftsmen is regulated by the day or by the piece ... The master-craftsmen know approximately how much work a journeyman can do every day in each trade, and they often pay them in proportion to the amount of work they perform; thus the journeymen do as much work as they can, in their own interest, and without needing any further supervision' ([Richard] Cantillon, *Essai sur la nature du commerce en général*, Amsterdam, 1756, pp. 185, 202. The first edition appeared in 1755). Cantillon, from whom Quesnay, Sir James Steuart and Adam Smith have largely drawn, here already presents the piece-wage as merely a modified form of the time-wage. The French edition of Cantillon professes in its title to be a translation from the English, but the English edition, *The Analysis of Trade, Commerce, etc., by Philip Cantillon, late of the City of London, Merchant*, is not only of later date (1759), but proves by its contents that it is a later and revised edition. For instance, in the French edition, Hume is not yet mentioned, while in the English edition, on the other hand, Petty hardly figures any longer. The English is of less theoretical significance, but it contains all kinds of details relating specifically to English commerce, bullion trade, etc. which are absent from the French text. The words on the title-page of the English edition, according to which the work is 'Taken chiefly from the manuscript of a very ingenious gentleman, deceased, and adapted, etc.', seem, therefore, a pure fiction, very customary at that time.

12. 'How often have we not seen many more workers taken on, in some workshops, than were needed actually to do the work? Workers are often set on in the expectation of work which is uncertain, or even completely imaginary; as they are paid piece-wages, the employers say to themselves that they run no risk, because any loss of working time will be at the expense of the workers who are unoccupied' (H. Grégoir, *Les Typographes devant le tribunal correctionnel de Bruxelles*, Brussels, 1865, p. 9).

wage is the form of wage most appropriate to the capitalist mode of production. Although by no means new – it figures officially side by side with time-wages in the French and English labour statutes of the fourteenth century – it only conquered a larger field of action during the period of manufacture properly so-called. In the stormy youth of large-scale industry, and particularly from 1797 to 1815, it served as a lever for the lengthening of the working day and the lowering of wages. Very important material bearing on the movement of wages during that period is to be found in the two Blue Books *Report and Evidence from the Select Committee on Petitions Respecting the Corn Laws* (Parliamentary Session of 1813–14), and *Report from the Lords' Committee, on the State of the Growth, Commerce, and Consumption of Grain, and all Laws Relating Thereto* (Session of 1814–15). Here we find documentary evidence of the constant lowering of the price of labour from the beginning of the Anti-Jacobin War. In the weaving industry, for example, piece-wages had fallen so low that in spite of the very great lengthening of the working day, the daily wage was then lower than it had been before. 'The real earnings of the cotton weaver are now far less than they were; his superiority over the common labourer, which at first was very great, has now almost entirely ceased. Indeed . . . the difference in the wages of skilful and common labour is far less now than at any former period.'[13] How little the increased intensity and extension of labour through piece-wages benefited the agricultural proletariat can be seen from the following passage from a pamphlet in favour of the landlords and farmers: 'By far the greater part of agricultural operations is done by people, who are hired for the day or on piece-work. Their weekly wages are about 12 shillings, and although it may be assumed that a man earns on piece-work under the greater stimulus to labour, 1 shilling, or perhaps 2 shillings more than on weekly wages, yet it is found, on calculating his total income, that his loss of employment, during the year, outweighs this gain . . . Further, it will generally be found that the wages of these men bear a certain proportion to the price of the necessary means of subsistence, so that a man with two children is able to bring up his family without recourse to parish relief.'[14] Malthus remarked at that time, with reference to the facts published by Parliament: 'I confess that I see,

13. *Remarks on the Commercial Policy of Great Britain*, London, 1815, p. 48.
14. *A Defence of the Landowners and Farmers of Great Britain*, London, 1814, pp. 4–5.

with misgiving, the great extension of the practice of piece-wage. Really hard work during 12 or 14 hours of the day, or for any longer time, is too much for any human being.'[15]

In those workshops which are subject to the Factory Act, the piece-wage becomes the general rule, because there capital can increase the yield of the working day only by intensifying labour.[16]

Changes in the productivity of labour mean that the same quantity of a given product represents an amount of labour-time which varies. Therefore, the piece-wage also varies, for it is the expression of the price of a definite amount of labour-time. In our earlier example, twenty-four pieces were produced in 12 hours, while the value-product of the 12 hours was 6 shillings, the daily value of the labour-power was 3 shillings, the price of an hour of labour was 3d., and the wage for one piece was $1\frac{1}{2}$d. Half an hour of labour was absorbed in one piece. If the productivity of labour is now doubled, so that the same working day supplies forty-eight pieces instead of twenty-four, and all other circumstances remain unchanged, then the piece-wage falls from $1\frac{1}{2}$d. to $\frac{3}{4}$d., as every piece now only represents $\frac{1}{4}$ instead of $\frac{1}{2}$ a working hour. $24 \times 1\frac{1}{2}$d. = 3s., and, similarly, $48 \times \frac{3}{4}$d. = 3s. In other words, the piece-wage is lowered in the same proportion as the number of pieces produced in the same time rises,[17] and therefore in the same proportion as the amount of labour-time employed on the same piece falls. This change in the piece-wage, so far purely

15. Malthus, *Inquiry into the Nature and Progress of Rent*, London, 1815 [p. 49, note].

16. 'Those who are paid by piece-work . . . constitute probably four-fifths of the workers in the factories' (*Reports of the Inspectors of Factories . . . 30 April 1858*, p. 9).

17. 'The productive power of his spinning-machine is accurately measured, and the rate of pay for work done with it decreases with, though not *as*, the increase of its productive power' (Ure, op. cit., p. 317). Ure himself later contradicts this last apologetic phrase. He admits that, for example, a lengthening of the mule causes some increase in the quantity of labour required. The amount of labour does not, therefore, diminish in the same ratio as its productivity increases. Further: 'By this increase the productive power of the machine will be augmented one-fifth. When this event happens the spinner will not be paid at the same rate for work done as he was before, but as that rate will not be diminished in the ratio of one-fifth, the improvement will augment his money earnings for any given number of hours of work,' but . . . 'the foregoing statement requires a certain modification . . . The spinner has to pay something additional for juvenile aid out of his additional sixpence' (ibid., p. 321). Improvements in machinery also 'displace a portion of adults' (ibid.) and this certainly does not tend to raise wages.

nominal, leads to constant struggles between the capitalist and the worker, either because the capitalist uses it as a pretext for actually lowering the price of labour, or because an increase in the productivity of labour is accompanied by an increase in its intensity, or because the worker takes the outward appearance of piece-wages seriously, i.e. he thinks his product is being paid for and not his labour-power, and he therefore resists any reduction of wages which is not accompanied by a reduction in the selling price of the commodity. 'The operatives . . . carefully watch the price of the raw material and the price of manufactured goods, and are thus enabled to form an accurate estimate of their master's profits.'[18]

The capitalist rightly rejects such pretensions as being gross errors as to the nature of wage-labour.[19] He cries out against this presumptuous attempt to lay taxes on the progress of industry, and declares roundly that the productivity of labour does not concern the worker in the least.[20]

18. H. Fawcett, *The Economic Position of the British Labourer*, Cambridge and London, 1865, p. 178.

19. In the London *Standard* of 26 October 1861, there is a report of proceedings taken by the firm of John Bright and Co. before the Rochdale magistrates, 'to prosecute for intimidation the agents of the Carpet Weavers Trades' Union. Bright's partners had introduced new machinery which would turn out 240 yards of carpet in the time and with the labour (!) previously required to produce 160 yards. The workmen had no claim whatever to share in the profits made by the investment of their employer's capital in mechanical improvements. Accordingly, Messrs Bright proposed to lower the rate of pay from 1½d. per yard to 1d., leaving the earnings of the men exactly the same as before for the same labour. But there was a nominal reduction, of which the operatives, it is asserted, had not fair warning beforehand.'

20. 'Trades' Unions, in their desire to maintain wages, endeavour to share in the benefits of improved machinery!' (*Quelle horreur!*) 'The demanding higher wages, because labour is abbreviated, is in other words the endeavour to establish a duty on mechanical improvements' (*On Combinations of Trades*, new edn, London, 1834, p. 42).

Chapter 22: National Differences in Wages

In Chapter 17 we were concerned with the manifold combinations which may bring about a change in the magnitude of the value of labour-power – this magnitude being considered either absolutely or relatively (i.e. as compared with surplus-value). We found also that the quantity of the means of subsistence in which the price of labour-power was realized might again undergo fluctuations independent of,[1] or different from, the changes in this price. As has been said already, the simple translation of the value, or respectively of the price, of labour-power, into the exoteric form of wages transforms all these laws into laws governing the movement of wages. What appears within the movement of wages as a series of varying combinations may appear for different countries as a set of simultaneous differences in national wage-levels. In comparing wages in different nations, we must therefore take into account all the factors that determine changes in the amount of the value of labour-power; the price and the extent of the prime necessities of life in their natural and historical development, the cost of training the workers, the part played by the labour of women and children, the productivity of labour, and its extensive and intensive magnitude. Even the most superficial comparison requires the prior reduction of the average daily wage for the same trades, in different countries, to a uniform working day. After this reduction of the daily wage to the same terms, the time-wage must again be translated into the piece-wage, as only the latter can be a measure both of the productivity and of the intensity of labour.

In every country there is a certain average intensity of labour, below which the labour for the production of a commodity re-

1. 'It is not accurate to say that wages' (he is dealing here with the price of labour-power) 'are increased, because they purchase more of a cheaper article' (David Buchanan, in his edition of Adam Smith's *Wealth of Nations*, 1814, Vol. I, p. 417, n.).

quires more than the time socially necessary, and therefore does not count as labour of normal quality. In a given country, only a degree of intensity which is above the national average alters the measurement of value by the mere duration of labour-time. It is otherwise on the world market, whose integral parts are the individual countries. The average intensity of labour changes from country to country; here is it greater, there less. These national averages form a scale whose unit of measurement is the average unit of universal labour. The more intense national labour, therefore, as compared with the less intense, produces in the same time more value, which expresses itself in more money.

But the law of value is yet more modified in its international application by the fact that, on the world market, national labour which is more productive also counts as more intensive, as long as the more productive nation is not compelled by competition to lower the selling price of its commodities to the level of their value.

In proportion as capitalist production is developed in a country, so, in the same proportion, do the national intensity and productivity of labour there rise above the international level.[2] The different quantities of commodities of the same kind, produced in different countries in the same working time, have, therefore, unequal international values, which are expressed in different prices, i.e. in sums of money varying according to international values. The relative value of money will therefore be less in the nation with a more developed capitalist mode of production than in the nation with a less developed capitalism. It follows then that nominal wages, the equivalent of labour-power expressed in money, will also be higher in the first nation than in the second; but this by no means proves that the same can be said of real wages, i.e. the means of subsistence placed at the disposal of the worker.

But even apart from these relative differences in the value of money in different countries, it will frequently be found that the daily or weekly wage in the first nation is higher than in the second while the relative price of labour, i.e. the price of labour as compared both with surplus-value and with the value of the product, stands higher in the second than in the first.[3]

2. We shall inquire, in another place, what circumstances in relation to productivity may modify this law for individual branches of production.

3. James Anderson remarks, in a polemic against Adam Smith: 'It deserves, likewise, to be remarked, that although the apparent price of labour is usually

J. W. Cowell, a member of the Factory Commission of 1833, came to the conclusion, after careful investigation of the spinning trade, that 'in England wages are *virtually* lower to the capitalist, though higher to the operative than on the Continent of Europe' (Ure, p. 314). The English factory inspector Alexander Redgrave, in his *Report* of 31 October 1866, proves, by comparing the statistics of Continental states, that in spite of lower wages and much longer hours of work, Continental labour is, in proportion to the product, dearer than English. The English manager of a cotton factory in Oldenburg declared that the working hours there were from 5.30 a.m. to 8 p.m., Saturdays included, and that the workers, when under English overseers, did not supply during this time quite so much of the product as the English in 10 hours, while they supplied much less when under German overseers. Wages are much lower than in England, in many cases lower by 50 per cent, but the number of 'hands' in proportion to the machinery is much greater, in certain departments in the proportion of 5:3. Mr Redgrave also gives very precise details as to the Russian cotton factories. The data were given him by an English manager until recently employed there. On this Russian soil, so fruitful of all infamies, the old horrors of the early days of English factories are in full swing. The managers are, of course, English, as the native Russian capitalist is incapable of handling factory business. Despite all the over-work, which continues throughout the day and the night, despite the most shameful under-payment of the workers, Russian manufacturing only manages to vegetate thanks to the prohibition of foreign competition. I give, in conclusion, a comparative table of Mr Redgrave's on the average number of

---

lower in poor countries, where the produce of the soil, and grain in general, is cheap; yet it is in fact for the most part really higher than in other countries. For it is not the wages that is given to the labourer per day that constitutes the real price of labour, although it is its apparent price. The real price is that which a certain quantity of work performed actually costs the employer; and considered in this light, labour is in almost all cases cheaper in rich countries than in those that are poorer, although the price of grain, and other provisions, is usually much lower in the last than in the first ... Labour estimated by the day, is much lower in Scotland than in England ... Labour by the piece is generally cheaper in England' (James Anderson, *Observations on the Means of Exciting a Spirit of National Industry, etc.*, Edinburgh, 1777, pp. 350–51). In fact, the inverse process also occurs: a low level of wages produces, in its turn, dearness of labour. 'Labour being dearer in Ireland than it is in England ... because the wages are so much lower' (N. 2074, in *Royal Commission on Railways, Minutes*, 1867).

spindles per factory and per spinner in the different countries of Europe. He himself remarks that these figures were collected a few years ago, and that since that time the size of the factories and the number of spindles per worker in England has increased. He assumes, however, that an approximately equal advance has been made in the Continental countries mentioned, so that the numbers given would still retain their value for purposes of comparison.

AVERAGE NUMBER OF SPINDLES PER FACTORY

England	12,600
France	1,500
Prussia	1,500
Belgium	4,000
Saxony	4,500
Austria	7,000
Switzerland	8,000

AVERAGE NUMBER OF SPINDLES PER PERSON
One person to:

France	14	spindles
Russia	28	,,
Prussia	37	,,
Bavaria	46	,,
Austria	49	,,
Belgium	50	,,
Saxony	50	,,
Switzerland	55	,,
Smaller German states	55	,,
Great Britain	74	,,

'This comparison,' says Mr Redgrave, 'is yet more unfavourable to Great Britain, inasmuch as there is so large a number of factories in which weaving by power is carried on in conjunction with spinning' (while in the table the weavers are not deducted) 'and the factories abroad are chiefly spinning factories; if it were possible to compare like with like, strictly, I could find many cotton spinning factories in my district in which mules containing 2,200 spindles are minded by one man (the "minder") and two assistants only, turning off daily 220 lb. of yarn, measuring 400 miles in length' (*Reports of the Inspectors of Factories . . . 31 October 1866*, pp. 31–7, passim).

It is well known that in Eastern Europe, as well as in Asia, English companies have undertaken the construction of railways, and have, in making them, employed a certain number of English workers side by side with the locals. Practical necessity has thus compelled them to take into account the national differences in the intensity of labour, but this has not brought them any loss. Their experience shows that even if the level of wages more or less corresponds with the average intensity of labour, the relative price of labour (i.e. the price of labour in relation to the product) generally varies in the inverse direction.

In an *Essay on the Rate of Wages*,[4] one of his first economic writings, H. Carey tries to prove that differences in national wage-levels are directly proportional to the degree of productivity of the working day of each nation, in order to draw from this international ratio the deduction that wages everywhere rise and fall in proportion to the productivity of labour. The whole of our analysis of the production of surplus-value shows that this deduction would be absurd even if Carey himself had demonstrated his premises, instead of shuffling a confused mass of statistical material to and fro in his usual uncritical and superficial manner. The best of all is that he does not assert that things actually are as they ought to be according to his theory. For state intervention has falsified the natural economic relation. The different national wages must therefore be calculated on the assumption that the part of them that goes to the state in the form of taxes was received by the worker himself. Ought not Mr Carey to consider further whether these 'state expenses' are not the 'natural fruits' of capitalist development? His reasoning is quite worthy of the man who, first of all, declared that capitalist relations of production were eternal laws of nature and reason, whose free and harmonious working was only disturbed by the intervention of the state, and then discovered afterwards that state intervention, i.e. the defence of those laws of nature and reason by the state, *alias* the system of protection, was necessitated by the diabolical influence of England on the world market, an influence which, it appears, does not spring from the natural laws of capitalist production. He discovered, further, that the theorems of Ricardo and others, in which existing social antagonisms and contradictions are formu-

4. *Essay on the Rate of Wages: With an Examination of the Causes of the Differences in the Condition of the Labouring Population throughout the World*, Philadelphia, 1835.

lated, are not the ideal product of the real economic movement, but, on the contrary, that the real antagonisms of capitalist production in England and elsewhere are the result of the theories of Ricardo and others! Finally he discovered that it is, in the last resort, trade which destroys the inborn beauties and harmonies of the capitalist mode of production. A step further, and he will perhaps discover that the one evil in capitalist production is capital itself. Only a man with such an atrocious lack of the critical faculty, and such spurious erudition, deserved, in spite of his Protectionist heresy, to become the secret source of the harmonious wisdom of a Bastiat, and of all the other free-trade optimists of the present day.

Part Seven

The Process of
Accumulation of Capital

The transformation of a sum of money into means of production and labour-power is the first phase of the movement undergone by the quantum of value which is going to function as capital. It takes place in the market, within the sphere of circulation. The second phase of the movement, the process of production, is complete as soon as the means of production have been converted into commodities whose value exceeds that of their component parts, and therefore contains the capital originally advanced plus a surplus-value. These commodities must then be thrown back into the sphere of circulation. They must be sold, their value must be realized in money, this money must be transformed once again into capital, and so on, again and again. This cycle, in which the same phases are continually gone through in succession, forms the circulation of capital.

The first condition of accumulation is that the capitalist must have contrived to sell his commodities, and to reconvert into capital the greater part of the money received from their sale. In the following pages, we shall assume that capital passes through its process of circulation in the normal way. The detailed analysis of the process will be found in Volume 2.

The capitalist who produces surplus-value, i.e. who extracts unpaid labour directly from the workers and fixes it in commodities, is admittedly the first appropriator of this surplus-value, but he is by no means its ultimate proprietor. He has to share it afterwards with capitalists who fulfil other functions in social production taken as a whole, with the owner of the land, and with yet other people. Surplus-value is therefore split up into various parts. Its fragments fall to various categories of person, and take on various mutually independent forms, such as profit, interest, gains made through trade, ground rent, etc. We shall be able to deal with these modified forms of surplus-value only in Volume 3.

On the one hand, then, we assume here that the capitalist sells the commodities he has produced at their value, and we shall not concern ourselves with their later return to the market, or the new forms that capital assumes while in the sphere of circulation, or the concrete conditions of reproduction hidden within those forms. On the other hand, we treat the capitalist producer as the owner of the entire surplus-value, or, perhaps better, as the representative of all those who will share the booty with him. We shall therefore begin by considering accumulation from an abstract point of view, i.e. simply as one aspect of the immediate process of production.

In so far as accumulation actually takes place, the capitalist must have succeeded in selling his commodities, and in reconverting the money shaken loose from them into capital. Moreover, the break-up of surplus-value into various fragments does not affect either its nature or the conditions under which it becomes an element in accumulation. Whatever the proportion of surplus-value which the capitalist producer retains for himself, or yields up to others, he is the one who in the first instance appropriates it. In our presentation of accumulation, then, we assume no more than is assumed by the actual process of accumulation itself. On the other hand, the simple, fundamental form of the process of accumulation is obscured both by the splitting-up of surplus-value and by the mediating movement of circulation. An exact analysis of the process, therefore, demands that we should, for a time, disregard all phenomena that conceal the workings of its inner mechanism.

Chapter 23: Simple Reproduction

Whatever the social form of the production process, it has to be continuous, it must periodically repeat the same phases. A society can no more cease to produce than it can cease to consume. When viewed, therefore, as a connected whole, and in the constant flux of its incessant renewal, every social process of production is at the same time a process of reproduction.

The conditions of production are at the same time the conditions of reproduction. No society can go on producing, in other words no society can reproduce, unless it constantly reconverts a part of its products into means of production, or elements of fresh products. All other circumstances remaining the same, the society can reproduce or maintain its wealth on the existing scale only by replacing the means of production which have been used up – i.e. the instruments of labour, the raw material and the auxiliary substances – with an equal quantity of new articles. These must be separated from the mass of the yearly product, and incorporated once again into the production process. Hence a definite portion of each year's product belongs to the sphere of production. Destined for productive consumption from the very first, this portion exists, for the most part, in forms which by their very nature exclude the possibility of individual consumption.

If production has a capitalist form, so too will reproduction. Just as in the capitalist mode of production the labour process appears only as a means towards the process of valorization, so in the case of reproduction it appears only as a means of reproducing the value advanced as capital, i.e. as self-valorizing value. The economic character of capitalist becomes firmly fixed to a man only if his money constantly functions as capital. If, for instance, a sum of £100 has this year been converted into capital, and has produced a surplus-value of £20, it must continue during the next year, and subsequent years, to repeat the same operation. As a periodic increment of the value of the capital, or a periodic fruit borne by capital-in-process, surplus-value acquires the form of a revenue arising out of capital.[1]

If this revenue serves the capitalist only as a fund to provide for his consumption, and if it is consumed as periodically as it is gained, then, other things being equal, simple reproduction takes place. And although this reproduction is a mere repetition of the process of production, on the same scale as before, this mere repetition, or continuity, imposes on the process certain new characteristics, or rather, causes the disappearance of some apparent characteristics possessed by the process in isolation.

The purchase of labour-power for a fixed period is the prelude to the production process; and this prelude is constantly repeated when the period of time for which the labour-power has been sold comes to an end, when a definite period of production, such as a week or a month, has elapsed. But the worker is not paid until after he has expended his labour-power, and realized both the value of his labour-power and a certain quantity of surplus-value in the shape of commodities. He has therefore produced not only surplus-value, which we for the present regard as a fund to meet the private consumption of the capitalist, but also the variable capital, the fund out of which he himself is paid, before it flows back to him in the shape of wages; and his employment lasts only as long as he continues to reproduce this fund. This is the reason for the formula of the economists, mentioned in Chapter 18, under II, which presents wages as a share in the product itself.[2] What flows back to the worker in the shape of wages is a portion of the product he himself continuously reproduces. The capitalist, it is true, pays him the value of the commodity in money, but this money is merely the transmuted form of the product of his labour. While he

1. 'The rich, who consume the products of the labour of others, can only obtain them by making exchanges' (purchases of commodities). 'They therefore seem to be exposed to an early exhaustion of their reserve funds ... But, in the social order, wealth has acquired the power of reproducing itself through the labour of others ... Wealth, like labour, and by means of labour, bears fruit every year, but this fruit can be destroyed every year without making the rich man any poorer thereby. This fruit is the revenue which arises out of capital' (Sismondi, *Nouveaux Principes d'économie politique*, Paris, 1819, Vol. 1, pp. 81–2).

2. 'Wages as well as profits are to be considered, each of them, as really a portion of the finished product' (Ramsay, op. cit., p. 142). 'The share of the product which comes to the worker in the form of wages' (J. Mill, *Élémens, etc.*, tr. Parisot, Paris, 1823, pp. 33–4).

is converting a portion of the means of production into products, a portion of his former product is being turned into money. It is his labour of last week, or of last year, that pays for his labour-power this week or this year. The illusion created by the money-form vanishes immediately if, instead of taking a single capitalist and a single worker, we take the whole capitalist class and the whole working class. The capitalist class is constantly giving to the working class drafts, in the form of money, on a portion of the product produced by the latter and appropriated by the former. The workers give these drafts back just as constantly to the capitalists, and thereby withdraw from the latter their allotted share of their own product. The transaction is veiled by the commodity-form of the product and the money-form of the commodity.

Variable capital is therefore only a particular historical form of appearance of the fund for providing the means of subsistence, or the labour-fund, which the worker requires for his own maintenance and reproduction, and which, in all systems of social production, he must himself produce and reproduce. If the labour-fund constantly flows to him in the form of money that pays for his labour, it is because his own product constantly moves away from him in the form of capital. But this form of appearance of the labour-fund makes no difference to the fact that it is the worker's own objectified labour which is advanced to him by the capitalist.[3] Let us take a peasant liable to do compulsory labour services. He works on his own land with his own means of production for, say, three days a week. The other three days are devoted to forced labour on the lord's domain. He constantly reproduces his own labour-fund, which never, in his case, takes the form of a money payment for his labour, advanced by another person. But in return his unpaid and forced labour for the lord never acquires the character of voluntary and paid labour. If one, fine morning, the landowner appropriates to himself the plot of land, the cattle, the seed, in short, the means of production of the peasant, the latter will thenceforth be obliged to sell his labour-power to the former. He will, other things being equal, labour six days a week as before, three for himself, three for his former lord, who thenceforth becomes a wage-paying capitalist. As before, he will

3. 'When capital is employed in advancing to the workman his wages, it adds nothing to the funds for the maintenance of labour' (Cazenove, in a note to his edition of Malthus's *Definitions in Political Economy*, London, 1853, p. 22).

use up the means of production as means of production, and transfer their value to the product. As before, a definite portion of the product will be devoted to reproduction. But from the moment that forced labour is changed into wage-labour, the labour-fund, which the peasant himself continues as before to produce and reproduce, takes the form of a quantity of capital advanced in the form of wages by the lord of the land. The bourgeois economist, whose limited mentality is unable to separate the form of appearance from the thing which appears within that form, shuts his eyes to the fact that even at the present time the labour-fund only crops up exceptionally on the face of the globe in the form of capital.[4]

Variable capital, it is true, loses its character of a value advanced out of the capitalist's funds[5] only when we view the process of capitalist production in the flow of its constant renewal. But that process must have had a beginning of some kind. From our present standpoint it therefore seems likely that the capitalist, once upon a time, became possessed of money by some form of primitive* accumulation [*ursprüngliche Akkumulation*] that took place independently of the unpaid labour of other people, and that this was therefore how he was able to frequent the market as a buyer of labour-power. However this may be, the mere continuity of the process of capitalist production, or simple reproduction, brings about other remarkable transformations which seize hold of not only the variable, but the total capital.

If a surplus-value of £200 is generated every year by the use of a capital of £1,000, and if this surplus-value is consumed every year, it is clear that when this process has been repeated for five years, the surplus-value consumed will amount to $5 \times £200$, or the £1,000 originally advanced. If only a part were consumed, say one-half, the same result would follow at the end of ten years, since $10 \times$

4. 'The wages of labour are advanced by capitalists in the case of less than one-fourth of the labourers of the earth' (Richard Jones, *Textbook of Lectures on the Political Economy of Nations*, Hertford, 1852, p. 36).

5. 'Though the manufacturer' (i.e. the worker engaged in manufacture) 'has his wages advanced to him by his master, he in reality costs him no expense, the value of those wages being generally restored, together with a profit, in the improved value of the subject upon which his labour is bestowed' (A. Smith, op. cit., Bk II, Ch. 3, [Vol. 2, p. 355 in Wakefield's edition of 1835–9.]

* We have preferred 'primitive accumulation' to 'original accumulation' as the phrase has become established by now as part of the English language.

£100 = £1,000. The following general formulation emerges: the value of the capital advanced divided by the surplus-value annually consumed gives the number of years, or periods of reproduction, at the expiration of which the capital originally advanced has been consumed by the capitalist and has disappeared. The capitalist thinks that he is consuming the produce of the unpaid labour of others, i.e. the surplus-value, and is keeping intact the value of his original capital; but what he thinks cannot alter the actual situation. After the lapse of a certain number of years, the value of the capital he possesses is equal to the sum total of the surplus-value he has appropriated during those years, and the total value he has consumed is equal to the value of his original capital. It is true that he has in hand a quantity of capital whose magnitude has not changed, and that part of it, such as buildings, machinery, etc., was already there when he began to conduct his business operations. But we are not concerned here with the material components of the capital. We are concerned with its value. When a person consumes the whole of his property, by taking upon himself debts equal to the value of that property, it is clear that his property represents nothing but the sum total of his debts. And so it is with the capitalist; when he has consumed the equivalent of his original capital, the value of his present capital represents nothing but the total amount of surplus-value appropriated by him without payment. Not a single atom of the value of his old capital continues to exist.

Therefore, entirely leaving aside all accumulation, the mere continuity of the production process, in other words simple reproduction, sooner or later, and necessarily, converts all capital into accumulated capital, or capitalized surplus-value. Even if that capital was, on its entry into the process of production, the personal property of the man who employs it, and was originally acquired by his own labour, it sooner or later becomes value appropriated without an equivalent, the unpaid labour of others materialized either in the money-form or in some other way. We saw in Chapter 4 that for the transformation of money into capital something more was required than the production and circulation of commodities. We saw that on the one hand the possessor of value or money, on the other hand the possessor of the value-creating substance – on the one hand, the possessor of the means of production and subsistence, on the other, the possessor of nothing but labour-power – must confront each other as buyer and seller.

A division between the product of labour and labour itself, between the objective conditions of labour and subjective labour-power, was therefore the real foundation and the starting-point of the process of capitalist production.

But what at first was merely a starting-point becomes, by means of nothing but the continuity of the process, by simple reproduction, the characteristic result of capitalist production, a result which is constantly renewed and perpetuated. On the one hand, the production process incessantly converts material wealth into capital, into the capitalist's means of enjoyment and his means of valorization. On the other hand, the worker always leaves the process in the same state as he entered it – a personal source of wealth, but deprived of any means of making that wealth a reality for himself. Since, before he enters the process, his own labour has already been alienated [*entfremdet*] from him, appropriated by the capitalist, and incorporated with capital, it now, in the course of the process, constantly objectifies itself so that it becomes a product alien to him [*fremder Produkt*]. Since the process of production is also the process of the consumption of labour-power by the capitalist, the worker's product is not only constantly converted into commodities, but also into capital, i.e. into value that sucks up the worker's value-creating power, means of subsistence that actually purchase human beings, and means of production that employ the people who are doing the producing.[6] Therefore the worker himself constantly produces objective wealth, in the form of capital, an alien power that dominates and exploits him; and the capitalist just as constantly produces labour-power, in the form of a subjective source of wealth which is abstract, exists merely in the physical body of the worker, and is separated from its own means of objectification and realization; in short, the capitalist produces the worker as a wage-labourer.[7] This incessant reproduction, this perpetuation of the worker, is the absolutely necessary condition for capitalist production.

6. 'This is a remarkably peculiar property of productive labour. Whatever is productively consumed is capital, and it becomes capital by consumption' (James Mill, op. cit., p. 242). James Mill, however, was never able to track down this 'remarkably peculiar property'.

7. 'It is true indeed, that the first introducing a manufacture emploies many poor, but they cease not to be so, and the continuance of it makes many' (*Reasons for a Limited Exportation of Wool*, London, 1677, p. 19). 'The farmer now absurdly asserts, that he keeps the poor. They are indeed kept in misery' (*Reasons for the late Increase of the Poor Rates: or a comparative view of the prices of labour and provisions*, London 1777, p. 31).

The worker's consumption is of two kinds. While producing he consumes the means of production with his labour, and converts them into products with a higher value than that of the capital advanced. This is his productive consumption. It is at the same time consumption of his labour-power by the capitalist who has bought it. On the other hand, the worker uses the money paid to him for his labour-power to buy the means of subsistence; this is his individual consumption. The worker's productive consumption and his individual consumption are therefore totally distinct. In the former, he acts as the motive power of capital, and belongs to the capitalist. In the latter, he belongs to himself, and performs his necessary vital functions outside the production process. The result of the first kind of consumption is that the capitalist continues to live, of the second, that the worker himself continues to live.

When dealing with the 'working day', we saw that the worker is often compelled to make his individual consumption into a merely incidental part of the production process. In such a case, he provides himself with means of subsistence in order to keep his labour-power in motion, just as coal and water are supplied to the steam-engine, and oil to the wheel. His means of consumption are then merely the means of consumption of a means of production; his individual consumption is directly productive consumption. This, however, appears to be an abuse, rather than an essential attribute of the capitalist process of production.[8]

The matter takes quite another aspect if we contemplate not the single capitalist and the single worker, but the capitalist class and the working class, not an isolated process of production, but capitalist production in full swing, and on its actual social scale. By converting part of his capital into labour-power, the capitalist valorizes the value of his entire capital. He kills two birds with one stone. He profits not only by what he receives from the worker, but also by what he gives him. The capital given in return for labour-power is converted into means of subsistence which have to be consumed to reproduce the muscles, nerves, bones and brains of existing workers, and to bring new workers into existence. Within the limits of what is absolutely necessary, therefore, the indi-

8. Rossi would not have declaimed so emphatically on this point if he had really penetrated the secret of 'productive consumption'.*

*Cf., for example, P. Rossi, *Cours d'économie politique*, Brussels, 1843, p. 370: 'To conceive capacity for labour in abstraction from the workers' means of subsistence during the production process is to conceive a phantom.'

vidual consumption of the working class is the reconversion of the means of subsistence given by capital in return for labour-power into fresh labour-power which capital is then again able to exploit. It is the production and reproduction of the capitalist's most indispensable means of production: the worker. The individual consumption of the worker, whether it occurs inside or outside the workshop, inside or outside the labour process, remains an aspect of the production and reproduction of capital, just as the cleaning of machinery does, whether it is done during the labour process, or when intervals in that process permit. The fact that the worker performs acts of individual consumption in his own interest, and not to please the capitalist, is something entirely irrelevant to the matter. The consumption of food by a beast of burden does not become any less a necessary aspect of the production process because the beast enjoys what it eats. The maintenance and reproduction of the working class remains a necessary condition for the reproduction of capital. But the capitalist may safely leave this to the worker's drives for self-preservation and propagation. All the capitalist cares for is to reduce the worker's individual consumption to the necessary minimum, and an immense distance separates his attitude from the crudeness of the South American mine-owners, who force their workers to consume the more substantial, rather than the less substantial, kind of food.[9]

Hence both the capitalist and his ideologist, the political economist, consider only that part of the worker's individual consumption to be productive which is required for the perpetuation of the working class, and which therefore must take place in order that the capitalist may have labour-power to consume. What the worker consumes over and above that minimum for his own pleasure is seen as unproductive consumption.[10] If the accumulation of capital were to cause a rise of wages and an increase in the worker's consumption unaccompanied by an increase in the consumption of labour-power by capital, the additional capital would be con-

9. 'The workers in the mines of South America, whose daily task (the heaviest perhaps in the world) consists in bringing to the surface on their shoulders a load of metal weighing from 180 to 200 pounds, from a depth of 450 feet, live on bread and beans only; they themselves would prefer the bread alone for food, but their masters, who have found out tha⁺ the men cannot work so hard on bread, treat them like horses, and compel them to eat beans; beans are relatively much richer in bone-ash than is bread' (Liebig, op. cit., Vol. 1, p. 194, n.).

10. James Mill, op. cit., pp. 238 ff.

sumed unproductively.[11] In reality, the individual consumption of the worker is unproductive even from his own point of view, for it simply reproduces the needy individual; it is productive to the capitalist and to the state, since it is the production of a force which produces wealth for other people.[12]

From the standpoint of society, then, the working class, even when it stands outside the direct labour process, is just as much an appendage of capital as the lifeless instruments of labour are. Even its individual consumption is, within certain limits, a mere aspect of the process of capital's reproduction. That process, however, takes good care to prevent the workers, those instruments of production who are possessed of consciousness, from running away, by constantly removing their product from one pole to the other, to the opposite pole of capital. Individual consumption provides, on the one hand, the means for the workers' maintenance and reproduction; on the other hand, by the constant annihilation of the means of subsistence, it provides for their continued re-appearance on the labour-market. The Roman slave was held by chains; the wage-labourer is bound to his owner by invisible threads. The appearance of independence is maintained by a constant change in the person of the individual employer, and by the legal fiction of a contract.

In former times, capital resorted to legislation, whenever it seemed necessary, in order to enforce its proprietary rights over the free worker. For instance, down to 1815 the emigration of mechanics employed in machine-making was forbidden in England, on pain of severe punishment.

The reproduction of the working class implies at the same time the transmission and accumulation of skills from one generation to another.[13] The capitalist regards the existence of such a skilled

11. 'If the price of labour should rise so high that, notwithstanding the increase of capital, no more could be employed, I should say that such increase of capital would be still unproductively consumed' (Ricardo, op. cit., p. 163).

12. 'The only productive consumption, properly so called, is the consumption or destruction of wealth' (he means the using up of the means of production) 'by capitalists with a view to reproduction ... The workman ... is a productive consumer to the person who employs him, and to the state, but not, strictly speaking, to himself' (Malthus, *Definitions, etc.*, p. 30).

13. 'The only thing, of which one can say, that it is stored up and prepared beforehand, is the skill of the labourer ... The accumulation and storage of skilled labour, that most important operation, is, as regards the great mass of labourers, accomplished without any capital whatever' (Hodgskin, *Labour Defended, etc.*, p. 13).

working class as one of the conditions of production which belong to him, and in fact views it as the real existence of his variable capital. This becomes very clear as soon as a crisis threatens him with its loss. As a result of the American Civil War and the accompanying cotton famine, the majority of the cotton workers of Lancashire were, as is well known, thrown out of work. Both from the working class itself, and from other social strata, there arose a cry for state aid, or voluntary national subscriptions, in order to make possible the emigration of those who were 'redundant' to the English colonies or to the United States. That was the time when *The Times* published a letter (24 March 1863) from Edmund Potter, a former President of the Manchester Chamber of Commerce. This letter was rightly described in the House of Commons as 'the manifesto of the manufacturers'.[14] We shall reproduce here a few characteristic passages, in which the proprietary rights of capital over labour-power are unblushingly asserted.

'He' (the man out of work) 'may be told the supply of cotton-workers is too large . . . and . . . must . . . in fact be reduced by a third, perhaps, and that then there will be a healthy demand for the remaining two-thirds . . . Public opinion . . . urges emigration . . . The master cannot willingly see his labour supply being removed; he may think, and perhaps justly, that it is both wrong and unsound . . . But if the public funds are to be devoted to assist emigration, he has a right to be heard, and perhaps to protest.' The same Potter then proceeds to point out how useful the cotton industry is, how 'it has undoubtedly drawn the surplus population from Ireland and from the agricultural districts', how immense is its extent, how it yielded $\frac{5}{13}$ths of total English exports in the year 1860, how, after a few years, it will again expand by the extension of the market, particularly of the Indian market, and by calling forth a plentiful supply of cotton at 6d. per lb. He then continues: '[It is not to be denied that] time – one, two, or three years it may be – will produce the quantity . . . The question I would put then is this – Is the trade worth retaining? Is it worth while to keep the machinery' (he means the living labour-machines) 'in order, and is it not the greatest folly to think of parting with that? I think it is. I allow that the workers are not a property, not the property of Lancashire and the masters; but they are the

14. 'That letter might be looked upon as the manifesto of the manufacturers' (Ferrand, 'Motion on the Cotton Famine', House of Commons, 27 April 1863).

strength of both; they are the mental and trained power which cannot be replaced for a generation; the mere machinery which they work might much of it be beneficially replaced, nay improved, in a twelvemonth.[15] Encourage or allow (!) the working-power to emigrate, and what of the capitalist?' This cry from the heart reminds one of Lord Chamberlain Kalb.* 'Take away the cream of the workers, and fixed capital will depreciate in a great degree, and the floating will not subject itself to a struggle with the short supply of inferior labour . . . We are told the workers wish it' (emigration). 'Very natural it is that they should do so . . . Reduce, compress the cotton trade by taking away its working power and reducing their wages expenditure, say one-fifth, or five millions, and what then would happen to the class above, the small shopkeepers; and what of the rents, the cottage rents . . . Trace out the effects upward to the small farmer, the better householder, and . . . the landowner, and say if there could be any suggestion more suicidal to all classes of the country than enfeebling a nation by exporting the best of its manufacturing population, and destroying the value of some of its most productive capital and enrichment . . . I advise a loan (of five or six millions sterling) . . . extending it may be over two or three years, administered by special commissioners added to the Boards of Guardians in the cotton districts, under special legislative regulations, enforcing some occupation or labour, as a means of keep-

15. It will not be forgotten that this same capital sings quite another tune under ordinary circumstances, when it is a question of reducing wages. Then the 'masters' exclaim with one voice (see above, p. 549): 'The factory operatives should keep in wholesome remembrance the fact that theirs is really a low species of skilled labour; and that there is none which is more easily acquired, or of its quality more amply remunerated, or which, by a short training of the least expert, can be more quickly, as well as abundantly, acquired . . . The master's machinery' (which we now learn can advantageously be replaced and improved within twelve months) 'really plays a far more important part in the business of production than the labour and skill of the operative' (who cannot now be replaced in less than thirty years), 'which six months' education can teach, and a common labourer can learn.'

*Kalb was a character in Schiller's tragedy *Kabale und Liebe*. In Act 3, Scene 2, Kalb, who is Lord Chamberlain of a petty German princely court, hears of the decision of the President (another court official) to resign, which would bring him down as well. 'But what of me? You can at least talk well' (he says, addressing the President), 'you are a man of learning. But what would become of me if his highness dismissed me?'

ing up at least the moral standard of the recipients of the loan ...
can anything be worse for landowners or masters than parting
with the best of the workers, and demoralizing and disappointing
the rest by an extended depletive emigration, a depletion of capital
and value in an entire province?'

Potter, the chosen mouthpiece of the cotton manufacturers,
distinguishes between two sorts of 'machinery'. Both belong to
the capitalist, but one stands in his factory, while the other is
housed in cottages outside the factory at night-time and on Sundays. The one is inanimate, the other living. The inanimate machinery not only wears out and loses value from day to day, but also
much of it becomes out of date so quickly, owing to constant
technical progress, that it can be replaced with advantage by new
machinery after a few months. With the living machinery the reverse is true: it gets better the longer it lasts, and in proportion as
the skill handed down from one generation to another accumulates. Here is the answer given by *The Times* to the cotton magnate:

'Mr Edmund Potter is so impressed with the exceptional and
supreme importance of the cotton masters that, in order to preserve this class and perpetuate their profession, he would keep half
a million of the labouring class confined in a great moral workhouse against their will. "Is the trade worth retaining?" asks Mr
Potter. "Certainly by all honest means it is," we answer. "Is it
worth while keeping the machinery in order?" again asks Mr
Potter. Here we hesitate. By the "machinery", Mr Potter means
the human machinery, for he goes on to protest that he does not
mean to use them as an absolute property. We must confess that
we do not think it "worth while", or even possible, to keep the
human machinery in order – that is to shut it up and keep it oiled
till it is wanted. Human machinery *will* rust under inaction, oil and
rub it as you may. Moreover, the human machinery will, as we
have just seen, get the steam up of its own accord, and burst or
run amuck in our great towns. It might, as Mr Potter says, require some time to reproduce the workers, but, having machinists
and capitalists at hand, we could always find thrifty, hard, industrious men wherewith to improvise more master-manufacturers
than we can ever want. Mr Potter talks of the trade reviving "in one,
two, or three years", and he asks us not "to encourage or allow(!)
the working power to emigrate". He says that it is very natural the
workers should wish to emigrate; but he thinks that in spite of
their desire, the nation ought to keep this half million of workers

with their 700,000 dependants, shut up in the cotton districts; and as a necessary consequence, he must of course think that the nation ought to keep down their discontent by force, and sustain them by alms – and upon the chance that the cotton masters may some day want them ... The time is come when the great public opinion of these islands must operate to save this "working power" from those who would deal with it as they would deal with iron, and coal, and cotton.'[16]

This article was only a *jeu d'esprit*. The 'great public opinion' was in fact of Mr Potter's own opinion, it too thought that the factory workers were movable accessories to the factories. Their emigration was prevented.[17] They were locked up in that 'moral workhouse', the cotton districts, and they form, as before, 'the strength' of the cotton manufacturers of Lancashire.

Capitalist production therefore reproduces in the course of its own process the separation between labour-power and the conditions of labour. It thereby reproduces and perpetuates the conditions under which the worker is exploited. It incessantly forces him to sell his labour-power in order to live, and enables the capitalist to purchase labour-power in order that he may enrich himself.[18] It is no longer a mere accident that capitalist and worker confront each other in the market as buyer and seller. It is the alternating rhythm of the process itself which throws the worker back onto the market again and again as a seller of his labour-power and continually transforms his own product into a means by which another man can purchase him. In reality, the worker belongs to capital before he has sold himself to the capitalist. His economic bondage[19] is

16. *The Times*, 24 March 1863.

17. Parliament did not vote a single farthing in aid of emigration, but simply passed some Act empowering the municipal corporations to keep the workers in a state of semi-starvation, i.e. to exploit them without paying the normal wages. On the other hand, when the cattle disease broke out three years later, Parliament hastened to break even its own normal customs, and immediately voted millions for the indemnification of the millionaire landlords, whose farmers in any event came out of it without losing anything, owing to the rise in the price of meat. The bestial howls of the landed proprietors at the opening of Parliament, in 1866, showed that a man can worship the cow Sabala without being a Hindu, and can change himself into an ox without being a Jupiter.

18. 'The worker asked for means of subsistence in order to live, the master asked for labour in order to make a profit' (Sismondi, op. cit., p. 91).

19. A clumsy agricultural form of this bondage exists in the county of Durham. This is one of the few counties in which circumstances do not

at once mediated through, and concealed by, the periodic renewal of the act by which he sells himself, his change of masters, and the oscillations in the market-price of his labour.[20]

The capitalist process of production, therefore, seen as a total, connected process, i.e. a process of reproduction, produces not only commodities, not only surplus-value, but it also produces and reproduces the capital-relation itself; on the one hand the capitalist, on the other the wage-labourer.[21]

---

secure to the farmer undisputed proprietary rights over the agricultural labourers. The existence of the mining industry allows the latter some freedom of choice. Here, therefore, and in contrast with the general rule which prevails elsewhere, the farmer rents only such farms as have on them labourers' cottages. The rent of the cottage forms part of the wage. These cottages are known as 'hinds' houses'. They are let to the labourers in consideration of certain feudal services, under a contract called 'bondage', which, among other things, binds the labourer, during the time he is employed elsewhere, to leave someone, say his daughter, etc., to fill his place. The labourer himself is called a 'bondsman'. This relationship also shows, from an entirely new angle, how individual consumption by the worker is consumption on behalf of capital, in other words productive consumption: 'It is curious to observe that the very dung of the hind and bondsman is the perquisite of the calculating lord . . . and the lord will allow no privy but his own to exist in the neighbourhood, and will rather give a bit of manure here and there for a garden than bate any part of his seigneurial right' (*Public Health, Seventh Report*, 1864, p. 188).

20. It will not be forgotten that, where the labour of children is concerned, even the formality of a voluntary sale vanishes.

21. 'Capital presupposes wage-labour; wage-labour presupposes capital. They reciprocally condition each other's existence; they reciprocally bring forth each other. Does a worker in a cotton factory merely produce cotton goods? No, he produces capital. He produces values which serve afresh to command his labour and by means of it to create new values' (Karl Marx, 'Lohnarbeit und Kapital', in *Neue Rheinische Zeitung*, No. 266, 7 April 1849) ['Wage Labour and Capital', in Karl Marx and Frederick Engels, *Selected Works* in three volumes, Vol. 1, p. 162]. The articles published under the above heading in the *Neue Rheinische Zeitung* are parts of some lectures given by me on that topic in 1847 in the *Deutscher Arbeiterverein* in Brussels;* their publication was interrupted by the February revolution.

*The *Deutscher Arbeiterverein* was founded in 1847 in Brussels by Marx and Engels, with the aim of educating the German workers living there in the principles of communism. In February 1848 the Belgian authorities compelled it to disband by arresting most of its leading members.

Chapter 24: The Transformation of Surplus-Value into Capital

1. CAPITALIST PRODUCTION ON A PROGRESSIVELY INCREASING SCALE. THE INVERSION WHICH CONVERTS THE PROPERTY LAWS OF COMMODITY PRODUCTION INTO LAWS OF CAPITALIST APPROPRIATION

Earlier we considered how surplus-value arises from capital; now we have to see how capital arises from surplus-value. The employment of surplus-value as capital, or its reconversion into capital, is called accumulation of capital.[1]

Let us first consider this process from the standpoint of the individual capitalist. Suppose a master-spinner has advanced a capital of £10,000, of which four-fifths (£8,000) is laid out in cotton, machinery, etc. and one-fifth (£2,000) in wages. Let him produce 240,000 lb. of yarn every year, and let the value of this yarn be £12,000. The rate of surplus-value being 100 per cent, the surplus-value is contained in the surplus, or net product, of 40,000 lb. of yarn, which is one-sixth of the gross product, and has a value of £2,000 which will be realized by a sale. £2,000 is £2,000. Neither seeing nor smelling will tell us that this sum of money is surplus-value. When we know that a given value is surplus-value, we know how its owner came by it; but that does not alter the nature either of value or of money.

In order to transform this newly acquired sum of £2,000 into capital, the master-spinner will, all circumstances remaining as before, advance four-fifths of it (£1,600) in the purchase of cotton, etc. and one-fifth (£400) in the purchase of additional spinning workers, who will find in the market the means of subsistence whose value the master has advanced to them. The new capital of

1. 'Accumulation of capital; the employment of a portion of revenue as capital' (Malthus, *Definitions, etc.*, ed. Cazenove, p. 11). 'Conversion of revenue into capital' (Malthus, *Principles of Political Economy*, 2nd edn, London, 1836, p. 320).

£2,000 then functions in the spinning-mill and in its turn brings in a surplus value of £400.

The capital-value was originally advanced in the form of money. The surplus-value, however, existed from the outset as the value of a definite portion of the gross product. If this gross product is sold, converted into money, the capital-value regains its original form. From this moment on, the capital-value and surplus-value are both sums of money, and their reconversion into capital takes place in precisely the same way. The one as well as the other is laid out by the capitalist in the purchase of commodities that place him in a position to start making his goods again, and indeed, on a larger scale this time. But in order to be able to buy these commodities, he must find them ready in the market.

His own yarn circulates only because he brings his annual product to market, as do all other capitalists with their commodities. But these commodities, before coming to market, were already part of the annual production fund, i.e. part of the total mass of objects of every kind into which the sum total of the individual capitals, or the total social capital, had been converted in the course of the year, and of which each capitalist had in hand only a small fraction. All the transactions in the market can accomplish is the interchange of the individual components of this annual product, their transfer from one hand to another. They cannot increase the total annual production, nor can they alter the nature of the objects produced. Hence the use that can be made of the total annual product depends entirely on its own composition, and in no way on circulation.

Annual production must in the first place furnish all those objects (use-values) from which the material components of capital, used up in the course of the year, have to be replaced. After we have deducted this, there remains the net or surplus product, which contains the surplus-value. And what does this surplus product consist of? Only of things destined to satisfy the needs and desires of the capitalist class, things which consequently enter into the consumption fund of the capitalists? If that were all, the cup of surplus-value would be drained to the very dregs, and nothing but simple reproduction would ever take place.

Accumulation requires the transformation of a portion of the surplus product into capital. But we cannot, except by a miracle, transform into capital anything but such articles as can be employed in the labour process (i.e. means of production), and such further articles as are suitable for the sustenance of the worker (i.e. means of subsistence). Consequently, a part of the annual surplus labour must have been applied to the production of additional means of production and subsistence, over and above the quantity of these things required to replace the capital advanced. In a word, surplus-value can be transformed into capital only because the surplus product, whose value it is, already comprises the material components of a new quantity of capital.[2]

Now, in order that these components may actually function as capital, the capitalist class requires additional labour. If the exploitation of the workers already employed does not increase, either extensively or intensively, additional labour-powers must be enlisted. The mechanism of capitalist production has already provided for this in advance, by reproducing the working class as a class dependent on wages, a class whose ordinary wages suffice, not only to maintain itself, but also to increase its numbers. All capital needs to do is to incorporate this additional labour-power, annually supplied by the working class in the shape of labour-powers of all ages, with the additional means of production comprised in the annual product, and the transformation of surplus-value into capital has been accomplished. Looked at concretely, accumulation can be resolved into the production of capital on a progressively increasing scale. The cycle of simple reproduction alters its form and, to use Sismondi's expression, changes into a spiral.[3]

Let us now return to our example. It is the old story: Abraham begat Isaac, Isaac begat Jacob and so on. The original capital of £10,000 brings in a surplus-value of £2,000, which is capitalized. The new capital of £2,000 brings in a surplus-value of £400, and this too is capitalized, transformed into a second additional

2. Here we take no account of the export trade, by means of which a nation can change articles of luxury either into means of production or means of subsistence, and *vice versa*. In order to examine the object of our investigation in its integrity, free from all disturbing subsidiary circumstances, we must treat the whole world of trade as one nation, and assume that capitalist production is established everywhere and has taken possession of every branch of industry.

3. Sismondi's analysis of accumulation suffers from the great defect that he contents himself, to too great an extent, with the phrase 'conversion of revenue into capital',* without trying to investigate the material conditions of this operation.

*Sismondi, *Nouveaux Principes d'économie politique*, Vol. 1, Paris, 1819, p. 119.

capital, which in its turn produces a further surplus-value of £80. And the process continues in this way.

We leave out of account here the portion of the surplus-value consumed by the capitalist. We are also not interested, for the moment, in whether the additional capital is joined on to the original capital, or separated from it so that it can valorize itself independently. Nor are we concerned whether the same capitalist employs it who originally accumulated it, or whether he hands it over to others. All we must remember is this: by the side of the newly formed capital, the original capital continues to reproduce itself and to produce surplus-value, and this is true of all accumulated capital in relation to the additional capital engendered by it.

The original capital was formed by the advance of £10,000. Where did its owner get it from? 'From his own labour and that of his forefathers', is the unanimous answer of the spokesmen of political economy.[4] And, in fact, their assumption appears to be the only one consonant with the laws of commodity production.

But it is quite otherwise with regard to the additional capital of £2,000. We know perfectly well how that originated. There is not one single atom of its value that does not owe its existence to unpaid labour. The means of production with which the additional labour-power is incorporated, as well as the necessaries with which the workers are sustained, are nothing but component parts of the surplus product, parts of the tribute annually exacted from the working class by the capitalist class. Even if the latter uses a portion of that tribute to purchase the additional labour-power at its full price, so that equivalent is exchanged for equivalent, the whole thing still remains the age-old activity of the conqueror, who buys commodities from the conquered with the money he has stolen from them.

If the additional capital employs the person who produced it, this producer must not only continue to valorize the value of the original capital, but must buy back the fruits of his previous labour with more labour than they cost. If we view this as a transaction between the capitalist class and the working class, it makes no difference that additional workers are employed by means of the unpaid labour of the previously employed workers. The capitalist may even convert the additional capital into a machine that throws the producers of that capital out of work, and replaces them with

4. 'The original labour, to which his capital owed its origin' (Sismondi, op. cit., Vol. 1, p. 109).

a few children. In every case, the working class creates by the surplus labour of one year the capital destined to employ additional labour in the following year.[5] And this is what is called creating capital out of capital.

The accumulation of the first additional capital of £2,000 presupposes that a value of £10,000 exists, advanced by the capitalist, and belonging to him by virtue of his 'original labour'. The second additional capital of £400 presupposes, on the contrary, only the prior accumulation of the £2,000, of which the £400 is the capitalized surplus-value. The ownership of past unpaid labour is thenceforth the sole condition for the appropriation of living unpaid labour on a constantly increasing scale. The more the capitalist has accumulated, the more is he able to accumulate.

The surplus-value that makes up additional capital no. 1 is the result of the purchase of labour-power with part of the original capital, a purchase which conformed to the laws of commodity exchange and which, from a legal standpoint, presupposes nothing beyond the worker's power to dispose freely of his own capacities, and the money-owner's or commodity-owner's power to dispose freely of the values that belong to him; equally, additional capital no. 2 is merely the result of additional capital no. 1, and is therefore a consequence of the relations described above; hence each individual transaction continues to conform to the laws of commodity exchange, with the capitalist always buying labour-power and the worker always selling it at what we shall assume is its real value. It is quite evident from this that the laws of appropriation or of private property, laws based on the production and circulation of commodities, become changed into their direct opposite through their own internal and inexorable dialectic. The exchange of equivalents, the original operation with which we started, is now turned round in such a way that there is only an apparent exchange, since, firstly, the capital which is exchanged for labour-power is itself merely a portion of the product of the labour of others which has been appropriated without an equivalent; and, secondly, this capital must not only be replaced by its producer, the worker, but replaced together with an added surplus. The relation of exchange between capitalist and worker becomes a mere semblance belonging only to the process of circulation, it becomes a mere form, which is alien to the content of the transaction itself,

5. 'Labour creates capital before capital employs labour' (E. G. Wakefield, *England and America*, London, 1833, Vol. 2, p. 110).

and merely mystifies it. The constant sale and purchase of labour-power is the form; the content is the constant appropriation by the capitalist, without equivalent, of a portion of the labour of others which has already been objectified, and his repeated exchange of this labour for a greater quantity of the living labour of others. Originally the rights of property seemed to us to be grounded in a man's own labour. Some such assumption was at least necessary, since only commodity-owners with equal rights confronted each other, and the sole means of appropriating the commodities of others was the alienation of a man's own commodities, commodities which, however, could only be produced by labour. Now, however, property turns out to be the right, on the part of the capitalist, to appropriate the unpaid labour of others or its product, and the impossibility, on the part of the worker, of appropriating his own product. The separation of property from labour thus becomes the necessary consequence of a law that apparently originated in their identity.[6]

Therefore,* however much the capitalist mode of appropriation may seem to fly in the face of the original laws of commodity production, it nevertheless arises, not from a violation of these laws but, on the contrary, from their application. Let us make this clear once more by briefly reviewing the consecutive phases of motion whose culminating point is capitalist accumulation.

We saw, in the first place, that the original transformation of a sum of values into capital was achieved in complete accordance with the laws of exchange. One party to the contract sells his labour-power, the other buys it. The former receives the value of his commodity, whose use-value – labour – is thereby alienated to the buyer. Means of production which already belong to the latter are then transformed by him, with the aid of labour equally belonging to him, into a new product which is likewise lawfully his.

The value of this product includes: first, the value of the means

6. The property of the capitalist in the product of the labour of others 'is a strict consequence of the law of appropriation, the fundamental principle of which was the reverse, the exclusive entitlement of the worker to the product of his own labour' (Cherbuliez, *Richesse ou pauvreté*, Paris, 1841, p. 58, where, however, the dialectical inversion is not correctly developed).

*This passage, up to p. 734, 'laws of capitalist appropriation', was added by Engels to the fourth German edition on the basis of a similar passage included by Marx in the French translation of 1872.

of production which have been used up. Useful labour cannot consume these means of production without transferring their value to the new product; but, to be saleable, labour-power must be capable of supplying useful labour in the branch of industry in which it is to be employed.

The value of the new product includes, further, the equivalent of the value of the labour-power together with a surplus-value. This is so because the value of the labour-power – sold for a definite length of time, say a day, a week, etc. – is less than the value created by its use during that time. But the worker has received payment for the exchange-value of his labour-power and by so doing has alienated its use-value – this being the case in every sale and purchase.

The fact that this particular commodity, labour-power, possesses the peculiar use-value of supplying labour, and therefore of creating value, cannot affect the general law of commodity production. If, therefore, the amount of value advanced in wages is not merely found again in the product, but augmented by a surplus-value, this is not because the seller has been defrauded, for he has really received the value of his commodity; it is due solely to the fact that this commodity has been used up by the buyer.

The law of exchange requires equality only between the exchange-values of the commodities given in exchange for one another. From the very outset, indeed, it presupposes a difference between their use-values and it has nothing whatever to do with their consumption, which begins only after the contract has been concluded and executed.

Thus the original transformation of money into capital takes place in the most exact accordance with the economic laws of commodity production and with the rights of property derived from them. Nevertheless, its result is:

(1) that the product belongs to the capitalist and not to the worker;
(2) that the value of this product includes, apart from the value of the capital advanced, a surplus-value which costs the worker labour but the capitalist nothing, and which none the less becomes the legitimate property of the capitalist;
(3) that the worker has retained his labour-power and can sell it anew if he finds another buyer.

Simple reproduction is only the periodic repetition of this first operation; each time, money is freshly transformed into capital. Thus the law is not broken; on the contrary, it gains the opportunity to operate continuously. 'Several successive acts of exchange have only made the last represent the first.'[7]

And yet we have seen that simple reproduction suffices to stamp this first operation, in so far as it is conceived as an isolated process, with a totally changed character. 'Of those who share the national income among themselves, the one side' (the workers) 'acquire each year a fresh right to their share by fresh labour; the others' (the capitalists) 'have already acquired, by their original labour, a permanent right to their share.'[8] It is indeed a well-known fact that the sphere of labour is not the only one in which primogeniture works miracles.

Nor does it matter if simple reproduction is replaced by reproduction on an extended scale, by accumulation. In the former case the capitalist squanders the whole of the surplus-value in dissipation, in the latter he demonstrates his bourgeois virtue by consuming only a portion of it and converting the rest into money.

The surplus-value is his property; it has never belonged to anyone else. If he advances it for the purposes of production, the advances made come from his own funds, exactly as on the day when he first entered the market. The fact that on this occasion the funds are derived from the unpaid labour of his workers makes absolutely no difference. If worker B is paid out of the surplus-value which worker A produced, then, in the first place, A furnished that surplus-value without having the fair price of his commodity cut by even a farthing, and, in the second place, the transaction is no concern of B's whatever. What B claims, and has a right to claim, is that the capitalist should pay him the value of his labour-power. 'Both of them still benefited: the worker because he was advanced the fruits of his labour' (should read: of the unpaid labour of other workers) 'before the work was done' (should read: before his own labour had borne fruit); 'the employer, because the labour of this worker was worth more than his wages' (should read: produced more value than the value of his wages).[9]

To be sure, the matter looks quite different if we consider capitalist production in the uninterrupted flow of its renewal, and if, in place of the individual capitalist and the individual worker, we view them in their totality, as the capitalist class and the working class confronting each other. But in so doing we should be applying standards entirely foreign to commodity production.

7. Sismondi, op. cit., Vol. 1, p. 70.   8. ibid., pp. 110, 111.
9. ibid., p. 135.

Only the mutually independent buyer and seller face each other in commodity production. Relations between them cease on the day when the term stipulated in the contract they concluded expires. If the transaction is repeated, it is repeated as the result of a new agreement which has nothing to do with the previous one and in which it is only an accident that brings the same seller together again with the same buyer.

If, therefore, commodity production, or one of its associated processes, is to be judged according to its own economic laws, we must consider each act of exchange by itself, apart from any connection with the act of exchange preceding it and that following it. And since sales and purchases are negotiated solely between particular individuals, it is not admissible to look here for relations between whole social classes.

However long a series of periodic reproductions and preceding accumulations the capital functioning today may have passed through, it always preserves its original virginity. As long as the laws of exchange are observed in every single act of exchange – taken in isolation – the mode of appropriation can be completely revolutionized without in any way affecting the property rights which correspond to commodity production. The same rights remain in force both at the outset, when the product belongs to its producer, who, exchanging equivalent for equivalent, can enrich himself only by his own labour, and in the period of capitalism, when social wealth becomes to an ever-increasing degree the property of those who are in a position to appropriate the unpaid labour of others over and over again.

This result becomes inevitable from the moment there is a free sale, by the worker himself, of labour-power as a commodity. But it is also only from then onwards that commodity production is generalized and becomes the typical form of production; it is only from then onwards that every product is produced for sale from the outset and all wealth produced goes through the sphere of circulation. Only where wage-labour is its basis does commodity production impose itself upon society as a whole; but it is also true that only there does it unfold all its hidden potentialities. To say that the intervention of wage-labour adulterates commodity production is to say that commodity production must not develop if it is to remain unadulterated. To the extent that commodity production, in accordance with its own immanent laws, undergoes a further development into capitalist production, the property laws of commodity production must undergo a dialectical inversion so that they become laws of capitalist appropriation.[10]

We have seen that even in the case of simple reproduction, all capital, whatever its original source, is transformed into accumulated capital, or capitalized surplus-value. But in the flood of production the total capital originally advanced becomes a vanishing quantity (*magnitudo evanescens* in the mathematical sense), in comparison with the directly accumulated capital, i.e. the surplus-value or surplus product that is reconverted into capital. This occurs whether the capital originally advanced is functioning in the hands of the man who accumulated it, or in the hands of other people. Hence the political economists describe capital in general as 'accumulated wealth' (transformed surplus-value or revenue) 'that is employed over again in the production of surplus-value',[11] and the capitalist himself as 'the owner of surplus-value'.[12] This same way of looking at things is merely expressed in another form in the statement that all existing capital is accumulated or capitalized interest, for interest is nothing but a fragment of surplus-value.[13]

2. THE POLITICAL ECONOMISTS' ERRONEOUS CONCEPTION OF REPRODUCTION ON AN INCREASING SCALE

Before we attempt to give a more detailed characterization of accumulation or the reconversion of surplus-value into capital, we must clear out of the way an ambiguity concocted by the classical economists.

The commodities the capitalist buys with a part of the surplus-value for his own consumption do not serve as means of produc-

10. We may well, therefore, feel astonished at the cleverness of Proudhon, who would abolish capitalist property – by enforcing the eternal laws of property which are themselves based on commodity production!

11. 'Capital, viz., accumulated wealth employed with a view to profit' (Malthus, op. cit. [p. 262]). 'Capital . . . consists of wealth saved from revenue, and used with a view to profit' (R. Jones, *Textbook of Lectures on the Political Economy of Nations*, Hertford, 1852, p. 16).

12. 'The possessors of surplus-produce or capital' (*The Source and Remedy of the National Difficulties. A Letter to Lord John Russell*, London, 1821 [p. 4]).

13. 'Capital, with compound interest on every portion of capital saved, is so all engrossing that all the wealth in the world from which income is derived, has long ago become the interest on capital' (*The Economist*, London, 19 July 1851).

tion or means of valorization; similarly, the labour he buys for the satisfaction of his natural and social requirements does not serve as productive labour. Instead of transforming surplus-value into capital, he rather consumes or expends it as revenue when he purchases those commodities and that labour. It was of decisive importance for the bourgeois economists, when confronted with the habitual mode of life of the old nobility, which, as Hegel rightly says, 'consists in consuming what is available',* and is displayed in particular in the luxury of personal retainers, to promulgate the doctrine that the accumulation of capital is the first duty of every citizen, and to preach unceasingly that accumulation is impossible if a man eats up all his revenue, instead of spending a good part of it on the acquisition of additional productive workers, who bring in more than they cost. On the other hand, the economists also had to contend against the popular prejudice which confuses capitalist production with hoarding,[14] and therefore imagines that accumulated wealth is either wealth that is rescued from destruction in its existing natural form, i.e. withdrawn from consumption, or wealth that does not enter into circulation. The exclusion of money from circulation would constitute precisely the opposite of its valorization as capital, and the accumulation of commodities in the sense of hoarding them would be sheer foolishness.[15] In fact the accumulation of commodities in great masses is the result either of a bottleneck in circulation or of over-production.[16] It is true that the popular mind is impressed, on the one hand, by the sight of the mass of goods that are stored up for gradual consumption by the rich,[17] and on the other hand by the

14. 'No political economist of the present day can by saving mean mere hoarding: and beyond this contracted and insufficient proceeding, no use of the term in reference to the national wealth can well be imagined, but that which must arise from a different application of what is saved, founded upon a real distinction between the different kinds of labour maintained by it' (Malthus, op. cit., pp. 38–9).

15. Thus for instance Balzac, who so thoroughly studied every shade of avarice, represents the old usurer Gobseck as being in his second childhood when he begins to create a hoard by piling up commodities.

16. 'Accumulation of stocks ... non-exchange ... over-production' (T. Corbet, op. cit., p. 104).

17. It is in this sense that Necker speaks of the 'articles of pomp and magnificence' whose 'accumulation has increased with time', and which 'the

*Hegel, *Philosophy of Right*, para. 203, addition (English edition, op. cit., p. 270).

formation of a reserve. The latter is a phenomenon which is common to all modes of production, and we shall dwell on it for a moment when we come to analyse the process of circulation.*

The classical economists are therefore quite right to maintain that the consumption of the surplus product by productive, instead of unproductive, workers is a characteristic feature of the process of accumulation. But at this point the mistakes also begin. Adam Smith has made it the fashion to present accumulation as nothing more than the consumption of the surplus product by productive workers. This amounts to saying that the capitalization of surplus-value consists merely in turning surplus-value into labour-power. Let us listen to Ricardo on this point: 'It must be understood that all the productions of a country are consumed; but it makes the greatest difference imaginable whether they are consumed by those who reproduce, or by those who do not reproduce another value. When we say that revenue is saved, and added to capital, what we mean is, that the portion of revenue, so said to be added to capital, is consumed by productive instead of unproductive labourers. There can be no greater error than in supposing that capital is increased by non-consumption.'[18] There can be no greater error than the one repeated after Adam Smith by Ricardo and all subsequent political economists, namely the view that 'the portion of revenue so said to be added to capital, is consumed by productive labourers'. According to this, all surplus-value that is transformed into capital becomes variable capital. However, in actual fact the surplus-value, like the value originally advanced, divides up into constant and variable capital, into means of production and labour-power. Labour-power is the form in which variable capital exists during the process of production. In this process the labour-power is itself consumed by the capitalist while the means of production are consumed by the labour-power in the exercise of its function, i.e. labour. At the same time, the money paid for the purchase of the labour-power is converted into

---

laws of property have assembled together in the hands of a single class of society' (*Œuvres de M. Necker*, Paris and Lausanne, 1789, Vol. 2, *De l'administration des finances de la France*, p. 291).*

18. Ricardo, op. cit., p. 163, note.

*This note is not in any of the German editions, but was included in the French translation of 1872.

---

*See *Capital*, Volume 2, Chapter 2, Section 4, 'Reserve Fund'.

means of subsistence, which are consumed, not by 'productive labour', but by the 'productive worker'. Adam Smith, at the end of a quite preposterous analysis, comes to the absurd conclusion that even though each individual capital is divided into a constant and a variable part, the capital of society can be entirely resolved into variable capital, i.e. it is laid out exclusively in the payment of wages.* For instance, suppose a cloth manufacturer converts £2,000 into capital. He lays out one part of the money in buying weavers, the other in woollen yarn, machinery, etc. But the people from whom he buys the yarn and the machinery themselves use a part of the purchase money to pay for labour, and so on until the whole £2,000 is spent in the payment of wages, i.e. until the entire product represented by the £2,000 has been consumed by productive workers. It is evident that the entire thrust of this argument lies in the words 'and so on', which send us from pillar to post. In fact, Adam Smith breaks off the investigation just where the difficulties begin.[19]

The annual process of reproduction is easily understood, as long as we look solely at the sum total of the year's production. But every single component of this annual product must be brought into the market as a commodity, and there the difficulties begin. The movements of the individual capitals and personal revenues cross and intermingle, and become lost in a general alternation of positions, i.e. in the circulation of society's wealth. This confuses the onlooker, and provides the investigation with very complicated problems to solve. In the third part of Volume 2 I shall give an analysis of the way the whole system is actually linked together. It is one of the great merits of the Physiocrats that in their *Tableau économique*† they were the first to attempt to depict the

---

[19]. In spite of his 'Logic' John Stuart Mill never manages to detect even such a faulty analysis as this on the part of his predecessors, even when it cries out for rectification from a purely technical standpoint, entirely within the bourgeois field of vision. In every case he registers the confusion of his masters with the dogmatism of a disciple. And so it is here: 'The capital itself in the long run becomes entirely wages, and when replaced by the sale of produce becomes wages again.'

---

*Adam Smith, *Wealth of Nations*, Bk II, Ch. 1. Smith, of course, refers not to constant and variable capital but to fixed and circulating capital.

† Marx discussed Quesnay's *Tableau économique* both in *Capital*, Volume 2, Chapter 19, and in *Theories of Surplus-Value*, Part I, Chapter 2, 'The Physiocrats'.

year's production in the shape in which it emerges from circulation.[20]

For the rest, it goes without saying that political economy has not failed to exploit, in the interests of the capitalist class, Adam Smith's doctrine that the whole of that part of the net product which is transformed into capital is consumed by the working class.

3. DIVISION OF SURPLUS-VALUE INTO CAPITAL AND REVENUE. THE ABSTINENCE THEORY

In the previous chapter, we treated surplus-value (or the surplus product) solely as a fund for satisfying the capitalist's individual consumption requirements. In this chapter, so far, we have treated it solely as a fund for accumulation. In fact, however, it is neither the one nor the other: it is both. One part of the surplus-value is consumed by the capitalist as revenue,[21] the other part is employed as capital, i.e. it is accumulated.

With a given mass of surplus-value, then, the larger the one part, the smaller the other. Other things being equal, the ratio of these parts determines the magnitude of the accumulation. But it is the owner of the surplus-value, the capitalist, who makes this division. It is an act of his will. That part of the tribute exacted by him which he accumulates is said to be saved by him, because he does

20. In his analysis of the process of reproduction, hence also that of accumulation, Adam Smith not only failed to advance, but even retrogressed considerably, in comparison with his predecessors, especially the Physiocrats. Connected with the illusion mentioned in the text is the really extraordinary dogma that the price of commodities is made up of wages, profit (interest) and ground rent, i.e. merely of wages and surplus-value.* Starting from this basis, Storch naïvely confesses, 'It is impossible to resolve the necessary price into its simplest elements' (Storch, op. cit., St Petersburg, 1815, Vol. 2, p. 141, note). A fine kind of economic science this is, which declares it impossible to resolve the price of a commodity into its simplest elements! This point will be further investigated in Part Three of Volume 2 and part seven of Volume 3.

21. The reader will notice that the word revenue is used in a double sense: first, to designate surplus-value, as the fruit periodically yielded by capital; and second, to designate the part of that fruit which is periodically consumed by the capitalist, or added to his private consumption-fund. I retain this double meaning because it harmonizes with the language of the English and French economists.

*'The whole price of the annual produce ... naturally divides itself into three parts; the rent of land, the wages of labour, and the profits of stock' (*Wealth of Nations*, Bk I, Ch. 11, Conclusion).

not consume it, i.e. because he performs his function as a capitalist, and enriches himself.

Except as capital personified, the capitalist has no historical value, and no right to that historical existence which, to use Lichnowsky's amusing expression, 'ain't got no date'.* It is only to this extent that the necessity of the capitalist's own transitory existence is implied in the transitory necessity of the capitalist mode of production. But, in so far as he is capital personified, his motivating force is not the acquisition and enjoyment of use-values, but the acquisition and augmentation of exchange-values. He is fanatically intent on the valorization of value; consequently he ruthlessly forces the human race to produce for production's sake. In this way he spurs on the development of society's productive forces, and the creation of those material conditions of production which alone can form the real basis of a higher form of society, a society in which the full and free development of every individual forms the ruling principle. Only as a personification of capital is the capitalist respectable. As such, he shares with the miser an absolute drive towards self-enrichment. But what appears in the miser as the mania of an individual is in the capitalist the effect of a social mechanism in which he is merely a cog. Moreover, the development of capitalist production makes it necessary constantly to increase the amount of capital laid out in a given industrial undertaking, and competition subordinates every individual capitalist to the immanent laws of capitalist production, as external and coercive laws. It compels him to keep extending his capital, so as to preserve it, and he can only extend it by means of progressive accumulation.

In so far, therefore, as his actions are a mere function of capital – endowed as capital is, in his person, with consciousness and a will – his own private consumption counts as a robbery committed against the accumulation of his capital, just as, in double-entry book-keeping, the private expenditure of the capitalist is placed on the debit side of his account against his capital. Accumulation is the conquest of the world of social wealth. It is the extension of the

* '*Keinen Datum nicht hat.*' This phrase was uttered in the Frankfurt National Assembly on 31 August 1848 by the reactionary Silesian landowner, Prince Felix von Lichnowsky, in the course of a speech attacking Poland's historical right to independence. Lichnowsky naturally became a byword for the intellectual narrowness and backwardness of the old Prussian nobility; he was greeted with laughter by most of the Assembly. The whole scene was described by Engels in the *Neue Rheinische Zeitung* (*MEW* 5, pp. 350–53).

area of exploited human material and, at the same time, the extension of the direct and indirect sway of the capitalist.[22]

But original sin is at work everywhere. With the development of the capitalist mode of production, with the growth of accumulation and wealth, the capitalist ceases to be merely the incarnation of capital. He begins to feel a human warmth towards his own Adam, and his education gradually enables him to smile at his former enthusiasm for asceticism, as an old-fashioned miser's prejudice. While the capitalist of the classical type brands individual consumption as a sin against his function, as 'abstinence' from accumulating, the modernized capitalist is capable of viewing

22. Taking the usurer, that old-fashioned but ever-renewed specimen of the capitalist, for his text, Luther shows very aptly that the love of power is an element in the desire to get rich. 'The heathen were able, by the light of reason, to conclude that a usurer is a double-dyed thief and murderer. We Christians, however, hold them in such honour, that we fairly worship them for the sake of their money ... Whoever eats up, robs, and steals the nourishment of another, that man commits as great a murder (so far as in him lies) as he who starves a man or utterly undoes him. Such does a usurer, and sits the while safe on his stool, when he ought rather to be hanging on the gallows, and be eaten by as many ravens as he has stolen guilders, if only there were so much flesh on him, that so many ravens could stick their beaks in and share it. Meanwhile, we hang the small thieves ... Little thieves are put in the stocks, great thieves go flaunting in gold and silk ... Therefore is there, on this earth, no greater enemy of man (after the devil) than a gripe-money, and usurer, for he wants to be God over all men. Turks, soldiers, and tyrants are also bad men, yet must they let the people live, and confess that they are bad, and enemies, and do, nay, must, now and then show pity to some. But a usurer and money-glutton, such a one would have the whole world perish of hunger and thirst, misery and want, so far as in him lies, so that he may have all to himself, and every one may receive from him as from a God, and be his serf for ever more. [This is what gladdens his heart, and also] to wear fine cloaks, golden chains, rings, to wipe his mouth, to be deemed and taken for a worthy, pious man ... Usury is a great huge monster, like a were-wolf, who lays waste all, more than any Cacus, Gerion or Antaeus. And yet decks himself out, and would be thought pious, so that people may not see where the oxen have gone, that he drags backwards into his den. But Hercules shall hear the cry of the oxen and of his prisoners, and shall seek Cacus even in cliffs and among rocks, and shall set the oxen loose again from the villain. For Cacus means the villain that is a pious usurer, and steals, robs, eats everything. And will not own that he has done it, and thinks no one will find him out, because the oxen, drawn backwards into his den, make it seem, from their foot-prints, that they have been let out. So the usurer would deceive the world, as though he were of use and gave the world oxen, which he, however, rends, and eats all alone ... And since we break on the wheel, and behead, highwaymen, murderers, and housebreakers, how much more ought we to break on the wheel and kill ... hunt down, curse, and behead all usurers' (Martin Luther, op. cit.).

accumulation as 'renunciation' of pleasure. 'Two souls, alas, do dwell within his breast; The one is ever parting from the other.'*

At the historical dawn of the capitalist mode of production – and every capitalist upstart has to go through this historical stage individually – avarice, and the drive for self-enrichment, are the passions which are entirely predominant. But the progress of capitalist production not only creates a world of delights; it lays open, in the form of speculation and the credit system, a thousand sources of sudden enrichment. When a certain stage of development has been reached, a conventional degree of prodigality, which is also an exhibition of wealth, and consequently a source of credit, becomes a business necessity to the 'unfortunate' capitalist. Luxury enters into capital's expenses of representation. Moreover, the capitalist gets rich, not, like the miser, in proportion to his personal labour and restricted consumption, but at the same rate as he squeezes out labour-power from others, and compels the worker to renounce all the enjoyments of life. Thus although the expenditure of the capitalist never possesses the *bona fide* character of the dashing feudal lord's prodigality, but, on the contrary, is always restrained by the sordid avarice and anxious calculation lurking in the background, this expenditure nevertheless grows with his accumulation, without the one necessarily restricting the other. At the same time, however, there develops in the breast of the capitalist a Faustian conflict between the passion for accumulation and the desire for enjoyment.

Dr Aikin says, in a work published in 1795: 'The trade of Manchester may be divided into four periods. First, when manufacturers were obliged to work hard for their livelihood.' They enriched themselves chiefly by robbing the parents whose children were bound as apprentices to them: the parents paid a high premium, while the apprentices were starved. On the other hand, the average profits were low, and, in order to accumulate, extreme parsimony was needed. They lived like misers, and were far from consuming even the interest on their capital. 'The second period, when they had begun to acquire little fortunes, but worked as hard as before' (for the direct exploitation of labour costs labour, as every slave-driver knows) 'and lived in as plain a manner as before . . . The third, when luxury began, and the trade was pushed by sending out riders for orders into every market town in the

* Cf. Goethe, *Faust*, Part I, Before the City Gate, lines 1112–13.

Kingdom . . . It is probable that few or no capitals of £3,000 to £4,000 acquired by trade existed here before 1690. However, about that time, or a little later, the traders had got money before-hand, and began to build modern brick houses, instead of those of wood and plaster.' Even in the early part of the eighteenth century, a Manchester manufacturer who placed a pint of foreign wine be-fore his guests exposed himself to the remarks and headshakings of all his neighbours. Before the rise of machinery, a manufacturer's evening expenditure at the public house where they all met never exceeded sixpence for a glass of punch, and a penny for a screw of tobacco. It was not till 1758, and this marks an epoch, that a person actually engaged in business was seen with a carriage of his own. 'The fourth period,' the last thirty years of the eighteenth century, 'is that in which expense and luxury have made great progress, supported by a trade extended by means of riders and factors through every part of Europe.'[23] What would the good Dr Aikin say if he could rise from the grave and see the Manchester of today?

Accumulate, accumulate! That is Moses and the prophets! 'Industry furnishes the material which saving accumulates.'[24] Therefore save, save, i.e. reconvert the greatest possible portion of surplus-value or surplus product into capital! Accumulation for the sake of accumulation, production for the sake of production: this was the formula in which classical economics expressed the historical mission of the bourgeoisie in the period of its domina-tion. Not for one instant did it deceive itself over the nature of wealth's birth-pangs.[25] But what use is it to lament a historical necessity? If, in the eyes of classical economics, the proletarian is merely a machine for the production of surplus-value, the capital-ist too is merely a machine for the transformation of this surplus-value into surplus capital. Classical economics takes the historical function of the capitalist in grim earnest. In order to conjure away

23. Dr Aikin, *Description of the Country from Thirty to Forty Miles round Manchester*, London, 1795, pp. 182 ff. [181, 188 as well].

24. Adam Smith, op. cit., Bk II, Ch. 3.

25. Even J. B. Say says: 'The savings of the rich are made at the expense of the poor.'* 'The Roman proletarian lived almost entirely at the expense of society . . . One might almost say that modern society lives at the expense of the proletarians, on the portion of the wages of labour which it withdraws from their pockets' (Sismondi, *Études etc.*, Vol. 1, p. 24).

*J. B. Say, *Traité d'économie politique*, 5th edn, Vol. 1, Paris, 1826, pp. 130–31.

the awful conflict between the desire for enjoyment and the drive for self-enrichment, Malthus, around the beginning of the 1820s, advocated a division of labour which assigned the business of accumulating to the capitalist actually engaged in production, and the business of spending to the other sharers in surplus-value, the landed aristocracy, the place-men, the beneficed clergy and so on. It is of the highest importance, he says, 'to keep separate the passion for expenditure and the passion for accumulation'.[26] The capitalists, who had long since turned themselves into good livers and men of the world, complained loudly at this. What, exclaimed one of their spokesmen, a follower of Ricardo, does Mr Malthus preach high rents, heavy taxation, etc. so that the industrious may constantly be kept up to the mark by the pressure of unproductive consumers? By all means let there be production, production on a constantly increasing scale, runs the shibboleth, but 'production will, by such a process, be far more curbed in than spurred on. Nor is it quite fair thus to maintain in idleness a number of persons, only to pinch others, who are likely, from their characters, if you can force them to work, to work with success.'[27] Though he finds it unfair to spur on the industrial capitalist by depriving his bread of its butter, he still thinks it necessary to reduce the worker's wages to a minimum, 'to keep him industrious'. Nor does he for a moment conceal the fact that the appropriation of unpaid labour is the secret of making a profit. 'Increased demand on the part of the labourers means nothing more than their disposition to take less of their own product for themselves, and leave a greater part of it to their employers; and if it be said, that this begets glut, by lessening consumption' (on the part of the workers) 'I can only reply that glut is synonymous with large profits.'[28]

The learned dispute between the industrial capitalist and the wealthy landowning idler as to how the booty pumped out of the workers may most advantageously be divided for the purposes of accumulation had to fall silent in the face of the July Revolution. Shortly afterwards, the urban proletariat sounded the tocsin of revolution at Lyons, and the rural proletariat began to set fire to farmyards and hayricks in England. On this side of the Channel Owenism began to spread; on the other side, Saint-Simonism and

26. Malthus, op. cit., pp. 319–20.
27. *An Inquiry into Those Principles, Respecting the Nature of Demand, etc.*, p. 67.
28. ibid., p. 59.

Fourierism. The hour of vulgar economics had arrived. Exactly a year before Nassau W. Senior discovered at Manchester that the profit (including interest) of capital is the product of the unpaid 'last hour of the twelve hours of labour',* he had announced to the world another discovery. 'I substitute,' he proudly says, 'for the word capital, considered as an instrument of production, the word abstinence.'[29] An unparalleled example of the 'discoveries' of vulgar economics! It replaces an economic category with a syco-phantic phrase, and that is all. 'When the savage,' says Senior, 'makes bows, he exercises an industry, but he does not practise abstinence.' This is supposed to explain how and why, in the earlier states of society, the implements of labour were constructed 'without the abstinence' of the capitalist. 'The more society pro-gresses, the more abstinence is demanded,'[30] namely from those whose business it is to appropriate the industry and the products of others. All the conditions necessary for the labour process are now converted into acts of abstinence on the part of the capitalist. If the corn is not all eaten, but in part also sown – abstinence of the capitalist. If the wine gets time to mature – abstinence of the capi-

29. Senior, *Principes fondamentaux de l'économie politique*, tr. Arrivabene, Paris, 1836, p. 309. This was rather too much for the adherents of the old classical school. 'Mr Senior has substituted for it' (the expression 'labour and profit') 'the expression Labour and Abstinence. He who converts his revenue abstains from the enjoyment which its expenditure would afford him. It is not the capital, but the use of the capital productively, which is the cause of profits' (John Cazenove, op. cit., p. 130, n.). John Stuart Mill, on the contrary, both copies Ricardo's theory of profit, and annexes to it Senior's 'remuneration of abstinence'. He is as much at home with absurd and flat contradictions as he is at sea with the Hegelian 'contradiction', which is the source of all dialectics. It has never occurred to the vulgar economist to make the simple reflection that every human action may be conceived as an 'abstin-ence' from its opposite. Eating is abstinence from fasting, walking is abstin-ence from standing still, working is abstinence from idling, idling is abstinence from working, etc. These gentlemen would do well to ponder occasionally over Spinoza's *'Determinatio est negatio'*.*

30. Senior, op. cit., pp. 342–3.

* Spinoza made this statement in a letter of 2 June 1674 to J. Jelles. But it should be noted that it is quoted and commented on a number of times by Hegel. The formulation in the *Logic* is particularly appropriate here: 'The foundation of all determinateness is negation' (*Logic*, para. 91, Addition). In this case, eating is not-fasting, working is not-idling, etc.

---

* See above, pp. 333–8, 'Senior's Last Hour'.

talist.[31] The capitalist robs himself whenever he 'lends (!) the instruments of production to the worker', in other words, whenever he valorizes their value as capital by incorporating labour-power into them instead of eating them up, steam-engines, cotton, railways, manure, horses and all; or, as the vulgar economist childishly conceives, instead of dissipating 'their value' in luxuries and other articles of consumption.[32] How the capitalist class can perform the latter feat is a secret which vulgar economics has so far obstinately refused to divulge. Enough that the world continues to live solely through the self-chastisement of this modern penitent of Vishnu, the capitalist. Not only accumulation, but the simple 'conservation of a capital requires a constant effort to resist the temptation of consuming it'.[33] The simple dictates of humanity therefore plainly enjoin the release of the capitalist from his martyrdom and his temptation, in the same way as the slave-owners of Georgia, U.S.A., have recently been delivered by the abolition of slavery from the painful dilemma over whether they should squander the surplus product extracted by means of the whip from their Negro slaves entirely in champagne, or whether they should reconvert a part of it into more Negroes and more land.

In economic formations of society of the most diverse kinds, there occurs not only simple reproduction but also, though in varying degrees, reproduction on an increasing scale. Progressively more is produced and consumed, and therefore more products have to be converted into means of production. However, this

31. 'No one ... will sow his wheat, for instance, and allow it to remain a twelvemonth in the ground, or leave his wine in a cellar for years, instead of consuming these things or their equivalent at once ... unless he expects to acquire additional value, etc.' (Scrope, *Political Economy*, ed. A. Potter, New York, 1841, pp. 133–4).*

32. 'The deprivation the capitalist imposes on himself by lending' (this euphemism is used, according to the approved method of vulgar economics, in order to identify the exploited wage-labourer with the industrial capitalist himself, who borrows money from other capitalists!) 'his instruments of production to the worker, instead of devoting their value to his own consumption, by transforming them into objects of utility or pleasure' (G. de Molinari, op. cit., p. 36).

33. Courcelle-Seneuil, op. cit., p. 20.

*This is in fact a reference to A. Potter's book, *Political Economy: Its Objects, Uses, and Principles*, New York, 1841. However, much of Potter's book is merely a reprint of Scrope's *Principles of Political Economy*, published in England in 1833.

process does not appear as an accumulation of capital, and consequently it does not appear as the function of a capitalist, as long as the worker's means of production, and with them his product and means of subsistence, do not confront him in the shape of capital.[34] Richard Jones, who died a few years ago, and was the successor of Malthus in the chair of Political Economy at Haileybury, the college that trains people for the Indian Civil Service, discusses this point well in the light of two important facts. Since the greater part of the Indian population are peasants cultivating their land themselves, their products, their instruments of labour and their means of subsistence never take 'the shape of a fund saved from revenue, which fund has, therefore, gone through a previous process of accumulation'.[35] On the other hand, in those provinces where English rule has least disturbed the old system, the non-agricultural workers are directly employed by the magnates, to whom a portion of the agricultural surplus product is rendered in the shape of tribute or rent. One part of this product is consumed by the magnates in its natural form, another part is converted by the workers into articles of luxury and other consumption goods for the use of the magnates, and the remainder forms the wage of the workers, who own their implements of labour. Here, production and reproduction on an increasing scale go on their way without any intervention from that peculiar saint, that knight of the woeful countenance, the 'abstaining' capitalist.

34. 'The particular classes of income which yield the most abundantly to the progress of national capital, change at different stages of their progress, and are, therefore, entirely different in nations occupying different positions in that progress ... Profits ... unimportant source of accumulation, compared with wages and rents, in the earlier stages of society ... When a considerable advance in the powers of national industry has actually taken place, profits rise into comparative importance as a source of accumulation' (Richard Jones, *Textbook, etc.*, pp. 16, 21).

35. ibid., pp. 36 ff. [Note by Engels to the fourth German edition: 'This must be an oversight, as the passage cannot be traced.'*]

*On the contrary, the passage is there on p. 36, but the quotation is highly compressed. It reads as follows, in full: 'The wages of the agriculturalists are not advanced out of funds which have been saved and accumulated from revenues.' (In other words) 'they have undergone no process of accumulation ... but are produced by the labourers themselves, and never exist in any other shape than that of a stock for their own immediate consumption.'

4. THE CIRCUMSTANCES WHICH, INDEPENDENTLY OF THE
PROPORTIONAL DIVISION OF SURPLUS-VALUE INTO
CAPITAL AND REVENUE, DETERMINE THE EXTENT OF
ACCUMULATION, NAMELY, THE DEGREE OF
EXPLOITATION OF LABOUR-POWER, THE PRODUCTIVITY
OF LABOUR, THE GROWING DIFFERENCE IN AMOUNT
BETWEEN CAPITAL EMPLOYED AND CAPITAL
CONSUMED, AND THE MAGNITUDE OF THE CAPITAL
ADVANCED

If we assume the proportion in which surplus-value breaks up into capital and revenue as a given factor, the magnitude of the capital accumulated clearly depends on the absolute magnitude of the surplus-value. Suppose that 80 per cent of the surplus-value is capitalized, and 20 per cent is eaten up, then the accumulated capital will be £2,400 or £1,200, according to whether the total amount of surplus-value was £3,000 or £1,500. Hence all the circumstances that determine the mass of surplus-value operate to determine the magnitude of the accumulation. Here we shall summarize them once again, but only in so far as they offer fresh material which relates to accumulation.

It will be remembered that the rate of surplus-value depends, in the first place, on the degree of exploitation of labour-power. Political economy lays such great stress on this point that it occasionally identifies the acceleration of accumulation which results from an increase in the productivity of labour with the acceleration which arises from an increase in the exploitation of the worker.[36] In the chapters on the production of surplus-value we constantly assumed that wages were at least equal to the value of labour-power. But the forcible reduction of the wage of labour beneath its value plays too important a role in the practical move-

36. 'Ricardo says: "In different stages of society the accumulation of capital or of the means of employing" (i.e. exploiting) "labour is more or less rapid, and must in all cases depend on the productive powers of labour. The productive powers of labour are generally greatest where there is an abundance of fertile land." If, in the first sentence, the productive powers of labour mean the smallness of that aliquot part of any produce that goes to those whose manual labour produced it, the sentence is nearly identical [i.e. tautologous], because the remaining aliquot part is the fund whence capital can, *if the owner pleases*, be accumulated. But then this does not generally happen, where there is most fertile land' (*Observations on Certain Verbal Disputes, etc.*, pp. 74–5).

ment of affairs for us not to stay with this phenomenon for a moment. In fact, it transforms the worker's necessary fund for consumption, within certain limits, into a fund for the accumulation of capital.

'Wages,' says John Stuart Mill, 'have no productive power; they are the price of a productive power. Wages do not contribute, along with labour, to the production of commodities, no more than the price of tools contributes along with the tools themselves. If labour could be had without purchase, wages might be dispensed with.'[37] But if the workers could live on air, it would not be possible to buy them at any price. This zero cost of labour is therefore a limit in a mathematical sense, always beyond reach, although we can always approximate more and more nearly to it. The constant tendency of capital is to force the cost of labour back towards this absolute zero. An eighteenth-century writer we have often quoted already, the author of the 'Essay on Trade and Commerce', actually reveals the innermost secret of English capital when he declares that England's historical mission is to force down English wages to the French and Dutch level.[38] He says, naïvely: 'But if our poor' (a technical term for the workers) 'will live luxuriously . . . then labour must, of course, be dear . . . One has only to consider what luxuries the manufacturing populace consume, such as brandy, gin, tea, sugar, foreign fruit, strong beer, printed linens, snuff, tobacco, etc.'[39] He quotes the work of a Northamptonshire manufacturer, who, with one eye on heaven, laments: 'Labour is one-third cheaper in France than in England; for their poor work hard, and fare hard, as to their food and clothing. Their chief diet is bread, fruit, herbs, roots, and dried fish; for they very seldom eat flesh; and when wheat is dear, they eat very little bread.'[40] 'To which may be added,' our essayist con-

37. John Stuart Mill, *Essays on Some Unsettled Questions of Political Economy*, London, 1844, p. 90.

38. *An Essay on Trade and Commerce*, London, 1770, p. 44. In December 1866 and January 1867 *The Times* published similar effusions by English mine-owners depicting the happy situation of the Belgian miners, who asked, and received, no more money than was strictly necessary to keep them alive for their 'masters'. The Belgian workers tolerate a great deal – but to figure in *The Times* as model proletarians! The answer came at the beginning of February 1867: a strike of Belgian mineworkers, at Marchienne, which was put down with powder and lead.

39. ibid., pp. 44, 46.

40. The Northamptonshire manufacturer commits a pious fraud, pardonable in one whose heart is so full. He pretends to compare the life of the

tinues, 'that their drink is either water or other small liquors, so that they spend very little money . . . These things are very difficult to be brought about; but they are not impracticable, since they have been effected both in France and in Holland.'[41] Twenty years later, an American humbug, the ennobled Yankee Benjamin Thompson (*alias* Count Rumford),* pursued the same line in philanthropy, to the great satisfaction of God and man. His *Essays* are a cookery book with recipes of all kinds for replacing the ordinary, but expensive food of the worker with various surrogates. The following is a particularly successful recipe issued by this remarkable 'philosopher': '5 lb. of barley-meal, 7½d.; 5 lb. of Indian corn, 6¼d.; 3d. worth of red herring, 1d. salt, 1d. vinegar, 2d. pepper and sweet herbs, in all 20¾d.; make a soup for 64 men, and at the medium price of barley and of Indian corn . . . this soup may be provided at ¼d. the portion of 20 ounces.'[42]

English and French manufacturing workers, but in the words just quoted he is in fact depicting the French agricultural labourers, as he himself later confesses in his confused way.

41. ibid., pp. 70–71. [Note by Engels to the third German edition:] Today, thanks to the competition on the world market which has grown up since then, we have advanced much further. 'If China,' says Mr Stapleton, M.P., to his constituents, 'should become a great manufacturing country, I do not see how the manufacturing population of Europe could sustain the contest without descending to the level of their competitors' (*The Times*, 3 September 1873, p. 8). The desired goal of English capital is no longer Continental wages, oh no, it is Chinese wages!

42. Benjamin Thompson, *Essays, Political, Economical, and Philosophical, etc.*, 3 vols., London, 1796–1802, Vol. 1, p. 294. In his book *The State of the Poor; or an History of the Labouring Classes in England, etc.*, Sir F. M. Eden strongly recommends the Rumfordian beggar-soup to workhouse overseers, and reproachfully warns the English workers that 'many poor people, particularly in Scotland, live, and that very comfortably, for months together, upon oat-meal and barley-meal, mixed with only water and salt' (Vol. 1, Bk I, Ch. 2, p. 503). The same sort of hints are made in the nineteenth century. 'The most wholesome mixtures of flour having been refused (by the English agricultural labourer) . . . in Scotland, where education is better, this prejudice is, probably, unknown' (Charles H. Parry, M.D., *The Question of the*

*Sir Benjamin Thompson (1753–1814) was born in Massachusetts, fought for England in the American War of Independence (which won him a knighthood), then spent the years between 1784 and 1795 in the service of the Elector of Bavaria. He eventually rose to the position of Minister of War. In 1790 the Elector created him Count von Rumford in the German imperial peerage, a title he continued to use for the rest of his life, which was spent in England and France.

With the advance of capitalist production, the adulteration of food has rendered Thompson's ideal superfluous.[43]

At the end of the eighteenth and during the first ten years of the nineteenth century, the English farmers and landlords enforced the absolute minimum of wages by paying the agricultural labourers less than the minimum in the actual form of wages, and the remainder in the form of parochial relief. Here is an example of the buffoonery of the English Dogberries, when they were 'legally' laying down a wage-tariff: 'The squires of Norfolk had dined, says Mr Burke, when they fixed the rate of wages; the squires of Berks evidently thought the labourers ought not to do so, when they fixed the rate of wages at Speenhamland, 1795 ... There they decided that, "income (weekly) should be 3s., for a man", when the gallon or half-peck loaf of 8 lb. 11 oz. is at 1s., and increase regularly till bread is 1s. 5d.; when it is above that sum, decrease regularly till it be at 2s., and then his food should be ⅕th less.'[44] Before the Committee of Inquiry of the House of Lords (1814) a certain A. Bennett, a big farmer, magistrate, poor-law guardian and wage-regulator, was asked: 'Has any proportion of the value of daily labour been made up to the labourers out of the poors' rate?' Answer: 'Yes, it has; the weekly income of every family is made up to the gallon loaf (8 lb. 11 oz.), and 3d. per head! ... The gallon loaf per week is what we suppose sufficient for the maintenance of every person in the family for the week; and the 3d. is for clothes, and if the parish think proper to find clothes, the 3d. is deducted. This practice goes through all the western part of Wiltshire, and, I believe, throughout the country.'[45]

Necessity of the Existing Corn Laws Considered, London, 1816, p. 69). This same Parry, however, complains that the English worker is now (1815) in a much worse condition than in Eden's time (1797).

43. From the reports of the most recent Parliamentary Commission on adulteration of the means of subsistence,* it will be seen that the adulteration even of medicines is the rule, not the exception, in England. For example, the examination of thirty-four specimens of opium, bought from the same number of different chemists in London, showed that thirty-one were adulterated with poppy heads, wheat-flour, gum, clay, sand, etc. Several specimens did not contain an atom of morphine.

44. G. L. Newnham (barrister-at-law), *A Review of the Evidence before the Committee of the Two Houses of Parliament on the Corn Laws*, London, 1815, p. 20, note.

45. ibid., pp. 19–20.

*This is the *Report from the Select Committee on the Working of the Adulteration of Food Act (1872)*, 1874.

'For years', exclaims a bourgeois writer of the time, 'they (the farmers) have degraded a respectable class of their countrymen, by forcing them to have recourse to the workhouse ... the farmer, while increasing his own gains, has prevented any accumulation on the part of his labouring dependants.'[46] The case of so-called 'domestic industry' shows the part played in our own time by direct robbery from the worker's necessary consumption-fund in the formation of surplus-value, and therefore in the formation of the fund for the accumulation of capital.* We shall give further facts on this subject later.

Although that portion of the constant capital which consists of the instruments of labour must, in all branches of industry, be sufficient for a certain number of workers (this number being determined by the size of the enterprise), it by no means always necessarily increases in the same proportion as the quantity of labour employed. Let us suppose that 100 workers, working 8 hours a day in a given factory, yield 800 hours of labour. If the capitalist wishes to raise this total by one half, he can employ 50 more workers; but then he must also advance more capital, not merely for wages, but for instruments of labour. But he might also let the 100 workers work 12 hours instead of 8, and then the instruments of labour already to hand would suffice. They would merely be consumed more rapidly. Thus additional labour, arising from a greater exertion of labour-power, can augment the surplus product and surplus-value, which is the substance of accumulation, without a proportional augmentation in the constant part of capital.

In the extractive industries, mines etc., the raw materials do not form part of the capital advanced. The object of labour is in this case not a product of previous labour, but something provided by nature free of charge, as in the case of metals, minerals, coal, stone, etc. Here the constant capital consists almost exclusively of instruments of labour which can very easily absorb an increased quantity of labour (day and night shifts, for example). All other

46. C. H. Parry, op. cit., pp. 77, 69. The landlords, on their side, not only 'indemnified' themselves for the Anti-Jacobin War, which they waged in the name of England, but enriched themselves enormously. Their rents doubled, trebled, quadrupled, 'and in one instance, increased sixfold in eighteen years' (ibid., pp. 100–101).

*See above, pp. 601–4.

things being equal, the mass and value of the product will rise in direct proportion to the labour expended. As on the first day of production, the two original agencies working to form the product, man and nature, continue to co-operate, and now, as creators of the products, they are also creators of the material elements of capital. Thanks to the elasticity of labour-power, the domain of accumulation has extended without any prior increase in the size of the constant capital.

In agriculture, the amount of land under cultivation cannot be increased without laying out more seed and manure. But once this has been done, the purely mechanical ploughing of the soil itself produces a marvellous effect on the size of the product. A greater quantity of labour, performed by the same number of workers as before, thus increases the fertility of the land without requiring any new contribution in the form of instruments of labour. It is once again the direct action of man on nature which becomes an immediate source of greater accumulation, without the intervention of any new capital.

Finally, in industry proper, every additional expenditure of labour presupposes a corresponding additional expenditure of raw materials, but not necessarily of instruments of labour. And as extractive industry and agriculture supply manufacturing industry both with its own raw materials and with those for its instruments of labour, the additional product provided by extractive industry and agriculture without any additional advance of capital also redounds to the advantage of manufacturing industry.

We arrive, therefore, at this general result: by incorporating with itself the two primary creators of wealth, labour-power and land, capital acquires a power of expansion that permits it to augment the elements of its accumulation beyond the limits apparently fixed by its own magnitude, or by the value and the mass of the means of production which have already been produced, and in which it has its being.

Another important factor in the accumulation of capital is the degree of productivity of social labour.

The mass of the products in which a certain value, and therefore a surplus-value of a given magnitude is embodied, increases along with the productivity of labour. If the rate of surplus-value remains the same (or even if it falls, provided that it falls more slowly than the productivity of labour rises), the mass of the surplus product increases. If the division of this product into revenue and additional capital remains the same, the consumption of the capitalist may accordingly increase without any decrease in the fund for accumulation. The relative magnitude of the accumulation-fund may even increase at the expense of the consumption-fund, while the cheapening of commodities places at the disposal of the capitalist as many means of enjoyment as formerly, or even more. But the increasing productivity of labour is accompanied by a cheapening of the worker, as we have seen, and it is therefore accompanied by a higher rate of surplus-value, even when real wages are rising. The latter never rise in proportion to the productivity of labour. The same value in variable capital therefore sets in motion more labour-power and, consequently, more labour. The same value in constant capital is embodied in more means of production, i.e. in more instruments of labour, materials of labour and auxiliary materials. It therefore supplies both more product-creating agencies and more value-creating agencies, in other words absorbers of labour. Therefore, even if the value of the additional capital remains the same or diminishes, accelerated accumulation still takes place. Not only does the scale of reproduction materially extend, but the production of surplus-value increases more rapidly than the value of the additional capital.

The growth of the productivity of labour also has an impact on the original capital, i.e. the capital which is already engaged in the production process. A part of the functioning constant capital consists of instruments of labour such as machinery, etc., which are not consumed, and therefore not reproduced or replaced, until long periods of time have elapsed. However, every year some of these instruments of labour perish, or reach the ultimate limit of their productive function. At this point, then, they reach the time for their periodic reproduction, for their replacement with other, similar machines. If the productivity of labour has increased in the place where these instruments of labour are constructed (and it does develop continually, owing to the uninterrupted advance of science and technology), the old machines, tools, apparatus, etc. will be replaced by more efficient and (considering their increased efficiency) cheaper ones. The old capital is replaced in a more productive form, not to mention continual improvements in the details of the instruments of labour actually in operation. The other part of the constant capital, raw material and auxiliary substances, is reproduced over and over again within the space of a year; the part of constant capital produced by agriculture is reproduced annually, by and large. Every time improved methods are introduced, therefore, this has an almost simultaneous impact on the new capital and the capital already engaged in its function. Every advance in chemistry not only multiplies the number of useful materials, and the useful applications of those already known, thus extending capital's sphere of investment along with its growth; it also teaches capital how to throw back the waste from the processes of production and consumption into the cycle of the process of reproduction, and thus, without any previous outlay of capital, it creates fresh materials for it. Like the increased exploitation of natural wealth resulting from the simple act of increasing the pressure under which labour-power has to operate, science and technology give capital a power of expansion which is independent of the given magnitude of the capital actually functioning. They react at the same time on that part of the original capital which has entered the stage of its renewal. This, in passing into its new shape, incorporates, free of charge, the social advances made while its old shape was being used up. Of course, this development of productivity is accompanied by a partial depreciation of the functioning capital; but in so far as this depreciation makes itself acutely felt in competition, the main burden falls on the worker, in whose increased exploitation the capitalist seeks compensation for his loss.

Labour transmits to the product the value of the means of production consumed by it. On the other hand, the value and mass of the means of production set in motion by a given quantity of labour increase as the labour becomes more productive. Although the same quantity of labour adds to its products only the same sum of new value, the old capital-value, transmitted by the labour to the products, nevertheless continues to increase in line with the growth in productivity.

An English spinner and a Chinese spinner, for example, may work the same number of hours with the same intensity; they will then both create equal values in the course of a week. But in spite of this equality, an immense difference exists between the value of the weekly product of the Englishman, who works with a mighty automatic machine, and that of the Chinese, who only has a spinning-wheel. In the same time as the Chinese spins one pound of cotton, the Englishman spins several hundreds of pounds. A sum of old values, many hundred times as great, swells the value of his product, for in that product the old values re-appear in a new useful form, and can thus function anew as capital. 'In 1782,' as

Friedrich Engels informs us, 'the whole wool crop of the preceding three years' (in England) 'lay unused for want of workers, and would have continued so to lie if the newly invented machinery had not come to its assistance and spun it.'[47] The labour which was objectified in the form of machinery did not of course directly cause men to spring out of the earth, but it made it possible for a smaller number of workers, adding relatively less living labour, not only to consume the wool productively, and put into it new value, but also to preserve its old value, in the form of yarn, etc. At the same time, it provided the means and the incentive for an increased reproduction of wool. It is the natural property of living labour to keep old value in existence while it creates new. Hence, with the increase in efficacy, extent and value of its means of production and therefore with the accumulation which accompanies the development of its productivity, labour maintains and perpetuates an always increasing capital-value in an ever-renewed form.[48] This natural power of labour appears as a power incorporated into capital for the latter's own self-preservation, just as

47. Friedrich Engels, *Lage der arbeitenden Klasse in England*, p. 20 [English translation, p. 44].

48. Classical economics, because of deficiencies in its analysis of the labour process and the valorization process, has never properly grasped this important aspect of reproduction. This can be seen from Ricardo, who says, for example, that whatever change may occur in productivity, 'a million men always produce in manufactures the same value'.* This is correct, if the extension and degree of intensity of their labour are constant. But what Ricardo overlooks in certain conclusions he draws is that the above fact does not prevent a million men, with different degrees of productivity in their labour, from turning into products very different masses of the means of production, and therefore preserving in their products very different masses of value; in consequence of which the values of the products yielded may vary considerably. It may be noted in passing that Ricardo tried in vain to make clear to J. B. Say, by that very example, the difference between use-value (which he here calls wealth or material riches) and exchange-value. Say answers: 'As for the difficulty raised by Ricardo when he says that, by using better methods of production, a million people can produce two or three times as much wealth, without producing any more value, this difficulty disappears when one bears in mind, as one should, that production is like an exchange in which a man contributes the productive services of his labour, his land, and his capital, in order to obtain products. It is by means of these productive services that we acquire all the products existing in the world. Therefore . . . we are the richer, our productive services have the more value, the greater the quantity of useful things they bring in through the exchange which is called production' (J. B. Say, *Lettres à M. Malthus*, Paris, 1820, pp. 168–9). The 'difficulty' – it exists for him, not for Ricardo – Say means to clear up is this: Why does the exchange-

* Ricardo, *On the Principles of Political Economy*, London, 1821, p. 320.

the productive forces of social labour appear as inherent characteristics of capital, and just as the constant appropriation of surplus labour by the capitalists appears as the constant self-valorization of capital. All the powers of labour project themselves as powers of capital, just as all the value-forms of the commodity do as forms of money. With the growth of capital, the difference between the capital employed and the capital consumed increases. In other words, there is an increase in the value and the material mass of the instruments of labour, such as buildings, machinery, drain-pipes, ploughing oxen, apparatus of every kind that functions for a longer or shorter time in constantly repeated processes of production, or serves for the attainment of particular useful effects, while the instruments of labour themselves only gradually wear out, therefore only lose their value piecemeal, and transfer

---

value of the use-values not increase, when their quantity increases in consequence of an increase in the productivity of labour? Answer: the difficulty is met by calling use-value exchange-value, if you please. Exchange-value is a thing which, one way or another, is connected with exchange. If therefore production is called an exchange of labour and means of production for the product, it is crystal-clear that you obtain more exchange-value in proportion as production yields more use-value. In other words, the more use-values, e.g. stockings, a working day yields to the stocking manufacturer, the richer is he in stockings. Suddenly, however, it occurs to Say that 'with a greater quantity' of stockings their 'price' (which of course has nothing to do with their exchange-value!) falls, 'because competition obliges them (the producers) to sell their products for what they cost to make'. But where does the profit come from if the capitalist sells the commodities at their cost price? Never mind! Say declares that, in consequence of increased productivity, everyone now receives in return for a given equivalent two pairs of stockings instead of one as before. The result he arrives at is precisely Ricardo's proposition, the proposition he aimed to disprove. After this mighty intellectual effort, he triumphantly exclaims to Malthus: 'This, Sir, is the well-founded doctrine without which it is impossible, I say, to explain the greatest difficulties in political economy, and, in particular, to explain why it is that a nation can be richer when its products fall in value, even though wealth is value' (ibid., p. 170). An English economist remarks on similar conjuring tricks which also appear in Say's *Lettres*: 'Those affected ways of talking make up in general that which M. Say is pleased to call his doctrine and which he earnestly urges Malthus to teach at Hertford, as it is already taught "in numerous parts of Europe". He says, "If all these propositions appear paradoxical to you, look at the things they express, and I venture to believe that they will then appear very simple and very rational." Doubtless, and in consequence of the same process, they will appear everything else, except original' (*An Inquiry into Those Principles Respecting the Nature of Demand, etc.*, pp. 116, 110).

that value to the product only bit by bit. In the same proportion as these instruments of labour serve as agencies in the formation of products without adding value to those products, i.e. in the same proportion as they are wholly employed but only partly consumed, to that degree do they perform, as we saw earlier, the same free service as the forces of nature, such as water, steam, air and electricity. This free service of past labour, when it is seized on and filled with vitality by living labour, accumulates progressively as accumulation takes place on a larger and larger scale.

Since past labour always disguises itself as capital, i.e. since the debts owed to the labour of A, B, C etc. are disguised as the assets of the non-worker X, bourgeois citizens and political economists are full of praise for the services performed by past labour, which, according to that Scottish genius MacCulloch, ought indeed to receive a special remuneration in the shape of interest, profit, etc.[49] The ever-growing weight of the assistance given by past labour to the living labour process in the form of means of production is therefore attributed to that form of past labour in which it is alienated [*entfremdet*], as unpaid labour, from the worker himself, i.e. it is attributed to its form as capital. The practical agents of capitalist production and their ideological word-spinners are as incapable of thinking of the means of production separately from the antagonistic social mask they wear at present as a slave-owner is of thinking of the worker himself as distinct from his character as a slave.

With a given degree of exploitation of labour-power, the mass of surplus-value produced is determined by the number of workers simultaneously exploited; this corresponds, although in varying proportions, with the magnitude of the capital. Thus the more that capital increases by means of successive accumulations, the more does the sum of value increase that is divided into a fund for consumption and a fund for accumulation. The capitalist can therefore live a more pleasant life, and at the same time 'renounce' more. And, finally, the more the scale of production extends, along with the mass of the capital advanced, the greater the expansive capacity of its driving forces.

49. MacCulloch took out a patent on the 'wages of past labour' long before Senior patented the 'wages of abstinence'.*

*J. R. MacCulloch, *The Principles of Political Economy*, London, 1825, p. 291: 'The profits of capital are only another name for the wages of accumulated labour.'

5. THE SO-CALLED LABOUR FUND

It has been shown in the course of this inquiry that capital is not a fixed magnitude, but a part of social wealth which is elastic, and constantly fluctuates with the division of surplus-value into revenue and additional capital. It has been seen further that, even with a given magnitude of functioning capital, the labour-power, science and land (which means, economically speaking, all the objects of labour furnished by nature without human intervention) incorporated in it form elastic powers of capital, allowing it, within certain limits, a field of action independent of its own magnitude. In this inquiry we have ignored all relations arising from the process of circulation, which may produce very different degrees of efficiency in the same mass of capital. And since we presupposed the limits set by capitalist production, i.e. we presupposed the social process of production in a form developed by purely spontaneous growth, we disregarded any more rational combination which could be effected directly and in a planned way with the means of production and the labour-power at present available. Classical political economy has always liked to conceive social capital as a fixed magnitude of a fixed degree of efficiency. But this prejudice was first established as a dogma by the arch-philistine, Jeremy Bentham, that soberly pedantic and heavy-footed oracle of the 'common sense' of the nineteenth-century bourgeoisie.[50] Bentham is among philosophers what Martin Tupper* is among poets. Both could only have been manufactured in England.[51]

50. Cf. among other passages, Jeremy Bentham, *Théorie des peines et des récompenses*, tr. Ét. Dumont, 3rd edn, Paris, 1826, Vol. 2, Bk IV, Ch. 2.

51. Bentham is a purely English phenomenon. Not even excepting our own philosopher, Christian Wolff,* in no time and in no country has the most homespun manufacturer of commonplaces ever strutted about in so self-satisfied a way. The principle of utility was no discovery made by Bentham. He simply reproduced in his dull way what Helvétius and other Frenchmen had said with wit and ingenuity in the eighteenth century. To know what is useful for a dog, one must investigate the nature of dogs. This nature is not

*Christian Wolff (1679–1754) was a German philosopher and mathematician, a disciple of Leibniz. His philosophy was in fact a common-sense adaptation and watering down of Leibniz's ideas, and it held the field in Germany from the 1730s until Kant's time.

*Martin Tupper (1810–89) was an English man of letters and poet. His fame in Victorian times rested on his *Proverbial Philosophy* (1838–67), a long series of commonplace didactic moralizings in blank verse.

This dogma in fact renders the commonest phenomena of the production process, for instance its sudden expansions and contractions, and even accumulation itself, absolutely incomprehensible.[52] It was used by Bentham himself, as well as by Malthus, James Mill, MacCulloch, etc., for apologetic purposes, and in particular so as to represent one part of capital, namely variable capital, or that part convertible into labour-power, as being of fixed size. Variable capital in its material existence, i.e. the mass of the means of subsistence it represents for the worker, or the so-called labour fund, was turned by this fable into a separate part of social wealth, confined by natural chains and unable to cross the boundary to the other parts. To set in motion the part of social wealth which is to function as constant capital, or, to express it in a material form, as means of production, a definite mass of living labour is required. This mass is given by technology. But the number of workers required to put this mass of labour-power in a fluid

---

itself deducible from the principle of utility. Applying this to man, he that would judge all human acts, movements, relations, etc. according to the principle of utility would first have to deal with human nature in general, and then with human nature as historically modified in each epoch. Bentham does not trouble himself with this. With the dryest naïveté he assumes that the modern petty bourgeois, especially the English petty bourgeois, is the normal man. Whatever is useful to this peculiar kind of normal man, and to his world, is useful in and for itself. He applies this yardstick to the past, the present and the future. The Christian religion, for example, is 'useful', 'because it forbids in the name of religion the same faults that the penal code condemns in the name of the law'. Art criticism is 'harmful' because it disturbs worthy people in their enjoyment of Martin Tupper, etc. This is the kind of rubbish with which the brave fellow, with his motto *'nulla dies sine linea'*,* has piled up mountains of books. If I had the courage of my friend Heinrich Heine, I should call Mr Jeremy a genius in the way of bourgeois stupidity.

52. 'Political economists are too apt to consider a certain quantity of capital and a certain number of labourers as productive instruments of uniform power, or operating with a certain uniform intensity ... Those ... who maintain ... that commodities are the sole agents of production ... prove that production could never be enlarged, for it requires as an indispensable condition to such an enlargement that food, raw materials, and tools should be previously augmented; which is in fact maintaining that no increase of production can take place without a previous increase, or, in other words, that an increase is impossible' (S. Bailey, *Money and Its Vicissitudes*, pp. 58, 70). Bailey criticizes the dogma mainly from the point of view of the process of circulation.

* 'No day without its line'. This statement was ascribed in antiquity to the painter Apelles, who (it is said) let no day go by without adding something to a painting. (Pliny the Elder, *Historia naturalis*, Bk XXXV, para. 84.)

state is not given, for it changes with the degree of exploitation of the individual labour-power. Nor is the price of this labour-power given, but only its minimum limit, which is moreover very elastic. The facts on which the dogma is based are these: on the one hand, the worker has no right to interfere in the division of social wealth into means of enjoyment for the non-worker and means of production. On the other hand, it is only in favourable and exceptional cases that he can enlarge the so-called 'labour fund' at the expense of the 'revenue' of the rich.[53]

How absurd a tautology results from the attempt to represent the capitalist limits of the labour fund as social barriers imposed by its very nature may be seen, for example, in Professor Fawcett.[54] 'The circulating capital of a country,' he says, 'is its wage-fund. Hence, if we desire to calculate the average money wages received by each labourer, we have simply to divide the amount of this capital by the number of the labouring population.'[55] That is to say, we first add together the individual wages actually paid, and then we assert that the sum thus obtained forms the total value of the 'labour fund' handed down to us by the grace of God and Nature. Lastly, we divide the sum thus obtained by the number of workers, in order to find out how much each is permitted to receive on the average. A very shrewd way of proceeding, this is. It does not prevent Mr Fawcett from saying, in the same breath: 'The aggregate wealth which is annually saved in England, is divided into two portions; one portion is employed as capital to

53. In his *Principles of Political Economy* [1868 edition, p. 128], John Stuart Mill says this: 'The produce of labour is apportioned at present in an inverse ratio to the labour – the largest portions to those who have never worked at all, the next largest to those whose work is almost nominal, and so in a descending scale, the remuneration dwindling as the work grows harder and more disagreeable, until the most fatiguing and exhausting bodily labour cannot count with certainty on being able to earn even the necessaries of life.' To avoid misunderstandings, let me say that, while it is quite right to rebuke men like John Stuart Mill for the contradiction between their traditional economic dogmas and their modern tendencies, it would be very unjust to lump them together with the herd of vulgar economic apologists.

54 H. Fawcett, Professor of Political Economy at Cambridge, *The Economic Position of the British Labourer*, London, 1865, p. 120.

55. Let me remind the reader here that I was the first to use the categories 'variable capital' and 'constant capital'. Political economy since the time of Adam Smith has confusedly mixed up the determining characteristics contained in these categories with the merely formal distinction, arising out of the process of circulation, between fixed and circulating capital. For further details on this point, see Volume 2, Part II.

maintain our industry, and the other portion is exported to foreign countries . . . Only a portion, and perhaps, not a large portion of the wealth which is annually saved in this country, is invested in our own industry.'[56]

The greater part of the yearly accruing surplus product, which is embezzled from the English workers without any equivalent being given in return, is thus used as capital, not in England, but in foreign countries. But with the additional capital thus exported, a part of the 'labour fund' invented by God and Bentham naturally also flows out of the country.[57]

56. Fawcett, op. cit., pp. 122–3

57. It might be said that not only capital but also workers, in the shape of emigrants, are annually exported from England. In the text, however, there is no question of the *peculium** of the emigrants, who are in great part not workers. Most of them are the sons of farmers. The additional capital annually transported abroad to be put out at interest is a much greater proportion of the annual accumulation than the yearly emigration is of the yearly increase of population.

*In Roman law, the small amount of property a father allowed his child, or a master his slave, to hold as his own. Here the meaning is the portion of the labour fund the emigrants have presumably left behind them, thus counterbalancing the loss of the capital exported, or rather the loss of that part of the capital exported which would have contributed to the labour fund if it had remained in the country.

Chapter 25: The General Law of Capitalist Accumulation

I. A GROWING DEMAND FOR LABOUR-POWER ACCOMPANIES ACCUMULATION IF THE COMPOSITION OF CAPITAL REMAINS THE SAME

In this chapter we shall consider the influence of the growth of capital on the fate of the working class. The most important factor in this investigation is the composition of capital, and the changes it undergoes in the course of the process of accumulation.

The composition of capital is to be understood in a twofold sense. As value, it is determined by the proportion in which it is divided into constant capital, or the value of the means of production, and variable capital, or the value of labour-power, the sum total of wages. As material, as it functions in the process of production, all capital is divided into means of production and living labour-power. This latter composition is determined by the relation between the mass of the means of production employed on the one hand, and the mass of labour necessary for their employment on the other. I call the former the value-composition, the latter the technical composition of capital. There is a close correlation between the two. To express this, I call the value-composition of capital, in so far as it is determined by its technical composition and mirrors the changes in the latter, the organic composition of capital. Wherever I refer to the composition of capital, without further qualification, its organic composition is always understood.

The many individual capitals invested in a particular branch of production have compositions which differ from each other to a greater or lesser extent. The average of their individual compositions gives us the composition of the total capital in the branch of production under consideration. Finally, the average of all the average compositions in all branches of production gives us the composition of the total social capital of a country, and it is with this alone that we are concerned here in the final analysis.

Growth of capital implies growth of its variable constituent, in other words, the part invested in labour-power. A part of the surplus-value which has been transformed into additional capital must always be re-transformed into variable capital, or additional labour fund. If we assume that, while all other circumstances remain the same, the composition of capital also remains constant (i.e. a definite mass of the means of production continues to need the same mass of labour-power to set it in motion), then the demand for labour, and the fund for the subsistence of the workers, both clearly increase in the same proportion as the capital, and with the same rapidity. Since the capital produces a surplus-value every year, of which one part is added every year to the original capital; since this increment itself grows every year along with the augmentation of the capital already functioning; and since, lastly, under conditions especially liable to stimulate the drive for self-enrichment, such as the opening of new markets, or of new spheres for the outlay of capital resulting from newly developed social requirements, the scale of accumulation may suddenly be extended merely by a change in the proportion in which the surplus-value or the surplus product is divided into capital and revenue – for all these reasons the requirements of accumulating capital may exceed the growth in labour-power or in the number of workers; the demand for workers may outstrip the supply, and thus wages may rise. This must indeed ultimately be the case if the conditions assumed above continue to prevail. For since in each year more workers are employed than in the preceding year, sooner or later a point must be reached at which the requirements of accumulation begin to outgrow the customary supply of labour, and a rise of wages therefore takes place. Complaints were to be heard about this in England during the whole of the fifteenth century, and the first half of the eighteenth. The more or less favourable circumstances in which the wage-labourers support and multiply themselves in no way alter the fundamental character of capitalist production. As simple reproduction constantly reproduces the capital-relation itself, i.e. the presence of capitalists on the one side, and wage-labourers on the other side, so reproduction on an expanded scale, i.e. accumulation, reproduces the capital-relation on an expanded scale, with more capitalists, or bigger capitalists, at one pole, and more wage-labourers at the other pole. The reproduction of labour-power which must incessantly be re-incorporated into capital as its means of valorization, which cannot get free of capital, and whose enslavement to capital is only concealed by the variety of individual capitalists to whom it sells itself, forms, in fact, a factor in the reproduction of capital itself. Accumulation of capital is therefore multiplication of the proletariat.[1]

Classical political economy grasped this fact so thoroughly that Adam Smith, Ricardo, etc., as mentioned earlier, inaccurately identified accumulation with the consumption, by productive workers, of the whole of the capitalized part of the surplus product, or with the transformation of the surplus product into additional wage-labourers. John Bellers was already saying this in 1696: 'For if one had a hundred thousand acres of land and as many pounds in money, and as many cattle, without a labourer, what would the rich man be, but a labourer? And as the labourers make men rich, so the more labourers there will be, the more rich men . . . the labour of the poor being the mines of the rich.'[2] So also Bernard de Mandeville at the beginning of the eighteenth century: 'It would be easier, where property is well secured, to live without money than without poor; for who would do the work? . . . As they [the poor] ought to be kept from starving, so they should receive nothing worth saving. If here and there one of the lowest class, by uncommon industry, and pinching his belly, lifts himself above the condition he was brought up in, nobody ought to hinder him; nay, it is undeniably the wisest course for every per-

1. Karl Marx, 'Wage Labour and Capital', op. cit.* 'If the masses are all oppressed equally, the more proletarians a country has, the richer it will be' (Colins, *L'Économie politique. Source des révolutions et des utopies prétendues socialistes*, Paris, 1857, Vol. 3, p. 331). 'Proletarian' must be understood to mean, economically speaking, nothing other than 'wage-labourer', the man who produces and valorizes 'capital', and is thrown onto the street as soon as he becomes superfluous to the need for valorization possessed by 'Monsieur Capital', as Pecqueur calls this person. 'The sickly proletarian of the primitive forest' is a pretty Roscherian fancy. The primitive forester is the owner of the primitive forest and uses it as his property, meeting as few obstacles to this as an orang-utang. He is not, therefore, a proletarian. This would only be the case if the primitive forest exploited him, instead of being exploited by him. As far as his health is concerned, such a man would well bear comparison, not only with the modern proletarian, but also with the syphilitic and scrofulous 'quality'. However, Herr Wilhelm Roscher no doubt means his native heath of Lüneburg when he talks about a 'primitive forest'.

2. John Bellers, op. cit., p. 2.

*Karl Marx and Frederick Engels, *Selected Works*, Vol. 1, p. 162.

son in the society, and for every private family to be frugal; but it is the interest of all rich nations, that the greatest part of the poor should almost never be idle, and yet continually spend what they get ... Those that get their living by their daily labour ... have nothing to stir them up to be serviceable but their wants which it is prudence to relieve, but folly to cure. The only thing then that can render the labouring man industrious, is a moderate quantity of money, for as too little will, according as his temper is, either dispirit or make him desperate, so too much will make him insolent and lazy ... From what has been said, it is manifest, that, in a free nation, where slaves are not allowed of, the surest wealth consists in a multitude of laborious poor; for besides that they are the never failing nursery of fleets and armies, without them there could be no enjoyment, and no product of any country could be valuable. To make the society' (which of course consists of non-workers) 'happy and people easier under the meanest circumstances, it is requisite that great numbers of them should be ignorant as well as poor; knowledge both enlarges and multiplies our desires, and the fewer things a man wishes for, the more easily his necessities may be supplied.'[3]

What Mandeville, an honest man with a clear mind, had not yet grasped was the fact that the mechanism of the accumulation process itself not only increases the amount of capital but also the mass of the 'labouring poor', i.e. the wage-labourers, who turn their labour-power into a force for increasing the valorization of the growing capital, and who are thereby compelled to make their relation of dependence on their own product, as personified in the capitalist, into an eternal relation. In reference to this relation of dependence, Sir F. M. Eden remarks, in his *The State of the Poor; or an History of the Labouring Classes in England*, 'the natural produce of our soil is certainly not fully adequate to our subsistence; we can neither be clothed, lodged nor fed but in consequence of some previous labour. A portion at least of the society must be indefatigably employed ... There are others who, though they "neither toil nor spin", can yet command the produce of industry,

3. Bernard de Mandeville, *The Fable of the Bees*, 5th edn, London, 1728, remarks, pp. 212–13, 328. 'Temperate living and constant employment is the direct road, for the poor, to rational happiness' (by which the author means the longest possible working days and the smallest possible amount of the means of subsistence), 'and to riches and strength for the state' (namely for the landowners, capitalists, and their political dignitaries and agents) (*An Essay on Trade and Commerce*, London, 1770, p. 54).

but who owe their exemption from labour solely to civilization and order ... They are peculiarly the creatures of civil institutions,[4] which have recognized that individuals may acquire property by various other means besides the exertion of labour ... Persons of independent fortune ... owe their superior advantages by no means to any superior abilities of their own, but almost entirely ... to the industry of others. It is not the possession of land, or of money, but the command of labour which distinguishes the opulent from the labouring part of the community ... This [the scheme approved by Eden] would give the people of property sufficient influence and authority over those who ... work for them; and it would place such labourers, not in an abject or servile condition, but in such a state of easy and liberal dependence as all who know human nature, and its history, will allow to be necessary for their own comfort.'[5] Sir F. M. Eden, it may be remarked in passing, was the only disciple of Adam Smith to have achieved anything of importance during the eighteenth century.[6]

4. Eden should have asked whose creatures 'the civil institutions' were. From the standpoint he adopts, that of juridical illusion, he does not regard the law as a product of the material relations of production, but rather the reverse: he sees the relations of production as products of the law. Linguet overthrew Montesquieu's illusory *'esprit des lois'* with one word: *'L'esprit des lois, c'est la propriété'*.*

5. Eden, op. cit., Vol. 1, Bk I, Ch. 1, pp. 1–2, and Preface, p. xx.

6. If the reader thinks at this point of Malthus, whose *Essay on Population* appeared in 1798, I would remind him that this work in its first form is nothing more than a schoolboyish, superficial plagiarism of Defoe, Sir James Steuart, Townsend, Franklin, Wallace, etc., declaimed in the manner of a sermon, but not containing a single original proposition of Malthus himself. The great sensation this pamphlet caused was due solely to the fact that it corresponded to the interests of a particular party. The French Revolution had found passionate defenders in the United Kingdom; the 'principle of population', slowly worked out in the eighteenth century, and then, in the midst of a great social crisis, proclaimed with drums and trumpets as the infallible antidote to the doctrines of Condorcet, etc., was greeted jubilantly by the English oligarchy as the great destroyer of all hankerings after a progressive development of humanity. Malthus, greatly astonished at his success, then set himself to the task of stuffing into the old framework of his book various bits of superficially compiled material, and adding to it new matter; but this new matter was not discovered by Malthus, it was merely annexed by him. Let us note incidentally that although Malthus was a parson of the Church of England he had taken the monastic vow of celibacy. For this is one of the conditions of holding a Fellowship in (Protestant) Cambridge University: *'Socios collegiorum*

*'The spirit of the laws is property'. S. Linguet, *Théorie des lois civiles, ou principes fondamentaux de la société*, Vol. 1, London, 1767, p. 236.

maritos esse non permittimus, sed statim postquam quis uxorem duxerit, socius collegii desinat esse '* (*Reports of Cambridge University Commission*, p. 172). This circumstance favourably distinguishes Malthus from other Protestant parsons, who have flung off the Catholic requirement of the celibacy of the priesthood, and taken 'Be fruitful and multiply' as their special Biblical mission to such an extent that they generally contribute to the increase of population to a really unbecoming extent, whilst at the same time preaching the 'principle of population' to the workers. It is characteristic that the fall of man, as economically travestied, the apple of Adam, the 'urgent appetite', 'the checks which tend to blunt the shafts of Cupid', as Parson Townsend waggishly puts it – it is characteristic that this delicate question was and is monopolized by the representatives of Protestant theology, or rather of the Protestant Church. With the exception of the Venetian monk Ortes, an original and clever writer, most of the population theorists are Protestant clerics. For instance, Bruckner's *Théorie du système animal* (Leyden, 1767), in which the whole of the modern theory of population is exhaustively treated, using ideas furnished by the passing dispute between Quesnay and his pupil, the elder Mirabeau;† then Parson Wallace, Parson Townsend, Parson Malthus and his pupil, the arch-Parson Thomas Chalmers, to say nothing of lesser reverend scribblers in this line. Originally, political economy was studied by philosophers such as Hobbes, Locke and Hume; by businessmen and statesmen, like Thomas More, Temple, Sully, De Witt, North, Law, Vanderlint, Cantillon and Franklin; and the theoretical aspects especially were studied, and with the greatest success, by medical men like Petty, Barbon, Mandeville and Quesnay. Even in the middle of the eighteenth century, the Rev. Mr Tucker, a notable economist for that time, made his excuses for meddling with Mammon. Later on, and indeed with the entry of the 'principle of population', the hour of the Protestant parsons struck. Petty, who regarded population as the basis of wealth, and was, like Adam Smith, an outspoken enemy of the parsons, said, as if he had a presentiment of their bungling interference, 'that Religion best flourishes when the Priests are most mortified, as was before said of the Law, which best flourisheth when lawyers have least to do'. He advises the Protestant priests, therefore, if they, once for all, will not follow the Apostle Paul and 'mortify' themselves by celibacy, 'not to breed more Churchmen than the Benefices, as they now stand shared out, will receive, that is to say, if there be places for about 12,000 in England and

---

* 'We do not permit the Fellows of the Colleges to be married, but rather, as soon as anyone takes a wife, he ceases to be a Fellow of his College.'

† Victor Riqueti, marquis de Mirabeau (1715–89), French economist, of the Physiocratic school. In *L'Ami des Hommes, ou traité de la population* (Avignon, 1756), the elder Mirabeau asserted that the level of population was always limited by the quantity of the means of subsistence. He differed from Quesnay in asserting that the decline of the population of France could be remedied by breaking up the great estates and making France a land of small proprietors, who would live frugally and be self-sufficient. Quesnay, on the other hand, supported large-scale agriculture, as he approached the question from the angle of agricultural production rather than that of population. The dispute was only temporary, for in 1763, in his *Philosophie rurale*, Mirabeau adopted all Quesnay's ideas, and disavowed his 'errors' of the past.

Under the conditions of accumulation we have assumed so far, conditions which are the most favourable to the workers, their relation of dependence on capital takes on forms which are endurable or, as Eden says, 'easy and liberal'. Instead of becoming more intensive with the growth of capital, this relation of dependence only becomes more extensive, i.e. the sphere of capital's exploitation and domination merely extends with its own di-

---

Wales, it will not be safe to breed up 24,000 ministers, for then the 12,000 which are unprovided for, will seek ways how to get themselves a livelihood, which they cannot do more easily than by persuading the people that the 12,000 incumbents do poison or starve their souls, and misguide them in their way to Heaven' (Petty, *A Treatise of Taxes and Contributions*, London, 1667, p. 57). Adam Smith's position with the Protestant priesthood of his time is shown by the following. In *A Letter to A. Smith, L.L.D., on the Life, Death, and Philosophy of His Friend, David Hume. By one of the People Called Christians*, 4th edn, Oxford, 1784, Dr Horne, Bishop of Norwich, reproves Adam Smith, because in a published letter to Mr Strahan, he 'embalmed his friend David' (i.e. Hume), because he told the world how 'Hume amused himself on his deathbed with Lucian and Whist', and because he even had the impudence to write of Hume: 'I have always considered him, both in his life-time and since his death, as approaching as nearly to the idea of a perfectly wise and virtuous man, as, perhaps, the nature of human frailty will permit.' The bishop cries out, in a passion: 'Is it right in you, Sir, to hold up to our view as "perfectly wise and virtuous" the *character* and *conduct* of one, who seems to have been possessed with an incurable antipathy to all that is called *Religion*; and who strained every nerve to explode, suppress and extirpate the spirit of it among men, that its very name, if he could effect it, might no more be had in remembrance?' (ibid., p. 8). 'But let not the lovers of truth be discouraged, Atheism cannot be of long continuance' (p. 17). Adam Smith 'had the atrocious wickedness to propagate atheism through the land' (namely by his *Theory of Moral Sentiments*). 'Upon the whole, Doctor, your meaning is good; but I think you will not succeed this time. You would persuade us, by the example of *David Hume, Esq.*, that atheism is the only cordial for low spirits, and the proper antidote against the fear of death ... You may smile over *Babylon* in ruins and congratulate the hardened *Pharaoh* on his overthrow in the Red Sea' (ibid., pp. 21–2). One orthodox individual among Adam Smith's college friends wrote after his death: 'Smith's well-placed affection for Hume ... hindered him from being a Christian ... When he met with honest men whom he liked ... he would believe almost anything they said. Had he been a friend of the worthy ingenious Horrocks he would have believed that the moon sometimes disappeared in a clear sky without the interposition of a cloud ... He approached to republicanism in his political principles' (*The Bee*, by James Anderson, 18 vols., Edinburgh, 1791–3, Vol. 3, pp. 166, 165). Parson Thomas Chalmers was inclined to suspect that Adam Smith invented the category of 'unproductive labourers' out of pure malice, so that he could put the Protestant parsons in it, in spite of their blessed work in the vineyard of the Lord.

mensions and the number of people subjected to it. A larger part of the worker's own surplus product, which is always increasing and is continually being transformed into additional capital, comes back to them in the shape of means of payment, so that they can extend the circle of their enjoyments, make additions to their consumption fund of clothes, furniture, etc., and lay by a small reserve fund of money. But these things no more abolish the exploitation of the wage-labourer, and his situation of dependence, than do better clothing, food and treatment, and a larger *peculium*, in the case of the slave. A rise in the price of labour, as a consequence of the accumulation of capital, only means in fact that the length and weight of the golden chain the wage-labourer has already forged for himself allow it to be loosened somewhat. In the controversies on this question, the essential fact has generally been overlooked, namely the *differentia specifica* of capitalist production. Labour-power is not purchased under this system for the purpose of satisfying the personal needs of the buyer, either by its service or through its product. The aim of the buyer is the valorization of his capital, the production of commodities which contain more labour than he paid for, and therefore contain a portion of value which costs him nothing and is nevertheless realized [*realisiert*] through the sale of those commodities. The production of surplus-value, or the making of profits, is the absolute law of this mode of production. Labour-power can be sold only to the extent that it preserves and maintains the means of production as capital, reproduces its own value as capital, and provides a source of additional capital in the shape of unpaid labour.[7] The conditions of its sale, whether more or less favourable to the worker, include therefore the necessity of its constant re-sale, and the constantly extended reproduction of wealth as capital. Wages, as we have seen, imply by their very nature that the worker will always provide a certain quantity of unpaid labour. Even if we leave aside the case where a rise of wages is accompanied by a fall in the price of labour, it is clear that at the best of times an increase in wages means only a quantitative reduction in the amount of unpaid labour the worker has to supply. This reduction can never go so

7. 'The limit, however, to the employment of both the operative and the labourer is the same; namely, the possibility of the employer realizing a *profit* on the produce of their industry. If the rate of wages is such as to reduce the master's gains below the average profit of capital, he will cease to employ them, or he will only employ them on condition of submission to a reduction of wages' (John Wade, op. cit., p. 241).

far as to threaten the system itself. Apart from violent conflicts over the rate of wages (and Adam Smith already showed that in such a conflict the master, by and large, remained the master) a rise in the price of labour resulting from accumulation of capital implies the following alternatives:

Either the price of labour keeps on rising, because its rise does not interfere with the progress of accumulation. There is nothing remarkable in this, for as Adam Smith says, 'after these' (profits) 'are diminished, stock may not only continue to increase, but to increase much faster than before ... A great stock, though with small profits, generally increases faster than a small stock with great profits' (op. cit., Vol. 1, p. 189). In this case it is evident that a reduction in the amount of unpaid labour in no way interferes with the extension of the domain of capital. Or, the other alternative, accumulation slackens as a result of the rise in the price of labour, because the stimulus of gain is blunted. The rate of accumulation lessens; but this means that the primary cause of that lessening itself vanishes, i.e. the disproportion between capital and exploitable labour-power. The mechanism of the capitalist production process removes the very obstacles it temporarily creates. The price of labour falls again to a level corresponding with capital's requirements for self-valorization, whether this level is below, the same as, or above that which was normal before the rise of wages took place. We see therefore that in the first case it was not the diminished rate, either of the absolute or of the proportional increase in labour-power, or the working population, which caused the excess quantity of capital, but rather the converse; the increase in capital made the exploitable labour-power insufficient. In the second case it was not the increased rate, either of the absolute or of the proportional increase in labour-power, or the working population, that made the capital insufficient, but rather the converse; the relative reduction in the amount of capital caused the exploitable labour-power, or rather its price, to be in excess. It is these absolute movements of the accumulation of capital which are reflected as relative movements of the mass of exploitable labour-power, and therefore seem produced by the latter's own independent movement. To put it mathematically: the rate of accumulation is the independent, not the dependent variable; the rate of wages is the dependent, not the independent variable. Thus, when the industrial cycle is in its phase of crisis, a general fall in the price of commodities is expressed as a rise in the relative value of money, and, in the phase of prosperity, a general rise in the price of commodities is expressed as a fall in the relative value of money. The so-called Currency School* conclude from this that with high prices too much money is in circulation, with low prices too little. Their ignorance and complete misunderstanding of the facts[8] are worthily paralleled by the economists, who interpret the above phenomena of accumulation by saying that in one case there are too few, and in the other, too many wage-labourers in existence.

The law of capitalist production which really lies at the basis of the supposed 'natural law of population' can be reduced simply to this: the relation between capital, accumulation and the rate of wages is nothing other than the relation between the unpaid labour which has been transformed into capital and the additional paid labour necessary to set in motion this additional capital. It is therefore in no way a relation between two magnitudes which are mutually independent, i.e. between the magnitude of the capital and the numbers of the working population; it is rather, at bottom, only the relation between the unpaid and the paid labour of the same working population. If the quantity of unpaid labour supplied by the working class and accumulated by the capitalist class increases so rapidly that its transformation into capital requires an extraordinary addition of paid labour, then wages rise and, all other circumstances remaining equal, the unpaid labour diminishes in proportion. But as soon as this diminution touches the point at which the surplus labour that nourishes capital is no longer supplied in normal quantity, a reaction sets in: a smaller part of revenue is capitalized, accumulation slows down, and the rising movement of wages comes up against an obstacle. The rise of wages is therefore confined within limits that not only leave intact the foundations of the capitalist system, but also secure its reproduction on an increasing scale. The law of capitalist accumulation, mystified by the economists into a supposed law of nature, in fact expresses the situation that the very nature of accumulation excludes every diminution in the degree of exploitation of labour, and every rise in the price of labour, which could seriously imperil

8. Cf. Karl Marx, *Zur Kritik der Politischen Ökonomie*, pp. 165 ff. [English edition, pp. 182–5].

*See above, p. 242, for a sketch of the doctrines of the Currency School, or adherents of the 'currency principle'.

the continual reproduction, on an ever larger scale, of the capital-relation. It cannot be otherwise in a mode of production in which the worker exists to satisfy the need of the existing values for valorization, as opposed to the inverse situation, in which objective wealth is there to satisfy the worker's own need for development. Just as man is governed, in religion, by the products of his own brain, so, in capitalist production, he is governed by the products of his own hand.[9]

2. A RELATIVE DIMINUTION OF THE VARIABLE PART OF CAPITAL OCCURS IN THE COURSE OF THE FURTHER PROGRESS OF ACCUMULATION AND OF THE CONCENTRATION ACCOMPANYING IT

According to the economists themselves, it is neither the actual extent of social wealth nor the magnitude of the capital already acquired that leads to a rise of wages, but only the constant growth of accumulation and the degree of rapidity of that growth (Adam Smith, Book I, Chapter 8). So far, we have considered only one special phase of this process, that in which the increase of capital occurs while the technical composition of capital remains constant. But the process goes beyond this phase.

Given the general basis of the capitalist system, a point is reached in the course of accumulation at which the development of the productivity of social labour becomes the most powerful lever of accumulation. 'The same cause,' says Adam Smith, 'which raises the wages of labour, the increase of stock, tends to increase its productive powers, and to make a smaller quantity of labour produce a greater quantity of work.'*

9. 'If we now return to our first inquiry, where we showed that capital itself is only a product of human labour ... it seems quite incomprehensible that man can have fallen under the domination of capital, his own product, and can be subordinated to it; and as in reality this is indisputably the case, the question involuntarily forces itself on us: How has the worker been able to pass from being the master of capital – as its creator – to being its slave?' (Von Thünen, *Der isolirte Staat*, Part II, Section 2, Rostock, 1863, pp. 5–6). It is to Thünen's credit that he asked this question. His answer is simply childish.

* Adam Smith, *Wealth of Nations*, Bk I, Cha. 8 (p. 142 of Volume 1 in the 1814 edition).

Apart from natural conditions, such as the fertility of the soil, etc., and apart from the skill of independent and isolated producers (shown rather qualitatively in the high standard of their products than quantitatively in their mass), the level of the social productivity of labour is expressed in the relative extent of the means of production that one worker, during a given time, with the same degree of intensity of labour-power, turns into products. The mass of means of production with which he functions in this way increases with the productivity of his labour. But those means of production play a double role. The increase of some is a consequence, that of the others is a condition, of the increasing productivity of labour. For example, the consequence of the division of labour (under manufacture) and the application of machinery is that more raw material is worked up in the same time, and therefore a greater mass of raw material and auxiliary substances enters into the labour process. That is the consequence of the increasing productivity of labour. On the other hand, the mass of machinery, beasts of burden, mineral manures, drain-pipes, etc. is a condition of the increasing productivity of labour. This is also true of the means of production concentrated in buildings, furnaces, means of transport, etc. But whether condition or consequence, the growing extent of the means of production, as compared with the labour-power incorporated into them, is an expression of the growing productivity of labour. The increase of the latter appears, therefore, in the diminution of the mass of labour in proportion to the mass of means of production moved by it, or in the diminution of the subjective factor of the labour process as compared with the objective factor.

This change in the technical composition of capital, this growth in the mass of the means of production, as compared with the mass of the labour-power that vivifies them, is reflected in its value-composition by the increase of the constant constituent of capital at the expense of its variable constituent. There may be, for example, originally 50 per cent of a capital laid out in means of production, and 50 per cent in labour-power; later on, with the development of the productivity of labour, 80 per cent may be laid out in means of production, 20 per cent in labour-power and so on. This law of the progressive growth of the constant part of capital in comparison with the variable part is confirmed at every step (as already shown) by the comparative analysis of the prices of commodities, whether we compare different economic epochs or different nations in the same epoch. The relative magnitude of the part of the price which represents the value of the means of production, or the constant part of the capital, is in direct proportion to the progress of accumulation, whereas the relative magnitude of the other part of the price, which represents the variable part of the capital, or the payment made for labour, is in inverse proportion to the progress of accumulation.

However, this diminution in the variable part of capital as compared with the constant part, or, in other words, this change in the composition of the value of the capital, provides only an approximate indication of the change in the composition of its material constituents. The value of the capital employed today in spinning is $\frac{7}{8}$ constant and $\frac{1}{8}$ variable, while at the beginning of the eighteenth century it was $\frac{1}{2}$ constant and $\frac{1}{2}$ variable.* Yet, in contrast to this, the mass of raw material, instruments of labour, etc. that a certain quantity of spinning labour consumes productively today is many hundred times greater than at the beginning of the eighteenth century. The reason is simple: with the increasing productivity of labour, the mass of the means of production consumed by labour increases, but their value in comparison with their mass diminishes. Their value therefore rises absolutely, but not in proportion to the increase in their mass. The increase of the difference between constant and variable capital is therefore much less than that of the difference between the mass of the means of production into which the constant capital, and the mass of the labour-power into which the variable capital, is converted. The former difference increases with the latter, but in a smaller degree.

The progress of accumulation lessens the relative magnitude of the variable part of capital, therefore, but this by no means thereby excludes the possibility of a rise in its absolute magnitude. Suppose that a capital-value† is divided at first into 50 per cent constant and 50 per cent variable capital, and later into 80 per cent constant and 20 per cent variable capital. If, in the meantime, the original capital, say £6,000, has increased to £18,000, its variable constituent has also increased, in fact by 20 per cent. It was £3,000, it is now £3,600. But whereas formerly an increase of capital by 20 per cent would have sufficed to raise the demand for labour by 20 per

* These proportions are notional ones, used for the purposes of illustration.
† *Kapitalwert*. This is a compressed way of saying: a quantity of capital possessing a given amount of value.

cent, now the original capital needs to be tripled to secure an increase of 20 per cent in the demand for labour.

We showed in Part IV how the development of the social productivity of labour presupposes co-operation on a large scale; how the division and combination of labour can only be organized on that basis, and the means of production economized by concentration on a vast scale; how instruments of labour which, by their very nature, can only be used in common, such as systems of machinery, can be called into existence; how gigantic natural forces can be pressed into the service of production; and how the production process can be transformed into a process of the technological application of scientific knowledge. When the prevailing system is the production of commodities, i.e. where the means of production are the property of private persons and the artisan therefore either produces commodities in isolation and independently of other people, or sells his labour-power as a commodity because he lacks the means to produce independently, the above-mentioned presupposition, namely co-operation on a large scale, can be realized only through the increase of individual capitals, only in proportion as the social means of production and subsistence are transformed into the private property of capitalists. Where the basis is the production of commodities, large-scale production can occur only in a capitalist form. A certain accumulation of capital in the hands of individual producers therefore forms the necessary pre-condition for a specifically capitalist mode of production. We had therefore to presuppose this when dealing with the transition from handicrafts to capitalist industry. It may be called primitive accumulation [*ursprüngliche Akkumulation*], because it is the historical basis, instead of the historical result, of specifically capitalist production. How it itself originates we need not investigate as yet. It is enough that it forms the starting-point. But all methods for raising the social productivity of labour that grow up on this basis are at the same time methods for the increased production of surplus-value or surplus product, which is in its turn the formative element of accumulation. They are, therefore, also methods for the production of capital by capital, or methods for its accelerated accumulation. The continual re-conversion of surplus-value into capital now appears in the shape of the increasing magnitude of the capital that enters into the production process. This is in turn the basis of an extended scale of production, of the methods for raising the productivity of labour that accompany it, and of an accelerated production of surplus-value. If, therefore, a certain degree of accumulation of capital appears as a pre-condition for the specifically capitalist mode of production, the latter reacts back to cause an accelerated accumulation of capital. With the accumulation of capital, therefore, the specifically capitalist mode of production develops, and, with the capitalist mode of production, the accumulation of capital. These two economic factors bring about, in the compound ratio of the impulses they give to each other, that change in the technical composition of capital by which the variable component becomes smaller and smaller as compared with the constant component.

Every individual capital is a larger or smaller concentration of means of production, with a corresponding command over a larger or smaller army of workers. Every accumulation becomes the means of new accumulation. With the increasing mass of wealth which functions as capital, accumulation increases the concentration of that wealth in the hands of individual capitalists, and thereby widens the basis of production on a large scale and extends the specifically capitalist methods of production. The growth of the social capital is accomplished through the growth of many individual capitals. All other circumstances remaining the same, the individual capitals grow, and with their growth the concentration of the means of production increases, in the proportion in which they form aliquot parts of the total social capital. At the same time offshoots split off from the original capitals and start to function as new and independent capitals. Apart from other causes, the division of property within capitalist families plays a great part in this. With the accumulation of capital, therefore, the number of capitalists grows to a greater or lesser extent. Two features characterize this kind of concentration, which grows directly out of accumulation, or rather is identical with it. Firstly: the increasing concentration of the social means of production in the hands of individual capitalists is, other things remaining equal, limited by the degree of increase of social wealth. Secondly: the part of the social capital domiciled in each particular sphere of production is divided among many capitalists who confront each other as mutually independent and competitive commodity-producers. Therefore not only are accumulation and the concentration accompanying it scattered over many points, but the increase of each functioning capital is thwarted by the formation of new capitals and the subdivision of old. Accumulation, therefore, presents itself on the one hand as increasing concentration of the means of production, and of the command over labour; and on the other hand as repulsion of many individual capitals from one another.

This fragmentation of the total social capital into many individual capitals, or the repulsion of its fractions from each other, is counteracted by their attraction. The attraction of capitals no longer means the simple concentration of the means of production and the command over labour, which is identical with accumulation. It is concentration of capitals already formed, destruction of their individual independence, expropriation of capitalist by capitalist, transformation of many small into few large capitals. This process differs from the first one in this respect, that it only presupposes a change in the distribution of already available and already functioning capital. Its field of action is therefore not limited by the absolute growth of social wealth, or in other words by the absolute limits of accumulation. Capital grows to a huge mass in a single hand in one place, because it has been lost by many in another place. This is centralization proper, as distinct from accumulation and concentration.

The laws of this centralization of capitals, or of the attraction of capital by capital, cannot be developed here. A few brief factual indications must suffice. The battle of competition is fought by the cheapening of commodities. The cheapness of commodities depends, all other circumstances remaining the same, on the productivity of labour, and this depends in turn on the scale of production. Therefore the larger capitals beat the smaller. It will further be remembered that, with the development of the capitalist mode of production, there is an increase in the minimum amount of individual capital necessary to carry on a business under its normal conditions. The smaller capitals, therefore, crowd into spheres of production which large-scale industry has taken control of only sporadically or incompletely. Here competition rages in direct proportion to the number, and in inverse proportion to the magnitude, of the rival capitals. It always ends in the ruin of many small capitalists, whose capitals partly pass into the hands of their conquerors, and partly vanish completely. Apart from this, an altogether new force comes into existence with the development of capitalist production: the credit system.* In its first stages, this

* [The passage which follows, from 'In its first stages' to 'movement towards centralization' (p. 780) was added by Engels to the fourth German

system furtively creeps in as the humble assistant of accumulation, drawing into the hands of individual or associated capitalists by invisible threads the money resources, which lie scattered in larger or smaller amounts over the surface of society; but it soon becomes a new and terrible weapon in the battle of competition and is finally transformed into an enormous social mechanism for the centralization of capitals.

Commensurately with the development of capitalist production and accumulation there also takes place a development of the two

edition, on the basis of the French translation of 1872. It replaces the following passage, written by Marx and retained throughout the first three German editions:] 'Not only is this itself a new and mighty weapon in the battle of competition. By unseen threads it also draws the disposable money, scattered in larger or smaller masses over the surface of society, into the hands of individual or associated capitalists. It is the specific machine for the centralization of capitals. The centralization of capitals, or the process of their attraction, becomes more intense in proportion as the specifically capitalist mode of production develops along with accumulation. In its turn, centralization becomes one of the greatest levers of this development. It shortens and quickens the transformation of separate processes of production into processes socially combined and carried out on a large scale. The increasing bulk of individual masses of capital becomes the material basis of an uninterrupted revolution in the mode of production itself. The capitalist mode of production continually conquers branches of industry not yet wholly, or only sporadically or formally, subjugated by it. At the same time there grow up on its soil new branches of industry, which could not exist without it. Finally, in the branches of industry already carried on upon the capitalist basis, the productivity of labour is made to ripen as in a hothouse. In all these cases, the number of workers falls in proportion to the mass of the means of production worked up by them. An ever increasing part of the capital is turned into means of production, an ever decreasing part into labour-power. The degree to which the means of production are means of employment for the workers lessens progressively as those means become more extensive, more concentrated, and technically more efficient. A steam plough is an incomparably more efficient means of production than an ordinary plough, but the capital-value laid out in it is an incomparably smaller means for employing men than if it were laid out in ordinary ploughs. At first, it is the mere adding of new capital to old which allows the objective conditions of the process of production to be extended and undergo technical transformations. But soon these changes of composition, and technical transformations, get a more or less complete grip on all the old capital that has reached the term of its period of reproduction and therefore has to be replaced. This metamorphosis of old capital is independent, to a certain extent, of the absolute growth of social capital, in the same way as is its centralization. But this centralization, which only redistributes the social capital already to hand, and melts a number of old capitals into one, works in its turn as a powerful agent in the metamorphosis of old capital.'

most powerful levers of centralization – competition and credit. At the same time the progress of accumulation increases the material amenable to centralization, i.e. the individual capitals, while the expansion of capitalist production creates, on the one hand, the social need, and on the other hand, the technical means, for those immense industrial undertakings which require a previous centralization of capital for their accomplishment. Today, therefore, the force of attraction which draws together individual capitals, and the tendency to centralization, are both stronger than ever before. But if the relative extension and energy of the movement towards centralization is determined, to a certain degree, by the magnitude of capitalist wealth and the superiority of the economic mechanism already attained, the advance of centralization does not depend in any way on a positive growth in the magnitude of social capital. And this is what distinguishes centralization from concentration, the latter being only another name for reproduction on an extended scale. Centralization may result from a mere change in the distribution of already existing capitals, from a simple alteration in the quantitative grouping of the component parts of social capital. Capital can grow into powerful masses in a single hand in one place, because in other places it has been withdrawn from many individual hands. In any given branch of industry centralization would reach its extreme limit if all the individual capitals invested there were fused into a single capital.[10] In a given society this limit would be reached only when the entire social capital was united in the hands of either a single capitalist or a single capitalist company.

Centralization supplements the work of accumulation by enabling industrial capitalists to extend the scale of their operations. Whether this latter result is the consequence of accumulation or centralization, whether centralization is accomplished by the violent method of annexation – where certain capitals become such preponderant centres of attraction for others that they shatter the individual cohesion of the latter and then draw the separate fragments to themselves – or whether the fusion of a number of capitals already formed or in process of formation takes place by the smoother process of organizing joint-stock companies – the

10. [Note by Engels to the fourth German edition:] The latest English and American 'trusts' are already striving to attain this goal by attempting to unite at least all the large-scale concerns in one branch of industry into a single great joint-stock company with a practical monopoly.

economic effect remains the same. Everywhere the increased scale of industrial establishments is the starting-point for a more comprehensive organization of the collective labour of many people, for a broader development of their material motive forces, i.e. for the progressive transformation of isolated processes of production, carried on by customary methods, into socially combined and scientifically arranged processes of production.

But accumulation, the gradual increase of capital by reproduction as it passes from the circular to the spiral form, is clearly a very slow procedure compared with centralization, which needs only to change the quantitative groupings of the constituent parts of social capital. The world would still be without railways if it had had to wait until accumulation had got a few individual capitals far enough to be adequate for the construction of a railway. Centralization, however, accomplished this in the twinkling of an eye, by means of joint-stock companies. And while in this way centralization intensifies and accelerates the effects of accumulation, it simultaneously extends and speeds up those revolutions in the technical composition of capital which raise its constant portion at the expense of its variable portion, thus diminishing the relative demand for labour.

The masses of capital welded together overnight by centralization reproduce and multiply as the others do, only more rapidly, and they thereby become new and powerful levers of social accumulation. Therefore, when we speak of the progress of social accumulation, we tacitly include – these days – the effects of centralization.

The additional capitals formed in the normal course of accumulation (see Chapter 24, Section 1) serve above all as vehicles for the exploitation of new inventions and discoveries, and industrial improvements in general. But in time the old capital itself reaches the point where it has to be renewed in all its aspects, a time when it sheds its skin and is reborn like the other capitals in a perfected technical shape, in which a smaller quantity of labour will suffice to set in motion a larger quantity of machinery and raw material. The absolute reduction in the demand for labour which necessarily follows from this is obviously so much the greater, the higher the degree to which the capitals undergoing this process of renewal are already massed together by virtue of the movement towards centralization.

On the one hand, therefore, the additional capital formed in the course of further accumulation attracts fewer and fewer workers in proportion to its magnitude. On the other hand, the old capital periodically reproduced with a new composition repels more and more of the workers formerly employed by it.

3. THE PROGRESSIVE PRODUCTION OF A RELATIVE SURPLUS POPULATION OR INDUSTRIAL RESERVE ARMY

The accumulation of capital, which originally appeared only as its quantitative extension, comes to fruition, as we have seen, through a progressive qualitative change in its composition, i.e. through a continuing increase of its constant component at the expense of its variable component.[11]

The specifically capitalist mode of production, the development of the productivity of labour which corresponds to it, and the change in the organic composition of capital which results from it, are things which do not merely keep pace with the progress of accumulation, or the growth of social wealth. They develop at a much quicker rate, because simple accumulation, or the absolute expansion of the total social capital, is accompanied by the centralization of its individual elements, and because the change in the technical composition of the additional capital goes hand in hand with a similar change in the technical composition of the original capital. With the progress of accumulation, therefore, the proportion of constant to variable capital changes. If it was originally say $1:1$, it now becomes successively $2:1$, $3:1$, $4:1$, $5:1$, $7:1$, etc., so that as the capital grows, instead of $\frac{1}{2}$ its total value, only $\frac{1}{3}$, $\frac{1}{4}$, $\frac{1}{5}$, $\frac{1}{6}$, $\frac{1}{8}$, etc. is turned into labour-power, and, on the other hand, $\frac{2}{3}$, $\frac{3}{4}$, $\frac{4}{5}$, $\frac{5}{6}$, $\frac{7}{8}$, into means of production. Since the demand for labour is determined not by the extent of the total capital but by its variable constituent alone, that demand falls progressively with the growth of the total capital, instead of rising in proportion to it, as was previously assumed. It falls relatively to the magnitude of the total capital, and at an accelerated rate, as this magnitude increases. With the growth of the total capital, its variable consti-

11. [Note by Engels to the third German edition:] In Marx's own copy there is here the marginal note: 'Note here for working out later: if the extension is only quantitative, then for a greater and a smaller capital in the same branch of business the profits are as the magnitudes of the capitals advanced. If the quantitative extension induces a qualitative change, then the rate of profit on the larger capital rises at the same time.'

tuent, the labour incorporated in it, does admittedly increase, but in a constantly diminishing proportion. The intermediate pauses in which accumulation works as simple extension of production on a given technical basis are shortened. It is not merely that an accelerated accumulation of the total capital, accelerated in a constantly growing progression, is needed to absorb an additional number of workers, or even, on account of the constant metamorphosis of old capital, to keep employed those already performing their functions. This increasing accumulation and centralization also becomes in its turn a source of new changes in the composition of capital, or in other words of an accelerated diminution of the capital's variable component, as compared with its constant one. This accelerated relative diminution of the variable component, which accompanies the accelerated increase of the total capital and moves more rapidly than this increase, takes the inverse form, at the other pole, of an apparently absolute increase in the working population, an increase which always moves more rapidly than that of the variable capital or the means of employment. But in fact it is capitalist accumulation itself that constantly produces, and produces indeed in direct relation with its own energy and extent, a relatively redundant working population, i.e. a population which is superfluous to capital's average requirements for its own valorization, and is therefore a surplus population.

If we consider the total social capital, we can say that the movement of its accumulation sometimes causes periodic changes, and at other times distributes various phases simultaneously over the different spheres of production. In some spheres a change in the composition of capital occurs without any increase in its absolute magnitude, as a consequence of simple concentration*; in others the absolute growth of capital is connected with an absolute diminution in its variable component, or in other words, in the labour-power absorbed by it; in others again, capital continues to grow for a time on its existing technical basis, and attracts additional labour-power in proportion to its increase, while at other times it undergoes organic change and reduces its variable component; in all spheres, the increase of the variable part of the capital, and therefore of the number of workers employed by it, is always connected with violent fluctuations and the temporary production of a surplus population, whether this takes the more striking form of the extrusion of workers already employed, or the

* The first three editions have here 'centralization' instead of 'concentration'.

less evident, but not less real, form of a greater difficulty in absorbing the additional working population through its customary outlets.[12] Owing to the magnitude of the already functioning social capital, and the degree of its increase, owing to the extension of the scale of production, and the great mass of workers set in motion, owing to the development of the productivity of their labour, and the greater breadth and richness of the stream springing from all the sources of wealth, there is also an extension of the scale on which greater attraction of workers by capital is accompanied by their greater repulsion; an increase takes place in the rapidity of the change in the organic composition of capital and in its technical form, and an increasing number of spheres of production become involved in this change, sometimes simultaneously, and sometimes alternatively. The working population therefore produces both the accumulation of capital and the means by which it is itself made relatively superfluous; and it does this to an extent which is always increasing.[13] This is a law of population peculiar

12. The census of England and Wales shows, for instance, all persons employed in agriculture (landlords, farmers, gardeners, shepherds, etc. included): 1851: 2,011,447; 1861: 1,924,110; a reduction of 87,337. Worsted manufacture, 1851: 102,714 persons; 1861: 79,242. Silk weaving, 1851: 111,940; 1861: 101,678. Calico-printing, 1851: 12,098; 1861: 12,556; a small increase, despite the enormous extension of this industry, which implies a great proportional reduction in the number of workers employed. Hat-making, 1851: 15,957; 1861: 13,814. Straw-hat and bonnet-making, 1851: 20,393; 1861: 18,176. Malting, 1851: 10,566; 1861: 10,677. Chandlery, 1851: 4,949; 1861: 4,686; this fall is due, among other things, to the increase in lighting by gas. Comb-making, 1851: 2,038; 1861: 1,478. Sawyers, 1851: 30,552; 1861: 31,647; a small increase, owing to the spread of sawing-machines. Nail-making, 1851: 26,940; 1861: 26,130; a fall, owing to the competition of machinery. Tin- and copper-mining, 1851: 31,360; 1861: 32,041. As against this, however, we have cotton-spinning and weaving, 1851: 371,777; 1861: 456,646; and coal-mining, 1851: 183,389; 1861: 246,613. 'The increase of labourers is generally greatest, since 1851, in those branches of industry in which machinery has not up to the present been employed with success' (*Census of England and Wales for the Year 1861*, Vol. 3, London, 1863, p. 36).

13. (The law of progressive diminution of the relative magnitude of variable capital, together with its effect on the situation of the class of wage-labourers, is suspected rather than understood by some of the prominent economists of the classical school. In this respect the greatest merit is due to John Barton, although he, like all the others, mixes up constant with fixed capital, and variable with circulating capital. He says:*) 'The demand for labour depends

*The passage in parentheses was added by Engels to the fourth German edition on the authority of changes made by Marx in the French edition. The whole of note 13 appears in fact in the main text of the French edition.

to the capitalist mode of production; and in fact every particular historical mode of production has its own special laws of population, which are historically valid within that particular sphere. An abstract law of population exists only for plants and animals, and even then only in the absence of any historical intervention by man.

But if a surplus population of workers is a necessary product of accumulation or of the development of wealth on a capitalist basis, this surplus population also becomes, conversely, the lever of capitalist accumulation, indeed it becomes a condition for the existence of the capitalist mode of production. It forms a disposable industrial reserve army, which belongs to capital just as absolutely as if the latter had bred it at its own cost. Independently of the limits of the actual increase of population, it creates a mass of human material always ready for exploitation by capital in the interests of capital's own changing valorization requirements. With accumulation, and the development of the productivity

---

on the increase of circulating, and not of fixed capital. Were it true that the proportion between these two sorts of capital is the same at all times, and in all circumstances, then, indeed, it follows that the number of labourers employed is in proportion to the wealth of the state. But such a proposition has not the semblance of probability. As arts are cultivated, and civilization is extended, fixed capital bears a larger and larger proportion to circulating capital. The amount of fixed capital employed in the production of a piece of British muslin is at least a hundred, probably a thousand times greater than that employed in a similar piece of Indian muslin. And the proportion of circulating capital is a hundred or thousand times less . . . the whole of the annual savings, added to the fixed capital, would have no effect in increasing the demand for labour' (John Barton, *Observations on the Circumstances which Influence the Condition of the Labouring Classes of Society*, London, 1817, pp. 161–7). 'The same cause which may increase the net revenue of the country may at the same time render the population redundant, and deteriorate the condition of the labourer' (Ricardo, op. cit., p. 469). With the increase of capital, 'the demand' (for labour) 'will be in a diminishing ratio' (ibid., p. 480, n.). 'The amount of capital devoted to the maintenance of labour may vary, independently of any changes in the whole amount of capital . . . Great fluctuations in the amount of employment, and great suffering may become more frequent as capital itself becomes more plentiful' (Richard Jones, *An Introductory Lecture on Political Economy*, London, 1833, p. 12). 'Demand' (for labour) 'will rise . . . not in proportion to the accumulation of the general capital . . . Every augmentation, therefore, in the national stock destined for reproduction, comes, in the progress of society, to have less and less influence upon the condition of the labourer' (Ramsay, op. cit., pp. 90–91).

of labour that accompanies it, capital's power of sudden expansion also grows; it grows, not merely because the elasticity of the capital already functioning increases, not merely because the absolute wealth of society expands (and capital only forms an elastic part of this), not merely because credit, under every special stimulus, at once places an unusual part of this wealth at the disposal of production in the form of additional capital; it grows also because the technical conditions of the production process – machinery, means of transport, etc. – themselves now make possible a very rapid transformation of masses of surplus product into additional means of production. The mass of social wealth, overflowing with the advance of accumulation and capable of being transformed into additional capital, thrusts itself frantically into old branches of production, whose market suddenly expands, or into newly formed branches, such as railways, etc., which now become necessary as a result of the further development of the old branches. In all such cases, there must be the possibility of suddenly throwing great masses of men into the decisive areas without doing any damage to the scale of production in other spheres. The surplus population supplies these masses. The path characteristically described by modern industry, which takes the form of a decennial cycle (interrupted by smaller oscillations) of periods of average activity, production at high pressure, crisis, and stagnation, depends on the constant formation, the greater or less absorption, and the re-formation of the industrial reserve army or surplus population. In their turn, the varying phases of the industrial cycle recruit the surplus population, and become one of the most energetic agencies for its reproduction.

This peculiar cyclical path of modern industry, which occurs in no earlier period of human history, was also impossible when capitalist production was in its infancy. The composition of capital at that time underwent only very gradual changes. By and large, therefore, the proportional growth in the demand for labour has corresponded to the accumulation of capital. Even though the advance of accumulation was slow in comparison with that of the modern epoch, it came up against a natural barrier in the shape of the exploitable working population; this barrier could only be swept away by the violent means we shall discuss later. The expansion by fits and starts of the scale of production is the precondition for its equally sudden contraction; the latter again evokes the former, but the former is impossible without disposable human material, without an increase in the number of workers, which must occur independently of the absolute growth of the population. This increase is effected by the simple process that constantly 'sets free' a part of the working class; by methods which lessen the number of workers employed in proportion to the increased production. Modern industry's whole form of motion therefore depends on the constant transformation of a part of the working population into unemployed or semi-employed 'hands'. The superficiality of political economy shows itself in the fact that it views the expansion and contraction of credit as the cause of the periodic alternations in the industrial cycle, whereas it is a mere symptom of them. Just as the heavenly bodies always repeat a certain movement, once they have been flung into it, so also does social production, once it has been flung into this movement of alternate expansion and contraction. Effects become causes in their turn, and the various vicissitudes of the whole process, which always reproduces its own conditions, take on the form of periodicity.* When this periodicity has once become consolidated, even political economy sees that the production of a relative surplus population – i.e. a population surplus in relation to capital's average requirements for valorization – is a necessary condition for modern industry.

'Suppose,' says H. Merivale, formerly Professor of Political Economy at Oxford, and later on employed at the Colonial Office, 'suppose that, on the occasion of some of these crises, the nation were to rouse itself to the effort of getting rid by emigration of some hundreds of thousands of superfluous arms, what would be the consequence? That, at the first returning demand for labour,

---

*The following passage is inserted at this point in the French edition: 'But only after mechanical industry had struck root so deeply that it exerted a preponderant influence on the whole of national production; only after foreign trade began to predominate over internal trade, thanks to mechanical industry; only after the world market had successively annexed extensive areas of the New World, Asia and Australia; and finally, only after a sufficient number of industrial nations had entered the arena – only after all this had happened can one date the repeated self-perpetuating cycles, whose successive phases embrace years, and always culminate in a general crisis, which is the end of one cycle and the starting-point of another. Until now the duration of these cycles has been ten or eleven years, but there is no reason to consider this duration as constant. On the contrary, we ought to conclude, on the basis of the laws of capitalist production as we have just expounded them, that the duration is variable, and that the length of the cycles will gradually diminish.'

there would be a deficiency. However rapid reproduction may be, it takes, at all events, the space of a generation to replace the loss of adult labour. Now, the profits of our manufacturers depend mainly on the power of making use of the prosperous moment when demand is brisk, and thus compensating themselves for the interval during which it is slack. This power is secured to them only by the command of machinery and of manual labour. They must have hands ready by them, they must be able to increase the activity of their operations when required, and to slacken it again, according to the state of the market, or they cannot possibly maintain that pre-eminence in the race of competition on which the wealth of the country is founded.'[14] Even Malthus recognizes that a surplus population is a necessity of modern industry, although he explains this, in his narrow fashion, not by saying that part of the working population has been rendered relatively superfluous, but by referring to its excessive growth. He says: 'Prudential habits with regard to marriage, carried to a considerable extent among the labouring class of a country mainly depending upon manufactures and commerce, might injure it ... From the nature of a population, an increase of labourers cannot be brought into market in consequence of a particular demand till after the lapse of 16 or 18 years, and the conversion of revenue into capital, by saving, may take place much more rapidly; a country is always liable to an increase in the quantity of the funds for the maintenance of labour faster than the increase of population.'[15] After political economy has thus declared that the constant production of a relative surplus population of workers is a necessity of capitalist accumulation, she very aptly adopts the shape of an old maid and puts into the mouth of her ideal capitalist the following words addressed to the 'redundant' workers who have been thrown onto the streets by their own creation of additional capital: 'We manufacturers do what we can for you, whilst we are increasing that capital on which you

14. H. Merivale, *Lectures on Colonization and Colonies*, London, 1841, Vol. 1, p. 146.

15. Malthus, *Principles of Political Economy*, pp. 215, 319–20. In this work Malthus finally discovers, with the help of Sismondi, the beautiful trinity of capitalist production: over-production, over-population and over-consumption. Three very delicate monsters, indeed! Cf. F. Engels, *Umrisse zu einer Kritik der Nationalökonomie*, op. cit., p. 107 ff. [English translation, pp. 437–40].

must subsist, and you must do the rest by accommodating your numbers to the means of subsistence.'[16]

Capitalist production can by no means content itself with the quantity of disposable labour-power which the natural increase of population yields. It requires for its unrestricted activity an industrial reserve army which is independent of these natural limits.

We have so far assumed that the increase or diminution of the variable capital corresponds precisely with the increase or diminution of the number of workers employed.

But the number of workers under the command of capital may remain the same, or even fall, while the variable capital increases. This is the case if the individual worker provides more labour, and his wages thus increase, although the price of labour remains the same or even falls, only more slowly than the mass of labour rises. Increase of variable capital, in this case, becomes an index of more labour, but not of more workers employed. It is the absolute interest of every capitalist to extort a given quantity of labour out of a smaller rather than a greater number of workers, if the cost is about the same. In the latter case, the outlay of constant capital increases in proportion to the mass of labour set in motion; in the former that increase is much smaller. The more extended the scale of production, the more decisive is this motive. Its force increases with the accumulation of capital.

We have seen that the development of the capitalist mode of production, and of the productivity of labour – which is at once the cause and the effect of accumulation – enables the capitalist, with the same outlay of variable capital, to set in motion more labour by greater exploitation (extensive or intensive) of each individual labour-power. We have further seen that the capitalist buys with the same capital a greater mass of labour-power, as he progressively replaces skilled workers by less skilled, mature labour-power by immature, male by female, that of adults by that of young persons or children.

On the one hand, therefore, with the progress of accumulation a larger variable capital sets more labour in motion without enlisting more workers; on the other, a variable capital of the same magnitude sets in motion more labour with the same mass of labour-power; and, finally, a greater number of inferior labour-powers is set in motion by the displacement of more skilled labour-powers.

16. Harriet Martineau, 'A Manchester Strike', 1832, p. 101.

The production of a relative surplus population, or the setting free of workers, therefore proceeds still more rapidly than the technical transformation of the process of production that accompanies the advance of accumulation and is accelerated by it, and more rapidly than the corresponding diminution of the variable part of capital as compared with the constant. If the means of production, as they increase in extent and effective power, become to a lesser extent means for employing workers, this relation is itself in turn modified by the fact that in proportion as the productivity of labour increases, capital increases its supply of labour more quickly than its demand for workers. The over-work of the employed part of the working class swells the ranks of its reserve, while, conversely, the greater pressure that the reserve by its competition exerts on the employed workers forces them to submit to over-work and subjects them to the dictates of capital. The condemnation of one part of the working class to enforced idleness by the over-work of the other part, and *vice versa*, becomes a means of enriching the individual capitalists,[17] and accelerates at the same time the production of the industrial reserve army on a

17. Even in the cotton famine of 1863, we find, in a pamphlet by the cotton-spinning operatives of Blackburn, fierce denunciations of over-work, which of course only affected adult male workers, as a result of the Factory Act. 'The adult operatives at this mill have been asked to work from 12 to 13 hours per day, while there are hundreds who are compelled to be idle who would willingly work partial time, in order to maintain their families and save their brethren from a premature grave through being over-worked ... We,' it goes on to say, 'would ask if the practice of working overtime by a number of hands, is likely to create a good feeling between masters and servants. Those who are worked overtime feel the injustice equally with those who are condemned to forced idleness. There is in the district almost sufficient work to give to all partial employment if fairly distributed. We are only asking what is right in requesting the masters generally to pursue a system of short hours, particularly until a better state of things begins to dawn upon us, rather than to work a portion of the hands overtime, while others, for want of work, are compelled to exist upon charity' (*Reports of the Inspectors of Factories ... 31 October 1863*, p. 8). The author of the *Essay on Trade and Commerce* grasps the effect of a relative surplus population on the employed workers with his usual unerring bourgeois instinct. 'Another cause of idleness in this kingdom is the want of a sufficient number of labouring hands ... Whenever from an extraordinary demand for manufactures, labour grows scarce, the labourers feel their own consequence, and will make their masters feel it likewise – it is amazing; but so depraved are the dispositions of these people, that in such cases a set of workmen have combined to distress the employer by idling a whole day together' (*Essay, etc.*, pp. 27–8). Those fellows were actually asking for a wage-increase!

scale corresponding with the progress of social accumulation. The importance of this element in the formation of the relative surplus population is shown by the example of England. Her technical means for the 'saving' of labour are colossal. Nevertheless, if tomorrow morning labour were universally to be reduced to a rational amount, and proportioned to the different sections of the working class according to age and sex, the available working population would be absolutely insufficient to carry on the nation's production on its present scale. The great majority of the now 'unproductive' workers would have to be turned into 'productive' ones.

Taking them as a whole, the general movements of wages are exclusively regulated by the expansion and contraction of the industrial reserve army, and this in turn corresponds to the periodic alternations of the industrial cycle. They are not therefore determined by the variations of the absolute numbers of the working population, but by the varying proportions in which the working class is divided into an active army and a reserve army, by the increase or diminution in the relative amount of the surplus population, by the extent to which it is alternately absorbed and set free. The appropriate law for modern industry, with its decennial cycles and periodic phases which, as accumulation advances, are complicated by irregular oscillations following each other more and more quickly, is the law of the regulation of the demand and supply of labour by the alternate expansion and contraction of capital, i.e. by the level of capital's valorization requirements at the relevant moment, the labour-market sometimes appearing relatively under-supplied because capital is expanding, and sometimes relatively over-supplied because it is contracting. It would be utterly absurd, in place of this, to lay down a law according to which the movement of capital depended simply on the movement of the population. Yet this is the dogma of the economists. According to them, wages rise as a result of the accumulation of capital. Higher wages stimulate the working population to more rapid multiplication, and this goes on until the labour-market becomes over-supplied, and hence capital becomes insufficient in relation to the supply of labour. Wages fall, and now we have the obverse side of the medal. The working population is, little by little, decimated by the fall in wages, so that capital is again in excess in relation to the workers, or, as others explain it, the fall in wages and the corresponding increase in the exploitation of the workers again accelerates accumulation, while, at the same time, the lower wages hold the growth of the working class in check. Then the time comes round again when the supply of labour is less than the demand, wages rise, and so on. This would indeed be a beautiful form of motion for developed capitalist production! Before the rise in wages could produce any positive increase of the population really fit for work, the deadline would long since have passed within which the industrial campaign would have to have been carried through, and the battle fought to a conclusive finish.

Between 1849 and 1859 a rise of wages which was in practice merely nominal, although it was accompanied by a fall in the price of corn, took place in the English agricultural districts. In Wiltshire, for example, the weekly wage rose from 7s. to 8s.; in Dorsetshire it rose from 7s. or 8s. to 9s., and so on. This was the result of an unusual exodus of the agricultural surplus population caused by wartime demands,* and by the vast extension of railways, factories, mines etc. The lower the wage, the higher is the proportion in which even a very insignificant increase is expressed. If the weekly wage, for instance, is 20s. and it rises to 22s., that is a rise of 10 per cent; but if it is only 7s., and it rises to 9s., that is a rise of $28\frac{4}{7}$ per cent, which sounds very fine. Anyway, the farmers howled, and the London *Economist*, with reference to these starvation wages, prattled quite seriously of 'a general and substantial advance'.[18] What did the farmers do now? Did they wait until the agricultural labourers had so increased and multiplied as a result of this splendid remuneration that their wages had to fall again, which is the way things are supposed to happen according to the dogmatic economic brain? No, they introduced more machinery, and in a moment the labourers were 'redundant' again to a degree satisfactory even to the farmers. There was now 'more capital' laid out in agriculture than before, and in a more productive form. With this the demand for labour fell, not only relatively, but absolutely.

The economic fiction we have been dealing with confuses the laws that regulate the general movement of wages, or the ratio between the working class – i.e. the total sum of labour-power – and the total social capital, with the laws that distribute the working

18. *The Economist*, 21 January 1860.

---

*The Crimean War took place between 1854 and 1856.

population over the different spheres of production. If, for example owing to a favourable conjuncture, accumulation in a particular sphere of production becomes especially active, and profits in it, being greater than the average profits, attract additional capital, then of course the demand for labour rises, and wages rise as well. The higher wages draw a larger part of the working population into the more favoured sphere until it is glutted with labour-power, and wages at length fall again to their average level or below it, if the pressure is too great. At that point the influx of workers into the branch of industry in question not only ceases, but gives place to an outflow of workers. Here the political economist thinks he can grasp the situation, he thinks he can see an absolute diminution of workers accompanying an increase of wages, and a diminution of wages accompanying an absolute increase of workers. But he really sees only the local oscillations of the labour-market in a particular sphere of production – he sees only the phenomena which accompany the distribution of the working population into the different spheres of outlay of capital, according to its varying needs.

The industrial reserve army, during the periods of stagnation and average prosperity, weighs down the active army of workers; during the periods of over-production and feverish activity, it puts a curb on their pretensions. The relative surplus population is therefore the background against which the law of the demand and supply of labour does its work. It confines the field of action of this law to the limits absolutely convenient to capital's drive to exploit and dominate the workers.

This is the place to return to one of the great exploits of economic apologetics. It will be remembered that if through the introduction of new machinery, or the extension of old, a portion of variable capital is transformed into constant capital, the economic apologist interprets this operation, which 'fixes' capital and by that very act 'sets free' workers, in exactly the opposite way, pretending that capital is thereby set free *for* the workers. Only now can one evaluate the true extent of the effrontery of these apologists. Not only are the workers directly turned out by the machines set free, but so are their future replacements in the rising generation, as well as the additional contingent which, with the usual extension of business on its old basis, would regularly be absorbed. They are now all 'set free' and every new bit of capital looking round for a function can take advantage of them. Whether it attracts them or

others, the effect on the general demand for labour will be nil, if this capital is just sufficient to take out of the market as many workers as the machines threw into it. If it employs a smaller number, the number of 'redundant workers' increases; if it employs a greater, the general demand for labour increases only to the extent of the excess of the employed over those 'set free'. The impulse that additional capital seeking an outlet would otherwise have given to the general demand for labour is therefore in every case neutralized until the supply of workers thrown out of employment by the machine has been exhausted. That is to say, the mechanism of capitalist production takes care that the absolute increase of capital is not accompanied by a corresponding rise in the general demand for labour. And the apologist calls this a compensation for the misery, the sufferings, the possible death of the displaced workers during the transitional period when they are banished into the industrial reserve army! The demand for labour is not identical with increase of capital, nor is supply of labour identical with increase of the working class. It is not a case of two independent forces working on each other. *Les dés sont pipés.**
Capital acts on both sides at once. If its accumulation on the one hand increases the demand for labour, it increases on the other the supply of workers by 'setting them free', while at the same time the pressure of the unemployed compels those who are employed to furnish more labour, and therefore makes the supply of labour to a certain extent independent of the supply of workers. The movement of the law of supply and demand of labour on this basis completes the despotism of capital. Thus as soon as the workers learn the secret of why it happens that the more they work, the more alien wealth they produce, and that the more the productivity of their labour increases, the more does their very function as a means for the valorization of capital become precarious; as soon as they discover that the degree of intensity of the competition amongst themselves depends wholly on the pressure of the relative surplus population; as soon as, by setting up trade unions, etc., they try to organize planned co-operation between the employed and the unemployed in order to obviate or to weaken the ruinous effects of this natural law of capitalist production on their class, so soon does capital and its sycophant, political economy, cry out at the infringement of the 'eternal' and so to speak 'sacred' law of supply and demand. Every combination between employed

* 'The dice are loaded'.

and unemployed disturbs the 'pure' action of this law. But on the other hand, as soon as (in the colonies, for example) adverse circumstances prevent the creation of an industrial reserve army, and with it the absolute dependence of the working class upon the capitalist class, capital, along with its platitudinous Sancho Panza, rebels against the 'sacred' law of supply and demand, and tries to make up for its inadequacies by forcible means.

4. DIFFERENT FORMS OF EXISTENCE OF THE RELATIVE SURPLUS POPULATION. THE GENERAL LAW OF CAPITALIST ACCUMULATION

The relative surplus population exists in all kinds of forms. Every worker belongs to it during the time when he is only partially employed or wholly unemployed. Leaving aside the large-scale and periodically recurring forms that the changing phases of the industrial cycle impress on it, so that it sometimes appears acute, in times of crisis, and sometimes chronic, in times when business is slack, we can identify three forms which it always possesses: the floating, the latent, and the stagnant.

In the centres of modern industry – factories, workshops, ironworks, mines, etc. – the workers are sometimes repelled, sometimes attracted again in greater masses, so that the number of those employed increases on the whole, although in a constantly decreasing proportion to the scale of production. Here the surplus population exists in the floating form.

Both in the factories proper, and in the large workshops, where machinery enters as one factor, or even where no more than a division of labour of a modern type has been put into operation, large numbers of male workers are employed up to the age of maturity, but not beyond. Once they reach maturity, only a very small number continue to find employment in the same branches of industry, while the majority are regularly dismissed. This majority forms an element of the floating surplus population, which grows with the extension of those branches of industry. Some of these workers emigrate; in fact they are merely following capital, which has itself emigrated. A further consequence is that the female population grows more rapidly than the male – witness England. That the natural increase of the number of workers does not satisfy the requirements of the accumulation of capital, and yet, at the same time, exceeds those requirements, is a contradiction inherent in capital's very movement. Capital demands more youthful workers, fewer adults. This contradiction is no more glaring than the other contradiction, namely that a shortage of 'hands' is complained of, while, at the same time, many thousands are out of work, because the division of labour chains them to a particular branch of industry.[19]

Moreover, the consumption of labour-power by capital is so rapid that the worker has already more or less completely lived himself out when he is only half-way through his life. He falls into the ranks of the surplus population, or is thrust down from a higher to a lower step in the scale. It is precisely among the workers in large-scale industry that we meet with the shortest life-expectancy. 'Dr Lee, Medical Officer of Health for Manchester, stated that the average age at death of the Manchester . . . upper middle class was 38 years, while the average age at death of the labouring class was 17; while at Liverpool those figures were represented as 35 against 15. It thus appeared that the well-to-do classes had a lease of life which was more than double the value of that which fell to the lot of the less favoured citizens.'[20] Under these circumstances, the absolute increase of this section of the proletariat must take a form which swells their numbers, despite the rapid wastage of their individual elements. Hence, rapid replacement of one generation of workers by another (this law does not hold for the other classes of the population). This social requirement is met by early marriages, which are a necessary consequence of the conditions in which workers in large-scale industry live, and by the premium that the exploitation of the workers' children sets on their production.

As soon as capitalist production takes possession of agriculture, and in proportion to the extent to which it does so, the demand for a rural working population falls absolutely, while the accumulation of the capital employed in agriculture advances, without this repulsion being compensated for by a greater attraction of workers,

19. During the last six months of 1866, 80–90,000 people in London were thrown out of work. This is what the Factory Report for that same half year says: 'It does not appear absolutely true to say that demand will always produce supply just at the moment when it is needed. It has not always done so with labour, for much machinery has been idle last year for want of hands' (*Reports of the Inspectors of Factories . . . 31 October 1866*, p. 81).

20. [Added by Engels to the third German edition:] Opening address to the Sanitary Conference, Birmingham, 14 January 1875, by J. Chamberlain, at that time Mayor of Birmingham, and now (1883) President of the Board of Trade.

as is the case in non-agricultural industries. Part of the agricultural population is therefore constantly on the point of passing over into an urban or manufacturing proletariat, and on the lookout for opportunities to complete this transformation. (The term 'manufacture' is used here to cover all non-agricultural industries.)[21] There is thus a constant flow from this source of the relative surplus population. But the constant movement towards the towns presupposes, in the countryside itself, a constant latent surplus population, the extent of which only becomes evident at those exceptional times when its distribution channels are wide open. The wages of the agricultural labourer are therefore reduced to a minimum, and he always stands with one foot already in the swamp of pauperism.

The third category of the relative surplus population is the *stagnant* population. This forms a part of the active labour army, but with extremely irregular employment. Hence it offers capital an inexhaustible reservoir of disposable labour-power. Its conditions of life sink below the average normal level of the working class, and it is precisely this which makes it a broad foundation for special branches of capitalist exploitation. It is characterized by a maximum of working time and a minimum of wages. We have already become familiar with its chief form under the rubric of 'domestic industry'. It is constantly recruited from workers in large-scale industry and agriculture who have become redundant, and especially from those decaying branches of industry where handicraft is giving way to manufacture, and manufacture to machinery. Its extent grows in proportion as, with the growth in the extent and energy of accumulation, the creation of a surplus population also advances. But it forms at the same time a self-reproducing and self-perpetuating element of the working class, taking a proportionally greater part in the general increase of that class than the other elements. In fact, not only the number of births and deaths, but the

21. The 781 towns enumerated in the census of England and Wales for 1861 'contained 10,960,998 inhabitants, while the villages and country parishes contained 9,105,226. In 1851, 580 towns were distinguished, and the population in them and in the surrounding country was nearly equal. But while in the subsequent ten years the population in the villages and the country increased half a million, the population in the 580 towns increased by a million and a half (1,554,067). The increase of the population of the country parishes is 6·5 per cent, and of the towns 17·3 per cent. The difference in the rates of increase is due to the migration from country to town. Three-fourths of the total increase of population has taken place in the towns' (*Census, etc.*, Vol. 3, pp. 11–12).

absolute size of families, stands in inverse proportion to the level of wages, and therefore to the amount of the means of subsistence at the disposal of different categories of worker. This law of capitalist society would sound absurd to savages, or even to civilized colonists. It calls to mind the boundless reproduction of animals individually weak and constantly hunted down.[22]

Finally, the lowest sediment of the relative surplus population dwells in the sphere of pauperism. Apart from vagabonds, criminals, prostitutes, in short the actual lumpenproletariat, this social stratum consists of three categories. First, those able to work. One need only glance superficially at the statistics of English pauperism to find that the quantity of paupers increases with every crisis of trade, and diminishes with every revival. Second, orphans and pauper children. These are candidates for the industrial reserve army, and in times of great prosperity, such as the year 1860, for instance, they are enrolled in the army of active workers both speedily and in large numbers. Third, the demoralized, the ragged, and those unable to work, chiefly people who succumb to their incapacity for adaptation, an incapacity which results from the division of labour; people who have lived beyond the worker's average life-span; and the victims of industry, whose number increases with the growth of dangerous machinery, of mines, chemical works, etc., the mutilated, the sickly, the widows, etc. Pauperism is the hospital of the active labour-army and the dead weight of the industrial reserve army. Its production is included in that of the relative surplus population, its necessity is implied by their necessity; along with the surplus population, pauperism forms a condition of capitalist production, and of the capitalist development of wealth. It forms part of the *faux frais** of capitalist production: but capital usually knows how to transfer these from its own shoulders to those of the working class and the petty bourgeoisie.

22. 'Poverty seems favourable to generation' (Adam Smith, *Wealth of Nations*, Bk I, Ch. 8). Indeed, according to the gallant and witty Abbé Galiani, this is a specially wise arrangement made by God. 'God has decreed that the men who carry on the most useful crafts should be born in abundant numbers' (Galiani, op. cit., p. 78). 'Misery up to the extreme point of famine and pestilence, instead of checking, tends to increase population' (S. Laing, *National Distress*, 1844, p. 69). After Laing has illustrated this by statistics, he continues: 'If the people were all in easy circumstances, the world would soon be depopulated.'

---

* 'Incidental expenses'.

The greater the social wealth, the functioning capital, the extent and energy of its growth, and therefore also the greater the absolute mass of the proletariat and the productivity of its labour, the greater is the industrial reserve army. The same causes which develop the expansive power of capital, also develop the labour-power at its disposal. The relative mass of the industrial reserve army thus increases with the potential energy of wealth. But the greater this reserve army in proportion to the active labour-army, the greater is the mass of a consolidated surplus population, whose misery is in inverse ratio to the amount of torture it has to undergo in the form of labour. The more extensive, finally, the pauperized sections of the working class and the industrial reserve army, the greater is official pauperism. *This is the absolute general law of capitalist accumulation.* Like all other laws, it is modified in its working by many circumstances, the analysis of which does not concern us here.

We can now understand the foolishness of the economic wisdom which preaches to the workers that they should adapt their numbers to the valorization requirements of capital. The mechanism of capitalist production and accumulation itself constantly effects this adjustment. The first word of this adaptation is the creation of a relative surplus population, or industrial reserve army. Its last word is the misery of constantly expanding strata of the active army of labour, and the dead weight of pauperism.

On the basis of capitalism, a system in which the worker does not employ the means of production, but the means of production employ the worker, the law by which a constantly increasing quantity of means of production may be set in motion by a progressively diminishing expenditure of human power, thanks to the advance in the productivity of social labour, undergoes a complete inversion, and is expressed thus: the higher the productivity of labour, the greater is the pressure of the workers on the means of employment, the more precarious therefore becomes the condition for their existence, namely the sale of their own labour-power for the increase of alien wealth, or in other words the self-valorization of capital. The fact that the means of production and the productivity of labour increase more rapidly than the productive population expresses itself, therefore, under capitalism, in the inverse form that the working population always increases more rapidly than the valorization requirements of capital.

We saw in Part IV, when analysing the production of relative surplus-value, that within the capitalist system all methods for raising the social productivity of labour are put into effect at the cost of the individual worker; that all means for the development of production undergo a dialectical inversion so that they become means of domination and exploitation of the producers; they distort the worker into a fragment of a man, they degrade him to the level of an appendage of a machine, they destroy the actual content of his labour by turning it into a torment; they alienate [*entfremden*] from him the intellectual potentialities of the labour process in the same proportion as science is incorporated in it as an independent power; they deform the conditions under which he works, subject him during the labour process to a despotism the more hateful for its meanness; they transform his life-time into working-time, and drag his wife and child beneath the wheels of the juggernaut of capital. But all methods for the production of surplus-value are at the same time methods of accumulation, and every extension of accumulation becomes, conversely, a means for the development of those methods. It follows therefore that in proportion as capital accumulates, the situation of the worker, be his payment high or low, must grow worse. Finally, the law which always holds the relative surplus population or industrial reserve army in equilibrium with the extent and energy of accumulation rivets the worker to capital more firmly than the wedges of Hephaestus held Prometheus to the rock. It makes an accumulation of misery a necessary condition, corresponding to the accumulation of wealth. Accumulation of wealth at one pole is, therefore, at the same time accumulation of misery, the torment of labour, slavery, ignorance, brutalization and moral degradation at the opposite pole, i.e. on the side of the class that produces its own product as capital.

This antagonistic character of capitalist accumulation[23] is enunciated in various forms by political economists, although they lump it together with other phenomena which are admit-

23. 'From day to day it thus becomes clearer that the relations of production in which the bourgeoisie moves do not have a simple, uniform character but rather a dual one; that in the same relations in which wealth is produced, poverty is produced also; that in the same relations in which there is a development of the forces of production, there is also the development of a repressive force; that these relations produce bourgeois wealth, i.e. the wealth of the bourgeois class, only by continually annihilating the wealth of the individual members of this class and by producing an ever-growing proletariat' (Karl Marx, *Misère de la philosophie*, p. 116) [English edition, p. 107].

tedly to some extent analogous, but nevertheless essentially distinct, since they appear only in pre-capitalist modes of production.

The Venetian monk Ortes, one of the great economic writers of the eighteenth century, regards the antagonism of capitalist production as a universal natural law of social wealth. 'In the economy of a nation, advantages and evils always balance each other' (*il bene ed il male economico in una nazione sempre all'istessa misura*): 'the abundance of wealth with some people is always equal to the lack of wealth with others' (*la copia dei beni in alcuni sempre eguale alla mancanza di essi in altri*): 'The great riches of a small number are always accompanied by the absolute deprivation of the essential necessities of life for many others. The wealth of a nation corresponds with its population, and its misery corresponds with its wealth. Diligence in some compels idleness in others. The poor and idle are a necessary consequence of the rich and active,' and so on.[24] About ten years after Ortes, the High Church Protestant parson, Townsend, glorified misery as a necessary condition of wealth in a thoroughly brutal way. 'Legal constraint' (to labour) 'is attended with too much trouble, violence, and noise, ... whereas hunger is not only a peaceable, silent, unremitted pressure, but as the most natural motive to industry and labour, it calls forth the most powerful exertions.' Everything therefore depends on making hunger permanent among the working class, and this is provided for, according to Townsend, by the principle of population, which is especially applicable to the poor. 'It seems to be a law of Nature that the poor should be to a certain degree improvident' (i.e. so improvident as to be born without silver spoons in their mouths) 'that there may always be some to fulfil the most servile, the most sordid, and the most ignoble offices in the community. The stock of human happiness is thereby much increased, whilst the more delicate are not only relieved from drudgery ... but are left at liberty without interruption to pursue those callings which are suited to their various dispositions ... it' (the Poor Law) 'tends to destroy the harmony and beauty, the symmetry and order of that system which God and Nature have established in the world.'[25] If the Venetian monk found in the

24. G. Ortes, *Della economia nazionale libri sei*, 1777, in Custodi, *Parte moderna*, Vol. 21, pp. 6, 9, 22, 25, etc. Ortes says, op. cit., p. 32: 'Instead of projecting useless systems for achieving the happiness of peoples, I shall limit myself to investigating the reasons for their unhappiness.'

25. *A Dissertation on the Poor Laws. By a Well-Wisher of Mankind* (the

fatal destiny that makes misery eternal a justification for the existence of Christian charity, celibacy, monasteries and pious foundations, the beneficed Protestant finds in it a pretext for condemning the laws by which the poor possessed a right to a miserable amount of public relief.

'The progress of social wealth,' says Storch, 'begets this useful class of society . . . which performs the most wearisome, the vilest, the most disgusting functions, which, in a word, takes on its shoulders all that is disagreeable and servile in life, and procures thus for other classes leisure, serenity of mind and conventional' (*c'est bon, ça*) 'dignity of character.'[26] Storch then asks himself what the actual advantage is of this capitalist civilization, with its misery and its degradation of the masses, as compared with barbarism. He can find only one answer: security!

'Thanks to the advance of industry and science,' says Sismondi, 'every worker can produce every day much more than he needs to consume. But at the same time, while his labour produces wealth, that wealth would, were he called on to consume it himself, make him less fit for labour.' According to him, 'men' (i.e. non-workers) 'would probably prefer to do without all artistic perfection, and all the enjoyments that industry procures for us, if it were necessary that all should buy them by constant toil like that of the worker . . . Exertion today is separated from its recompense; it is not the same man that first works, and then reposes; but it is because the one works that the other rests . . . The indefinite multiplication of the productive powers of labour can have no other

---

Rev. J. Townsend), 1786, republished London, 1817, pp. 15, 39, 41. This 'delicate' parson, from whose work just quoted, as well as from his *Journey through Spain*, Malthus often copies whole pages, himself borrowed the greater part of his doctrine from Sir James Steuart, though distorting Steuart's views in the process. For example, Steuart says: 'Here, in slavery, was a forcible method of making mankind diligent' (in the interests of the non-workers) . . . 'Men were then forced to work' (i.e. to work for others without return) 'because they were slaves of others; men are now forced to work' (i.e. to work for non-workers without return) 'because they are the slaves of their necessities.'* But, unlike our fat benefice-holder, he does not conclude from this that the wage-labourer must always go fasting. He wishes, on the contrary, to multiply their needs, and to make the increasing number of their needs a stimulus to their labour on behalf of the 'more delicate'.

26. Storch, op. cit., Vol. 3, p. 223.

*Sir James Steuart, *An Inquiry into the Principles of Political Economy*, Vol. 1, Dublin, 1770, pp. 39–40.

result than the increase of luxury and enjoyment on the part of the idle rich.'[27]

And finally, that fish-blooded bourgeois doctrinaire Destutt de Tracy makes the point in the most brutal fashion: 'In poor nations the people are comfortable, in rich nations they are generally poor.'[28]

5. ILLUSTRATIONS OF THE GENERAL LAW OF CAPITALIST ACCUMULATION

(a) England from 1846 to 1866

No period of modern society is so favourable for the study of capitalist accumulation as the period of the last twenty years. It is as if Fortunatus's purse* had been discovered. But of all countries England again provides the classical example, because it holds the foremost place in the world market, because capitalist production is fully developed only in England, and finally because the introduction of the free-trade millennium since 1846 has cut off the last retreat of vulgar economics. We have already sufficiently indicated the titanic progress of production in Part IV; in fact, in the latter half of the twenty-year period under discussion it has gone far beyond its progress in the former half.

Although the absolute growth of the English population in the last half century has been very great, the relative increase or rate of growth has fallen constantly, as is shown by the following table, borrowed from the census, which gives the average annual increase of the population of England and Wales over successive ten-year periods:

	per cent
1811–21	1·533
1821–31	1·446
1831–41	1·326
1841–51	1·216
1851–61	1·141

27. Sismondi, op. cit., pp. 79–80, 85.
28. Destutt de Tracy, op. cit., p. 231: *'Les nations pauvres, c'est là où le peuple est à son aise; et les nations riches, c'est là où il est ordinairement pauvre.'*

---

* See above, p. 586.

Let us now, on the other hand, consider the increase of wealth. Here the movement of profits, ground rent, etc., which are subject to income tax, provides the surest basis. The increase of profits liable to income tax in Great Britain from 1853 to 1864 (farmers and some other categories not included) amounted to 50·47 per cent (or an annual average of 4·58 per cent),[29] while the population itself increased during the same period by about 12 per cent. The augmentation of the rent of land subject to taxation (including houses, railways, mines, fisheries, etc.) amounted for 1853 to 1864 to 38 per cent, or $3\frac{5}{12}$ per cent annually. Under this heading, the following categories showed the greatest increase:[30]

	Percentage excess of annual income of 1864 over that of 1853	Percentage increase per year
Houses	38·60	3·50
Quarries	84·76	7·70
Mines	68·85	6·26
Ironworks	39·92	3·63
Fisheries	57·37	5·21
Gasworks	126·02	11·45
Railways	83·29	7·57

If we compare the years from 1853 to 1864 in three sets of four consecutive years each, the rate of increase of these incomes accelerates constantly. Incomes arising from profits increased between 1853 and 1857 at 1·73 per cent a year; 1857–61, 2·74 per cent, and 1861–4, 9·30 per cent a year. The sum of the incomes of the United Kingdom that come under the income tax was, in 1856, £307,068,898; in 1859, £328,127,416; in 1862, £351,745,241; in 1863, £359,142,897; in 1864, £362,462,279; in 1865, £385,530,020.[31]

29. *Tenth Report of the Commissioners of H. M. Inland Revenue*, London, 1866, p. 38.

30. ibid.

31. These figures are sufficient for comparison, but taken absolutely they are false, since some £100,000,000 of income is not declared every year. The complaints of the Inland Revenue Commissioners about systematic fraud, especially on the part of the commercial and industrial classes, are repeated in each of their reports. For example: 'A joint-stock company returns £6,000 as assessable profits, the surveyor raises the amount to £88,000, and upon that sum duty is ultimately paid. Another company which returns £190,000 is finally compelled to admit that the true return should be £250,000' (ibid., p. 42).

The accumulation of capital was accompanied at the same time by its concentration and centralization. Although no official statistics of agriculture existed for England (they did for Ireland) they were voluntarily given in ten counties. It emerged from these statistics that between 1851 and 1861 the number of farms of less than 100 acres had fallen from 31,583 to 26,597, so that 5,016 had been thrown together into larger farms.[32] From 1815 to 1825 no personal estate of more than £1,000,000 came under the succession duty; from 1825 to 1855, however, eight did; and from 1856 to June 1859, i.e. in 4½ years, four did.[33] The centralization will best be seen, however, from a short analysis of the Income Tax Schedule D (profits, exclusive of farms, etc.), in the years 1864 and 1865. I note in advance that incomes from this source pay income tax on everything over £60. These taxable incomes amounted in England, Wales and Scotland in 1864 to £95,844,222, and in 1865 to £105,435,579.[34] The number of persons taxed was, in 1864, 308,416 out of a population of 23,891,009; in 1865, 332,431 out of a population of 24,127,003. The following table shows the distribution of these incomes in the two years:

	Year ending 5 April 1864		Year ending 5 April 1865	
	Income from profits £	Persons	Income from profits £	Persons
Total income of persons in this category	95,844,222	308,416	105,435,738	332,431
„ „	57,028,289	23,334	64,554,297	24,265
„ „	36,415,225	3,619	42,535,576	4,021
„ „	22,809,781	832	27,555,313	973
„ „	8,744,762	91	11,077,238	107

In 1855 there were produced in the United Kingdom 61,543,079 tons of coal, of value £16,113,167; in 1864, 92,787,873 tons, of

32. *Census, etc.*, op. cit., p. 29. John Bright's assertion that 150 landlords own half the soil of England, and twelve own half the soil of Scotland, has never been refuted.

33. *Fourth Report of the Commissioners of H.M. Inland Revenue*, London, 1860, p. 17.

34. These are the net incomes after certain legally authorized abatements.

value £23,197,968; in 1855, 3,218,154 tons of pig-iron, of value £8,045,385; in 1864, 4,767,951 tons, of value £11,919,877. In 1854 the length of railways in use in the United Kingdom was 8,054 miles, with a paid-up capital of £286,068,794; in 1864 the length was 12,789 miles, with a paid-up capital of £425,719,613. In 1854 the total sum of the exports and imports of the United Kingdom was £268,210,145; in 1865, £489,923,285. The following table shows the movement of exports:

1846	£58,842,377
1849	£63,596,052
1856	£115,826,948
1860	£135,842,817
1865	£165,862,402
1866	£188,917,563[35]

After these few examples one understands the cry of triumph uttered by the Registrar-General: 'Rapidly as the population has increased, it has not kept pace with the progress of industry and wealth.'[36]

Let us now turn to the direct agents of this industry, or the producers of this wealth, the working class. 'It is one of the most melancholy features in the social state of this country,' says Gladstone, 'that we see, beyond the possibility of denial, that while there is at this moment a decrease in the consuming powers of the people, an increase of the pressure of privations and distress' (upon the working class) 'there is at the same time a constant accumulation of wealth in the upper classes, an increase of the luxuriousness of their habits, and of their means of enjoyment' (and a constant increase of capital).[37] Thus spake this unctuous minister in the House of Commons on 13 February 1843. On 16 April 1863, twenty years later, in the speech in which he introduced his Budget, he said: 'From 1842 to 1852 the taxable income of the

35. At this moment, in March 1867, the Indian and Chinese markets are again overstocked by the consignments of the British cotton manufacturers. In 1866 a reduction in wages of 5 per cent took place among the cotton workers. In 1867, as a result of a similar operation, there was a strike of 20,000 men at Preston. [Added by Engels to the fourth German edition:] That was the prelude to the crisis which broke out immediately afterwards.*

36. *Census, etc.*, op. cit., p. 11.

37. Gladstone, in the House of Commons, on 13 February 1843, reported in *The Times*, 14 February 1843.

*The financial and economic crisis of 1866–8.

country increased by 6 per cent . . . In the eight years from 1853 to 1861 it had increased from the basis taken in 1853 by 20 per cent! The fact is so astonishing as to be almost incredible . . . this intoxicating augmentation of wealth and power . . . entirely confined to classes of property . . . must be of indirect benefit to the labouring population, because it cheapens commodities of general consumption. While the rich have been growing richer, the poor have been growing less poor. At any rate, whether the extremes of poverty are less, I do not presume to say.'[38] How lame an anticlimax! If the working class has remained 'poor', only 'less poor' in proportion as it produces for the wealthy class 'an intoxicating augmentation of wealth and power', then it has remained relatively just as poor. If the extremes of poverty have not lessened, they have increased, because the extremes of wealth have. As for the cheapening of the means of subsistence, the official statistics, for instance the accounts of the London Orphan Asylum, show an increase in price of 20 per cent over the last ten years, if we compare the average of the three years 1860 to 1862 with the average of 1851 to 1853. In the following three years, 1863 to 1865, there was a progressive rise in the price of meat, butter, milk, sugar, salt, coal and a number of other necessary means of subsistence.[39] Gladstone's next Budget speech of 7 April 1864 is a Pindaric dithyramb on the progress of surplus-value extraction and the happiness of the people, moderated by 'poverty'. He speaks of masses 'on the border of pauperism', of branches of trade in which 'wages have not increased', and finally sums up the happiness of the working class in the words: 'human life is but, in nine cases out of ten, a struggle for existence'.[40] Professor Fawcett,

38. Gladstone, in the House of Commons, 16 April 1863, reported in the *Morning Star*, 17 April 1863.

39. See the official accounts in the Blue Book entitled *Miscellaneous Statistics of the United Kingdom*, Part VI, London, 1866, pp. 260–73, passim. Instead of the statistics of orphan asylums, etc., the declamations of the ministerial journals in recommending dowries for the royal children might also serve. The greater dearness of the means of subsistence is never forgotten there.

40. Gladstone, in the House of Commons, 7 April 1864. The Hansard version of the last sentence is 'Again, and yet more at large, what is human life, but, in the majority of cases, a struggle for existence.' The continual crying contradictions in Gladstone's Budget speeches of 1863 and 1864 were characterized by an English writer with the following quotation from Boileau:

> *Voilà l'homme en effet. Il va du blanc au noir,*
> *Il condamne au matin ses sentiments du soir.*

not bound like Gladstone by official considerations, declares roundly: 'I do not, of course, deny that money wages have been augmented by this increase of capital' (in the last ten years) 'but this apparent advantage is to a great extent lost, because many of the necessaries of life are becoming dearer' (he believes that this is because of the fall in value of the precious metals) ... 'the rich grow rapidly richer, whilst there is no perceptible advance in the comfort enjoyed by the industrial classes ... They' (the workers) 'become almost the slaves of the tradesman, to whom they owe money.'[41]

In the chapters on the 'Working Day' and 'Machinery' the reader has seen the circumstances under which the British working class created an 'intoxicating augmentation of wealth and power' for the possessing classes. There we were chiefly concerned with the worker while he was exercising his social function. But for a full elucidation of the law of accumulation, his condition outside the workshop must also be looked at, his condition as to food and accommodation. The limits of this book compel us to concern ourselves chiefly with the worst paid part of the industrial proletariat and the agricultural labourers, who together form the majority of the working class.

But before this, just one word about official pauperism, or the part of the working class which has forfeited its condition of existence (the sale of labour-power), and vegetates on public alms. The official list of paupers in England[42] numbered 851,369 persons in 1855; 877,767 in 1856; and 971,433 in 1865. As a result of the cotton famine, it swelled to 1,079,382 in 1863 and 1,014,978 in 1864. The crisis of 1866, which hit London most severely, created there, in the centre of the world market, a city with more inhabitants than the kingdom of Scotland, an increase of pauperism

---

Importun à tout autre, à soi-même incommode,
*Il change à tout moment d'esprit comme de mode.***

([H. Roy,] *The Theory of Exchanges, etc.*, London, 1864, p. 135).

41. H. Fawcett, op. cit., pp. 67–82. As far as the increasing dependence of workers on the retail shopkeepers is concerned, this is the consequence of the frequent oscillations and interruptions in their employment.

42. Wales is here always included in England.

*'Such is the man: he goes from black to white. He condemns in the morning what he felt in the evening. A nuisance to everyone else, and an inconvenience to himself, he changes his way of thinking as easily as he changes his way of dressing.'

for the year 1866 of 19·5 per cent compared with 1865, and of 24·4 per cent compared with 1864, and a still greater increase for the first months of 1867 as compared with 1866. Two points emerge clearly when we analyse the statistics of pauperism. On the one hand, the rise and fall of the number of paupers reflects the periodic changes of the industrial cycle. On the other, the official statistics become more and more misleading as to the actual extent of pauperism in proportion as, with the accumulation of capital, the class struggle develops, and hence the class-consciousness of the workers as well. For example, the barbarous nature of the treatment of the paupers, at which the English press (*The Times*, *Pall Mall Gazette*, etc.) has cried out so loudly during the last two years, is in fact of ancient date. F. Engels, in 1844, demonstrated exactly the same horrors, and exactly the same transient, canting outcries of 'sensational literature'.* But the frightful increase in the number of deaths by starvation in London during the last ten years proves beyond doubt the growing horror in which the workers hold the slavery of the workhouse,[43] that place of punishment for poverty.

(b) The Badly Paid Strata of the British Industrial Working Class

During the cotton famine of 1862[-3], Dr Edward Smith was charged by the Privy Council to make an investigation into the conditions of nourishment of the distressed cotton workers of Lancashire and Cheshire. His observations during many preceding years had led him to the conclusion that 'to avert starvation diseases' the daily food of an average woman ought to contain at least 3,900 grains of carbon and 180 grains of nitrogen; the daily food of an average man, at least 4,300 grains of carbon and 200 grains of nitrogen; for women, about the same quantity of nutritive elements as are contained in 2 lb. of good wheaten bread, for men $\frac{1}{9}$ more; for the weekly average of adult men and women, at

43. A peculiar light is thrown on the advances made since the time of Adam Smith by the fact that he still occasionally uses the word 'workhouse' as a synonym for 'manufactory'. For example, the opening of his chapter on the division of labour: 'those employed in every different branch of the work can often be collected into the same workhouse.'*

*Adam Smith, *Wealth of Nations*, Vol. 1, Edinburgh, 1814, p. 6.

---

*In his *The Condition of the Working Class in England*, published in 1845, but written over the years 1844 and 1845.

least 28,600 grains of carbon and 1,330 grains of nitrogen. His calculation was practically confirmed in a surprising manner by its agreement with the miserable quantity of nourishment to which the emergency had reduced the consumption of the cotton workers. This was, in December 1862, 29,211 grains of carbon and 1,295 grains of nitrogen a week.

In 1863, the Privy Council ordered an investigation into the state of distress of the worst-nourished part of the English working class. Dr Simon, medical officer to the Privy Council, chose for this work the above-mentioned Dr Smith. His inquiry covers on the one hand the agricultural labourers, on the other hand silk-weavers, needlewomen, kid-glovers, stocking-weavers, glove-weavers and shoemakers. The latter categories are, with the exception of the stocking-weavers, exclusively town-dwellers. It was made a rule in the inquiry to select in each category the most healthy families, and those comparatively in the best circumstances.

As a general result it was found that 'in only one of the examined classes of indoor operatives did the average nitrogen supply just exceed, while in another it nearly reached, the estimated standard of bare sufficiency' (i.e. sufficient to avert starvation diseases) 'and that in two classes there was defect – in one, a very large defect – of both nitrogen and carbon. Moreover, as regards the examined families of the agricultural population, it appeared that more than a fifth were with less than the estimated sufficiency of carbonaceous food, that more than one-third were with less than the estimated sufficiency of nitrogenous food, and that in three counties (Berkshire, Oxfordshire, and Somersetshire), insufficiency of nitrogenous food was the average local diet.'[44] Among the agricultural labourers, those of England, the wealthiest part of the United Kingdom, were the worst fed.[45] The insufficiency of food among the agricultural labourers fell as a rule chiefly on the women and children, for 'the man must eat to do his work'. Still greater penury ravaged the urban workers he examined. 'They are so ill fed that assuredly among them there must be many cases of severe and injurious privation.'[46] (This is all 'abstinence' on the part of the capitalist! For it is 'abstinence' from paying for the means of subsistence absolutely necessary for the mere vegetation of his 'hands'.)

The following table shows the conditions of nourishment of the

44. *Public Health, Sixth Report, 1863*, London, 1864, p. 13.
45. ibid., p. 17.   46. ibid., p. 13.

above-named categories of purely town-dwelling workers, as compared with the minimum assumed by Dr Smith, and with the food-allowance of the cotton workers during the time of their greatest distress:[47]

(Both sexes)	Average weekly carbon (in grains)	Average weekly nitrogen (in grains)
Five indoor occupations	28,876	1,192
Unemployed Lancashire operatives	28,211	1,295
Minimum quantity to be allowed to the Lancashire operatives, equal number of males and females	28,600	1,330

Just under one-half ($\frac{60}{125}$) of the categories of industrial worker investigated had absolutely no beer, and 28 per cent no milk. The weekly average of liquid means of nourishment in the families varied from seven ounces in the case of the needlewomen to 24¾ ounces in the case of the stocking-makers. The majority of those who did not obtain milk were needlewomen in London. The quantity of bread consumed weekly varied from 7¾ lb. for the needlewomen to 11½ lb. for the shoemakers, and gave a total average of 9·9 lb. per adult weekly. Sugar (treacle, etc.) varied from 4 ounces weekly for the kid-glovers to 11 ounces for the stocking-makers; and the total average per week for all categories was 8 ounces per adult per week. The total weekly average butter intake (fat, etc.) was 5 ounces per adult. The weekly average of meat (bacon, etc.) varied from 7¼ ounces for the silk-weavers to 18¼ ounces for the kid-glovers; total average for the different categories, 13·6 ounces. The weekly cost of food per adult was expressed in the following average figures: silk-weavers 2s. 2½d., needlewomen 2s. 7d., kid-glovers 2s. 9½d., shoemakers 2s. 7¾d., stocking-weavers 2s. 6¼d. For the silk-weavers of Macclesfield the average was only 1s. 8½d. The worst-nourished categories were the needlewomen, silk-weavers and kid-glovers.[48]

In his General Health Report, Dr Simon says this about the state of nourishment: 'That cases are innumerable in which defective diet is the cause or the aggravator of disease can be affirmed

47. *Public Health, Sixth Report, 1863,* London, 1864, Appendix, p. 232.
48. ibid., pp. 232–3.

by any one who is conversant with poor law medical practice, or with the wards and out-patient rooms of hospitals ... Yet in this point of view there is, in my opinion, a very important sanitary context to be added. It must be remembered that privation of food is very reluctantly borne, and that as a rule great poorness of diet will only come when other privations have preceded it. Long before insufficiency of diet is a matter of hygienic concern, long before the physiologist would think of counting the grains of nitrogen and carbon which intervene between life and starvation, the household will have been utterly destitute of material comfort; clothing and fuel will have been even scantier than food – against inclemencies of weather there will have been no adequate protection – dwelling space will have been stinted to the degree in which over-crowding produces or increases disease; of household utensils and furniture there will have been scarcely any – even cleanliness will have been found costly or difficult, and if there still be self-respectful endeavours to maintain it, every such endeavour will represent additional pangs of hunger. The home, too, will be where shelter can be cheapest bought; in quarters where commonly there is least fruit of sanitary supervision, least drainage, least scavenging, least suppression of public nuisances, least or worst water supply, and, if in town, least light and air. Such are the sanitary dangers to which poverty is almost certainly exposed, when it is poverty enough to imply scantiness of food. And while the sum of them is of terrible magnitude against life, the mere scantiness of food is in itself of very serious moment ... These are painful reflections, especially when it is remembered that the poverty to which they advert is not the deserved poverty of idleness. In all cases it is the poverty of working populations. Indeed, as regards the indoor operatives, the work which obtains the scanty pittance of food, is for the most part excessively prolonged. Yet evidently it is only in a qualified sense that the work can be deemed self-supporting ... And on a very large scale the nominal self-support can be only a circuit, longer or shorter, to pauperism.'[49]

The intimate connection between the pangs of hunger suffered by the most industrious layers of the working class, and the extravagant consumption, coarse or refined, of the rich, for which capitalist accumulation is the basis, is only uncovered when the economic laws are known. It is otherwise with the housing situation. Every unprejudiced observer sees that the greater the centrali-

49. ibid., pp. 14–15.

zation of the means of production, the greater is the corresponding concentration of workers within a given space; and therefore the more quickly capitalist accumulation takes place, the more miserable the housing situation of the working class. 'Improvements' of towns which accompany the increase of wealth, such as the demolition of badly built districts, the erection of palaces to house banks, warehouses etc., the widening of streets for business traffic, for luxury carriages, for the introduction of tramways, obviously drive the poor away into even worse and more crowded corners. On the other hand, everyone knows that the dearness of houses stands in inverse ratio to their quality, and that the mines of misery are exploited by house speculators with more profit and at less cost than the mines of Potosí were ever exploited. The antagonistic character of capitalist accumulation, and thus of capitalist property-relations in general,[50] is here so evident that even the official English reports on this subject teem with heterodox onslaughts on 'property and its rights'. This evil makes such progress alongside the development of industry, the accumulation of capital and the growth and 'improvement' of towns that the sheer fear of contagious diseases, which do not spare even 'respectable people', brought into existence from 1847 to 1864 no less than ten Acts of Parliament on sanitation, and that the frightened middle classes in certain towns, such as Liverpool, Glasgow and so on, took strenuous measures to deal with the problem through their municipalities. Nevertheless, Dr Simon says in his report of 1865: 'Speaking generally, it may be said that the evils are uncontrolled in England.' By order of the Privy Council, in 1864, an inquiry was made into the condition of the housing of agricultural labourers, and in 1865 the same thing was done for the poorer classes of the towns. The results of the admirable work of Dr Julian Hunter are to be found in the seventh (1865) and eighth (1866) Reports on Public Health. I shall come back to the agricultural labourers later on. On the condition of urban dwellings, I quote, as a preliminary, a general remark made by Dr Simon. 'Although my official point of view,' he says, 'is one exclusively physical, common humanity requires that the other aspect of this

50. 'In no particular have the rights of *persons* been so avowedly and shamefully sacrificed to the rights of *property* as in regard to the lodging of the labouring class. Every large town may be looked upon a place of human sacrifice, a shrine where thousands pass yearly through the fire as offerings to the moloch of avarice' (S. Laing, op. cit., p. 150).

evil should not be ignored . . . In its higher degrees it' (i.e. over-crowding) 'almost necessarily involves such negation of all delicacy, such unclean confusion of bodies and bodily functions, such exposure of animal and sexual nakedness, as is rather bestial than human. To be subject to these influences is a degradation which must become deeper and deeper for those on whom it continues to work. To children who are born under its curse, it must often be a very baptism into infamy. And beyond all measure hopeless is the wish that persons thus circumstanced should ever in other respects aspire to that atmosphere of civilization which has its essence in physical and moral cleanliness.'[51]

London takes the first place in overcrowded habitations, absolutely unfit for human beings. 'I feel clear,' says Dr Hunter, 'on two points; first, that there are about twenty large colonies in London, of about 10,000 persons each, whose miserable condition exceeds almost anything I have seen elsewhere in England, and is almost entirely the result of their bad house accommodation; and second, that the crowded and dilapidated condition of the houses of these colonies is much worse than was the case twenty years ago.'[52] 'It is not too much to say that life in parts of London and Newcastle is infernal.'[53]

Furthermore, the better-off part of the working class, together with the small shopkeepers and other elements of the lower middle class, falls in London more and more under the curse of these vile housing conditions, in proportion as 'improvements', and with them the demolition of old streets and houses, advance, in proportion as factories spring up and the influx of people into the metropolis grows, and finally in proportion as house rents rise owing to increases in urban ground rent. 'Rents have become so heavy that few labouring men can afford more than one room.'[54] There is almost no house property in London that is not over-

51. *Public Health, Eighth Report*, 1866, p. 14, n.
52. ibid., p. 89. With reference to the children in these 'colonies' Dr Hunter says: 'People are not now alive to tell us how children were brought up before this age of dense agglomerations of poor began, and he would be a rash prophet who should tell us what future behaviour is to be expected from the present growth of children, who, under circumstances probably never before paralleled in this country, are now completing their education for future practice, as "dangerous classes" by sitting up half the night with persons of every age, half naked, drunken, obscene, and quarrelsome' (ibid., p. 56).
53. ibid., p. 62.
54. *Report of the Officer of Health of St Martin's in the Fields*, 1865.

burdened with a number of middlemen. For the price of land in London is always very high in comparison with its yearly revenue, and therefore every buyer speculates on getting rid of it again at a 'jury price' (the expropriation valuation fixed by jurymen), or on pocketing an extraordinary increase of value arising from the proximity of some large-scale undertaking. As a result of this, there is a regular trade in the purchase of 'fag-ends of leases'. 'Gentlemen in this business may be fairly expected to do as they do – get all they can from the tenants while they have them, and leave as little as they can for their successors.'[55]

The rents are weekly, and these gentlemen run no risk. Owing to the construction of railways within the city, 'the spectacle has lately been seen in the East of London of a number of families wandering about some Saturday night with their scanty worldly goods on their backs, without any resting place but the workhouse.'[56] The workhouses are already overcrowded, and the 'improvements' already sanctioned by Parliament have only just begun. If the workers are driven away by the demolition of their old houses, they either do not leave the old parish, or at the most they settle down on its borders, as near as they can get to it. 'They try, of course, to remain as near as possible to their workshops. The inhabitants do not go beyond the same or the next parish, parting their two-room tenements into single rooms, and crowding even those . . . Even at an advanced rent, the people who are displaced will hardly be able to get an accommodation so good as the meagre one they have left . . . Half the workmen . . . of the Strand . . . walked two miles to their work.' This same Strand, a main thoroughfare which gives strangers an imposing idea of the wealth of London, may serve as an example of the way human beings are packed together in that city. In one of its parishes, the Public Health Officer reckoned 581 persons per acre, although half the width of the Thames was included in the parish. It will of course be understood that all the measures for the improvement of public health which have been taken so far in London have in fact, by demolishing uninhabitable houses, driven the workers out of some districts only to crowd them together still more closely in other districts. 'Either,' says Dr Hunter, 'the whole proceeding will of necessity stop as an absurdity, or the public compassion (!) be effectually

55. *Public Health, Eighth Report*, 1866, p. 91.
56. ibid., p. 88.

aroused to the obligation which may now be without exaggeration called national, of supplying cover to those who will provide it for them.'[57] Capitalist justice is truly to be wondered at! The owner of land and houses, the businessman, when expropriated by 'improvements' such as railways, the building of new streets, etc., does not just receive full compensation. He must also be comforted, both according to human law and divine law, by receiving a substantial profit in return for his compulsory 'abstinence'. The worker, with his wife and child and chattels, is thrown out into the street, and, if he crowds in too large numbers near districts where the local authority insists on decency, he is prosecuted in the name of public health!

Except London, there was at the beginning of the nineteenth century no single town in England of more than 100,000 inhabitants. Only five had more than 50,000. Now there are twenty-eight towns with more than 50,000 inhabitants. 'The result of this change is not only that the class of town people is enormously increased, but the old close-packed little towns are now centres built round on every side, open nowhere to air, and being no longer agreeable to the rich are abandoned by them for the pleasanter outskirts. The successors of these rich are occupying the larger houses at the rate of a family to each room ... and find accommodation for two or three lodgers ... and a population, for which the houses were not intended and quite unfit, has been created, whose surroundings are truly degrading to the adults and ruinous to the children.'[58] The more rapidly capital accumulates in an industrial or commercial town, the more rapidly flows the stream of exploitable human material, the more miserable are the improvised dwellings of the workers.

Newcastle-on-Tyne, as the centre of a coal and iron district which is becoming more and more productive, takes second place after London in the housing inferno. Not less than 34,000 persons live there in single rooms. Because of their absolute danger to the community, houses in great numbers have recently been pulled down by the authorities in Newcastle and Gateshead. The building of new houses progresses very slowly, business very quickly. The town was therefore more full than ever in 1865. There was scarcely a room to let. Dr Embleton, of the Newcastle Fever Hospital,

57. ibid., p. 89.
58. ibid., pp. 55–6.

says: 'There can be little doubt that the great cause of the continuance and spread of the typhus has been the over-crowding of human beings, and the uncleanliness of their dwellings. The rooms, in which labourers in many cases live, are situated in confined and unwholesome yards or courts, and for space, light, air, and cleanliness, are models of insufficiency and insalubrity, and a disgrace to any civilized community; in them, men, women, and children lie at night huddled together; and as regards the men, the night-shift succeed the day-shift, and the day-shift the night-shift, in unbroken series for some time together, the beds having scarcely time to cool; the whole house badly supplied with water and worse with privies; dirty, unventilated, and pestiferous.'[59] The price per week of such lodgings ranges from 8d. to 3s. 'The town of Newcastle-on-Tyne,' says Dr Hunter, 'contains a sample of the finest tribe of our countrymen, often sunk by external circumstances of house and street into an almost savage degradation.'[60]

As a result of the ebb and flow of capital and labour, the state of the dwellings of an industrial town may today be tolerable, tomorrow frightful. Or the local magistracy of the town may have summoned up the energy to remove the most shocking abuses. The next day, masses of ragged Irishmen or decayed English agricultural labourers may come crowding in, like a swarm of locusts. They are stowed away in cellars and lofts, or a hitherto respectable working-class dwelling is transformed into a lodging-house whose personnel changes as quickly as soldiers' quarters in the Thirty Years War. Take Bradford for example. There the municipal philistine had just been engaged in making improvements to the town. Besides, there were still 1,751 uninhabited houses in Bradford in 1861. But now comes that revival of trade which the sweet-natured Liberal Mr Forster, the Negro's friend, recently crowed over so gracefully.* With the revival of trade there naturally occurred an overflow from the wages of the ever-fluctuating 'reserve army' or 'relative surplus population'. The

59. *Public Health, Eighth Report*, 1866, p. 149.
60. ibid., p. 50.

---

*William Edward Forster (1818–86), son of a Quaker minister, leading Bradford wool manufacturer, Liberal M.P. for that city from 1861 to 1886. He spent much of the 1850s campaigning on the issue of American slavery, and was strongly in favour of the North in the Civil War.

frightful cellar habitations and rooms registered in the list,[61] which Dr Hunter obtained from the agent of an insurance company, were for the most part inhabited by well-paid workers. They declared that they would willingly pay for better dwellings if they were to be had. Meanwhile they become degraded and fall ill, every man jack of them, while that sweet-natured Liberal, Forster M.P., sheds tears of joy over the blessings of free trade, and the profits of the eminent men of Bradford who deal in worsted. In the report of 5 September 1865, Dr Bell, one of the poor law doctors of Bradford, ascribes the frightful mortality of fever patients in his district to the conditions in which they live. 'In one small cellar measuring 1,500 cubic feet ... there are ten persons ... Vincent Street, Green Aire Place, and the Leys include 223 houses having 1,450 inhabitants, 453 beds, and 36 privies ... The beds – and in that term I include any roll of dirty old rags, or an armful of

61. Here is the Bradford collecting agent's list:

(1) Houses

Vulcan Street, No. 122	1 room	16 persons
Lumley Street, No. 13	1 „	11 „
Bower Street, No. 41	1 „	11 „
Portland Street, No. 112	1 „	10 „
Hardy Street, No. 17	1 „	10 „
North Street, No. 18	1 „	16 „
North Street, No. 17	1 „	13 „
Wymer Street, No. 19	1 „	8 adults
Jowett Street, No. 56	1 „	12 persons
George Street, No. 150	1 „	3 families
Rifle Court, Marygate, No. 11	1 „	11 persons
Marshall Street, No. 28	1 „	10 „
Marshall Street, No. 49	3 „	3 families
George Street, No. 128	1 „	18 persons
George Street, No. 130	1 „	16 „
Edward Street, No. 4	1 „	17 „
George Street, No. 49	1 „	2 families
York Street, No. 34	1 „	2 „
Salt Pie Street (bottom)	2 „	26 persons

(2) Cellars

Regent Street	1 cellar	8 persons
Acre Street	1 „	7 „
33 Roberts Court	1 „	7 „
Back Pratt Street, used as a brazier's shop	1 „	7 „
27 Ebenezer Street	1 „	6 „

(List taken from ibid., p. 111)

shavings – have an average of 3·3 persons to each, many have 5 and 6 persons to each, and some people, I am told, are absolutely without beds; they sleep in their ordinary clothes, on the bare boards – young men and women, married and unmarried, all together. I need scarcely add that many of these dwellings are dark, damp, dirty, stinking holes, utterly unfit for human habitations; they are the centres from which disease and death are distributed amongst those in better circumstances, who have allowed them thus to fester in our midst.'[62]

Bristol takes the third place after London in the misery of its dwellings. 'Bristol, where the blankest poverty and domestic misery abound in the wealthiest town of Europe.'[63]

(c) The Nomadic Population

We now turn to a group of people whose origin is rural, but whose occupation is for the most part industrial. They are the light infantry of capital, thrown from one point to another according to its present needs. When they are not on the march they 'camp'. Nomadic labour is used for various building and draining works, for brick-making, lime-burning, railway-making, etc. A flying column of pestilence, it carries smallpox, typhus, cholera and scarlet fever into the places in whose neighbourhood it pitches its camp.[64] In undertakings which involve a large outlay of capital, such as railways etc., the contractor himself generally provides his army with wooden huts and so on, thus improvising villages which lack all sanitary arrangements, are outside the control of the local authorities, and are very profitable to the gentleman who is doing the contracting, for he exploits his workers in two directions at once – as soldiers of industry, and as tenants. Depending on whether the wooden hut contains one, two or three holes, its inhabitant, the navvy or whatever he may be, has to pay 2, 3 or 4 shillings a week.[65] One example will suffice. Dr Simon reports that in September 1864 the Chairman of the Nuisances Removal Committee of the parish of Sevenoaks sent the following denunciation to Sir George Grey, the Home Secretary: 'Small-pox cases were

62. *Public Health, Eighth Report,* 1866, p. 114.
63. ibid., p. 50.
64. *Public Health, Seventh Report,* 1865, p. 18.
65. ibid., p. 165.

rarely heard of in this parish until about twelve months ago. Shortly before that time, the works for a railway from Lewisham to Tunbridge were commenced here, and, in addition to the principal works being in the immediate neighbourhood of this town, here was also established the depot for the whole of the works, so that a large number of persons was of necessity employed here. As cottage accommodation could not be obtained for them all, huts were built in several places along the line of the works by the contractor, Mr Jay, for their especial occupation. These huts possessed no ventilation nor drainage, and, besides, were necessarily over-crowded, because each occupant had to accommodate lodgers, whatever the number in his own family might be, although there were only two rooms to each tenement. The consequences were, according to the medical report we received, that in the night-time these poor people were compelled to endure all the horror of suffocation to avoid the pestiferous smells arising from the filthy, stagnant water, and the privies close under their windows. Complaints were at length made to the Nuisances Removal Committee by a medical gentleman who had occasion to visit these huts, and he spoke of their condition as dwellings in the most severe terms, and he expressed his fears that some very serious consequences might ensue, unless some sanitary measures were adopted. About a year ago, Mr Jay promised to appropriate a hut, to which persons in his employ, who were suffering from contagious diseases, might at once be removed. He repeated that promise on the 23rd July last, but although since the date of the last promise there have been several cases of small-pox in his huts, and two deaths from the same disease, yet he has taken no steps whatever to carry out his promise. On the 9th September instant, Mr Kelson, surgeon, reported to me further cases of small-pox in the same huts, and he described their condition as most disgraceful. I should add, for your' (the Minister's) 'information that an isolated house, called the Pest-house, which is set apart for parishioners who might be suffering from infectious diseases, has been continually occupied by such patients for many months past, and is also now occupied; that in one family five children died from small-pox and fever; that from the 1st April to the 1st September this year, a period of five months, there have been no fewer than ten deaths from small-pox in the parish, four of them being in the huts already referred to; that it is impossible to ascertain the exact number of persons who have suffered from that disease although they are known to be many, from the fact of the families keeping it as private as possible.'[66]

Workers in coal and other mines belong to the best paid categories of the British proletariat. The price they pay for their wages was shown on an earlier page.[67] Here I shall merely glance at their housing conditions. As a rule, the exploiter of a mine, whether he is the proprietor or a tenant, builds a number of cottages for his 'hands'. They receive cottages and coal for firing 'for nothing' – i.e. these form part of their wages, paid in kind. Those who cannot be housed in this way receive in compensation £4 per annum. The mining districts rapidly attract a large population, made up of the miners themselves and the artisans, shopkeepers, etc. who group themselves around them. The ground rent is high, as it generally is where population is dense. The mining employer therefore tries to put up, within the smallest space possible at the entrance to the pit, exactly the number of cottages necessary to pack together his workers and their families. If new mines are opened in the neighbourhood, or old ones are again set working, the pressure increases. In the construction of the cottages, only one point of view is of significance, the 'abstinence' of the capitalist from all expenditure that is not absolutely unavoidable. 'The lodging which is obtained by the pitmen and other labourers connected with the collieries of Northumberland and Durham,' says Dr Julian Hunter, 'is perhaps, on the whole, the worst and the dearest of which any large specimens can be found in England, the similar parishes of Monmouthshire excepted ... The extreme badness is in the high number of men found in one room, in the smallness of the ground-plot on which a great number of houses are thrust, the want of water, the absence of privies, and the frequent placing of one house on the top of another, or distri-

66. *Public Health, Seventh Report*, 1865, p. 18, n. The Relieving Officer of the Chapel-en-le-Frith Union reported to the Registrar General as follows: 'At Doveholes, a number of small excavations have been made into a large hillock of lime ashes, which are used as dwellings, and occupied by labourers and others employed in the construction of a railway now in course of construction through that neighbourhood. The excavations are small and damp, and have no drains or privies about them, and not the slightest means of ventilation except up a hole pushed through the top, and used for a chimney. In consequence of this defect, small-pox has been raging for some time, and some deaths' (amongst the troglodytes) 'have been caused by it' (ibid., note 2).

67. The details given on pp. 626–34 refer especially to the coal-miners. On conditions in the metal mines, which are even worse, see the very conscientious report of the Royal Commission of 1864.

bution into flats, ... the lessee acts as if the whole colony were encamped, not resident.'[68] 'In pursuance of my instructions,' says Dr Stevens, 'I visited most of the large colliery villages in the Durham Union ... With very few exceptions, the general statement that no means are taken to secure the health of the inhabitants would be true of all of them ... All colliers are bound' ('bound', an expression which, like 'bondage', dates from the age of serfdom) 'to the colliery lessee or owner for twelve months ... If the colliers express discontent, or in any way annoy the "viewer", a mark of memorandum is made against their names, and, at the annual "binding", such men are turned off ... It appears to me that no part of the "truck system" could be worse than what obtains in these densely-populated districts. The collier is bound to take as part of his hiring a house surrounded with pestiferous influences; he cannot help himself, and it appears doubtful whether anyone else can help him except his proprietor (he is, to all intents and purposes, a serf), and his proprietor first consults his balance-sheet, and the result is tolerably certain. The collier is also often supplied with water by the proprietor, which, whether it be good or bad, he has to pay for, or rather he suffers a deduction for from his wages.'[69]

In a conflict with 'public opinion', or even with the Officers of Health, capital has no difficulty in 'justifying' the partly dangerous and partly degrading conditions to which it confines the working and domestic life of the mine-worker, on the ground that they are necessary for profitable exploitation. It is the same thing when capital 'abstains' from protective measures against dangerous machinery in the factory, from safety appliances and means of ventilation in the mines, and so on. It is the same here with the housing of the miners. Dr Simon, medical officer of the Privy Council, says in his official report: 'In apology for the wretched household accommodation ... it is alleged that mines are commonly worked on lease; that the duration of the lessee's interest (which in collieries is commonly for twenty-one years), is not so long that he should deem it worth his while to create good accommodation for his labourers, and for the tradespeople and others whom the work attracts; that even if he were disposed to act liberally in the matter, this disposition would commonly be defeated by his landlord's tendency to fix on him, as ground-rent, an exorbitant additional charge for the privilege of having on the

68. ibid., pp. 180, 182.   69. ibid., pp. 515, 517.

surface of the ground the decent and comfortable village which the labourers of the subterranean property ought to inhabit, and that prohibitory price (if not actual prohibition) equally excludes others who might desire to build. It would be foreign to the purpose of this report to enter upon any discussion of the merits of the above apology. Nor here is it even needful to consider where it would be that, if decent accommodation were provided, the cost . . . would eventually fall – whether on landlord, or lessee, or labourer, or public. But in presence of such shameful facts as are vouched for in the annexed reports' (those of Dr Hunter, Dr Stevens, etc.) 'a remedy may well be claimed . . . Claims of landlordship are being so used as to do great public wrong. The landlord in his capacity of mine-owner invites an industrial colony to labour on his estate, and then in his capacity of surface-owner makes it impossible that the labourers whom he collects, should find proper lodging where they must live. The lessee' (the capitalist exploiter of the mine) 'meanwhile has no pecuniary motive for resisting that division of the bargain; well knowing that if its latter conditions be exorbitant, the consequences fall not on him, that his labourers on whom they fall have not education enough to know the value of their sanitary rights, that neither obscenest lodging nor foulest drinking water will be appreciable inducements towards a "strike".'[70]

(d) Effect of Crises on the Best Paid Section of the Working Class

Before I turn to the agricultural labourers, I shall just show, by one example, how crises have an impact even on the best paid section of the working class, on its aristocracy. It will be remembered that the year 1857 brought one of the gigantic crises with which the industrial cycle always terminates. The next crisis was due in 1866. Already discounted in the actual factory districts by the cotton famine, which threw much capital from its accustomed sphere into the great centres of the money-market, the crisis assumed this time a predominantly financial character. Its outbreak in May 1866 was signalled by the failure of a giant London bank, immediately followed by the collapse of countless swindling companies. One of the great London branches of industry involved in the catastrophe was iron shipbuilding. The magnates of this trade had not

70. *Public Health, Seventh Report,* 1865, p. 16.

only overproduced beyond all measure during the swindling period,* but they had, apart from this, entered into enormous contracts on the speculative assumption that credit would be forthcoming to an equivalent extent. A terrible reaction then set in, which continues even now (at the end of March 1867) both in shipbuilding and in other London industries.[71] Let me characterize the situation of the workers by quoting the following from a very detailed report by a correspondent of the *Morning Star*, who visited the chief centres of distress at the end of 1866 and the beginning of 1867: 'In the East End districts of Poplar, Millwall, Greenwich, Deptford, Limehouse and Canning Town, at least 15,000 workmen and their families were in a state of utter destitution, and 3,000 skilled mechanics were breaking stones in the workhouse yard (after distress of over half a year's duration) . . . I had great difficulty in reaching the workhouse door, for a hungry crowd besieged it . . . They were waiting for their tickets, but the time had not yet arrived for the distribution. The yard was a great square place with an open shed running all round it, and several large heaps of snow covered the paving-stones in the middle. In the middle, also, were little wicker-fenced spaces, like sheep pens, where in finer weather the men worked; but on the day of my visit the pens were so snowed up that nobody could sit in them. Men were busy, however, in the open shed breaking paving-stones into macadam. Each man had a big paving-stone for a seat, and he chipped away at the rime-covered granite until he had broken up, and think! five bushels of it, and then he had done his day's work, and got his day's pay – threepence and an allowance of food. In another part of the yard

71. 'Wholesale starvation of the London Poor . . . Within the last few days the walls of London have been placarded with large posters, bearing the following remarkable announcement: "Fat oxen! Starving men! The fat oxen from their palace of glass have gone to feed the rich in their luxurious abode, while the starving men are left to rot and die in their wretched dens." The placards bearing these ominous words are put up at certain intervals. No sooner has one set been defaced or covered over, than a fresh set is placarded in the former, or some equally public place . . . this . . . reminds one of the secret revolutionary associations which prepared the French people for the events of 1789 . . . At this moment, while English workmen with their wives and children are dying of cold and hunger, there are millions of English gold – the produce of English labour – being invested in Russian, Spanish, Italian, and other foreign enterprises' (*Reynolds' Newspaper*, 20 January 1867).

* A reference to the period of unsound speculation which immediately preceded the collapse of Overend and Gurney in 1866.

was a rickety little wooden house, and when we opened the door of it, we found it filled with men who were huddled together shoulder to shoulder, for the warmth of one another's bodies and breath. They were picking oakum and disputing the while as to which could work the longest on a given quantity of food – for endurance was the point of honour. Seven thousand ... in this one workhouse ... were recipients of relief ... many hundreds of them ... it appeared, were, six or eight months ago, earning the highest wages paid to artisans ... Their number would be more than doubled by the count of those who, having exhausted all their savings, still refuse to apply to the parish, because they have a little left to pawn. Leaving the workhouse, I took a walk through the streets, mostly of little one-storey houses, that abound in the neighbourhood of Poplar. My guide was a member of the Committee of the Unemployed ... My first call was on an ironworker who had been seven and twenty weeks out of employment. I found the man with his family sitting in a little back room. The room was not bare of furniture, and there was a fire in it. This was necessary to keep the naked feet of the young children from getting frost bitten, for it was a bitterly cold day. On a tray in front of the fire lay a quantity of oakum, which the wife and children were picking in return for their allowance from the parish. The man worked in the stone yard of the workhouse for a certain ration of food, and three-pence per day. He had now come home to dinner quite hungry, as he told us with a melancholy smile, and his dinner consisted of a couple of slices of bread and dripping, and a cup of milkless tea ... The next door at which we knocked was opened by a middle-aged woman, who, without saying a word, led us into a little back parlour, in which sat all her family, silent and fixedly staring at a rapidly dying fire. Such desolation, such hopelessness was about these people and their little room, as I should not care to witness again. "Nothing have they done, sir," said the woman, pointing to her boys, "for six and twenty weeks; and all our money gone – all the twenty pounds that me and father saved when times were better, thinking it would yield a little to keep us when we got past work. Look at it," she said, almost fiercely, bringing out a bank-book with all its well-kept entries of money paid in, and money taken out, so that we could see how the little fortune had begun with the first five shilling deposit, and had grown by little and little to be twenty pounds, and how it had melted down again till the sum in hand got from pounds to shillings, and the last entry made the book as worthless as a blank sheet. This family received relief from the workhouse, and it furnished them with just one scanty meal per day ... Our next visit was to an iron labourer's wife, whose husband had worked in the yards. We found her ill from want of food, lying on a mattress in her clothes, and just covered with a strip of carpet, for all the bedding had been pawned. Two wretched children were tending her, themselves looking as much in need of nursing as their mother. Nineteen weeks of enforced idleness had brought them to this pass, and while the mother told the history of that bitter past, she moaned as if all her faith in a future that should atone for it were dead ... On getting outside a young fellow came running after us, and asked us to step inside his house and see if anything could be done for him. A young wife, two pretty children, a cluster of pawn-tickets, and a bare room were all he had to show.'*

On the after-pains of the crisis of 1866, we shall quote an extract from a Tory newspaper. It must not be forgotten that the East End of London, which is dealt with here, is not only the location of the iron shipbuilding mentioned above, but also of the so-called domestic industry, which is always paid less than the minimum wage. 'A frightful spectacle was to be seen yesterday in one part of the metropolis. Although the unemployed thousands of the East-end did not parade with their black flags *en masse*, the human torrent was imposing enough. Let us remember what these people suffer. They are dying of hunger. That is the simple and terrible fact. There are 40,000 of them ... In our presence, in one quarter of this wonderful metropolis, are packed – next door to the most enormous accumulation of wealth the world ever saw – cheek by jowl with this are 40,000 helpless, starving people. These thousands are now breaking in upon the other quarters; always half-starving, they cry their misery in our ears, they cry to Heaven, they tell us from their miserable dwellings, that it is impossible for them to find work, and useless for them to beg. The local ratepayers themselves are driven by the parochial charges to the verge of pauperism' (*Standard*, 5 April 1867).

As it is the fashion amongst English capitalists to quote Belgium as the workers' paradise, because 'freedom of labour' or, what is the same thing, 'freedom of capital' is there limited neither by the despotism of the trade unions nor by the shackles of the Factory

*Morning Star, 7 January 1867.

Acts, we shall say a word or two here about the 'good fortune' of
the Belgian worker. Assuredly no one was more thoroughly
initiated into the mysteries of this good fortune than the late
M. Ducpétiaux, inspector-general of Belgian prisons and charit-
able institutions, and member of the Central Statistical Commission of Belgium. Let us take his work *Budgets économiques des
classes ouvrières de la Belgique* (Brussels, 1855). Here we find,
among other things, a discussion of a normal Belgian worker's
family, whose yearly income and expenditure he calculates on
very exact data, and whose conditions of nourishment are then
compared with those of the soldier, the sailor and the prisoner.
The family 'consists of father, mother, and four children'. Of
these six persons, 'four may be usefully employed the whole year
through'. It is assumed that 'there is no sick person among them,
or anyone incapable of work', nor are there 'expenses for religious,
moral and intellectual purposes, except a very small sum for
church pews', nor contributions to savings banks or benefit
societies, 'nor expenses due to luxury or the result of improvidence'. The father and eldest son, however, allow themselves 'the
use of tobacco', and on Sundays 'go to the ale-house', for which a
whole 86 centimes a week are reckoned. 'From a general compilation of wages allowed to workers in different trades, it follows that
the highest average daily wage is 1 franc 56 centimes for men, 89
centimes for women, 56 centimes for boys, and 55 centimes for
girls. Calculated at this rate, the resources of the family would
amount, at the maximum, to 1,068 francs a year . . . In the family
taken as typical we have calculated all possible resources. In
ascribing wages to the mother of the family, however, we thereby
remove the household from her management. But who will look
after the house and the young children? Who will prepare the
meals, do the washing and mending? This is the dilemma presented every day to the workers.' According to this the budget of
the family is:

The father 300 working days at fr. 1.56	fr.	468
The mother 300 working days at fr. 89	fr.	267
The boy 300 working days at fr. 56	fr.	168
The girl 300 working days at fr. 55	fr.	165
Total	fr.	1,068

The annual expenditure of the family would result in the follow-ing deficits, according to whether the worker has the food of:

The sailor in the fleet fr. 1,828		Deficit fr. 760
The soldier fr. 1,473		Deficit fr. 405
The prisoner fr. 1,112		Deficit fr. 44

'We see that few workers' families can reach, we will not say the average of the sailor or soldier, but even that of the prisoner. The general average (of the cost of each prisoner in the different prisons during the period 1847 to 1849), has been 63 centimes for all prisons. This figure, compared with that of the daily mainten-ance of the worker, shows a difference of 13 centimes. It must be remarked further that if in the prisons it is necessary to set down in the account the expenses of administration and surveillance, on the other hand, the prisoners do not have to pay for their lodgings ... How does it happen, then, that a great number, we might say the great majority of workers, live even more economically than prisoners? It is because they adopt expedients whose secrets are only known by the workers: they reduce their daily rations; they substitute rye-bread for wheat; they eat less meat, or even none at all, and the same with butter and condiments; they content them-selves with one or two rooms where the family is crammed to-gether, where boys and girls sleep side by side, often on the same mattress; they economize on clothing, washing, and decency; they give up the diversions of Sunday; in short, they resign themselves to the most painful privations. Once this extreme limit has been reached, the least rise in the price of food, the shortest stoppage of work, the slightest illness, increases the worker's distress and brings him to complete disaster: debts accumulate, credit fails, the most necessary clothes and furniture are pawned, and finally the family asks to be enrolled on the list of paupers.'[72]

In fact, in this 'paradise for capitalists', the smallest change in the prices of the most essential means of subsistence is followed by a change in the number of deaths and crimes! (See *Manifest der Maatschappij 'De Vlamingen Vooruit!'*, Brussels, 1860, pp. 15–16.)*

72. Ducpétiaux, op. cit., pp. 151, 154, 155–6.

---

*This is the manifesto of the Association 'Forward the Flemings!', an early Flemish nationalist group.

There are 930,000 families in Belgium, of whom, according to the official statistics, 90,000 are wealthy and on the list of voters, i.e. 450,000 persons; 390,000 families of the lower middle class in towns and villages, the greater part of them constantly sinking into the proletariat, i.e. 1,950,000 persons. Finally, 450,000 working-class families, i.e. 2,250,000 persons, of whom the model ones enjoy the good fortune depicted by Ducpétiaux. Of the 450,000 working-class families, over 200,000 are on the pauper list!

(e) The British Agricultural Proletariat

Nowhere does the antagonistic character of capitalist production and accumulation assert itself more brutally than in the progress of English agriculture (including cattle-breeding) and the retrogression of the English agricultural labourer. Before I turn to his present situation, a rapid look back. Modern agriculture dates in England from the middle of the eighteenth century, although the revolution in property relations on the land which is the basis of the altered mode of production occurred much earlier.

If we take the statements of Arthur Young, a careful observer though a superficial thinker, about the agricultural labourer of 1771, the latter plays a very pitiable role as compared with his predecessor of the end of the fourteenth century, 'when the labourer ... could live in plenty, and accumulate wealth',[73] not to speak of the fifteenth century, 'the golden age of the English labourer in town and country'. We need not, however, go back as far as that. In a very instructive book produced in 1777 we read: 'The great farmer is nearly mounted to a level with him' (the gentleman); 'while the poor labourer is depressed almost to the earth. His unfortunate situation will fully appear, by taking a comparative view of it, only forty years ago, and at present ... Landlord and tenant ... have both gone hand in hand in keeping the labourer down.'[74] It is then proved in detail that real agricultural wages fell by nearly $\frac{1}{4}$, or 25 per cent, between 1737 and 1777.

73. James E. Thorold Rogers (Professor of Political Economy in the University of Oxford), *A History of Agriculture and Prices in England*, Oxford, 1866, Vol. 1, p. 690. This work, the fruit of diligent labour, comprises only the period from 1259 to 1400, in the two volumes that have so far appeared, and the second volume consists exclusively of statistical material. It is the first authentic 'history of prices' that we have for that time.

74. *Reasons for the Late Increase of the Poor-Rates: Or a Comparative View of the Prices of Labour and Provisions*, London, 1777, pp. 5, 11.

'Modern policy,' as Dr Richard Price was saying at the same time, 'is, indeed, more favourable to the higher classes of people; and the consequences may in time prove that the whole kingdom will consist of only gentry and beggars, or of grandees and slaves.'[75]

Nevertheless, the position of the English agricultural labourer from 1770 to 1780, with respect to his food and dwelling, as well as his self-respect, amusements, etc., is an ideal never attained again since that time. His average wage expressed in pints of wheat was, from 1770 to 1771, 90 pints, in Eden's time (1797) only 65, and in 1808, 60.[76]

The state of the agricultural labourer at the end of the Anti-Jacobin War, during which landed proprietors, farmers, manufacturers, merchants, bankers, stockbrokers, army contractors and so on enriched themselves to such an enormous extent, has been already indicated above. The nominal wage rose, partly as a result of the depreciation of banknotes, and partly owing to a rise in the prices of the primary means of subsistence which occurred independently of this depreciation. But the real movement of wages can be demonstrated quite simply, without entering into details that are unnecessary here. The Poor Law was the same, and was administered in the same way, in 1795 and in 1814. It will be remembered how this law was put into effect in the country districts: in the form of alms, the parish made up the nominal wage to the nominal sum required for the simple vegetation of the labourer. The ratio between the wage paid by the farmer and the wage-deficit made good by the parish shows us two things. First, the fact that wages had fallen below their minimum; second, the degree to which the agricultural labourer was a combination of wage-labourer and pauper, or the degree to which he had been turned into a serf of his parish. Let us take one county that represents the average situation in all counties. In North-

75. Dr Richard Price, *Observations on Reversionary Payments*, 6th edn, by W. Morgan, London, 1803, Vol. 2, pp. 158–9. Price remarks on p. 159: 'The nominal price of day-labour is at present no more than about four times, or, at most five times higher than it was in the year 1514. But the price of corn is seven times, and of flesh-meat and raiment about fifteen times higher. So far, therefore, has the price of labour been even from advancing in proportion to the increase in the expenses of living, that it does not appear that it bears now half the proportion to those expenses that it did bear.'

76. Barton, op. cit., p. 26. For the end of the eighteenth century, cf. Eden, op. cit.

amptonshire, in 1795, the average weekly wage was 7s. 6d.; the total yearly expenditure of a family of six persons, £36 12s. 5d.; their total income, £29 18s.; deficit made good by the parish, £6 14s. 5d. In 1814, in the same county, the weekly wage was 12s. 2d.; the total yearly expenditure of a family of five persons £54 18s. 4d.; their total income, £36 2s.; deficit made good by the parish, £18 6s. 4d.[77] In 1795 the deficit was less than a quarter of the wage, in 1814 it was more than a half. It is self-evident that under these circumstances the meagre comforts that Eden still found in the cottage of the agricultural labourer had vanished by 1814.[78] Of all the animals kept by the farmer, the labourer, the *instrumentum vocale*,* was thenceforth the most oppressed, the worst nourished, the most brutally treated.

This state of affairs continued quietly until 'the Swing riots, in 1830, revealed to us' (i.e. to the ruling classes) 'by the light of blazing corn-stacks, that misery and black mutinous discontent smouldered quite as fiercely under the surface of agricultural as of manufacturing England.'[79] It was at this time that Sadler, in the House of Commons, christened the agricultural labourers 'white slaves', and a bishop echoed the epithet in the House of Lords. The most notable political economist of that period – E. G. Wakefield – says: 'The peasant of the South of England . . . is not a freeman, nor is he a slave; he is a pauper.'[80]

The time just before the repeal of the Corn Laws threw new light on the condition of the agricultural labourers. On the one hand, it was in the interest of the middle-class agitators to prove how little the Corn Laws protected the actual producers of the corn. On the other hand, the industrial bourgeoisie was seething with wrath at the denunciations of the factory system made by the landed aristocracy, at the affectation of sympathy displayed by those utterly corrupt, heartless and genteel idlers for the woes of the factory workers, and at their 'diplomatic zeal' for factory legislation. There is an old English proverb to the effect that when thieves fall out, honest men come into their own, and in fact the noisy and passionate dispute between the two factions of the

77. Parry, op. cit., p. 80.
78. op. cit., p. 213.
79. S. Laing, op. cit., p. 62.
80. *England and America*, London, 1833, Vol. 1, p. 47.

* 'Speaking implement'. See above, p. 303, n. 18.

ruling class as to which of them exploited the workers more shamelessly was the midwife of truth on both sides of the question. Earl Shaftesbury, then Lord Ashley, was the protagonist of the aristocratic philanthropic campaign against the factories. He therefore formed a favourite target for the revelations of the *Morning Chronicle* in 1844 and 1845 on the condition of the agricultural labourers. This newspaper, at that time the most important Liberal organ, sent special commissioners into the agricultural districts, commissioners who did not content themselves with mere general descriptions and statistics, but published the names both of the families of labourers examined and of their landlords. The following list [p. 832] gives the wages paid in three villages in the neighbourhood of Blandford, Wimborne and Poole. The villages are the property of Mr G. Bankes and the Earl of Shaftesbury. It will be noted that, just like Bankes, the pope of the Low Church, the head of the English pietists, also pockets a large part of the miserable wages of the labourers under the pretext of the rent of their houses.

The repeal of the Corn Laws gave a marvellous impulse to English agriculture. Drainage on the most extensive scale,[82] new methods of stall-feeding and the artificial cultivation of green crops, the introduction of mechanical manuring apparatus, new treatment of clay soils, increased use of mineral manures, employment of the steam-engine and all kinds of new machinery, more intensive cultivation in general, are all characteristic of this epoch. Mr Pusey, Chairman of the Royal Agricultural Society, declares that the (relative) expenses of farming have been reduced nearly 50 per cent by the introduction of new machinery. On the other hand, the actual productive return of the soil rose rapidly. Greater outlay of capital per acre, and as a consequence more rapid concentration of farms, were essential conditions of the new method.[83] At the same time, the area under cultivation increased,

82. To do this, the landed aristocracy gave themselves an advance, through Parliament of course, of funds from the Treasury, at a very low rate of interest, which the farmers have to return to them at double the rate.

83. The decline of the medium-sized farmer can be seen especially in the census category 'Farmer's son, grandson, brother, nephew, daughter, granddaughter, sister, niece', in other words, the members of his own family employed by the farmer. This category numbered 216,851 persons in 1851 and only 176,151 in 1861. From 1851 to 1871, farms of under 20 acres fell by more than 900; those of between 50 and 75 acres fell from 8,253 to 6,370; the same thing occurred with all other farms of under 100 acres. On the other

First Village [81]

Children (a)	Number of Members in Family (b)	Weekly Wage of the Men (c) s. d.	Weekly Wage of the Children (d)	Weekly Income of the Whole Family (e) s. d.	Weekly Rent (f) s. d.	Total Weekly Wage After Deduction of Rent (g) s. d.	Weekly Income per Head (h) s. d.
2	4	8 0	—	8 0	2 0	6 0	1 6
3	5	8 0	—	8 0	1 6	6 6	1 3½
2	4	8 0	—	8 0	1 0	7 0	1 9
2	4	8 0	1/6, 2/0	8 0	1 0	7 0	1 9
6	8	7 0	—	10 6	2 0	8 6	1 0¼
3	5	7 0	—	7 0	1 4	5 8	1 1½

Second Village

Children (a)	Number of Members in Family (b)	Weekly Wage of the Men (c) s. d.	Weekly Wage of the Children (d)	Weekly Income of the Whole Family (e) s. d.	Weekly Rent (f) s. d.	Total Weekly Wage After Deduction of Rent (g) s. d.	Weekly Income per Head (h) s. d.
6	8	7 0	1/6, 1/6	10 0	1 6	8 6	1 0¾
6	8	7 0	—	7 0	1 3½	5 8½	0 8½
8	10	7 0	—	7 0	1 3½	5 8½	0 7
4	6	7 0	—	7 0	1 6½	5 5½	0 11
3	5	7 0	—	7 0	1 6½	5 5¼	1 1

Third Village

Children (a)	Number of Members in Family (b)	Weekly Wage of the Men (c) s. d.	Weekly Wage of the Children (d)	Weekly Income of the Whole Family (e) s. d.	Weekly Rent (f) s. d.	Total Weekly Wage After Deduction of Rent (g) s. d.	Weekly Income per Head (h) s. d.
4	6	7 0	2/0, 2/6	7 0	1 0	6 0	1 0
3	5	7 0	—	11 6	0 10	10 8	2 1½
0	2	5 0	—	5 0	1 0	4 0	2 0

81. London *Economist*, 29 March 1845, p. 290.

from 1846 to 1856, by 464,119 acres, without counting the large part of the eastern counties which was transformed from rabbit warrens and poor pastures into magnificent corn-fields. It has already been seen that, simultaneously with this, the total number of persons employed in agriculture fell. As far as the actual agricultural labourers of both sexes and all ages are concerned, their number fell from 1,241,396 in 1851 to 1,163,217 in 1861.[84] The English Registrar General rightly remarks: 'The increase of farmers and farm-labourers, since 1801, bears no kind of proportion ... to the increase of agricultural produce,'[85] and this disproportion is even more noticeable for the last period, when a positive decrease of the agricultural population went hand in hand with an increase in the cultivated area and in the intensity with which it was cultivated, an unheard-of accumulation of the capital incorporated with the soil and devoted to its cultivation, an augmentation of the product of the soil unparalleled in the history of English agriculture, abundant rent-rolls for the landowners, and growing wealth for the capitalist farmers. If we take this together with the swift, unbroken extension of the market, i.e. the growth of the towns, and the reign of free trade, then the agricultural labourer was at last, *post tot discrimina rerum*,* placed in circumstances that ought, *secundum artem*,† to have made him drunk with happiness.

But Professor Rogers comes to the conclusion that the situation of the English agricultural labourer of today, in comparison with his predecessor from 1770 to 1780, not to speak of his predecessor in the last half of the fourteenth and in the fifteenth century, has changed for the worse to an extraordinary extent, that 'the peasant has again become a serf', and a serf worse fed and worse clothed.[86]

---

hand, during the same twenty years, the number of large farms increased; those of 300 to 500 acres rose from 7,771 to 8,410, those of more than 500 acres from 2,755 to 3,914, those of more than 1,000 acres from 492 to 582.

84. The number of shepherds increased from 12,517 to 25,559.

85. *Census, etc.*, op. cit., p. 36.

86. Rogers, op. cit., pp. 693, 10. Mr Rogers belongs to the Liberal school of thought, is a personal friend of Cobden and Bright, and therefore no *laudator temporis acti*.*

* 'Singer of praises of times gone by' (Horace, *Ars poetica*, verse 173).

---

* 'After so many vicissitudes'.
† 'According to the orthodox rules'.

Dr Julian Hunter, in his epoch-making report on the dwellings of the agricultural labourers, says: 'The cost of the hind' (a name for the agricultural labourer, inherited from the time of serfdom) 'is fixed at the lowest possible amount on which he can live . . . the supplies of wages and shelter are not calculated on the profit to be derived from him. He is a zero in farming calculations.'[87] 'The means' (of subsistence) 'are always supposed to be a fixed quantity.'[88] 'As to any further reduction of his income, he may say, *nihil habeo nihil curo*.* He has no fears for the future, because he has now only the spare supply necessary to keep him. He has reached the zero from which are dated the calculations of the farmer. Come what will, he has no share either in prosperity or adversity.'[89]

In the year 1863, an official inquiry took place into the conditions of nourishment and work of the criminals condemned to transportation and penal servitude. The results are recorded in two voluminous Blue Books. Among other things it is said: 'From an elaborate comparison between the diet of convicts in the convict prisons in England, and that of paupers in workhouses and of free labourers in the same country . . . it certainly appears that the former are much better fed than either of the two other classes,'[90] while 'the amount of labour required from an ordinary convict under penal servitude is about one-half of what would be done by an ordinary day-labourer.'[91] Here are a few characteristic depositions of witnesses. No. 5056: 'The diet of the English prisons is superior to that of ordinary labourers in England'. No. 5075: 'It is the fact . . . that the ordinary agricultural labourers in Scotland very seldom get any meat at all.' Answer No. 3047: 'Is there anything that you are aware of to account for the necessity of feeding them very much better than ordinary labourers? – Certainly not.' No. 3048: 'Do you think that further experiments

87. *Public Health, Seventh Report*, 1865, p. 242. It is therefore by no means unusual either for the landlord to raise a labourer's rent as soon as he hears that he is earning a little more, or for the farmer to lower the wage of the labourer, 'because his wife has found a trade' (ibid.).

88. ibid., p. 135.

89. ibid., p. 134.

90. *Report of the Commissioners . . . Relating to Transportation and Penal Servitude*, London, 1863, pp. 42, 50.

91. ibid., p. 77, 'Memorandum by the Lord Chief Justice'.

* 'I have nothing, and I do not care about anything.'

ought to be made in order to ascertain whether a dietary might not be hit upon for prisoners employed on public works nearly approaching to the dietary of free labourers?'[92] ... 'He' (the agricultural labourer) 'might say: "I work hard, and have not enough to eat, and therefore it is better for me to be in prison again than here."'[93] From the tables appended to the first volume of the Report I have compiled this comparative summary.[94]

Weekly Amount of Nutriment

	Quantity of nitrogenous ingredients	Quantity of non-nitrogenous ingredients	Quantity of mineral matter	Total
	(Ounces)	(Ounces)	(Ounces)	(Ounces)
Portland (convict)	28·95	150·06	4·68	183·69
Sailor in the Navy	29·63	152·91	4·52	187·06
Soldier	25·55	114·49	3·94	143·98
Working coach-maker	24·53	162·06	4·23	190·82
Compositor	21·24	100·83	3·12	125·19
Agricultural labourer	17·72	118·06	3.29	139·08

The general result of the inquiry by the medical commission of 1863 into the state of nourishment of the worst fed classes of the people is already known to the reader. He will remember that the diet of a great part of the families of agricultural labourers is below the minimum necessary 'to avert starvation diseases'. This is especially the case in all the purely rural districts of Cornwall, Devon, Somerset, Wiltshire, Staffordshire, Oxfordshire, Berkshire and Hertfordshire. 'The nourishment obtained by the labourer himself,' says Dr E. Smith, 'is larger than the average quantity indicates, since he eats a larger share ... necessary to enable him to perform his labour ... of food than the other members of the family, including in the poorer districts nearly all the meat and bacon ... The quantity of food obtained by the wife and also by the children at the period of rapid growth, is in many cases, in almost every county, deficient, and particularly in nitrogen.'[95] The male and female servants who live

92. ibid., Vol. 2, Minutes of Evidence.
93. ibid., Vol. 1, Appendix, p. 280.
94. ibid., pp. 274–5.
95. *Public Health, Sixth Report*, 1864, pp. 238, 249, 261–2.

with the farmers themselves are sufficiently nourished. Their number fell from 288,277 in 1851 to 204,962 in 1861. 'The labour of women in the fields,' says Dr Smith, 'whatever may be its disadvantages ... is under present circumstances of great advantage to the family, since it adds that amount of income which ... provides shoes and clothing and pays the rent, and thus enables the family to be better fed.'[96] One of the most remarkable findings of the inquiry was that the agricultural labourer of England, as compared with other parts of the United Kingdom, 'is considerably the worst fed', as the appended table shows:[97]

Quantities of carbon and nitrogen consumed every week by an average adult agricultural labourer

	Carbon, grains	Nitrogen, grains
England	46,673	1,594
Wales	48,354	2,031
Scotland	48,980	2,348
Ireland	43,366	2,434

96. *Public Health, Sixth Report*, 1864, p. 262.

97. ibid., p. 17. The English agricultural labourer receives only a quarter as much milk, and half as much bread, as the Irish. Arthur Young already noticed the better nourishment of the latter when making his 'tour through Ireland' at the beginning of this century.* The reason is simply this, that the poor Irish farmer is incomparably more humane than the rich English. With reference to Wales, what is said in the text† does not hold for the south-west of that country. 'All the doctors there agree that the increase of the death-rate through tuberculosis, scrofula, etc., increases in intensity with the deterioration of the physical condition of the population, and all ascribe this deterioration to poverty. His' (the farm labourer's) 'keep is reckoned at about 5d. a day, but in many districts it was said to be of much less cost to the farmer' (himself very poor) ... 'A morsel of the salt meat or bacon ... salted and dried to the texture of mahogany, and hardly worth the difficult process of assimilation ... is used to flavour a large quantity of broth or gruel, of meal and leeks, and day after day this is the labourer's dinner.' The advance of industry resulted for him, in this harsh and damp climate, in 'the abandonment of the solid homespun clothing in favour of the cheap and so-called cotton goods', and of stronger drinks for so-called tea. 'The agriculturalist, after several hours' exposure to wind and rain, gains his cottage, to sit by a fire of peat or of balls of clay and small coal kneaded together, from which volumes of carbonic and sulphurous acids are poured forth. His walls are of mud and stones, his floor the bare earth which was there before the hut was built, his roof a mass of loose and sodden thatch. Every crevice is stopped to

*Arthur Young in fact made his tours in Ireland between 1776 and 1779. His book first appeared in 1780.

†This refers to the implication in the text that the Welsh agricultural labourer is better off than the English.

'To the insufficient quantity and miserable quality of the house accommodation generally had by our agricultural labourers,' says Dr Simon, in his official Health Report, 'almost every page of Dr Hunter's report bears testimony. And gradually, for many years past, the state of the labourer in these respects has been deteriorating, house-room being now greatly more difficult for him to find, and, when found, greatly less suitable to his needs than, perhaps, for centuries had been the case. Especially within the last twenty or thirty years, the evil has been in very rapid increase, and the household circumstances of the labourer are now in the highest degree deplorable. Except in so far as they whom his labour enriches, see fit to treat him with a kind of pitiful indulgence, he is quite peculiarly helpless in the matter. Whether he shall find house-room on the land which he contributes to till, whether the house-room which he gets shall be human or swinish, whether he shall have the little space of garden that so

---

maintain warmth, and in an atmosphere of diabolic odour, with a mud floor, with his only clothes drying on his back, he often sups and sleeps with his wife and children. Obstetricians who have passed parts of the night in such cabins have described how they found their feet sinking in the mud of the floor, and they were forced (an easy task!) to drill a hole through the wall to effect a little private respiration. It was attested by numerous witnesses in various grades of life, that to these insanitary influences, and many more, the underfed peasant was nightly exposed, and of the result, a debilitated and scrofulous people, there was no want of evidence ... The statements of the relieving officers of Carmarthenshire and Cardiganshire show in a striking way the same state of things. There is besides a plague more horrible still, the great number of idiots.' Now a word on the climatic conditions. 'A strong south-west wind blows over the whole country for 8 or 9 months in the year, bringing with it torrents of rain, which discharge principally upon the western slopes of the hills. Trees are rare, except in sheltered places, and where not protected, are blown out of all shape. The cottages generally crouch under some bank, or often in a ravine or quarry, and none but the smallest sheep and native cattle can live on the pastures ... The young people migrate to the eastern mining districts of Glamorgan and Monmouth. Carmarthenshire is the breeding ground of the mining population and their hospital. The population can therefore barely maintain its numbers.' Thus in Cardiganshire:

	1851	1861
Males	45,155	44,446
Females	52,459	52,955
Total	97,614	97,401

(Dr Hunter's Report, in *Public Health, Seventh Report, 1864*, London, 1865, pp. 498–502 passim.)

vastly lessens the pressure of his poverty – all this does not depend on his willingness and ability to pay reasonable rent for the decent accommodation he requires, but depends on the use which others may see fit to make of their "right to do as they will with their own". However large may be a farm, there is no law that a certain proportion of labourers' dwellings (much less of decent dwellings) shall be upon it; nor does any law reserve for the labourer ever so little right in that soil to which his industry is as needful as sun and rain ... An extraneous element weighs the balance heavily against him ... the influence of the Poor Law in its provisions concerning settlement and chargeability.[98] Under this influence, each parish has a pecuniary interest in reducing to a minimum the number of its resident labourers: – for, unhappily, agricultural labour instead of implying a safe and permanent independence for the hard-working labourer and his family, implies for the most part only a longer or shorter circuit to eventual pauperism – a pauperism which, during the whole circuit, is so near, that any illness or temporary failure of occupation necessitates immediate recourse to parochial relief – and thus all residence of agricultural population in a parish is glaringly an addition to its poor-rates ... Large proprietors[99] ... have but to resolve that there shall be no labourers' dwellings on their estates, and their estates will thenceforth be virtually free from half their responsiblity for the poor. How far it has been intended, in the English constitution and law, that this kind of unconditional property in land should be acquirable, and that a landlord, "doing as he wills with his own", should be able to treat the cultivators of the soil as aliens, whom he may expel from his territory, is a question which I do not pretend to discuss ... For that power of eviction ... does not exist only in theory. On a very large scale it prevails in practice – prevails ... as a main governing condition in the household circumstances of agricultural labour ... As regards the extent of the evil, it may suffice to refer to the evidence which Dr Hunter has compiled from the last census, that destruction of houses, notwithstanding increased local demands for them,

98. In 1865 this law was improved to some extent.* It will soon be learned from experience that this kind of tinkering is no use.

99. To understand what follows, we must bear in mind that 'close villages' are villages owned by one or two big landowners, and 'open villages' are villages whose soil belongs to many small proprietors. It is in villages of the second kind that building speculators can build cottages and lodging-houses.

  *By the Union Chargeability Act, 28 and 29 Victoria, c. 79.

had, during the last ten years, been in progress in 821 separate parishes or townships of England, so that irrespectively of persons who had been forced to become non-resident (that is in the parishes in which they work), these parishes and townships were receiving in 1861, as compared with 1851, a population 5⅓ per cent greater, into house-room 4½ per cent less . . . When the process of depopulation has completed itself, the result, says Dr Hunter, is a show-village where the cottages have been reduced to a few, and where none but persons who are needed as shepherds, gardeners, or game-keepers, are allowed to live; regular servants who receive the good treatment usual to their class.[1] But the land requires cultivation, and it will be found that the labourers employed upon it are not the tenants of the owner, but that they come from a neighbouring open village, perhaps three miles off, where a numerous small proprietary had received them when their cottages were destroyed in the close villages around. Where things are tending to the above result, often the cottages which stand, testify, in their unrepaired and wretched condition, to the extinction to which they are doomed. They are seen standing in the various stages of natural decay. While the shelter holds together, the labourer is permitted to rent it, and glad enough he will be to do so, even at the price of decent lodging. But no repair, no improvement shall it receive, except such as its penniless occupants can supply. And when at last it becomes quite uninhabitable – uninhabitable even to the humblest standard of serfdom – it will be but one more destroyed cottage, and future poor-rates will be somewhat lightened. While great owners are thus escaping from poor-rates through the depopulation of lands over which they have control, the nearest town or open village receives the evicted labourers; the nearest, I say, but this "nearest" may mean three or four miles distant from the farm where the labourer has his daily toil. To that daily toil there will then have to be added, as though it were nothing, the daily need of walking six

1. A show-village of this kind looks very nice, but is as unreal as the villages that Catherine II saw on her journey to the Crimea. In recent times even the shepherd has often been banished from these show-villages; e.g. near Market Harborough there is a sheep-farm of about 500 acres, which only employs the labour of one man. To reduce the long trudges over these wide plains, over the beautiful pastures of Leicestershire and Northamptonshire, the shepherd used to get a cottage on the farm. Now they give him a thirteenth shilling a week for lodgings, which he must find at a great distance away in an 'open village'.

or eight miles for power of earning his bread. And whatever farm-work is done by his wife and children, is done at the same disadvantage. Nor is this nearly all the toil which the distance occasions him. In the open village, cottage-speculators buy scraps of land, which they throng as densely as they can with the cheapest of all possible hovels. And into those wretched habitations (which, even if they adjoin the open country, have some of the worst features of the worst town residences) crowd the agricultural labourers of England[2] . . . Nor on the other hand must it be supposed that even when the labourer is housed upon the lands which he cultivates, his household circumstances are generally such as his life of productive industry would seem to deserve. Even on princely estates . . . his cottage . . . may be of the meanest description. There are landlords who deem any stye good enough for their labourer and his family, and who yet do not disdain to drive with him the hardest possible bargain for rent.[3] It

2. 'The labourers' houses' (in the open villages, which of course are always overcrowded) 'are usually in rows, built with their backs against the extreme edge of the plot of land which the builder could call his, and on this account are not allowed light and air, except from the front' (Dr Hunter's Report, op. cit., p. 135). Very often the beer-seller or grocer of the village is at the same time the man who lets its houses. In this case the agricultural labourer finds in him a second master, besides the farmer. He must be the grocer's customer as well as his tenant. 'The hind with his 10s. a week, minus a rent of £4 a year . . . is obliged to buy at the seller's own terms, his modicum of tea, sugar, flour, soap, candles, and beer' (ibid., p. 132). These open villages form in fact 'penal settlements' for the English agricultural proletariat. Many of the cottages are simply lodging-houses, and all the rabble of the neighbourhood passes through them. The countryman and his family, who had often preserved, under the foulest conditions, a capacity for work and a purity of character which were truly to be wondered at, now, in these lodging-houses, go utterly to the devil. It is of course the fashion among the Shylocks of the aristocracy to shrug one's shoulders pharisaically at the building speculators, the small landlords and the 'open villages'. They know well enough that their 'close villages' and 'show-villages' are the places where the 'open villages' originate, and could not exist without them. 'The labourers . . . were it not for the small owners, would, for the most part, have to sleep under the trees of the farms on which they work' (ibid., p. 135). The system of 'open' and 'closed' villages obtains in all the Midland counties and throughout the east of England.

3. 'The employer . . . is . . . directly or indirectly securing to himself the profit on a man employed at 10s. a week, and receiving from this poor hind £4 or £5 annual rent for houses not worth £20 in a really free market, but maintained at their artificial value by the power of the owner to say "Use my house, or go seek a hiring elsewhere, without a character from me" . . . Does a man wish to better himself, to go as a plate-layer on the railway, or to begin

may be but a ruinous one-bedroomed hut, having no fire-grate, no privy, no opening window, no water supply but the ditch, no garden – but the labourer is helpless against the wrong . . . And the Nuisances Removal Acts . . . are . . . a mere dead letter . . . in great part dependent for their working on such cottage-owners as the one from whom his' (the labourer's) 'hovel is rented . . . From brighter, but exceptional scenes, it is requisite in the interests of justice, that attention should again be drawn to the over-whelming preponderance of facts which are a reproach to the civilization of England. Lamentable indeed, must be the case, when, notwithstanding all that is evident with regard to the quality of the present accommodation, it is the common con-clusion of competent observers that even the general badness of dwellings is an evil infinitely less urgent than their mere numerical insufficiency. For years the overcrowding of rural labourers' dwellings has been a matter of deep concern, not only to persons who care for sanitary good, but to persons who care for decent and moral life. For, again and again in phrases so uniform that they seem stereotyped, reporters on the spread of epidemic disease in rural districts have insisted on the extreme importance of that overcrowding, as an influence which renders it a quite hopeless task, to attempt the limiting of any infection which is introduced. And again and again it has been pointed out that, notwithstanding the many salubrious influences which there are in country life, the crowding which so favours the extension of contagious disease, also favours the origination of disease which is not contagious. And those who have denounced the over-crowded state of our rural population have not been silent as to a further mischief. Even where their primary concern has been only with the injury to health, often almost perforce they have been referred to other relations on the subject. In showing how frequently it happens that adult persons of both sexes, married and unmarried, are huddled together in single small sleeping rooms, their reports have carried the conviction that, under the circumstances they describe, decency must always be outraged,

---

quarry-work, the same power is ready with "Work for me at this low rate of wages, or begone at a week's notice; take your pig with you, and get what you can for the potatoes growing in your garden." Should his interest appear to be better served by it, an enhanced rent is sometimes preferred in these cases by the owner' (or, as the case may be, the farmer) 'as the penalty for leaving his service' (Dr Hunter, op. cit., p. 132).

and morality almost of necessity must suffer.[4] Thus, for instance, in the appendix of my last annual report, Dr Ord, reporting on an outbreak of fever at Wing, in Buckinghamshire, mentions how a young man who had come thither from Wingrave with fever, "in the first days of his illness slept in a room with nine other persons. Within a fortnight several of these persons were attacked, and in the course of a few weeks five out of the nine had fever, and one died." ... From Dr Harvey, of St George's Hospital, who, on private professional business, visited Wing during the time of the epidemic, I received information exactly in the sense of the above report ... "A young woman having fever, lay at night in a room occupied by her father, and mother, her bastard child, two young men (her brothers), and her two sisters, each with a bastard child – ten persons in all. A few weeks ago thirteen persons slept in it."[5]

Dr Hunter investigated 5,375 agricultural labourers' cottages, not only in the purely agricultural districts, but in all the counties of England. 2,195 out of the 5,375 had only one bedroom (often used at the same time as a living-room), 2,930 only two, and 250 more than two. I give below a short selection of examples, gathered from a dozen counties.

(1) Bedfordshire

Wrestlingworth. Bedrooms about 12 feet long and 10 broad, although many are smaller than this. The small, one-storied cots* are often divided by partitions into two bedrooms, one bed frequently in a kitchen, 5 feet 6 inches in height. Rent, £3 a year. The tenants have to make their own privies, the landlord

---

4. 'New married couples are no edifying study for grown-up brothers and sisters; and though instances must not be recorded, sufficient data are remembered to warrant the remark, that great depression and sometimes death are the lot of the female participator in the offence of incest' (Dr Hunter, op. cit., p. 137). A rural policeman, who had for many years been a detective in the worst quarters of London, says of the girls of his village: 'Their boldness and shamelessness I never saw equalled during some years of police life and detective duty in the worst parts of London ... They live like pigs, great boys and girls, mothers and fathers, all sleeping in one room, in many instances' (*Children's Employment Commission, Sixth Report*, 1867, Appendix, p. 77, n. 155).

5. *Public Health, Seventh Report*, 1865, pp. 9–14 passim.

---

* Cottages.

only supplies a hole. As soon as one has made a privy, it is made use of by the whole neighbourhood. One house, belonging to a family called Richardson, was of quite unapproachable beauty. 'Its plaster walls bulged very like a lady's dress in a curtsey. One gable end was convex, the other concave, and on this last, unfortunately, stood the chimney, a curved tube of clay and wood like an elephant's trunk. A long stick served as prop to prevent the chimney from falling. The doorway and window were rhomboidal.' Of seventeen houses visited, only four had more than one bedroom, and those four overcrowded. The cots with one bedroom sheltered three adults and three children, a married couple with six children, etc.

Dunton. High rents, from £4 to £5, weekly wages of the men, 10s. They hope to pay the rent by the straw-plaiting of the family. The higher the rent, the greater the number that must work together to pay. Six adults, living with four children in one sleeping apartment, pay £3 10s. for it. The cheapest house in Dunton, 15 feet long externally, 10 broad, let for £3. Only one of the houses investigated had two bedrooms. A little outside the village, a house whose 'tenants dunged against the house-side', the lower 9 inches of the door eaten away through sheer rottenness; the doorway, a single opening closed at night by a few bricks, ingeniously pushed up after shutting and covered with some matting. Half a window, with glass and frame, had gone the way of all flesh. Here, without furniture, huddled together were three adults and five children. Dunton is not worse than the rest of the Biggleswade Union.

(2) Berkshire

Beenham. In June 1864 a man, his wife and four children lived in a cot (one-storied cottage). A daughter came home from service with scarlet fever. She died. One child sickened and died. The mother and one child were down with typhus when Dr Hunter was called in. The father and one child slept outside, but the difficulty of securing isolation was seen here, for in the crowded market of the miserable village lay the linen of the fever-stricken household, waiting for the wash. The rent of H's house, 1s. a week; one bedroom without window, fire-place, door, or opening, except into the lobby; no garden. A man lived here for a little while, with two grown-up daughters and one grown-up son;

father and son slept on the bed, the girls in the passage. Each of the latter had a child while the family was living here, but one went to the workhouse for her confinement and then came home.

(3) Buckinghamshire

Thirty cottages – on 1,000 acres of land – contained here about 130–140 persons. The parish of *Bradenham* comprises 1,000 acres; it numbered, in 1851, thirty-six houses and a population of 84 males and 54 females. This inequality of the sexes was partly remedied in 1861, when they numbered 98 males and 87 females; an increase in ten years of 14 men and 33 women. Meanwhile, the number of houses had declined by 1.

Winslow. Great part of this newly built in good style; demand for houses appears very marked, since very miserable cots let at 1s. to 1s. 3d. per week.

Water Eaton. Here the landlords, in view of the increasing population, have destroyed about 20 per cent of the existing houses. A poor labourer, who had to go about 4 miles to his work, answered the question whether he could not find a cot nearer: 'No; they know better than to take a man in with my large family.'

Tinker's End, near Winslow. A bedroom in which were four adults and four children; 11 feet long, 9 feet broad, 6 feet 5 inches high at its highest part; another 11 feet 3 inches by 9 feet, 5 feet 10 inches high, sheltered six persons. Each of these families had less space than is considered necessary for a convict. No house had more than one bedroom, not one of them a back door; water very scarce; weekly rent from 1s. 4d. to 2s. In sixteen of the houses visited, only one man that earned 10s. a week. The quantity of air for each person under the circumstances just described corresponds to that which he would have if he were shut up in a box of 4 feet measuring each way, the whole night. But then, the ancient dens afforded a certain amount of unintentional ventilation.

(4) Cambridgeshire

Gamlingay belongs to several landlords. It contains the wretchedest cots to be found anywhere. Much straw-plaiting. 'A deadly lassitude, a hopeless surrendering up to filth', reigns in Gamlingay. The neglect in its centre becomes mortification at its extremities, north and south, where the houses are rotting to pieces. The absentee landlords bleed this poor rookery too freely. The rents are very high; eight or nine persons packed in one sleeping apartment, in two cases six adults, each with one or two children in one small bedroom.

(5) *Essex*

In this county, decline in the number of persons and of cottages goes hand in hand in many parishes. In not less than twenty-two parishes, however, the destruction of houses has not prevented increase of population, or has not brought about that expulsion which, under the name 'migration to towns', generally occurs. In Fingringhoe, a parish of 3,445 acres, there were 145 houses in 1851, and only 110 in 1861. But the people did not wish to go away, and managed even to increase under these circumstances. In 1851, 252 persons inhabited 61 houses, but in 1861, 262 persons were squeezed into 49 houses. In Basildon, in 1851, 157 persons lived on 1,827 acres, in 35 houses; at the end of ten years, 180 persons lived in 27 houses. In the parishes of Fingringhoe, South Farnbridge, Widford, Basildon and Ramsden Crags, in 1851, 1,392 persons were living on 8,449 acres in 316 houses; in 1861, on the same area, 1,473 persons in 249 houses.

(6) *Herefordshire*

This little county has suffered more from the 'eviction spirit' than any other in England. At Madley, overcrowded cottages generally, with only two bedrooms, belonging for the most part to the farmers. They can let them very easily for £3 or £4 a year, and pay a weekly wage of 9s.!

(7) *Huntingdonshire*

Hartford had, in 1851, 87 houses; shortly after this, nineteen cottages were destroyed in this small parish of 1,720 acres; population in 1831, 452; in 1851, 832; and in 1861, 341. Fourteen cottages, each with one bedroom, were visited. One of these rooms, in which eight people slept, was 12 feet 10 inches long, 12 feet 2 inches broad, 6 feet 9 inches high: the average, without making any deductions for projections into the apartment, comes to about 130 cubic feet per head. In the fourteen sleeping rooms, thirty-four

adults and thirty-three children. These cottages are seldom provided with gardens, but many of the inmates are able to farm small
allotments at 10s. or 12s. per rood ($\frac{1}{4}$ acre). These allotments are at
a distance from the houses, which are without privies. The family
'must either go to the allotment to deposit their ordures', or, as
happens in this place, if the reader will permit the reference, 'use
a closet with a trough set like a drawer in a chest of drawers, and
drawn out weekly and conveyed to the allotment to be emptied
where its contents were wanted'. In Japan the cyclical movement
of the conditions of human life proceeds more cleanly and more
decently than this.

(8) Lincolnshire

Langtoft. A man lives here, in Wright's house, with his wife, her
mother, and five children; the house has a front kitchen, scullery,
bedroom over the front kitchen; front kitchen and bedroom, 12
feet 2 inches by 9 feet 5 inches; the whole ground floor, 21 feet
2 inches by 9 feet 5 inches. The bedroom is a garret; the walls run
together into the roof like a sugar-loaf, a dormer-window opening
in front. 'Why did he live here? On account of the garden? No; it
is very small. Rent? High, 1s. 3d. per week. Near his work? No;
6 miles away, so that he walks daily, to and fro, 12 miles. He lived
there, because it was a tenantable cot,' and because he wanted to
have a cot for himself alone, anywhere, at any price, and in any
conditions. The following are the statistics of twelve houses in
Langtoft, with twelve bedrooms, thirty-eight adults, and thirty-six
children.

Twelve Houses in Langtoft

Houses	Bedrooms	Adults	Children	Number of persons
No. 1	1	3	5	8
No. 2	1	4	3	7
No. 3	1	4	4	8
No. 4	1	5	4	9
No. 5	1	2	2	4
No. 6	1	5	3	8
No. 7	1	3	3	6
No. 8	1	3	2	5
No. 9	1	2	0	2
No. 10	1	2	3	5
No. 11	1	3	3	6
No. 12	1	2	4	6

(9) Kent

Kennington, very seriously over-populated in 1859, when diph-theria appeared, and the parish doctor instituted a medical inquiry into the conditions of the poor classes. He found that in this locality, where much labour is employed, various cots had been destroyed and no new ones built. In one district, there stood four houses, named birdcages; each had four rooms of the following dimensions in feet and inches:

> Kitchen: 9 ft 5 by 8 ft 11 by 6 ft 6.
> Scullery: 8 ft 6 by 4 ft 6 by 6 ft 6.
> Bedroom: 8 ft 5 by 5 ft 10 by 6 ft 3.
> Bedroom: 8 ft 3 by 8 ft 4 by 6 ft 3.

(10) Northamptonshire

Brinworth, Pickford and *Floore*: in these villages in the winter twenty to thirty men were lounging about the streets from lack of work. The farmers do not always till the corn and turnip lands sufficiently, and the landlord has found it best to throw all his farms together into two or three. Hence the shortage of employ-ment. While on one side of the wall the land is crying out to be worked, on the other side the defrauded labourers are casting longing glances at it. Feverishly over-worked in summer, and half-starved in winter, it is no wonder if they say in their own local dialect, 'the parson and gentlefolks seem frit to death at them'.

At Floore there are cases, in one bedroom of the smallest size, of couples with four, five, six children; three adults with five children; a couple with grandfather and six children down with scarlet fever, etc.; in two houses with two bedrooms, two families of eight and nine adults respectively.

(11) Wiltshire

Stratton. Thirty-one houses visited, eight with only one bedroom. Pen Hill, in the same parish: a cot let at 1s. 3d. a week with four adults and four children, had nothing good about it, except the walls, from the floor of rough-hewn pieces of stones to the roof of worn-out thatch.

(12) Worcestershire

House-destruction here not quite so excessive; yet from 1851 to 1861, the number of inhabitants to each house, on the average, has risen from 4·2 to 4·6.

Badsey. Many cots and little gardens here. Some of the farmers declare that the cots are 'a great nuisance here, because they bring the poor'. In the view of one gentleman: 'The poor are none the better for them; if you build 500 they will let fast enough, in fact, the more you build, the more they want' (according to him the houses give birth to the inhabitants, who then by a law of nature put pressure on 'the means of housing'). Dr Hunter remarks: 'Now these poor must come from somewhere, and as there is no particular attraction, such as doles, at Badsey, it must be repulsion from some other unfit place, which will send them here. If each could find an allotment near his work, he would not prefer Badsey, where he pays for his scrap of ground twice as much as the farmer pays for his.'*

The continual emigration to the towns, the continual formation of a surplus population in the countryside through the concentration of farms, the conversion of arable land into pasture, the introduction of machinery, etc., are things which go hand in hand with the continual eviction of the agricultural population by the destruction of their cottages. The more empty the district of people, the greater is its 'relative surplus population'; the greater their pressure on the means of employment, the greater is the absolute excess of the agricultural population over the means for housing it, and the greater, therefore, is the local surplus population in the villages and the pestilential herding together of human beings. The creation of dense knots of humanity in scattered little villages and small country towns corresponds to the forcible draining of men from the surface of the land. The continuous conversion of the agricultural labourers into a surplus population, in spite of their diminishing number and the increasing mass of their products, is the cradle of pauperism. The pauperism of the agricultural labourers is ultimately a motive for their eviction; it is also the chief source of their miserable housing, which breaks down

---

* The above description of housing conditions is extracted from Dr Hunter's report, op. cit., pp. 148–302.

their last power of resistance, and makes them mere slaves of the landed proprietors[6] and the farmers. Thus the minimum of wages becomes a law of nature for them. On the other hand, the land, in spite of its constant 'relative surplus population', is at the same time under-populated. This is not only seen locally, at the points where the flow of men to towns, mines, railway constructions, etc. is most marked. It is to be seen everywhere, at harvest-time as well as in spring and summer, on those numerous occasions when English agriculture, careful and intensive as it is, needs extra hands. There are always too many agricultural labourers for the ordinary needs of cultivation, and too few for exceptional and temporary requirements.[7] Hence we find in the official documents

6. 'The heaven-born employment of the hind gives dignity even to his position. He is not a slave, but a soldier of peace, and deserves his place in married men's quarters to be provided by the landlord, who has claimed a power of enforced labour similar to that the country demands of the soldier. He no more receives market-price for his work than does the soldier. Like the soldier he is caught young, ignorant, knowing only his own trade, and his own locality. Early marriage and the operation of the various laws of settlement affect the one as enlistment and the Mutiny Act affect the other' (Dr Hunter, op. cit., p. 132). Sometimes an exceptionally soft-hearted landlord relents at the solitude he has created. 'It is a melancholy thing to stand alone in one's country,' said Lord Leicester,* when complimented on the completion of Holkham. 'I look around and not a house is to be seen but mine. I am the giant of Giant Castle, and have eat up all my neighbours.'†

7. Similar developments have taken place in France in the last few decades: there, in proportion as capitalist production takes possession of agriculture, it drives the 'surplus' agricultural population into the towns. Here also we find deterioration in the housing, and other conditions, at the source of the 'surplus population'. On the peculiar *'prolétariat foncier'*‡ which has arisen out of the fragmentation of holdings, see the work by Colins, already quoted, and also Karl Marx, *Der Achtzehnte Brumaire des Louis Bonaparte*, 2nd edn, Hamburg, 1869, pp. 88 ff.§ In 1846, the urban population of France constituted 24·42 per cent of the total, the rural 75·58 per cent; in 1861, the urban population was 28·86 per cent, the rural 71·14 per cent. During the last five years, the decline of the agricultural percentage of the population has been still more marked. As early as 1846, Pierre Dupont wrote, in *Le Chant des ouvriers*,

> Mal vêtus, logés dans des trous,
> Sous les combles, dans les décombres,

*Thomas William Coke of Holkham, Earl of Leicester (1752–1842), was a very successful capitalist farmer in the county of Norfolk.

†Dr Hunter, op. cit., p. 135, n.

‡'Landowning proletariat'.

§English translation, Karl Marx, *Surveys from Exile*, Pelican Marx Library, 1973, pp. 240–45.

contradictory complaints from the same places of a simultaneous deficiency and excess of labour. A temporary and local shortage of labour does not bring about a rise in wages, but rather forces the women and children into the fields, and constantly lowers the age at which exploitation begins. As soon as the exploitation of women and children takes place on a large scale, it becomes in turn a new means of making the male agricultural labourer 'redundant' and keeping down his wage. The finest fruit of this vicious circle thrives in the east of England – this is the so-called gang-system, to which I must briefly return here.[8]

The gang-system obtains almost exclusively in the counties of Lincolnshire, Huntingdonshire, Cambridgeshire, Norfolk, Suffolk and Nottinghamshire, and sporadically in the neighbouring counties of Northamptonshire, Bedfordshire and Rutland. Lincolnshire will serve as an example. A large part of this county is new land, formerly marsh, or even, as in others of the eastern counties just mentioned, recently won from the sea. The steam-engine has worked wonders in the way of drainage. What were once fens and sandbanks now bear a luxuriant sea of corn, and very high ground rents. The same thing is true of the alluvial lands won by human endeavour, as in the island of Axholme and other parishes on the banks of the Trent. Not only were no new cottages built there but, in proportion as the new farms arose, old cottages were demolished and the supply of labour had to come from 'open villages' miles away, by long roads that wound along the sides of the hills. There alone had the population formerly found shelter from the incessant floods of winter. The labourers who live on the farms of 400–1,000 acres (they are called 'confined labourers') are solely employed on agricultural work which is permanent, difficult and requires the aid of horses. For every 100 acres there is, on an average, scarcely one cottage. A fenland farmer, for instance, gave this evidence before the Commission of Inquiry: 'I farm 320

---

*Nous vivons avec les hiboux
Et les larrons, amis des ombres.* *

8. The sixth and last† Report of the Children's Employment Commission, published at the end of March 1867, deals solely with the agricultural gang-system.

*'Badly clothed, living in holes, under the eaves, in the ruins, with the owls and the thieves, companions of the shadows.'

† The Children's Employment Commission issued its fifth and final report in 1866. It was however requested to produce an extra report on the gang-system.

acres, all arable land. I have not one cottage on my farm. I have only one labourer on my farm now. I have four horsemen lodging about. We get light work done by gangs.'[9] The soil requires a great deal of light field labour, such as weeding, hoeing, certain processes of manuring, removing of stones, and so on. This is done by the gangs, or in other words the organized bands who live in the open villages.

The gang consists of from ten to forty or fifty persons, women, young persons of both sexes (13–18 years of age, although the boys are for the most part eliminated at the age of 13), and children of both sexes (6–13 years of age). At the head of the gang is the gang-master, always an ordinary agricultural labourer, and usually what is called a bad lot, a rake, unsteady, drunken, but with a dash of enterprise and *savoir faire*. He is the recruiting-sergeant for the gang, which works under him, not under the farmer. He generally negotiates with the latter over piece-work, and his income, which on the average is not very much above that of an ordinary agricultural labourer,[10] depends almost entirely on the dexterity with which he manages to extract the greatest possible amount of labour from his gang within the shortest time. The farmers have discovered that women only work steadily under the direction of men, but that women and children, when once set going, spend their vital forces impetuously – as Fourier already knew in his time – whereas the adult male worker is shrewd enough to economize on his strength as much as he can. The gang-master goes from one farm to another, and thus employs his gang for from six to eight months in the year. Employment by him is therefore much more lucrative and more certain for the labouring families than employment by the individual farmer, who only employs children occasionally. This circumstance so completely rivets his influence in the open villages that children can in general be hired only through his agency. The lending-out of the latter, individually and independently of the gang, is a subsidiary trade for him.

The 'drawbacks' of this system are the over-working of the children and young persons, the enormous marches that they make every day to and from the farms, which are five, six and sometimes seven miles away, and finally the demoralization of the 'gang'. Although the gang-master, who is called 'the driver' in some dis-

9. *Children's Employment Commission, Sixth Report*, Evidence, p. 37, n. 173.
10. Some gang-masters, however, have worked up to the position of farmers of 500 acres, or proprietors of whole rows of houses.

tricts, is armed with a long stick, he seldom uses it, and complaints of brutal treatment are exceptional. He is a democratic emperor, or a kind of Pied Piper of Hamelin. He must therefore be popular with his subjects, and he binds them to himself by the charms of the gipsy life which flourishes under his auspices. Coarse freedom, noisy jollity and the obscenest kind of impertinence give attractions to the gang. Generally the gang-master pays up in a public house; then he returns home at the head of the procession of gang members, reeling drunk, and propped up on either side by a stalwart virago, while children and young persons bring up the rear, boisterously, and singing mocking and bawdy songs. On the return journey what Fourier calls '*phanerogamie*'* is the order of the day. Girls of 13 and 14 are commonly made pregnant by their male companions of the same age. The open villages, which supply the contingents for the gangs, become Sodoms and Gomorrahs,¹¹ and have twice as high a rate of illegitimacy as the rest of the kingdom. The moral character of girls bred in these schools, when they become married women, was shown above. Their children, when opium does not finish them off entirely, are born recruits for the gang.

The gang in its classical form, as we have just described it, is called the public, common or tramping gang. For there also exist private gangs. These are made up in the same way as the common gang, but count fewer members, and work, not under a gang-master, but under some old farm servant, whom the farmer does not know how to employ in any better way. The gipsy fun has vanished in this case, but, according to all the witnesses, the payment and treatment of the children is worse.

The gang-system, which has steadily expanded during the most recent years,¹² clearly does not exist for the sake of the gang-

11. 'Half the girls of Ludford have been ruined by going out' (in gangs) (loc. cit., ibid., p. 6, n. 32).

12. 'They' (the gangs) 'have greatly increased of late years. In some places they are said to have been introduced at comparatively late dates; in others where gangs ... have been known for many years ... more and younger children are employed in them' (ibid., p. 79, n. 174).

---

*Charles Fourier, *Le Nouveau Monde industriel et sociétaire*, Paris, 1829, Part 5, Supplement to Chapter 36, and Part 6, Summary. Here Fourier describes '*phanerogamie*' as a means of limiting the population. It is a form of polyandry practised within the phalanx, that is, the communal unit which was to replace the family, and is compared explicitly by Fourier himself with the sexual behaviour of various tribes in Java and Tahiti.

master. It exists for the enrichment of the large-scale farmers[13] and indirectly for the landowners.[14] For the farmer, there is no more ingenious method of keeping his labourers well below the normal level, and yet of always having an extra hand ready for extra work, of extracting the greatest possible amount of labour with the least possible expenditure of money,[15] and of making adult male labour 'redundant'. From the foregoing exposition it will be understood why, on the one hand, a greater or lesser lack of employment for the agricultural labourer is admitted, while, on the other, the gang-system is at the same time declared 'necessary' on account of the shortage of adult male labour and its migration to the towns.[16] The cleanly weeded land and the unclean human weeds of Lincolnshire are pole and counterpole of capitalist production.[17]

13. 'Small farmers never employ gangs.' 'It is not on poor land, but on land which affords rent of from 40 to 50 shillings, that women and children are employed in the greatest numbers' (ibid., pp. 17, 14).

14. One of these gentlemen found the taste of his rents so delicious that he indignantly declared to the Commission of Inquiry that the whole hullabaloo was only due to the name of the system. If, instead of 'gang', it were to be called 'the Agricultural Juvenile Industrial Self-Supporting Association', everything would be all right.

15. 'Gang work is cheaper than other work; that is why they are employed,' says a former gang-master (ibid., p. 17, n. 14). 'The gang-system is decidedly the cheapest for the farmer, and decidedly the worst for the children,' says a farmer (ibid., p. 16, n. 3).

16. 'Undoubtedly much of the work now done by children in gangs used to be done by men and women. More men are out of work now where children and women are employed than formerly' (ibid., p. 43, n. 202). On the other hand, 'the labour question in some agricultural districts, particularly the arable, is becoming so serious in consequence of emigration, and the facility afforded by railways for getting to large towns that I' (the 'I' in question is the steward of a great lord) 'think the services of children are most indispensable' (ibid., p. 80, n. 180). The 'labour question' in English agricultural districts, unlike the rest of the civilized world, means the 'landlords' and farmers' question', namely how, despite an always increasing exodus of the agricultural folk, can a sufficient relative surplus population be kept up in the country, thereby keeping the wages of the agricultural labourer at a minimum?

17. The *Public Health Report* already cited, in which the gang-system is treated in passing, in connection with the subject of the mortality of children, remains unknown to the press, and therefore unknown to the English public. The last Report of the Children's Employment Commission, however, afforded the press sensational and welcome copy. While the Liberal press asked how the fine gentlemen and ladies, and well-paid clergy of the state Church, with whom Lincolnshire swarms, people who expressly send out missions to the antipodes 'for the improvement of the morals of South Sea Islanders',

(f) Ireland

In concluding this section, we must travel for a moment to Ireland. First, the main facts of the case.

The population of Ireland had, by 1841, grown to 8,222,664. In 1851 it had dwindled to 6,623,985; in 1861, to 5,850,309; and in 1866, to 5½ millions, approximately its level in 1801. The decrease in population began with the famine year of 1846, so that Ireland has lost more than $\frac{5}{16}$ of its people in less than twenty years.[18] Total emigration from May 1851 to July 1865 numbered 1,591,487. During the years between 1861 and 1865 the emigration was more than half a million. The number of inhabited houses fell, from 1851 to 1861, by 52,990. From 1851 to 1861 the number of holdings of from 15 to 30 acres increased by 61,000, that of holdings of over 30 acres by 109,000, while the total number of all farms fell by 120,000. This fall was therefore solely due to the suppression of farms of less than 15 acres, in other words it was due to their centralization.

---

could allow such a system to arise on their estates, under their very eyes, the more refined newspapers confined themselves to reflections on the coarse degradation of an agricultural population which was capable of selling its children into such slavery! Under the accursed conditions to which these 'delicate' people condemn the agricultural labourer, it would not be surprising if he ate his own children. What is really wonderful is the healthy integrity of character he has largely retained. The official reports prove that the parents, even in the gang districts, loathe the gang-system. 'There is much in the evidence that shows that the parents of the children would, in many instances, be glad to be aided by the requirements of a legal obligation, to resist the pressure and the temptations to which they are often subject. They are liable to be urged, at times by the parish officers, at times by employers, under threats of being themselves discharged, to be taken to work at an age when . . . school attendance . . . would be manifestly to their greater advantage . . . All that time and strength wasted; all the suffering from extra and unprofitable fatigue produced to the labourer and to his children; every instance in which the parent may have traced the moral ruin of his child to the undermining of delicacy by the over-crowding of cottages, or to the contaminating influences of the public gang, must have been so many incentives to feelings in the minds of the labouring poor which can be well understood, and which it would be needless to particularize. They must be conscious that much bodily and mental pain has thus been inflicted upon them from cases for which they were in no way answerable; to which, had it been in their power, they would have in no way consented; and against which they were powerless to struggle' (ibid., p. xx, n. 82, and xxiii, n. 96).

18. Population of Ireland in 1801: 5,319,867; in 1811: 6,084,996; in 1821: 6,869,544; in 1831: 7,828,347; in 1841: 8,222,664.

The decrease of the population was naturally accompanied by a decrease in the mass of products. For our purpose it is sufficient to consider the five years from 1861 to 1865, years during which over half a million emigrated and the absolute number of people sank by more than ⅓ of a million.

Table A: Livestock

Year	Horses			Cattle		
	Total Number	Decrease	Total Number	Decrease	Increase
1860	619,811		3,606,374		
1861	614,232	5,993	3,471,688	138,316	
1862	602,894	11,338	3,254,890	216,798	
1863	579,978	22,916	3,144,231	110,695	
1864	562,158	17,820	3,262,294		118,063
1865	547,867	14,291	3,493,414		231,120

Year	Sheep			Pigs		
	Total Number	Decrease	Increase	Total Number	Decrease	Increase
1860	3,542,080			1,271,072		
1861	3,556,050		13,970	1,102,042	169,030	
1862	3,456,132	99,819		1,154,324		52,282
1863	3,308,204	147,982		1,067,458	86,866	
1864	3,366,941		58,737	1,058,480	8,978	
1865	3,688,742		321,801	1,299,893		241,413

The following results emerge from the above table: an absolute decrease of 72,358 in the number of horses, an absolute decrease of 116,626 in the number of cattle, an absolute increase of 146,608 in the number of sheep and an absolute increase of 28,819 in the number of pigs.[19]

Let us now turn to the produce of agriculture proper, which provides the means of subsistence for cattle and for men. In the

19. The result would be still more unfavourable if we went further back. Thus: sheep in 1865, 3,688,742, but in 1856, 3,694,554. Pigs in 1865, 1,299,893, but in 1858, 1,409,883.

Table B: Increase or Decrease in the Area Under Crops and Grass (in Acres)

Year	Cereal Crops	Green Crops		Grass and Clover		Flax		Total Cultivated Land	
	Decrease	Decrease	Increase	Decrease	Increase	Decrease	Increase	Decrease	Increase
1861	15,701	36,974		47,969			19,271	81,873	
1862	72,734	74,785			6,623		2,055	138,841	
1863	144,719	19,358			7,724		63,922	92,431	
1864	122,437	2,317			47,486		87,761		10,493
1865	72,450		25,241		68,970	50,159		28,218	
1861–5	428,041	107,984			82,834		122,850	330,860	

Table C: Increase or Decrease in the Area Under Cultivation, Product Per Acre, and Total Product of 1865 Compared with 1864[20]

Product	Acres of Cultivated Land			Product	Per Acre	Increase or Decrease	Total Product (Qrs)		Increase or Decrease, 1865
	1864	1865	Increase or Decrease, 1865	1864	1865	1865	1864	1865	
Wheat	276,483	266,989	9,494	(Cwt) 13·3	13·0	−0·3	875,782	826,783	−48,999
Oats	1,814,886	1,745,228	69,658	(Cwt) 12·1	12·3	+0·2	7,826,332	7,659,727	−166,605
Barley	172,700	177,102	4,402	(Cwt) 15·9	14·9	−1·0	761,909	732,017	−29,892
Bere }	8,894	10,091	1,197	(Cwt) 16·4	14·8	−1·6	15,160	13,989	−1,171
Rye }				(Cwt) 8·5	10·4	+1·9	12,680	18,364	+5,684
Potatoes	1,039,724	1,066,260	26,536	(Tons) 4·1	3·6	−0·5	4,312,388	3,865,990	−446,398
Turnips	337,355	334,212	3,143	(Tons) 10·3	9·9	−0·4	3,467,659	3,301,683	−165,976
Mangel-wurzels	14,073	14,839	316	(Tons) 10·5	13·3	+2·8	147,284	191,937	+44,653
Cabbages	31,821	33,622	1,801	(Tons) 9·3	10·4	+1·1	297,375	350,252	+52,877
Flax	301,693	251,433	50,260	(St.) 34·2	25·2	−9·0	64,506	39,561	−24,945
Hay	1,609,569	1,678,492	68,924	(Tons) 1·6	1·8	+0·2	2,607,153	3,068,707	+461,554

20. The data in the text have been put together from the material provided by the *Agricultural Statistics, Ireland. General Abstracts*, Dublin, for the years 1860 ff., and the *Agricultural Statistics, Ireland. Tables Showing the Estimated Average Produce, etc.*, Dublin, *1866*. These statistics are official, and are laid before Parliament every year. The official statistics for the year 1872 show a decrease in the area under cultivation of 134,915 acres, as compared with 1871. An increase occurred in the cultivation of green crops, turnips, mangel-wurzels and so on; a decrease in the area over which wheat was cultivated of 16,000 acres; oats, 14,000; barley and rye, 4,000; potatoes, 66,632; flax, 34,667; grass, clover, vetches and rape-seed, 30,000. The area of land on which wheat is cultivated has undergone a series of diminutions over the last five years, as can be seen from these figures: area of wheat in 1868, 285,000 acres; in 1869, 280,000; in 1870, 259,000; in 1871, 244,000; and in 1872, 228,000. For 1872 we find, in round numbers, an increase of 2,600 horses, 80,000 horned cattle, 68,609 sheep, and a decrease of 236,000 pigs.

Table D: The Income Tax on the Subjoined Incomes, in Pounds Sterling[21]

	1860	1861	1862	1863	1864	1865
Schedule A 1. Rent of Land	13,893,829	13,003,554	13,398,938	13,494,091	13,470,700	13,801,616
Schedule B 2. Farmers' Profits	2,765,387	2,773,644	2,937,899	2,938,823	2,930,874	2,946,072
Schedule D 3. Industrial, etc. Profits	4,891,652	4,836,203	4,858,800	4,846,497	4,546,147	4,850,199
4. Total Schedules A to E	22,962,885	22,998,394	23,597,574	23,658,631	23,236,298	23,230,340

21. *Tenth Report of the Commissioners of Inland Revenue*, London, 1866.

following table we have computed the decrease or increase for each separate year, as compared with its immediate predecessor. The cereal crops include wheat, oats, barley, rye, beans and peas; the green crops, potatoes, turnips, mangolds, beetroot, cabbages, carrots, parsnips, vetches, etc. (See Table B.)

In the year 1865, 127,470 additional acres came under the heading 'grass land', chiefly because the area under the heading of 'unoccupied bog and waste' decreased by 101,543 acres. If we compare 1865 with 1864, there is a decrease in cereals of 246,667 quarters, of which 48,999 were wheat, 160,605 oats, 29,892 barley and so on: the decrease in potatoes was 446,398 tons, although the area of their cultivation increased in 1865. (See Table C.)

From the movement of population and of agricultural production in Ireland, we pass to the movement of the incomes of its landlords, larger farmers and industrial capitalists. This movement is reflected in the rise and fall of the income tax (see Table D).

Table E: Schedule D Income from Profits (over £60) in Ireland[22]

	1864		1865	
	Pounds Sterling	Divided among these Persons	Pounds Sterling	Divided among these Persons
Total yearly income	4,368,610	17,467	4,669,979	18,081
Yearly income over £60 and under £100	238,626	5,015	222,575	4,703
Of the total yearly income	1,979,066	11,321	2,028,471	12,184
Remainder of the total yearly income	2,150,818	1,131	2,418,933	1,194
	1,083,906	910	1,097,937	1,044
	1,066,912	121	1,320,996	186
Of these	430,535	105	584,458	122
	646,377	26	736,448	28
	262,610	3	274,528	3

22. The total yearly income under Schedule D is different in this table from that which appears in the preceding ones, because of certain deductions allowed by law.

It may be recalled that Schedule D (profits with the exception of those of farmers) also includes so-called 'professional' profits – i.e. the incomes of lawyers, doctors, etc.; and Schedules C and E, in which no details are given, include the incomes of civil servants, officers, state sinecurists, creditors of the state, etc.

Under Schedule D the average annual increase of income from 1853 to 1864 was only 0·93 per cent in Ireland, whereas in the same period in Great Britain it was 4·58 per cent. Table E shows the distribution of the profits (with the exception of those of farmers) for the years 1864 and 1865.

England, a pre-eminently industrial country with fully developed capitalist production, would have bled to death under such a population drain as Ireland has suffered. But Ireland is at present merely an agricultural district of England which happens to be divided by a wide stretch of water from the country for which it provides corn, wool, cattle and industrial and military recruits.

The depopulation of Ireland has thrown much of the land out of cultivation, greatly diminished the produce of the soil,[23] and in spite of the greater area devoted to cattle breeding, brought about an absolute decline in some of its branches, and in others an advance scarcely worth mentioning, and constantly interrupted by retrogressions. Nevertheless, the rents of the land and the profits of the farmers increased along with the fall in the population, though not so steadily as the latter. The reason for this will easily be understood. On the one hand, with the throwing together of smallholdings and the change from arable to pasture land, a larger part of the total product was transformed into a surplus product. The surplus product increased although there was a decrease in the total product of which the surplus product formed a fraction. On the other hand, the monetary value of this surplus product increased still more rapidly than its actual quantity, owing to the rise in the price of meat, wool, etc. on the English market during the last twenty years, and especially during the last ten.

The scattered means of production that serve the producers themselves as means of employment and subsistence, without valorizing themselves through the incorporation of the labour of others, are no more capital than a product consumed by its pro-

23. If the product also diminishes relatively, per acre, it must not be forgotten that for a century and a half England has indirectly exported the soil of Ireland, without even allowing its cultivators the means for replacing the constituents of the exhausted soil.

ducer is a commodity. If the mass of the means of production employed in agriculture diminished along with the mass of the population, the mass of the capital employed in agriculture increased, because a part of the means of production that were formerly scattered was turned into capital.

The total capital of Ireland outside agriculture, employed in industry and trade, accumulated only slowly during the last two decades, and with great and constantly recurring fluctuations. So much the more rapidly did the concentration of its individual constituents develop. And, however small its absolute increase, its relative growth, in proportion to the diminishing population, was tremendous.

Here then, under our own eyes, and on a large scale, there emerges a process which perfectly corresponds to the requirements of orthodox economics for the confirmation of its dogma, the dogma that misery springs from an absolute surplus of population, and that equilibrium is re-established by depopulation. This is a far more important experiment than the mid-fourteenth-century plague* so celebrated by the Malthusians. Let us remark in passing: if it required the naïveté of a schoolmaster to apply the standard of the fourteenth century to the relations of production prevailing in the nineteenth century, and the corresponding relations of population, the error was compounded by overlooking the difference between its consequences in England and in France. On this side of the Channel, the plague and the decimation that accompanied it was followed by the enfranchisement and enrichment of the agricultural population; whereas on the other side, in France, it was followed by a greater degree of enslavement and an increase in misery.[24]

The Irish famine of 1846 killed more than 1,000,000 people, but it killed poor devils only. It did not do the slightest damage to the

24. As Ireland is regarded as the promised land of the 'principle of population', Thomas Sadler, before publishing his work on population,* issued the famous book *Ireland: Its Evils, and Their Remedies* (2nd edn, London, 1829). Here, by comparing the statistics of the individual provinces and the individual counties in each province, he proves that the misery there is not, as Malthus would have it, in proportion to the level of the population, but in inverse ratio to this.

* Sadler's attack on the Malthusian theory, published in 1830 as *The Law of Population* (2 vols.).

*The Black Death of 1347 to 1350.

wealth of the country. The exodus of the next twenty years, an exodus which still continues to increase, did not, as for instance the Thirty Years' War did, decimate the means of production along with the human beings. The Irish genius discovered an altogether new way of spiriting a poor people thousands of miles away from the scene of its misery. The exiles transplanted to the United States send sums of money home every year as travelling expenses for those left behind. Every troop that emigrates one year draws another after it the next. Thus, instead of costing Ireland anything, emigration forms one of the most lucrative branches of its export trade. Finally, it is a systematic process, which does not simply make a passing gap in the population, but sucks out of it every year more people than are replaced by births, so that the absolute level of the population falls year by year.[25]

What were the consequences for the Irish labourers left behind and freed from the surplus population? These: the relative surplus population is as great today as it was before 1846; wages are just as low; the oppression of the labourers has increased; misery is forcing the country towards a new crisis. The reasons are simple. The revolution in agriculture has kept pace with emigration. The production of a relative surplus population has more than kept pace with the absolute depopulation. A glance at Table B will show that the change from arable to pasture land must work still more acutely in Ireland than in England. In England the cultivation of green crops increases with the breeding of cattle; in Ireland, it decreases. While a large number of acres that were formerly tilled lie idle or are turned permanently into grass land, a great part of the waste land and peat bogs that were formerly unused becomes of service for the extension of cattle-breeding. The smaller and the medium farmers – I reckon among these all who do not cultivate more than 100 acres – still make up about $\frac{8}{10}$ of the whole number.[26] They are, one after the other, and with a degree of force unknown before, crushed by the competition of an agriculture managed by capital, and thus they continually furnish new recruits to the class of wage-labourers. The one great industry of Ireland, the manufacture of linen, requires relatively few adult men, and

25. Between 1851 and 1874 the total number of emigrants amounted to 2,325,922.

26. According to a table in Murphy's *Ireland, Industrial, Political and Social*, [London,] 1870, 94·6 per cent of the farms are smaller than 100 acres, while 5·4 per cent exceed that amount.

only employs altogether, in spite of its expansion since the price of cotton increased in the years from 1861 to 1866, a comparatively insignificant portion of the population. Like all other large-scale industries, it constantly produces, owing to its incessant fluctuations, a relative surplus population within its own sphere, despite the absolute increase in the mass of human beings absorbed by it. The misery of the agricultural population forms the pedestal for gigantic shirt-factories, whose armies of workers are, for the most part, scattered over the country. Here we again encounter the system of 'domestic industry' already described, which possesses its own systematic means of rendering workers 'redundant' in the form of under-payment and over-work. Finally, although the depopulation does not have such destructive consequences as would result in a country where capitalist production is fully developed, it does not proceed without constantly reacting back onto the home market. The gap caused by emigration limits not only the local demand for labour, but also the incomes of small shopkeepers, artisans and tradesmen in general. Hence the decrease in incomes between £60 and £100 indicated in Table E.

A clear presentation of the condition of agricultural labourers in Ireland is to be found in the *Reports of the Irish Poor Law Inspectors* (1870).[27] As officials of a government which is maintained only by bayonets and by a state of siege sometimes open and sometimes disguised, they have to observe all the linguistic precautions their English colleagues disdain. In spite of this, however, they do not let their government cradle itself in illusions. According to them, the rate of wages in the country, still very low, has risen by 50 to 60 per cent within the last twenty years, and stands now at an average of 6s. to 9s. a week. But this apparent rise hides an actual fall in wages, for it by no means cancels out the rise in the price of

Average Weekly Cost of Maintenance Per Head

Year ended	Provisions and necessaries	Clothing	Total
29 September 1849	1s. 3¼d.	3d.	1s. 6¼d.
29 September 1869	2s. 7¼d.	6d.	3s. 1¼d.

27. *Reports from the Poor Law Inspectors on the Wages of Agricultural Labourers in Ireland*, Dublin, 1870. See also *Agricultural Labourers (Ireland). Return, etc., 8 March 1861*, London, 1862.

the necessary means of subsistence that has taken place in the meantime. The proof is the above extract from the official accounts of an Irish workhouse.

The price of the necessary means of subsistence is thus approximately twice as high, and the price of clothing exactly twice as high, as twenty years before.

Even if we leave aside this disproportion, a mere comparison of the rate of wages expressed in money would give a far from accurate result. Before the famine, the great mass of agricultural wages was paid in kind, and only the smallest part in money; today, payment in money is the rule. It follows from this that, whatever movement has taken place in the real wage, its money rate must have risen. 'Previous to the famine, the labourer enjoyed his cabin ... with a rood, or half-acre or acre of land, and facilities for ... a crop of potatoes. He was able to rear his pig and keep fowl ... But they now have to buy bread, and they have no refuse upon which they can feed a pig or fowl, and they have consequently no benefit from the sale of a pig, fowl, or eggs.'[28] In fact the agricultural labourers were formerly indistinguishable from the smallest of the small farmers, and they formed for the most part a kind of rear-guard of the medium and large farms on which they found employment. Only since the catastrophe of 1846 have they begun to form a section of the class of pure wage-labourers, a special estate which is now connected with its masters only by monetary relations.

We know what their living conditions were in 1846. Since then they have grown still worse. Some of the agricultural day-labourers (though their number grows smaller day by day) continue to live on the holdings of the farmers, in overcrowded huts whose hideousness far surpasses the worst examples the agricultural districts of England can offer, And this holds generally, with the exception of certain tracts of Ulster. It holds in the south, in the counties of Cork, Limerick, Kilkenny, etc.; in the east, in Wicklow, Wexford, etc.; in the centre, in King's County and Queen's County, Dublin, etc.; in the north, in Down, Antrim, Tyrone, etc.; and in the west, in Sligo, Roscommon, Mayo, Galway, etc. 'The agricultural labourers' huts,' an inspector cries out, 'are a disgrace to the Christianity and to the civilization of this country.'[29] To make these holes more attractive for the day-

28. *Reports from the Poor Law Inspectors, etc.*, pp. 29, 1.
29. ibid., p. 12.

labourers, the pieces of land which have belonged to them from time immemorial are systematically confiscated. 'The mere sense that they exist subject to this species of ban, on the part of the landlords and their agents, has . . . given birth in the minds of the labourers to corresponding sentiments of antagonism and dissatisfaction towards those by whom they are thus led to regard themselves as being treated as . . . a proscribed race.'[30]

The first act of the agricultural revolution was to sweep away the huts situated at the place of work. This was done on the largest scale, and as if in obedience to a command from on high. Thus many labourers were compelled to seek shelter in villages and towns. There they were thrown like refuse into garrets, holes, cellars and corners, in the worst slum districts. Thousands of Irish families who, even on the testimony of the English, blinded as the latter are by nationalist prejudices, are notable for their rare attachment to the domestic hearth, for the gaiety and the purity of their home life, suddenly found themselves transplanted into hotbeds of vice. The men are now obliged to seek work from the neighbouring farmers, and are only hired by the day, and therefore under the most precarious form of wage. Hence 'they sometimes have long distances to go to and from work, often get wet, and suffer much hardship, not infrequently ending in sickness, disease and want'.[31]

'The towns have had to receive from year to year what was deemed to be the surplus-labour of the rural division'[32] and then people still wonder that 'there is still a surplus of labour in the towns and villages, and either a scarcity or a threatened scarcity in some of the country divisions'.[33] The truth is that this scarcity only becomes perceptible 'in harvest-time, or during spring, or at such times as agricultural operations are carried on with activity; at other periods of the year many hands are idle';[34] that 'from the digging out of the main crop of potatoes in October until the early spring following . . . there is no employment for them';[35] and further, that during the active times they 'are subject to broken days and to all kinds of interruptions'.[36]

These results of the agricultural revolution – i.e. the change of arable into pasture land, the use of machinery, the most rigorous

30. ibid., p. 12.
32. ibid., p. 27.
34. ibid., p. 1.
36. ibid., p. 25.

31. ibid., p. 25.
33. ibid., p. 26.
35. ibid., p. 32.

economy of labour, etc. – are still further aggravated by the model landlords, who, instead of spending their rents in other countries, condescend to live in Ireland on their demesnes. In order that the law of supply and demand may not be infringed, these gentlemen draw their 'labour-supply . . . chiefly from their small tenants, who are obliged to attend when required to do the landlords' work, at rates of wages, in many instances, considerably under the current rates paid to ordinary labourers, and without regard to the inconvenience or loss to the tenant of being obliged to neglect his own business at critical periods of sowing or reaping'.[37]

The uncertainty and irregularity of employment, the constant return and long duration of gluts of labour, are all symptoms of a relative surplus population, and they therefore figure in the reports of the Poor Law inspectors as so many hardships suffered by the Irish agricultural proletariat. It will be recalled that we met with similar phenomena among the English agricultural proletariat. But the difference is that in England, an industrial country, the industrial reserve is recruited from the countryside, whereas in Ireland, an agricultural country, the agricultural reserve is recruited from the towns, the places of refuge of the agricultural labourers who have been driven from the land. In England, the surplus rural labourers are transformed into factory workers; in Ireland, those forced into the towns remain agricultural labourers even while they exert a downward pressure on urban wages, and are constantly sent back to the countryside in search of work.

The official inspectors sum up the material condition of the agricultural labourer as follows: 'Though living with the strictest frugality, his own wages are barely sufficient to provide food for an ordinary family and pay his rent, and he depends upon other sources for the means of clothing himself, his wife, and his children . . . The atmosphere of these cabins, combined with the other privations they are subjected to, has made this class particularly susceptible to typhus and consumption.'[38] In view of this, it is no wonder that, according to the unanimous testimony of the inspectors, a sombre discontent runs through the ranks of this class, that they long for the return of the past, loathe the present, despair of the future, give themselves up 'to the evil influence of agitators', and have only one fixed idea, to emigrate to America. This is the

37. *Reports from the Poor Law Inspectors, etc.*, p. 30.
38. ibid., pp. 21, 13.

land of Cockaigne, into which depopulation, the great Malthusian panacea, has transformed green Erin!

One example will be sufficient to show what a prosperous life is led by the Irish factory worker. 'On my recent visit to the North of Ireland,' says the English factory inspector Robert Baker, 'I met with the following evidence of effort in an Irish skilled workman to afford education to his children; and I give his evidence verbatim, as I took it from his mouth. That he was a skilled factory hand, may be understood when I say that he was employed on goods for the Manchester market. "Johnson: I am a beetler* and work from 6 in the morning till 11 at night, from Monday to Friday. Saturday we leave off at 6 p.m., and get three hours of it (for meals and rest). I have five children in all. For this work I get 10s. 6d. a week; my wife works here also, and gets 5s. a week. The oldest girl, who is 12, minds the house. She is also cook, and all the servant we have. She gets the young ones ready for school. A girl going past the house wakes me at half past five in the morning. My wife gets up and goes along with me. We get nothing (to eat) before we come to work. The child of 12 takes care of the little children all the day, and we get nothing till breakfast at 8. At 8 we go home. We get tea once a week; at other times we get stirabout, sometimes of oatmeal, sometimes of Indian meal, as we are able to get it. In the winter we get a little sugar and water to our Indian meal. In the summer we get a few potatoes, planting a small patch ourselves; and when they are done we get back to stirabout. Sometimes we get a little milk as it may be. So we go on from day to day, Sunday and week day, always the same the year round. I am always very much tired when I have done at night. We may see a bit of flesh meat sometimes, but very seldom. Three of our children attend school, for whom we pay 1d. a week a head. Our rent is 9d. a week. Peat for firing costs 1s. 6d. a fortnight at the very lowest." '[39] Such are Irish wages, such is Irish life!

In fact, the misery of Ireland is once again a daily theme of discussion in England. At the end of 1866 and the beginning of 1867, one of the Irish land magnates, Lord Dufferin, set about solving

39. *Reports of the Inspectors of Factories ... 31 October 1866*, p. 96.

---

* A man employed in embossing fabrics under the pressure of a set of rollers known as a beetling-machine.

the problem in *The Times*. '*Wie menschlich von solch' grossem Herrn!*'*

We saw from Table E that during 1864, out of a total profit of £4,368,610, three money-grubbers pocketed only £262,610; that in 1865, however, out of a total profit of £4,669,979, the same three virtuosos of 'abstinence' pocketed £274,528; in 1864, 26 money-grubbers took £646,377; in 1865, 28 money-grubbers took £736,448; in 1864, 121 money-grubbers took £1,066,912; in 1865, 186 money-grubbers took £1,320,996; in 1864, 1,131 money-grubbers took £2,150,818, nearly half of the total annual profit; and in 1865, 1,194 money-grubbers took £2,418,933, more than half of the total annual profit. But the lion's share of the yearly national rental which an inconceivably small number of land magnates in England, Scotland and Ireland swallow up is so monstrous that English statesmanship finds it inappropriate to afford the same statistical materials about the distribution of rents as about the distribution of profits. Lord Dufferin is one of those land magnates. That rent-rolls and profits can ever be 'excessive', or that the plethora of rent-rolls and profits is in any way connected with the plethora of popular miseries, is, of course, an idea as 'disreputable' as it is 'unsound'. Dufferin keeps to the facts. The fact is that, as the Irish population diminishes, the Irish rent-rolls swell; that depopulation benefits the landlords, thus also benefits the soil and therefore the people, that mere accessory of the soil. He declares, therefore, that Ireland is still over-populated, and the stream of emigration still flows too sluggishly. To be perfectly happy, Ireland must get rid of at least one-third of a million working men. Let no one imagine that this lord, who is also a poet, is a physician of the school of Sangrado,† who, if he failed to find an improvement in the condition of his patient, ordered blood-letting after blood-letting, until the patient lost his sickness when he had lost his blood. Lord Dufferin demands a new blood-letting of one-third of a million only, instead of about two millions; but in fact, unless these two millions are got rid of, the millennium cannot come to pass in Erin. The proof is easily given.

---

*'What humanity from such a great lord!' The quotation comes, in altered form, from Goethe's *Faust*, where the words of Mephistopheles in the 'Prologue in Heaven' (lines 352–3) are '*Es ist gar hübsch von einem grossen Herrn, So menschlich mit dem Teufel selbst zu sprechen*' ('It is indeed civil on the part of a great lord, to speak so nicely to the devil himself').

†A character from the novel *Gil Blas*, by Lesage.

Number and Extent of Farms in Ireland in 1864

1		2		3		4	
Farms not over 1 acre		Farms over 1, not over 5 acres		Farms over 5, not over 15 acres		Farms over 15, not over 30 acres	
No.	Acres	No.	Acres	No.	Acres	No.	Acres
48,653	25,394	82,037	288,916	176,368	1,836,310	136,578	3,051,343

5		6		7		8
Farms over 30, not over 50 acres		Farms over 50, not over 100 acres		Farms over 100 acres		Total area
No.	Acres	No.	Acres	No.	Acres	Acres
71,961	2,906,274	54,247	3,983,880	31,927	8,227,807	26,319,924[40]

Centralization has from 1851 to 1861 mainly destroyed farms of the first three categories, under 1 and not over 15 acres. This gives 307,058 'surplus' farmers, and, reckoning a low average of four persons per family, 1,228,232 persons. On the extravagant assumption that a quarter of these can again be absorbed after the completion of the agricultural revolution, there remain for emigration 921,174 persons. Categories 4, 5 and 6, including farms of between 15 and 100 acres, are, as has long been known in England, too small for the capitalist cultivation of corn, and almost infinitesimal from the point of view of sheep-breeding. On the same assumptions as before, therefore, there are a further 788,761 persons to emigrate: grand total, 1,709,532. And, as appetite grows with eating, Rent Roll's eyes will soon discover that Ireland with 3½ millions, still continues to be miserable, miserable because she is overpopulated. Therefore her depopulation must go still further, in order that she may fulfil her true destiny, to be an English sheep-walk and cattle pasture.[41]

40. The total area includes also peat, bogs and waste-land.
41. The famine and its consequences have been deliberately exploited both by the individual landlords and by the English Parliament through legislation so as to accomplish the agricultural revolution by force and to thin down the population of Ireland to the proportion satisfactory to the landlords. I shall show more fully in Volume 3 of this work, in the section on landed property, how this has been done. There also I shall return to the condition of the small

Like all good things in the world, this profitable mode of proceeding has its drawbacks. The accumulation of the Irish in America keeps pace with the accumulation of rents in Ireland. The Irishman, banished by the sheep and the ox, re-appears on the other side of the ocean as a Fenian. And there a young but gigantic republic rises, more and more threateningly, to face the old queen of the waves:

> *Acerba fata Romanos agunt*
> *Scelusque fraternae necis.**

---

farmers and the agricultural labourers.* For the present, just one quotation. Nassau W. Senior says the following, among other things, in his posthumous work, *Journals, Conversations, and Essays Relating to Ireland* (2 vols., London, 1868), ' "Well," said Dr G., "we have got our Poor Law and it is a great instrument for giving the victory to the landlords. Another, and a still more powerful instrument is emigration . . . No friend to Ireland can wish the war to be prolonged" (between the landlords and the small Celtic farmers) " – still less, that it should end by the victory of the tenants. The sooner it is over – the sooner Ireland becomes a grazing country, with the comparatively thin population which a grazing country requires, the better for all classes"' (op. cit., Vol. 2, p. 282). The English Corn Laws of 1815 secured to Ireland the monopoly of the free importation of corn into Great Britain. They therefore artificially encouraged the cultivation of corn. With the abolition of the Corn Laws in 1846, this monopoly was suddenly removed. Apart from all other circumstances, this event alone was sufficient to give a great impulse to the conversion of Irish arable land into pasture, to the concentration of farms, and to the eviction of small-scale cultivators. Having praised the fruitfulness of the Irish soil between 1815 and 1846, and proclaimed it loudly as destined for the cultivation of wheat by nature herself, English agronomists, economists and politicians suddenly discovered that it was good for nothing but the production of forage. M. Léonce de Lavergne has hastened to repeat this on the other side of the Channel.† It takes a 'serious' man, à la Lavergne, to be caught by such childishness.

*There is very little about Ireland in *Capital*, Vol. 3, as finally published, but Chapters 37 and 47 contain some comments on the situation of the small farmers.

† In his book *Économie rurale de l'Angleterre* (Paris, 1854), translated into English in 1855 as *The Rural Economy of England, Scotland, and Ireland.*

---

* 'A cruel fate torments the Romans, and the crime of fratricide' (Horace, *Epodes*, 7).

Part Eight

So-Called Primitive Accumulation

Chapter 26: The Secret of Primitive Accumulation

We have seen how money is transformed into capital; how surplus-value is made through capital, and how more capital is made from surplus-value. But the accumulation of capital presupposes surplus-value; surplus-value presupposes capitalist production; capitalist production presupposes the availability of considerable masses of capital and labour-power in the hands of commodity producers. The whole movement, therefore, seems to turn around in a never-ending circle, which we can only get out of by assuming a primitive accumulation (the 'previous accumulation' of Adam Smith*) which precedes capitalist accumulation; an accumulation which is not the result of the capitalist mode of production but its point of departure.

This primitive accumulation plays approximately the same role in political economy as original sin does in theology. Adam bit the apple, and thereupon sin fell on the human race. Its origin is supposed to be explained when it is told as an anecdote about the past. Long, long ago there were two sorts of people; one, the diligent, intelligent and above all frugal élite; the other, lazy rascals, spending their substance, and more, in riotous living. The legend of theological original sin tells us certainly how man came to be condemned to eat his bread in the sweat of his brow; but the history of economic original sin reveals to us that there are people to whom this is by no means essential. Never mind! Thus it came to pass that the former sort accumulated wealth, and the latter sort finally had nothing to sell except their own skins. And from this original sin dates the poverty of the great majority who, despite all their labour, have up to now nothing to sell but themselves, and the wealth of the few that increases constantly, although they have long ceased to work. Such insipid childishness is every day preached

* 'The accumulation of stock must, in the nature of things, be previous to the division of labour' (Adam Smith, *Wealth of Nations*, Bk II, Introduction).

to us in the defence of property. M. Thiers, for example, still repeats it with all the solemnity of a statesman to the French people, who were once so full of wit and ingenuity. But as soon as the question of property is at stake, it becomes a sacred duty to proclaim the standpoint of the nursery tale as the one thing fit for all age-groups and all stages of development. In actual history, it is a notorious fact that conquest, enslavement, robbery, murder, in short, force, play the greatest part. In the tender annals of political economy, the idyllic reigns from time immemorial. Right and 'labour' were from the beginning of time the sole means of enrichment, 'this year' of course always excepted. As a matter of fact, the methods of primitive accumulation are anything but idyllic.

In themselves, money and commodities are no more capital than the means of production and subsistence are. They need to be transformed into capital. But this transformation can itself only take place under particular circumstances, which meet together at this point: the confrontation of, and the contact between, two very different kinds of commodity owners; on the one hand, the owners of money, means of production, means of subsistence, who are eager to valorize the sum of values they have appropriated by buying the labour-power of others; on the other hand, free workers, the sellers of their own labour-power, and therefore the sellers of labour. Free workers, in the double sense that they neither form part of the means of production themselves, as would be the case with slaves, serfs, etc., nor do they own the means of production, as would be the case with self-employed peasant proprietors. The free workers are therefore free from, unencumbered by, any means of production of their own. With the polarization of the commodity-market into these two classes, the fundamental conditions of capitalist production are present. The capital-relation presupposes a complete separation between the workers and the ownership of the conditions for the realization of their labour. As soon as capitalist production stands on its own feet, it not only maintains this separation, but reproduces it on a constantly extending scale. The process, therefore, which creates the capital-relation can be nothing other than the process which divorces the worker from the ownership of the conditions of his own labour; it is a process which operates two transformations, whereby the social means of subsistence and production are turned into capital, and the immediate producers are turned into wage-labourers. So-called primitive accumulation, therefore, is nothing else than the historical process of divorcing the producer from the means of production. It appears as 'primitive' because it forms the pre-history of capital, and of the mode of production corresponding to capital.

The economic structure of capitalist society has grown out of the economic structure of feudal society. The dissolution of the latter set free the elements of the former.

The immediate producer, the worker, could dispose of his own person only after he had ceased to be bound to the soil, and ceased to be the slave or serf of another person. To become a free seller of labour-power, who carries his commodity wherever he can find a market for it, he must further have escaped from the regime of the guilds, their rules for apprentices and journeymen, and their restrictive labour regulations. Hence the historical movement which changes the producers into wage-labourers appears, on the one hand, as their emancipation from serfdom and from the fetters of the guilds, and it is this aspect of the movement which alone exists for our bourgeois historians. But, on the other hand, these newly freed men became sellers of themselves only after they had been robbed of all their own means of production, and all the guarantees of existence afforded by the old feudal arrangements. And this history, the history of their expropriation, is written in the annals of mankind in letters of blood and fire.

The industrial capitalists, these new potentates, had on their part not only to displace the guild masters of handicrafts, but also the feudal lords, who were in possession of the sources of wealth. In this respect, the rise of the industrial capitalists appears as the fruit of a victorious struggle both against feudal power and its disgusting prerogatives, and against the guilds, and the fetters by which the latter restricted the free development of production and the free exploitation of man by man. The knights of industry, however, only succeeded in supplanting the knights of the sword by making use of events in which they had played no part whatsoever. They rose by means as base as those once used by the Roman freedman to make himself the master of his *patronus*.

The starting-point of the development that gave rise both to the wage-labourer and to the capitalist was the enslavement of the worker. The advance made consisted in a change in the form of this servitude, in the transformation of feudal exploitation into capitalist exploitation. To understand the course taken by this change, we do not need to go back very far at all. Although we come across the first sporadic traces of capitalist production as early as the fourteenth or fifteenth centuries in certain towns of the Mediterranean, the capitalist era dates from the sixteenth century. Wherever it appears, the abolition of serfdom has long since been completed, and the most brilliant achievement of the Middle Ages, the existence of independent city-states, has already been on the wane for a considerable length of time.

In the history of primitive accumulation, all revolutions are epoch-making that act as levers for the capitalist class in the course of its formation; but this is true above all for those moments when great masses of men are suddenly and forcibly torn from their means of subsistence, and hurled onto the labour-market as free, unprotected and rightless proletarians. The expropriation of the agricultural producer, of the peasant, from the soil is the basis of the whole process. The history of this expropriation assumes different aspects in different countries, and runs through its various phases in different orders of succession, and at different historical epochs. Only in England, which we therefore take as our example, has it the classic form.[1]

1. In Italy, where capitalist production developed earliest, the dissolution of serfdom also took place earlier than elsewhere. There the serf was emancipated before he had acquired any prescriptive right to the soil. His emancipation at once transformed him into a 'free' proletarian, without any legal rights, and he found a master ready and waiting for him in the towns, which had been for the most part handed down from Roman times. When the revolution which took place in the world market at about the end of the fifteenth century had annihilated northern Italy's commercial supremacy, a movement in the reverse direction set in. The urban workers were driven *en masse* into the countryside, and gave a previously unheard-of impulse to small-scale cultivation, carried on in the form of market gardening.

Chapter 27: The Expropriation of the Agricultural Population from the Land

In England, serfdom had disappeared in practice by the last part of the fourteenth century. The immense majority of the population[1] consisted then, and to a still larger extent in the fifteenth century, of free peasant proprietors, however much the feudal trappings might disguise their absolute ownership. In the larger seigniorial domains, the old bailiff, himself a serf, was displaced by the free farmer. The wage-labourers of agriculture were partly peasants, who made use of their leisure time by working on the large estates, and partly an independent, special class of wage-labourer, relatively and absolutely few in numbers. The latter were also in practice peasants, farming independently for themselves, since, in addition to their wages, they were provided with arable land to the extent of four or more acres, together with their cottages. Moreover, like the other peasants, they enjoyed the right to exploit the common land, which gave pasture to their cattle, and furnished them with timber, fire-wood, turf, etc.[2] In all countries

1. 'The petty proprietors who cultivated their own fields with their own hands, and enjoyed a modest competence ... then formed a much more important part of the nation than at present. If we may trust the best statistical writers of that age, not less than 160,000 proprietors who, with their families, must have made up more than a seventh of the whole population, derived their subsistence from little freehold estates. The average income of these small landlords ... was estimated at between £60 and £70 a year. It was computed that the number of persons who tilled their own land was greater than the number of those who farmed the land of others' (Macaulay, *History of England*, 10th edn, London, 1854, Vol. 1, pp. 333, 334). Even in the last third of the seventeenth century, four-fifths of the English people were agriculturalists (loc. cit., p. 413). I quote Macaulay, because as a systematic falsifier of history he minimizes facts of this kind as much as possible.

2. We must never forget that even the serf was not only the owner of the piece of land attached to his house, although admittedly he was merely a tribute-paying owner, but also a co-proprietor of the common land. 'The peasant' (in Silesia) 'is a serf.' Nevertheless these serfs possess common lands. 'It has not yet been possible to persuade the Silesians to partition the common

of Europe, feudal production is characterized by division of the soil amongst the greatest possible number of sub-feudatories. The might of the feudal lord, like that of the sovereign, depended not on the length of his rent-roll, but on the number of his subjects, and the latter depended on the number of peasant proprietors.[3] Thus although the soil of England, after the Norman conquest, was divided up into gigantic baronies, one of which often included some 900 of the old Anglo-Saxon lordships, it was strewn with small peasant properties, only interspersed here and there with great seigniorial domains. Such conditions, together with the urban prosperity so characteristic of the fifteenth century, permitted the development of that popular wealth Chancellor Fortescue depicted so eloquently in his *De laudibus legum Angliae*, but they ruled out wealth in the form of capital.

The prelude to the revolution that laid the foundation of the capitalist mode of production was played out in the last third of the fifteenth century and the first few decades of the sixteenth. A mass of 'free' and unattached proletarians was hurled onto the labour-market by the dissolution of the bands of feudal retainers, who, as Sir James Steuart correctly remarked, 'everywhere uselessly filled house and castle'.* Although the royal power, itself a product of bourgeois development, forcibly hastened the dissolution of these bands of retainers in its striving for absolute sovereignty, it was by no means the sole cause of it. It was rather that the great feudal lords, in their defiant opposition to the king and Parliament, created an incomparably larger proletariat by forcibly driving the peasantry from the land, to which the latter had the same feudal title as the lords themselves, and by usurpation of the common lands. The rapid expansion of wool manufacture in Flanders and the corresponding rise in the price of wool in

---

lands, whereas in the *Neumark* there is scarcely a village where this partition has not been implemented with very great success' (Mirabeau, *De la monarchie prussienne*, London, 1788, Vol. 2, pp. 125–6).

3. Japan, with its purely feudal organization of landed property and its developed small-scale agriculture, gives a much truer picture of the European Middle Ages than all our history books, dictated as these are, for the most part, by bourgeois prejudices. It is far too easy to be 'liberal' at the expense of the Middle Ages.

---

* James Steuart, *An Inquiry into the Principles of Political Economy*, Vol. 1, Dublin, 1770, p. 52.

England provided the direct impulse for thes eevictions. The old nobility had been devoured by the great feudal wars. The new nobility was the child of its time, for which money was the power of all powers. Transformation of arable land into sheep-walks was therefore its slogan. Harrison, in his *Description of England, prefixed to Holinshed's Chronicles*, describes how the expropriation of small peasants is ruining the country. 'What care our great incroachers?' The dwellings of the peasants and the cottages of the labourers were razed to the ground or doomed to decay. 'If,' says Harrison, 'the old records of euerie manour be sought . . . it will soon appear that in some manour seventeene, eighteene, or twentie houses are shrunk . . . that England was neuer less furnished with people than at the present . . . Of cities and townes either utterly decaied or more than a quarter or half diminished, though some one be a little increased here or there; of townes pulled downe for sheepe-walks, and no more but the lordships now standing in them . . . I could saie somewhat.'* The complaints of these old chroniclers are always exaggerated, but they faithfully reflect the impression made on contemporaries by the revolution in the relations of production. A comparison between the writings of Chancellor Fortescue and Thomas More reveals the gulf between the fifteenth and the sixteenth centuries. As Thornton rightly says, the English working class was precipitated without any transitional stages from its golden age to its iron age.†

Legislation shrunk back in the face of this immense change. It did not yet stand at that high level of civilization where the 'wealth of the nation' (i.e. the formation of capital and the reckless exploitation and impoverishment of the mass of the people) figures as the *ultima Thule‡* of all statecraft. In his history of Henry VII Bacon says this: 'Inclosures at that time' (1489) 'began to be more frequent, whereby arable land, which could not be manured§ without people and families, was turned into pasture, which was easily rid by a few herdsmen; and tenancies for years, lives, and at will, whereupon much of the yeomanry lived, were turned into demesnes. This bred a decay of people, and, by consequence, a decay of towns, churches, tithes, and the like . . . In remedying of

* William Harrison, *Description of England*, Chapter 19, 'Of Parks and Warrens', ed. G. Edelen, Ithaca, N.Y., 1968, pp. 257–8.
† W. T. Thornton, op. cit., p. 185.
‡ 'uttermost limit'.
§ i.e. cultivated.

this inconvenience the king's wisdom was admirable, and the parliament's at that time ... They took a course to take away depopulating inclosures, and depopulating pasturage.'* An Act of Henry VII, 1489, c. 19, forbade the destruction of all 'houses of husbandry' possessing 20 acres of land. By another Act, 25 Henry VIII [c. 13], this law was renewed. It recites, among other things, that 'many farms and large flocks of cattle, especially of sheep, are concentrated in the hands of a few men, whereby the rent of land has much risen, and tillage has fallen off, churches and houses have been pulled down, and marvellous numbers of people have been deprived of the means wherewith to maintain themselves and their families.' The Act therefore ordains the re-building of the decayed farmsteads, and fixes a proportion be-tween corn land and pasture land, etc. The same Act recites that some owners possess 24,000 sheep, and limits the number to be owned to 2,000.[4] The cries of the people and the legislation directed, for 150 years after Henry VII, against the expropriation of the small farmers and peasants, were both equally fruitless. Bacon, without knowing it, reveals to us the secret of their lack of success. 'The device of King Henry VII,' says Bacon, in the twenty-ninth of his *Essays, Civil and Moral*, 'was profound and admirable, in making farms and houses of husbandry of a standard; that is, maintained with such a proportion of land unto them as may breed a subject to live in convenient plenty and no servile condition, and to keep the plough in the hands of the owners and not mere hirelings.'[5] What the capitalist system demanded was

4. In his *Utopia*, Thomas More speaks of the curious land where 'sheep ... swallow down the very men themselves' (*Utopia*, tr. Robinson, ed. Arber, London, 1869, p. 41).

5. Elsewhere, Bacon discusses the connection between a free, well-to-do peasantry, and good infantry. 'This did wonderfully concern the might and mannerhood of the kingdom to have farms as it were of a standard sufficient to maintain an able body out of penury, and did in effect amortise a great part of the lands of the kingdom unto the hold and occupation of the yeomanry or middle people, of a condition between gentlemen, and cottagers and peasants ... For it hath been held by the general opinion of men of best judgment in the wars ... that the principal strength of an army consisteth in the infantry or foot. And to make good infantry it requireth men bred, not in a servile or indigent fashion, but in some free and plentiful manner. Therefore, if a state run most to noblemen and gentlemen, and that the husbandmen and plough-

*F. Bacon, *The Reign of Henry VII, Verbatim Reprint from Kennet's 'England'*, ed. 1719, London, 1870, p. 307.

the reverse of this: a degraded and almost servile condition of the mass of the people, their transformation into mercenaries, and the transformation of their means of labour into capital. During this transitional period, legislation also strove to retain the four acres of land by the cottage of the agricultural wage-labourer, and forbade him to take lodgers into his cottage. In the reign of Charles I, in 1627, Roger Crocker of Fontmill was condemned for having built a cottage on the manor of Fontmill without four acres of land attached to the same in perpetuity. As late as 1638, in the same reign, a royal commission was appointed to enforce the implementation of the old laws, especially the law referring to the four acres of land. Even Cromwell forbade the building of a house within four miles of London unless it was endowed with four acres of land. As late as the first half of the eighteenth century, complaint is made if the cottage of the agricultural labourer does not possess an adjunct of one or two acres of land. Nowadays the labourer is lucky if it is furnished with a small garden, or if he may rent a few roods of land at a great distance from his cottage. 'Landlords and farmers,' says Dr Hunter, 'work here hand in hand. A few acres to the cottage would make the labourers too independent.'[6]

The process of forcible expropriation of the people received a new and terrible impulse in the sixteenth century from the Reformation, and the consequent colossal spoliation of church property. The Catholic church was, at the time of the Reformation, the feudal proprietor of a great part of the soil of England. The dissolution of the monasteries, etc., hurled their inmates into the proletariat. The estates of the church were to a large extent given away to rapacious royal favourites, or sold at a nominal price to speculating farmers and townsmen, who drove out the

---

men be but as their workfolks and labourers, or else mere cottagers (which are but hous'd beggars), you may have a good cavalry, but never good stable bands of foot . . . And this is to be seen in France, and Italy, and some other parts abroad, where in effect all is noblesse or peasantry . . . insomuch that they are inforced to employ mercenary bands of Switzers and the like, for their battalions of foot; whereby also it comes to pass that those nations have much people and few soldiers' (F. Bacon, op. cit., p. 308).

6. Dr Hunter, op. cit., p. 134. 'The quantity of land assigned' (under the old laws) 'would now be judged too great for labourers, and rather as likely to convert them into small farmers' (George Roberts, *The Social History of the People of the Southern Counties of England in Past Centuries*, London, 1856, pp. 184–5).

old-established hereditary sub-tenants in great numbers, and threw their holdings together. The legally guaranteed property of the poorer folk in a part of the church's tithes was quietly confiscated.[7] '*Pauper ubique jacet*'* cried Queen Elizabeth, after a journey through England. In the forty-third year of her reign it finally proved necessary to recognize pauperism officially by the introduction of the poor-rate. 'The authors of this law seem to have been ashamed to state the grounds of it, for' (contrary to traditional usage) 'it has no preamble whatever.'[8] The poor-rate was declared perpetual by 16 Charles I, c. 4, and in fact only in 1834 did it take a new and severer form.[9] These immediate results

---

7. 'The right of the poor to share in the tithe, is established by the tenour of ancient statutes' (Tuckett, op. cit., Vol. 2, pp. 804–5).

8. William Cobbett, *A History of the Protestant 'Reformation'*, para. 471.

9. The 'spirit' of Protestantism may be seen from the following, among other things. In the south of England certain landed proprietors and well-to-do farmers put their heads together and propounded ten questions as to the right interpretation of the Elizabethan Poor Law. These they laid before a celebrated jurist of that time, Sergeant Snigge (later a judge under James I), for his opinion. 'Question 9 – Some of the more wealthy farmers in the parish have devised a skilful mode by which all the trouble of executing this Act might be avoided. They have proposed that we shall erect a prison in the parish, and then give notice to the neighbourhood, that if any persons are disposed to farm the poor of this parish, they do give in sealed proposals, on a certain day, of the lowest price at which they will take them off our hands; and that they will be authorised to refuse to any one unless he be shut up in the aforesaid prison. The proposers of this plan conceive that there will be found in the adjoining counties, persons, who, being unwilling to labour and not possessing substance or credit to take a farm or ship, so as to live without labour, may be induced to make a very advantageous offer to the parish. If any of the poor perish under the contractor's care, the sin will lie at his door, as the parish will have done its duty by them. We are, however, apprehensive that the present Act will not warrant a prudential measure of this kind; but you are to learn that the rest of the freeholders of the county, and of the adjoining county of B, will very readily join in instructing their members to propose an Act to enable the parish to contract with a person to lock up and work the poor; and to declare that if any person shall refuse to be so locked up and worked, he shall be entitled to no relief. This, it is hoped, will prevent persons in distress from wanting relief, and be the means of keeping down parishes' (R. Blakey, *The History of Political Literature from the Earliest Times*, London, 1855, Vol. 2, pp. 84–5). In Scotland, the abolition of serfdom took place some centuries later than in England. Fletcher of Saltoun declared as late as 1698, in the Scottish Parliament, 'The number of beggars in Scotland is reckoned at not less than 200,000. The only remedy that I, a republican on principle, can suggest, is to restore the old state of serfdom, to make slaves of all those

---

*'The poor man is everywhere in subjection' (Ovid, *Fasti*, Bk I, verse 218).

of the Reformation were not its most lasting ones. The property of the church formed the religious bulwark of the old conditions of landed property. With its fall, these conditions could no longer maintain their existence.[10]

Even in the last few decades of the seventeenth century, the yeomanry, the class of independent peasants, were more numerous than the class of farmers. They had formed the backbone of Cromwell's strength, and, on the admission of Macaulay himself, stood in favourable contrast to the drunken squires and their servants, the country clergy, who had to marry their masters' cast-off mistresses. By about 1750 the yeomanry had disappeared,[11] and so, by the last decade of the eighteenth century, had the last trace of the common land of the agricultural labourer. We leave on one side here the purely economic driving forces behind the agricultural revolution. We deal only with the violent means employed.

After the restoration of the Stuarts, the landed proprietors carried out, by legal means, an act of usurpation which was effected everywhere on the Continent without any legal formality. They abolished the feudal tenure of land, i.e. they got rid of all its obligations to the state, 'indemnified' the state by imposing taxes on the peasantry and the rest of the people, established for

who are unable to provide for their own subsistence.' Eden (op. cit., Bk I, Ch. 1, pp. 60–61) says: 'The decrease of villeinage seems necessarily to have been the era of the origin of the poor. Manufactures and commerce are the two parents of our national poor.' Eden, like our Scottish republican on principle, is only wrong on this point: not the abolition of villeinage, but the abolition of the property of the agricultural labourer in the soil made him a proletarian, and eventually a pauper. In France, where the expropriation was effected in another way, the Ordinance of Moulins, 1571, and the Edict of 1656, correspond to the English Poor Laws.

10. Mr Rogers, although he was at the time Professor of Political Economy in the University of Oxford, the very centre of Protestant orthodoxy, emphasized the pauperization of the mass of the people by the Reformation in his preface to the *History of Agriculture*.

11. *A Letter to Sir T. C. Bunbury, Bart., on the High Price of Provisions. By a Suffolk Gentleman*, Ipswich, 1795, p. 4. Even that fanatical advocate of the system of large farms, the author of the *Inquiry into the Connection between the Present Price of Provisions, and the Size of Farms, etc.*, London, 1773 [J. Arbuthnot], says on p. 139: 'I most lament the loss of our yeomanry, that set of men who really kept up the independence of this nation; and sorry I am to see their lands now in the hands of monopolizing lords, tenanted out to small farmers, who hold their leases on such conditions as to be little better than vassals ready to attend a summons on every mischievous occasion.'

themselves the rights of modern private property in estates to which they had only a feudal title, and, finally, passed those laws of settlement which had the same effect on the English agricultural labourer, *mutatis mutandis*, as the edict of the Tartar Boris Godunov had on the Russian peasantry.*

The 'glorious Revolution' brought into power, along with William of Orange,[12] the landed and capitalist profit-grubbers. They inaugurated the new era by practising on a colossal scale the thefts of state lands which had hitherto been managed more modestly. These estates were given away, sold at ridiculous prices, or even annexed to private estates by direct seizure.[13] All this happened without the slightest observance of legal etiquette. The Crown lands thus fraudulently appropriated, together with the stolen Church estates, in so far as these were not lost again during the republican revolution, form the basis of the present princely domains of the English oligarchy.[14] The bourgeois capita-

12. On the private morality of this bourgeois hero, among other things: 'The large grant of lands in Ireland to Lady Orkney, in 1695, is a public instance of the king's affection, and the lady's influence ... Lady Orkney's endearing offices are supposed to have been – *foeda labiorum ministeria*.'* (In the Sloane Manuscript Collection, at the British Museum, No. 4224. The manuscript is entitled: *The Character and Behaviour of King William, Sunderland, etc., as Represented in Original Letters to the Duke of Shrewsbury from Somers, Halifax, Oxford, Secretary Vernon, etc.* It is full of *curiosa*.)

13. 'The illegal alienation of the Crown Estates, partly by sale and partly by gift, is a scandalous chapter in English history ... a gigantic fraud on the nation' (F. W. Newman, *Lectures on Political Economy*, London, 1851, pp. 129–30). [Added by Engels to the fourth German edition:] For details as to how the present large landed proprietors of England came into their possessions, see *Our Old Nobility. By Noblesse Oblige* (N. H. Evans), London, 1879.

14. Read for example Edmund Burke's pamphlet† on the ducal house of Bedford, whose offshoot was Lord John Russell, the 'tomtit of liberalism'.‡

*'Base services performed with the lips'.

† This was the pamphlet produced by Burke in 1796, entitled *A Letter from the Right Honourable Edmund Burke to a Noble Lord, on the Attacks Made upon Him and His Pension, in the House of Lords, by the Duke of Bedford and the Earl of Lauderdale, Early in the Present Session of Parliament*. In it he turned on his former Whig allies, from whom he had parted over the question of the war with France, and demonstrated that the Russells had wrested from the English people a 'quite incredible' number of estates over the centuries.

‡ Cobbett compared Lord John Russell with a tom-tit 'endeavouring to put all right with the old oak of the British Constitution by picking at a nest of

---

*This was the Edict of 1597, by which peasants who had fled from their lords could be pursued for five years and forcibly returned to them when caught.

lists favoured the operation, with the intention, among other things, of converting the land into a merely commercial commodity, extending the area of large-scale agricultural production, and increasing the supply of free and rightless proletarians driven from their land. Apart from this, the new landed aristocracy was the natural ally of the new bankocracy, of newly hatched high finance, and of the large manufacturers, at that time dependent on protective duties. The English bourgeoisie acted quite as wisely in its own interest as the Swedish burghers, who did the opposite: hand in hand with the bulwark of their economic strength, the peasantry, they helped the kings in their forcible resumption of crown lands from the oligarchy, in the years after 1604 and later on under Charles X and Charles XI.

Communal property – which is entirely distinct from the state property we have just been considering – was an old Teutonic institution which lived on under the cover of feudalism. We have seen how its forcible usurpation, generally accompanied by the turning of arable into pasture land, begins at the end of the fifteenth century and extends into the sixteenth. But at that time the process was carried on by means of individual acts of violence against which legislation, for a hundred and fifty years, fought in vain. The advance made by the eighteenth century shows itself in this, that the law itself now becomes the instrument by which the people's land is stolen, although the big-farmers made use of their little independent methods as well.[15] The Parliamentary form of the robbery is that of 'Bills for Inclosure of Commons', in other words decrees by which the landowners grant themselves the people's land as private property, decrees of expropriation of the people. Sir F. M. Eden refutes his own crafty special pleading, in which he tries to represent communal property as the private

15. 'The farmers forbid cottagers to keep any living creatures besides themselves and children, under the pretence that if they keep any beasts or poultry, they will steal from the farmers' barns for their support; they also say, keep the cottagers poor and you will keep them industrious, etc., but the real fact, I believe, is that the farmers may have the whole right of common to themselves' (*A Political Inquiry into the Consequences of Enclosing Waste Lands*, London, 1785, p. 75).

animalculae seated in the half-rotten bark of one of the meanest branches'. This apt characterization of Russell's efforts at parliamentary reform between 1813 and 1830 was adopted by Marx as the keynote for his article 'Lord John Russell' in the *New York Daily Tribune* of 28 August 1855.

property of the great landlords who have taken the place of the feudal lords, when he himself demands a 'general Act of Parliament for the enclosure of Commons' (thereby admitting that a parliamentary *coup d'état* is necessary for their transformation into private property), and moreover calls on the legislature to indemnify the expropriated poor.[16]

While the place of the independent yeoman was taken by tenants at will, small farmers on yearly leases, a servile rabble dependent on the arbitrary will of the landlords, the systematic theft of communal property was of great assistance, alongside the theft of the state domains, in swelling those large farms which were called in the eighteenth century capital farms,[17] or merchant farms,[18] and in 'setting free' the agricultural population as a proletariat for the needs of industry.

The eighteenth century, however, did not yet recognize as fully as the nineteenth the identity between the wealth of the nation and the poverty of the people. Hence the very vigorous polemic, in the economic literature of that time, on the 'enclosure of commons'. From the mass of material that lies before me, I give a few extracts chosen for the strong light they throw on the circumstances of the time. 'In several parishes of Hertfordshire,' writes one indignant person, 'twenty-four farms, numbering on the average 50 to 150 acres, have been melted up into three farms.'[19] 'In Northamptonshire and Leicestershire the enclosure of common lands has taken place on a very large scale, and most of the new lordships, resulting from the enclosure, have been turned into pasturage, in consequence of which many lordships have not now 50 acres ploughed yearly, in which 1,500 were ploughed formerly. The ruins of former dwelling-houses, barns, stables, etc.' are the sole traces of the former inhabitants. 'An hundred houses and families have in some open field villages . . . dwindled to eight or ten . . . The landholders in most parishes that have been enclosed only fifteen or twenty years, are very few in comparison of the

16. Eden, op. cit., Preface [pp. xvii, xix].

17. *Two Letters on the Flour Trade, and the Dearness of Corn. By a Person in Business*, London, 1767, pp. 19–20.

18. *An Enquiry into the Causes of the Present High Price of Provisions*, London, 1767, p. 111, note. This good book, published anonymously, was written by the Rev. Nathaniel Forster.

19. Thomas Wright, *A Short Address to the Public on the Monopoly of Large Farms*, 1779, pp. 2, 3.

numbers who occupied them in their open-field state. It is no un-common thing for four or five wealthy graziers to engross a large enclosed lordship which was before in the hands of twenty or thirty farmers, and as many smaller tenants and proprietors. All these are hereby thrown out of their livings with their families and many other families who were chiefly employed and supported by them.'[20] It was not only land that lay waste, but often also land that was still under cultivation, being cultivated either in common or held under a definite rent paid to the community, that was annexed by the neighbouring landowners under pretext of enclosure. 'I have here in view enclosures of open fields and lands already improved. It is acknowledged by even the writers in defence of enclosures that these diminished villages increase the monopolies of farms, raise the prices of provisions, and pro-duce depopulation . . . and even the enclosure of waste lands (as now carried on) bears hard on the poor, by depriving them of a part of their subsistence, and only goes towards increasing farms already too large.'[21] 'When,' says Dr Price, 'this land gets into the hands of a few great farmers, the consequence must be that the little farmers' (previously described by him as 'a multitude of little proprietors and tenants, who maintain themselves and families by the produce of the ground they occupy by sheep kept on a common, by poultry, hogs, etc., and who therefore have little occasion to purchase any of the means of subsistence') 'will be converted into a body of men who earn their subsistence by working for others, and who will be under a necessity of going to market for all they want . . . There will, perhaps, be more labour, because there will be more compulsion to it . . . Towns and manu-factures will increase, because more will be driven to them in quest of places and employment. This is the way in which the engrossing of farms actually operates. And this is the way in which, for many years, it has been actually operating in this kingdom.'[22] He sums up the effect of the enclosures in this way: 'Upon the whole, the circumstances of the lower ranks of men

20. Rev. Addington, *Inquiry into the Reasons for or against Inclosing Open Fields*, London, 1772, pp. 37–43 passim.

21. Dr R. Price, op. cit., Vol. 2, pp. 155–6. Forster, Addington, Kent, Price and James Anderson should be read and compared with the miserable prattle of the sycophantic MacCulloch, in his catalogue *The Literature of Political Economy*, London, 1845.

22. Price, op. cit., p. 147.

are altered in almost every respect for the worse. From little occupiers of land, they are reduced to the state of day-labourers and hirelings; and, at the same time, their subsistence in that state has become more difficult.'[23] In fact, the usurpation of the common lands and the accompanying revolution in agriculture had such an acute effect on the agricultural labourers that, even according to Eden, their wages began to fall below the minimum between 1765 and 1780, and to be supplemented by official Poor Law relief. Their wages, he says, 'were not more than enough for the absolute necessaries of life'.

Let us hear for a moment a defender of enclosures and an opponent of Dr Price. 'Nor is it a consequence that there must be depopulation, because men are not seen wasting their labour in the open field ... If, by converting the little farmers into a body of men who must work for others, more labour is produced, it is an advantage which the nation' (to which, of course, the people who have been 'converted' do not belong) 'should wish for ... the produce being greater when their joint labours are employed on one farm, there will be a surplus for manufactures, and by this means

23. Price, op. cit., p. 159. We are reminded of ancient Rome. 'The rich had got possession of the greater part of the undivided land. They were confident that, in the conditions of the time, these possessions would never be taken back again from them, and they therefore bought some of the pieces of land lying near theirs, and belonging to the poor, with the acquiescence of the latter, and the rest they took by force, so that now they were cultivating widely extended domains, instead of isolated fields. Then they employed slaves in agriculture and cattle-breeding, because the free men had been taken away from labour to do military service. The possession of slaves brought great gains to them, in that the slaves, on account of their exemption from military service, could multiply without risk and therefore had great numbers of children. Thus the powerful men drew all wealth to themselves, and the whole land swarmed with slaves. The Italians, on the other hand, were always decreasing in number, worn down as they were by poverty, taxation, and military service. Even in times of peace, they were doomed to complete inactivity, because the rich were in possession of the soil, and used slaves instead of free men to cultivate it' (Appian, *The Roman Civil Wars*, Bk I, Ch. 7). This passage refers to the time before the Licinian Law.* Military service, which hastened to so great an extent the ruin of the Roman plebeians, was also the chief means by which, as in a forcing-house, Charlemagne brought about the transformation of free German peasants into serfs and bondsmen.

*The Licinian Law, passed in 367 B.C., was an attempt to remedy these inequalities. Appian says it provided that 'nobody should hold more than 500 *jugera* of public land, or pasture on it more than 100 cattle or 500 sheep' (*The Roman Civil Wars*, Bk. I, Ch. 8).

manufactures, one of the mines of the nation, will increase, in proportion to the quantity of corn produced.'[24]

The stoical peace of mind with which the political economist regards the most shameless violation of the 'sacred rights of property' and the grossest acts of violence against persons, as soon as they are necessary in order to lay the foundations of the capitalist mode of production, is shown by Sir F. M. Eden, who is, moreover, Tory and 'philanthropic' in his political colouring. The whole series of thefts, outrages and popular misery that accompanied the forcible expropriation of the people, from the last third of the fifteenth to the end of the eighteenth century, leads him merely to this 'comfortable' concluding reflection: 'The due proportion between arable land and pasture had to be established. During the whole of the fourteenth and the greater part of the fifteenth century, there was 1 acre of pasture to 2, 3, and even 4 of arable land. About the middle of the sixteenth century the proportion was changed to 2 acres of pasture to 2, later on, to 2 acres of pasture to 1 of arable, until at last the just proportion of 3 acres of pasture to 1 of arable land was attained.'

By the nineteenth century, the very memory of the connection between the agricultural labourer and communal property had, of course, vanished. To say nothing of more recent times – have the agricultural population received a farthing's compensation for the 3,511,770 acres of common land which between 1801 and 1831 were stolen from them and presented to the landlords by the landlords, through the agency of Parliament?

The last great process of expropriation of the agricultural population from the soil is, finally, the so-called 'clearing of estates', i.e. the sweeping of human beings off them. All the English methods hitherto considered culminated in 'clearing'. As we saw in the description of modern conditions given in a previous chapter, when there are no more independent peasants to get rid of, the 'clearing' of cottages begins; so that the agricultural labourers no longer find on the soil they cultivate even

24. [J. Arbuthnot,] *An Inquiry into the Connection between the Present Price of Provisions, etc.*, pp. 124, 129. Here is a similar argument, but with an opposite tendency: 'Working-men are driven from their cottages and forced into the towns to seek for employment; but then a larger surplus is obtained, and thus capital is augmented' ([R. B. Seeley,] *The Perils of the Nation*, 2nd edn, London, 1843, p. xiv.)

the necessary space for their own housing. But what 'clearing of estates' really and properly signifies, we learn only in the Highlands of Scotland, the promised land of modern romantic novels. There the process is distinguished by its systematic character, by the magnitude of the scale on which it is carried out at one blow (in Ireland landlords have gone as far as sweeping away several villages at once; but in the Highlands areas as large as German principalities are dealt with), and finally by the peculiar form of property under which the embezzled lands were held.

The Highland Celts were organized in clans, each of which was the owner of the land on which it was settled. The representative of the clan, its chief or 'great man', was only the titular owner of this property, just as the Queen of England is the titular owner of all the national soil. When the English government succeeded in suppressing the intestine wars of these 'great men', and their constant incursions into the Lowland plains, the chiefs of the clans by no means gave up their time-honoured trade as robbers; they merely changed its form. On their own authority, they transformed their nominal right to the land into a right of private property, and as this came up against resistance on the part of their clansmen, they resolved to drive them out openly and by force. 'A king of England might as well claim to drive his subjects into the sea,' says Professor Newman.[25] This revolution, which began in Scotland after the last rising of the followers of the Pretender,* can be followed through its first phases in the writings of Sir James Steuart[26] and James Anderson.[27] In the eighteenth century the Gaels were both driven from the land and forbidden to emigrate, with a view to driving them forcibly to

25. F. W. Newman, op. cit., p. 132.

26. Steuart says: 'If you compare the rent of these lands' (he erroneously includes in this economic category the tribute paid by the taksmen* to the chief of the clan) 'with the extent, it appears very small. If you compare it with the numbers fed upon the farm, you will find that an estate in the Highlands maintains, perhaps, ten times as many people as another of the same value in a good and fertile province' (op. cit., Vol. 1, Ch. 16, p. 104).

27. James Anderson, *Observations on the Means of Exciting a Spirit of National Industry, etc.*, Edinburgh, 1777.

*The taksmen were the immediate subordinates of the laird, or chief, of the clan. They were the actual holders of the land, the 'tak', and paid a nominal sum to the laird in recognition of his suzerainty.

*The rising of 1745–6 in favour of the Young Pretender, Charles Edward Stuart.

Glasgow and other manufacturing towns.[28] As an example of the method used in the nineteenth century,[29] the 'clearings' made by the Duchess of Sutherland will suffice here. This person, who had been well instructed in economics, resolved, when she succeeded to the headship of the clan, to undertake a radical economic cure, and to turn the whole county of Sutherland, the population of which had already been reduced to 15,000 by similar processes, into a sheep-walk. Between 1814 and 1820 these 15,000 inhabitants, about 3,000 families, were systematically hunted and rooted out. All their villages were destroyed and burnt, all their fields turned into pasturage. British soldiers enforced this mass of evictions, and came to blows with the inhabitants. One old woman was burnt to death in the flames of the hut she refused to leave. It was in this manner that this fine lady appropriated 794,000 acres of land which had belonged to the clan from time immemorial. She assigned to the expelled inhabitants some 6,000 acres on the sea-shore – 2 acres per family. The 6,000 acres had until this time lain waste, and brought in no income to their owners. The Duchess, in the nobility of her heart,

28. In 1860 some of the people who had been expropriated by force were exported to Canada under false pretences. Others fled to the mountains and neighbouring islands. They were followed by the police, came to blows with them and escaped.

29. 'In the Highlands of Scotland,' says Buchanan, in his commentary on Adam Smith, published in 1814, 'the ancient state of property is daily subverted . . . The landlord, without regard to the hereditary tenant' (this too is a wrongly applied category in this case) 'now offers his land to the highest bidder, who, if he is an improver, instantly adopts a new system of cultivation. The land, formerly overspread with small tenants or labourers, was peopled in proportion to its produce, but under the new system of improved cultivation and increased rents, the largest possible produce is obtained at the least possible expense; and the useless hands being, with this view, removed, the population is reduced, not to what the land will maintain, but to what it will employ . . . The dispossessed tenants . . . seek a subsistence in the neighbouring towns, etc.' (David Buchanan, *Observations on, etc.*, *A. Smith's Wealth of Nations*, Edinburgh, 1814, Vol. 4, p. 144). 'The Scotch grandees dispossessed families as they would grub up coppice-wood, and they treated villages and their people as Indians harassed with wild beasts do, in their vengeance, a jungle with tigers . . . Man is bartered for a fleece or a carcase of mutton, nay, held cheaper . . . Why, how much worse is it than the intention of the Moguls, who, when they had broken into the northern provinces of China, proposed in council to exterminate the inhabitants, and convert the land into pasture. This proposal many Highland proprietors have effected in their own country against their own countrymen' (George Ensor, *An Inquiry Concerning the Population of Nations*, London, 1818, pp. 215–16).

actually went so far as to let these waste lands at an average rent of 2s. 6d. per acre to the clansmen, who for centuries had shed their blood for her family. She divided the whole of the stolen land of the clan into twenty-nine huge sheep farms, each inhabited by a single family, for the most part imported English farm-servants. By 1825 the 15,000 Gaels had already been replaced by 131,000 sheep. The remnant of the original inhabitants, who had been flung onto the sea-shore, tried to live by catching fish. They became amphibious, and lived, as an English writer says, half on land and half on water, and withal only half on both.[30]

But the splendid Gaels had now to suffer still more bitterly for their romantic mountain idolization of the 'great men' of the clan. The smell of their fish rose to the noses of the great men. They scented some profit in it, and let the sea-shore to the big London fishmongers. For the second time the Gaels were driven out.[31]

Finally, however, part of the sheep-walks were turned into deer preserves. Everyone knows that there are no true forests in England. The deer in the parks of the great are demure domestic cattle, as fat as London aldermen. Scotland is therefore the last refuge of the 'noble passion'. 'In the Highlands,' reports Somers in 1848, 'new forests are springing up like mushrooms. Here, on one side of Gaick, you have the new forest of Glenfeshie; and there on the other you have the new forest of Ardverikie. In the same line you have the Black Mount, an immense waste also recently erected. From east to west – from the neighbourhood of

30. When the present Duchess of Sutherland entertained Mrs Beecher Stowe, authoress of *Uncle Tom's Cabin*, with great magnificence in London to show her sympathy for the Negro slaves of the American republic – a sympathy she prudently forgot, along with her fellow-aristocrats, during the Civil War, when every 'noble' English heart beat for the slave-owners – I gave the facts about the Sutherland slaves in the *New York Tribune*.* (Some extracts from this were printed by Carey in *The Slave Trade*, Philadelphia, 1853, pp. 202–3.) My article was reprinted in a Scottish newspaper, and it called forth a nice polemic between that newspaper and the sycophants of the Sutherlands.

31. Interesting details on this fish trade will be found in Mr David Urquhart's *Portfolio, New Series*. Nassau W. Senior, in his posthumous work, already quoted, describes 'the proceedings in Sutherlandshire' as 'one of the most beneficent clearings since the memory of man' (op. cit., p. 282).

*'The Duchess of Sutherland and Slavery', *New York Daily Tribune*, 9 February 1853. This article was published in almost identical form on 12 March 1853 in the Chartist *People's Paper*, from where it is reprinted in Karl Marx and Frederick Engels, *Articles on Britain*, Moscow, 1971, pp. 143–9.

Aberdeen to the crags of Oban – you have now a continuous line of forests; while in other parts of the Highlands there are the new forests of Loch Archaig, Glengarry, Glenmoriston, etc. Sheep were introduced into glens which had been the seats of communities of small farmers; and the latter were driven to seek subsistence on coarser and more sterile tracts of soil. Now deer are supplanting sheep; and these are once more dispossessing the small tenants, who will necessarily be driven down upon still coarser land and to more grinding penury. Deer-forests[32] and the people cannot co-exist. One or other of the two must yield. Let the forests be increased in number and extent during the next quarter of a century, as they have been in the last, and the Gaels will perish from their native soil ... This movement among the Highland proprietors is with some a matter of ambition ... with some love of sport ... while others, of a more practical cast, follow the trade in deer with an eye solely to profit. For it is a fact, that a mountain range laid out in forest is, in many cases, more profitable to the proprietor than when let as a sheep-walk ... The huntsman who wants a deer-forest limits his offers by no other calculation than the extent of his purse ... Sufferings have been inflicted in the Highlands scarcely less severe than those occasioned by the policy of the Norman kings. Deer have received extended ranges, while men have been hunted within a narrower and still narrower circle ... One after one the liberties of the people have been cloven down ... And the oppressions are daily on the increase ... The clearance and dispersion of the people is pursued by the proprietors as a settled principle, as an agricultural necessity, just as trees and brushwood are cleared from the wastes of America or Australia; and the operation goes on in a quiet, business-like way, etc.'[33]

32. The deer-forests of Scotland do not contain a single tree. The sheep are driven from, and then the deer driven to, the naked hills, and this is then called a deer-forest. Not even timber-planting and real forest culture.

33. Robert Somers, *Letters from the Highlands; or the Famine of 1847*, London, 1848, pp. 12–28 passim. These letters originally appeared in *The Times*. The English economists of course explained the famine of the Gaels in 1847 by referring to – over-population. At all events, they were 'pressing' on their food supply. The 'clearing of estates', or as it is called in German, '*Bauernlegen*', made its influence felt in Germany especially after the Thirty Years' War, and, as late as 1790, led to peasant revolts in Electoral Saxony. *Bauernlegen* was particularly prevalent in the-eastern part of Germany. In most of the Prussian provinces, Frederick II for the first time secured property rights for the peasants. After the conquest of Silesia, he forced the landowners

to rebuild huts, barns, etc. and to provide the peasants with cattle and implements. He wanted soldiers for his army, and taxpayers for his treasury. For the rest, the pleasant life led by the peasant under Frederick's financial system and his governmental hotch-potch of despotism, bureaucracy and feudalism may be seen from the following quotation from his admirer Mirabeau: 'Flax represents one of the greatest sources of wealth for the peasant of North Germany. Unfortunately for the human race, this is only a resource against misery and not a means towards well-being. Direct taxes, forced labour services, obligations of all kinds, crush the German peasant, especially as he still has to pay indirect taxes on everything he buys . . . and to complete his ruin he dare not sell his produce where and as he wishes; he dare not buy what he needs from the merchants who could sell it to him at a cheaper price. He is slowly ruined by all these factors, and when the direct taxes fall due, he would find himself incapable of paying them without his spinning-wheel; it offers him a last resort, while providing useful occupation for his wife, his children, his maids, his farm-hands, and himself; but what a painful life he leads, even with this extra resource! In summer, he works like a convict with the plough and at harvest; he goes to bed at nine o'clock and rises at two to get through all his work; in winter he ought to be recovering his strength by sleeping longer; but he would run short of corn for his bread and next year's sowing if he got rid of the products that he needs to sell in order to pay the taxes. He therefore has to spin to fill up this gap . . . and indeed he must do so most assiduously. Thus the peasant goes to bed at midnight or one o'clock in winter, and gets up at five or six; or he goes to bed at nine and gets up at two, and this he does every day of his life except Sundays. These excessively short hours of sleep and long hours of work consume a person's strength, and hence it happens that men and women age much more in the country than in the towns' (Mirabeau, op. cit., Vol. 3, pp. 212 ff.). In March 1866, eighteen years after the publication of the work of Robert Somers quoted above, Professor Leone Levi gave a lecture before the Society of Arts on the transformation of sheep-walks into deer-forests, in which he depicted the further progress in the devastation of the Scottish Highlands. He says, among other things: 'Depopulation and transformation into sheep-walks were the most convenient means for getting an income without expenditure . . . A deer-forest in place of a sheep-walk was a common change in the Highlands. The landowners turned out the sheep as they once turned out the men from their estates, and welcomed the new tenants – the wild beasts and the feathered birds . . . One can walk from the Earl of Dalhousie's estates in Forfarshire to John o' Groats, without ever leaving forest land . . . In many of these woods the fox, the wild cat, the marten, the pole-cat, the weasel and the Alpine hare are common; whilst the rabbit, the squirrel and the rat have lately made their way into the country. Immense tracts of land, much of which is described in the statistical account of Scotland as having a pasturage in richness and extent of very superior description, are thus shut out from all cultivation and improvement, and are solely devoted to the sport of a few persons for a very brief period of the year.' The London *Economist* of 2 June 1866 says, 'Amongst the items of news in a Scotch paper of last week, we read . . . "One of the finest sheep farms in Sutherlandshire, for which a rent of £1,200 a year was recently offered, on the expiry of the existing lease this year, is to be converted into a deer-forest." Here we see the modern instincts of feudalism . . . operating

The spoliation of the Church's property, the fraudulent alienation of the state domains, the theft of the common lands, the usurpation of feudal and clan property and its transformation into modern private property under circumstances of ruthless terrorism, all these things were just so many idyllic methods of primitive accumulation. They conquered the field for capitalist agriculture, incorporated the soil into capital, and created for the urban industries the necessary supplies of free and rightless proletarians.

---

pretty much as they did when the Norman Conqueror . . . destroyed thirty-six villages to create the New Forest . . . Two millions of acres . . . totally laid waste, embracing within their area some of the most fertile lands of Scotland. The natural grass of Glen Tilt was among the most nutritive in the county of Perth. The deer-forest of Ben Aulder was by far the best grazing ground in the wide district of Badenoch; a part of the Black Mount forest was the best pasture for black-faced sheep in Scotland. Some idea of the ground laid waste for purely sporting purposes in Scotland may be formed from the fact that it embraced an area larger than the whole county of Perth. The resources of the forest of Ben Aulder might give some idea of the loss sustained from the forced desolations. The ground would pasture 15,000 sheep, and as it was not more than one-thirtieth part of the whole forest ground in Scotland . . . (the amount of pasture lost can be imagined). All that forest land is totally unproductive . . . It might just as well have been submerged under the waters of the North Sea . . . Such extemporized wildernesses or deserts ought to be put down by the decided interference of the Legislature.'

Chapter 28: Bloody Legislation against the Expropriated since the End of the Fifteenth Century. The Forcing Down of Wages by Act of Parliament

The proletariat created by the breaking-up of the bands of feudal retainers and by the forcible expropriation of the people from the soil, this free and rightless* proletariat could not possibly be absorbed by the nascent manufactures as fast as it was thrown upon the world. On the other hand, these men, suddenly dragged from their accustomed mode of life, could not immediately adapt themselves to the discipline of their new condition. They were turned in massive quantities into beggars, robbers and vagabonds, partly from inclination, in most cases under the force of circumstances. Hence at the end of the fifteenth and during the whole of the sixteenth centuries, a bloody legislation against vagabondage was enforced throughout Western Europe. The fathers of the present working class were chastised for their enforced transformation into vagabonds and paupers. Legislation treated them as 'voluntary' criminals, and assumed that it was entirely within their powers to go on working under the old conditions which in fact no longer existed.

In England this legislation began under Henry VII.

Henry VIII, 1530: Beggars who are old and incapable of working receive a beggar's licence. On the other hand, whipping and imprisonment for sturdy vagabonds. They are to be tied to the cart-tail and whipped until the blood streams from their bodies, then they are to swear on oath to go back to their birthplace or to where they have lived the last three years and to 'put themselves to labour'. What grim irony! By 27 Henry VIII [c. 25] the previous statute is repeated, but strengthened with new clauses. For the second arrest for vagabondage the whipping is to be repeated and half the ear sliced off; but for the third relapse the

---

*Here, as elsewhere in this context, Marx uses the word *'vogelfrei'*, literally 'as free as a bird', i.e. free but outside the human community and therefore entirely unprotected and without legal rights.

offender is to be executed as a hardened criminal and enemy of the common weal.

Edward VI: A statute of the first year of his reign, 1547,* ordains that if anyone refuses to work, he shall be condemned as a slave to the person who has denounced him as an idler. The master shall feed his slave on bread and water, weak broth and such refuse meat as he thinks fit. He has the right to force him to do any work, no matter how disgusting, with whip and chains. If the slave is absent for a fortnight, he is condemned to slavery for life and is to be branded on forehead or back with the letter S; if he runs away three times, he is to be executed as a felon. The master can sell him, bequeath him, let him out on hire as a slave, just as he can any other personal chattel or cattle. If the slaves attempt anything against the masters, they are also to be executed. Justices of the peace, on information, are to hunt the rascals down. If it happens that a vagabond has been idling about for three days, he is to be taken to his birthplace, branded with a red hot iron with the letter V on the breast, and set to work, in chains, on the roads or at some other labour. If the vagabond gives a false birthplace, he is then to become the slave for life of that place, of its inhabitants, or its corporation, and to be branded with an S. All persons have the right to take away the children of the vagabonds and keep them as apprentices, the young men until they are 24, the girls until they are 20. If they run away, they are to become, until they reach these ages, the slaves of their masters, who can put them in irons, whip them, etc. if they like. Every master may put an iron ring round the neck, arms or legs of his slave, by which to know him more easily and to be more certain of him.[1] The last part of this statute provides that certain poor people may be employed by a place or by persons who are willing to give them food and drink and to find them work. Slaves of the parish of this kind were still to be found in England in the mid nineteenth century under the name of 'roundsmen'.

Elizabeth, 1572:† Unlicensed beggars above 14 years of age are to be severely flogged and branded on the left ear unless some-

1. The author of the *Essay on Trade, etc.*, 1770, says: 'In the reign of Edward VI indeed the English seem to have set, in good earnest, about encouraging manufactures and employing the poor. This we learn from a remarkable statute which runs thus: "That all vagrants shall be branded, etc." ' (p. 5).

---

*An Act for the Punishing of Vagabonds, 1 Edward VI, c. 3.

†An Act for the Punishment of Vagabonds, 14 Elizabeth I, c. 5.

one will take them into service for two years; in case of a repetition of the offence, if they are over 18, they are to be executed, unless someone will take them into service for two years; but for the third offence they are to be executed without mercy as felons. Similar statutes: 18 Elizabeth, c. 13, and another of 1597.[2]

James I: Anyone wandering about and begging is declared a rogue and a vagabond. Justices of the peace in Petty Sessions are authorized to have them publicly whipped and to imprison them for six months for the first offence, and two years for the second. While in prison they are to be whipped as much and as often as the justices of the peace think fit . . . Incorrigible and dangerous rogues are to be branded with an R on the left shoulder

2. Thomas More says in his *Utopia*: 'Consequently, in order that one insatiable glutton and accursed plague of his native land may join field to field and surround many thousand acres with one fence, tenants are evicted. Some of them, either circumvented by fraud or overwhelmed by violence, are stripped even of their own property, or else, wearied by unjust acts, are driven to sell. By hook or by crook the poor wretches are compelled to leave their homes – men and women, husbands and wives, orphans and widows, parents with little children and a household not rich but numerous, since farm work requires many hands. Away they must go, I say, from the only homes familiar and known to them, and they find no shelter to go to. All their household goods which would not fetch a great price if they could wait for a purchaser, since they must be thrust out, they sell for a trifle. After they have soon spent that trifle in wandering from place to place, what remains for them but to steal and be hanged – justly, you may say! – or to wander and beg. And yet even in the latter case they are cast into prison as vagrants for going about idle when, though they most eagerly offer their labour, there is no one to hire them.' Out of these poor fugitives, of whom Thomas More says that they were forced to steal, '72,000 great and petty thieves were put to death,' in the reign of Henry VIII (Holinshed, *Description of England*, Vol. 1, p. 186).* In Elizabeth's time, 'rogues were trussed up apace, and there was not one year commonly wherein three or four hundred were not devoured and eaten up by the gallowes' (Strype, *Annals of the Reformation and Establishment of Religion, and Other Various Occurrences in the Church of England during Queen Elizabeth's Happy Reign*, 2nd edn, 1725, Vol. 2). According to this same Strype, in Somersetshire in one year 40 persons were executed, 35 robbers burnt in the hand, 37 whipped and 183 discharged as 'incorrigible vagabonds'. Nevertheless, he is of the opinion that this large number of prisoners does not comprise 'even a fifth of the actual criminals, thanks to the negligence of the justices and the foolish compassion of the people', and that the other counties of England were not better off in this respect than Somersetshire, while some were even worse off.

* This is in fact the *Description of England* by William Harrison (referred to earlier), Ch. 11, 'Of Sundry Kinds of Punishments Appointed for Malefactors', p. 193.

and set to hard labour, and if they are caught begging again, to be executed without mercy. These statutes were legally binding until the beginning of the eighteenth century; they were only repealed by 12 Anne, c. 23.

There were similar laws in France, where by the middle of the seventeenth century a kingdom of vagabonds (*royaume des truands*) had been established in Paris. Even at the beginning of the reign of Louis XVI, the Ordinance of 13 July 1777 provided that every man in good health from 16 to 60 years of age, if without means of subsistence and not practising a trade, should be sent to the galleys. The Statute of Charles V for the Netherlands (October 1537), the first Edict of the States and Towns of Holland (10 March 1614) and the *Plakaat* of the United Provinces (26 June 1649) are further examples of the same kind.

Thus were the agricultural folk first forcibly expropriated from the soil, driven from their homes, turned into vagabonds, and then whipped, branded and tortured by grotesquely terroristic laws into accepting the discipline necessary for the system of wage-labour.

It is not enough that the conditions of labour are concentrated at one pole of society in the shape of capital, while at the other pole are grouped masses of men who have nothing to sell but their labour-power. Nor is it enough that they are compelled to sell themselves voluntarily. The advance of capitalist production develops a working class which by education, tradition and habit looks upon the requirements of that mode of production as self-evident natural laws. The organization of the capitalist process of production, once it is fully developed, breaks down all resistance. The constant generation of a relative surplus population keeps the law of the supply and demand of labour, and therefore wages, within narrow limits which correspond to capital's valorization requirements. The silent compulsion of economic relations sets the seal on the domination of the capitalist over the worker. Direct extra-economic force is still of course used, but only in exceptional cases. In the ordinary run of things, the worker can be left to the 'natural laws of production', i.e. it is possible to rely on his dependence on capital, which springs from the conditions of production themselves, and is guaranteed in perpetuity by them. It is otherwise during the historical genesis of capitalist production. The rising bourgeoisie needs the power of the state, and uses it to 'regulate' wages, i.e. to force them into the limits suitable for making a profit, to lengthen the working day, and to keep the worker himself at his normal level of dependence. This is an essential aspect of so-called primitive accumulation.

The class of wage-labourers, which arose in the latter half of the fourteenth century, formed then and in the following century only a very small part of the population, well protected in its position by the independent peasant proprietors in the countryside and by the organization of guilds in the towns. Masters and artisans were not separated by any great social distance either on the land or in the towns. The subordination of labour to capital was only formal, i.e. the mode of production itself had as yet no specifically capitalist character. The variable element in capital preponderated greatly over the constant element. The demand for wage-labour therefore grew rapidly with every accumulation of capital, while the supply only followed slowly behind. A large part of the national product which was later transformed into a fund for the accumulation of capital still entered at that time into the consumption-fund of the workers.

Legislation on wage-labour, which aimed from the first at the exploitation of the worker and, as it progressed, remained equally hostile to him,[3] begins in England with the Statute of Labourers issued by Edward III in 1349. The Ordinance of 1350 in France, issued in the name of King John, corresponds to it. The English and French laws run parallel and are identical in content. Where these labour-statutes aim at a compulsory extension of the working day, I shall not return to them, as we discussed this point earlier (in Chapter 10, Section 5).

The Statute of Labourers was passed at the urgent insistence of the House of Commons. A Tory says naïvely: 'Formerly the poor demanded such *high* wages as to threaten industry and wealth. Next, their wages are so *low* as to threaten industry and wealth equally and perhaps more, but in another way.'[4] A tariff of wages was fixed by law for town and country, for piece-work and day-

3. 'Whenever the legislature attempts to regulate the differences between masters and their workmen, its counsellors are always the masters,' says Adam Smith.* 'The spirit of the laws is property,' says Linguet.†

4. [J. B. Byles,] *Sophisms of Free Trade. By a Barrister*, London, 1850, p. 206. He adds maliciously: 'We were ready enough to interfere for the employer, can nothing now be done for the employed?'

* Adam Smith, *Wealth of Nations*, Vol. 1, Edinburgh, 1814, p. 142.

† S.-N.-H. Linguet, *Théorie des lois civiles, ou principes fondamentaux de la société*, Vol. 1, London, 1767, p. 236.

work. The agricultural labourers were to hire themselves out by the year, the urban workers were to do so 'on the open market'. It was forbidden, on pain of imprisonment, to pay higher wages than those fixed by the statute, but the taking of higher wages was more severely punished than the giving of them (similarly, in Sections 18 and 19 of Elizabeth's Statute of Apprentices, ten days' imprisonment is decreed for the person who pays the higher wages, but twenty-one days for the person who receives those wages). A statute of 1360 increased the penalties and authorized the masters to extort labour at the legal rate of wages by using corporal punishment. All combinations, contracts, oaths, etc. by which masons and carpenters reciprocally bound themselves were declared null and void. Workers' combinations are treated as heinous crimes from the fourteenth century until 1825, the year of the repeal of the laws against combinations. The spirit of the Statute of Labourers of 1349 and its offshoots shines out clearly in the fact that while the state certainly dictates a maximum of wages, it on no account fixes a minimum.

In the sixteenth century, as we know, the condition of the workers became much worse. The money wage rose, but not in proportion to the depreciation of money and the corresponding rise in the prices of commodities. Real wages therefore fell. Nevertheless, the laws for keeping them down remained in force, together with the ear-clipping and branding of those 'whom no one was willing to take into service'. By 5 Elizabeth, c. 3 (the Statute of Apprentices), the justices of the peace were given the power to fix certain wages and to modify them according to the time of the year and the current prices of commodities. James I extended these labour regulations to weavers, spinners and indeed to all other possible categories of worker.[5] George II extended

5. From a clause in the statute 2 James I, c. 6, we see that certain clothiers took it upon themselves, in their capacity of justices of the peace, to dictate the official tariff of wages in their own workshops. In Germany, especially after the Thirty Years' War, statutes for keeping down wages are met with frequently. 'The shortage of servants and labourers was very troublesome to the landed proprietors in the depopulated districts. All villagers were forbidden to let rooms to single men and women; all the latter were to be reported to the authorities and thrown into prison if they were unwilling to become servants, even if they were employed at any other work, such as sowing seeds for the peasants at a daily wage, or even buying and selling corn (*Kaiserliche Privilegia und Sanctiones für Schlesien*, I, 125). For a whole century the decrees of the German princelings contain bitter and repeated complaints about the wicked and impertinent rabble, which will not reconcile itself to its

the laws against combinations of workers to all manufactures.*

In the period of manufacture properly so called, the capitalist mode of production had become sufficiently strong to render legal regulation of wages as impracticable as it was unnecessary; but the ruling classes were unwilling to be without the weapons of the old arsenal in case some emergency should arise. Hence, even in the eighteenth century, 7 George I, c. 13, forbade a daily wage higher than 2s. 7½d. for journeymen tailors in and around London, except in cases of general mourning; 13 George III, c. 68, handed over to the justices of the peace the task of regulating the wages of silk-weavers; in 1796 it required two judgements of the higher courts to decide whether the orders made by justices of the peace as to wages also held good for non-agricultural workers; and in 1799 Parliament confirmed that the wages of mining workers in Scotland should continue to be regulated by a statute of Elizabeth and two Scottish Acts of 1661 and 1671. How completely the situation had been transformed in the meantime is proved by a hitherto unheard-of occurrence in the House of Commons. There, where for more than 400 years laws had been made for the maximum beyond which wages absolutely must not rise, Whitbread in 1796 proposed a legal minimum wage for agricultural labourers. Pitt opposed this, but conceded that the 'condition of the poor was cruel'. Finally, in 1813, the laws for the regulation of wages were repealed. They became an absurd anomaly as soon as the capitalist began to regulate his factory by his own private legislation, and was able to make up the wage of the agricultural labourer to the indispensable minimum by means of the poor-rate. The provisions of the statutes of labourers as to contracts between master and workman, regarding giving notice and the like, which allow only a civil action against the master

---

harsh conditions, and will not be content with its wage as laid down by law. The individual landowners are forbidden to pay more than the state has fixed by a tariff. And yet the conditions of service were at times better after the war than 100 years later; the farm servants of Silesia had meat twice a week in 1652, whereas even in our century there are districts where they have it only three times a year. Moreover, wages after the war were higher than in the succeeding centuries' (G. Freytag).*

*G. Freytag, *Neue Bilder aus dem Leben des deutschen Volkes*, Leipzig, 1862, pp. 35–6.

---

*By 22 George II, c. 27.

who breaks his contract, but permit, on the contrary, a criminal action against the worker who breaks his contract, are still in full force at this moment.*

The barbarous laws against combinations of workers collapsed in 1825 in the face of the threatening attitude of the proletariat. Despite this, they disappeared only in part. Certain pretty survivals of the old statutes did not vanish until 1859. Finally, the Act of 29 June 1871 purported to remove the last traces of this class legislation by giving legal recognition to trade unions.† But another Act, of the same date ('An act to amend the criminal law relating to violence, threats and molestation'),‡ in fact re-established the previous situation in a new form. This Parliamentary conjuring-trick withdrew the means the workers could use in a strike or lock-out from the common law and placed them under exceptional penal legislation, the interpretation of which fell to the manufacturers themselves in their capacity of justices of the peace. Two years earlier, the same House of Commons, and the same Mr Gladstone, in the customary honourable fashion, had brought in a bill for the removal of all exceptional penal legislation against the working class. But it was never allowed to go beyond the second reading, and the matter was drawn out in this way until at length the 'great Liberal party', by an alliance with the Tories, found the courage to turn decisively against the very proletariat that had carried it into power. Not content with this betrayal, the 'great Liberal party' allowed the English judges, ever ready to wag their tails for the ruling classes, to exhume the earlier laws against 'conspiracy' and apply them to combinations of workers. It is evident that only against its will, and under the pressure of the masses, did the English Parliament give up the laws against strikes and trade unions, after it had itself, with shameless egoism, held the position of a permanent trade union of the capitalists against the workers throughout five centuries.

During the very first storms of the revolution, the French bourgeoisie dared to take away from the workers the right of association they had just acquired. By a decree of 14 June 1791, they declared that every combination by the workers was 'an assault on liberty and the declaration of the rights of man',

* Until the passing of the Employers and Workmen Act in 1875 (38 and 39 Victoria, c. 90).

† Trade Union Act, 34 and 35 Victoria, c. 31.

‡ Criminal Law Amendment Act, 34 and 35 Victoria, c. 32.

punishable by a fine of 500 livres, together with deprivation of the rights of an active citizen for one year.[6] This law, which used state compulsion to confine the struggle between capital and labour within limits convenient for capital, has outlived revolutions and changes of dynasties. Even the Terror left it untouched. It was only struck out of the Penal Code quite recently. Nothing is more characteristic than the pretext for this bourgeois *coup d'état*. 'Granting,' says Le Chapelier, the *rapporteur* of the Committee on this law, 'that wages ought to be a little higher than they are ... that they ought to be high enough for him that receives them to be free from that state of absolute dependence which results from the lack of the necessaries of life, and which is almost a state of slavery,' granting this, the workers must nevertheless not be permitted to inform themselves about their own interests, nor to act in common and thereby lessen their 'absolute dependence', 'which is almost a state of slavery', because by doing this they infringe 'the liberty of their former masters, who are the present *entrepreneurs*', and because a combination against the despotism of the former masters of the corporations is – guess what! – a restoration of the corporations abolished by the French constitution![7]

6. Article I of this law runs: 'As the abolition of any form of association between citizens of the same estate and profession is one of the foundations of the French constitution, it is forbidden to re-establish them under any pretext and in any form, whatever this might be.' Article IV declares that if 'citizens belonging to the same profession, craft, or trade have joint discussions and make joint decisions with the intention of refusing together to perform their trade or insisting together on providing the services of their trade or their labours only at a particular price, then the said deliberations and agreements ... shall be declared unconstitutional, derogatory to liberty and the declaration of the rights of man, etc.'; this is made a felony, therefore, just as in the old statutes of labourers. (*Révolutions de Paris*, Paris, 1791, Vol. 3, p. 523.)

7. Buchez and Roux, *Histoire parlementaire*, Vol. 10, pp. 193–5 passim.

Chapter 29: The Genesis of the Capitalist
Farmer

Now that we have considered the forcible creation of a class of free and rightless proletarians, the bloody discipline that turned them into wage-labourers, the disgraceful proceedings of the state which employed police methods to accelerate the accumulation of capital by increasing the degree of exploitation of labour, the question remains: where did the capitalists originally spring from? For the only class created directly by the expropriation of the agricultural population is that of the great landed proprietors. As far as the genesis of the farmers is concerned, however, we can so to speak put our finger on it, because it is a slow process evolving through many centuries. The serfs, as well as the free small-scale proprietors, held land under very different tenures, and were therefore emancipated under very different economic conditions.

In England, the first form of the farmer is the bailiff, himself a serf. His position is similar to that of the *villicus* in ancient Rome, only in a more limited sphere of action. During the second half of the fourteenth century he is replaced by a farmer, whom the landlord provides with seed, cattle and farm implements. The farmer's condition is not very different from that of the peasant, but he exploits more wage-labour. Soon he becomes a *métayer*, a share-cropper. He advances one part of the agricultural stock, the landlord the other. The two divide the total product in proportions determined by contract. This form disappears quickly in England, and gives place to the form of the farmer properly so called, who valorizes his own capital by employing wage-labourers, and pays a part of the surplus product, in money or in kind, to the landlord as ground rent.

During the fifteenth century the independent peasant, and the farm-labourer working for himself as well as for wages, enriched themselves by their own labour; and as long as this was the case, both the farmer's circumstances and his field of production remained mediocre. But the agricultural revolution which began in the last third of the fifteenth century, and continued during the bulk of the sixteenth (excepting, however, its last few decades), enriched him just as quickly as it impoverished the mass of the agricultural folk.[1] The usurpation of the common lands allowed the farmer to augment greatly his stock of cattle, almost without cost, while the cattle themselves yielded a richer supply of manure for the cultivation of the soil.

A further factor, of decisive importance, was added in the sixteenth century. At that time the contracts for farms ran for a long time, often for ninety-nine years. The progressive fall in the value of the precious metals, and therefore of money, brought golden fruit to the farmers. Apart from all the other circumstances discussed above, it lowered wages. A portion of the latter was now added to the profits of the farm. The continuous rise in the prices of corn, wool, meat, in short of all agricultural products, swelled the money capital of the farmer without any action on his part, while the ground rent he had to pay diminished, since it had been contracted for on the basis of the old money values.[2] Thus he grew

---

1. Harrison, in his *Description of England*, says: 'although peradventure £4 of old rent be improved to £40, £50, or £100, yet will the farmer ... think his gains very small toward the end of his term if he have not six or seven years' rent lying by him.'*

2. On the influence of the depreciation of money in the sixteenth century on the different classes of society, see *A Compendious or Briefe Examination of Certayne Ordinary Complaints, of Divers of Our Country Men in These Our Days*, By W. S., Gentleman, London, 1581. The dialogue form of this work led people for a long time to ascribe it to Shakespeare, and it was re-published under his name as late as 1751. Its author is William Stafford. In one place the knight reasons as follows:

'Knight: You, my neighbour, the husbandman, you Maister Mercer, and you Goodman Cooper, with other artificers, may save yourself metely well. For as much as all things are dearer than they were, so much do you arise in the pryce of your wares and occupations that ye sell agayne. But we have nothing to sell whereby we might advance ye price there of, to countervaile those things that we must buy agayne.' In another place the knight asks the doctor: 'I pray you, what be those sorts that ye meane. And first, of those that ye thinke should have no losset hereby? Doctor: I mean all those that live by buying and selling, for as they buy deare, they sell thereafter. Knight: What is the next sort that ye say would win by it? Doctor: Marry, all such as have takings of fearmes in their owne manurance [cultivation] at the old rent,

*Chapter 12, 'Of the Manner of Building and Furniture of Our Houses', p. 202.

rich at the expense both of his labourers and his landlords. No wonder, therefore, that England, at the end of the sixteenth century, had a class of capitalist farmers who were rich men in relation to the circumstances of the time.[3]

---

for where they pay after the olde rate they sell after the newe – that is, they paye for theire lande good cheape, and sell all things growing thereof deare. Knight: What sorte is that which, ye sayde should have greater losse hereby, than these men had profit? Doctor: It is all noblemen, gentlemen, and all other that live either by a stinted rent or stypend, or do not manure [cultivate] the ground, or doe occupy no buying and selling.'

3. In France, the *régisseur*, or steward, who collected the dues for the feudal lords during the earlier part of the Middle Ages, soon became an *homme d'affaires*, or man of business, who by means of extortion, cheating and so on swindled his way into the position of capitalist. The *régisseurs* were themselves sometimes men of quality. For instance: 'This is the account given by M. Jacques de Thoraisse, knight, and lord of a manor near Besançon, to the lord who administers the accounts at Dijon for his highness the Duke and Count of Burgundy, of the rents appurtenant to the above-mentioned manor, from the 25th day of December 1359 to the 28th day of December 1360' (Alexis Monteil, *Traité de matériaux manuscrits de divers genres d'histoire*, Vol. 1, Paris, 1835, pp. 234–5). It is already evident here how in all spheres of social life the lion's share falls to the middleman. In the economic domain, for example, financiers, stock-exchange speculators, merchants and shop-keepers skim the cream; in questions of litigation the lawyer fleeces his clients; in politics the representative is more important than the voters, the minister more important than the sovereign; in religion God is pushed into the background by the 'mediator',* and the latter is again shoved back by the priests, who are the inevitable mediators between the good shepherd and his flock. In France, as in England, the great feudal territories were divided into innumerable small homesteads, but under conditions incomparably more unfavourable for the people. During the fourteenth century arose the 'farms' (*fermes* or *terriers*). Their number grew constantly, far beyond 100,000. They paid rents varying from one-twelfth to one-fifth of the product in money or in kind. These farms were fiefs, sub-fiefs etc. (*fiefs, arrière-fiefs*) according to the value and extent of the domains, many of which only contained a few acres (*arpents*). But all these *terriens* (farmers) had rights of jurisdiction to some degree over those who dwelt on the soil; there were four grades. The oppression suffered by the agricultural folk under all these petty tyrants will be understood. Monteil says that there were once 160,000 courts in France, whereas today 4,000 tribunals (including local courts) are sufficient.

* In Christian theology, Jesus Christ is the mediator between God and man.

Chapter 30: Impact of the Agricultural Revolution on Industry. The Creation of a Home Market for Industrial Capital

The intermittent but constantly renewed expropriation and expulsion of the agricultural population supplied the urban industries, as we have seen, with a mass of proletarians standing entirely outside the corporate guilds and unfettered by them; a fortunate circumstance which makes old A. Anderson* (not to be confused with James Anderson) express a belief in the direct intervention of Providence, in his *History of Commerce*. We must still pause a moment on this element of primitive accumulation. The thinning-out of the independent self-supporting peasants corresponded directly with the concentration of the industrial proletariat, in the way that Geoffroy Saint-Hilaire explained the condensation of cosmic matter at one place by its rarefaction at another.[1] But this was not the only consequence. In spite of the smaller number of its cultivators, the soil brought forth as much produce as before, or even more, because the revolution in property relations on the land was accompanied by improved methods of cultivation, greater co-operation, a higher concentration of the means of production and so on, and because the agricultural wage-labourers were made to work at a higher level of intensity,[2] and the field of production on which they worked for themselves shrank more and more. With the 'setting free' of a part of the agricultural population, therefore, their former means of nourishment were also set free. They were now transformed into material

1. In his *Notions de philosophie naturelle*, Paris, 1838.
2. A point that Sir James Steuart emphasizes.*
*In *An Inquiry into the Principles of Political Economy*, Vol. 1, Dublin, 1770, Bk I, Ch. 16.

---

*Adam Anderson (1692–1765), Scottish historian of commerce. He wrote only one book, *An Historical and Chronological Deduction of the Origin of Commerce*, 2 vols., London, 1764. For forty years he was a clerk in a London business house.

elements of variable capital. The peasant, expropriated and cast adrift, had to obtain the value of the means of subsistence from his new lord, the industrial capitalist, in the form of wages. And the same thing happened to those raw materials of industry which depended on indigenous agriculture. They were transformed into an element of constant capital.

Suppose, for example, that one part of the Westphalian peasantry, who, at the time of Frederick II, all span flax, are forcibly expropriated and driven from the soil; and suppose that the other part, who remain behind, are turned into the day-labourers of large-scale farmers. At the same time, large establishments for flax-spinning and weaving arise, and in these the men who have been 'set free' now work for wages. The flax looks exactly as it did before. Not a fibre of it is changed, but a new social soul has entered into its body. It now forms a part of the constant capital of the master manufacturer. Formerly it was divided among a mass of small producers, who cultivated it themselves and span it with their families in small portions. Now it is concentrated in the hands of one capitalist, who sets others to spin and weave it for him. The extra labour expended in flax-spinning was realized formerly in extra income to numerous peasant families, or perhaps, in the time of Frederick II, in taxes *pour le roi de Prusse*.* Now it is realized in profit for a few capitalists. The spindles and looms, formerly scattered over the face of the countryside, are now crowded together in a few great labour-barracks, together with the workers and the raw material. And spindles, looms and raw material are now transformed from means for the independent existence of the spinners and weavers into means for commanding[3] them and extracting unpaid labour from them. You cannot tell from looking at the large factories and the large farms that they have originated from the combination of many small centres of production, and have been built up by the expropriation of many small independent producers. Nevertheless, unprejudiced observers did not allow themselves to be deceived. In the time of

3. 'I will allow you,' says the capitalist, 'to have the honour of serving me, on condition that, in return for the pains I take in commanding you, you give me the little that remains to you' (J.-J. Rousseau, *Discours sur l'économie politique*, Geneva, 1760, p. 70).

---

* 'For the King of Prussia'. In other words, for a man who will give nothing in return. Here, of course, the literal sense is also intended.

Mirabeau, the 'lion of the revolution',* the great factories were still called *manufactures réunies*, or workshops thrown into one, as we speak of fields thrown into one. Says Mirabeau: 'We only pay attention to the large-scale factories, in which hundreds of men work under a director, and which are commonly called *manufactures réunies*. Those where a very large number of workers work in isolation and on their own account are hardly considered worthy of a glance. They are put entirely into the background. This is a very great mistake, as the latter alone form a really important component of the national wealth . . . The combined workshop (*fabrique réunie*) will prodigiously enrich one or two *entrepreneurs*, but the workers will only be journeymen, paid more or less [according to circumstances], and will not have any share in the success of the undertaking. In the isolated workshop (*fabrique séparée*), on the contrary, no one will become rich, but many workers will be comfortable. The number of hard-working and economical workers will grow, because they will see in good conduct, and in activity, a means of substantially improving their situation, and not of obtaining a small increase of wages that can never be of any importance for the future, and whose sole result is to place men in the position to live a little better, but only from day to day . . . The isolated, individual workshops, for the most part combined with the cultivation of smallholdings, are the only free ones.'[4] The expropriation and eviction of a part of the agricultural population not only set free for industrial capital the workers, their means of subsistence and the materials of their labour; it also created the home market.

In fact, the events that transformed the small peasants into wage-labourers, and their means of subsistence and of labour into material [*sachliche*] elements of capital, created, at the same time, a home market for capital. Formerly, the peasant family produced means of subsistence and raw materials, which they themselves

4. Mirabeau, op. cit., Vol. 3, pp. 20–109 passim. The fact that Mirabeau considers the separate workshops to be more economical and more productive than the 'combined' ones, and sees in the latter merely artificial and exotic products of intensive government cultivation, can be explained by the contemporary position of a large part of the Continental manufactures.

*This is the younger Mirabeau (Honoré-Gabriel-Victor Riqueti, comte de Mirabeau, 1749–91), who played a great part in the early years of the French Revolution.

for the most part consumed. These raw materials and means of subsistence have now become commodities; the large-scale farmer sells them, he finds his market in the manufactures. Yarn, linen, coarse woollen stuffs – things whose raw materials had been within the reach of every peasant family, had been spun and woven by the family for its own use – are now transformed into articles of manufacture, the markets for which are found precisely in the country districts. Previously a mass of small producers, working on their own account, had found their natural counterpart in a large number of scattered customers; but now these customers are concentrated into one great market provided for by industrial capital. [5] Thus the destruction of the subsidiary trades of the countryside, the process whereby manufacture is divorced from agriculture, goes hand in hand with the expropriation of the previously self-supporting peasants and their separation from their own means of production. And only the destruction of rural domestic industry can give the home market of a country that extension and stability which the capitalist mode of production requires.

Still, the manufacturing period, properly so called, does not succeed in carrying out this transformation radically and completely. It will be remembered that manufacture conquers the domain of national production only very partially, and always rests on the handicrafts of the towns and the domestic subsidiary industries of the rural districts, which stand in the background as its basis. If it destroys these in one form, in particular branches at certain points, it resurrects them again elsewhere, because it needs them to some extent for the preparation of raw material. It produces, therefore, a new class of small villagers who cultivate the soil as a subsidiary occupation, but find their chief occupation in industrial labour, the products of which they sell to the manufacturers directly, or through the medium of merchants. This is

5. 'Twenty pounds of wool converted unobtrusively into the yearly clothing of a labourer's family by its own industry in the intervals of other work – this makes no show; but bring it to market, send it to the factory, thence to the broker, thence to the dealer, and you will have great commercial operations, and nominal capital engaged to the amount of twenty times its value ... The working class* is thus amerced to support a wretched factory population, a parasitical shop-keeping class, and a fictitious commercial, monetary, and financial system' (David Urquhart, op. cit., p. 120).

* By 'working class' Urquhart means those people who work on the land.

one cause, though not the chief one, of a phenomenon which at first puzzles the student of English history. From the last third of the fifteenth century we find continual complaints, only interrupted at certain intervals, about the encroachment of capitalist farming in the country districts and the progressive annihilation of the peasantry. On the other hand, we always find that this peasantry turns up again, although in diminished number, and in a progressively worse situation.[6] The chief cause is this: England is at certain epochs mainly a corn-growing country, at others mainly a cattle-breeding country. These periods alternate, and the alternation is accompanied by fluctuations in the extent of peasant cultivation. A consistent foundation for capitalist agriculture could only be provided by large-scale industry, in the form of machinery; it is large-scale industry which radically expropriates the vast majority of the agricultural population and completes the divorce between agriculture and rural domestic industry, tearing up the latter's roots, which are spinning and weaving.[7] It therefore also

6. Cromwell's time forms an exception. As long as the Republic lasted, the mass of the English people of all levels rose from the degradation into which they had sunk under the Tudors.

7. Tuckett knew that the large-scale wool industry had sprung, with the introduction of machinery, from manufacture proper and from the destruction of rural or domestic manufactures (Tuckett, op. cit., Vol. 1, pp. 139-44). 'The plough, the yoke, were the invention of gods, and the occupation of heroes; are the loom, the spindle, the distaff, of less noble parentage? You sever the distaff and the plough, the spindle and the yoke, and you get factories and poor-houses, credit and panics, two hostile nations, agricultural and commercial' (David Urquhart, op. cit., p. 122). But now along comes Carey, and accuses England, surely not without reason, of trying to turn every other country into a purely agricultural nation, whose manufacturer is to be England. He asserts that Turkey has been ruined in this way, because 'the owners and occupants of land have never been permitted by England to strengthen themselves by the formation of that natural alliance between the plough and the loom, the hammer and the harrow' (*The Slave Trade*, p. 125). According to him, Urquhart himself is one of the chief agents in the ruin of Turkey, because he made free-trade propaganda there in the English interest. The joke here is that Carey (who is, incidentally, an abject servant of the Russians)* wants to prevent the process of separation between agriculture and domestic industry by means of that very system of protection which accelerates it.

*This passage alludes to the controversy of the 1850s between pro-Turks (such as Urquhart) and pro-Russians over responsibility for the outbreak of the Crimean War, and more generally over the possibility of reforming the Ottoman Empire.

conquers the entire home market for industrial capital, for the first time.[8]

8. The philanthropic English economists, such as Mill,* Rogers, Goldwin Smith, Fawcett, etc., and liberal manufacturers like John Bright & Co., ask English landed proprietors, as God asked Cain about Abel, 'Where are our thousands of freeholders gone?' But where do *you* come from, then? From the destruction of those freeholders. Why don't you go further, and ask where the independent weavers, spinners and handicraftsmen have gone to?
    *The context would suggest John Stuart Mill, not James Mill.

Chapter 31: The Genesis of the Industrial Capitalist

The genesis of the industrial[1] capitalist did not proceed in such a gradual way as that of the farmer. Doubtless many small guild-masters, and a still greater number of independent small artisans, or even wage-labourers, transformed themselves into small capitalists, and, by gradually extending their exploitation of wage-labour and the corresponding accumulation, into 'capitalists' without qualification. In the period when capitalist production was in its infancy things often happened as they had done in the period of infancy of the medieval town, where the question as to which of the escaped serfs should be master and which servant was in great part decided by the earlier or later date of their flight. The snail's pace of advance under this method by no means corresponded with the commercial requirements of the new world market, which had been created by the great discoveries of the end of the fifteenth century. But the Middle Ages had handed down two distinct forms of capital, which ripened in the most varied economic formations of society, and which, before the era of the capitalist mode of production, nevertheless functioned as capital – usurer's capital and merchant's capital.

'At present, all the wealth of society goes first into the possession of the capitalist . . . he pays the landowner his rent, the labourer his wages, the tax and tithe gatherer their claims, and keeps a large, indeed the largest, and a continually augmenting share, of the annual produce of labour for himself. The capitalist may now be said to be the first owner of all the wealth of the community, though no law has conferred on him the right to this property . . . this change has been effected by the taking of interest on capital . . . and it is not a little curious that all the law-givers of Europe endeavoured to prevent this by statutes, viz., statutes against

1. 'Industrial' here as opposed to 'agricultural'. In the strict sense the farmer is just as much an industrial capitalist as the manufacturer.

usury ... The power of the capitalist over all the wealth of the country is a complete change in the right of property, and by what law, or series of laws, was it effected?'[2] The author should have reminded himself that revolutions are not made with laws.

The money capital formed by means of usury and commerce was prevented from turning into industrial capital by the feudal organization of the countryside and the guild organization of the towns.[3] These fetters vanished with the dissolution of the feudal bands of retainers, and the expropriation and partial eviction of the rural population. The new manufactures were established at sea-ports, or at points in the countryside which were beyond the control of the old municipalities and their guilds. Hence, in England, the bitter struggle of the corporate towns against these new seed-beds of industry.

The discovery of gold and silver in America, the extirpation, enslavement and entombment in mines of the indigenous population of that continent, the beginnings of the conquest and plunder of India, and the conversion of Africa into a preserve for the commercial hunting of blackskins, are all things which characterize the dawn of the era of capitalist production. These idyllic proceedings are the chief moments of primitive accumulation. Hard on their heels follows the commercial war of the European nations, which has the globe as its battlefield. It begins with the revolt of the Netherlands from Spain, assumes gigantic dimensions in England's Anti-Jacobin War, and is still going on in the shape of the Opium Wars against China, etc.

The different moments of primitive accumulation can be assigned in particular to Spain, Portugal, Holland, France and England, in more or less chronological order. These different moments are systematically combined together at the end of the seventeenth century in England; the combination embraces the colonies, the national debt, the modern tax system, and the system of protection. These methods depend in part on brute force, for instance the colonial system. But they all employ the power of the state, the concentrated and organized force of society, to hasten, as in a hothouse, the process of transformation of the feudal mode of

2. *The Natural and Artificial Rights of Property Contrasted*, London, 1832, pp. 98–9. Author of this anonymous work: Thomas Hodgskin.

3. Even as late as 1794, the small cloth-makers of Leeds sent a deputation to Parliament, with a petition for a law to forbid any merchant from becoming a manufacturer (Dr Aikin, op. cit. [pp. 564–5]).

production into the capitalist mode, and to shorten the transition. Force is the midwife of every old society which is pregnant with a new one. It is itself an economic power.

W. Howitt, a man who specializes in being a Christian,* says of the Christian colonial system, 'The barbarities and desperate outrages of the so-called Christian race, throughout every region of the world, and upon every people they have been able to subdue, are not to be paralleled by those of any other race, however fierce, however untaught, and however reckless of mercy and of shame, in any age of the earth.'[4] The history of Dutch colonial administration – and Holland was the model capitalist nation of the seventeenth century – 'is one of the most extraordinary relations of treachery, bribery, massacre, and meanness'.[5] Nothing is more characteristic than their system of stealing men in Celebes, in order to get slaves for Java. Man-stealers were trained for this purpose. The thief, the interpreter and the seller were the chief agents in this trade, the native princes were the chief sellers. The young people thus stolen were hidden in secret dungeons on Celebes, until they were ready for sending to the slave-ships. An official report says: 'This one town of Macassar, for example, is full of secret prisons, one more horrible than the other, crammed with unfortunates, victims of greed and tyranny fettered in chains, forcibly torn from their families.' In order to get possession of Malacca, the Dutch bribed the Portuguese governor. He let them into the town in 1641. They went straight to his house and assassinated him, so as to be able to 'abstain' from paying the £21,875 which was the amount of his bribe. Wherever they set foot, devastation and depopulation followed. Banjuwangi, a province of Java, numbered over 80,000 inhabitants in 1750 and only 18,000 in 1811. That is peaceful commerce!

4. William Howitt, *Colonisation and Christianity: A Popular History of the Treatment of the Natives by the Europeans in All Their Colonies*, London, 1838, p. 9. There is a good compilation on the treatment of slaves in Charles Comte, *Traité de la législation*, 3rd edn, Brussels, 1837. This stuff ought to be studied in detail, to see what the bourgeois makes of himself and of the worker when he can model the world according to his own image without any interference.

5. Thomas Stamford Raffles, late Lieut.Gov. of that island, *The History of Java*, London, 1817 [Vol. 2, pp. 190–91].

*William Howitt (1792–1879), a prolific writer on many topics, was a leading Spiritualist in the 1860s, and published numerous accounts of spiritual experiences he claimed to have undergone.

The English East India Company, as is well known, received, apart from political control of India, the exclusive monopoly of the tea trade, as well as of the Chinese trade in general, and the transport of goods to and from Europe. But the coasting trade round India and between the islands,* as well as the internal trade of India, was the monopoly of the higher officials of the Company. The monopolies of salt, opium, betel and other commodities were inexhaustible mines of wealth. The officials themselves fixed the price and plundered the unfortunate Hindus at will. The Governor-General took part in this private traffic. His favourites received contracts under conditions whereby they, cleverer than the alchemists, made gold out of nothing. Great fortunes sprang up like mushrooms in a day; primitive accumulation proceeded without the advance of even a shilling. The trial of Warren Hastings swarms with such cases. Here is an instance. A contract for opium was given to a certain Sullivan at the moment of his departure on an official mission to a part of India far removed from the opium district. Sullivan sold his contract to one Binn for £40,000; Binn sold it the same day for £60,000, and the ultimate purchaser who carried out the contract declared that he still extracted a tremendous profit from it. According to one of the lists laid before Parliament, the Company and its officials obtained £6,000,000 between 1757 and 1766 from the Indians in the form of gifts. Between 1769 and 1770, the English created a famine by buying up all the rice and refusing to sell it again, except at fabulous prices.[6]

The treatment of the indigenous population was, of course, at its most frightful in plantation-colonies set up exclusively for the export trade, such as the West Indies, and in rich and well-populated countries, such as Mexico and India, that were given over to plunder. But even in the colonies properly so called, the Christian character of primitive accumulation was not belied. In 1703 those sober exponents of Protestantism, the Puritans of New England, by decrees of their assembly set a premium of £40 on every Indian scalp and every captured redskin; in 1720, a premium

6. In the year 1866 more than a million Hindus died of hunger in the province of Orissa alone. Nevertheless, an attempt was made to enrich the Indian treasury by the price at which the means of subsistence were sold to the starving people.

---

* i.e. the East Indian islands.

of £100 was set on every scalp; in 1744, after Massachusetts Bay had proclaimed a certain tribe as rebels, the following prices were laid down: for a male scalp of 12 years and upwards, £100 in new currency, for a male prisoner £105, for women and children prisoners £50, for the scalps of women and children £50. Some decades later, the colonial system took its revenge on the descendants of the pious pilgrim fathers, who had grown seditious in the meantime. At English instigation, and for English money, they were tomahawked by the redskins. The British Parliament proclaimed bloodhounds and scalping as 'means that God and Nature had given into its hand'.

The colonial system ripened trade and navigation as in a hothouse. The 'companies called Monopolia' (Luther)* were powerful levers for the concentration of capital. The colonies provided a market for the budding manufactures, and a vast increase in accumulation which was guaranteed by the mother country's monopoly of the market. The treasures captured outside Europe by undisguised looting, enslavement and murder flowed back to the mother-country and were turned into capital there. Holland, which first brought the colonial system to its full development, already stood at the zenith of its commercial greatness in 1648. It was 'in almost exclusive possession of the East Indian trade and the commerce between the south-east and the north-west of Europe. Its fisheries, its shipping and its manufactures surpassed those of any other country. The total capital of the Republic was probably greater than that of all the rest of Europe put together'.† Gülich forgets to add that by 1648 the people of Holland were more over-worked, poorer and more brutally oppressed than those of all the rest of Europe put together.

Today, industrial supremacy brings with it commercial supremacy. In the period of manufacture it is the reverse: commercial supremacy produces industrial predominance. Hence the preponderant role played by the colonial system at that time. It was the 'strange God' who perched himself side by side with the old divinities of Europe on the altar, and one fine day threw them all overboard with a shove and a kick. It proclaimed the making of profit as the ultimate and the sole purpose of mankind.

*See above, p. 424.
†G. von Gülich, *Geschichtliche Darstellung des Handels, der Gewerbe und des Ackerbaus der bedeutendsten handeltreibenden Staaten unsrer Zeit*, Vol. 1, Jena, 1830, p. 371.

The system of public credit, i.e. of national debts, the origins of which are to be found in Genoa and Venice as early as the Middle Ages, took possession of Europe as a whole during the period of manufacture. The colonial system, with its maritime trade and its commercial wars, served as a forcing-house for the credit system. Thus it first took root in Holland. The national debt, i.e. the alienation [*Veräusserung*]* of the state – whether that state is despotic, constitutional or republican – marked the capitalist era with its stamp. The only part of the so-called national wealth that actually enters into the collective possession of a modern nation is – the national debt.[7]

Hence, quite consistently with this, the modern doctrine that a nation becomes the richer the more deeply it is in debt. Public credit becomes the *credo* of capital. And with the rise of national debt-making, lack of faith in the national debt takes the place of the sin against the Holy Ghost, for which there is no forgiveness.

The public debt becomes one of the most powerful levers of primitive accumulation. As with the stroke of an enchanter's wand, it endows unproductive money with the power of creation and thus turns it into capital, without forcing it to expose itself to the troubles and risks inseparable from its employment in industry or even in usury. The state's creditors actually give nothing away, for the sum lent is transformed into public bonds, easily negotiable, which go on functioning in their hands just as so much hard cash would. But furthermore, and quite apart from the class of idle *rentiers* thus created, the improvised wealth of the financiers who play the role of middlemen between the government and the nation, and the tax-farmers, merchants and private manufacturers, for whom a good part of every national loan performs the service of a capital fallen from heaven, apart from all these people, the national debt has given rise to joint-stock companies, to dealings in negotiable effects of all kinds, and to speculation: in a word, it has given rise to stock-exchange gambling and the modern bankocracy.

At their birth the great banks, decorated with national titles, were only associations of private speculators, who placed themselves by the side of governments and, thanks to the privileges

7. William Cobbett remarks that in England all public institutions are designated as 'royal'; in compensation, however, there is the 'national' debt.

---

*Alienation by sale.

they received, were in a position to advance money to those governments. Hence the accumulation of the national debt has no more infallible measure than the successive rise in the stocks of these banks, whose full development dates from the founding of the Bank of England in 1694. The Bank of England began by lending its money to the government at 8 per cent; at the same time it was empowered by Parliament to coin money out of the same capital, by lending it a second time to the public in the form of bank-notes. It was allowed to use these notes for discounting bills, making advances on commodities and buying the precious metals. It was not long before this credit-money, created by the bank itself, became the coin in which the latter made its loans to the state, and paid, on behalf of the state, the interest on the public debt. It was not enough that the bank gave with one hand and took back more with the other; it remained, even while receiving money, the eternal creditor of the nation down to the last farthing advanced. Gradually it became the inevitable receptacle of the metallic hoard of the country, and the centre of gravity of all commercial credit. The writings of the time (Bolingbroke's, for instance) show what effect was produced on their contemporaries by the sudden emergence of this brood of bankocrats, financiers, *rentiers*, brokers, stock-jobbers, etc.[8]

Along with the national debt there arose an international credit system, which often conceals one of the sources of primitive accumulation in this or that people. Thus the villainies of the Venetian system of robbery formed one of the secret foundations of Holland's wealth in capital, for Venice in her years of decadence lent large sums of money to Holland. There is a similar relationship between Holland and England. By the beginning of the eighteenth century, Holland's manufactures had been far outstripped. It had ceased to be the nation preponderant in commerce and industry. One of its main lines of business, therefore, from 1701 to 1776, was the lending out of enormous amounts of capital, especially to its great rival England. The same thing is going on today between England and the United States. A great deal of capital, which appears today in the United States without any birth-certificate, was yesterday, in England, the capitalized blood of children.

8. 'If the Tartars were to flood into Europe today, it would be a difficult job to make them understand what a financier is with us' (Montesquieu, *Esprit des lois*, Vol. 4, p. 33, London, 1769).

As the national debt is backed by the revenues of the state, which must cover the annual interest payments etc., the modern system of taxation was the necessary complement of the system of national loans. The loans enable the government to meet extra-ordinary expenses without the taxpayers feeling it immediately, but they still make increased taxes necessary as a consequence. On the other hand, the raising of taxation caused by the accumulation of debts contracted one after another compels the government always to have recourse to new loans for new extraordinary expenses. The modern fiscal system, whose pivot is formed by taxes on the most necessary means of subsistence (and therefore by increases in their price), thus contains within itself the germ of automatic progression. Over-taxation is not an accidental occurrence, but rather a principle. In Holland, therefore, where this system was first inaugurated, the great patriot, De Witt, extolled it in his *Maxims** as the best system for making the wage-labourer sub-missive, frugal, industrious . . . and overburdened with work. Here, however, we are less concerned with the destructive influence it exercises on the situation of the wage-labourer than with the forcible expropriation, resulting from it, of peasants and artisans, in short, of all the constituents of the lower middle class. There are no two opinions about this, even among the bourgeois economists. Its effectiveness as an expropriating agent is heightened still further by the system of protection, which forms one of its integral parts.

The great part that the public debt and the fiscal system corresponding to it have played in the capitalization of wealth and the expropriation of the masses, has led many writers, like Cobbett,† Doubleday‡ and others, to seek here, incorrectly, the fundamental cause of the misery of the people in modern times.

The system of protection was an artificial means of manufacturing manufacturers, or expropriating independent workers, of capitalizing the national means of production and subsistence,

*P. de la Court, *Political Maxims of the State of Holland* (1669), English translation, London, 1743, Part I, Ch. 24, p. 92: 'All the said ways of raising money will excite the commonalty to ingenuity, diligence, and frugality.'

† In a pamphlet published in London in 1817, entitled: 'Paper against Gold: containing the history and mystery of the Bank of England, the funds, the debt, the sinking fund . . . and shewing that taxation, pauperism, poverty, misery, and crimes ever must increase with a funding system'.

‡ Thomas Doubleday, *A Financial, Statistical, and Monetary History of England from 1688*, London, 1847.

and of forcibly cutting short the transition from a mode of production that was out of date to the modern mode of production. The European states tore each other to pieces to gain the patent of this invention, and, once they had entered into the service of the profit-mongers, they did not restrict themselves to plundering their own people, indirectly through protective duties, directly through export premiums, in the pursuit of this purpose. They also forcibly uprooted all industries in the neighbouring dependent countries, as for example England did with the Irish woollen manufacture. On the Continent of Europe the process was much simplified, following the example of Colbert. The original capital for industry here came in part directly out of the state treasury. 'Why,' cries Mirabeau, 'why go so far to seek the cause of the manufacturing glory of Saxony before the war? One hundred and eighty millions of debts contracted by the sovereigns!'[9]

Colonial system, public debts, heavy taxes, protection, commercial wars, etc., these offshoots of the period of manufacture swell to gigantic proportions during the period of infancy of large-scale industry. The birth of the latter is celebrated by a vast, Herod-like slaughter of the innocents. Like the royal navy, the factories were recruited by means of the press-gang. Though Sir F. M. Eden is indifferent to the horrors of the expropriation of the agricultural population from the soil, from the last third of the fifteenth century up to his own time; though he shows great self-satisfaction in congratulating his country on this process, which was 'essential' in order to establish capitalist agriculture and 'the due proportion between arable and pasture land'; despite this, he does not show the same economic insight into the necessity of child-stealing and child-slavery for the transformation of manufacturing production into factory production and the establishment of the true relation between capital and labour-power. He says: 'It may, perhaps be worthy the attention of the public to consider, whether any manufacture, which, in order to be carried on successfully, requires that cottages and workhouses should be ransacked for poor children; that they should be employed by turns during the greater part of the night and robbed of that rest which, though indispensable to all, is most required by the young; and that numbers of both sexes, of different ages and dispositions, should be collected together in such a manner that the contagion of example

9. Mirabeau, op. cit., Vol. 6, p. 101.

cannot but lead to profligacy and debauchery; will add to the sum of individual or national felicity?'[10]

'In the counties of Derbyshire, Nottinghamshire, and more particularly in Lancashire,' says Fielden, 'the newly-invented machinery was used in large factories built on the sides of streams capable of turning the water-wheel. Thousands of hands were suddenly required in these places, remote from towns; and Lancashire, in particular, being, till then, comparatively thinly populated and barren, a population was all that she now wanted. The small and nimble fingers of little children being by very far the most in request, the custom instantly sprang up of procuring apprentices (!) from the different parish workhouses of London, Birmingham, and elsewhere. Many, many thousands of these little, hapless creatures were sent down into the north, being from the age of 7 to the age of 13 or 14 years old. The custom was for the master' (i.e. the child-stealer) 'to clothe his apprentices and to feed and lodge them in an "apprentice house" near the factory; overseers were appointed to see to the works, whose interest it was to work the children to the utmost, because their pay was in proportion to the quantity of work that they could exact. Cruelty was, of course, the consequence ... In many of the manufacturing districts, but particularly, I am afraid, in the guilty county to which I belong (Lancashire), cruelties the most heart-rending were practised upon the unoffending and friendless creatures who were thus consigned to the charge of master-manufacturers; they were harassed to the brink of death by excess of labour ... were flogged, fettered and tortured in the most exquisite refinement of cruelty; ... they were in many cases starved to the bone while flogged to their work and ... even in some instances ... were driven to commit suicide ... The beautiful and romantic valleys of Derbyshire, Nottinghamshire and Lancashire, secluded from the public eye, became the dismal solitudes of torture, and of many a murder. The profits of manufacturers were enormous; but this only whetted the appetite that it should have satisfied, and therefore the manufacturers had recourse to an expedient that seemed to secure to them those profits without any possibility of limit; they began the practice of what is termed "night-working", that is, having tired one set of hands, by working them throughout the day, they had another set ready to go on working throughout the night; the day-set getting

10. Eden, op. cit., Vol. 1, Bk II, Ch. 1, p. 421.

924   *So-Called Primitive Accumulation*

into the beds that the night-set had just quitted, and in their turn again, the night-set getting into the beds that the day-set quitted in the morning. It is a common tradition in Lancashire, that the beds *never get cold.*'[11]

With the development of capitalist production during the period of manufacture, the public opinion of Europe lost its last remnant of shame and conscience. The nations bragged cynically of every infamy that served them as a means to the accumulation of capital. Read, for example, the naïve commercial annals of the worthy A. Anderson.* Here it is trumpeted forth as a triumph of English statesmanship that, at the Peace of Utrecht, England extorted from the Spaniards, by the Asiento Treaty, the privilege of being allowed to ply the slave trade, not only between Africa and the English West Indies, which it had done until then, but also between Africa and Spanish America. England thereby acquired the right to supply Spanish America until 1743 with 4,800 Negroes a year. At the same time this threw an official cloak over British smuggling. Liverpool grew fat on the basis of the slave trade. This was its method of primitive accumulation. And even to the present day, the Liverpool 'quality' have remained the Pindars of the slave

---

11. John Fielden, op. cit., pp. 5–6. On the earlier infamies of the factory system, cf. Dr Aikin (1795), op. cit., p. 219, and Gisborne, *Enquiry into the Duties of Men*, 1795, Vol. 2. When the steam-engine transplanted the factories from the waterfalls of the countryside into the centres of the towns, the 'abstemious' profit-monger found his childish material ready to hand, without having to bring slaves forcibly from the workhouses. When Sir R. Peel (father of the 'minister of plausibility') brought in his bill for the protection of children, in 1815, Francis Horner, luminary of the Bullion Committee and intimate friend of David Ricardo, said in the House of Commons: 'It is notorious, that with a bankrupt's effects, a gang, if he might use the word, of these children had been put up to sale, and were advertised publicly as part of the property. A most atrocious instance had been brought before the Court of King's Bench two years before, in which a number of these boys, apprenticed by a parish in London to one manufacturer, had been transferred to another, and had been found by some benevolent persons in a state of absolute famine. Another case more horrible had come to his knowledge while on a [Parliamentary] Committee . . . that not many years ago, an agreement had been made between a London parish and a Lancashire manufacturer, by which it was stipulated, that with every twenty sound children one idiot should be taken.' [Horner's speech of 6 June 1815.]

---

*See above, p. 908.

trade,* which – as noted in the work by Dr Aikin we have just quoted – 'has coincided with that spirit of bold adventure which has characterized the trade of Liverpool and rapidly carried it to its present state of prosperity; has occasioned vast employment for shipping and sailors, and greatly augmented the demand for the manufactures of the country'.† In 1730 Liverpool employed 15 ships in the slave trade; in 1751, 53; in 1760, 74; in 1770, 96; and in 1792, 132.

While the cotton industry introduced child-slavery into England, in the United States it gave the impulse for the transformation of the earlier, more or less patriarchal slavery into a system of commercial exploitation. In fact the veiled slavery of the wage-labourers in Europe needed the unqualified slavery of the New World as its pedestal.[12]

Tantae molis erat‡ to unleash the 'eternal natural laws' of the capitalist mode of production, to complete the process of separation between the workers and the conditions of their labour, to transform, at one pole, the social means of production and subsistence into capital, and at the opposite pole, the mass of the population into wage-labourers, into the free 'labouring poor', that artificial product of modern history.[13] If money, according to

12. In 1790 there were in the English West Indies ten slaves to one free man, in the French fourteen to one, and in the Dutch twenty-three to one (Henry Brougham, *An Inquiry into the Colonial Policy of the European Powers*, Edinburgh, 1803, Vol. 2, p. 74).

13. The expression 'labouring poor' is found in English legislation from the moment when the class of wage-labourers becomes noticeable. This term is used in opposition, on the one hand, to the 'idle poor', beggars etc., and, on the other, to those workers who are not yet plucked fowl but rather the possessors of their own means of labour. From the statute book the expression passed into political economy, and was handed down by Culpeper, J. Child, etc to Adam Smith and Eden. After this, one can estimate the good faith of the 'execrable political cantmonger' Edmund Burke, when he called the expression 'labouring poor' – 'execrable political cant'. This sycophant, who, in the pay of the English oligarchy, played the part of romantic opponent of

*Pindar (522–442 B.C.) was a Greek lyric poet famous above all for his triumphal odes to the victors in the Olympic games; hence here the Liverpool bourgeoisie continues to celebrate its own triumphs in the era of the slave trade.

†Aikin, op. cit., p. 339.

‡The full quotation is *'Tantae molis erat Romanam condere gentem'* ('So great was the effort required to found the Roman race'), from Virgil, *Aeneid*, Bk I, line 33.

Augier,[14] 'comes into the world with a congenital blood-stain on one cheek,' capital comes dripping from head to toe, from every pore, with blood and dirt.[15]

---

the French Revolution, just as, in the pay of the North American colonies at the beginning of the troubles in America, he had played the liberal against the English oligarchy, was a vulgar bourgeois through and through. 'The laws of commerce are the laws of Nature, and therefore the laws of God' (E. Burke, op. cit., pp. 31–2). No wonder then that, true to the laws of God and Nature, he always sold himself in the best market! A very good portrait of this Edmund Burke, during his liberal time, is to be found in the writings of the Rev. Mr Tucker, who, though a parson and a Tory, was, apart from that, an honourable man and a competent political economist. In face of the infamous moral cowardice that prevails today, and believes so devoutly in 'the laws of commerce', it is our duty to brand again and again the Burkes of this world, who only differ from their successors in one thing – talent!

14. Marie Augier, *Du crédit public*, Paris, 1842, p. 265.

15. 'Capital is said by a Quarterly Reviewer to fly turbulence and strife, and to be timid, which is very true; but this is very incompletely stating the question. Capital eschews no profit, or very small profit, just as Nature was formerly said to abhor a vacuum. With adequate profit, capital is very bold. A certain 10 per cent will ensure its employment anywhere; 20 per cent certain will produce eagerness; 50 per cent positive audacity; 100 per cent will make it ready to trample on all human laws; 300 per cent, and there is not a crime at which it will scruple, nor a risk it will not run, even to the chance of its owner being hanged. If turbulence and strife will bring a profit, it will freely encourage both. Smuggling and the slave-trade have amply proved all that is here stated' (T. J. Dunning, op. cit., pp. 35, 36).

Chapter 32: The Historical Tendency of Capitalist Accumulation

What does the primitive accumulation of capital, i.e. its historical genesis, resolve itself into? In so far as it is not the direct transformation of slaves and serfs into wage-labourers, and therefore a mere change of form, it only means the expropriation of the immediate producers, i.e. the dissolution of private property based on the labour of its owner. Private property, as the antithesis to social, collective property, exists only where the means of labour and the external conditions of labour belong to private individuals. But according to whether these private individuals are workers or non-workers, private property has a different character. The innumerable different shades of private property which appear at first sight are only reflections of the intermediate situations which lie between the two extremes.

The private property of the worker in his means of production is the foundation of small-scale industry, and small-scale industry is a necessary condition for the development of social production and of the free individuality of the worker himself. Of course, this mode of production also exists under slavery, serfdom and other situations of dependence. But it flourishes, unleashes the whole of its energy, attains its adequate classical form, only where the worker is the free proprietor of the conditions of his labour, and sets them in motion himself: where the peasant owns the land he cultivates, or the artisan owns the tool with which he is an accomplished performer.

This mode of production presupposes the fragmentation of holdings, and the dispersal of the other means of production. As it excludes the concentration of these means of production, so it also excludes co-operation, division of labour within each separate process of production, the social control and regulation of the forces of nature, and the free development of the productive forces of society. It is compatible only with a system of production and a society moving within narrow limits which are of natural origin. To perpetuate it would be, as Pecqueur rightly says, 'to decree universal mediocrity'.* At a certain stage of development, it brings into the world the material means of its own destruction. From that moment, new forces and new passions spring up in the bosom of society, forces and passions which feel themselves to be fettered by that society. It has to be annihilated; it is annihilated. Its annihilation, the transformation of the individualized and scattered means of production into socially concentrated means of production, the transformation, therefore, of the dwarf-like property of the many into the giant property of the few, and the expropriation of the great mass of the people from the soil, from the means of subsistence and from the instruments of labour, this terrible and arduously accomplished expropriation of the mass of the people forms the pre-history of capital. It comprises a whole series of forcible methods, and we have only passed in review those that have been epoch-making as methods of the primitive accumulation of capital. The expropriation of the direct producers was accomplished by means of the most merciless barbarism, and under the stimulus of the most infamous, the most sordid, the most petty and the most odious of passions. Private property which is personally earned, i.e. which is based, as it were, on the fusing together of the isolated, independent working individual with the conditions of his labour, is supplanted by capitalist private property, which rests on the exploitation of alien, but formally free labour.[1]

As soon as this metamorphosis has sufficiently decomposed the old society throughout its depth and breadth, as soon as the workers have been turned into proletarians, and their means of labour into capital, as soon as the capitalist mode of production stands on its own feet, the further socialization of labour and the further transformation of the soil and other means of production into socially exploited and therefore communal means of production takes on a new form. What is now to be expropriated is not the self-employed worker, but the capitalist who exploits a large number of workers.

1. 'We are in a situation which is entirely new for society ... we are striving to separate every kind of property from every kind of labour' (Sismondi, *Nouveaux Principes d'économie politique*, Vol. 2, p. 434).

*C. Pecqueur, *Théorie nouvelle d'économie sociale et politique*, Paris, 1842, p. 435.

This expropriation is accomplished through the action of the immanent laws of capitalist production itself, through the centralization of capitals. One capitalist always strikes down many others. Hand in hand with this centralization, or this expropriation of many capitalists by a few, other developments take place on an ever-increasing scale, such as the growth of the co-operative form of the labour process, the conscious technical application of science, the planned exploitation of the soil, the transformation of the means of labour into forms in which they can only be used in common, the economizing of all means of production by their use as the means of production of combined, socialized labour, the entanglement of all peoples in the net of the world market, and, with this, the growth of the international character of the capitalist regime. Along with the constant decrease in the number of capitalist magnates, who usurp and monopolize all the advantages of this process of transformation, the mass of misery, oppression, slavery, degradation and exploitation grows; but with this there also grows the revolt of the working class, a class constantly increasing in numbers, and trained, united and organized by the very mechanism of the capitalist process of production. The monopoly of capital becomes a fetter upon the mode of production which has flourished alongside and under it. The centralization of the means of production and the socialization of labour reach a point at which they become incompatible with their capitalist integument. This integument is burst asunder. The knell of capitalist private property sounds. The expropriators are expropriated.

The capitalist mode of appropriation, which springs from the capitalist mode of production, produces capitalist private property. This is the first negation of individual private property, as founded on the labour of its proprietor. But capitalist production begets, with the inexorability of a natural process, its own negation. This is the negation of the negation. It does not re-establish private property, but it does indeed establish individual property on the basis of the achievements of the capitalist era: namely co-operation and the possession in common of the land and the means of production produced by labour itself.

The transformation of scattered private property resting on the personal labour of the individuals themselves into capitalist private property is naturally an incomparably more protracted, violent and difficult process than the transformation of capitalist private property, which in fact already rests on the carrying on of production by society, into social property. In the former case, it was a matter of the expropriation of the mass of the people by a few usurpers; but in this case, we have the expropriation of a few usurpers by the mass of the people.[2]

2. 'The advance of industry, whose involuntary but willing promoter is the bourgeoisie, replaces the isolation of the workers, due to competition, with their revolutionary combination, due to association. The development of large-scale industry, therefore, cuts from under its feet the very foundation on which the bourgeoisie produces and appropriates products for itself. What the bourgeoisie, therefore, produces, above all, are its own gravediggers. Its fall and the victory of the proletariat are equally inevitable ... Of all the classes which confront the bourgeoisie today, the proletariat alone is a really revolutionary class. The other classes decay and disappear in the face of large-scale industry, the proletariat is its most characteristic product. The lower middle classes, the small manufacturers, the shopkeepers, the artisans, the peasants, all these fight against the bourgeoisie in order to save from extinction their existence as parts of the middle class ... they are reactionary, for they try to roll back the wheel of history' (Karl Marx and F. Engels, *Manifest der Kommunistischen Partei*, London, 1848, pp. 11, 9) [English translation: Karl Marx, *The Revolutions of 1848*, Pelican Marx Library, pp. 79, 77].

Chapter 33: The Modern Theory of Colonization[1]

Political economy confuses, on principle, two different kinds of private property, one of which rests on the labour of the producer himself, and the other on the exploitation of the labour of others. It forgets that the latter is not only the direct antithesis of the former, but grows on the former's tomb and nowhere else.

In Western Europe, the homeland of political economy, the process of primitive accumulation has more or less been accomplished. Here the capitalist regime has either directly subordinated to itself the whole of the nation's production, or, where economic relations are less developed, it has at least indirect control of those social layers which, although they belong to the antiquated mode of production, still continue to exist side by side with it in a state of decay. To this ready-made world of capital, the political economist applies the notions of law and of property inherited from a pre-capitalist world, with all the more anxious zeal and all the greater unction, the more loudly the facts cry out in the face of his ideology.

It is otherwise in the colonies. There the capitalist regime constantly comes up against the obstacle presented by the producer, who, as owner of his own conditions of labour, employs that labour to enrich himself instead of the capitalist. The contradiction between these two diametrically opposed economic systems has its practical manifestation here in the struggle between them. Where the capitalist has behind him the power of the mother country, he tries to use force to clear out of the way the modes of production and appropriation which rest on the personal labour of the independent producer. The same interest which, in

1. We are dealing here with true colonies, i.e. virgin soil colonized by free immigrants. The United States is, economically speaking, still a colony of Europe. Apart from this, old plantations where the abolition of slavery has completely revolutionized earlier relationships also belong here.

the mother country, compels the sycophant of capital, the political economist, to declare that the capitalist mode of production is theoretically its own opposite, this same interest, in the colonies, drives him 'to make a clean breast of it', and to proclaim aloud the antagonism between the two modes of production. To this end he demonstrates that the development of the social productivity of labour, co-operation, division of labour, application of machinery on a large scale, and so on, are impossible without the expropriation of the workers and the corresponding transformation of their means of production into capital. In the interest of the so-called wealth of the nation, he seeks for artificial means to ensure the poverty of the people. Here his apologetic armour crumbles off, piece by piece, like rotten touchwood.

It is the great merit of E. G. Wakefield to have discovered, not something new *about* the colonies,[2] but, *in* the colonies, the truth about capitalist relations in the mother country. Just as the system of protection originally[3] had the objective of manufacturing capitalists artificially in the mother country, so Wakefield's theory of colonization, which England tried for a time to enforce by Act of Parliament, aims at manufacturing wage-labourers in the colonies. This is what he calls 'systematic colonization'.

First of all, Wakefield discovered that, in the colonies, property in money, means of subsistence, machines and other means of production does not as yet stamp a man as a capitalist if the essential complement to these things is missing: the wage-labourer, the other man, who is compelled to sell himself of his own free will. He discovered that capital is not a thing, but a social relation between persons which is mediated through things.[4] A Mr Peel, he complains, took with him from England to the Swan River district of Western Australia means of subsistence and of production to

2. Wakefield's few insights into the nature of modern colonization are fully anticipated by Mirabeau *père*, the Physiocrat,* and even much earlier by English economists.

3. Later, it became a temporary necessity in the international competitive struggle. But whatever its motive, the consequences remain the same.

4. 'A negro is a negro. In certain relations he becomes a slave. A mule is a machine for spinning cotton. Only in certain relations does it become capital. Outside these circumstances, it is no more capital than gold is intrinsically money, or sugar is the price of sugar ... Capital is a social relation of production. It is a historical relation of production' (Karl Marx, 'Lohnarbeit und Kapital', *Neue Rheinische Zeitung*, No. 266, 7 April 1849) [English translation, *Karl Marx and Frederick Engels, Selected Works*, Vol. I, pp. 159–60].

* In *L'Ami des hommes* (1756).

the amount of £50,000. This Mr Peel even had the foresight to bring besides, 3,000 persons of the working class, men, women and children. Once he arrived at his destination, 'Mr Peel was left without a servant to make his bed or fetch him water from the river.'[5] Unhappy Mr Peel, who provided for everything except the export of English relations of production to Swan River!

For the understanding of the following discoveries of Wakefield, let us make two preliminary remarks: We know that the means of production and subsistence, while they remain the property of the immediate producer, are not capital. They only become capital under circumstances in which they serve at the same time as means of exploitation of, and domination over, the worker. But this, their capitalist soul, is so intimately wedded, in the mind of the political economist, to their material substance, that he christens them capital under all circumstances, even where they are its exact opposite. Thus it is with Wakefield. Further: he describes the splitting-up of the means of production into the individual property of many mutually independent and self-employed workers as equal division of capital. The political economist is like the feudal jurist, who used to attach the labels supplied by feudal law even to relationships which were purely monetary.

'If,' says Wakefield, 'all the members of the society are supposed to possess equal portions of capital ... no man would have a motive for accumulating more capital than he could use with his own hands. This is to some extent the case in new American settlements, where a passion for owning land prevents the existence of a class of labourers for hire.'[6] So long, therefore, as the worker can accumulate for himself – and this he can do so long as he remains in possession of his means of production – capitalist accumulation and the capitalist mode of production are impossible. The class of wage-labourers essential to these is lacking. How then, in old Europe, was the expropriation of the worker from his conditions of labour brought about? In other words, how did capital and wage-labour come into existence? By a social contract of a quite original kind. 'Mankind have adopted a ... simple contrivance for promoting the accumulation of capital,' which, of course, had dangled in front of them since the time of Adam as the ultimate and only goal of their existence, 'they have divided

5. E. G. Wakefield, *England and America*, Vol. 2, p. 33.
6. ibid., Vol. 1, p. 17.

themselves into owners of capital and owners of labour . . . This division was the result of concert and combination.'[7] In short: the mass of mankind expropriated itself in honour of the 'accumulation of capital'. Now one would think that this instinct of self-denying fanaticism would especially run riot in the colonies, the only places where the men and the conditions exist to turn a social contract from a dream into a reality. So why should 'systematic colonization' be called in to replace its opposite, spontaneous and unregulated colonization? Here is one reason: 'In the Northern States of the American Union, it may be doubted whether so many as a tenth of the people would fall under the description of hired labourers . . . In England . . . the labouring class compose the bulk of the people.'[8] Indeed, the drive to self-expropriation for the glory of capital exists so little in the case of working humanity, that slavery, according to Wakefield himself, is the sole natural basis of colonial wealth. His systematic colonization is a mere makeshift, resulting from the fact that he has free men, not slaves, to deal with. 'The first Spanish settlers in Saint Domingo did not obtain labourers from Spain. But, without labourers', (i.e. without slavery) 'their capital must have perished, or, at least, must soon have been diminished to that small amount which each individual could employ with his own hands. This has actually occurred in the last colony founded by Englishmen – the Swan River Settlement – where a great mass of capital, of seeds, implements, and cattle, has perished for want of labourers to use it, and where no settler has preserved much more capital than he can employ with his own hands.'[9]

We have seen that the expropriation of the mass of the people from the soil forms the basis of the capitalist mode of production. The essence of a free colony, on the contrary, consists in this, that the bulk of the soil is still public property, and every settler on it can therefore turn part of it into his private property and his individual means of production, without preventing later settlers from performing the same operation.[10] This is the secret both of the prosperity of the colonies and of their cancerous affliction – their resistance to the establishment of capital. 'Where land is

7. E. G. Wakefield, *England and America*, Vol. 1, p. 18.
8. ibid., pp. 42–4.   9. ibid., Vol. 2, p. 5.
10. 'Land, to be an element of colonization, must not only be waste, but it must be public property, liable to be converted into private property' (ibid., Vol. 2, p. 125).

very cheap and all men are free, where every one who so pleases can easily obtain a piece of land for himself, not only is labour very dear, as respects the labourer's share of the produce, but the difficulty is to obtain combined labour at any price.'[11]

In the colonies the separation of the worker from the conditions of labour and from the soil, in which they are rooted, does not yet exist, or only sporadically, or on too limited a scale. Hence the separation of agriculture from industry does not exist either, nor have any of the domestic industries of the countryside been destroyed. Whence then is to come the home market for capital? 'No part of the population of America is exclusively agricultural, excepting slaves and their employers who combine capital and labour in particular works. Free Americans, who cultivate the soil, follow many other occupations. Some portion of the furniture and tools which they use is commonly made by themselves. They frequently build their own houses, and carry to market, at whatever distance, the produce of their own industry. They are spinners and weavers, they make soap and candles, as well as, in many cases, shoes and clothes for their own use. In America the cultivation of land is often the secondary pursuit of a blacksmith, a miller or a shopkeeper.'[12] Where, among such curious characters, is the 'field of abstinence' for the capitalists?

The great beauty of capitalist production consists in this, that it not only constantly reproduces the wage-labourer as a wage-labourer, but also always produces a relative surplus population of wage-labourers in proportion to the accumulation of capital. Thus the law of supply and demand as applied to labour is kept on the right lines, the oscillation of wages is confined within limits satisfactory to capitalist exploitation, and lastly, the social dependence of the worker on the capitalist, which is indispensable, is secured. At home, in the mother country, the smug deceitfulness of the political economist can turn this relation of absolute dependence into a free contract between buyer and seller, between equally independent owners of commodities, the owner of the commodity capital on one side, the owner of the commodity labour on the other. But in the colonies this beautiful illusion is torn aside. There, the absolute numbers of the population increase much more quickly than in the mother country, because many workers enter the colonial world as ready-made adults,

11. ibid., Vol. 1, p. 247.   12. ibid., pp. 21–2.

and still the labour-market is always understocked. The law of the supply and demand of labour collapses completely. On the one hand, the old world constantly throws in capital, thirsting after exploitation and 'abstinence'; on the other, the regular reproduction of the wage-labourer as a wage-labourer comes up against the most mischievous obstacles, which are in part insuperable. And what becomes of the production of redundant wage-labourers, redundant, that is, in proportion to the accumulation of capital? Today's wage-labourer is tomorrow's independent peasant or artisan, working for himself. He vanishes from the labour-market – but not into the workhouse. This constant transformation of wage-labourers into independent producers, who work for themselves instead of for capital, and enrich themselves instead of the capitalist gentlemen, reacts in its turn very adversely on the conditions of the labour-market. Not only does the degree of exploitation of the wage-labourer remain indecently low. The wage-labourer also loses, along with the relation of dependence, the feeling of dependence on the abstemious capitalist. Hence all the inconveniences depicted so honestly, so eloquently and so movingly by our friend E. G. Wakefield.

The supply of wage-labour, he complains, is neither constant, nor regular, nor sufficient. 'The supply of labour is always, not only small, but uncertain.'[13] 'Though the produce divided between the capitalist and the labourer be large, the labourer takes so great a share that he soon becomes a capitalist ... Few, even of those whose lives are unusually long, can accumulate great masses of wealth.'[14] The workers most emphatically refuse to let the capitalist abstain from paying for the greater part of their labour. It is of no assistance to him if he cunningly imports his own wage-labourers from Europe, with his own capital. They soon 'cease ... to be labourers for hire; they ... become independent land-owners, if not competitors with their former masters in the labour-market.'[15] Horror of horrors! The excellent capitalist has imported bodily from Europe, with his own good money, his own competitors! The end of the world has come! No wonder Wakefield laments the absence both of relations of dependence and feelings of dependence on the part of the wage-labourers in the colonies. On account of the high wages, says his disciple Merivale, there is in the colonies an urgent desire for cheaper and more sub-

13. E. G. Wakefield, *England and America,* Vol. 2, p. 116.
14. ibid., Vol. 1, p. 131.   15. ibid., Vol. 2, p. 5.

servient workers, for a class of people to whom the capitalist may dictate his terms, instead of having his terms dictated by them . . . In the old civilized countries the worker, although free, is by a law of nature dependent on the capitalist; in colonies this dependence must be created by artificial means.[16]

What now is the consequence of this regrettable state of affairs in the colonies, according to Wakefield? A 'barbarizing tendency of dispersion' of producers and of the wealth of the nation.[17] The fragmentation of the means of production among innumerable owners, working on their own account, annihilates, along with the centralization of capital, all the foundations of combined labour. Every lengthy undertaking, extending over several years and demanding the outlay of fixed capital, is prevented from being carried out. In Europe, capital does not hesitate for a moment, for the working class forms its living appendage, always present in excess, always at its disposal. But not in the colonies! Wakefield recounts the following exceedingly painful anecdote. He was talking with some capitalists of Canada and the state of New York, where moreover the wave of immigration often sticks,

16. Merivale, op. cit., Vol. 2, pp. 235–314 passim. Even that mild, free-trading, vulgar economist Molinari says this: 'In the colonies where slavery has been abolished without the compulsory labour being replaced with an equivalent quantity of free labour, there has occurred the opposite of what happens every day before our eyes. Simple workers have been seen to exploit in their turn the industrial *entrepreneurs*, demanding from them wages which bear absolutely no relation to the legitimate share in the product which they ought to receive. The planters were unable to obtain for their sugar a sufficient price to cover the increase in wages, and were obliged to furnish the extra amount, at first out of their profits, and then out of their very capital. A considerable number of planters have been ruined as a result, while others have closed down their businesses in order to avoid the ruin which threatened them. . . It is doubtless better that these accumulations of capital should be destroyed than that generations of men should perish' (how generous of M. Molinari) 'but would it not be better if both survived?' (Molinari, op. cit., pp. 51–2). M. Molinari, M. Molinari! What then becomes of the ten commandments, of Moses and the Prophets, of the law of supply and demand, if in Europe the '*entrepreneur*' can cut down the worker's 'legitimate share' and in the West Indies the workers can cut down the *entrepreneur*'s? And what, if you please, is this 'legitimate share', which, according to your own admission, the capitalist in Europe daily neglects to pay? Over yonder, in the colonies, where the workers are so 'simple' as to 'exploit' the capitalist, M. Molinari feels a powerful itch to use police methods to set on the right road that law of supply and demand which works automatically everywhere else.

17. Wakefield, op. cit., Vol. 2, p. 52.

depositing a sediment of 'redundant' workers. 'Our capital,' says one of the characters in the melodrama, 'was ready for many operations which require a considerable period of time for their completion; but we could not begin such operations with labour which, we knew, would soon leave us. If we had been sure of retaining the labour of such emigrants, we should have been glad to have engaged it at once, and for a high price: and we should have engaged it, even though we had been sure it would leave us, provided we had been sure of a fresh supply whenever we might need it.'[18]

After Wakefield has contrasted English capitalist agriculture and its 'combined' labour with the scattered cultivation of American peasants, he unwittingly shows us the obverse of the medal. He depicts the mass of the American people as well-to-do, independent, enterprising and comparatively cultured, whereas 'the English agricultural labourer is a miserable wretch, a pauper ... In what country, except North America and some new colonies, do the wages of free labour employed in agriculture, much exceed a bare subsistence for the labourer? ... Undoubtedly, farm-horses in England, being a valuable property, are better fed than English peasants.'[19] But never mind, the wealth of the nation is once again, by its very nature, identical with the misery of the people.

How then can the anti-capitalist cancer of the colonies be healed? If men were willing to turn the whole of the land from public into private property at one blow, this would certainly destroy the root of the evil, but it would also destroy – the colony. The trick is to kill two birds with one stone. Let the government set an artificial price on the virgin soil, a price independent of the law of supply and demand, a price that compels the immigrant to work a long time for wages before he can earn enough money to buy land[20] and turn himself into an independent farmer. The

18. Wakefield, *England and America*, Vol. 2, pp. 191–2.
19. ibid., Vol. 1, pp. 47, 246.
20. 'It is, you add, a result of the appropriation of the soil and of capital that the man who has nothing but the strength of his arms finds employment and creates an income for himself ... but the opposite is true, it is thanks to the individual appropriation of the soil that there exist men who only possess the strength of their arms ... When you put a man in a vacuum, you rob him of the air. You do the same, when you take away the soil from him ... for you are putting him in a space void of wealth, so as to leave him no way of living except according to your wishes' (Colins, op. cit., Vol. 3, pp. 268–71).

fund resulting from the sale of land at a price relatively prohibitory for the wage-labourers, this fund of money extorted from the wages of labour by a violation of the sacred law of supply and demand, is to be applied by the government, in proportion to its growth, to the importation of paupers from Europe into the colonies, so as to keep the wage-labour market full for the capitalists. Under these circumstances, 'everything will be for the best in the best of all possible worlds'. This is the great secret of 'systematic colonization'. Under this plan, Wakefield exclaims triumphantly, 'the supply of labour *must* be constant and regular, because, first, as no labourer would be able to procure land until he had worked for money, all immigrant labourers, working for a time for wages and in combination, would produce capital for the employment of more labourers; secondly, because every labourer who left off working for wages and became a landowner, would, by purchasing land, provide a fund for bringing fresh labour to the colony.'[21] The land-price laid down by the state must of course be 'sufficient', i.e. it must be high enough 'to prevent the labourers from becoming independent landowners until others had followed to take their place'.[22] This 'sufficient price for the land' is nothing but a euphemistic circumlocution for the ransom which the worker must pay to the capitalist in return for permission to retire from the wage-labour market to the land. First, he must create for the capitalist the 'capital' which enables him to exploit more workers; then, at his own expense, he must put a 'substitute' in the labour-market, who is dispatched across the sea by the government, again at the worker's expense, for his old master, the capitalist.

It is extremely characteristic that the English government for years practised this method of 'primitive accumulation' prescribed by Mr Wakefield expressly for use in the colonies. The resulting fiasco was of course as ignominious as the fate of Peel's Bank Act.* The stream of emigration was simply diverted from the English colonies to the United States. Meanwhile, the advance of capitalist

21. Wakefield, op. cit., Vol. 2, p. 192.
22. ibid., p. 45.

---

*Sir Robert Peel's Bank Act of 1844. The 'fiasco' referred to here is the suspension of the Act in November 1857 owing to the onset of the commercial crisis of that year. See *A Contribution to the Critique of Political Economy*, p. 185.

production in Europe, accompanied by increasing government pressure, has rendered Wakefield's recipe superfluous. On the one hand, the enormous and continuous flood of humanity, driven year in, year out, onto the shores of America, leaves behind a stationary sediment in the East of the United States, since the wave of immigration from Europe throws men onto the labour-market there more rapidly than the wave of immigration to the West can wash them away. On the other hand, the American Civil War has brought in its train a colossal national debt and, with it, a heavy tax-burden, the creation of a finance aristocracy of the vilest type, and the granting of immense tracts of public land to speculative companies for the exploitation of railways, mines, etc. In short, it has brought a very rapid centralization of capital. The great republic has therefore ceased to be the promised land for emigrating workers. Capitalist production advances there with gigantic strides, even though the lowering of wages and dependence of the wage-labourer has by no means yet proceeded so far as to reach the normal European level. The shameless squandering of uncultivated colonial land on aristocrats and capitalists by the English government, so loudly denounced even by Wakefield, has, especially in Australia,[23] in conjunction with the stream of men attracted by the gold-diggings, and the competition from imported English commodities which affects everyone down to the smallest artisan, produced an ample 'relative surplus population of workers', so that almost every mail-boat brings ill tidings of a 'glut of the Australian labour-market', and prostitution flourishes there in some places as exuberantly as in the Haymarket in London.

However, we are not concerned here with the condition of the colonies. The only thing that interests us is the secret discovered in the New World by the political economy of the Old World, and loudly proclaimed by it: that the capitalist mode of production and accumulation, and therefore capitalist private property as well, have for their fundamental condition the annihilation of that private property which rests on the labour of the individual himself; in other words, the expropriation of the worker.

23. As soon as Australia became her own law-giver, she naturally passed laws favourable to the settlers, but the squandering of the land, already accomplished by the English government, stands in the way. 'The first and main object at which the new Land Act of 1862 aims is to give increased facilities for the settlement of the people' (*The Land Law of Victoria*, by the Hon. C. G. Duffy, Minister of Public Lands, London, 1862 [p. 3]).

Appendix

Results of the Immediate Process of Production

Our knowledge and understanding of *Capital* has been significantly advanced during the last decades as a result of the publication in the thirties of two previously unknown major texts by Marx. The first of these was, of course, the *Grundrisse*, which the Pelican Marx Library has now made available to English-speaking readers in a separate volume. The second was an originally planned Part Seven of Volume 1 of *Capital*, published here for the first time in an English translation. Entitled 'Resultate des unmittelbaren Produktionsprozesses' ('Results of the Immediate Process of Production'), and hereafter referred to as the *Resultate*, it was first published in 1933, simultaneously in Russian and German, by Adoratsky in Volume II of *Arkhiv Marksa i Engelsa* (*Marx-Engels Archives*), printed in Moscow. Only when it was reprinted in German and other Western European languages in the late sixties did it become an object of intense study by Marxists and academic 'Marxologists' alike.

It seems to have been written between June 1863 and December 1866,[1] that is after the 1861–3 manuscript (the enormous twenty-three notebooks) was completed. Indeed, Kautsky published an excerpt from notebook 18 (undated, but which he supposes to have been written in December 1862) in which the final draft contents for Volume 1 of *Capital* are listed. After the first five parts, which are maintained in the final version, it reads as follows:

6. Reconversion of surplus-value into capital. Primitive accumulation. Wakefield's colonial theory.
7. Result of the production process. – The change in the form of the law of appropriation can be shown either under 6 or under 7.
8. Theories of surplus-value.
9. Theories of productive and unproductive labour.[2]

1. This suggestion is put forward by Bruno Maffi, in his interesting 'Presentation' to the recent Italian translation (Marx, *Il Capitale: Libro I, capitolo VI inedito*, Florence, 1969).
2. Karl Kautsky, 'Vorrede', in Karl Marx, *Theorien über den Mehrwert*, Vol. 3, Stuttgart, 1910, p. viii.

We know that 8 and 9 were relegated by Marx from Volume 1 to Volume 4. A new Part Six was introduced into the final version of Volume 1, entitled 'Wages' ('Arbeitslohn'). The original 6 thus became Part Seven, with a new and striking title: 'The Accumulation of Capital'. We know already that the new Part Six on wages was introduced as a result of the change made by Marx in the plan for the whole of *Capital*, when he abandoned his intention to deal with wage-labour in a later and separate volume. But why was the originally planned Part Seven discarded? (As written, it is entitled 'Chapter Six'. 'Seven' was changed into 'Six' because Marx intended at the time to publish the present Part One as an introduction. 'Chapter' was the term he was using at the time for what in the published version became 'Part'.) For the time being, it is impossible to give a definitive answer to that question, on the basis of the knowledge which we possess about the development of Marx's thought between 1863 and 1866. Possibly the reason lay in Marx's wish to present *Capital* as a 'dialectically articulated artistic whole'.[3] He may have felt that, in such a totality, 'Chapter Six' would be out of place, since it had a double *didactic* function: as a summary of Volume 1 and as a *bridge* between Volumes 1 and 2.

Be that as it may, in the light of this intended double function, the *Resultate* contains many illuminating insights, not only regarding Volume 1 but also regarding Volume 2. I shall just mention in this respect the *explicit* statement by Marx, so often contested by his critics and by some of his followers too, that he considered the *constant expansion of the capitalist market as absolutely necessary for the survival of the capitalist mode of production*. For precisely because capitalist production is production through a growing mass of machinery, a growing fixed capital, a growing organic composition of capital, it is also of necessity mass production of commodities on a constantly increasing scale, whose sale demands a constantly growing market.

The key aspect of the *Resultate* relates to the synthesis of the capitalist mode of production as production of surplus-value and production of commodities produced by capital, and to the interconnected problem of the origin and content of the increased productivity of labour without which no increase in surplus-value production would be possible in the long term. For this purpose, Marx introduces a distinction between what he calls the formal and the real 'subsumption of labour under capital'. Formal subsumption is characteristic of the period of manufacture; real subsumption is characteristic of the modern factory, with its constant revolution of production techniques and methods. Using this distinction, he unfolds the particular inner logic of capitalism in pages which have an 'up-to-date' ring matched by few other writings by nineteenth-century economists. The search for a constant increase in surplus-value production implies a search for constant

3. Karl Marx, letter to Engels of 31 July 1865, in *MEW* 31, p. 132.

reductions in cost price, a constant cheapening of commodities. Thereby capital, rather than adapting itself to a given structure of demand or socially acknowledged needs, by revolutionizing production revolutionizes demands and needs themselves, expanding markets, provoking new needs, creating new products and new spheres into which production of exchange values for more value, production for profit, makes its appearance.

This leads to a constant expansion of technology, of the use of and search for scientific discoveries applicable in the production process itself. These discoveries too become a business subsumed under capital. So a new and formidable source of increased productivity of labour appears, unknown before the modern factory. Marx denounces the mystification which consists in considering science both as a 'source of value' and as a 'proof' that 'capital is productive'. He stresses the fact that, under capitalism, labour should not be seen as manual labour only, but as the *combined or collective labour potential* (*kombiniertes Arbeitsvermögen*, *Gesamtarbeitsvermögen*) of all those whose labour is indispensable to produce the final product. He even uses the concept of the 'collective worker', the 'global worker' (*Gesamtarbeiter*), in this respect. The value-producing process is the manifestation of labour-time spent by all those who co-operate in production while selling their labour-power to the capitalist. This 'global worker' explicitly included, for Marx, engineers, technologists and even managers.[4]

It would be possible, at this point, to deal with the important controversy still raging among students and followers of Marx concerning the exact definition of, and distinction between, 'productive' and 'unproductive' labour. I prefer, however, to relegate this discussion to the introduction to Volume 2. For the real difficulty in establishing the distinction does not, in fact, hinge so much upon what occurs *inside* the process of production – this problem is adequately clarified in the *Resultate* – as upon the distinction *between* production and circulation of commodities and upon the problem of the so-called service industries. The final version of Marx's opinion in that respect (his initial views had been expressed in *Theories of Surplus-Value*) can be found in *Capital* Volume 2.

What is necessary, however, is to stress that what we find extensively dealt with in the *Resultate* is nothing but a further development of one of the most striking aspects of the *Grundrisse*, namely Marx's theory of the *objective socialization of labour by capitalism*. For what Marx sketches in these pages – summarizing what is already developed in Chapter 15 of Volume 1 – is the way in which the integration of science and production, the development of technology and of machinery, has a twofold way of objectively denying the private character *of work and of labour* which is the very essence of commodity production.

4. See below, pp. 1052–5.

On the one hand, inside the factory, the individual labourer and the individual scientist alike can work only as part of a team. They can no longer do individual jobs in function of individual inclinations, regardless of the activities of other members of the team. Their jobs have become part of a *co-operative totality* which, potentially, once capitalism has been superseded by the reign of the associated producers, will open up undreamt-of possibilities for the development of individual talents and capacities too, precisely because this high level of objective co-operation of labour immensely widens the general scope of human endeavour and potential self-development.

On the other hand, between factories, branches of industry, countries, the more the centralization of capital advances, the more technical and economic integration advances also, creating closer and closer bonds of objective co-operation between producers who are still living hundreds if not thousands of miles apart. In this way too, capitalism prepares the ground for both the real unity of the human race and the real universality of the individual, made materially possible by this objective socialization of labour.

But under the capitalist mode of production this objective socialization of labour cannot free itself from the shackles of capitalist relations of production. This whole gigantic machinery can function under capitalism only for the purpose and with the goal of private appropriation of profit, of profit maximization by each individual firm, which is something quite distinct from optimum economic development (and even from the optimization of the division and growth of social material resources). The conflict between, on the one hand, the development of the objectively more and more socialized productive forces and, on the other, the capitalist relations of production based upon private appropriation determines both recurrent economic crises and a potential social crisis, which becomes terrifyingly explosive as soon as bourgeois society has fulfilled its progressive mission and enters its period of historical decline.

In this connection, a word is necessary about the fragments published here as 'Isolated Fragments'. Found in the same notebook of Marx's and included in the German manuscript published in 1933, they are not, properly speaking, part of the original Part Seven ('Chapter Six'). Adoratsky entitled them 'Einzelne Seiten' (separate pages). Two of these are especially significant, one discussing the importance and function of trade unions and the second on the function of emigration. Both confirm the interpretation of Marx's theory of wages put forward in the introduction to this volume.

In the first fragment Marx insists on the fact that a trade union is a combination of sellers of the commodity labour-power, which enables them to negotiate the price of this commodity with the capitalists under more equal conditions than if they were to negotiate on an individual basis. As is the case with all commodities, this price can never for very long radically depart from the axis of the value of labour-power around which it oscillates. However, by preventing the capitalists from lowering the value of labour-power, trade unions can at least prevent all the results of increased productivity of labour from automatically accruing to the former: in other words they can achieve an increase in real wages, through the inclusion in the value of labour-power (in its moral-historical element) of the counter-value of new mass-produced commodities satisfying newly acquired needs.

The second fragment emphasizes the limits of emigration from Europe (especially from Britain) overseas, states that the international mobility of labour is inferior to the international mobility of capital, but adds that *if Britain's overseas emigration significantly increased, this would destroy its dominant position on the world market.* This is exactly what did in fact happen.[5] As a result of a significant increase both in British exports of commodities and in British exports of redundant labour, a secular decline of the industrial reserve army occurred, which explains the secular rise in real wages.

5. Between 1841 and 1881, the net outflow of population from Britain was practically nil, Irish and Scottish immigration offsetting English overseas emigration. In the period 1881–91 this net outflow was over 600,000 and in the period 1881–1911 nearly 1·2 million (A. K. Cairncross, *Home and Foreign Investment*, Cambridge, 1953, p. 70).

ERNEST MANDEL

Appendix: Results of the
Immediate Process of Production

441 The subject-matter of this chapter falls into three parts:

(1) *Commodities* as the *product of capital*, of capitalist production;

(2) Capitalist production is the *production of surplus-value*;

(3) It is, finally, the production and reproduction of the total relationship by virtue of which this immediate process of production defines itself as specifically capitalist.

Of these three topics, (1) should be placed last, and not first, in the final revision before printing, because it forms the *transition* to Volume 2 – 'The Circulation Process of Capital'. For the sake of convenience, however, we begin with it here.*

I: COMMODITIES AS THE PRODUCT OF CAPITAL

As the elementary form of bourgeois wealth, the *commodity* was our point of departure, the prerequisite for the emergence of capital. On the other hand, *commodities* appear now as the *product of capital*.

The circular nature of our argument corresponds to the *historical development* of capital. Capital is predicated on the *exchange of commodities, trade in commodities*, but it may be formed at various stages of production, common to all of which is the fact that capitalist production does not yet exist, or only exists sporadically. On the other hand, a highly developed commodity exchange and the *form of the commodity* as the universally necessary social form of the product can only emerge as the *consequence of the capitalist mode of production*.

However, if we consider societies where *capitalist production* is *highly developed*, we find that the commodity is both the constant elementary premiss (precondition) of capital and also the immediate result of the capitalist process of production.

Both money and commodities are elementary preconditions of capital, but they develop into capital only under certain circumstances. Capital cannot come into being except on the foundation of the circulation of commodities (including money), i.e. where trade has already grown to a certain given degree. For their part, however, the production and circulation of commodities do not at all imply the existence of the capitalist mode of production. On the contrary, as I have already shown,[1] they may be found

1. *Zur Kritik der politischen Ökonomie*, Berlin, 1859, p. 74 [English edition, p. 95].

---

*The German and Russian editions, following Marx's hint, changed the order of the three sections, and placed the first, 'Commodities as the Product of Capital', at the end. We have chosen to follow the French edition (*Un Chapitre inédit du Capital*, ed. and trans. by R. Dangeville, Paris, 1971), which retains the original order, partly because Marx never undertook the 'final revision' which would justify the change, and partly because the subject-matter as it stands unfolds more naturally and logically in this way. The numbers in the left-hand margins refer to the pagination of the manuscript.

even in 'pre-bourgeois modes of production'. They constitute the *historical premiss* of the capitalist mode of production. On the other hand, however, once the commodity has become the *general form of the product*, then everything that is produced must assume that form; sale and purchase embrace not just excess produce, but its very substance, and the various conditions of production themselves appear as *commodities* which leave circulation and enter production only on the foundations of capitalist production. Hence if the *commodity* appears on the one hand as the premiss of the formation of capital, it is also essentially the result, the product of capitalist production once it has become the *universal elementary form of the product*. At earlier stages of production *a part* of what was produced took the form of commodities. Capital, however, necessarily produces its product as a *commodity*.[2] This is why as capitalist production, i.e. capital, develops, the general laws governing the commodity evolve in proportion; for example, the laws affecting value develop in the distinct form of the circulation of money.

We see here how even economic categories appropriate to earlier modes of production acquire a new and specific historical character under the impact of capitalist production.

The transformation of money, itself only a different form of the commodity, into capital occurs only when a worker's labour-power* has been converted into a commodity for him. This implies that the category of trade has been extended to embrace a sphere from which it had previously been excluded or into which it had made only sporadic inroads. In other words the working population must have ceased either to be part of the *objective* conditions of labour, or to enter the market-place as the producer of commodities; instead of selling the products of its labour it must sell that labour itself, or more accurately, its labour-power. Only then can it be said that production has become the *production of commodities* through its entire length and breadth.

2. Sismondi.

---

*Throughout this appendix Marx uses *Arbeitsvermögen* (capacity for labour) instead of *Arbeitskraft* (labour-power), the term which he finally settled on in the published version of *Capital*. Since 'labour-power' is more natural in English and since it has gained general acceptance it has been used here except for a few instances where the idea of 'capacities' or 'faculties' is emphasized.

Only then does all produce become commodity and the objective conditions of each and every sphere of production enter into it as commodities themselves. Only on the basis of capitalist production does the commodity actually become the *universal elementary form of wealth*. For example, where capital has not yet taken over agriculture, a large proportion of agricultural produce is still used directly as means of subsistence and not as a commodity. In that event a large proportion of the working population will not have been transformed into wage-labourers and a large proportion of the conditions of labour will not yet have become capital. It is implicit in this situation that the developed division of labour which appears *by chance* within society, and the capitalist division of labour within the workshop, are things that mutually condition and produce each other. For the *commodity* as the necessary form of the product, and hence the alienation of the product as the necessary means of appropriating it, entail a fully developed *division of social labour*. While, conversely, it is only on the basis of capitalist production, and hence of the *capitalist division of labour* within the workshop, that all produce necessarily assumes the form of the commodity and hence all producers are necessarily commodity producers. Therefore, it is only with the emergence of capitalist production that use-value is universally mediated by exchange-value.

These three points are crucial:

(1) Capitalist production is the first to make the commodity into the general form of all produce.

(2) The production of commodities leads inexorably to capitalist production, once the worker has ceased to be a part of the conditions of production (as in slavery, serfdom), or once primitive common ownership has ceased to be the basis of society (India). In short, from the moment when labour-power in general becomes a commodity.

(3) Capitalist production destroys the basis of commodity production in so far as the latter involves independent individual production and the exchange of commodities between owners or the exchange of equivalents. The formal exchange of capital and labour-power becomes general.

From this standpoint it is immaterial in what form the conditions of production enter into the *labour process*. It is unimportant whether, like a part of the constant capital, the machinery, etc.,

443   they only yield up a part of their value to the product by degrees, or are entirely absorbed into it, like the raw material; whether, as in the case of seed in farming, a portion of the product is at once employed by the producer as the means of labour, or whether it is first sold and then converted back into a means of labour. Apart from the service they perform as use-values in the process of production, all the means of labour that have been produced now also serve as ingredients in the *valorization process*. Where they are not changed into actual money, they are converted into accounting money; in short, they are used as exchange-values and the element of value that they add to the product in one way or another is precisely calculated. And to the extent to which agriculture, for example, becomes a capitalistically run branch of industry (capitalist production sets up its stall in the countryside), to the extent to which agriculture produces for the market, i.e. produces *commodities*, articles for sale and not for its own immediate consumption – so too, and to the same degree, it calculates its costs, treats each item as a commodity (regardless of whether it buys it from another or from itself, i.e. from *production*). In other words, then, inasmuch as the commodity is treated as an autonomous exchange-value, it acts as *money*. Thus since wheat, hay, cattle, seed of all kinds, etc. are *sold* as commodities – and since without the sale they cannot be regarded as products – it follows that they enter production as *commodities*, i.e. as money. Like the *products*, and *as their ingredients*, the *conditions of production* are indeed themselves products and they too are thus reduced to *commodities*. And as a consequence of the valorization process they are included in the calculations as *sums of money*, i.e. in the autonomous form of exchange-value. Here then the immediate process of production is always an indissoluble union of *labour process* and *valorization process*, just as the product is a whole composed of *use-value* and *exchange-value*, i.e. the *commodity*. But there is more to the matter than these formal aspects: as the farmer *buys* what he has to *lay out*, we witness the development of a trade in seed, in manure, in breeding cattle, etc. – while he *sells* his income. Thus for the individual farmer these conditions of production pass from circulation into his process of production; circulation thus becomes in effect the precondition of his production since they [the conditions of production] increasingly become commodities he has *bought* (or that *can be bought*). They have long since become commodities in his eyes, since they are articles,

means of labour, that are at the same time *values* forming part of his capital. (When he returns them to production in nature he therefore includes them in his calculations as things sold him qua *producer*.) And moreover all this keeps pace with the growth of the capitalist mode of production in agriculture, which therefore is increasingly put on a factory basis.

As the *universally necessary form of the product*, as the specific characteristic of capitalist production, the commodity palpably comes into its own in the large-scale production that emerges in the course of capitalist production. The product becomes increasingly one-sided and *massive in nature*. This imposes upon it a social character, one which is closely bound up with existing social relations, while its immediate use-value for the gratification of the needs of its producer appears wholly adventitious, immaterial and inessential. This mass product must be realized as exchange-value, it must undergo the metamorphosis of the commodity, not only because the producer who produces as a capitalist must ensure his own survival, but also because the process of production

444   must itself be contained and renewed. It is therefore absorbed into commerce. Its purchaser is not the immediate consumer, but the merchant whose business it is to bring about the metamorphosis of the commodity (Sismondi).* Finally, then, the product develops its commodity character, and hence its exchange-value, since with capitalist production the spheres of production become increasingly diversified and hence the possibilities of exchanging products are steadily multiplied.[3]

The *commodity* that emerges from capitalist production is different from the commodity we began with as the element, the precondition of capitalist production. We began with the individual commodity viewed as an autonomous article in which a specific amount of labour-time is objectified and which therefore has an exchange-value of a definite amount.

The commodity may now be further defined as follows:

(1) What is objectified in it – apart from its use-value – is a specific quantum of socially necessary labour. But whereas in the

---

3. Cf. *Zur Kritik der politischen Ökonomie*, p. 17 [English edition, p. 42]. See also Wakefield.

---

* This sentence is a summary and at the same time an interpretation of Sismondi's argument in *Nouveaux Principes*, Vol. 1, Paris, 1827, p 90.

commodity regarded by itself it remains quite undecided (and is in fact a matter of indifference) from whom this objectified labour is derived, the *commodity* as the *product of capital* can be said to contain both paid and unpaid labour. It has already been mentioned that this is not strictly true since the labour itself is not bought or sold directly. But the commodity contains a specific overall quantity of *objectified* labour. A portion of this objectified labour (aside from constant capital for which an equivalent has been paid) is exchanged for the equivalent of the worker's wages; another portion is appropriated by the capitalist without any equivalent being paid. Both portions are objectified and so present as parts of the value of the commodity. And it is a convenient abbreviation to describe the one as paid and the other as unpaid labour.

445   (2) The individual commodity does not only appear materially as a part of the total produce of capital, but as an aliquot part of the total produced by it. We are now no longer concerned with the individual autonomous commodity, the single product. The result of the process is not individual goods, but a *mass of commodities* in which the value of the capital invested together with the surplus-value – i.e. the surplus labour appropriated – has reproduced itself, and each one of which is the incarnation of both the value of the *capital* and the surplus-value it has produced. The labour expended on each commodity can no longer be calculated – except as an average, i.e. an ideal estimate. The calculation begins with that portion of the constant capital which only enters into the value of the total product in so far as it is used up; it continues with the conditions of production that are consumed communally, and ends with the direct social contribution of many co-operating individuals whose labour is averaged out. This labour, then, is reckoned *ideally* as an aliquot part of the total labour expended on it. When *determining the price* of an individual article it appears as a merely ideal fraction of the total product in which the capital reproduces itself.

(3) As the product of capital, the commodity embodies the total value of the capital together with the surplus-value, unlike the original commodity which appeared to us as an autonomous thing. *The commodity* is a transfiguration of capital that has valorized itself, and its sale must now be organized on the *scale* and in the *quantities* necessary to realize the old capital value and the old surplus-value it has created. To achieve this it is by no

means sufficient for the individual commodities or a portion of them to be sold at their value.

We have already seen that the commodity must acquire a two-fold mode of existence if it is to be rendered fit for the circulation process. It is not enough for it to appear to the buyer as an article with particular useful qualities, i.e. as a specific *use-value* which can gratify specific needs whether of individual or of productive consumption. Its exchange-value must also have acquired a definite, independent, *form*, distinct, albeit ideally, from its use-value. It must represent both the unity and the duality of use-value and exchange-value. Its exchange-value acquires this distinctive form independent of its use-value, as the pure form of materialized social labour-time, i.e. its *price*. For the price is the expression of exchange-value as exchange-value, i.e. as *money*, and more precisely as *money of account*.

Now there exist in reality individual commodities such as railways, large building complexes, etc. which are so continuous in nature and on such a grand scale that the entire product of the capital invested appears to be a *single* product. In such cases we should apply the law relevant in the case of single commodities; in other words *price* is nothing but value as expressed in money terms. The total value of the capital + surplus-value would then be contained within the single commodity and could be expressed in terms of money of account. The actual price of such a commodity would not be otherwise different from what we have said about individual commodities, since the *total product* of capital really would be present in this case as a *single* commodity. It is unnecessary therefore to dwell on the matter further.

The majority of commodities, however, are discrete in nature (and even those that are continuous can for the most part be considered as discrete quantities). In other words, viewed as quantities of a given article, they are divisible in terms of *measures* traditionally appropriate to them as use-values. Thus we deal with (*a*) wheat by the quarter, (*b*) coffee by the hundredweight, (*c*) linen by the ell, (*d*) knives by the dozen – and in all these cases the single commodity is a unit of the measure, etc.

We have now to consider that *total product* of capital which can always be regarded as a *single* commodity, irrespective of its scale, and whether it is discrete or continuous, a product which can be considered as a single use-value and whose exchange-value therefore also appears in the *total price* as the expression of the total value of this total product.

In our examination of the *valorization process*, it turned out that a part of the constant capital invested, such as buildings, machinery, etc., transfers to the product only the determinate portion of value that it loses while functioning as a means of labour during the labour process. It never enters the product materially in the form of its own use-value. It continues to assist the production of commodities over a long period of time and the value that it transfers to the objects produced during their production is measured in terms of the relationship of that time-span to the total period during which it is used up as a means of labour, that is to say, a period in which its total value is consumed and transferred to the product. Thus if it lasts for ten years we may average it out and say that it transfers $\frac{1}{10}$ of its value each year to the product, $\frac{1}{10}$ of its value to the annual product of the capital. Once a given quantity of products has been disposed of, a part of the constant capital may continue to be used as a means of labour and so continue to represent a certain value on the average basis as just calculated, since it does not form part of the value of the mass of products so disposed of. Its total value is only of importance to the value of the mass of products disposed of, i.e. the products to whose production it had contributed; that is to say, the value it transfers over a definite period is deducted as an aliquot part of its total value, i.e. the given period in which it is utilized is related to the overall time during which it is employed and in which it transfers its total value to the product. For the rest, any value it still retains is irrelevant to the valuation of the mass of values already disposed of. As far as they are concerned, it can be set at nought. Or, and it amounts to the same thing, we can for the sake of simplicity treat the matter as if the *entire capital*, including the constant portion which is only absorbed into the product over a long period of time, were contained in and had entered into the product of the total capital under consideration.

Let us assume, therefore, that the total product = 1,200 ells of linen. The capital invested = £100, of which £80 is constant capital and £20 variable. The rate of surplus-value = 100 per cent, so that the worker labours for half the working day for himself, and the other half gratis for the capitalist. In this case the surplus-value produced = £20 and the total value of the 1,200 ells = £120, of which £80 represents the constant capital invested, and £40 comes from the additional living labour. Of this latter, half goes as wages 147 to the worker and the other half represents surplus labour or constitutes surplus-value.

Since, with the exception of the additional labour, the elements of capitalist production already enter the process of production as commodities, i.e. with specific prices, it follows that the value added by the constant capital is already given in terms of a *price*. For example, in the present case it is £80 for flax, machinery, etc. As for the additional labour, however, if the wage as determined by the necessary means of subsistence = £20, and the surplus labour is as great as the paid labour, it must be expressed at a price of £40, since the value expressing the additional labour depends on its quantity and by no means on the circumstances in which it is paid. Hence the total price of the 1,200 ells produced by a capital of £100 = £120.

How are we to determine the value of the individual commodity, in this case the ell of linen? Obviously, by dividing the total price of the aggregate product by the number of units as divided into aliquot parts in accordance with a given measure. In other words, the *total price* is divided by the *number of measured units* in which the use-value is expressed. In the present case then, $\frac{£120}{1,200 \text{ ells}}$.
This results in a price of 2s. per ell of linen. If the ell which serves as a measure in the case of linen is now further defined, i.e. if it is broken down into smaller aliquot parts, we can go on to determine the price of half an ell, etc., in the same way. The price of the individual commodity is determined, then, by expressing its use-value as an aliquot part of the aggregate product, and its price as the corresponding aliquot part of the total value generated by the capital invested.

We have seen that as the *productivity* or *productive power of labour* varies, the same labour-time will result in the production of very different quantities of a product, or in other words equal exchange-values will be expressed in quite different quantities of use-values. Let us assume, in the present instance, that the linen weaver's productivity is increased fourfold. The constant capital, i.e. the flax, machinery, etc. set in motion by the labour expressed as £40, was = £80. If the weaver's productivity increases fourfold it will set four times as much capital in motion, i.e. £320 worth of flax, etc. And the number of ells produced would also increase in proportion, viz. from 1,200 to 4,800. The additional weavers' labour, however, would still be expressed as £40, since its quantity remains unaltered. Thus the total price of the 4,800 ells is now = £360, and the price of each ell = $\dfrac{£360}{4,800 \text{ ells}}$ = 1s. 6d. per ell. Thus the price of each ell would have fallen from 2s. or 24d. to $1\frac{1}{2}$s. or 18d., i.e. by $\frac{1}{4}$, because the constant capital in each ell had absorbed $\frac{1}{4}$ less additional living labour in the process of converting that labour into linen. Or in other words the same amount of weaving had been distributed over a larger amount of the product. For our present purposes, however, it is better to take an example where the total money invested remains the *same* while the productivity of labour produces very different amounts of the same use-value, for example wheat, merely as the result of varying natural conditions, such as more or less favourable weather. Let us assume that £7 represents the *amount* of work spent on an acre of land, in the production of wheat for instance. Of this sum £4 is additional labour and £3 is labour already objectified in constant capital. Of this £4, let £2 be employed for wages and £2 remains as surplus labour, at the rate of 100 per cent already assumed.

The crop however is to vary with the variation of the seasons.

Total in quarters	One quarter	Value or price of the total produced
'When the farmer has 5	he can sell at 28s.	£7
4½	at about 31	„
4	35	„
3½	40	„
3	46s. 8d.	„
2½	56	„
2	70	„ '4

The *value* or *price* of the aggregate product yielded by the capital of £5 invested in each acre remains £7, since the invested quantities of objectified and additional living labour remain

4. *An Inquiry into the Connection between the Present Price of Provisions, and the Size of Farms. With Remarks on Population as Affected Thereby. To Which are Added, Proposals for Preventing Future Scarcity. By a farmer.* [The author is John Arbuthnot.]

constant. However, this same labour results in very different quantities of wheat, and the individual quarter of wheat, therefore, the same aliquot part of the aggregate product, has very different prices. This variation in the prices of the individual commodities produced with the same capital has absolutely no *effect* on the rate of surplus-value, .or the proportion of surplus-value to variable capital, or the way in which the working day is divided into paid and unpaid labour. The total value in which the additional labour is expressed remains unchanged because now, as previously, the same amount of living labour is added to the constant capital; that is to say, the relation of surplus-value to wages, or of paid to unpaid labour remains the same, irrespective of whether the ell costs 2s. or, with the growing productivity of labour, 1½s. All that has changed as far as the individual ell is concerned is the total amount of weavers' work applied to it; but the proportions of paid and unpaid labour into which this total amount is broken down remain the same for every aliquot part of that total contained in each ell, however big or small the total may be. Likewise, in the situation *given* in our other example, i.e. with the declining productivity of labour, the situation in which the newly added labour is distributed among fewer quarters so that a larger proportion of additional labour is attributed to each quarter, the increase in price per quarter in the second case would not affect in the slightest the proportions in which this greater or smaller amount of labour absorbed by each quarter is distributed between paid and unpaid labour. It makes not the slightest difference either to the total surplus-value that the capital has produced or to the aliquot part of surplus-value contained in the value of each quarter relative to the value newly added to it. Under the given conditions, if more living labour is added to a specific amount of the means of labour, then more paid and unpaid labour is added in the same proportions, and if less, then less paid and unpaid labour, likewise in the same proportions. But in either case, the *proportions* of these two ingredients of the newly added labour remain *unaltered*.

Apart from certain extraneous factors irrelevant for our present purposes, the tendency and the result of the capitalist mode of production is steadily to increase the productivity of labour. Hence it also increases the mass of the means of production converted into products by the use of the same quantity of additional labour. This additional labour is then distributed progressively over a greater mass of products, thus reducing the *price* of each individual commodity and commodity prices in general. In and for itself, however, this reduction in the prices of commodities introduces no change either in the *mass* of the surplus-value produced by the same variable capital, or in the proportional division into paid and unpaid of the labour newly added to each individual commodity, or in the rate of surplus-value valorized in each individual commodity. When a specific quantity of flax or number of spindles requires less labour to produce an ell of linen, the fact of a greater or lesser amount of labour does not affect the proportions of paid to unpaid labour. The *absolute amount* of living labour newly added to a specific amount of already objectified labour does not affect the *proportions* in which this greater or lesser quantity breaks down into paid and unpaid labour when applied to the individual commodity. Despite the variation in the price of a commodity arising from a variation in the productive capacity of labour, i.e. despite the reduction in prices and the cheapening of commodities, the relation between paid and unpaid labour and in general the rate of surplus-value valorized by capital can remain *constant*. Even if there were no variation in the productivity of the labour newly added to the means of labour, but only in the productivity of the labour that creates the means of labour, bringing about a rise or fall in their prices, it is equally obvious that the resultant change in the *prices* of the commodities concerned would have no effect on the constant division of the newly added labour they contain into paid and unpaid labour.

And conversely, a *variation in the price of commodities* does not preclude a constant rate of surplus-value, a constant division of the newly added labour into paid and unpaid. And by the same token, *constancy in the price of commodities* does not of itself prevent a variation in the rate of surplus-value, nor a modification in the proportions of paid to unpaid labour. For simplicity's sake let us assume that in the branch of industry under discussion there is no *variation in the productivity of any of the labour within it*. Thus in the above-mentioned case there is no variation in the productivity of the weaving or the labour involved in producing the flax, the spindles, etc. On the assumption previously made, £80 is invested in constant capital, and £20 in variable. This £20 is to represent 20 days (i.e. weekdays) for twenty weavers. On our hypothesis they produced £40, working half the day for themselves and half for the capitalist. But also we shall assume that instead of a working day of 10 hours, this is now extended to 12, so that the surplus labour is now increased by 2 hours per man. The total working day has now grown by $\frac{1}{5}$, from 10 hours to 12. Since $10:12=16\frac{2}{3}:20$, only $16\frac{2}{3}$ weavers would now be required to set the same constant capital of £80 in motion and hence to produce 1,200 ells of linen. (For twenty men working 10 hours = 200 hours, and $16\frac{2}{3}$ men working 12 hours also = 200). Alternatively, if we retain all twenty workers, they will now put in 240 hours work, instead of 200. And since the value of 200 hours daily amounts to £40 per week, 240 hours daily will amount to £48 per week. However, since the productivity of labour, etc. has remained static and since £40 corresponded to £80 constant capital, it follows that £48 requires £96 constant capital. The capital laid out, therefore, amounts to £116 and the value of the commodities produced by it = £144. However, since £120 = 1,200 ells, £144 = 1,440 ells. The cost of one ell would be: $\frac{£144}{1,440} = \frac{£1}{10} = $ 2s. The price of a single ell would remain unchanged because it would still have cost the same total amount in terms of additional labour and labour objectified in the means of labour. But the amount of surplus-value contained in each ell would have increased. Previously, there was £20 surplus-value on 1,200 ells. On one ell, therefore, the surplus-value would be $\frac{£20}{1,200} = \frac{2}{120} = £\frac{1}{60} = \frac{1}{3s.} = $ 4d. Now, however, for 1,440 ells there is £28; for 1 ell, therefore, $4\frac{2}{3}$d., since $4\frac{2}{3}$d. × 1,440 = £28 which is the real sum of the surplus-value in the 1,440 ells. In the same way there is an additional £8 surplus-value (= 80 ells at 2s. per ell), and in fact the number of ells has grown from 1,200 to 1,440.

In this example, then, the *price of the commodity* remains the same. So do the productivity of labour and the capital employed in paying wages. Nevertheless, the amount of surplus-value rises from 20 to 28, or by 8, which is $\frac{2}{5}$ of 20, since $8 \times \frac{5}{2} = \frac{40}{2} = 20$; i.e. by 40 per cent. This is the percentage by which the total surplus-value has grown. As for the rate of surplus-value, then, it has risen from 100 per cent to 140 per cent.

These damned figures can be corrected later on.* For the mom-

---

*Marx's figures have been corrected where necessary.

ent it is sufficient to note that with *prices constant* the surplus-value grows because the same variable capital sets *more* labour in motion and this means not only that *more* goods are produced at the same *cost* but that more goods are produced containing a *greater* proportion of unpaid labour.

451   The *correct calculation* is shown in the following comparison to which I would only preface this note:

If the original £20 *v* [variable capital] is = 20 10-hour days (as weekdays can be multiplied by six, it does not affect the situation) and the working day = 10 hours, then the total labour performed = 200 hours.

Now if the day is lengthened from 10 to 12 hours (and the surplus labour from 5 to 7) then the total labour of the 20 [days] = 240.

If 200 hours' labour represents £40, then 240 = £48.

If 200 hours set £80 worth of constant capital in motion, then 240 will transform a capital of £96.

If 200 hours produce 1,200 ells, then 240 hours will yield 1,440 ells.

And now for our comparison:

	c	v	s	Value of total product	Rate of surplus-value	Sum of surplus-value	Ells	Price per ell	Amount of labour per ell	Surplus labour [per ell]	Rate of surplus labour
I	£80	£20	£20	£120	100%	£20	1200	2s.	8d.	4d.	4:4 = 100%
II	£96	£20	£28	£144	140%	£28	1440	2s.	8d.	$4\frac{2}{3}$d.	$4\frac{2}{3} : 3\frac{1}{3}$ = 140%
											7:5 = the number of hours increased from 5 to 7

In consequence of the increase in the *absolute surplus-value*, i.e. as the result of the prolongation of the working day, the proportions in the total amount of labour worked have altered from 5:5 to 7:5, i.e. from 100 per cent to 140 per cent, a proportion also reflected *pari passu* in *each* ell. However, the total amount of surplus-value is determined by the *number* of workers employed at this higher rate. If there had been a reduction in their number following the extension of the working day, i.e. if the same amount of work were performed, but using fewer workers on account of the longer working day, then the rate of surplus-value would show the *same* increase, but its absolute yield would not.

Conversely, let us now proceed from the assumption that the *working day remains the same*, i.e. 10 hours, but that the necessary labour is reduced from 5 hours to 4 because of *increased productivity* not in the constant capital employed in weaving, or in the weaving itself, but in other branches of industry whose products form part of the working wage. This means that the workers now work 6 hours for the capitalist, instead of 5, and 4 for themselves instead of 5. The ratio of surplus labour to necessary had been 5:5, i.e. 100 per cent. It is now 6:4, i.e. 150 per cent.

Now as previously, twenty men are employed for 10 hours, which gives 200 hours. In both cases they set the same constant capital of £80 in motion. The value of the total product remains £120, the number of ells still stands at 1,200, and the price of each ell is still 2s. – since nothing has changed in the price of production. The total product (in terms of value) of 1 man [-day] = £2, and 20 = £40. But whereas formerly it took 5 hours per day, i.e. £20 per week to buy his means of subsistence, it now takes only 4 hours, = £16 per week, to buy the same amount. The payment of the twenty who now perform only 16 hours of necessary labour is now £16 as against £20 previously. The variable capital has fallen from £20 to £16, but still sets the same amount of absolute labour in motion. But this amount is now distributed differently. Before, $\frac{1}{2}$ had been paid, and $\frac{1}{2}$ unpaid. Now out of 10 hours 4 are paid and 6 unpaid, i.e. $\frac{2}{5}$ are paid and $\frac{3}{5}$ unpaid. Instead of a ratio of 5:5 the present ratio is 6:4, and the rate of surplus-value has risen from 100 per cent to 150 per cent. The rate of surplus-value has increased by 50 per cent. Per ell, then, $3\frac{1}{5}$d. would be paid, and $4\frac{4}{5}$d. would be unpaid labour; this is $\frac{24}{5}:\frac{16}{5}$ or 24:16, as above. Thus the total picture is as follows:

	c	v	s	Value of total product	Rate of surplus-value	Sum of surplus-value	Ells	Price per ell	Amount of labour per ell	Surplus labour [per ell]	Rate of surplus labour
III	£80	£16	£24	£120	150%	£24	1200	2s.	8d.	$4\frac{4}{5}$d.	$4\frac{4}{5}:3\frac{1}{5} =$ 24:16 = 150%

It will be observed here that the sum of surplus-value is only £24 instead of £28 as in Table II. But if in III the same variable capital £20 had been laid out, the *total amount* of labour employed would have risen, since it remains the same with a variable capital of £16. In fact, since 20 is $\frac{1}{4}$ more than 16, it would have increased by $\frac{1}{4}$. In that event the *total amount of labour employed would have risen and not just the ratio of surplus labour to paid labour*. Since, given the new rate, £16 yields £40, then £20 would yield £50, of which £30 would be surplus-value. If £40 = 200 hours, then £50 would equal 250 hours. And if 200 hours set £80 *c* in motion, then 250 hours would transform £100 *c*. And finally, if 200 hours produced 1,200 ells, then 250 hours would yield 1,500 ells. The calculation works out as follows:

	c	v	s	Value of total product	Rate of surplus-value	Sum of surplus-value	Ells	Price per ell	Amount of labour per ell	Surplus labour [per ell]	Rate of surplus labour
IIIa	£100	£20	£30	£150	150%	£30	1500	2s.	8d.	4$\frac{4}{5}$d.	150%

This should be noted in general: as a result of a fall in wages (the consequence here of increased productivity) *less variable capital* is required to put the same amount of labour to work, i.e. to put the *same amount of labour to work at greater advantage* to capital (since the paid portion of the same amount falls in relation to the unpaid portion). Therefore, the capitalist who continues to lay out the *same* amount of *variable capital* will gain doubly. For he is able not only to gain a *higher rate of surplus-value* for the same total amount, but he is able to exploit a *larger quantity of labour at this higher rate*, although his variable capital has not increased in magnitude.

453   We have seen then:
    (1) where *commodity prices vary* the rate and quantity of surplus-value can *remain constant*; and
    (2) where *commodity prices are constant* the rate and quantity of surplus-value can *vary*.

In general, as we have shown in our discussion of the production of surplus-value, the prices of commodities only exert an influence to the extent that they enter into the costs of reproducing labour-power, thus affecting *its* value, an effect that can be nullified in the short term by contrary influences.

It follows from (1) that if we ignore here that sector of produce which, by becoming cheaper, makes labour-power cheaper too (just as by becoming dearer, it makes it more expensive) the fall in prices, the cheapening of goods, resulting from the increase in the productivity of labour means that less labour is materialized in particular commodities, or that the same labour gives rise to a greater quantity of goods so that a smaller aliquot part of labour is needed to produce the individual product. However, it does not necessarily mean any change in the relative distribution between the *paid* and *unpaid* labour that has gone into any given article. The two laws here shown apply generally to all commodities including those that do not enter directly or indirectly into the reproduction of labour-power and whose price therefore, whether high or low, is irrelevant to the determination of the *value* of labour-power itself.

It follows from (2) (see Tables III and IIIa) that although the *prices* of commodities, and the productivity of living labour employed directly in the branch of industry which creates those commodities, remain constant, the *rate and quantity of surplus-value can rise*. (By the same token, we might have demonstrated the *converse*, namely that they can fall if the total working day is curtailed or if the *necessary labour time* grows (the working day itself remaining constant) because of other goods becoming dearer.) This is the case where a *variable capital of given magnitude* occupies very *unequal* amounts of labour of a *given productivity*. (While the prices of commodities remain constant as long as there is no change in the productivity of labour.) Alternatively, a *variable capital of varying size can occupy equal amounts* of labour of a given productivity. In short a variable capital of a certain given size does not always set the same amount of living labour in motion, and if we regard it as a symbol of the amounts of labour it sets in motion, it must be considered to be a symbol of *variable magnitude*.

This latter observation (*ad* Table II and the second law) shows how the commodity must be thought of very differently from the way in which we conceived of it at the outset of our discussion of the individual independent product – for here it appears as the product of capital, as the aliquot component of capital, as the depository of capital that has valorized itself and hence contains an aliquot part of the surplus-value generated by capital.

(When we speak of the price of commodities, it is always implicitly assumed that the *total price* of the quantity of goods produced by capital = its *total value*, and hence the *price* of the aliquot part of the individual commodity = the aliquot part of that total value. *Price* in this context is in general just the money-expression of *value*. Prices differing from the underlying values have not yet entered into our discussions.)

[454] The *individual commodity* viewed as the product, the actual elementary component of capital that has been generated and reproduced, differs then from the individual commodity with which we began, and which we regarded as an *autonomous* article, as the premiss of capital formation. It differs not only in the question of price as already noted, but also in the fact that even if the commodity is sold at its price, the *value* of the capital invested in its production may not be realized, and the *surplus-value* created by that capital even less so. Indeed, as the mere depository of capital, not only materially, i.e. as a part of the use-value of which the capital consists, but as the depository of the *value* of which the capital consists, it is possible for the capitalist to sell commodities at prices corresponding to their individual value, and nevertheless at *less than* their value as *products of capital* and as *components of the aggregate product in which the capital that has been valorized actually has its being*.

In the instance given above, a capital of £100 reproduced itself in the form of 1,200 ells of linen at a price of £120. Since in our previous discussion we used the figures $\frac{c}{80} \frac{v}{20} \frac{s}{20}$, we can now represent the situation by assuming that the £80 constant capital is embodied in 800 ells, or $\frac{2}{3}$ of the aggregate product; £20 variable capital or wages amount to 200 ells, or $\frac{1}{6}$ of the total, and £20 surplus-value is likewise the equivalent of 200 ells or $\frac{1}{6}$. If we now suppose that not one ell, but let us say 800 ells were sold at the right price, i.e. £80, and the other two portions were unsaleable, then only $\frac{2}{3}$ of the original capital value of £100 would have been reproduced. As the depository of the total capital, i.e. as the only *actual* product of the total capital of £100, the 800 ells would have been sold at *less than* their value, at $\frac{2}{3}$ of their value, to be precise, since the value of the whole product = 120 and 80 is but $\frac{2}{3}$ of that, the missing 40 being the remaining third. These 800 ells, taken by themselves, could conceivably also be sold for *more than* their true value, and as the depositories of the total capital they might still be sold at the right price, e.g. if they were sold for £90 and the remaining 400 ells for £30. For our present purposes, however, we intend to disregard the sale of different fractions of the total quantity of goods at prices *higher* or *lower* than their value, since our premiss is precisely that they should be sold *at their correct value*.

55   What is at issue here is not just that the commodity's sale price should reflect its value, as in the case of the commodity conceived as an autonomous thing, but that, as a depository of the capital invested in it, its sale price should also reflect the fact that it is an *aliquot part of the total product of that capital*. If only 800 ells are sold out of a total product of $1,200 = £120$, then these 800 ells do not represent $\frac{2}{3}$ of the total value, but the total value itself, i.e. they represent the value of £120 and not £80, and the individual commodity does not $= \dfrac{£80}{800} = \dfrac{8}{80} = \dfrac{4}{40} = \dfrac{2}{20} = 2s.$, but $\dfrac{£120}{800} = \dfrac{12}{80} = \dfrac{3}{20} = 3s.$ Thus as an individual product it would have been sold 50 per cent too dear, if it had been sold at 3s. instead of 2s. As an aliquot part of the total value the individual product must be sold at the correct price and hence as the *aliquot part* of the total product sold. It may not be sold, therefore, as an independent article, but, e.g., as 1/1,200 of the total product, in relation therefore to the remaining 1,199/1,200. What is at issue is that the single article should be sold at the correct price multiplied by the *number* which forms its denominator as the aliquot part of a whole.

(It follows from this that, with the *development of capitalist production* and the resultant reduction in prices, there must be an increase in the *quantity of goods*, in the *number* of articles that must be sold. That is to say, a constant *expansion of the market* becomes a necessity for capitalist production. But this point is better left to the subsequent book.) (It also explains why the capitalist cannot sell 1,300 ells at 2s., even though he could supply 1,200 at that price. For the additional 100 might well require extensions of the constant capital which would be able to provide another 1,200 at that price, but not an extra 100, etc.)

We can see from this how an article regarded as the *product of capital* is to be distinguished from an *individual article treated as an independent object*, and this distinction will increasingly make itself felt. The more we advance into the processes of capitalist production and circulation, the more its impact on the real price of the commodity will be observed.

The point, however, to which I wish particularly to draw attention is this:

It was seen in Chapter 2, Section 3, of this first book,* how the various elements of value in the product of capital – the value of constant capital, that of variable capital and surplus-value – are to be found, and are, as it were, repeated, on the one hand, in the same proportions in every single commodity, both as aliquot parts of the *total use-value produced*, and as aliquot parts of the *total (exchange-)value produced*. On the other hand, the total product can be divided up into certain portions of the use-value or article produced, one part of which represents only the value of the constant capital, a second that of the variable capital and the third the surplus-value. Although both these descriptions are essentially identical, they *contradict* each other in their form of expression. For in the latter account the individual articles that belong to, say, lot 1, i.e. that reproduce only the value of the constant capital, represent only labour that has been objectified prior to the process of production. For example, the 800 ells = £80 = the value of the constant capital invested – they represent only the value of the cotton yarn, oil, coal and machinery consumed, but not a jot of the additional labour of weaving. On the other hand, *regarded as a use-value*, each ell of linen contains not only flax, but also a definite quantity of labour which is what gave it the form of linen. Similarly, in its price of 2s., it contains 16d. as reproduction of the constant capital it has consumed, 4d. for wages and 4d. of unpaid labour embodied in it.

The failure to solve this apparent contradiction can lead, as will be seen, to fundamental blunders in analysis. It is at first sight just as *confusing* for the person who only considers the *price* of the individual commodity as our earlier proposition that the individual commodity or a specific proportion of the total product can be sold both at the right price and below it, at the right price and above it, and even at more than its right price even though it is below it. For an example of this confusion see Proudhon (*verte*).†

* Chapter 9 in the present edition of *Capital*, Vol. 1.
† This refers to p. 457 in the MS; see p. 971 of the present edition.

(In the above example, the price of the ell is determined not in isolation but as an aliquot part of the total product.)

456 I have earlier given a similar account of the foregoing argument about the *determination of prices* (particular formulations from the original discussion should perhaps be interpolated here):

Originally, we considered the *individual commodity in isolation*, as the result and the direct product of a specific quantity of labour. Now, as the *result*, the *product of capital*, the commodity changes in form (and later on, in the price of production, it will be changed in *substance* too). The difference is as follows: The mass of use-values produced represents a *quantity of labour* equal to *the value of the constant capital contained in and consumed by the product* (of the *quantity of labour objectified and transferred* from it to the product) + the value of the *quantity of labour* exchanged for variable capital. A part of this labour goes to replace the value of the variable capital and the remainder constitutes the *surplus-value*. If we express the labour-time contained in the capital as = £100 of which £40 is variable capital and the rate of surplus-value = 50 per cent, then the total quantity of labour contained in the product comes to £120. Before the commodity can circulate, its *exchange-value* must be previously converted into the *price*. Therefore, if the total product is not a single continuous thing, so that the entire capital is reproduced in a *single* commodity, such as a house – then the capitalist must calculate the *price* of the individual commodity, i.e. he must represent the *exchange-value* of the individual commodity in terms of money of account. Then depending on the various rates of productivity of labour the *total value* of £120 will be *shared out* among a greater or smaller number of products, and the *price* of the individual article will stand *in inverse ratio* to the total number of articles, and each item will represent a larger or smaller aliquot part of the £120. For example, if the total product is 60 tons of coal, then 60 tons = £120 = £2 per ton $= \dfrac{£120}{60}$; if it is 75 tons of coal, then each ton $= \dfrac{£120}{75} = £1$ 12s.; if it is 240 tons, then $\dfrac{£120}{240} = \dfrac{12}{24} = £\frac{1}{2}$, and so on. The price of the individual article then $= \dfrac{\text{the total price of the product}}{\text{the total number of products}}$, the total price divided by the total number of products as measured in the various units of measure, depending on the use-value of the product.

So if the price of the individual article is equal to the total price of the quantity of goods (total number of tons) produced by the capital of £100 *divided* by the total number of articles (here in tons), then on the other hand, the *total price* of the total product is equal to the price of the individual article *multiplied* by the *total number* of articles produced. If the quantity of goods has increased with productivity, then the number will also increase and the price of the individual article will fall. The converse holds good where productivity has declined; there the one factor, the price, will rise, and the other factor, the number, will fall. As long as the *amount of labour employed* remains steady it will end up with the same total price of £120, regardless of how much of it accrues to the individual article which is produced in varying quantities depending on the productivity of the labour.

If the fraction of the price assigned to the individual article – the aliquot part of the total value – becomes smaller because of the greater number of articles produced, i.e. because of the greater productivity of labour, then it follows that the portion of surplus-value that accompanies it will be smaller, i.e. the aliquot part of the total price to which the surplus-value of £20 has become attached. Nevertheless, this does not introduce any change in the *relation* between the part of the price of the article representing surplus-value and that part which represents wages or the payment of labour.

It is perfectly true, however, as our examination of the capitalist process of production has shown, that – quite apart from the prolongation of the working day – there is a definite tendency for labour-power itself to become cheaper. This stems from the fall in the prices of the goods that determine the value of labour-power and enter into the necessary consumption of the labourer. Hence also there is at the same time a trend towards curtailing the *paid* part of his work and extending the *unpaid* part while keeping the working day constant.

Thus, on our earlier assumption, the price of the individual article participated in the *surplus-value* in the same proportions in which it shared in the total value and in the total price. The position now, however, is that despite the falling price the fraction of the price that represents the surplus-value increases. However, this occurs only because the surplus-value becomes proportionately greater in the *total price* of the product because the productivity of labour has increased. For the same reason – the greater productivity of labour (and the opposite would hold good if productivity were to decline) – the *value of labour-power is reduced*, since the same quantity of labour, the same value of £120, is spread over a larger quantity of goods, thus causing the price of each article to fall. Hence, even though the *price of the individual article falls*, and even though the total amount of labour declines, and with it the value contained in it, the amount of surplus-value in the price increases relatively. In other words, in the smaller total amount of labour to be found in the individual article, e.g. the ton, there is a larger *amount of unpaid labour* than before when the labour was less productive, the quantity of the product was smaller and the price of the individual article higher. The *aggregate price* of £120 now contains more unpaid labour than before and the same is true of each aliquot part of that £120.

457 It is puzzles of this sort that lead Proudhon astray, since he looks only at the price of the individual article in isolation, and not the commodity as the *product of a total capital*. Hence he ignores the overall situation within which the total product is divided up into its various components with regard to price.

'*Il est impossible que* l'intérêt du capital' (this is just one particular named part of the surplus-value) '*s'ajoutant dans le commerce au* salaire de l'ouvrier *pour* composer le prix de la marchandise, *l'ouvrier puisse racheter ce qu'il a lui-même produit. Vivre en travaillant est un principe qui, sous le régime de l'intérêt, implique contradiction*' ['Since in commerce the *interest on capital* is added to the *labourer's wages* to *make up the price of commodities*, it is impossible for the labourer to buy back his own product. To live by working is a principle which, under the regimen of interest, entails a contradiction'] (*Gratuité du crédit. Discussion entre M. Fr. Bastiat et M. Proudhon*, Paris, 1850, p. 105).

This is quite right: to make the matter clear let us assume that the worker, *l'ouvrier*, under discussion is the working class as a whole. The weekly payment it receives and with which it has to buy the means of subsistence, etc., is spent on a mass of commodities. Whether we take each separately or every one together, their price contains one part = wages and another = *surplus-value* (of which the interest mentioned by Proudhon is but one and perhaps a relatively insignificant element). How then is it possible for the working class to use its weekly income, which consists just of '*salaire*', to buy a quantity of goods that consists of '*salaire*' + surplus-value? Since the week's wages, taking the class as a whole, equal only the weekly aggregate of the means of subsistence, it is as clear as day that with the money he has received the worker *cannot* possibly buy the means of subsistence he requires. For the sum of money he has received equals his week's wages, the price paid each week for his labour, whereas the price of the provisions he requires for a week = the price of the labour they contain + the price represented by the unpaid surplus labour. Ergo: 'Il est impossible que . . . l'ouvrier puisse racheter ce qu'il a lui-même produit. *Vivre en travaillant*' under these conditions therefore really does entail '*contradiction*'. Proudhon is quite right as far as *appearances go*. But if, instead of considering the commodity in isolation, he were to view it as the product of capital, he would discover that the week's product breaks down into one part whose price = the weekly wage, = the variable capital laid out during the week and containing no *surplus-value*, etc., and another part whose price consists entirely of surplus-value. And even though the price of the commodity includes all these elements, it is in fact only the first part that the worker buys back (and in the present context it is irrelevant that he can be swindled by the grocer in the process, etc.).

This is what generally turns out to be the case with Proudhon's apparently profound and insoluble economic paradoxes. They consist in the fact that he regards the confusion wrought by economic phenomena in his own mind as the laws governing those phenomena.

(Indeed, his assertion here is even more misleading than suggested above, since it entails the assumption that the true price of the commodity = the wages contained in it = the amount of *paid* labour contained in it, while the *surplus-value*, interest, etc. is no more than a *surcharge*, an arbitrary extra on top of the true price of the commodity.)

But the criticism levelled at him by the vulgar economists is even worse. For example, M. Forcade points out that his assertion proves too much on the one hand, since he shows that, according to it, the working class could not survive at all; while on the other hand, he does not press the paradox far enough since the price of the commodities the buyer purchases includes not just wages + interest but also the cost of the raw materials etc. (i.e. the elements of constant capital in the price). Quite right, Forcade. But what then? He shows that the problem is even more intractable than Proudhon had implied – but in his eyes this is a pretext for providing a *non*-solution to the problem on a scale even smaller than that on which Proudhon had tackled the matter, and instead he just fudges the issue, dismissing it with a hollow rhetoric.*

158   And in fact it is the virtue of Proudhon's approach that he frankly expresses the confusions in the realities of the economic phenomena, airing them with sophistical self-satisfaction, but re-

---

*Marx took up Forcade's criticism of Proudhon in Vol. 3 of *Capital*: 'Proudhon exposes his inability to grasp this in the ignorant formulation: *"l'ouvrier ne peut pas racheter son propre produit"* (the labourer cannot buy back his own product), because the interest which is added to the *prix-de-revient* (cost price) is contained in the product. But how does M. Eugène Forcade teach him to know better? "If Proudhon's objection were correct, it would strike not only the profits of capital, but would eliminate the possibility even of industry. If the labourer is compelled to pay 100 for each article for which he has received only 80, if his wages can buy back only the value which he has put into a product, it could be said that the labourer cannot buy back anything, that wages cannot pay for anything. In fact, there is always something more than the wages of the labourer contained in the cost price, and always more than the profits of enterprise in the selling price, for instance, the price of raw materials, often paid to foreign countries . . . Proudhon has forgotten about the continual growth of national capital; he has forgotten that this growth refers to all labourers, whether in an enterprise or in handicrafts" (*Revue des Deux Mondes*, 1848, Vol. 24, p. 998). Here we have the optimism of bourgeois thoughtlessness in the form of sagacity that most corresponds to it. M. Forcade first believes that the labourer could not live did he not receive a higher value than that which he produces, whereas conversely the capitalist mode of production could not exist were he really to receive all the value which he produces. Secondly, he correctly generalizes the difficulty, which Proudhon expressed only from a narrow viewpoint. The price of commodities contains not only an excess over wages, but also over profit, namely, the constant portion of value. According to Proudhon's reasoning, then, the capitalist too could not buy back the commodities with his profit. And how does Forcade solve this riddle? By means of a meaningless phrase: the growth of capital. Thus the continual growth of capital is also supposed to be substantiated, among other things, in that the analysis of commodity prices, which is impossible for the political economist as regards capital of 100, becomes superfluous in the case of a capital of 10,000. What would be said of a chemist, who, on being asked: How is it that the product of the soil contains more carbon than the soil? were to answer: it comes from the continual increase in agricultural production. The well-meaning desire to discover in the bourgeois world the best of all possible worlds replaces in vulgar economy all need for love of truth and inclination for scientific investigation' (*Capital*, Vol. 3, Moscow, 1962, p. 822, n. 53).

vealing them in all their theoretical impoverishment. This contrasts sharply with the vulgar economists who attempt to hush things up but are incapable of comprehending them. Thus Herr W. Thucydides Roscher dismisses Proudhon's *Qu'est-ce que la propriété?* as 'confused and confusing'. The word 'confusing' suggests the impotence of the vulgar economists in the face of this confusion. They are incapable of resolving the contradictions of capitalist production even in the confused, superficial and sophistical form in which Proudhon wraps them and hurls them at their heads. Nothing remains for them but to recoil from a sophistry they cannot disentangle and to launch an appeal to 'commonsense' relying on the notion that things will take their course. A great consolation for the would-be 'theorist'.

(N.B. This entire section on Proudhon should probably go into Book II, Chapter [i.e. Part] III, or even later.)

At the same time we find here the solution to the problem presented in Chapter 1.* If the *commodities* that form the product of capital are sold at prices determined by their value, in other words, if the entire capitalist class sells commodities *at their true value*, then each of its members realizes a surplus-value, i.e. he sells a portion of the value of a commodity which has cost him nothing and which he has not paid for. The profit they each make is not achieved at each other's expense – that would only be the case where one managed to grab the share of surplus-value due to another – nor is it achieved by their selling their goods at more than their value. On the contrary, they sell their produce *at its true value*. The hypothesis that commodities are sold at prices corresponding to their values forms the basis of the investigations to be carried out in the next volume.

Commodities are the first result of the immediate process of capitalist production, its product. In the price of these commodities we find not merely a replacement of the value of the capital invested in them and consumed in the course of their production, but also the materialization, the objectification as surplus-value of the surplus labour consumed during that same process of production. As a *commodity*, the product of capital must enter the process of exchange, and this means not merely the actual physical process, but also that it must submit to the various changes in form that we have specified as the metamorphosis of the commodity. As far as

*Presumably Chapter 5 in the present edition.

the purely formal changes are concerned – the transformation of these commodities into money and their reversion into commodities – this process is already present in our account of what we designated as 'simple circulation' – the circulation of commodities as such. But these commodities are at the same time the depositories of capital; they are capital that has been valorized, impregnated with surplus-value. And in this respect their circulation, which is simultaneously the reproduction process of capital, entails further determinations alien to the abstract description of the circulation of commodities. For this reason our next task is to turn to an examination of the *circulation process of capital*. This we shall do in the next volume.*

II: CAPITALIST PRODUCTION AS THE PRODUCTION OF SURPLUS-VALUE

459   Where capital still appears only in its elementary forms, such as commodities or money, the capitalist manifests himself in the already familiar character of the owner of money or commodities. But such a person is no more a capitalist in himself than money or commodities are capital in themselves. They become translated into capital only in certain specific circumstances and their owners likewise become capitalists only when these circumstances obtain.

Originally, capital became manifest as *money*, as something to be transformed into capital, or which was only potentially capital.

The economists have made the blunder of confusing these elementary forms of capital – money and commodities – with capital as such. They have also made the further blunder of equating capital with its mode of existence as use-value – the means of labour.

In what we may call its first, provisional form of *money* (the point of departure for the formation of capital), capital exists as yet only as money, i.e. as a *sum of exchange-values* embodied in the *self-subsistent form of exchange-value*, in its *expression as money*. But the task of this money is to generate value. The exchange-value must serve to create still more exchange-value. The *quantity of value* must be increased, i.e. the available value must not only be maintained; it must yield an increment, Δ value, a surplus-value,

---

*This is in fact the subject of *Capital*, Vol. 2, so presumably Marx would have finished the present chapter at this point when he had finally revised it.

so that the value given, the particular sum of money, can be viewed as *fluens** and the increment as fluxion. We shall come back to the self-subsistent expression of capital as money when we come to consider its process of circulation. Here, where we are concerned with money only as the *point of departure* for the *immediate process of production*, we can confine ourselves to this observation: capital exists here as yet only as a *given quantum of value* = M (money), in which all use-value is extinguished, so that nothing but the monetary form remains. The *magnitude* of this quantum of value is limited by the *amount* or *quantity* of the *money* to be transformed into capital. So this value becomes capital by *increasing* its *size*, by transforming itself into a *changing quantity*, by being, from the very outset, a *fluens* that must engender a fluxion. *In itself* this sum of money may only be *defined* as capital if it is employed, spent, with the aim of *increasing* it, if it is spent expressly in order to *increase* it. In the case of the sum of value or money this phenomenon is its *destiny*, its inner law, its tendency, while to the *capitalist*, i.e. the owner of the sum of money, in whose hands it shall acquire its function, it appears as *intention, purpose*. Thus in this originally simple expression of capital (or of the capital to be) as money or value, every link with use-value has been broken and entirely destroyed. But even more striking is the elimination of every unwelcome sign, all potentially confusing evidence of the *actual process of production* (production of commodities, etc.). It is for this reason that the character, the specific nature of capitalist production, appears to be so simple and abstract. If the original capital is a quantum of value = x, it becomes capital and fulfils its purpose by changing into $x + \Delta x$, i.e. into a quantum of money or value = the original sum + a balance over the original sum. In other words, it is transformed into the given amount of money + additional money, into the *given value + surplus-value*. The *production of surplus-value* – which includes the preservation of the value originally advanced – appears therefore as the determining purpose, the driving force and the *final result* of the capitalist process of production, as the means through which the original value is transformed into capital. *How* this is brought about, the real procedure by means of which x is changed into $x + \Delta x$, does not affect the purpose and result of the process in the least. It is true that x can be changed into $x + \Delta x$ even in the absence of the capi-

*Something liable to change.

talist process of production, but not if we *postulate* that the rival members of society confront each other as persons, that they deal with each other only as the *owners of commodities*, and that they come into contact with each other only in this capacity (this excludes slavery, etc.). And secondly, if we postulate further that the social product should be produced as a *commodity*. (This excludes all social formations in which the use-value is the main point as far as the immediate producers are concerned, and the excess produce at most is transformed into a commodity.)

460   The fact that the purpose of the process is that x should be transformed into $x+\Delta x$ also points to the path our own investigations should take. The result must be expressed as the function of a variable quantity, or be transformed into one during the process. As a *given sum of money*, x is a constant from the outset and hence its increment $= O$. In the course of the process, therefore, it must be changed into another amount which contains a variable element. Our task is to discover this component and at the same time to identify the mediations by means of which a constant magnitude becomes a variable one. Now since, as we can see from our further inspection of the actual process of production, a part of x is transformed back into a constant magnitude – namely, into the means of labour; and since a part of the *value* of x is to be found only in the form of specific use-values, instead of in their money form (a change which has no effect on the constant nature of the quantum of value and in fact has no effect of any kind on this aspect of it in so far as it is exchange-value), it follows that x can be represented as c (constant magnitude)$+v$ (variable magnitude) $= c+v$. But now the difference $\Delta(c+v) = c+(v+\Delta v)$ and since $c = 0$, the result is $v+\Delta v$. So what appeared originally as Δx is in reality Δv. And the relation of this increment of the original x to the part of x of which it really is the increment must be as follows: $\Delta v = \Delta x$ (since $\Delta x = \Delta v$), $\dfrac{\Delta x}{v} = \dfrac{\Delta v}{v}$ which is in fact the formula of the *rate of surplus-value*.

Since the total capital $C = c+v$, where c is constant and v is variable, C can be regarded as a function of v. If v is increased by Δv, then $C = C'$.

What we have then is:
(1) $C = c+v$
(2) $C = c+(v+\Delta v)$.

If we subtract the first equation from the second, the difference is $C'-C$, the increment of $C = \Delta C$.

(3) $C'-C = c+v+\Delta v-c-v = \Delta v$

(4) $\Delta C = \Delta v$

So this gives us (3) and hence (4) $\Delta C = \Delta v$. But $C'-C = $ the amount by which C has changed $(= \Delta C)$, $=$ the increment of C or ΔC, i.e. (4). In other words, the increment of the total capital $=$ the increment of the variable part of it, such that ΔC or the change in the constant part of the capital $= 0$. Hence in this investigation of ΔC or Δv the constant capital is given as $= 0$, i.e. it must be left out of account.

The proportion by which v has grown $= \dfrac{\Delta v}{v}$ (the *rate of surplus-value*). The proportion by which C has grown $= \dfrac{\Delta v}{C} = \dfrac{\Delta v}{c} + v$ (*rate of profit*).

Thus the actual function specific to capital as such is the *production of surplus-value* which, as will be shown later, is nothing but the production of *surplus labour*, *the appropriation of unpaid labour* in the course of the actual process of production. This labour manifests itself, objectifies itself, as *surplus-value*.

It has also been seen that if x is to be changed into capital, into $x+\Delta x$, the value or sum of money represented by x has to be transformed into the *factors of the production process*, and above all into the *factors of the actual labour process*. In some branches of industry a part of the means of production – the *object of labour* – may possibly have no value, may possibly not be a *commodity*, although it is a use-value. In that event only a portion of x will be transformed into the means of production, and if we consider the transformation of x, i.e. the use of x to purchase commodities destined for the labour process, then the value of the object of labour – which is nothing but the means of production that have been purchased – is $= 0$. But we shall only consider the matter in its complete form where the object of labour $=$ the commodity. Where this is not the case this factor is to be deemed $= 0$, as far as value is concerned, so as to rectify the calculation.

Like the commodity, which is an immediate unity of use-value and exchange-value, the process of production, which is the process of the production of commodities, is the immediate unity of the processes of labour and valorization. Just as *commodities*, i.e. the immediate unities of use-value and exchange-value, emerge from the process as *result*, as product, so too do they enter into it as its constituent parts. And in general nothing can ever emerge from the process of production which did not enter into it as conditions of production in the first place.

The transformation of the sum of money invested, of the money to be expanded and changed into capital, into the *factors of the production process*, is an act of the circulation of the commodity, of the process of exchange, and it breaks down into a series of purchases. This *act*, then, does not yet enter *into* the immediate production process. It only inaugurates it, though it is its *necessary precondition*, and if we look beyond the immediate process of production, and consider the whole continuous process of capitalist production, we find that this transformation of money into the *factors of the production process*, the purchase of the means of production and labour power, itself constitutes an *immanent moment of the overall process.*

61   If we now turn to the form assumed by capital *within* the immediate process of production we find that, like the simple commodity, it possesses the *double shape* of *use-value* and *exchange-value*. But both forms are characterized by further, more highly developed determinations than those we found in the simple commodity considered as a thing in its own right.

To take the *use-value* first, its particular content, its further determination, was completely irrelevant to the definition of the commodity. The article destined to be a commodity, and hence the incarnation of exchange-value, had to gratify some social want or other, and had therefore to possess some useful qualities. *Voilà tout.** It is otherwise with the *use-value* of the commodities functioning within the process of production. Owing to the nature of the *labour process* the means of production are first sundered into the *object* and the *means of labour*, or to define it more closely, *raw material* on the one hand, and *instruments, aids*, etc. on the other. These are the *formal determinations of use-value* as they emerge from the nature of the labour process itself, and they constitute the further definition of use-value – as far as the means of production are concerned. This *formal definition of use-value* is essential to the

*'That's all.'

further analysis of *economic relationships*, of *economic categories*.

Furthermore, the use-values entering into the labour process are also sundered into two strictly different conceptual moments, two opposing spheres (analogous to those we have just revealed in the case of the *material* means of production). On the one hand, we find the material means of production, the *objective* conditions of production, and on the other hand, the active capacities for labour, labour-power expressing itself purposively: the *subjective* condition of labour. This is a further formal determinant of capital considered as use-value in the immediate process of production. In the simple commodity specific purposive labour, such as spinning, weaving, etc., is embodied, objectified, in the yarn or fabric. The purposive form of the product is the only trace left behind by the purposive labour, and these traces can themselves be obliterated if the product has the form of a natural product, such as cattle, wheat, etc. In the commodity the use-value is present directly, immediately, whereas in the labour process it becomes manifest as the *product*. The individual commodity is in fact a finished article, which has left its mode of origin behind it and which contains preserved within itself the process in which particular useful labour was performed and objectified. From the production process the commodity is born. It is constantly precipitated from the process as its product, in such a way that the product appears to be a mere moment of that process. A portion of the *use-value* in which capital appears in the process of production is the *living labour-power itself*. But this labour-power has definite *specifications*, stemming from the particular use-value of the means of production; it is a *self-activating capacity*, a *labour-power that expresses itself* purposively by converting the means of production into the material objects of its activity, *transforming* them from their original form into the new form of the product. Thus in the course of the labour process use-values undergo a *genuine transformation,* whether of a mechanical, chemical or physical nature. In the commodity the use-value is a given thing with definite characteristics. Now, however, in the labour process, we find the *transformation* of things, use-values, functioning as raw materials or means of labour, into a new use-value – the *product*. This is effected by the living labour activating itself in and through them, a labour which is simply labour-power in action. So we may say that the form assumed by capital as a *use-value* in the labour process may be broken down

462 firstly into the means of production sundered into conceptually distinct but interrelated parts; secondly, into a conceptual division, arising from the nature of the labour process, between the *objective* conditions of labour (the means of production) and its *subjective* conditions, purposively active *capacity for labour*, i.e. labour itself. Thirdly, however, taking the process as a whole, the use-value of capital appears here as a process that creates use-values. In this process the means of production function in accordance with this specificity as the means by which to produce the purposively active, *specific labour-power* their determinate nature requires. Or, in other words, we may say that the total *labour process* as such, with the totality of its objective and subjective interactions, appears as the total manifest form of the use-value, i.e. as the *real* form of capital in the process of production.

Looking at the process of production from its real side, i.e. as a process which creates new use-values by performing useful labour with existing use-values, we find it to be a *real labour process*. As such its elements, its conceptually specific components, are those of the labour process itself, of any *labour process*, irrespective of the mode of production or the stage of economic development in which they find themselves. Now this real form, the form of the objective use-values in which *capital is incorporated,* its material substratum, is necessarily the form assumed by the means of production – the means and object of labour – which are required for the creation of new products. Furthermore, these use-values are already present (on the market) in the circulation process, in the form of commodities, i.e. in the possession of the capitalist as the owner of commodities, even before they become active in the labour process in fulfilment of their specific purpose. In view of this, and since, therefore, capital – to the extent to which it manifests itself in the *objective* conditions of labour – *consists* of *means of production*, raw materials, auxiliary materials, means of labour, tools, buildings, machines etc., people tend to conclude that all means of production are capital *potentially*, and that they are so *actually* when they function as means of production. Capital then is held to be a necessary feature of the *human labour process as such*, irrespective of the historical forms it has assumed; it is consequently something permanent, determined by the nature of human labour itself. In the same way, it is urged that because the process of production of capital in general is the labour process, the *labour process as such*, it follows that the labour process in all forms of society is necessarily capitalist in nature. Thus capital comes to be thought of as a *thing*, and as a thing it plays a certain role, a role appropriate to it as a thing in the process of production. It is the same logic that infers that because money is gold, gold is intrinsically money; that because wage-labour is labour, all labour is necessarily wage-labour. The *identity* is proved by holding fast to the features common to all processes of production, while neglecting their *specific differentiae*. The identity is demonstrated by abstracting from the distinctions. We shall return to this crucial point in greater detail in the course of this chapter. For the present we shall merely note:

First, the commodities purchased by the capitalist for consumption as the *means of production* in the production process or labour process are his own property. They are in fact no more than his money transformed into commodities and they are just as much the existing reality of his capital as that money. Even more so, indeed, since they have been changed into the form in which they will really function as *capital*, i.e. as the means of creating value, of valorizing, i.e. expanding, its value. These means of production are therefore *capital*. On the other hand, with the remaining portion of the money invested, the capitalist has purchased labour-power, workers, or, as we have shown in Chapter IV,* he has purchased *living labour*. This belongs to him just as effectively as do the objective conditions of the labour process. Nevertheless, a specific difference becomes apparent here: real labour is what the worker really gives to the capitalist in exchange for the purchase price of labour, that part of capital that is translated into the wage. It is the expenditure of his life's energy, the realization of his productive faculties; it is his movement and not the capitalists'. Looked at as a personal function, in its reality, labour is the function of the worker, and not of the capitalist. Looked at from the standpoint of exchange, the worker represents to the capitalist what the latter receives from him, and not what he is *vis-à-vis* the capitalist in the course of the labour process. So here we find that, within the labour process, the objective conditions of labour, as capital, and to that extent, as the capitalist, stand in opposition to the subjective conditions of labour, i.e.

463

*Presumably Chapter 6 in the present edition.

labour itself, or rather the worker who works. This is how it comes about that from the standpoint of both capitalist and worker, the *means of production* as an existing form of capital, as eminently the capital of labour, confront the other component in which capital has been invested and hence appear potentially to have a specific mode of existence as capital even outside the production process. As we shall see, this can be further analysed, partly in the context of the capitalist process of valorization in general (in the role of the means of production as devourers of living labour), and partly in the development of the specifically capitalist mode of production (in which machinery, etc. becomes the real master of living labour). This is why we find in the capitalist process of production this *indissoluble fusion of use-values* in which capital subsists in the form of the *means of production* and *objects* defined as capital, when what we are really faced with is a definite social relationship of production. In consequence the *product* embedded in this mode of production is equated with the commodity by those who have to deal with it. It is this that forms the foundation for the fetishism of the political economists.

Second, the means of production leave circulation and enter into the labour process as specific commodities, e.g. cotton, coal, spindles, etc. In so doing, they still possess the *shape of the use-values* they had while they were circulating as commodities. Once they have entered the process, they proceed to function with the qualities that cotton, etc. has as cotton, corresponding to their use-values, to the characteristics appropriate to them as *things*. The position is otherwise with that portion of capital we have called *variable* but which only becomes the really *variable portion of capital* when it has been exchanged for *labour-power*. In reality, *money* – the portion of capital that the capitalist expends on the purchase of labour-power – is *nothing* but the *means of subsistence available on the market* (or dumped on it on certain terms), and destined for the individual consumption of the workers. Money then is only the transmuted form of these means of subsistence which the worker immediately transforms back into means of subsistence as soon as he receives it. Both this transformation and the subsequent consumption of these commodities as use-values constitute a process that has no *direct* bearing on the immediate process of production, or, more precisely, the labour process, and which in fact operates outside its limits. One part of the capital, and thereby the capital in its entirety, is transformed into a *variable magnitude* by the fact that instead of money – which is a constant magnitude – or the means of subsistence as which it may appear and which are likewise constant magnitudes, it is exchanged for *living labour-power* – a value-creating force, something which can be smaller or greater, which can manifest itself as a variable magnitude and which in fact always enters the process of production as a fluctuating, *developing* magnitude and hence as one contained within different limits, rather than as a *magnitude* that has become *fixed*. It is true enough in reality that the consumption of the means of subsistence by the worker can be included (calculated) in the labour process, just as the consumption of *matières instrumentales** by the machinery is reckoned along with the machinery itself. In that event the worker appears merely as an instrument purchased by capital, an instrument that requires a certain quantity of provisions as his *matières instrumentales*, if he is to perform his functions in the labour process. This happens to a greater or lesser degree, depending on the extent and the ruthlessness with which the worker is exploited. But it is not, strictly speaking, included in the definition of capitalist relations. (We shall consider its further implications in Section III below in our discussion of the reproduction of the entire relationship.) Normally the worker consumes his provisions during pauses in the labour process, whereas the *machine* consumes what is essential to it *while it is still functioning*. (Like an animal?) But taking the working class as a whole, a portion of these means of subsistence is consumed by members of the family who either do not yet work, or have ceased to do so. In practice then the difference between a worker and a machine can effectively be reduced to the distinction between an animal and a machine, as far as *matières instrumentales* and their consumption are concerned. But this is not necessary and hence it does not form part of the definition of capital. At all events, the capital earmarked for wages appears formally as something that has *ceased to exist* in the eyes of the capitalist, but which belongs to the *worker* as soon as it has assumed its true shape of the means of subsistence destined to be consumed by him. Thus the *form of the use-value* as a commodity, before it is absorbed into the process of production – i.e. as *means of subsistence* – is quite different from its form *within* that process

*'Accessory materials'.

which is that of *labour-power actively expressing itself*, and hence
of living labour itself. Thus this portion of capital is specifically
distinguished from the capital present in the form of means of production, and this is yet another reason why in the capitalist mode
of production the *means of production* appear as capital in and for
themselves in *distinction* from, and in *contrast* to, the *means of
subsistence*. This appearance is dispelled quite simply – even ignoring for the moment our later arguments – by the circumstance that
the *form of the use-value* in which capital exists at the conclusion
of the production process is that of the *product*, and this product
can be found embodied both as *means of production* and as *means
of subsistence*. Thus both are *capital* to an equal extent and so both
are present in opposition to the living labour-power.

Let us now turn to the *valorization process* [*Verwertungsprozess*].
As far as *exchange-value* is concerned, we again see the distinction between the *commodity* and the capital involved in valorization.
The *exchange-value* of the capital entering into the process of
production is smaller than the exchange-value of capital placed or
invested in the market. In fact, the only *value* that enters the process of production is that of the *commodities* which operate as the
means of production (i.e. the value of the *constant* part of capital).
Instead of the value of the variable portion we now have *valorization* as a process, labour in the act of realizing itself constantly as
value, but also flowing beyond already existing values to create
new ones.

As far as the *old value* is concerned, namely the value of the
constant portion, this depends for its maintenance on the value of
the means of production entering the process not being greater
than necessary. The commodities of which they are made up
should contain in objectified form, i.e. as buildings, machinery,
etc., no more than the *socially necessary labour-time* essential for
their production. And it is the task of the capitalist to see to it
when purchasing these means of production that their use-values
have no more than the average quality needed to manufacture the
product. This applies both to raw materials and to machinery, etc.
They must all function with average quality and not present labour,
the living factor, with any abnormal obstacles. For example the
quality of the raw material implies among other things that the

machinery used should not produce more than the average amount of waste, etc. The capitalist must attend to all these things. Even beyond that, however, if the value of constant capital is not to be eroded, it must as far as possible be consumed productively and not squandered, since in that case the product would contain a greater amount of objectified labour within it than is *socially necessary*. In part this depends on the workers themselves, and it is here that the *supervisory responsibility of the capitalist* enters. (He secures his position here through piece-work, deductions from wages, etc.) He must also see to it that the work is performed in an orderly and methodical fashion and that the use-value he has in mind actually emerges *successfully* at the end of the process. At this point too the capitalist's ability to *supervise* and enforce *discipline* is vital. Lastly, he must make sure that the process of production is not interrupted or disturbed and that it really does proceed to the creation of the product within the time allowed for by the particular labour process and its objective requirements. This depends partly on the *continuity of work* which is introduced by capitalist production, partly however on uncontrollable external factors. Because of this latter aspect each process of production entails a risk for the values introduced into it, a risk however to which (1) they are exposed even *outside* the process of production, and which (2) is a feature of *every* process of production and not merely that of capitalism. (Capital protects itself against such risks by *association*. The immediate producer who works with his own means of production is subject to the same risk. There is nothing in this peculiar to the capitalist process of production. If the risk falls on the capitalist himself, this is only the consequence of his having usurped the ownership of the means of production.)

As to the vital element in the valorization process we may say that the *value* of the variable capital can be maintained (1) if it is replaced, reproduced, i.e. if care is taken to ensure that the means of production are augmented by a quantity of labour as great as that of the value of the variable capital or of the wages of labour; (2) if an *increment* of its value, i.e. surplus-value, is created by objectifying in the product an *additional quantum of work*, an amount of work in excess of that contained in wages.

In this the distinction between the *use-value* of the capital employed or of the commodities in which it is invested, and the *form* assumed by the *use-values of capital* in the labour process, corres-

465

ponds to the *distinction* between the exchange-value of the capital employed and the form assumed by the *exchange-value* of capital in the valorization process. In the *former* case, the instrument of production, the constant capital, enters the process without alteration to the form of its *use-values*, while the finished *use-values* of which the variable capital was composed are replaced by the living factor of real labour, of the labour-power that valorizes itself in new use-values. In the *latter* case, however, the value of the means of production, of the constant capital, enters the valorization process in its own right, while the *value* of the variable capital does not so enter, but is instead replaced by the value-creating activity, the activity of the living factor embodied in the valorization process.

If the *labour-time* of the worker is to create value in proportion to its duration, it must be *socially necessary labour-time*. That is to say, the worker must perform the *normal social* quantity of useful labour in a given time. The capitalist therefore compels him to work at the normal social *average* rate of intensity. He will strive as hard as possible to raise his output above this *minimum* and to extract as much work from him as is possible in a given time. For every intensification of work above the *average rate* creates surplus-value for him. Furthermore, he will attempt to extend the labour process as far as possible beyond the limits which must be worked to make good the value of the variable capital invested, i.e. the wages of labour. Where the intensity of the labour process is given, he will seek to increase its duration, and conversely, where the duration is fixed he will strive to increase its intensity. The capitalist *forces* the worker where possible to exceed the normal rate of intensity, and he forces him as best he can to extend the process of labour beyond the time necessary to replace the amount laid out in wages.

Thanks to this feature peculiar to the capitalist valorization process, the *real form* of capital in the process of production, its *form as use-value*, receives further modifications. *First*, the means of production must be present in a *quantity* adequate to absorb not only the necessary labour, but also the surplus labour. *Second*, the intensity and duration of the actual labour process are subject to change.

The means of production made use of by the worker in the actual labour process are, it is true, the property of the capitalist, and they therefore confront his labour, which is the only expression of his life, as *capital* – as we have already shown. On the other hand, however, it is he who makes use of them in the course of his work. In the actual process, the worker uses the means of labour as his tools, and he uses up the object of labour in the sense that it is the material in which his labour manifests itself. It is by this means that he transforms the means of production into the appropriate form of the product. The situation looks quite different in the valorization process. Here it is not the worker who makes use of the means of production, but the means of production that make use of the worker. Living labour does not realize itself in objective labour which thereby becomes its objective organ, but instead objective labour maintains and fortifies itself by drawing off living labour; it is thus that it becomes *value valorizing itself, capital*, and functions as such. The means of production thus become no more than leeches drawing off as large an amount of living labour as they can. Living labour for its part ceases to be anything more than a means by which to increase, and thereby capitalize, already existing values. And quite apart from what has already been shown, it is precisely for this reason that the means of production appear *éminemment** as the effective form of *capital* confronting living labour. And they now manifest themselves moreover as the rule of past, dead labour over the living. It is precisely as *value-creating* that living labour is continually being absorbed into the valorization process of objectified labour. In terms of effort, of the expenditure of his life's energy, work is the personal activity of the worker. But as something which *creates value*, as something involved in the process of objectifying labour, the worker's labour becomes one of the *modes of existence* of capital, it is incorporated into capital as soon as it enters the production process. This power which *maintains old values* and *creates new ones* is therefore the power of capital, and that process is accordingly the process of its *self-valorization*. Consequently it spells the impoverishment of the worker who creates value as *value alien to himself*.

466   Within the framework of capitalist production this ability of objectified labour to transform itself into *capital*, i.e. to transform the means of production into the means of controlling and exploiting living labour, appears as something utterly appropriate

*'Eminently'.

to them (just as within that framework it is potentially bound up with it), as inseparable from them and hence as a *quality* attributable *to them as things, as use-values, as means of production.* These appear, therefore, intrinsically as capital and hence as capital which expresses a *specific relationship of production,* a specific social relationship in which the owners of the conditions of production treat living labour-power as a *thing,* just as value had appeared to be the attribute of a thing and the *economic definition* of the thing as a *commodity* appeared to be an aspect of its thinghood [*dingliche Qualität*], just as the social form conferred on labour in the shape of money presented itself as the *characteristics of a thing.** In fact the rule of the capitalist over the worker is nothing but the rule of the independent *conditions of labour* over the *worker,* conditions that have made themselves independent of him. (These embrace not only the objective conditions of the process of production – the means of production – but also the objective prerequisites for the sustenance and effectiveness of labour-power, i.e. its *means of subsistence.*) And this is the case even though this relationship comes into existence only in the course of the actual process of production, which, as we have seen, is in essence the *process of creating surplus-value* (including the maintenance of the old value), the process of *valorizing the capital invested.* In circulation the capitalist and the worker confront each other only as the *vendors of commodities,* but owing to the specific, opposed nature of the commodities they sell to each other, the worker necessarily enters the process of production as a component of the *use-value,* the *real existence,* of capital, its *existence as value.* And this remains true even though that relationship only constitutes itself *within* the process of production, and the capitalist, who exists only as a potential purchaser of labour, becomes a real capitalist only when the worker, who can be turned into a *wage-labourer* only through the sale of his capacity for labour, *really* does submit to the commands of capital. The *functions* fulfilled by the capitalist are no more than the functions of capital – viz. the valorization of value by absorbing living labour – executed *consciously* and *willingly.* The capitalist functions only as *personified* capital, capital as a person, just as the worker is no more than *labour* personified. That labour is for him just effort and torment,

---

*The number (2) appears in the MS. at this point, but there is no corresponding (1).

whereas it belongs to the capitalist as a substance that creates and increases wealth, and in fact it is an element of capital, incorporated into it in the production process as its living, variable component. Hence the rule of the capitalist over the worker is the rule of things over man, of dead labour over the living, of the product over the producer. For the commodities that become the instruments of rule over the workers (merely as the instruments of the rule of *capital* itself) are mere consequences of the process of production; they are its products. Thus at the level of material production, of the life-process in the realm of the social – for that is what the process of production is – we find the *same* situation that we find in *religion* at the ideological level, namely the inversion of subject into object and *vice versa*. Viewed *historically* this inversion is the indispensable transition without which wealth as such, i.e. the relentless productive forces of social labour, which alone can form the material base of a free human society, could not possibly be created by force at the expense of the majority. This antagonistic stage cannot be avoided, any more than it is possible for man to avoid the stage in which his spiritual energies are given a religious definition as powers independent of himself. What we are confronted by here is the *alienation* [*Entfremdung*] of man from his own labour. To that extent the worker stands on a higher plane than the capitalist from the outset, since the latter has his roots in the process of alienation and finds absolute satisfaction in it whereas right from the start the worker is a victim who confronts it as a rebel and experiences it as a process of enslavement. At the same time the process of production is a real labour process and to the extent to which that is the case and the capitalist has a definite function to perform within it as 467 *supervisor* and *director*, his activity acquires a specific, many-sided content. But the *labour process itself* is no more than the *instrument* of the *valorization process*, just as the use-value of the product is nothing but a repository of its exchange-value. The self-valorization of capital – the creation of surplus-value – is therefore the determining, dominating and overriding purpose of the capitalist; it is the absolute motive and content of his activity. And in fact it is no more than the rationalized motive and aim of the hoarder – a highly impoverished and abstract content which makes it plain that the capitalist is just as enslaved by the relationships of capitalism as is his opposite pole, the worker, albeit in a quite different manner.

In the original situation the would-be capitalist purchases labour ('labour-power' would be more accurate after Chapter 4*) from the worker in order to capitalize a sum of money, and the worker sells his labour, the right to dispose of his labour-power, in order to prolong his life. This situation is the essential prelude and pre condition of the actual process of production in which the commodity owner becomes a capitalist, capital personified, and the worker becomes the mere personification of labour for capital. This first relationship, in which each confronts the other apparently on equal terms as the *owner of a commodity*, is the premiss of the capitalist process of production, but, as we shall see in due course, it is also its result and product. But it follows that both acts must be sharply distinguished from each other. The first belongs to circulation. The second only develops in the actual process of production on the basis of the first.

The process of production is the *immediate* unity of labour process and valorization process, just as its immediate result, the commodity, is the *immediate* unity of use-value and exchange-value. But the labour process is only the means whereby the valorization process is implemented and the valorization process is essentially the *production of surplus-value*, i.e. the *objectification of unpaid labour*. We have thus arrived at a definition of the specific characteristics of the process of production as a whole.

Even though we have considered the process of production from two distinct points of view: (1) as *labour process*, (2) as *valorization process*, it is nevertheless implicit that the labour process is single and indivisible. The work is not done twice over, once to produce a suitable product, a use-value, to *transform* the means of production into products, and a second time to generate *value* and *surplus-value*, to *valorize value*. Work is contributed only in the definite, concrete, specific form, manner, mode of existence in which it is the purposive activity that can convert the means of production into a specific product, spindle and cotton, for instance, into *yarn*. All that is contributed is the labour of spinning, etc., and through this contribution more yarn is continually produced. This *real* work creates value only if it is performed at a normally defined rate of intensity (or in other words it only *pays* as long as it achieves this)

* i.e. 'The Sale and Purchase of Labour-Power', Chapter 6 in the present edition.

and if this *real work* of given intensity and of given quantity as measured in terms of time actually materializes as a product. *If the labour process stops short* at the point where the amount of labour contributed in the form of spinning = the work contained in wages, then no surplus-value would be generated. The *surplus-value*, then, manifests itself in a *surplus-product*, in the present case as an amount of yarn over and above the amount whose value = the value of the worker's wages. Therefore, the labour process becomes a valorization process by virtue of the fact that the concrete labour invested in it is a quantity of *socially necessary* labour (thanks to its intensity), = a certain quantity of average social labour, and by virtue of the further fact that this quantity represents an *excess* over the amount contained in wages. It is the *quantitative* calculation of the particular concrete amount of labour as *average, necessary social labour*. What corresponds to this calculation, however, is the real element, firstly, of the normal intensity of work (i.e. that to produce a product in a certain quantity only the socially necessary labour-time is consumed) and [secondly] of the extension of the labour process beyond the *time* necessary to replenish the value of the variable capital invested.

468   It follows from our arguments hitherto that the expression 'objectified labour', and the opposition established between *capital* as *objectified labour* and *living labour* is open to grave misunderstanding.

I have already shown earlier on[5] that the analysis of the commodity in terms of 'labour' has been carried out only imperfectly and ambiguously by all previous economists. It is not sufficient to reduce the commodity to 'labour'; labour must be broken down into its twofold form – on the one hand, into *concrete labour in the use-values of the commodity*, and on the other hand, into *socially necessary labour* as calculated in *exchange-value*. In the first case everything depends on the particular use-values, their specific nature, which is what confers on the use-values such labour as creates their distinctive character and makes them into concrete use-values to be distinguished from others, into this particular

5. In the absence of this confusion it would not have been possible to embark on a dispute about whether nature contributes to the manufacture of a product quite apart from labour. Here we are concerned only with *concrete* labour.

article. In the second case we entirely ignore their particular utility, their specific nature and mode of being, for such labour is regarded solely in its importance as a *value-creating* factor, and the commodity as its objective form. As such it is undifferentiated, *socially necessary general* labour, utterly indifferent to any particular content. For that very reason, even in its most independent form as *money*, or *price* in the case of the commodity, it is defined in a manner common to all commodities and is distinguished from others only quantitatively. In its first aspect, then, labour presents itself as a given *use-value* of the commodity, its given *existence as a thing*; in its second, it appears as *money*, either as money proper or as a mere calculation of the price of a commodity. In the first case we are concerned exclusively with the *quality*, in the second, with the *quantity* of labour. In the first case the different modes of concrete labour are expressed in the division of labour, in the second we find only an undifferentiated expression in terms of money. Now within the process of production this distinction confronts us *actively*. It is no longer we who make it; instead it is created in the process of production itself.

The distinction between *objectified* and *living labour* manifests itself in the actual *process of labour*. The means of production, cotton, spindles, etc., are products, use-values, which *embody* definite, useful, concrete acts of labour – the planting of cotton, construction of machinery, etc. The *work of spinning,* on the other hand, although a mode of labour included in the means of production, is nevertheless a distinctive, specific mode of labour, and as living labour it is in the process of realizing itself, it continuously gives birth to its products and thus stands in contrast to labour which has already acquired objective form in the shape of products peculiar to it. From this vantage-point, too, we see the antagonism between capital in an established form on the one hand and living labour as the immediate life task of the worker on the other. Furthermore, in the labour process, objectified labour constitutes an *objective factor*, an element for the *realization of living labour*.

The position is quite otherwise, however, when we come to consider the valorization process, the formation and creation of new value.

The labour contained in the means of production is a *specific quantity of general social labour* and it may be represented, therefore, as a certain *amount of value* or *sum of money*, the *price* in fact of these means of production. The work that is added to this is a *specific additional quantity of general social labour* and may be represented as an additional *amount of value* or *sum of money*. The labour already contained in the means of production is identical to what is now added. The two kinds of labour are distinguished only by the fact that the one is already *objectified* in use-values while the other is in the process of being so *objectified*. The one is in the past, the other in the present; the one dead, the other living; the one *objectified* in the past, the other *objectifying* itself in the present. To the extent to which past labour replaces living labour, it itself becomes a process, *valorizes itself*; it becomes a *fluens* that creates a fluxion. This absorption into itself of additional living labour is its *process of self-valorization*, its authentic *transformation into capital*, into value generating itself, its transformation from a *constant amount of value* into a variable value in a state of *process*. Admittedly, this additional labour can appear only in the shape of concrete labour and hence it can be added to the means of production only in its specific form, as particular use-values. And by the same token the value contained in these means of production can *endure* only if it is consumed by concrete labour as part of *its* means. Nevertheless, this is not to deny that the *value actually present*, the labour *objectified* in the means of production, can only be increased, and increased not only beyond its own previous value but beyond the amount of labour objectified in variable capital, to the extent to which it sucks in living labour and objectifies it as *money*, as *general social labour*. It is therefore preeminently in this sense – which pertains to the *valorization process* as the authentic aim of capitalist production – that capital as *objectified* labour (accumulated labour, pre-existent labour and so forth) may be said to confront *living* labour (immediate labour, etc.), and is so contrasted by the economists. However, the latter constantly lapse into contradictions and ambiguity – even Ricardo – because they have failed to work out a clear analysis of the commodity in terms of the dual form of labour.

With the original exchange between capitalist and worker – both as commodity owners – the only real component of capital to enter the process of production is the living factor, labour-power itself. But it is only in the actual process of production that *objectified labour* is transformed into capital by absorbing living labour and hence it is only then that *labour transforms itself into* capital.*

*

469a   The capitalist process of production is the unity of labour process and valorization process. In order to translate money into capital it is transformed into commodities which constitute *factors of the labour process*. The money must be used first to buy labour-power and, after that, the things without which labour-power cannot be *consumed*, i.e. cannot *work*. Within the *labour process* the sole significance of these things is as the *means of subsistence of labour, use-values for labour*. *Vis-à-vis* living labour itself they are materials and means, *vis-à-vis* the product of labour they are the means of production, and *vis-à-vis* the circumstance that these means of production are themselves products, they are products as the means of production of yet another, new product. It is not the case, however, that these things play this role in the labour process because the capitalist purchases them, because they are the metamorphosis of his money, but rather the opposite: he buys them because they play this role in the labour process. For the pro-

* At this point Marx inserted the following note: 'The contents of pp. 96–107 under the heading "*The immediate process of production*" belong here; they should be blended in with the foregoing so that each acts as a corrective to the other. The same applies to pp. 262–4 of this book.' – In accordance with Marx's instruction we print both the passages he mentions here. No changes were made ('so that each acts as a corrective to the other'). The pages to be inserted (originally pp. 96–107) were subsequently renumbered by Marx as 469a–469m. On p. 469a (96) itself the text begins with the continuation of a paragraph deleted by Marx (it is struck through by four diagonal lines), which established continuity with the now lost pp. 1–95. At the top of the first page Marx wrote: 'This belongs to p. 496' [an error for 469]. The text that follows on from the deleted passage carries the title, superfluous in the present context: '*The immediate process of production*.' The passage omitted reads as follows:

  '. . . for the capital used to purchase the capacity for labour is embodied in fact in the means of subsistence although these means of subsistence are transferred to the worker in the form of money. Like the supporters of the monetary system the worker might well answer the question: What is capital? with the words: *Capital* is *money*. For while in the labour process capital is to be found physically in the form of raw materials, the instruments of labour, etc., in the circulation process it takes the form of money. In the same way, if an economist of antiquity had been asked: What is a worker? he would have had to answer, following the identical logic: A worker is a slave (because the slave was the worker in the labour process of antiquity).'

cess of spinning as such, for example, it is immaterial that cotton and spindles *represent* the capitalist's money, i.e. *capital*, and that the money invested is capital by definition. They become the means and materials of labour only in the hands of the spinner as he works, and they become so because he spins, and not because he takes some cotton which belongs to another person and makes it into yarn for that same other person with the aid of a spindle which likewise belongs to that person. Commodities do not become capital by being consumed or used up in production during the labour process; this only makes of them the elements of the labour process. In so far as these material elements of the labour process have been purchased by the capitalist, they represent his capital. But the same applies to labour itself. It too represents his capital, for the owner of the capacity for labour owns that labour just as effectively as he owns the other material conditions of labour that he has bought. And he does not just own the particular elements of the labour process; the entire process belongs to him. The capital that had been money previously now assumes the form of the labour process. But the fact that capital has taken over the labour process and the worker therefore works for the capitalist instead of himself does not mean any change in the *general nature* of the labour process itself. The fact that when money is transformed into capital it is simultaneously transformed into the elements of the labour process, and hence necessarily assumes the shape of the materials and means of labour, does not mean that the materials and means of labour are *capital* by their very nature, any more than gold and silver are *money* by their very nature, merely because gold and silver are among the forms assumed by money. Modern economists deride the simple-mindedness of the monetary system when it responds to the question: What is money? with the answer: gold and silver are money. But these self-same economists do not blush to respond to the question: What is capital? with the reply: Capital is cotton. Yet this is what they do when they declare that the materials and means of labour, the means of production or products that serve in the creation of new products, in short, all the *material conditions of labour* are *capital* by their very nature, and that they are capital because, and to the extent that, they participate in the labour process by virtue of their physical qualities as use-values. It is in order if others add to their list: Capital is meat and bread, for even though the capitalist purchases labour-power with money, this money in fact only repre-

469b sents bread, meat and, in short, all the means of subsistence of the worker.[6]

Under certain circumstances a chair with four legs and a velvet covering may be used as a *throne*. But this same chair, a thing for sitting on, does not become a throne by virtue of its use-value. The most essential factor in the labour process is the worker himself, and in antiquity this worker was a slave. But this does not imply that the worker is a *slave* by nature (though this latter view is not entirely foreign to Aristotle), any more than spindles and cotton are *capital* by nature just because they are consumed nowadays by

6. '*Capital* is that part of the wealth of a country which is employed in production and consists of food, clothing, tools, raw materials, machinery, etc. necessary to give effect to labour' (Ricardo, op. cit. [*On the Principles of Political Economy and Taxation*], p. 89). '*Capital* is a portion of the national wealth, employed or meant to be employed, in favouring reproduction' (G. Ramsay, op. cit., p. 21). '*Capital* . . . a particular species of wealth . . . destined . . . to the obtaining of other articles of utility' (R. Torrens, op. cit.) [*An Essay on the Production of Wealth*, pp. 69–70] '*Capital* . . . *produit* . . . *comme moyen d'une nouvelle production*' ['*Capital* . . . produces . . . as the means of new production'] (Senior, op. cit. [*Principes fondamentaux de l'économie politique*], p. 318). '*Lorsqu'un fonds est consacré à la production matérielle, il prend le* nom de capital' ['When a fund is devoted to material production it takes the *name of capital*'] (H. F. Storch, *Cours d'économie politique*, Paris edition, 1823, p. 207). '*Le* capital *est cette portion de la richesse produite qui est destinée à la reproduction*' ['*Capital* is that portion of wealth *produced* that is destined for reproduction'] (Rossi, *Cours d'économie politique*, 1836–7, Brussels edition, 1842, p. 364). Rossi racks his brains over the 'difficulty' about whether 'raw materials' can be counted as capital. He thinks one can indeed distinguish between '*capital-matière*' and '*capital-instrument*', but '*est-ce (la matière première) vraiment là un instrument de production? N'est-ce pas plutôt l'objet sur lequel les instruments producteurs doivent agir?*' ['but are the raw materials really an instrument of production? Are they not rather the objects on which the instruments of production must operate?'] (p. 367). He does not realize that once he confuses capital with its physical manifestations and hence calls the objective conditions of labour capital, they do indeed break down into the materials and the instruments of labour, but are all equally means of production as far as the product is concerned. Thus on p. 372 he refers to capital simply as '*les moyens de production*', '*Il n'y a aucune différence entre un* capital *et tout autre portion de richesse: c'est seulement par l'emploi qui en est fait, qu'une* chose *devient* capital, *c'est à dire lorsqu'elle est employée dans une opération productive, comme matière première, comme instrument ou comme approvisionnement*' ['There is no difference between capital and any other fraction of wealth: it is only by virtue of the use that is made of it that an *article* becomes *capital*, that is to say, it must be employed in a productive operation, as raw materials, as an instrument or as a means of supply'] (Cherbuliez, *Riche ou pauvre*, Paris, 1840, p. 18).

the *wage-labourer* in the labour process. The folly of identifying a specific *social relationship of production* with the thing-like [*dingliche*] qualities of certain articles simply because it represents itself in terms of certain articles is what strikes us most forcibly whenever we open any textbook on economics and see on the first page how the elements of the process of production, reduced to their basic form, turn out to be land, *capital* and labour.[7] One might just as well say that they were *landed property*, knives, scissors, spindles, cotton, grain, in short, the *materials* and *means of labour*, and – *wage-labour*. On the one hand, we name the elements of the labour process combined with the *specific social characteristics* peculiar to them in a given *historical* phase, and on the other hand we add an element which forms an integral part of the *labour process* independently of any particular social formation, as part of an eternal commerce between man and nature. By confusing the appropriation of the labour process by capital with the labour process itself, the economists transform the *material elements* of the labour process into capital, simply because capital itself changes into the material elements of the labour process *among other things*. We shall see below that these illusions only last as long as the classical economists look at the process of capitalist production exclusively from the standpoint of the labour process and that they then subsequently correct them. And we shall see above all that this illusion is one that springs from the nature of capitalist production itself. But it is evident even now that this is a very convenient method by which to demonstrate the eternal validity of the capitalist mode of production and to regard *capital* as an *immutable natural element* in human production as such. Work is the eternal natural condition of human existence. The process of labour is nothing but work itself, viewed at the moment of its creative activity. Hence the universal features of the labour process are independent of every specific social development. The materials and means of labour, a proportion of which consists of the products of previous work, play their part in every labour process in every age and in all circumstances. If, therefore, I label them 'capital' in the confident knowledge that '*semper aliquid haeret*',*

7. See, for example, John Stuart Mill, *Principles of Political Economy*, Vol. 1, Bk 1.

***

*'Something always sticks.'

then I have *proved* that the existence of capital is an eternal law of
nature of human production and that the Kirghiz who cuts down
rushes with a knife he has stolen from a Russian so as to weave
them together to make a canoe is just as true a capitalist as Herr
von Rothschild. I could prove with equal facility that the Greeks
and Romans celebrated communion because they drank wine and
ate bread, and that the Turks sprinkle themselves daily with holy
water like Catholics because they wash themselves daily. This is
the sort of impertinent and superficial rubbish that one finds doled
out with self-important complacency not only by the likes of
F. Bastiat* or the little economic pamphlets of the Society for the
469c Advancement of Useful Knowledge, or the nursery stories of a
Mother Martineau,† but even in the writings of reputable authorities. Far from demonstrating, as they hope, that capital is an
eternal natural necessity, all they succeed in doing is to *refute* that
necessary existence in the case of a specific historical phase of the
social process of production. For if it is claimed that capital is
nothing but the material and instruments of labour or that the
material elements of the labour process are capital by nature, one
may rightly riposte that in that event we do indeed require capital
but no capitalists, or alternatively that capital is nothing but a
name invented to deceive the masses.[8]

8. 'We are told that Labour cannot move one step without Capital – that
Capital is as a shovel to a man who digs – that Capital is just as necessary to
production as Labour itself is. The working man knows all this, for its truth
is daily brought home to him; but this mutual dependency between Capital
and Labour has nothing to do with the relative position of the capitalist and
the working man; nor does it show that the former could be maintained by
the latter. Capital is but so much unconsumed produce; and that which is at
this moment in being, exists now independent of, and is in no way identified
with, any particular individual or class. Labour is the parent of it, on the one
side, and mother earth upon the other; and were every capitalist and every
rich man in the United Kingdom to be annihilated in one moment, not a
single particle of wealth or capital would disappear with them; nor would the
nation itself be less wealthy, even to the amount of one farthing. It is the
capital, and not the capitalist, that is essential to the operations of the producer; and there is as much difference between the two, as there is between
the actual cargo and the bill of lading' (J. F. Bray, *Labour's Wrongs and
Labour's Remedy, etc.*, Leeds, 1839, p. 59).
   'Capital is a sort of *cabalistic word* like church or state, or any other of

* e.g. *Sophismes économiques*, Paris, 1846–8.
† Harriet Martineau, *Illustrations of Political Economy*, 9 vols., London,
1832–4.

The failure to comprehend the labour process as an independent thing and at the same time as an aspect of capitalist production becomes even more strikingly obvious when Mr F. Wayland, for example, tells us that *raw materials* are *capital* and that it is by treating them that we arrive at the product. Thus leather is the *product* of the currier and the *capital* of the shoemaker. Both 'raw material' and 'product' are terms referring to things in the *labour process* and in itself neither has anything to do with *capital* although both raw material and product represent *capital* the moment the labour process is appropriated by the capitalist.[9]

M. Proudhon has exploited all this with his customary 'profundity'. 'How does the *concept of a product* suddenly become transformed into the *concept of capital*? Through the *idea of value*. That is to say, in order to become capital the product must have undergone an authentic process of valuation, it must have been bought or sold, its price debated and established by a sort of legal convention. When a hide comes from a butcher it is the *product of the butcher*. Suppose the hide be now purchased by a currier. The latter immediately enters it or its value in his exploitation fund. Then, through the labour of the currier, this *capital* becomes a *product* once again.'[10] M. Proudhon distinguishes himself here by the apparatus of false metaphysics by means of which he first enters the most elementary notions as capital in his 'exploitation fund' and then sells them to the public as a high-sounding pro-

---

those general terms which are invented by those who fleece the rest of mankind to conceal the hand that shears them' (*Labour Defended against the Claims of Capital etc.*, London, 1825, p. 17). The author of this pamphlet is Th. Hodgskin, one of the most important modern English economists. Some years after its publication, the work cited, whose importance is still acknowledged (see, for example, John Lalor, *Money and Morals etc.*, London, 1852), was the occasion of an anonymous counter-pamphlet by Lord Brougham, whose response was noteworthy for the same superficiality that marks all the economic productions of that windbag.

9. 'The material which . . . we obtain for the purpose of combining it with *our own* (!) industry, and forming it into a product, is called *capital*; and, after the labour has been exerted, and the value created, it is called a *product*. Thus the same article may be *product* to one, and *capital* to another. Leather is the product of the currier, and the capital of the shoemaker' (F. Wayland, op. cit., p. 25).

10. There now follows the above-quoted shit from Proudhon, *Gratuité du Crédit. Discussion entre M. Fr. Bastiat et M. Proudhon*, Paris, 1850, pp. 179, 180 and 182.

duct. The question of how *products* can be turned into *capital* is essentially nonsensical, but the answer proves worthy of the question. In actual fact M. Proudhon merely informs us of two fairly well-known facts: first, that products sometimes serve as raw materials to be processed, and second, that *products* are also *commodities*, i.e. they possess a *value* which has to withstand the ordeal of an interchange between buyer and seller before it can be realized. The same 'philosopher' remarks: '*La différence, pour la société, entre capital et produit n'existe pas. Cette différence est toute subjective aux individus.*' He calls the abstract social form 'subjective' and his subjective abstraction he calls 'society'.

As long as the economist looks at the process of capitalist production only in the context of the *labour process*, he declares that capital is a mere *article*, raw material, an instrument, etc. But it then occurs to him that the process of production is also the valorization process and that in the latter the articles come into consideration only as a *value*. 'The same capital exists now in the form of a sum of money, now in the form of raw material, an instrument, a finished product. These *articles* are not actually *capital*; capital resides in the *value* they possess.'[11] In so far as this value 'maintains itself, endures, multiplies itself, detaches itself from the commodity that has created it and remains, like a metaphysical and insubstantial quality, always in the possession of the same producer (i.e. the capitalist)'[12] the same thing which was just declared to be an *article*, is now deemed 'a *commercial idea*'.

The product of capitalist production is neither a mere *product* (a use-value), nor just a *commodity*, i.e. a product with an exchange-value, but a *product specific to itself*, namely *surplus-value*. Its product is *commodities* that possess more exchange-value, i.e. represent more labour than was invested for their production in the shape of money or commodities. In capitalist production the

11. Cf. J. B. Say, op. cit. [*Traité d'économie politique*], Vol. II, p. 429, note. When Carey says, '*Capital* . . . all articles possessing exchangeable value' (H. C. Carey, *Principles of Political Economy*, Part I, Philadelphia, 1837, p. 294) this lapses into the explanation of capital referred to in Chapter I*: 'Capital – is commodities', an explanation that can only refer to the manifestation of capital in the process of circulation.

12. Sismondi, *Nouv. Princ. etc.*, Vol. I, p. 89. Cf. also '*Le capital est une idée commerciale*' ['Capital is a commercial idea'] (Sismondi, *Études, etc.*, Vol. II, p. 389).

* See above, p. 255, n. 13.

labour process is only the *means*; the end is supplied by the *valorization process* or the *production of surplus-value*. As soon as this occurs to the economist he declares capital to be wealth which is used in production to make a 'profit'.[13]

We have seen that the transformation of money into capital breaks down into two wholly distinct, autonomous spheres, two entirely separate processes. The first belongs to the realm of the *circulation of commodities* and is acted out in the *market-place*. It is the *sale and purchase of labour-power*. The second is the *consumption* of *the labour-power that has been acquired*, i.e. the process of production itself. In the first process the capitalist and the worker confront one another merely as the owners respectively of money and commodities, and their transactions, like those of all buyers and sellers, are the exchange of equivalents. In the second process the worker appears *pro tempore* as the living component of capital itself, and the category of exchange is entirely excluded here since the capitalist has acquired by purchase all the factors of the production process, both material and personal, before the negotiations begin. However, although the two processes subsist independently side by side, each conditions the other. The first introduces the second and the second completes the first.

The first process, the *sale and purchase of labour-power*, displays to us the capitalist and the worker only as the buyer and seller of commodities. What distinguishes the worker from the vendors of other commodities is only the *specific nature*, the *specific use-value*, of the commodity he sells. But the particular use-value of a commodity does not affect the economic form of the transaction; it does not alter the fact that the purchaser represents money, and the vendor a commodity. In order to *demonstrate*, therefore, that the relationship between capitalist and worker is nothing but a relationship between commodity owners who exchange money and commodities with a free contract and to their mutual advantage, it suffices to isolate the first process and to cleave to its formal character. This simple device is no sorcery, but it contains the entire wisdom of the vulgar economists.

13. '*Capital*. That portion of the stock of a country which is kept or employed with a view to profit in the production and distribution of wealth' (T. R. Malthus, *Definitions in Political Economy*, new edition, etc. by John Cazenove, London, 1853, p. 10). 'Capital is the part of wealth employed for production and generally for the purpose of obtaining profit' (Th. Chalmers, *On Political Economy, etc.*, London, 1832, 2nd edn, p. 75).

We have seen that the capitalist must transform his money not only into labour-power, but into the material factors of the labour process, i.e. the means of production. However, if we think of the whole of capital as standing on one side, i.e. the totality of the purchasers of labour-power, and if we think of the totality of the vendors of labour-power, the totality of workers on the other, then we find that the worker is compelled to sell not a commodity but his own labour-power as a commodity. This is because he finds on the other side, opposed to him and confronting him as alien property, all the means of production, all the material conditions of work together with all the means of subsistence, money and means of production. In other words, all *material wealth confronts* the worker as the property of the *commodity possessors*. What is proposed here is that he works as a *non-proprietor* and that the *conditions of his labour confront* him as *alien property*. The fact that Capitalist No. 1 owns money and that he buys the means of production from Capitalist No. 2, who owns them, while the worker buys the means of subsistence from Capitalist No. 3 with the money he has obtained from Capitalist No. 2, does not alter the fundamental situation that Capitalists Nos. 1, 2 and 3 are together the exclusive possessors of money, means of production and means of subsistence. Man can only live by producing his own means of subsistence, and he can produce these only if he is in possession of the means of production, of the material conditions of labour. It is obvious from the very outset that the worker who is denuded of the means of production is thereby deprived of the means of subsistence, just as, conversely, a man deprived of the means of subsistence is in no position to create the means of production. Thus even in the first *process*, what stamps money or commodities as *capital* from the outset, even before they have been really transformed into *capital*, is neither their money nature nor their commodity nature, nor the material use-value of these commodities as means of production or subsistence, but the circumstance that this money and this commodity, these means of production and these means of subsistence confront *labour-power*, stripped of all material wealth, as autonomous powers, personified in their owners. The objective conditions essential to the realization of labour are *alienated* from the worker and become manifest as *fetishes* endowed with a will and a soul of their own. *Commodities*, in short, appear as the purchasers of *persons*. The buyer of labour-power is nothing but the personification of *objectified* labour which cedes a part of itself to the worker in the form of the means of subsistence in order to annex the living labour-power for the benefit of the remaining portion, so as to keep itself intact and even to grow beyond its original size by virtue of this annexation. It is not the worker who buys the means of production and subsistence, but the means of production that buy the worker to incorporate him into the means of production.

The *means of subsistence* are a particular form of material existence in which capital confronts the worker before he acquires them through the sale of his labour-power. But by the time the process of production begins the labour-power has already been sold and hence the means of subsistence have passed *de jure* at least into the consumption fund of the worker. These means of subsistence themselves form no part of the labour process, which, apart from the presence of effective labour-power, requires nothing but the materials and means of labour. In fact, of course, the worker must sustain his capacity for work with the aid of means of subsistence, but this, his private consumption, which is at the same time the reproduction of his labour-power, falls outside the process of producing commodities. It is possible that in capitalist production the entire available time of the worker is actually taken up by capital and that the consumption of the means of subsistence is actually no more than an incident in the labour process, like the consumption of coal by the steam-engine, of oil by the wheel, of hay by the horse and like the entire private consumption of the labouring slave. It is in keeping with this that Ricardo, for instance (see note 6 above), lists 'food and clothing' alongside raw materials and tools, as things which 'give effect to labour' and hence serve as 'capital' in the labour process. However that may be

469f *in fact*, the means of subsistence that the worker consumes are commodities that he has *purchased*. As soon as they pass into his hands, and even more evidently, as soon as he has consumed them, they cease to be capital. They form no part of the *physical elements* in which capital manifests itself in the *immediate process of production*, even though they constitute the *physically existing form* of *variable capital* which enters the market place as the purchaser of labour-power within the *sphere of circulation*.[14]

14. This is the valid point underlying Rossi's polemic against the inclusion of the means of subsistence among the components of productive capital. How wide he is of the mark in his interpretation, however, and the extent

When a capitalist takes 500 thalers and invests 400 of them in the means of production and 100 in the acquisition of labour-power, these 100 thalers constitute his *variable* capital. With them the workers buy the means of subsistence, either from the same capitalist or from another. These 100 thalers are nothing but the *money-form* of the means of subsistence which in fact constitute the *physical manifestation* of the variable capital. Within the *immediate process of production* the variable capital has ceased to exist: it exists neither in the form of money, nor of commodities, but in the form of *living labour* which the capitalist has acquired through the purchase of labour-power. And it is only by virtue of this transformation of variable capital into labour that the quantum of value invested in money or commodities can be converted into *capital*. Thus when we look at the process of capitalist production as a *whole* and not merely at the immediate production of commodities, we find that although the *sale and purchase of labour-power* (which itself conditions the transformation of a part of the capital into variable capital) is entirely separate from the immediate production process, and indeed precedes it, it yet forms the *absolute foundation* of capitalist production and is an integral *moment* within it. Material wealth transforms itself into capital simply and solely because the worker sells his labour-power in order to live. The *articles* which are the material conditions of labour, i.e. the *means of production*, and the articles which are the precondition for the survival of the worker himself, i.e. the *means of subsistence*, both become *capital* only because of the phenomenon of *wage-labour*. Capital is not a *thing*, any more than money is a *thing*. In capital, as in money, certain *specific social relations of production between people* appear as *relations of things to people*, or else certain social relations appear as the *natural properties of things in society*. Without a *class dependent on wages*, the moment individuals confront each other as free persons, there can be no production of surplus-value; without the production of surplus-value there can be no capitalist production, and hence no capital and no capitalist! Capital and wage-labour (it is thus we designate the labour of the worker who sells his own labour-power) only express two aspects

of the confusion introduced by his rationalizations, is something we shall return to in a later chapter.*

*This point is dealt with in *Grundrisse*, pp. 591–4. Marx did not however return to it anywhere in *Capital*, or in *Theories of Surplus-Value*.

of the self-same relationship. Money cannot become capital unless it is exchanged for labour-power, a commodity sold by the worker himself. Conversely, work can only be wage-labour when its *own* material conditions confront it as autonomous powers, alien property, value existing for itself and maintaining itself, in short as capital. If capital in its material aspect, i.e. in the use-values in which it has its being, must depend for its existence on the material conditions of labour, these material conditions must equally, on the formal side, confront labour as *alien, autonomous powers*, as value – objectified labour – which treats living labour as a mere means whereby to maintain and increase itself. Thus wage-labour, the wages system, is a social form of work indispensable to capitalist production, just as capital, i.e. potentiated value, is an indispensable social form which must be assumed by the material conditions of labour in order for the latter to be wage-labour. Wage-labour is then a necessary condition for the formation of capital and remains the essential prerequisite of capitalist production. Therefore, although the primary process, the exchange of money for labour-power, or the sale of labour-power, does not as such enter the immediate process of production, it does enter into the production of the relationship as a whole.[15]

As we have seen, the first process, the sale and purchase of labour-power, presupposes that the means of production and subsistence have become autonomous objects confronting the worker, i.e. it presupposes the *personification* of the means of production and subsistence which, as purchasers, negotiate a contract with the

15. We may readily deduce what an F. Bastiat understands about the nature of capitalist production when he declares the wages system to be an external and irrelevant formality in capitalist production, and discovers the truth '*que ce n'est pas la* forme de remunération *qui crée pour lui* (*l'ouvrier*) *cette dépendance*' ['it is not the *form of remuneration* that creates his (the worker's) dependence'] (*Harmonies économiques*, Paris, 1851, p. 378). This is a discovery – and moreover a piece of misinterpreted plagiarism taken over from real economists – altogether worthy of the eloquent ignoramus who discovered in the same work, i.e. in 1851 '*ce qui est plus décisif et infaillible encore, c'est* la disparition des grandes crises industrielles *en Angleterre*' ['what is still more decisive and incontestable is the *disappearance of major industrial crises* in England'] (p. 396). Although F. Bastiat had eliminated great crises from England by decree as early as 1851, England enjoyed a great crisis no later than 1857, and, as we can read in the official reports of the English Chambers of Commerce, a further industrial crisis of hitherto unprecedented dimensions was averted in 1861 only by the outbreak of the American Civil War.

workers as vendors. When we leave this process which is enacted in the *market-place*, in the *sphere of circulation*, and proceed directly to the *immediate process of production*, we find that it is primarily a *labour process*. In the labour process the worker enters as worker into a normal active relationship with the means of production determined by the nature and the purpose of the work itself. He takes possession of the means of production and handles them simply as the means and materials of his work. The autonomous nature of these means of production, the way they hold fast to their independence and display a mind of their own, their separation from labour – all this is now *abolished* [*aufgehoben*] in practice. The material conditions of labour now enter into a normal unity with labour itself; they form the material, the organs requisite for its creative activity. The worker treats the hide he is tanning simply as the object of his creative activity, and not as capital. He does not tan the hide for the capitalist.[16] If we consider production just as a labour process, the worker consumes the means of production as the *mere means of subsistence of labour*. But production is also a process of *valorization*, and here the capitalist devours the labour-power of the worker, or appropriates his living labour as the life-blood of capitalism. Raw materials and the object of labour in general exist only to *absorb* the work of others, and the instrument of labour serves only as a conductor, an agency, for this *process of absorption*. By incorporating living labour-power into the material constituents of capital, the latter becomes an animated monster and it starts to act 'as if consumed by love'.* Since work creates value only in a definite useful form, and since every particular useful form of work requires materials and instruments with specific use-values, spindles and cotton, etc. for spinning, hammer, anvil and iron for forging metal, etc., labour can only be drained off if capital assumes the shape of the means of production required for the particular labour process in question, and only in this shape can it annex living labour. This is the reason, then, why the capitalist, the worker and the political economist,

16. 'We see further from the explanations of the economist himself, that *in the process of production*, capital, the result of labour, is immediately transformed again into the substratum, into the material of labour; and how therefore the momentarily postulated *separation of capital from labour* is immediately *superseded by the unity of both*' (F. Engels, *Deutsch-französische Jahrbücher, etc.*, p. 99) [English translation, p. 430].

*Goethe, *Faust*, Part I, Auerbach's Cellar, line 2141.

who is only capable of conceiving the labour process as a process owned by capital, all think of the *physical* elements of the labour process as *capital* just because of their physical characteristics. This is why they are incapable of detaching their physical existence as mere elements in the labour process from the *social* characteristics amalgamated with it, which is what really make them *capital*. They are unable to do this because in reality the labour process that employs the physical qualities of the means of production as the means of subsistence of labour is identical with the labour process that converts these self-same means of production into means for living labour. In the labour process looked at purely for itself the worker utilizes the means of production. In the labour process regarded also as a capitalist process of production, the means of production utilize the worker, so that work appears only as an instrument which enables a specific *quantum of value*, i.e. a specific mass of *objectified* labour, to suck in living labour in order to sustain and increase itself. Regarded thus, the labour process is the *self-valorization process* of objectified labour through the agency of living labour.[17] *Capital* utilizes the *worker*, the *worker* does not utilize *capital*, and only *articles which utilize the worker* and hence possess *independence*, a consciousness and a will of their own in the capitalist, are *capital*.[18]

17. 'Labour is the *agency* by which capital is made productive of ... profit' (John Wade, op. cit., p. 161). 'In bourgeois society, living labour is but a means to increase accumulated labour' (*Manifesto of the Communist Party*, 1848, p. 12) [see *The Revolutions of 1848*, Pelican Marx Library, 1973, p. 81].

18. The fact that the *means of subsistence* have the particular *economic* characteristic that they purchase workers, or that the *means of production*, such as leather and lasts, *utilize cobbler's assistants* – this inversion of *person and thing* has become an inseparable part of the *physical* character of the elements of production both in capitalist production itself and in the imagination of the economists. So much so in fact that when Ricardo, for example, deems it necessary to give an analysis of the physical elements of capital, he *naturally* without scruples or reflection of any kind makes use of the *correct* economic expressions. Thus he talks of 'capital, or the *means of employing labour*' (i.e. not 'means employed by labour' but 'means of employing labour') (op. cit., p. 92); 'quantity of labour employed by a capital' (ibid., p. 419); 'the fund which is to employ them' (the labourers) (p. 252, etc.). Likewise in modern German the capitalist, the personification of *things* which take labour, is called an '*Arbeitgeber*' [employer, literally a giver of work], while the actual worker who gives his labour is called an '*Arbeitnehmer*' [employee, literally a taker of work]. 'In bourgeois society capital is independent and has individuality, while the living person is dependent and has no individuality' (*Manifesto of the Communist Party*, op. cit.).

Since the labour process is only the instrument and the actual form of the *valorization process*, i.e. since its purpose is to employ the labour materialized in wages to objectify in commodities an *extra quantity of unpaid labour, surplus-value,* i.e. to *create surplus-value,* the crux of the entire process is the exchange of *objectified labour* for *living labour,* of less *objectified labour* for more *living labour.* In the course of the exchange an amount of labour objectified in money as a commodity is exchanged for an equal amount of labour objectified in living labour.

-69h   In accordance with the laws of commodity exchange equivalent values change hands, i.e. *equal amounts* of objectified labour, although the one amount is objectified in a thing, the other in flesh and blood. But this exchange only inaugurates the *process of production* through whose agency in fact more labour in living form is given up than was supplied in its objectified form. It is therefore greatly to the credit of the classical economists that they portrayed the entire process of production in terms of a commerce between *objectified* and *living labour,* and that they accordingly defined capital only as *objectified labour* in contrast to living labour. That is to say, they depict capital as *value* which makes use of living labour to *valorize* itself. Their only failings are firstly that they were unable to show how this exchange of more living labour for less objectified labour could be reconciled with the laws of commodity exchange and the definition of the value of commodities in terms of labour-time. And this led to their second failure of confusing the exchange of a definite quantity of *objectified labour* for labour-power in the *process of circulation,* with what takes place in the process of production, namely, the drawing off of living labour by labour *objectified* in the means of production. They confound the *exchange process* that takes place between variable capital and labour-power with the process in which living labour finds itself sucked up and absorbed by constant capital. This failure, too, is rooted in their 'capitalist' blinkers, since for the capitalist himself, who pays for labour only after it has been valorized, the exchange of a small amount of objectified labour for a large amount of living labour appears to be a *single unmediated process.* Therefore, when the modern economist contrasts capital as *objectified labour* to living labour, what he understands by objectified labour is not *products of labour* in the sense that they have a use-value and embody certain useful acts of labour, but *products of labour* in the sense that they are the material base of a certain *amount* of general social labour and hence *value*, money that valorizes itself by acquiring the *living* labour of others. This process of acquisition is mediated by the exchange that takes place in the open market between variable capital and labour-power, but is only completed in the actual process of production.[19]

The subordination of the labour process to capital does not at first affect the actual mode of production and its only practical effects are these: the worker bows to the command, the direction and the supervision of the capitalist, although naturally only in

19. Immediate labour and objectified labour, labour present and past, living and hoarded labour, etc., all these are forms which the economists use to express the relations of capital and labour. 'Labour and capital . . . the one *immediate* labour . . . the other *hoarded labour*' (James Mill, *Elements of Political Economy*, London, 1821, p. 75). '*Antecedent labour* (capital) . . . *present labour*' (E. G. Wakefield in his edition of Adam Smith, London, 1835, Vol. 1, p. 231, note). '*Accumulated labour* (capital) . . . *immediate labour*' (Torrens, op. cit., Ch. 1, p. 31). '*Labour* and *Capital*, that is, *accumulated labour*' (Ricardo, op. cit., p. 499). 'The *specific* advances of the capitalist do not consist of cloth' (or of any use-values as such), 'but of *labour*' (Malthus, *The Measure of Values, etc.*, London, 1823, pp. 17–18).

'*Comme tout homme est forcé de consommer avant de produire, l'ouvrier pauvre se trouve dans la* dépendance *du riche, et ne peut ni vivre ni travailler, s'il n'obtient de lui des denrées et des marchandises existantes, en retour de celles qu'il promet de produire par son travail . . . pour l'y (id est le riche) faire consentir, il a fallu convenir que toutes les fois qu'il échangerait du* travail fait contre du *travail* à faire, *le dernier aurait une valeur supérieure au premier*' ['Just as everyone is forced to consume before he produces, the poor worker finds himself in a state of *dependence* upon the rich man and can neither live nor work without obtaining existing produce and commodities from him, in exchange for those which he pledges to produce by his own labour . . . to induce him (i.e. the rich man) to consent to this, it was necessary to agree that whenever *labour already performed* was exchanged for *labour yet to be done*, the latter would be worth more than the former'] (Sismondi, *De la richesse commerciale*, Paris, 1803, Vol. 1, pp. 36–7).

Herr W. Roscher, who evidently has not the faintest idea what the English economists are saying and who has belatedly recollected that Senior christened capital 'abstinence', has the following professorial comment to make, a comment remarkable incidentally for its grammatical 'dexterity': 'The school of Ricardo is also wont to subsume capital under the concept of labour, under the heading of "hoarded labour". This is *inept* because of course (!) the owner of capital has surely (!) done *more* (!) than merely (!) producing (!) and maintaining (!) it; he abstains namely from enjoying it himself, in return for which he requires e.g. interest' (W. Roscher, op. cit.)*. [The 'dexterity' which Marx mentions is a reference to Roscher's play on '*Er*haltung' (maintaining) and '*Ent*haltung' (abstaining).]

*See above p. 314, n. 3.

respect of his labour which belongs to capital. The capitalist makes sure that he wastes no time and sees to it, for example, that he hands over the product of an hour's work every hour, that he only spends the average labour-time necessary for producing the product. Since the relations of capital are essentially concerned with controlling production and since therefore the worker constantly appears in the market as a seller and the capitalist as a buyer, the labour process itself is *continuous* for the most part. It is not interrupted as it would be if the worker were an independent producer of commodities, who depended on selling his wares to individual customers, because the minimum capital must be large enough to occupy the worker continuously and to ensure that there is no necessity to sell the goods in a hurry.[20] Lastly, the capitalist forces the workers to extend the duration of the labour process as far as possible beyond the limits of the labour-time needed to reproduce the amount paid in wages, since it is just this *excess labour* that supplies him with the *surplus-value*.[21]

469i

20. 'If in the progress of time a change takes place in their (i.e. the workmen's) economic position, if they become the workmen of a capitalist who advances their wages beforehand, two things take place. First, they can now labour continuously; and, secondly, an agent is provided, whose office and whose interest it will be, to see that they *do* labour continuously ... Here, then, is an increased continuity in the labour of all this class of persons. They labour daily from morning to night, and are not interrupted by waiting for or seeking the customer ... But the continuity of labour, thus made possible, is secured and improved by the superintendence of the capitalist. He has advanced their wages; he is to receive the produce of their labour. It is his interest and his privilege to see that they do not labour interruptedly or dilatorily' (R. Jones, *Textbook, etc.*, pp. 37 ff. passim).

21. '*Un axiome généralement admis par les économistes est que tout travail doit laisser un excédant. Cette proposition est pour moi d'une vérité universelle et absolue: c'est le corollaire de la loi de la proportionalité (!), que l'on peut regarder comme le sommaire de toute la science économique. Mais, j'en demande pardon aux économistes, le principe que* tout travail doit laisser un excédant *n'a pas de sens dans leur théorie, et n'est pas susceptible d'aucune* démonstration' ['An axiom generally admitted by economists is that all labour must leave a surplus. In my opinion this proposition is universally and absolutely true: it is the corollary of the law of proportion, which may be regarded as the summary of the whole of economic science. But, if the economists will permit me to say so, the principle that *all labour must leave a surplus* is meaningless according to their theory, and is not susceptible of any demonstration.'] (Proudhon, *Philosophie de la misère*). In my work *Misère de la philosophie. Réponse à la Philosophie de la misère de M. Proudhon,* Paris, 1847, pp. 76–91 [English edition, pp. 78–89], I have shown that M. Proudhon has not the slightest idea what this '*excédant du travail*' is, namely

Just as the commodity owner is interested only in the use-value of a commodity as the depository of its exchange-value, so too the capitalist is interested only in the labour process as the depository and instrument of the valorization process. And within the production process too – in so far as it is a valorization process – the means of production continue to be nothing but monetary value, indifferent towards the particular physical form, the specific use-value in which the exchange-value is clothed. Similarly, labour does not count as productive activity with a specific utility, but simply as value-creating substance, as social labour in general which is in the act of objectifying itself and whose sole feature of interest is its *quantity*. Hence in the eyes of capital each sphere of production is simply a sphere in which capital is invested in order to produce more money, in order to maintain and increase already existing money or to acquire *surplus labour*. In every sphere of production the labour process is different, and so too are the factors in that process. Boots cannot be produced with the aid of spindles, cotton and spinners. But the investment of capital in this or that branch of production, the quantities in which the total capital of society is distributed among the various spheres of production, and lastly the conditions in which it emigrates from one type of production to another – all this is determined by the changing conditions according to the needs of society for the products of this or that industry. That is to say, it is determined by society's need of the use-values of the commodities they create. For although it is only the exchange-value of the product that is paid for, products are only ever bought for their use-value. (Since the immediate product of the process of production is the *commodity*, it is only by finding purchasers for his wares that the capitalist can realize the capital which at the end of the process is located in the *commodity*, i.e. realize the *surplus-value* it contains.)

469j

But capital is in itself indifferent to the *particular* nature of every sphere of production. Where it is invested, how it is invested and

the *surplus product* in which the surplus labour or unpaid labour of the worker becomes manifest. Since he finds that all labour in fact produces such an '*excédant*' in capitalist production he attempts to explain this fact by reference to some mysterious natural attribute of labour, and to shout his way out of the difficulty with such '*sesquipedalia verba*'* as 'corollaire de la loi de la proportionalité', etc.

*'Many-syllabled words'.

to what extent it is transferred from one sphere of production to another or redistributed among the various spheres of production – all this is determined only by the greater ease or difficulty of selling the commodities manufactured. In reality the mobility of capital is impeded by obstacles which we cannot consider in the present context. But on the one hand, as we shall see, it creates means by which to overcome obstacles that spring from the nature of production itself, and on the other hand, with the development of the mode of production peculiar to itself, it eliminates all the legal and extra-economic impediments to its freedom of movement in the different spheres of production. Above all it overturns all the legal or traditional barriers that would prevent it from buying this or that kind of labour-power as it sees fit, or from appropriating this or that kind of labour. Furthermore, although labour-power assumes a distinctive form in every particular sphere of production, as a capacity for spinning, cobbling, metal-working, etc., so that every sphere of production requires a capacity for labour that is developed in a specific direction, a *distinctive* capacity for labour, it remains true that the flexibility of capital, its indifference to the particular forms of the labour process it acquires, is extended by capital to the worker. He is required to be capable of the same flexibility or *versatility* in the way he applies his labour-power. As we shall see, the capitalist mode of production itself raises obstacles in the way of its own tendency, but it pushes to one side all *legal* and other *extra-economic* obstructions standing in the way of this versatility.[22] Just as capital, as value valorizing itself, views with indifference the particular physical guise in which labour appears in the labour process, whether as a steam-engine, dung heap or silk, so too the worker looks upon the *particular content* of his labour with equal indifference. His work belongs to capital, it is only the use-value of the commodity that he has sold, and he has only sold it to acquire money and, with the money, the means of subsistence. A change in his mode of labour interests him only because every specific mode of labour requires a different development of his labour-power. If his indifference to the particular content of his work does not give him the power to vary his labour-power to order, he will express his indifference by inducing his replacements,

22. 'Every man, if not restrained by law, would pass from one employment to another, as the various turns in trade should require' (*Considerations Concerning Taking Off the Bounty on Corn Exported, etc.*, London, 1753, p. 4).

the rising generation, to move from one branch of industry to the next, depending on the state of the market. The more highly capitalist production is developed in a country, the greater the demand will be for *versatility* in labour-power, the more indifferent the worker will be towards the *specific content* of his work and the more fluid will be the movements of capital from one sphere of production to the next. Classical economics regards the versatility of labour-power and the *fluidity* of capital as axiomatic, and it is right to do so, since this is the tendency of capitalist production which ruthlessly enforces its will despite obstacles which are in any case largely of its own making. At all events, in order to portray the laws of political economy in their purity we are ignoring these sources of friction, as is the practice in mechanics where the frictions that arise have to be dealt with in every particular application of its general laws.[23]

4691   Although capitalist and worker confront each other in the market-place only as *buyer*, money, on the one hand, and *seller*, commodity, on the other, this relationship is coloured in advance by the peculiar content of their dealings. This is particularly true since both sides appear *constantly*, repeatedly in the market-place playing the *same* opposed roles. If we consider the relations of commodity-owners in general in the market-place we see that the same man appears alternately as the buyer and seller of wares.

23. Nowhere does the fluidity of capital, the versatility of labour and the indifference of the worker to the content of his work appear more vividly than in the United States of North America. In Europe, even in England, capitalist production is still affected and distorted by hangovers from feudalism. The fact that baking, shoemaking, etc. are only just being put on a *capitalist* basis in England is entirely due to the circumstance that English capital cherished feudal preconceptions of 'respectability'. It was 'respectable' to sell Negroes into slavery, but it was not respectable to make sausages, boots or bread. Hence all the machinery which conquers the 'unrespectable' branches of industry for capitalism in Europe comes from America. By the same token, nowhere are people so indifferent to the type of work they do as in the United States, nowhere are people so aware that their labour always produces the same product, money, and nowhere do they pass through the most divergent kinds of work with the same nonchalance. This 'versatility' appears to be a quite distinctive mark of the free worker, in contrast to the working slave, whose labour-power is stable and capable of being employed in a manner determined by local custom. 'Slave labour is eminently defective in point of versatility . . . if tobacco be cultivated, tobacco becomes the sole staple, and tobacco is produced whatever be the state of the market, and whatever be the condition of the soil' (Cairnes, op. cit., pp. 46–7).

The fact that two men differ from each other as buyer and seller is of ever diminishing significance since in the course of time everyone assumes all the roles in the sphere of circulation. Now it is also true that once the worker has sold his labour-power and transformed it into money, he too becomes a buyer, and the capitalists appear to him as the mere sellers of goods. But in his hand money is nothing but a means of circulation. In the actual *commodity-market*, then, it is quite true that the worker, like any other owner of money, is a buyer and is distinguished by that fact alone from the commodity owner as seller. But on the *labour-market*, *money* always confronts him as *capital* in the form of money, and so the owner of money appears as capital personified, as a *capitalist*, and he for his part appears to the owner of money merely as the personification of labour-power and hence of labour, i.e. as a *worker*.[24] The two people who face each other on the market-place, in the sphere of circulation, are not just a *buyer* and a *seller*, but *capitalist* and *worker* who confront each other as *buyer* and *seller*. Their relationship as *capitalist* and *worker* is the precondition of their relationship as *buyer* and *seller*. Unlike the situation in the case of other sellers, the relationship does not arise directly from the nature of commodities. This derives from the fact that no one directly produces the products he needs in order to live, so that each man only produces a single product as a *commodity* which he then sells in order to be able to acquire the products of others. Here, however, we are not concerned with the merely *social division of labour* in which each branch of labour is autonomous, so that, for example, a cobbler becomes a seller of boots but a buyer of leather or bread. What we are concerned with here is the *division* of the *constituents of the process of production* itself, constituents that really belong together. This division leads to the progressive *separation* of these elements and their personification *vis-à-vis* each other, so that *money* as the general form of *objectified labour* becomes the *purchaser* of labour-power, the living source of *exchange-value* and hence of wealth. *Real* wealth (from the standpoint of exchange-value), *money* (from the standpoint of use-value), i.e. the *means of subsistence and the means of production*, make their appearance as persons in opposition to the *possibility* of wealth, i.e. labour-power, which appears as a different person.

24. 'The relation of the manufacturer to his operatives ... is purely economic. The manufacturer is Capital, the operative "Labour"' (F. Engels, *Lage der arbeitenden Klassen, etc.*, p. 329) [English edition, op. cit., p. 302].

469m   Since *surplus-value* is the product specific to the production
process, what is produced is not just a commodity, but also *capital*.
Within the production process labour is transformed into capital.
The activity of labour-power, i.e. labour, *objectifies* itself in the
course of production and so becomes value. But since the labour
has ceased to belong to the worker even before he starts to work,
what objectified itself for him is *alien labour* and hence a value,
capital, independent of his own labour-power. The *product* belongs
to the capitalist and in the eyes of the worker it is as much a part of
capital as the *elements of production*. On the other hand, an existing amount of value – money – becomes *real* capital only when, in
the first place, it begins to realize itself, to become part of a *process*,
and this it achieves when the activity of labour-power, namely
labour, is incorporated in the production process and becomes its
property. And secondly, it must yield *surplus-value* as distinct
from its original value, and this in turn is again the product of the
objectification of surplus labour.

In the process of production labour becomes *objectified labour*,
i.e. capital in opposition to living labour-power, and, in the second
place, by absorbing labour into production, by thus appropriating
it, the original value becomes value in *process* and hence value that
creates surplus-value different from itself. It is only because labour
is changed into capital in the course of production that we can say
that the original quantum of value valorizes itself, that what was at
first *potentially* capital has become *capital in actual fact*.[25]*

*

263   [. . .] i.e. to obtain a higher value from the process of production
than the sum of the values invested in it and for it (i.e. the production process) by the capitalist. The production of commodities is

25. 'They' (the workers) 'exchange their labour' (i.e. their labour-power)
'for corn' (i.e. means of subsistence). 'This constitutes their revenue' (i.e.
their individual consumption) '. . . whereas their *labour* has become *capital*
for their master' (Sismondi, *Nouveaux Principes*, Vol. 1, p. 90). 'The workers
who give up their labour in the process of exchange transform it [the product
of the whole year] into *capital*' (ibid., p. 105).

*At this point the first interpolated passage, consisting of MS. pp. 469a–
469m, breaks off. Following Marx's own directions (see our note on p. 995)
it is to be succeeded by a second interpolation which Marx numbered pp.
262–4. Page 262 is missing.

simply a means to this end, as indeed the labour process itself is no more than the instrument of the valorization process – in the sense of the process of creating surplus-value, and not, as previously, in the sense of simply creating value.

This result is brought about only as long as the living labour, which the worker has at his disposal and which therefore is objectified in the product of his labour, is greater than the labour contained in the variable capital or laid out in wages, or, in other words, required in the reproduction of his labour-power. Since the production of surplus-value is the means by which the money invested becomes capital, the origins of capital, like the process of capitalist production itself, are based on two factors in the first instance:

First, the *purchase and sale of labour-power*, an act which falls within the sphere of circulation but which, viewed in the context of *capitalist production as a whole*, is not merely an aspect of it and its precondition, but also its continuous result. This purchase and sale of labour power implies that the objective conditions of labour – i.e. the *means of subsistence* and the *means of production* – are separated from the living labour-power itself, so that the latter becomes the sole property at the disposal of the worker and the sole commodity which he has to sell. This separation is so radical that these conditions of labour appear as *independent persons* confronting the worker, for as their owner the capitalist is merely their personification, in opposition to the worker who is the owner of nothing but his labour-power. This separation and independence is the premiss on the basis of which the sale and purchase of labour-power can proceed and living labour can be absorbed into dead labour as a means of maintaining and increasing it, i.e. of enabling it to valorize itself. Without the *exchange* of variable capital for labour-power the total capital could not valorize itself and so the formation of capital and the transformation of the means of production and means of subsistence into capital could not take place. The second factor then is the actual process of production, i.e. the actual consumption of the labour-power purchased by the owner of money or commodities.*

* The following quotation, the first part of which is missing, occurs in the MS. immediately after the above text, to which it has no relation. It is in fact the continuation of a footnote referring to the missing text on p. 262: '... to

264   In the actual process of production the objective conditions of labour – its materials and instruments – serve to ensure not just that living labour objectifies itself, but that *more* labour objectifies itself than was contained in variable capital. They therefore act as the means by which the surplus labour which appears in the form of surplus-value (and surplus produce) is extorted and absorbed. If, therefore, we take the two factors together: first, the exchange of labour-power for variable capital, and second, the process of production proper (in which living labour is incorporated as an *agens** into capital), the entire process has the following characteristics. (1) Less objectified labour is exchanged for more living labour, since what the capitalist receives *realiter* for wages is living labour. And (2) the objective forms in which capital manifests itself directly in the labour process, the means of production (once again: objectified labour), are the instruments by means of which living labour is extorted and absorbed. Thus the entire process is a traffic between objectified and living labour in which living labour is transformed into objectified labour and in which at the same time objectified labour is transformed into capital. So that in the upshot living labour is transformed into capital. Hence the process is one which produces surplus-value and hence *capital*, as well as actual produce. (Cf. pp. 96–108.)†

---

three capital workmen or to four ordinary ones ... If the three could be hired at £3 10s. apiece, while the four required £3 apiece, though the wages of the three would be higher, the price of the work done by them would be lower. It is true that the causes which raise the amount of the labourers' wages often raise the rate of the capitalist's profit. If, by increased industry, one man performs the work of two, both the amount of wages, and the rate of profits will generally be raised; not by the rise of wages, but *in consequence of the additional supply of labour having diminished its price*, or having diminished the period for which it had previously been necessary to advance that price. The labourer, on the other hand, is principally interested in the *amount of wages*. The amount of his wages being given, it is certainly his interest that the *price of labour should be high*, for on that depends the degree of exertion imposed on him' (op. cit., pp. 14, 5).

And from the same work: 'The labourer's situation does not depend on the amount which he receives at any one time, but on his average receipts during a given period ... The longer the period taken, the more accurate will be the estimate' (ibid., p. 7). 'The year is the best period to take. It includes both summer and winter wages' (ibid., p. 7).

---

*'Effective force'.

† These figures refer to MS. pp. 469a–469m, i.e. pp. 995–1016 of the present text.

Hence we may say that the means of production appear not just as the means for accomplishing work, but as the means for *exploiting the labour of others*.*

*

469 One further point remains to be made about value or money as the objectification of an average measure of general social labour. If we take spinning, for example, we see that it may be performed at a rate that either falls *below* or rises *above* the social average. That is to say, a certain quantity of spinning may be equal to, greater or less than the same quantity of the average, e.g. it may be the same magnitude (length) as the labour-time objectified in a certain amount of gold. But if the spinning is carried out with a degree of intensity normal in its particular *sphere*, e.g. if the labour expended on producing a certain amount of yarn in an hour = the normal quantity of yarn that an hour's spinning will produce on average in the given social conditions, then the labour objectified in the yarn is *socially necessary labour*. As such it has a quantitatively determinate relation to the social average in general which acts as the standard, so that we can speak of the same amount or a greater or smaller one. It itself therefore expresses a *definite quantum* of average social labour.

THE FORMAL SUBSUMPTION OF LABOUR UNDER CAPITAL

The labour process becomes the instrument of the valorization process, the process of the self-valorization of capital – the manufacture of surplus-value. The labour process is subsumed under capital (it is its *own* process) and the capitalist intervenes in the process as its director, manager. For him it also represents the direct exploitation of the labour of others. It is this that I refer to as the *formal subsumption of labour under capital*. It is the general form of every capitalist process of production; at the same time, however, it can be found as a *particular* form alongside the *specifically capitalist mode of production* in its developed form, because although the latter entails the former, the converse does not necessarily obtain [i.e. the formal subsumption can be found in the absence of the specifically capitalist mode of production].

*At this point the second interpolated passage comes to an end. What follows is the continuation of p. 469 of the MS.

470   The process of production has become the process of capital itself. It is a process involving the *factors of the labour process* into which the capitalist's money has been converted and which proceeds under his direction with the sole purpose of using money to make more money.

When a peasant who has always produced enough for his needs becomes a day labourer working for a farmer; when the hierarchic order of guild production vanishes making way for the straightforward distinction between the capitalist and the wage-labourers he employs; when the former slave-owner engages his former slaves as paid workers, etc., then we find that what is happening is that production processes of varying social provenance have been transformed into capitalist production. The changes delineated above then come into force. A man who was formerly an independent peasant now finds himself a factor in a production process and dependent on the capitalist directing it, and his own livelihood depends on a contract which he as commodity owner (viz. the owner of labour-power) has previously concluded with the capitalist as the owner of money. The slave ceases to be an instrument of production at the disposal of his owner. The relationship between master and journeyman vanishes. That relationship was determined by the fact that the former was the master of his craft. He now confronts his journeyman only as the owner of capital, while the journeyman is reduced to being a vendor of labour. Before the process of production they all confront each other as commodity owners and their relations involve nothing but *money*; *within* the process of production they meet as its components personified: the capitalist as 'capital', the immediate producer as 'labour', and their relations are determined by labour as a mere constituent of capital which is valorizing itself.

Furthermore, the capitalist takes good care that the labour adheres to the normal standards of quality and intensity, and he extends its duration as far as possible in order to increase the surplus-value that it yields. The *continuity* of labour increases when producers dependent on individual customers are supplanted by producers who, bereft of wares to sell, have a constant paymaster in the shape of the capitalist.

The mystification inherent in the *capital-relation* emerges at this point. The value-sustaining power of labour appears as the self-supporting power of capital; the value-creating power of labour as the self-valorizing power of capital and, in general, in accordance with its concept, *living* labour appears to be put to work by *objectified* labour.

All this notwithstanding, this change does not in itself imply a fundamental modification in the real nature of the labour process, the actual process of production. On the contrary, the fact is that capital subsumes the labour process as it finds it, that is to say, it takes over an *existing labour process*, developed by different and more archaic modes of production. And since that is the case it is evident that capital took over an *available, established labour process*. For example, handicraft, a mode of agriculture corresponding to a small, independent peasant economy. If changes occur in these traditional established *labour processes* after their takeover by capital, these are nothing but the gradual consequences of that subsumption. The work may become more intensive, its duration may be extended, it may become more continuous or orderly under the eye of the interested capitalist, but in themselves these changes do not affect the character of the actual labour process, the actual mode of working. This stands in striking contrast to the development of a *specifically capitalist mode of production* (large-scale industry, etc.); the latter not only transforms the situations of the various agents of production, it also *revolutionizes* their actual mode of labour and the real nature of the labour process as a whole. It is in contradistinction to this last that we come to designate as the *formal subsumption of labour under capital* what we have discussed earlier, viz. the takeover by capital of a mode of labour developed before the emergence of capitalist relations. The latter as a form of *compulsion* by which surplus labour is exacted by extending the duration of labour-time – a *mode of compulsion* not based on personal relations of domination and dependency, but simply on differing economic functions – this is common to both forms. However, the specifically capitalist mode of production has yet other methods of exacting surplus-value at its disposal. But given a pre-existing mode of labour, i.e. an *established* development of the productive power of labour and a mode of labour corresponding to this productive power, surplus-value can be created only by lengthening the working day, i.e. by increasing *absolute surplus-value*. In the *formal* subsumption of labour under capital, this is the *sole* manner of producing surplus-value.

The general features of the labour process as described in

Chapter II,* for example, the sundering of the objective conditions of labour into materials and instruments on the one hand, and the living activity of the workers on the other, are all independent of every historical and specifically social conditioning and they remain valid for all possible forms and stages in the development of the processes of production. They are in fact immutable natural conditions of human labour. This is strikingly confirmed by the fact that they hold good for people who work independently, i.e. for those, like Robinson Crusoe, who work not in exchange with society, but only with nature. Thus they are in fact absolute determinations of *human* labour as such, as soon as it has evolved beyond the purely animal.

The way in which even the merely formal subsumption of labour under capital begins to become differentiated within itself – and does so increasingly as time goes on, even on the basis of the old, traditional mode of labour – is in terms of the *scale* of production. That is to say, differences appear later in the volume of the means of production invested, and in the number of workers under the command of a single employer. For example, what appeared to be the maximum attainable in the mode of production of the guilds (let us say, in reference to the number of journeymen employed) can scarcely serve as a minimum for the relations of capital. For the latter can achieve no more than a nominal existence unless the capitalist can employ at the very least enough workers to ensure that the surplus-value he produces will suffice for his own private consumption and to fill his accumulation fund. Only then will he be relieved of the need to work directly himself and be able to content himself with acting as *capitalist*, i.e. as supervisor and director of the process, as a mere function, as it were, endowed with consciousness and will, of the capital engaged in the process of valorizing itself. This enlargement of *scale* constitutes the real foundation on which the specifically capitalist mode of production can arise if the historical circumstances are otherwise favourable, as they were for instance in the sixteenth century. Of course, it may also occur *sporadically*, as something which does not dominate society, at isolated points within earlier social formations.

The distinctive character of the *formal* subsumption of labour under capital appears at its sharpest if we compare it to situations

*In Chapter 7 of the present edition.

in which capital is to be found in certain specific, subordinate functions, but where it has not emerged as the direct purchaser of labour and as the immediate owner of the process of production, and where in consequence it has not yet succeeded in becoming the dominant force, capable of determining the form of society as a whole. In India, for example, the capital of the *usurer* advances raw materials or tools or even both to the immediate producer in the form of money. The exorbitant interest which it attracts, the interest which, irrespective of its magnitude, it extorts from the primary producer, is just another name for surplus-value. It transforms its money into capital by extorting unpaid labour, surplus labour, from the immediate producer. But it does not intervene in the process of production itself, which proceeds in its traditional fashion, as it always had done. In part it thrives on the *withering* away of this mode of production, in part it is a means to make it *wither* away, to force it to *eke out* a vegetable existence in the most unfavourable conditions. But here we have *not yet* reached the stage of the formal subsumption of labour under capital. A further example is *merchant's capital*, which commissions a number of immediate producers, then collects their produce and sells it, perhaps making them advances in the form of raw materials, etc., or even money. It is this form that provides the soil from which modern capitalism has grown and here and there it still forms the transition to capitalism proper. Here too we find no formal subsumption of labour under capital. The immediate producer still performs the functions of selling his wares and making use of his own labour. But the transition is more strongly marked here than in the case of the usurer. We shall return later to these forms, both of which survive and reproduce themselves as transitional subforms within the framework of capitalist production.

72 THE REAL SUBSUMPTION OF LABOUR UNDER CAPITAL OR THE SPECIFIC MODE OF CAPITALIST PRODUCTION

We have demonstrated in detail in Chapter III* the crucial importance of *relative surplus-value*. This arises when the individual capitalist is spurred on to seize the *initiative* by the fact that value = the socially necessary labour-time objectified in the product and that therefore *surplus-value* is created for him as soon as the *in-*

* Presumably Part Four of the present edition.

dividual value of his product falls *below* its social value and can be sold accordingly at a price *above* its individual value. With the production of relative surplus-value the entire real form of production is altered and a *specifically capitalist form of production* comes into being (at the technological level too). Based on this, and simultaneously with it, the corresponding *relations of production* between the various agents of production and above all between the capitalist and the wage-labourer, come into being for the first time.

The *social* productive forces of labour, or the productive forces of directly social, *socialized* (i.e. collective) labour come into being through co-operation, division of labour within the workshop, the use of *machinery*, and in general the transformation of production by the conscious *use* of the sciences, of mechanics, chemistry, etc. for specific ends, technology, etc. and similarly, through the enormous increase of *scale* corresponding to such developments (for it is only socialized labour that is capable of applying the *general* products of human development, such as mathematics, to the immediate processes of production; and, conversely, progress in these sciences presupposes a certain level of material production). This entire development of the productive forces of *socialized labour* (in contrast to the more or less isolated labour of individuals), and together with it the *use of science* (the *general* product of social development), in the *immediate process of production*, takes the form of the *productive power of capital*. It does not appear as the productive power of labour, or even of that part of it that is identical with capital. And least of all does it appear as the productive power either of the individual worker or of the workers joined together in the process of production. The mystification implicit in the relations of capital as a whole is greatly intensified here, far beyond the point it had reached or could have reached in the merely formal subsumption of labour under capital. On the other hand, we here find a striking illustration of the historic significance of capitalist production in its specific form – the transmutation of the immediate process of production itself and the development of the social forces of production of labour.

It has been shown (Chapter III)* how not merely at the level of ideas, but also in reality, the social character of his labour con-

---

* Presumably Part Three, in this case.

fronts the worker as something not merely alien, but hostile and antagonistic, when it appears before him objectified and personified in capital.

If the production of absolute surplus-value was the material expression of the formal subsumption of labour under capital, then the production of relative surplus-value may be viewed as its real subsumption.

At any rate, if we consider the two forms of surplus-value, absolute and relative, separately, we shall see that absolute surplus-value always precedes relative. To these two forms of surplus-value there correspond two separate forms of the subsumption of labour under capital, or two distinct forms of capitalist production. And here too one form always precedes the other, although the second form, the more highly developed one, can provide the foundations for the introduction of the first in new branches of industry.

473 ADDITIONAL REMARKS ON THE FORMAL SUBSUMPTION OF LABOUR UNDER CAPITAL

Before proceeding to a further examination of the real subsumption of labour under capital, here are a few additional reflections from my notebooks.

The form based on absolute surplus-value is what I call the *formal subsumption of labour under capital*. I do so because it is only *formally* distinct from earlier modes of production on whose foundations it arises spontaneously (or is introduced), either when the producer is self-employing or when the immediate producers are forced to deliver surplus labour to others. All that changes is that compulsion is applied, i.e. the method by which surplus labour is extorted. The essential features of *formal subsumption* are:

1. The pure money relationship between the man who appropriates the surplus labour and the man who yields it up: subordination in this case arises from the *specific content* of the sale – there is not a subordination underlying it in which the producer stands in a relation to the exploiter of his labour which is determined not just by money (the relationship of one commodity owner to another), but, let us say, by political constraints. What

brings the seller into a relationship of dependency is *solely* the fact that the buyer is the owner of the conditions of labour. There is no fixed political and social relationship of supremacy and subordination.

2. This is implicit in the first relationship – for were it not for this the worker would not have his labour-power to sell: it is that his *objective conditions of labour* (the means of production) and the *subjective conditions of labour* (the means of subsistence) confront him as *capital*, as the monopoly of the buyer of his labour-power. The more completely these *conditions of labour* are mobilized against him as alien property, the more effectively the *formal* relationship between capital and wage-labour is established, i.e. the more effectively the formal subsumption of labour under capital is accomplished, and this in turn is the premiss and precondition of its *real* subsumption.

There is no change as yet in the mode of production itself. *Technologically speaking*, the *labour process* goes on as before, with the proviso that it is now *subordinated* to capital. Within the production process, however, as we have already shown, two developments emerge: (1) an *economic* relationship of supremacy and subordination, since the consumption of labour-power by the capitalist is naturally supervised and directed by him; (2) labour becomes far more continuous and intensive, and the conditions of labour are employed far more economically, since every effort is made to ensure that no more (or rather even less) *socially necessary* time is consumed in making the product – and this applies both to the living labour that is used to manufacture it and to the *objectified* labour which enters into it as an element in the means of production.

With the *formal* subsumption of labour under capital the *compulsion* to *perform surplus labour*, and to create the *leisure time* necessary for development independently of material production, differs only in form from what had obtained under the earlier mode of production. (Even though, be it noted, this compulsion implies also the necessity of forming needs, and creating the means of satisfying them, and of supplying quantities of produce well in excess of the traditional requirements of the worker.) But this formal change is one which increases the continuity and intensity of labour; it is more favourable to the development of *versatility among the workers*, and hence to increasing diversity in modes of working and ways of earning a living. Lastly, it dissolves the relationship between the owners of the conditions of labour and the workers into a *relationship of sale and purchase, a purely financial relationship*. In consequence the process of exploitation is stripped of every patriarchal, political or even religious cloak. It remains true, of course, that the *relations of production* themselves create a new relation of *supremacy and subordination* (and this also has a *political* expression). But the more capitalist production sticks fast in this formal relationship, the less the relationship itself will evolve, since for the most part it is based on small capitalists who differ only slightly from the workers in their education and their activities.

474   The variations which can occur in the relation of *supremacy and subordination* without affecting the mode of production can be seen best where *rural* and *domestic* secondary industries, undertaken primarily to satisfy the needs of individual families, are transformed into autonomous branches of capitalist industry.

The distinction between labour *formally* subsumed under capital and previous modes of labour becomes more apparent, the greater the increase in the *volume of capital* employed by the individual capitalist, i.e. the greater the increase in the *number of workers employed by him at any one time*. Only with a certain minimum capital does the capitalist cease to be a worker himself and [begin] to concern himself entirely with directing work and organizing sales. And the *real* subsumption of labour under capital, i.e. *capitalist production proper*, begins only when capital sums of a certain magnitude have directly taken over control of production, either because the merchant turns into an industrial capitalist, or because larger industrial capitalists have established themselves on the basis of the *formal subsumption*.[26]

If supremacy and subordination come to take the place of slav-

26. [The text of this footnote is to be found on an extra unnumbered sheet added subsequently. Since the passage to which the footnote refers was followed on the MS. p. 474 by another short paragraph, Marx preceded the footnote with the remark: '(a) This (a) refers not to the last passage, but to the preceding one.' This comment is followed by the footnote itself:]

474a   (a) 'A free labourer has generally the liberty of changing his master: this liberty distinguishes a slave from a free labourer, as much as an English man-of-war sailor is distinguished from a merchant sailor ... The condition of a labourer is superior to that of a slave, because a labourer *thinks* himself *free*; and this conviction, however erroneous, has no small influence on the character of a population' (T. R. Edmonds, *Practical, Moral and Political*

ery, serfdom, vassallage and other patriarchal forms of subjection, the change is *purely one of form*. The form becomes *freer*,
because it is objective in nature, voluntary in appearance, *purely
economic*. (Verte.)*

475   Alternatively, supremacy and subordination in the *process of
production* supplant an earlier state of *independence*, to be found,
for example, in all self-sustaining peasants, farmers who only have

---

Economy, London, 1828, pp. 56–7). 'The motive that drives a free man to
work is much more violent than what drives the slave: a free man has to choose
between hard labour and *starvation* (check the passage), a slave between . . .
and a good whipping' (ibid., p. 56). 'The difference between the conditions
of a slave and a labourer under the money system is very inconsiderable; . . .
the master of the slave understands too well his own interest to weaken his
slaves by stinting them in their food; but the master of a free man gives him as
little food as possible, because the *injury done to the labourer does not fall on
himself alone, but on the whole class of masters*' (ibid.).
    'In antiquity, *to make mankind laborious beyond their wants*, to make one
part of a state work, to *maintain the other part gratuitously*', was only to be
achieved through slaves: hence slavery was introduced generally. 'Slavery
was then as necessary towards multiplication, as it would now be destructive
of it. The reason is plain. *If mankind be not forced to labour, they will only
labour for themselves*; and if they have few wants, there will be few who labour.
But when states come to be formed and have occasion for idle hands to defend
them against the violence of their enemies, food at any rate must be procured
for those *who do not labour*; and as by the supposition, the wants of the
labourers are small, a method must be found to *increase their labour above the
proportion of their wants*. For this purpose *slavery* was calculated . . . The
slaves were forced to labour the soil which fed both them and the idle free-
men, as was the case in Sparta; or they filled all the servile places which free-
men fill now, and they were likewise employed, as in Greece and in Rome, in
supplying with manufactures those whose service was necessary for the state.
Here then was a *violent method of making mankind laborious* in raising food . . .
Men were then forced to labour, because *they were slaves to others*; men are
now forced to labour because they are *slaves of their own wants*' (J. Steuart,
Dublin edition, Vol. 1, pp. 38–40).
    In the sixteenth century, the same Steuart says, 'while on the one hand the
lords dismissed their retainers, the farmers' (who were transforming themselves
into industrial capitalists) 'dismissed the idle mouths. From a *means of subsistence* agriculture was transformed into a *trade*.' The consequence was,
'The withdrawing . . . of a number of hands from a trifling agriculture *forces*
in a manner, the *husbandmen to work harder*; and *by hard labour upon a small
spot, the same effect* is produced as *with slight labour upon a great extent*'
(ibid., p. 105).

---

* This refers to the remark quoted in footnote 26.

to pay a rent on what they produce, either to the state or a land-lord; rural or domestic secondary industry or *independent handicraft*. Here then we encounter the loss of an earlier *independence* in the process of production, and the relation of supremacy and subordination is itself the result of the rise of capitalist production.

Lastly, the relation of capitalist and wage-labourer can replace that of the guild master and his journeyman and apprentices, a situation found to some extent in urban manufacture. The *medieval guild system*, of which analogous forms were developed to a limited extent in both Athens and Rome, and which was of such crucial importance in Europe for the evolution of both capitalists and free labourers, is a *limited* and as yet inadequate form of the relationship between capital and wage-labour. It involves relations between buyers and sellers. Wages are paid and masters, journeymen and apprentices encounter each other as free persons. The technological basis of their relationship is *handicraft*, where the more or less sophisticated use of *tools* is the decisive factor in production; independent personal labour, and hence its professional development, which requires a longer or shorter spell as an apprentice–these are what determine the results of labour. The master does indeed own the conditions of production – tools, materials, etc. (although the tools may be owned by the journeyman too) – and he owns the product. To that extent he is a *capitalist*. But it is not as capitalist that he is *master*. He is an *artisan* in the first instance and is supposed to be a master of his craft. Within the process of production he appears as an artisan, like his journeymen, and it is he who initiates his apprentices into the mysteries of the craft. He has precisely the same relationship to his apprentices as a professor to his students. Hence his approach to his apprentices and journeymen is not that of a capitalist, but of a *master* of his craft, and by virtue of that fact he assumes a position of superiority in the corporation and hence towards them. It follows that his capital is restricted in terms of the *form it assumes*, as well as in *value*. It is far from achieving the freedom of capital proper. It is not a *definite quantum of objectified labour*, value in general, at liberty to assume this or that form of the conditions of labour depending on the form of living labour it acquires in order to produce surplus labour. Before he can invest money in *this particular* branch of trade, in his own craft, before he can set about purchasing either the objective conditions of labour, or acquiring the necessary journeymen and apprentices, he has to pass through the prescribed stages of apprentice and journeyman and even produce his own masterpiece. He can transform money into capital only in his own craft, i.e. not merely as the means of his own labour, but as the means of exploiting the labour of others. His capital is bound to a definite kind of *use-value* and hence does not confront his own workers directly as *capital*. The methods of work that he employs are laid down not just by tradition, but by the guild – they are thought of as indispensable, and so, from this point of view too, it is the use-value of labour, rather than its exchange-value, that appears to be the ultimate purpose. It does not remain at the discretion of the master to produce work of this or that standard; all the arrangements of the guild are designed to ensure that work of a *definite quality* is produced. He has as little control over the price as over the methods of work. The *restrictions* that prevent his wealth from functioning as capital also ensure that this capital does not exceed a certain *maximum*. He may not employ more than a *certain number* of journeymen, since the guild guarantees that all the masters earn a certain amount from their trade. Lastly, there is the relationship of the master to the other masters in the guild. As a master he belonged to a corporation which [enforced] certain collective conditions of production (guild restrictions, etc.) and possessed political rights, a share in municipal administration, etc. He worked to order – with the exception of what he produced for merchants – and produced goods for immediate use. The number of masters too was restricted as a result. He did not confront his workers *merely as a merchant*. Even less could the merchant convert his money into productive capital; he could only 'commission' the goods, not produce them himself. Not exchange-value as such, not enrichment as such, but a life appropriate to a certain *status or condition* – this was the purpose and result of the exploitation of the labour of others. The *instrument* of labour was the crucial factor here. In many trades (e.g. tailoring) the master was supplied with raw materials by his clients. The limits on production were kept by regulation within the limits of actual consumption. That is to say, production was not restricted by the confines of capital itself. In capitalist production these barriers are swept away along with the socio-political limits in which capital was confined. In short, what we see here is not yet *capital* proper.

476   The purely formal conversion of production based on handicraft into capitalist production, i.e. a change in which for the time
being the technological process remains the same, is achieved by
the *disappearance of all these barriers*. And this in turn brings about
changes in the relations of supremacy and subordination. The
master now ceases to be a capitalist because he is a master, and becomes a master because he is a capitalist. The limits on his production are no longer determined by the limits imposed on his capital.
His capital (money) can be freely exchanged for labour, and hence
the conditions of labour of any kind whatever. He can cease to be
an artisan. With the sudden expansion of trade and consequently
of the demand for goods on the part of the merchant class, the
production of the guilds is driven beyond its limits by its own
momentum and hence is converted formally into capitalist production.
    Compared to the independent artisan who makes goods for
other customers, we observe a great increase in the continuity of
labour of the man who works for a capitalist whose production is
not limited by the haphazard requirements of isolated customers
but only by the limits of the capital that employs him. In contrast
to the slave, this labour becomes more productive because more
intensive, since the slave works only under the spur of external fear
but not for *his existence* which is *guaranteed* even though it does
not belong to him. The free worker, however, is impelled by his
wants. The consciousness (or better: the *idea*) of free self-deter-
mination, of liberty, makes a much better worker of the one than
of the other, as does the related feeling (sense) of *responsibility*;
since he, like any seller of wares, is responsible for the goods he
delivers and for the quality which he must provide, he must strive
to ensure that he is not driven from the field by other sellers of the
same type as himself. The *continuity in the relations* of slave and
slave-owner is based on the fact that the slave is kept in his situation by *direct compulsion*. The free worker, however, must maintain his own position, since his existence and that of his family
depends on his ability continuously to renew the sale of his labour-
power to the capitalist.

    In the eyes of the slave a *minimal wage* appears to be a constant
quantity, independent of his work. For the free worker, however,
the *value of his labour-power* and the average wage *corresponding to
it* does not appear to him as something predestined, as something

independent of his own labour and determined by the mere needs of his physical existence. The *average* for the class as a whole remains more or less *constant*, like the value of all commodities; but this is not how it immediately appears to the *individual* worker whose wages may stand above or below this minimum. The *price of labour* sometimes sinks below and sometimes rises above the *value of labour-power*. Furthermore, there is scope for variation (within narrow limits) to allow for the worker's *individuality*, so that partly as between *different* trades, partly in the *same* one, we find that wages vary depending on the diligence, skill or strength of the worker, and to some extent on his actual personal achievement. Thus the size of his wage packet appears to vary in keeping with the results of his own work and its individual quality. This is particularly evident in the case of *piece rates*. Although, as we have shown, the latter do not affect the general relationship between capital and labour, between necessary labour and surplus labour, the result differs for the individual worker, and it does so in accordance with his particular achievement. In the case of the slave, great physical strength or a special talent may enhance his value to a *purchaser*, but this is of no concern to him. It is otherwise with the free worker who is the owner of *his labour-power*.

477   The higher value of his labour-power must accrue to him and it is expressed in the form of higher wages. So there are great variations in the wages paid, depending on whether a particular type of work requires a more highly developed labour-power at greater cost or not. And this gives scope for individual variation while, at the same time, it also provides the worker with an incentive to develop his own labour-power. Certain though it be that the mass of work must be performed by more or less unskilled labour, so that the vast majority of wages are determined by the *value of simple labour-power*, it nevertheless remains open to individuals to raise themselves to higher spheres by exhibiting a particular talent or energy. In the same way there is an abstract possibility that this or that worker might conceivably become a capitalist and the exploiter of the labour of others. The slave is the property of a particular *master*; the worker must indeed sell himself to capital, but not to a particular capitalist, and so within certain limitations he may choose to sell himself to whomever he wishes; and he may also change his master. The effect of all these differences is to make the free worker's work more intensive, more continuous, more

flexible and skilled than that of the slave, quite apart from the fact that they fit him for quite a different historical role. The slave receives the means of subsistence he requires in the form of *naturalia* which are fixed both in kind and quantity – i.e. he receives *use-values*. The free worker receives them in the shape of *money*, *exchange-value*, the abstract social form of wealth. Even though his wage is in fact nothing more than the *silver* or *gold* or *copper* or *paper* form of the necessary means of subsistence into which it must constantly be dissolved – even though money functions here only as a *means of circulation*, as a vanishing form of exchange-value, that *exchange-value, abstract wealth*, remains in his mind as something more than a particular use-value hedged round with traditional and local restrictions. It is the worker himself who converts the money into whatever use-values he desires; it is he who buys commodities as he wishes and, as the *owner of money*, as the buyer of goods, he stands in precisely the same relationship to the sellers of goods as any other buyer. Of course, the conditions of his existence – and the limited amount of money he can earn – compel him to make his purchases from a fairly restricted selection of goods. But some variation is possible as we can see from the fact that newspapers, for example, form part of the essential purchases of the urban English worker. He can save or hoard a little. Or else he can squander his money on drink. But even so he acts as a free agent; he must pay his own way; he is responsible to himself for the way he spends his wages. *He learns to control himself, in contrast to the slave*, who needs a master. Admittedly, this is valid only if we consider the transformation from serf or slave into free worker. In such cases the capitalist relationship appears to be an improvement in one's position in the social scale. It is otherwise when the independent peasant or artisan becomes a wage-labourer. What a gulf there is between the proud yeomanry of England of which Shakespeare speaks and the English agricultural labourer! Since the sole purpose of work in the eyes of the wage-labourer is his wage, money, a specific quantity of exchange-value from which every particular mark of use-value has been expunged, he is wholly indifferent towards the *content* of his labour and hence his own particular form of activity. While he was in the guild or caste system his activity was a calling, whereas for the slave, as for the beast of burden, it is merely something that befalls him, something forced on him, it is the mere activation of his labour-power. Except where labour-power has been rendered quite one-sided by the division of labour, the free worker is *in principle* ready and willing to accept every possible variation in his labour-power and activity which promises higher rewards (as we can see from the way in which the surplus population on the land constantly pours into the towns). Should the worker prove more or less incapable of this versatility, he still regards it as open to the next generation, and the new generation of workers is infinitely distributable among, and adaptable to, new or expanding branches of industry. We can see this *versatility*, this perfect indifference towards the particular content of work and the free transition from one branch of industry to the next, most obviously in North America, where the development of wage-labour has been relatively untrammelled by the vestiges of the guild system etc. This *versatility* stands in stark contrast to the utterly monotonous and traditional nature of *slave labour*, which does not vary with changes in production, but which requires, on the contrary, that production be adapted to whatever mode of work has once been introduced and carried on from one generation to the next. All American commentators point to this phenomenon as illustrating the distinction between the free labour of the North and the slave labour of the South. (See Cairnes.)* The constant development of *new forms of work*, this continual change – which corresponds to the diversification of use-values and hence represents a real advance in the nature of exchange-value – and in consequence the progressive division of labour in *society as a whole*: all this is the product of the capitalist mode of production. It starts with free production on the basis of the guild and handicraft system wherever this is not thwarted by the ossification of a particular branch of trade.

478   After these additional comments on the *formal subsumption of labour by capital*, we come now to:

THE REAL SUBSUMPTION OF LABOUR UNDER CAPITAL

The general features of the *formal subsumption* remain, viz. the direct *subordination of the labour process to capital*, irrespective of the state of its technological development. But on this foundation there now arises a technologically and otherwise *specific mode of production – capitalist production –* which transforms the nature *of*

*See above, p. 1014, n. 23.

the labour process and its actual conditions. Only when that happens do we witness the *real subsumption of labour under capital.*

'*Agriculture for subsistence* . . . changed for *agriculture for trade* . . . the *improvement of the national territory* . . . proportioned to this *change*' (A. Young, *Political Arithmetic*, London, 1774, p. 49, note).

The real subsumption of labour under capital is developed in all the forms evolved by relative, as opposed to absolute surplus-value.

With the real subsumption of labour under capital a complete (and constantly repeated)[27] revolution takes place in the mode of production, in the productivity of the workers and in the relations between workers and capitalists.

With the real subsumption of labour under capital, all the changes in the labour process already discussed now become reality. The *social forces of production* of labour are now developed, and with large-scale production comes the direct application of science and technology. On the one hand, *capitalist production* now establishes itself as a mode of production *sui generis* and brings into being a new mode of material production. On the other hand, the latter itself forms the basis for the development of capitalist relations whose adequate form, therefore, presupposes a definite stage in the evolution of the productive forces of labour.

It has already been noted that a definite and constantly *growing minimum amount of capital* is both the necessary precondition and the constant result of the *specifically* capitalist mode of production. The capitalist must be the owner or proprietor of the means of production on a *social* scale and in quantities that beggar comparison with the possible production of the individual and his family. The *minimum amount of capital* in an industry increases in proportion to its penetration by capitalist methods and the growth in the social productivity of labour within it. Capital must increase the value of its operations to the point where it assumes social dimensions, and so sheds its *individual* character entirely. It is precisely the productivity of labour, the mass of production, of population and of surplus population created by this mode of production that constantly calls new branches of industry into being once labour and capital have been set free. And in these new branches of

27. *Manifesto of the Communist Party* (1848). [*The Revolutions of 1848*, Pelican Marx Library, p. 70.]

industry capital can once more operate on a small scale and pass through the various phases until this new industry too can be operated on a social scale. This process is continuous. At the same time, *capitalist production* has a tendency to take over all *branches of industry* not yet acquired and where only *formal subsumption* obtains. Once it has appropriated agriculture and mining, the manufacture of the principal textiles etc., it moves on to other sectors where the artisans are still *formally* or even genuinely independent. It has already been remarked, in our discussion of machinery, that the introduction of machinery into one industry leads to its introduction into other industries and other branches of the same industry. Thus spinning machines led to power-looms in weaving; machinery in cotton spinning to machinery in the woollen, linen and silk etc. industries. The increased use of machinery in the mines, cotton mills etc. made the introduction of large-scale production in machine tools inevitable. Quite apart from the improved means of transport rendered necessary by large-scale production, it was also only the introduction of machinery in engineering itself – especially the rotary prime movers – which made steamships and railways a possibility and revolutionized the whole of shipbuilding. Large-scale industry hurls such huge masses of people into industries as yet unsubjugated, or creates such relative surplus populations with them as are required to transform handicraft or small formally capitalist workshops into large-scale concerns. Here the following Tory Jeremiad is relevant:

'In the good old times, when "Live and let live" was the general motto, every man was contented with one avocation. In the cotton trade, there were weavers, cotton-spinners, blanchers, dyers and several other independent branches, all living upon the profits of their respective trades, and all, as might be expected, contented and happy. By and by, however, when the downward course of trade had proceeded to some extent first one branch was adopted by the capitalist and then another, till in time, the whole of the people were ousted, and thrown up on the market of labour, to find out a livelihood in the best manner they could. Thus, although *no charter* secures to these men the right to be cotton-spinners, manufacturers, printers etc., yet the course of events has invested them *with a monopoly of all* . . . They have become Jack-of-all trades, and as far as the country is concerned in the business, it is to be feared, they are masters of none' (*Public Economy Concentrated etc.*, Carlisle, 1833, p. 56).

The material result of capitalist production, if we except the development of the *social productive forces of labour*, is to *raise the quantity of production* and *multiply* and *diversify the spheres of production* and their sub-spheres. For it is only then that the corresponding development of the *exchange-value* of the products emerges – as the realm in which they can operate or realize themselves as *exchange-value*.

'*Production for production's sake*' – production as an end in itself – does indeed come on the scene with the *formal subsumption of labour under capital*. It makes its appearance as soon as the immediate purpose of production is to produce *as much surplus-value as possible*, as soon as the exchange-value of the product becomes the deciding factor. But this *inherent* tendency of capitalist production does not become *adequately realized* – it does not become *indispensable*, and that also means *technologically* indispensable – until the *specific mode of capitalist production* and hence the *real subsumption of labour under capital* has become a reality.

480   The latter has already been argued in detail, so that we may be quite brief here. It is a form of production not bound to a level of needs laid down in advance, and hence it does not predetermine the course of production itself. (Its contradictory character includes a *barrier to production* which it is constantly striving to overcome. Hence crises, over-production etc.) This is one side, in contrast to the former mode of production; if you like, it is the positive side. On the other hand, there is the negative side, its contradictory character: production in contradiction, and indifference, to the *producer*. The real producer as a mere means of production, material wealth as an end in itself. And so the growth of this material wealth is brought about in contradiction to and at the expense of the individual human being. *Productivity of labour* in general = the *maximum of profit* with the *minimum of work*, hence, too, goods constantly become cheaper. This becomes a *law*, independent of the will of the individual capitalist. And this law only becomes reality because instead of the scale of production being controlled by existing needs, the quantity of products made is determined by the constantly increasing scale of production dic-

tated by the mode of production itself. Its aim is that the individual product should contain as *much unpaid labour as possible*, and this is achieved only by *producing for the sake of production*. This becomes manifest, on the one hand, as a law, since the capitalist who produces on too small a scale puts more than the socially necessary quantum of labour into his products. That is to say, it becomes manifest as an adequate embodiment of the *law of value* which develops fully only on the foundation of capitalist production. But, on the other hand, it becomes manifest as the desire of the individual capitalist who, in his wish to render this law ineffectual, or to *outwit it* and turn it to his own advantage, reduces the *individual* value of his product to a point where it falls *below* its socially determined value.

Apart from the increase in the minimum amount of *capital necessary for production*, all these forms of production (of relative surplus-value) have one feature in common. This is that the rationalization of *conditions* for many workers co-operating together directly permits economies. And this contrasts with the fragmentation of conditions in small-scale production, since the *effectiveness* of these collective conditions of production does not bring about a proportionate increase in their quantity and *value*. The fact that they are *employed simultaneously and collectively* causes their *relative* value to sink (with reference to the product), however much their absolute value grows.

PRODUCTIVE AND UNPRODUCTIVE LABOUR

I should like to deal with this briefly before taking a further look at the *changed form of capital* resulting from the capitalist mode of production.

Since the immediate purpose and the *authentic product* of capitalist production is *surplus-value, labour is only productive,* and an exponent of labour-power is only a *productive worker,* if it or he creates *surplus-value* directly, i.e. the only productive labour is that which is directly *consumed* in the course of production for the valorization of capital.

Looked at from the simple standpoint of the *labour process*, labour seemed *productive* if it realized itself in a *product*, or rather a commodity. From the standpoint of capitalist production we may add the qualification that labour is productive if it directly valorizes capital, or creates surplus-value. That is to say, it is productive if it is *realized* in a surplus-value without any equivalent for the worker, its creator; it must appear in surplus produce, i.e. an *additional increment of a commodity* on behalf of the monopolizer of the means of labour, the capitalist. Only the labour which posits the variable capital and hence the total capital as $C+\Delta C = C+\Delta v$ is productive. It is therefore labour which directly serves capital as the agency of its *self-valorization*, as means for the production of surplus-value.

The capitalist labour process does not cancel the general definitions of the labour process. It produces both product and commodity. Labour remains productive as long as it objectifies itself in *commodities*, as the unity of exchange-value and use-value. But the labour process is merely a means for the self-valorization of capital. Labour is productive, therefore, if it is converted into *commodities*, but when we consider the individual commodity we find that a certain proportion of it represents *unpaid* labour, and when we take the *mass of commodities as a whole* we find similarly that a certain proportion of that also represents unpaid labour. In short, it turns out to be a product that costs the capitalist nothing.

The *worker* who performs *productive work* is *productive* and the work he performs is productive if it directly creates *surplus-value*, i.e. if it *valorizes* capital.

481   It is only bourgeois obtuseness that encourages the view that capitalist production is production in its absolute form, the unique form of production as prescribed by nature. And only the bourgeoisie can confuse the questions: what is productive labour? and what is a productive worker from the standpoint of capitalism? with the question: what is *productive* labour as such? And they alone could rest content with the tautological answer that all labour is productive if it produces, if it results in a product or some other use-value or in anything at all.

The only productive worker is one whose labour = the *productive consumption* of labour-power – of the bearer of that labour – on the part of capital or the capitalist.

Two things follow from this:

First, with the development of the *real subsumption of labour under capital*, or the *specifically capitalist mode of production*, the *real lever* of the overall labour process is increasingly not the individual worker. Instead, *labour-power socially combined* and the various competing labour-powers which together form the entire production machine participate in very different ways in the immediate process of making commodities, or, more accurately in this context, creating the product. Some work better with their hands, others with their heads, one as a manager, engineer, technologist, etc., the other as overseer, the third as manual labourer or even drudge. An ever increasing number of types of labour are included in the immediate concept of *productive labour*, and those who perform it are classed as *productive workers*, workers directly exploited by capital and *subordinated* to its process of production and expansion. If we consider the aggregate *worker*, i.e. if we take all the members comprising the workshop together, then we see that their *combined activity* results materially in an *aggregate* product which is at the same time a *quantity of goods*. And here it is quite immaterial whether the job of a particular worker, who is merely a limb of this aggregate worker, is at a greater or smaller distance from the actual manual labour. But then: the activity of this aggregate labour-power is its *immediate productive consumption by capital*, i.e. it is the self-valorization process of capital, and hence, as we shall demonstrate, the immediate production of surplus-value, the *immediate conversion of this latter into capital*.

Second, the more detailed definition of productive labour follows from the characteristic features of capitalist production as we have described them. In the first place, the owner of labour-power confronts capital or the capitalist, irrationally, as we have seen it expressed, as the *seller* of his property. He is the direct vendor of *living labour, not of a commodity*. He is a *wage-labourer*. This is the *first premiss*. Secondly, however, once this preliminary process (which is really part of circulation) has been initiated, his labour-power, his labour, is directly incorporated into the production process of capital as a *living factor*; it becomes one of its *components*, a variable component, moreover, which partly maintains and partly reproduces the capital values invested. It goes even further; it *augments* them and, through the creation of surplus-value, it transforms them into value valorizing itself, into capital. This labour *objectifies* itself directly during the labour process as a *fluid quantum of value*.

It is possible for the *first condition to be fulfilled and not the second*. A worker can be a wage-labourer, a day labourer etc. This happens whenever the second moment is absent. Every productive worker is a wage-labourer, but not every wage-labourer is a productive worker. Whenever labour is purchased to be consumed as a *use-value*, as a *service* and not to replace the value of variable capital with its own *vitality* and be incorporated into the capitalist process of production – whenever that happens, labour is not productive and the wage-labourer is no productive worker. His work is consumed for its *use-value*, not as *creating exchange-value*; it is consumed unproductively, not productively. Hence the capitalist does not encounter it in his role of capitalist, a representative of capital. The money that he pays for it is *revenue*, not *capital*. Its consumption is to be formulated not as M–C–M, but as C–M–C (the last being the *labour* or *service* itself). The money functions here only as a means of circulation, not as capital.

The *services* that the capitalist buys freely or under compulsion (for example from the state) for their use-value are not consumed productively and cannot become *factors of capital*, any more than the *commodities* he buys for his personal consumption. They do not become factors of capital; they are therefore not productive labour and those who carry them out are not *productive workers*.

The more production becomes the production of commodities, the more each person has to, and wishes to, become a *dealer in commodities*, then the more everyone wants to make money, either from a product, or from his *services*, if his product only exists naturally in the form of a service, and this *money-making* appears as the ultimate purpose of activity of every kind.[28] In capitalist production the tendency for all products to be commodities and all labour to be *wage-labour*, becomes absolute. A whole mass of functions and activities which formerly had an aura of sanctity about them, which passed as ends in themselves, which were performed for nothing or where payment was made in roundabout ways (like all the professions, barristers, doctors, in England where the barrister and the physician neither could nor can sue for payment to this very day) – all these become directly converted into *wage-labourers*, however various their activities and *payment*

28. Aristotle. [See above, p. 253, n. 6.]

may be.[29] And, on the other hand, their valuation – the *price* of these different *activities* from the prostitute to the king – becomes subject to the *laws that govern the price of wage-labour*. The implications of this last point should be explored in a special treatise on wage-labour and wages, rather than here. Now the fact that with the growth of capitalist production all *services* become transformed into *wage-labour*, and those who perform them into *wage-labourers*, means that they tend increasingly to be confused with the productive worker, just because they share this characteristic with him. This confusion is all the more tempting because it arises from *capitalist production* and is typical of it. On the other hand, it also creates an opening for its apologists to convert the productive worker, simply because he is a wage-labourer, into a worker who only exchanges his *services* (i.e. his labour as a use-value) for *money*. This makes it easy for them to gloss over the specific nature of this 'productive worker' and of capitalist production – as the production of surplus-value, as the self-valorization of capital in which living labour is no more than the agency it has embodied in itself. A soldier is a wage-labourer, a mercenary, but this does not make a productive worker of him.

Further error springs from two sources.

First, within capitalist production there are always certain parts of the productive process that are carried out in a way typical of *earlier modes of production*, in which the relations of *capital and wage-labour* did not yet exist and where in consequence the capitalist concepts of *productive* and unproductive labour are quite inapplicable. But in line with the dominant mode of production, even those kinds of labour which have not been subjugated by capitalism in reality are so in thought. For example, the self-employing worker is his own wage-labourer; his own means of production appear to him in his own mind as capital. As his own capitalist he puts himself to work as wage-labourer. Such anomalies provide welcome opportunities for all sorts of hot air about the difference between productive and unproductive labour.

483   *Second*, certain kinds of *unproductive work* may be incidentally connected to the process of production and their *price* may even enter into the *price of the commodity*. In consequence the money laid out for them may form part of the *capital invested* and the

29. *Manifesto of the Communist Party* (1848). [*The Revolutions of 1848*, ibid.]

labour they require may appear to be labour exchanged not for *revenue* but directly for *capital*.

As an example of this, let us consider *taxes*, the price for government services. But taxes belong to the *faux frais de production** and as far as capitalist production is concerned they are utterly *adventitious* and anything but a necessary, intrinsic phenomenon *resulting* from it. If, for example, all *indirect* taxes are converted into *direct* ones, the taxes will be paid now as before, but they will cease to be capital investment and will instead be the disbursement of *revenue*. The fact that this metamorphosis is possible shows its superficial, external and incidental nature as far as it touches the capitalist process of production. A comparable metamorphosis in productive labour on the other hand would mean the end of the revenue from capital and of capital itself.

Further examples are legal proceedings, contractual agreements, etc. All matters of this sort are concerned with stipulations between commodity owners as buyers and sellers of goods, and have nothing to do with the relations between capital and labour. Those engaged on them may become the wage-labourers of capital; but this does not make productive workers of them.

Productive labour is merely an abbreviation for the entire complex of activities of labour and labour-power within the capitalist process of production. Thus when we speak of *productive labour* we mean *socially determined* labour, labour which implies a quite specific relationship between the buyer and seller of labour. Productive labour is exchanged directly for *money as capital*, i.e. for money which is intrinsically capital, which is destined to function as capital and which confronts labour-power as capital. Thus productive labour is labour which for the worker only reproduces the value of his labour-power as determined beforehand, while as a value-creating activity it valorizes capital and *confronts* the worker with the values so created and transformed into *capital*. The specific relationship between *objectified* and *living* labour that converts the former into capital also turns the latter into *productive labour*.

The specific product of the capitalist process of production, surplus-value, is created only through an exchange with *productive labour*.

*'Incidental costs of production'.

What gives it a *specific use-value* for capital is not its particular utility, any more than the particular useful qualities of the product in which it is objectified. Its use to capital is its ability to generate exchange-value (surplus-value).

The capitalist process of production does not just involve the production of commodities. It is a process which absorbs unpaid labour, which makes the means of production into the means for extorting unpaid labour.

From the foregoing it is evident that for *labour to be designated productive*, qualities are required which are utterly unconnected with the *specific content* of the labour, with its particular utility or the use-value in which it is objectified.

484 Hence labour with *the same content* can be either productive or unproductive.

For instance, Milton, who wrote *Paradise Lost*, was an unproductive worker. On the other hand, a writer who turns out work for his publisher in factory style is a productive worker. Milton produced *Paradise Lost* as a silkworm produces silk, as the activation of *his own* nature. He later sold his product for £5 and thus became a merchant. But the literary proletarian of Leipzig who produces books, such as compendia on political economy, at the behest of his publisher is pretty nearly a productive worker since his production is taken over by capital and only occurs in order to increase it. A singer who sings like a bird is an unproductive worker. If she sells her song for money, she is to that extent a wage-labourer or merchant. But if the same singer is engaged by an entrepreneur who makes her sing to make money, then she becomes a productive worker, since she *produces* capital directly. A schoolmaster who instructs others is not a productive worker. But a schoolmaster who works for wages in an institution along with others, using his own labour to increase the money of the entrepreneur who owns the knowledge-mongering institution, is a productive worker. But for the most part, work of this sort has scarcely reached the stage of being subsumed even formally under capital, and belongs essentially to a transitional stage.

On the whole, types of work that are consumed as services and not in products separable from the worker and hence not capable of existing as commodities independently of him, but which are yet capable of being directly exploited in *capitalist* terms, are of microscopic significance when compared with the mass of capitalist production. They may be entirely neglected, therefore, and can be dealt with under the category of wage-labour that is not at the same time productive labour.

It is possible for work of one type (such as gardening, tailoring etc.) to be performed by the same working man either in the service of an industrial capitalist or on behalf of the immediate consumer. He is a wage-labourer or day labourer in either situation, only he is a *productive* worker in the one case and *unproductive* in the other, because in the one he produces capital and in the other not; because in the one case his work is a factor in the self-valorization process of capital and in the other it is not.

A large part of the annual product which is consumed as revenue and hence does not re-enter production as its means, consists of the most tawdry products (use-values) designed to gratify the most impoverished appetites and fancies. As far as the question of productive labour is concerned, however, the nature of these objects is quite immaterial (although obviously the development of wealth would inevitably receive a check if a disproportionate part were to be reproduced in this way instead of being changed back into the means of production and subsistence, to become absorbed once more – productively consumed, in short – into the process of reproduction either of commodities or of labour-power). This sort of productive labour produces use-values and objectifies itself in products that are destined only for unproductive consumption. In their reality, as articles, they have no *use-value* for the process of reproduction. (For they could acquire this only through *metabolism*, through the exchange with productive use-values; but this is only a displacement. Somewhere they must be consumed unreproductively. Other such articles falling into the category of unproductive consumption could, if need be, also function again as capital. More about this in Bk II, Chapter III,* on the process of reproduction. We would make only one comment here in anticipation: ordinary economic theory finds it impossible to utter a single sensible word on the barriers to the production of luxuries even from the standpoint of capitalism itself. The matter is very simple, however, if the elements of the process of reproduction are examined systematically. If the process of reproduction suffers a check, or if its progress, in so far as this is already determined by

*i.e. Vol. 2, Part Four.

the natural growth of the population, is held up by the disproportionate diversion of *productive labour* into unreproductive
articles, it follows that the means of subsistence or production will
not be reproduced in the necessary quantities. In that event it is
possible to condemn the manufacture of luxury goods from the
standpoint of capitalist production. For the rest, however, luxury
goods are absolutely necessary for a mode of production which
creates wealth for the non-producer and which therefore must
provide that wealth in forms which permit its acquisition only by
those who enjoy.)

For the worker himself this productive labour, like any other, is
simply a means of reproducing the means of subsistence he requires. For the capitalist to whom both the nature of the use-value
and the character of the actual concrete labour employed are
matters of complete indifference, it is simply *un moyen de battre
monnaie, de produire la survalue.**

485   The desire to define *productive* and *unproductive* labour in terms
of their *material* content has a threefold source.

(1) The fetishism peculiar to the capitalist mode of production
from which it arises. This consists in regarding *economic* categories, such as being a *commodity* or *productive* labour, as qualities inherent in the material incarnations of these formal determinations or categories;

(2) Looking at the labour process as such, labour is held to be
productive only if it results in a *product* (and since we are concerned
here only with material wealth, it must be a material product);

(3) In the *actual* process of reproduction – considering only its
real moments – there is a vast difference which affects the formation of wealth, between labour which is engaged on articles essential to reproduction and labour concerned purely with luxuries.

(*Example*: It is a matter of complete indifference to me whether
I buy a pair of trousers or whether I just buy the cloth and have a
tailor's assistant come into my house and pay him for his *services*
(i.e. making it up). I buy it from the merchant tailor because it is
cheaper. In either case I convert the money I spend into a use-
value that forms part of my individual consumption, and that is
designed to gratify my individual need, and not into capital. The
tailor's assistant performs the identical *service* for me irrespective

*'A means of coining money, of producing surplus-value'.

of whether he works for the merchant tailor, or in my home. On the other hand, when the same tailor's assistant is employed by a merchant tailor the service he performs for that capitalist is that he does 12 hours' work and is paid only for 6. The service he performs, then, is that he does 6 hours' work for nothing. The fact that this transaction is embodied in the action of making trousers only *conceals* its real nature. As soon as he can, the merchant tailor seeks to convert the trousers back into money, i.e. into a form in which the distinctive character of the work of tailoring has totally disappeared, and the service performed becomes embodied in the fact that one thaler has become two.)

In general, we may say that *service* is merely an expression for the particular use-value of labour where the latter is useful not as an article, but as an activity. *Do ut facias, facio ut facias, facio ut des, do ut des** – all these are interchangeable formulae for the same situation, whereas in capitalist production the *do ut facias* expresses a highly specific relationship between material wealth and living labour. Since, therefore, in this *purchase of services* the specific relation of capital and labour is not contained – it is either obliterated or simply absent – it is naturally the form preferred by Say, Bastiat and Co. to express the *relation of capital and labour*.†

The worker, too, purchases *services* with his money. This is a form of expenditure, but it is no way to turn money into capital.

No one buys medical or legal 'services' as a means of converting the money laid out into capital.

A large proportion of *services* belongs with the costs of consuming produce. Cooks for example.

The distinction between *productive* and *unproductive* labour depends merely on whether labour is exchanged for *money as money* or for *money as capital*. For instance, if I buy *produce* from a self-employing worker, artisan, etc., the category does not enter into the discussion because there is no direct exchange between money and labour of any kind, but only between *money* and *produce*.

86   In the case of non-material production there are two possibili-

---

*'I give so that you may do, I do so that you may do, I do so that you may give, I give so that you may give.'

† See above, p. 300, n. 17.

ties, even where it is undertaken purely for the sake of exchange, producing goods, etc:

(1) It results in commodities which exist separately from the producer, i.e. they can circulate in the interval between production and consumption as commodities, e.g. books, paintings and all products of art as distinct from the artistic achievement of the practising artist. Here capitalist production is possible only within very narrow limits. Apart from such cases as, say, sculptors who employ assistants, these people (where they are not independent) mainly work for merchant's capital, e.g. booksellers, a pattern that is only transitional in itself and can only lead to a *capitalist mode of production in the formal* sense. Nor is the position altered by the fact that exploitation is at its greatest precisely in these transitional forms.

(2) The product is not separable from the act of producing. Here too the capitalist mode of production occurs only on a limited scale and in the nature of the case it can operate only in certain areas. (I want *the doctor* and not his errand boy.) For example, in teaching institutions the teachers can be no more than wage-labourers for the entrepreneur of the learning factory. Such peripheral phenomena can be ignored when considering capitalist production as a whole.

'*The productive labourer* [is one who] directly increases *his master's wealth*' (Malthus, *Principles of Political Economy,* 2nd edn, London, 1836 [p. 47, note]).

The distinction between *productive* and *unproductive labour* is vital for accumulation since only the exchange for productive labour can satisfy one of the conditions for the reconversion of surplus-value into capital.

As the representative of *productive capital* engaged in the process of self-expansion, the capitalist performs a *productive* function. It consists in the direction and exploitation of productive labour. In contrast to his fellow-consumers of *surplus-value* who stand in no such immediate and active relationship to their production, his class is the *productive* class par excellence. (As the director of the labour process the capitalist performs *productive labour* in the sense that his labour is involved in the total process that is realized in the product.) We are concerned here only with capital within the immediate process of production. The other functions of capital and the agents which it employs within them form a subject to be left for later.

The definition of *productive labour* (and hence of its opposite, *unproductive* labour) is based on the fact that the production of capital is the production of surplus-value and the labour it employs is labour that produces surplus-value.

87 NET AND GROSS PRODUCT

(This fits better perhaps in Bk III, Chapter III.)
Since the purpose of capitalist production (and hence of *productive* labour) is not the existence of the producer, but the production of surplus-value, it follows that all necessary labour which does not produce surplus labour is superfluous and worthless to capitalist production. The same holds good for a nation of capitalists. All *produit brut* [gross produce] which merely reproduces the worker, i.e. which creates no *produit net* [surplus produce] is just as superfluous as the worker himself. Thus workers who were indispensable for the creation of *produit net*, at a certain stage of development, can become superfluous at a more advanced stage of production which has no need of their services. In other words, only the number of people profitable to capitalism is necessary. The same holds good for the nation of capitalists. 'Is not the real interest of a nation similar' to the interest of a private capitalist for whom 'it would be a matter quite indifferent whether his capital would employ a hundred or a thousand men . . . provided his profits on a capital of £20,000 were not diminished below £2,000'? 'Provided its net real income, its rents and profits be the same, it is of no importance whether the nation consists of ten or of twelve millions of inhabitants . . . If five millions of men could produce as much food and clothing as was necessary for ten millions, food and clothing for five millions would be the net revenue. Would it be of any advantage to the country, that to produce this same net revenue, seven millions of men should be required, that is to say, that seven millions should be employed to produce food and clothing sufficient for twelve millions? The food and clothing of five millions would still be the net revenue.'*

Even the philanthropists can have no objection to bring forward against this statement of Ricardo's. For it is always better that of

* Ricardo, *On the Principles of Political Economy*, pp. 416–17.

ten million people only 50 per cent should vegetate as pure pro-
duction-machines for five millions, than that of twelve millions,
seven or $58\frac{3}{4}$ per cent should vegetate as such.

'Of what use in a modern kingdom would be a whole province
thus divided (between self-sustaining little farmers as in the first
times of ancient Rome), however well cultivated, except for the
mere purpose of breeding men, which singly taken, is a most useless purpose' (Arthur Young, *Political Arithmetic, etc.*, London,
1774, p. 47).

Since capitalist production is *essentiellement* the *production of
surplus-value,* its aim is *net produce* and that is to say the form of
surplus-produce in which *surplus-value* is embodied.

All this conflicts with, for example, the antiquated view typical
of earlier modes of production according to which the city authorities would, for instance, prohibit inventions so as not to deprive
workers of their livelihood. In such a society the worker was an
end in himself and appropriate employment was his privilege, a
right which the entire order was concerned to maintain. It conflicts, moreover, with the idea of the protectionist system (as opposed to free trade), an idea tinged with nationalism, which holds
that industries should be protected since they form the source of
income for a mass of people. They should therefore be protected
on a national basis against foreign competition. Finally, it conflicts with the view of Adam Smith that, for example, the investment of capital in agriculture is 'more productive' because the
same capital provides work for more hands. From the perspective
of an advanced form of capitalist production these are all antiquated and erroneous ideas. A large gross product (as far as the
variable part of capital is concerned) standing in proportion to a
small net product = a reduction in the productive power of
labour and therefore of capital.

488   Traditionally, however, all sorts of confused ideas are current in
connection with the gross and net product. They stem in part from
the Physiocrats (see Book IV), and in part from Adam Smith who
still here and there confuses capitalist production with production
on behalf of the immediate producers.

The individual capitalist who sends his money abroad and receives 10 per cent interest for it, whereas by keeping it at home he

could employ a mass of surplus people, deserves from the stand-point of capitalism to be crowned king of the bourgeoisie. For this man of virtue simply implements the law which distributes capital on the world market, just as it does within the bounds of the domestic market, viz. in tune with the rate of profit yielded by the various spheres of production: it has the effect of balancing them out and regulating production. (It is irrelevant whether the money goes, for instance, to the Tsar of Russia to finance wars against Turkey. In acting thus the individual capitalist only obeys the immanent law, and hence the moral imperative, of capital to produce as much surplus-value as possible.) However, this has no connection with our examination of the immediate process of production.

Furthermore, the contrast is often made between *capitalist* and *non-capitalist production*. For example, agriculture for subsistence in which hands are occupied, is distinguished from agriculture for trade, which places a much greater product on the market and hence allows people formerly engaged in agriculture to recover a net product in manufacturing. But this distinction has no application *within* capitalist production itself.

On the whole, we have seen that the law of capitalist production is to increase constant capital at the expense of variable, that is, to increase surplus-value, net produce. Secondly, net produce is to be increased in relation to the part of the product that replenishes capital, i.e. wages. Now these two things are frequently confused. If the aggregate product is called the gross product, then in capitalist production it grows in relation to the net product; if we call that portion of the product that can be broken down into wages+ net produce the net product, then the net product grows in relation to the gross product. Only in agriculture (owing to the conversion of cultivated land into pasture) does the net product often grow at the expense of the gross product (the overall mass of products) in consequence of certain features peculiar to rent which cannot be discussed in this context.

In other respects the theory of the *net product* as the last and highest purpose of production is no more than the brutal but ac-curate expression of the fact that the *valorization of capital*, and hence the creation of surplus-value without heed to the worker, is the driving force behind capitalist production.

Its loftiest ideal – corresponding to the relative growth of the *produit net* – is the greatest possible reduction of wages, the greatest possible increase in the number of those living off *produit net*.

MYSTIFICATION OF CAPITAL ETC.

Since – within the process of production – living labour has already been absorbed into capital, all the *social productive forces of labour* appear as the *productive forces* of capital, as intrinsic attributes of capital, just as in the case of money, the creative power of labour had seemed to possess the qualities of a thing. What was true of money is even truer of capital because:

(1) although labour is an *expression of labour-power*, although it represents the effort of the *individual worker*, and so belongs to him (it is the substance with which he pays the capitalist for what he receives from him), it nevertheless objectifies itself in the product and so belongs to the capitalist. – Even worse, the *social configuration* in which the individual workers exist, and within which they function only as the particular organs of the total labour-power that makes up the workshop as a whole, does not belong to them either. On the contrary, it confronts them as a *capitalist arrangement* that is *imposed* on them;

(2) these *social productive forces of labour*, or *productive forces of social labour*, came into being historically only with the advent of the specifically capitalist mode of production. That is to say, they appeared as something intrinsic to the relations of capitalism and inseparable from them;

(3) with the development of the capitalist mode of production the *objective conditions of labour* take on a different form owing to the scale on which, and the economy with which, they are employed (quite apart from the form of the machinery itself). As they develop they become increasingly concentrated; they represent *social* wealth and, to put the matter in a nutshell, their scope and their effect is that of the *conditions of production* of labour *socially* combined. And quite apart from the combination of labour, the *social character of the conditions of labour* – and this includes machinery and *capitale fixe* of every kind – appears to be entirely autonomous and independent of the worker. It appears to be a *mode of existence of capital* itself, and therefore as something ordered by *capitalists* without reference to the workers. Like the *social character* of their own labour, but to a far greater extent, the *social character* with which the conditions of production are en-

dowed, as the conditions of production of the combined labour of the *community*, appears as *capitalistic*, as something independent of the workers and intrinsic to the conditions of production themselves.

ad (3) we should at once add the following rider which to some extent anticipates later discussion:

Profits as distinct from surplus-value can rise as a result of the economical use of *collective* conditions of labour, such as saving in overheads, for example heating, lighting, etc. The fact that the value of the prime mover does not increase at the same rate as its power: economies in the price of raw materials, recycling of waste, reduction in administrative costs, or in storage costs as the result of mass production, etc. – all these *relative* savings accruing to constant capital and coinciding with the absolute growth in its value are based on the fact that these means of production, i.e. both the means and the materials of labour, are used *collectively*. This *collective* use in its turn is based on the absolute premiss of the co-operation of an agglomeration of workers. It is itself, therefore, only the objective expression of the *social character of labour* and the social forces of production arising from it, just as the particular form assumed by these conditions, the machinery for instance, cannot possibly be used other than for work on a co-operative basis. To the worker who enters into these relations, however, they appear as *given* conditions, *independent* of himself; they are the *forms of capital*. In consequence, all these economies (and the resultant growth in profits and reductions in the price of goods) seem to be something quite separate from the *surplus labour* of the worker. They appear to be the direct *act* and *achievement of the capitalist*, who functions here as the personification of the *social* character of labour, of the *workshop as a whole*. In the same way, *science*, which is in fact the general intellectual product of the social process, also appears to be the direct offshoot of capital (since its application to the material process of production takes place in isolation from the knowledge and abilities of the individual worker). And since society is marked by the exploitation of labour by capital, its development appears to be the productive force of capital as opposed to labour. It therefore appears to be the *development of capital*, and all the more so since, for the great majority, it is a process with which the *drawing-off of labour-power* keeps pace.

90   The capitalist himself wields power only inasmuch as he is the

personification of capital. (It is for this reason that he always appears in a dual role in Italian book-keeping. For instance, as the debtor of his own capital.)

As regards capital in the context of the *formal* mode of subsumption, its *productivity* consists in the first instance only in the *compulsion to perform surplus labour*. This compulsion is one which it shares with earlier modes of production, but in capitalism it is more favourable for production.

Even if we consider just the *formal* relation, the *general* form of capitalist production, which is common to both its more and its less advanced forms, we see that the *means of production*, the *material conditions of labour*, are not subject to the worker, but he to them. Capital *employs* labour. This in itself exhibits the relationship in its simple form and entails the personification of things and the reification [*Versachlichung*] of persons.

The relationship becomes more complicated, however, and apparently more mysterious, with the emergence of the specifically capitalist mode of production. Here we find that it is not only such things – the products of labour, both use-values and exchange-values – that rise up on their hind legs and face the worker and confront him as '*Capital*'. But even the social form of labour appears as a *form of development of capital*, and hence the productive forces of social labour so developed appear as the *productive forces of capitalism*. *Vis-à-vis* labour such social forces are in fact '*capitalized*'. In fact *collective* unity in co-operation, combination in the division of labour, the use of the forces of nature and the sciences, of the products of labour, as *machinery* – all these confront the individual workers as something *alien, objective, ready-made*, existing without their intervention, and frequently even hostile to them. They all appear quite simply as the prevailing forms of the instruments of labour. As objects they are independent of the workers whom they *dominate*. Though the workshop is to a degree the product of the workers' combination, its entire intelligence and will seem to be incorporated in the capitalist or his under-strappers [Marx's word], and the workers find themselves confronted by the *functions* of the capital that lives in the capitalist. The social forms of their own labour – both subjectively and objectively – or, in other words, the forms of *their own* social labour, are utterly independent of the individual workers. Subsumed under capital the workers become components of these social formations, but these social formations do not belong to them and so rise up against them as the *forms* of capital itself, as if they belonged to capital, as if they arose from it and were integrated within it, in opposition to the isolated labour-power of the workers. And this entire process is progressively intensified as their labour-power is itself modified by these forms to such an extent that it is rendered impotent even when it exists autonomously. In other words its independent productive capacities are destroyed once it finds itself outside the framework of capitalism. And on the other hand, with the development of machinery there is a sense in which the conditions of labour come to dominate labour even technologically and, at the same time, they replace it, suppress it and render it superfluous in its independent forms. In this process, then, the *social* characteristics of their labour come to confront the workers so to speak in a *capitalized* form; thus machinery is an instance of the way in which the visible products of labour take on the appearance of its masters. The same transformation may be observed in the forces of nature and science, the products of the general development of history in its abstract quintessence. They too confront the workers as the *powers* of capital. They become separated effectively from the skill and the knowledge of the individual worker; and even though ultimately they are themselves the products of labour, they appear as an *integral* part of capital wherever they intervene in the labour process. The capitalist who puts a machine to work does not need to understand it. (See Ure.) But the science realized *in the machine* becomes manifest to the workers in the form of *capital*. And in fact every such application of *social labour* to science, the forces of nature and the products of labour on a large scale, appears as no more than the *means for the exploitation of labour*, as the means of appropriating surplus labour, and hence it seems to deploy *forces* distinct from labour and integral to capital. Of course, capital makes use of these means only in order to exploit labour, but if it is to exploit it, it must apply them to production itself. And so the development of the *social* productive forces of labour and the conditions of that development come to appear as the *achievement of capital*, an achievement which the individual worker endures passively, and which progresses at his expense.

Since capital consists of commodities, it appears in twofold form:

(1) *Exchange-value* (money), but value *valorizing* itself, value

that creates value, *grows as value*, receives an increment simply because it is *value*. This resolves itself into the exchange of a given quantity of objectified labour for a larger amount of living labour.

(2) *Use-value,* and here capital conforms to the specific nature of the labour process. And precisely here it is not limited to the materials or means of labour to which *labour* belongs, which have absorbed labour. But along with labour it has also appropriated its network of *social relations* and the level of development of the means of labour corresponding to them. Capitalist production is the first to develop the conditions of the labour process, both its objective and subjective ones, on a large scale – it tears them from the hands of the individual independent worker, but develops them as powers that control the individual *worker* and are *alien* to him.

In this way capital becomes a highly mysterious thing.

491   The conditions of labour pile up in front of the worker as *social forces*, and they assume a *capitalized* form.

Thus capital appears *productive*:

(1) as the *compulsion to surplus labour*. Now if labour is *productive* it is precisely as the agent that performs this surplus labour, as the result of the difference between the actual value of labour-power and its valorization.

(2) as the *personification and representative*, the reified form of the 'social productive forces of labour' or the productive forces of social labour. How the law of capitalist production – the creation of surplus-value, etc. – achieves this has already been discussed. It takes the form of a compulsion which the capitalists impose upon the workers and on each other: – in reality, then, it is the law of capital as enforced against both. Labour as a social and natural force does not develop within the valorization process as such, but within the *actual labour process*. It presents itself therefore as a set of attributes that are intrinsic to capital as a thing, as its use-value. Productive labour – as something productive of value – continues to confront capital as the labour of the *individual* workers, irrespective of the social combinations these workers may enter into in the process of production. Therefore whereas capital always represents the social productivity of labour *vis-à-vis* the workers, productive labour itself never represents more than the labour of the *individual* worker *vis-à-vis* capital.

We have already seen in our discussion of the *process of accumulation* how past labour, i.e. labour in the form of the forces and conditions of production already produced, intensifies reproduction both as use-value and exchange-value; i.e. both in terms of the mass of value which a specific quantum of living labour *sustains*, as also the *mass of use-values* it creates anew. And we have seen how this manifests itself as a *force immanent in capital*, because the *objectified labour* always functions as capitalized labour *vis-à-vis* the worker.

'*Le capital c'est la puissance démocratique philanthropique et égalitaire par excellence*' ['Capital is the democratic, philanthropic and egalitarian power par excellence'] (F. Bastiat, *Gratuité du crédit, etc.*, Paris, 1850, p. 29).

'Stock cultivates land: stock employs labour' (Adam Smith, op. cit., Bk V, Ch. 2, ed. Buchanan, 1814, Vol. 3, p. 309).

'Capital is ... collective force' (John Wade, *History of the Middle and Working Classes etc.*, 3rd edn, London, 1835, p. 162). 'Capital is only another name for civilization' (ibid., p. 104).

'*La classe des capitalistes, considérée en bloc, se trouve dans une position normale, en ce que son bien-être suit la marche du progrès social*' (Cherbuliez, *Riche ou pauvre*, p. 75). '*Le capitaliste est l'homme social par excellence, il représente la civilisation*' (ibid., p. 76). ['The class of capitalists, considered as a whole, finds itself in a normal situation when its well-being keeps pace with the march of social progress ... The capitalist is social man par excellence: he represents civilization.]

Superficial: 'The *productive power of capital* is nothing but the quantity of real productive power which the capitalist can command by virtue of his capital' (John Stuart Mill, *Essays on Some Unsettled Questions of Political Economy*, London, 1844, p. 91).

'The accumulation of capital, or of the means of employing labour ... must in all cases depend on the *productive powers of labour*' (Ricardo, *Principles*, 3rd edn, 1821, p. 92). A commentator on Ricardo made the following observation on this point: '*If the productive powers of labour mean the smallness of that aliquot part of any produce that goes to those whose manual labour produced it*, the sentence is nearly identical' (*Observations on Certain Verbal Disputes in Political Economy*, London, 1821, p. 74).

The constant transposition of labour into capital is well formulated in the following naïve statements of *Destutt de Tracy*:

'*Ceux qui vivent de profits* (*les capitaux industrieux*) *alimentent tous les autres, et seuls augmentent la fortune publique et créent tous nos moyens de jouissance. Cela doit être*, puisque le travail est la source de toute richesse, *et puisque eux seuls donnent une* direction utile au travail actuel, *en faisant un usage utile du travail accumulé*' ['They' (the industrial capitalists) 'who live on profits maintain all the others and alone augment the public fortune and create all our means of enjoyment. That must be so, *because labour is the source of all wealth* and because they alone give a *useful direction to current labour*, by making a useful application *of accumulated labour*'] (Destutt de Tracy, *Traité d'économie politique*, p. 242). Because labour is the source of all wealth, capital is the augmenter of all wealth. '*Nos facultés sont notre seule richesse originaire, notre travail produit tous les autres, et tout travail bien dirigé est productif*' ['Our faculties are our only original wealth; our labour produces all other wealth, and all labour, properly directed, is productive'] (ibid., p. 243). Our capacities are our only original wealth. Hence the capacity for labour is no wealth. Labour produces all other forms of wealth; that is to say, it produces wealth for all others but itself, and it is not even wealth itself, but merely the product of wealth. All well-directed labour is productive; in other words, all productive labour, all labour that yields profit for the capitalist, is well directed.

The transposition of the social productivity of labour into the material attributes of capital is so firmly entrenched in people's minds that the advantages of machinery, the use of science, invention, etc. are *necessarily* conceived in this *alienated* form, so that all these things are deemed to be the *attributes of capital*. The basis for this is (1) the form in which objects appear in the framework of capitalist production and hence in the minds of those caught up in that mode of production; (2) the historical fact that this development first occurs in capitalism, in contrast to earlier modes of production, and so its *contradictory character appears* to be an integral part of it.

TRANSITION FROM SECTIONS II AND III TO SECTION I*

We have seen that capitalist production is the production of surplus-value, and as such (in the process of *accumulation*), it is at the

* Marx actually gave this section the heading 'Transition from Sections I and II of This Chapter to Section III, Originally Treated as Section I',

same time the *production of capital* and the *production* and reproduction of the entire capitalist relation on a steadily increasing (expanding) scale. But the surplus-value is produced only as a part of the value of commodities and it appears in a specific quantum of commodities or surplus produce. Capital produces only *surplus-value* and reproduces itself only in its capacity as the *producer of commodities*. It is therefore with the *commodity* as its *immediate product* that we must concern ourselves once more. However, as we have seen, *commodities* are *incomplete results* regarded *formally* (i.e. as economic forms). Before they can function again as wealth (whether as money or as use-values), they must undergo certain formal changes and they must re-enter the process of exchange in order to do so. We must therefore take a closer look at the *commodity* as the first result of the capitalist process of production and then consider the further processes that it has to undergo. (Commodities are the elements of capitalist production, and commodities are its *product*; they are the form in which capital re-appears at the end of the process of production.)

44   We begin with the commodity, with this specific social form of the product – for it is the foundation and premiss of capitalist production. We take the individual product in our hand and analyse the formal determinants that it contains as a commodity and which stamp it as a commodity. Prior to capitalist production a large part of what was produced did not take the form of commodities, nor was it produced for that purpose. What is more, a large proportion of the products that went into production were not commodities and did not go into the process of production as commodities. The transformation of produce into commodities occurred only at isolated points; it affected only the surplus produce, or only particular sectors (such as manufactured goods). Produce as a whole did not enter into the process as merchandise, nor did it emerge as such from the process.[30] Nevertheless, within certain limits both goods and money were circulated and hence there was a certain evolution of trade: this was the *premiss* and *point of departure for the formation of capital* and the capitalist

30. See the French work of around 1752 where it is alleged that before . . . only wheat was regarded as merchandise in France.

following his intention to re-arrange the order of sections as explained on p. 949. To avoid confusion we have retitled it to conform with the order in which the three sections are presented here.

mode of production. We regard the commodity as just such a premiss and we proceed from the commodity as capitalist production in its simplest form. On the other hand, however, the *commodity* is a product, a result of capitalist production. What began as one of its components turns out later to be its own product. Only on the basis of capitalist production will the commodity become the general form of the product. And the more it evolves the more will all the ingredients of production become absorbed into the process.*

III: CAPITALIST PRODUCTION IS THE PRODUCTION AND REPRODUCTION OF THE SPECIFICALLY CAPITALIST RELATIONS OF PRODUCTION

The product of capitalist production is not only *surplus-value*; it is also *capital*.

Capital is, as we have seen, M–C–M, i.e. *value valorizing itself*, value that gives birth to value.

In the first instance, even after its conversion into the factors of the labour process (i.e. into the means of production, *constant* capital on the one hand – and *labour-power* into which the variable capital has been transformed, on the other), the value or money invested is only capital *in itself*, only *potentially*. And this was even truer before it was transposed into the factors of the actual process of production. Only when it finds itself within that process, only when living labour is *really* incorporated into the objectively existent forms of capital, only when additional labour is sucked into the process, only then do we find that *this labour* is converted into capital. And furthermore, we then find that the amounts of potential capital, of what has been capital in intention, what has actually been invested, have also been transformed into capital in actuality and in effect. What took place in this process as a whole? The worker sold the right to control his labour-power in exchange for the necessary means of subsistence. He did so for a specific value which was determined by the value of his labour-power. Looking at him, what is the result? *Simplement et purement* the reproduction of his labour-power. So what did he part with? The activity that maintains value, that creates and augments it: his

*After the heading to the two foregoing paragraphs Marx made the note: 'Cf. p. 444'. It is for this reason that we have inserted the text of this last paragraph here. In the MS. it is emphasized by a number of brackets.

labour. Thus, if we ignore the exhaustion of his labour-power, he emerges from the process as he entered it, namely as a merely subjective labour-power which must submit itself to the same process once more if it is to survive.

In contrast to this, capital does not emerge from the process as it entered it. It only becomes real capital, value valorizing itself, *in the course* of the process. It now exists as capital realized in the form of the aggregate product, and as such, as the property of the capitalist, it now confronts labour once more as an autonomous power even though it was created by that very labour. Hence the process does not reproduce just capital, but also the product. Previously, the conditions of production confronted the worker as capital only in the sense that he *found* them existing as *autonomous* beings opposed to himself. What he now finds so opposed to him is the product of his own labour. What had been the premiss is now the result of the process of production.

To say that the process of production creates *capital* is, to that extent, just another way of saying that it has created *surplus-value*.

But the matter does not rest there. The surplus-value is changed back into additional capital; it manifests itself as the formation of new capital or of enlarged capital. Hence *capital* has created *capital*; it has not just realized itself as capital. The *process of accumulation* is itself an intrinsic feature of the capitalist process of production. It entails the *new creation of wage-labourers*, of the means to realize and increase the available amount of capital. It does this either by extending its rule to sections of the population not previously subject to itself, such as women or children; or else it subjugates a section of the labouring masses that has accrued through the natural growth of the population. On closer inspection it becomes evident that capital itself *regulates* this production of labour-power, the production of the mass of men it intends to exploit in accordance with its own needs. Hence capital not only produces capital, it produces a growing mass of men, the material through which alone it can function as additional capital. Therefore, it is not only true to say that labour produces on a constantly increasing scale the conditions of labour in opposition to itself in the *form* of *capital*, but equally, capital produces on a steadily increasing scale the productive wage-labourers it requires. Labour produces the conditions of its production in the form of *capital*, and capital produces labour, i.e. as wage-labour, as the means towards its own realization as *capital*. Capitalist production is not merely the reproduction of the relationship: it is its reproduction on a steadily increasing scale. And just as the social productive forces of labour develop in step with the capitalist mode of production, so too the heaped-up wealth confronting the worker grows apace and confronts him as *capital*, as *wealth that controls him*. The world of wealth expands and faces him as an alien world dominating him, and as it does so his subjective poverty, his need and dependence grow larger in proportion. His *deprivation* and its *plenitude* match each other exactly. And at the same time, there is a corresponding increase in the mass of this living means of production of capital: the labouring proletariat.

493   The *growth of capital* and the *increase in the proletariat* appear, therefore, as interconnected – if opposed – *products* of the same process.

This relation is not merely reproduced, it is produced on a steadily more massive scale, so that it creates ever new supplies of workers and encroaches on branches of production previously independent. In addition, as we have seen in our account of the mode of production specific to capitalism, the relation is reproduced in a fashion increasingly favourable to the one side, the capitalists, and increasingly unfavourable to the other side, the wage-labourers.

If we consider the continuity of the process of production, the labourer's wage is only that *part* of the product constantly produced by the worker, who converts it into the means of subsistence and hence into the means for the preservation and increase of the labour-power which capital requires to valorize value for itself, i.e. for its own life-process. The maintenance and increase of labour-power appear therefore merely as the reproduction and extension of its own conditions of reproduction and accumulation. (See the Yankee.)*

This destroys the last vestiges of the *illusion*, so typical of the relationship when considered superficially, that in the circulation process, in the market-place, two equally matched *commodity owners* confront each other, and that they, like all other *commodity owners*, are distinguishable only by the material content of their

* H. C. Carey, in *Principles of Political Economy*, Part I, pp. 76–8.

goods, by the specific use-value of the goods they desire to sell each other. Or in other words, the *original* relation remains intact, but survives only as the *illusory* reflection of the *capitalist* relation underlying it.

There are two distinct features here: the *reproduction of the relation itself* on a steadily increasing scale as the result of the capitalist process of production, and the original form in which it first appears *historically*, and then constantly renews itself on the surface of a developed capitalist society.

(1) *First, with regard to the initial process* within the sphere of circulation, *the sale and purchase of labour-power*.

The capitalist process of production is not just the *conversion* into *capital* of the value or of the commodity which the capitalist partly puts on the market and partly retains within the labour process. On the contrary, these products *transformed* into capital are not *his* products, but the products of the worker. He constantly sells him a portion of his product – the necessities of life for his labour – in order to maintain and increase the labour-power, i.e. the purchaser himself. And he borrows from him in return another portion of his product, the objective conditions of labour, as *capital*, as the means whereby capital can valorize itself. Thus, while the worker produces his produce as *capital*, the capitalist reproduces the worker as a *wage-labourer* and hence as the vendor of his labour. The relation of people who merely sell commodities is that they exchange *their own labour* objectified in different use-values. However, the sale and purchase of labour-power, as the constant result of the capitalist process of production, implies that the worker must constantly *buy back* a portion of his own produce in exchange for his living labour. This *dispels* the illusion that we are concerned here merely with *relations between commodity owners*. This constant sale and purchase of labour-power, and the constant entrance of the commodity produced by the worker himself as *buyer of* his labour-power and as constant capital, appear merely as *forms which mediate* his subjugation by capital. Living labour is no more than the means of maintaining and increasing the *objective* labour and making it independent of him. This form of mediation is intrinsic to this mode of production. It perpetuates the relation between capital as the buyer and the worker as the seller of labour. It is a form, however, which can be distinguished only formally from other more direct forms of the enslavement of labour and the *ownership of it* as perpetrated by the owners of the means of production. Through the mediation of this sale and purchase it *disguises* the real transaction, and the perpetual dependence which is constantly renewed, by presenting it as nothing more than a financial relationship. Not only are the conditions of this *commerce* constantly reproduced, but the object which the one must sell and which the other uses in order to buy 494 are themselves the result of the process. The constant renewal of the relationship of *sale and purchase* merely ensures the perpetuation of the specific relationship of dependency, endowing it with the deceptive *illusion* of a transaction, of a contract between equally free and equally matched *commodity owners*. This *initial* relationship itself now appears as an integral feature of the rule of objectified labour over living labour that is created in capitalist production.

It follows that two widely held views are in error:

There are firstly those who consider that wage-labour, the sale of labour to the capitalist and hence the *wage form*, is something only *superficially* characteristic of capitalist production. It is, however, one of the *essential* mediating forms of capitalist relations of production, and one constantly reproduced by those relations themselves.

Secondly, there are those who regard this superficial relation, this *essential formality*, this *deceptive appearance* of capitalist relations as its true *essence*. They therefore imagine that they can give a true account of those relations by classifying both workers and capitalists as *commodity owners*. They thereby gloss over the essential nature of the relationship, extinguishing its *differentia specifica*.

(2) For capitalist relations to establish themselves at all presupposes that a certain historical level of social production has been attained. Even within the framework of an earlier mode of production certain needs and certain means of communication and production must have developed which go beyond the old relations of production and coerce them into the capitalist mould. But for the time being they need to be developed only to the point that permits the formal subsumption of labour under capital. On the basis of that change, however, specific changes in the mode of production are introduced which create new forces of production, and these in turn influence the mode of production so that new real

conditions come into being. Thus a complete economic revolution is brought about. On the one hand, it creates the real conditions for the domination of labour by capital, perfecting the process and providing it with the appropriate framework. On the other hand, by evolving conditions of production and communication and productive forces of labour antagonistic to the workers involved in them, this revolution creates the real premises of a new mode of production, one that abolishes the contradictory form of capitalism. It thereby creates the material basis of a newly shaped social process and hence of a new social formation.

The view outlined here diverges sharply from the one current among bourgeois economists imprisoned within capitalist ways of thought. Such thinkers do indeed realize how production takes place *within* capitalist relations. But they do not understand how these *relations* are themselves produced, together with the material preconditions of their dissolution. They do not see, therefore, that their *historical justification* as a *necessary form* of economic development and of the production of social wealth may be undermined. Unlike them, we have seen both how capital produces, and how it is itself produced, and we have seen also how it emerges from the process of production as something essentially different from the way it entered into it. On the one hand, it transforms the existing mode of production; on the other hand, this change in the mode of production, the particular stage reached in the evolution of the material forces of production, is itself the basis and precondition – the premiss of its own formation.

95 RESULTS OF THE IMMEDIATE PROCESS OF PRODUCTION

It is not just the objective conditions of the process of production that appear as its result. The same thing is true also of its *specific social* character. The social relations and therefore the social position of the agents of production in relation to each other, i.e. the *relations of production*, are themselves produced: they are also the constantly renewed result of the process.*

---

*The text of the manuscript breaks off at this point. What follows now are isolated fragments which were evidently meant to be revised and incorporated in the present version. We print them in the arbitrary order that results from following Marx's own pagination, which contains lacunae of considerable magnitude. Titles in square brackets have been added by the present editor.

IV: [ISOLATED FRAGMENTS]

[THE SALE OF LABOUR-POWER AND THE TRADE UNIONS]

24 [temporary control over] his labour-power. By the time his labour actually begins it has already ceased to belong to the worker and as a result can no longer be *sold* by him.

In consequence of the peculiar nature of this particular commodity, namely labour-power, the commodity sold only passes into the hands of the purchaser* as a use-value after the conclusion of the contract between buyer and seller. Its exchange-value, like that of every other commodity, is determined before it goes into circulation, since it is sold as a capacity, a power, and a specific amount of labour-time was required to produce this capacity, this power. The exchange-value of this commodity existed, therefore, before its sale, while its use-value consists only in the subsequent expression of its power. That is to say, the alienation of the power and its actual expression, i.e. its existence as a use-value, do not coincide in time. It is the same as with a house whose use has been sold to me for a month. In such a case the use-value has been transferred to me only when I have lived there for a month. In the same way, the use-value of labour-power is transferred to me only after I have used it up, i.e. after I have caused it to work for me. However, where the formal alienation of the commodity through sale does not coincide in time with the real transfer of its use-value to the purchaser, the buyer's money functions as we have seen in the first instance as a *means of payment*. The labour-power is *sold* for a day, a week, etc., but it is *paid for* only after it has been consumed for a day or a week, etc. In all countries where capitalist relations are in the process of development, labour-power is only *paid for* after it has been used up. As a rule, then, the worker *advances* the use of his commodity to the capitalist. He permits its consumption by the buyer, he allows him *credit*, before he receives its exchange-value in payment. At times of crisis and even in the event of individual bankruptcies we can see that, because of the special nature of the use-value sold, the idea that the worker constantly gives credit to the capitalist is no empty delusion.[31]†

31. *'L'ouvrier* prête *son industrie'* ['The worker *lends* his industry'] (Storch, *Cours d'économie politique*, St Petersburg edition, 1815, Vol. 2, p. 36).

*The MS. had 'vendor'.

† The above paragraph was included in *Capital*, along with n. 31. See above, p. 278.

However, whether money is used as a means of purchase or a means of payment is immaterial to the nature of commodity exchange itself. The price of labour-power is fixed contractually in the purchase even though it is only realized later. Nor does this form of payment influence the fact that the price pertains to the *value of the labour-power* and is unrelated either to the *value of the product* or to the *value of the labour* which as such is not a commodity at all.

As has been shown, the *exchange-value* of labour-power is paid for when the price paid is that of the means of subsistence that is customarily held to be essential in a given state of society to enable the worker to exert his labour-power with the necessary degree of strength, health, vitality, etc. and to perpetuate himself by producing replacements for himself.[32]

However, Storch adds slyly 'he *risks nothing*' but 'perdre son salaire ... *l'ouvrier ne transmet* rien de matériel' ['*to lose his wages* ... the working man transmits *nothing material*'] (ibid., p. 37). 'All labour is paid after it has ceased' (*An Inquiry into Those Principles, Respecting the Nature of Demand, etc.*, London, 1821, p. 104). Other practical consequences arising from this mode of payment, which is incidentally founded in the nature of the relationship, cannot detain us here. However, one example may be in place. In London there are two sorts of bakers, the 'full-priced' who sell bread at its *full price* and the *undersellers* who sell it at *less*. The latter comprise more than ¾ of all bakers (report of the Government Commissioner, H. S. Tremenheere, on the *Grievances Complained of by the Journeymen Bakers, etc.*, London, 1862, p. xxxii). These 'undersellers' mostly sell bread adulterated with alum, soap, pearl-ashes, chalk, Derbyshire stone-dust, etc. (Vide the above-mentioned Blue Book, and also the *Report of the Committee of 1855 on the Adulteration of Bread* and C. Hassall's *Adulterations Detected*, 2nd edn, London, 1861.) Sir John Gordon stated before the Committee of 1855 that because of these adulterations 'the poor men who lived on 2 lb. of bread a day did not take in one-fourth of that amount of nutrition', to say nothing of the 'deleterious effects on health'. Tremenheere explains (ibid., p. xlviii) why 'a very large part of the working class' accepted the alum, stone-dust, etc., although they were aware of the adulteration: he points out that for them it was 'a matter of necessity to take from their baker, or from the chandler's shop such bread as they choose to supply'. Since they receive their wages only at the end of the week they can 'only pay for the week's supply to the family at the week's end'. And Tremenheere adds, citing the testimony of eye-witnesses, that 'it is notorious that *bread composed of those mixtures, is made expressly for sale in this manner*'.

32. *Petty* defines the value of the daily working wage as the value of the 'daily food' sufficient for the worker 'so as to live, labour and generate' (*Political Anatomy of Ireland*, London, 1672, edn of 1691, p. 64. Quoted

Man is distinguished from all other animals by the limitless and flexible nature of his needs. But it is equally true that no animal is able to restrict his needs to the same unbelievable degree and to reduce the conditions of his life to the absolute minimum. In a word, there is no animal with the same talent for 'Irishing' himself. Such a reduction to the bare *physical minimum* is not at issue when we are discussing the *value* of labour-power. As with every commodity so it is true of labour-power that its price can rise *above* its value or fall *beneath* it, i.e. its value can deviate in either direction from the price, which is only the monetary expression of its value. The level of the necessaries of life whose total value

25

---

from Dureau de la Malle). 'The price of labour is always constituted of the price of necessaries.' The worker does not receive the corresponding wage 'whenever the price of necessaries is such, that the labouring man's wages will not, *suitably* to his low rank and station, as a labouring man, support *such a family* as is often the lot of many of them to have' (Jacob Vanderlint, *Money Answers All Things*, London, 1734, p. 15).

'*Le simple ouvrier, qui n'a que ses bras et son industrie, n'a* rien *qu'autant qu'il parvient à vendre à d'autres sa peine* ... *En tout genre de travail* il doit arriver et il arrive en effet, *que le salaire de l'ouvrier se borne à ce qui lui est nécessaire pour lui procurer sa subsistance'* ['This simple worker, with only his limbs and his industry, has *only* what he manages to sell his labour for. For every kind of labour *it must result, and it does in fact result*, that what he receives is limited to the sum necessary for his means of subsistence.'] (Turgot, *Réflexions sur la formation et la distribution des Richesses* (1766), *Œuvres*, Vol. 1, p. 10, ed. Daire, Paris, 1844).

'The price of the necessaries of life is, in fact, the cost of producing labour' (Malthus, *Inquiry into, etc. Rent*, London, 1815, p. 48, note). 'Another inference we may draw from a review comparing the price of corn and the wages of labour since the reign of Edward III, is that during the course of nearly 500 years, the earnings of a day's labour in this country have probably been more frequently below than above a peck of wheat (= $\frac{1}{4}$ bushel); that a peck of wheat may be considered as something like a middle point, or a point rather above the middle, about which the corn wages of labour, varying according to the demand and supply, have oscillated' (Malthus, *Principles of Political Economy*, 2nd edn, London, 1836, p. 254).

'The natural price of any article is that ... bestowed upon its production ... Its' (labour's) 'natural price ... consists of such a quantity of the necessaries and comforts of life, as, from the nature of the climate and the habits of the country, are necessary to support the labourer, and to enable him to rear such a family as may preserve, *in the market*, an undiminished supply of labour ... The natural price of labour ... though it varies under different climates, and with the different stages of national improvement, may, in any given time and place, be regarded as very nearly stationary' (R. Torrens, *An Essay on the External Corn Trade*, London, 1815, pp. 55–65 passim).

constitutes the value of labour-power can itself rise or fall. The analysis of these variations, however, belongs not here but in the theory of wages.[33] It will become apparent in the course of these discussions that for the analysis of capital it is a matter of complete indifference whether the level of the worker's needs is assumed to be high or low. In practice, as in theory, the point of departure is the *value* of labour-power regarded as a *given quantity*. Thus, for example, the owner of money who desires to convert his money into capital, let us say into the industrial capital of a cotton factory, will inquire above all into the average wages paid in the locality where he intends to set up his factory. He knows full well that wages, like cotton, continually diverge from that average, but he knows too that these variations cancel each other out. For this reason wages enter his calculations as a *given value*. On the other hand, the *value of labour-power* constitutes the conscious and explicit foundation of the *trade unions*, whose importance for the English working class can scarcely be overestimated. The *trade unions* aim at nothing less than to prevent the *reduction of wages* below the level that is traditionally maintained in the various branches of industry. That is to say, they wish to prevent the *price* of labour-power from falling below its *value*. They are aware, of course, that if there is a change in the relations of supply and demand, this results in a change in the market price. But on the one hand this change is a very different thing from the one-sided claim of the buyer, in this case the capitalists, that such a change has taken place. And on the other hand, there is 'a great distinction between the level of wages as determined by supply and demand, i.e. by the level produced by the fair operation of exchange that exists when buyer and seller *negotiate on equal terms*, and the level of wages which the seller, the labourer, must put up with when the capitalist negotiates with each man *singly*, and dictates a reduction

33. 'When corn forms a part of the subsistence of the labourer, an increase in its natural price necessarily occasions an increase in the natural price of labour; or, in other words, when it requires a greater quantity of labour to procure subsistence, a greater quantity of labour, or of its produce, must remain with the labourer, as his wages. But, as a greater quantity of his labour, or (what is the same thing) of the produce of his labour, becomes necessary to the subsistence of the labouring manufacturer, and is consumed by him while at work, a smaller quantity of the productions of labour will remain with the employer' (R. Torrens, *An Essay on the External Corn Trade*, 1815, pp. 325, 236). [Marx marked this passage as a footnote to a now lost p. 244; we have inserted it here, where it seems apposite.]

by exploiting the chance need of individual workers (which exists independently of the general relations of supply and demand). The workers *combine* in order to achieve *equality* of a sort with the capitalist in their *contract concerning the sale of their labour*. This is the *rationale* (the logical basis) of the *trade unions*.'[34] What they purpose is that 'the accidental immediate neediness of a labourer should not compel him to make do with a smaller wage than supply and demand has *already* established in a particular branch of labour'[35] and thus depress the *value* of labour-power in a particular area below its customary level. The *value* of labour-power is 'regarded by the workers themselves as the *minimum wage* and by the capitalist as the *uniform rate of wages* for all workers in the same trade'.[36] For this reason the unions never allow their members to work for *less* than this minimum.[37] They are insurance societies formed by the workers themselves. An example may explain the purpose of these combinations formed by the workers

34. T. J. Dunning (Secretary to the London Consolidated Society of Bookbinders), *Trades' Unions and Strikes: Their Philosophy and Intention*, London, 1860, pp. 6, 7.

35. ibid., p. 7.

36. ibid., p. 17.

37. It is obvious that the capitalists will denounce this *'uniform rate of labour'* as an attack on the personal freedom of the worker, as an obstacle which prevents the capitalists from following the promptings of their hearts and rewarding a special talent with a special wage. Mr Dunning, whose book, just cited, not only hits the nail on the head but also treats the subject with an apt turn of irony, retorts that the trade unions are happy to permit the capitalist 'to pay for superior skill, or working ability, as much more as he pleases', but would prevent him from depressing 99/100 of the mass of wages, i.e. the wages of 'the common run of men', the average worker in each trade, beneath the *'minimum wage'*. That is to say, they would prevent him from reducing the normal value of average labour-power. It is of course quite in order when the combinations of workers against the despotism of capital are denounced by an Edinburgh Reviewer (Concerning the Combinations of Trade, 1860)* as a slavery which these free-born Englishmen submit to in consequence of incomprehensible delusion. In war it is always desirable for an enemy to refuse to subject itself to the despotism of discipline. The morally indignant Reviewer uncovers even more odious facts. The trade unions are a *sacrilege* for they offend against the laws of *free trade*! *Quelle horreur*! Mr Dunning replies *inter alia*: 'It would not be a *free exchange* of blows if one of the parties were to have one arm disabled or tied down, while the other had the free use of both ... the employer wishes to deal with his men singly, so that he, whenever he pleases, may give the "sweaters" price for their labour;

*This is in fact a reference to the article 'Secret Organization of Trades' which appeared in No. 224 of the *Edinburgh Review* (October 1859).

for the protection of the *value* of their labour-power. In all branches of trade in London there are so-called 'sweaters'. A *sweater* is someone who undertakes to deliver a certain quantity of work at normal prices to an entrepreneur, but who then has it carried out for a lower price by others. The difference, which goes to make up his profit, is *sweated out* of the workers who actually perform the labour[38] and represents nothing but the difference between the *value* of the labour-power that is *paid* by the first entrepreneur and the price which is equivalent to *less than* the value of that labour-power and which is paid by the *sweater* to the actual workers.[39]

Incidentally, it is a highly characteristic*...

*

259   The form of *piece wages* is used for example in the English potteries to engage young apprentices (in their thirteenth year) at a low rate so that they overwork themselves 'for the great benefit of their masters' in the very period of their own development. This is given officially as one of the reasons for the degeneration of the population in the pottery factories.[40]

---

their right arm as bargainers being tied down by their necessities in its sale. This he calls *free trade*, but the freedom is all on his own side. Call it *trade*, if you will, it is not free *exchange*' (op. cit., p. 47).

38. ibid., p. 6.

39. 'A philanthropic association has been formed in London for the purpose of contracting to deliver military clothing at prices identical with those paid at present to contractors by the government, while paying the starving semp-stresses an extra 30 per cent on top of their present wages. This result is achieved by eliminating the "middleman" whose profits will go to the human material from which he has hitherto carved them. With all the benefits that the associa-tion can afford, a sempstress cannot earn more than 1 shilling for 10 hours' uninterrupted work on military shirts, namely at a rate of two shirts per day, and in the case of other articles of clothing not more than 1s. 6d. a day, for a day of 12 hours' work. At the present time their wages vary from 5d. to 8d. for 10 hours' work, for which moreover they have to supply their own yarn, etc.' (*The Times*, 13 March 1860).

40. 'There are, in the employ of the manufacturer, many youths who are taken as apprentices at the early ages of 13 and 14 as flat-ware pressers and hollow-ware pressers. For the first two years they are paid weekly wages of 2s. to 3s. 6d. per week. After that they begin to work on the *piece-work system,*

---

*At this point the MS. of p. 25 breaks off.

The raising of the overall wage (the weekly wage, for example) frequently occurs in branches of industry where piece-work has been freshly introduced. But as soon as it has reached a certain rate, this rise which has been brought about by the increased intensity of labour becomes itself a reason for the masters to reduce wages, since they regard them as higher than is good for the worker. Piece-work as a means for depressing wages is to be denounced directly.[41]

It must be made perfectly clear that the way *in which* wages are paid out does not affect the situation in the least, although one mode of payment may well favour the development of the capitalist process of production more than another and we may note in passing that the technical nature of the process may sometimes permit only one or the other mode.

It is clear that *individual* variations in wages, variations which have greater scope in wages by piece than in wages by time, are only deviations from the level of wages in general. However, wages by the piece if not prevented by other circumstances tend to depress the general level.*

Wages as the *aggregate price* of the average daily labour contradict the concept of value. Every price must be reducible to *value*, since the price is in itself nothing but the monetary expression of value and the fact that actual prices may stand above or below the price corresponding to their value does not alter the fact that they are a quantitatively incongruent expression of the value of the commodity – even if in the situation assumed they may be *quantitatively*

---

earning journeymen's wages. "The practice," as Longe says, "of employing a great number of apprentices and taking them at the age of 13 and 14 is very common in a certain class of manufactories, a practice which is not only very prejudicial to the interests of the trade, but is probably another great cause to which the *bad constitutions of the potters are to be attributed.* This system, *so advantageous to the employer*, who requires quantity rather than quality of goods, tends directly to encourage the young potter *greatly to overwork himself* during the four or five years during which he is employed on the piece-work system, but at low wages." The consequences of over-work in the hot stoves at that early age may readily be anticipated' (*Children's Employment Commission, First Report*, London, 1863, p. xiii).

41. 'Indeed, the main objection in different trades to *working by the piece*, is the complaint that, when men are found to earn good wages at it, the *employer wishes to reduce the price* of the work, and that *it is so often made use of as a means of reducing wages*' (Dunning, op. cit., p. 22).

---

*This paragraph is crossed through once in the MS.

too great or too small. But here in the *price of labour* the lack of congruence is *qualitative*.

60   Since the value of a commodity equals the necessary labour it contains, then the value of a day's labour – a day's labour performed under adequate conditions of production and with the average *normal* social measure of intensity and skill – would be equal to the day's labour contained in it, which is nonsense and affords no definition. The *value of labour* – i.e. the price of labour (qualitatively) stripped of its monetary expression – is then an irrational expression and in fact is no more than a disguised and inverted form for the *value of labour-power*. (*Price* which is not reducible to *value*, whether immediately or through a series of mediations, expresses a merely accidental exchange of something for money. In this way articles which are not *commodities* in themselves, and which therefore are in this sense *extra commercium hominum*,* may be converted into commodities by being exchanged for money. Hence the connection between venality and corruption and the money relationship. Since money is the transformed shape of the commodity it does not reveal what has been transformed into it: whether conscience or virginity or horse dung.)

But just as irrational as time-wages, the most immediate form of wages, are piece-wages, which are supposed to be the immediate expression of a value relationship. For example, suppose that one hour's labour, equal to 6d., let us say, is objectified in a piece of a given commodity (setting aside the constant capital it contains). The worker receives 3d., since otherwise the *value of this piece* is not determined *vis-à-vis* the worker by the *value* contained in it as measured by the labour-time consumed. In fact, therefore, this piece-wage does not express any value relationship *directly*. The point, therefore, is not to measure the value of the piece by the amount of labour-time contained in it. On the contrary, the necessary labour-time performed by the worker must be measured by the piece. *The wage the worker receives*, therefore, *is a time-wage*, since the piece only has the task of measuring the time for which he receives his wages and of acting as a guarantee that he uses only *necessary labour time*, i.e. that he has worked at the right intensity and that his labour (as a use-value) is of the appropriate quality. *Piece-wages*, then, are nothing but a *specific form* of time-wages, which in their turn are nothing but the disguised form of the

*'Outside human commerce'.

value of labour-power, alternatively of the *price of labour-power* corresponding quantitatively to or deviating from that value. If it is true that piece-wages tend to leave great scope for the individual worker to rise more or less above the general level, then it is no less true that they reduce the wages of other workers below that level and that the level itself tends to fall as a result of the extremely intense competition among the workers that piece-wages inspire.

In a comparison between the time-wages in different countries (i.e. the wage for a working day of given length), in so far as the intensity of labour is measured – other things being equal – by the mass of the product yielded by the worker in a given time, one must at the same time compare these wages in terms of piece rates. This is the only way to discover the true relation between necessary and surplus labour, or between wages and surplus-value. It will then often turn out that although the apparent time-wages are higher in rich countries, piece-wages are higher in poorer ones. Hence, in the latter, the worker requires a greater portion of the working day to reproduce his salary than in the former, i.e. the rate of surplus-value is smaller in the latter than the former and the relative wage is therefore greater. So in fact the real price of labour is higher in poor countries than in rich ones. Looking at various nations we find that, apart from the duration and the productivity independent of the individual worker, there is as great a variation in the intensity as in the duration of the working day. The more intensive national working day may be equated to the less intensive one $+x$. If we take the working day of the countries that produce gold and silver as the standard of the international working day, then the more intensive English working day of 12 hours can be expressed in more gold than the less intensive Spanish day. That is to say, it will stand higher in comparison to the medium working day as expressed in terms of gold and silver. A higher national working wage, assuming an aggregate day of fixed length, will stand higher then, both in terms of use-value and of exchange-value, and hence also in terms of its monetary expression. (Assuming a given value in gold and silver, a higher monetary expression must always express more value, and a lower, less: looking at the money-wages of workers in different countries *simultaneously*, the *value of gold and silver* is assumed to be constant as even a change in their value would mean a simultaneous change for all the nations concerned, so that as far as their relative positions are concerned *no* change occurs at all.) The fact of a higher national wage, then, does not imply a higher *price for labour* as the price of a certain amount of labour. Given the greater duration of work, or, what amounts to the same thing internationally, a greater intensity of labour, the wage can be higher in one country than another, but it may firstly occupy a smaller portion of the aggregate day, i.e. be smaller relatively speaking, and secondly it may represent a lower *price*. For example, if the worker receives 3s. daily for 12 hours' work, this is less than if his day's wages were 2½s. for 11 hours. For the one hour of surplus labour involves far more wear and tear, i.e. a speedier reproduction of labour-power. The difference would be even greater in the event of his receiving 2½s. for 10 and 3 for* . . .

[DIFFERENT MODES OF CENTRALIZATION OF THE MEANS OF PRODUCTION IN DIFFERENT COUNTRIES]

379 'Although skill and mechanical science may do much, the preponderance of the *vital element is essential in the extension of manufactures.* The system of *morcellement,*† in preventing a rapid development of the population, has thus tended indirectly to retard the extension of manufactures. It has also had that effect in a direct manner. It has retained a large population attached to and occupied upon the soil. The cultivation of the soil is their primary occupation – the one which they follow with pride and contentment. Their employment in spinning, weaving and the like is but a subsidiary one necessary for their support. Their savings are hoarded for the purpose of increasing their inheritance and they are not prone to wander from home in search of fresh occupation or new habits.' (So precisely here – where saving equals hoarding, and still exists to a relatively high degree and is able to exist under the given circumstances – the *formation of capital*, relatively speaking, and the *development of capitalistic* production are prevented in comparison to England, by the very same economical conditions that are favourable to hoarding, etc.) 'The position of a proprietor, the possession of a house, of a plot of ground, is the chief object also of the factory operative, and of almost every poor

_____
*Pages 261 and 262 are missing. In their place is a sheet numbered 379, titled as shown, which in subject-matter follows on more or less naturally from the preceding text.
†'Parcellation'.

man who has not already a property; in fact, all look to the land . . .
From this description of the character and occupations of a very
numerous class of the French people, it will be readily inferred that
unlike that of England, the manufacturing industry of France is
represented by small establishments,' (this shows how necessary
the expropriation of land is for the development of large-scale
industry) 'some moved by steam and water, many dependent for
their moving power upon animal labour and many factories still
entirely employing manual labour only. The *characteristic of
French industry* is well described by Baron C. Dupin, as *consequent
upon the system of the tenure of land*. He says: "As France is the
country of divided properties, that of small holdings, so it is the
country of the division of industry, and of small workshops" ' (*Reports of Inspectors of Factories . . . 31 October 1855*, pp. 67–8).
The same factory inspector (A. Redgrave) provides a survey (for
1852) of French textile manufactures of whatever importance from
which it appears that the source of power employed was as follows:
steam 2,053 (h.p.), water 959 and other mechanical power 2,057
(ibid., p. 69).[42] He compares this return with the return of the
number of factories, etc., presented to the House of Commons in
1850 and uses them to show 'the following remarkable difference
between the system of textile manufacture of England and France'.
The result is as follows:

380   'The *number* of factories in France is *three times as large* as
those in England, while the number of persons employed in them
is only $\frac{1}{2}$ greater; but the very different proportions of machinery
and moving power will best be shown by the following comparison:

42. What appears as the preliminary (primitive) accumulation of capital is
in reality only the process by which the conditions of production become
independent – they break loose from the self-employing producer who is
transformed into a wage-labourer. In the text this is shown in the case of
manufacturing. But it is also evident, for example, in the relations between the
farming capitalist and the peasant etc. *'La grande culture n'exige pas une
plus grande masse de capitaux que la petite ou la moyenne culture; elle en
exige moins au contraire,* but in these different systems capital must be vari-
ously distributed; *dans la grande culture les capitaux appliqués à l'agriculture
doivent se trouver entre les mains d'un petit nombre d'hommes qui salarient les
bras qu'ils emploient'* ['Large-scale agriculture does not require a greater
amount of capital than cultivation on a small or medium scale. On the
contrary, it requires less . . . in large-scale agriculture the capital sums invested must be retained in the hands of a small number of men who pay the
wages of the men they employ'] (Mathieu de Dombasle, *Annales agricoles de
Roville*, 2-ème livraison, 1825, p. 218).

	France	England	
Number of factories	12,986	4,330	
Number of persons employed	706,450	596,082	In fact the figures for France include as factories what would not be counted as such in England
Average number of persons in each factory	54	137	
Average number of spindles to each person employed	7	43	i.e. six times as many in England as in France
Average number of persons to each loom	2 (power and handloom)	2 (powerloom only)	

Hence there are in France *more* people employed than in England but only because all handloom weaving is excluded in the English return. But in the average establishment there are more than twice as many people than in France ($\frac{54}{136} = \frac{27}{68} = \frac{13}{34} =$ almost $\frac{1}{3}$), i.e. there is a much larger number of people brought together under the command of the same capital. In France there are three times as many factories, but only $\frac{1}{5}$ more people employed in them, i.e. *fewer* persons in proportion to the *number of establishments*. Furthermore, with regard to the mass of machinery falling to each person, there are six times as many spindles in England as in France. If all the persons employed were spinners there would be 4,945,150 spindles in France and in England $\frac{1}{5}$ fewer. So in England there is one power loom between two people, in France one power or one handloom. Thus in England there are 25,631,526 spindles. Furthermore, the steam power employed in factories of Great Britain = 108,113 h.p., the proportion of persons employed about $5\frac{1}{2}$ persons to each horse-power of steam; the proportions in France upon this estimate should give a steam power = 128,409 h.p. whereas the *whole* of the steam power of France was only = 75,518 h.p. in 1852, produced by 6,080 steam-engines, of an average power of less than $12\frac{1}{2}$ h.p. each; while the number of steam-engines employed in the textile

Persons   596,082
                  43
         _____
         1 788 246
         2 384 328
         _____
         25,631,526

factories of France appears to have been 2,053 in 1852 and the power of those engines to be equal to 20,282 h.p., distributed as follows:

		Factories	Horse-power
Employed in	spinning only	1,438	16,494
,, ,,	weaving only	101	1,738
,, ,,	finishing etc.	242	612
,, . ,,	other processes	272	1,438
		2,053	20,282

(ibid., p. 70).

'The absence in France of the bones and sinews of manufactures, coal and iron, must ever retard her progress as a manufacturing country' (ibid.).

For each worker in an English factory, compared to the Frenchmen, there is far more machinery for working and also far more power-driving machinery (mechanic power), and hence, too, far more raw materials are processed by him in the *same* time. The productive power of his labour is, therefore, much greater, as is the capital that employs him. The number of establishments is much smaller in England than in France. The number of working men employed on the average, in one single establishment, is much greater in England than in France, although the total number employed in France is greater than England, although in a small proportion only, compared to the number of establishments.

It becomes quite plain to see here that because of historical and other circumstances which have had a varying effect upon the *relative magnitude of the concentration of the means of production,* there is a correspondingly greater or smaller *expropriation* of the mass of immediate producers. In the same way, there is a very different development of the forces of production and of the *capitalist mode of production* in general. And this stands in inverse ratio to the 'saving' and 'hoarding' of the immediate producer himself, which in France is huge in comparison with England. The scale on which the surplus labour of the producers can be 'saved' and 'hoarded' and 'accumulated' and brought together in greater masses, i.e. *concentrated*, can be used as capital, corresponds exactly to the degree in which their surplus labour is hoarded, etc., by their employers instead of by themselves; it corresponds, therefore, to the degree in which the great mass of the real producers is precluded from the capacity and the conditions of 'saving', 'hoarding', 'accumulating', is, in one word, precluded from all power of appropriating its own surplus labour to any important degree, because of its more or less complete *expropriation* from its *means of production*. Capitalist accumulation and concentration are based upon, and correspond to, the facility of *appropriating other people's surplus labour in great masses* and the corresponding inability of these people themselves to lay any claim to their own surplus labour. It is, therefore, the most ludicrous delusion, fallacy or imposture to explain and account for this capitalist accumulation by confounding it with, and, as far as the phraseology is concerned, converting it into, a process quite its opposite, exclusive of it, and corresponding to a mode of production upon whose ruins alone capitalist production can be reared. This is one of the delusions carefully nurtured by Political Economy. The truth is this, that in this bourgeois society every workman, if he is an exceedingly clever and shrewd fellow, and gifted with bourgeois instincts and favoured by an exceptional fortune, can possibly be converted himself into an *exploiteur du travail d'autrui*.* But where there was no *travail* to be *exploité*, there would be no capitalist nor capitalist production.

*

75.† In fact Ricardo consoles the workers by saying that, as a result of the mounting productivity of labour, the increase in the aggregate capital grows as opposed to its variable part, and so does the part of the surplus-value that is consumed as revenue. There is accordingly an increased demand for menial servants. (Ricardo, *Principles*, p. 473.)

76. 'Property ... is essential to preserve the common unskilled worker from falling into the condition of a piece of machinery, bought at the *minimum* market price at which it can be produced, that is at which labourers can be got to exist and propagate their species, to which he is *invariably* reduced sooner or later, when the interests of capital and labour are quite distinct, and are left to adjust themselves under the sole operation of the law of supply and demand' (Samuel Laing, *National Distress*, London, 1844, p. 46).

*'Exploiter of others' labour'.
† This number and the following ones are not page numbers but refer instead to indented footnotes which form the rest of the text. The pages on which they are to be found are not paginated.

IRELAND. EMIGRATION

77. In so far as the real increase or decrease of the working population could exert any perceptible influence on the labour market
over the ten-year industrial cycle, this could happen only in
England and we therefore take it as our model. For the capitalist
mode of production is fully developed in England, unlike on the
Continent, where it still functions on the foundations of an agricultural economy alien to it. We may therefore consider in isolation
the influence which the need of capital to expand exercises upon
the expansion or contraction of emigration. We should begin by
noting that the emigration of capital, i.e. of that part of annual
revenue which is invested abroad, particularly in the colonies and
the United States of America, is far greater in proportion to the
annual accumulation fund than is the number of emigrants in
proportion to the annual growth in the population. And indeed a
part does in fact follow the capital abroad. Furthermore, emigration from England consists if we consider its principal part, the
agricultural sector, not of working men, but of tenant-farmers' sons,
etc. Hitherto it was more than made good by immigration from
Ireland. The periods of stagnation and crisis where the impulse
to emigrate is at its height are identical with those periods in which
more surplus capital is sent abroad, and conversely, the periods in
which emigration declines correspond to those where the emigration of surplus capital is in decline. Hence the absolute relation
between labour-power and the capital *employed* in the country is
largely unaffected by the fluctuations in emigration. If emigration
from England were really to swell to serious dimensions in relation
to the annual growth in the population, it would spell the end of its
dominance of the world market. The Irish emigration since 1848
has robbed the Malthusians of all their hopes and expectations. In
the first place, they had declared that an emigration on a scale that
exceeded the growth of the population was an impossibility. The
Irish solved the problem despite their poverty. People who have
already emigrated for the most part send back each year the means
to enable those who are left behind to emigrate in their turn.
Secondly, however, these gentlemen had prophesied that the
famine that carried off a million and the exodus that succeeded it
would have the same effect in Ireland as the Black Death in England in the mid fourteenth century. Exactly the opposite has
occurred. Production has declined faster than the population, and

so have the means of occupying the agricultural labourers, even though their wages are no higher now, if we take the differences in the price of necessaries into account, than they were in 1847. The population, however, has diminished from 8 million to around 4½ million in 15 years. It is true, indeed, that the production of cattle has increased somewhat, and Lord Dufferin, who wishes to transform Ireland into pasture land for sheep, is quite right when he says that the people are still far too numerous. The Irish, meanwhile, take not only their bones to America but also themselves, and the terrible threat of the *Exoriare aliquis ultor** will one day be fulfilled on the other side of the Atlantic.

If we examine the last two years 1864 and 1865 we discover the following figures for the chief crops:

	1864 (qrs)	1865 (qrs)	Decrease
Wheat	875,782	826,783	48,999
Oats	7,826,332	7,659,727	166,605
Barley	761,909	732,017	29,892
Bere	15,160	13,989	1,171
Potatoes	4,312,388	3,865,990	446,398
Turnips	3,467,659	3,301,683	165,976
Flax	64,506	39,561	29,945

(The official *Agricultural Statistics of Ireland*, Dublin, 1866, p. 4.)

This does not prevent individuals from enriching themselves at the cost of ruining the country as a whole. For example, the number of persons whose annual income ranged between £900 and £1,000 was 59 in 1864 and 66 in 1865; for those between £1,000 and £2,000, 315 in 1864 and 342 in 1866. Other incomes were as follows:

	1864	1865
Incomes between £3,000–4,000	46	50
£4,000–5,000	19	28
£5,000–10,000	30	44
£10,000–50,000	23	25

And there were three persons each of whom had £87,706 and three each of whom had £91,509 (*Income and Property Tax*

---

* '*Exoriare aliquis nostris ex ossibus ultor*' (Virgil, *Aeneid*, Bk IV, line 625). 'May an avenger one day arise from our bones.'

Returns, 7 August 1866).* Lord Dufferin, who is himself one of the 'supernumeraries', finds, rightly, that Ireland still has far too many inhabitants.

[EXPROPRIATION AND DEPOPULATION IN EASTERN GERMANY DURING THE EIGHTEENTH CENTURY]

'Not until the reign of Frederick II were Prussian subjects (peasants) granted security of tenure and the right to inherit their land in the majority of the provinces of the Kingdom. The decree authorizing this helped put an end to a grievance on the part of the rural population that was threatening to *depopulate* the countryside. For earlier in the (eighteenth) century, ever since the landlords had begun to concentrate their efforts on *raising the yield of their properties*, they found it to their advantage *to drive out many of their subjects and to add their fields to their own estates*. The people thus expropriated, having no home of their own, became destitute; those who remained were now overwhelmed by the burdens imposed on them, since the lords of the manor now required them to till the fields that had formerly been worked by the tenants whose labour had previously greatly facilitated the cultivation of the lords' fields. This process of enclosure, known as "*Bauernlegen*", was especially severe in the *eastern parts of Germany*. When Frederick II conquered Silesia there were many thousands of farms without farmers; the huts lay in ruins, the fields were in the hands of the lords of the manor. *All confiscated land* had to be reorganized, farmers had to be found, cattle and equipment provided and the land redistributed among the peasantry with the right of tenure and to pass the land on to their heirs. In *Rügen*, even during the boyhood of Ernst Moritz Arndt, the same abuses led to uprisings on the part of the rural populace, troops had to be sent, rebels imprisoned: the peasants then sought to avenge themselves, they ambushed individual noblemen and murdered them. Similarly, in the *Electorate of Saxony*, the same abuses led to an uprising as late as 1790' (Gustav Freytag).‡

What the noble feelings of the feudal lords really amounted to was made perfectly clear here!†

* The more detailed analysis of these statistics in *Capital* makes it clear that three persons each received an average of £87,606 in 1864 and an average of £91,509 in 1865. See above, p. 859.

† The text on this page is crossed out with one vertical line.

‡ Freytag, op. cit., pp. 38–9.

[PROPERTY AND CAPITAL]

Although the formation of capital and the capitalist mode of production are essentially founded not merely on the abolition of feudal production but also on the *expropriation of the* peasantry, craftsmen and in general of the mode of production based on the *private ownership by the immediate producer of his conditions of production*; although, once capitalist production has been introduced, it continues to develop at the same rate as that private property and the mode of production based on it is destroyed, so that those immediate producers are expropriated in the name of the *concentration of capital* (centralization); although the subsequent systematic repetition of the process of *expropriation* in the 'clearing of estates' is in part the act of violence that *inaugurates* the capitalist mode of production – although all this is the case, both the *theory of capitalist production* (political economy, philosophy of law, etc.) and the capitalist himself in *his own mind* is pleased to confuse his mode of property and appropriation, which is based on the expropriation of the immediate producer in its origins, and on the acquisition of the labour of others in its further progress, with its opposite: with a mode of production that presupposes that the *immediate producer privately owns his own conditions of production* – a premiss which would actually render capitalist production in agriculture and manufacture, etc. impracticable. In consequence he regards every attack on this latter *form of appropriation* as an attack on the former and indeed as an attack on *property as such*. Not unnaturally, the capitalist always finds it extremely difficult to represent the expropriation of the working masses as the precondition of property based on labour. (Incidentally, in private property of every type the *slavery* of the members of the family at least is always implicit since they are made use of and exploited by the head of the family.) Hence, the general juridical notion from Locke to Ricardo is always that of *petty-bourgeois ownership*, while the relations of production they describe belong to the *capitalist mode of production*. What makes this possible is the relationship of *buyer* and *seller* which *formally* remains the same in both cases. In all these writers the following dualism is apparent:

(1) *Economically* they are opposed to *private property based on labour*; they present the advantages of the *expropriation of the masses* and the *capitalist mode of production*;

(2) *Ideologically* and *juridically* the ideology of private property founded on labour is transferred without more ado to property founded on the *expropriation of the immediate producers*.

79. Thus, for example, the talk of eliminating present burdens by means of government debts which put them on the shoulders of future generations. When B lends A goods either in reality or in appearance, A can give him a promissory note on the *products of the future*, just as there are poets and composers of the future. But A and B together never consume an atom of the produce of the future. Every age must pay its own way. A worker, on the other hand, is able to spend in advance this year the labour of the next three.

'In pretending to stave off the expenses of the present hour to a future day, in pretending that you can burthen posterity to supply the wants of the existing generation', the absurd claim is made 'that you can consume what does not yet exist, that you can feed on provisions before their seeds have been sown in the earth ... All the wisdom of our statesmen will have ended in a great transfer of property from one class of persons to another, in creating an enormous fund for the rewards of jobs and peculation' (Piercy Ravenstone, M.A., *Thoughts on the Funding System and Its Effects*, London, 1824, pp. 8, 9).

THE COLLIERS

73. What the colliers' dependence on the exploiters for their homes means in practice can be seen in any strike. For example, the strike in Durham in November 1863. The people were evicted, wives and children included, in the harshest weather; and their furniture was put into the street. Their first problem then was to find shelter from the cold nights. A large number slept in the open; some broke into their evacuated dwellings and occupied them during the night. The next day the mine-owners had the doors and windows barred and nailed up, to deprive the evicted people of the luxury of sleeping through ice-cold nights on the bare floors of the empty cottages. The people then took refuge in setting up wooden cabins, and wigwams made of peat, but these were torn down by the owners of the fields they had entered. A host of children died or were broken during this campaign of labour against capital. (*Reynolds' Newspaper*, 29 November 1863.)

Quotations in Languages other than English and German

p. 126, n. 6 'La valeur consiste dans le rapport d'échange qui se trouve entre telle chose et telle autre, entre telle mesure d'une production et telle mesure d'une autre.'

p. 130, n. 10 'Toutes les productions d'un même genre ne forment proprement qu'une masse, dont le prix se détermine en général et sans égard aux circonstances particulières.'

p. 133, n. 13 'Tutti i fenomeni dell'universo, sieno essi prodotti della mano dell'uomo, ovvero delle universali leggi della fisica, non ci danno idea di attuale creazione, ma unicamente di una modificazione della materia. Accostare e separare sono gli unici elementi che l'ingegno umano ritrova analizzando l'idea della riproduzione; e tanto è riproduzione di valore' (. . .) 'e di ricchezza se la terra, l'aria e l'acqua ne' campi si trasmutino in grano, come se colla mano dell'uomo il glutine di un insetto si trasmuti in velluto ovvero alcuni pezzetti di metallo si organizzino a formare una ripetizione.'

p. 175, n. 35 'Les économistes ont une singulière manière de procéder. Il n'y a pour eux que deux sortes d'institutions, celles de l'art et celles de la nature. Les institutions de la féodalité sont des institutions artificielles, celles de la bourgeoisie sont des institutions naturelles. Ils ressemblent en ceci aux théologiens, qui eux aussi établissent deux sortes de religions. Toute religion qui n'est pas la leur est une invention des hommes, tandis que leur propre religion est une émanation de dieu. – Ainsi il y a eu l'histoire, mais il n'y en a plus.'

p. 183, n. 6 'I metalli . . . naturalmente moneta.'

p. 184, n. 8 'Il danaro è la merce universale.'

p. 185, n. 10 'L'oro e l'argento hanno valore come metalli anteriore all'essere moneta.'

p. 185, n. 11 'L'argent en' (des denrées) 'est le signe.'

'Comme signe il est attiré par les denrées.'

'L'argent est un signe d'une chose et la représente.'

'L'argent n'est pas simple signe car il est lui-même richesse; il ne représente pas les valeurs, il les équivaut.'

'Qu'aucun puisse ni doive faire doute, que à nous et à notre majesté royale n'appartienne seulement . . . le mestier, le fait, l'état, la provision et toute l'ordonnance des monnaies, de donner tel cours, et pour tel prix comme il nous plaît et bon nous semble.'

p. 194, n. 9 'Le monete le quali oggi sono ideali sono le più antiche d'ogni nazione, e tutte furono un tempo reali, e perchè erano reali con esse si contava.'

p. 196, n. 14 'Ou bien, il faut consentir à dire qu'une valeur d'un million en argent vaut plus qu'une valeur égale en marchandises,' and hence 'qu'une valeur vaut plus qu'une valeur égale'.

p. 203, n. 17 'Toute vente est achat.' 'Vendre est acheter.'

p. 204, n. 18 'Le prix d'une marchandise ne pouvant être payé que par le prix d'une autre marchandise.'

p. 204, n. 19 'Pour avoir cet argent, il faut avoir vendu.'

p. 205, n. 21 'Si l'argent représente, dans nos mains, les choses que nous pouvons désirer d'acheter, il y représente aussi les choses que nous avons vendues pour . . . cet argent.'

p. 206, n. 22 'Il y a donc . . . quatre termes et trois contractants, dont l'un intervient deux fois.'

p. 212, n. 26 'Il' (l'argent) 'n'a d'autre mouvement que celui qui lui est imprimé par les productions.'

p. 215, n. 27 'Ce sont les productions qui le' (l'argent) 'mettent en mouvement et le font circuler . . . La célérité de son mouvement' (i.e. de l'argent) 'supplée à sa quantité. Lorsqu'il en est besoin, il ne fait que glisser d'une main dans l'autre sans s'arrêter un instant.'

p. 221, n. 31 'Si l'on compare la masse de l'or et de l'argent qui est dans le monde, avec la somme des marchandises qui y sont, il est certain que chaque denrée ou marchandise, en particulier, pourra être comparée à une certaine portion . . . de l'autre. Supposons qu'il n'y ait qu'une seule denrée ou marchandise dans le monde, ou qu'il n'y ait qu'une seule qui s'achète, et qu'elle se divise comme l'argent: cette partie de cette marchandise répondra à une partie de la masse de l'argent; la moitié du total de l'une à la moitié du total de l'autre etc. . . . l'établissement du prix des choses dépend toujours fondamentalement de la raison du total des choses au total des signes.'

p. 227, n. 37 'Une richesse en argent n'est que . . . richesse en productions, converties en argent.'

'Une valeur en productions n'a fait que changer de forme.'

p. 230, n. 43 'οὐδὲν γὰρ ἀνθρώποισιν οἷον ἄργυρος κακὸν νόμισμ' ἔβλαστε τοῦτο καὶ πόλεις πορθεῖ, τόδ' ἄνδρας ἐξανίστησιν δόμων. τόδ' ἐκδιδάσκει καὶ παραλλάσσει φρένας χρηστὰς πρὸς αἰσχρὰ πράγμαθ' [ἵστασθαι βροτῶν.]

[πανουργίας δ'ἔδειξεν] ἀνθρώποις ἔχειν καὶ παντὸς ἔργου δυσσέβειαν εἰδέναι.'

p. 230, n. 44 ''Ελπιζούσης τῆς πλεονεξίας ἀνάξειν ἐκ τῶν μυκῶν τῆς γῆς αὐτόν τὸν πλούτωνα.'

p. 231, n. 45 'Accrescere quanto più si può il numero de' venditori d'ogni merce, diminuire quanto più si può il numero dei compratori, questi sono i cardini sui quali si raggirano tutte le operazioni di economia politica.'

p. 239, n. 56 'L'argent . . . est devenu le bourreau de toutes les choses.'
. . . 'alambic qui a fait évaporer une quantité effroyable de biens et de denrées pour faire ce fatal précis.' 'L'argent déclare la guerre . . . à tout le genre humain.'

p. 243, n. 63 'L'argent se partage entre les nations relativement au besoin qu'elles en ont . . . étant toujours attiré par les productions.'

p. 248, n. 2 'Avec de l'argent on achète des marchandises, et avec des marchandises on achète de l'argent.'

p. 251, n. 4 'On n'échange pas de l'argent contre de l'argent.'
'Le commerce est un jeu . . . et ce n'est pas avec des gueux qu'on peut gagner. Si l'on gagnait long-temps en tout avec tous, il faudrait rendre de bon accord les plus grandes parties du profit, pour recommencer le jeu.'

p. 254, n. 8. 'Il mercante non conta quasi per niente il lucro fatto, ma mira sempre al futuro.'

p. 255, n. 11 'Questo infinito che il cose non hanno in progresso, hanno in giro.'

p. 255, n. 12 'Ce n'est pas la matière qui fait le capital, mais la valeur de ces matières.'

p. 260, n. 3 'Que l'une de ces deux valeurs soit argent, ou qu'elles soient toutes deux marchandises usuelles, rien de plus indifférent en soi.'

p. 260, n. 4 'Ce ne sont pas les contractants qui prononcent sur la valeur; elle est décidée avant la convention.'

p. 261, n. 6 'L'échange devient désavantageux pour l'une des parties, lorsque quelque chose étrangère vient diminuer ou exagérer le prix: alors l'égalité est blessée, mais la lésion procède de cette cause et non de l'échange.'

p. 261, n. 7 'L'échange est de sa nature un contrat d'égalité qui se fait de valeur pour valeur égale. Il n'est donc pas un moyen de s'enrichir, puisque l'on donne autant que l'on reçoit.'

p. 262, n. 9 'Dans la société formée il n'y a pas de surabondant en aucun genre.'

p. 263, n. 12 'Si l'on est forcé de donner pour 18 livres une quantité de telle production qui en valait 24, lorsqu'on employera ce même argent à acheter, on aura également pour 18 l. ce que l'on payait 24.'

p. 263, n. 13 'Chaque vendeur ne peut donc parvenir à renchérir habituellement ses marchandises, qu'en se soumettant aussi à payer habituellement plus cher les marchandises des autres vendeurs; et par la même raison, chaque consommateur ne peut . . . payer habituellement moins cher ce qu'il achète, qu'en se soumettant aussi à une diminution semblable sur le prix des choses qu'il vend.'

p. 266, n. 18 'L'échange qui se fait de deux valeurs égales n'augmente ni ne diminue la masse des valeurs subsistants dans la société. L'échange de deux valeurs inégales . . . ne change rien non plus à la somme des valeurs sociales, bien qu'il ajoute à la fortune de l'un ce qu'il ôte de la fortune de l'autre.' 'On n'achète des produits qu'avec des produits.' 'Les productions ne se paient qu'avec des productions.'

p. 278, n. 12 'Le crédit commercial a dû commencer au moment où l'ouvrier, premier artisan de la production, a pu, au moyen de ses économies, attendre le salaire de son travail jusqu'à la fin de la semaine, de la quinzaine, du mois, du trimestre etc.'

p. 278, n. 13 'L'ouvrier prête son industrie' . . . 'de perdre son salaire . . . l'ouvrier ne transmet rien de matériel.'

p. 298, n. 14 'Cette façon d'imputer à une seule chose la valeur de plusieurs autres' (par example au lin la consommation du tisserand), 'd'appliquer, pour ainsi dire, couche sur couche, plusieurs valeurs sur une seule, fait que celle-ci grossit d'autant . . . Le terme d'addition peint très-bien la manière dont se forme le prix des ouvrages de main d'oeuvre; ce prix n'est qu'un total de plusieurs valeurs consommées et additionnées ensemble; or, additionner n'est pas multiplier.'

p. 318, n. 8 'Toutes les productions d'un même genre ne forment proprement qu'une masse, dont le prix se détermine en général et sans égard aux circonstances particulières.'

p. 342, n. 5 'Si le manouvrier libre prend un instant de repos, l'économie sordide qui le suit des yeux avec inquiétude, prétend qu'il la vole.'

p. 430, n. 1 'Le simple ouvrier, qui n'a que ses bras et son industrie, n'a rien qu'autant qu'il parvient à vendre à d'autres sa peine . . . En tout genre de travail il doit arriver et il arrive en effet, que le salaire de l'ouvrier se borne à ce qui lui est nécessaire pour lui procurer la subsistance.'

p. 431, n. 2 'Quando si perfezionano le arti, che non è altro che la scoperta di nuove vie, onde si possa compiere una manufattura con meno gente o (che è lo stesso) in minor tempo di prima.' 'L'économie sur les frais de production ne peut être autre chose que l'économie sur la quantité de travail employé pour produire.'

p. 438, n. 8 'Ces speculateurs si économes du travail des ouvriers qu'il faudrait qu'ils payassent.'

p. 444, n. 8 'On doit encore remarquer que cette division partielle du travail peut se faire quand même les ouvriers sont occupés d'une même besogne. Des maçons par exemple, occupés de faire passer de mains en mains des briques à un échafaudage supérieur, font tous la même besogne, et pourtant il existe parmi eux une espèce de division de travail, qui consiste en ce que chacun d'eux fait passer la brique par un espace donné, et que tous ensemble la font parvenir beaucoup plus promptement à l'endroit marqué qu'ils ne feraient si chacun d'eux portait sa brique séparément jusqu'à l'échafaudage supérieur.'

p. 445, n. 9 'Est-il question d'exécuter un travail compliqué, plusieurs choses doivent être faites simultanément. L'un en fait une pendant que l'autre en fait une autre, et tous contribuent à l'effet qu'un seul homme n'aurait pu produire. L'un rame pendant que l'autre tient le gouvernail, et qu'un troisième jette le filet ou harponne le poisson, et la pêche a un succès impossible sans ce concours.'

p. 447, n. 13 'La forza di ciascuno uomo è minima, ma la riunione delle minime forze forma una forza totale maggiore anche della somma delle forze medesime fino a che le forze per essere riunite possono diminuire il tempo ed accrescere lo spazio della lore azione.'

p. 456, n. 1 '. . . est toute patriarcale; elle emploie beaucoup de femmes et d'enfants, mais sans les épuiser ni les corrompre; elle les laisse dans leurs belles vallées de la Drôme, du Var, de l'Isère, de Vaucluse, pour y élever des vers et dévider leurs cocons; . . . jamais elle n'entre dans une véritable fabrique. Pour être aussi bien observé . . . le principe de la division du travail, s'y revêt d'un caractère spécial. Il y a bien des dévideuses, des moulineurs, des teinturiers, des encolleurs, puis des tisserands; mais ils ne sont pas réunis dans un même établissement, ne dépendent pas d'un même maître; tous ils sont indépendants.'

p. 471, n. 25 'Nous rencontrons chez les peuples parvenus à un certain degré de civilisation trois genres de divisions d'industrie: la première, que nous nommons générale, amène la distinction des producteurs en agriculteurs, manufacturiers et commerçans, elle se rapporte aux trois principales branches d'industrie nationale; la seconde, qu'on pourrait appeler spéciale, est la division de chaque genre d'industrie en espèces . . . la troisième division d'industrie, celle enfin qu'on devrait qualifier de division de la besogne ou du travail proprement dit, est celle qui s'établit dans les arts et les métiers séparés . . . qui s'établit dans la plupart des manufactures et des ateliers.'

p. 477, n. 36 'On peut . . . établir en règle générale, que moins l'autorité préside à la division du travail dans l'intérieur de la société, plus la division du travail se développe dans l'intérieur de l'atelier, et plus elle y est soumise à l'autorité d'un seul. Ainsi l'autorité dans l'atelier et celle dans la société, par rapport à la division du travail, sont en raison inverse l'une de l'autre.'

p. 481, n. 39 'La concentration des instruments de production et la division du travail sont aussi inséparables l'une de l'autre que le sont, dans le régime politique, la concentration des pouvoirs publics et la division des intérêts privés.'

p. 482, n. 42 'L'ouvrier qui porte dans ses bras tout un métier, peut aller partout exercer son industrie et trouver des moyens de subsister: l'autre . . . n'est qu'un accessoire qui, séparé de ses confrères, n'a plus ni capacité, ni indépendance, et qui se trouve forcé d'accepter la loi qu'on juge à propos de lui imposer.'

p. 486, n. 54 'Ciascuno prova coll'esperienza, che applicando la mano e l'ingegno sempre allo stesso genere di opere e di produtti, egli più facili, più abbondanti e migliori ne trova i resultati, di quello che se ciascuno isolatamente le cose tutte a sé necessariamente soltanto facesse . . . Divendosi in tal maniera per la comune e privata utilità gli uomini in varie classe e condizioni.'

p. 513, n. 27 'Il est possible . . . de parvenir à des connaissances fort utiles à la vie, et qu'au lieu de cette philosophie spéculative qu'on enseigne dans les écoles, on en peut trouver une pratique, par laquelle, connaissant la force et les actions du feu, de l'eau, de l'air, des astres, et de tous les autres corps qui nous environnent, aussi distinctement que nous connaissons les divers métiers de nos artisans, nous les pourrions employer en même façon à tous les usages auxquels ils sont propres, et ainsi nous rendre comme maîtres et possesseurs de la nature . . . contribuer au perfectionnement de la vie humaine.'

p. 548, n. 5 'Un homme s'use plus vite en surveillant quinze heures par jour l'évolution uniforme d'un mécanisme, qu'en exerçant dans le même espace de temps, sa force physique. Ce travail de surveillance, qui servirait peut-être d'utile gymnastique à l'intelligence, s'il n'était pas trop prolongé, détruit à la longue, par son excès, et l'intelligence et le corps même.'

p. 555, n. 14 'In hac urbe . . . ante hos viginti circiter annos instrumentum quidam invenerunt textorium, quo solus quis plus panni et facilius conficere poterat, quam plures aequali tempore. Hinc turbae ortae et querulae textorum, tandemque usus hujus instrumenti a magistratu prohibitus etc.'

p. 556, n. 16 'Je considère donc les machines comme des moyens d'augmenter (virtuellement) le nombre des gens industrieux qu'on n'est pas obligé de nourrir . . . En quoi l'effet d'une machine diffère-t-il de celui de nouveaux habitants?'

p. 575, n. 48 'Les classes condamnées à produire et à consommer diminuent, et les classes qui dirigent le travail, qui soulagent, consolent et éclairent toute la population, se multiplient . . . et s'approprient tous les bienfaits qui résultent de la diminution des frais du travail, de l'abondance des productions et du bon marché des consommations. Dans cette direction, l'espèce humaine s'élève aux plus hautes conceptions du génie, pénètre dans les profondeurs mystérieuses de la religion, établit les principes salutaires de la morale' (de 's'approprier tous les bienfaits etc.'), 'les lois tutélaires de la liberté' (. . . liberté pour 'les classes condamnées à produire'?) 'et du pouvoir, de l'obéissance et de la justice, du devoir et de l'humanité.'

p. 649, n. 6 'Le solstice est le moment de l'année où commence la crue du Nil, et celui que les Égyptiens ont dû observer avec le plus d'attention . . . C'était cette année tropique qu'il leur importait de marquer pour se diriger dans leurs opérations agricoles. Ils durent donc chercher dans le ciel un signe apparent de son retour.'

p. 650, n. 9 'Chaque travail doit . . . laisser un excédant.'

p. 672, n. 4 '. . . une richesse indépendante et disponible, qu'il n'a point achetée et qu'il vend.'

p. 676, n. 4 'Il a fallu convenir . . . que toutes les fois qu'il échangerait du travail fait contre du travail à faire, le dernier' (le capitaliste) 'aurait une valeur supérieure au premier' (le travailleur).

p. 677, n. 6 ' "Le travail est dit valoir, non pas en tant que marchandise lui-même, mais en vue des valeurs qu'on suppose renfermées puissanciellement en lui. La valeur du travail est une expression figurée etc . . ." Dans le travail-marchandise, qui est d'une réalité effrayante, il ne voit qu'une ellipse grammaticale. Donc toute la société actuelle, fondée sur le travail-marchandise, est désormais fondée sur une licence poétique, sur une expression figurée. La société veut-elle "éliminer tous les inconvénients" qui la travaillent, eh bien! qu'elle élimine les termes malsonnants, qu'elle change de langage, et pour cela elle n'a qu'à s'adresser à l'Académie pour lui demander une nouvelle édition de son dictionnaire.'

'C'est ce qu'une chose vaut.' 'La valeur d'une chose exprimée en monnaie.' And why has 'le travail de la terre . . . une valeur? Parce qu'on y met un prix.'

p. 694, n. 4 'Le salaire peut se mesurer de deux manières; ou sur la durée du travail, ou sur son produit.'

p. 697, n. 12 'Combien de fois n'avons-nous pas vu, dans certains ateliers, embaucher, beaucoup plus d'ouvriers que ne demandait le travail à mettre en main? Souvent, dans la prévision d'un travail aléatoire, quelquefois même imaginaire, on admet des ouvriers: comme on les paie aux pièces, on se dit qu'on ne court aucun risque, parce que toutes les pertes de temps seront à la charge des inoccupés.'

p. 723, n. 18 'L'ouvrier demandait de la subsistance pour vivre, le chef demandait du travail pour gagner.'

p. 728, n. 4 'Le travail primitif auquel son capital a dû sa naissance.'

p. 735, n. 17 'Objets de faste et de somptuosité' dont 'le tems a grossi l'accumulation' et que 'les loix de la propriété ont rassemblés dans une seule classe de la société.'

p. 738, n. 20 'Il est impossible de résoudre le prix nécessaire dans ses éléments les plus simples.'

p. 742, n. 25 'Les épargnes des riches se font aux dépens des pauvres.'

p. 745, n. 32 'La privation que s'impose le capitaliste, en prêtant . . . ses instruments de production au travailleur au lieu d'en consacrer la valeur à son propre usage, en la transformant en objets d'utilité ou d'agrément.'

p. 745, n. 33 'La conservation d'un capital exige . . . un effort constant pour résister à la tentation de le consommer.'

p. 755, n. 48 'Quant à la difficulté qu'élève Mr Ricardo en disant que, par des procédés mieux entendus, un million de personnes peuvent produire deux fois, trois fois autant de richesses, sans produire plus de valeurs, cette difficulté n'est pas une lorsque l'on considère, ainsi qu'on le doit, la production comme un échange dans lequel on donne les services productifs de son travail, de sa terre, et de ses capitaux, pour obtenir des produits. C'est par le moyen de ces services productifs que nous acquérons tous les produits qui sont au monde . . . Or . . . nous sommes d'autant plus riches, nos services productifs ont d'autant plus de valeur, qu'ils obtiennent dans l'échange appelé production, une plus grande quantité de choses utiles.'

'. . . parce que la concurrence les' (les producteurs) 'oblige à donner les produits pour ce qu'ils leur coûtent.'

'Telle est, monsieur, la doctrine bien liée sans laquelle il est impossible, je le déclare, d'expliquer les plus grandes difficultés de l'économie politique et notamment, comment il se peut qu'une nation soit plus riche lorsque ses produits diminuent de valeur, quoique la richesse soit de la valeur.'

'. . . Si vous trouvez une physionomie de paradoxe à toutes ces propositions, voyez les choses qu'elles expriment, et j'ose croire qu'elles vous paraitront fort simples et fort raisonnables.'

p. 764, n. 1 'À égalité d'oppression des masses, plus un pays a de prolétaires et plus il est riche.'

p. 797, n. 22 'Iddio fa che gli uomini che esercitano mestieri di prima utilità nascono abbondantemente.'

p. 799, n. 23 'De jour en jour il devient donc plus clair que les rapports de production dans lesquels se meut la bourgeoisie n'ont pas un caractère uni, un caractère simple, mais un caractère de duplicité; que dans les mêmes rapports dans lesquels se produit la richesse, la misère se produit aussi; que dans les mêmes rapports dans lesquels il y a développement des forces productives, il y a une force productive de répression; que ces rapports ne produisent la richesse bourgeoise, c'est à dire la richesse de la classe bourgeoise, qu'en anéantissant continuellement la richesse des membres intégrants de cette classe et en produisant un prolétariat toujours croissant.'

p. 800, n. 24 'In luoco di progettar sistemi inutili per la felicità de'popoli, mi limiterò a investigare la ragione della loro infelicità.'

p. 877, n. 2 'Le paysan y' (en Silésie) 'est serf.' 'On n'a pas pu encore engager les Silésiens au partage des communes, tandis que dans la nouvelle Marche, il n'y a guère de village où ce partage ne soit exécuté avec le plus grand succès.'

p. 894, n. 33 'Le lin fait donc une des grandes richesses du cultivateur dans le Nord de l'Allemagne. Malheureusement pour l'espèce humaine, ce n'est qu'une ressource contre la misère, et non un moyen de bien-être. Les impôts directs, les corvées, les servitudes de tout genre, écrasent le cultivateur allemand, qui paie encore des impôts indirects dans tout ce qu'il achète ... et pour comble de ruine, il n'ose pas vendre ses productions où et comme il le veut; il n'ose pas acheter ce dont il a besoin aux marchands qui pourraient le lui livrer au meilleur prix. Toutes ces causes le ruinent insensiblement, et il se trouverait hors d'état de payer les impôts directs à l'échéance sans la filerie; elle lui offre une ressource, en occupant utilement sa femme, ses enfants, ses servants, ses valets, et lui-même: mais quelle pénible vie, même aidée de ce secours! En été, il travaille comme un forçat au labourage et à la récolte; il se couche à neuf heures et se lève à deux, pour suffire aux travaux; en hiver il devrait réparer ses forces par un plus grand repos; mais il manquera de grains pour le pain et les semailles, s'il se défait des denrées qu'il faudrait vendre pour payer les impôts. Il faut donc filer pour suppléer à ce vide ... il faut y apporter la plus grande assiduité. Aussi le paysan se couche-t-il en hiver à minuit, une heure, et se lève à cinq ou six; ou bien il se couche à neuf, et se lève à deux, et cela tous les jours de sa vie si ce n'est le dimanche. Cet excès de veille et de travail usent la nature humaine, et de là vient qu'hommes et femmes vieillissent beaucoup plutôt dans les campagnes que dans les villes.'

p. 904, n. 6 'L'anéantissement de toutes espèces de corporations du même état et profession étant l'une des bases fondamentales de la constitution française, il est défendu de les rétablir de fait sous quelque prétexte et sous quelque forme que ce soit ...' '[Si] des citoyens attachés aux mêmes professions, arts et métiers prenaient des délibérations, faisaient entre eux des conventions tendantes à refuser de concert ou à n'accorder qu'à un prix déterminé le secours de leur industrie ou de leurs travaux, les dites délibérations et conventions ... seront déclarées inconstitutionelles, attentatoires à la liberté et à la déclaration des droits de l'homme etc.'

p. 907, n. 3 'C'est li compte que messire Jacques de Thoraisse, chevalier chastelain sor Besançon rent es seigneur tenant les comptes à Dijon pour monseigneur le duc et comte de Bourgoigne, des rentes appartenant à la dite chastellenie, depuis XXVe jour de décembre MCCCLIX jusqu'au XXVIIIe jour de décembre MCCCLX.'

p. 909, n. 3 'Je permettrai ... que vous ayez l'honneur de me servir, à condition que vous me donnez le peu qui vous reste pour la peine que je prends de vous commander.'

p. 920, n. 8 'Si les Tartares inondaient l'Europe aujourd'hui, il faudrait bien des affaires pour leur faire entendre ce que c'est un financier parmi nous.'

p. 922, n. 9 'Pourquoi aller chercher si loin la cause de l'éclat manufacturier de la Saxe avant la guerre? Cent quatre-vingt millions de dettes faites par les souverains!'

p. 928, n. 1 'Nous sommes ... dans une condition tout-à-fait nouvelle de la société . . . nous tendons à séparer . . . toute espèce de propriété d'avec toute espèce de travail.'

p. 937, n. 16 'Dans les colonies où l'esclavage a été aboli sans que le travail forcé se trouvait remplacé par une quantité équivalente de travail libre, on a vu s'opérer la contrepartie du fait qui se réalise tous les jours sous nos yeux. On a vu les simples travailleurs exploiter à leur tour les entrepreneurs d'industrie, exiger d'eux des salaires hors de toute proportion avec la part légitime qui leur revenait dans le produit. Les planteurs, ne pouvant obtenir de leurs sucres un prix suffisant pour couvrir la hausse de salaire, ont été obligés de fournir l'excédant, d'abord sur leurs profits, ensuite sur leurs capitaux mêmes. Une foule de planteurs ont été ruinés de la sorte, d'autres ont fermé leurs ateliers pour échapper à une ruine imminente . . . Sans doute, il vaut mieux voir périr des accumulations de capitaux, que des générations d'hommes . . . mais ne vaudrait-il pas mieux que ni les uns ni les autres périssent?'

p. 938, n. 20 'C'est, ajoutez-vous, grâce à l'appropriation du sol et des capitaux que l'homme, qui n'a que ses bras, trouve de l'occupation, et se fait un revenu . . . c'est au contraire, grâce à l'appropriation individuelle du sol qu'il se trouve des hommes n'ayant que leurs bras . . . Quand vous mettez un homme dans le vide, vous vous emparez de l'atmosphère. Ainsi faites-vous, quand vous vous emparez du sol . . C'est le mettre dans le vide de richesses, pour ne le laisser vivre qu'à votre volonté.'

Index of Authorities Quoted

[*Titles as given here may differ in detail from those in the text, since the latter follows Marx's own versions.*]

I. BOOKS BY NAMED OR ANONYMOUS AUTHORS

Addington, Stephen, *An Inquiry into the Reasons for and against Inclosing Open Fields*, 2nd edn, London, 1772. 886–7

Advantages of the East-India Trade to England, The, London, 1720. 436, 458, 463, 465, 467, 486, 553, 647

Aikin John, *Description of the Country from Thirty to Forty Miles round Manchester*, London, 1795. 741–2, 915, 924, 925

Anderson, Adam, *An Historical and Chronological Deduction of the Origin of Commerce from the Earliest Accounts to the Present Time*, 2 vols., London, 1764. 908, 924

Anderson, James, *The Bee, or Literary Weekly Intelligencer*, Vol. 3, Edinburgh, 1791. 768

Observations on the Means of Exciting a Spirit of National Industry; Chiefly Intended to Promote the Agriculture, Commerce, Manufactures, and Fisheries of Scotland. In a Series of Letters to a Friend. Written in the Year 1775, Edinburgh, 1777. 702–3, 890

Appian of Alexandria, *The Roman Civil Wars*. 888

Arbuthnot, John, *An Inquiry into the Connection between the Present Price of Provisions, and the Size of Farms. With remarks on Population as Affected Thereby. To Which are Added, Proposals for Preventing Future Scarcity. By a Farmer*, London, 1773. 423, 444, 446, 883, 889, 958

Aristotle, *Nicomachean Ethics*. 151

Politics. 179, 253–4, 267, 444, 532, 1041

Ashley, Lord Anthony, *Ten Hours' Factory Bill. The Speech in the House of Commons, on Friday, 15 March*, London, 1844. 526, 538,

Athenaeus, *Deipnosophistae*. 195, 230

Augier, Marie, *Du Crédit public et de son histoire depuis les temps anciens jusqu'à nos jours*, Paris, 1842. 926

Babbage, Charles, *On the Economy of Machinery and Manufactures*, London, 1832. 466, 469, 497, 514, 528–9

Bacon, Francis, *The Essays or Counsels Civil and Moral*, London, 1625. 880–81

*The Reign of Henry VII. Verbatim Reprint from Kennet's 'England',
1719*, London, 1870. 879–80

Bailey, Samuel, *A Critical Dissertation on the Nature, Measures, and
Causes of Value: Chiefly in Reference to the Writings of Mr Ricardo
and His Followers. By the Author of Essays on the Formation and
Publication of Opinions*, London, 1825. 155, 177, 675

*Money and Its Vicissitudes in Value; as They Affect National Industry
and Pecuniary Contracts: with a Postscript on Joint Stock Banks*,
London, 1837. 141, 759

Barbon, Nicholas, *A Discourse Concerning Coining the New Money
Lighter. In Answer to Mr Locke's Considerations about Raising the
Value of Money*, London, 1696. 125–8, 226, 242, 244

Barton, John, *Observations on the Circumstances which Influence the
Condition of the Labouring Classes of Society*, London, 1817. 783–4,
829

Bastiat, Frédéric, *Harmonies économiques*, Paris, 1851. 1006

Bastiat, Frédéric, and Proudhon, Pierre-Joseph, *Gratuité du Crédit*,
Paris, 1850. 971, 1000, 1057

Baynes, John, *The Cotton Trade. Two Lectures on the Above Subject,
Delivered before the Members of the Blackburn Literary, Scientific, and
Mechanics' Institution, Blackburn*, London, 1857. 511.

Beccaria, Cesare, *Elementi di economia pubblica* (1772), in *Scrittori
classici italiani di economia politica, Parte moderna*, ed. Custodi,
Vol. 11, Milan, 1804. 486

Beckmann, Johann, *Beyträge zur Geschichte der Erfindungen*, Vol. 1,
Leipzig, 1786. 554

Bellers, John, *Essays about the Poor, Manufactures, Trade, Plantations,
and Immorality*, London, 1699. 228, 244, 553, 609

*Proposals for Raising a Colledge of Industry of All Useful Trades and
Husbandry*, London, 1696. 236, 443, 619, 764

Bentham, Jeremy, *Théorie des peines et des récompenses, ouvrage extrait
des manuscrits de M. Jérémie Bentham*, 3rd edn, Paris, 1826. 758

Berkeley, George, *The Querist*, London, 1750. 453, 474

Bidaut, J. N., *Du monopole qui s'établit dans les arts industriels et le
commerce, au moyen des grands appareils de fabrication. 2e livraison:
Du monopole de la fabrication et da la vente*, Paris, 1828. 438

Biese, Franz, *Die Philosophie des Aristoteles*, Berlin, 1842. 532

Blakey, Robert, *The History of Political Literature from the Earliest
Times*, Vol. 2, London, 1855. 882

Blanqui, Jérôme-Adolphe, *Cours d'économie industrielle. Recueilli et
annoté par A. G. Blaise*, Paris, 1838–9. 456

Des classes ouvrières en France, pendant l'année 1848, Paris, 1849.
389

Block, Maurice, *Les Théoriciens du socialisme en Allemagne. Extrait du
Journal des économistes*, Paris, 1872. 100

Boileau, Étienne, *Règlemens sur les arts et métiers de Paris, rédigés au XIII siècle, et connus sous le nom du Livre des métiers*, Paris, 1837. 616

Boileau-Despréaux, Nicolas, Satire VIII. 806–7

Boisguillebert, Pierre le Pesant, *Le Détail de la France* (1695) In: *Économistes financiers du XVIIIe siècle. Précédes de notices historiques sur chaque auteur, et accompagnés de commentaires et de notes explicatives, par Eugène Daire*, Paris, 1843. 227.

Dissertation sur la nature des richesses, de l'argent et des tributs où l'on découvre la fausse idée qui règne dans le monde à l'égard de ces trois articles (1707), in *Économistes financiers du XVIIIe siècle*, ed. E. Daire, Vol. 1, Paris, 1843. 239

Boxhorn, Marcus Zuerius, *Marci Zuerii Boxhornii institutionum politicarum liber primus*, Amsterdam, 1663. 555

Bray, John Francis, *Labour's Wrongs and Labour's Remedy*, Leeds, 1839. 999

Broadhurst, J., *Political Economy*, London, 1842. 147

Brougham, Henry, *An Inquiry into the Colonial Policy of the European Powers*, Vol. 2, Edinburgh, 1803. 925

Bruckner, John, *Théorie du système animal*, Leyden, 1767. 767

Buchanan, David, *Inquiry into the Taxation and Commercial Policy of Great Britain; with Observations on the Principles of Currency, and of Exchangeable Value*, Edinburgh, 1844. 233

Observations on the Subjects Treated of in Dr Smith's Inquiry into the Nature and Causes of the Wealth of Nations, Edinburgh, 1814. 891

Buchez, Philippe, and Roux-Lavergne, Pierre, *Histoire parlementaire de la Révolution Française, ou journal des assemblées nationales depuis 1789 jusqu'en 1815*, Vol. 10, Paris, 1834. 904

Burke, Edmund, *A Letter from the Right Honourable Edmund Burke to a Noble Lord, on the Attacks Made upon Him and His Pension in the House of Lords, by the Duke of Bedford and the Earl of Lauderdale. Early in the Present Session of Parliament*, London, 1796. 884

Thoughts and Details on Scarcity, Originally Presented to the Rt Hon. W. Pitt in the Month of November 1795, London, 1800. 315, 344, 440, 925–6

Butler, Samuel, *Hudibras*. 126

Byles, John Barnard, *Sophisms of Free Trade and Popular Political Economy Examined. By a Barrister.* 7th edn, London, 1850. 383, 900

Cairnes, John Elliott, *The Slave Power*, London, 1862. 304, 377, 450, 1014, 1034

Campbell, George, *Modern India: A Sketch of the System of Civil Government*, London, 1852. 479

Cantillon, Philip, *The Analysis of Trade, Commerce, Coin, Bullion, Banks, and Foreign Exchanges*, London, 1759. 697

Fielden, John, *The Curse of the Factory System; or, A Short Account of the Origin of Factory Cruelties*, London, 1836. 527, 537, 923–4

Fleetwood, William, *Chronicon Preciosum: or, An account of English Money, the Price of Corn, and Other Commodities, for the Last 600 Years*, London, 1707, and 2nd edn, London, 1745. 384

Fonteret, Antoine-Louis, *Hygiène physique et morale de l'ouvrier dans les grandes villes en général, et dans la ville de Lyon en particulier*, Paris, 1858. 484

Forbonnais, François-Véron de, *Élémens du commerce*, Leyden, 1766. 185

Forcade, Eugène, 'La Guerre du socialisme', *Revue des Deux Mondes*, Vol. 4, Brussels, 1848. 973

Forster, Nathaniel, *An Enquiry into the Causes of the Present High Price of Provisions*, London, 1767. 386, 554, 649, 886

Fortescue, John, *De laudibus legum Angliae* (1469), London, 1537. 878

Fourier, Charles, *La Fausse Industrie morcelée, répugnante, mensongère, et l'antidote, l'industrie naturelle, combinée, attrayante, véridique, donnant quadruple produit*, Paris, 1835–6. 553

Le Nouveau Monde industriel et sociétaire, ou invention du procédé d'industrie attrayante et naturelle distribuée en séries passionnées, Paris, 1829. 403, 506, 852

Franklin, Benjamin, *A Modest Inquiry into the Nature and Necessity of a Paper Currency* (1729), in *The Works of Benjamin Franklin*, ed. J. Sparks, Vol. 2, Boston, 1836. 142

Positions to be Examined, Concerning National Wealth (1769), in *The Works of Benjamin Franklin*, Vol. 2. 267

Freytag, Gustav, *Neue Bilder aus dem Leben des deutschen Volkes*, Leipzig, 1862. 901–2, 1082

Fullarton, John, *On the Regulation of Currencies*, 2nd edn, London, 1845. 225, 240, 243

Galiani, Ferdinando, *Della moneta* (1750), in *Scrittori classici italiani di economia politica, Parte moderna*, ed. Custodi, Vols. 3 and 4, Milan, 1803. 167, 183, 185, 194, 255, 261, 431, 797

Ganilh, Charles, *Des Systèmes d'économie politique*, 2nd edn, Vols. 1–2, Paris, 1821. 153, 278, 575

La Théorie de l'économie politique, Vols. 1–2, Paris, 1815. 285

Garnier, Germain, *Abrégé élémentaire des principes de l'économie politique*, Paris, 1796. 694

Gaskell, Peter, *The Manufacturing Population of England*, London, 1833. 563, 572

Genovesi, Antonio, *Lezioni di economia civile* (1766–7), in *Scrittori classici italiani di economia politica, Parte moderna*, ed. Custodi, Vols. 7–9, Milan, 1803. 254

Geoffroy Saint-Hilaire, Étienne, *Notions synthétiques, historiques, et physiologiques de philosophie naturelle*, Paris, 1838. 908

Gisborne, Thomas, *An Enquiry into the Duties of Men in the Higher and Middle Classes of Society in Great Britain*, 2nd edn, Vol. 2, London, 1795. 924

Goethe, Johann Wolfgang von, 'An Suleika', in *West-östlicher Diwan*. 381

Faust. 161, 180, 302, 741, 868

Gray, John, *The Essential Principles of the Wealth of Nations, Illustrated, in Opposition to Some False Doctrines of Dr Adam Smith and Others*, London, 1797. 263

Greg, Robert Hyde, *The Factory Question, Considered in Relation to Its Effects on the Health and Morals of Those Employed in Factories: and 'The Ten Hours Bill', in Relation to Its Effect upon the Manufactures of England, and Those of Foreign Countries*, London 1837. 404

Grégoir, Henri, *Les Typographes devant le tribunal correctionnel de Bruxelles*, Brussels, 1865. 697

Grove, William Robert, *On the Correlation of Physical Forces*, 5th edn, London, 1867. 664

Gülich, Gustav von, *Geschichtliche Darstellung des Handels, der Gewerbe und des Ackerbaus der bedeutendsten handeltreibenden Staaten unsrer Zeit*, 5 vols., Jena, 1830–45. 95, 918

Haller, Ludwig von, *Restauration der Staatswissenschaften*, 4 vols., Winterthur, 1816–20. 512

Hamm, Wilhelm, *Die landwirthschaftlichen Geräthe und Maschinen Englands. Ein Handbuch der landwirthschaftlichen Mechanik und Maschinenkunde*, 2nd edn, Brunswick, 1856. 636

Hanssen, Georg, *Die Aufhebung der Leibeigenschaft und die Umgestaltung der gutsherrlich-bäuerlichen Verhältnisse überhaupt in den Herzogthümern Schleswig und Holstein*, St Petersburg, 1861. 346

Harris, James, *Dialogue Concerning Happiness*, in *Three Treatises*, 3rd edn, London, 1772. 487

Harris, James, Earl of Malmesbury, *Diaries and Correspondence*, ed. by his grandson the Third Earl of Malmesbury, 4 vols., London, 1844. 486–7

Harrison, William, *The Description of England*, in Holinshed's *Chronicles*, London, 1587. 879, 898, 906

Hassall, Arthur Hill, *Adulterations Detected, or Plain Instructions for the Discovery of Frauds in Food and Medicine*, 2nd edn, London, 1861. 278, 358, 1067

Hegel, Georg Wilhelm Friedrich, *Encyclopädie der philosophischen Wissenschaften im Grundrisse. Erster Theil. Die Logik*. In *Werke*, Vol. 6, Berlin, 1840. 285, 373

the *Necessity of Consumption, Lately Advocated by Mr Malthus*, London, 1821. 265, 278, 568, 743, 756, 1067
Isocrates, *Busiris*. 489

Jacob, William, *An Historical Enquiry into the Production and Consumption of the Precious Metals*, 2 vols., London, 1831. 130
A Letter to Samuel Whitbread, Esq., Being a Sequel to Considerations on the Protection Required by British Agriculture, London, 1815. 328
Jerome, *Letters*. 197
Jones, Richard, *An Essay on the Distribution of Wealth, and on the Sources of Taxation*, London, 1831. 446
An Introductory Lecture on Political Economy, London, 1833. 784
Textbook of Lectures on the Political Economy of Nations, Hertford, 1852. 115, 423, 438, 452, 714, 734, 746, 1011

Kaufmann, I. I. 'Tochka zreniya politiko-ekonomicheskoi kritiki u Karla Marksa', in *Vyestnik Evropi*, Vol. 3, St Petersburg, 1872. 100–102
Kopp, Hermann, *Entwickelung der Chemie*, in *Geschichte der Wissenschaften in Deutschland. Neuere Zeit*, Vol. 10, Part 3, Munich, 1873. 424

Laborde, Alexandre de, *De l'esprit d'association dans tous les intérêts de la communauté, ou essai sur le complément du bien-être et de la richesse en France par le complément des institutions*, Paris, 1818. 671
Laing, Samuel, *National Distress. Its Causes and Remedies*, London, 1844, 305, 797, 812, 830, 1079
Lalor, John, *Money and Morals*, London, 1852. 1000
Lancellotti, Secondo, *L'hoggidì; overo Gl'ingegni non inferiori à'passati*, Venice, 1637. 554
Lassalle, Ferdinand, *Herr Bastiat-Schulze von Delitzsch, derök onomische Julian, oder Capital und Arbeit*, Berlin, 1864. 89
Die Philosophie Herakleitos des Dunklen von Ephesos, Vol. 1, Berlin, 1858. 200
Law, John, *Considérations sur le numéraire et le commerce* (1705), in *Économistes financiers du XVIIIe siècle*, ed. E. Daire, Paris, 1843. 185
Le Trosne, Guillaume-François, *De l'intérêt social par rapport à la valeur, à la circulation, à l'industrie, et au commerce intérieur et extérieur* (1777), in *Physiocrates*, ed. E. Daire, Part 2, Paris, 1846. 126, 130, 185, 196, 206, 212, 215, 243, 260, 261, 263, 266, 318
Letter to Sir T. C. Bunbury on the Poor Rates, and the High Price of

Varro, *Rerum Rusticarum Libri Tres.* 303
Verri, Pietro, *Meditazioni sulla economia politica* (1771), in *Scrittori Classici italiani di economia politica, Parte moderna,* ed. Custodi, Vol. 15, Milan, 1804. 133, 134, 184, 231, 447
Virgil, *Aeneid.* 416, 925, 1081
Vissering, Simon, *Handboek van Praktische Staathuishoudkunde,* Amsterdam, 1860–62. 635

Wade, John, *History of the Middle and Working Classes,* 3rd edn, London, 1835. 353, 383–4, 769, 1008, 1057
Wakefield, Edward Gibbon, *England and America,* Vols. 1–2, London, 1833. 380, 729, 830, 932–9
  A View of the Art of Colonization, with Present Reference to the British Empire, London, 1849. 443
Ward, John, *The Borough of Stoke-upon-Trent,* London, 1843. 378
Watson, John Forbes, 'A Paper, delivered to the Society of Arts', *Journal of the Society of Arts,* 17 April 1860. 514
Watts, John, *The Facts and Fictions of Political Economists,* Manchester, 1842. 692
  Trade Societies and Strikes, Machinery and Co-operative Societies, Manchester, 1865. 692, 695
Wayland, Francis, *The Elements of Political Economy,* Boston, 1843. 266, 316, 1000
West, Edward, *Essay on the Application of Capital to Land, By a Fellow of University College, Oxford,* London, 1815. 665, 684
  Price of Corn and Wages of Labour, London, 1826. 683–4
Wilks, Mark, *Historical Sketches of the South of India,* Vol. 1, London, 1810. 479
Wright, Thomas, *A Short Address to the Public on the Monopoly of Large Farms,* London, 1779. 886

Xenophon, *Cyropaedia.* 488

Young, Arthur, *Political Arithmetic,* London, 1774. 219, 339, 386, 1035, 1050
  A Tour in Ireland, 2nd edn, 2 vols., London, 1780. 836

2. PARLIAMENTARY REPORTS AND OTHER OFFICIAL PUBLICATIONS

Act for Regulating the Hours of Labour for Children, Young Persons, and Women Employed in Workshops, 21 August 1867. 624–5
Act to Limit the Hours of Labour, and to Prevent the Employment of Children in Factories under Ten Years of Age. Approved 18 March 1851 by the seventy-fifth legislature of the state of New Jersey. 383

3. NEWSPAPERS AND PERIODICALS

Bengal Hurkaru, Calcutta, 22 July 1861. 446
Bury Guardian, 12 May 1860. 379

Concordia. Zeitschrift für die Arbeiterfrage, Berlin, 7 March 1872. 115
    4 July 1872. 116
    11 July 1872. 117

Daily Telegraph, London, 17 January 1860. 354
Demokratisches Wochenblätt. Organ der deutschen Volkspartei, Leipzig.
    1 August 1868, 22 August 1868, 29 August 1868, and 4 September
    1868. 99

Economist, London, 29 March 1845. 832
    15 April 1848. 338
    19 July 1851. 734
    21 January 1860. 791
    2 June 1866. 894
Edinburgh Review, October 1859. 1070
Evening Standard, London, 1 November 1886. 112
Glasgow Daily Mail, Glasgow, 25 April 1849. 426

Journal of the Society of Arts, London, 9 December 1859. 497–8
    17 April 1860. 514
    23 March 1866. 894
    5 January 1872. 542

Macmillan's Magazine, London and Cambridge, August 1863. 366
Manchester Guardian, Manchester, 15 January 1875. 795
Morning Advertiser, London, 17 April 1863. 117
Morning Star, London, 17 April 1863. 117, 806
    23 June 1863. 365
    7 January 1867. 823–5

Neue Rheinische Zeitung. Politisch-ökonomische Revue, Hamburg, April
    1850. 366

Observer, London, 24 April 1864. 237

Philosophie Positive. Revue, La, Paris, November–December 1868. 99
Portfolio. Diplomatic Review (New Series), London. 892

Révolutions de Paris, 11–18 June 1791. 904

General Index

Abstinence, theory of, 9, 61, 298–9, 338, 343, 809, 1010
Abstract human labour, 142, 150
Abstract social labour, 42, 308
Abstraction, levels of, 29–32
Accessory materials, 288, 984
Accidents, in coal mines, 632; in factories, 552–3, 611; on railways, 363–4
Accumulation of capital, 60–65, 725–34, 742–3; antagonistic character of, 799; extent of, 747; general law of, 798, 802–70; natural barriers to, 785; necessary conditions for, 709–10; worsening of worker's situation in proportion to, 799
Adoratsky, Vladimir Viktorovich, 943
Adulteration of food, 358–9, 750, 1067
Aggregate product of capital. See Total product of capital
Agricultural labourers, 363, 634, 723–4; dwellings of 834, 836–48; emigration of to towns, 572; nourishment of, 809, 834–6; surplus labour of, 670; surplus population of, 796; wages of, 517, 698, 750, 791, 831; working day of, 386–8; worsening of situation of, 828–30, 833
Agricultural production, increase in, 833
Agriculture, 453–4, 752, 1051; application of machinery to, 636–7, 831; capitalist production

in, 952–3; large-scale industry and, 636–8; revolutions in the mode of production in, 556–7, 828, 906
Alchian, Armen Albert, 53
Alien labour 357, 508, 672, 928, 1016, 1024–5
Alien product, 716
Alien property, 1003, 1026
Alien value, 988, 1006
Alienation (*Entfremdung*), 34, 203, 716, 757, 799, 1003, 1054, 1058; contrast between attitude of capitalist and attitude of worker to, 990
Alienation by sale (*Veräusserung*), 182, 204, 232, 271, 277, 301, 919, 1066
Althusser, Louis, 14
Alum, 358
American Civil War, 91, 113, 298, 398, 517, 546, 680
Amin, Samir, 64
Anarchy of capitalist production, 477, 635, 667
Anatomy, 12
Anderson, Adam, 908, 924
Anderson, James, 639, 887
Anne, Queen of England, 899
Anti-Corn Law League, 97
Anti-Jacobin War, 698, 751, 829
Antipater of Thessalonica, 532
Apelles, 619, 759
Apocalypse, 181
Appearance, forms of, 127, 128, 188, 433, 677, 682; in relation to essence, 20–22
Appropriation, 729–30, 756
Approvisionnement, 292

Deutsch, Hans, 73
Deutscher Arbeiterverein, 724
Devil's dust, 313
De Witt, Johan, 921
Dialectical inversion, 423, 425, 532, 533, 729, 798, 990
Dialectical method, 17–25, 100–103
Diamonds, 130
Dietzgen, Joseph, 98
Direct exchange of products, 181–2
Discipline, 489–90, 549–51
Dissolution of the monasteries, 881
Divestiture (*Entäusserung*), 204
Division of labour, 132, 171, 201–3; in antiquity, 486–9; in the factory, 547, 615, 951; in manufacture, 456–91; in society, 471–3, 475–7, 572, 616, 951
Dobb, Maurice, 59
Domestic industry, so-called, 590, 595–9, 620, 796, 825
Doubleday, Thomas, 921
Doveholes, 820
Drafts on the social product, 713
Dressmaking, 364–5
Dual character of the commodity, 125–31, 153, 199, 209, 952
Dufferin, Lord. *See* Hamilton-Temple-Blackwood
Dureau de la Malle, Adolphe, 1068
Durham, 723, 820–21, 1084

East End of London, 823, 825
East India Company, 917
East Indies, 650–51
Economic crisis of 1825, 97
Economic crisis of 1857, 822, 1006
Economic crisis of 1866, 805, 807, 822–3; effect of on skilled workers, 823–5
Economic formations of society, 273, 286
Economic laws, relativity of, 13
Economy in the use of the means of production, 442
Eden, Sir Frederick Morton, 765–6, 889
Education, 628–9; factory legislation relating to, 523–6, 613–14
Edward VI, King of England, 897

Egypt, 451–2, 459, 489, 648
Eleatics, 358
Elizabeth I, Queen of England, 881, 882, 897, 898, 901
Ellis, Charles Augustus, Baron Howard de Walden and Seaford, 389
Emigration, 379, 588, 720, 723, 761, 786; from Britain, 947; from England, 1080; from Ireland, 862, 1080–81
Emmanuel, Arghiri, 64
Employers and Workmen Act (1875), 903
Enclosures, 879, 885–9
Engels, Friedrich, 14, 19, 28, 35, 52, 349, 523, 808; as editor of *Capital*, 27, 31, 46, 57, 87, 170, 212, 325, 346, 424, 471, 511, 624, 635, 669, 777
Engineers, 545–6
Envelope manufacture, 500
Epicurus, 172
Equality, 280, 520, 621
Eschwege, Wilhelm Ludwig von, 130
Essen, 513
Everett, William, of Horningsham, Wiltshire, 554
Exchange of commodities, 178–87, 259–60
Exchange of objectified labour for living labour, 1009
Exchange of products, 182, 472
Exchange-value, 126–8; has to acquire a form distinct from use-value, 955
Exeter Hall, 376
Exploitation, 518, 569, 769, 1048; naked, 1027
Expropriation of the expropriators, 929–30
Expropriation of the immediate producers, 875, 927–8, 1078–9, 1083

Factory, 34, 477, 544–53, 576
Factory Act of 1833, 333, 384, 390–3; of 1844, 393–5, 523; of 1847, 395–8, 539, 688; of 1850, 349, 405; of 1860, 409; of 1861,

1132   General Index

Quakers, 351–2

Quesnay, François, 97, 203, 437, 737, 767

Quételet, Lambert-Adolphe-Jacques, 440

Rag trade, 592

Railways, over-work on, 363

Raw material, 284, 287–9, 311, 579; in technical sense, 285

Redgrave, Alexander, 688, 703–4, 1076

Redskins. *See* North American Indians

Reformation of the sixteenth century, 881

Régisseur, 907

Règlement organique, 347–8

Reification (*Versachlichung*), 209, 1054, 1056

Relations of production, production of the, 1065

Relative surplus population, 786, 789, 848, 862; floating, 794–5; latent, 795–6; reproduction of, 797; stagnant, 796–7

Relay system, 391–3, 400–404, 426, 546

Religion, 165, 172, 175, 493–4, 907; inversion of subject into object in, 990

Reproduction, extended, 732; simple, 711–24

Reproduction process, 1045–6

Reserve Army of labour, 64, 781–94

Reserve fund, 736

Resultate. See *Capital*, Unpublished 'Chapter Six'

Revenue, 738

Rhodes, 269

Ribbon-loom, 554

Ribbon trade, 582, 589, 614, 697

Ricardians, 155, 177, 265, 421, 568

Ricardo, David, 26, 42, 46, 66, 68, 74, 96; on the accumulation of capital, 736, 1057; on capital, 997, 1004, 1008; on labour, 1079; on machinery, 510, 516, 532, 557, 565; on money, 242; on population, 1049–50; on profit,

651–2, 657, 665; on rent, 639; on Robinson Crusoe, 169; on the surplus product, 339; on value, 173–5, 269, 755

Robinson, Joan, 30, 38, 59

Rodbertus-Jagetzow, Johann Karl, 669

Roll, Sir Eric, 70

Roman Law, 185–6, 761

Romania, 271

Rome, 193, 233, 265, 275, 400, 888, 1050

Roscher, Wilhelm Georg Friedrich, 314, 325–6, 485, 974, 1010

Rosdolsky, Roman, 28, 31, 38, 69, 73

Rosenberg, David I., 21

Rossi, Pellegrino, 997, 1004–5

Roundsmen, 897

Rowthorn, Bob, 72

Roy, Joseph, 87, 105, 110

Rubel, Maximilien, 31

Rubin, Isaak Illich, 14, 73

Rural domestic industry, 911; destruction of by large-scale industry, 912

Russell, Lord John, 884

Russia, 703, 884

Russian Revolution, 85

Saddlery shops, 692–3

Sadler, Michael Thomas, 830, 861

Sago, 650–51

St John, Henry, Viscount Bolingbroke, 920

Sale, 200

Sale and purchase, 208, 248–50, 258–66, 681

Samuelson, Paul, 23, 39, 52, 81

Sanderson Bros. and Co., 372–4

Saving, 254, 735

Saw-mill, 554

Saxony, 922, 1082

Say, Jean-Baptiste, 26; on crises, 210; on exchange, 266; on machinery, 568; on surplus-value, 314; on value, 174, 677, 755–6

Scale of production, 1022, 1035–6

Schmidt, Conrad, 19

Note on Previous Editions of the Works of Marx and Engels

Until recently there existed no complete edition of the works of Marx and Engels in any language. The Marx-Engels Institute, under its director D. Riazanov, began to produce such an edition in the late 1920s. For reasons never since made clear, the project did not survive the mid-1930s. However, eleven indispensable volumes did emerge between 1927 and 1935, under the title *Karl Marx – Friedrich Engels: Historisch-Kritische Gesamtausgabe*, commonly referred to as the *MEGA* edition. The *MEGA* contains the works of both men down to 1848, and their correspondence, but nothing more. For the next thirty years, the field was held by the almost inaccessible Russian edition, the Marx-Engels *Sochineniya* (twenty-nine volumes, 1928–46).

Only in 1968 did the East Germans complete the first definitive edition in the German language, the forty-one volume *Marx-Engels Werke* (*MEW*). Until then, the works of Marx and Engels existed only in separate editions and smaller collections on specific themes. For this reason, the translations into English have followed the same pattern – the only general selection being the *Marx-Engels Selected Works* (*MESW*), now expanded to a three-volume edition. Recently, however, the major gaps in the English translations have begun to be filled up. Lawrence and Wishart have produced a complete translation of *Theories of Surplus-Value*, as well as the first adequate translation of *A Contribution to the Critique of Political Economy* and Marx's book on *The Cologne Communist Trial*. They plan to issue a complete English-language edition of even greater scope than the *MEW*, though this will inevitably take many years to complete. The Pelican Marx Library occupies an intermediate position between the *MESW* and the complete edition. It brings together the most important of Marx's larger works, the three volumes of *Capital* and the *Grundrisse*, as well as three volumes of political writings and a volume of early writings.

Chronology of Works by Marx and Engels

Date[1]	Author[2]	Title	English edition[3]
1843	M	*Critique of Hegel's Doctrine of the State*	P *EW*
1843	M	*On the Jewish Question*	P *EW*
1843–4	M	*A Contribution to the Critique of Hegel's Philosophy of Right. Introduction*	P *EW*
1844	M	*Excerpts from James Mill's* Elements of Political Economy	P *EW*
1844	E	*Outlines of a Critique of Political Economy*	P. Engels
1844	M	*Economic and Philosophical Manuscripts*	P *EW*
1844	M	*Critical Notes on the Article 'The King of Prussia and Social Reform. By a Prussian'*	P *EW*
1844	M & E	*The Holy Family, or a Critique of Critical Critique*	LW 1957
1844–5	E	*Condition of the Working Class in England*	Blackwell 1958

1. Date of composition, except for *Capital*, where the date of first publication is given.

2. M = Marx, E = Engels.

3. The following abbreviations are used:

P. Engels: Engels, *Selected Writings*, Harmondsworth, 1967.

LW: Lawrence and Wishart.

MESW: *Karl Marx and Frederick Engels, Selected Works in Three Volumes*, Progress Publishers, 1969.

P: Pelican Marx Library.

P *EW*: *Early Writings* (Pelican Marx Library).

P *FI*: *The First International and After* (Pelican Marx Library).

P *R1848*: *The Revolutions of 1848* (Pelican Marx Library).

P *SE*: *Surveys from Exile* (Pelican Marx Library).

Date	Author	Title	English edition
1845	M	*Theses on Feuerbach*	P *EW*
1845–6	M & E	*The German Ideology*	LW 1964
1846–7	M	*The Poverty of Philosophy*	LW 1956
1847	M & E	*Speeches on Poland*	P *R1848*
1847	M	*Wage Labour and Capital*	*MESW I*
1847–8	M & E	*Manifesto of the Communist Party*	P *R1848*
1848	M & E	*Speeches on Poland*	P *R1848*
1848	M & E	*Demands of the Communist Party in Germany*	P *R1848*
1848–9	M & E	*Articles in the* Neue Rheinische Zeitung	P *R1848* (selection)
1850 (March)	M & E	*Address of the Central Committee to the Communist League*	P *R1848*
1850 (June)	M & E	*Address of the Central Committee to the Communist League*	P *R1848*
1850	M & E	*Reviews from the* Neue Rheinische Zeitung Revue	P *R1848*
1850	M	*The Class Struggles in France: 1848 to 1850*	P *SE*
1850	E	*The Peasant War in Germany*	LW 1956
1851–2	E	*Revolution and Counter-Revolution in Germany*	*MESW I*
1852	M	*The Eighteenth Brumaire of Louis Bonaparte*	P *SE*
1852	M	*Revelations of the Cologne Communist Trial*	LW 1970
1856	M	*Speech at the Anniversary of the* People's Paper	P *SE*
1857–8	M	*Grundrisse*	P
1859	M	*A Contribution to the Critique of Political Economy*	LW 1971
1852–61	M & E	*Articles in the* New York Daily Tribune	P *SE* (selections)
1861	M	*Articles in* Die Presse *on the Civil War in the United States*	P *SE* (selections)
1861–3	M	*Theories of Surplus-Value,* Vol. 1	LW 1967
		Vol. 2	LW 1970
		Vol. 3	LW 1972
1863	M	*Proclamation on Poland*	P *SE*
1864	M	*Inaugural Address of the International Working Men's Association*	P *FI*
1864	M	*Provisional Rules of the International Working Men's Association*	P *FI*

Date	Author	Title	English edition
1865	E	*The Prussian Military Question and the German Workers' Party*	P *FI* (extract)
1865	M	*Wages, Prices, and Profit*	*MESW II*
1866	E	*What Have the Working Classes to Do with Poland?*	P *FI*
1867	M	*Capital*, Vol. 1	P
1867	M	*Instructions for Delegates to the Geneva Congress*	P *FI*
1868	M	*Report to the Brussels Congress*	P *FI*
1869	M	*Report to the Basel Congress*	P *FI*
1870	M	*The General Council to the Federal Council of French Switzerland (a circular letter)*	P *FI*
1870	M	*First Address of the General Council on the Franco-Prussian War*	P *FI*
1870	M	*Second Address of the General Council on the Franco-Prussian War*	P *FI*
1871	M	First draft of *The Civil War in France*	P *FI*
1871	M & E	*On the Paris Commune*	LW 1971
1871	M	*The Civil War in France*	P *FI*
1871	M & E	*Resolution of the London Conference on Working-Class Political Action*	P *FI*
1872	M & E	*The Alleged Splits in the International*	P *FI*
1872	M	*Report to the Hague Congress*	P *FI*
1872–3	E	*The Housing Question*	*MESW II*
1874	M	*Political Indifferentism*	P *FI*
1874	E	*On Authority*	*MESW II*
1874–5	M	*Conspectus of Bakunin's Book* Statism and Anarchy	P *FI* (extract)
1875	M & E	*For Poland*	P *FI*
1875	M	*Critique of the Gotha Programme*	P *FI*
1876–8	E	*Anti-Dühring*	LW 1955
1879	M & E	*Circular Letter to Bebel, Liebknecht, Bracke*, et al.	P *FI*
1879–80	M	*Marginal Notes on Adolph Wagner's* Lehrbuch der politischen Ökonomie	P *Capital*
1880	E	*Socialism: Utopian and Scientific*	*MESW III*
1880	M	*Introduction to the Programme of the French Workers' Party*	P *FI*
1873–83	E	*Dialectics of Nature*	LW 1954
1884	E	*The Origin of the Family, Private Property, and the State*	*MESW III*

Date	Author	Title	English edition
1885	M	*Capital*, Vol. 2	P
1886	E	*Ludwig Feuerbach and the End of Classical German Philosophy*	*MESW III*
1894	M	*Capital*, Vol. 3	P

More About Penguins and Pelicans

For further information about books available from Penguins please write to Dept EP, Penguin Books Ltd, Harmondsworth, Middlesex UB7 0DA.

In the U.S.A.: For a complete list of books available from Penguins in the United States write to Dept CS, Penguin Books, 625 Madison Avenue, New York, New York 10022.

In Canada: For a complete list of books available from Penguins in Canada write to Penguin Books Canada Ltd, 2801 John Street, Markham, Ontario L3R 1B4.

In Australia: For a complete list of books available from Penguins in Australia write to the Marketing Department, Penguin Books Australia Ltd, P.O. Box 257, Ringwood, Victoria 3134.

In New Zealand: For a complete list of books available from Penguins in New Zealand write to the Marketing Department, Penguin Books (N.Z.) Ltd, P.O. Box 4019, Auckland 10.